SUPPLEMENT XVII
Max Apple to Franz Wright

American Writers
A Collection of Literary Biographies

JAY PARINI
Editor in Chief

SUPPLEMENT XVII
Max Apple to Franz Wright

CHARLES SCRIBNER'S SONS
An imprint of Thomson Gale, a part of The Thomson Corporation

Detroit • New York • San Francisco • New Haven, Conn. • Waterville, Maine • London

American Writers, Supplement XVII
Jay Parini, Editor in Chief

Project Editors
James E. Person, Robert James Russell

Copyeditors
Melissa A. Dobson, Gretchen Gordon

Proofreaders
Susan Barnett, Jane Spear

Permission Researchers
Aja Perales, Sue Rudolph, Tim Sisler, Julie Van Pelt

Indexer
Katharyn Dunham

Compositor
Tracey L. Matthews

Publisher
Frank Menchaca

© 2008 The Gale Group

Thomson and Star Logo are trademarks and Gale and Charles Scribner's Sons are trademarks used herein under license.

For more information, contact
Thomson Gale
27500 Drake Rd.
Farmington Hills, MI 48331-3535
Or you can visit our Internet site at
http://www.gale.com

ALL RIGHTS RESERVED
No part of this work covered by the copyright hereon may be reproduced or used in any form or by any means—graphic, electronic, or mechanical, including photocopying, recording, taping, Web distribution, or information storage retrieval systems—without the written permission of the publisher.

For permission to use material from this product, submit your request via Web at http://www.gale-edit.com/permissions, or you may download our Permissions Request form and submit your request by fax or mail to:

Permissions Department
Thomson Gale.
27500 Drake Rd.
Farmington Hills, MI 48331-3535
Permissions Hotline:
248 699-8006 or 800 877-4253, ext. 8006
Fax: 248 699-8074 or 800 762-4058

Since this page cannot legibly accommodate all copyright notices, the acknowledgments constitute an extension of the copyright notice.

LIBRARY OF CONGRESS CATALOGING-IN-PUBLICATION DATA

American writers : a collection of literary biographies / Leonard Unger, editor in chief.
  p. cm.
  The 4-vol. main set consists of 97 of the pamphlets originally published as the University of Minnesota pamphlets on American writers; some have been rev. and updated. The supplements cover writers not included in the original series.
  Supplement 2, has editor in chief, A. Walton Litz; Retrospective suppl. 1, c1998, was edited by A. Walton Litz & Molly Weigel; Suppl. 5-7 have as editor-in-chief, Jay Parini.
  Includes bibliographies and index.
  Contents: v. 1. Henry Adams to T.S. Eliot — v. 2. Ralph Waldo Emerson to Carson McCullers — v. 3. Archibald MacLeish to George Santayana — v. 4. Isaac Bashevis Singer to Richard Wright — Supplement[s]: 1, pt. 1. Jane Addams to Sidney Lanier. 1, pt. 2. Vachel Lindsay to Elinor Wylie. 2, pt. 1. W.H. Auden to O. Henry. 2, pt. 2. Robinson Jeffers to Yvor Winters. — 4, pt. 1. Maya Angelou to Linda Hogan. 4, pt. 2. Susan Howe to Gore Vidal — Suppl. 5. Russell Banks to Charles Wright. — Suppl. 6. Don DeLillo to W.D.Snodgrass _ Suppl. 7. Julia Alvarez to Tobias Wolff _ Suppl. 8. T.C. Boyle to August Wilson. _ Suppl. 11 Toni Cade Bambara to Richard Yares.
  ISBN 0-684-19785-5 (set) — ISBN 0-684-13662-7
  1. American literature—History and criticism. 2. American literature—Bio-bibliography. 3. Authors, American—Biography. I. Unger, Leonard. II. Litz, A. Walton. III. Weigel, Molly. IV. Parini, Jay. V. University of Minnesota pamphlets on American writers.

PS129 .A55
810'.9
[B]   73-001759

ISBN-13: 978-0-684-31517-1
ISBN-10: 0-684-31517-3

Printed in the United States of America
10 9 8 7 6 5 4 3 2 1

Acknowledgments

Acknowledgment is gratefully made to those publishers and individuals who have permitted the use of the following material in copyright. Every effort has been made to secure permission to reprint copyrighted material.

MAX APPLE Apple, Max. From *The Oranging of America.* Grossman Publishers, 1976. Copyright © 1974, 1975, 1976 by Max Apple. Used by permission of Viking Penguin, a division of Penguin Group (USA) Inc. and the author. All rights reserved. / Max Apple, From "The Jew as Writer/The Writer as Jew: Reflections on Literature and Identity," in *Writing the Jewish Future,* February 1, 1998. Reproduced by permission of the author. / Liz Rahaim, From "An Interview with Max Apple," in *Kelly Writers House,* spring, 2002. Reproduced by permission of Max Apple.

CHARLES BAXTER Baxter, Charles. From *Chameleon.* New Rivers Press, 1970. Poems Copyright © 1970 by Charles M. Baxter. Reproduced by permission of the author. / Baxter, Charles. From "Hoarfrost," in *Slow Loris Broadsides, Series III.* Slow Loris Press, 1973. Reproduced by permission of the author. / *Poetry,* for "Midwestern Poetics" by Charles Baxter. Reproduced by permission of the author. / *Ploughshares,* v. 25, fall, 1999 for "About Charles Baxter" by Don Lee. Copyright © 1999 by Emerson College. Reproduced by permission of the author. / *Tin House,* v. 2, spring, 2001 for "Interview with Charles Baxter" by Jennifer Levasseur and Kevin Rabalais. Reproduced by permission. / Baxter, Charles. From "The Breath of Life," in *A William Maxwell Portrait: Memories and Appreciations.* Edited by Charles Baxter, Michael Collier, and Edward Hirsch. W. W. Norton, 2004. Copyright © 2004 by Charles Baxter, Michael Collier, and Edward Hirsch. All rights reserved. Used by permission of W. W. Norton & Company, Inc. / *Star Tribune,* July 7, 2006. Copyright © 2006 Star Tribune. All rights reserved. Reproduced with permission of Star Tribune, Minneapolis-St. Paul.

LINDA BIERDS Bierds, Linda. From *First Hand.* G. P. Putnam's Sons, 2004. Copyright © 2004 by Linda Bierds. Used by permission of Marion Wood Books an imprint of G.P. Putnam, a division of Penguin Group (USA) Inc. / Bierds, Linda. From *Flights of the Harvest-Mare.* Ahsahta Press, Boise State University, 1985. Copyright © 1985 by Linda Bierds. Reproduced by permission. / Bierds, Linda. From *The Stillness, The Dancing.* Henry Holt, 1988. Copyright © 1988 by Linda Bierds. All rights reserved. Reproduced by permission of the author. / Bierds, Linda. From *Heart and Perimeter.* Henry Holt, 1991. Copyright © 1991 by Linda Bierds. All rights reserved. Reproduced by permission of the author. / Bierds, Linda. From *The Ghost Trio.* Henry Holt, 1994. Copyright © 1994 by Linda Bierds. All rights reserved. Reproduced by permission of the author. / Bierds, Linda. From *The Profile Makers.* Henry Holt, 1997. Copyright © 1997 by Linda Bierds. All rights reserved. Reproduced by permission of the author. / *Seattle Weekly,* March 25, 1999. Copyright 1999 Stern Publishing, Inc. Reproduced by permission. / Bierds, Linda. From *The Seconds.* G. P. Putnam's Sons, 2001. Copyright © 2001 by Linda Bierds. All rights reserved. Used by permission of Marion Wood Books an imprint of G.P. Putnam, a division of Penguin Group (USA) Inc. / Marshall, Tod. From *Range of the Possible: Conversations with Contemporary Poets.* Eastern Washington University Press, 2002. Copyright © 2002 Eastern Washington University Press. Reproduced by permission. / Bierds, Linda. From *First Hand.* G. P. Putnam's Sons, 2004. Copyright © 2004 by Linda Bierds. Used by permission of Marion Wood Books an imprint of G.P. Putnam, a division of Penguin Group (USA) Inc.

MELVIN BUKIET Melvin Jules Bukiet, "Acceptance speech for Edward Lewis Wallant Prize," 1993. Reproduced by permission of the author. / Excerpts from "The Library of Moloch" in *While the Messiah Tarries.* Copyright © 1995, 1991, 1986 by Melvin Jules Bukiet. Reprinted by permission Harcourt, Inc. This material may not be reproduced in any form or by any means without the prior written permission of the publisher. All rights reserved. / Bukiet, Melvin Jules. From *Nothing Makes You Free: Writings by Descendents of Jewish Holocaust Survivors.* W. W. Norton, 2002. Copyright © 2002 by Melvin Jules Bukiet. All rights reserved. Used by permission of W. W. Norton & Company, Inc.

GUY ENDORE *New York Times,* May 10, 1933. Copyright © 1933 by The New York Times Company. Reproduced by permission.

ANNIE FINCH Finch, Annie. From *The Ghost of Meter.* University of Michigan Press, 1993. Copyright © 1993 by the University of Michigan. All rights reserved. Reproduced by permission. / *Eugene Weekly,* December, 1994. Reproduced by permission. / Finch, Annie. From *Eve.* Story Line Press, 1997. All rights reserved. Reproduced by permission. / *Bloomsbury Review,* spring, 1998 for review of "Eve" by C. L. Rawlins. Reproduced by permission of the author. / Finch, Annie. From "A Carol for Carolyn," in *Carolyn Kizer: Perspectives on Her Life and Work.* Edited by Annie Finch, Johanna Keller & Candace McClelland. CavanKerry Press, 2001. Copyright © 2000 by Annie Finch. Reproduced by permission of Tupelo Press. / *The Sewanee Review,* v. CIX, winter 2001. Copyright © 2001 by The University of the South. Reprinted with permission of the editor. / Finch, Annie. From *Calendars.* Tupelo Press, 2003. Copyright

© 2003 Annie Finch. Reproduced by permission of Tupelo Press. / Finch, Annie. From *Encyclopedia of Scotland*. Salt Publishing, 2004. Copyright © 2004 Annie Finch. Reproduced by permission. / *Blue Mesa Review,* spring, 2005. Reproduced by permission.

HUTCHINS HAPGOOD Hapgood, Hutchins. From *A Victorian in the Modern World*. Harcourt, Brace and Company, 1939. Reproduced by permission of the author. / Theodore Dreiser, "Letter to Hapgood," *Hapgood Family Papers in the Yale Collection of American Literature, Beinecke Rare Book and Manuscript Library, at Yale University,* December 15, 1921. Reproduced by permission of the author. / Rischin, Moses. From an Introduction to *The Spirit of the Ghetto* by Hutchins Hapgood. Edited by Moses Rischin. Cambridge, Mass.: The Belknap Press of Harvard University Press, 1967. Copyright © 1967 by the President and Fellows of Harvard College. All rights reserved. Reproduced by permission of Harvard University Press. / Hutchins Hapgood, "Letter to Fanny Powers Hapgood," *Hapgood Family Papers in the Yale Collection of American Literature, Beinecke Rare Book and Manuscript Library, at Yale University,* May 15, 1898. Reproduced by permission of the author.

DENIS JOHNSON "Vespers", "The Incognito Lounge," from *The Incognito Lounge* by Denis Johnson, © 1974, 1976, 1977, 1978, 1979, 1980, 1981, 1982 by Denis Johnson. Used by permission of Random House, Inc.

BRIGIT PEGEEN KELLY Kelly, Brigit Pegeen. From *To the Place of Trumpets*. Yale University Press, 1988. Copyright © 1988 by Yale University. All rights reserved. Reproduced by permission of the publisher and author. / *Northwest Review,* vol. 25, 1987. Copyright © 1987 by Northwest Review. Reproduced by permission. / *Poetry Northwest,* vol. XXVIII, spring, 1987. Reproduced by permission. / *Ironwood,* vol. 29, 1987. Copyright © 1987 by Ironwood Press. Reproduced by permission of the author and publisher. / Kelly, Brigit Pegeen. From *Song*. BOA Editions, 1995. Copyright © 1995 by Brigit Pegeen Kelly. All rights reserved. Reproduced by permission of BOA Editions, Ltd., www.boaeditions.org. / *Northwest Review,* vol. 31, 1993. Copyright © 1993 by Northwest Review. Reproduced by permission. / *Kenyon Review,* vol. XIII, summer, 1991, for "Dead Doe" by Brigit Pegeen Kelly. Copyright © 1991 by Kenyon College. All rights reserved. Reproduced by permission of BOA Editions, Ltd., www.boaeditions.org. / *Kenyon Review,* vol. XXIII, winter, 2001, for "Windfall" by Brigit Pegeen Kelly. Copyright © 2000 by Kenyon College. All rights reserved. Reproduced by permission of BOA Editions, Ltd., www.boaeditions.org. / *Kenyon Review,* vol. XXIII, winter, 2001, for "Rose of Sharon" by Brigit Pegeen Kelly. Copyright © 2000 by Kenyon College. All rights reserved. Reproduced by permission of BOA Editions, Ltd., www.boaeditions.org. / *The Yale Review,* vol., 79, no. 2, winter, 1990. Copyright © 1990 by Yale University. Reproduced by permission of Blackwell Publishers. / *New England Review,* vol. 14, fall, 1991, for "Silverlake" by Brigit Pegeen Kelly. Copyright © 1991 by Middlebury College Publications. Reproduced by permission of BOA Editions, Ltd. / *Booklist,* v. 91, February 1, 1995. Copyright © 1995 by the American Library Association. Reproduced by permission. / Kelly, Brigit Pegeen. From *The Orchard*. BOA Editions, 2004. Copyright © 2004 by Brigit Pegeen Kelly. All rights reserved. Reproduced by permission of BOA Editions, Ltd., www.boaeditions.org. / *Antioch Review,* v. 62, fall, 2004. Copyright © 2004 by the Antioch Review Inc. Reproduced by permission of the Editors.

MARK JARMAN Jarman, Mark. From *Tonight is the Night of the Prom*. Three Rivers Press, 1974. Copyright © 1974 by Three Rivers Press. Reproduced by permission of the author. / *Field: Contemporary Poetry and Poetics,* no. 15, fall, 1976; no. 24, spring, 1981. Copyright © 1976, 1981 by Oberlin College. Both reproduced by permission. / Jarman, Mark. From *North Sea*. Cleveland State University Poetry Center, 1978. Copyright © 1978 by Mark Jarman. Reproduced by permission. / *The Chowder Review,* no. 13, fall-winter, 1979, for "Address to the Devil," by Mark Jarman. Copyright © 1979. Reproduced by permission of the author. / *Poetry Northwest,* vol., XX, winter, 1979-80. Copyright © 1979 by the University of Washington. Reproduced by permission. / Mark Jarman, *The Rote Walker,* Pittsburgh, PA: Carnegie-Mellon University Press, 1981. Copyright © 1981 Mark Jarman. All rights reserved. Reproduced by permission. / Jarman, Mark. From *Far and Away*. Carnegie-Mellon University Press, 1985. Copyright © 1985 by Mark Jarman. All rights reserved. Reproduced by permission of the author. / Jarman, Mark. From *Black Riviera*. Wesleyan University Press, 1990. Copyright © 1986 by the Mark Jarman. All rights reserved. Reproduced by permission of the publisher and author. / Jarman, Mark. From *Iris*. Story Line Press, 1992. Copyright © 1992 by Mark Jarman. All rights reserved. Reproduced by permission of the author. / Jarman, Mark. From *Questions for Ecclesiastes*. Story Line Press, 1997. Copyright © 1997 by Mark Jarman. All rights reserved. Reproduced by permission of the publisher and author. / Jarman, Mark. From Unholy Sonnets. Story Line Press, 2000. Copyright © 2000 by Mark Jarman. All rights reserved. Reproduced by permission of the author. / *The Hudson Review,* vol. XLVII, no. 3, autumn, 1994. Copyright © 1994 by Mark Jarman. Reprinted by permission from The Hudson Review. / *Denver Quarterly,* vol. 31, no. 2, fall, 1996, for "Unholy Sonnet" by Mark Jarman. Reproduced by permission of the author. / *Slate,* March 11, 2003. Copyright © 2003 Washington Post, Newsweek Interactive Co. LLC. All rights reserved. Distributed by United Feature Syndicate, Inc. Reproduced by permission of the author. / *The Atlantic Monthly,* vol. 283, May, 1999, for "In the Tube" by Mark Jarman. Copyright © 1999, by The Atlantic Monthly Company. All rights reserved. Reproduced by permission of the author. / Jarman, Mark. From *To the Green Man*. Sarabande Books, 2004. Copyright © 2004 by Mark Jarman. All rights reserved. Reproduced by permission of the author. / *Shenandoah,* vol. 47, no. 2, summer, 1997, for "Unholy Sonnet" by Mark Jarman. Copyright © 1997 by Shenandoah. Reproduced by permission of the publisher and author.

DAVID MARKSON Yeats, William Butler. From *The Collected Works of W.B. Yeats, Volume 1: The Poem*. Revised edited by Richard J. Finneran. Copyright © 1940 by Georgie Yeats, copyright renewed 1968 by Bertha Georgie Yeats, Michael Butler Yeats & Anne Yeats. All rights reserved. Reproduced by permission of A. P. Watt Ltd., on behalf of Grainne Yeats, and reprinted with the permission of Scribner, an imprint of Simon & Schuster Adult Publishing Group.

Acknowledgments / vii

WILLARD MOTLEY Motley, Willard. From *Knock on Any Door.* Northern Illinois University Press, 1989. Copyright © 1947 by Willard Motley. Copyright © 1989 by Northern Illinois University Press, renewed copyright © 1975 by Frederica Westbrooke. Reproduced in North America by permission of Penguin Putnam, Inc. Reprinted in the UK by permission of Harold Matson Co., Inc. Used by permission of Dutton Signet, a division of Penguin Group (USA) Inc.

AANNA QUINDLEN Quindlen, Anna. From *Living Out Loud.* Random House, 1988. Copyright © 1988 by Anna Quindlen. All rights reserved. Reproduced by permission of Random House, Inc. / *Commonweal,* v. 121, January 14, 1994. Copyright © 1994 Commonweal Publishing Co., Inc. Reproduced by permission of Commonweal Foundation. / *New York Times Book Review,* September 11, 1994. Copyright © 1994 by The New York Times Company. Reprinted with permission. / *Los Angeles Times,* March 4, 1998 for "From Discord, a Wife Makes a Nice New Life—Too Nice" by Susie Linfield. All rights reserved. Reproduced by permission. / *America,* v. 178, June 6, 1998. Copyright © 1998 www.americamagazine.org. All rights reserved. Reproduced by permission of America Press. For subscription information, visit www.americamagazine.org. / *Kirkus Reviews,* v. LXXII, February 1, 2004. Copyright © 2004 by The Kirkus Service, Inc. All rights reserved. Reproduced by permission of the publisher, Kirkus Reviews and Kirkus Associates, L.P.

SCOTT TUROW *Bookpage,* www.bookpage.com/ 9910bp/scott_turow.html, October, 1999. Copyright © 1999 ProMotion, Inc. Reproduced by permission.

WILLIAM VOLLMANN *Review of Contemporary Fiction,* v. 13, summer, 1993. Copyright © 1993 The Review of Contemporary Fiction. Reproduced by permission.

FRANZ WRIGHT Wright, Franz. From *God's Silence.* Alfred A. Knopf, 2006. Copyright © 2006 by Franz Wright. All rights reserved. Reproduced by permission of Alfred A. Knopf, a division of Random House, Inc. / Bly, Robert. From *The Light Around the Body.* Harper & Row Publishers, 1967. Copyright © 1959, 1960, 1961, 1962, 1963, 1964, 1965, 1966, 1967 by Robert Bly. All rights reserved. Reprinted by permission of HarperCollins Publishers Inc. / Wright, James. From *Shall We Gather at the River.* Wesleyan University Press, 1968. Copyright © 1960, 1961, 1962, 1963, 1964, 1965, 1966, 1967, 1968 by James Wright. Reproduced by permission of Wesleyan University Press. www.wesleyan.edu/wespress / Bukowski, Charles. From *The Last Night of the Earth Poems.* Black Sparrow Press, 1992. Copyright © 1992 by Charles Bukowski. All rights reserved. Reprinted by permission of HarperCollins Publishers Inc. / / *Field: Contemporary Poetry and Poetics,* no. 70, spring, 2004. Copyright © 2004 by Oberlin College. Reproduced by permission. / *Field: Contemporary Poetry and Poetics,* no. 72, spring, 2005. Copyright © 2005 by Oberlin College. Reproduced by permission. / *Oberlin Review,* v. 129, March 16, 2001. Reproduced by permission.

List of Subjects

Introduction	xi	BRIGIT PEGEEN KELLY Kim Bridgford	123
List of Contributors	xiii	DAVID MARKSON Peter Dempsey	135
MAX APPLE Sanford Pinsker	1	WILLARD MOTLEY James A. Lewin	149
CHARLES BAXTER Jen Hirt	13	ANNA QUINDLEN Angela Garcia	165
LINDA BIERDS Judith Kitchen	25	JOANNA SCOTT D. Quentin Miller	183
MELVIN BUKIET Sanford Pinsker	39	GAY TALESE Susan Butterworth	199
GUY ENDORE Robert Niemi	53	SCOTT TUROW Nancy L. Bunge	213
ANNIE FINCH Claire Keyes	69	WILLIAM T. VOLLMANN J. M. Tyree	225
M. F. K. FISHER Susan Butterworth	81	FRANZ WRIGHT Ernest Hilbert	239
HUTCHINS HAPGOOD Robert M. Dowling	95	*Cumulative Index*	251
MARK JARMAN Kim Bridgford	109		

Introduction

In one of his most provocative but interesting statements, D.H. Lawrence wrote: "Never trust the artist. Trust the tale." He continued on the subject further, talking about critics in relation to the work of art: "The proper function of a critic is to save the tale from the artist who created it." The essays in this seventeenth supplement of *American Writers* are focused with considerable intensity on the language of some our most contemporary writers, as well as a couple from the past. In each case they are written by critics put a great deal of trust in the tale (or poem, or play) itself, trusting the work of art more than the artist, with the aim of bringing the reader closer to the text at hand.

American Writers had its origin in a series of monographs that appeared between 1959 and 1972. The *Minnesota Pamphlets on American Writers* were incisively written and informative, treating ninety-seven American writers in a format and style that attracted a devoted following of readers. The series proved invaluable to a generation of students and teachers, who could depend on these reliable and interesting critiques of major figures. The idea of reprinting these essays occurred to Charles Scribner, Jr., an innovative publisher during the middle decades of the twentieth century. The series appeared in four volumes entitled *American Writers: A Collection of Literary Biographies* (1974).

Since then, seventeen supplements have appeared, treating well over two hundred American writers: poets, novelists, playwrights, essayists, critics and autobiographers. The idea has been consistent with the original series: to provide clear, informative essays aimed at the general reader. These essays often rise to a high level of craft and critical vision, but they are meant to introduce a writer of some importance in the history of American literature, and to provide a sense of the scope and nature of the career under review. A certain amount of biographical and historical context is also offered, giving a context for the work itself. It will, I think, be easier to "trust the tale," as Lawrence puts it, if one at least knows something of the teller of that tale. Poems and novels do not, indeed, come out of nowhere.

The authors of these critical articles are mostly teachers, scholars, and writers. Most have published articles (even books) in their field. As anyone glancing through this volume will see, they are held to the highest standards of good writing and sound scholarship. The essays each conclude with a select bibliography intended to direct the reading of those who want to pursue the subject further.

Supplement XVII focuses intensely on contemporary writers, many of whom have received little sustained attention from critics. Fiction writers Max Apple, Charles Baxter, Joanna Scott, Scott Turow, William T. Vollmann, David Markson, Melvin Bukiet, and Anna Quindlen have written substantial novels. They have been written about in the review pages of newspapers and magazines, and their fiction has acquired a following of enthusiastic readers, but their work has yet to attract significant scholarship. The same may be said for poets like Linda Bierds Mark Jarman, Brigit Pegeen Kelly Franz Wright, Annie Finch, each of whom has published a good deal but remain in mid-career. Their work is only beginning to attract substantial criticism, and these essay may be thought of as early attempts to take the measure of their writing lives.

Gay Talese is included here for the first time, and he represents one of the most important voices in nonfiction writing over the past half a century, being one of the founders of what is called the New Journalism. A few writers here may be considered authors from the near past: Guy Endore, Willard Motley, and M. F. K. Fisher wrote mainly in the postwar era, and it is time their lives and works received the kind of attention we devote to them in this supplement. Hutchins Hapgood is the only writer here with his roots in the deeper past—he was born in the nineteenth century—and we are pleased to have an essay on this influential journalist and autobiographer, a major figure in the early twentieth century.

The critics who contributed to this collection represent a catholic range of backgrounds and critical approaches, although the baseline for inclusion was that each essay should be accessible to the non-specialist reader or beginning student, the reader that Virginia Woolf once addressed as the Common Reader. The creation of culture involves the continuous reassessment of interesting and important texts produced by its writers, and my belief is that this supplement performs a useful service here, providing substantial introductions to American writers who matter, and it will assist readers in the difficult but rewarding work of learning to trust the tale.

——*JAY PARINI*

Contributors

Kim Bridgford. Professor of English at Fairfield University and editor of *Dogwood* and *Mezzo Cammin*. Her books include *Undone*, nominated for the Pulitzer Prize; *Instead of Maps*, nominated for the Poets’ Prize; and *In the Extreme: Sonnets about World Records*, winner of the Donald Justice Prize. She is currently working on a three-book poetry/photography project with visual artist Jo Yarrington, focusing on journey and sacred space in Iceland, Venezuela, and Bhutan. MARK JARMAN, BRIGIT PEGEEN KELLY

Nancy Bunge. Professor at Michigan State University. She has held Fulbright lectureships at the University of Vienna, the Free University of Brussels, the University of Ghent and the University of Siegen. She is the interviewer and editor of *Master Class: Lessons from Leading Writers* (University of Iowa Press, 2005) and *Finding the Words: Conversations with Writers who Teach* (Swallow/Ohio University Press, 1985), the editor of *Conversations with Clarence Major* (University Press of Mississippi, 2002), and the author of *Nathaniel Hawthorne: a Study of the Short Fiction* (Macmillan, 1991). SCOTT TUROW

Susan Butterworth. is a professor of English at Salem State College in Salem, Massachusetts. She enjoys teaching and reading aloud and has a commitment to keeping the written and spoken word alive. She has written numerous reference articles and is also a freelance writer with an interest in creative nonfiction, travel and memoir writing, and literary biography. M. F. K. FISHER

Peter Dempsey. Teaches American literature at the University of Sunderland in the United Kingdom. He has published essays on a number of American authors and has recently co-edited a collection of essays on Richard Powers. DAVID MARKSON

Robert M. Dowling. Assistant Professor of English at Central Connecticut State University. His first book is entitled *Slumming in New York: From the Waterfront to Mythic Harlem* (Illinois 2007), which includes a chapter on Hutchins Hapgood and Abraham Cahan. He is currently working on his next book project *Critical Companion to Eugene O'Neill: A Literary Reference to His Life and Work* (Facts on File, 2008) and co-editing a critical anthology on O'Neill's early bohemian and radical influences. HUTCHINS HAPGOOD

Angela Garcia. Received her MA in English from UC Davis. She has worked as a teacher for five years in San Francisco, and more recently, for two years in San Salvador, El Salvador. She now lives in Corvallis, Oregon with her husband and two young children, where she plans to pursue a Master's in Library Science. ANNA QUINDLEN **Ernest Hilbert.** Editor of the *Contemporary Poetry Review*. He was educated at Oxford University, where he was the editor of the *Oxford Quarterly*. He later became the poetry editor for Random House's magazine Bold Type in New York and edited the magazine *nowCulture* for several years. He publishes reviews in the *New York Sun* and essays for the Academy of American Poets, and his poetry has appeared in *The New Republic*, *New Criterion*, and *The American Scholar*. He composes libretti and song texts for the composers Daniel Felsenfeld and Mark Adamo. He also works as an antiquarian book dealer and lives in Philadelphia with his fiancée, an archaeologist. FRANZ WRIGHT

Jen Hirt. teaches English at Harrisburg Area Community College in Pennsylvania. She also writes reference articles, has done editing work, and writes creative nonfiction. She grew up in Valley City, Ohio, and holds degrees from

Hiram College, Iowa State University, and the University of Idaho. Learn more about her work at her website, www.geocities.com/jenszijen. CHARLES BAXTER

Claire Keyes. Professor Emerita at Salem State College in Massachusetts, where she served as English Department Chair and Coordinator of the Graduate English Programs. She is the author of *The Aesthetics of Power: The Poetry of Adrienne Rich*. Her reviews and poems have appeared in *Calyx*, *ReviewRevue*, *The Women's Review of Books*, *Spoon River Poetry Review*, *Zone 3*, *The Georgia Review*, and *Blueline*, among others. Her chapbook, *Rising and Falling*, won the Foothills Poetry Competition. She lives in Marblehead, Massachusetts with her husband, Jay Moore. ANNIE FINCH

Judith Kitchen. Lives in Port Townsend, WA, and teaches in the Rainier Writing Workshop low-residency MFA at Pacific Lutheran University in Tacoma, WA. She is the author of two books of essays, a novel, a collection of poems, and a critical study of William Stafford. She regularly reviews poetry for *The Georgia Review* where she serves as an Advisory and Contributing Editor. LINDA BIERDS

James A. Lewin. 1967 graduate of Oberlin College, received his M.A. in Creative Writing in 1985 and his Ph.D. in English Literature in 1994 from the University of Illinois at Chicago. Since 1995, he has been on the faculty at Shepherd University in Shepherdstown, West Virginia. His academic publications include articles on Shakespeare as well as previous American Writers entries on Nelson Algren and Isaac Bashevis Singer. He lives in Frederick, Maryland with his wife, Carolyn Snyder, and their cat Simone. WILLARD MOTLEY

D. Quentin Miller. Associate Professor of English at Suffolk University in Boston. His books include *Prose and Cons* (2005), *The Generation of Ideas* (2005), *John Updike and the Cold War* (2001), and *Re-Viewing James Baldwin* (2000). His essays have appeared in journals such as *American Literature*, *Legacy*, and *American Literary Realism*, and he is one of the editors of the *Heath Anthology of American Literature*. JOANNA SCOTT

Robert Niemi. Associate Professor of English and Coordinator of the American Studies Program at St. Michael's College. Colchester, VT. Niemi has published extensively on American literary and cultural topics. His books are: *The Bibliography of Weldon Kees* (Parrish House, 1997); *Russell Banks* (Simon & Schuster/Macmillan, 1997); *History in the Media: Film and Televsion* (ABC-Clio, 2006). GUY ENDORE

Sanford Pinsker. Shadek Professor of Humanities at Franklin and Marshall College. He is the author of numerous books, articles, and reviews, including *The Schlemiel as Metaphor* and *Bearing the Bad News*. He has been named the U.S. literature editor for a revised version of the *Encyclopedia Judaica*. MAX APPLE, MELVIN BUKIET **J. M. Tyree.** Wallace Stegner Fellow in Fiction at Stanford University. His book, *BFI Film Classics: The Big Lebowski* (co-author, Ben Walters), is forthcoming from the British Film Institute, and will be distributed in the USA by the University of California Press. WILLIAM T. VOLLMANN

SUPPLEMENT XVII
Max Apple to Franz Wright

MAX APPLE
(1941—)

Sanford Pinsker

IN AN ESSAY titled "The Jew as Writer/The Writer as Jew: Reflections on Literature and Identity," Max Apple insists that "identity is someone's else's problem." For him, all the fuss about defining a "Jewish identity" or, worse, who is, or is not, a "Jewish—American writer" falls on deaf ears. He knows who he is, and always has. But he quickly adds there are in fact two persons hidden inside his undersized body: there is Max and there is his alter ego, Mottele—two distinctly different cultural types sharing the same skin.

So far as Apple is concerned, one could think of these inner personalities as "the American and the Jew" but none of these categories precisely fit: "Mottele," Apple opines in the same essay, who "knows almost nothing about the real America of politics and economics, is uncritically in love with Yankee ways, while Max [his English—speaking double] who does understand America is a European socialist." Furthermore, Apple informs us that "Mottele isn't really a citizen," but, rather, the son of immigrants: "He grew up among Yiddish—speaking parents and grandparents in a place called Michigan that he thinks is a province of Lithuania."

Apple's bifurcated sensibility is best revealed in the warmhearted way he sees the world. Max knows full well that there is something empty at the core of American popular culture, and that wheeler—dealers such as Walt Disney or Howard Johnson are, at bottom, no better than the Wizard of Oz when the curtain is yanked aside and he is revealed as a colossal fake. Mottele looks at America with the oversized eyes of the immigrant: everything he sees, the more dazzling the better, is filled with wonderment and opportunity.

Dr. Samuel Johnson, the eighteenth—century critic and consummate tastemaker, dismissed the metaphysical poets of the seventeenth century as people who yoked together heterogeneous elements "by violence." He was referring to such poets as John Donne and Andrew Marvell, who often built their metaphorical constructions by juxtaposing radically different images and forcing them to share floor space in the same stanza. Apple does much the same thing when he surveys his fictional landscape, with one eye belonging to Max while the other is that of Mottele.

The result, often as odd as it is hilarious, keeps Apple from joining those who produce their satire "straight," with no chasers or mediating elements; and despite many academic critics who once regularly compared Apple's buoyant style with such postmodernist experimenters as John Barth, Donald Barthelme, and Robert Coover, the plain truth is that Apple never joined the fashionable movement to push the envelope's edges by exploring the fictionality of fiction—that is, writing about writing—and, as a result, his work is as readable today as it was three decades ago. The same cannot be said of other writers who themselves got "lost in the funhouse" (a Barth title) of their own making.

Apple's fiction is built on three supporting columns: a high regard for "story" largely inherited from his grandparents; a reverence for "language" (in Apple's words, it was his "fascination with the English language that made me a writer"); and a deep belief in the power of the imagination. For Apple, popular culture, looked at from oblique angles and always with a warm—ish regard for its cultural power, triggered his quirky, entirely lovable imagination.

Compared with writers of similar reputation, Apple's oeuvre from the years 1976–2006 seems decidedly limited: two novels, two collections of short stories, and two memoirs, but if he had only published his 1976 short story collection *The Oranging of America* and his 1994 memoir

1

MAX APPLE

Roommates, his place in contemporary American letters would be assured. During the middle 1970s, *The Oranging of America* replaced J. D. Salinger's 1951 novel, *The Catcher in the Rye,* in its ubiquity on college campuses and in student backpacks. For one thing, most students identified with Salinger's hypersensitive protagonist, Holden Caulfield, while they were in high school (it became a de facto, and underground, rite of passage); for another, the war in Vietnam had concluded, however ambivalently, and Apple's stories were a better fit for an age that no longer swelled the numbers at antiwar marches. The protest era of the 1960s had frowned on the indulgent distraction of humor; but by the 1970s college students, and general readers as well, were ready to enjoy social satire with more than merely a whiff of humor.

Max Apple was born on 23 October 1941 in Grand Rapids, Michigan, the son of Samuel Apple, a baker, and Betty Goodstein Apple. His memoirs often return to a childhood richer in love—and in the anecdotes of his maternal grandparents, who were Lithuanian Jews—than in money. When Apple was growing up, Grand Rapids had a tiny Jewish population but there is as much truth as there is poetry in Apple's claim that he might as well have been raised in his grandparents' place of origin: Serei, Lithuania, a shtetl (townlet) steeped in Old World customs and manners. To the people of Grand Rapids, he was known as Max; but as the grandchild called "Mottele," he knew every nook, every cranny, every Jewish citizen, in Serei.

Apple did not imagine that he would attend college, much less become a writer and a teacher of creative writing. As he told the interviewer Liz Rahaim, "I grew up in a poor neighborhood in the Midwest, and the idea of being a writer, or of being anything other than a factory worker, didn't occur to most people, nor did it occur to me." Although Apple's imagination did not announce itself during high school, the stories he heard around the kitchen table were piling up inside his unconscious. They would eventually come out years later.

Apple fell in love with written (rather than oral) stories and novels when he attended the University of Michigan. He received his BA degree from the University of Michigan in 1963 and entered a writing program at Stanford the following year but dropped out when his father died. When he returned to the University of Michigan for graduate school, Apple took his grandfather with him and later drew from those experiences in *Roommates.*

The mid-1960s were turbulent times on U.S. college campuses, but during the days in Michigan, Apple's grandfather would often lug a bulky volume of the Talmud to the quad, find a shady spot, and proceed to study. Unfortunately for him, this was also a popular place for Frisbee throwers and other groups of students noisily enjoying themselves. Apple's grandfather would scream at them in Yiddish to be quiet, but they didn't understand nor did they pay much attention to this odd, out-of-place duck. Apple received his PhD in 1970; his grandfather did the best he could to plow through the Talmud.

After a brief stint (1970–1971) as an assistant professor of literature and humanities at Reed College in Portland, Oregon, Apple moved to Rice University in Houston, Texas, where he taught for the next twenty-nine years. Apple rose through the ranks and became a full professor of English in 1980. By all accounts, he was a popular, effective teacher of creative writing.

Many cultural commentators thought of Apple as a "Texas academic," He had no problem with the first adjective but strongly objected to the second. He spent the bulk of his life teaching creative writing (in fall 2001 he became a part-time teacher at the University of Pennsylvania, where his second wife works as an administrator), always insisting that this work is best done by approaching students with the right posture and tone: "When I teach," Apple told Liz Rahaim, "I think it's important to be a friend, an ally to students." But, he quickly added, "The best way that I can be their friend is to help them clean up their style, get rid of what they don't need, and show them, in as kindly a way as possible, a straight path through all this confusion that is in our lives and in our narratives." To know what is necessary for a story and what is merely ballast is crucially important in a genre where every paragraph must pull its weight. Apple is an effective teacher of creative writing not only because he is a friendly, likable person, but because he crafts his own prose with a gift for the operations—cleaning up, and paring down—that make for successful fiction, and he can "coach" undergraduates to learn how to bring such operations to their own work.

THE ORANGING OF AMERICA

The ten short stories contained in Apple's 1976 collection *The Oranging of America, and Other Stories* gave him wide visibility. Early reviewers agreed that he wrote with both precision and charm. With the possible exception of two stories—"Inside Norman Mailer" and "The Yogurt of Vasirin Kefirovsky"—Apple chooses allusions and plot situations with which general readers can readily identify. The stories in *The Oranging of America* follow the motel kingpin Howard Johnson down America's highways, put Apple in the boxing ring with none other than Norman Mailer, give us a black donut-maker's memoir about his early years as President Gerald Ford's closest pal, and revolve around other equally whacky examples of Apple taking his measure of contemporary American culture.

Apple's title story is a (playful) echo of Charles Reich's *The Greening of America* (1970), which was a radical manifesto in the spirit of the LSD guru Timothy Leary's mantra, "turn on, tune in, drop out." Reich's book made the argument that people in their early twenties should consider making sandals in Encino, California, rather than following in Daddy's footsteps to a seat on the stock exchange. Reich's vision of a new, greener America did not take into account, however, that Encino (or anywhere else for that matter) can support only a limited number of sandal makers and that there are plenty of college students (who grew up poor) willing to risk whatever disappointments Reich ticked off in his book to become part of the stock market and its potential for personal wealth.

Apple's "oranging," however, refers to the orange pins that dot the map of the ever-growing Howard Johnson ice cream empire and to the orange roofs of his inns. (At one point, Howard Johnson eateries dominated the turnpike rest stops throughout the United States, and their many flavors of ice cream were a staple of weary highway travelers. This is no longer the case, so at least a portion of the easy cultural recognition Apple counted on may be lost.) "The Oranging of America" gave the raspberry to corporate America-as personified by the ice cream empire that Howard Johnson painstakingly built—but with a lighthearted humor and a refreshing zaniness noticeably absent in the radical reassessments of American culture that were being produced by pinch-faced people like Reich. Part research and part a loosening of the imagination, Apple's stories give us a comic look at the culture's movers and shakers, but it is a look that knows where the warts are and, more important, how to reveal them.

Whatever else Apple's prose might be, it is not cruel. He takes oversized figures down a peg or two, but he does not aim at the jugular or relish the prospect of chopping their heads off. Apple lets his historical figures live and breathe and reveal themselves in small, telling details. "The Oranging of America" opens with sentences that make the virtues of Apple's style clear. Mr. HJ is surrounded by corporate flunkies who hand him reports from food chemists and marketing analysts, but he puts his trust in Otis's ice-cream sensitive tongue. And so it was, because HJ, a man who restricted his own ice-cream eating to vanilla, is also a man who knows instinctively who he can trust, and who he can't.

Howard Johnson triggers Apple's imagination, and in other stories so do Fidel Castro, Albert Einstein, and Norman Mailer. Apple once told a writing class at Oklahoma State that historical figures appeal to him as a writer because they have so much cultural recognition attached to them; using such characters means that there is much that a writer does not have to describe. In "The Oranging of America," Howard Johnson—a cultural figure who became a brand name—is yoked by comic insistence to his secretary, Mildred ("Millie") Bryce. A passionate believer in cryonics, the (pseudo-) science of deep-freezing bodies after death in order that they might be reanimated years in the future, Millie spent her time seeking out the right place to freeze herself; but it was HJ himself who came up with the perfect solution. Freezing is the central metaphor of the story, but the odd juxtaposition, what Apple means by the "imagination," puts a deadly spin on the ice cream flavors that are never far from the inquisitive HJ.

"The Yogurt of Vasirin Kefirovsky" substitutes Albert Einstein for Howard Johnson and, this time, aims its gentle, satiric barbs at science. The story suggests something of the world Apple knew as the child Mottele, but Apple insists that what triggered his imagination in this tale was the fact that Rice University is heavy on the sciences and that many of his students were biophysicists and biochemists. The result is a complicated story but not one unavailable to those who grew up repeating Einstein's famous formula about mass and energy, even if they didn't understand exactly what squaring c had to do with anything.

The story "Inside Norman Mailer," however, packs so much literary gossip into its paragraphs that readers not intimately familiar with names such as Philip Rahv, Kenneth Burke, or Gore Vidal are likely to feel left out. The setting is a boxing ring in which Apple is pitted against the old warhorse Norman Mailer. Again, Apple's method is juxtaposition; here he takes two utterly different languages and makes them coexist inside the ring ropes:

> For countless hours I have trained before a mirror with his snapshot taped to the middle. I had blown up to poster size that old *Esquire* pose of him in the ring, and I am ready for what I know will be the first real encounter…. I see indifferent eyes and gay youthful glances. Checkbook eyes. Evelyn Wood eyes. Then suddenly he blinks and I have my first triumph. Fear pops out. Plain old-fashioned fear. Not trembling, not panic, just a little fear. And I've found it in the eyes, exactly like the nineteenth-century writers used to before Mailer switched it to the asshole.

One of Mailer's major influences was Ernest Hemingway, who took an enormous pride in the he-mannish and ultracompetitive way he took on the world. Norman Mailer, in his love for boxing as an image and a metaphor, follows in his master's steps. No doubt Apple was familiar with the many photographs of Mailer in the ring, often sparring with fighters who could easily have floored this short-of-stature writer with the small hands. Apple is even shorter than Mailer and he weighs far less, but that's where fantasy comes into play-not as James Thurber did it when he limned the "secret life" of his thoroughly domestic antihero, Walter Mitty, but as Apple explores what might happen if he and Mailer ever met in the ring.

Apple describes his adversary on fight night: "You stand in your corner like Walt Whitman. No electric outlets, cheap cotton YMCA trunks, even your gloves look used." As the author brings his "fight" to its surprising but inevitable conclusion, the problem, Apple tells us, "is as old as realism": "You don't want all the grunts, the shortness of breath, the sound of leather on skin." And if Apple is too busy taking the measure of his opponent, then he advises that "you [the reader] put it in." What Apple does provide, however, are descriptions of the final moments he spends between rounds in Mailer's corner (which much upsets his second, the literary theorist, Richard Poirier), his punch to Mailer's stomach that sends him to the canvas for a ten-count, and Mailer's final words: "I am the Twentieth Century…. Go forth from here toward the east and earn your bread by the sweat of your brow. Never write another line nor raise a fist to any man." And so Apple went forth, "a seer."

No doubt "Inside Norman Mailer" was delicious fun to write; it is certainly delicious fun to read. Some of the other stories in Apple's first collection (for example, "Vegetable Love" or "Gas Stations") are less impressive, but as a whole, *The Oranging of America* introduced a new voice—and a new talent—to American letters.

ZIP

In *Zip: A Novel of the Left and Right*, which appeared in 1978, Apple's infectious style continued to charm readers. Perhaps Apple had set the bar too high with his early stories, and his novel could not meet the challenges of being equally successful; perhaps a larger canvas simply gave Apple organizational trouble. In any case, in *Zip* there are simply too many plots working against, rather than with, each other. Part of the novel was premised on depicting the lovable flop, the beautiful loser, the schlemiel, who was a staple ingredient of Jewish American fiction of the 1950s; another part took the political temperature of the 1960s and 1970s. Both themes were parodied, but the send-ups did not work effectively.

For critics who felt that, unlike short stories, novels should take on larger themes and fulfill larger expectations, *Zip* disappointed in this respect as well. Terence Winch voiced a majority opinion when he argued that Apple was a good writer but "in *Zip* he seems to be taking on too much in too brief a novel. Apple could learn a lesson from Henry James who, it has been said, 'chewed more than he bit off.'" Whatever else *Zip* is, it is not a Jamesian novel—not only because Apple's congenial style does not render consciousness in long, meandering sentences interrupted by a series of sentiments set aside by commas, but also because he cannot resist the zany. Apple's "house of style" is a much more freewheeling place, one where rapid-fire juxtapositions can spoil the solemn coherence of a Jamesian structure.

Writing in the *New York Times*, the reviewer Jerome Charyn argued that *Zip* has more than its fair share of rough edges, especially in terms of plot coherence, but he quickly went on to add perhaps the most important thing a reader can say about a comic novel: "Max Apple makes me laugh." Consider, for example, the fact that the novel's protagonist, Ira Goldstein, is, in Charyn's words, "locked in some autistic daydream. He can take lead from smashed batteries and weigh it on a scale, but do little else: 'It's as if between me and the world there is a sheet of Saran Wrap.'"

Those critics who argue that *Zip* fits into the larger framework of Jewish American fiction, a tradition that includes not only Philip Roth, Bernard Malamud, and Stanley Elkin but also Edward Lewis Wallant and the early Saul Bellow, make a valid point. But the downside of lumping Apple with this already well-defined tradition is that he operates well outside—and beyond—its borders. *Zip* is about certain Jewish families, and about the politics of the 1960s, but most of all, *Zip* is about energy—because that is precisely what "*Zip*" is. Any serious consideration of the morality or immorality of the 1960s, as in *Zip*—says Stevick—must give room to the possibility that amorality was in fact much more significant in achieving the adrenaline rush that is at *Zip*'s center. At one point, for instance, the character Goldstein describes a living room that is a study in radical contradictions. On Debbie Silvers' living room wall is a picture of Ho Chi Minh and napalmed children; on her waterbed Debbie herself sits, incongruously, munching M&Ms and reading *The Structure of Music*. What's wrong with this picture? Everything, which is precisely Apple's point about the excesses, on both the left and right, during the 1960s.

Zip is narrated by the twenty-four-year-old Ira Goldstein, the manager of a middleweight prizefighter named Jesus Martinez (nicknamed "the Crab"), a Marxist Puerto Rican. As the novel unfolds, sports and politics are juxtaposed, each one presumably reinforcing the other. Apple's zany plot (or plots, to be more accurate) eventually takes us to Cuba for the title fight; along the way, there are cameo performances by Jane Fonda, Fidel Castro, and J. Edgar Hoover, as Apple continues to juxtapose real personalities with purely fictional characters.

In *Zip*, Apple fires off a number of well-aimed satiric shots. Unfortunately, they do not add up to a novel.

FREE AGENTS

The twenty stories collected in *Free Agents* (1983) allow Apple to range widely in search of material that is a good fit for his oddball sense of humor. Even in "Eskimo Love," with its odd locale and even odder humor, Apple's wife Debby, who died from multiple sclerosis, is never far away from his paragraphs. She haunts this story as well as others (for example, "Bridging"), as Apple enters the perplexing territory of single parenthood.

There is nothing funny about death (even Apple has wondered, in print, about the phrase "comic death"), but it is also true that humor can be a weapon as well as a shield when life forces us to confront the unsettling dark. Apple's quirky sense of humor has its gentle sides, but it also has an ability to wrap the imagination around terrible events.

Some of the stories look forward to sections of his 1987 novel *The Propheteers* (for example, "Walt and Will," Apple's rumination on the facts—and fiction—of how Disneyland went from dream to reality); some to Jewish-black relations as evidenced in his wealthy Uncle Jake's odd decision to live among his tenants in a poor black neighborhood ("Blood Relatives"); and some to his oddball family history ("The Eighth Day" is probably the funniest circumcision story ever written). "Walt and Will" examines the peculiar use to which Walt Disney put the thoroughly American theme of observing nature closely. In "Blood Relatives," Max is afraid for his uncle's life but he learns, as the story deepens, that the people he thought of simply hustlers as may have other, more charitable dimensions, especially when Uncle Jake is dying.

In "The Eighth Day," Max, encouraged by his girlfriend, a devotee of cutting-edge psychoanalysis, finds himself trying to remember earliest experience. He gives primal therapy his best shot but is stopped, again and again, at the eighth day—when he was ritually circumcised.

Apple's best stories transcend the merely falldown funny (however fall—down funny they in fact are) because the pratfalls and comic takes are part of a larger picture. His earliest stories took a measure of American culture, much as his immigrant grandparents did, but always with a gentle understanding of human foibles; the stories in *Free Agents* do much the same thing.

THE PROPHETEERS

The *New York Times* book critic Michiko Kakutani suggests that Apple's 1987 novel, *The Propheteers,* departs from the familiar contours of literary satire. She pointed to Robert Coover's 1977 novel *The Public Burning* as a perfect example of the no-holds-barred literary furor that a Richard Nixon could ignite. By contrast, the animating impulse in Max Apple's *The Propheteers* is not white-hot rage but, rather, what Kakutani called his capacity for "amused reverence." Mottele is never far away from Max's paragraphs; he is the conscience that keeps his alter ego in check.

For Max/Mottele, the mythic figures most responsible for the contemporary American fast-food landscape are Howard Johnson, C. W. Post, and Walt Disney, men who are visionaries, prophets (of a sort) rather than profiteers. Money alone does not motivate their rise to corporate life. No doubt many would disagree with Apple's charitable assessment, but as he sees it, his propheteers were people who had a dream about what a changed America could look like—and the dream came true. Money beyond their wildest dreams also followed, along with fame and dizzying corporate responsibility. As he weaves the stories of the three cultural figures together, Howard Johnson emerges as the one most willing to give himself over to an instinctual knowledge. Apple reprises many details from his early story "The Oranging of America," where we first met Howard Johnson and the ice cream freezer fitted into his 1964 Cadillac. In the late 1920s, however, HJ was "a young man with a few restaurants and a dream of hospitality." His dream energizes his quest for the perfect sites on which to build his future empire.

By contrast, C. W. Post, the cereal king, is more messianic, and harsher. A devout Nazarite and vegetarian, Post believes in nothing less than "feeding the world" by weaning the world's hungry masses from eating meat to eating something more healthful, and to his mind, more holy: breakfast cereal. Other men would have been content with Post's enormous commercial success, but not Post himself. He began an evangelical mission to remove the images of wine and meat from the world's art. Post was longer on convictions than he was on learning.

MAX APPLE

Walt Disney, the third propheteer, was, in Kakutani's words, a "divine innocent," a man who not only watched the movements of ants when a child but who also dreamed about translating such movements into film. Walt got his wish, but in ways he had not bargained for. Will Disney, his ambitious brother, didn't give a fig about art, other than to be impressed by its worth in hard cash. It is Will who pushes Walt to build the first Disneyland in California and to expand the empire to the swamps of Florida.

The Propheteers brings together Howard Johnson, C. W. Post, and Walt and Will Disney in a complicated plot that sends all the giant dreamers into deep conflict with each other. Will Disney wants to build a second Disneyland in the Florida swamps, on a piece of Orlando real estate where Howard Johnson is likewise dreaming of building a park (his based on nature rather than technology); meanwhile Margery Post, C. W.'s strong-willed daughter, wants the Florida she came to for peace and quiet to remain unspoiled. Adding to Apple's comic complications is the entirely fictional character Bones Jones, a wacky inventor who erroneously believes that the Disney brothers ruined him by destroying his own cartoon creation, Perky Parrot. Sometimes the confrontations that result work effectively, but the character sketches of HJ and the Disney team are more effective in the original short stories than they are in a novel with too much repetition, too much padding, and far too much of the discursive.

ROOMMATES

The Oranging of America includes the odd, memoir—like "Patty-Cake, Patty-Cake...A Memoir." Purportedly a story of Gerald Ford's early friendship with "Sonny Mammy" Williams, a black baker who supplies him with donuts, the fiction is a parody of memoir itself. As witty as it is incisive, the male-bonding tale includes scenes in which "Sonny," the black man, cannot get a haircut cut at the same barbershop as GR. Why so? Because, as the exasperated barber tries to explain, they don't cut "colored hair." GR is furious, and wants to know why these people think Sonny is colored. He never saw him that way.

Much of the memoir is devoted to Sonny's reminiscences of GR, who, we learn near the end of the memoir, is none other than President Gerald R. Ford. Interspersing historical figures among fictional creations is a common thread in Apple's first collection, but with *Roommates: My Grandfather's Story* (1994), he tries his hand at memoir in earnest.

Much had changed in the literary landscape since Apple's early stories, and nothing more so than the tell-all nature of memoir. Tales of how one escaped a probable fate, whether told by blacks trapped in urban ghettoes or housewives suffering (almost) silently in the suburbs, flew off the bookshelves and made their way to the bestseller lists. Afternoon television shows could not get enough of authors who chronicle their misery in lurid detail and then go on to show the audience how they became survivors. Literary culture since the 1970s has been awash in memoirs—some distinguished, many mediocre, and a few built from willful exaggerations and downright lies. Seldom does a week go by without at least one memoir being singled out for commentary in the *New York Times Book Review*. If there was once a time when the average Joe or Jane seriously pondered making good on the proposition that everybody has a novel inside him or her, that person now dreams about turning toward the writing of a memoir. A recent *New Yorker* cartoon gives a fair, if satiric, assessment of the current situation. In it, a boy, probably a fifth or sixth grader, faces the class to read his composition. The caption reads: "Gameboy: The Memoir of an Addict."

Memoir, like any other art, is made from selection, from aesthetic shaping, from knowing how to distinguish the quick of one's life from what is dead. With *Roommates*, Apple entered the fray on just such literary terms. His memoir about his ninety-seven-year-old grandfather coming to share his apartment at the University of Michigan so mixes humor with sadness, a certain amount of exasperation with large measures of love, that the result is far removed from the crop of contemporary memoirs that pile one grief upon another. Apple is a seasoned writer, one who knows that well-crafted scenes will accrete meanings and that the impulse toward treacle must be resisted. The result is crisp, clean prose and a pervasive understatement that nonetheless allows deep sentiment to surface.

Roommates is focused on both Debby, Apple's first wife who died of multiple sclerosis, and Herman (Rocky) Goodstein, Apple's cranky yet lovable grandfather. Rocky had always lived with his grandson: they shared an apartment over the garage when Apple was seven, and when Apple went off to graduate school at the University of Michigan after his father's death, Rocky tagged along.

On one level, the story of Max Apple's relationship with his grandfather might bring to mind Neil Simon's mismatched roommates in *The Odd Couple;* on another, the memoir speaks to the durability of families, despite bouts of what certain psychologists would call "dysfunctional behavior." But in times of great family stress, when his grandson's wife dies young, and horribly, from the ravages of multiple sclerosis, Rocky is there, as solid a "rock" as his nickname implies, helping others to cope and then to survive.

Rocky, a lifelong baker, brings aspects of his trade to his flinty, no-nonsense view of life: "Doughnuts," he pronounces with a certainty that simultaneously charms and annoys. At Ann Arbor, where Rocky is sharing his grandson's graduate school apartment, it does not take him long to interfere with Apple's love life. Debby, a young college radical Max had met at an Eldridge Cleaver rally and brought back to the apartment, meets Rocky under bad circumstances. As she and Apple share a kiss, his ninety-three-year-old roommate suddenly appears, full of fire, brimstone, and kvetching.

It takes the despondent Apple a few days to find Debby and to rekindle the romance Rocky has tried to ruin. The couple continues to date and as their love affair flourishes, the two get married. Rocky, however, refuses to attend the ceremony. In the essential rhythm of the Rocky-Apple relationship, Apple forgives his grandfather. A job at Rice University takes the new couple to Houston, where Apple's mother joins them—and later, so does Rocky himself.

Thus far, *Roommates* sounds like a thrice-told tale of smothering Jewish families, rebellious Jewish sons, and the tensions that naturally result. But *Roommates* is not Philip Roth's *Portnoy's Complaint* (1969) or the dozens of imitators that followed. Rather, *Roommates* adds layers of family tragedy to the story of Rocky and his long-suffering, deeply loving, grandson. When Debby's condition worsens, the illness takes a predictable, entirely understandable toll on Apple's two children, Jessica and Sam. Memoirs that make their way by limning such scenes in ham-fisted, purple prose cannot match the effect that Apple produces more economically and more powerfully. One day Apple discovers Jessica, age eight, throwing stones with all the force her small body can muster.

Apple's clear, simple prose, his ability to pare away the unnecessary and to focus on the essential—and to do both with utter honesty—is the foundation of his ability to produce both fiction and nonfiction that is eminently readable. (Curiously, "nonfiction" has become a slippery term, especially as applied to the memoir; to feed the reading public's appetite for the sensational, writers have sometimes felt at liberty to add material more invented than real. But although Apple is an inventive writer of fiction, in this relatively quiet memoir of his grandfather the truth proves more affecting than anything Apple could "make up.") As it turns out, Sam Apple became a first-rate nonfiction writer, whose first book, *Schlepping Through the Alps* (2005), was published to acclaim.

Roommates soon joined *The Oranging of America* as a favorite Apple book, but when Rocky's story appeared in a film adaptation in 1995, many fans were disappointed. In the Max Apple–Stephen Metcalfe screenplay, Rocky, played by Peter Falk, was transmogrified from a Lithuanian Jew into a Polish Catholic. Falk turned in a masterly performance as the curmudgeonly Rocky, but the film, unlike the book, was often strained and unconvincing. Apple received scores of letters from Jewish Americans disappointed by the film version of *Roommates*. In

MAX APPLE

"The Jew as Writer/The Writer as Jew," Apple presents a typical complaint: "So, if you weren't ashamed for the *Reader's Digest*," a Brooklyn rabbi asks, "why were you ashamed for the movies?" The reply from Max Apple is eloquent: "There is no shame," he writes to the rabbi,

> in imagining what it's like to be someone else. That's what I do for a living. The world is full of writers writing about characters like themselves—lawyers writing about lawyers, alcoholics about alcoholics, Jews about Jews. There's no danger that this will come to an end. Our likenesses will always be among us. The writer's job is to make you believe a character is real, not Jewish. This is called "verisimilitude," and it evokes empathy, the attempt to put yourself in someone else's skin.... This is what writing is all about and in order to do it, the writer must be free to imagine anything, even a non-Jewish version of himself and his grandfather.

Apple's alter ego, Mottele, however, responds to such criticism more bluntly. "Dear Rabbi," he writes, "Business is business. The movie people wanted goyim. They thought that would sell more tickets...If they had left us alone, we could have made a nice Jewish picture." Both letters are torn up, Apple says, and the rabbi is still waiting for a reply.

Apple had already experienced the dust a film can kick up, after writing the screenplay for a 1994 film, *The Air Up There,* which features a frustrated college coach who goes to Africa in search of tall young man who can learn how to dunk. He finds a six-foot-nine candidate who ultimately makes it big on American basketball courts. A sportswriter took offense from a line in the film's press kit, which quotes Apple, a five-foot-four white writer, as saying that he liked to imagine himself as a tall black power forward. Like some Jewish Americans who raised objections to the screenplay for *Roommates,* the sportswriter could not imagine Apple imagining himself as a black basketball player, and he deeply resented the attempt. Only Apple's first screenplay, the mediocre 1981 action comedy *Smokey Bites the Dust,* which contained enough car chase scenes to entertain and turn a profit, embroiled Apple in no controversies whatsoever.

I LOVE GOOTIE

I Love Gootie: My Grandmother's Story (1995), introduces us to the warm and interesting character of Apple's grandmother; small wonder that he loves her. If Gootie was not, now or then, what one would consider a "beauty," she told beautiful stories: she created a "bubble" for her grandson, Mottele. Never comfortable in America, Gootie wears clothing in varying shades of gray, dispenses home remedies for colds, bits of wisdom for spiritual troubles, and old stories about her life in Lithuania that, over time, evolve into new ones. Apple learned a great deal at his grandmother's knee but nothing more important than what he assimilated about the art of telling a story.

I Love Gootie is in fact built on a structure of one anecdote after another. Given the warm-hearted way that Gootie triumphs over the challenges of American culture (she is a portrait of anti-assimilation), one is reminded of Leo Rosten's irascible night-school student, Hyman Kaplan, who cleverly rules the roost in tales collected in 1937 as *The Education of H*y*m*a*n K*a*p*l*a*n*. As quick-witted as he is unflappable, Mr. Kaplan turns the tables on his exasperated instructor, no matter what the lesson in English might be.

Warm accounts of growing up in an immigrant household are hardly limited to Jewish Americans. Hearty perennials such as Betty Smith's *A Tree Grows in Brooklyn* (1943) or Kathryn Forbes's *Mama's Bank Account* (1943) make clear the intricate ways that adults hide strapped circumstances from their children. However different they may be in ethnic particulars, the youngsters these books describe know what it is like to grow up loved, protected, and cared for. Even if there is no actual money in Mama's bank account, that hard fact need not matter as the family learns to pull together. The same thing is true on the streets of Betty Smith's Brooklyn—and in the Goodstein household in Grand Rapids, Michigan.

Despite any comparison to Leo Rosten's passive-aggressive Hyman Kaplan, Gootie is not likely to show up in an English-as-a-second-language class; Yiddish is sufficient for her needs, which are entirely circumscribed by the four walls of the Goodstein home. But this does not mean she is a shrinking violet. Far from it. Gootie can explain anything.

Gootie is as feisty as she is tenderhearted. Ever suspicious of non-Jews and ever on her guard against what she regards as unwanted intrusions by American culture, Gootie can be her husband's sharpest critic and his best friend, and she is surely the best grandmother the imaginative Max Apple can imagine; but she does not fill up the pages with the same fierce intensity as does her husband, Rocky. There comes a point when her Old World wisdom, dispensed around the kitchen table turns both predictable and tiresome.

Apple's memoirs are a welcome counterbalance to the themes of "mommy dearest" (and, yes, even "grandma dearest") that are so common in the genre, because it successfully argues that real people can be as capable of love as they are of wickedness. And, more important, that the past cannot only be recaptured but also that it can be passed on to a grandchild.

Selected Bibliography

WORKS OF MAX APPLE

NOVELS AND SHORT STORY COLLECTIONS
The Oranging of America, and Other Stories. New York: Grossman, 1976.
Zip: A Novel of the Left and the Right. New York: Viking, 1978.
Free Agents. New York: Harper & Row, 1984.
The Propheteers. New York: Perennial, 1987.

MEMOIRS
Roommates: My Grandfather's Story. New York: Warner, 1994.
I Love Gootie: My Grandmother's Story. New York: Warner, 1998.

SCREENPLAYS
Smokey Bites the Dust. Directed by Charles B. Griffith. New World Pictures, 1981.

The Air Up There. Directed by Paul Michael Glaser. Hollywood Pictures, et. al., 1994.
Roommates. Directed by Peter Yates. Hollywood Pictures, 1995.

OTHER WORK
"The Jew as Writer/The Writer as Jew: Reflections on Literature and Identity." National Foundation for Jewish Culture, *Writing the Jewish Future: A Global Conversation* (http://www2.jewishculture.org/publications/wtjf/publications_wtjf_apple.html).
Mom, the Flag, and Apple Pie: Great American Writers on Great American Things. Editor. Garden City, N.Y.: Doubleday, 1976.

CRITICAL AND BIOGRAPHICAL STUDIES
"Koret Foundation Jewish Book Awards." *Princeton University Library Chronicle* 63, nos. 1–2: 33–39 (2001).
Klinkowitz, Jerome. "Max Apple." In *Contemporary Jewish-American Novelists: A Bio-Critical Sourcebook.* Edited by Joel Shatzky and Michael Taub. Westport, Conn.: Greenwood Press, 1997. Pp. 8–12.
Plymell, Charles. "Max Apple." In *American Short Story Writers Since World War II.* Edited by Patrick Meanor. Detroit: Gale, 1993.
Wilde, Alan. "Irony in the Postmodern Age: Toward a Map of Suspensiveness." *Boundary 2* 9, no. 1: 5–46 (autumn 1980).
———. "Dayanu: Max Apple and the Ethics of Sufficiency." *Contemporary Literature* 26, no. 3: 254–285 (autumn 1985).
———. "Max Apple and the American Nightmare." *Critique* 30, no. 1: 27–47 (fall 1988).

REVIEWS AND INTERVIEWS
Charyn, Jerome. *New York Times,* 16 July 1978.
Delbanco, Nicholas. *New Republic,* 24 June 1978.
Goodman, Andrew. *New York Times,* 19 June 1994. (Review of *Roommates.*)
Goodman, Walter. "I Remember Grandma." *New York Times,* 10 May 1998.
Hundley, Patrick D. "Triggering the Imagination: An Interview with Max Apple." *Southwest Review* 64, no. 3: 230–237 (summer 1979).
Leonard, John. *New York Times,* 17 July 1979.
Mauer, Robert. *New Yorker,* 22 July 1978.
Rahaim, Liz. "An Interview with Writer Max Apple." *Kelly Writers House* (http://www.writing.upenn.edu~wh/news/maxapple.html), spring 2002.

Stevick, Philip. *Nation,* 19–26 August 1978.

Sukenick, Lynn Luria. *Partisan Review* 1980.

Vorda, Allan, ed. "A Continuing Act of Wonder: An Interview with Max Apple." In *Face to Face Interviews with Contemporary Novelists.* Houston, Texas: Rice University Press, 1993.

Wincelberg, Shimon. *New Leader,* 9–23 July 1978.

Winch, Terence. *Washington Post,* 6 August 1978.

CHARLES BAXTER

(1947—)

Jen Hirt

To read the fiction of Charles Baxter is to read about the quiet impulsiveness of Midwesterners. In his fictional town of Five Oaks, Michigan, characters can slip into tiny moments of triumph, but more often they are coping with the consequences of mistakes—their own, their families', or the world's. Mistakes get made, for the most part, when a character does something on impulse, something banal but risky, one step out of the ordinary—the ordinary that blankets the Midwest like corn. As a result, the ordinary stands in stark relief, and Baxter's writing has found a readership with anyone who has taken stock of the irregular in the day-to-day routine. His characters are distinct, yet we recognize ourselves in them. His recurrent setting of Five Oaks helps that identity emerge, in the tradition of Sherwood Anderson's many stories about Winesburg, Ohio.

In an online interview with Jennifer Levasseur and Kevin Rabalais in *Tin House* magazine, Baxter explained what he thinks about his characters' motivations:

> What people want on the surface is often not particularly interesting. What's more telling is the congested subtext, which is what they really want underneath what they say they want. It's congested in the sense that the more you unpack it, the less clear it gets. This can be both comic and tragic: you wanted love, but you got fame; you wanted fame, but you got money.... People don't always get what they want, but what they do get creates the story.

Astute observations such as that have sustained Baxter through eight works of fiction (short story collections, a novella, and novels). Along with appearances in the *Best American Short Stories* series, his work has won Pushcart Prizes and the Award in Literature from the American Academy of Arts and Letters. He has received grants from the National Endowment for the Arts, the Guggenheim Foundation, and the Lila Wallace–Reader's Digest Fund, among others. His novel *The Feast of Love* (2000) was a finalist for the National Book Award.

While noted for his skills and grasp of craft as a writer, he has also earned a reputation as an excellent teacher, due to his nonfiction book *Burning Down the House* (1997), a series of essays on craft that is now a standard requirement in many writing programs. He headed the Master of Fine Arts writing program at the University of Michigan–Ann Arbor, taught in the esteemed Warren Wilson College graduate program, and since 2003 has taught at the University of Minnesota, where he is the Edelstein-Keller Professor in Creative Writing.

WORLD'S END, WORLD'S BEGINNING

Charles Baxter was born on May 13, 1947, in Minneapolis, Minnesota, to Mary (Eaton) Baxter and John T. Baxter. While neither parent was a writer, they nonetheless cultivated a circle of artistic friends. Don Lee, in a profile for *Ploughshares,* noted that Baxter's parents "had befriended many musicians and writers, including Sinclair Lewis...His aunt Helen's confidants were artists and bohemians as well. Brenda Ueland, the author of *If You Want to Write,* was among them." (p. 211)

In 1948 his father died of a heart attack, leaving a widow and three sons. Three years after the loss Mary wedded Loring Staples, Sr. The family shifted economic classes: Baxter's father had been an insurance salesman, but Staples was a well-heeled attorney. The family moved to Staples' idyllic country estate, World's End, in Excelsior, Minnesota. When his two older brothers grew up and left home, Baxter was left with a secluded, rural childhood. In the interview with Lee, Baxter commented that "there often wasn't much for me to do except go out into these woods or fields or watch the sheep or read. I did a great deal of that." (p. 210)

The financial shift Baxter experienced under the income of his stepfather was paired with a shift in attitudes toward intellectual development. While he stayed in touch with Aunt Helen's informal circle of luminaries, he also had an academically intimidating stepfather who appreciated the complicated, transgressive writing of European thinkers. In *Ploughshares,* Lee wrote that

> Loring Staples, a forbidding, erudite man who modeled himself after English country gentlemen, had collected an enormous library of first editions. An entire shelf was occupied by a complete set of Nietzsche, about whom Staples would lecture during dinner.... Staples would also recite, by memory, long swatches of poetry, especially Swinburne. "It was *very* disconcerting to hear him do this," Baxter says. (pp. 210–211)

Reflecting on his early years, Baxter told Lee he realized he had to negotiate two complex worlds. There was the world of his father's and aunt's artist friends who appointed themselves as guardians of Baxter's aesthetic development. Ueland's mentorship, for example, consisted of her telling Baxter he should be ashamed of his lack of plans. In comparison was "this other strange world on the estate that was more like *The Turn of the Screw* than anything else—[the two worlds]were almost mutually exclusive. They must have affected the way I turned out." (p. 212)

COLLEGE YEARS: POETRY AND TEACHING

Baxter began to get a sense of how he would "turn out" when he studied literature as an undergraduate at Macalester College in Saint Paul, Minnesota. Baxter's proximity to another up-and-coming American writer at that time is a popular piece of trivia in his interviews. Baxter went to college with Tim O'Brien, author of the immensely popular Vietnam-era novel *The Things They Carried.* Baxter was the editor of Macalester's literary journal, and O'Brien was on the student council, which meant that Baxter's goals for that year's journal were subject to O'Brien's approval of the journal's budget. It's a story Baxter has recounted with downplayed delight, given the status both writers have since achieved.

After graduating in 1969, Baxter sought a draft deferment by teaching fourth grade in Pinconning, Michigan. He told Lee, "It was kind of an exotic experience for me...and I came to feel it was one of the most important things that happened to me in my life. I was enraged at the [Vietnam] war and was trying not to bring the war into the classroom and sometimes failed." (p. 212) That year set the foundation for a future short story, "Gryphon," that would earn Baxter some of his earliest praise; at the time, however, Baxter considered himself a poet and a literary critic, and he would not switch to short stories until later in the next decade.

New Rivers Press, based in New York and Minnesota and still in business today as one of the oldest small presses in the nation, published Baxter's first book, a poetry chapbook titled *Chameleon,* in 1970. Some of the poems had already been published by respected journals such as *Poetry Northwest* and the *Minnesota Review*. The poems, some illustrated with bleak black-and-white drawings by Baxter's teaching colleague Mary Miner, read like communications from a series of private histories. On his website Baxter calls them "examples of peculiar lyricism." People are struggling to cope, and no one has it as easy as the chameleon who can simply change color to match his background. For the pedestrian masses, it's a life of stark contrast.

In "Do-It-Yourself," Baxter writes:

> Our minds are made up
> By gnats flying in and out
> Of our ears, chewing the old desperate thoughts
> And coughing them up as jingles. Every piano
> is pneumatic and plays these tunes
> just when we need nocturnes.
> (p. 71)

The poem has a tone of desperation and confusion that is emblematic of the collection. Baxter

14

visits and revisits the anxiety of observation, juxtaposing metaphors in a steady tone. A specific touchstone theme is evident: references to ice.

All eight poems in the first section mention ice. Two use ice in the title: "The Idea of Ice" and "The Ice Fisherman." "Release" personifies the ice, describing how it "walks in from shore" to greet a dark bird. Ice is a threat, an intrigue, a punishment, a challenge, and a temptation—all themes that would be echoed and focused in his various short stories and novel chapters that also reference ice. However, the forty-nine poems in *Chameleon,* while competent, garnered little public or critical reaction, and Baxter soon enrolled in graduate school at the State University of New York at Buffalo.

In 1974 he earned a PhD in literature. That same year, New Rivers Press published his second book of poetry, *The South Dakota Guidebook*. The book contains fifty poems and a few old photos provided by the Minnesota Historical Society.

Of all of Baxter's early work sought by collectors, *The South Dakota Guidebook* has the improbable status of being the jackpot find. Of the press run of six hundred copies (four hundred paperbacks, two hundred bound in cloth), Baxter signed and numbered fifteen. The rarity of the book, and the further rarity of the signed editions, has resulted in high prices for the remaining copies. (For example, in September 2006, copies available through online bookstores had price tags starting at $100 and topping out at $400 for a clothbound copy in pristine condition.) The perceived value of *The South Dakota Guidebook* is countered by Baxter, who states on his website that the book contains "wild, misguided stuff. Don't read it."

Are the poems wild and misguided? A successful fiction writer looking back on his early attempts in the genre he eventually abandoned might certainly think so, given the sobering clarity of hindsight. But much like the lyricism in *Chameleon,* the poems in *The South Dakota Guidebook* look at people struggling to figure it all out—the very observation that would guide Baxter in his fiction. In "Hoarfrost," Baxter writes:

Inside the poem,
planes are taking off frantically.
I am worrying about your departures
And what to say of your loss.
(p. 50)

A few stanzas later, he notes:

And so I imagine
hoarfrost, a shadowless glaze
that never arrives or originates anywhere
but is defined
as it falls, as the wind strikes the branches
to which it clings.
until it drops, it is mistaken for snow.
under a glass, it has my face.
(p. 50)

The ice theme enjoys a reprise, and in this early poem Baxter flirts with the image of shadows and the thing defined by its action, themes that will pervade his fiction, most notably his novels *First Light* and *Shadowplay,* whose titles alone emphasize the importance of the shadow/light contrast. If anything, the real value of *The South Dakota Guidebook* is not in its rarity but in how Baxter was starting to make thematic connections that would develop to full force in his fiction.

That Baxter began his creative writing career in one genre and shifted to another is hardly unusual, since it is a typical mode of exploration for talented writers trying to find which genre best suits their goals. For the generation of writers coming of age in the late 1960s to mid-1970s, colleges offered little in the way of creative writing classes, and graduate degrees in creative writing were far from the mainstream. So for many years Baxter had to set aside his creative writing as the thing he would do while not studying literature or teaching.

TAKING UP FICTION

Wayne State University in Detroit, Michigan, hired Baxter as a literature instructor in 1974, the same year he earned his PhD. Two years later he married Martha Ann Hauser, and they had one son, Daniel. In the interview with Lee, Baxter explains that one summer, as he tried to continue with his poetry, he found himself struggling. "It was as if the knowledge of how to do it had somehow left me, and I found myself ill-equipped to write [poetry]. I was becoming more interested in sequences, characters, and characterizations, the rickrack of detail surrounding people." (p. 213)

So in the early 1980s Baxter began writing novels. Initially he wrote and discarded three of them. "They were very abstract, these novels, very schematic, in some sense like bad postmodernism." (p. 213) Two remain completely unpublished, and an excerpt of the third, *In Hibernation,* is on Baxter's Web site. When he was on the verge of abandoning writing altogether, Baxter had the idea to condense his three failed novels into short stories. As Lee writes in his profile:

> He took apart his baroque, experimental style and taught himself craft. In rereading Joyce, Chekhov, O'Connor, Woolf, Porter, and Evan S. Connell, he also learned something else: "that fiction didn't need to be about extraordinary things. It could be about ordinary things, ordinary lives that I spent my adult life observing." It was a long apprenticeship—his friend, the novelist Robert Boswell, has admitted him into a club called The Slow Learners—but Baxter was disciplined and diligent, and eventually his work began receiving attention.
> (p. 214)

The result put him on the path to his first short story collection, *Harmony of the World,* published in 1984. The book won the sixth annual Associated Writing Programs Award Series in Short Fiction, an award that frequently launches successful writing careers.

Harmony of the World contains ten short stories. The title story received the most critical attention—it appeared in *Best American Short Stories 1982* (having first been published by the *Michigan Quarterly Review*) and *The Pushcart Prize VII.* The story is a first-person account of Peter Jenkins, a once-prodigal pianist from a small Ohio town who thinks he is special until he realizes "apparently there were other small towns." The strict practice regime, tough college competition from players with more natural talent, and the intense doubts of his instructor at a prestigious music school send him to the edge of quitting the only thing he has ever been good at. But instead of abandoning music he gets a journalism job covering a small-town orchestra; when Paul Hindemith's *Harmony of the World* symphony makes the year's playlist, Peter takes the opportunity to introduce his readership to the disappointing story behind the symphony. At the same time, he signs on as an accompanist to a second-rate singer, Karen Jensen, and they strike up a relationship, even though he has nothing but contempt for her singing (and can't recognize himself as second-rate).

The story alternates between the relationship and the real story behind Hindemith's symphony, which traces its origins to the scientist Johannes Kepler's 1619 publication *Harmonice Mundi.* The townspeople give a tepid response to the performance (which was how audiences in Hindemith's time reacted), and one man even boos, despite the detailed intellectual article Peter wrote in promotion.

The story comes to a climax when Karen gives her mediocre recital, with Peter accompanying, and afterward he criticizes her mistakes as "a public disgrace." We learn that Hindemith, after the failure of his symphony, had a nervous breakdown. Then Karen tricks Peter into thinking she has hanged herself due to his criticisms. But Peter remains coldly aloof, citing Dante's understanding of "grief without torment" and how it fits into the elusive harmony of life.

The complexity of this story showcases Baxter's budding talent. There is an unreliable, egotistic narrator who gets wrapped up telling the story of Hindemith's story, which was in turn telling Kepler's story. Add to that a failed relationship and a town that supports the arts but doesn't "get" the arts, and you have a heavy, tangled tale that would be a burden in the hands of a novice writer.

"Harmony of the World" isn't the only story dealing with people who have reached an inability to continue functioning in day-to-day activities. In "Weights," a man confronts his midlife crisis with weightlifting, then ends up instigating a randomly violent situation, yet is still able to peacefully crawl into his girlfriend's bed afterward, bloody hands and all. "The Cliff" is Baxter's single magical realism story. An old man with knowledge of a spell for flying initiates a young man, who promptly decides to use flying for his own hedonistic pursuits. "Horace and Margaret's Fifty-second" follows the elderly Margaret through one day of disconcerting senility.

Just one year later, Baxter released his second collection, *Through the Safety Net*. It was another solid set of realistic, character-driven stories, many set in Five Oaks, Michigan. The collection is generally recognized for two things. First, it contains the initial "Saul and Patsy" story, one in a series of stories that would eventually become an entire novel. Second, it contains the story "Gryphon," which is Baxter's most anthologized (and some say most taught) short story. It currently exists in its original story form, as a radio play, and as a made-for-television movie that aired on public television.

"Gryphon" is the short story that came out of Baxter's experiences as an elementary school teacher back in 1970. The story is so successful because of one unusual character whose decisions create a startling situation. It is an example of Baxter's short story strategy distilled and refined and distilled once again. It first appeared in *Epoch* and was later selected for *Best American Short Stories 1986*.

The story is set in Mr. Hibler's fourth-grade classroom in the town of Five Oaks. One day, when Mr. Hibler is sick, a substitute teacher named Miss Ferenczi arrives. She seems suspicious from the outset. Tommy, the first-person narrator, has never seen her before, nor has he seen someone with such odd affectations. She draws a tree on the board to make herself feel better, unfurls a fancy hankie from her ruffled sleeves, uses a made-up word when a student misbehaves, has a warbling voice, and eats figs and raw spinach for lunch.

Things take a turn toward the inexplicable when Miss Ferenczi claims that eleven times six can sometimes equal sixty-eight, not always sixty-six. When the befuddled fourth graders press her for an explanation, she calls the answer a "substitute fact" that is allowable because she is a substitute teacher. After lunch she teaches a fanciful, imaginary unit on the Egyptians, full of substitute facts, including her own visit to the pyramids where, she claimed, she saw a live gryphon.

The narrator remains in doubt but later looks up "gryphon" in the dictionary. Surprised to find an entry at all, he becomes an immediate convert to Miss Ferenczi's world. The next day, Miss Ferenczi abandons Mr. Hibler's lesson plans and simply tells amazing stories all day: meat-eating trees, angels on Earth, perpetual fires under Ohio, and planets controlling behavior. The class loves it. When Mr. Hibler returns, the daily routine feels more drab than ever.

Miss Ferenczi subs again a few months later. This time she brings her tarot cards. When reading for Wayne Razmer, she draws the Death card. The story ends with Wayne telling the principal about the tarot cards and Miss Ferenczi heading home in the middle of the day. Tommy (the narrator) gets in a fight with Wayne when he realizes what Wayne has done. The students get crammed into the other fourth-grade classroom, where they learn facts about insects and are warned about tomorrow's test about the material.

A year after *Through the Safety Net* was published Baxter's talent was evident in the tiers of creative writing, and he was invited to teach in the MFA Program for Writers at Warren Wilson College in North Carolina. It is a unique and selective program that does not require students or instructors to be on campus year-round; instead, the instructors (all successful writers) correspond one-on-one with students throughout the semester, and they meet for ten-day intensive seminars. The appointment at Warren Wilson allowed Baxter to continue his full-time teaching at Wayne State University, and it allowed him to start teaching fiction in a serious capacity.

BECOMING A NOVELIST

Baxter published his first novel, *First Light*, in 1987. In addition to being an all-around good story with interesting characters, the chronology of events is reversed, yet the book is written in present tense. An epigraph from the Danish philosopher Søren Kierkegaard explains the underlying theory at work in *First Light:* "Life can only be understood backwards, but it must be lived forwards."

The novel starts with a Fourth of July celebration. Car salesman Hugh Welch and his family (wife, two daughters) are hosting Hugh's astrophysicist sister, Dorsey, who has arrived with her new husband, Simon (an actor), and her deaf son, Noah. Dorsey's family lives in Buffalo, New York, but Simon is headed to Minneapolis for an acting job, and Dorsey, after dropping him off, will return with Noah to Buffalo, where she teaches at a local college.

The story unfolds, or refolds, from alternating third-person viewpoints: sometimes Hugh, sometimes Dorsey. Bit by backstory bit, we learn why it is they act as they do at the summer celebration that begins the book. Hugh is anxious about the future and has a need for practical hands-on carpentry projects as a way to keep his present under control; Hugh can also cold-read, a parlor game that, when done smoothly, makes him seem like he has psychic-level powers of perception. He loves his wife, but not passionately, so he is having an affair. Dorsey, meanwhile, is estranged from Noah's father, a pedantic old physics professor who tapped into Dorsey's sublime love of astronomy when she was just a student. Simon is a self-absorbed actor who does a ferocious parody of Hugh. Simon hates to follow driving directions, and Hugh despises Simon.

In terms of action, the novel starts with the celebration, then moves back to the road trip Hugh agreed to when Dorsey and her family needed to move from California to New York because Dorsey had to get away from Noah's father, the overbearing professor. It jumps further back to when Hugh found out that his sister was suddenly pregnant, out of wedlock. Then the narrative slips into Dorsey's story, as she recounts her college days as an intelligent woman with an uncanny grasp of astronomy, physics, and science in general. She was obsessed with the origins of the universe, the moment of first light. Hugh, meanwhile, didn't finish college. The final chapters trace their high school days, their childhood, and finally, Dorsey's birth.

Throughout the novel there are references to cosmic origins and light-related phenomena-atomic bomb tests, stars, light shining through photo negatives, fireworks, floodlights, lightning. There are also references to how we struggle with understanding time.

The book, despite being a first novel from a little-known writer, earned notable reviews in major publications such as *Time* and the *New York Times Book Review*. By chance it also got a write-up in the April 1988 issue of *Astronomy* because the astronomer and writer Richard Preston also released a book that year titled *First Light*. Preston's was a nonfiction scientific look at the origins of the universe, while Baxter's was a fictional look at the origins of personality and private worlds. The reviewers were pleased to see complicated scientific theories made accessible by the characters in Baxter's novel.

The year 1989 brought big changes for Baxter. First, he left Wayne State University, where he had taught for fourteen years, to head the MFA program at the University of Michigan at Ann Arbor. Second, two stories that would eventually appear in a future collection won awards: "Westland" was selected for inclusion in *Pushcart Prize XIV* and "Fenstad's Mother" earned Baxter an appearance in *Best American Short Stories 1989*. Third, he published his final book of poetry, *Imaginary Paintings*.

By now Baxter was fully in touch with his status as a Midwest writer, and he deconstructed the region in "Midwest Poetics," a poem that might read as a chorus for his novels:

The unpromising meets the unexotic,
and we are home again, alone,
There is time, and more time
and more time after that to learn to love
the mild gifts—these apple trees these
sparrows—in this marriage with a woman
who knows you, but will not kiss you back.
(pp. 20–21)

Despite Baxter's doubts about the quality of his poetry, *Imaginary Paintings* got the attention of the critic Stephen Burt, who included the work in "Charles Baxter, August Kleinzahler, Adrienne

Rich: Contemporary Stevensians and the Problem of 'Other Lives.'" Burt argued that Baxter was the latest descendant to "add narrative time" to certain Midwest scenes.

Baxter's third collection of short stories, *A Relative Stranger,* was published in 1990. Of the thirteen stories all but one received prior publication in competitive magazines and journals that had a reputation for publishing only the best writers. "Snow," for example, first appeared in *The New Yorker;* "Westland" first found a readership at the *Paris Review;* and "Scissors" was accepted by *Story.* By this time Baxter had solidified himself as a skilled writer of the realistic American short story.

All the stories in *A Relative Stranger* are worth commentary, but a few stand out. "Snow" is the short story whose climax hinges on ice—the way some of Baxter's poems from the 1970s meditated on ice. "Snow" is told from the first person point of view of a twelve-year-old, Russell, who learns from his older brother, Ben, that two nights ago a car fell through the ice on the lake near their house. When Russell expresses doubt the boys head out in Ben's car to take a look for themselves. Ben picks up his girlfriend, Stephanie, who flirts with Russell because she knows he's too young to understand, and the three drive to the edge of the lake. They crawl out to where the ice has created a ridge due to pressure, and yes, there's a two-door Impala down in the frozen depths.

When Ben lies about someone dying in the accident, Stephanie gets mad at him for not being more normal. Russell watches them have a private conversation, which, as a twelve-year-old, he only feels angry about because he doesn't understand love. Then Ben decides he will drive his *own* car across the ice to get home. While Russell and Stephanie wait for Ben to arrive with the car, Stephanie confesses that she doesn't know how to make Ben really notice her. Russell suggests she take off her shoes and socks, which she does. Ben picks her up, but Russell refuses to get in the car, opting for the safer activity of walking home. Later, when he arrives at his house, he stands outside and plunges his bare hand into the snow until it hurts. He wants to grow up, and he sees that risky judgment has something to do with it, but he doesn't know how it all fits together.

"Snow" features Baxter's trademark technique of having characters do something on impulse, and other stories in the collection do the same. In "Westland," the first-person narrator, Warren Banks, crosses paths with a runaway girl, then impulsively asks her to come get a meal with him. The decision leads him to a friendship with the runaway's father, which sets the action for the rest of the story. In "Shelter," Cooper, a baker, struggles with guilt about the local homeless people. He makes an irrational decision to bring home a transient, Billy Bell, who ends up antagonizing Cooper's wife. Later, Cooper's bakery is robbed. In "The Disappeared," a Swedish businessman's goal is to sleep with an American woman. Being naive, he ends up in a dangerous part of town, gets mugged, and goes to the hospital. While lingering outside the nursery window, he gets mistaken for a new father, and, impulsively, he points to a baby and pretends it is his.

The second novel, *Shadow Play,* came out in 1993. Baxter told Paul that it was more challenging to write than *First Light.* Set in the town of Five Oaks, it is mostly the story of Wyatt Palmer, assistant city manager. Wyatt is the hub for a starburst of complicated relationships and decisions that make up the conflicts in the book. Wyatt's father is long dead (much like Baxter's own father), and Wyatt has been left to ponder two things: his father's unfinished project made out of wood and his father's enigmatic Thought Drawer, a collection of musings written on scraps of paper. Wyatt's mother has been institutionalized (she's off-kilter and makes up words); his aunt is deep into an obscure research project because she wants to write her own version of the Bible. Wyatt's old friend Jerry Schwartzwalder has reappeared and wants Wyatt to facilitate approval of a new chemical plant that is shady from the outset but promises to bring jobs. And finally there's Wyatt's cousin Cyril, who's constantly in a cycle of setbacks (such as jail time for drunk driving, or losing his job) and self-improvement (creating his own junk-hauling business).

Wyatt strikes an unethical deal with Schwartzwalder regarding the new chemical plant—Wyatt agrees to overlook possible pollution violations if Schwartzwalder gives Cyril a job. (Many critics have noted that this is basically a deal-with-the-devil scenario.) Later, Cyril gets lung cancer (from the unchecked pollution) and commits suicide by drowning himself—a drowning that Wyatt has to assist in and cover up. At the same time, Wyatt learns some unknown family history; he almost drowned as a child. Wyatt gets Cyril's name as a tattoo, impulsively pretending to be Cyril while at the tattoo parlor. Then he attempts to burn down Schwartzwalder's house but fails. He finally succumbs to a brewing affair with a coworker. He moves his family to Brooklyn and recedes into a deep contemplation.

There is much in *Shadow Play* that doesn't get explained, in particular Wyatt's father's unfinished wooden contraption. Wyatt's mother makes up a word for it, "carthiger," but that seems to make it even more inexplicable.

Shadow Play is, in part, sociopolitical cultural commentary as well. Various reviews noted that the novel uses the consequences of unchecked environmental pollution as a major turning point in the lives of two unsuspecting men.

During the early 1990s Baxter was teaching graduate fiction workshops at Warren Wilson College. He turned many of his lectures into nonfiction essays about topics and challenges faced by most fiction writers. The essays, noted for their understated humor and their clarity, were roundly applauded and quickly incorporated into the required reading lists at many colleges. They first appeared in journals such as the *Gettysburg Review, Harper's,* and *Ploughshares.* Baxter collected them in the book *Burning Down the House,* which was published by Graywolf Press (out of Baxter's college town of Saint Paul, Minnesota) in 1997.

"Against Epiphanies" is one of the better-known essays. Baxter explains the origins of the epiphany in fiction, that sudden moment of revelation or understanding. He gives examples of notable epiphanies and laments their current state of prolific blandness.

While disintegrating the formulaic suggestions of "how to write fiction" manuals, Baxter also offers a theory behind bad fiction. In "Dysfunctional Narratives: Or, 'Mistakes Were Made,'" he notes that his students are creating characters who are passive victims embracing bad consequences. Baxter blamed the Reagan-Bush era for promoting this passivity, and he defines the dysfunction narrative as one we can't leave alone because we can't figure it out, because no one is stepping up to actively accept blame. He cites the making of mistakes as a classically great generator of tension, and tension can drive a short story the way that a description of a passive victim cannot.

If Baxter's characters embody the essence of impulse, they just as frequently end up with their arms full over the consequences of a misstep. In 1997's *Believers,* characters do just that.

Believers contains seven short stories and one novella. The recurring characters Saul and Patsy give another episode in their lives in "Saul and Patsy Are in Labor." They are new parents, but Saul, a high school teacher, is struggling with himself as an authority figure. One of his at-risk students gives him trouble, but Saul, wrapped in his new status of father, continues to believe that he is always doing the right thing until it's almost too late to correct the mistakes he has made.

In "Kiss Away," Jodie thinks she's found the perfect man until a jilted ex-girlfriend contacts her with a claim that the man is abusive. Who will Jodie believe—the boyfriend, who does have some peculiar habits, or the ex-girlfriend, who might be right but might be jealous? The story had already won an O. Henry award in 1995, and many readers cite it as one of the best in the collection.

"Time Exposure," originally titled "Super Night," also won an award, earning Baxter a spot in *Pushcart Prize XX*. It's the story of a lapsed Jehovah's Witness housewife, Irene, whose husband, Walter, comes home from the bar one night with alarming news: their neighbor, Burt Mink, confessed to Walter that he killed a boy.

Irene doubts Walter on two counts: first, he's been drinking; second, Irene and Walter had watched a television murder mystery about a neighbor who killed a boy. She thinks he's confused, but true to the title of the book, she doesn't know what to believe. But Walter is sure, and he takes justice into his own hands. He tinkers with Burt's brakes, resulting in an accident that sends Burt to the hospital with broken bones. While Burt is laid up at home Irene visits him out of sympathy. Earlier she had taken a carefully planned photo of a red maple tree and submitted it to the local television news channel's contest. She sees the photo on Burt's poorly adjusted TV, but it looks purple, not red, and Burt is color-blind anyway. What people choose to see, and what they end up believing, comes to a lyric end as Irene is left still not knowing quite what to believe about her neighbor. Furthermore, since she sees her award-winning photo misrepresented by an aging television set, she questions perception in general.

Finally, the book contains a novella, also titled "Believers." The novella steps away from the Midwest setting of the short stories, and away from the frequent couple-in-conflict setup, and instead delves into how the narrator's father had a brush with fascism in pre–World War II Germany. The narrator tells about his father, a former Catholic priest known as Father Pielke, who befriended a British couple in rural America long before the narrator's birth. They invite Pielke to Germany, with the pretense that he will act as their translator. But when he gets there, Pielke learns that the wife is fluent in German and that they are really there to witness the beginnings of the Holocaust. For the British couple, they are there to cheer it on. It's a sorrowful novella about the lure of charisma and fallen beliefs in God, embodying all the complicated nuances of what it means to believe.

Baxter closed out his prolific decade in 1999 as editor of a nonfiction collection of essays titled *The Business of Memory*. Baxter oversaw the lineup of contributors, who include Patricia Hampl, Richard Bausch, and Lydia Davis. He also wrote the introduction and one essay, "Shame and Forgetting in the Information Age."

The essay begins with a sketch about his forgetful brother, Tom, who had recently died of a heart attack, and moves through other topics such as shame, innocence, and how we handle the glut of information we are supposed to remember. His essay presents a sweeping scope of literary examples of memory, along with interpretations of their meaning.

Take *Burning Down the House* and *The Business of Memory* as a duo, and one thing becomes clear: Baxter is good at explaining writing because he coins smart phrases. Since the late 1990s, what Baxter has to say about writing has emerged as a focal point of study in creative writing classes. In *The Business of Memory* he introduced his idea of "strategic amnesia," which is a sort of subconscious forgetting on purpose. He also uses "dysfunctional narrative," which was originally coined in *Burning Down the House* but applies just as well to memoir. Also in the fiction essays, he introduced "rhyming action" or "narrative echo," "defamiliarization," and "stillness."

LATER WORKS

In 2000, a full thirty years after his first publication, Baxter's next novel, *The Feast of Love,* was a finalist for the National Book Award. The French translation was awarded the Prix St. Valentine.

The Feast of Love is about a circle of acquaintances, all experiencing some form of love: the passion of the young; the stigmatized love of divorced people; the displaced love of estranged parents and children. Each chapter is from the first-person point of view of a different character, and they are often retelling, revising, and countering each other's claims as they justify their lovelorn actions over the course of three sections ("Beginnings," "Middles," and "Ends").

The frame for all these stories is that they are being told to another narrator, one "Charlie Baxter," an insomniac who is trying to write a novel and has taken a late—night break to walk in the park (picture Shakespeare's instigator, Puck). Charlie's neighbor, Bradley, comes up with the "title," the rotating stories, and then sends people

Charlie's way so he can write about them. Bradley, for example, is twice divorced, and one of his ex-wives left him not for a man but for a woman. Bradley owns the coffeehouse where another character, Chloe, works. She and Oscar are the hip youngsters who are consumed with each other's physical passion. Bradley's neighbor, Harry Ginsberg, is a professor who references Søren Kierkegaard as a way to explain much of love's turmoil—and to find resolution regarding his troubled son, Aaron. It was an epigraph from Kierkegaard that opened Baxter's first novel, *First Light,* and another maxim guides this novel: "Søren Kierkagaard maintained that everyone intuits what love is, and yet it cannot be spoken of directly." Bradley's two ex-wives make appearances, as does Oscar's creepy father, known as "the Bat." Their stories cycle through the events of any relationship—misunderstandings, exhilaration, grudges, a pregnancy, and even a death.

The Feast of Love, with its rotating narrators and its story within a story with a character who is, but isn't, the author, could be considered metafiction (fiction that is aware of itself as fiction). However, it enjoyed a popularity and wide readership that metafiction usually does not. Scriptwriters and film studios showed interest. As of September 2006, filming was in progress for a version of *The Feast of Love* based on a screenplay cowritten by Baxter and Allison Burnett. Greg Kinnear had been cast as Bradley and Morgan Freeman as Harry. In a brief interview with Kristen Tillotsson for the *Star Tribune* newspaper in his hometown of Minneapolis, Baxter said that he felt the script was satisfactory, in light of Hollywood's frequently weak revamping of literature. "My novel is not the most cinematic thing in the world, and they've found a way of structuring it. Many different characters all have stories of their own, so the problem is finding the through-lines to connect them all." (p. 2F)

With the critical acclaim of *The Feast of Love* encouraging him, Baxter stepped down from his full-time position in the MFA program at the University of Michigan–Ann Arbor in order to devote more time to writing. He stayed at the university but as an adjunct instructor. He worked on projects as an editor: *Best American New Voices 2001* and *Bringing the Devil to His Knees,* another collection of essays about writing fiction (but unlike *Burning Down the House,* these were written by a roster of contributors.)

In 2003 he left the University of Michigan–Ann Arbor for a position at the University of Minnesota, back in his home state. The university's Edelstein-Keller Professorship in Creative Writing allowed him the flexibility to teach there and travel to other universities as a visiting writer yet still have time to work on his own projects.

Saul and Patsy, his next novel, was published in 2003. It uses the earlier stories about the couple ("Saul and Patsy Are Getting Comfortable in Michigan" from *Through the Safety Net;* "Saul and Patsy Are Pregnant" from *A Relative Stranger;* and "Saul and Patsy Are in Labor" from *Believers*) as a cornerstone for an expanded narrative. These earlier stories are, in fact, obviously recognizable as chapters in the novel.

Saul Bernstein teaches history, journalism, and speech at Five Oaks High School. Patsy Bernstein works at a bank. They've bought a farmhouse and are adjusting to the Midwest (they are from the East Coast). Patsy gets pregnant, and a daughter is born. Meanwhile, a troubled student, Gordy Himmelman, starts to lurk at their farmhouse, where he antagonizes Saul over all sorts of issues, including the fact that Saul is Jewish. Saul and Patsy move, but Gordy follows them and continues to just stand around in their yard, "their local acned Bartleby." Various subplots develop around Saul's mother, Delia, and Saul's brother, Howie, who each have their own peculiarities, but the second part of the novel starts with the sudden suicide of Gordy. He shoots himself under the tree in Saul's front yard. The problem is that "Gordy hadn't been suicidal. Still, he had committed suicide. The logic of this confounded everybody." The remainder of the book deals with the community's reaction to the suicide. A group of teenage misfits creates a spooky and improbable cult following, even creating a shrine to Gordy. Local anti-Semites harass Saul and Patsy. He quits teaching and starts to write an opinion column for the newspaper, which only inflames his opponents. Narratives shift in the end, and chapters are written from the point of view of one of Gordy's classmates and from Saul's mother and brother.

Saul and Patsy received the most reviews of any of Baxter's books, but they were mixed, both in terms of the merits of the novel and the intentions of the novel.

In 2004 Baxter honored one of his main influences, the fiction writer and *New Yorker* editor William Maxwell, with *A William Maxwell Portrait: Memories and Appreciations*. Along with coeditors Michael Collier and Edward Hirsch, Baxter commissioned major American writers to reflect on the impact Maxwell had on fiction. Baxter contributed a chapter titled "The Breath of Life." In it, he analyzes *So Long, See You Tomorrow* as an example of excellent authorial "displacement" in a novel. "This is not just a triumph of writerly technique and emotional balance; the displacement has something to do with the capaciousness—a word he liked—of his imaginative sympathies." (pp. 88–89) Baxter also describes some of his visits with Maxwell, compares him to poet James Wright, and brings up instructive parts of Maxwell's letters. The chapter ends on a note about Maxwell's generosity: "At the end of *So Long, See You Tomorrow*, you feel that you have been given considerably more of what is precious to its author than is often the case in novels of many hundreds of pages. What Maxwell has loved, he gives away in that book. 'If Schubert ever came back to Earth,' he once said to me, 'he could come into my house and take anything.'" (pp. 105–106)

As of September 2006 Baxter was still at the University of Minnesota and teaching as a guest lecturer at a number of universities around the nation. He reportedly had shelved a novel that he had started after the success of *Saul and Patsy*: in July 2006 Kristen Tillotson wrote in the *Star-Tribune* that he was "taking *The Silence Cure* for most of this year, because he needs utter quiet in which to work and wasn't happy with the last novel he wrote (and abandoned before publication)." (p. 2F) He's not afraid to stop a novel that isn't meeting his satisfaction. His long list of successes have proven that he can accomplish his goal in many forms and will likely continue to do so in future novels, essays, and short stories.

Selected Bibliography

WORKS OF CHARLES BAXTER

NOVELS
First Light. New York: Penguin, 1988.
Shadow Play. New York: Norton, 1993.
The Feast of Love. New York: Pantheon, 2000.
Saul and Patsy. New York: Pantheon, 2003.

SHORT STORY COLLECTIONS
Harmony of the World. Columbia: University of Missouri Press, 1984.
Through the Safety Net. New York: Viking, 1985.
A Relative Stranger. New York: Norton, 1990.
Believers. New York: Pantheon, 1997.

POETRY
Chameleon. New York: New Rivers Press, 1970.
The South Dakota Guidebook. New York: New Rivers Press, 1974.
Imaginary Paintings. Latham, New York: Paris Review Editions, 1989.

NONFICTION
"The Drowned Survivor: The Fiction of J. R. Salamanca." *Critique* 19, no. 1:75–89 (1977).
"Nabokov, Idolatry, and the Police State." *Boundary* 5, no. 3:813–828 (spring 1977).
"The Bureau of Missing Persons: Notes on Paul Auster's Fiction." *Review of Contemporary Fiction* 14, no. 1:40–44 (spring 1994).
Burning Down the House: Essays on Fiction. Saint Paul, Minn.: Graywolf Press, 1997.
"Greetings from the Swing States: Along I-35, Even the Cornfields Disagree." *New York Times,* November 1, 2004, p. A25.
"Our Happy Warriors." *New York Times,* August 6, 2006, section 4, p. 13.
www.charlesbaxter.com. (Baxter's website.)

AS EDITOR
The Business of Memory: The Art of Remembering in an Age of Forgetting. Saint Paul, Minn.: Graywolf Press, 1999.

Ploughshares 25, nos. 2–3 (fall 1999). (Guest editor.)

Best New American Voices 2001. New York: Harvest, 2001. (Guest editor.)

Bringing the Devil to His Knees. Ann Arbor: University of Michigan Press, 2001. (With Peter Turchi.)

A William Maxwell Portrait: Memories and Appreciations. New York: Norton, 2004. (With Michael Collier and Edward Hirsh.)

CRITICAL AND BIOGRAPHICAL STUDIES

Brock, James. "Through the Safety Net." *Studies in Short Fiction*. 23, no. 4:459–460 (fall 1986). (Review.)

Burt, Stephen. "Charles Baxter, August Kleinzahler, Adrienne Rich; Contemporary Stevensians and the Problem of 'Other Lives.'" *Wallace Stevens Journal* 24, no. 2:115–134 (fall 2000).

Caesar, Terry. "Knowledge, Home, and Gender in Charles Baxter's Short Fiction." *Revista UNIMAR* 16, no. 1:217–228 (April 1994).

Caldwell, Gail. "Seeking the Light." *Boston Globe,* January 3, 1993, p. A12. (Review of *Shadow Play*.)

———. "These Mortals Be by Tale or History." *Boston Globe,* June 25, 2000, p. M1. (Review of *The Feast of Love*.)

Davis, Robert Murray. "Harmony of the World/Freedom and Other Fictions/The Invention of Flight." *Studies in Short Fiction* 22, no. 3:358–360 (summer 1985). (Review.)

Eakin, Emily. "Quiet Midwest Novelist Is Making a Little Noise." *New York Times,* September 4, 2003, pp. E1, E4.

Ferguson, William. "The Timid Life." *New York Times Book Review,* October 21, 1990, p. 18. (Review of *A Relative Stranger*.)

Fitzgerald, Carol Ann. "Poppy Love: Fathers Find Salvation in Two New Novels." *Gettysburg Review* 17, no. 1: 151–157 (spring 2004). (Review of *Saul and Patsy*.)

Gray, Paul. "Regressions First Light." *Time,* September 14, 1987.

Harmon, Josh. "The Unfamiliar Truth: Three Recent Books of Fiction." *Sewanee Review* 112, no. 3:456–463 (summer 2004). (Review of *Saul and Patsy*.)

Kellman, Steven. "Cardiograms from the Heartland." *Michigan Quarterly Review* 43, no. 3:467–476 (summer 2004). (Review of *Saul and Patsy*.)

Lee, Don. "About Charles Baxter." *Ploughshares* 25, nos. 2–3:210–217 (fall 1999).

Livingood, Jeb. "Charles Baxter: Fiction Resisting the Corilineal." *Hollins Critic* 37, no. 5:1–18 (October 2000).

Marcus, James. "Encore." *Atlantic Monthly,* September 2003, p. 152. (Review of *Saul and Patsy*.)

McGraw, Erin. "Larger Concerns." *Georgia Review* 51, no. 4:782–793 (winter 1997). (Review of *Burning Down the House* and *Believers*.)

Mifflin, Margot. "First Light." *New York Times Book Review,* October 4, 1987, p. 18.

Mitgang, Herbert. "*First Light* Author Begins at the End." *New York Times,* September 7, 1987, p. 14. (Review of *First Light*.)

Prose, Francine. "Midwestern Civ." *New York Times Book Review,* April 6, 1997, section 7, p. 7. (Review of *Believers*.)

Reinsmith, William A. "Gryphon: Taming the Fabulous Beast." *Eureka Studies in Teaching Short Fiction* 5, no. 1:140–146 (fall 2004).

Tillotson, Kristen. "Baxter Novel Headed for the Big Screen." *Star Tribune* (Minneapolis–Saint Paul), July 30, 2006, p. 2F.

Wachtel, Chuck. "Borders and Mirrors." *Nation,* April 7, 1997, pp. 33–36. (Review of *Believers*.)

Weinberger, Eric. "Control Yourself!" *New York Times Book Review,* September 14, 2003, p. 8. (Review of *Saul and Patsy*.)

Winans, Molly. "Bigger Than We Think: The World Revealed in Charles Baxter's Fiction." *Commonweal* 124, no. 19:12–16 (November 7, 1997).

INTERVIEWS

Bowers, James, and Scott Rhoden. "An Interview With Charles Baxter." *Indiana Review* 19, no. 2:64–79 (fall 1997).

Hogan, Ron. "Charles Baxter." *Beatrice* (beatrice.com/interviews/baxter). 1997.

Levasseur, Jennifer, and Kevin Rabalais. "Interview with Charles Baxter." *Tin House* 2, no. 3: (spring 2001). http://tinhouse.com/mag/back_issues/archive/issues/issue_7/baxter.html.

"Meet the Writers: Charles Baxter." (http://www.barnesandnoble.com/writers/writer.asp?z=y&cid=342911). Fall 2003.

Paul, Donald. "Chiaroscuro." *San Francisco Review of Books* 18, no. 2:8–9 (March-April 1993).

"A Son of the Middle Border." *Michigan Today* (http://www.umich.edu~newsinfo/MT/97/Spr97/mta7s97.html). Spring 1997.

FILMS AND DRAMATIC READINGS BASED ON THE WORKS OF CHARLES BAXTER

"Gryphon." Television screenplay by Manuel Arce and Carl Haber. Directed by Mark Cullingham. Wonderworks, 1990.

"Gryphon." Radio reading on WBEZ Chicago. Read by Scott Parkinson. Directed by Abigail Deser. Part of the *Stories on Stage* series. Originally broadcast November 9, 2002.

The Feast of Love. Screenplay by Charles Baxter and Allison Burnett. Directed by Robert Benton. Forthcoming in 2007.

LINDA BIERDS
(1945—)

Judith Kitchen

FOR OVER THIRTY years Bierds has been assembling a poetry scrapbook, photocopying poems she especially likes and collecting them under one cover. There, Thomas Wyatt flirts with Amy Clampitt and poets speak to each other across the ages in odd juxtapositions. Bierds herself rarely looks at more than one poem at a time, choosing each for singular reasons, studying each for what it reveals on its own terms. "The only commonality they share is the consciousness that selected them," she stated in an interview with Tod Marshall published in 2002, and then added wryly, "At nineteen, in love with lost romance, I'm sure I was drawn to those naked feet stalking in Wyatt's chamber. At fifty-plus, I'm drawn to the metrical reversal in that second line!" (p. 19)

Her use of the scrapbook speaks to her own working methods as well. Bierds rarely works on more than one poem at a time; she writes not in drafts but line by line, never moving on until she has completed the lines to her satisfaction, two or three lines per day until the poem is finally realized. She emphasized this process in her interview with Marshall: "I have an absolute fear of letting a poem close, even by draft, before its time…. When I have the first two lines, I have a distant, preverbal shadow of the rest of the poem; I feel it there, an entity beyond language." (p. 27)

LIFE

Shortly after her birth in Wilmington, Delaware, On April 20, 1945, Bierds's father, an airline executive with Alaska Airlines, moved the family to Anchorage, Alaska, where she spent her formative years. She ascribes much of her attention to image to the changing quality of light (the short days of winter, the peculiar brightness and length of the summer evenings) that made up her first impressions of the world. Add to that physical geography the emotional geography of a family for whom silence was the norm and you have someone removed from family narrative, attuned to nuance. In addition, an early diagnosis of degenerative myopia meant that, from girlhood on, she understood her vision would slowly fade. The confluence of these forces has made her keenly aware of the ineffable; her struggle to discover pattern or to articulate an intuitive sense of order may come, in part, from such emphasis on the solitary and the ephemeral.

Memory, for Bierds, is often hazy and insubstantial; she is more likely to recall the "feel" of a place or event than to re-experience its details or chronology. She attributes this in some measure to the lack of "story" in her childhood. This is a possible reason for the dearth of autobiography in her poems, though she also claims that she had so worked over her psyche in therapy sessions that she had no further interest in the self. An equally valid explanation might be that Bierds quite simply elects to retain some privacy, and she relies on her forays into science and history to yield a more comprehensive sense of discovery.

When she was seven-years-old the family moved to Seattle, where Linda and her brother attended public schools. She became the first member of her family to receive a university education, earning both her BA (1969) and MA (1971) degrees in English, with a concentration on fiction writing, from the University of Washington. For nine years after her graduation Bierds worked as an editor for Credit Northwest Corporation in Seattle and as a Washington State Poet in the Schools, and it was during that time that she refined her craft and began publishing poems in a series of prestigious small literary magazines. In the ensuing years her work has appeared in a cross section of the nation's most influential literary journals, including over twenty publications in *The New Yorker*.

In 1982 Bierds's first collection—a thirty-page chapbook of poetry, *Snaring the Flightless Birds*—was published by Allegany Mountain Press in Olean, New York. At around the same time, she became a part-time information specialist at the University of Washington Women's Information Center. In 1989 she began to teach as a part-time lecturer in the university's English Department. Following her initial chapbook, in approximately three-year intervals, she has published seven full-length collections; in addition, she has been awarded numerous prizes and fellowships, including four Pushcart Prizes, fellowships from the National Endowment for the Arts, the Ingram Merrill Foundation, the Guggenheim Foundation, the Wolfers-O'Neill Foundation, and, in 1998, the John D. and Catherine T. MacArthur Foundation. That same year she received the Washington State Governor's Writers Award and a PEN Center USA West Poetry Award. In 1996 she became an associate professor at the University of Washington and was rapidly promoted to professor in 1998, holding the named chair of Lockwood Professor in the Humanities from 2003 to 2006. But prized among her many honors are the three times she received the Special Recognition for Teaching Award from the English Department, an indication of her dedication to her students and their individual endeavors.

In her interview with Tod Marshall, Bierds stated her poetic objectives. "I share Richard Wilbur's feelings about poetry: 'The poem is an effort to express a knowledge imperfectly felt, to articulate relationships not quite seen, to make or discover some pattern in the world. It is a conflict with disorder.' And when it's done well, it takes us to a place that is perfectly unseen or unseen perfectly." (p. 19) She went on to elaborate: "But the ordering of chaos isn't isolated to the physical making of the poem for me—it's also the subject of many of my poems. And the perfectly unseen is always preceded by the precisely seen, by my dependence on the visual image. I'm certain, in thinking more about my scrapbook poems, a commonality shared by the majority would be the luminosity of their visual images." (p. 19)

FLIGHTS OF THE HARVEST-MARE *AND* THE STILLNESS, THE DANCING

The epigraph for Bierds's first full-length book, *Flights of the Harvest-Mare* (1985), is taken from Sir James George Frazer's *The Golden Bough:* "I am not one, as you think, but two." If there is something to "get," she all but announces, it will be multifaceted, complex, sparked by more than one way of seeing.

True, *Flights of the Harvest-Mare* does not delve into the autobiographical material so common to many first books of poetry. In a collection filled with the lives of others—from fur traders to an ancient Zuni potter to a farmer on the Great Plains to nineteenth-century painters and scientists—even the occasional poem about her mother or her father might be considered to be imagined, invoked as representative of an emotional state, illustrative rather than literal. However, in some way we do come to know the poet—or what the poet finds of interest, which is as valid a way of knowing someone as knowing intimate details and personal psychology.

The poems in this introductory collection ask more questions than they answer; they focus not so much on active transformation as on moments of conversion—places where one thing simply, even quietly, becomes another. Sometimes this happens in the imagery itself, or in its repetition, as in "Zuni Potter: Drawing the Heartline," where the reader is taken into the process:

Coil to coil, paddle to anvil,
the bowl on her palm-skin blossoms,
the bowl on her lap
blossoms, the lap blossoms
in its biscuit of bones.
  (p. 23)

Bowl and lap become indivisible, fused by their shared shape and the repetition of "blossom," before they fall back to their separate entities—clay and bone.

At other times the poet's imaginative entry into the life of another, her attention to imagined detail, allows her to revive a time and a place—and therefore a *context*—for discovery. Perhaps most representative is the poem entitled "In Prague, in Montmarte" where we watch Eduard Adolf Strasburger and Walther Flemming as they first see chromosomes through a microscope and wonder at the suggestions of genetics, while Edgar Degas, in France, is putting the finishing touches on a painting, stepping back to see the dancers come into focus. His "yes" of recognition speaks simultaneously for the scientists in Prague, speaks across centuries to clarify that instant of perception.

Often the reader is invited to participate in the poem's inherent dualities as a not-quite-dispassionate onlooker pulled inexorably into the scene, stepping in and out of the time of the poem. For example, at the conclusion of "Elegy for 41 Whales Beached in Florence, Oregon, June 1979," the reader is both in the scene and of it, participant and whale. Then, with its quick shift of tense, its short statement of fact, the poem consigns them to their fate.

A second book allows for a more thorough assessment of the first, and the publication of *The Stillness, the Dancing* in 1988 revealed the extent to which the earlier publication had been the work of a fully mature poet, already caught up in what would be her lifelong quest to bring order out of chaos, already working with what can now be seen to be her characteristic stanzaic structure, her attention to nuance in repetition, her keen reproduction of detail. It also reinforced Bierds' absorption with duality, this time pairing motion with potential, consequence with source. Once again the poet enters history, this time at moments of convergence. The title poem enacts a moment in a Federico Fellini film when the actors were reenacting their own filming; the poem's focus is on the congruence of imagery in the fan of intertwined bones of a mother and child who died during childbirth seen from the window of a passing train and the fanned tail of the peacock who inadvertently wandered onto the movie's set, displaying his ecstasy of color in a reversal that startles the reader/observer much as it must have quickened the pulse of the poet who perceived the likeness. Death and life hold the same shape.

Over and over, Bierds discovers such congruencies, but the reader does not become lulled into acceptance; instead, each poem brings its own surprise, triggered by images that pay such attention to historical detail that they seem to swim into view like recovered items from the hulls of shipwrecks, reminding us of the specificity of other times and places. "The Claude Glass: 1890" reminds us that discovery comes from within the ordinary: "The world swirls on its axis, science / blooms, cream is dipped from saucers / with knuckles of ginger-cake." (p. 34) Thus the reader is taken into underground mines, Victorian parlors, ships' galleys, Conestoga wagons, each rendered with the precision of memory, locked in its sounds ("the snap / and whisper of cards") and its sensations ("a certain musk-brush of velvet"). As a result, we fully grasp how the Horse Latitudes received their name as, under stilled sails, twenty horses are sent to their deaths:

There is shouting, the command of gunfire,
black hooves clacking past a gap in the railing,
then stroking, mid-air, even before
the bodies submerge,
surface to become their own pure symbols:
chaos and instinct.
(p. 9)

An epigraph from Captain Matthew Baird in 1750 reminds us that this scene—so fully realized in its combination of stasis and motion—is grounded in historical fact. Then the imagination fills in the gaps; the sailors return to the hold, to the odor of horses and the memory of fields, a felt sense of horses pressing against the emptiness as though their absence were a paddock to contain the "perfect silence." (p. 10)

The concept of perfection—an underlying order that momentarily emerges from chaos—haunts these poems as they dissect the moments of their being, their "small, individual teeth." In "The Anatomy Lesson of Dr. Nicholaas Tulp, Amsterdam, 1632," just as Rembrandt watches the anatomy lesson, we watch Rembrandt watching; we hear the sputter of wagon wheels and feel the cold settle into the room as he readies his canvas:

there will be umber
and madder root, yellow ochre, bone-black,
the scorch of sulfur, from
the oils of walnut and linseed—all things of the earth—
that forearm, that perfect ear.
 (p. 59)

The poem stops there at the cusp, wedding stasis with action, teetering on the knife edge of Rembrandt's notion that the painting might be able to capture the unruliness of life even as it holds it, motionless and perfected.

A similar moment happens in "Stradivari" as the artisan senses the potential in the wood and hears his dead son's voice emanating from the human figures ("pale ear with its mussel-shell of blood") of the violins. In his grief, he is already aware of, and aspiring to, the moment when the wood will return to "simple wood, / the sound, just sound." In this instance Bierds relies on our knowledge of perfected sound to peel it back to its inception.

Bierds adopts the sensibility of historical figures but she does not pretend to speak *as* those personages, or even *for* them; instead she fits herself into their circumstance, letting it flow about her as weightlessly as the Aleut vessels of her poem "The Skin-Boats: 1830." The voice of the poems remains remarkably consistent—a narrating observer who speaks in what can only be identified as the poet's voice, carefully reconstructing a time and a place where questions hover. There is no sense of a predetermined conclusion. Bierds builds the moment line by line and image by image to where history is, for want of a better word, "remembered." Yet these moments are not the product of memory as such but a rendition of shared memory, made personal and particular. This treatment of the material is quite unlike the more traditional persona poem, and this binary sensibility is where her poetry is most original.

HEART AND PERIMETER

Linda Bierds's third book, *Heart and Perimeter* (1991), adds to the dualities of its title the concept of interval—the time between the clapper's poised movement and the bell's resonant response. In "Ringing," a child reading about bells hears a sound outside the window—a "tap-scratch" she imagines to be a trapped rabbit, so much so that she almost can't bear to look, but when she does go to the window, she sees her brother with his slingshot pelting the sugar maples.

Heart and Perimeter examines the time between the release and the answering, emphasizing and elongating the indefinable separation between dancer and dance. Feeling the pulse of cause and effect, it becomes the tribute of the held note to the longing that spawned it. In many ways the collection as a whole is a study in correspondence. Its twenty-six poems are linked by an intricate threadwork of image and vocabulary-bells, music, snow, wind, bees—and a succession of verbs unite these images in their instants of lifting, melding, braiding. Individual phrases repeat themselves from poem to poem, call and echo, until the book resonates in a bell of its own making. It culminates with a description of ringing the changes. Within a matrix of slant rhymes delineating its regular five-line stanzas, "The Grandsire Bells" mirrors the permutations of the changes; the five bell ringers come face to face with five miners and they peal out a sound whose resultant absence resounds in the morning air.

Mining the past as in her earlier books, Bierds looks to such figures as Meriwether Lewis, Wilbur Wright, and Robert Schumann to probe the heart of aspiration, and she creates others—the boy who sketches John James Audubon's borders, the men who built the tunnel beneath the Thames in a version of Edmond Halley's complicated diving bell, the trio in the underwater capsule retrieving items from the *Titanic,* the white bears of Leo Tolstoy's imagination—to skirt the edges of a mirroring desire. Thus, for example, the men in the capsule, manipulating their mechanical joystick to pick through the wreckage, do not turn into the three men of the painting by James Abbott McNeill Whistler that frames the poem but function instead as a kind of ghostly reflection—and the painting reminds us that there was a real man who lifted his brush to the canvas. So too the notations for the gridwork of Shaker dances remind us of the extinct dancers.

To the sounding note of the past, however, Bierds adds flickering tones of the present so that, in "April," the crow looks down at the plowed fields to see the emphasized contour of the land as fingerprint patterns. Throughout the book, intimations of the present are superimposed on the past, exposing it to the X-ray film or sonar blip that will reveal its interior spaces.

These inner lives are given to us sometimes in third person as though watching a character on a screen, sometimes in a first-person accounting that takes on the trappings of individuality, but always with the tracking consciousness of the poet as an accompanying presence, allowing her characters to arrive at moments of deep awareness. It seems accurate to say that she chooses to dramatize instances of receptivity—the moment when the concept slips into being. Here, for example, the young woman of "In the Beeyard" steps through snow toward the hives, hears their "deep hummings," and is suddenly transported:

Then salt pillars, headless horsemen
turned white by some stark moonlight.
In a flurry the images reach her,
their speed almost frightening, splendid,
as if the myths and fables of her life are a blizzard
drawn suddenly to her, drawn suddenly visible
through some brief interaction of temperature, light.
   (pp. 21–22)

The reader is invited to participate in the act of imagination. Such words as "flurry" and "blizzard" wed the snow and the bees, conjure the salt and the moonlight. This is the pathway to insight, and intuition is made tangible in the image of the hive, its shape suddenly made visible through its hundreds of living parts.

Bees flit in and out of these pages. The hive with its core of combs, the workers with their singular, obsessive determination, become emblematic as we watch the intricate interconnections of a society in flux. We learn the facts of beekeeping so well that when the swarm appears in other forms, as in "Apisculptures," their transformation to the human shape seems, somehow, expected. The revelation of contemporary knee surgery transports the bee images into the present, fusing image, object, and duration, as everything merges into one.

THE GHOST TRIO *AND* THE PROFILE MAKERS

In her next two books Bierds continued to explore the past for how it might instruct the present. By now she had established what might be termed a "characteristic" poem: taking as its central figure an isolated consciousness from the past, it unfolds as a lyrical narrative of approximately fifty to seventy lines, organized in uneven stanzas, and making use of counterpoint and enjambment to heighten the narrative flow. Bierds sees some fundamental metrical differences in the way these voices are presented. As she noted in the interview with Tod Marshall in the summer of 2001, "When I use the third person point of view, iambs predominate. The voice within my persona poems is more malleable with the cadences of anapest and dactyl. Everyone argues that the rhythm of familiar speech is iambic. Evidently not for my characters." (p. 27)

This type of poem posed particular problems, however: how to make the information accessible in order to avoid charges of deliberate obscurity and, at the same time, how to move the poem beyond mere biography. Bierds decided against relying on footnotes, choosing to imbed the information in the poem with carefully orchestrated descriptive detail so that the reader can infer what is needed through context and connotation. Further, she made use of an associative vocabulary and a consistent inquisitive tone that allowed her to step seamlessly in and out of other lives and other times.

Bierds conveys that distance with such precision that intimacy is inevitable, but both *The Ghost Trio* (1994) and *The Profile Makers* (1997) introduce a new element: they are conceived as unified statements that center around an idea—what might be thought of as conceptual metaphor. The working method of these poems is a kind of triangulation—past, present, and circumstance—so that the metaphor communicates in two directions at once and the reader is forced to read both forward and backward.

In *The Ghost Trio,* Bierds amasses detail, exploring the interrelationships of three central characters as they lead, inevitably, toward a culminating figure in history. The "ghost trio" comprises Erasmus Darwin (grandfather of Charles Darwin), Josiah Wedgwood (founder of the famous English pottery works), and James Whitfield (an eighteenth-century miner, hired to mine coal for the kilns), whose lives are connected through friendship, marriage, and economics. The figures beget the concept, and the originating trio expands to encompass the lineage of the Darwin and Wedgwood families and a long line of miners down the centuries.

Each of the three men is given his own first-person moment and these are then joined through image and metaphor. For example, each man, in his own way, goes into the ground. Through a series of associative moves and linked images, the child Erasmus imagines a pond in winter as some "strange heaven" the stilled fish will rise to when it thaws; Whitfield describes surfacing from the mines, coming up through icicles in the drift tunnels; Josiah Wedgwood comes out of drugged surgery to see the world shatter in a burst of light.

Because Charles Darwin is such a significant historical figure, the poems all point to his theories, even as they are not "about" him. In fact, Bierds deflects our attention away from his scientific achievement, as in "Hunter," where the young boy's mother has just recently died. Inside, his father begins telling a story, perhaps about Beethoven, then the drowning of an uncle, and the boy watches the candle flame flicker until it resembles the red coats of hunters and he can hear the baying of the distant hounds, a ghost music that takes him farther and farther away from—and into—his loss. He cannot distinguish grief from the story of grief, so seamlessly does one evolve into the other.

Bierds follows this extended "family" in a similar way until the images haunt the poems across time and circumstance; thus she chronicles the plight of miners over centuries, coming eventually to the loss of twenty-six miners in Nova Scotia in the early 1990s. Time and earth collapse simultaneously for the lost men while, above, the crickets drone on, their song of life going on heedless of time and human tragedy:

Today. Tomorrow. In that May Nova Scotia darkness
when the earth flared and collapsed.
Before that May. After that darkness.
On the larch bud. On the fire station.
On shale and the grind-steps of magma.
On the gold straining in its seam bed.
On the coal straining. On the twenty-six headlamps
swaying through the drift tunnels.
 (p. 42)

Another element is the appearance of a seemingly more autobiographical "I" who makes the occasional casual appearance, especially in the third section of *The Ghost Trio.* The Northwestern landscape of the Stillaguamish River makes its way into the poems, and the headlamps of miners of an earlier time rise and dip the way the "white stomachs" of the field birds "flash in unison" while the speaker's father, wearing his nitroglycerin patch, watches from his "sunlit chair." Their flashing, in turn, is mirrored in a vivid memory of fish in the seine nets "turning together, flashing / together in the early sun." (p. 46) They rise in the present as a mirror image of the stilled fish in Erasmus Darwin's winter pond:

And although
we knew they traveled to us
by a net of our own making,
still we stood spellbound in their unified light.
 (p. 46)

The patch, recurring in a subsequent poem, creates a contemporary meditation on mortality, spawning recollection of an ancestor who escaped wildfire by lying down in a burned patch of his own making. The fish, recurring in a subsequent poem spoken by the character of Charles Darwin, prefigures the conclusion he has not yet made. As Darwin watches a cormorant catch and release a single fish eight separate times, he considers the fish's survival. With hindsight, the reader witnesses the concept of evolution appear on the horizon.

The Profile Makers reverses the process, starting from one known fact—that some of the glass plate negatives of Mathew Brady's photographs of the Civil War had been used to replace broken greenhouse windows—and extends the concept of the captured image to fashion a broader landscape. Thus the concept begets the figures, and Bierds invents a family posed by one of Brady's aides, interspersing a sequence of seven italicized poems spoken by one of the children (each entitled "Six in All") across the collection. The Civil War is over, the fields returned to stillness, and the photographs in the recycled plates seem incongruous, out of context. The speaker (not identified as male or female) discovers in the greenhouse wall a dead sister's waving fist, a mother's calm profile, and enough memory to elegize their drowned father's unrealized potential. Bierds pays close attention to the qualities of a negative, the ways the reversal of dark and light provokes imagination, and she meticulously reminds us of the lush, fertile greenery that forms a background—and a foreground—for the static images imprisoned in the glass:

Within the glass plate negative, he waits
near summer oaks: coat sharp, shirt sharp, but face
dissolved to clouds. Across the plate's transparent sky
the hothouse air has spawned an emerald scum,
a silken vegetation that spreads
its spidered reach. He stands below, coat sharp,
shirt sharp, his head dissolved to clouds.
It will support him soon, the green.

(p. 6)

This central speaker is surrounded by other figures from the past, especially photographers, and their concerns begin to overlap. In "Balance," L. J. M. Daguerre remembers his boyhood attempts at walking a tightrope, the precipitous falls where a verbal exchange of image predicts his later art:

I would hang inverted as Yesterday—just over
the present, just under the past—
with the flagstones at my back a kind of sky,
and above me, which was now below,
the balcony bottoms. And farther, below, where
the late sky offered its fresh earth,
the rooflines and eaves,
all the doves in their darkening chambers.

(p. 24)

The image of suspension—in water, in air, in time—repeats itself throughout *The Profile Makers*, harking back to the extended interval of the earlier books, demarcating the infinitesimal moves from cause to effect much as the activated series of still shots defines motion pictures.

Further complicating the exchange, a sequence of first-person poems has been shaken loose from any marks that might identify them with a particular person or time in history, almost as though the speaker of the six italicized poems has stepped forth as a representative contemporary speaker. A second invented family (one that lives on a farm with fields bordered by six greenhouses) intertwines with the lived lives—and deaths—of Brady and Thomas Edison and Clover Adams so that the imagined informs the actual. Samuel F. B. Morse speaks for all of them: "Often, I think of our lives / as distinctions, quick breaking-aways. From some vast, celestial streaming / we are particles. The splendid particulars." (p. 45) Like the eerie images that appear and disappear on the greenhouse wall depending on the season or the shift of light, it becomes almost impossible to differentiate the interior from the exterior, the imagined real from the really imagined.

"After–Image" opens with "Three weeks after my father's death," and we might very well be back at the greenhouse, in an image-induced reverie. But the second line—"his surgeons, in pond-green smocks, linger" (p. 61);—hauls us into the twentieth century, when green displaced white for surgeons' coats. But the lingering image is so intense that one senses the poem has stepped completely over the artificial boundaries and become a personal elegy. All its imagery belongs to the Northwest. As its (implied) speaker considers the spawning salmon, she reiterates the grief of an imagined child in an earlier time:

I think I will gather them soon, deep
in the eye, red and red and red,
then turn to the canopy of sky and cedars.
It will support them soon, the green.

(p. 61)

The final line substitutes "them" for the "him" of the earlier poem, but the repeated observation demonstrates how tightly knit the images are in this collection. Such repetitions reinforce the idea that coincidence is an important element in creative insight. When the stars—or the words—are aligned, congruence alerts the mind to possibility.

THE SECONDS *AND* FIRST HAND

As Linda Bierds added a sixth book—and then a seventh—to her list of accomplishments, it became clear that her poetic venture was one ongoing oeuvre. By bringing to vivid life an invented model of the earth peopled by distinctive individuals, she was making a statement about the human condition. However, she had some concerns about the nature of her project. Not only did she have to worry about historical accuracy, but she could be seen to be appropriating the lives of her subjects, twisting them to fit her preconceptions or working them to her own ends. Certainly the narrative devices and the almost palpable details present a fiction as though it were fact, and while Bierds does not pretend to assume her characters' actual voices or circumstance, she does provide a sensibility and a perspective that is uniquely theirs for the duration of the poem. It takes a sensitive reader to understand the symbolic nature of the inquiry.

Bierds is acutely aware of this issue, and it seems increasingly to worry her. In the interview with Tod Marshall, she made a clear distinction between her persona poems and those of Ezra Pound's *Personae*:

> The poems there, like many of Browning's, are ultimately "self"—striving or self—revelatory, either within their contexts or as a result of the act of their composition. Their focus is the self, and their inquiry is primarily psychological; my focus is, quite often, communal—that is, how the individual character is representative of the larger community—and my inquiry is primarily spiritual.
> (p. 21)

Earlier, in 1999, she touched on this concern in a discussion with Bruce Barcott and Adrienne Rich for the *Seattle Weekly*:

> Rich: I've been working more and more with what I think of as a "theater of voices," working away from the restricted "I" poem, the poem that begins and ends at the poet's consciousness. I'm trying to create fictional characters in my poems, go back to historical figures, and try to bring their voices into this theater.
>
> Bierds: I'd like to ask you about this because of how it affects my own work....
>
> Rich: I think I was interested in recuperating these women of the past whose work, at the time I was writing the poems at least, was little known. To imagine myself into the skin of another woman artist. But...it began to seem like something...almost *tricky*. You know what I'm talking about. You've done that kind of thing very, very well.
>
> Bierds: I think the difference is that when I'm speaking as Dorothy Wordsworth or any other person, I'm not doing it in the tradition of the dramatic monologue—to reveal character attributes—but to advance a philosophical or spiritual inquiry.
>
> Rich: That's something I admire about your poetry, you see. You may be feeling it as a defect, but I admire it very much.
>
> Bierds: Thank you. It's a way that I'm able to get outside the self, and be transported, and try to empathize with another. But not to the extent I think that I could claim that person's personality. The context of the individual poem would be far too short to do that. It has to advance a greater vision. And that is a kind of appropriation, and I do find myself [wondering about that] and thinking, *Is that the right thing to do?*

In addition, Bierds has sometimes been accused of making her poems so dense and difficult that they are "exclusionary." Difficult, yes, she admits in the interview with Marshall, but not exclusionary: "[That's] a political phrase, and the rhetoric that surrounds it has elements that are chilling to me.... Art thrives on diversity, not conformity." (p. 24) A more pertinent concern comes from the very strength and consistency of her endeavor. With the accumulation of poems, they can begin to repeat strategies or to sound familiar. Since her voice has been so consistent and her method has been so uniform, that may be a valid complaint, though there is evidence of more formal experimentation in later collections.

Bierds has begun slowly to ring some changes of her own. Most noticeable is even more acute attention to how enjambment functions to interrupt or propel the poem. For the moment, she uses the line break more to enhance the narrative elements of the poem. Further, the intrusion of an "I" who stands in for the poet's self allows the dimensions of the poem to grow ever more complex and interesting as she speaks not only to the past but also to the future.

The Seconds (2001) takes up where *The Profile Makers* leaves off, and indeed it seems as though some of the concerns—and even the imagery—of the previous book are carried over into the new poems. The careful orchestration of concept remains, but Bierds allows herself more flexibility by wedding her inquiry to a particular word—"second"—rather than to the captured images in the greenhouse glass.

Time asserts itself in the opening poem, "Dementia Translucida," in which Philip V of Spain has taken to his bed, surrounded himself with clocks, and does not shake himself from his melancholy until he hears the castrato Farinelli singing an aria outside his window. For the next two years he summoned Farinelli every night to sing to him. The words of the aria wind through the centuries, touching the lives of many characters.

Although all the books deal with this sense of precarious wonder, *The Seconds* embodies it more fully. For instance, Bierds seems more willing to follow the poems' formal challenges and her own experimentation with language to discover, *along with* her characters, what it means to skirt the edges of madness or to wrestle with implications of mortality. Occasionally she experiments with bringing the reader intimately into the poem, as in the final stanza of "Testament: Vermeer in December." Vermeer wills his belongings to his family and, in doing so, imagines his funeral:

And to you, in half-rings around me, your faces
spaced like pearls...imagine that moment
when the ropes are lowered and something begins
on the lit walls, shape over shape. I leave it to you,
that shadowed conjunction of matter and light
that flies, in its fashion, between us.
(p. 19)

With this inclusive gesture, Bierds bequeaths to us her sense of how a poem can arc between writer and reader, offering up something akin to magic.

Throughout, the word "seconds" is sifted through its many definitions. Time ticks on, through the biography of the composer of the aria, through the singing of the last castrato in 1904, through Zelda Fitzgerald listening to the opera and asking her answerless question: "into what shape / will our shapelessness flow?" With an exchange of adjectives, sky and sea become indistinguishable and time brings its radium-blue light into the consciousness of Marie Curie:

When the oriole stops its aria—and the minute—hand
  stalls
between rising and falling—its body withdraws
in an instant of color,
like a scarf snapped back through a wizard's sleeve....
(p. 51)

Curie embodies what unites the disparate characters in *The Seconds*—a quickening urge to investigate. In fact, she senses herself a part of something larger: "I think we are one, harmonious voice, one set // of days circling." (p. 49)

The images feel fresh, as though Bierds intuitively trusts her metaphorical connections. Limes, transported from the greenhouse of the previous book, serve as a metaphor for the osteogenesis imperfecta, or "glass-bone disease," of the young jazz pianist Michel Petrucciani, who died at age thirty-six. To prevent spoilage by frost, water is cast on the trees so that the coating of ice will protect the fruit. The young man identifies—"And how perfect / the brindles of ice, he might say, curved like ribs / to those greening hearts" (p. 37)—then, from his frailty, addresses Fitzgerald's turbulent question:

Imagine how fiercely they dip the cups,
the lift of their arms, the falling,
how the horse's throat—deep, rhythmic sighs,
and the vapory mist of each dipper's breath,
step forth, take their shapes, and are gone.
(p. 37)

A reversal, of sorts, can be found in the book's most arresting image—that of the lifeless weight of a bird falling through the airlessness of the newly invented vacuum tube. A man imagining such a moment would be struck by the absence of movement—"no papery sway, no tumble"—and the poet writing such an imagination is able to bring the bird to life even as she folds it back into the finality of death:

—a movement so still
in its turbulence, he can find in his world no
correspondent: not the wavering journeys of snow
or sound, not the half-steps of dust or moonlight—
and the bird not *beauty*, the movement not *fear*,
although there in the candle's copper light, both
fall equally across his upturned face.
(p. 17)

New to this collection are poems with clearly defined formal strategies. Several poems have regular stanzas, and "Organmeister: Hasse After Marienkirche" plays with terza rima to fashion a nontraditional villanelle. "Grand Forks" recounts the North Dakota flood of 1997 in a modified, slant-rhymed villanelle that is so subtle it almost goes unnoticed. The repetitions here are linguistically induced, and the exploration feels somehow more elastic. With hindsight it becomes clear that already Bierds was moving into the territory of her subsequent volume.

First Hand (2005) opens with a prose description of visiting a biochemistry lab to view, in the microscope's light, the chromosomes of a living cell. The ensuing poems look to those moments at the brink of the discoveries that form the foundation for contemporary exploration: Archimedes, Sir Isaac Newton, Gregor Mendel, Marie Curie, and James D. Watson, along with more obscure scientists, as well as a number of artists and inventors—those whose explorations also realigned our sights. From electricity to moving pictures, from the chiseled stone of Gian Lorenzo Bernini to the chiseled words of John Keats, Bierds looks through all the "if onlys" that lead to new technology, to the ever-increasing rate of change as the cloned lamb (now old hat) leads us back down into the dark world of doubt.

In the articulated facts of their lives, the poet's potent inquiry probes at the roots of their curiosity. The inquisitive voices chime across the centuries; their individual, lonely pursuits fit neatly together as one fact informs another over time and space. The butterflies heard by Bishop Berkeley as "shifting, clicking tines" fall to the forest floor in modern Mexico. In "Ecstasy," the eerie fact that the actress Hedy Lamarr invented a magnetic code for torpedo guidance systems is played against her filmy magnetism on the screen:

Look, she whispered,
there is nothing between us—until nothing
stopped her airy touch, and nothing
stirred, and nothing cast its rhythmic clicks
high in the darkness above them.
(p. 39)

Taking as its representative figure that of the Moravian monk Gregor Mendel (1822–1884), whose experimentation with pea plants led to an understanding of genetic heredity, *First Hand* delves into the twin impulses of science and religion. From matins to vespers, Mendel prays to a God he takes on faith; from morning to evening, he thwarts the natural propagation of the peas (some called it heresy) in order to see behind their mysteries. Bierds captures his voice and his meditative mind so that he emerges wholly human in his complex needs. Nothing—not the abbot tending his sheep, not the cat with its sleep-filled eyes, not the patternless petals spilling on the floor-escapes his notice. One good example is "Spillikins: Gregor Mendel at the Table." The poem—in its mapping of the elaborate spill of the pick-up sticks, in its hesitant, hovering dashes—hints at the helical structure intimated by Mendel's rudimentary experiments:

On the table, a nest of fretted sticks:
trefoil, knife blade, horse head, bell,
snake on a staff, bird on a branch,
miter, bucket-yoke, fork.
And at my elbow, black tea,
the mahogany sheen of contentment.
All afternoon, to train the hand,
I lifted the snake from the branch,
the yoke from the horse,
the bird from the yoke,
each carved bone such weighted weightlessness.
And then, through the window, it came—
for a moment, through the window—
that silence so still it is holy. That stillness

when the world's swirl suddenly stops
and everything—wind and whinny and cough—
is gripped by respite's harmony.
Then the grip loosened
and all down the hillsides the church bells spilled.
And under the bells, the birds,
and under the birds, the metallic chitter
of knife blades, forks,
and I rose
for the body's sustenance.
  (pp. 25–26)

World and representation shimmer in the hologram until, with a flick of the wrist, the world emerges in the vibrant energy of sounds repeated (still/stillness, gripped/grip, hillsides/bells/spilled/bells) and sound itself is sustenance.

More than in her earlier collections, Bierds (in the guise of Mendel) seems willing to follow sound toward meaning. Perhaps because she is sustaining an individual character across a number of poems, she relaxes the content and allows him a kind of linguistic freedom that quickens the ear.

Three-quarters of the way through the book Bierds enters these poems as a speaking persona in her own right, and this changes the equation. Addressing the contemporary concerns raised in her preface, she becomes our representative; we are asked to consider not only past and present but also the future. The poems suddenly have the potential for prediction or, at the very least, forewarning.

Bierds displays the like instrument of her own mind in the measured cadences of the penultimate poem, "Sonnet Crown for Two Voices," a tightly sung descant between herself and Mendel, her century and his, as she comes full circle to the moment in the biochemistry lab where a "gloved guide" reveals to her the microscopic world.

The scientist within me watched the desk
withdraw, and then the scope's glass stage, and then
a pocked, nucleic wall, as down we spun,
the shapes that hold the shapes all slipping back,
peripheral.
  (p. 65)

Speaking first for the self in an almost iambic octet, and then for Mendel in the more closely iambic sestet, each sonnet balances the scales of what is known—the cyclone of 1870, the cyclone-spun chromatin of 2004—against an unknown future. Just as the cyclone gave Mendel a glimpse of symmetries yet to be discovered, Bierds looks deep into the nucleus and senses the ultimate mystery. As she gives Mendel's enduring faith the final word, even the fact of death takes on a kind of incandescence:

Silence, then through the frost of shattered glass
an afterglow arose—or pressed—fully formed
but borderless. As I will be, the swirling world
subtracted from the I of me: wind, chalice,
heartbeat, hand...Weightless, measureless, but beautiful
the glow. How can I express it, my God?
  (p. 67)

For Bierds, the quest is not religious but spiritual in a much broader sense. Twenty years later Bierds is still pushing the poem to the brink of the ineffable, and then beyond. The future takes on significance as new technologies engender new misgivings. Will we respect what is most human in our moments of discovery, or will we evade the ethical questions in our race to further invention?

In the end, the nature of Bierds' inquiry is symbolized by Mendel's realization that steam is what cannot be seen, is only known through the evidence of its condensation. Faith is expressed first in the negative and then, through faith, as the positive of what is yet to be known:

*Not plume. Not plume. Not
shape—Holy Father—but gap.*

"Gap," ultimately, is Linda Bierds' territory. In the book's "epilogue," a collage of detail links Ortelius with Pieter Bruegel the Elder in order to reflect on the first tulips brought from Constantinople to Antwerp with the rising tide of invaders. The poem's final image—the Nuremberg Peace Fair of 1650 where fifteen hundred boys on wooden horses rocked in the square, filling it with color—reveals the subtle moiré patterns of history. With an austere elegance worthy of a mathematician, Linda Bierds communicates her own wonder at the natural design, repeatedly achieving "that sudden click of harmony" where the intellect and the lived fact find congruence.

CONCLUSION

Linda Bierds is not yet at the end of her poetic project, and it is impossible to assess her place in the history of American letters. But it is possible to predict that her poems will continue to insist themselves on readers, somewhat the way Elizabeth Bishop's continue to stir us with their immaculate precisions. Bierds elected not to follow in the confessional strain of most of her peers but instead finds a more sympathetic resonance with the philosophical concerns of the modernists. In her work one finds echoes of Wallace Stevens and Robert Frost, W. B. Yeats and T. S. Eliot, as well as an attention to orchestrated cadence inherited from William Carlos Williams. More, her aesthetic considerations clearly match her description of modernism, found in *Range of the Possible:* a belief "that language could be crafted to produce a poetry whose path-work of lines could lead to the ineffable.... It resulted in, or strove for, a condition of wholeness." (p. 18)

Unless Bierds makes radical changes, one could only expect further incremental adjustments in her basic approach to her craft. This is borne out in two poems that appeared in the September 2006 issue of *Poetry.* More important for her future explorations, "Flight" uses its two regular ten-line stanzas to explore the way an astronaut's body can slowly recover from weightlessness-induced atrophy. The poem opens on the sound of the heart beating and reproduces his seamless devolution toward the embryo and back. The formal constraints of "Flight" appear to give Bierds the freedom to fly. One feels the weighted weightlessness of this poem as it adds to her continuing vision.

Bierds's accomplishment is cumulative; no one poem stands out as fully emblematic; yet in the aggregate she is perhaps poetic proof that ontogeny begets ontology. Within the larger scope of her poetic tapestry she attains the fusion of times she feels in the writing. Individual poems grow organically until they transcend the temporal and the physical; the universe coheres, briefly, in a moment of reflective ecstasy—a rational equivalent of mysticism. And yet it is the act of the mind that creates and offers up the universe.

It is altogether possible that the lack of narrative memory in Linda Bierds's childhood home is poetry's genuine gain. The world of her poems cannot be drawn from vivid personal memory, so she pieces together the puzzle of collective memory, conceiving an invented map of the earth, spinning in actual, tenuous time, filled with human uncertainty and awe. In the end, the world has been her theater, and the set she has designed (with its familiar blue-green glow) is one of intricate wonder and unique perception.

Selected Bibliography

WORKS OF LINDA BIERDS

Poetry Collections

Snaring the Flightless Birds (chapbook). Olean, N.Y.: Allegany Mountain Press, 1982.

Flights of the Harvest-Mare. Boise, Idaho: Ahsahta Press, Boise State University, 1985.

Off the Aleutian Chain (chapbook). Seattle: L'Epervier Press, 1985.

The Stillness, the Dancing. New York: Henry Holt, 1988.

Heart and Perimeter. New York: Henry Holt, 1991.

Companions for the Slow Rowing (chapbook). Seattle: Sea Pen Press & Paper Mill, 1991.

The Ghost Trio. New York: Henry Holt, 1994.

The Profile Makers. New York: Henry Holt, 1997.

The Seconds. New York: Putnam, 2001.

First Hand. New York: Putnam, 2005.

Essays and Anthologized Works

American Alphabets: 25 Contemporary Poets. Edited by David Walker. Oberlin, Ohio: Oberlin College Press, 2006. (Features generous selections of the work of twenty-five poets born since World War II, with thoughtful introductions and annotations.)

"The Journal and the Poem." In *The Writer's Journal: 40 Contemporary Authors and Their Journals.* Edited by Sheila Bender. New York: Delta, 1997.

Poets of the New Century. Edited by Roger Weingarten and Richard Higgerson. Boston: Godine, 2001.

CRITICAL AND BIOGRAPHICAL STUDIES

Baker, David. "Kinds of Knowing: Eric Pankey, Louise Gluck and Linda Bierds." *Kenyon Review* 15, no. 1:184–192 (winter 1993).

Brahic, Beverley Bie. "Linda Bierds: *The Profile Makers* and *The Seconds*." *Borderlands: Texas Poetry Review* 20:92 (spring-summer 2003).

Curdy, Averill. "Reading Guide: Linda Bierds." Poetryfoundation.org (http://www.poetryfoundation.org/features/feature.guidebook.html?id=178020).

Encke, Jeff. "On Linda Bierds: Unwinding the Given." *Octopus Magazine* (http://www.octopusmagazine.com/issue04/html/main.html). Also found at Poets.org/viewmedia.php/prmMID/19302.

Kitchen, Judith. "The Fact of the Room." *Georgia Review* 59, no. 3:672–690 (fall 2005).

"Portraits of the Artist." *Washington Post,* December 22, 1991, p. 11. Veale, Scott. "Captured Images." *New York Times Book Review,* January 4, 1998, p. 16.

Walker, David. "Making History: Linda Bierds, *The Stillness, the Dancing*." *Field* 40:86–93 (spring 1989).

Warn, Emily. "The Immortality We Imagine." *Bloomsbury Review* 7, no. 4:28–29 (July-August 1987).

Wright, Carolyne. "Dream, Desire, Delight: A Review of Recent Poetry." *New England Review/Bread Loaf Quarterly* 12, no. 1:203–207 (winter 1989).

———. "Persona Grata." *Women's Review of Books,* May 1996, 19–20.

INTERVIEWS

Barcott, Bruce. "Poetic Conversation: Adrienne Rich and Linda Bierds Talk Poetry, Persona, and Politics." *Seattle Weekly* (http://www.seattleweekly.com/arts/9912books-barcott.php). March 24, 1999.

Beason, Tyrone. "Poetry in Moments." *Seattle Times: Pacific Northwest Magazine* (http://seattletimes.nwsource.com/pacificnw/2002/0616/cover.html). 2002.

Bradfield, Elizabeth. "Wary Awe." *Anchorage Press* (http://www.anchoragepress.com/archives-2005/featurevol14ed13.shtml). March 31–April 6, 2005.

Marshall, John. "Unassuming Linda Bierds a 'Genius' in Our Midst." *Seattle Post-Intelligencer* (http://seattlepi.nwsource.com/books/bier20.shtml). April 20, 2000.

Marshall, Tod. *Range of the Possible: Conversations with Contemporary Poets.* Spokane: Eastern Washington University Press, 2002. Pp. 16–29.

Slease, Marcus, and Jennifer Whetham. "The Grand Outline: Interview with Linda Bierds." *Bellingham Review* 51:19–24 (fall 2002).

MELVIN JULES BUKIET
(1953—)

Sanford Pinsker

IN HIS INTRODUCTION to the anthology *Scribblers on the Roof: Contemporary American Jewish Fiction* (2006), Melvin Jules Bukiet includes a sentence guaranteed to make readers squirm: "Jews are good at two things: being killed and writing about it." Small wonder that Bukiet is such a controversial figure. Many would insist that the sweep of Jewish history includes much more than oceans of blood and that the contributions Jews have made to Western civilization go far beyond writing about being killed. But Bukiet refuses to deflect attention from the murdered and the murderers. Nor will he engage, even for a moment, in platitudes designed to make Jews feel better about their place in the world. Instead, Bukiet prefers to fashion paragraphs as stark and as uncompromising as possible.

To write as he does about the aftermath of the Holocaust is less a choice than it is the case of an irresistible subject choosing him. As the child of a survivor, a member of what has come to be known as the Second Generation, Bukiet seems more connected with Mitteleurope than with most of contemporary America. He may wear baseball caps and live on Manhattan's Upper West Side, but his imagination is tied to Jewish life in the Old World. Being so deeply tied to a past he did not experience firsthand makes Bukiet an odd sort of "witness," because what he offers up as testimony is not the world of his father but, rather, the world that a child discovers from a father's stories.

Growing up in a family forever scarred by the Holocaust of World War II cannot help but alter one's perceptions. Alan Berger's study of the Second Generation is aptly titled *The Children of Job* (1997), a way of linking the suffering of the war generation with that of the God-tormented Job and of noting the special plight of the Second Generation as youngsters who "both rebel against and identify with their parents' victimization." The "2Gs" differ in terms of how much rebellion, how much identification, is packed into their lives (Bukiet, for example, is longer on identification), but the ambivalence Berger points toward is always hardwired into their genes. This accounts for the fact that so many 2Gs unroll their tensions in memoirs, scholarly studies of survivor trauma, or fiction.

In the introduction to his anthology *Nothing Makes You Free: Writings by Descendants of Jewish Holocaust Survivors* (2002), Bukiet provides an overview that is as accurate as it is unnerving. "What the Second Generation knows better than anyone else is the First Generation," he says. "Other kids' parents didn't have numbers on their arms. Other kids' parents didn't talk about massacres as easily as baseball. Other kids' parents had parents." (p.14) The stark staccato sentences, as confident as they are grimly evocative, identify Bukiet's style as recognizably as a thumbprint. Although he appears to go out of his way to infuriate readers, his agenda includes much more than merely shocking the complacent. Bukiet suggests that feel-good slogans such as the omnipresent "Never again!" buttons; sentimental readings of Anne Frank's iconic *Diary;* or popular films such as Steven Spielberg's Academy Award–winning *Schindler's List* (1993) all become mere bandages that cover wounds in an effort to heal them; by contrast, Bukiet feels that some wounds cannot ever heal, indeed, should not ever heal. Bukiet's fiction and opinion pieces call an appropriately somber attention to the Holocaust; he insists that the stakes are simply too high to have the Holocaust become domesticated, trivialized, and eventually turned into "Holocaust chic."

Bukiet is aware that the popular culture packs an enormous power and that seriousness of the right sort is hard to spread. That is one of the reasons he has tried to bring the best writers of the Second Generation to wide attention. As his introduction to *Nothing Makes You Free* makes clear, dealing with childhoods marked by confusion, trauma, doubt, and words whispered late at night behind thin walls took a wide variety of forms. Not all of those in the Second Generation became writers, but most of them gravitated toward professions that somehow reflect the role that, being children of Holocaust survivors, they feel obliged to play. "So, what do you do with this cosmic responsibility?" Bukiet asks at a later point in his introduction. "You were born in the fifties so you smoked dope and screwed around like everyone else. But your rebellion was pretty halfhearted, because how could you rebel against these people who endured such loss? Compared to them, what did you have to complain about?" (p. 14)

Bukiet may enjoy playing the *enfant terrible* to some extent, especially by crafting paragraphs designed to destabilize the status quo, but the deeper truth is that he realizes, as the sentences quoted above reveal, that he is destined to be a stranger in a strange land, and that his role as a Second Generation writer and as an anthologist and publicist for the wider movement, however much he might "halfheartedly" resist it, is to speak on behalf of those whose suffering will always exceed his. One might not use the word "humble" to describe Bukiet's opinion pieces, his appearances on television shows such as *Charlie Rose*, or his role in the 2005 British Broadcasting Corporation documentary (shown in the United States on the Public Broadcasting System) *Auschwitz: The Nazis and the "Final Solution,"* but the term accurately describes the adult Bukiet as he compares his essentially sheltered life with that of his father's, and even as his theological speculations become as complicated as they are angry.

BIOGRAPHY

Melvin Jules Bukiet was born on September 21, 1953, the son of Joseph Bukiet—a survivor of the concentration camps at Auschwitz, Buchenwald, and finally Theresienstadt—and his American-born wife, Rose Small. Official records list Bukiet's birthplace as Far Rockaway, New York, but in a playful interview Bukiet insists that Far Rockaway, Poland, is more correct—and in a deep, imaginative sense he is right, for Poland, and especially the townlet of Proszowice (near Krakow), where his father was born, became his true home

The stories his father told about Proszowice were infectious, and as Bukiet once told an interviewer, for a long time he thought "the great capitals of the Europe were Rome, Paris, London, and Proszowice." Wonderful, even magical things happened in this place—that is, until it was swallowed up by the Holocaust. Survivors deal with the deaths of parents, uncles and aunts, siblings, and extended family members along a wide continuum of response: some question God but continue to observe His commandments, others abandon the God who presumably abandoned them, while still others find ways to survive their own survival.

Joseph Bukiet belongs to the last group. In America, anything is possible, and his life as a successful house builder in New Jersey (the setting of Melvin Bukiet's first novel, *Sandman's Dust,* 1985) proves the premise, at least in his case. For Joseph Bukiet, the "impossible" had already happened, and no matter how bad things got, nothing could be worse. From such bedrock beliefs, a powerful optimism was born, one that enabled the elder Bukiet to become wealthy beyond his wildest Proszowice dreams.

In telling his stories, despite some dips into the terrible, Bukiet's father transmogrified events, with his upbeat attitude, until they took surprising turns. He had a spectacular sense of humor long before the Holocaust darkened the Polish landscape, but it is also true that, as was the case with many others caught up in the mortal pangs of history, the grim was transformed into the darkly comic, a resource to which those without power have always turned. The humor generated in the concentration camps might embarrass some timid American readers, but a darkly comic vision helped many in the camps to survive. Their humor was both a shield and a weapon—not as life-sustaining perhaps as an extra crust of bread, but invaluable nonetheless

His father's stories never left Bukiet's consciousness, and indeed, as Bukiet began working on the stories that would one day become his second book—the 1992 collection *Stories of an Imaginary Childhood*—neither father nor son was completely sure about whose "story" this or that one was. No doubt elements of both storytellers were fused into the edgy, unsettling tales about coming of age in a world on the brink of destruction. "What harm could possibly come to us in 1928?" one story asks—but meanwhile, the narrator's tone, drawn from the well of retrospective knowledge, understands full well that the answer is "Everything"—the imaginable as well as things that are not.

As the young Bukiet added stories he read to those he heard from his father, the result was a volatile mixture of boundless curiosity and endless page turning. During the awkward years of middle school, Bukiet was so undersized that playground bullies ignored him. Meanwhile, he continued to read, and to read voraciously—everything from Sinclair Lewis to Kurt Vonnegut, Jr., but, interestingly enough, not any books by Jewish authors.

His interest in writers such as Isaac Babel and Bruno Schulz, Israel Joshua Singer and Chaim Grade—figures who loomed importantly over his early fiction—would come later, when he enrolled at Sarah Lawrence College (1970–1974) in Bronxville, New York. Bukiet not only breathed in the rarified air at Sarah Lawrence, a school especially strong in the arts, but he also rediscovered nineteenth-century British and European novels in classes with the legendary Sarah Lawrence professor Ilja Wachs. Bukiet already knew how to devour books, but Wachs turned him into a close reader. More important, Wachs taught him, in Bukiet's words, "how to live."

From Sarah Lawrence (where he eventually returned as a teacher in his own right), Bukiet enrolled in the MFA program at Columbia (1974–1976), where, after several false starts, he began writing the stories set in Proszowice that later appeared as *Stories of an Imaginary Childhood*. His apprenticeship—short if one calculates it from his years at Sarah Lawrence and at Columbia, long if one begins counting at birth, or possibly even earlier—positioned him to move from arranging used volumes at the Strand bookstore to writing books of his own that would be sold in mainstream venues farther uptown.

STORIES OF AN IMAGINARY CHILDHOOD

Melvin Jules Bukiet may have been ready for the publishing world, but in the early 1980s the publishing world was not ready for him. Bukiet spent the summer of 1982 at the Yaddo writers colony revising his Proszowice stories—this after discovering that his creative juices seemed to flow much better when the draft of a so-so story was moved backward in time to the place where his father once resided. In 1983 he married Jill Goldman, an attorney; and in 1985 he published *Sandman's Dust,* a family novel set in Vineland, New Jersey, in 1941. Bukiet's extended family had roots in Vineland, a town that had attracted many European Jews during the middle 1930s and then, after the end of World War II, many Holocaust survivors. The area had first been populated as an agricultural colony funded by the nineteenth-century philanthropist Baron Maurice de Hirsch for the purpose of Jewish immigration, and the majority of those who found themselves living in Vineland, New Jersey, in the twentieth century became poultry farmers with the help of the Baron de Hirsch Fund. In *Sandman's Dust,* this sleepy town is visited by a fantastical circus, and soon the real and the surreal become indistinguishable. (Many readers saw the science fiction writer Ray Bradbury as an influence in Bukiet's novel.) *Sandman's Dust* did not put Bukiet on the literary map, but it did have some of the features critics would notice in his later work; In her entry on Bukiet for *Dictionary of Literary Biography,* Janet Burstein points out the novel's "elongated, elaborate sentences." But more important, the fact that Bukiet had published a novel made it easier for an agent to place his second book.

The twelve interrelated stories that make up *Stories of an Imaginary Childhood* brought Bukiet to wide attention and won the 1992

Edward Lewis Wallant Prize. The voice in these stories is engaging, and altogether infectious: "Show me a Jewish home without a prodigy and I'll show you an orphanage. So thought the great sage and musician of Proszowice, me, as I made sounds like the slaughter of swine on my new violin." At the same time, for those who regarded Jewish American literature as inextricably wedded to social realism and, more important, to the comic battles that pit sexually rebellious sons against their well-meaning but ultimately castrating mothers, the unsettling fiction of Melvin Jules Bukiet came as a surprise, perhaps even as a shock. Part experimentation in the manner of magical realism, part a relentless, often pitiless consideration of the post-Holocaust universe, Bukiet's work fixes its gaze neither on Jewish mommas nor on the affluent Jewish suburbs but, rather, on God and his complicity in the history of Jewish persecution.

The English physicist and futurist Freeman Dyson coined the word "theofiction" in the early 2000s to describe writing that uses the conventions of science fiction to address questions of theology—and one could say that with *Stories of an Imaginary Childhood,* Bukiet took his place as a leading practitioner of theofiction, Jewish style. A list of other notable "Jewish theofictionists" might include Cynthia Ozick (whose 1987 novel *The Messiah of Stockholm* is, among other thing, about a quest to find Bruno Schulz's lost manuscript, "The Messiah"), Steve Stern (*Lazar Malkin Enters Heaven,* 1986). and Allen Hoffman (*Kagan's Superfecta,* 1981, a little known but spectacular novella). Despite wide differences in style and technique, what these writers have in common is a sense of the interplay between man and God, and of how the "inviolate realms" of memory and theology conspire to reveal glimpses of perfection amid the impurities that surround us.

Bukiet's *Stories of an Imaginary Childhood* involve an unflagging, protracted quarrel with God, usually focused on the Holocaust but also extending backward (as if to link arms) with such traditional figures of Jewish protest as Levi Isaac of Berdychev (1740–1809), the Hasidic *rebbe* whose famous "*Din* Torah with God" summoned God to a court of judgment, and perhaps even to the Hebrew Bible's Job. What each insists on is nothing more nor less than God's obligation to behave as a *mensch,* a human being in the fullest sense of the term. At the same time, Bukiet sharply reacts against those contemporary fictionists whose minimalism systematically shrinks our humanity until it threatens to vanish altogether, or whose fascination with the "fictionality of fiction" reduces the literary enterprise to a philosophical parlor game. Dispensing with the steady, nearly fifty-year diet of *schlemiels* and assorted crybabies in Jewish literature, Bukiet is a writer more interested in the Jewish soul than in the ethnic foods that pass Jewish lips on the way to Jewish bellies.

Stories of an Imaginary Childhood confirms Bukiet as a new Jewish voice in a tradition of American essayists, poets, novelists, and short story writers whose work is grounded in theology as an essential focus. Addressing the Harvard Divinity School in 1839, for example, Ralph Waldo Emerson insisted that the missing ingredient in religious life was "first, soul, and second, soul, and evermore, soul" yet when it came to speaking about God directly, his language dissolved into transcendental vapor: it was the Oversoul, rather than God, who shaped Emerson's literary consciousness. Other American writers from Walt Whitman to Wallace Stevens thought about divinity in the metaphors of pantheism, either energized by the giddy language of democratic celebration (what Whitman called the "body electric") or the gradual blend of Nature and naked men dancing in a ring that brings Stevens' magnificent poem "Sunday Morning" to its quasi-religious closure.

Few American writers were as God-haunted, as God-obsessed, as were Nathaniel Hawthorne and Herman Melville; but what pulsed at the core of their respective visions was a brooding Calvinism, a sense of living in the dark shadow of Adam's Fall, albeit systematically stripped of Calvinist theology. This compulsion is significant because the bulk of our most notable American writers charted out the tensions between society and self, freedom and restraint, the adult obligation of the hearth and the giddy promises of a wilder, essentially lawless frontier. All of which may make Flannery O'Connor the United States's first genuine "theofictionist," because her fierce, uncompromising Catholicism did not require the trappings of the Church or the appearance of priests to buttress the stern, philosophical vision of damnation, grace, and redemption that plays out in her haunting fiction. Her violent, shocking tales were so unflinching, so dipped in the acid of irony, that it is hardly surprising that the morally complacent were made uncomfortable by them. (By contrast, the stories of J. F. Powers often deal with priests and an insider's sense of convent life, but one does not think of his fiction as God-obsessed in same way that one recognizes immediately in O'Connor.) For O'Connor, theology mattered more than metaphor, as her famous retort to Mary McCarthy suggests. When McCarthy reluctantly admitted that the Holy Ghost might indeed be a useful metaphor, O'Connor exploded: "If it's just a symbol, the hell with it."

The same observations could be made, with an adjustment here, a modification there, about the essential differences between Jewish theofictionists and more secularly minded chroniclers of the Jewish American scene. Philip Roth fits easily into the latter camp: his earliest stories were slabs of social realism, filled to the brim with sharp, often satirical jabs at the life assimilated, newly affluent Jews made in the American suburbs. Like J. F. Powers, he knew the details, and even more impressive, he knew how to weave them into impressive art. But Roth's protagonists tend to quarrel with nagging Jewish mothers (*Portnoy's Complaint,* 1969) or overly cautious tribal spokesmen (*The Ghost Writer,* 1979) rather than with God-quarrels that reduce themselves, with book after book, to a long irritating whine.

Roth's near contemporary Cynthia Ozick, by comparison, came to the writing of fiction with a moral gravitas and a much richer sense of what "Jewishness" means. As she put it in the introductory remarks to an early story: "I believe that stories ought to judge and interpret the world." The result was fiction that changed the way we define Jewish American writing and, more important, the way that Jewish American writing defines itself. Ozick is an inveterate "explainer," at one point talking about the creation of a "new Yiddish," at another, about the necessity of exploring fiction's "liturgical" dimensions, but what she set into motion with stories such as "The Pagan Rabbi" and "Bloodshed" was writing that riddled about God-as-riddle.

Melvin Bukiet's ruminations about a possibly unjust God continues the tradition of writers such as Ozick and O'Connor, who are as unflinching about consequences as they are inclined toward theology. In *Stories of an Imaginary Childhood,* he re-creates the world of Proszowice, Poland, as seen through the eyes of an unnamed twelve-year-old protagonist; and in his 1995 collection, *While the Messiah Tarries,* the stories move effortlessly from Manhattan to the Soviet Union.

What Bukiet will not do is confront the Holocaust experience directly. The title of his third novel, *After* (1996), says it all. Bukiet's imagination will only deal with the world that Holocaust survivors encountered—and in a wide variety of ways, made their own—after the camps were liberated. Using what happened in the camps for art's minor purposes strikes Bukiet as inappropriate, if not downright obscene. Nonetheless, the power his fictions pack may reveal more about the situation of Jewry in a nightmarish century than tales of barbed wire and gas chambers ever could.

Bukiet aims at "revelations" of a peculiarly gritty sort. As he put it in his 1993 Edward Lewis Wallant Prize acceptance speech: "Fiction is the language of revelation in our time, and that may be a modern heresy. As the Bible ceases to satisfy and Biblical parables to soothe, fiction provides the stories we need to tell ourselves." Even more important, the "stories we need to tell ourselves" must take both God and history into full account—they cannot escape being unsettling. Fiction, Bukiet insists, is "the voice of God within us enabling a creation from nothing"; it is, therefore, an attempt "to make the world as it should be." But Bukiet also goes on to point out that "as God failed at Auschwitz, fiction becomes the world that is, flawed, degenerated from the first idyll."

MELVIN JULES BUKIET

Stories of an Imaginary Childhood has a shadowy resemblance to a world that did exist; it is, an effort to reinscribe what the Nazis obliterated into the Book of Life. Memory, however, often takes peculiar, even disturbing turns in Bukiet's fiction, for he is less concerned about getting the details exactly right, in the manner of social realism, than he is with evoking a shivery, theological brooding. The result mixes that which was with that which is imagined, and in the process, contemporary touches were juxtaposed—often in jarring ways—with the dirt streets of a small Polish town.

In the course of reviewing a novel by Allen Hoffman for *Commentary* magazine in December 1996, David Roskies takes Bukiet and others to task for fiction that includes details about Old World Jewish life that are wildly inaccurate. Roskies complains that authors such as Rebecca Goldstein (*Mazel,* 1994), Allen Hoffman (*Small Worlds,* 1996), and Melvin Jules Bukiet blur the distinction between what "was" and what they invent. As such, readers who rely on their fiction for accurate renderings of life in the Old World are being misled. This, of course, assumes that readers come to a novel in the same way that they come to a sociological study, and that the literal counts for more than the literary.

In Bukiet's case, throwing in what Roskies regards as inappropriate data is precisely what gives *Stories of an Imaginary Childhood* both its tension and its charm. The novel's unnamed protagonist has a vivid, but largely "imaginary" childhood. In one scene, an old-fashioned, unfamiliar (at least in Proszowice) bicycle makes its way across the streets of the shtetl in ways that juxtapose contemporary prose rhythms with a sleepy, early-twentieth-century landscape.

The literary critic Janet Burstein, in her 2006 study, *Telling the Little Secrets,* says that *Stories of an Imaginary Childhood* ultimately offers "the emergence—from the pieties and simplicities of the European past—of a singular artistic voice." Although Bukiet's narrator must liberate himself from Proszowice to discover a voice that is fully his, it is also true that the stories he spins are deeply woven into the fabric of the shtetl he experienced growing up. In this sense, Bukiet's protagonist is not essentially different from James Joyce's literary alter ego Stephen Dedalus, who must leave Dublin in order to write but who finds that Ireland is inevitably the subject of his work.

But the interconnected stories of Bukiet's "imaginary" childhood contain more than the appearance of a bicycle (wonderfully rendered in postmodernist fashion) or the ringing of an out-of-place doorbell, but passages that take us to the very heart of what a theofictionist such as Bukiet can do. Here, for example, is a selection taken from the collection's concluding tale. "Torquemada" is, at its most literal level, a feverish dream in which Bukiet's young protagonist imagines that he is the Grand Inquisitor; but it is also a relentless brooding about history's mortal pang, its bloodthirsty darkness.

At this point, Bukiet's youthful protagonist begins to cry, and the dybbuk of Torquemada is replaced by a growing sense of his Jewishness. The worried elders who have been clustered around him feel that, at last, everything is all right. History will prove them tragically wrong.

Bukiet's Eastern European Jews cannot imagine the night and fog, the fire and ash, destined to consume them. In *Stories of an Imaginary Childhood,* as Bukiet broods about the place that nurtured his father as well as about the role that God played (or did not play) in the unfolding of unspeakable horrors, he gives the traditional initiation story a new spin, not in the way he deals with a largely innocent world about to be stripped of its innocence but also because his stories speak to the special burdens and obligations of being a member of the Second Generation.

Bukiet's subsequent work would continue his explorations of "inner turmoil" in the post-Holocaust world, albeit without the quiet subtlety Cheyette claims he saw in *Stories of an Imaginary Childhood.*

AFTER

If Bukiet is unwilling to confront the concentration camp universe directly, he is hardly shy about treating the chaotic years between 1945 and 1947 with an unflinching, go-for-broke candor. *Stories of an Imaginary Childhood* "imagined" the world before the Nazi juggernaut destroyed the universe of small Jewish villages, and most of eastern European Jewry. *After* (1996) concerns itself with the wide range of human adjustment to inhumanity—from the noble to the base, from those who felt themselves free to fully engage their libidos to those who engaged in postwar profiteering, to survive and then to prosper.

Bukiet's vision of the post-Holocaust world is bitterly comic and relentlessly ironic. His band of merry forgers and black-market mavens understands that, after Auschwitz, it is money, rather than "work," that makes you free. Bukiet uses the term "crackpot realism" to describe the ways that his fiction is related to magical realism in general and to the work of Gabriel García Márquez in particular. A more relevant antecedent, however, might be the nineteenth-century Russian writer Nikolay Gogol. What Bukiet does is raise the ante until a world made weird really *is* weird.

The long string of descriptive phrases reveals much about the characters in *After* but even more about Bukiet's style. Elements of the picaresque attach themselves to *After's* dizzying plot but always in ways that suggest how unstable the world's landscape has become. Rather than the saintly Holocaust survivor—victim that is a favorite emblem of American popular culture, Bukiet insists on throwing up all manner of schemers, some comic and some decidedly less so. His survivors know how to survive—by using their wits and by taking advantage of opportunities.

Bukiet means to scour a number of targets—from the do-gooders of Jewish relief agencies to Jewish intellectuals from the *Partisan Review*—but he reserves his deepest, most passionate quarrels for the God of Jewish history. If *After's* style is "crackpot realism," its modus operandi is theofiction. What he refuses to do is turn a brief against God into the stuff of sentimentality. There may be glimmers of something akin to hope in the novel's last pages, but most of the time *After* drives home its point by assaulting our sense of the tasteful, as if decorum were the same thing "after" that it had been before.

After has highbrow antecedents (Pynchon, Heller), but it owes many of its more outrageous scenes to the Broadway musical *Cabaret* and especially to its sardonic Emcee. If Bukiet's willfully offensive song does not quite rise to the level of the famous musical number "Springtime for Hitler" in Mel Brooks's 1968 film *The Producers,* it packs enough power to make readers wince.

But for all its grim humor, the engine of Bukiet's complicated plot keeps chugging toward the discovery of a huge cache of gold (extracted from millions of Jewish teeth) and the effort of a small group of survivors steal it back. In this endeavor, profit matters less than an appropriate reburial in a place that honors the dead, a reburial that makes perfect sense within the contours of *After's* imaginatively altered landscape. *After* brings us closer to closer to the world that Holocaust survivors found, and made, in the slippery surfaces of Mitteleurope. It is a daring, often disturbing, tour de force.

SIGNS AND WONDERS

Bukiet's 1999 novel *Signs and Wonders* is a wickedly sardonic parody of the life of Jesus Christ. Set in Germany on the edge of the second and third millennia, *Signs and Wonders* allows Bukiet an enormous amount of imaginative freedom. Sometimes the result is as witty as the story line is entertaining, but there are also times when his Christ figure, Ben Aleph, seems little more than a one-dimensional cartoon.

Ben Aleph (in English, "son of the First One," or God) belongs to a long line of false messiahs, but in much the same way that Bukiet shies away from describing the years between 1939 and 1945 he cannot put flesh and blood around Ben Aleph's bones. He is, according to Neuert, a character of "little interest"; Ben Aleph's disciples occupy the novel's center stage. Ultimately Ben Aleph is betrayed by one of his disciples and is assassinated. *Signs and Wonders* may have brought Bukiet's "crackpot realism" to its logical end, proving both its assets and its liabilities.

Bukiet's looping prose is well-served by the patina of science fiction, but there is simply too much "crackpot" in this novel's pages.

STRANGE FIRE

Bukiet writes what can only be called odd novels, but *Strange Fire,* which appeared in 2001, may be the oddest of the bunch. It is energized by conspiracy theories piled atop conspiracy theories and centered on a protagonist who is blind, gay, and a Russian-born Israeli immigrant. Bukiet had never written a political thriller before, but the change of genre, and pace, make for an exciting novel.

Bukiet's protagonist is the wisecracking, utterly audacious Nathan Kazakov. While Bukiet shares neither blindness nor sexual orientation with his lead character, the author and Kazakov have much in common, not least of which is their ability to speak in eminently quotable sound bites.

Thrillers generally start by plunging us into the middle of the action, and *Strange Fire* is no exception. Kazakov has been hit by a bullet (bad enough), but even more perplexing, by a bullet perhaps meant for somebody else. Who that person is sets the novel's mystery into motion.

A failed poet, Kazakov is now a speechwriter for the charismatic Prime Minister Simon ben Levi, a character loosely modeled on former Israeli prime minister Benjamin Netanyahu. Kazakov is a man who knows deep in his bones about the power that language packs. When he is shot at a press conference, the list of possible attackers is long, including the prime minister's advisors, the secret service, a legendary female Arab arms dealer, and a group of militant Orthodox Jewish settlers led by a rabbi named "Moshe X." Once again, Bukiet pushes the envelope, but this time in a land where excess and inhibition live side by side, and where intrigues are brewed along with strong cups of coffee.

Was the bullet, fired by one of Moshe X's followers, meant for Kazakov, or, rather, for the prime minister, a man who has the "morals of a guided missile"? Or was it meant for the prime minister's son, Gabriel, an idealistic figure who opposes his father's hawkishness by numbering himself with the nation's doves?

Kazakov soon discovers that the prime minister's son was the real object of the attack that set *Strange Fire* into motion. He enlists the aid of a Russian doctor. He suffers a wide variety of misfortunes (being scalded with boiling oil, shot at twice, and burnt by the sun); and in each case, the doctor pleads with Kazakov to go get treatment at a hospital, but in each case, Kazakov refuses. As Bukiet's plot continues to thicken, we learn that Gabriel is entwined in a larger conspiracy-code name, "strange fire"—that widens to include arms sales, real-estate deals, archeological finds, and a collection of long-simmering Arab-Israeli grievances.

Ultimately, Bukiet gives us a "scorecard" of sorts: the villains are identified and the clues to "strange fire," hidden in Leviticus, are (partially) explained. In much the same way that a Euro-Disney theme park is the apotheosis of *Signs and Wonders,* Bukiet orchestrates an appropriate setting for a big finish. Kazakov's tale is part stand-up comedy (Bukiet simply cannot resist playing the wise guy) and part a serious commentary on the way that Middle Eastern power corrupts virtually everything it touches.

OTHER STORIES

The nine stories collected in 1995 as *While the Messiah Tarries* give the resolution of intellectual conflicts outlined in the twelfth century by the philosopher-theologian Moses Maimonides. But Bukiet's tales put a contemporary spin on Maimonides' *Guide for the Perplexed* (a comparative study of Jewish mysticism and Aristotelian philosophy)—not only because Bukiet suggests that the messiah "tarries" for an inordinately long time but also because his tone implies that He might not come at all.

Fiction is, for Bukiet, a proper place to raise questions that were once the province of theology. One of Maimonides' thirteen attributes—the one many pious Jews recited as they entered the gas chambers—provides the title for Bukiet's collection, *While the Messiah Tarries.* In the post—

Holocaust world, theofiction offers a consolation uniquely its own—not the bromide of sermons or the consolation of answers where none exist.

"The Library of Moloch," widely anthologized and the best-known story of the collection, is a devastating critique of a project designed to collect videotapes of Holocaust survivors, and especially a critique of the project's earnest, well-meaning director. Bukiet's title is, of course, taken from Jorge Luis Borges' "The Library of Babel," arguably the Argentine writer's most representative tale about the labyrinthine world of fictions-within-fictions and the magical realism he spins about them. By contrast, Bukiet's story drives toward more palpable conclusions, as the director finds himself tormented by a reluctant witness who accuses him of jealousy ("You are jealous of the Holocaust. Jealous of having a reason to hate.... Jealous of those who adhere to a broken covenant. Jealous of the sacred." (p. 196)) and then confronted by a fire that systematically destroys the videotapes he has amassed:

> In his delirium, he wondered if fire was the fate of all libraries. First, there was the Library of Alexandria with the wisdom of the ancient world, and now, the Library of Moloch containing what its keeper truly believed was the wisdom of the modern world. Perhaps, he thought crazily amid the mounting flames, the fate was not inappropriate, for Moloch was the god of fire to whom children were routinely sacrificed. Moloch, the Lord of Gehenna, lived outside of Jerusalem in what was the valley of the damned, forever exiled in sight of the heavenly city.
> (p. 196)

Earlier, the director's antagonist had told him that there were two inviolate realms. One is memory. The other—which the director only discovers in the story's final word—is theology. Theofiction such as Bukiet's, one might argue, concerns itself with both, and, moreover, in ways that are likely to disturb those accustomed to more conventional Jewish American fiction.

When Bukiet isn't being a theofictional scold, he enjoys playing the role of literary scamp—and it is this Bukiet, the writer of wild imagination, whose hand is most evident in the eleven stories collected as *A Faker's Dozen* in 2003. No doubt some may moan at the play of words in Bukiet's title: unlike a baker's dozen that throws an extra item in free of charge, a faker's dozen comes out one short. But in this case, there are other possibilities as well, including faker spelled as "fakir," and "faker" as in somebody who not what he appears to be. Fiction writers are first-rate "liars" who (temporarily) convince us that their characters are real people whose lives often matter more than they should.

About a third of the stories in *Faker's Dozen* deal with writers, academics, or both. Take, "Squeak, Memory," for example, a title that riffs on Vladimir Nabokov's memoir, *Speak, Memory* (1951) and that concerns a young writer who stalks the author of *Lolita* across Manhattan during the summer of 1973. Bukiet's premise seems almost recklessly fanciful, but what the story ultimately explores tells us much about Nabokov and even more about the making of fiction. "The Return of Eros to Academe" is the tale of an elderly philosophy professor and the young student who both manipulates and liberates him into giving her an A. But to feel Bukiet's subversive bent at its most unrestrained, one needs to follow the wacky logic that pulses just underneath "Splinters," a story about how various religious groups got into a bidding war for pieces of the True Cross. This is Bukiet at his purest, which some would argue is the same thing as saying at his most offensive.

"Tongue of the Jews" is even more subversive. The character Simon Keeper is a Holocaust survivor (clearly modeled on Elie Wiesel). But Simon Keeper is also a sexual outlaw and a man cloaked in deception. At the end of this improbable tale, Keeper performs a crude circumcision on a gentile scholar who has converted to Judaism. Wrinkled into the final paragraph is a scene set in a Manhattan coffee shop where the newly circumcised Nathan (formerly "Ned") Hawkins has gone to recover.

Bukiet's short fictions are as unsparing as they are taut, despite the fact that his most congenial canvas is what Henry James called "the loose baggy monster" of the novel.

MELVIN JULES BUKIET

ANTHOLOGIES

Literary anthologies require an editor with an organizing principle and an ability to round up contributors who will flesh out what began its life as an idea. Melvin Jules Bukiet has a notable record on both fronts. His 1999 anthology, *Neurotica: Jewish Writers on Sex,* not only had an eye-catching title but also pieces by Woody Allen, Philip Roth, Steve Stern, and others. As people who wrote, and often lived, under the long shadow cast by Sigmund Freud, it is hardly surprising that, in the selected pieces, laughter coexisted with trembling.

Bukiet's next anthology, *Nothing Makes You Free: Writing by the Descendants of Jewish Holocaust Survivors,* appeared in 2002. Writing in the *Forward,* Janet Burstein calls attention to Helen Epstein's *Children of the Holocaust* (1976), a study that marked the decade in which children of survivors began to identify their common—but uncommon—"emotional and historical baggage." To take ownership of a tragic inheritance is not an easy task but many have found their way to selfhood through imaginative writing. Bukiet's anthology marks an effort to catalog the most interesting writers of the Second Generation. As Bukiet puts it: "If a chasm opened in the case of the First Generation, they could nevertheless sigh on the far side and recall the life Before, but for the Second Generation there is no Before. In the beginning was Auschwitz." (p. 13)

The cover of Bukiet's canon—making effort on behalf his fellow 2Gs makes it clear that he is a tough, uncompromising cookie: while the jacket photo shows a huge wrought iron entry gate bearing the words "Arbeit Macht Frei" ("Work Makes You Free"), the horrific lie that greeted the Jews as they were herded into Nazi concentration camps, the book's title offers a rewording that is more chillingly correct: *Nothing Makes You Free.* What the parents suffered, and what the children can never know, is the unspeakable reality of the camps, but the 2Gs' fate as the survivors of survivors nonetheless has been hardwired into their genes. That is the condition Bukiet explores with his introduction and with the thirty pieces of fiction and nonfiction he has collected in this volume, a compilation long overdue and singularly important.

"Much congratulatory celebration is made of [the survivors'] vigor, their character, and their mere existence," Bukiet says bluntly in his introduction, "but let's keep one terrible truth on the table. In fact, Hitler won. The Jews lost, badly. [Europe] is morally, culturally, essentially Judenrein." (p. 12) Those who managed to escape the nights of fog and systematic death were expected to be unobtrusive, to refrain from disturbing the normal world with what Bukiet calls "the clanking of their chains and their alarming stories." (p. 12) For the most part, this is what the survivors did. There were a few exceptions (Bukiet mentions Elie Wiesel and Primo Levi) but, in the 1950s, the word "Holocaust" (with all the problems that would swirl around the term) had not yet entered the public consciousness, and the survivors recounted their stories largely to themselves and to the captive audience of their children.

In conveying their relationship to the events of the Holocaust, writers of the Second Generation substituted their imaginations for the memories of their survivor parents. As the selections in Bukiet's anthology amply demonstrate, what fierce imaginations they have been. Bukiet includes a snippet from Art Spiegelman's *Maus II: And Here My Troubles Began* (1991), at the point in 1982 when Spiegelman's father, Vlatek, dies; he samples the strange magic realism of Joseph Skibell's 1997 novel, *A Blessing on the Moon,* in which a grandfather steps out of a grave and a rabbi turns into a crow; and he includes Thane Rosenbaum's short story "Cattle Car Complex," about a young lawyer who is trapped in a faulty elevator that gradually propels him in time to the days of crowded boxcars and death camps. These are haunted, angry imaginations. Rage is what the works, however disparate, have in common. As Bukiet, a rager of the first order, puts it:

> In imagining, a particular tone bleeds through in all but the mildest of Second Generation writers. Though often literarily exuberant and sometimes "experimental," they are viciously unredemptive, scoured of weakness, they look atrocity straight in

48

the face with barely contained rage. Despite today's insipid fetish for "healing," frequently engaged in by the social workers of the Second Generation, the writers heal nothing and comfort no one with their work. Healing is another word for forgetting. (pp. 21–22)

Don't look in this collection for the upbeat messages of such mawkish films as the 1997 crowd-pleaser *Life Is Beautiful*. "Instead of closure," he says, "the writers prefer the open wound. And should that wound threaten to close, they rip out the stitches." (p. 22) Bukiet may not be accurately describing *every* Second Generation writer, but he is certainly describing himself (see the absolutely chilling, absolutely unforgiving, "The Library of Moloch," which he rightly includes in the collection).

Bukiet also suggests that the Holocaust has, unfortunately, become a kind of Rorschach blot in which people see what they wish: "If you're depressive, you can justify despair. If you're hopeful, you can find redemption. If you're stupid, you can discern the triumph of the spirit." (p. 15) But the writers of the Second Generation know that they cannot know. They understand that the Holocaust cannot be explained nor can it be realistically rendered. "All you know," Bukiet argues, "is that you've received a tainted inheritance, secondhand knowledge of the worst event in history." (p. 18)

From that legacy writers have no choice but to write. And in *Nothing Makes You Free,* Bukiet cobbles together the best examples of a group of writers who deserve the attention of anyone living in what Elie Wiesel once called "the Holocaust universe."

Scribblers on the Roof: Contemporary American Jewish Fiction (2006), edited with David G. Roskies, was Bukiet's next offering in the realm of literary anthology. American Jews have always been crazy for culture. At the turn of the last century, New York City's Lower East Side was more crowded than Calcutta, and out of that tenement squalor came an astonishing number of Yiddish writers and dramatists. Granted, most of the newly arrived immigrants were busy with the business of making a living—in the newly emerging garment industry or in various other small trades—but the extraordinary thing about these people, bone tired after a long workday, was their addiction to lectures (about socialism, or Darwinism, or any topic vaguely erudite—just so long as it was delivered in Yiddish); to the melodramatic, often boisterous Yiddish theater; or to following the spats between competing Yiddish newspapers. The result was a culture fairly bursting at its seams, and also a culture that knew full well that the English language lessons offered up at the Education Alliance building would simultaneously allow their children access into a larger America and sound a death knell for the Yiddish-speaking ethos they so loved.

Flash forward to 1999 and the Upper West Side, an area of some three square miles that rivals, if not surpasses, the heyday of the Lower East Side for cultural institutions, and of course for writers. The adult education committee of Congregation Ansche Chesed (located at West 100th Street and West End Avenue) came up with what it thought would be a nice program to fill up the empty spaces in the summer cultural calendar: writers reading, al fresco, on the synagogue's roof. "Scribblers on the Roof" seemed to be the perfect title for what, in fact, became a wildly popular event, one that featured a wide range of American Jewish writers. Some were known commodities, others largely unfamiliar names, but, taken together, the scribblers on the roof made for first-rate evenings. People looked forward to them because what remained constant, week after week, and then year after year, was the high quality of the readers and what they read.

The makers of anthologies—in this case, Melvin Jules Bukiet and David Roskies—engage in risky work, often thankless work. Leave out a friend and you soon discover that you have made a lifelong enemy. By contrast, include everyone and the result will be a book that no printer could bind and no publisher would put under contract. The twenty pieces that made it into the first *Scribblers on the Roof* anthology (other volumes seem likely to follow) run the gamut from A (Pearl Abraham) to S (Aryeh Lev Stollman), and from already established writers such as Cynthia Ozick, Norma Rosen, Steve Stern, and Max

Apple to representatives of what are often called "emerging writers": Jon Papernick, Jonathan Rosen, and perhaps the most promising of the bunch, Dara Horn.

With the exception of two stories set in Israel (Jon Papernick's "An Unwelcome Guest" and Aryeh Lev Stollman's "Mr. Mitochondria") and Ken Kalfus's "Pu-239 (set in present-day Russia), the remaining fictions take place in America, and often in Manhattan. Among the many occasions to say "mazel tov" are Cynthia Ozick's "Stone," a story (about a statue of Mohammed) that has never been republished since its initial appearance in 1957; the fact that Norma Rosen and her son Jonathan both have selections in the anthology; or a reminder that Steve Stern was the first scribbler to read on Ansche Chesed's roof.

Nonetheless, *Scribblers on the Roof* must make its way into the literary world as more than an elaborate way of celebrating an Upper West Side landmark and the readings this shul hosted. What Bukiet's introduction promises is an anthology that puts the best contemporary American Jewish writing between hard covers—not only stories or sections of novels with overt Jewish content, but also stories that demonstrate the truth of a quip by the late Irving Howe about Jewish literature being easy to recognize but hard to define.

The mixture provides an accurate picture of the wide-ranging nature of contemporary American Jewish fiction: A story such as Ken Kalfus's nightmarish tale about a nuclear disaster in Russia, with nothing explicitly "Jewish" about its content, is allowed to coexist with a selection from Jonathan Rosen's 2004 novel *Joy Comes in the Morning,* about the travails, some comic, of a very human, very vulnerable female rabbi out on a first date. Pages from Dara Horn's 2006 novel *The World to Come* move us from considerations of the art made in this world to a vivid, imaginative rendering of the world to come. Sonia Pilcer's "Paskudnyak" is a powerful story about children of Holocaust survivors.

Other stories fall nicely between the cracks. From the popular culture of Elvis sightings and pop star worship, Eidus fashions a very contemporary—and very contemporary American Jewish—story that yokes together disparate elements into a satisfying whole. Other notable stories include Max Apple's "The Eighth Day," a fall-down-funny story about circumcision, and Pearl Abraham's "The Seven Fat Brides," an ambitious remodeling of a parable by the Hasidic *rebbe* Nachman of Bratslav.

Melvin Jules Bukiet's introduction to this volume is pure Bukiet—out to shock and out to get as quickly to the bottom line as possible. David Roskies, the anthology's coeditor, comes off as a more temperate fellow, especially when he falls into remembrances of his Montreal childhood and emphasizes what has come to be known as the "place of place." Manhattan turned out to be that place—for him, for Bukiet, for the members of Congregation Ansche Chesed, and for the twenty writers we meet between the pages of *Scribblers on the Roof.*

Melvin Jules Bukiet is a prominent figure in New York City's cultural scene, not only because of his shaping role in the Scribblers on the Roof series, but also because he was a founding member of KGB, a bar in the East Village that sponsors literary evenings with poets, fiction writers, and critics. And, of course, he continues to write.

Selected Bibliography

WORKS OF MELVIN JULES BUKIET

NOVELS AND SHORT STORY COLLECTIONS
Sandman's Dust. New York: Arbor House, 1985.
Stories of an Imaginary Childhood. Evanston, Il.: Northwestern University Press, 1992.
While the Messiah Tarries: Stories. New York: Harcourt Brace, 1995.
After. New York: St. Martin's, 1996.
Signs and Wonders. New York: Picador USA, 1999.
Strange Fire. New York: Norton, 2001.
A Faker's Dozen: Stories. New York: Norton, 2003.

ANTHOLOGIES
Neurotica: Jewish Writers on Sex. New York: Norton, 1999.
Nothing Makes You Free: Writings by Descendants of Jewish Holocaust Survivors. New York: Norton, 2002.

Scribblers on the Roof: Contemporary American Jewish Fiction. Coedited with David G. Roskies. New York: Perseus, 2006.

CRITICAL AND BIOGRAPHICAL STUDIES

"Authenticity and Marginality: Conversation Between Melvin Jules Bukiet, Ilan Stavans, and Cynthia Ozick." *Jewish Quarterly,* fall 1999, pp. 47–52. (Interview.)

Berger, Alan. *Children of Job: American Second-Generation Witnesses to the Holocaust.* Albany: State University of New York Press, 1997. Pp. 47–52.

Burstein, Janet. "Traumatic Memory and American Jewish Writers: One Generation After the Holocaust." *Modern Jewish Studies* 11, nos. 3–4: 188–198 (1999).

———. *Telling the Little Secrets: American Jewish Writing Since the 1980s.* Madison: University of Wisconsin Press, 2006. Pp. 48–75.

———. "Melvin Jules Bukiet." Dictionary of Literary Biography. Vol. 299, *Holocaust Novelists*. Edited by Efraim Sicher. Detroit: Gale, 2004. Pp. 65–69.

Furman, Andrew. *Contemporary Jewish American Writers and the Multicultural Dilemma: The Return of the Exiled.* Syracuse, NY: Syracuse University Press, 2000. Pp. 40–57.

Pinsker, Sanford. "American Literature, Jewish Writers, and Something Called 'Theo-Fiction.'" *Philadelphia Exponent,* 12 December 1996, p. 1.

———. "Jewish Novelists: 'The Next Generation.'" *Reform Judaism* 25, no. 3: 61–66 (spring 1997).

Sucher, Cheryl Pearl. "The Jewish Imagination Before and After the Holocaust." *Poets & Writers,* January–February 1999, pp. 37–41.

GUY ENDORE

(1900–1970)

Robert Niemi

BORN IN BROOKLYN on the Fourth of July, 1900, six months before the beginning of the twentieth century, Samuel Guy Endore, was, in many ways, prototypically American. Optimistic, energetic, and possessed of a formidable work ethic, Endore forged a successful life as a professional writer against considerable odds. In a more fundamental way, though, Guy Endore always considered himself a man without a country. A Jew, an orphan and exile in his youth, fluent in three languages, a radical intellectual and activist, a biographer, a pamphleteer, a writer of horror and mystery fiction, a Hollywood screenwriter, Endore inhabited a number of remarkable identities quite apart from mainstream America and its cherished values and attitudes.

Guy Endore's deeply ingrained sense of the fragility of the self in a vast, ever-changing, and tumultuous world inspired a body of work remarkable for its diversity, political commitment, and compassion. The man and his writings deserve to be rescued from obscurity.

YOUTH AND EDUCATION

By his own account, Guy Endore was "born under a sinister star." His mother, Malka Goldstein, was afflicted with what is now referred to as bipolar disorder. In 1904 she committed suicide—a fact not known to Guy Endore until thirteen years later, when he was seventeen-years-old. In the aftermath of his mother's death, Guy's father, Isadore Goldstein (who adopted the surname Endore to disguise the family's Jewish roots) hastily remarried and subsequently sent Guy and his four siblings—Rae, Celia, Mark, and Ataline—to Tuscarora Home for Children, a Methodist Church orphanage in eastern Ohio. The five Endore children remained at Tuscarora until 1908, at which time their father briefly took them home to live with him in Pittsburgh, Pennsylvania. Isadore Endore then took his children to Vienna, Austria, to obtain what he considered to be a respectable European education. Upon arrival he abruptly left them in the care of Mademoiselle Boiedec, a French nanny from Brittany, and then returned to the United States.

In Vienna from 1908 until 1913—oddly enough an aspiring artist named Adolf Hitler lived in Vienna during those very same years—Guy and his siblings learned French at home and German in public school. Various prominent Jewish families in Vienna expressed an interest in adopting the five Endore children, but an investigation revealed that they had a father living in Pittsburgh, whereupon the American consulate repatriated the children to the United States at taxpayer expense. When the Endore brood arrived in Pittsburgh by train from Toronto after their Atlantic crossing, there was no one there to meet them at the station—an all-too-common occurrence for them. Eventually located, the elusive Isadore Endore reluctantly took in his offspring. The repeated episodes of abandonment that Guy Endore experienced as a child understandably imbued him with deep-seated insecurities and manifested in recurrent headaches and a poor appetite.

In Pittsburgh with his father and siblings during the World War I, Guy Endore spent the 1916–1917 academic year studying art at the Carnegie Institute of Technology. Accustomed to being at the head of his class, Endore made the disillusioning discovery that his classmates had studied art much longer than he had and were generally more talented. Discouraged, he quit Carnegie Tech at the end of the year. Meanwhile, Guy's older brother, Mark, had won a scholar-

53

ship to attend the two-year program at Columbia University's School of Optometry. Relocating to New York City in 1918, Guy joined Mark at Columbia. Endore later admitted that he was lost at Columbia. Without an academic advisor (unaware that he even needed one) and very often broke, Endore struggled to support himself by working low-paying jobs, for example, at the post office—which he hated—or as a deliveryman. Indeed, he was so poor that he was forced to rent floor space in the corner of a dorm room to shelter from the elements. Despite the hardships, Endore excelled at his studies and sometimes helped other students with their academic work. One of the students he tutored repaid the favor with cash and, even more importantly, urged Endore to adopt a healthier diet and get regular exercise. Though he was not very bright, the young man's crude but deeply savvy brand of existentialism hit Endore like a thunderclap. Thereafter he would often grapple with the religious indoctrination that dominated his childhood and would follow a strict physical health regimen (that included vegetarianism) for the rest of his life.

After five years of penury, confusion, and tentative self-discovery, Endore managed to graduate from Columbia in 1923 with an AB in French. Not knowing what to do after he graduated, Endore stayed on at Columbia and began to work toward a master's degree in French. Awarded a prestigious University Scholar Fellowship for 1924–1925, Endore was able to study at the Sorbonne in Paris for five months. Although Paris was then the celebrated center of literary modernism and a large, boisterous American expatriate community, it held no fascination for Endore. For Endore, the one bright spot of his Paris sojourn was to meet and befriend the American poet and Ezra Pound biographer, Charles Norman (1904–1996). For a short time the two young men shared a villa, complete with an orange grove, in Juan-les-Pins, a small seaside village a few miles east of Cannes on the French Riviera. After he returned from France, Endore finished his master's degree, in 1925, but discovered that he could not get a job teaching French at Columbia because the head of the department was anti-Semitic. Angered, Endore complained to the dean, who persuaded him not to take the matter to the newspapers.

EARLY LITERARY ENDEAVORS

Stymied in academe and not wanting to leave New York, Endore was referred by a friend to an editor at *Vanity Fair* magazine named William A. Drake (1899–1965). Drake did translations of European literature on the side and had more work than he could handle. Endore met with Drake and agreed to take on his backlog: a nonfiction book and an Arthur Schnitzler play from German and some novels in French, all to be translated into English under Drake's name. A number of other (credited) translation projects followed. Endore's personal life also took an upward turn when he happened to set eyes on a beautiful young woman at the New York Public Library. Instantly smitten, Endore had a mutual acquaintance introduce him, and he and the woman—whose name was Henrietta Portugal—began dating. In 1927 they married. The Endores initially settled into an apartment in Queens and later moved to the Bronx.

Besides giving Endore gainful employment as a translator, William Drake also introduced him to Guy Holt, an editor at John Day publishers on Thirty-sixth Street in Manhattan. After several meetings with Holt to discuss book ideas, Endore proposed a biography of Giacomo Girolamo Casanova (1725–1798), the infamous Italian rake and adventurer for whom no modern, full-length biography existed. Holt liked the idea and sold John Day on funding the project by suggesting they give Endore a sort of package deal whereby he would contract to translate a book for a larger-than-usual fee so that he could use the extra money to live on while he wrote the Casanova book. Endore's translation for John Day—Hanns Heinz Ewers' novel of supernatural horror, *Alraune*—came out in 1929, as did his Casanova biography—*Casanova: His Known and Unknown Life*. (The Endores' first child, Marcia, was born on October 16, 1929—eight days before the stock market crash.) Despite disaster on Wall Street, Endore's *Casanova* sold fairly well. The modest success of the book also prompted a two-book contract offer from Farrar & Rinehart. The first of Endore's two books for Farrar & Rinehart was a novel titled *The Man From Limbo* (1930), the first-person narrative of Harry Kling, an ineffectual dreamer obsessed with a particularly virulent form of the delusion that he will escape poverty and obtain great wealth and power—Endore's critique of the pernicious effect of "American dream" ideology on ordinary citizens. The second book was the biography of a much more effectual dreamer: Joan of Arc (*The Sword of God: Jeanne D'Arc*, 1931). Both books flopped, a result not unrelated to the onset of the Great Depression.

In the spring of 1932 Endore applied for a five-week residency at Yaddo, the four-hundred-acre writers' colony in Saratoga Springs, two hundred miles north of New York City. Accepted at Yaddo through the auspices of his friend Lewis Mumford, Endore wrote—in longhand and with almost no revisions—most of the eighty-thousand-word manuscript of his fifth book, *The Werewolf of Paris,* there in the early fall of 1932. The myth of lycanthropy (that is, the transformation of a human being into a wolf) dates back to the folklore of ancient Greece and has been a staple of European folktales for many centuries. Toward the end of the seventeenth century C. F. Paullini's *Lycographia* (1694) presented a pseudoscientific survey of human-animal transformations of all kinds. Frederick Marryat's *The Phantom Ship* (1839) contained numerous stories of werewolves, and the motif quite naturally became a commonplace of nineteenth-century gothic literature. Among other books, Clemence Housman's *The Were-Wolf* (1896) and Montague Sommers' *Werewolf* (1933) brought the myth into the modern era.

Though hardly original, Guy Endore's rendition of the werewolf story was innovative insofar as it employed a terse, naturalistic prose style. In an interview with a *New York Times* reporter (10 May 1933), Endore admitted that he "found that a great many authors doing the weird type of story decorate too much, put in too much fine writing. They string a small idea too long and too thin. A great part of good writing, particularly in stories of this type, is to know when not to write expansively." Another innovative feature of *Werewolf of Paris* was that it employed a very specific and politically evocative socio-historical backdrop-the Franco-Prussian War of 1870–1871, which resulted in the seventeen-week-long siege of Paris (19 September 1870–28 January 1871), the defeat of France, the rebellion of the Parisian proletariat (which engendered the legendary but short-lived Paris Commune), and the incredibly brutal counterrevolutionary repression that followed. Indeed, *The Werewolf of Paris* is most profitably read as thinly veiled political allegory in which the grotesque crimes of Bertrand Caillet, the werewolf of the book's title, stand for the disastrous consequences of a needless war unleashed on France by its corrupt and conniving bourgeoisie.

Upon his return to New York City in October 1932, Endore discovered that his second child (a boy, born that summer) had been seriously ill while he was gone. A blood test revealed that the infant had syphilis, and a further test seemed to indicate that the disease had been contracted from the infant's mother (though a second test was negative, suggesting that the first test might have produced a false positive). The boy soon died, and Henrietta Endore offered to let her husband divorce her. He adamantly refused to believe she had a venereal disease and refused her offer of divorce. Though the test results had been ambiguous, Henrietta Endore took the precaution of seeking treatment for the disease and the Endores decided not to have any more children—and did not, until further tests, in 1943, again proved inconclusive, prompting them to risk another pregnancy.

The Werewolf of Paris came out in the spring of 1933 but failed to find much of an audience.

Endore's assessment is unnecessarily dour; *The Werewolf of Paris* did sell six thousand copies in six weeks under the very worst economic conditions in American history. Moreover, it cemented Endore's reputation as a writer. Universal Pictures even offered to buy the screen rights but Endore refused the offer, a paltry $1,000. Years later he sold the rights to Anthony Hinds at Hammer Productions for $10,000; the British studio subsequently turned the book into a 1961 film, *The Curse of the Werewolf.*

Endore's next book project was hatched while he was reading a history of the French Revolution. Endore's interest was piqued by an account of a 1791 meeting between Louis XVI's queen, Marie Antoinette, and a delegation of sugar plantation owners from the French colony of Saint-Domingue (the island now shared by Haiti and the Dominican Republic). The plantation owners sought royal protection from their black slaves, who were fomenting a full-scale insurrection that threatened white property interests. Marie Antoinette reputedly shed tears over the plantation owners' dilemma: a fact that angered Endore not only because the slave owners deserved no sympathy but also because history had so little to say about the slaves' suffering. Fluent in French (so he could read primary documents) and just a five-cent subway ride from his apartment in the Bronx to the main branch of the New York Public Library at Forty-second Street in Manhattan, Endore began to research the fascinating history of the Haitian Revolution (1791–1803).

He soon discovered that the revolt started in a forest clearing at Bois Caïman (that is, Gator Woods, southwest of Cap Haitian) on Saturday night, 13 August 1791, with a *voudou* ceremony attended by some two hundred black slaves. Presiding over the rite—during which a pig was sacrificed—was a charismatic, towering Dahomey-born slave and *papaloa* (*voudon* priest) named Boukman (also known as Dutty Boukman or Zamba Boukman), who passionately declaimed the need to rise up and destroy the white oppressor. Although Boukman was soon captured in battle and beheaded by the French, he is generally credited with igniting the spark that touched off the Haitian Revolution.

Endore decided to write a novel based on the life and death of Dutty Boukman: a choice that allowed for considerable poetic license inasmuch as Boukman's story is largely lost to history—and the accounts that do exist tend to contradict each other. To flesh out his protagonist, whom he calls Babouk, and to make his novel, *Babouk*—which appeared in 1934—as historically accurate as possible, Endore traveled to Haiti and did extensive reading on the conquest and settlement of the New World, on every facet of the transatlantic slave trade, and on the operations of the sugar and indigo industries on Saint-Domingue at the end of the eighteenth century.

Babouk begins near what is now Dakar, Senegal, on the west coast of sub-Saharan Africa. Captured in the interior and marched hundreds of miles to the Atlantic coast as part of a large caravan, Babouk is sold to French slavers on the small but infamous island of Gorée, from whence he and his fellow captives are deported—as were millions of others over a three-hundred-year period. Loaded on a slave ship ironically called the *Prie-Dieu* ("Pray God"), Babouk and his fellow captives endure the stark horrors of the Middle Passage: chained together in pairs in incredibly cramped quarters, minimal food, virtually no sanitation. Those who die from disease are simply tossed overboard.

Upon his arrival at Cap Français in Saint-Domingue, the first thing that Babouk witnesses is the gruesome spectacle of three black captives—two men and a woman—being burned alive at the stake for some unknown crime against the established order. Though Endore provides few specifics he gives enough hints to identify the incident as one that actually occurred. On 20 January 1758, French authorities, in the exactly the manner described by Endore, executed a maroon (that is, an escaped slave) rebel leader named Macandal and two of his followers who were attempting to foment a full-scale black rebellion against the French planters. Besides illustrating the resolute brutality of the colonial powers, the incident acts as a foreshadowing of Babouk's own fate thirty-three years later. (Indeed, Babouk's historical model, Boukman, is thought to have inaugurated his revolt in Bois Caïman in homage to Macandal, who died nearby.)

Assigned to the sprawling Galifet sugar plantation, in the northwestern part of the island, Babouk works as a field slave and soon acquires fame among his fellow slaves for his fierce mien, physical stature, storytelling abilities, and his powers as a *papaloa*. Recapturing him after an escape attempt, Babouk's colonial masters exact the standard retribution by amputating one of his ears. Over the years, Babouk becomes increasingly embittered and radicalized by the sordid cruelties he witnesses. With tensions on the island at fever pitch following an unsuccessful revolt in the fall of 1790 by a mulatto leader named Ogé, Babouk quite naturally steps into a leadership role. A week after the notorious *voudon* ceremony mentioned above, Babouk leads a massive slave revolt in the north. The rampaging rebels (perhaps 100,000 in number) burn plantations by the score and kill their white overseers wherever they find them—women and children included. Armed with superior weaponry, including cannon, the French soon rally and crush the rebellion. In the midst of leading a charge against enemy artillery batteries, Babouk is blown apart by a cannonball. To discourage further insurrection the French put Babouk's head on a pike with a placard that reads, "Babouk, chief of the rebels."

Though Babouk's rebellion ultimately fails, the end of the novel makes it clear that black revolutionary fervor is far from quelled—not only in Saint-Domingue, which will soon succeed in expelling the French—but in the modern world, where racism, imperialism, and widespread oppression of blacks is a far from passé phenomenon.

Quite justifiably, Endore was proud of what he had accomplished with *Babouk*. And writing the book affected profound changes in him; Endore was forever radicalized by what he had discovered about the monstrous evil that was the transatlantic slave trade. Because of his book's assuredly radical politics, Endore's contracted publisher, Crown, refused to put it out. Passed from one publisher to another all over New York like a hot potato, *Babouk* finally found a home with Vanguard, a progressive press willing to take a chance on an unusually provocative book. Twenty years ahead of its time in its unflinching treatment of the racism and class oppression, *Babouk* garnered mixed reviews and ended up selling only four hundred copies. The printing plates were subsequently destroyed. (The book remained in limbo until Monthly Review Press published a new edition fifty-seven years later, in 1991.)

HOLLYWOOD SCREENWRITER AND ACTIVIST

Occurring as it did in the depths of the Great Depression, the commercial failure of *Babouk* convinced Endore that writing fiction was no way to make a living, at least not at that time. In the fall of 1934 he did what scores of American writers at loose ends did; he sought work as a Hollywood screenwriter. Almost as soon as he settled himself and his family in Los Angeles, Endore joined an organization called the American League Against War and Fascism. With Hitler in power, Benito Mussolini adopting a more aggressively nationalistic stance, and the Japanese having conquered a good part of Manchuria, it was clear to thinking persons that fascist militarism was a looming international threat and that a major, perhaps even another global, war might be inevitable. In subsequent years Endore would devote countless hours in service to the League as a writer, editor, organizer, and speaker. Indeed for the next several years his life would be starkly bifurcated: a hack studio writer by day and an impassioned political activist by night and on weekends. In the late 1930s the League Against War and Fascism was absorbed into the American Communist Party, so Endore "became" a Communist by default.

As a screenwriter, Endore's first Hollywood assignment was to co—write, with former silent film star Seena Owen, a B—movie treatment for Paramount that Howard J. Green, Frank Partos, Harry Ruskin, and Paul Gerard Smith turned into a tepid William LeBaron musical titled *Rumba* (1935), starring George Raft and Carole Lombard. For some reason—perhaps owing to Raft's reputed underworld connections—the Catholic Legion of Decency designated *Rumba* "as suited for adults only."

As befitting the author of a werewolf novel, the next four films that Endore worked on were all in the horror genre, which was enjoying great popularity in the wake of such successful films as *Dracula* (1931), *Frankenstein* (1931), *Dr. Jekyll and Mr. Hyde* (1931), *The Mummy* (1932), and *King Kong* (1933). On his first studio assignment, for Metro-Goldwyn-Mayer (MGM), Endore joined the screenwriter-playwright Bernard L. Schubert to collaborate with the horror-picture legend Tod Browning (*Freaks,* 1932*; Dracula*), on *Mark of the Vampire* (1935), a remake of Browning's Lon Chaney silent film classic (now lost), *London After Midnight* (1927). Starring Bela Lugosi as Count Mora, a rather pompous vampire; Carroll Borland as his weird daughter, Luna (also a vampire); Lionel Barrymore as Mora's nemesis, Professor Zelen; and Elizabeth Allan as Irena Borotyn, the damsel menaced by Mora, *Mark of the Vampire* is a fairly conventional vampire story until its entire premise is overturned by a surprise ending. For his part Endore wanted to explain the relationship between Mora and his daughter, Luna, by strongly suggesting that the two had committed incest: a story element rejected and expunged by the studio. Even without Endore's incest theme, the film evidently still packed a punch.

For his next assignment Endore joined a half dozen other Universal studio writers, all uncredited, who assisted the screenwriter David Boehm in "adapting" Edgar Allan Poe's most famous poem, "The Raven" (1845) into a low-budget sixty-minute film that bears the same title but none of the poem's actual content or anything else even remotely similar to Poe's work. Produced by Carl Laemmle, Jr. (the son of Universal's founder), and helmed by the then-neophyte director, Louis Friedlander (also known as Lew Landers), *The Raven* starred a scenery-chewing Bela Lugosi as Dr. Richard Vollin, a diabolical neurosurgeon, and Boris Karloff as Edmond Bateman, Vollin's demented, disfigured sidekick, in an unholy plot to rehabilitate and possess a beautiful but crippled dancer played by Irene Ware.

Immediately after *The Raven,* Endore returned to his home studio, MGM, to help adapt a French horror novel, Maurice Renard's *Les Mains d'Orlac* (1920), which had already been made into a haunting silent film, *Orlacs Hände* (1924), in Weimar Germany by Robert Weine. Working with Florence Crewe—Jones's 1929 English translation of Renard's book, *The Hands of Orlac*—though he could have done a far better translation himself—Endore's job was to help screenwriters Pincus J. Wolfson and John L. Balderston distill Renard's prose narrative into a what was then called a "photoplay." Also assisting were Wolfson's brother, Leon, Edgar Allan Woolf, Gladys von Ettinghausen, and Leon Gordon (all of whom were uncredited). The premise of the resulting 1935 film, released with the title *Mad Love,* involves two venerable horror subgenres: the mad scientist and transplanted body parts that have a mind of their own. Stephen Orlac (Colin Clive) is a famous pianist whose hands are crushed in a train accident. Dr. Gogol (Peter Lorre), a brilliant but psychotic surgeon, replaces Orlac's hands with the hands of Rollo (Edward Brophy), a recently executed murderer whose specialty in life was knife throwing in a circus. Gogol's motive in transplanting the evil hands is to ruin Orlac so that he can have Orlac's wife, Yvonne (Frances Drake) to himself. In the end, and with appropriate irony, Orlac saves his wife from Gogol's clutches by hurling a knife into the back of the love-crazed surgeon.

The fourth and last horror picture Guy Endore worked on was Tod Browning's *The Devil-Doll,* released by MGM in 1936. Working closely with Browning; the legendary writer-director-actor Erich Von Stroheim; Garrett Fort, a screenwriter; and the dialogue specialist Richard Schayer, Endore helped turn Abraham Merritt's novel *Burn Witch Burn!* (1933) into a film that melds the revenge-tragedy plot with the mad-scientist motif. Lionel Barrymore plays Paul Lavond, a man wrongly imprisoned on Devil's Island. Lavond escapes with Marcel (Henry B. Walthall), a mad scientist who has perfected a way to reduce animals to one sixth of their natural size, supposedly in order to save the world (in some way). After Marcel dies, Lavond joins forces with Marcel's widow, Malita (Rafaela Ottiano), not to use Marcel's process for good but to use it to exact revenge on his three former partners who betrayed him and sent him to Devil's Island. Accordingly, Lavond, disguised as a frail, old woman, opens a doll shop in Paris and uses Marcel's process to create miniature people who proceed to dispatch his former partners. Though the premise was typically absurd, the miniaturization theme allowed for some dazzling special effects.

By the late 1930s the horror-picture vogue had cooled off and Endore was assigned to other genres. His next credited work was for *Carefree* (1938), a routine RKO musical directed by Mark Sandrich and starring Fred Astaire and Ginger Rogers (in their eighth film together since 1933). Once again Endore worked with a half dozen other studio staff writers to come up with a suitably flimsy plot that functioned as nothing more than narrative scaffolding for the Irving Berlin song-and-dance numbers that the film showcased.

In marked contrast to his studio hackwork, Endore played a key role in Hollywood's response to a notorious criminal trial. On March 25 1931, a fight had broken out between white and black hobos riding a freight train through northeastern Alabama. Stopped by a posse, nine black teenagers were charged with assault—and rape, after two white women also on the train leveled highly dubious charges against them. Tried before an all—white jury, eight of the nine young men were convicted of rape and sentenced to death less than three weeks after the alleged incidents occurred. The racial character of the case, the youth of the defendants, the harshness of the penalties, and the extreme swiftness of the legal process instigated impassioned protests and "the Scottsboro case" soon became a major cause célèbre among progressive and civil rights groups throughout the country. Numerous legal challenges to the verdicts resulted in an agonizing series of retrials that dragged on through the 1930s. In 1938 Endore added his voice to the choir of protest by helping to form the Hollywood Scottsboro Committee and by authoring an eloquent pamphlet in defense of the "Scottsboro Boys": *The Crime at Scottsboro*.

Endore's next screen credit after *Carefree* was *Lady from Louisiana* (1941), a John Wayne vehicle from Republic Pictures that was produced and directed by Bernard Vorhaus (a director who later ran afoul of the Hollywood blacklist). Teaming with veteran screenwriters Vera Caspary and Michael Hogan, Endore helped to fashion a screenplay from a story written by Edward James and Francis Edward Faragoh. To wit: Blanche Brunot (Helen Westley), a New Orleans dowager, summons family friend (and lawyer) John Reynolds (John Wayne) from Memphis to clean up the corrupt city lottery. In transit down the Mississippi by riverboat, Reynolds meets the beautiful Julie Mirbeau (Ona Munso) and they begin a smoldering infatuation. Unbeknownst to Reynolds, Julie is the daughter of General Anatole Mirbeau (Henry Stephenson), the man who runs the lottery. After Reynolds discovers that the lottery has ties to organized crime, his aggressive crusade against it brings him into inevitable conflict with Miss Mirbeau—until he discovers that the source of the corruption is not General Mirbeau but a crooked assistant named Blackie Williams (Ray Middleton). After General Mirbeau fires Williams, Williams exacts revenge by having his henchmen murder the general. Blaming Reynolds for her father's death, Julie Mirbeau ill-advisedly takes up with Blackie Williams—until she discovers him in the arms of anther woman. In the end, Miss Mirbeau reunites with Reynolds and helps him prosecute Blackie Williams and his nefarious associates.

In 1940, A. J. Cronin, a British physician turned writer, completed his first stage play, *Jupiter Laughs,* and sold the film rights to Hal B. Wallis at Warner Bros., which also produced the stage version. The play centers on Dr. Paul Venner, a gruff but brilliant medical scientist who is unjustly exiled from Budapest after Von Reiter, a rival scientist, steals his research on a cure for dementia praecox (schizophrenia) and arranges Venner's deportation. Venner starts over at a small sanitorium in Scotland, assisted by the young and beautiful Dr. Mary Murray. Suffice to say that, in the end, despite the usual travails, Venner achieves his medical breakthrough and "gets the girl." *Jupiter Laughs* opened at the Biltmore Theatre, West Forty-seventh Street, New York City, on 9 September 1940, but was harshly reviewed and closed on 28 September after only twenty-four performances. Despite the work's poor showing on Broadway, Warner Bros. immediately went ahead with a film version starring James Stephenson as Venner and Geraldine Fitzgerald as Mary Murray (Jessica Tandy played

Murray on stage). Howard Koch (who went on to write *Casablanca* with Julius and Philip Epstein) joined Anne Froelich in turning Cronin's script into a screenplay. Endore's role was relatively minor; he and Warren Duff acted as uncredited script doctors. The 1941 film, released as *Shining Victory,* was moderately successful.

In the summer of 1942 Endore and likeminded progressives were presented with another cause célèbre to rival the Scottsboro case. On August 2, the body of a twenty-two-year-old Mexican American farmworker named José Díaz was found at an isolated irrigation reservoir in East Los Angeles colloquially known (after a popular song) as Sleepy Lagoon. Though it was not at all clear that Díaz had been murdered—his injuries suggested that he might have been run over by a car while lying in the road, drunk—the *Los Angeles Times,* the *Los Angeles Examiner,* the Hearst—owned *Evening Herald-Express,* and other area newspapers whipped up racial prejudice with inflammatory headlines and hysterical editorials regarding the perceived public menace of Chicano youth gangs, whose members were known as "zoot-suiters" or "*pachucas/os.*" Responding to the hue and cry, the Los Angeles Police Department rounded up and arrested several hundred Mexican American youths. Eventually twenty-two Chicanos were indicted for the Díaz "murder" and placed on mass trial, the largest in California history, before an all-white jury. Presiding over the trial was Judge Charles W. Fricke, a bigot who refused to allow the defendants to change out of their gang-associated zoot suits (consisting of baggy pants, oversized suit jackets with long watch chains, and wide-brimmed fedoras), or even to consult with their defense attorneys. In January 1943, after a three-month trial marked by the presentation of woefully flimsy evidence, lurid press coverage, and outrageous procedural irregularities, three of the defendants were convicted of first-degree murder and sentenced to life in prison; nine others were convicted of second-degree murder and sentenced to five-to-life terms; five were convicted of assault and soon released for time served, and the remaining five were acquitted of all charges.

Just as the Díaz trial was getting under way, Hispanic and African American community leaders, civil rights advocates, clergy, leftists, and other interested persons formed the Sleepy Lagoon Defense Committee and appointed the author-historian Carey McWilliams as its chairman. Initially, the purpose of the committee was to raise money for the defendants' legal expenses and to publicize the injustice of the proceedings. After the convictions were handed down, the committee focused on providing emotional and material support to the dozen defendants sentenced to long prison terms and to work to secure their exoneration and freedom. Guy Endore's very visible role was to write *The Sleepy Lagoon Mystery,* a forty-eight-page pamphlet published by the Sleepy Lagoon Defense Committee in June 1944. Therein, Endore rather dubiously argued that the newspaper mogul William Randolph Hearst deliberately fanned anti-Mexican hysteria in order to sow American civil strife and abet the German war effort, which he allegedly favored. (Hearst did indeed engage in his usual rabble-rousing but probably for the more pedestrian purpose of increasing newspaper sales.) Endore was on firmer ground when he quoted from the trial transcripts to point up numerous, blatant instances of judicial misconduct. At any rate, *The Sleepy Lagoon Mystery* sold over twenty-five thousand copies in just three months and was a crucial part of the committee's efforts to sway public opinion and pressure state officials to reconsider the Díaz convictions. In October 1944, twenty-one months after the guilty verdicts, the California Court of Appeals reversed the convictions.

In late 1942 officials at the newly established Office of War Information (OWI) approached MGM mogul Louis B. Mayer and requested that his studio make a propaganda movie that would glorify America's key ally, the Soviet Union, in its struggle against Nazi Germany. MGM somewhat reluctantly obliged with *The Song of Russia* (1944). Directed by Gregory Ratoff (and László Benedek after Ratoff took ill), *Song of Russia* stars Robert Taylor as an American symphony conductor named John Meredith who falls in love with and marries a classical music enthusiast named Nadya Stepanova (Susan Peters) while on a triumphant forty-city concert tour of Russia in the spring and summer of 1941. When Hitler invades Russia (22 June 1941), Nadya returns to her village and Meredith dutifully continues his tour to help bolster Russian morale. In the end, Meredith and Nadya Stepanova are tearfully reunited. Guy Endore's role in the creation of *The Song of Russia* was to help write the story upon which the screenplay was based: a role that would come back to haunt him after the war. Though perfectly acceptable in 1944, the film's highly adulatory and fanciful depiction of Soviet society—as deliriously happy, harmonious, and culturally sophisticated—expressed a viewpoint that was not only a bit silly but one that was starkly out of synch with the anti-Communist fervor at the onset of the Cold War.

In ideological terms Endore was on much firmer ground when he collaborated with Leopold Atlas and Philip Stevenson in penning *The Story of G.I. Joe* (1945), a screen adaptation of the writings of the famed war correspondent Ernie Pyle (1900–1945). Always at the front to cover the experiences of ordinary U.S. infantrymen as they pushed forward into North Africa, Sicily, Italy, France, the Low Countries, and Germany in the last three years of the war, Pyle published regular dispatches in Scripps Howard newspapers back in the States. Two book-length compilations of Pyle's columns—*Here Is Your War* (1943) and *Brave Men* (1944)—became national bestsellers and Pyle won a Pulitzer Prize for Journalism in 1944. Rightly concluding that Ernie Pyle's realistic, unpretentious depictions of frontline American soldiers had the makings of a stirring film that would be patriotic without being cloying, Hollywood producer Lester Cowan won Pyle's support to make a movie version. Under the watchful eye of director William "Wild Bill" Wellman, Endore, Atlas, and Stevenson carefully preserved Pyle's ground-level point of view and the episodic nature of his dispatches to create a screenplay that avoided the usual, bombastic war movie clichés in favor of an honest and historically accurate portrayal of the G.I. as a weary, grimy, fatalistic soul hoping not for martial glory but only to survive the war and return home to his family in one piece. Starring Burgess Meredith as Ernie Pyle, Robert Mitchum in his breakout role, and many real combat veterans and war correspondents, *The Story of G.I. Joe* was released after the defeat of Nazi Germany but before the capitulation of Japan. A box office success, the film won critical acclaim and four Oscar nominations, including one for best screenplay.

Not having published a novel since *Babouk,* Endore broke his eleven-year silence in the fiction arena with *Methinks the Lady...* (1945), a highly original psychological thriller. Mrs. Spence Gillian, the young and beautiful wife of a prominent psychoanalyst, seems to be some sort of schizoid personality totally unaware of the Mr. Hyde part of her psyche that is demonstrably a kleptomaniac—she is caught stealing a mermaid brooch at a department store. Worse still, she is possibly also a nymphomaniac and perhaps even a murderer.

The narrative that decides these questions is divided into three sections. The first section consists of conversations between Mrs. Gillian and her analyst as she tries, with scant success, to fathom the symbolic workings of her subconscious. The second section recounts an inconclusive conversation between three analysts—two Freudians and one non-Freudian-appointed to examine Mrs. Gillian and determine her fitness to stand trial (again) for the murder of a woman who sought to be one of her husband's patients. The third section consists of a summary of the case by Mrs. Gillian that quotes liberally from the examination and cross-examination of her husband at her second trial. After much reader confusion as to Mrs. Gillian's possible guilt or innocence—confusion that enacts and matches her own—the reader is apprised of Dr. Gillian's theory, no doubt correct, that it was not his wife who is the murderer but Dave Jenkins, the department store detective who arrested her for stealing the mermaid pin and uses the arrest to wield power over her.

It turns out that Jenkins suffers from an affliction known as satyriasis (that is, hypersexuality) and has killed his victim with the mermaid pin during a tryst that went out of his control. Jenkins's panicked reaction in the courtroom seals his guilt—and Mrs. Gillian's innocence. Beyond its narrative function as a thriller, *Methinks the Lady...* allowed Endore a means to explore psychoanalytic theories and methods and to advance his own notion that there is no such thing as insanity, only "confusion" (a theory that uncannily anticipates Thomas S. Szasz's controversial book, *The Myth of Mental Illness* (1960).

Endore subsequently sold the film rights to the producer-director Otto Preminger and *Methinks the Lady...* was made into a Preminger film titled *Whirlpool* (Twentieth Century Fox, 1949), starring Gene Tierney, Richard Conte—and José Ferrer as an evil hypnotist (a character entirely invented for the movie). In a later interview Endore pronounced *Whirlpool* "bad."

While *The Story of G.I. Joe* marked the high point of Endor's career in Hollywood, his next film credit, *The Vicious Circle* (1948), marked a low point. Produced and directed by Wilhelm "Willie" Wilder, the estranged and relatively untalented older brother of the great Billy Wilder, *The Vicious Circle* was adapted by Endore and the playwright Heinz Herald from *The Burning Bush,* an obscure two-act play written by Herald and Geza Herczeg. The play was, in turn, loosely based upon a historical incident known as the Tiszaeszár "blood libel" or the "Tiszaeszár affair." In the spring of 1882, Hungarian anti-Semites blamed Jews for the murder of a fourteen-year-old Christian peasant girl named Eszter Solymosi. The alleged motive: to use the slain girl's blood to prepare matzos for Passover. Four Jews were indicted for murder and eleven others for abetting the crime. Though all fifteen defendants were eventually acquitted, they were forced to spend fifteen months in jail awaiting trial. Predictably anti-Semites in Hungary and throughout Europe hysterically denounced the "not guilty" verdicts. Coming in the immediate wake of the Holocaust, *The Vicious Circle* seemed tame and not a little irrelevant given much more recent and hideous examples of European anti-Semitism.

In 1948 the independent producer Irving Starr and John Wayne's favorite screenwriter, James Edward Grant, approached Columbia Pictures with an action story Grant had written about a reformed criminal turned undercover Treasury agent whose mission is to penetrate and destroy a massive counterfeiting operation. The consensus at Columbia was that Grant's treatment would make a good vehicle for the actor George Raft, who had decided a few years before to quit playing gangsters in order to present a better role model to America's youth. Along with staff screenwriter Karen De Wolf, Endore was assigned to turn Grant's story into a full-fledged screenplay. The resulting picture, *Johnny Allegro* (Columbia, 1949), was an unremarkable potboiler that starred Raft, George Macready as the villain, and Nina Foch as the hero's love interest.

Left to his own devices Guy Endore could fashion a film narrative that easily exceeded, in psychological complexity and dramatic impact, the banal fare the studios usually assigned to him. Such was the case with *Tomorrow Is Another Day* (Warner Brothers, 1951), for which Endore wrote the treatment and then, with Art Cohn, wrote the screenplay. Drawing on his own, emotionally stunted youth and late blooming, Endore created Bill Clark, also known as Mike Lewis (played by Steve Cochran in the film), a thirty-one-year-old parolee who has spent eighteen years in prison for having killed his brutally abusive father. Institutionalized during his prime formative years, Bill Clark is volatile, undersocialized, and naive—especially around women. In keeping with the plot requisites of film noir, Clark quite naturally casts his lot with his polar opposite: a cynical, street-smart taxi dancer named Catherine "Cay" Higgins (Ruth Roman). After a fracas during which Cay accidentally shoots her cop boyfriend, Bill and Cay must seek the anonymous refuge of the road and end up working on a farm. The film's couple-on-the-run-from-the-law motif was a stock feature of noir most recently reprised in the 1949 United Artists film *Deadly Is the Female* and was oft repeated in years to come. Endore's innovation is to dispense with the femme fatale trope, make both of his protagonists essentially innocent, and to have their innocence confirmed by the movie's conclusion, thus transforming the nihilistic premises of film noir into something resembling a romantic melodrama with soap opera overtones.

BLACKLISTED

On Monday, 20 October 1947, after thirteen years in Hollywood, Guy Endore was one of dozens of studio personnel served notice that their professional careers were in jeopardy. On that day three powerful Hollywood moguls-studio heads Louis B. Mayer (MGM) and Jack Warner (Warner Bros.) and the independent producer-director Sam Wood—all testified as "friendly" (that is, cooperative) witnesses before the House Un-American Activities Committee (HUAC) in Washington. Also read into the record that day were pages of preliminary testimony from Jack Warner taken some months earlier in which he named sixteen writers whose contracts he refused to renew "because of lack of sympathy with their [leftist political] views." As reported in the *New York Times,* these writers were: Irwin Shaw, Clifford Odets, Alvah Bessie, Gordon Kahn, Guy Endore, Howard Koch, Ring Lardner, Jr., Robert Rosson, Emmett Lavery, Albert Maltz, Sheridan Gibney, Julius and Philip Epstein, John Wexley, Dalton Trumbo, and John Howard Lawson. In his testimony on 20 October, Warner voiced second thoughts about four of the writers he had named earlier and now felt their names should be deleted from the list. Endore was one of the four writers Warner exonerated: a fact that probably spared him from having to testify before HUAC and kept his career afloat, though suspect, for another four years. Indeed, Endore was "clean" enough politically for blacklisted writers Dalton Trumbo and Hugo Butler to use him as a front for their 1951 film, *He Ran All the Way.*

Though he was under suspicion, not to mention FBI surveillance, Endore refused to shrink from activist causes. In the wake of the Sleepy Lagoon trial of 1942 and the so-called zoot-suit riots that occurred the following summer, tensions between white and Mexican Angelenos continued unabated. Another racial flare-up occurred in 1948 when William J. Keyes, a white LAPD officer, shot and killed a young Mexican named Augustine Salcido under very dubious circumstances. Despite compelling evidence that pointed to official misconduct, Keyes was exonerated. Under the auspices of the Civil Rights Congress of Los Angeles—an outgrowth of the Sleepy Lagoon Defense Committee—Endore wrote *Justice for Salcido,* a thirty-two-page pamphlet that succinctly laid out the facts pointing to a racially motivated killing and subsequent cover-up.

Two months after the publication of *Justice for Salcido* in 1948, Endore's radical politics finally caught up with him. One shoe having dropped in October 1947, the other one finally fell on 19 September 1951 when the screenwriter Martin Berkeley "named names" while testifying before a second set of public hearings held in Los Angeles by the HUAC on Communist influence in Hollywood. One of the more than one hundred names that Berkeley disclosed was Endore's. Eleven days later a screenwriter named Roy Huggins appeared before the committee, admitted Communist party membership in the 1940s, and named a dozen former comrades, Endore included. In the wake of the 1951 HUAC hearings, the studios were under tremendous pressure from nervous stockholders to fire the artists and writers publicly implicated as current or former "Reds." The blacklist was immediately put into full force, and Endore suddenly found himself unemployed. The irony of Endore being blacklisted is that he always had pronounced differences with Communist party officials—especially the Hollywood apparatchik John Howard Lawson—over ideological questions and issues of personal artistic autonomy. Joseph Stalin's pact with Hitler and the later, horrible revelations about Stalin's mass purges in the 1930s only added to Endore's disgust with Communism. By the 1950s he was a thoroughly and bitterly disillusioned former Party member. Hollywood's political quarantine of Endore (and many of his contemporaries) proved to be quite unnecessary, except perhaps as retribution.

Frozen out of his chosen profession, Endore publicly protested (with an article titled "Life on the Black List" for the *Nation* in December 1952) and joined a class-action lawsuit against the blacklist even though he felt it would probably fail—which it eventually did. In the meantime, though, there was the pressing problem of making a living to support himself, his wife, and his second daughter, Gita (born in 1944, fifteen years to the day after the birth of Marcia). The breadwinner role shifted somewhat to Endore's wife, Henrietta, who had proven to be a resourceful teacher of young children while working for the School for Nursery Years in the Brentwood suburb of Los Angeles. She soon branched out to provide daycare for a few children in the Endore home. After Endore was blacklisted, he and his wife decided to start a small private school that would be based upon theories of childhood development advanced by Anna Freud.

The idea was a good one but the execution proved to be disastrous. The Endores sold their house and bought another one that they intended to renovate and turn into a residence and school. Unfortunately they discovered to their dismay that they had purchased the new house in a part of the city not zoned for schools. An attempt to obtain a zoning variance failed when a mysterious stranger burst into the zoning board meeting and vigorously denounced Endore as a "Red." To add insult to injury, the two men Endore hired to work on the new house proved to be grossly dishonest and incompetent. In the end the school idea failed miserably and cost the Endores thousands of dollars. Next, Endore was invited to New York to work on a book about the Alger Hiss case. (In 1950 Hiss, a former State Department official, was sentenced to five years in prison after being convicted of perjury in a notorious Soviet espionage case.) The Hiss book project failed to materialize. By this point Endore was becoming increasingly desperate.

Near the end of his rope financially, Endore avoided bankruptcy by reverting to the kinds of historical fiction he wrote before he went off to Hollywood in the early 1930s. He managed to wrangle an advance from Simon & Schuster for a fictionalized biography of Alexandre Dumas, pére (1802–1870), the fabulously popular French author of the D'Artagnan romances, *The Count of Monte Cristo,* and countless other works. Dumas appealed to Endore in several ways. First, there was the family's connection to Saint-Dominigue and the transatlantic slave trade: a subject area Endore had explored in depth with *Babouk*. Dumas's grandfather, the Marquis Antoine-Alexandre Davy de la Pailleterie, who served as a government official on Saint-Domingue, married Marie-Césette Dumas, a black slave, in 1761. Second, there was Dumas' fondness for historical fiction, which Endore shared. Third, there was the figure of Dumas himself, which was larger than life. Alexandre Dumas was a self-made man of vast appetites and passions who had risen from poverty to become one of the most popular writers of his day. He wrote prodigiously (some five hundred works), earned millions of francs and squandered it all, quarreled constantly with his contemporaries, was married but had hundreds of mistresses, and had a tumultuous love-hate relationship with his illegitimate son, Alexandre, *fils,* also a famous writer. In short, Dumas lived life with great gusto, even abandon. *King of Paris* (1956), Endore's rollicking, five-hundred-page account of Dumas' life, though heavily fictionalized and embellished with imagined episodes and fabricated dialogue, was based on Endore's typically extensive and careful research. A great read about an exuberant, fascinating life, *King of Paris* garnered glowing reviews, became a best seller, and was chosen as a selection for the Book-of-the-Month Club for October 1956.

Representing a change of pace was Endore's fifth and final work of pure fiction, *Detour at Night* (1959), a mystery yarn about Professor Frank Willis, a linguist who narrowly escapes a murder conviction. Really a novel of linguistics and semantics masquerading as a mystery, the book quickly sank out of sight. It remains interesting as Endore's exploration of the ways in which human beings reify words-which are, after all, merely symbols-into living things that shape experience.

After completing *Detour at Night,* Endore tried to repeat the success he had with *King of Paris* by undertaking a fictionalized duel biography of François-Marie Arouet, known as Voltaire (1694–1778), and Jean-Jacques Rousseau (1712–1778) that focused on the intellectual rivalry that existed between these two giants of the French

Enlightenment. Unfortunately the breezy style that so well suited Dumas was not appropriate to the more cerebral likes of Voltaire and Rousseau. Nor was their story even remotely as colorful as the story of Dumas, *pére* and *fils*. Not surprisingly, *Voltaire! Voltaire!* (1961) received harsh reviews and sold poorly.

DE SADE, SHAKESPEARE, AND SYNANON

The weak showing of *Voltaire! Voltaire!* was disappointing but hardly crushing; Endore had already pocketed a hefty advance for it. Also, by the time it was published, Endore had already immersed himself in a daring new book project: a fictionalized biography of the Marquis de Sade (1740–1814) that would enable him to explore human sexuality and the taboos that surround its more outré manifestations. He also wrote *Call Me Shakespeare* (1966), a play that surveys the longstanding debate about Shakespeare's true identity, pays tribute to Shakespeare's art, and explores the Bard's socio-historical milieu. Beyond these new literary projects, Endore also discovered a cause that would captivate him until the end of his life. Some time in 1960 Endore and his wife had dinner with Bernard Brandchaft, a noted Los Angeles psychiatrist, and Brandchaft's wife, Elaine. The dinner conversation turned to a revolutionary drug rehabilitation program in Santa Monica run by a group called the Synanon Foundation. Intrigued, Endore had Elaine Brandchaft take him down to the old armory building at 1351 Ocean Front in Santa Monica to experience Synanon firsthand. Founded in the summer of 1958 by a recovering alcoholic named Charles "Chuck" Dederich, Sr. (1913–1997), Synanon used a "therapeutic community model" to treat heroin addicts that mandated comprehensive lifestyle changes, complete segregation from the wider world, and regular group sessions (called "The Game") that stressed harsh confrontation and criticism by peer counselors. Synanon was initially envisioned as a two-year residence program, but Dederich soon came to the conclusion that residents could never "graduate" because addiction recovery is a never-ending process.

Possessed of a utopian temperament and fascinated by collectivist alternatives to capitalist society's lonely, competitive, atomistic status quo, Endore was naturally drawn to the therapeutic, communitarian experiment that was Synanon. It reminded him of John Humphrey Noyes' Oneida Community (1848–1881) in upstate New York: a Christian-communist sect also founded and lorded over by a charismatic patriarchal figure that likewise stressed economic self-sufficiency, isolation from worldly influence, harsh mutual criticism, and a belief in ultimate human perfectibility. (More problematically, Oneida also engaged in a host of unorthodox sexual practices including polygamous marriage and a primitive sort of eugenics.)

Guy Endore's somewhat idealized attraction to Synanon was immediately reciprocated by an opportunistic Chuck Dederich, who invited Endore to collaborate with two men already working on a film about the foundation: Barry Orringer, a young, inexperienced Israeli screenwriter, and Fredric Gadette, an obscure independent writer-producer-director who made *This Is Not a Test* (1962), a film about a fictional nuclear attack on the United States. However, Orringer and Gadette were not keen on sharing credit. For his part, Endore was reluctant to participate because he feared his political notoriety would have an adverse affect on the project. Ultimately he served only as an unofficial script consultant and Hollywood talent matchmaker. The producer Ronald Lubin (*Billy Budd,* 1962) was briefly attached to the project but, through Endore's auspices, ultimately the producer-director Richard Quine signed on, secured a film deal with Columbia Pictures, and made *Synanon* (1965), a rather mediocre docudrama written by Orringer, Ian Bernard, and S. Lee Pogostin and starring the veteran character actor Edmund O'Brien as Chuck Dederich; the film had a supporting cast including Chuck Connors, Stella Stevens, Alex Cord, Richard Conte, Eartha Kitt, and Alejandro Rey.

Endore served Synanon in other ways, by writing *Synanon City* (1968), an adulatory publicity pamphlet, and *Synanon* (1968), an equally adulatory full-length study that presents Synanon's philosophy, details the daily workings of the commune, and recounts the often harrowing life stories of many of its members. In a way it is fortunate that Guy Endore died of a heart attack, at the age of sixty-nine, on 12 February 1970. His death spared him a series of disillusioning revelations in the mid-1970s that Chuck Dederich had relapsed into alcoholism, had grown increasingly paranoid and dictatorial, and had turned Endore's beloved Synanon into a mean-spirited, corrupt, violence-prone cult that ultimately self-destructed. Endore, an idealist and romantic who always believed in the amelioration of the human condition, would have been crushed.

Selected Bibliography

WORKS OF GUY ENDORE

First Editions
Casanova: His Known and Unknown Life. New York: John Day, 1929.
The Man from Limbo. New York: Farrar & Rinehart, 1930.
The Sword of God: Jeanne d'Arc. New York: Farrar & Rinehart, 1931.
The Werewolf of Paris. New York: Farrar & Rinehart, 1933.
Babouk. New York: Vanguard, 1934.
Methinks the Lady.... New York: Duell, Sloan and Pearce, 1945.
King of Paris. New York: Simon & Schuster, 1956.
Detour at Night. New York: Simon & Schuster, 1959.
Voltaire! Voltaire! New York: Simon & Schuster, 1961.
Satan's Saint: A Novel About the Marquis de Sade. New York: Crown, 1965.
Synanon. Garden City, NY: Doubleday, 1968.

Pamphlets
The Crime at Scottsboro. Hollywood, Calif.: Hollywood Scottsboro Committee, 1938.
The Sleepy Lagoon Mystery. Los Angeles, Calif.: Sleepy Lagoon Defense Committee, 1944.
Justice for Salcido. Los Angeles, Calif.: Civil Rights Congress of Los Angeles, 1948.
War Yes, Sex No. New York: Push Pin Studios, 1963. (From a talk given by Guy Endore to the graduating class of the School of Library Service, University of California, Los Angeles, 25 May 1962.)
Synanon City. Santa Monica, Calif.: Synanon Foundation, 1968.

Translations and Edited Work
Blei, Franz. *Fascinating Women, Sacred & Profane.* Translated from the German by Guy Endore. New York: Simon & Schuster, 1928.
Ewers, Hanns Heinz. *Alraune.* Translated from the German by Guy Endore. New York: John Day, 1929.
Demaison, André. *Beasts Called Wild.* Translated from the French by Guy Endore. New York: Farrar & Rinehart, 1930.
Picard, Max. *The Human Face.* Translated from the German by Guy Endore. New York: Farrar & Rinehart, 1930.
Loti, Pierre. *An Iceland Fisherman.* Translated from the French by Guy Endore. Stockholm: Norstedt, 1931.
Schenzinger, Karl A. *Fired!* Translated from the German by Guy Endore. New York: Century, 1932.
Kisch, Egon Erwin. *Sensation Fair.* Translated from the German by Guy Endore. New York: Modern Age, 1941.
Weirauch, Anna Elisabet. *The Outcast.* Translated from the German by Guy Endore. New York: Willey, 1948.
Dumas, Alexandre, 1802–1870. *An Autobiography-Anthology Including the Best of Dumas.* Edited by Guy Endore. Garden City, N.Y.: Doubleday, 1962.

Screenwriting
Mad Love. Directed by Karl Freund. MGM, 1935. (Adaptation.)
Mark of the Vampire. Directed by Tod Browning. MGM, 1935. (Screenplay.)
The Raven. Directed by Louis Friedlander. Universal, 1935. (Contributing writer, uncredited.)
Rumba. Directed by Marion Gering. Paramount, 1935. (Story.)
The Devil-Doll. Directed by Tod Browning. MGM, 1936. (Screenplay.)
Carefree. Directed by Mark Sandrich. RKO, 1938. (Story.)
Lady from Louisiana. Directed by Bernard Vorhaus. Republic, 1941. (Screenplay.)
Shining Victory. Directed by Irving Rapper. Warner Bros., 1941. (Contributing writer, uncredited.)
Song of Russia. Directed by Gregory Ratoff. MGM, 1944. (Story.)
The Story of G.I. Joe. Directed by William Wellman. United Artists, 1945.
El hombre que amé. Directed by Alberto de Zavalia. Andes Films (Argentina), 1947. (Story.)
The Vicious Circle. Directed by W. Lee Wilder. United Artists, 1948. (Screenplay.)

Johnny Allegro. Directed by Ted Tetzlaff. Columbia, 1949.

Whirlpool. Directed by Otto Preminger. Twentieth Century-Fox, 1949. (Novel, *Methinks the Lady...*)

Tomorrow Is Another Day. Directed by Felix E. Feist. Warner Bros., 1951. (Story.)

The Curse of the Werewolf. Directed by Terence Fisher. Hammer (U.K.), 1961. (Novel, *The Werewolf of Paris.*)

Captain Sindbad. Directed by Byron Haskin. MGM, 1963. (Under the pseudonym Harry Relis.)

Fear No Evil. Directed by Paul Wendkos. NBC Television, 1969. (Story.)

ARTICLES, STORIES, AND PLAY

"Cataract." In *The New American Caravan: A Yearbook of American Literature.* Edited by Alfred Kreymborg et al. New York: Macaulay, 1929.

"A Christmas Story." In *American Caravan IV.* Edited by Alfred Kreymborg et al. New York: Macaulay, 1931.

"Lazarus Returns." In *A Century of Horror Stories.* Edited by Dennis Wheatley. London: Hutchison, 1935.

"Night Thoughts." *Clipper: A Western Review,* 1940, pp. 20–24.

"Men of Iron." *Fantasy & Science Fiction,* fall 1949.

"The Day of the Dragon." In *Avon Fantasy Reader.* New York: Avon, 1950.

"Life on the Black List." *Nation,* 20 December 1952, p. 568.

"Shoulder of a Giant." *Library Journal,* 1 June 1962.

Call Me Shakespeare. New York: Dramatists Play Service, 1966.

"Changeling." In *The Monster Makers: Creators and Creations of Fantasy and Horror.* Edited by Peter Haining. New York: Taplinger, 1974.

MANUSCRIPTS, JOURNALS, AND CORRESPONDENCE

The S. Guy Endore Papers are held at the University of California, Los Angeles, Library, Department of Special Collections.

CRITICAL AND BIOGRAPHICAL STUDIES

Dixon, Elizabeth. "Reflections of Guy Endore." 1964. A 321-page transcript of interviews conducted by Elizabeth Dixon with Endore in 1961–1962. (Quotes throughout this essay are used with permission of the Regents of the University of California and the UCLA Oral History Program, Department of Special Collections, Charles E. Young Research Library.)

"Ideal Horror Tale Defined By Writer." *New York Times,* 10 May 1933.

Stableford, Brian. "Guy Endore." *St. James Guide to Horror, Ghost, and Gothic Writers.* Detroit: St. James Press, 1998.

The author wishes to thank Guy Endore's daughters, Marcia Endore Goodman and Gita Endore, for sharing reminiscences of their father.

ANNIE FINCH
(1956—)

Claire Keyes

ANNIE FINCH HAS made a place for herself in contemporary literature as a poet, essayist, and editor of anthologies of poetry and poetics. Among the new formalist poets, she has distinguished herself by focusing on the contributions of contemporary American women and also by assembling definitive essays about the nature of formalism and specific types of formal poetry. Her poetry and essays are all of a piece. Discovering that she was a formalist in an age that seemed to focus primarily on free verse, she determined to create a context for her poetry and the poetry of other formalists by doing significant work in poetics and poetic theory.

CENTRAL THEMES AND SUBJECTS

Annie Finch believes that poetry speaks to the body as much as to the mind. To that end, her poetry lends itself to performance, to incantation, and to ritual. She gravitates toward myths for her subjects; in myth she locates her earth-centered, goddess-centered spirituality. The mother of two children, she writes about sex, love, and motherhood. A strong current in her work is the decentering of the self, a theme that stems from her deep connection with the natural world and her perception of the self as part of nature.

Finch's writings in poetic theory complement her poetry and help create an artistic climate for others wanting to write in form, especially women. In establishing a critical context for her own work in formal verse, she creates a more positive environment for all contemporary poets drawn to patterning their poetry. The female poetic tradition would include such poets as Sara Teasdale and Edna St. Vincent Millay, as well as numerous nineteenth-century women poets. Finch's focus on women poets and the female poetic tradition distinguishes her work in theory from that of other new formalists, including, for example, Dana Gioia.

BIOGRAPHY

Annie Finch was born in New Rochelle, New York, on October 13, 1956. Her father, Henry Leroy (Roy) Finch, was a professor of philosophy at nearby Sarah Lawrence College and Hunter College as well as the author of books on Ludwig Wittgenstein and Simone Weil. As a teenager at the family's summer camp in Maine, Annie would discuss literature, religion, and philosophy with her father. Her mother, Margaret Rockwell Finch, is a poet and a maker of fine art dolls. At Annie's urging, she published her first book of poetry, *Davy's Lake,* in 1996 with Caribou Press. Both parents were political activists and pacifists. Annie Finch has four siblings: Julie, Marta, Dabney, and Roy.

Poetry played a large part in Finch family life. Both parents loved poetry and hearing poems read or recited was part of Finch's childhood. Her mother would recite Edna St. Vincent Millay's sonnets; her father gave a dramatic rendition of "The Night Before Christmas" each year, and Finch has said that she recalls loving the rhythm of that poem. Finch began memorizing poems herself: Robert Louis Stevenson's "Where Go the Boats," Walter de la Mare's "The Listeners," and E. A. Robinson's "Luke Havergal."

The Finch summer place in Maine, Camp Caribou, was central to Annie Finch's deep feeling for the natural world, to her strong bond with her parents, and to her growth as a poet. Here a theme central to her work emerged: the erasure of the line between subject and object as the boundaries of self loosened. In her 2005 volume

ANNIE FINCH

The Body of Poetry: Essays on Women, Form, and the Poetic Self, she describes long conversations with her father on the porch. Out of these conversations and her own experiences in the natural world she came to believe she was not separate from nature, but part of it. Honoring this belief in her poetry, she would abandon the stance of the primary observer. Finch was on the path to embracing a woman's poetic tradition that she would discover in the "poetesses" of the nineteenth and early twentieth centuries.

Finch studied at Yale University in the late 1970s, receiving her BA in 1979. Two courses that made a mark on her were Louis Martz's in modern poetry and a course on versification taught by Penelope Laurens. Passionate about language and poetry, she learned at Yale to read "Beowulf," Chaucer, and Homer in the original versions. At the same time, Yale was a hotbed of literary theory, and she studied with Harold Bloom and Paul De Man. From them, she learned new ways of looking at language and the poetic tradition. Such issues were not as set as she had thought, but in flux.

Postcollege, she lived in New York City, where she got involved in the performance poetry scene. Poetry took on a vital existence when audiences were involved and when words were combined with music. At this time, she began writing a long performance poem she titled "The Encyclopedia of Scotland," heavily influenced by the surrealists and the Beats.

When she enrolled in the graduate program in creative writing at the University of Houston, she discovered that her poetry workshops were dominated by a focus on free verse and confessional-style poetry. Feeling alienated from the emphasis on free verse, she had to stake out her own territory as a formalist poet. Working with the poet and dramatist Ntozake Shange, she composed her thesis, a verse drama, and received her MA in 1986. In Houston, she married her husband, Glen Brand, an environmentalist.

Stanford University's PhD program in English and American literature followed Houston and was a more congenial poetic environment. Finch focused on poetics and versification. In California, she entered a remarkably creative period in her life, engendering projects that led to books of poetry and studies in poetics, and she received her PhD in 1990. She also started a family. Glen Brand and Annie Finch have two children, Julian and Althea. After completing her degrees, she taught at the University of Northern Iowa, then became a member of the creative writing faculty at Miami University in Ohio. In 2005 she became the director of the Stonecoast master of fine arts program in creative writing at the University of Southern Maine in Portland.

EARLY POETRY: THE ENCYCLOPEDIA OF SCOTLAND

The Encyclopedia of Scotland (2004) is Annie Finch's "youthful longpoem." When her father inherited some money, he offered to help her publish a book of her poems. *Scotland* is the result. The original text was too long for a modest publication so she produced what she terms "an abridged libretto" in 1982. The full text was published in 2004. The mere printing of this long poem is by no means the whole story. *The Encyclopedia of Scotland* is a performance piece.

When the abridged version was available, Finch writes in her "Introductory Narrative," she gathered together performers and served as director and chief performer. The performance aspect of this early work is central to some of the themes and concerns that have remained important to her. Finch says that *Scotland* was, in essence, a pagan ritual. "Pagan" refers primarily to worship of the earth and the processes of nature.

Whatever the conflicts in the poem, the critics are in agreement about its effect. The poet and editor Jennifer Moxley describes Finch's libretto as "fanciful" in her jacket blurb. In other words, this is a young woman's poem. The poet Ron Silliman, in his weblog *Silliman's Blog* of August 23, 2005, also picks up on the sensual quality of Finch's verse, but with a different emphasis. He quotes, as illustration, a passage from "Recessional," which is striking for its use of anaphora, its lines beginning in the same pattern until the pattern is broken and a new one evolves:

Left these hills
Left the green hills to the night-time,

Left these hills
Left them for another
Left these hills
Left them a harmonica
Howling at the ocean
Left them green
but I am there, chinning the windowsill,
I call from the doors,
I meet in the walls
I laugh on the sills,
I dance on these hills
   (p. 77)

Silliman's allegiance is to the language of poetry, and he admires poets who place language first over, say, an expression of emotion. Thus he admires Finch and her "commitment to language."

THE GHOST OF METER

Finch's first published work in poetics, *The Ghost of Meter* (1993), was written originally as her PhD thesis at Stanford. Although it is not overtly feminist, there is a definite subtext. Finch's title comes from T. S. Eliot, who defined "good free verse as poetry that uses, not meter, but the 'ghost' of meter." Finch got the idea for this book while in a University of Houston poetry workshop.

Finch looks for and finds the "ghost of meter" in what she terms "the metrically variable verse of Dickinson," as well as in the free verse of Whitman, Stephen Crane, Eliot, and two contemporary American poets, Audre Lorde and Charles Wright. In the works of these poets, Finch "explains and illustrates a new idea about the relationship between meter and meaning in poetry, the metrical code." Her book, she goes on to say,

> proposes that meter can constitute a crucial aspect of the meaning of poems written during times of metrical crisis-periods of deep change in the prosodic foundations of poetry. The words in such poems comment, on one level, on their own meter, just as meter enriches the meaning of the words. Metered lines of metrically variable verse can reveal the poet's attitudes toward the meter's cultural and literary connotations.
> (p. 1)

Finch points out how the iambic pentameter line was associated with the authority and power of patriarchal structures. Both Dickinson and Whitman refused to adopt the iambic as a basic meter, but reverted to it at key moments. Whitman also would set off his iambic pentameter with dactylics, termed by Finch the "falling meter" (long-short-short).

Finch points out how American poets have resisted iambic pentameter because of its dominance in English literature. Her knowledge and use of dactylic meter is, however, not simply a matter of definitions. Her study of dactylic meter in Whitman, Dickinson, and others convinced her of the power of what she saw as a vital and life-affirming rhythm. She determined to use such meter in her own poetry and literally had to teach herself to write in dactyls. *The Ghost of Meter,* begun in a poetry workshop, transformed into a doctoral dissertation and then a book, led to metric transformations in her poetry that connected to her sense of the women's poetic tradition and of herself as a woman.

A FORMAL FEELING COMES

Finch was definitely on the right track in her next book, an anthology of poems in form by contemporary women. *A Formal Feeling Comes* (1994) derives its title from Emily Dickinson and became her most successful book.

This anthology, with an introduction by Finch, collects poems in form by sixty women, from more famous names like Maxine Kumin, Carolyn Kizer, May Sarton, Rita Dove (the former poet laureate of the United States), and Marilyn Hacker to women poets just emerging and those in between. Each poet writes a brief introduction to her poems, commenting on her choice of formal strategies. The critic Alice Evans notes that "ethnic diversity is one of the highlights of this book.... Poets whose work is represented include Mexican American writer Sandra Cisneros, Dominican Republic native Julia Alvarez,

Asian American poet Nellie Wong and other women of color."

Evans also confesses to her own preference for free verse and says that she opened *A Formal Feeling Comes* with "a sense of hesitance, even alarm." As with Finch (and many, many others), Evans had "absorbed the in-vogue dictum of the 1970s and 1980s that said formal poetry, particularly poetry rhymed and strictly metered, is something modern poets must evolve beyond." But she was won over by Finch's book, with poet after poet "singing the praises of form, giving testimony to its lasting beauty." Plus, they were all women.

The praise for the prose introductions to each set of poems is particularly ironic, for getting the poets to delve into their reasons for writing in form was an onerous task for Finch. Some were reluctant to discuss their poetic process, and she had to coax them over the phone and record what they had to say. It was worth it.

Finch's own contribution to the volume includes a two-paragraph introduction in which she celebrates the impact of meter on her own verse. Her introduction is followed by four poems, among which "For Grizzel McNaught (1709–1792)" appears as perhaps the most relevant to Finch's development as a poet. The poem concerns the speaker's connection with Grizzel, who was considered a witch. A terza rima, "For Grizzel" contains twelve lines. A slightly different form of the poem appears in her 1997 volume, *Eve,* as "Ancestor." What remains the same in both are lines where Finch employs dactyls.

EVE

Avid readers of free verse would find Annie Finch's *Eve,* her first full book of poems, somewhat daunting. Finch prefers writing in a variety of forms from terza rima to the sonnet to Sapphics. If the reader lacks acquaintance with these forms, then a great deal of the pleasure of the poems is missed. Finch's poetry can be best understood if the reader is familiar with her work in poetics.

Before *Eve,* Finch published a poetry chapbook, *Catching the Mermother,* with Aralia Press in 1997. Aralia is a fine art press located in West Chester, Pennsylvania; it has also published chapbooks by Dana Gioia, another new formalist. In fact, Gioia was an advisor to the press in the 1990s, and he decided upon the order of Finch's poems. Aralia printed 150 copies with a hand-painted cover illustration. The twelve poems in *Catching the Mermother* were incorporated into *Eve*. These poems, according to Finch's acknowledgment in *Eve,* are: "Running in Church," "Being a Constellation," "Mermother," "Coy Mistress," "Diving Past African Violets," "Lucid Waking," "Tribute," "My Raptor," "No Snake," "Pearls," "Samhain," and "Sapphics for Patience." These poems appear in various sections in *Eve*.

Finch dedicates *Eve* to C. A. K., Carolyn Kizer, who also wrote a review of the book. Finch is one of the editors of a celebratory volume of essays about Kizer that appeared in 2001, and she also includes poems by Kizer in *A Formal Feeling Comes*. Their bond is deep. In Kizer's review, she says that all looked forward to the publication of *Eve* and "liked the use of myth in modern contexts." One can see the aptness of Kizer's remarks in a poem like "Running in Church," which contains the subheading "for Marie," whom the poet describes as

...a hot-thinking, thin-lidded tinderbox.
Losing your balance meant nothing at all. You would
pour through the aisles in the highest cathedrals,
careening deftly as patriarchs brooded.
(p. 2)

Like Kizer, C. L. Rawlins praises *Eve,* finding it "the most delightful and original poetry I've run across in years." Rawlins also finds the book's organization elegant and compelling: "Starting with nine ancestral goddesses, [Finch] composes for each a section-opening poem that reflects not only the content, but the style of the original." Rawlins goes on to point out how the poem "'Inanna' adopts from Sumerian myths a four-beat accentual line divided into two parts. "For example, the first line: "A young goddess, full of love, fresh with the touch of a husband."

The poem that follows "Inanna" is "The Last Mermother," and in it Rawlins finds not "idle folkloric invention," but imaginative risk-taking of the highest order. The poem begins simply enough with a direct statement in the poem's governing metric, iambic pentameter: "I used to fish in San Francisco Bay." From this bland opening comes a wild encounter, not with a mermaid, but with a "mermother":

She howled, stretching her hand to mine,
floating her tail in the rocking of the tide
as she clung to the slippery post below. I tried
to look at her. I saw that it was true.
Well, what would you have done? I helped her through
(p. 14)

In lines 1–3 quoted above, the iambic meter gives way to the dactylic as the wild, nonrational being emerges: "stretching her hand" and "floating her tail in the rocking of the tide." In this movement of meters, Finch enacts her thesis from *The Ghost of Meter.*

Where Kizer "liked the use of myth in modern contexts," Rawlins goes a little further: "Finch uses myth and archetype in a present way, to illuminate life." But what aspect of life does the mermother illuminate? Finch writes in the first stanza how her speaker used to enjoy fishing "until the day I was destroyed." In stanza four, she writes, "that was the day I lost my mind." (p. 15) By the last stanza, the emphasis has shifted from the speaker of the poem to the child of the mermother:

A mother! I still can't say
if my fishing hook killed it, or if she
dropped it in the struggle, but of course it died that
   day.
   (p. 15)

The child is the "it"; "it died that day" just as the speaker knew that she "was destroyed." Primitive, violent, if anything, the mermother reminds us of Grendel's mother in the poem *Beowulf.* Overwhelming in her physicality, she dwarfs the speaker's sense of personal identity. Her "I" exists no longer but is subsumed in this ancient archetype—the Great Goddess of pagan religion. To be "destroyed" by such a being is not such a bad thing. In stanza 3, when the speaker looks directly at the mermother: "I saw that it was true." In other words, the subjective gets annihilated in this encounter and the speaker releases the boundaries of the self. Recognizing this theme is essential to understanding the work of Annie Finch.

Although Rawlins confesses that he has not read Finch's scholarly prose, he praises her for having "a knowing way with sound. What she proves is that rhyme-and-meter isn't just a formerly fashionable sort of bondage, the equivalent of a whalebone corset, but is instead a bio-acoustic key to memory and emotion, which existed prior to the written word. And it still works."

Taking a different perspective from Kizer and Rawlins, C. G. Macdonald notes the numerous transformations that occur in *Eve.* In "Three Generations of Secrets," for example, the speaker, a pregnant woman, becomes a bell. This transformation is conscious and willed: "I think I will turn metal, like a bell." Her purpose is maternal; she wants her unborn child to hear and reciprocate:

so you can clapper my voice out, to where
the silent memories will echo care
and speak again.
   (p. 26)

This sonnet concludes with a vision of the mother and child coming together in their sounding, but ultimately separating:

But we'll speak, and you will live,
tolling and striking what we know at last,
until you ring aloud with newer sounds
   (p. 26)

In commenting on "Tribute," written to Emily Dickinson, MacDonald finds many qualities in Finch's *Eve* that he also locates in Emily Dickinson, one of Finch's foremothers in verse. Macdonald grants that Finch does not have the "oceanic amplitude" of Dickinson, but that like her foremother she is "gnomic, lyrical, intricate, and deft." MacDonald then praises Finch for her "post-feminist jauntiness and a theoretical and cultural sweep that were unavailable to

Dickinson." The latter part of this comment is entirely justifiable and pertains to Finch's work in poetics; the first part underrates one of the central aspects of Finch's work: her feminism.

Annie Finch is feminist to the core, meaning that the fact of her womanhood is central to all her poems, to her subject matter, and even to her style. She embraces the Great Goddess in her many manifestations in the *Eve* poems. She locates her influences in women artists, from Carolyn Kizer to Emily Dickinson to Sappho. She is not interested in overthrowing the patriarchy; she takes that as a given. Finch even labels herself as a feminist and a "postmodern poetess," with all that implies.

AFTER NEW FORMALISM

Over the years, Annie Finch has served as editor and coeditor of several scholarly texts dealing with aspects of new formalism, projects that are a measure of her status, credibility, and the depth of her knowledge. The reviewer Carmine Starnino speculates on the first word of the title of a 1999 collection of essays for which Finch served as editor—*After New Formalism*—saying that it is: "a suggestion of the movement's new phase." He goes on to say that he "regard[s] the 'after' as a subliminal reassurance, a message that the new formalism has survived its fugitive status and can now enjoy the calmer civic life of self-appraisal and reassessment." (p. xiii) Finch's introduction is a useful guide to the collection of essays on form, narrative, and tradition. In opening, she identifies herself as a formalist poet and then goes on to say how uncomfortable she is with the images that have become associated with new formalist poetry. She feels that such poetry is viewed, wrongly, as "insular and reactionary." The essays she has collected in *After New Formalism* are intended to squash these stereotypes.

Beginning the volume with Adrienne Rich's "Format and Form" is certainly a deliberate ploy to shatter the stereotype of formalism. Although Rich began her poetic career in the 1950s as a writer of formalist verse, she broke with that tradition as she became more overtly feminist in her politics and her poetry. Her essay, like many others in the volume, is a reprint and was published first in her 1993 collection, *What Is Found There: Notebooks on Poetry and Politics*. In this essay, Rich cites examples of poems by the Jewish Muriel Rukeyser, homoerotic poems of Alarçon, and poems by poets of color such as Claude McKay.

While the reviewer Starnino does not include Rich's essay in his list of the "best essays" in the volume, he praises the work of James Cummins, Marilyn Nelson, Molly Peacock, Christian Wiman, Agha Shahid Ali, and Anne Stevenson for the freshness of language "brightened by...aplomb and finesse." He is scathing, however, about other essays in the volume, which he finds stodgy "in their joylessly schematic and cerebral approach to formalism." (p. xiv) Starnino, a Montreal poet, critic, and editor concludes his review with a prescription for new formalist criticism. He feels that what "many readers (and poets) need when it comes to formal poetry is [criticism] that's able to return life to the poems, to give readers a sense of the poetry moving inside its own warm-blooded immediacy and vigor." Starnino states bluntly that "*After New Formalism* does not accomplish this enough." (p. xiv)

ON CAROLYN KIZER

Carolyn Kizer: Perspectives on Her Life and Work (2001) was begun as a way for Finch to honor the woman poet who had offered her "warm and supportive response" to her own poetry. From Finch's preface to the book, we learn that she and her coeditors "discovered the extent of Carolyn's support of younger poets, especially women." The book is divided into three sections: 1) essays, articles, and reviews; 2) poems for Kizer; and 3) interviews. Finch herself contributes an essay, titled "Carolyn Kizer and the Chain of Women," and a poem, "A Carol for Carolyn."

Finch's essay, a tribute to Kizer, provides a clear sense of the path that Finch has pursued in her own poetry. For Finch, Kizer provides a significant link to the tradition of women poets in America. While Kizer disparages these women poets (among whom Finch locates Phyllis Wheatley, Frances Osgood, Emily Dickinson, Alice Dunbar Nelson, Sara Teasdale, Edna St. Vincent Millay, Anna Hampstead Beach, Louise Bogan and Leonie Adams), Finch esteems them as "emotionally astute, poetically exacting, [and] passionate." (p. 85)

Finch is not put off by Kizer's disparagement of the poetesses and their "sentimentist" techniques. She uses this term to distinguish the women poets from the Romantics of the nineteenth century. In sum, they wrote the poetry to which Finch also aspired.

Finch's essay is a brilliant exposition of how Kizer balances this responsibility to the aesthetic of the poetesses while surpassing their limitations. Likewise, Finch's poetry displays this same balance. What she brings to the poetry table is a grasp of the whole tradition and her compelling theoretical acumen.

Finch's poem "A Carol for Carolyn" joins together poetic theory and practice. In honoring Kizer, she builds upon an epigraph from Kizer's poem, "In the First Stanza": "It is easy to be a poet, / Brim with transparent water." Finch's two stanzas explore the relationship between the poet and "transparent water." Both stanzas develop a rhyme scheme of ABABCCC; both rely chiefly upon the short-long-short meter of amphibrachs. Finch tells the interviewer Brendan Kiely: "That was the hardest meter I knew and I wanted to write [Carolyn] something special." Here is the first stanza:

I dreamed of a poet who gave me a whale
that shadowed clear pools through the sea-weeded shade.
When beached sea-foam dried on the rocks, it would sail
down currents that gathered to pool and cascade
with turbulent order.
She brims with transparent water,
as mother and poet and daughter.
   (p. 163)

The reader can follow the image of the whale and its actions, although the context is a bit otherworldly. When we come to the last two lines, we see how Finch has conjoined the whale image with the woman poet: "She brims with transparent water, / as mother and poet and daughter." The verb "brims" connotes both the amazing spectacle of a whale surfacing and the generous spilling forth of the "mother and poet and daughter" who is Carolyn Kizer.

In "A Carol for Carolyn," Finch, like her sentimentist predecessors, metaphorizes the self—in this case the self of Kizer imaged as a whale. Although the poem begins with the "I" as the locus of the dream, the "I" is relatively unimportant. Stanza 2 focuses more on the effect of the poet: "The ocean she's authored / brims, with transparent water / for poet and mother and daughter." (p. 163) Slight word changes and word order indicate Finch's esteem for Kizer. The water in the second stanza is not "for" herself alone—as in stanza 1—but others. There is a diffusion of the self of Carolyn Kizer and this diffusion spreads into a womanly world of poets and mothers and daughters—the female poetic tradition. Finch is consistent. With her, theory and practice are one.

LOFTY DOGMAS

In her preface to *Lofty Dogmas* (2005), Maxine Kumin explains how for years she had been "carrying around in my head" the concept of the book. What she wanted was a book on poetics by practicing poets and not theoreticians. She felt such a book would be eminently useful, particularly for students. She located Deborah Brown, a neighbor of hers who is a poet-professor, and then Annie Finch. The resulting book, edited by the three women, pulls together in remarkable fashion statements in prose and poetry from practitioners throughout the ages with a special emphasis on English and American poetry in the modern era.

Perhaps the most significant aspect of the book is how eclectic it is. No particular school of poetry dominates *Lofty Dogmas*. Readers can attend to John Milton or John Keats, William Carlos Williams or T. S. Eliot, Edna St. Vincent Millay or Adrienne Rich—and everyone in between. The editors may have missed a poet or two, but the volume is truly comprehensive. It speaks of a largeness of vision for poetry.

ANNIE FINCH

Annie Finch contributes a segment from her essay "Coherent Decentering: Towards a New Model of the Poetic Self," a piece that is central to an understanding of Finch's strategies in her own poetry. She begins with a disavowal of the Romantic poetic stance in which the poetic self is "fixed" and "central"—for example, Keats contemplating the Grecian urn. Finch's goal is to write poems from the "true self" and to embody it.

Finch is not alone in embracing the "decentered self" as a valid point of departure. She separates herself, however, from those in the avant-garde who write poetry that is deliberately scattered and incoherent. She tried such tactics herself and gave them up, preferring the challenge of working with ordinary syntax. Within those constraints she would perform the requisite "twisting and turning" to work the limitations to her own advantage. She admits that her most common technique is the use of forms or patterns. Finch's focus upon the decentered self and the techniques she used to achieve such a self in poetry are enormously useful in reading her second book of poems, *Calendars*.

CALENDARS

Finch's widely reviewed book of poetry *Calendars* (2003), which was short-listed for the Forward Poetry Prize, crystallizes themes and strategies that Annie Finch has expressed in her theoretical prose and edited collections. Randall D'Arcy usefully articulates the structure and theme of the book:

> This is a book of life seasons, organized loosely around the Celtic or Wiccan calendar. Poems celebrating Winter Solstice, Imbolc, Spring Equinox, Summer Solstice, and Lammas serve as keystones for each section; together they establish a theme of cyclical time. Within this framework, the poems vary in theme and style. Many participate in feminist poetic and critical conversations concerning women's creative and procreative authority. In *Calendars,* a woman's cycles, her lovers, her pregnancies, her losses, her relationship with her own parents, and her muses are interrelated. Some poems are set in the domain of myth; others, like

"Elegy for My Father" or "Epithalamium," appear to be written for or inspired by contemporary occasions. All of the poems, however, can be classified as "formal." For the reader, the challenge to determine *what* forms, and how they work, is one of the book's many charms.

Adrian Oktenberg's reading of *Calendars* puts Finch in the company of "Elizabeth Bishop [and] Marilyn Hacker" because her formal poems are contemporary. Oktenberg quotes the first poem in the volume, "Landing Under Water, I See Roots":

All the things we hide in water
hoping we won't see them go—
(forests growing under water
press against the ones we know)—
and they might have gone on growing
and they might now breathe above
everything I speak of sowing
(everything I try to love).
(p. 3)

Oktenberg praises Finch's ear and eye. Instead of logical meaning, Finch aims for an aural environment captured in the rhythm of her words and the patterning of the lines. The emphasis on the underworld may suggest that Finch is dealing here with elements of the subconscious, that fertile birthplace of the imagination. The penultimate line refers to "everything I speak of sowing," initiating an image pattern in the book of seeds and fruition in nature and the human being.

Patricia Monaghan focuses upon the element of tradition in *Calendars,* and finds that Finch's poems show "an embrace of traditional subject as well as form." Finch, however, puts a little spin on the subject of nature and it cycles. As if to underline this point of view, Finch, at the end of the volume, includes a list of all the poems and their approximate year of completion. The dates run from 1970 through 2000, yet the poems appear in vastly different order in the collection. Finch has a nonlinear view of her own poems, perceiving them as having their own meaningful order unrelated to date of composition.

"Caribou Kitchen" can help clarify this point about a nonlinear structuring of time:

Most things have vanished
while we were talking

(the dents in a pitcher
gleam by the gas lamp),
but nothing is lost
(cups in far corners).
Arms still lean
over the table
(shadows on the oilcloth).
   (p. 21)

The first two lines mingle the past and the present. Lines 3 and 4 introduce what Tad Richards terms the "counter-voice" in parentheses. A concrete image countering the abstraction of the opening lines, these lines seem to introduce a continuous present, something always there in the place Finch has known as Caribou Camp in Maine since her early childhood. The paradox of line 5: "But nothing is lost" seemingly negates the opening line: "Most things have vanished." Concreteness wins out: "Arms still lean / over the table." Although they may not be the same arms that leaned in the past, the poet only suggests this. The counter-voice comes back at the end to introduce "shadows on the oilcloth," perhaps of those no longer present.

Jack Foley, in a review of *Calendars* is also intrigued by Finch's sonnet "Watching the Oregon Whale." He draws some interesting comparisons between it and D. H. Lawrence's "Whales Weep Not!" This comparison is illuminating because it helps to highlight Finch's strategies and themes. The feminine pronouns are clear, as in "I follow her fill / into and out of green light in the depth she has spun." (p. 8) Although Foley does not use the phrase "metaphorizing the self," he finds significant the turn in the poem when the speaker "becomes a cormorant":

I trail her, spun
down through my life in the making of her difference,
fixing my mouth, with the offerings of silence,
on her dark whale-road...
   (p. 8)

An excellent reader, Jack Foley establishes many connections between Finch's statements on poetics and the poems in *Calendars*. He intuits a connection between Finch's poetry and the sentimentist tradition. Foley quotes Crapsey's poem "Grain Field" to make his point:

Scarlet the poppies
Blue the corn-flowers,
Golden the wheat.
Gold for The Eternal:
Blue for Our Lady:
Red for the five
Wounds of her Son.
   (p. 77)

Granted, the overtly Christian references in this poem are not likely to appear in Finch's poetry. Foley finds a link, however, between "Our Lady" and Finch's allusions to the pagan Great Goddess. Jack Foley, in sum, gets Annie Finch.

Silliman calls attention to Finch's six-line poem "Moon," finding it comparable to the work of H.D. (Hilda Doolittle) in its timing.

Then are you the dense everywhere that moves,
the dark matter they haven't yet walked through?
(No, I'm not. I'm just the shining sun,
sometimes covered up by the darkness.)
But in your beauty—yes, I know you see—
There is no covering, no constant light.
   (p. 4)

The fact that Finch draws readers like Foley and Silliman into precise and nuanced discussions of her work is, of course, to her great credit. She is taken seriously. She has accomplished what she wished: to create a context for the poetry she chooses to write.

THE BODY OF POETRY

Annie Finch has a strong attraction to the body of poetry, its form, its shape. She wrote the essays in *The Body of Poetry* (2005) to help nurture a similar love in other poets and readers. She feels that free verse, the dominant mode of American poetry since at least the middle of the twentieth century, denies the appeal of poetry's body. An aspect of this denial extends back to a distaste for the "pre-Modernist women's poetic tradition," as Finch says in her preface to this volume. She embraces that tradition and asserts her identity as a "postmodern poetess."

Julie Kane, in her review of *The Body of Poetry,* credits Finch as a leader of the New Formalist movement and also with making a solid argument for the "timelessness and timeliness of formal verse." Finch, it must be noted, does not limit formal verse to prescribed structures such as the sonnet or villanelle, but enlarges the definition of "formal" to include any sort of obvious patterning or repetition. Finch's championing of formal poetry and her role as one of the leading poet—critics of new formalism are deeply connected to her own spirituality. For Finch, exercising her poetic craft is an aspect of "goddess poetics."

Finch's criticism exhilarates because she takes on the potentially "stodgy" subject of meter and elevates it from the counting of stresses to aesthetic metamorphosis. In other words, Finch lays out the case for creating in poetry the experience of the diffusion of the self.

Although Finch has made the case elsewhere in her work, she articulates her theme with great precision in *The Body of Poetry.* The poet attends to something larger or other than him or herself in working with forms. The poet is also engaging with tradition. In writing a sonnet the poet reaches back through time and shares the experience of a Keats or a Shakespeare or an Edna St. Vincent Millay.

In the section of *The Body of Poetry* titled "Confessions of a Postmodern Poetess," Finch expands upon her appreciation for the poetess tradition. Central to her defense of the poetess tradition is her belief that modern Western culture needs an experience in art that is more communal and that would at the same time reconnect us with nature.

CONCLUSION

Readers will derive more from Annie Finch's poetry if they also sample her work in poetics. Because her work in poetic theory and practice is so rich in ideas, so penetrating in its cultural criticism, and so accessible compared to most work in theory, it becomes not just a guide to her own poetry but also a way of seeing the larger trends in poetry from the nineteenth century to the present day.

Finch is right about the dominance of free verse and the risk to poetry of that dominance. She is right about the poetess tradition and the undercurrent of misogyny in throwing off this tradition. She is right about the enduring pleasure of "the body of poetry." Whether her own poetry can engage readers in rejoicing in that body is an open question. Her own "ear" for poetic rhythm and sound may be the most significant element of her poetry and her poetics. It will take a while, however, for the collective "ear" of the poetry-loving public to catch up with her. As passionate as she is about poetry's body, as sustained as her effort is to bring that passion forth in her books of poetry and poetics, hers is clearly a poetic voice that challenges our assumptions about poetry just as it exhilarates.

Selected Bibliography

WORKS OF ANNIE FINCH

POETRY

The Encyclopedia of Scotland. Abridged libretto. New York: Caribou Press, 1982; complete edition, Cambridge, U.K.: Salt Publishing, 2004.

Catching the Mermother. West Chester, Penn.: Aralia Press, 1995.

Eve. Brownsville, Ore.: Story Line Press, 1997.

Season Poems. San Francisco: Calliope Press, 2001.

Calendars. Manchester, Vt.: Tupelo Press, 2003.

Home-Birth. Cincinnati, Ohio: Dos Madres Press, 2004.

Annie Finch: Greatest Hits. Columbus, Ohio: Pudding House Press, 2006.

POETICS AND TRANSLATION

The Ghost of Meter: Culture and Prosody in American Free Verse. Ann Arbor: University of Michigan Press, 1993; paperback edition with new preface, 2001.

A Formal Feeling Comes: Poems in Form by Contemporary Women. Brownsville, Ore.: Story Line Press, 1994.

After New Formalism: Poets on Form, Narrative, and Tradition. Brownsville, Ore.: Story Line Press, 1999.

Carolyn Kizer: Perspectives on Her Life and Work. Coeditor with Johanna Keller and Candace McClelland. Fort Lee,

N.J.: CavanKerry Press, 2001.

An Exaltation of Forms: Contemporary Poets Celebrate the Diversity of Their Art. Coeditor with Kathrine Varnes. Ann Arbor: University of Michigan Press, 2002.

The Body of Poetry: Essays on Women, Form, and the Poetic Self. Poets on Poetry Series. Ann Arbor: University of Michigan Press, 2005.

Lofty Dogmas: Poets on Poetics. Coeditor with Maxine Kumin and Deborah Brown. Fayetteville: University of Arkansas Press, 2005.

Louise Labé: Complete Poetry and Prose: A Bilingual Edition. Poetry translations by Annie Finch. Edited and with translations by Deborah Lesko Baker. Chicago: University of Chicago Press, 2006.

Multiformalisms: Postmodern Poetics of Form. Coeditor with Susan Schultz. Cincinnati: Textos Books (Wordtech Editions), 2008.

Annie Finch maintains a Web site at http://www.usm.maine.edu~afinch, containing many links to articles, reviews, and interviews.

CRITICAL AND BIOGRAPHICAL STUDIES

Articles and Reviews

Adams, Stephen J. Review of *The Ghost of Meter. Canadian Review of American Studies* 25, no. 2: 142, 4p (spring 1995).

Barron, Jonathan. "Annie Finch." *Dictionary of Literary Biography.* Vol. 282, *New Formalist Poets.* Edited by Jonathan N. Barron and Bruce Meyer. Detroit: Gale, 2003. Pp. 91–101.

Brock, J. Review of *An Exaltation of Forms. Choice Magazine,* September 2002. (Reprinted at Annie Finch's Web site.)

Caplan, David. Review of *An Exaltation of Forms. South Atlantic Review* 69:1 Fall 2004: 142–146.

Evans, Alice. "Women Poets, Formally Speaking." *Eugene Weekly,* 1 December 1994.

Foley, Jack. Review of *Calendars. Alsop Review* (http://www.alsopreview.com/columns/foley/jfFinch.html)

Gwynn, R. S. "Proseurs." *Sewanee Review* 104, no. 1: 142, 8p (winter 1996). (Review of The Ghost of Meter)

Kane, Julie. Review of *The Body of Poetry. Consciousness, Literature, and the Arts* 7, no. 2 (August 2006). (Available at http://www.aber.ac.uk/cla/current/finch.html.)

Kizer, Carolyn. "Four Smart Poets." *Michigan Quarterly Review* 39, no. 1: 167 (winter 2000). (Review of *Eve.*)

Lamoureaux, Mark. Review of *The Body of Poetry. Art New England,* (June/July 2005) 6.

MacDonald, C. G. Review of *Eve. Poetry Flash* (December 1998). (Reprinted at Annie Finch's Web site.)

Monaghan, Patricia. "Review of Annie Finch, *Calendars.*" *Web del Sol Review of Books* (http://www.webdelsol.com/WDSRB/Monaghan.html).

Morris, Timothy. Review of *The Ghost of Meter. Style* 28, no.1: 125–127 (spring 1994).

Oktenberg, Adrian. "Formal but Unconstrained." *Women's Review of Books* 20, nos. 10–11: 36, 2p (July 2003). (Review of *Calendars.*)

"Poetics After New Formalism: Poets on Form, Narrative and Tradition." *Publishers Weekly,* 26 July 1999: 87.

D'Arcy, Randall. Review of *Calendars. Blue Mesa Review* (spring 2005).

Rawlins, C. L. Review of *Eve. Bloomsbury Review* (spring 1998).

Richards, Tad. Review of *Calendars. Jacket* 26 (http://jacketmagazine.com/26/rich-finch.html), October 2004.

Scharf, Michael. Review of Calendars. *Publishers Weekly,* 23 June 2003: 63, 1/5p.

Silliman, Ron. Review of *Calendars. Silliman's Blog* (www.ronsilliman.blogspot.com), 13 October 2002.

———. Review of *The Encyclopedia of Scotland. Silliman's Blog* (www.ronsilliman.blogspot.com), 23 August 2005. (Available via link at Annie Finch's Web site)

Standing, Sue. Review of *A Formal Feeling Comes. Boston Review* 20, no. 3 (summer 1995) 40–41.

Stanford, Donald E. "American Formalism." *Southern Review* 31, no. 2: 381, 7p (spring 1995).

Starnino, Carmine. "The Multiformalist Approach to New Formalism." *Sewanee Review* 109, no. 1: 12, 3p (winter 2001).

Wagner-Lawlor, Jennifer. Review of *A Formal Feeling Comes* and *The Ghost of Meter. ANQ* 10, no. 4: 57 (fall 1997).

Interviews

Gwynn, R. S. "Giving Back to the World Its Lost Heart." *Ablemuse* (http://www.ablemuse.com/v5/a-finch.htm), winter 2002.

Kiely, Brendan. "Pattern and Poetic Creativity: An Interview with Annie Finch." *Writer's Chronicle* 37, no. 3: 42–47 (December 2004).

Maas, Tomma Lou. "Multiformalisms: An Interview with Annie Finch." *Poetry Flash* (September 1994). (Reprinted at Annie Finch's website.)

Murray, Chris. "A Conversation with Annie Finch." *Znine: Words, Words, Words* (http://www.uta.edu/english/zninef03/interview1.html), 2003.

M. F. K. FISHER

(1908–1992)

Susan Butterworth

THE ESSAYIST M.F.K. (Mary Frances Kennedy) Fisher is known primarily for her particular blend of food, travel, and memoir writing. She came from a family of journalists, and considered herself a journalist all her life. Late in life she commented that she had earned her living from writing freelance articles, never from books. Fisher wrote for a commercial market rather than a literary one, yet she created a genre of literature about cuisine that included personal voice and wider significance, a literature that equated good cooking with love and shelter.

Fisher lived a rich and unconventional life, a life that was a well of material for her memoir-infused stories, articles, and books. Her scenes and sketches of the art of good eating and good living offer glimpses of moments in her life, glimpses that allow the reader to piece together the story of her life without that story becoming confessional, without revealing details that she chooses to leave unspoken. Several themes and motifs recur throughout Fisher's life and work: journeying, being alone, returning to beloved places, a sense of joie de vivre in spite of an underlying sadness that grows more poignant with the passage of time and accumulation of experience. Many of her experiences center on food and eating, and on hunger in a larger sense; hunger for love as well as for food. Her writing displays a simple, natural, yet witty and sophisticated style, a personal voice that evokes the mood of a place through her careful selection of detail and experience.

Mary Frances Kennedy was born on 3 July 1908 in Albion, Michigan, where her father, Rex Brenton Kennedy, owned and edited a newspaper with his brother. Her mother, Edith Oliver Holbrook, was an educated and cultivated woman who had studied music in Europe. A younger sister, Anne, was born two years later, and the two girls were inseparable for their first twenty years. The young Anne appears in many of Fisher's stories of her early life.

In 1911, Rex Kennedy sold his share in the Albion newspaper and moved the family to Whittier in southern California. He was the editor and publisher of the *Whittier News* for the rest of his life. The family grew to include Grandmother Holbrook, and then a third daughter, Norah, nine years younger than Mary Frances, and a son, David, two years later. As characters in Fisher's stories and memoirs, each of these family members become vividly real to her readers.

The family valued education, literature, and ideas. Young Mary Frances learned to read at the age of five and had the run of a large family library. As a young girl in the Kennedy home, she also learned to cook, to respect and appreciate older people, and to breathe in the atmosphere of journalism. She and her father were close, and she liked to spend afternoons in the newsroom with him.

Mary Frances was precocious, enjoying the attention she received from cooking for the family and for the stories she began to write to entertain her sister Anne. She has said that she was a natural writer. She began as a child, and kept writing. It never occurred to her not to write. The two sisters attended local schools in Whittier, and then private boarding schools elsewhere in California. Mary Frances worked hard in English classes and wrote and edited for her school yearbook and literary magazine. She spent the summer of her fifteenth year working for her father's newspaper, writing sports, society, and news stories as needed.

After graduation from Miss Harker's, a preparatory school attached to Stanford University, in 1927, Mary Frances, unsure of what she wanted to do next, and a year ahead of her sister at school, attended a semester at Illinois College with a cousin, then returned home for a semester at Whittier College. The following summer, needing to make up some lost credits so she could enter Occidental College as a sophomore in the fall, she took courses at University of California in Los Angeles. While at UCLA, she met Al Fisher.

Alfred Young Fisher was a Princeton-educated literature scholar and poet who was teaching at a boarding school to earn money before pursuing an advanced degree abroad. Mary Frances Kennedy was an intelligent and attractive twenty-year-old who lacked direction and was eager to leave home. The two corresponded after Al returned to his school in Wyoming and the two Kennedy sisters began the year at Occidental College. At Occidental, Mary Frances met some lifelong literary friends and wrote for the campus newspaper. By the end of the year, however, Al had asked her to join him in France, where he would be studying for his doctorate at a French university. Mary Frances and Al were married on 5 September 1929, and they sailed for France almost immediately. Less than two weeks later, they were in Dijon.

DIJON, 1929–1932

Fisher would write frequently and fondly about the years she spent in Dijon with Al. It is evident from her letters, stories, and autobiographical essays that it was an idyllic time. The couple was young, fortunate, and in love. Not only was she in love with Al, but she also fell in love with the food and culture of France. She was introduced to gastronomy, the art of eating and of the table.

The young couple lived as pensionnaires, renting two rooms and eating their meals in a family home. In this way, there were introduced to the rich culture and cuisine of Burgundy. At the table of the Ollagniers, and their successors the Rigoulets, they ate elaborate multi-course meals, drank the wines of the region, and learned to enjoy local specialties. They became *clients habituels,* regular diners, at Aux Trois Faisans, a fine Dijon restaurant, and immersed themselves in the art of dining in France. Monsieur Ollagnier introduced them to the members of the Club Alpine, and they hiked around the region, becoming familiar with the countryside and eating at the best country inns in the company of the local people.

While Al worked on his degree in literature at the University of Dijon, Mary Frances took courses in art and the French language. Monsieur Ollagnier introduced her to the French writer Jean Anthelme Brillat-Savarin and his book *Physiologie du goût* (*The Physiology of Taste,* 1825). She lived and breathed French language, culture, and food. All of this became material for the work she would do later, for anecdotes and stories and recipes that she would draw on for the rest of her life.

After two years in Dijon, Mary Frances returned to California for a summer to visit with her family. She brought her fourteen-year-old sister Norah back to France with her and enrolled her in a convent school in Dijon, beginning a pattern that she would continue years later with her own daughters. Leaving their rooms at the Rigoulets, Mary Frances and Al found a small apartment with a tiny kitchen. Her days were spent experimenting with writing, which she seemed to take for granted would become her métier, and shopping for the exquisite fresh produce, meats, and dairy products that she would serve later: to friends from the university; to their friend Larry Powell from Occidental, also studying in Dijon; and to her sister Norah on the days when she was free from the convent school where she lived. In Dijon, Mary Frances began to develop a personal style of cooking, of food presentation, and of eating with friends, influenced both by what she had learned and by what she rejected of her experiences eating with the Ollagniers and the Rigoulets, and by the necessities of the very limited and simple kitchen she worked in. Already her life was becoming her art.

RETURN TO CALIFORNIA, 1932–1936

When Al completed his doctorate in 1932, the couple left France with Norah and returned to California, planning to write and look for an academic position for Al. Jobs were scarce during the Depression, and they were dependent on Mary Frances' family, who had been subsidizing them since their marriage. They moved into the family's second home in Laguna Beach, and became part of a beach community of un- and underemployed artists, writers, and actors, some of them friends from her days at Occidental. They worked at odd jobs, and money was tight. Earning a few dollars seems to have been the motivation for Mary Frances' first magazine article, as it would be so often in the future. Although journalism was in her blood, she had been working on fiction while Al wrote poetry. "Pacific Village," published in *Westways* in 1934, was a sketch of the changes wrought by development in Laguna Beach. She signed her article "M. F. K. Fisher," and her professional persona was born. Thrilled with the money she earned, Fisher realized that writing about a place was one of her strengths, and it was marketable.

Finally Al was offered a position teaching at Occidental College. In Laguna Beach, they had met Dillwyn and Gigi Parrish. Dillwyn Parrish, fifteen years older than she, and an artist, writer, and entrepreneur, became her mentor, encouraging her writing at the same time as she was falling in love with him. Parrish's young wife was in the process of leaving him for another man, Al Fisher was preoccupied with his teaching, and Mary Frances Fisher was uninterested in being a faculty wife. She and Dillwyn Parrish become lovers. Meantime, she was spending her days at the Los Angeles Public Library, searching through old books on cooking and gastronomy, gathering old recipes, and writing sketches based on her research as well as sketches about her own personal experiences with food. With Parrish's encouragement and publishing contacts, this material would become her first book, *Serve It Forth* (1937).

LE PAQUIS, SWITZERLAND, 1937–1939

In 1936, Fisher accepted an invitation to travel to Europe with Dillwyn Parrish and his mother, as his mother's companion. For the first time, she saw the land Parrish and his sister had bought near Vevey in Switzerland, a meadow with a stone cottage called Le Paquis. She returned to California and to Al Fisher, but the marriage was strained not only by her defection to Dillwyn Parrish, but by Al Fisher's own dissatisfaction with his career. By the end of 1936, the Fishers had been invited to join a literary and artistic community envisioned by Parrish and his sister at Le Paquis, and an awkward ménage a trois developed in Switzerland. It is likely that the three never openly admitted to themselves that Mary Frances and Dillwyn were lovers, but certainly Al was bitterly disappointed. When Al left Le Paquis to accept a teaching position at Smith College, it became more difficult to keep up the fiction that their marriage was intact. In 1937, Mary Frances returned to California to tell her family that she had decided to divorce Al, and *Serve It Forth* was published.

Serve It Forth is a small book, and Fisher was still a very young woman, yet in this work she manages to present herself as a philosopher of food and an advocate of intelligent eating. The book establishes her style and form, historical information mingled with personal anecdotes. She writes about eating, about what to eat, and where to eat, and people who eat. There is some highly sensual writing in the book; for instance, a vignette about roasting tangerine sections on the radiator in a pension in Strasbourg that is quite sexy. Al Fisher is all through the book, along with their shared experiences of learning to eat in France and M. F. K. Fisher's own childhood experiences. "The Standing and the Waiting" is an poignant travel essay, about returning to Aux Trois Faisans after six years, this time with Parrish (called Chexbres in her essays), and finding her favorite waiter old and drunk. She cries at the end, for the passage of time, and the sadness of change. "On Dining Alone," written at this early stage of her career, foreshadows some of her subsequent thoughts about keeping her own company.

Dillwyn Parrish was the love of M. F. K. Fisher's life. The period of a little over a year that they spent at Le Paquis from the spring of 1937 until late summer 1938 was the happiest of her life. At Le Paquis the lovers developed a routine of writing, painting, gardening, and entertaining that provided more material for Fisher's writing and continued to establish her convictions about the art of eating and entertaining. Using the pseudonym Victoria Berne, together they wrote and published *Touch and Go* (1939), a slight novel of manners.

Sadly, at the end of the summer of 1938, Parrish and his sister decided they must sell Le Paquis, which was expensive to maintain. Shortly afterward, on a weekend trip to Bern, Parrish was stricken with severe leg pain. He entered the hospital, where he was operated on for blood clots in his leg. A difficult and lengthy hospital stay ensued, during which the leg was amputated.

Parrish's illness, coinciding with the beginning of the war in Europe, was a turning point in Fisher's life. After months during which Parrish was in the hospital grappling with the pain of phantom limb syndrome, and with war gathering in Europe, Parrish and Fisher sailed home to the United States for more medical advice. By now Parrish was dependent on painkilling drugs that Fisher would inject between rolls of the ship on the rough crossing. They made a final Atlantic voyage over and back to Switzerland in May 1939, to close their apartment in Switzerland and to obtain a supply of Analgeticum, a pain reliever not available in the United States, which was the only drug that offered Parrish any relief. They were realistic and fatalistic, knowing that the supply would run out, and that Parrish would not be able to live without the drug. On 1 September 1939, France and Britain declared war on Germany, and the war in Europe began. The sadness of the loss of that period of happiness, of the art of living as she had known it, in France and Switzerland, with both Al Fisher and Dillwyn Parrish, would pervade the autobiographical volume *The Gastronomical Me* (1943).

BAREACRES, CALIFORNIA, 1939–1941

Fisher and Parrish settled in the San Jacinto Hills in California, buying land and renovating a cabin they called Bareacres. Parrish was diagnosed with Buerger's disease, a chronic phlebitis, with a prognosis that foretold the eventual amputation of his remaining leg and both his arms. He continued to endure extreme pain throughout his illness. Fisher and Parrish established a life of writing, painting, and entertaining family and friends at Bareacres, a life that was made poignant by the awareness that Parrish's supply of drugs would inevitably run out. Money grew short as their savings were depleted, and Fisher turned away from attempts at fiction and turned to what would become her cash crop, writing about food. The sensuous *Consider the Oyster* (1941), only sixty pages long, was written to amuse Parrish. Fisher's blend of history, anecdote, recipes, and experiences, written with charm and humor, makes the reader yearn for oysters and champagne. Fisher creates a connection with the reader, as her oyster-related experiences awaken the reader's own memories.

By mid-1941, Parrish had grown much worse, and on 6 August 1941, he shot himself at Bareacres. Fisher would write with simplicity, restraint, and great poignancy of her life with him, and the loss of her great love, in *The Gastronomical Me* (1943), and an element of sadness and loss would infuse many of her sketches for the rest of her career.

HOLLYWOOD, 1942–1945

On 7 December 1941, the Japanese bombed Pearl Harbor and the United States entered the war. Fisher left Bareacres, where she had been living by herself and struggling with the trauma of Parrish's death, and, needing to support herself by her writing once again, moved to an apartment in Hollywood, taking a job as a writer for Paramount Pictures.

Living alone in Hollywood during the war after the death of her beloved Dillwyn, Fisher began to shape the book that would become *How to Cook a Wolf* (1942). This book, which offers recipes and a philosophy of how to live and eat well in the face of wartime shortages and conditions, is entertaining and practical. *How to Cook a Wolf* was the first introduction to M. F. K. Fisher for many readers, and it enhanced her reputation as a different kind of cookbook writer, offering advice on life and living as well as recipes. Simple recipes for simple food are offered in chapters with titles like "How to Be Cheerful Though Starving" and "How to Practice True Economy." Emphatic ideas on food and nutrition, the balanced diet, and a simple, nutritious diet were lifelong convictions for Fisher. Ahead of her time, she advocated a diet of whole grains, fresh organic vegetables, and organic meat. Not only is such a diet simple and healthy, in her opinion, but it recalls the honest flavors of her years in France, flavors she found difficult to duplicate in America. *How to Cook a Wolf* was timely and well received, and she began to attract attention as the writer of a hybrid genre, one that combined recipes and food writing with stories, a personal voice, and a simple, elegant, evocative style.

In 1942, the thirty-four-year-old Fisher, divorced and widowed, found herself a career woman, earning her living by her writing and her philosophy of the art of eating. Intelligent, attractive, cosmopolitan, experienced, and accustomed to living by her own rules, she had several affairs while living in Hollywood. By December 1942, she discovered that she was pregnant. She never revealed the identity of her child's father. Instead she hinted to family and friends that she was going undercover for the duration of a secret government publicity job, and quietly spent the months of her pregnancy working on articles for food magazines and writing *The Gastronomical Me*, her gastronomical autobiography. In her letters, she speaks of finishing her government job by August and adopting a child. On 15 August 1943, Fisher gave birth to a daughter, Anne Kennedy Parrish, called Anna, and brought her "adopted" daughter home to Bareacres.

While critics and friends urged her to write novels, as fiction was generally considered artistically superior to writing food articles, Fisher made no apologies for the commercial assignments she took to support herself, her daughter, and her home. Working at Paramount part of the year and freelancing for magazines as often as she could, she wrote quickly and continuously. In the foreword to *The Gastronomical Me* she wrote what amounts to a manifesto of her philosophy of writing.

The Gastronomical Me begins with her earliest memories of food, continues through her childhood and youth, and then recounts the years in Dijon with Al Fisher and at Le Paquis with Parrish/Chexbres. Fisher tells her story through a series of vignettes centered on experiences with food and travel. Her genius for capturing the spirit of place is always evident, as are her strong ideas about preparing and serving food.

Love leaps from the pages of *The Gastronomical Me*. Love for her parents and sisters, love for Al Fisher—and sadness at hurting him when she knew she would divorce him—and most of all, love for Parrish—and the poignant sadness after his death. The final section of the book is set in Mexico, where she went to stay with her brother David and sister Norah in late 1941 after Parrish's suicide. The ending is painful. In a haunting and trance-like sequence, she writes of a mariachi singer named Juanito, a young boy who is revealed to be actually a young woman suffering from unrequited love for David. The bereaved Fisher ends the book on a note of secrets hidden and revealed, of hunger unfed.

The trauma of Parrish's suicide, the suicide of her brother David on the eve of the day he was to report for military service in 1942, and the strain and fatigue of single parenthood and supporting herself and her daughter took a toll. In April 1945, experiencing anxiety attacks and needing a change of scene, Fisher took Anna and her nurse to stay at a friend's apartment in New York City for the summer.

NEW YORK CITY AND BAREACRES, 1945–1949

Within days of settling into her temporary apartment in New York, Fisher was introduced to Donald Friede at a dinner party. Friede, a colorful editor and publisher, wined and dined her and urged her to marry him immediately. Impulsively, she agreed, and they were married on 19 May 1945.

The household, now consisting of Fisher, Donald Friede, Anna, and her nurse, spent the summer in a sublet apartment in Greenwich Village. Fisher was offered a contract for an anthology on the subject of banquets and feasting in literature and history. She spent her days doing research at the New York Public Library and her evenings socializing and dining with a variety of friends and acquaintances in the publishing community in New York. By the fall of 1945, Fisher was pregnant and the household moved back to Bareacres.

Here Let Us Feast (1946) was completed in January 1946. Bowing to pressure from Donald Friede and her writing friends to write fiction, she began work on the novel that would become *Not Now but Now* (1947). Fisher's second daughter, Kennedy Friede, was born on March 12, 1946. Donald Friede had legally adopted Anna and was looking for work in Hollywood while working on a memoir at Bareacres. Money was tight, Friede was not earning, and once again Fisher was hard at work supporting her family as a freelance writer for magazines such as *Gourmet* and *House Beautiful,* while working on book projects at the same time. Like Colette, one of her favorite writers and models, she wrote steadily, quickly, and with a minimum of revision.

Here Let Us Feast is another instance of Fisher's wide-ranging knowledge of the literature of gastronomy and ability to add pleasing commentary drawn from her own experience, creating a sensuous mood of well-being based on good eating and drinking. As always, Fisher's personal voice and imaginative selection of recipes add charm and depth and a singular sense of connection with the reader.

The novel *Not Now but Now* is less successful. As Fisher's heroine Jennie moves through a succession of romantic encounters with both men and women in different historical time periods, the comparison with Virginia Woolf's *Orlando* (1928) is inevitable. Fiction was never Fisher's natural voice. Her fiction style is unconvincing, her dialogue stilted, and her plotting unoriginal, although her language is always sophisticated and her voice charming.

The early-nineteenth-century French writer and gastronomer Jean Anthelme Brillat-Savarin had influenced Fisher since her days in Dijon. In *Serve It Forth,* she had acknowledged this artist of fine eating, whose writing she describes as "a masterpiece of clarity and charm." This would be her own goal, Brillat-Savarin her model. That Brillat-Savarin's style and material had influenced her own work was evident from *Serve It Forth* through *Here Let Us Feast* and throughout her career. She had contemplated writing a new translation of his *Physiology of Taste* for years, and in 1946 she was offered a contract for the project.

While continuing to do commercial work, she used her intelligence and wide knowledge of the literature of gastronomy in her books. She began an abecedary, a series of monthly ABC sketches for *Gourmet*. These sketches, which would be published as *An Alphabet for Gourmets* (1949), are a window into Fisher's life in the mid-1940s, her experiences in Hollywood and with Donald Friede, as always centered on food. "A is for dining Alone," she writes of her early years in Hollywood after Parrish's death. "B is for Bachelors," she writes of her would-be seducers in Hollywood, ending with a dinner for two with Donald Friede. "S is for Sad," she writes of the hunger of the bereaved, continuing her commentary on the way food feeds more than physical hunger.

WHITTIER, 1949–1953

Fisher's impulsive marriage to Donald Friede did not last long. After her mother died in early 1949, she and Friede separated. With two young children, still struggling financially, she closed Bareacres and moved in with her father. She would spend the next four years in Whittier, caring for her father and raising her daughters.

Her translation of Brillat-Savarin, *The Physiology of Taste; or, Meditations on Transcendent Gastronomy,* appeared at the end of 1949 in a deluxe volume published by the Limited Editions Club. Only M. F. K. Fisher had the combination of appreciation of the language, the gastronomy, and the wit of Brillat-Savarin to create such an excellent translation in the spirit of the original work. Her most scholarly work, the translation is embellished with hundreds of glosses, marginal notes, and commentary, which make the work a conversation between herself and Brillat-

Savarin. It is a work that she would be proud of for the rest of her life.

In 1950, Fisher revised *How to Cook a Wolf*. Her parenthetical comments inserted within the text of the 1941 version create a conversation with her younger self. While the book was originally conceived as a wartime cookbook and survival manual, the revision lifts the work into the realm of a guide to living with economy, dignity, and grace at any time—this was a realm in which Fisher was at home in her life as well as her work.

Fisher's divorce from Donald Friede became final in August 1950. This period of her life was a lonely one. She continued in her role as a journalist, however, taking charge of the *Whittier News*, the family newspaper, as her father became increasingly ill. Always practical, always capable, she managed to hire and supervise household and nursing help, take the children to school, cook for the family, and manage and edit the paper. She wrote columns and editorials, attended board meetings, and took over her father's community responsibilities as publisher of the local daily newspaper. She suffered from fatigue, anxiety, and depression, and underwent time-consuming psychoanalysis. Immersed in caring for the children and the household, as well as the newspaper, she had little time or energy for any new writing of her own beyond a few magazine articles.

Fisher's father, Rex Kennedy, died on June 2, 1953. Shortly afterward, she moved with the children to St. Helena in California's Napa Valley. At the same time, her publisher conceived the idea of a collection of five of her early gastronomic works, published as *The Art of Eating* (1954). *The Art of Eating* was the culmination of over fifteen years of writing about gastronomy and is considered by many her best work. Fisher had proved the depth of her expertise with *Here Let Us Feast* and the Brillat-Savarin translation. The collection of *Serve It Forth, Consider the Oyster*, the revised *How to Cook a Wolf, The Gastronomical Me,* and *An Alphabet for Gourmets*, with an introduction by the literary critic Clifton Fadiman, proved that her gastronomical writing wore well with time and needed no apology.

Fadiman praised Fisher's writing style, introducing Fisher as a philosopher of food. *The Art of Eating* was praised by critics and the public for its personal voice, its simplicity, and its practicality, as well as for Fisher's evocative, novelistic style of writing about food. Collected together, the five books piece together a picture of her life through the years, her particular brand of subtle, veiled autobiography that hides as much as it reveals. Her early genuine love for Al Fisher, her happiness and then her grief for Parrish, the war years in Hollywood, and the excitement of the early time with Friede are all there, demonstrated through her experiences with food and with travel. But in her writing Fisher is always the star, adored by her husbands, waiters, innkeepers, and all who cross paths with her charming, gastronomical self.

PROVENCE AND THE NAPA VALLEY, 1954–1960

When the sale of the *Whittier News* became final in 1954, Fisher's money worries eased. She decided to take the two girls to France for a few months, to learn the language and revisit the culture that had so influenced her twenty years earlier.

A few months stretched into two years. Reminiscent of the time that she had responsibility for her young sister Norah, she put the children into convent schools while she lived as a pensionnaire in Aix-en-Provence. The children spoke French, and became familiar with the landscapes of the provincial city. The family became *clients habituels* at the Deux Garcons. Once again Fisher was adored by waiters, observed the locals, composted material for future stories, sketches, and books. She seems to have been unconcerned about consistency in the girls' education, taking them out of school to live in the country outside town, exploring countryside, chateaux, and markets. Together they roamed Marseilles at Christmas, blended into the crowded pre-Lenten Carnival in Aix, and attended performances during the summer music festival, observing the seasonal rhythms of the place, always eating, always commenting. Fisher had the advantage of perspective; she had known France before the war. Fisher found France and the French much changed by the occupation, as much changed as she herself was by time and sad experience. A few years later she would notice a shift toward relative ease and security.

While food would always be present in her writing, the writing that emerged from the years in Aix-en-Provence and Marseilles initiated a new period in M. F. K. Fisher's work. The stories and sketches about Provence center around place and experience. Her daughters emerge as characters, replacing Al and Chexbres. The experiences that begin with "The Weather Within" (collected in *Sister Age*, 1983), the story about the voyage to Europe with the children and the death of an elderly passenger on the ship, and that continue through a series of stories including "The Mahogany Tree," about a Christmas in spent in Marseilles, and "Two Kitchens in Provence" (collected in *As They Were*, 1982), where she races against the decay of her exquisitely fresh fruits and vegetables, when published would be among her best travel writing. As always, by piecing together the vignettes, the reader discovers a great deal about Fisher's life in Provence but is still left with the sense that much more has not been told. The sketches are unconnected by transitions and mundane details.

Fisher, Anna, and Kennedy returned to St. Helena in 1956. She became involved in the community and her girls' lives, and struggled to reinvent herself as a writer. She felt that she needed to escape her former professional persona, the "M. F. K. Fisher" of the 1940s, but other than some magazine writing she drifted from project to project without completing anything. She had sketched some stories set in Provence, but they were not yet finished and published. She loved the Napa Valley and became involved in the wine industry, organizing wine tastings and a wine library. As always, she entertained in her own style, with simple good food, good friends, and good conversation.

In late 1959, Fisher and her daughters returned to Europe. With her sister Norah and Norah's sons, they traveled to Lugano, Italy. The girls learned Italian and once again attended convent schools. Returning to Aix in the spring of 1960, Fisher began to write again. *A Cordiall Water: A Garland of Odd & Old Receipts To Assuage the Ills of Man and Beast* (1961) is a collection of healing recipes and cures, ancient and unconventional alternative remedies, folklore and comforting foods, drawing on a wide variety of sources—from her grandmother, to scholarly research, to her own interest in healing diets. Fisher was pleased with the book, feeling that writing in English while speaking French was good for the purity and simplicity of her style.

FOOD AND WINE, 1961–1970

Returning to St. Helena in the summer of 1961, Fisher turned to her interest in the wine industry of the region for material. An awareness of California wines became another thread in the Fisher legacy. Through the 1960s, she was frequently asked to speak and to write about California wines and about pairing wines with food. *The Story of Wine in California* (1962), published by University of California Press, is a volume of photographs of the vineyards and the winemaking process of the region, accompanied by a text by M. F. K. Fisher.

By 1963, Fisher had pulled together her Aix material to her satisfaction. *Map of Another Town: A Memoir of Provence* (1964) was the result. Critics and the public enjoyed this new side of M. F. K. Fisher. Food is ever present, but the book also serves as a guidebook of sorts, with information on the history and culture of the region, as well as the restaurants, markets, and festivals. Who, having read *Map of Another Town*, can stop in Aix-en-Provence without visiting the Deux Garcons, Fisher's favorite café? The presence of M. F. K. Fisher, and her two girls, is so immediate that one looks for them on the Cours Mirabeau or at the Glaciers, where they would meet after school.

Fisher's personal life continued to be both rich and complicated. She had had a long relationship with a woman, Marietta Voorhees, in St. Helena, followed by a long-term, long-distance affair with the writer and publisher Arnold Gingrich. She spent the summer and fall of 1964 teaching

English to educationally disadvantaged black students at the Piney Woods School in Mississippi. Her somewhat unstable daughter Anna, later diagnosed as manic-depressive, gave birth to a son, Jean-Christophe, in 1965. Her younger daughter, Kennedy, had departed for Russell Sage College in New York State. Fisher lost her sister Anne to cancer, also in 1965.

America in the 1960s was the scene of a growing awareness of food, and American cooks and cooking writers began to rise in prestige. This was the era of Julia Child's *Mastering the Art of French Cooking* (1961), which gave rise to her popular television series, *The French Chef*. James Beard and Craig Claiborne were household names. Fisher's expertise was in demand. In 1964, Fisher's agent had negotiated a contract with the *New Yorker* for a minimum of four or five articles a year. The prestige of Fisher's *New Yorker* publications, which included excerpts from *Map of Another Town* as well as fiction, had renewed her reputation as a food expert and a writing stylist.

She was offered, and accepted, a contract to write the first in a Time-Life series called Foods of the World. Fisher traveled to France with a staff of cooks, editors, and photographers on a Time-Life expense account, beginning a long friendship with Julia Child and further solidifying her attachment to Provence, where the Childs had a house. The resulting book, *The Cooking of Provincial France* (1968), with its professional full-page, full-color photographs of food and regional scenes—in addition to Fisher's always knowledgeable and stylish prose and accompanying recipes—was a popular success, and further secured her position as a member of the food establishment in the United States.

Fisher had written about and reviewed many cookbooks through the years, and she had always included recipes in her books and articles. While exploring the idea of writing a cookbook herself, she published a number of chapters of what would become *With Bold Knife and Fork* (1969) in the *New Yorker*. The volume, while it includes hundreds of recipes, is not exactly a cookbook but rather a collection of essays on hunger, ingredients, and reflections on how she liked to cook. Fisher drew on childhood memories for the book, and a nostalgic thread of the relationship between food and memory, of the associations among food, friends, and family, runs through the book. This nostalgia appealed to her readers, and her popularity, reputation, and fan mail continued to increase.

LAST HOUSE, 1971–1992

Fisher drew on this thread of memory and nostalgia for her next book, *Among Friends* (1971). A memoir about her childhood in Whittier, California, *Among Friends* describes her life as a minority Episcopalian in a predominantly Quaker town. A selection of vignettes about family and small-town life, the volume became a sourcebook about her childhood for the growing numbers of Fisher fans. As always, however, Fisher reveals only what she chooses, and her point of view upset many of her old associates and the Whittier community. Even some old friends commented that they did not remember certain events as Fisher told them. The fictive nature of memory aside, it has been said that M. F. K. Fisher never let the truth stand in the way of a good story.

In the late 1960s, Fisher made the acquaintance of David Bouverie of Glen Ellen in California's Sonoma Valley. Bouverie was a wealthy English aristocrat who had settled on a large acreage and designed and built a compound where he entertained an eclectic literary and artistic circle. With her children grown and gone, Fisher decided to sell her three-story Victorian house in St. Helena and build a two-room cottage on Bouverie's land. She moved into the house she would call "Last House" in April 1971.

While the smaller house was being built, she and her sister Norah traveled again to France, to revisit Dijon and Provence and their friends Paul and Julia Child. The very sad and beautiful essay "About Looking Alone at a Place: Arles" (later collected in *As They Were*) describes her Christmas alone there in 1970, after Norah had returned to California.

By the 1970s, M. F. K. Fisher had a wide network of contacts in publishing and in the increasingly trendy food world on both coasts. *The Art of Eating* was reissued in 1971 with an appreciation by James Beard in addition to the original Clifton Fadiman introduction. She lived at Last House, organizing her notes, papers, and journals, which she had arranged to donate to the Schlesinger Library at Radcliffe College, at Julia Child's suggestion. At the center of a growing culinary circle in California, she gave lectures and entertained guests, fans, and a new generation of cooks, including Alice Waters of San Francisco's Chez Panisse. Her name added cachet to both food-related and writing-related projects. She was asked to write a number of introductions to the books of others.

But Fisher had still another major project of her own to complete, a book about Marseilles, the complex southern port that had captured her heart. She had spent memorable holidays there, beginning with her first husband, Al Fisher; with Dillwyn Parrish; with Donald Friede; with her sister Norah; and with her two daughters. In 1973, Fisher and Norah rented a studio apartment in Marseilles, experiencing once again the sights, sounds, smells, and food of the Old Port while Fisher worked on her book.

Now in her mid-sixties, Fisher's health had begun to decline. She had long struggled with anxiety and depression, had been hospitalized with bouts of illness, and at times had been too tired and ill to write. She suffered from arthritis as well. She found it increasingly difficult to travel alone. She had always been the caretaker of others: her parents, her younger siblings, her husbands, her children, her wide circle of neighbors and friends. She was comfortable at Last House, surrounded by Parrish's paintings and her large collection of books, with fewer people and a smaller house to care for, and with the selected company of good and valuable friends nearby. In 1976, and again in 1978, with Norah, she returned to Aix, a place that had long made her feel vivid and alive.

A Considerable Town, the Marseilles book, was published in 1978, when Fisher was seventy years old. It was her last great effort, her last book that is not mainly a reconfiguration of previously written and published material. In this series of moments from her first visit with Al in 1929 to her residence there with Norah in 1973, Fisher is an observer-participant of life in Marseilles. Her descriptions of people and places, history and scenes, as always from her personal point of view, draw the reader into the sensual appeal of the place. She approaches Marseilles as a mysterious, even mystical, and ancient place that is often shunned as dangerous, but which she explores with a comfort and appreciation unusual in "an obvious Anglo-Saxon of American citizenship and birth." Her Marseilles is eccentric and exotic. Her reader is not warned to avoid the rough and sinister port city; the reader is urged to enjoy the fish markets and seafood restaurants, and is welcomed at Christmastime to admire the clay Nativity figures of the *santons* fair and attend midnight mass at the basilica Notre-Dame de la Garde. The passage of time is a theme of her book about the ancient city: the passage of history, and also, from her perspective of a woman of seventy in declining health, the passage of her own life.

Fisher continued to be in demand for introductions, forewords, afterwords, and blurbs for other people's books. Her name drew crowds at lectures and dinners, and sold books. She continued to widen her experience of food and culture. She was invited to Osaka, Japan, to learn more about Japanese cooking so that she could write an introduction to Shizuo Tsuji's *Japanese Cooking: A Simple Art,* which first appeared in English in 1980. With her sister Norah, Fisher enjoyed two weeks in October 1978 deepening her appreciation of that subtle cuisine.

Fisher's health worsened during the 1980s. As her eyesight began to fail, she endured a hip replacement, and then two subsequent hip dislocations. She was unsteady and shaking and was diagnosed with Parkinson's disease. By 1986 she used a wheelchair and was dependent on household help.

Nevertheless, she continued to work, and her reputation reached even greater heights. The new Berkeley-based North Point Press reissued several of her out-of-print early books in tasteful, quality paperback editions, including *A Cordiall Water,* the novel *Not Now but Now, Among*

Friends, and *The Physiology of Taste,* as well as the five books that constituted *The Art of Eating,* issued as individual slim volumes. Interviews and articles about her appeared in a wide variety of magazines and newspapers. Some of her individual essays and stories were published as limited editions by fine arts presses. The Aix and Marseilles books were reissued together as *Two Towns in Provence* in 1983, keeping Fisher's travel books in print and in the public eye.

A collection of twenty pieces, all previously written, some of them previously published, appeared with the title *As They Were* in 1982. All the essays in this collection are about places that had meaning for Fisher, the scenes frequently centered around food. Burgundy, Provence, California, and New York are represented. *As They Were* is the condensed essence of Fisher's essays about place. "Two Kitchens in Provence," "On Looking Alone at a Place," "I Was Really Very Hungry," and "Gare de Lyon" are among her most representative, beautiful, and evocative writing about food, cooking, and places in France, ranging over fifty years of experience. Reading only the early work *The Gastronomical Me* and the late work *As They Were* would offer the reader the essential M. F. K. Fisher, the full range and flavor of her life and work. As always, in the memoir-based essays in *As They Were,* Fisher withholds background and transitions, leaving only the kernel, the sensory essence of her experience.

Fisher had been collecting the material she referred to as "the old age project" for decades. *Sister Age* appeared in 1983, and included a number of stories and essays that had been previously published in the *New Yorker.* The volume demonstrates Fisher's strengths and her weaknesses. The essays based on experience, such as "The Weather Within," which is the account of the death of a fellow passenger at the end of her first voyage to Europe with her daughters, and "The Oldest Man," about a trip to an old friend's ancestral home in Languedoc, are Fisher at her best. The fiction, even the fictionalized third-person stories based on her own experience, feel stiff and contrived. The book is a fine collection, but emphasizes that Fisher's true voice lies in memoir-based writing.

M. F. K. Fisher had always been an industrious researcher, spending time in libraries in Los Angeles, New York, and France uncovering and rediscovering forgotten culinary books, and then including their material in her own books that blended experience, culinary history, and recipes. One of those books was the California writer Catherine Plagemann's *Fine Preserving,* which had appeared in 1967. Fisher's own copy of the book was on the shelves at Last House, with her detailed annotations in the margins, and in 1986 Plagemann's book was reissued as *Fine Preserving: M. F. K. Fisher's Annotated Edition of Catherine Plagemann's Cookbook,* continuing Fisher's ongoing conversation with the culinary writers of the past.

Fisher was still publishing in her eighties, with the help of her sister Norah and a part-time secretary. *Dubious Honors,* a collection of twenty of her introductions to other writers' works and the introductions to her own earlier books, came out in 1988. *The Boss Dog,* a fictional story set in Aix, with herself and her daughters as characters, had been written years before and was finally published in 1991. The book succeeds better than much of her fiction because setting, always her strength, is emphasized over plot. *Long Ago in France: The Years in Dijon,* published in 1991, brings together Dijon-based selections from *Serve It Forth, The Gastronomical Me,* and *With Bold Knife and Fork,* connecting the scattered vignettes to create a unified memoir of that pivotal time in Fisher's life.

M. F. K. Fisher grew steadily weaker through early 1992. On 22 June 1992, just a few days short of her eighty-fourth birthday, she died of Parkinson's disease, in her own bed at Last House, with her sister Norah, her daughter Kennedy, and a few close friends at her side. Her daughter Anna had visited for the last time in January 1992 and begged her mother once to more to reveal the name of her father. Fisher refused.

Her final project, which she worked on until she became too weak to continue, was a series of selections from her journals. The three volumes were published posthumously as *To Begin Again:*

Stories and Memoirs, 1908–1929 (1992), *Stay Me, Oh Comfort Me: Journals and Stories, 1933–1941* (1993), and *Last House: Reflections, Dreams, and Observations, 1943–1991* (1995).

THE M. F. K. FISHER LEGACY

M. F. K. Fisher was always the charming heroine of her own story; her personal voice and vision illuminates her recipes and travels. Over the more than fifty years of her writing career, she wrote much of her own story, her autobiography. Yet she never wrote a sustained narrative, revealing herself only in fragments, through recipes and vignettes. In *Serve It Forth, The Gastronomical Me,* and *Among Friends* she wove stories of her childhood and life with her first two husbands among the recipes and tales of the art of eating; in *An Alphabet for Gourmets*, she wrote about her years in Hollywood and life with her third husband; she wrote about motherhood and her travels with her two daughters in *Map of Another Town*. She wrote about her life as a gastronomer and about her life as a writer. Sometimes what is left unspoken provokes curiosity; sometimes what is left unspoken is heartbreaking. Always she writes of hunger, satisfied and unsatisfied.

With her command of tone and mood, her fine-tuned ability to express the essence of a place as well as create a mood, M. F. K. Fisher raised writing about food to a new level of art. She brought the literature of gastronomy to the attention of the American public, pioneering a genre that is neither cookbook, nor memoir, nor travel book, but a subtle blend of all these and more. By the end of her life, there was no need to apologize for the commercial nature of her work, for its origins in journalism, in magazine food writing, in her need to earn a living. She had been a part of the rise of gastronomy, the art of eating, as a serious genre of nonfiction prose in America. Her books are shelved under the label "belles lettres."

Selected Bibliography

WORKS OF M. F. K. FISHER
Serve It Forth. New York: Harper, 1937.

Touch and Go. (Written with Dillwyn Parrish and published under the pseudonym Victoria Berne). New York and London: Harper & Brothers, 1939.

Consider the Oyster. New York: Duell, Sloan and Pearce, 1941.

How to Cook a Wolf. New York: Duell, Sloan and Pearce, 1942.

The Gastronomical Me. New York: Duell, Sloan and Pearce, 1943.

Here Let Us Feast: A Book of Banquets. New York: Viking, 1946.

Not Now but Now. New York: Viking, 1947.

An Alphabet for Gourmets. New York: Viking, 1949.

The Physiology of Taste; or, Meditations on Transcendental Gastronomy by Jean Anthelme Brillat-Savarin. New York: Limited Editions Club, 1949. (Translation, along with preface and annotations by M. F. K. Fisher of *Physiologie du goût*, 1825; illustrations by Sylvain Sauvage.)

The Art of Eating. New York: Macmillan, 1954.

A Cordiall Water: A Garland of Odd & Old Receipts to Assuage the Ills of Man & Beast. Boston: Little, Brown, 1961.

The Story of Wine in California. Berkeley: University of California Press, 1962.

Map of Another Town: A Memoir of Provence. Boston: Little, Brown, 1964.

The Cooking of Provincial France. New York: Time-Life Books, 1968.

With Bold Knife and Fork. New York: Putnam, 1969.

Among Friends. New York: Knopf, 1971.

A Considerable Town. New York: Knopf, 1978.

As They Were. New York: Knopf, 1982.

Two Towns in Provence. New York: Vintage, 1983.

Sister Age. New York: Knopf, 1983.

Fine Preserving: M. F. K. Fisher's Annotated Edition of Catherine Plagemann's Cookbook. Berkeley, Calif.: Aris, 1986.

Dubious Honors. San Francisco: North Point Press, 1988.

The Boss Dog: A Story of Provence. San Francisco: North Point Press, 1991.

Long Ago in France: The Years in Dijon. New York: Prentice-Hall, 1991.

To Begin Again: Stories and Memoirs, 1908–1929. New York: Pantheon, 1992.

Stay Me, Oh Comfort Me: Journals and Stories, 1933–1941. New York: Pantheon, 1993.

Last House: Reflections, Dreams, and Observations, 1943–1991. New York: Pantheon, 1995.

The Measure of Her Powers: An M. F. K. Fisher Reader. Edited by Dominique Gioia. Washington, DC: Counterpoint, 1999.

JOURNALS AND LETTERS
M. F. K. Fisher: A Life in Letters: Correspondence, 1929–1991. Edited by Norah Barr, Marsha Moran, and Patrick

Moran. Washington. D.C.: Counterpoint, 1997.

From the Journals of M. F. K. Fisher. New York: Pantheon, 1999.

Home Cooking: An Excerpt from a Letter to Eleanor Friede. Pasadena, Calif.: Weatherbird Press, 2000.

CRITICAL AND BIOGRAPHICAL STUDIES

Ferrary, Jeannette. *Between Friends: M. F. K. Fisher and Me.* New York: Atlantic Monthly Press, 1991.

Fussell, Betty. *Masters of American Cookery: M. F. K. Fisher, James Andrews Beard, Raymond Craig Claiborne, Julia McWilliams Child.* New York: Times Books, 1983.

Gioia, Dominique, ed. *A Welcoming Life: The M. F. K. Fisher Scrapbook.* Washington, DC: Counterpoint, 1997.

Lazar, David, ed. *Conversations with M. F. K. Fisher.* Jackson: University Press of Mississippi, 1992.

Reardon, Joan. *M. F. K. Fisher, Julia Child, and Alice Waters: Celebrating the Pleasures of the Table.* New York: Harmony Books, 1994.

Reardon, Joan. *Poet of the Appetites: The Lives and Loves of M. F. K. Fisher.* San Francisco: North Point Press, 2004.

Tucher, Andie, ed. *Bill Moyers: A World of Ideas II.* "M. F. K. Fisher: Essayist." New York: Doubleday, 1990.

HUTCHINS HAPGOOD

(1869–1944)

Robert M. Dowling

THE JOURNALIST AND author Hutchins Hapgood is best-known for his sociological explorations into the inner worlds of immigrants, labor unionists, bohemians, prostitutes, former convicts, and anarchists, among scores of disenfranchised or otherwise maligned groups of his era. Counting among his many prominent friends and associates the philosophers William James and George Santayana, the painters Pablo Picasso and Henri Matisse, the playwrights Susan Glaspell and Eugene O'Neill, the fiction writers Theodore Dreiser and Ernest Hemingway, and the political activists John Reed and Emma Goldman, Hapgood appears, Zelig-like, right on the ground floor of virtually every major intellectual achievement of the late nineteenth and early twentieth centuries. Indeed, the title of his 1939 autobiography, *A Victorian in the Modern World,* fittingly indicates that the story of Hutchins Hapgood is the story of modernism itself. And like his longtime friend the novelist Gertrude Stein, he had something of a talent for being at just the right place at just the right time. Stein's highly experimental fiction made a sizable impact on literary culture, however, whereas Hapgood's style never quite caught on until the rise of New Journalism in the 1960s. Hapgood is now considered, if considered at all, little more than an early Greenwich Village radical who dabbled in urban sociology, the avant-garde, and the labor movement. At the time, however, Hapgood's was a strong voice of opposition in a period of enormous change: "I had many readers in New York City," he wrote in *A Victorian in the Modern World,* looking back nostalgically on his early years as a journalist, "especially those coming from the east side, and from the socialists, anarchists, suffragists; from all varieties of liberals and radicals; all those people who felt the esthetic or moral need of fresh interpretations of social and political forms." (p. 275) Along with an enormous body of journalistic pieces, Hapgood published eight books that together are unique in their prismatic renderings of the clangor of the period's social terrain.

Hapgood might profitably be called a "rebel by profession," in the mode of Jean Genet or Hunter S. Thompson, insofar as he made his living fomenting the annihilation of traditional values. Nevertheless, Hapgood confessed late in life that he never fully severed his emotional connection to his first thirty-odd years, deeply embedded as they were in Victorian culture. The modern world ushered in "vast and excited changes," Hapgood wrote in the preface of his autobiography, changes that

> brought new color and significance into social life, great dangers, possibilities of ultimate destruction of the whole order. I was so sensitive to these, so impressionable and sympathetic, that if it hadn't been for the crystallized background of Victorian time, I would have been like a rudderless ship in a stormy sea, with the winds blowing in all directions at once.
> (p. vii)

Today, Hapgood is mainly associated with the 1910s rise of bohemian culture in Greenwich Village, though much of his best work was behind him by then. He was well into his forties and something of a radical icon when the major Greenwich Village institutions—the Liberal Club, the *Masses,* Mabel Dodge's salon parties, and the Provincetown Players—came to fruition. But with his experiences abroad, his network of contacts, his sociable manner, and his knowledge of unconventional subjects—the Jewish Lower East Side, the Bowery district, the penitentiary system, the downtown barrooms and dance halls, Tammany leaders, and the labor movement—he gave invaluable breadth to New York bohemian life. In an *Atlantic Monthly* article on the "mayor of Chinatown," Chuck Connors, Hapgood demonstrated an understanding and appreciation for life principles that inspired him to defend radicals and outcasts throughout his writing career. The term the "real thing" connotes a certain frankness and authenticity in action and word, traits that Hapgood believed the staid Victorian middle class sorely lacked. The candid articulations of political and social viewpoints he overheard in the taverns of New York at the turn of the century led him to both continue his pursuit of the "real thing" and apply that philosophy to his writing. Some scholars suggest Hapgood exploited the working poor, and, professionally speaking, there is no disputing this. But it is also true that he was uncompromising in his mission to author books like *The Spirit of the Ghetto* (1902), *The Autobiography of a Thief* (1903), and *The Spirit of Labor* (1907) in an effort to overstep generations of closed-minded stereotyping in the mainstream American mind.

Hapgood and other Greenwich Village radicals, including Alfred Stieglitz, Edna St. Vincent Millay, Carl Van Vechten, Floyd Dell, George Cram "Jig" Cook, John Reed, Eugene O'Neill, Mabel Dodge, Emma Goldman, and Max Eastman, were largely unified throughout the 1910s in their belief that if enough individuals relieved themselves from outside expectations, then society would be compelled to loosen its tightening grip. Many scholars have read this modernist obsession with the "self" as encouraging a "culture of narcissism," scholar Elen Kay Trimberger has noted, and Hapgood was unquestionably narcissistic. But for all his lofty professional goals, Hapgood was a model underachiever in life. His wife, Neith Boyce (1872–1951), was the finer writer of the two; his older brother, Norman, was his superior in political and professional standing, most famously as the liberal editor at the muckraking periodical *Collier's* (1903–1912) and later at *Harper's Weekly* (1913–1916); and his younger brother, William, who owned a progressively run packing company in Indiana, was more successful financially.

Hapgood's prose is unremarkable on the whole, often falling into sentimental hyperbole and long-winded philosophical digression. No one could argue credibly for his literary prowess. But his ideas are so sincerely presented, they inspire us to read on. What most impressively remains of Hapgood's literary legacy was his gift for cultivating intimate friendships, and his social philosophy reflects this inclination. Hapgood never compromised critical acclaim to his passionate embrace of all things radical. Though he refused to subordinate to one political or philosophical ideology, if Hapgood can be pigeonholed at all, he might most usefully be considered a "philosophical anarchist." And like other self-proclaimed philosophical anarchists, rather than joining any particular party or syndicate, Hapgood relied upon one-on-one interactions to spread the good word of moral and spiritual freedom.

Friendship is a persistent theme in Hapgood's personal and professional life, and among the American intellectual elite, he was a social catalyst. He entranced Mabel Dodge, whose Greenwich Village salon parties at 23 Fifth Avenue attracted scores of New York radicals and artists in the 1910s.

In kind, the rabble-rousing anarchist Emma Goldman addressed him in her letters as "My Dear Old Hutch." With a good deal of help from Hapgood, Theodore Dreiser's play *The Hand of the Potter* was produced in New York by the Provincetown Players in 1921, and well before he and Dreiser had a high-profile falling out (in 1933 Hapgood publicly accused Dreiser and the editorial staff at the *American Spectator* of anti-Semitism), Dreiser wrote Hapgood in a letter from his home in Los Angeles dated December 15, 1921:

Despite the sunshine and the flowers and the blue mountains of this favored land I miss the sombre [sic] common places of the village [Greenwich Village] and the faces and forms of mental strugglers whose dispairs [sic] and passions as well as enthusiasms and fol-de-rols [sic] I can honestly respect. I grow so weary of those whom a placid fortune has blessed with an urbane mediocrity. And

I wish for all the land that there were a thousand Hapgoods or his ilk, where now there is one.

And finally, though by no means exhaustively, nearly twenty years later the art critic and novelist Carl Van Vechten wrote a letter to Hapgood congratulating him on the publication of his autobiography.

DEVELOPMENTAL YEARS AND "MODERN" MARRIAGE

The first Hapgood to settle in the New World was Shadrach Hapgood, who came to the Massachusetts Bay Colony in 1656 on a ship called the *Speedwell*. Ultimately, according to Hapgood in his autobiography, Shadrach was "killed and scalped by Indians." The family survived, however, and prospered in the New England area until the end of the Civil War. Hapgood's father, Charles Hutchins Hapgood, an agnostic follower of the freethinker politician and orator Robert Ingersoll, relocated his family to Chicago to start a plow manufacturing company. There Hutchins Hapgood was born on 21 May 1869. Charles's business was tragically destroyed by the Great Chicago Fire of 1871, and he and his wife, Fanny Louise Powers Hapgood, transferred their family to Alton, Illinois, a burgeoning town along the Mississippi where "Hutch," as he was known, spent a restless, lonely childhood. Hapgood's wife, Neith Boyce, recorded the complete saga of the Hapgoods in her late book *The Story of an American Family* (completed in 1940; published privately in 1953). The Hapgoods were a progressive and industrious Victorian family, and by all accounts Charles and Fanny were fine parents. Charles was strict, but unconcerned with money and sympathetic to his boys' progressive natures; Fanny was an outgoing, cultured woman of Irish descent who raised her sons on Shakespeare and lively conversation. In spite of his solid upbringing, Hapgood showed traits of nervousness, sensitivity, and alienation throughout his formative years, traits that persisted throughout his life and were later reflected in his work. (He bizarrely attributed much of his premature sexual awareness, as early as six years of age, to an unusually "tight foreskin," a detail he included in his autobiography that speaks to his genuine openness, but also may have been a preemptive strike against meddling biographers.)

Along with his older brother, Norman, and younger brother, William, Hapgood attended Harvard University from 1889 to 1892 and was strongly influenced by the unorthodox moral philosophies of Professors William James, Josiah Royce, and George Santayana. His stay at Harvard, where he was elected to Phi Beta Kappa, was a life-defining experience for the young midwesterner. One telling day in the fall semester of 1889, Hapgood stepped quietly into James's office, but seeing his professor was hard at work, he respectfully withdrew. James, who had just that year been granted an endowed chair in the incipient field of psychology, might well have been revising the second volume of *The Principles of Psychology*, published the following year. *The Principles* stands large as a work of undisputed genius, one that revolutionized the field of psychology and made a colossal impact on the history of Western thought. In *A Victorian in the Modern World*, Hapgood recounts that James stopped what he was doing, called his student back, and offered a piece of advice that would characterize Hapgood's worldview to his death in 1944:

> I never allow myself to be too busy to make room for any demand upon me. If I did not accept all challenges, it would mean that the reservoirs of my nature, which are unplumbed and unfathomable, would tend to dry up. We are all of us capable of far more than we think and if we keep our minds and hearts open to every new appeal and influence, we grow constantly in power and consciousness. Any moment you or another sophomore might contribute something of great importance to me.
> (p. 70)

Growing up in Alton, Hapgood always considered himself a kind of closet deviant. In a 1977 biography, Michael Marcaccio says that at Harvard, where Hutchins Hapgood developed a strong proclivity for romanticism in an age heavily dominated by realism and pragmatic thought, he discovered ways to redefine his deviance as "a healthy and artistic sensitivity." Hapgood spent a year at Harvard graduate school studying modern literature and fine art, then continued postdoctoral study at the University of Berlin. While at Berlin, along with drinking beer and engaging in countless sexual encounters with prostitutes, barmaids, and the occasional "middle-class girl on a lark" (as he reports in *A Victorian*), Hapgood studied sociology under Georg Simmel, whose idealistic theories on human "sociability" and "symbolic play" must have had an enormous impact on Hapgood's consciousness; Simmel's concepts, when one looks at Hapgood's life as a whole, virtually drove his every personal and professional endeavor.

While in Germany, Hapgood suffered from a condition of what was then called "neurasthenia"; today we call it "clinical depression." He returned to Alton in the summer of 1895, but at the behest of his parents, he soon after embarked on a world tour through the South Pacific, Asia, the Middle East, and Europe (a trip Charles Hapgood financed). Some of this experience he shared with the novelist Gertrude Stein's brother, Leo Stein. For a time, the two renegade Americans abroad rented a property in Kyoto, Japan, where they had many servants and married two Japanese women in order to enjoy their sexual favors in a veil of cultural approval. Back in the United States, he attended Harvard for another year to complete his graduate work; he received his MA in the spring of 1897. In the summer of 1897, he taught English at the University of Chicago and planned to return to Harvard in the fall to carry on teaching there indefinitely. A visit to his brother, Norman, however, who was then working as a journalist under Lincoln Steffens (the famous muckraker and author of the groundbreaking exposé *The Shame of the Cities*, 1904) at the *New York Commercial Daily Advertiser*, changed his life course utterly. New York to him was an enchanting playground, offering the experiential variety he discovered in Europe and on his world tour. The possibilities of experience New York contained electrified him and far outweighed the prospect of a career plan in which he would live out the rest of his life in comfortable bourgeois complacency as a Harvard don in Cambridge, Massachusetts.

At the *Commercial Advertiser*, Steffens, a brilliantly innovative city desk editor, urged Hapgood and his other recruits to report on New York life at its grittiest. It was a revolutionary method of reportage that may seem rather old hat more than a century later, but in its time this approach to journalism shocked its genteel public into a new awareness of their cohabitation with prostitutes, gangsters, immigrants, anarchists, and the like. It was at the *Commercial Advertiser*, where he spent three years as a reporter, that Hapgood met his future wife, Neith Boyce, in 1897. A sphinx like presence about the office, Boyce was a highly independent, quiet, and introverted twenty-seven-year-old and the only woman on Steffens' staff. Born in Franklin, Indiana, Boyce moved with her family to Los Angeles, where her father, the Civil War hero Henry Harrison Boyce, cofounded the *Los Angeles Times*. Though she never attended college, she began writing fiction and journalism at an early age. When Henry Boyce sold his holdings in the newspaper, he relocated his family to New York, where Neith Boyce took an apartment on Washington Square, the heart of Greenwich Village. As a lifetime mate, she could scarcely have been less suitable for the intensely voluble Hapgood, but for him it was love at first sight. In the introduction to her 2003 collection of the autobiographical writings of Neith Boyce, Carol DeBoer-Langworthy quotes a letter that Hapgood wrote to his mother in 1898:

> there is a girl in N.Y. who has been much more to me than any other girl I ever knew. We are not engaged and it is practically sure that we never shall be. She is a "new woman," ambitious and energetic, a hard worker, more or less disliked by all my friends that know her, and she has no idea of getting married, at any rate to me.
> (p. 6)

To the consternation of Hapgood's social circle, they married less than a year later.

He and Neith Boyce had four children—Boyce, nicknamed "Harry" to avoid confusion (born in 1901); Charles (born in 1904); Miriam (born in 1906); and Beatrix (born in 1910). Their marriage was characterized by spatial and sexual mobility, though the combination nearly tore them apart and contributed to a number of nervous breakdowns on both sides. They first moved abroad in May 1903, and after living with Bernard Berenson (who introduced them to the local literati and expatriate art communities), they settled into a country villa in Settignano, near Florence, Italy. But in 1904 they returned to New York and then on to Chicago, where Hapgood collected material for his book on syndicalist-anarchist movement, *The Spirit of Labor*.

While in Chicago, Hapgood cavorted with various labor leaders and anarchists and openly practiced "varietism," a philosophy that promoted extramarital affairs as strengthening, rather than degrading, the marital bond. Both *The Story of a Lover* and Boyce's autobiographical novel *The Bond* (1908) treat the good intentions and devastating outcomes of their extramarital affairs. Hapgood initially encouraged Boyce to enjoy sexual relations with other men, but when she took him up on it, he turned resentful and abusive. In one instance, recounted in *The Story of a Lover,* when Boyce confessed to an affair while Hapgood was off wandering on his own, Hapgood, in his own words, "took her by the throat." In the short run at least, Boyce's affairs agitated Hapgood enough to relocate his family from the United States back to Florence, Italy, where they lived from 1906 to 1908.

Not long after, Boyce fell in love with the political scientist Arthur F. Bentley, a married man and a close friend of Hapgood's from his Harvard years. (DeBoer-Langworthy writes that Boyce reportedly proposed a ménage à trois; Hapgood's daughters Miriam and Beatrix recalled letters, all but a few of them destroyed, that provide evidence for this.) Outraged by the revelation that Boyce could love another man as passionately as she loved him, Hapgood relocated the family in a desperate act of jealousy from Europe to Indianapolis, Indiana, the headquarters of his brother William's Progressive-era experiments in "industrial democracy." That winter, 1908–1909, Boyce suffered a complete nervous breakdown. In 1911, Charles Hapgood bought his son a house in Dobbs Ferry, New York. From that location, Hapgood continued his ramblings through New York's underbelly, and as one consequence, hired the notorious anarchist agitator Hippolyte Havel as his cook in Dobbs Ferry. Much later, in 1917, Hapgood in his turn fell in love with Mary Pyne, an actress for the Provincetown Players who was twenty-five years younger than he. Though Neith insisted she didn't want to interfere, Pyne's husband, Harry Kemp, a well-known Greenwich Village poet and at one point a great friend of Hapgood's, threatened to beat him up over the embarrassingly public affair.

The summer of 1911 was one of the hottest on record. On the advice of a close friend, the novelist Mary Heaton Vorse, Hapgood and Boyce rented a cottage in Provincetown, Massachusetts, a remote fishing village at the end of Cape Cod. More writers and artists trickled in, and the family began summering there regularly. The summer crowd included the Hapgoods, Havel, Vorse, George Cram "Jig" Cook, Susan Glaspell, and John Reed, among others. Together they formed the experimental theater group known as the Provincetown Players. The Players are most famous for first discovering the talents of Eugene O'Neill, widely regarded today as America's foremost playwright. In the summer of 1916, one of Hapgood's anarchist subjects, Terry Carlin, introduced the as-yet-unknown O'Neill to Hapgood, who in turn introduced him to the Provincetown Players. The genesis of this introduction is the stuff of legend: Carlin and O'Neill had met at a Greenwich Village dive called the Golden Swan, a popular spot among gangsters, pickpockets, prostitutes, and bohemians, known affectionately to them all as the Hell Hole. At the time, O'Neill was profoundly depressed, as up to that very moment, his life had amounted to virtually nothing of consequence. Carlin, a loquacious ne'er-do-well, convinced his new drinking partner to join him on a lark to Provincetown. Once the two arrived—drunk, exhausted, and broke—Carlin suggested they "put the bite" on Hapgood for ten dollars, according to Doris Alexander in *The Tempering of Eugene O'Neill* (1962). Hapgood gave them the money, introduced O'Neill to the Provincetown Players, and American drama was born. (By 1939, after winning three Pulitzer

Prizes and the Nobel Prize in Literature, the only American playwright ever to be awarded that honor, O'Neill still owed Hapgood the ten-spot.) By that time, however, the Players had already begun their movement to transform American theater, saturated as it was with plot-driven melodramas and musical extravaganzas. The Players followed the European models of Henrik Ibsen, George Bernard Shaw, and August Strindberg by infusing psychology, symbolism, and "true" experience on the American stage.

In 1915, the summer before O'Neill arrived, Neith Boyce wrote *Constancy,* the Players' first production ever. Lacking an appropriate venue (which they would later find at the Wharf Theater), the one-act play was performed on the Hapgoods' porch. *Constancy* is based on the love affair between the radical journalist John Reed and the activist socialite Mabel Dodge. The following summer Boyce and Hapgood collaborated on *Enemies,* a one-act dialogue between husband (He) and wife (She) in which they explore their actual relationship in the context of modern marriage. *Enemies,* along with its unproduced first draft, *Dialogue,* discusses Hapgood's propensity, in direct opposition to Boyce, for actual life over imaginary stories, real people over fictional characters, and lived experience over vicarious consumption. Hutchins later wrote (in *A Victorian*) that *Enemies* mainly concerned the uncomfortable fact that he and Neith, "like many other couple [sic] who on the whole were good fathers and mothers, were conscious of the latent feminism urging men to give up the ascendancy which women thought they had, and women to demand from men that which they didn't really want, namely so-called freedom from the ideal of monogamy." (p. 395) *Enemies* was later produced in New York and is notable for being one of the first plays ever to be broadcast on radio.

The Hapgood-Boyce marriage, clearly, was an artistic as well as a domestic partnership. According to Hapgood (in *The Story of a Lover*), each adopted the role of wife and husband, mother and father, nurturer and provider. Boyce took the craft of writing more seriously than did her husband and wrote a series of novels, including *The Folly of Others* (1904), *The Eternal Spring* (1906), and *The Bond,* all of which explore the intricate balancing act of modern marriage. (Hers is a lost literary voice that richly deserves rediscovery, and the critic Carol DeBoer-Langworthy has made ample strides in that direction.) *The Bond* especially testifies to her ability. In this autobiographical novel, Boyce unpacks the difficulties and rewards of maintaining an intimate marital bond, particularly with a spouse who has a penchant for nightlong drinking binges in seedy dive bars and conducts plenteous affairs with other women. Though Hapgood never quite relinquished his need for the attentions of other women, in *The Story of a Lover* he muses that this woman was the only woman he had ever loved. Despite years of marital strife punctuated by threats of divorce, Hapgood and Boyce remained together until Hapgood's death on 26 November 1944.

PRODUCTIVE YEARS

In 1900, the Riverside Press commissioned Hapgood, after reading his *Atlantic Monthly* piece on the New York roustabout Chuck Connors, to contribute a concise biography of the Revolutionary War naval hero John Paul Jones. This eventually became his first book, *Paul Jones* (1901). Hapgood acknowledged that the biography was written and researched in a "hack spirit," but it is distinct from overly patriotic biographies of the legendary naval commander. Hapgood perceived something of his own desire for fame, rank, and adventure in the career of the renegade Scotsman. Indeed, it does not appear, in this book anyway, that Jones particularly cared one way or the other about "democracy," "patriotism," "freedom," and the rest of the Revolutionary War cant—he liked a good fight, he reveled in glory, and he was a wizard on the open sea. After the government's lackluster post-revolution treatment of the war hero, he became a kind of mercenary for the British navy. (The British naval commanders compelled to fight alongside a man they considered nothing less than one of the world's most vile terrorists did not appreciate the irony.) Indeed, two lines from *Paul Jones* are uncannily predictive of the final years of the author's own life: as Hapgood proved with *Victorian*, "Jones himself...if proper allowance is made for the effects of his vanity, is, as a rule, his own best biographer"; and also like Jones, though with none of the legend that followed, "circumstances allowed him to accomplish little...before he died he was a genuinely pathetic figure."

Hapgood's second book, drawn from a series of articles he wrote from 1898 to 1902 on the Jewish Lower East Side for the *Commercial Advertiser* and *Atlantic Monthly,* among others, is *The Spirit of the Ghetto: Studies of the Jewish Quarter of New York* (1902). Just as the novelist and critic Carl Van Vechten, another close friend, would later promote Harlem in the 1920s to middle-class white New Yorkers, Hapgood, an Anglo-Saxon with ancestral ties to Puritan New England, celebrated the Jewish Lower East Side. Moses Rischin's 1967 introduction to *The Spirit of the Ghetto* quotes Abraham Cahan, who worked alongside Hapgood at the *Commercial Advertiser* and affectionately considered him "the only Gentile who knows and understands the spirit of the Ghetto." (p. xxviii) An immigrant from Lithuania and the only Jew on Steffens' staff, Cahan acted as Hapgood's insider informant on the Lower East Side and provided him with introductions and a sense of credibility among the inhabitants of that quarter of the city. Adding a further note of authenticity to the volume, the Jewish artist Joseph Epstein, soon to become a world-renowned sculptor, provided the illustrations. Hapgood took from his experiences in that district a vitalizing cultural and literary model that reflected what he describes as the Jewish "love of truth." "Modernity" implied a cosmopolitan sense of cultural acceptance and adaptation to Hapgood, and he argued that the United States should encourage cultural diversity if it wished to adapt to the modern world. He called for a rejuvenated American "spirit" in *The Spirit of the Ghetto* and argued that the arrogant ethnocentrism of Victorian America had hobbled cultural expression.

By "spirit" Hapgood essentially means the ghetto's psychosocial culture, and the spirit he discovered in the ghetto, as he explains in a 1917 essay, "The Picturesque Ghetto," for *Century* magazine, "is the spirit of seriousness, of melancholy, of a high idealism, which, when interpreted by the sympathetic artist, illuminates even the sweat-shop, the push-cart market, and the ambitious businessman." (p. xxiii) Hapgood encourages reverse acculturation in *The Spirit of the Ghetto,* figuratively presenting himself as an emigrant in the cloistered neighborhood, writing home to his people uptown. "Hapgood] has painted for us," wrote one reviewer for *Bookman,* "a large community of Jews who are not primarily interested in the dollar, and who, in the midst of poverty and squalor, give more strenuous activity to the discussing of abstract principles, of theories of universal brotherhood, of philosophies of life, than questions of how to gain a livelihood" (quoted in Rischin's 1967 introduction). (p.xxviii) The famed "slum journalist" Jacob Riis had already published a considerable number of accounts of ghetto life in the years immediately preceding Hapgood's book. Rischin points out the distinction between the journalistic methods of the two men, positing that while

> Riis consorted with the president of the Board of Health, the chief inspector of the New York police force, the registrar of vital statistics, and the Reverend Charles Parkhurst of the Society for the Prevention of Crime in his concern for immigrant bodies, Hapgood searched out the poets, scholars, dramatists, actors, and artists in his eagerness to register immigrant souls.
> (p. xxiv)

"Geographically," Rischin continues, 'Riis' 'Jewtown' and Hapgood's ghetto were identical worlds. Spiritually, however, they were worlds apart." Many books had been written about iniquitous, poverty-stricken New York neighborhoods, notably the Five Points in lower Manhattan, but none had yet produced a comprehensive ethnography of a distinct immigrant culture.

Hapgood's next two books, *The Autobiography of a Thief* (1903) and *The Spirit of Labor* (1907), are social biographies of a New York pickpocket, Jim Caulfield, and a Chicago labor leader, Anton Johannsen, respectively. The famous "hobo journalist" Josiah Flynt introduced Hapgood to

Caulfield one evening at a Bowery dive, and the reporter and the former convict soon became inseparable drinking partners. Caulfield, a skilled pickpocket, spent much of his life in the Sing-Sing and Auburn penitentiaries, degrading experiences that did little but exacerbate his criminality with taxpayer money. On one of their nights out on the Bowery, Hapgood suggested they collaborate on a book-length study of Caulfield's life, which became *The Autobiography of a Thief*. Hapgood's anthropological approach toward criminality in that book appears in a self-reflexive passage near the end of the book:

> In writing a book on crime, one ought to have in mind to give the public a truthful account of a thief's life, his crimes, habits, thoughts, emotions, vices and virtues, and how he lives in prison and out. I believe this ought to be done, and the man who does it well must season his writings with pathos, humor, sarcasm, tragedy, and thus give the real life of the grafter.

Strangely, *The Autobiography* is written in the first person, though Hapgood's name is the only one to appear on the cover. Nevertheless, they signed a contract that stipulated Caulfield would receive half of the royalties. Throughout the book, Caulfield's exciting lifestyle among the grafters in Bowery saloons leads him to crave stimulants for enhancing the experience—opium, morphine, whiskey, tobacco, among other "necessaries of life." By the final pages of the book, one gets the impression that Caulfield finally rehabilitated after spending a horrific stint at the Dannemora asylum for the criminally insane. His rehabilitation at Dannemora did not take hold for long, however, and Caulfield applied his share of the book's proceeds to feed a growing cocaine addiction. In spite of this unfortunate reality—and notwithstanding the former criminal's failure to succeed at a manual trade school—Hapgood convinced his brother William, then operating the Columbia Conserve Company in Indianapolis, to hire him on as a laborer. William soon dismissed Caulfield on the grounds that he was consistently late for work, perpetually inebriated on the job, and demonstrated a generally lazy disposition. Caulfield and Hapgood fell out over the incident, and their friendship never recovered. This estrangement with Caulfield may have affected Hapgood's later rejection of the criminal element as a subject, as he articulated the switch in *The Spirit of Labor*.

Hapgood and his family arrived in Chicago in 1904, when the city was one of the fastest growing industrial societies in the world. A friend secured him a position on the *Chicago Evening Telegraph* under the editorship of the Irish American columnist and fiction writer Finley Peter Dunne, but his real interests lay in his next group of study—the industrial laborer. Hapgood soon discovered that breaking into working-class saloon culture in Chicago was substantially more difficult than in New York. The workers first looked upon Hapgood as an effete "parasite," and, calling to mind Hunter S. Thompson's similar encounter with the Hell's Angels in the 1960s, a group of steelworkers jumped him in a neighborhood bar. Through further efforts, he acquainted himself with Anton Johannsen, then the president of the Chicago labor union. Johannsen considered himself an anarchist and held an abiding interest in European philosophy. *The Spirit of Labor* is essentially a memoir of Johannsen's extraordinary rise from German immigrant to vagabond hobo to woodworker to powerful labor leader. The editor of the *San Francisco Bulletin,* Freemont Older, and John Chamberlain, a reviewer for the *New York Times,* both hailed the book as a revelation. Chamberlain years later praised *The Spirit of Labor* as the only book he had seen prior to World War I that fully captured the radical side of labor politics. But in a parallel with his earlier interest in the criminal life of Caulfield, Hapgood's interest in his subject lay not so much in labor reform or social justice, but rather in establishing models among outcast societies for self-realization and cultural salvation.

Hapgood's fifth book, *An Anarchist Woman* (1909), draws even closer to this goal. Still in Chicago, Hapgood attended an "anarchist ball" with Johannsen, where he fell in with another unorthodox figure—one of the most unorthodox private citizens in U.S. history—Terry Carlin (née Terence O'Carolan). A follower of the German philosophers Max Stirner and Friedrich Nietzsche, the Irish-born Carlin was an "individualist" or "philosophical" anarchist in the mode of the American publisher Benjamin R. Tucker and, even earlier, before the term "anarchism" was coined, Henry David Thoreau. Outlining the distinction between communist-anarchism and individualist-anarchism, Hapgood admitted that most of the American anarchists he knew were of the first stripe, activists who believed in political "revolution" and the use of violence rather than social "insurrection." The "anarchist woman" of the title is Carlin's girlfriend Marie, who, along with Carlin, supplied Hapgood with an extensive correspondence delineating her working-class upbringing, her life as a chambermaid, and her eventual turn to prostitution. As a philosophical anarchist, Carlin's chief method of conversion was, like Hapgood's, through intimate relations, what he called "unconscious propaganda," and Marie, only seventeen years old (Carlin was thirty-five), became his pupil and longtime lover.

An Anarchist Woman portrays Carlin as a man who (again like Hapgood) "consorted with thieves, prostitutes, with all low human types." But Carlin had no interest in career building; in fact, he absolutely refused to work for money. Hapgood voices a similar sentiment in *A Victorian,* where he explains one aspect of philosophical anarchism as "a willingness to receive hospitably whatever dawning forces there may be in the submerged; a refusal to deny their possible validity in a more complex society." Eventually, however, Carlin, whom Eugene O'Neill famously immortalized in the character Larry Slade in his late masterpiece *The Iceman Cometh* (1939), became mentally unwound by the effects his philosophy had on himself and those close to him.

Hapgood ends *An Anarchist Woman* with Marie going her own way, and Terry continuing his parasitic existence (in one telling instance, Eugene O'Neill was forced to evict him from his Provincetown home when O'Neill's housekeeper lay down the ultimatum that either Carlin left or she did). *An Anarchist Woman* is significant in American literary history in that it inverts the nineteenth-century formula of the fallen woman who descends into prostitution after society casts her out. Rather than committing suicide or seeking help at a settlement house as the sentimental formula would have it, the heroine redeems her sordid past by forming an open relationship with an anarchist free-love advocate; by thus drawing Marie into his philosophical world, Carlin effectively rescued her from a life of prostitution.

In his next book, a collection of New York sketches, *Types from City Streets* (1910), the titles of his essays—all taken from feature articles he wrote for the *Atlantic Monthly, Harper's Weekly, Leslie's Monthly,* the *New York Daily Telegraph,* the *New York Evening Post,* and the *New York Daily Commercial Advertiser*—reveal a good deal about the author's personal predilections: "Literature in Low Life," "The Real Bowery," "The Thief's Philosophy of Life," "The Tammany Man," "The Bohemian," and so forth. His essay "The Pathos of Low Life" is telling in that he claims his subjects have influenced his writing style, as the succeeding generations of New Journalists would later assert. He acknowledges that it is not his choice of subject his critics will condemn, as the literature of "low life" has enjoyed a long tradition, but rather his affirmation of it.

No matter the innovative energy unleashed sporadically throughout the book, Hapgood's critical reputation, largely based on the initial success of *The Spirit of the Ghetto,* no longer prevailed. By 1910, Moses Rischin suggests (in his 1967 introduction), critics simply categorized Hapgood as a washed-up writer who held a "morbid sympathy for low life."

Soon after *Types from City Streets* appeared, Hapgood agreed to supply an introduction for Alexander Berkman's *Prison Memoirs of an Anarchist* (1912). Berkman composed the memoir after fourteen years of incarceration for the attempted assassination of the millionaire industrialist Henry Clay Frick. Berkman, Emma Goldman's longtime lover and fellow anarchist agitator, had tried to gun down Frick in retaliation for Frick's brutal treatment of steel workers during the infamous Homestead Strike of 1892. He believed that Berkman's memoir exposed prison life at its most authentic. The year he wrote the Berkman preface, Hapgood was back in New York working at the *Commercial Advertiser,* now called the *Globe* (among many of his accomplishments during his tenure there, he interviewed the presidents Theodore Roosevelt and Woodrow Wilson). His editor H. J. Wright received some disturbing letters from his subscribers accusing Hapgood, one of his most widely read writers, of being an anarchist sympathizer. And Berkman was not only controversial among social conservatives: while Emma Goldman passed around a petition for Berkman's release, the philosophical anarchist Benjamin R. Tucker—an uncompromising passivist—refused outright to sign.

Hapgood was not strictly an anarchist, nor was he an official member of any political faction. His political ambivalence is clear from the opening remarks to the Berkman memoir. He admits that his reasons for writing the piece stem from a passionate desire to reveal "truth." He was not a Marxist like so many of his Greenwich Village associates; Robert Allen Skotheim has discussed the way Hapgood contested the Marxist preoccupation with materialism. What does appear time and again in his work is the proposition that the lower classes can instill healthy psychological and cultural models for the middle class. He was firmly convinced that what he called the "'low' forms of human life" lay bare a consummate self-esteem and cultural tolerance that was in stark contrast to the United States's querulous middle class.

FINAL YEARS

Hapgood and Boyce separated indefinitely in the summer of 1914. Boyce accompanied Mabel Dodge to Florence to hobnob with Europe's burgeoning artists and writers, while Hapgood fled to Provincetown to write and drink in solitude. Boyce and her companions had not, unfortunately, anticipated the eruption of the World War I. and she and Van Vechten made a harrowing trip back to the United States, which she recorded in her "War Diary" (first published in DeBoer-Langworthy's collection of Boyce's autobiographical writing). During this time, Hapgood wrote *The Story of a Lover,* his last book before the publication of his autobiography decades later. An anonymously published memoir, *The Story of a Lover* did not actually appear until 1919, a year after the loss of his eldest son Harry to influenza (Neith Boyce published a memoir of his life entitled *Harry: A Portrait* in 1923). *The Story of a Lover* is a highly sentimental account of his relations with Neith Boyce and their children from 1906 to 1908, and it also dwells on the incredibly painful period in Italy when Boyce fell in love with Arthur Bentley. As such, it is a confession in which Hapgood attempts to come to grips with the disparities between the love he felt for his wife and his own philandering tendencies. He also recognized the "shameful impossibility" of Boyce sharing his enthusiasm for pickpockets, Yiddish poets, drunks, and even "the careless girl of my acquaintance."

The Story of a Lover (a book, in truth, only a biographer could love) is at its core a long-winded apology to Neith Boyce, filled with heavy-handed exclamation points and question marks to bring home the sincerity of his claims. The work was completed a few days before the outbreak of the World War I., timing that Hapgood described in his autobiography as a "rather strange coincidence," as the story revolved around a topic he often compared to warfare—the institution of marriage. He contended, in *The Story of a Lover,* that in fact it was the "friction," of their relationship that fueled their passion for one another. *The Story of a Lover* never explicitly condemns extramarital relations; and for this and other reasons, the courts deemed the book obscene, the publisher was charged with indecency, and all copies were provisionally removed from the shelves by the police (the ban was officially repealed a year later).

Hapgood's writing career effectively ended with the tragic death of his son Harry, who at age seventeen fell victim to the catastrophic 1918 influenza epidemic while working as a cowboy in New Mexico. Hapgood's father died the year before and his mother soon after, in 1921. Mary Pyne, probably the only other woman in Hapgood's female repertoire who came close to the spiritual intimacy he shared with Neith Boyce, died from tuberculosis in 1919. In 1922, Hapgood and Boyce, emotionally and professionally incapacitated by this series of devastating losses, sold the Dobbs Ferry house and moved to France, where they distracted themselves by attending Gertrude Stein's famous Paris salon gatherings. The horrors of World War I had finally come to an end, and a large group of expatriates from the United States began pouring into Paris—including F. Scott Fitzgerald, John Dos Passos, and Ezra Pound, among many other disillusioned Americans who collectively formed what Gertrude Stein labeled "The Lost Generation." At one point during their stay, a young journalist named Ernest Hemingway, who was then reporting for the *Toronto Star*, plied Hapgood for his opinion on a short story he was then struggling over. Though only twenty-three years old, Hemingway was already a seasoned reporter but had yet to achieve his great ambition—to publish a work of fiction. He had recently developed a crush on Hapgood's sixteen-year-old daughter Miriam, and the attraction seemed mutual. Hapgood didn't think much of the story, but considered the young aspirant a "sound journalist and a charming person" (as he recalls in *A Victorian*), so he encouraged him nonetheless. As far as Hapgood knew, Hemingway never acted on his infatuation with his daughter, but he definitely continued writing. His first book, *Three Stories and Ten Poems,* came out the following year.

After a brief stint in Switzerland, Boyce and Hapgood returned to the United States in 1925 and bought a farm near Richmond, New Hampshire. Hapgood lost most of his inheritance in the stock market crash of 1929. The couple then lived a vagabond existence but retained the farm as Boyce's haven from Hapgood's erratic lifestyle through the 1940s. Over this period they traveled intermittently from New York to Provincetown to Key West, Florida. In 1932, Hapgood wrote the draft of a thirty-thousand-word memoir titled "My Forty Years of Drink," which still resides unpublished and unrevised in the Hapgood Family Papers at Yale University's Beinecke Rare Book and Manuscript Library. After a series of rejections from publishers, he sent Theodore Dreiser the manuscript, hoping it might be published in serial form. Dreiser mentions that he passed the manuscript along to an editor, but whether he did or did not, the book was never published.

Hapgood's last true moment in the cultural spotlight, also involving Dreiser but in a far less congenial way, took place from 1933 to 1934. In 1933, when the high-profile literary journal the *American Spectator*—edited by a cabal of intellectual giants, including Dreiser, O'Neill, and Sherwood Anderson—published a symposium on the Jews in America they flippantly titled "Editorial Conference (with Wine)." Their consensus on the Jews reflected the larger American public's view, at a time when Jews were reading the writing on the walls of Hitler's Germany, that Jews as a "race" were too smart for their own good. Hapgood wrote a scathing response to Ernest Boyd, another editor at the *Spectator,* who then sent it on to Dreiser. Dreiser responded, on October 10, 1933, with an even more anti-Semitic letter to Hapgood, in which he exaggerated and decried the rise of the United States's Jewish population and voiced his belief in creating a Jewish state (to check them from becoming too dominant internationally). Hapgood demanded of the *Spectator* that it publish the letters in their entirety, but the editorial board declined, and a year and a half later, after the *Spectator* went defunct, he persuaded the editors of the *Nation* to print the contentious exchange of October 1933. In spite of the fact that Dreiser substantially revised his letter for publication, softening the anti-Semitic impact of the original, the affair struck a national chord and received a good deal of press defending both sides.

Hapgood remained depressed, transient, and professionally inactive until Boyce urged him to start writing his autobiography in 1936. Though published by the preeminent imprint Harcourt, Brace, *A Victorian in the Modern World* received tepid reviews and low sales. Hapgood attributed the poor reception to the fact that the title contained the unfashionable word "Victorian" along with the fact that the poet Carl Sandburg had published his Pulitzer Prize–winning four-volume biography of *Abraham Lincoln: The War Years* through the same publisher in the same year. Two years before Hapgood's death, he drafted a frantic appeal to Abraham Cahan—a letter that remains in the Hapgood family papers, as he apparently couldn't lower himself to send it—asking his longtime friend to recommend him for a position in any active Jewish organization during the World War II. By this time, however, Hapgood was seventy-three years old and his despondency had effectively alienated him from useful service in any quarter of American life.

CRITICAL RECEPTION AND CULTURAL LEGACY

There remain two schools of Hapgood criticism, meager as it is. One holds him up as a near evangelical celebrant of marginal societies, chiefly of radical labor movements and the Jewish immigrant classes, and the other critiques his personal life in the context of 1910s Greenwich Village bohemian culture, his marriage to Neith Boyce, and his near pathological inclination for extramarital relations and "self-abuse" (both literally and figuratively).

Hutchins Hapgood's only biographer is Michael Marcaccio, who in 1977 made available a proficient comparative study titled *The Hapgoods: Three Earnest Brothers*. In Moses Rischin's invaluable introduction to the 1967 reprint of Hapgood's bestseller, *The Spirit of the Ghetto: Studies of the Jewish Quarter of New York* (1902), he applauds Hapgood for sidestepping the anti-Semitic, dispassionate reform-writing tradition of Jacob Riis and his ilk. The journalism historian Thomas B. Connery has pointed out Hapgood's correlation to the so-called New Journalism that emerged later in the century—the melding of subject and style, fact and fiction.

Ellen Kay Trimberger edited a remarkable, if psychologically distressing, selection of fiction, memoir, poetry, letters, and drama by Hapgood and Neith Boyce concerning their turbulent relationship; in it, she intermingles a number of astute essays by and about the bohemian couple in the context of early-twentieth-century marriages, demonstrating the extent to which sex was seen as a tool for effecting social change. Christine Stansell in her history of early-twentieth-century American bohemianism, *American Moderns: Bohemian New York and the Creation of a New Century* (2000), correspondingly argues that Hapgood and other moderns used sex to break down class and gender barriers.

The only truly comprehensive study is Hapgood's chatty and at times brilliantly written autobiography, *A Victorian in the Modern World*, an exceptional document in that Hapgood attempts to reconcile his generation's Victorian-modernist contradiction.

As a whole, the life of Hutchins Hapgood corresponds to the historical transition from Victorianism to modernism in American culture, from what Trimberger has described as a national commitment to "self-sacrifice" to one of a "self-realization." Though a self-professed product of the Victorian era, Hapgood believed that sacrificing the needs of the individual hindered the democratic and spiritual progress of the United States. As such, he was one of the first public critics of the Victorian "cult of respectability," along with George Santayana, Harold Stearns, and H. L. Mencken. The term "Victorian," like its close cousin "Puritan," became forever associated with conventional conservatism in American life. But Hapgood's ideas took hold in the popular imagination well after his career was over, and he received little credit for their provenance. In *A Victorian,* Hapgood quotes Lincoln Steffens as having aptly told him, on more than one occasion, "You are always in the lead, but too far for you to do very much about it. You will leave that for those who come after you." In one revealing passage from his autobiography, he explains what he derived from years of exploring America's underworld:

> I preferred for many years the society of outcasts, men and women, and the dramshops of life to the respectable people and their social resorts. I don't know why it was, entirely, but even from the beginning I felt something limited and repressive in morality as it is ordinarily conceived. It seemed to say, "Thou shalt not," but only rarely, "Thou shalt,"

and then faintheartedly. I felt that the lid shut away from the human social center a large number of the people who also belonged there, whom we call the submerged...I am aware, of course, of my own rationalization of my personal inclinations. It is easy of course to live, during the period of youth especially, with loose and lawless bohemians. It is natural to desire the freedom which is generally and sometimes legitimately denied. In other words, I am sure that I had a more than normal desire to be with the dissipated and self-indulgent gang. But why the mental and temperamental excitement that I felt? It was not sensuality only, it was something of the opposite of nature. It was a spiritual and esthetic excitement that one feels in the hope of a less boring, more enhancing existence.
(pp. 325–326)

Hapgood ignited this "spiritual and esthetic excitement" through extensive wanderings among the tenements of Manhattan's Jewish Lower East Side and the billiard halls of Chicago; through intimate conversations in the saloons of the Bowery and the cafés of Greenwich Village; and through his groundbreaking reportage from the dance halls of Harlem and the opium dens of Chinatown. As such, his modernist philosophy foresaw the interests of younger, far more prominent authors whose careers emerged from the social chaos following the World War I.—John Dos Passos, Eugene O'Neill, Gertrude Stein, and Ernest Hemingway, just to name a few, all of whom were close Hapgood associates from the start of their brilliant careers. Along with having an obvious influence on radical movements that occurred well after his death—the beat generation of the 1950s, the cultural rebellion of the 1960s, Generation X of the 1990s—whether one considers Hapgood an avant-garde reporter of the disenfranchised or merely a self-absorbed epicurean, this American writer played an integral role in defining what it means to be "modern." Most important of all, he left behind a body of work that gives form and definition to the social conflicts and psychological tensions that produced a culture of tolerance and multiculturalism through the twentieth and into the early twenty-first centuries. But the fact is, regardless of his tireless networking and topical subject matter, not one of his books has remained in print.

Selected Bibliography

WORKS OF HUTCHINS HAPGOOD

SELECTED VOLUMES

Paul Jones. Boston: Houghton, Mifflin and Co., 1901.

The Spirit of the Ghetto: Studies of the Jewish Quarter in New York. New York: Funk & Wagnalls, 1902; rev. ed., New York: Funk & Wagnalls, 1909; new ed. with a preface by Harry Golden, New York: Funk & Wagnalls, 1965; reprint, with an introduction by Moses Rischin, Cambridge, Mass.: Belknap Press of Harvard University Press, 1967.

The Autobiography of a Thief. New York: Fox, Duffield & Company, 1903.

The Spirit of Labor. New York: Duffield & Company, 1907.

An Anarchist Woman. New York: Duffield & Company, 1909.

Types from City Streets. New York: Funk & Wagnalls, 1910.

The Story of a Lover, anonymous. New York: Boni & Liveright, 1919.

A Victorian in the Modern World. New York: Harcourt, Brace, 1939; reprint, with an introduction by Robert Allen Skotheim, Seattle: University of Washington Press, 1972.

OTHER WRITING

Introduction. In *Prison Memoirs of an Anarchist*, by Alexander Berkman. New York: Mother Earth Publishing Association, 1912.

Dialogue. With Neith Boyce. 1915. In *Intimate Warriors: Portraits of a Modern Marriage, 1899–1944*. Edited by Ellen Kay Trimberger. New York: Feminist Press at the City University of New York, 1991. Pp. 180–185.

Enemies: A Play in One Act. 1916. With Neith Boyce. In *Intimate Warriors: Portraits of a Modern Marriage, 1899–1944*. Edited by Ellen Kay Trimberger. New York: Feminist Press at the City University of New York, 1991. Pp. 186–195.

"The Picturesque Ghetto." *Century*, July 1917.

Foreword. In *The Provincetown Plays*. Edited by George Cram Cook and Frank Shay. Cinncinnati, Ohio: Stewart Kidd, 1921.

"Hutchins Hapgood." In *Twentieth Century Authors: A*

Biographical Dictionary of Modern Literature. Edited by Stanley J. Kunitz and Howard Haycraft. New York: H. W. Wilson, 1942. P. 614. (Autobiographical sketch.)

The primary archive of Hutchins Hapgood's miscellaneous papers is collected with the Hapgood Family Papers in the Yale Collection of American Literature, Beinecke Rare Book and Manuscript Library, at Yale University in New Haven, Conn. (Includes the essay "A Liberal Radical" and correspondence with Abraham Cahan and Theodore Dreiser.)

CRITICAL AND BIOGRAPHICAL STUDIES

Connery, Thomas B. "Hutchins Hapgood and the Search for a 'New Form of Literature.'" *Journalism History* 13: 2–9 (spring 1986).

DeBoer-Langworthy, Carol, ed. *The Modern World of Neith Boyce: Autobiography and Diaries.* Albuquerque: University of New Mexico Press, 2003.

Dowling, Robert M. "Hutchins Hapgood." *The Oxford Encyclopedia of American Literature.* Edited by Jay Parini. Vol. 2. New York: Oxford University Press, 2004. Pp. 144–146.

———. "Hutchins Hapgood." *The Dictionary of Literary Biography, Vol. 303: American Radical and Reform Writers, First Series.* Edited by Steven Rosendale. Farmington Hills, Mich.: Gale, 2005. Pp. 192–199.

———. "On Eugene O'Neill's 'Philosophical Anarchism.'" *Eugene O'Neill Review* 30 (Spring 2007).

———. *Slumming in New York: From the Waterfront to Mythic Harlem.* Forthcoming. Champaign: University of Illinois Press, 2007.

Filler, Louis. "Hutchins Hapgood." In *Dictionary of American Biography: Supplement Three, 1941–1945.* Edited by Edward T. James. Charles Scribner's Sons, 1973. Pp. 329–330.

Humphrey, Robert E. *Children of Fantasy: The First Rebels of Greenwich Village.* New York: Wiley, 1978.

Luhan, Mabel Dodge. *Movers and Shakers.* New York: Harcourt, Brace, 1936. (Vol. 3 of *Intimate Memories.*)

Madison, Charles A. "Benjamin R. Tucker: Individualist and Anarchist." *The New England Quarterly*, Vol. 16, No. 3. (September 1943): 444–467.

Marcaccio, Michael. *The Hapgoods: Three Earnest Brothers.* Charlottesville: University Press of Virginia, 1977.

Minter, David. "Hutchins Hapgood." In *American National Biography.* Edited by Mark C. Carnes and John A. Garraty. New York: Oxford University Press, 1997.

Rischin, Moses. "Abraham Cahan and the *New York Commercial Advertiser.*" *Publications of the American Jewish Historical Society* 43: 10–36 (September 1953).

———. Introduction. In *The Spirit of the Ghetto*, by Hutchins Hapgood. 1902. Cambridge, Mass.: Belknap Press of Harvard University Press, 1967.

Sanders, Ronald. "Reformers in the Ghetto." *Commentary* 40: 78–93 (1965).

Skotheim, Robert Allen. Introduction. In *A Victorian in the Modern World*, by Hutchins Hapgood. 1939. Seattle: University of Washington Press, 1972.

Stansell, Christine. *American Moderns: Bohemian New York and the Creation of a New Century.* New York: Metropolitan, 2000.

Trimberger, Ellen Kay. *Intimate Warriors: Portraits of a Modern Marriage, 1899–1944.* New York: Feminist Press at the City University of New York, 1991.

Share, Allen J., and Stephen Weinstein. "Hutchins Hapgood." In *The Encyclopedia of New York City.* Edited by Kenneth T. Jackson. New Haven, Conn.: Yale University Press, 1995. P. 926.

OTHER WORKS CITED

Alexander, Doris. *The Tempering of Eugene O'Neill.* New York: Harcourt, Brace, and World, 1962.

———. *Eugene O'Neill's Last Plays: Separating Art from Autobiography.* Athens: University of Georgia Press, 2005.

O'Neill, Eugene. *Selected Letters of Eugene O'Neill.* Edited by Travis Bogard and Jackson R. Bryer. 1988. New York: Limelight Editions, 1994.

Van Vechten, Carl. Letter to Hutchins Hapgood, 13 December 1939. In *Letters of Carl Van Vechten.* Edited by Bruce Kellner. New Haven, Conn.: Yale University Press, 1987.

MARK JARMAN
(1952—)

Kim Bridgford

ARGUABLY ONE OF the best contemporary religious poets, Mark Foster Jarman (not to be confused with the Canadian novelist Mark Anthony Jarman) is a central figure in the new formalist movement, which, in the 1980s, advocated a return to traditional forms. A central part of this movement was a return to narrative poetry, and Jarman, along with his friend Robert McDowell, made this a particular mission, founding a magazine called the *The Reaper,* which ran from 1980 to 1989 and took issue with the direction of contemporary poetry. As a regular contributor to *The Hudson Review,* he has gone on to further this mission, favoring poetry rich in imagery and storytelling. With David Mason, he published the most notable anthology of the new formalist movement, *Rebel Angels: Twenty-five Poets of the New Formalism* (1996), which created a surprisingly heated response in the poetry community, bringing the tension between free-verse and formal poets to the forefront. Finally, along with McDowell, he founded Story Line Press, an Oregon-based publishing company that has published some of the primary figures of new formalism, including David Mason and Kate Light. Although Jarman has written striking narrative poetry, most notably in *The Black Riviera* (1990), he is equally well known for his sonnets; in fact, he is one of the strongest living practitioners of the sonnet sequence. His central topic is religion. The son of a preacher, Jarman has always been fascinated with issues of belief, but it is the poems in *Questions for Ecclesiastes* (1997) and *Unholy Sonnets* (2000; the title a take on John Donne's "Holy Sonnets") that, at mid career, are his legacy. He does not offer easy answers, but his poems indicate that wrestling with the issues is well worth the effort.

BIOGRAPHY

The son of Donald R. Jarman and Bo Dee (Foster) Jarman, Mark Foster Jarman (named for Mark Twain) was born on June 5, 1952, in Mount Sterling, Kentucky, where his father received theological training. He was the eldest of three children. His father's ministry took the family to a range of locales—from the harsh, cold landscape of Scotland to the easygoing surf of Redondo Beach, California. While Jarman credits his interest in writing to his maternal grandmother, he owes his complex relationship to religion to his father and his paternal grandfather, also a preacher.

The relationship to the father—God, his own father, and his grandfather—is pivotal in Jarman's work. Since his father and grandfather were both preachers, Jarman had to examine his own place in that lineage. He did not choose to be a preacher, but a poet; however, all three struggled with issues of religion, language, and audience. His earlier religious poetry is bitter and continually returns to the nothingness that he suspected was underneath the enterprise of Christianity. It was only later in life that Jarman returned to Christianity and could offer praise in the midst of a complicated religious faith.

Jarman's educational experiences were important not only because he loved school but because of the relationships he formed there. Jarman graduated from the University of California at Santa Cruz summa cum laude, with a BA in English literature, in 1974. While there, he met Robert McDowell, with whom he was to form a lifelong friendship, and during his senior year, he met Amy Kane, whom he married on December 28, 1974. She was instrumental in helping Jarman to return to his religious faith in 1986. Jarman and Kane have two daughters: Claire Marie (born in 1980) and Zoe Anne (born in 1982). The two daughters have chosen the stage over their parents' professions (Claire a stage manager and Zoe an actress), but shared a close family life, including common interests in baseball (Jarman is a Los Angeles Dodgers fan) and Scrabble. Jarman went on to receive an MFA in poetry writing from the University of Iowa in 1976. At Iowa, he studied with Donald Justice, one of the most famous teachers at the workshop and a formalist poet. Jarman said in an interview with Mary Flinn that the chance to study with Justice was his impetus for going to Iowa.

Jarman has spent his life as an academic, teaching at Indiana State University, the University of California at Irvine, and Murray State University in Kentucky, before settling down at Vanderbilt University in Nashville, Tennessee, in 1983, where he has been a full professor since 1992. He is the author of numerous books of poetry—*Tonight Is the Night of the Prom* (1974), *North Sea* (1978), *The Rote Walker* (1981), *Far and Away* (1985), *The Black Riviera* (1990), *Iris* (1992), *Questions for Ecclesiastes* (1997), *Unholy Sonnets* (2000), and *To the Green Man* (2004); three books of criticism—*The Reaper Essays* (with Robert McDowell; 1996), *The Secret of Poetry: Essays* (2001), and *Body and Soul: Essays on Poetry* (2002); as well as a noted anthology, *Rebel Angels: Twenty-five Poets of the New Formalism* (with David Mason; 1996).

He has thrice received fellowships from the National Endowment for the Arts, and he has been the recipient of a Guggenheim fellowship. He received the Academy of American Poets' Prize for *The Black Riviera,* and *Questions for Ecclesiastes* was a finalist for the National Book Critics Circle Award, the winner of the Lenore Marshall Poetry Prize, and chosen by the editors of the journal *Image* as one of the One Hundred Top Books of the Century.

JARMAN THE CRITIC

The Reaper, the provocative magazine that Jarman published with Robert McDowell from 1980 to 1989, eighteen issues in all, took as its mission a revitalization of narrative poetry and the death of the mediocre in contemporary poetry.

With McDowell's urging, they founded *The Reaper* in the manner of *kayak,* the iconoclastic journal edited by their former teacher George Hitchcock at the University of California at Santa Cruz. The figure of the Grim Reaper in one guise or another appeared on every cover. McDowell and Jarman cowrote *The Reaper* essays, which appeared alongside poetry, fiction, and essays by others in each issue. They used them as a playful opportunity both to assert a personality for *The Reaper* and as a serious opportunity to air their poetic philosophy.

In her introduction to the volume of collected essays from *The Reaper,* Meg Schoerke underscores the revolutionary character of the journal, placing it alongside such groundbreakers as *Blast* and *kayak.*

Jarman and McDowell feel that metrical poetry has been unjustly maligned and that the craft of poetry requires understanding how to write in traditional meters. They also feel that much of what passes for poetry is "navel gazing" and that one way to fix this problem is through narrative. They go on to stipulate that narrative in contemporary poetry is not narrative at all but the germ of a narrative. Their preferences include such poets as Wallace Stevens, Robert Frost, Philip Larkin, Larry Levis, Tess Gallagher, and Chase Twichell. The magazine published such poets as Jared Carter (the most frequent contributor), Rita Dove, Michael Collier, and Jorie Graham.

They do not hesitate to use humor to make a point, as with the figure of the Grim Reaper himself, who travels to conferences, conducts fictitious interviews, and does surveys. Jarman and McDowell are quick to parody the self-absorption of the poetry establishment and the lack of appeal of poetry to the general reader. For example, in "*The Reaper* Interviews Jean Doh and Sean Dough," the fictitious poets being interviewed are frustrated screenwriters who have turned to teaching but cannot remember their students and who write books about pointless topics such as "slug death" and with inane titles such as "*Bones Through Their Noses.*" Jarman and McDowell are not afraid to take on some of the big names in contemporary poetry, like Robert Hass and Charles Simic, or to take issue with a well-circulated poetry magazine like the *American Poetry Review* or with noted anthologies like *New American Poets of the 80s* and *The Morrow Anthology of Younger American Poets*. In the essay "Forever Young," *The Reaper* editors respond to a disappointed (fictitious) reader of these anthologies, Nora Bodie, by cherry-picking the anthologies for poems of which they approve. While Jarman and McDowell most often take on contemporary, or at least twentieth-century, poetry, no poet is off limits for humor. An excellent case in point is an epistolary argument between Homer and Dante, "The Dogtown Letters," in which they postulate whose poetic philosophy is best. As might be expected, Homer prefers outward, earth-oriented poems, Dante spiritual, afterlife poems. (*The Reaper* seems to favor Homer.)

While some readers might have felt that *The Reaper* died too soon, it did serve its purpose in bringing narrative poetry to the fore and using a unique medium to do it.

Jarman's next collection of essays was a 2001 volume titled *The Secret of Poetry*. As might be expected, both from the title of the collection and the difference in venue, the tone of this volume of essays is different from those published in *The Reaper*. There is a more intimate, personal tone to the book. Nonetheless, some things remain the same: a preference for form and narrative, a love of precision, a frustration with muddled writing and thinking. New to the discussion is an attention to religion and the role it plays in poetry. Jarman lays the groundwork for what would grow to preoccupy him as a poet.

In "Poetry and Religion," Jarman illustrates different ways in which contemporary poets approach the issue of religion. Unlike earlier poets, like John Donne or Emily Dickinson, contemporary poets struggle to find a sense of belief in an age of disbelief. Jarman describes how contemporary poets address the violence of religion, such as the crucifixion of Jesus, by breaking apart its elements—violence, forgiveness, salvation—or how poets seek oneness in a larger natural world, whose vastness mimics the vastness of God. Robinson Jeffers, a favorite of Jarman, literally worships nature. One other poet with whom Jarman is preoccupied is T. S. Eliot (and what poet wouldn't be?). However, it is human suffering, as handled by Eliot, that becomes of issue to him. In laying out these alternatives, Jarman chooses his particular preoccupations: nature and suffering. Jay Twomey takes issue with the way in which Jarman addresses religion, finding that in evaluating poems—Mary Oliver's and Clare Rossini's, for example—Jarman blends aesthetic and religious judgment, finding the more traditionally religious poem preferable. Yet Jarman is more interested in the parts than he is in the whole.

While Jarman discusses famous poets in this volume, he follows his own advice by addressing an unexpected topic in relation to them—Eliot's and Ezra Pound's "Americanness"; the respective "playwright" and "psychoanalyst" styles of John Berryman and Randall Jarrell. At the same time, he brings a new depth and open affection to topics that may be familiar.

Jarman has a gift for sentences that sum up the crux of his review. Although he uses new formalism as the center of his poetic taste, he likes poets as diverse as Andrew Hudgins and Jorie Graham. The *Booklist* critic Ray Olson cites the essay on Graham as "one of the best pieces" in the book.

The 2002 volume *Body and Soul*, which collected more of Jarman's essays on poetry and appeared in the prestigious University of Michigan Poets on Poetry series, shows a new ease with his role as critic, although in many ways it is an extension of his work in *The Secret of Poetry*, especially his work on religion and Robinson Jeffers. The book, which is dedicated to Donald Davie, Jarman's colleague at Vanderbilt, is largely about the nature of devotion, and how this plays out through body and soul. This devotion might be illustrated in a variety of ways: through friendship, through religion, through one's literary taste, and through one's past and one's family.

The four most striking essays in the collection are the preface; "The Body on Fire, the Soul in Flight"; "Slip, Shift, and Speed Up: The Influence of Robinson Jeffers's Narrative Syntax";

and "Body and Soul: Parts of a Life," but for different reasons. The preface is important because it underscores Jarman's relationship to Davie and the way in which he learned to appreciate Davie's point of view. He had criticized Davie in *The Reaper,* and, over time, Davie forgave him. Three parts of Davie's poetic philosophy would grow to be important to Jarman.

"The Body on Fire, the Soul in Flight," a discussion of the poetry of Michelangelo and St. John of the Cross, is important for its emphasis on the body and the soul. While Jarman also evaluates the translations of these voices—John Frederick Nims's overly rollicking translation of the poems of Michelangelo and Ken Krabbenhoft's rather remote take on the poetry of St. John of the Cross, without the rhyme and meter that would make the poems more musical—the essay is an occasion to examine the relationship to God, and which Jarman sees as charged with the sexuality represented in traditional love poems. Because there is no other way to express one's love than through the physical body, Jarman sees this situation as inevitable.

"Slip, Shift, and Speed Up" is memorable as Jarman's furthering of Jeffers' reputation. Jarman takes Jeffers' poem "Apology for Bad Dreams" and uses it as a model from which poems by C. K. Williams, Garrett Hongo, Chase Twichell, and Kate Daniels flow. While the argument for Chase Twichell is the least convincing, Jarman does trace a connection to the type of long free—verse line that makes its way from the Bible, to Walt Whitman, to Jeffers, and to these other poets. Yet whether Jeffers is essential to that lineage as an intermediary is arguable.

The last essay in the collection, "Body and Soul," is important not only because it continues to emphasize the connection between the physical body and spirituality, but because it is a rare glimpse at Jarman's life. This autobiographical essay discusses not only Jarman's childhood but also his significant relationships: with family members, teachers, landscapes, and his wife and daughters. The essay is more affectionate about the past than some of Jarman's poems are, and thus "Body and Soul" provides a fascinating counterpoint to what he has written elsewhere.

JARMAN THE ANTHOLOGIST

With David Mason, Mark Jarman edited an anthology titled *Rebel Angels: Twenty-five Poets of the New Formalism,* which appeared in 1996. The title comes from a quote by John Keats, "I feel I should have been a Rebel Angel had the opportunity been mine." The idea of poet—and person—as rebel has appeal for Jarman and is an idea that he explores in his poetry. It goes on to imply, in this context, how one rebels against the "heavenly" sameness of free verse. The imagery also refers to an essay by Diane Wakoski titled "The New Conservatism in American Poetry" (published in the *American Poetry Review,* May-June, 1986), in which John Hollander, an earlier formalist, is called "Satan." The new formalists are, by extension, his followers. In addition to having an adherence to new formalism as a criterion for a poet's inclusion in the book, Jarman and Mason also use year of birth as a criterion. This anthology includes some of the finest poets of the new formalist movement, including Julia Alvarez, Rafael Campo, Dana Gioia, Marilyn Hacker, Andrew Hudgins, Brad Leithauser, Charles Martin, Marilyn Nelson, Mary Jo Salter, and Timothy Steele.

However, many critics took issue with the collection, with Ray Olson in *Booklist* preferring the humorous poetry over the serious, and others taking issue with both its stance and poetry. The tone of response tended toward the vitriolic.

JARMAN THE POET

Jarman's first book of poetry, *Tonight Is the Night of the Prom,* a chapbook, was published while he was still an undergraduate. It illustrates both his prodigious talent—he had already published in such journals as *Antaeus* and *Poetry*—and his preoccupations, particularly with time and loss. While the poems are less specific than they would grow to be, some of the work is memorable, particularly the title poem and two others: "The Phone Booths," and "Elegy for Redondo Beach."

While in the age of cell phones, the experience described in "The Phone Booths" can feel dated, there is something magical about the way in which phone booths serve as vehicles of love for the poem's speaker: "casual as time machines, unnoticed / as angels, until they are paid attention." (p. 6) The sense of intimacy of the moment is remarkable: "I pay to smuggle myself to you," and "it *is* the smoothest way / to migrate out of here for awhile: / talking to you in a box of light." (p. 6)

Light is a way to illuminate the moment; Jarman uses it in all three poems under discussion here. Yet while the light is magical in "Tonight Is the Night of the Prom" and "The Phone Booths," it is intrusive in "Elegy for Redondo Beach," where the intimacy of darkness is preferable. The preferable light to Jarman is one that illuminates his own private spotlight for the moment, one that is soon to be lost.

Jarman's first full-length collection, *North Sea*, was published in 1978, when he was only twenty-six. The primary emphasis of the book is the land of Scotland: the first important landscape in Jarman's life. The opening epigraph of the book establishes the mood of the book and underscores Jarman's preoccupation with the past.

The first poem in the book, "Dead Reckoning," establishes the mood of return and remembrance. Spinning the globe, returning to the scene of an earlier life that once brought him pain, the speaker addresses his younger self:

You lived here once
Not choosing to
In winter, which was hard.
Now, to come to it again.
To have chosen to come to it again.
  (p. 11)

Important to the book is setting, and Jarman underscores both interior and exterior landscapes, from "the stone kitchen [with] The open jar...clotted with wasps," in the poem "Foreigners," to the road in the poem "The Close"—

This is a good road to climb,
If wind is rising with you.
Behind are the park and bomb shelter,
Shelled chestnuts and those
Still in their husks
  (p. 16)

While most of the poems have a bruised melancholy, there is joyfulness in some scenes, as in "My Parents Have Come Home Laughing" and "Kicking the Candles Out." In fact, the mood and shape of the latter are reminiscent of William Carlos Williams' "The Dance."

The second section of the book does not stay focused on Scotland, but contains other landscapes, such as Los Angeles. The issue here is less the physical setting than salvation, and Jarman's situation as the child of a traveling minister underscores that preoccupation. The book ends with the poem "Lullaby for Amy," in which Jarman is traveling with his wife and asserting that even though "We are here, in another provisional city," one thing is certain: "The earth is a wave that will not set us down"

Religion is the central concern of Jarman's next collection, published in 1981 and titled *The Rote Walker*, an allusion to Jarman's grandfather's habit of memorizing scripture by walking back and forth. Jarman in his autobiographical essay "Body and Soul" says that the collection is dedicated to both his grandfather and his father, and is the first time Jarman addresses the subject of religion at length. The book's epigraph by John Logan—"When we speak of God, is it God we speak of?"—indicates the searching quality of the collection. Just as Jarman's grandfather was obsessed by memorizing texts, Jarman is obsessed by investigating faith. Yet, while for his grandfather text was the means, for Jarman it is the end.

Intertwined with the notion of religion is the notion of memory. One way to trigger memory is through music. The bookends of the text use the song "Greensleeves" as a way of approaching memory. While the first poem, "Greensleeves," is about how memory comes to us in fragments. The second poem, "What Child Is This?" addresses the grandfather made childlike by age. The first poem shows the bitterness we can have if we hold on to memories we suffer over; the second shows that, at a certain point, those who have made us suffer are absorbed by their own inability to be blamed:

And it's like talking to the one-sided past,
telling him he's released, his God is walking
and hearing only his silence.
  (p. 51)

Jarman's rebellious attitude toward religion is evident in his poems about his grandfather. For example, his poem "The Ritual" is framed by the Catholic writer Flannery O'Connor: "If it's only a symbol, then I say to hell with it." The messianic fervor of this grandfather is what makes people give money to the congregation:

Nothing was anything much
but Grandfather made men cry, guided
clenched hands to the plate,
and when they opened hypnotically,
everything meant something. Even the air was
  negotiable.
  (p. 27)

However, once his grandfather suffers from a sequence of strokes, the magic of the experience is lost.

Jarman struggles to know what is at the heart of religion. Is it so simple as a cult of personality? He even writes a poem "Address to the Devil," as he thinks about these issues. The poem provides an interesting comparison with "Satan Says," by Sharon Olds, which appeared in 1980; however, while the speaker in Olds's poem is tempted by Satan to turn away from her parents and say unspeakable things about them (she ultimately chooses love over Satan), the speaker in Jarman's poem does not deal with the issue of family (although it is implied, given Jarman's family history). Rather he is interested in the absence of God and religion:

I have shrugged off God, that nonentity.
Like a stranger done with pleasantries
who returns to his drink, I turn to
a privacy no one else is part of,
and find you thorny, well-groomed, waiting.
  (p. 35)

While Olds in "Satan Says" presents Satan as a being that gives her permission to unloose hateful feelings, feelings she is ultimately repulsed by, Jarman's "Address to the Devil" is more civilized:

You appear in the last crack of light,
draw up my boredom like a chair,
and begin your cool confiding.
  (p. 35)

The temptation Satan presents to Jarman is a poetic legacy: "You have me convinced that death / becomes fame, when you end." (p. 35) Yet Jarman's Satan is ultimately left alone with himself, just as human beings are, just as Jarman is; Olds, by contrast, is abandoned, as the struggle to present a complicated family history is pursued. *"It's your coffin now,* Satan says."

Jarman's relationship with his father furthers his personal struggle with religion, and on a more intimate level. In "Comparisons of Wonder," Jarman describes his father taking him to visit the physically handicapped—"the boy / of bandages, of folded, flaccid arms," "the grown children, / with beards and breasts like costumes" (p. 39)—and tries to come to terms with how the physically challenged have a different relationship with religion:

You know that every escape clause
is always the heart of the matter
unlike those bedded, braced, blanked out here
who knew or never knew
and crossed over into this life.
  (p. 39)

His fatherly relationship is as close as his own palm, as he writes in "To Answer Your Question":

In my palms, the damp shrine
where moths died and prayer hid,
I have put my face out of sight.
  (p. 47)

While other religious experiences do appear in the book—the relationship that older women have with the cross that Jarman does not, Jarman's intense relationship with the city of Los Angeles—the book is primarily about fathers, and how fathering—both through religion and through family—carries with us through our lives. As the title poem tells us, "What you inherit / in turn was inherited." It is what you do with that inheritance that is important, whether your memories are good or not, painful or not. While Jarman is describing the degeneration of his grandfather in "What Child Is This?"—"But when he sighs and smacks his lips / the sounds are so personal, I jump"—the phrase "the sounds are so personal, I jump" (p. 51) is an apt way to describe how the words of religion and of the fathers penetrate Jarman's consciousness.

The Rote Walker was followed in 1985 by a volume titled *Far and Away*, in which Jarman's topic is California; the book has been described by Richard Flynn as a "watershed collection," Here Jarman brings his characteristic power of observation to his subject matter; the end of "Far and Away," the title poem, is an excellent example:

Think of the Pacific on that night,
like a deceptive Spanish dancing skirt
that shimmers and almost seems too short,
but when twirled flares out and fills your sight.
    (p. 13)

The waves become a way of achieving perspective on life. The speaker of "The Supremes" is eager for the excitement of life—he even sees Diana Ross filming on the beach—but finds a different emphasis when measured by the waves, especially from the altitude of a plane.

Far and Away is largely about Jarman's adolescence, so distance is not only a factor with regard to man and nature but in terms of past and present. Occasionally Jarman attempts to recapture the past as if he is reliving it in the present, as the present: for example, in "Long Stemmed Roses" Jarman uses present tense to establish the moment:

Mist clings tonight,
    and the hiss of passing cars
is like the release of pressure
    as pressure builds.
    (p. 18)

However, by the end of the poem, the speaker is using the language of remembrance:

I remember the scent
    of low tide, Jody Portillo nicked
under the left nipple
    and the first string center in the thigh,
and feel the thorn on the stalk
    leading back to such
blossoms of memory,
    when we were young.
    (p. 19)

There are some surprises in the book, such as "Ballad of Larry and Club," written in traditional ballad stanzas. Though less successful than many of the poems in the book, the poem illustrates Jarman's dedication to bringing the oral tradition back in poetry, one of the tenets of new formalism. Stanza 10 is a typical example of both the strengths and weaknesses of the poem:

Larry, high on the shaggy scent
    of eucalyptus and power,
made each of us climb as high as he went,
    near the dinner hour.
    (p. 35)

Also surprising is the series of "Half Sonnets," seven-line poems that read like a combination of the Zen koan and the love poem. "To the Reader" describes the process of the speaker's devolving from his current age of eighty-three, and as he moves backward through important moments in his life he has new knowledge: "I understand the room-building / of marriage now." Yet as the world continues to devolve, the speaker disappears, and understands how death operates in the present: "I am lost / And it is not to death." (pp. 60–61)

Jarman's next book, *The Black Riviera* (1990), won the 1991 Poets Prize, given to the best book of poetry by an American, and put Jarman's philosophy about the importance of narrative poetry into action. Flynn writes that *The Black Riviera* "shows Jarman in full command of his narrative power." In the manner of Frost, whom he admires, Jarman tells a series of stories about teenagers buying marijuana, old people who don't want to move to a new nursing home because it overlooks a graveyard, and a child kidnapped by her own father. Yet while the narrative strategy is similar to that of Frost, and at times the voice is as well, the locale is different. While Frost's landscape is New England, Jarman's is most typically the gritty streets of Los Angeles. A common theme in the poems is time, and how it slips away from us.

In fact, the first poem in the collection, which is less narrative and more lyrical than many of the rest, announces this theme. In "The Children," Jarman describes the way young people understand the nature of time in a way that adults do not. Adults, by contrast, look forward to the future and thus miss the present, which so quickly becomes the past. In the poems that follow in the collection, characters often are fascinated by this "soft fruit" of the past.

One way in which Jarman examines the past is through examining and re-telling its truth. The speaker of "Human Geography" keeps returning to the event of a friend's stepping on a piece of glass and having to go to a stranger's house to ask for a needle. This story morphs not only as it is retold later to friends, but as the story is presented to the reader. Is the woman inside the house a photographer? Is she clothed or not? Is the friend male or female? Such is the nature of narrative—and of time—that there is a truth beyond the truth. Another way in which Jarman examines the past is through a shifting of images that are related through association, not through linearity. From the speaker seeing some boys burn the tire of a bicycle, to an image of a poet reading, to Janis Joplin singing, "The Shrine and the Burning Wheel" illustrates a relationship with other people based on a burning circle of experience and feeling.

The unexpectedness of the topics is one strength of the book. Although a religious poem like "Good Friday" is not unexpected, the way in which Jarman relates the suffering of Christ to the suffering of men in his own family does surprise, as does his preoccupation with the narrative of Christ, which suddenly shifts to his daughter's blowing the head off a dandelion and not thinking of Christ at all. The way in which a younger Jarman listens through the wall, in "Story Hour," to the

> storytellers
> The newsbringers, the parablists,
> The fabulists, the gathered tribe
> Of the living room
> (p. 23)

makes him other, like the ant, termite, or snake. The speaker tells us,

> I believe there is a secret to life
> Because my earliest memories are
> Of hearing secrets muffled by a wall,
> Coming to me in pieces like dust
> Sliding down a shaft of sunlight.
> (p. 27)

Yet while many reincarnations of Jarman populate the book, there are many other characters as well. Three particularly compelling poems are "The Gift," the story of a girl kidnapped by her father, only to be returned to her mother; "The Home" involving a nursing home manager attempting to convince visitors, the patients, and himself that the move to a new home is the right thing; and "Miss Urquhart's Tiara," involving a story the speaker attempts to remember about a woman who, in order to soothe two children she is taking care of, tells them the story of her life, the story of a man who gave her a tiara as he was to marry her, then asked for it back in order to sell the tiara so that he could go to Australia. In all these cases, Jarman illustrates that the truth is slippery—whether it is in terms of our relationships, our wishing something to be true that is not, or believing that something fictional has a greater truth than physical reality. To live, we create myths for ourselves, and the black Riviera of the title emblemizes that. While literally it houses the drug dealer from whom some teenagers buy marijuana, it is

> The apotheosis of wet asphalt
> And smeary—silvery glare
> And plush inner untouchability.
> (p. 4)

The 1992 volume *Iris* was the first of Jarman's books published by Story Line Press and is the culmination of his narrative concerns; it is a book-length poem about a woman named Iris, a battered wife whose journey takes her home to her birth family, and then after a catastrophic event—her brothers and her mother's boyfriend are brutally shot to death, and her mother is wounded—she makes her way to California, where she finally goes to the home of the poet who haunts her: Robinson Jeffers. As Terri Witek points out, the journey parallels Jarman's own—from western Kentucky, to California, and back again, and Iris's preoccupation with Jeffers mirrors Jarman's own.

Jarman struggles with the formal issues surrounding the book-length poem, whose genesis was in Homer with *The Iliad* and *The Odyssey*. Recent uses of the form have been few, with Vikram Seth's book-length poem *The Golden Gate* (1986) one of the most well-known examples. Jarman develops his book in the manner of a novel, with three sections illustrating three journeys: the first the journey back to Kentucky, the second the journey to California, and the last the journey to Jeffers's house. There are some parallels with Homer's work, particularly *The Odyssey*; both poems are about journeys, although Iris's journey is by land, and Ulysses's is by sea. Both cover great spans of time; both demand difficult choices and tests. However, Iris's choices are determined by the fact that she is a wife, mother, and daughter, Ulysses's by the fact that he is a man and a warrior. In writing the poem, Jarman uses the long sweeping line preferred by Jeffers.

The book has as its core the plot of a potboiler novel, or the plot of poems from the oral tradition in English literature: the world of dramatic events. Iris, whose husband Cale has beaten her one time too often, returns home to western Kentucky—in fact, the physical landscape mirrors the landscape around Murray State, where Jarman once taught—to live with her mother and two brothers, who are secretly raising a crop of marijuana to make money that they cannot make otherwise. Intermingled with a world made up of fatty beef poured on overcooked macaroni, a rabid dog, and too much drinking is the contemplative world of Robinson Jeffers. Iris escapes from the family to go to the library. She does not think that she and Jeffers would understand each other's lives:

Iris tried to imagine the life her poet would write for
    her, but the one place he described—
Bare silos, meager grasses, rock like pointed fire that
    she could hardly picture, sea
Underscoring it all with mud-gray body and snarling
    teeth—
    that place was too noble.
She withdrew from there.
(p. 28)

While she is at the grocery store one day with her daughter, her family is visited by gunmen, presumably over the marijuana crop: "She heard a doglike moan turn human. There they lay, the four of them, face down, arms bound / Like chicken wings, in the living area." (p. 39) Ultimately she leaves for California, with her daughter and her wounded mother.

Iris is a survivor who takes on the responsibility for finding her mother and daughter a new life. She does that, with a man named Smith, whom she meets upon her arrival in California. He runs a salvage shop, salvaging junk the way that Iris does her life, and they make a life together. Over time, Smith and Iris grow apart, but three pivotal events mark Iris's next journey: her daughter's wedding and her mother's wedding (both on the same day), and Smith's burning of his shop.

Iris' last journey is personal and literary. Finally she makes her way to Jeffers' home, but on the way she meets the hitchhiker Nora (aptly named for Jarman's grandmother, his storyteller model), who was raised on a turkey farm and provides a parallel to Iris, in also depending on women, and ultimately herself, for survival. The two exchange stories, and Iris explains,

I've kept my real life a secret—
    reading Jeffers
And trying to imagine him imagining someone like
    me. It's
    when he says
He has been saved from human illusion and foolish-
    ness
    and passion and wants to be like rock
That I miss something.
(p. 119)

When she arrives at his house, homeless, she finds her true home: "The house where pain and pleasures had turned to poetry / and stone, and a family had been happy." (p. 126)

Even with Jarman's obvious success as a writer both of free verse and narrative poetry, most critics see *Questions for Ecclesiastes,* published in 1997, as Jarman's religious breakthrough book and cite his strengths as a practitioner of the sonnet, particularly the sonnet series. However, there was disagreement about whether the collection was entirely successful, depending on which side of the poetic fence one was on.

The poet's voice has a new wise, preacherly tone in these poems, even in those not about religion. The book's prefatory poem is titled "Ground Swell," which takes as its premise the lived moments that mean the most to us: "You write about the life that's vividest. / And if that is your own, that is your subject." (p. 13) Here Jarman is a teenager, who is acknowledged by a boy who is older than he:

To be identified by one like him—
The easy deference of a kind of god
Who also went to church where I did—made me
Reconsider my worth.
    (p. 14)

The boy is later killed in Vietnam, and Jarman finds himself returning to that time:

Yes, I can write about a lot of things
Besides the summer that I turned sixteen.
But that's my ground swell. I must start
Where things began to happen and I knew it.
    (p. 14)

In the first section of the book, Jarman uses his poem "Transfiguration" in order to examine the notion of suffering. The poem, which is written in alternating long and short lines, has a meditative quality. The speaker, in hypothesizing about the transfiguration of Jesus, thinks of another type of transfiguration, that of "resistance":

I want to believe he resisted at that moment, when he
    appeared glorified
Because he could not reconcile the contradictions
    and suspected
That love had a finite span and was merely the comfort
    of the lost
I know he must have acceded to his duty, but I want
    to believe

He was transfigured by resistance, as he listened,
    and they talked.
    (p. 21)

Yet his poem "Proverbs" takes on a more positive tone of celebration. What unites the poems is the wise voice of the poet, and the sense that even joy is complicated and tinged with sadness. Using the echo of "Three things are too wonderful for me. / Four I do not understand" from Proverbs 30 as a way to unify the beginning of the stanzas of the poem (although there are some variations), Jarman knits together lovemaking, the aging of children, the cycle of day, and the presence of God. While most of the poem underscores what Jarman says here, "This is the way with daily life— / From waking to sleeping is like this," (p. 23) the ending of the poem trembles with the reality of death and the possibility of eternal life:

Three things name God—
    Four establish God's presence:
The inner voice saying *Live;*
    The outer voice saying *Live;*
The voice saying, "Oh, my God
    At the abrupt stoppage of time;
And repeating, like a psalm,
    "My whole body is moving."
    (p. 24)

The centerpiece of the book is the series "Unholy Sonnets," twenty sonnets in all. While there is not as much versatility in tone within this section of poems as there would be in his next book, an entire volume of "unholy sonnets," this series establishes Jarman's skill with the sonnet and sonnet series, as well as his ability to wrestle with religious issues in this form. While not all sonnets are love poems, of course, Jarman's relationship with God in his religious poems can be described as a love relationship, even when he is angry, frustrated, or questioning, just as earthly relationships are not based entirely on praise but also on emotional investment and longing. Three poems deserve special mention: sonnets 9, 10, and 14. While sonnet 9 illustrates the longing of people, sonnet 10 illustrates the speaker's use of art as religious activity.

Also noteworthy in the collection are Jarman's poems about his children, especially "After

Disappointment." He is reverential about this place he escapes to, his daughter's bed, and by using a "you strategy" implicates us all in this experience. Not only is it a wonderful place to be alone, but it promises company:

there remain these places, occupied
By children, yours if lucky, like the girl
Who finds you here and lies down by your side.
   (p. 31)

This is the kind of unexpected religious gift that Jarman finds in life.

In 2000 Jarman produced an entire volume of poems in sonnet form. The rebellious attitude with which Jarman examines faith, however—as in the earlier "resistance" of the poem "Transfiguration"—is evident not only in the cover, which includes a painting by William Blake, another religious iconoclast, but also throughout the poems, as Jarman attempts to find his own sense of the religion apart from the religion he experienced as a child.

That Jarman's God is different from the traditional conception is evident in the prologue to the book. The speaker asks God to

Please be the driver bearing down behind,
Or swerve in front and slow down to a crawl,
Or leave a space to lure me in, then pull
Ahead, cutting me off, and blast your horn.
   (p. 15)

That Jarman's desire is for a God struck by road rage rather than a benevolent voice out of the clouds is telling. What Jarman is looking for is engagement, not distance. Ray Olson finds that the use of slant rhyme helps to emphasize this engagement, and Peggy Rosenthal finds this particularly effective in the world post–September 11th.

And Jarman's sonnets are all about engagement. In sonnet 3, a take on John Donne's "Batter My Heart, Three—Personed God," the speaker does not want to receive life's blows—or God's—but if he has to, he wants to resist:

But if I'm to be bent back like the pole
A horseshoe clangs against and gives a kink to,
Then take me like the grinning iron monger
I saw once twist a bar that made him sink to
His knees. His tongue was like a hot pink coal
As he laughed and said he thought that he was
   stronger.
   (p. 23)

As is evident in Jarman's famous anthology, he understands the situation of the rebel angel. He abjures passivity, wants action.

Many of the poems in the book take this "devil's advocate" position. In sonnet 7, which examines the aftermath of an accident, the speaker of the poem asks,

In which of these details does God inhere?
The woman's head in the boy's lap? His punctured
   lung?
The place where she had bitten through her tongue?
The drunk's truck in three pieces? The drunk's beer,
Tossed from the cooler, made to disappear?
   (p. 27)

And in sonnet 9, in the face of a plane crash, the speaker thinks, "Surely, someone was praying. And the prayer / Struck the blank face of earth."

Sometimes it is not a devil's advocate position that Jarman assumes, but simply a different way of seeing. In sonnet 16, the speaker examines the notion that while Mary, like any mother, would want Jesus, her son, to live; her son would prefer to have his mother die and go to heaven. In sonnet 17, Jarman carries these parent-child dynamics to their real-world context, illustrating how this relationship is at the center of all existence.

Yet there is joy in these poems, too. There is more range here than in the sonnets in *Questions for Ecclesiastes*. In sonnet 13, the speaker discusses the notion of being blessed:

Blessèdness—not only in a face
But in the air surrounding everybody,
The charged air that makes me see a body
As blessed just because it has a face.
   (p. 35)

In this book, Jarman occasionally repeats end-words—in sonnet 16, for example—in order to underscore a deep relationship among the parts of his subject matter and to further the feeling of natural speech. Another poem that underscores the positive is sonnet 25, a poem about pleasure, drinking, eating, making love. He also finds joy in nature, as in sonnet 41:

Fallen persimmons among the dew-bent grasses,
...
And the opossum in the predawn hours
Who, when the headlights catch her feeding, scuttles
On pink feet down the driveway to the shadows.
   (p. 71)

To the Green Man, published in 2004, has a gentler approach than *Unholy Sonnets,* and has more of an emphasis on nature. While the book includes poems about Jarman's daughters, it continues to return to his characteristic subject matter: his religion and his youth.

The book opens with a quotation from Donald Justice, "Whisper to me some beautiful secret that you remember from life," which, while also apt with regard to Jarman's collection of essays *The Secret of Poetry,* is apt in terms of the dailiness of life that Jarman worships and praises. It is no surprise that at the center of this worship is nature. The title poem takes the god of nature, the green man, and speaks of both his fertility and his pleasure. The book is, in large part, a discussion of these beautiful surprises, from the glories of appetite ("Testimonies of a Roasted Chicken"), to a man's single-minded obsession with watching ants move ("Butterflies Under Persimmon"), to the nobility of a meeting with a fox ("Fox Night"). Everything speaks its own language, even out of silence, for instance in "As Close as Breathing":

A spider's dragline, glinting like a thought,
Trolls through depths of shade and morning light.
The hemlock limbs bob as if at anchor.
And a pair of downy woodpeckers swoops up
To the seed bell at my study window. Everything
 answers.
   (p. 13)

The pleasures of life naturally extend to his daughters, but he is aware in the book of how time has passed in terms of his relationship with them. In "The Secret Ocean" he says that "When you were little girls, I brought you here," (p. 61) but they didn't know why:

   Neither of you knew that we were there
To calm and change the color of my thought,
   To ease its glaring pressure for a moment.
   (p. 62)

There the two girls learned

that these private walks
To places like the secret ocean
...
Were preparations for new valleys of the shadow,
   Fearing no evil, because someone was with you.
   (p. 63)

The book ends with the poem "Prayer for Our Daughters," which combines both his fatherly feelings and his religious ones. It is a warm Polonius-like list of advice and prayer for the twenty-first century:

May they never be lonely at parties
Or wait for mail from people they haven't written
Or still in middle age ask God for favors.
   (p. 74)

He wishes a life of possibility and not regret: "May they enter the coming century / Like swans under a bridge into enchantment" and "May they find a place to love, without nostalgia / For some place else that they can never go back to." (p. 74) This is what he wants for them: a life of hope. Ned Balbo says that Jarman's "approachable, unforced voice is perhaps his greatest asset."

His religious poems in this collection, furthermore, have a sense of hopefulness. In "Five Psalms," Jarman suggests,

let us think of kissing
   God with the kisses
Of our mouths, of lying with God,
   As sea worms lie,
Snugly petrifying
   In their coral shirts.
   (p. 43)

Even the disturbing poem about Jarman's grandfather, "The Excitement," describing the ghost that haunts him, is hopeful in the sense that the grandfather is spiritually visited; he wants the importance of this friendship with Christ, even though it drives him mad.

Yet always underneath these poems there is a kind of sadness—found in such a poem as "In the Tube," where three friends carry home their dead friend, who has died of a drug overdose. Filled with sadness as they bear his body home—the image is reminiscent of that in A. E. Housman's "To an Athlete Dying Young"—they are nonetheless also young and full of vitality; they are surfers. Even in this death, there is a terrible beauty in life:

> where the sharp
>   New light would score
>   The wave crests and they
> Would ride below them,
>   Dodging the onrush.
>   (p. 17)

We are reminded of the line in "Lullaby for Amy": "The earth is a wave that will not set us down."

CONCLUSION

The author of twelve books and one anthology, Mark Jarman is not only a prolific writer but also one who has struggled with some of the central issues of human existence. As he has dealt with these concerns, he has moved from the specific facts of his religious upbringing and line of religious fathers, to his own sense of nothingness, to his own poetic power, and finally achieved his combination of poetry and religion, in the manner of his poetic father, Donald Davie. He is recognized as one of the central religious poets of his generation, and perhaps of the twentieth century. His position as one of the most well-known new formalist poets has enabled him to argue for the importance of narrative poetry, through *The Reaper*, on the one hand, and for the importance of metrical poetry, on the other hand, through his affiliation with Story Line Press and through his controversial anthology, *Rebel Angels*. While ultimately he sides with the angels, his rebellious side understands the complications in life that are to be embraced precisely because we are earthbound, because to live is to wrestle and to strive to understand. Often we have to do this by looking back on our past and attempting to understand it from a position in the future. Memory is faulty; the past slips through our fingers. Yet the beauty and difficulty of this enterprise is all there is.

Selected Bibliography

WORKS OF MARK JARMAN

ANTHOLOGIES AND CRITICISM

"The Reaper" Essays. With Robert McDowell. Brownsville, Ore.: Story Line Press, 1996.

Rebel Angels: Twenty-five Poets of the New Formalism. Edited with David Mason. Brownsville, Ore.: Story Line Press, 1996.

The Secret of Poetry: Essays. Ashland, Ore.: Story Line Press, 2001.

Body and Soul: Essays on Poetry. Ann Arbor: University of Michigan Press, 2002.

POETRY

Tonight Is the Night of the Prom. Pittsburgh, Pa.: Three Rivers Press, 1974. (Chapbook.)

North Sea. Cleveland, Ohio: Cleveland State University Poetry Center, 1978.

The Rote Walker. Pittsburgh, Pa.: Carnegie-Mellon University Press, 1981.

Far and Away. Pittsburgh, Pa.: Carnegie-Mellon University Press, 1985.

The Black Riviera. Middletown, Conn.: Wesleyan University Press, 1990.

Iris. Ashland, Ore.: Story Line Press, 1992.

Questions for Ecclesiastes. Brownsville, Ore.: Story Line Press, 1997.

Unholy Sonnets. Ashland, Ore.: Story Line Press, 2000.

To the Green Man: Poems. Louisville, Ky.: Sarabande, 2004.

CRITICAL AND BIOGRAPHICAL STUDIES

ARTICLES

Flinn, Mary. "An Interview with Mark Jarman." *Blackbird: An Online Journal of Literature and the Arts* 1, no. 2 (http://www.blackbird.vcu.edu/v1n2/features/jarman_m_120202/jarman_m.htm), 2 December 2002.

Flynn, Richard. "Mark Jarman." In *Dictionary of Literary Biography*. Vol. 120, *American Poets Since World War II, Third Series*. Edited by R. S. Gwynn. Detroit: Gale, 1992. Pp. 156–161.

Schneiderman, Jason. "The Holy Forms of Mark Jarman." *Frigate* 2 (www.frigatezine.com/review/poetry/rpy02sch.html), November 2000–September 2001.

Schoerke, Meg. Introduction. *The Reaper Essays*. By Mark Jarman and Robert McDowell. Brownsville, Ore.: Story Line Press, 1996. Pp. vii–xiv.

Spalding, J. M. "Mark Jarman." *Cortland Review* (www.cortlandreview.com/features/99/01/index.html), January 1999.

Twomey, Jay. "Reading a Christian Reading: Mark Jarman, T. S. Eliot, and the Aesthetic Strategies of Religious Faith." *Religion and the Arts* 8, no. 2: 223–243 (2004).

Walzer, Kevin. "Bold Colors: Jarman, Nelson, Peacock, Turner." In his *The Ghost of Tradition: Expansive Poetry and Postmodernism*. Ashland, Ore.: Story Line Press, 1998. Pp. 85–121.

Witek, Terri. "Mark Jarman." In *Dictionary of Literary Biography*. Vol. 282, *New Formalist Poets*. Edited by Jonathan N. Barron and Bruce Meyer. Detroit: Gale, 2003. Pp. 165–172.

REVIEWS

Balbo, Ned. Review of *To the Green Man*. *Antioch Review* 63, no. 3: 600–601 (summer 2005).

Bledsoe, C. L. Review of *To the Green Man*. *Hollins Critic* 42, no. 3 (June 2005).

Coyle, Bill. Review of *Questions for Ecclesiastes*. *First Things*, no. 84: 48–51 (http://www.firstthings.com/ftissues/ft9806/reviews/coyle.html), June–July 1998.

deNiord, Chard. Review of *To the Green Man*. *Harvard Review*, no. 28: 179ff. (June 2005).

Hatch, James. Letter to *PN Review*. *PN Review* 24, no. 3: 2–3 (January–February 1998).

Kirby, David. Review of *The Secret of Poetry*. *Library Journal*, 1 May 2001, p. 84.

Olson, Ray. Review of *Rebel Angels: Twenty-five Poets of the New Formalism*. *Booklist*, 15 October 1996, p. 399.

———. Review of *Questions for Ecclesiastes*. *Booklist*, 1 January 1997, p. 809.

———. Review of *Unholy Sonnets*. *Booklist*, 15 April 2000, p. 1517.

———. Review of *The Secret of Poetry*. *Booklist*, 1 April 2001, p. 1443.

Ratner, Rochelle. Review of *Questions for Ecclesiastes*. *Library Journal* 12, no. 1: 103 (Jan 1997).

Review of *Questions for Ecclesiastes*. *Publishers Weekly* 30 December 1996, p. 62.

Review of *Rebel Angels: Twenty-five Poets of the New Formalism*. *Publishers Weekly* 30 September 1996, p. 82.

Review of *Unholy Sonnets*. *Publishers Weekly*, 24 April 2000, p. 84.

Rosenthal, Peggy. "Easter Sonnet: Poetry Reading." *Christian Century*, 27 March 2002, p. 10. (Review of *Unholy Sonnets*.)

Schoerke, Meg. "The Secret Service: Mark Jarman's Quest for a Poetics." *Hudson Review* 55, no. 1: 137ff. (spring 2002).

Whited, Stephen. Review of *Unholy Sonnets*. *Book*, March–April 2001, p. 84.

BRIGIT PEGEEN KELLY

(1951—)

Kim Bridgford

A POET WHO explores myth, archetype, and fairy tale, Brigit Pegeen Kelly is known for writing about transcendent moments in a symbolic landscape. In deserted windy gardens, her speakers share the stage with broken statuary, gravestones, swans, deer, dogs, children, and the haunting notes of music. Given the recurrent setting of the garden, it is not surprising that her central theme is loss of innocence. She is a religious poet, but one that operates outside conventional religion. At the same time, her speakers must revisit the choices emblematic of the garden, and because mankind lives in a fallen world there is always the bitter aftertaste of loss. What makes loss bearable is the human capacity for love and the sheer virtuosity of experience. Over the years Kelly's preoccupations have not changed but deepened.

In addition to exploring symbolic landscapes, she is known for her lush imagery. Patricia Monaghan wrote in *Booklist:* "Imagine a tapestry in which every color, itself resplendent, is couched next to another, equally brilliant hue. Such is Kelly's work—so gorgeous in its language, so vivid in its sonorousness." (p. 988)

BIOGRAPHY

A native of Palo Alto, California, Brigit Pegeen Kelly was born on April 21, 1951. A private person, she would prefer to discuss her work over her biography. In fact not much is known about Kelly's personal life. She grew up in Indiana, the daughter of an Indiana University English professor and poet, Robert Kelly. Her father both read to the children and had them write, teaching them discipline at an early age. Yet Kelly also had control issues. Given her fascination with extremes, it is not surprising that she suffered from an eating disorder when she was an adolescent, nor that she yearned for the order of the religious life (her parents were Catholic, but not regular churchgoers).

After leaving the convent Kelly lived variously in England, Indiana, Oregon, and New Jersey. She has practiced such professions as nursing, printmaking, and acting (often being cast as a villain because of her deep voice) and currently is a professor at the University of Illinois at Urbana—Champaign, where she has received college-wide recognition for her teaching. She has two children, Huck and Maria, has been once divorced, and is currently married to poet Michael Madonick.

She is the author of three books of poetry, *To the Place of Trumpets* (1988), published by Yale University Press and winner of the Yale Younger Poets Prize; *Song (1995),* published by BOA editions and the Lamont Poetry Selection for 1994; and *The Orchard,* a finalist for the *Los Angeles Times* Book Award in Poetry, the Pulitzer Prize, and the National Book Critics Circle Award. Her fellowships include a Whiting Writer's Award and a poetry fellowship from the National Endowment from the Arts. The winner of the "Discovery"/*The Nation* Award, she has appeared in five Pushcart Prize anthologies and in six editions of *Best American Poetry.*

TO THE PLACE OF TRUMPETS

In his introduction to Kelly's Yale Younger Poets volume, James Merrill emphasizes both the influence of Kelly's Catholicism and the folk aspects of her poetry, describing the way in which she has taken her religion and reshaped it. He provided the lead for the critical reception of the volume and for ways of interpreting it. Critics were positive about the book, emphasizing both Kelly's religious subject matter and the elements of the folktale. Ironically, even though Kelly's poems are symbolic and otherworldly, they are more narrative and autobiographical than they would grow to be in later collections.

To the Place of Trumpets, like all of Kelly's books, is divided into four sections. The first section introduces many of Kelly's central concerns: containment, the body, truth and perception, nature, religion, childhood, and music. She interweaves these ideas in different combinations in order to emphasize the nature of mortality and loss and the sometimes indecipherable border between reality and the dream.

The first poem, "After Your Nap," dedicated to Kelly's daughter Maria and written in jagged couplets, shows the body in its literal, mortal sense and in its sense of the symbolic. For Kelly, the body is intimate and distancing; she holds her daughter and says, "I cradle my marriage gentle in my lap— / a quiet thing, small, a thing barely breathing, / like those curtains rising." (p. 3) Her daughter is a paradox, vulnerable and sturdy, "contained":

I run my hand over the neat purse of your small belly
the hard knot of your pubis
and think how surely we are contained
how well our small boundaries love us.
(p. 3)

Yet, followed as this poem is by "Music School," there is the implication that we must try to transcend the limits of the body, for the birds in that poem confuse their bodies with their music:

They are dazed by the sun that presses its belly against them,
convincing them that they are their songs
and that they will never again inhabit their shabby bodies.
(p. 4)

The crease between the body and transcendence is one which Kelly continues to explore, the dreamy interlace between what one perceives and what one is.

Two poems that explore the nature of perception are "Sundays" and "Queen Elizabeth and the Blind Girl or Music for the Dead Children." "Sundays," which is in four sections (a favorite way of organizing for Kelly) is filtered. There is a sense of discombobulation, as if the world as we know it is itself and not itself. One technique is to zoom in on an unexpected detail: "Under the black walnuts on the church lawn, / Anna wears her face / like a new hat." (p. 9) Another technique is to build upon her images in a variety of ways. One way is to use a list in order to underscore the subtleties of the image she is picturing:

And over her shoulders the beautiful
nubbed shawl, gray as doves'
bellies all together, or the rose-noted
dove's song, or the priest's
Irish vowels.
(p. 9)

Another is to extend the image by association and hyperbole. The end of the first section is an excellent example:

And her husband's teeth
are whale-bone
perfect, a wrist band hoop, tight
and right and singing
of seas and salt. And when he smiles
his head comes forward
and his teeth come forward
as if he brought his fence out farther
to make the yard larger
to let more people in.
(p. 9)

Kelly is a poet who values discovery, an accumulation of details for a slow realization of context, so while the reader understands the strangeness of perspective in the poem's first section, it becomes clearer in the second section. The perspective is that of a child. It is a world of repetition, television, and Elmer Fudd:

It is hard to be a hunter,
over and over, always the kite
snagged in the tree, always the balloon
just out of reach.
(p. 10)

She is fascinated and repelled by confinement: "Always to be caught in Sam's broken t.v. / under the dimestore counter." Sight and sound and association gather together in order to reconfigure levels of experience and perception:

And the cash register bangs gold.
And Elmer's gun bangs red.
And the door to the store bangs black.
And talcum settles
like incense over the polished wood floor.
   (p. 10)

The short lines, combined with the repetition of "and" at the beginning of each line, add to the frenetic quality of the section.

Section 3 connects images through movement and sound, the gathering of which reaches its apotheosis in the middle of the section:

Bird calls
and man calls
and calls that are not,
cats—eating—tin calls,
the calls of martins in flight,
calls that roll orange groves out in the night.
   (p. 11)

The language of the poem takes on the frenetic otherworldly nature of the cartoon. Yet, while other poets might try to replicate the actual cartoon world more exactly, Kelly is not so literal.

The poem ends with an image of innocence: "the lost calf." The camera lens of Kelly's poetry shifts, and we are left with detail: "little / lily-breathed, tufted-bird-feather / furred." Kelly leaves this bovine Icarus of the landscape ready to experience life and nature, as she regularly does her characters and speakers. Even if life can be strange and disorienting, it is still something to desire and to seize. On a sensory level to be sure, Kelly is a carpe diem poet.

It is the juxtaposition of different economic situations that gives "Queen Elizabeth and the Blind Girl or Music for the Dead Children" its power; at the same time the two sections of the poem are linked by death, confusion, irony, music, and a breathlessness of language. The first section describes the baptism of Queen Elizabeth's godson, who has died; however, the queen has not been told about this in order to preserve the celebration and ceremony of the baptism. Here Kelly underscores the macabre nature of the situation, because the reader has knowledge that the queen does not:

In the tapestried hall
partridges dropped golden grease, a jester
shrieked, black and white robed singers opened their
moist mouths in perfect halos of sound.
   (p. 16)

We are left to hear what the dead cannot.

The second section of the poem is about a blind girl involved in her own scene of death, burying her son. While she does so, she listens to a boy who runs a stick along a fence, creating his own scene of song and happiness while the burial of the dead boy takes place. The sound of his stick becomes the impetus for the rest of the poem, like a match to a larger flame. In fact Kelly uses an image of fire, a cause and effect, or sound and effect, showing how one cry can set a whole series of events in motion. A woman yelling "Fire" can create a context of fire trucks and escaping people, and so the boy with his stick can start a series of associations, like the widening sounds of a rung bell. The poem moves, then, to the bells rung in honor of the dead boy, but because the bell ringer is deaf the baptismal bells are rung instead of the dead bells (linking the first and second sections of the poem as well). Because it is his greatest wish, he longs to give the blind girl the gift of sound: the sounds of birds in a bird shop. And yet ironically, as he looks down from his tower, he does not hear birds but sees them "as they wake / like a hundred green candles in a field."

"The Thief's Wife," one of the best persona poems in contemporary poetry, is an excellent early example of Kelly's preoccupation with the line between good and evil. The speaker is drawn to her husband because of his power—over her, over others, and over the material world. So exciting is this power to the speaker that she wills a kind of blindness; when her husband makes love to her outside, she says that she "keep[s] her eyes shut, thinking / that the world when my eyes were shut / was a world that would forgive those who could not see." (p. 24) When her husband tells her he has committed incest, she is "drawn even more toward / that body which made another body lie down / in darkness under it and die." It is the things he steals that underscore his love for her. Yet because she takes them, she is guilty too:

Your hand passes over something
that is stolen and settles on it—the way
chicken feathers settled this morning in the honey
I spilled on the table—and then forever
your hand is one with that thing, forever that thing is
in your room.
 (p. 25)

After a long first stanza, rich in lists of stolen objects, the second stanza reconfirms the speaker's guilt by outlining her interaction with people who stop by her house in order to convert her. When she dreams, she imagines these figures are insects. Yet the speaker commits acts of kindness in order to atone. However, there is evidence to suggest that she has not mended her ways. Her son is just like the father, and she herself admits that, if her husband could steal the moon for her, she would take it, and "put [her] hands / all over it—and never let it go." The sticky, honey-sweet feeling of guilty pleasure has not left her. While the image is a hyperbolic gesture of love, there is also the suggestion that she would steal time from others, wrapped in her private world of desire.

What links the poems in this second section is loss, which is often mixed up with guilt. While the literal betrayal of Jesus occurs in "Garden Among Tombs," a vague, and more physically menacing betrayal is evident in "Dog": "the foul dog walking / up the corn row of your spine." (p. 28) This haunting ghost dog is a reminder of a real dog that was maltreated by the "you" in the poem:

you kicked him to stop the noise
kicked and kicked, as if you were kicking
the loud wheel of the truck that struck him,
as if you were that wheel itself.
 (pp. 28–29)

The "you strategy" of the poem indicates that none of us is blameless. In Kelly's work, people are guilty both of specific acts of cruelty and of inaction, and of the fact of being human. The dreamy horror of the situation is undeniable:

But now where you sit
at your desk overlooking the wet fields
something scratches at the base of your neck
and pulls your head up, so that you see coming
toward you with dead calm through the dusk
a forest-dark and limbless.
 (p. 29)

One last poem in the section that emphasizes loss is "The Cruel Mother," based on the famous anonymous ballad of that name. Here, after giving birth and leaving her babies to die, the speaker is an outcast, shunned by the better side of herself as well as by the town, illustrating that often what we see as universal condemnation may be exacerbated by the manifestation of our conscience. She cannot move on from her deed. She is like the carp,

telling the same
sad story again and again—
that what begins in brackish waters
comes to a butcher's end,
 (p. 33)

or like the sparrow, "sing[ing] what is lost." At the end of the poem, her body broken, she distances herself from her own lost beauty, ironically thinking:

The woman
with hair like a thrush's breast and rose perfume
came in with a different man tonight,
her finger like a petal on his arm, her smile
a crimson wing; he bowed low to her. I
would not for the world again
have such a fine shoe upon my foot.
 (p. 34)

The staggering costs of beauty and desire have been too high.

The poems in the third section are defined by relationships, particularly relationships between elders and young people, and more clearly delineated real-world settings, although even here there is a dreamy folktale cast to the poems. One characteristic poem is "Imagining Their Own Hymns." The speaker in the poem, who is poor, is bitter about the townswomen who condescend to her and her poverty. She allies herself instead with the angels in the church window. She envisions herself, like the angels, breaking away from their stained-glass confines into another life.

Kelly's actions always have consequences, which are often intermingled with, or illustrated by, a connection with the natural world. In "The Leaving" the speaker decides to test her father's view of her: that she cannot pick all the peaches in the orchard. She is funneled down to this one purpose: "I had only one [ladder] and a long patience with lit hands / and the looking of the stars which moved right through me." (p. 42) She collects these peaches and puts them in the pond by the orchard. Yet at the end she is faced not only by her desire to prove her father wrong but by another hunger:

The light came over the orchard.
The canals were silver and then were not,
and the pond was—I could see as I laid
the last peach in the water—full of fish and eyes.
   (p. 42)

"The House on Main Street" underscores another kind of longing: that for a strong relationship with community. The poem is organized around the notion of the butterfly effect: that if the speaker and her family had bought this house, the speaker would know the person in town who had died and would not be an outsider. The irony is that in setting up the poem the speaker reveals a knowledge of the town and yet insists upon a different intimacy with the town, that of insider. From a distance—in time and space—she writes a poem with another kind of intimacy, and yet she wants to know something that eludes her: she wants a moment lost in time, the person she might have been, in the context of the community she is not a part of.

"The Place of Trumpets," in the last section of the book, illustrates another type of moment in her project: the moment outside time. In tracing the journey to heaven, to paradise, outside the body, the speaker envisions a place "Where all who wake, wake undone." The tone of the poem recalls both the air of a song and a fairy tale, the "tra la la" of optimism: "To the place of trumpets / We are going. To the sweet / Beggar's pipes blowing." (p. 64) This is where "time will / Split and spill its tattered toys." It is a religious vision of rest and peacefulness, at the foot of God. With Kelly there is always hope—whether in the fulsome presence of God or in a priceless nugget of language.

SONG

While *To the Place of Trumpets* ends in heaven, *Song* begins in the garden with original sin. Reviews of her work were more mixed than they were earlier. The primary reason was opacity. Certainly this had always been an issue. In *Booklist,* Patricia Monaghan called *Song* "lavish but demanding." The book, with its emphasis on song and myth, starts the quiet journey away from literalism into an actualized dreamscape, or, as Carol Moldaw was to write later in the *Antioch Review* about *The Orchard,* "a recurrent real garden with imaginary toads." (p. 775)

The title poem of the collection is a good way of approaching Kelly's project. In it, some neighborhood boys steal and kill a young girl's goat and then are haunted by their deed. When the boys cut the goat's head off, they physically emphasize the wrongness of separating one's mind from one's body: "The head called to the body. The body to the head." (p. 15) The girl who owns the goat has called it "Broken Thorn Sweet Blackberry," and the lost sweetness of her interaction is destroyed by the boys who do not fully understand their own cruelty until they are haunted by the cry of the goat. They put the goat's head in a tree—a joke at first. However, guilt overcomes them: "What they didn't know / Was that the goat's head would go on singing, just for them." (p. 16) There is something lost in the voice that they can never get back:

The low song a lost boy sings remembering his
   mother's call.
Not a cruel song, no, no, not cruel at all. This song
Is sweet. It is sweet. The heart dies of this sweetness.
   (p. 16)

"Courting the Famous Figures at the Grotto of Improbable Thought" underscores Kelly's fascination with statuary and is another way of emblemizing human loss. The style of the poem illustrates her move toward a slightly arch, fanciful postulation. The poem takes place in a grotto filled with statues, and the speaker asks, "A jester might deliver a benediction but who would believe him? / Would God? Would God in his sad figure here? Would you?" (p. 22) Intermingled with this tone is a world-weary matter-of-factness. A statue mother holds her dead son in her lap: "the mother's face afflicted / With the indecency of it all: the undressed moment: / The exposure of the broken motion." (p. 22) Kelly is fascinated with this type of moment. She attempts to isolate it, study it, and hypothesize around it in the way that it can be difficult to do in the blur of regular life. Because moss has grown around the statue, it looks as if the boy has a beard before his time, and this juxtaposition bothers the speaker: "vaguely indecent," "The story seems to be about overblown failure." As she steps through this garden of statues, the speaker exhibits a need that the grotto underscores, as visitors want to feed their religious longing: "We came with our orders ... We had practiced / Our roles ... The whole bag of tricks designed to catch God off guard / And relieve him of one or two of his multitudinous gifts. / We followed the rules." (p. 23) Finally the speaker visits the Lady, the centerpiece of the visit. In the lines underscoring origin, we hear echoes of William Blake's "The Tyger": "High-wrought hand ... How many hammer blows to uncover the brow? The neck?" (p. 24) And yet there is no epiphanic culmination:

A field of disinterest. But still we push forward.
We bow, we bend. We keep moving. *Though we feel nothing.*
We keep moving. Here in the theater of public longing.
(p. 25)

"Garden of Flesh, Garden of Stone" continues Kelly's fascination with statuary, the garden, and her interest in the interrelationship between the animate and inanimate. One thing leads to another thing—not necessarily in physical terms, as a sparrow is exploring the ear of a statue boy, but rather in terms of the hypothetical cause-and-effect waterfall of language. Kelly writes,

Maybe he has found some seed in it. Or maybe he is telling the boy a secret, some sweet nothing.
Or maybe he has mistaken the rimmed flesh, taut and sweet as the skin of a fig, for his bathing dish,
and is about to dive through the pale sky reflected in it.
(p. 30)

Kelly imagines the response of the boy,

as if he likes the soft sewing motion of the beak
within his ear, the delicate morse of the white throat,
a bird plain as dust, but swift-witted and winged,
and the possessor of the saddest of all calls,
five slow notes that bring to mind a whole garden.
(p. 30)

This last line could sum up Kelly's vision: although then she would go on to write the symphony.

As the sparrow hops around the boy, Kelly meditates upon various points—the physical location of the sparrow, the physical attributes of the boy—but returns to "Five notes. Five slow notes. / This is the song of the white throat." (p. 31) These notes seem to awaken some place in the stone boy, the sound that makes him human. Yet when the sparrow starts darting about the boy's body, the stone boy is irritated in the way a human boy might be. The sparrow alerts him to be something more, to yearn, to question his maker. He is left with the dissatisfaction of being more than stone and less than flesh:

Why did he listen to the bird's song? What is this weight of stone in his belly? Where is the one
with heavy hands? How will he call him?
And what, when he raises his small voice
for the first time, will that voice sound like?
(p. 32)

In short, what does it mean to have a voice?

To have a voice means, among other things, to give voice to unspoken truths in the world. In "Dead Doe," written for her son Huck, Kelly attempts to address the subject of death. This is a hard fact to say "yes" to, and there is a refrain throughout the poem of "yes" and "no": "The doe lay dead on her back in a field of asters: no. / The doe lay dead on her back beside the school bus stop: yes." (p. 37) There is a biblical sonorousness about some of the writing in the poem, giving weight to its subject matter. At the same time, the long lines in the poem are often broken up and scattered across the page in order to stress the breathless grief of the situation: "The doe lay dead: she lent / her deadness to the morning, that the morning might have weight, that / our waiting might matter: be upheld by significance." (p. 38) This death raises issues of mothering because the speaker cannot protect her son from certain facts of life; yet there are certain facts of creative possibility that even the dead can "mother," although physically, of course, they are powerless to do so: "The dead can mother nothing ... nothing / but our sight: they mother that, whether they will or no / they mother our looking." In a trick of vision, the deer with its four legs standing straight up looks like "two swans ... fighting," and this vision is emblematic, in its blur, of the soul emerging from the body. As Kelly writes, "And this is the soul: like it or not. Yes: the soul comes down: yes: comes / into the deer: yes: who dies: yes: and in her death twins herself into swans: / fools us with mist and accident into believing." (p. 39) The ending of the poem is awe mixed with dread, a kind of "slouching toward Bethlehem": "Child. We are done for / in the most remarkable ways."

Both "Arguments of Everlasting" and "Wild Turkeys: Dignity of the Damned" explore through exuberance of language and association two remarkably different pictures of the natural world: gladiolas and wild turkeys. One poem explores a frenzied beauty, undercut by loss; the other abject shame. While Kelly is most taken by the taste of nothingness in the fallen world, there is a spectrum of experience in her vision. Although there is a range of feeling about her objects, she brings an explosion of language to each; there is no glass half full for Kelly in terms of language. Or to put it another way, whether she perceives an empty, half empty, or full glass, her linguistic cup runneth over. Kelly responds to the world with an Edenic linguistic wonder, which, as Patricia Monaghan points out, makes it difficult to quote Kelly: "It's tempting to cite great swatches, for although a single line is beautiful, the one after it reflects additional brilliance, and the next expands into luminosity." (p. 988)

In addition to exploring a rush of language funneled through different moods and subject matter, Kelly explores through metaphorical language the connections that human beings have with the natural world. It is a web of connection that ultimately cannot sustain itself, when different species pool into their differences inside themselves. But as we move outward through language and connection, we can maintain the illusion for a while, and sometimes that illusion can have substance. A good poem to look at with this framework is "Pipistrelles."

The speaker uses bats as a way to establish the setting of the poem:

In the damp dusk
The bats playing spies and counterspies by the river's
Bankrupt water station
Look like the flung hands of deaf boys, restlessly
Signing the dark.
 (p. 45)

The personification implied in these comparisons humanizes the bats, making them emissaries for the "Lost fluting of the outcast heart." The speaker asks what we perceive: "But do we see now / The world as it actually is? Or merely another world? / A world within a world?" (p. 45) This perception inside of perception is an echo of Wallace Stevens.

The second section of the poem begins to peel apart the differences between the layers of images: "The bats resemble the deaf. / But they are not deaf." (p. 46) Although the bats are tested to see what they will do in man-made contexts—tempted by the tricks of piano wire, fingernail polish, and blindfolds—they still make music and only occasionally are tripped up by the nature of their own fear in these bizarre circumstances. Kelly explains,

But it is different with us. Fear in us
Is central. Of the bone. It is our inheritance.
Our error. What flies back at us
From rocks and trees, from the emptiness.
 (p. 46)

She sees the heart as "a shadow, a domed dark / Hung with remembered doings." (p. 47) This heart is capable of, among other things, violence and loss.

What we share with the bats is that "we are not birds." Although we are not bats either, the two species share "high-strung skin" and a penchant for flight. Ultimately, we share "illusion" with the bats, and perhaps this yearning to take to the skies makes the slippery nature of metaphor into something paradoxically more solid.

As one moves through Kelly's project one becomes increasingly aware of her position as voyeur. The speaker in her poems is often generalized; she is there less as player in the poems than as the filtering consciousness attempting to make sense of things. Yet she is physically present, often interested in intimate, unselfconscious moments. In "Silver Lake" she addresses a man fishing. Later in the poem she visits an antique shop, and as the shopkeeper shows her his wares, she focuses on his eyes: "very red / And it was impossible not to look at that soreness." The poem returns to the speaker watching the man she is with "paying [his] line out slow as a delicious thought / Into the circled dark." (p. 61) Although Kelly is always interested in observation this poem in particular is about the differences between men and women, and she enters the world of men briefly through observation and touch:

And when you put your hand on the fish
I felt how it burned your flesh, burned for the two
    worlds to meet.
I don't lie to myself. This is what men love the best.
The thoughts they deal from the dark. Better than any
    woman's flesh.
    (p. 61)

Wallace Stevens' "Thirteen Ways of Looking at a Blackbird" might stand as a model for the way in which Kelly approaches experience, although one might jokingly say that, in her exuberance, Kelly's might be called "A Thousand Ways of Looking at the Garden." Her project is so multitudinous it makes her gasp.

Kelly also agrees with Stevens that "Death is the mother of beauty." As fascinated as she is by peacock colors of life (as much as she is preoccupied by swans), she needs the chill of death as a counterpoint, and it is this knowledge, reflected in the gaze, that she is interested in.

THE ORCHARD

Of her three books, *The Orchard* has received the most acclaim, being a finalist for both the *Los Angeles Times* Book Prize and the Pulitzer Prize. At the same time critics were more vocal about Kelly's difficulty as a poet. Carol Moldaw's response in the *Antioch Review* is an excellent example: "Syntactical complexities, circling repetitions, parallel construction, close sounds, expert pacing, are all hallmarks of her polished style, but the mastery that bedazzles and gives the poems their luminous depth is the way her finely wrought comparisons extend outward one from the other, so that worlds interpenetrate worlds." (p. 775)

"Black Swan" is arguably one of the best poems about lost innocence in contemporary poetry. The speaker explains that she has woven a fanciful tale about her son's birth:

I told the boy I found him under a bush.
What was the harm? I told him he was sleeping
And that a black swan slept beside him,
The swan's feathers hot, the scent of the hot feathers
And of the bush's hot white flowers
As rank and sweet as the stewed milk of a goat.
The bush was in a strange garden, a place
So old it seemed to exist outside time.
    (p. 11)

The boy and swan lay interwoven together, but the mother has claimed the son, "slipped him into my belly / The way one might slip something stolen / Into a purse." In the same way that the mother has stolen this mythological innocence by birthing him into the fallen world, so the boy finds his own innocence stolen by boys who pick on him, so much so that he says, "I wish I had never / Been born. I wish I were back under that bush." (p. 12) But of course as Thomas Wolfe says, we can't go home again, nor can we return to the garden. When the mother and son revisit this fairy-tale place:

There was no black swan. And beneath
The sound of the wind, I could hear, dark and low,
The great stone hooves of the horses,
Striking and striking the hardening ground.
 (p. 12)

While she wishes to, the mother cannot protect her son from life; worse still, from the thundering sound of death.

The poems in the first section of *The Orchard* are preoccupied with loss of innocence, and often this is underscored through another species or another perspective. "The Garden of the Trumpet Tree" is a prose poem, a form used more than once in the collection, and its blockiness lends an additional density to an already dense poem. The speaker comes across an apple, which someone has placed in the mouth of a statue. Next to it is a "tree out of time, the smoldering center of some medieval dream." (p. 15) Here the apple in the garden gets symbolic representation. Kelly freezes this moment: "The garden stood perfectly still. And for a moment in that garden it seemed as if sound and silence were the same thing." (p. 16) When she pictures what will happen—a crow will eat the apple, and things will change—she plucks the fruit herself, and this transferal signifies a reverence and also death: "I took the apple out. There was no sound. It was like closing the eyes of the dead."

"Blacklegs" is told through the innocence of a boy, and yet there is a recognition of the hunger reflected in all of nature. After plaintively singing his descriptions of sheep, bee, and horse—"The sheep has nipples … / And fur all around," "The bee has a suffering softness," "The horse runs hard / As sorrow, or a storm, or a man / With a stolen purse in his shirt" (p. 17)—he describes the way in which animals will turn on him with their own hungers, and this sense of desire is what makes him sing:

My legs are two,
And they shine black as the arrows
That drop down on my throat
And my chest to draw out the blood
The bright animals feed on.
 (p. 17)

The speaker admits that their "Hunger is a dress for my song." (p. 18)

This collection crystallizes Kelly's preoccupation not only with mythological moments but moments outside time. In fact, she herself as poet becomes the vehicle through which these moments can be observed and articulated, and her poems increasingly become ways of shaping Marianne Moore's "imaginary gardens with real toads." As she describes in "Brightness from the North,"

It seems as if
This might be what forever is, the presence of time
Overriding the body of time, the fullness of time
Not a moment but a being, watchful and unguarded,
Unguarded and gravely watched this garden.
 (p. 20)

One might say she is the caretaker of the garden.

Although Kelly may be such a caretaker and may experiment with a variety of perspectives, ultimately focusing on a godlike moment outside time (in which she can make what the Maker makes in a poem), she of course is not God the father but the poet mother, and her poem "Sheep Child" is a mother's take on James Dickey's "The Sheep Child." While Dickey's poem focuses on an imaginary offspring that results from the union of a farm boy and sheep, Kelly's focuses on the attempt of a human mother to merge her consciousness with that of the sheep. The fact that it is a sheep is not happenstance, as the sheep is a symbol of innocence. Yet the attempt to explain the world is difficult: "And that black thing spinning in the dung / Is a truck tire stuffed with hay." (p. 22) While the mother merges to the point that she can intuit what the sheep is thinking, she ultimately cannot become the sheep, just as a mother cannot become her own child. It is the role of a mother to leave a child to the world, and this mother does the same for the sheep. At a certain point this mother love is monstrous, and this point is exacerbated by the difference in species. Moreover, there is a subtle commentary about the nature of poetry, that however much we see the moments outside time, or from another's perspective, we must fall back into our own bodies. There can be a kind of weepy frustration about writing poetry, the "foolishness" of it in trying to hold, and preserve, something lasting:

Oh, Sheep, Sheep,
This is my undoing, that you have a thought
And I *can* read it. Dear Monstrous Child, I would
Nurse you if I could. But you are far too large,
And I am far too old for such foolishness.
 (p. 23)

"The Satyr's Heart," because it is one of Kelly's most accessible poems, is one most frequently approached by students, and it contains all the usual Kelly signifiers: the garden, a statue, the interconnection between humans and nature, the living and dead. While the poem shows Kelly's love of language, it is less extravagant than most of her others. The posture of the speaker, with her head against the heart of the statue, says something about the posture Kelly herself takes, a careful listening to the breath of the animate and inanimate world. One thinks of Emily Dickinson sewing her fascicles, but also of the meek living creatures on the earth, following their instincts, doing their work. Hunger exists in the natural realm, however much we want to carve it into stony perfection.

While Kelly can ascribe a life force to inanimate objects, she can also layer a thought process on living things incapable of thought. In a questioning poem reminiscent of Robert Frost's "Design," Kelly wonders about the interrelationship of natural forces and what the individual participants know. After delighting in the orgasmically beautiful rose of Sharon—"The wind kicking up skeins / Of scented foam. High-kicking waves. Or laughing / Dancers" (p. 32)—the rose of Sharon tree is destroyed by an ice storm. Because the speaker is so engaged with the tree, its beautiful life, she wonders, "Did the bush fear the ice? Did it know of the ice's / Black designs? Did its featherweight nature darken / Just before it was felled? Was it capable of darkening?" (p. 32) There is a knowledge for man that comes out of the garden, and so, the logic goes, it may be in what makes up the garden itself.

One particularly memorable poem in the section, "Windfall," is reminiscent of "The Leaving" in *To the Place of Trumpets*. The fish in "Windfall" emblemize the story of the garden, the meeting of mind and appetite, with appetite being the victor. A man has left an ornamental garden, with pond, to go its own way. The carp inside the pond have wildly multiplied so that they fill the pond in large, hungry layers of fish: "The pond was full of ornamental carp, and they were large, larger than the carp I have seen in museum pools, large as trumpets, and so gold they were almost yellow." (p. 33) When the speaker throws bread to them, "they fought each other for the bread, and they were not like fish but like gulls or wolves, biting and leaping. Again and again, I threw the bread. Again and again, the fish leaped and wrestled." (p. 34) There is something horrifically mesmerizing about this spectacle for the speaker, the fascination with hyperbole, with monstrous hunger. Swimming underneath these fish is a bigger fish: "A thing both fragrant and foul. A lily and a man's brain bound together in one body." (p. 34)

Although Kelly is fascinated with dichotomies, she is also interested in the power of transformation, which can be both beautiful and horrifying. In "Pale Rider," Kelly describes a doe who has died, its legs chopped off, and then the winter following that summer sees a disembodied face shining in the woods: "And I knew it was that doe." (p. 40) Then it turns out that this face is not one face but four,

Attached to one legless body, one golden swollen body
That smelled of fallen fruit splitting in the sun and
 shone
The way an image from a dream will darkly shine,
Floating up from childhood, ...
 (p. 41)

But this is not all. The four-headed doe is attempting to give birth to a grown human child:

I knew that the child would never
Be born, but must ride always with her, his body
Embedded in hers, his head up to the sky. I wanted
To reach up and touch that head.
 (p. 41)

Eventually the doe disappears, "Pale rider, lost in the woods where I was lost." (p. 42) This vision of the ghostly embodiment of suffering, of motherly vulnerability, cannot be sustained, but in the moment outside time suggests a Christlike nobility, floating above the footfalls of the earth.

The relationship between the hunter and hunted, man and beast, is the focus as well in the title poem, "The Orchard." A ghostly dog eats a dead doe, and the speaker, who is both horrified and interested, says, "Maybe / I wanted a piece of the dog's feasting, / The way the hunter wanted a piece / Of the doe's improbable swiftness." (p. 51) One thing gives itself to another thing. What Kelly explores is whether this is the heart of religion, the heart of the beast, or both:

And it was as if, on that hill,
While the dog fed and the lake lay
Frozen, I was holding in my hand,
Against my lips, not a piece of fruit,
Not a piece of bitter, half-eaten fruit,
But the still warm and almost beating
Heart of some holy being.
(p. 52)

Perhaps, in her efforts at transformation, she is attempting to merge everything into an unexpected holiness, as she writes in "Plants Fed On by Fawns":

And then the water that does not exist opening up
Before one, dark as wine, and the unveiled figure
Of the self stepping unclothed, sweetly stripped
Of its leaf, into starlight and the shadow of night,
The cold water warm around the narrow ankles,
The body at its most weightless, a thing so durable
It will—like the carved stone figures holding up
The temple roof—stand and remember its gods
Long after those gods have been forsaken.
(p. 55)

"Lion" picks up the four-headed image of "Pale Rider" with a four-headed lion on a body with four legs, and this lion is emblematic, as things are

in a museum ... where things which are part of a bigger picture are pulled away from that picture and made to stand outside of time, all alone, apart from their given function and the things to which they were born: they stand and stand so that we can stare at them until the mind goes blank.
(p. 55)

How to make sense of this? It is the spectacle rather than complete understanding that fascinates Kelly, or if it is understanding, it is an intuited understanding rather than any kind of argument that can be explained: "a wild dance here in this little yard, a mad dance, a sweet disfigured dance that cannot be deciphered, but still delights, as such things on some days delight." (p. 56)

The last poem in the collection, a long poem called "The Sparrow's Gate," with its darting glints of images and thought, has the sonorousness of a poet like Stevens and the stream—of—consciousness water—over—rock brilliance of a poet like Jorie Graham. A sparrow flies through the missing arms of a statue, and the poem becomes a meditation on the relationship between presence and absence, between art and the natural world. The poem is organized around all the things that absence is not and then what it is, the anaphora of Whitman, and it is this that makes her stunning streams of thought hang together. Is life chaos upon which a poet imposes a pattern, or does the poet in doing so replicate the universal moments beneath the veil? There are moments that always stay with us, good and bad, and they make up the pattern of our lives.

And yet, while these moments crystallize for us in the windy dreamscape of the imagination, hope prevails. There is a prayerfulness with which Kelly approaches life through her poetry, an awe at transcendence, the way in which art's beautiful and stony expanse meets the lion and the lamb. There may be nothingness and lack of breath on the one hand, and there may be blood and savagery on the other: Ozymandias meets the lion "slouching toward Bethlehem." Yet ultimately as life calls in all its brilliant hues, she claps her hands. With the virtuosity of her language, Kelly claps her hands.

Selected Bibliography

WORKS OF BRIGIT PEGEEN KELLY

POETRY
To the Place of Trumpets. Foreword by James Merrill. New Haven, Conn.: Yale University Press, 1988.
Song. Brockport, N.Y.: BOA, 1995.
The Orchard. Rochester, N.Y.: BOA, 2004.

CRITICAL AND BIOGRAPHICAL STUDIES

Blevins, Adrian. "'The Satyr's Heart': Human Consciousness and Animal Instincts." *Poetry for Students*. Vol. 22. Detroit: Thomson Gale, 2005.

Donnelly, Patrick. "'The Satyr's Heart.' in the Context of the Collection *The Orchard* as a Whole." *Poetry for Students*. Vol. 22. Detroit: Thomson Gale, 2005.

"Kelly, Brigit Pegeen." *Contemporary Authors*. Vol. 219. Detroit: Thomson Gale. Pp. 207–209.

Merrill, James. Foreword to *To the Place of Trumpets*. New Haven, Conn.: Yale University Press, 1988. Pp. x–xii.

Newman, Judith P. "Poetic License." *Horizon* 30, no. 9:39–40 (November 1987).

Trudell, Scott. "Critical Essay on 'The Satyr's Heart.'" *Poetry for Students*. Vol. 22. Detroit: Thomson Gale, 2005.

Williams, Lisa. "The Necessity of Song: The Poetry of Brigit Pegeen Kelly." *Hollins Critic* 39, no. 3:1–17 (June 2002).

REVIEWS

Collins, Floyd. "Mythic Resonances." *Gettysburg Review* 11, no. 2:344–361 (summer 1998). (Review of *Song*.)

Kitchen, Judith. "Speaking Passions." *Georgia Review* 407–422 (summer 1988). (Review of *To the Place of Trumpets*.)

Leuzzi, Tony. *Double Room* 5 (http://www.webdelsol.com/Double_Room/issue_five/Brigit_Pegeen_Kelly.html). Winter-spring 2005. (Review of *The Orchard*.)

Lund, Elizabeth. "Weaving Words into Tapestries: Where a Boy Can Be a Swan and the Language Is a Delight." *Christian Science Monitor* (http://www.csmonitor.com/2005/0426/p16s01—bogn.html). April 26, 2005. (Review of *The Orchard*.)

Manguso, Sarah. *Believer* 3, no. 3 (April 2005). (Review of *The Orchard*.)

Moldaw, Carol. *Antioch Review* 62, no. 4:775 (fall 2004). (Review of *The Orchard*.)

Monaghan, Patricia. *Booklist* 91, no. 11:988 (February 1, 1995). (Review of *Song*.)

Shoaf, Diann Blakely. "Plucking After Mystery." *Antioch Review* 55, no. 2:206–212 (spring 1997). (Review of *Song*.)

Williams, Susan Settlemyre. *Blackbird* (http://www.blackbird.vcu.edu/v3n1/features/williams_ss_081504.kelly_bp.htm). (Review of *The Orchard*.)

DAVID MARKSON

(1927—)

Peter Dempsey

DAVID MARKSON IS both one of the most adventurous and one of the most readable of American novelists of his era, a writer whose contemporaries admire his work profoundly. Markson's novels have won praise from the likes of Kurt Vonnegut, William Kennedy, and Frederick Exley. *Wittgenstein's Mistress* itself has been reprinted half a dozen times after being rejected by a staggering fifty-four publishers.

Markson published his first novel in 1959, but it is his later work that has cemented his literary reputation as an innovator of the novel form. Indeed, concern with finding a form, there from the beginning of his writing career, takes up a good deal of the content of these extraordinary works. Markson has produced work in a variety of styles and genres, from crime fiction and westerns, film scripts and poetry, to the most rigorous of literary experimentalism, but there is also a surprising thematic continuity to his work. His early fiction has the trace elements of literary techniques and concerns found throughout his work: his interest in the lives of artists and writers; his attraction to the catalog or list; and an ambiguous, reflexive celebration of, and skepticism toward, the creative act itself.

Markson's first two books were detective novels, where death initiates the plot but isn't really part of the subject matter of the book. In his later work, death becomes its subject; the deaths of authors and artists, the death also of hope and of forms of success. With references to Troy, Nanking, the Crusades, and (in the 2004 novel *Vanishing Point*) the terrorist attacks on the World Trade Center, the fiction dwells upon death on a personal, national, and international scale. While Markson's first four books were plot-driven genre novels, the later novels enact in their structure and subject matter another death—seemingly that of the novel form itself. In this later work, Markson walks a literary tightrope, without the safety net of plot, yet through some form of literary alchemy, he is able to produce books that are compelling and oddly haunting, remembered long after they have been put down or, more likely, pressed enthusiastically into the hands of friends.

EARLY LIFE AND WORK

David Merrill Markson was born in Albany, New York, on December 20, 1927. His father, Samuel A. Markson, was for many years a newspaper editor, and his mother, Florence Stone Markson, was a high school teacher. Both were originally from Kingston, New York, a location that crops up in *Wittgenstein's Mistress*. Markson became a sports writer and reporter while at high school, and after serving in the army from 1946 to 1948, he returned to journalism while studying for his BA, which he received from Union College in Schenectady, New York, in 1950. Markson gained an MA from Columbia University, New York, in 1952. It was while studying for his MA that Markson began a correspondence with Malcolm Lowry, whose 1947 novel *Under the Volcano* was the subject of Markson's MA thesis (in 1978 the thesis was published in much-expanded form and was a pioneering critical study). Markson became close to Lowry, who stayed at the Marksons' apartment when he visited New York City in 1954. It was in the early 1950s that Markson got to know a number of other important writers of the time, including Conrad Aiken, Dylan Thomas, and Jack Kerouac, who spent time on the Marksons' living room couch and whose style is playfully sent up in one of Markson's early novels.

After spending the summer of 1952 as a logger in Oregon, and after a week's visit to Lowry in British Columbia, Markson moved to New York City and became an editor first at Dell Publishing and then at Lion Books. He married Elaine Kretchmar in 1956, and that same year he edited *Women and Vodka*, a selection of classic Russian short stories, under the pseudonym Mark Merrill. Around this time, also pseudonymously, he published westerns and other genre stories in men's magazines. The first work to which he attached his own name, "White Apache," a western story, appeared in the 29 September 1956 edition of the popular *Saturday Evening Post*. Markson and his wife spent 1958 to 1961 in Mexico, where he was supported by a writer's fellowship as he wrote his first two novels (detective fiction published in 1959 and 1961) and where he completed a very long draft of *Going Down*, his first serious novel, which would eventually be published many drafts later in 1970.

The 1950s, when Markson was beginning to write, edit, and meet other writers, was a period of unparalleled prosperity in the United States. Between 1947 and 1960 the average real income for American workers increased by as much as it had in the previous half-century. Soldiers returning from World War II took advantage of the GI Bill, which gave a massive kick-start to the postwar building boom and the economy generally. There was social mobility too, with the growth of a salaried middle-class workforce in the fast-growing corporations. This in turn created what sociologists such as David Riesman and C. Wright Mills called a new managerial or corporate personality.

Furthermore, behind the Eisenhower years of ever-growing economic prosperity was the cold-war dread of nuclear annihilation and communist infiltration. Secrecy and fear became the ambient noise of the 1950s. After the spy trials of Alger Hiss and the Rosenbergs, and the emergence on the national stage of Senator Joe McCarthy, stories of political treachery were part of the media's daily bread. In a society where the vast majority of citizens were hidebound by social taboos and driven by the desire to conform, notions of secrecy and betrayal took on a political hue.

It may be fitting, in this context that Markson's first two novels—*Epitaph for a Tramp* (1959) and *Epitaph for a Dead Beat* (1961)—were detective stories, a genre that takes secrets and lies as its starting point. Within that genre, Markson wrote in the hard-boiled tradition, where personal betrayal, at the heart of the work of early practitioners such as Dashiell Hammett and Raymond Chandler, plays such an important part.

Epitaph for a Tramp (1959) introduces the protagonist of both Markson's hard-boiled books, Harry Fannin, a World War II veteran whose mortally wounded former wife turns up at his New York City apartment in the middle of a hot August night. The novel follows Fannin's attempts to find her killer. Fannin is that familiar figure, the laconic private eye, and a good deal of the first two novels' pleasure comes from their Chandleresque verbal humor and the way they are peppered with different types of discourses: criminal argot; Greenwich Village hipster-speak; police procedural language; letters and telegrams; quotations from other books; advertisements and jingles; street and shop signs; parodies of Beat poetry and prose; lists and catalogs of sportsmen, singers, actors, military men; and much more. We can also see Markson's playful allusiveness at work in *Epitaph for a Tramp*. To take one small example, standing in an apartment block stairwell, Fannin hears someone singing "Vesti la giubba," the most famous aria from *Pagliacci*, Ruggiero Leoncavallo's popular opera about adultery. This is a rueful comment on the conduct of Fannin's ex-wife, Cathy Hawes, there for the reader to notice or not.

While he wrote these books for money, Markson also crafted them with considerable care, and they have well-shaped plots, convincing characterization and satisfying twists for their denouements. Many of the texts Fannin reads or finds on the shelves of Greenwich Village apartments as he goes about his job form a kind of running commentary both on the times and the very book we are reading. The books Fannin reads or finds are often the kinds of works to whose scope and high ambition the young Markson aspired; ambitions that cannot easily be contained within the detective story.

Epitaph for a Tramp is therefore an unusual mystery novel. It is a book knowingly at odds with itself, consciously straining at the self-imposed boundaries of the genre. As the novel opens, Fannin is lying awake in bed reading *The Magic Mountain* (1924), by Thomas Mann, which, he says, contains "hardly any shooting at all." We know of course that a shooting is a virtual necessity for a mystery novel. The implication is that the novel we are reading has been written for money, while Mann's modernist masterpiece has been written with a higher aesthetic end in mind. We might like to draw the familiar parallel between self-employed author, writing for a living, and self-employed private eye. Such a parallel also hints at what might well be the novelist's ultimate subject: the fiscal and literary trials and tribulations of the inferred author of Markson's own oeuvre. In fact, Thomas Mann's novel does have deaths galore. On top of the "magic mountain" of the title sits a sanatorium, and in a striking early scene we witness bodies dead from tuberculosis being transported down the mountainside on sledges. There is actually shooting, too; a duel takes place between two patients. And, finally, there is the slaughter of World War I at the novel's end. Markson will quote Mann's comments on death in *Vanishing Point,* and illness and mortality are constant themes in the two books that precede *Vanishing Point.*

Right from his first novel, then, the question of literary form is central to Markson's aesthetic concerns. Even in the pulp fictions that make up his early work, Markson is writing a species of metafiction (a term the novelist dislikes), that is, fiction which, directly or indirectly, reflects on the nature of fiction itself, and which in Markson's work becomes a continuous quest for the form most appropriate for his literary ambitions.

Markson's two hard-boiled novels are broad satires on the 1950s Greenwich Village scene of pretentious and self-regarding poseurs living the bohemian life and producing second-rate works of art or, more usually, nothing at all, justifying their hedonism as a heroic disregard for the social conventions of Eisenhower's America. The origins of such behavior, however, were a genuine response to the stifling moral and political world of 1950s America, and the characters that Markson sends up in his early novels actually embody a complex international cross-fertilization of European existentialist philosophy and a literary mode in U.S. fiction established by the most famous American novelist of the time, Ernest Hemingway. In *Epitaph for a Dead Beat* a publisher is, he says, having "dinner with Papa," using Hemingway's affectionate nickname to suggest his own status and influence. The allusions are self-referential, acknowledging Hemingway's influence on the hard-boiled literary style that Markson is appropriating. In the mid-1920s, Dashiell Hammett took Hemingway's laconic style and adapted it for crime fiction. In the late 1930s, Chandler added an ironic tone and the distinctive style of the hard-boiled first person narrator had been firmly established. In Hemingway's major characters and in the characters of a number of the hard-boiled U.S. crime writers influenced by him, postwar French thinkers such as Jean-Paul Sartre and Albert Camus saw prefigured the isolated, antiauthoritarian existentialist hero of postwar French philosophy and fiction.

Conversely, the existentialism of Sartre and Camus became an important ingredient in the makeup of the independent-minded, sceptical PI of the postwar hard-boiled detective novel. In the mid-1950s, everyone who considered themselves interested in new ideas read Walter Kaufmann's *Existentialism from Dostoevsky to Sartre* (1956), Markson among them. Existentialist philosophy suggests that human beings have no pre-given essence or destiny, that we are born as free-thinking creatures with a finite life and we are therefore responsible for our actions, and that we should aim to live in the most authentic and fulfilling way we can, which often means resisting calls to conform, to follow what Friedrich Nietzsche called "the herd." It is easy to see the attraction of such a philosophy in the 1950s, with its cold-war obsession with anticommunism, its stifling work ethic, and its will to conformity.

The detective novel is a form of quest story, one of the oldest forms of narrative. While early quest stories had knights in search of grails and princesses, in the hard-boiled novel the search is for a murderer, but ultimately for the truth. Detective fiction has been accused of trivializing issues of both knowledge and mortality, and, to be sure, the discovery of the dead body is usually no more than a device to get the plot going. For Markson, these hard-boiled novels were escapes from literature inasmuch as they have no real literary ambition, but paradoxically for this kind of escapist fiction, Markson has woven literary allusions into their very fabric. Questions of knowledge are a key component of any mystery story's plot, but philosophical questions are on the tips of the tongues of many of Markson's characters in the Greenwich Village that is their setting.

In *Epitaph for a Dead Beat*, Fannin investigates a series of murders among the bohemian set in Greenwich Village, and this gives Markson a chance to satirize both those who see themselves as free-spirited young artistic types in the style of Jack Kerouac and Allen Ginsberg and the more somber existentialists. The biggest irony in the novel, however, is that, as Fannin observes it, all these seekers after freedom of expression and authentic action are by and large following the latest fashion, in other words the Nietzschean herd. Markson builds the notion of the inauthentic into the very structure of the novel by having an act of literary theft, of fake authorship, at the heart of the murder mystery.

What galvanized the serious thinker's interest in the emerging philosophy of existentialism was its absolute commitment to freedom, its facing up to personal finitude—that is, the inevitability of death—and its grappling with questions about what freedom meant in the face of such knowledge. Existentialist ideas made the pressure to follow social conventions seem like very small beer indeed, and thus were virtually a poison injected into the very veins of Eisenhower's superficially optimistic America. While it might be said that existentialism has come and gone as a fashionable philosophical interest, it has remained a central concern of Markson's most serious fiction for over fifty years, from the first drafts of *Going Down,* on which he had been working since the mid-1950s, right through to the novels in his distinctive late style, such as 2004's *Vanishing Point*.

But with a young family—his children Johanna and Jed were born in 1963 and 1964 respectively—Markson needed to earn some money through his writing. Returning to New York from Mexico in late 1961, Markson worked on a screenplay for a never-to-be-made film that was abandoned in 1962. He worked the material up into the last of his pulp crime fictions, while also teaching at the University of Long Island in Brooklyn. Probably the slightest of Markson's works, the lively *Miss Doll, Go Home* was published in 1965. It tells the story of expatriate American artists in a small town near Mexico City living lives, as one character points out, of Thoreauvian "quiet desperation." Three strangers turn up and (though it seems unlikely) a number in the colony suspect correctly that they are bank robbers. In a series of increasingly tense and comic episodes, the expats attempt to rob the robbers, while the robbers, through greed and well-founded mutual suspicion, eventually kill each other off. While none of the expats profits financially, by the end long-hidden feelings of love are expressed between two of the characters and another comes to accept what the world has to offer him.

Although this book has little in the way of the literary allusiveness of Markson's previous two novels, *Miss Doll, Go Home* does have, in the Geek, a character reminiscent of Benji in William Faulkner's *The Sound and The Fury* (1929). As with Markson's two hard-boiled novels, this book too is concerned with how to make a living as an artist or writer and explores to what kinds of fantasies and temptations desperate and impoverished artists and writers are prone.

The notion that the strangers in town have a vast sum of cash seems at first a possibility beyond dreaming. As a piece of pulp fiction, the novel needs this to be true, to engender the action necessary to fulfill the requirements of the crime novel genre, just as the previous two hard-boiled novels needed their murders. In a final comic irony, the expats inadvertently dispose of the stolen money and find on the shelves of the robbers' house not books, and not the money they so ardently seek, but instead, rather funereally, dust.

Still struggling with the manuscript of *Going Down*, Markson next turned to work on a western, the genre that first got him published and seemed to have the best chance of earning him some money. *The Ballad of Dingus Magee* (1966) began as a conventional western genre novel, but soon became a eupeptic parody of the gunslinger adventure story. Nineteen-year-old Dingus Magee never kills anyone, but through an intuitive understanding of the process of western mythmaking, he becomes the most wanted man in the American Southwest, with a huge bounty on his head. With the pace of the baroquely intricate plot allowing no time for reflection, the novel consists of a series of comic adventures involving mistaken identity, jokey near-deaths, and miraculous escapes as parodic resurrections. Markson deals with death by defying it through comedy and sensuality. Repeatedly Dingus finds himself facing death, and always, through his own wiles and finally through the love of a lost mother, escapes it.

The story shows us the triumph of the young over the old and the clever over the stupid. There is also a satiric, demythologizing element to the book, in which we witness the shabby origins of almost-mythic figures such as Wyatt Earp and Doc Holliday. The novel was filmed in 1970 as *Dirty Dingus Magee,* starring a fifty-odd-year-old Frank Sinatra as the teen-aged Dingus. Even with the hand of Joseph Heller in the screenplay, the film was box-office poison, but it miraculously fulfilled Markson's financial hopes for the book: the rights were sold for a reported $100,000. The money allowed the Marksons to live in Europe for over two years, including a year in London, where Markson once again put considerable energy into screenplay writing. This time he worked on a contracted treatment of his own novel, *Epitaph for a Dead Beat,* and once again the project never saw the light of day. However, the money from the *Dingus* film rights allowed Markson to abandon genre fiction and finally to finish what he considered his first serious work of fiction, the formidable *Going Down* (1970).

As a student at Columbia University between 1951 and 1952, Markson wrote his MA thesis on Malcolm Lowry's 1947 novel *Under the Volcano.* It was unheard of to write on such a recently published text, as the novel had yet to establish itself as the modern classic it has now become. With no critical commentary available on such an allusive and complex book, Markson wrote for advice to the author himself. Touched by the young man's interest and obvious seriousness, Lowry wrote back at considerable length and a kinship was established that lasted until Lowry's premature death in 1957. One Lowry critic has described Markson as Lowry's "spiritual son," and the relationships between master and pupil, between artistic father and disciple, between legitimacy and illegitimacy, together with questions of legacy, became important elements of Markson's work. Such questions become quite pointed when reading Markson's *Going Down*, a novel that is co-dedicated to Lowry and is set, like Lowry's novel, in Mexico

Going Down tells the story of Steve Chance, an embryonic, unpublished writer; Fern Winters, a budding painter; and Lee Suffridge, the wife of Chance's mentor, the painter Ferrin Priest. To the scandal of the locals, the three live together in a house in a small Mexican village. The novel opens with Fern holding a bloody machete, but it is many pages before we find out who the victim is and, more important, why the murder took place. This mystery element seems absolutely organic to the structure of the novel. At a formal level, the novel is a miracle of nonlinear narrative, with a shape of high aesthetic beauty. The spinning, looping plot folds back on itself to bring each character up to the present of the opening scene with an Aristotelian tightness of temporal unity, with the main action taking place (as in Markson's first two novels) over one day. The command of the material is quite staggering.

Markson uses a panoply of literary techniques to describe forms of loss and the abysmal meaninglessness of existence from which the expatriate characters seem to suffer; there are passages in italics, streams of consciousness, flashbacks, speeches cut off before being completed, biblical and poetic prose, and allusions and quotations from a huge range of texts in literature, philosophy, and culture, both Eastern and Western, as well as motifs drawn from Mexican myth along with a sympathetic realism in the depiction of the lives of the Mexican villagers. *Going Down*, then, is excessive in every way, like the Mexico it depicts: the heat, the poverty; death cults, and the main characters' unconventional sexual relations. The troubled Steve Chance and the psychologically fragile Fern see themselves in a whole range of literary characters, and the proliferation of references and allusions are their attempt to paper over the suspicion that the world appears to have no intrinsic meaning, that reality itself may either be a solipsistic fantasy or that human beings are unknowingly playing parts in some larger fiction.

It is Markson's most mysterious and in some ways most forbidding novel. *Going Down* is a powerful blend of an obviously ambitious literary novel and a mystery novel. Markson also takes advantage of the loosening of taboos around the representation of sexuality at this time, in his frank portrayal of sometimes-unconventional sexual behavior. The novel was written and revised from the mid-1950s, when there were abundant strictures on the human activities that could be directly portrayed in art, until the late 1960s, when there came a huge explosion of work that attempted to break down those taboos. It could be said that, in the spirit of the late 1960s, when the manuscript was going through its final revisions, in this remarkable novel the unconventional sexual activity initiated by Steve Chance with Fern and Lee becomes an emblem of his disregard for social conventions of any kind. And while his motives in confessing to a murder he didn't commit and in taking his own life are deeply ambiguous, part of the meaning of these acts is that they stand as a challenge to those conventions.

At one point a character places a book on a shelf between *Ulysses* and Edgar Allan Poe, and that description serves to give something of the flavor of Markson's own allusive, challenging and at times rather gothic work. This is a mystery novel in many senses. Though we find out who did it and why, the larger motivations of the two main characters, Fern and Steve Chance, remain profoundly mystifying, and this goes some way to explaining why *Going Down* retains its power decades after its first publication. The novel's occasional verbal excesses are the result of ambitious overreaching and are quickly forgotten when there is so much achievement elsewhere in the book. Its reissue in 2005 confirmed its lasting power.

The novel is death-obsessed; there are bullfights, murders, and fatally bungled operations, along with images of death and decay in every chapter. The novel opens with the young woman Fern standing in an abandoned cemetery holding a bloody machete. Someone has been killed, and it will take most of the rest of the novel until we are told who committed the crime. But Steve Chance, innocent of the crime, decides to take responsibility for the death, confesses to it, and later hangs himself. The reader suspects that he has made an existential choice to end his life, and while the novel offers us a number of reasons why he might have done so, his choice is ultimately mysterious as is much human motivation. But the novel also offers us alternative attitudes we might take in the face of an indifferent universe. The stoicism of the Mexican peasants, brilliantly rendered and not a whit romanticized, is one.

MIDCAREER: OUT FROM UNDER MODERNISM

T. S. Eliot's *The Waste Land* and James Joyce's *Ulysses*—both published in 1922 and both central texts of literary modernism—and late-modern works such as Lowry's *Under the Volcano* were all profound influences on Markson, in particular the way the authors use a series of overarching myths to underpin the fragmentary, parodic, and heterogeneous surface of their work. *Going Down*, too, uses this kind of strategy, but it brings the epistemological questions found both in modernist and detective fiction together in one novel. Also, by the end of *Going Down*, the desire to find something meaningful in the plethora of religious and cultural parallels breaks down; such is the pressure of the torque applied to them by the characters in the book. Acutely conscious of his literary forebears, Markson's fiction up to this point is deeply marked by a sense of literary belatedness, a self-consciousness about those who have gone before and who, in this novel and its predecessors, are dealt with through homage, pastiche, and parody.

Going Down is both an original work of art and also a work produced from within what would be seen as a modernist aesthetic, that is, a richly symbolic and allusive manner of writing. In his aesthetic restlessness and ambition, Markson by 1970 had taken this kind of writing as far as he could. The novels he went on to produce would finally get him out from under his influences, without forgetting them. In other words, these volumes began to be postmodern in the sense that they recognized the enormous legacy of earlier influences, while wanting to do something new. Markson in his later novels surmounts what might loosely be called, after Harold Bloom, "the anxiety of influence," and he begins by writing a novel in which the hero is the writing itself.

Meanwhile, in 1972, Markson finally got a screenplay made into a film. *Face to the Wind* was an original screenplay and was made into a very low-budget film, which, after a brief release, disappeared into obscurity. Its re-release under such titles as *Naked Revenge* and *Count Your Bullets* have not altered its initial fate.

Markson's next novel, *Springer's Progress,* was published in 1977 and marks both many continuities with his earlier work and a significant break with it too. It is a melancholic New York comedy about Lucien Springer, a middle-aged writer, creatively blocked and married with children, who has an affair with Jessica Cornford. In other words, a young woman much like those found in Markson's early Greenwich Village mystery novels. As the story concludes, Springer breaks his writer's block by writing the novel we are reading. What Markson has produced is a self-engendering novel, a comic work that eventually has mortality as its subject. The novel is metafiction *in excelsis*; a celebration of creative power cashed out in erotically charged prose, and a celebration of language itself.

While suffering from concussion in *Epitaph for a Dead Beat*, Fannin free–associates, linking books, writers, and films together through similarities of themes and names. The scene is a way for Markson, through the literary expedient of his detective's concussion, to push at the realist boundaries of the genre. In *Springer's Progress*, a much more exuberantly literary work, the novelist can give his protagonist—a novelist too—his head. Here be obscure learning, cloacal swivings; congeries of long-whiskered, sesquipedalian words; satirical shafts; spectacularly bad puns; catalogs; and melancholic apostrophes. But unlike in *Going Down*, where the allusions rage around, larding every act with a multitude of possible meanings, trying to make sense of a yawning metaphysical absence, in *Springer's Progress* they are all in the service of serious play. The comic celebration of the triumph of life over death found in *Dingus Magee* is tempered in this novel.

Like Springer's lover's firm but flexible neck, the novel's prose is cartilaginous, too, full of casual pastiches and poetic foreshortenings. While the novel is written in the third person, the "center of consciousness" is Springer; we see things from his perspective. Will Springer be able to write, in the midst of love and death? The catalog performs a number of functions in Markson's work and is there from the very beginning. On the first page of Markson's first novel, there's the list of the linemen of the 1940 Chicago Bears. In the second novel, Fannin recites a list of historical facts to avoid the dawning of an awful truth. But it is in *Springer's Progress* that Markson's love of the catalog is given full rein at last. The catalog is an ancient form, going back as far as Genesis, where the generations of the sons of Noah are listed. Famously in classical writing are the Homeric and Virgilian lists of heroes. In the Renaissance the catalog was known as a *blason*, a list usually of a woman's attributes. So in this novel, one chapter near the end consists of nothing more than the opening lines of classic poems, plays, and novels. In the following chapter, Springer begins his novel, and we realize with a shock that it is a shadowy first draft of the very book we are reading. In a piece of dizzying metafictional panache, we apprehend, with an aesthetic thrill, that Springer, formally a character in the novel, is its *author*.

The process of the story leading the reader to its own beginning echoes the form of Markson's first two novels and *Going Down*. A body is found. Who did it? In the opening chapter of *Epitaph for a Tramp*, Cathy Hawes dies in Fannin's apartment. The novel is complete when Fannin figures out how and why that happened, when he is able to trace the story back until it reaches the moment of its beginning, with Cathy's death in his apartment. A similar process is at work in *Springer's Progress*, except that to complete the circular movement described above, the narrative has to shift levels, where the protagonist, Springer, becomes the author of the work.

The vertiginous shift in narrative levels, what critics call "metalepsis," is also there by implication in Markson's first two books, in the parallel we might draw between detective and author, and in *Going Down*'s disturbing suggestion that the characters might be dimly aware of their status as characters in a novel. In Markson's next book, *Wittgenstein's Mistress,* one sign of the narrator's mental fragility will be her inability at times to keep levels of fiction and reality separate.

Markson's four early genre novels are plot driven. *Going Down* combines elements of a whodunit with a richly symbolic and temporally fragmented narrative. *Springer's Progress* is circular and self-engendering. But with *Wittgenstein's Mistress,* published in 1988, Markson begins more aggressively stripping away the accepted conventions of fiction, while still aiming to produce something recognizable as a novel. That he succeeded, but that it was no easy task, can be seen by the trouble the novelist had in placing the book with a publisher and the impressive reception the book got when it finally did appear. Once again, a comment by one of Markson's characters regarding a rejected manuscript was prescient about the career of his creator; Markson sustained fifty-four rejections for what many now regard as his finest achievement, a prize-winning novel that was many critics' 1988 novel of the year and one that has been reprinted half a dozen times.

The ten-year gap between *Springer's Progress* and *Wittgenstein's Mistress* can be a little misleading about the extent of Markson's contributions to the literary world in the years directly after 1977. With its origins in Markson's MA thesis of 1952, his critical study *Malcolm Lowry's "Volcano": Myth Symbol Meaning* came out in 1978, although it had been completed several years before it was published. On and off during the 1980s, Markson ran fiction-writing workshops at Columbia University in New York City, and he led a similar class at the West Side YMCA during 1985. *Wittgenstein's Mistress* itself was completed in 1983, but then began its epic journey around the U.S. publishing houses.

Markson's private life changed too. He separated from his wife in 1982 and began a ten-year relationship with the painter Joan Semmel, to whom *Wittgenstein's Mistress* is dedicated. The Marksons were officially divorced in 1994. Elaine Markson had set up a successful literary agency in the early 1970s and was by now representing a number of leading writers, but even her efforts for her former husband's extraordinary new novel came to nothing. In the end Steven Moore, a perceptive critic of contemporary fiction and a recently appointed editor at the enterprising avant-garde publishing house the Dalkey Archive, was the fifty-fifth professional reader of the manuscript and got the book into print.

In *Going Down*, the painter Fern Winters free-associates, remembering stories of artists and writers; she often misremembers and then corrects herself. She is the center of consciousness for the majority of that novel. In her we can see the germ of the method of narration developed in *Wittgenstein's Mistress*, while the trauma-induced amnesia suffered by Fannin's exwife Cathy in *Epitaph for a Tramp* is here shaped into something much more rich and strange. In this plangent novel, a painter, Kate Winter, appears, by her own first person account, to have awoken one day to find that she is the only person in the world left alive. Living in a Long Island beach house, in between getting on with the tasks of everyday life, Kate is writing a fragmented, speculative, and often very funny account of her current and past life. At first it seems she has traveled across most of Europe and Russia, stopping in major European cities and visiting art galleries. She writes up her experiences without revision, and as the novel progresses, we begin to wonder whether she really is alone or whether she has had some form of mental breakdown and just cannot see those around her.

Mysteriously, Kate finds that boats and cars have seemingly moved of their own accord; meanwhile we notice how she misremembers or reinvents episodes from the immediate past. At the heart of her suffering is the memory of the death of her young son, an event we suspect is quite capable of triggering a possible mental collapse. Yet we cannot be certain about this. Cars parked on hills will eventually move when their brakes wear out. Boats occasionally break free of their moorings and are moved by the winds and tides The novel, therefore, maintains a balancing act between reality and imagination with immense skill, recalling the undecidable ambiguity in relation to reality in such great American work as Henry James's "The Turn of the Screw" and Nathaniel Hawthorne's *The Scarlet Letter*.

Kate writes and reconsiders what she has written, sometimes weeks later, so we can see what her preoccupations are and what might have brought her to where she now finds herself. We cannot be sure what Kate has experienced and what she has merely imagined, the event and the representation of the event; she discovers this is something built into the way we use language itself. It is her self-consciousness about the way language represents the world that accounts for the novel's title, as well as the short paragraphs of which the novel is made, which has loose echoes of the declarative style of Ludwig Wittgenstein's early philosophical work, the *Tractatus* of 1921. As the novel progresses, these distinctions between world and representation become more and more porous.

A cat seen in the Colosseum in Rome is at first russet-colored, then orange, then black, taking on the colors and qualities of cats she has seen in paintings. In *Reader's Block* we learn that, dying, Honoré de Balzac called for Doctor Bianchon, a character from one of his novels, unable to make the distinction between fiction and reality.

This moving novel of isolation and loss ends fugue-like, with Kate repeating lines and refrains from earlier in the work, her words forming a textual collage that is both an index of and a sign of resistance to mental disintegration. And it is the use of literary quotations and biographical anecdotes that Markson turns into a novelistic method for his next fiction.

LATE STYLE: MARKSON'S POSTMODERN FICTION

At the end of the 1980s, Markson had bouts of serious illnesses, including both lung cancer and a prostate cancer still being treated in the mid-1990s. As a consequence, the novelist had a number of major operations in 1989. But it was also around this time that he began to get some serious critical attention. In 1990 Markson was awarded a $20,000 National Endowment for the Arts and a set of laudatory essays on his work was published in the *Review of Contemporary Fiction*. In 1992, volume 67 of the reference work *Contemporary Literary Criticism* included a seventeen-page section on Markson's work and its reception. *Springer's Progress* was reprinted and the witty *Collected Poems* was published in 1993. Who then could have guessed at this point in his career—and in his mid-sixties, when others are thinking of retirement-that Markson's most original work was still to come?

The first of these later works, and possibly the best, is *Reader's Block*, an original work of art and that rarest of beasts, an addictively readable experimental novel. The effacement of plot that began in *Wittgenstein's Mistress* is taken further here. An elderly writer, known as Reader, considers composing a novel. How much of his own experience will his character, known only as Protagonist, have? Where will it be set? By the sea? Overlooking a graveyard? Who will his character meet? Will he have family or friends? As the bifurcating narrative unfolds, Reader shows Protagonist's life both by the sea and in a house contiguous to a graveyard. Both Reader and Protagonist, seem to live, like Kate Winter before them, in virtual isolation. By the end, we witness the fate of Protagonist, whether he lives by the sea or by the graveyard, in an act that pushes his isolation as far as it is physically possible.

The story of Protagonist's sojourn by the sea and by the graveyard takes up roughly 20 percent of the text. The rest of the novel is made up of a series of short anecdotes, some a line or two, others a paragraph, largely about the difficulties of the imaginative life. There are 333 unattributed fragments of texts, titles, and quotations.

The fragments Markson includes of the lives of artists, writers, and musicians tell of success, fame, and riches, but more often of failure, madness, poverty, and principally of death. They are fascinating in themselves, but while we learn that Gioacchino Rossini, for instance, wore a wig—two on cold days—and that Aristotle presumed that women had fewer teeth than men, we also begin to realize that many of these seemingly unconnected stories begin to form patterns—and one pattern in particular, about deaths more serious than that of the individual.

A "*shlemiel* of shreds and patches," the character Springer calls himself. If we ignore the self-deprecating element of the description, the phrase describes the author of a novel like *Reader's Block* as well as any. The work that seems closest in complexion to the novel is Eliot's *The Waste Land*, an oft-quoted reference point in Markson's fiction. A substantial part of Eliot's poem quotes the work of others, as does *Reader's Block*. But Markson's method is much looser than that of Eliot's modernist poem, and rather than being metaphorical, that is, symbolist, his is a metonymic method. Markson exploits the art of juxtaposition, of contiguity, to address his themes. While *Going Down*'s welter of literary references and complex, recursive narrative announced its seriousness, *Reader's Block*, along with the novels that have followed it, wears its thematic seriousness much more lightly. Markson gives his readers a fragment of verse and then, a few lines or pages later, an anecdote about the writer of the verse. Often this is playful; but at the center of *Reader's Block* is the use of this postmodern technique for more somber purposes: to address what in his Lowry book Markson calls "a subject as grave as anti-Semitism."

How is a novelist to deal with this topic with some sense of tact? Markson's method is oblique juxtaposition. Here is one example from dozens, an unattributed quotation from William Butler Yeats's "John Kinsella's Lament for Mrs Mary Moore": "What shall I do for pretty girls / Now my old Bawd is dead?" (p. 23) Scattered throughout the novel, we find a similar formula, used to describe Seneca, T. S. Eliot, Roald Dahl, Edgar Degas, Jean-Jacques Rousseau, Carl Jung, Rudyard Kipling, Geoffrey Chaucer, and upwards of seventy others.

These lines are part of the novel's representation of death and loss, but they also obliquely reinforce the work's concern with anti-Semitism. By quoting just two lines of the poem, readers are encouraged to seek out the whole work. If we do, we find: "Though stiff to strike a bargain / Like an old Jew man." (p. 23) Which takes us back to the bare phrase found early in the novel: "William Butler Yeats was an anti-Semite."

The repetition of this formula is relentless, and its implications for Western culture are profoundly enervating, but anti-Semitism is called out along with parallel, more affirming stories. Elsewhere in the novel we learn that Joyce helped a dozen or more Jews, including the novelist Hermann Broch, escape the Nazis, and that when the Nazis ordered the roundup of Denmark's eight thousand Jews, nearly every one of them was smuggled into neutral Sweden by fishing boat. It should be said, however, that we can understand *Reader's Block* perfectly well without recognizing the allusions and quotations; they are there to reinforce what is clear to any reader of the novel.

Reader's Block constantly switches from the public and political to the personal, and it is as much a story about loneliness and memory as anything else. Be he near the graveyard or by the sea, Protagonist makes an existential choice at the end of the novel, obliquely evoking the most famous question in English literature, that of

Hamlet's in act 3, scene 1, of Shakespeare's play. A page or two before Protagonist answers the question "to be or not to be" for himself, we are presented with one of the author's beloved *blasons,* or catalogs, this time of more than fifty fictional suicides, from Emma Bovary to Launcelot, by way of Ophelia and Seymour Glass. With Markson's characteristic interest in the shifting levels of fiction, Protagonist's fate has chilling implications both for his creator, Reader, and as we have seen before, by extension, for the shadowy implied author of the novel itself, the creator of both Reader and Protagonist, and of the first person "I" on the novel's opening page.

In gerontology, the study of aging, researchers use the term "next to death" in a variety of contexts. Fannin, as a private investigator in a mystery novel, finds himself regularly "next to death" in two senses. First, he is simply contiguous to it. People around him get killed. Second, in crucial scenes his life is under threat. In reality, the kinds of deaths that are found in mystery novels are rare and are usually there to generate plot movement of one kind of another. Springer's life-affirming desires are initially brought up sharp by the death of his past love Maggie Oldring, who, in a bitter irony early in the book, Springer describes as a "terminal case" when it comes to romance. Springer is "next to death" in another sense here. He loses a loved one and therefore is touched by death. Death takes a definitive step closer in *Reader's Block* and the novels that follow it. At the conclusion of *Reader's Block*, Protagonist preempts nature, but old, poor, and isolated, what choices are left open to him? The heroic, convention-defying existential choices made by the young Greenwich Village intellectuals seem in this new context much narrower. And while his first two novels are titled epitaphs, it is in the later books that death becomes a serious concern for Markson and his characters.

While about 20 percent of *Reader's Block* concerned itself with Reader and his Protagonist, in *This Is Not a Novel*, published in 2001, there is only a character called "Writer". The rigorous formal task Writer has set himself is to write a novel that is "Plotless." The title begs the question; if *This Is Not a Novel* lacks many of the elements of conventional fiction, do we take the title seriously? The answer is a serious yes and no.

The title alludes to the famous René Magritte painting of a pipe titled *This Is Not a Pipe* and to Denis Diderot's statement in his novel *Jacques le fataliste* (1796) that "this is not a novel," both quoted in the text. The Magritte painting is a picture of a pipe, so it is not a real pipe, as *Wittgenstein's Mistress*'s Kate Winter would point out, whereas the Diderot book is in fact a novel, though denies it is one. However, *This Is Not a Novel* is not merely concerned with its status as fiction. The novel quotes Heraclitus: "We are and we are not." This is not just a comment on the identity of the book we are reading, but also a comment on Writer and, by extension, on the nature of the human character, seen in its most bizarre manifestations in the comic, tragic, and sometimes cruel episodes in the lives of the artists depicted in the book.

As the novel winds down there can only be one fate in store for Writer; we learn of his cancer. But of course there is always the work. Markson's later fiction is much exercised about the fragility and contingency of posterity. We hear of works famous in the ancient world that have disappeared, others reappearing hundreds of years later; artistic reputations that are made and lost; artists neglected by their contemporaries who have had lasting posthumous fame. We learn that Ovid, Horace, and Pindar believed in their own literary immortality, but Markson is nowhere near as arrogant as they; *Going Down* ends with Steve Chance's literary notebook used as toilet paper, and *Reader's Block* concludes with the word "Wastebasket." Still, there is the possibility of literary survival or rediscovery.

In *Vanishing Point*, Burton's book furnishes the reader with a way of thinking about Markson's own heterogeneous later work. *Vanishing Point* paradoxically continues the paring away of the narrative elements begun in the earlier books, while retaining the rich mix of anecdote and reference.

A writer, here called Author, procrastinates over beginning a new work; whether he is unable to get started because of old age, general tiredness, or something else, he isn't sure. This is a complex, ambiguous, aesthetically rather beautiful attempt to discuss mastery, authorship, and the art of fiction. While the prose here again demonstrates a concern with anti-Semitism, in this novel it is placed in a larger context of racism in America. *Vanishing Point* is also a post–September 11th novel, both in its references to religious, political, and artistic responses to the atrocity and in the way it juxtaposes that event with past mass slaughters carried out for ostensibly religious purposes, from the Crusades onward.

Finally, once more, *Vanishing Point* is a personal book. Author experiences gaps in consciousness, while all around him in the book the famous are dying. If *Reader's Block* deals largely with suicides and *This Is Not a Novel* describes how large numbers of artists and writers die, then *Vanishing Point* is threaded through with references to the places where people died. Near the novel's end there is a catalog of places, time of day, day of the month, and year. It is only necessary to recognize one of these pieces of information to grasp what is going on, and most readers will be familiar with at least one: we realize that even the greatest of us will be cut down, for it turns out that the catalog is of the moments *in articulo mortis,* at the point of death, of well-known writers and artists.

Read with the proceeding novels, *Vanishing Point* gives us a fragmented though affecting portrait of a marriage, growing children, and lack of financial success. Markson's own children had grown up by then and were having children of their own. They are the dedicatees of *This Is Not a Novel*. In *Springer's Progress*, one of the novelist's small children calls out, "Hey Dad, can I borrow your scissors?" By *Vanishing Point*, the children are fully grown. The children's voices are the only occurrences of direct speech in these novels. This is speech from the world outside the ruminations, quotations, and stories of the creative life. While there is no suggestion of any kind of transcendence in the novel, it ends with a careful ambiguity. Either Author dies or is silent, lost, maybe only temporarily, to serious illness. But of course, Author is "next to death" and the end cannot be far away.

Markson's fiction is unillusioned, bleak, and finally deeply moving. It runs against the grain of a generally upbeat American culture and is therefore part of that great tradition of nay-saying American literature.

Selected Bibliography

WORKS OF DAVID MARKSON

Novels

Epitaph for a Tramp. New York: Dell, 1959; reissued with *Epitaph for a Dead Beat* in a single volume. Emeryville, Calif.: Shoemaker & Hoard, 2007.

Epitaph for a Dead Beat. New York: Dell, 1961.

Miss Doll, Go Home. New York: Dell, 1965.

The Ballad of Dingus Magee. Indianapolis, Ind.: Bobbs-Merrill, 1966.

Going Down. New York: Holt, Rinehart and Winston, 1970; Emeryville, Calif.: Shoemaker & Hoard, 2005.

Springer's Progress. Holt, Rinehart and Winston, 19871977; Elmwood Park, Ill.: Dalkey Archive, 1990.

Wittgenstein's Mistress. Elmwood Park, Ill.: Dalkey Archive, 1988.

Reader's Block. Normal, Ill.: Dalkey Archive, 1996.

This Is Not a Novel. Washington, D.C.: Counterpoint, 2001.

Vanishing Point. Washington, D.C.: Shoemaker & Hoard, 2004.

The Last Novel. Washington D.C.: Shoemaker & Hoard, 2007.

Short Stories and Poems

"White Apache." *Saturday Evening Post*, 29 September 1956, pp. 30, 135–139.

"All My Sins Remembered." *Review of Contemporary Fiction* 10, no. 2: 145–156 (1990). (Written in 1955.)

"Healthy Kate." *Review of Contemporary Fiction* 10, no. 2: 131–144 (1990). (Written in 1986.)

Collected Poems. Normal, Ill.: Dalkey Archive, 1993.

Other Works

Women and Vodka. Edited under the pseudonym Mark Merrill. New York: Pyramid, 1956; reprinted as *Great Tales of Old Russia.* New York: Pyramid, 1963. (An anthology of Russian short stories.)

Malcolm Lowry's "Volcano": Myth Symbol Meaning. New York: Times Books, 1978.

ARTICLES AND ESSAYS

"A Day for Addie Joss." *Atlantic Monthly*, August 1974, pp. 36–40.

"Reviewers in Flat Heels: Being a Postface to Several Novels." *Review of Contemporary Fiction* 10, no. 2: 124–130 (1990).

CRITICAL AND BIOGRAPHICAL STUDIES

CRITICISM

Denham, Alice. *Sleeping with Bad Boys,* New York: Book Republic, 2006. (A memoir about literary New York in the 1950s and 1960s featuring a number of appearances by Markson himself.)

Elias, Camelia. "The Graveyard of Genre: David Markson's Postmodern Epitaphs." *Reconstruction* 5, no. 1 (winter 2005). (Available at http://reconstruction.eserver.org/051/elias.shtml.)

Gessen, Keith. "Writing for No One." *Feed,* March 2001.

Green, Jeremy. *Late Postmodernism: American Fiction at the Millenium.* New York: Palgrave, 2005. (See chapter 4.)

Tabbi, Joseph. *Cognitive Fictions.* Minneapolis: University of Minnesota Press, 2002. (See chapter 5.)

———, ed. John Barth–David Markson special issue. *Review of Contemporary Fiction* 10, no. 2 (1990).

———. "Reading David Markson." In *Context,* no. 1: 1–7 (fall 1999). (Available at http://www.centerforbookculture.org/context/no1/tabbi.htm.)

———. "Solitary Inventions: David Markson at the End of the Line." *Modern Fiction Studies* 43, no. 3: 745–772 (1997).

INTERVIEWS

Burn, Stephen. "Reading the Archive: An Interview with David Markson." *Rain Taxi* 9, no. 3: 50–51 (2004).

McEvoy, Dermot. "Wittgenstein's Author." *Publishers Weekly,* 1 March 2004 (http://www.publishersweekly.com).

Tabbi, Joseph. "Interview with David Markson." *Review of Contemporary Fiction* 10, no. 2: 104–117 (1990). (Available at http://www.centerforbookculture.org/interviews/interview_markson.html.)

WILLARD MOTLEY

(1909–1965)

James A. Lewin

THE CENTRAL TENET of Willard Motley's literary mission is that there is no race except the human race. As an African American author, Motley made an artistic decision to write about white ethnic characters in the urban slums of Chicago. His work exalts the vitality of a sprawling, brawling underclass striving for self-realization, although the author himself was brought up in a middle-class home, protected from the systemic injustice his books portray. Forces of evil, random chance, and ruthless indifference dominate Motley's world, determined by social hierarchy and biological need. Yet he never surrenders an implicit belief in the inherent goodness of the human spirit.

LIFE

Born in Chicago, Willard Motley grew up in a black family living in what was then an all-white neighborhood on the city's South Side. When Motley was inducted into the International Literary Hall of Fame for Writers of African Descent in October 2001, his nephew Archie Motley confirmed the clarification of the author's birth date as July 14, 1909, although some sources have incorrectly cited the same date in 1912. He was raised by his maternal grandparents, evidently believing they were his parents. As a child he was also led to consider his uncle, the painter Archibald Motley, Jr., to be his older brother and to think of his biological mother, Florence Motley, as his sister. The identity of his biological father is not included in any of his available biographical data.

His grandfather, Archibald Motley, Sr., earned a respectable income as a Pullman railroad porter, while his grandmother, Mary "Mae" Motley, was the dominant influence on his early years. As a token black family in an otherwise segregated white enclave, the Motley household was spared the brunt of racial prejudice. During the Chicago race riots of 1919, for example, white neighbors protected the Motley home as one of their own.

The author began his career as a teenage prodigy. After winning a contest sponsored by the city's black newspaper, the *Chicago Defender,* he wrote a series of children's columns under the pseudonym "Bud Billiken," published along with a picture of the young scribe looking very studious in a suit and tie, with heavy-framed glasses and an editor's eyeshade. (Subsequently his pen name, based on a Chinese good luck figure, was adopted as the logo for a yearly parade in Chicago's black community, though many participants have probably never heard of Willard Motley.)

At racially mixed Englewood High School, Motley played halfback on the football team and earned the sobriquet "Little Iron Man." He also worked for the student newspaper and yearbook. After high school graduation, however, he was unable to afford to go to college. Instead he took off on an adventurous bicycle trip to New York City, arriving in thirteen days. One ulterior motive for the odyssey may have been to visit his biological mother, as he now recognized her, who had moved to New York. She encouraged him to pursue his ambition to become a writer.

Continuing his education in the wide world, he took two car trips to the West Coast, during which he gathered material that he would incorporate into his first novel. In 1936 he was arrested for stealing gas and spent a month in the Cheyenne, Wyoming, jail. Returning to his home in Chicago, Motley began to churn out stories and nonfiction articles that were rejected by editors of leading magazines. Instead of giving up on his writing career, however, the author became involved with the Hull House community project begun by Jane Addams. Moving into an apartment in Chicago's worst skid row slums near West Madison Street, he collected the background he would use for his novels about the city's backstreets and alleys. With two friends, in 1939, he helped to found the *Hull-House Magazine,* which gave him the chance to develop both his style and his substance as a writer. In 1940 he was hired by the Works Progress Administration Writers' Project, which provided an income and the chance to continue to develop his writing.

Registering as a conscientious objector, he did not serve in the military during World War II. With the assistance of grants from the Newberry Library and the Rosenwald Fund, he completed his first novel, *Knock on Any Door,* published in 1947, to considerable critical acclaim and popular success. He published three more novels as well as shorter pieces, but his later work did not receive the same level of attention as his first book. Two of his books, *Knock on Any Door* and *Let No Man Write My Epitaph* (1958), were made into successful Hollywood films. Leaving Chicago, Motley lived his last years in Mexico with an adopted son, still writing but increasingly impoverished. He had trouble collecting royalties from his books because he owed back taxes to the Internal Revenue Service and evidently depended on earnings from European translations of his work. He died March 4, 1965, of intestinal gangrene in a Mexican hospital, an illness that might have been cured if treated in its earlier stages.

KNOCK ON ANY DOOR *(1947)*

Although his first novel took many years of evolution and painstaking revision, his career began with a bang. If he had never written another novel after *Knock on Any Door,* Motley would still have earned a niche in the canon of American naturalist fiction. Thematically the novel is an extended argument against capital punishment. In more general terms Motley presents as his central thesis the contention that the criminal justice system merely creates more criminals. Yet Motley does not make his task easy on himself. Not only has Nick Romano committed homicide, he is convicted of killing a police officer. That puts him beyond the outer limits of social sympathy from the red-white-and-blue mainstream voting public.

Nick Romano is far from innocent. Is the twenty-one-year-old Nick's life, the reader is led to ask, therefore expendable? Even the lowest criminal, Motley suggests, retains enough humanity to be worth rescuing from capital punishment. The novel assumes an underlying goodness of humanity, even though that goodness has been perverted by cruelty, lust, apathy, and despair. Nick is a fellow human being; we are collectively responsible for his fate. If we condemn Nick, the author implies, we condemn a part of ourselves.

Reform is obviously needed in the society Motley portrays. But the nature of that reform is far from obvious. Other than questioning the righteous certainty that sends a twenty-one-year-old to the electric chair, the novel weaves a web of despair, built on economic and cultural factors as well as individual failings, leaving a sense of tragic awe at the lost potential of humanity. Elements of melodrama and sentimentality contend with an unsparing account of a reverse pilgrimage from childhood innocence to indelible degradation. Nick becomes an unrepentant rebel against established authority and a hardened petty criminal, whose whole life leads by a perverse logic, step by step, to his legally sanctioned execution.

At first Nick is portrayed as an altar boy, full of prayerful compassion for the weak and victimized. His immigrant parents consider themselves fortunate and successful. His older brother and sister seem well adjusted. Until his twelfth birthday he remains pious, meek, mild, almost saintly. His parents plan for him to grow up to become a priest, his father sternly announcing their intention to give Nick to the church. His mother loves to tell the story of how, as a little boy, Nick saved a mouse from a cat. Nick's identification with the mouse becomes emblematic of his thwarted compassion and his victimization by forces beyond his control, a screen memory which continues to haunt him through the rest of his short life.

Walking, head down, through a crowd of curiosity seekers watching this sidewalk melodrama, little Nick rescues the mouse from both the natural cruelty of the cat and the cultivated indifference of the onlookers.

Innocence remains Nick's birthright, even as he becomes increasingly brutalized and corrupted by his experience of the world. The downward spiral begins when Nick's father loses his business in the Depression, and the family moves to the slums. Nick must transfer to a different school, where the priests and nuns are not the gentle mentors he has known and where the students make discipline a constant problem. When the class troublemaker shoots a pin from a rubber-band slingshot, Nick takes the blame to keep his friend from being expelled. Falsely accused and punished, Nick begins to turn against all that he had, until then, revered.

With his newfound friends from the wrong side of town, Nick learns how to play hooky, steal pies from a bakery truck and baskets of apples from a produce truck, then run from the cops. When these older, tougher kids rob a pawnshop, Nick waits outside. He is still innocent. But he is soon drawn deeper into their world of petty crimes.

His first serious trouble with the law begins with the fatal flaw of loyalty, when he obeys the first commandment of the underworld: Thou shalt not squeal. Intimidated by an older, bigger, meaner boy, Nick agrees, against his better judgment, to hide a stolen bicycle. When the cops show up, he refuses to inform on the other kid. Nick Romano, the former altar boy, winds up in reform school. From that point on his doom is sealed.

The reform school is presided over by a one-armed sadist named Fuller. The superintendent's handicap seems to embody the deformed nature of his power over the boys under his control. Within its hierarchy, a pecking order of cruelty descends from the official authorities paid to run the institution to the strongest and meanest inmates who dominate those who are less aggressive. In this regimented jungle, survival depends on becoming tougher and fighting harder than the oppressor, or else submitting to the tyranny of the strong over the weak.

Yet noble heroism and friendship remain possible, even at the bottom of this seemingly bottomless pit. Nick's first real friend is Rocky, who teaches him the tricks of getting by. Rocky helps him to obtain cigarettes and to avoid detentions. Nick's first hero is Tommy, a younger and smaller kid, who refuses to be intimidated by anyone, no matter how big or powerful. Tommy sets an example, first by defying the bully Bricktop, who threatens him for being friends with a black kid and then by stoically holding back his tears when he is brutally whipped and humiliated by Superintendent Fuller. For Nick, the injustice done to Tommy is a turning point. Between the authority of Fuller and the rebellion of Tommy, Nick chooses defiance.

While in reform school, Nick also meets the writer and sociologist Grant Holloway who is doing research for a study of such penal institutions. An immediate rapport between Nick and Grant becomes a painful lost hope that Nick might yet prove society wrong about his unredeemable badness.

By the time he gets out of the reform school Nick has become a devoted enemy of the status quo. No longer impressed by the pieties of church, school, or courts of law, Nick seems predestined to a life of crime.

His family moves to the Near Southside of Chicago. But Nick finds his way from their Taylor Street neighborhood of poor working-class families to West Madison Street, the central thoroughfare of Chicago's skid row, where life-after-death continues on earth.

Motley's strength lies in his detailed description of life in the gutter. He knows the world of West Madison Street in the depths of its degradation only a few blocks away from the rough-and-tumble families like Nick's struggling for survival. Motley does not shirk from portraying violence and corruption, but he also records redeeming notes of a slum culture that has progressed toward embracing the equality of all colors and creeds, if only because they share in similar misfortune. The author explicitly portrays a breaking down of barriers to cultural diversity.

In the Maxwell Street melting pot, all nationalities mingle and intertwine. Racism and prejudice persist, but there seems more hope for humanity in the underclass of the city than in its respectable counterpart.

For Nick, the street is a realm of both life and death. When the mayor visits, the police block off the street and the neighborhood becomes a carnival. After the mayor leaves, a band plays jitterbug music and there is dancing on the pavement, along with craps games, prostitution, and street fights. On his way home Nick passes the body of a dog, carrion for flies, still lying where he had seen it run over by a truck earlier in the day, as newspapers swirl in the air.

In the taverns and pool halls of West Madison Street, the education Nick began to acquire in reform school progresses. He lives between the Nickel Plate, an all-night diner with coffee at three cents a cup, and the Pastime, a poolroom and bar.

He learns the techniques of jack-rolling: how to spot a likely victim by his pressed pants and shined shoes, how to wait in the shadows, how to hook the guy around the neck and press your knees against the back of his knees, how to slug him, bring him down, and then empty his pockets. Easy money.

He also learns how to hustle homosexuals, leading them on and then turning on them, threatening and beating them until they give up their money. Cast into the lower depths of society by his association with criminals, Nick is brought ever lower because of his one great asset, his seemingly innocent good looks. Seduced by both men and women, Nick becomes a bisexual hustler, playing on his ability to attract the attention of everyone he meets. Arousing the lustful desires of others, Nick becomes increasingly unable to feel anything but contempt for himself and other people.

Through it all, however, Nick retains his ability to put on a mask of utter innocence, a trick he uses to avoid the consequences of his immorality without alleviating his own guilt.

Arrested for stealing a violin in a mugging, Nick refuses to confess. In the back of the police station Nick experiences Chicago-style interrogation techniques: blows aimed for the maximum pain while leaving the least evidence of injury on the suspect, fists slammed into the hollow above the hipbone and rabbit punches aimed at the back of the neck by his arch-nemesis Officer Riley. But no matter how badly Riley beats him, Nick defies his power. With three notches in his belt, one for each of the three men he has killed in the line of duty. In the person of Officer Riley, Nick sees the embodiment of systematic injustice.

The more he is brutalized by the legal authorities, the more readily he succumbs to depravity. The one inhibition that remains in him is the sense of shame for seducing a "nice" girl, Rosemary. In his mind, sexual fulfillment becomes, by definition, dirty. Haunted by a sense of guilt, he becomes unable to form normal sexual relationships. This shameful inhibition becomes crippling impotence when he finally meets the girl of his dreams, Emma. After they are married, Nick is unable to be an adequate husband to his wife, either in terms of providing for Emma economically or giving her the sexual satisfaction she needs, not to mention the baby she desperately wants. Increasingly he sneaks back to his underworld haunts, committing crimes, getting drunk, indulging in promiscuity, and then guiltily returning to his wife.

When Emma commits suicide Nick blames himself for killing her. Convinced that he is "no good" and the cause of destruction for anyone who tries to get close to him, he abandons himself utterly to despair. After Emma's suicide Nick loses all vestiges of moral constraint. As he accelerates on his downward slide from altar boy to reform school punk to street criminal and androgynous hustler, Nick's self-disgust becomes too heavy to bear. Even his friends from West Madison Street, without comprehending, sense Nick's broken psyche as he blames himself for Emma's death. Inevitably, he commits the crime that leads to his demise.

He holds up a bar. Officer Riley chases him through the street. Turning, Nick shoots the officer, killing him, and then hurls his gun into the dead policeman's face. He exults in his crime, convinced that he has fulfilled his purpose in life.

Standing over the corpse, he kicks Riley, paying him back for the beatings Riley had given him. Looking up, Nick realizes that a crowd is staring at him from the end of the alley. He tries to escape but is finally caught and enclosed in the condemnation he has come to expect as his destiny.

Contemptible even to himself, Nick risks losing the sympathy, if not the empathy, of the reader. The one quality that keeps him from being utterly pathetic is his ability to take the punishment without surrendering his own honor. The more brutally the cops beat him, the more he regains a certain status as a potentially tragic rather than a merely pathetic individual. And the cops beat him without mercy or remorse. Refusing to confess to any involvement in Riley's death, Nick is subjected to the collective wrath of a police force avenging the death of one of its own.

Like the protagonist of a traditional morality play, Nick is surrounded by a cast of characters who either undermine or support his hopes for redemption. But unlike the struggle over the souls of everyman and mankind, the bad angels triumph over the good in the psychodrama of Nick. In addition to villains such as Fuller and Riley, secondary vice figures also play their parts as false friends aiding and abetting in Nick's demise.

For example, a distinctive West Madison Street hustler, the Kid, a.k.a. "Kid Fingers," lives by panhandling money from friends and strangers when he cannot pick somebody's pocket in Jefferson Park. Promising to teach him the ropes, the Kid wises up Nick to his method of operations. Later, both the Kid and Squint (another false friend) testify against Nick in his murder trial. The novel implies that they have been encouraged by the district attorney to perjure themselves. But that seems to be business as usual in Motley's Chicago.

On the other side of the equation, Nick's loyal friends stick by him in the trial that will decide if he lives or dies, even if they also perjure themselves in bending the truth in Nick's favor. Called by the prosecution, Juan switches his testimony on the stand to support Nick's innocence. Also on Nick's side is Sunshine—the token Negro in Nick's entourage. Nick wins Sunshine's friendship with a coin for a meal when Sunshine had not eaten in two days. After that Sunshine becomes Nick's most loyal ally, always ready to watch his back or concoct an alibi. On the stand, Sunshine claims that Nick was with him at the time of Riley's murder. And of all his associates, Nick seems to have the most genuine concern for Sunshine.

Another of Nick's benefactors is a lonely individual named Owen, first introduced, without a name, as the "unhappy man" who "sat at his table by the window" of the Nickel Plate. Seeing that Nick needs new shoes, this anonymous good Samaritan puts five dollars on the table and walks away. The following day, in the same place, Nick lifts one of his new shoes for his benefactor's inspection. When Squint cuts Nick's hand in a knife fight late one night, the same individual appears, takes Nick to his apartment, bandages the wound, and seems to ask for nothing in return. Impressed, Nick finally asks him his name. Owen becomes one of his most faithful friends. A repressed homosexual, Owen loves Nick for his beauty and grace, without expecting anything in return.

Nick's doomed wife, Emma, is a girl his sister knows from the factory where they both work. Invited to Sunday dinner, she meets him and is immediately smitten, as are all women when they first meet Nick, by his preternatural good looks. For Nick, however, Emma is in a class of her own. Unlike the girls he is used to treating with contempt, Nick puts Emma on a pedestal all by herself. He seems to adore her.

In contrast, Nellie Watkins is just one of the girls on the street. Nick takes her for granted, uses her for sex, takes money from her, sometimes sleeps in her apartment, and then turns around and tells her to get lost. There is no hint in Motley's first novel of what a significant role Nellie will play, as the mother of Nick's child, in the book's sequel.

The structure of *Knock on Any Door* will be familiar to viewers of the television series *Law and Order*. The first part of the plot concerns an act of homicide, followed by a courtroom drama to resolve questions of guilt or innocence. But

Motley tells the story from the point of view of the perpetrator rather than the cops and the district attorney, and he takes five hundred pages, allowing much more time to develop his characters and the setting. In many ways, setting becomes the focus of interest. Chicago is represented as the microcosm of a world that is only half civilized, ruled by the laws of the jungle slightly modified to appease the sensitivities of courtroom procedure.

The last third of the novel is taken up by Nick's trial, conviction, and execution in the electric chair. Nick himself becomes almost a secondary figure as the drama focuses on the two lawyers, Morton for the defense (the part played by Humphrey Bogart in the film version) and Kerman for the prosecution, the good and evil angels in mortal combat. Nick's fate seems to hang in the balance. He still wants to live. But the courtroom and the law are far from him. On the outside he plays the role of "Pretty Boy Romano" created for him by the newspapers, the tough guy who feels no remorse. Inside, however, he is suffering for the death of Emma. The court accuses him of killing a policeman. His own heart convicts him for murdering the only person he ever tried to love.

Morton does his best to save Nick's life. He even sets up an alibi to try to convince the jury Nick is innocent. In knowingly concocting a false version of events, with the help of Nick's loyal friends, Morton seems to betray his professional ethics as a lawyer. The implication is that, in the legal apparatus, conscience and empathy may trump even a true indictment. Morton also calls Nick to the stand in his own defense. Calling Nick to testify may be unwise in terms of legal strategy, but it is an effective maneuver for the author of the novel.

Motley could have had his protagonist convicted unjustly, as happened often enough in Chicago courts, or Nick could have conceded his guilt grudgingly, with emphasis on the extenuating circumstances. Instead the author suggests that Nick is convicted for the death of Officer Riley because he feels guilty for the death of his love.

In the other corner, Kerman sneers and insinuates and bullies until he gets his way. The prosecutor wants the conviction in order to burnish his record as a crime-fighter, without any serious consideration for the consequences of sending Nick, who is less than nobody in Kerman's view, to his death.

The fatal turning point comes when Kerman questions Nick about Emma. Until then Nick sticks to his story through Kerman's browbeating, insults, and insinuations. The jury seems to buy Nick's baby-faced stare and stubborn refusal to admit involvement in Officer Riley's death. Insidiously, and against the rule of the court, Kerman slips in references to Emma, even though her death has no direct bearing on the evidence. Finally Nick's resistance snaps. Tough enough to stand up to the cops' brutal physical abuse, he breaks under the weight of Kerman's verbal assault.

Despite the fact that he has lost the gamble he took in putting Nick on the witness stand, Morton pursues the archetypal liberal argument that "Society" is to blame for the crimes that have been perpetrated.

The narrative is on the side of Morton's defense. But the plot is stacked against Nick. After Nick confesses on the witness stand, there is nothing in the text to refute Kerman's claim. The jurors nevertheless have a hard time reaching a unanimous verdict. Some sympathetic jurors seem worn down rather than persuaded by the evidence.

The author seems to believe in the natural innocence of humanity and blames the corruption of the soul on the perversions of power. Figures of authority, such as the one-armed reform school superintendent Fuller, use their positions of dominance to inflict their deformity on those who fall under their control. Power of one individual over another creates the imbalance that results in man's inhumanity to his fellow. Although the message of the novel is stark, the author lets his story write its own moral:

The city doesn't change. The people come and go, the visitors. They see the front yard.

But what of the city's back yard, and the alley? Who knows the lives and minds of the people who live in the alley?

Knock on any door down this street, in this alley.

Motley's best-known book owes a debt to the influence of Theodore Dreiser's *An American Tragedy,* Richard Wright's *Native Son,* and Fyodor Dostoevsky's *Crime and Punshishment.* But as an African American author writing about whites to prove the universality of the human condition, Motley does not fit into preconceived categories. Working in the naturalist tradition, Motley hits hard and he keeps hitting with subject-verb sentences accumulating body blows to the reader's subconscious.

WE FISHED ALL NIGHT *(1951)*

Although not as well received by critics, Motley's second book, *We Fished All Night,* expanded his horizons as a writer. The novel features excellent character development and a convincing representation of Chicago's corrupt political machine. Its main problem is a shifting point of view, involving three central characters, resulting in a somewhat disjointed narrative with a weakness for didactic sermonizing.

In his first book Motley tackled the issue of capital punishment. His second, far more ambitious novel espouses the cause of pacifism. Again, while projecting his topic in terms of a thesis novel, the author does not make his own task easy for himself by following the path of least resistance. In *Knock on Any Door,* Motley wrote about a seemingly hardened criminal who had slain a police officer, the type of defendant most likely to serve as the poster boy for the death penalty. In writing what could seem to have been intended as an antiwar tract, Motley takes on U.S. participation in World War II, the single historical event most often cited as proof of the ultimate necessity and irreducible value of armed conflict to solve problems of national and international policy. Motley raises doubts about claiming a virtuous cause, however justified, to answer violence with violence. The consequences, the author suggests, cannot be either rationalized or ignored.

To make his point, the narrator follows the paths of three individuals before, during, and after the war. The first, Don Lockwood, an amateur thespian before the war, loses one of his legs as a result of an injury, then uses the status of a wounded veteran to launch a successful career as an increasingly corrupt and cynical politician. The second, Jim Norris, a union activist motivated by the highest ideals, returns without a scratch, at least externally, but his experiences of war have brutalized him and summoned forth inner demons he never knew existed. The third, Aaron Levin, an aspiring poet, suffers a mental breakdown from which he never recovers, left as a lost soul wandering the urban landscape.

As the noted Motley scholar Robert E. Fleming has pointed out, the title of *We Fished All Night* is based on a statement made by Peter to Jesus in the New Testament (Luke 5:5). The downbeat application of this reference is echoed in other purposefully ironic biblical allusions the author uses to define his characters as unheroic paradigms of humanity. The underlying implication throughout is that though the war has been won, the aftermath leaves unresolved residual societal problems.

The most effective parts of the book focus on Don Lockwood, originally Chet Kosinski. Raised in the slums, Don is too ashamed of his origins to let anyone know his real name and address. His mother, while raising Don and his sisters on her own, supplements a meager income with money earned as a part-time prostitute. Don's elderly grandfather, who shares the family apartment, spends most of his time bemoaning the fact that he ever left his native land. As much as his grandfather tries to instill Polish pride in him, Don switches his ethnic Polish birth name to a vaguely British and upper-class-sounding pseudonym, first for the benefit of stagebills and then legally to establish his political identity. A hypocrite who aspires to greatness but settles for crass success, Don is the embodiment of a culture that rewards phony opportunists in the name of idealistic values.

Motley portrays Don as an understandable, almost sympathetic scoundrel who knows his inner emptiness so well that he is ready to follow any lead that could provide hope of an escape from his sense of despair. First he becomes the protégé of amateur director, Sue Carroll, who offers him a previously unimaginable alternative reality. Although his talent is limited, Don persuades Sue to cast him as the lead in Shakespeare's *Hamlet*. Encouraged by Sue, who falls in love with him despite her own better judgment, Don begins to fantasize his future as star of stage and screen. As the older woman infatuated with a younger man, Sue seems to see her own unrealized ambitions in Don. Far better educated than Don, Sue is grounded in a genuine appreciation for high culture. She is also committed to supporting progressive liberal causes. As he strives to internalize Sue's knowledge of theater, Don also begins to mirror her liberal ideology. The war seems a distant and vaguely menacing background shadow until he is called up for military service.

In the army Don again attaches himself to a stronger and more fully developed personality. To his own amazement he becomes buddies with a soldier named Wayne who represents the American dream to Don. Not only has he had the advantages, unlike Don, of coming from an upper-class family, Wayne is also handsome, educated, and idealistic. As in his relationship with Sue, Don adopts Wayne's point of view as his own. When Wayne dies in battle, Don makes a conscious decision to carry on the American idealism that Wayne represents to him. As much as he becomes compromised and corrupted, Don still clings to an inner image of himself acting as Wayne would have done if he had survived.

Don's political career begins at Chicago's "Bughouse Square," a small park across from the Newberry Library where speakers of all persuasions can exercise their democratic freedom of speech. When hecklers in the crowd shout bigoted remarks at a black speaker, Don pushes his way to the front and confronts the crowd. In a spontaneous moment Don improvises what he had long dreamed of: the performance of his life. Dramatically calling attention to his own artificial leg and striking a dramatic pose, he defines himself as a veteran who has sacrificed for American ideals. Invoking the heroic memory of his dead friend Wayne, while projecting his voice as he had done onstage, Don declares that those who fought the war did so to create a world free of prejudice and inequality.

It turns out that Thomas McCarren, ward committeeman of the Democratic Party, happens to be present to hear Don's speech. Before he knows what has happened, Don finds himself running for state senate. Under the tutelage of this new mentor, Don again adapts himself in the familiar role as the follower of a stronger personality. Oblivious of the political realities that have created his candidacy, Don is told—and believes implicitly—that he cannot lose the election. He loses all the same. Still, he finds consolation in becoming the ward boss's right-hand man, collecting the bribes and delivering the favors that turn the gears of the political machine.

Unconstrained by the nonfiction writer's limitation to verifiable allegations, Motley can portray the intimate relationship between a criminal underworld of vice and organized crime with the official political hierarchy. Motley's Chicago is not undermined by corruption; rather, the city is built on a foundation designed by and for corrupted interests. The police function as enforcers of illegal understandings that allow gangsters and elected leaders to coexist in mutual interdependence. For this intimate snapshot of Chicago politics at its worst, *We Fished All Night* deserves a wider audience.

The plot thickens when Don belatedly realizes that he has been played for a stooge by Committeeman McCarren. Having learned his lessons well, Don stages a coup, running for election as committeeman with the aid of all the disgruntled operatives in McCarren's own organization. Suddenly Don steps up as ward boss, with all the accoutrements of his new position: the diamond ring, the shiny new car, the great wads of cash, and the power to make or break the lives of others with a nod or shake of his head.

He marries the spoiled but beautiful daughter of a rich capitalist, moves into a Gold Coast apartment, and seems to have utterly betrayed his motives of liberal idealism. But Don does not see himself in that light. He is convinced that he still stands for progressive and enlightened American idealism in the mold of his dead war buddy Wayne. And in perhaps the most poignant and textured aspect of the novel, Don continues a lifelong love affair with his first mentor, Sue Carroll, who is still living in her walk-up flat off Division Street, still plugging away at little theater productions, still working tirelessly for political reform, even as she finds herself unable to stop loving Don any more than he is unable to stop needing her.

On this private island of Don the politician and Sue the theater type, the novel might have explored inner realities that would have made a great work of art. Unfortunately the world of Don and Sue is swamped by a vast wave of events and characters that do have inherent interest but lack the subtle, intimate, psychological complexity of fully developed individuals.

Not that the author lacks imagination or energy. His characters all have a remarkable quality of verisimilitude, even as they approach the outer limits of abnormal behavior. The problem seems to be a predetermined intention to prove a point, namely that war is no way to achieve peace. Rather than following real people through the experiences of real life toward the inevitable finality of human fate, the author intrudes himself with an ideology of well-intentioned moral certitude.

Aaron Levin is perhaps the most pathetic character of the book. An aspiring writer, Aaron inhabits the no-man's-land between genius and insanity. As a big and strong-looking young man he is all the more a candidate for the draft because of his half-Jewish ancestry. His father shows Aaron the scars he carries on his body from a pogrom he survived as a boy in eastern Europe and tells Aaron that it is his duty to redeem the suffering of his people. At the battlefront, Aaron has a mental breakdown. He winds up in an asylum, is treated with electroshock therapy, and receives a dishonorable discharge from the military. Psychologically vulnerable even before the war, Aaron returns home shattered by the trauma he has suffered and haunted by a sense of dishonor he cannot overcome.

His only place of refuge is a cafeteria on Chicago Avenue where artists, writers, and union organizers congregate. Before the war, the circle of friends he makes at the cafeteria seems to provide Aaron a spiritual and intellectual oasis. After he returns, however, he is increasingly alienated even from them. He seeks a new beginning, first in the Communist Party, but finds himself unable to accept the ideological dictates of party discipline. Then he attempts, briefly, to find solace in religion. But neither Judaism nor Christianity seem to have the answers to his tormented doubts. Slowly Aaron comes under the influence of Steve, a psychopathic nihilist he meets in the cafeteria, who seems to take a sadistic pleasure in dragging Aaron down into the despair and disgust he feels for humanity.

Yet through it all, Aaron is loved by Rebecca, an attractive and sensitive girl he grew up with but had always ignored. Eventually Aaron and Rebecca begin a relationship and start living together, but it is too late for Aaron to be redeemed even by love. As they sink deeper into poverty and neglect, Rebecca, who is pregnant with their child, turns to drink. Aaron, meanwhile, wanders the streets, scribbling phrases and images on scraps of paper that he stuffs in his pockets, imagining himself a great poet.

Motley's third main character, Jim Norris, seems an all-American guy with an optimistic personality. Handsome and athletic, Jim is nice to the point of being boring, except for his deep commitment to union activism. After the war, however, Jim brings home a hidden scar on his psyche that his wife and children will never understand. Brutalized by his experiences in combat, Jim cannot stop himself from having fantasies of raping young women, whom he begins to follow compulsively along dark streets at night.

In the end Jim is saved from himself by an ironic plot twist that brings together all the strands of the novel in a confrontation between striking workers and the evil capitalist empire of Emerson Bradley, owner of the Haines Company. While Don Lockwood convinces himself that it is his duty as a good American to help break the union, Aaron wanders in the vicinity of the strike aware only of his own internal nightmare world, and Jim suffers a fatal blow on the skull by a policeman's club. The war is over, yet the war goes on.

As the narrative develops, the book seems to get diverted from Motley's original conception. Rather than an antiwar tract, *We Fished All Night* is a compendium of liberal issues all raised simultaneously. Despite vivid characterizations and convincing vignettes, the novel does not hold together as an integrated work of art. It reads like two or three different novels, none of which is completed, stitched together as one. Nevertheless, Motley's second book helped him to develop his craft as a writer.

LET NO MAN WRITE MY EPITAPH (1958)

Motley's third novel, *Let No Man Write My Epitaph,* is a sequel to *Knock on Any Door.* It focuses primarily on Nick Romano, Jr., son of the protagonist of Motley's first book. His mother is Nellie Watkins, one of Nick Romano's casual sexual conquests, who testifies for the defense in his trial for the murder of a police officer. In the first novel Nellie is a shadowy if sympathetic woman whom Nick Senior treats with cavalier contempt. Only when she takes the witness stand does Nick seem to realize that Nellie is anything more than an object to be used when convenient and scorned for her devotion.

In *Let No Man Write My Epitaph,* Nellie (played by Shelley Winters in the movie version) becomes a major character as the mother to Nick Junior and as the paradigmatic example of the novel's theme. Again the author organizes his plot around a controversial issue; in this case the issue is drug addiction. Although it has some of the flaws common to a sequel, *Let No Man Write My Epitaph* includes much of Motley's best work, further developing his ability to juxtapose intertwined plots involving an extended cast of characters. Yet *Let No Man Write My Epitaph* also strikes some false notes. While the characters and action are strong and believable, the treatment of addiction as a social problem is reminiscent of a narcotics detective's lecture to high school students. Mixing valid insights with bogus assumptions, Motley's portrayal of illegal drug use seems to be based on an outsider's view of the addict's vicious cycle of dependency and escape. As the novel progresses, drug use becomes secondary to the quest for identity in an urban jungle dominated by the sheer struggle for survival.

In addition to a number of sympathetic characters, Motley introduces his most terrifying villain, the embodiment of Chicago's evil instincts. At first the reader experiences this spirit as "the great beast of the city." Gradually this blue-black panther bestial spirit of the city at night manifests itself in the character of Frank Ramponi, nicknamed "The Wolf." First introduced as a nameless figure standing in the shadows, his favorite sport is to throw coins on the sidewalk for kids on the street to fight over, as he encourages them not to let the others snatch the pennies, nickels, and dimes without a struggle.

Early in the novel the Wolf proves himself as a cold-blooded killer. In a chilling back-alley switchblade crucifixion, he executes an anonymous black teenager. Once he collars his prey in the dark shadows, the Wolf stabs him, with remorseless persistence, again and again and again. As he dies, the victim kisses his assailant's shoes, begging for mercy. Without emotion, the Wolf leaves the body for dead.

Although the killing is for an alleged infraction of gang etiquette, it turns out that the victim is the "wrong guy." Not that the Wolf cares one way or the other: a black kid dead in an alley off Halsted and Maxwell Streets is of little concern to the greater society of Chicago.

The Wolf, who is always high on marijuana, initiates Nellie to heroin use simply as a way of establishing his power over her. Attracted to him sexually, even as she is repulsed by his crude bestiality, Nellie reluctantly takes Frank Ramponi as a lover but rejects him for the sake of Nick Junior. But she then finds that she cannot free herself from his insidious presence as she becomes increasingly hooked on drugs: the pusher is the Wolf.

Although she is not the chief protagonist of the plot, Nellie Watkins is, from the opening pages, in many ways the central presence of the book. In *Knock on Any Door* she is barely identified by name. Representing one of Nick Romano's many sexual conquests, she is most notable for following him doggedly from bar to bar, no matter how much he scorns her. Allowing Nick to use her bed and herself as a fallback when the streets become too hectic, Nellie seems to live in a fantasy of romantic love that she refuses to surrender. She is most memorable, in Motley's first novel, for taking the stand in Nick's defense, risking charges of perjury to provide him an alibi for the crime of which he is, as she realizes belatedly, in fact, guilty. At that time there is no hint in the narrative that she may be carrying Nick's child.

In *Let No Man Write My Epitaph* the reader learns of Nellie's dreadful childhood, abandoned by a mother she barely remembers and raised by foster parents. She recalls being seduced by her Uncle Clarence when she was barely a teenager as one of her few memories of anyone caring for her at all. Her Aunt Martha, unaware of her husband's philandering, ships Nellie off to other distant relatives simply because she resents having her sister's illegitimate daughter as an extra mouth to feed. Eventually Nellie runs away and comes to the big city of Chicago, finding work as a waitress at a greasy-spoon restaurant and settling into the lower depths of West Madison Street. Expecting to be exploited and abused as if it were her predestined fate, Nellie somehow finds the strength to survive in a world that seems to have been made without a place for her to call her own.

When she gives birth to Nick Romano's son and namesake, however, Nellie tries to turn her life around. She is determined to provide her child with the love and attention she never had, following the prescriptions she reads in books by experts on baby care with zealous devotion. Her life finds meaning in her son, and she constructs an alternative history of her relationship with his father, in which Nick loved her as she loved him.

Yet Nellie does find a network of support to assist her in her role as a single parent earning a meager wage in a menial occupation. Her shift as a waitress is from 6 in the evening until 3 A.M., but her boss lets her arrive for work a few minutes late so that she does not miss feeding her baby at the prescribed time. While Nellie works, the infant sleeps in the back of the restaurant in an improvised crib of an unused dishpan lined with blankets.

Even more important for Nick Junior's future development, an unlikely group of male role models form a protective circle to shield the child from the harsh realities of the urban lower depths. Each of them is a survivor of the school of hard knocks. The first of Nick's surrogate uncles is Judge Sullivan, a graduate of Yale Law School and former justice of the New Jersey circuit court who has been brought down to the level of wandering from bar to bar on skid row peddling razor blades, needles, thread, and costume jewelry from a cigar box to pay for his next drink. Nellie hopes he will be able to help her teach young Nick to speak educated English. For his part, Judge Sullivan (played by Burl Ives in the film) finds a small miracle of meaning in the chance encounter that gives him the opportunity to be more than just another bum on the street, if only for a few moments at a time. Yet the author is careful not to sentimentalize the aged alcoholic too much. Judge Sullivan needs his drink first. Only then can he pay attention to Nick. As the child grows, Judge Sullivan becomes an integral part of Nick's life, relating to him without condescension and broadening his horizons with excursions to the Field Museum.

Introduced by Judge Sullivan, three younger men also make young Nick their favorite. Max, Phil, and Norman are drinking companions, each with his own story of survival. Max, a hard-drinking Mexican cabdriver and World War II veteran, is first introduced by Motley as a minor character in *We Fished All Night*. In *Let No Man Write My Epitaph,* Max represents a working-class hero and exemplar of Motley's belief in the basic goodness of humanity. Phil, a reformed gang member, tells his story of lethal street fights and explains the protocols of gang membership in a set piece within the longer narrative. Finally, Norman is described as a gay man who is fully accepted by his straight friends, provided that he does not hold his cigarette in *too* effeminate a style.

Max, Phil, and Norman buy Nick candy and when they find out that he likes to draw, they encourage him, giving him crayons and watercolors. For Christmas they chip in to buy Nick an electric train. To share their sense of celebration, as a huge turkey roasts in the electric-plate burner in Nellie's flat, they decide to each bring a guest from the street. The dinner party includes Helen Kosinski, sister to Don Lockwood from *We Fished All Night,* as well as a prostitute, a panhandler, and a young hobo from Tennessee. They all drink wine from gallon jugs and eat the turkey with their fingers. For the first time in her life, Nellie feels a sense of belonging to a happy extended family.

Her happiness does not endure. Frank Ramponi, a.k.a. The Wolf, makes Nellie's misery his pet project, first seducing her sexually and then intentionally getting her hooked on heroin out of sheer spite, because Nellie makes it clear that her son Nick is more important to her than he can ever be. As Nellie descends into a spiral of addiction, she neglects Nick and becomes a walking zombie, prostituting herself for money, associating only with other addicts, living from drug fix to drug fix. For her, there is no hope. She misses attending her son's high school graduation because of her drug habit. When Nick buys a train ticket for her to go to a treatment center in Lexington, Kentucky, Nellie sneaks back, unable to endure the treatment.

Motley represents addiction as a metaphor for human weakness and social decay, with convincing vignettes of the drug underworld. But the author's attitude is filtered through the perspective of the writer Grant Holloway, a character who played an integral role in *Knock on Any Door.* In this novel, however, Grant's presence seems an artificial authorial device to explain heroin addiction to the presumably uninformed reader. Along the way Motley mixes useful information with stereotypes and debatable assumptions. Marijuana is portrayed not only as the first step to almost inevitable heroin addiction but also as a stimulant to criminal violence. In contrast, alcohol use by Grant and others, even to excess, seems a natural antidote to a materialistic society poisoned by individual competition.

Other characters are also brought back from *Knock on Any Door,* including the first Nick Romano's friend Juan, who becomes Nick Junior's skeptically self-conscious yet caring godfather. Wise old Aunt Rosa returns to introduce young Nick to his father's family and to prevent Louie Romano, the first Nick's younger brother, from following in his older brother's footsteps to the electric chair. Squint, Kid Fingers, and other known perpetrators still lurk around the fringes of the neighborhood. Also, returning from his major role in *We Fished All Night,* Don Lockwood shows up as a shady political overlord of the drug trade.

As heirs of the handsome, doomed antihero of *Knock on Any Door,* young Nick and his uncle Louie Romano each must find a way to rewrite the destiny that looms over them. Young Nick, unlike his father, grows up to be slight of build and shy, with a burning aspiration to become an artist. Louie, on the other hand, seems like an exact replica of his older brother. What saves him is falling in love with an African American waitress. Neither for young Nick nor for Louie Romano is there any easy path out of the inferno of the Chicago slums. But Motley concludes his third novel on a hopeful note. Blended with the naturalist's concern for environment and genetics as deterministic factors, Motley introduces the possibility of gradual self-awareness as an alternative individual destiny. Despite false images the author creates in his effort to paint a realistic picture of the drug scene, Motley continues his development as a novelist in *Let No Man Write My Epitaph,* making it perhaps the best entry place for a reader who has never read any of his other books to appreciate Motley's sense of shared humanity.

LET NOON BE FAIR *(1966)*

The author's last major work of fiction was published posthumously, following his untimely death. In a shift of setting, *Let Noon Be Fair* brings the author's eye for social upheaval in Chicago's backstreets to a tourist town in Mexico. In many ways it is Motley's most subtle and dynamic novel. It is, unfortunately, also perhaps his most disappointing. While a broad canvas of indigenous Mexicans and tourists from the United States interacting across a period of years is portrayed with verve, imagination, and profound sensibility, the text seems in need of more thorough editing and detailed revision. The native Mexican characters are for the most part sharply delineated in their strengths and weaknesses, but they tend toward stereotypes, including a decadent scion of Spanish ancestry, a self-serving hypocritical leader of the community, and an illiterate Indian who outsmarts all the others. The tourists, on the other hand, blur together, with a few exceptions, into a bland, pleasure-seeking crowd of names and faces without distinction.

In his last book Motley shows himself still developing as a writer, finding a new level of awareness in the interplay of innocence and cynicism. For example, when an utterly unscrupulous politician assumes he can not only steal the native Indians' land but also corner the market on their home-brewed liquor, he is chased out of the province by an uprising he had never expected or was equipped to put down. Similarly, when a corrupted priest who joins the church for mercenary motives spurns the love of his childhood soul mate, she turns around and becomes a prostitute with a genius for business.

As in his earlier works, the author focuses on a central theme, in this case the corruption of a Mexican fishing village as it becomes a tourist attraction. With a greater spectrum of colors in his palette, the author creates a more nuanced picture of the conflict between the individual and society as compared with his film-noir-style black-and-white portrayal of Chicago. He immerses himself in the fictional representation of a Mexican village much as he does in the urban slums, but Motley probably never understood the social mores and unstated assumptions of individual behavior among his Mexican characters as he did with his denizens of West Madison Street. The episodic plot is filled with dramatic turns and unexpected events, and the shifting focus on a variety of characters can be disorienting. Still, the book deserves attention as a portrayal of the relationship between an affluent but unsatisfied North American culture and its hungry Mexican counterpart.

In addition to his four novels Motley also published short fiction as well as nonfiction magazine articles. The diaries he kept for most of his life were edited and published in 1979. He also left a large collection of papers and manuscripts at Northern Illinois University and the University of Wisconsin. One of these manuscripts is a long narrative account of the adventures he had during his youthful travels through Oregon and California. The Yale University Library also has the typed original manuscript of *Knock on Any Door*, running to more than a thousand pages. An intriguing enigma, however, remains concerning a novella Motley wrote based on the history of his own family. Although the manuscript "Remember Me to Mama" was submitted and rejected by at least one publisher, there is no copy available to Motley scholars. Apparently the Motley family has chosen to keep its contents private.

Whether Motley fulfilled his own romantic self-definition can be debated by critics of his work. Devoted to his craft, Motley did not compromise his talents. But as Blanche Gelfant has pointed out, Motley lacked some of the imagination and poetic vision of Nelson Algren, who also wrote about Chicago's underworld. Motley may never have been the heavyweight champion of Chicago writers. But he was a serious contender. On his own terms Motley produced a solid body of work, rooted in the naturalist tradition of American fiction. For that, he should not only be honored. His books deserve to be read.

Selected Bibliography

WORKS OF WILLARD MOTLEY

NOVELS AND MEMOIR
Knock on Any Door. New York: Appleton-Century, 1947.

We Fished All Night. New York: Appleton-Century—Crofts, 1951.

Let No Man Write My Epitaph. New York: Random House, 1958.

Let Noon Be Fair. New York: Putnam, 1966.

The Diaries of Willard Motley. Edited by Jerome Klinkowitz; foreword by Clarence Majors. Ames: Iowa State University Press, 1979.

SHORT STORIES AND MAGAZINE ARTICLES
"The Boy." *Ohio Motorist,* August 1938, pp. 30–31.

"'Religion' and the Handout." *Commonweal* 24, no. 20:14, 30–31 (March 10, 1939).

"The Boy Grows Up." *Ohio Motorist,* August 1939.

"Hull-House Neighborhood." *Hull-House Magazine* 1, no. 1 (November 1939), pp. 5–7.

"Pavement Portraits." *Hull-House Magazine* 1, no. 2:2–6 (December 1939).

"Handfuls." *Hull-House Magazine* 1, no. 3:9–11 (January 1940).

"The Education of a Writer." *New Idea,* winter 1961, pp. 11–13, 15, 18, 20, 26, 28. (Transcript of a lecture.)

"Let No Man Write Epitaph of Hate for His Chicago." *Chicago Sunday Sun Times,* August 11, 1963, section 2, pp. 1–4.

"The Almost White Boy." In *Soon One Morning.* Edited by Herbert Hill. New York: Knopf, 1963. Pp. 389–400.

"A Kilo of Tortillas, A Guajae of Pulque." *Rogue,* August 1964, pp. 46–48, 75.

"Give the Gentleman What He Wants." *Rogue,,* October 1964, pp. 14–16, 75.

"Christmas in Mexico." *Rogue,* December 1964.

"Death Leaves a Candle." *Rogue,* August 1965, pp. 19–22, 79.

MANUSCRIPT COLLECTIONS
Motley Collection. Swen Franklin Parson Library, Northern Illinois University, DeKalb, Ill. Loaned by the Estate of Willard Motley.

Motley Collection. Memorial Library, University of Wisconsin, Madison, Wis. Donated by the author.

James Weldon Johnson Memorial Collection. Beinecke Rare Book and Manuscript Library, Yale University Library, New Haven, Conn. Donated by the author.

CRITICAL AND BIOGRAPHICAL STUDIES

Bayliss, John F. "Nick Romano: Father and Son." *Negro American Literature Forum* 3, no. 1:18–21, 32 (spring 1969).

Bone, Robert A. *The Negro Novel in America.* Rev. ed. New Haven, Conn., and London: Yale University Press, 1965.

Bontemps, Arna. "Famous WPA Authors." *Negro Digest,* June 1950, pp. 43–47.

Breit, Harvey. "James Baldwin and Two Footnotes." In *The Creative Present: Notes on Contemporary American Fiction.* Edited by Nona Balakian and Charles Simmons. Garden City, N.Y.: Doubleday, 1963.

Eisinger, Chester E. *Fiction of the Forties.* Chicago: University of Chicago Press, 1963.

Ellison, Bob. "Three Best-Selling Authors: Conversations." *Rogue,* December 1963, pp. 20, 22, 24, 75.

Fleming, Robert E. "Willard Motley's Urban Novels." *Umoja: Southwestern Afro-American Journal* 1:15–19 (summer 1973).

———. "Willard Motley's Date of Birth: An Error Corrected." *American Notes & Queries* 13, no. 1:8–9 (September 1974).

———. "The First Nick Romano: The Origins of *Knock on Any Door.*" *MidAmerica 2,* 1975. Pp. 80–87.

———. *Willard Motley.* Boston: Twayne, 1978.

Gelfant, Blanche Houseman. *The American City Novel.* Norman: University of Oklahoma Press, 1954.

Giles, James R. "Willard Motley's Concept of 'Style' and 'Material': Some Comments Based upon the Motley Collection at the University of Wisconsin." *Studies in Black Literature* 4, no. 1:4–6 (spring 1973).

Giles, James R., and Jerome Klinkowitz. "The Emergence of Willard Motley in Black American Literature." *Negro American Literature Forum* 4, no. 2:31–34 (summer 1972).

Giles, James R., and N. Jill Weyant. "The Short Fiction of Willard Motley." *Negro American Literature Forum* 9, no. 1:3–10 (spring 1975).

Grenander, M. E. "Criminal Responsibility in *Native Son* and *Knock on Any Door.*" *American Literature* 49:221–233 (May 1977).

Hoffman, F. J. *The Modern Novel in America: 1900–1950.* Chicago: Henry Regnery, 1951.

Hughes, Carl Milton. *The Negro Novelist: A Discussion of the Writings of American Negro Novelists, 1940–1950.* New York: Citadel, 1953.

Jarrett, Thomas D. "Sociology and Imagery in a Great American Novel." *English Journal* 38:518–520 (November 1949).

Klinkowitz, Jerome, James Giles, and John T. O'Brien. "The

Willard Motley Papers at the University of Wisconsin." *Resources for American Literary Study* 2:218–273 (autumn 1972).

Major, Clarence. *The Dark and Feeling: Black American Writers and Their Work.* New York: Third Press, 1974.

Rayson, Ann L. "Prototypes for Nick Romano of *Knock on Any Door.*" *Negro American Literature Forum* 8, no. 3:248–251 (fall 1974).

"The Return of Willard Motley." *Ebony,* December 1958, pp. 84–88.

Rideout, Walter B. *The Radical Novel in the United States: 1900–1954.* Cambridge, Mass.: Harvard University Press, 1956.

Weyant, N. Jill. "Lyrical Experimentation in Willard Motley's Mexican Novel: *Let Noon Be Fair.*" *Negro American Literature Forum* 10, no. 1:95–99 (spring 1976).

———. "Willard Motley's Pivotal Novel: *Let No Man Write My Epitaph.*" *Black American Literature Forum* 11, no. 2:56–61 (summer 1977).

Wood, Charles. "*Adventure* Manuscript: New Light on Willard Motley's Naturalism?" *Negro American Literature Forum* 6, no. 2:35–38 (summer 1972).

FILMS BASED ON WORKS BY WILLARD MOTLEY

Knock on Any Door. Starring Humphrey Bogart and John Derek. Screenplay by Willard Motley and John Monks, Jr. Directed by Nicholas Ray. Columbia Pictures, 1949.

Let No Man Write My Epitaph. Starring Burl Ives and Shelley Winters. Screenplay by Willard Motley and Robert Presnell, Jr. Directed by Philip Leacock. Columbia Pictures, 1960.

ONLINE SOURCES

"Willard Motley Collection." Northern Illinois University Rare Books and Special Collections. http://www.ulib.niu.edu/rbsc/motley/htm Posted 3/25/2005.

ANNA QUINDLEN
(1952—)

Angela Garcia

A POPULAR AUTHOR grounded in feminist ideals, Anna Quindlen remains one of the few American writers to have succeeded in the twin worlds of journalism and fiction. Since the late 1980s, her books—written in a variety of different genres, fiction and nonfiction alike—have consistently graced the *New York Times* best-seller lists, and in 1992 she won the Pulitzer Prize for Commentary. Quindlen's emphasis on the home or family environment under duress, along with her remarkable ability to humanize serious sociopolitical issues, are the foundation of her novels' importance in contemporary American literature; as social and feminist realism, they push the limits of domestic fiction.

Quindlen began her career as a reporter at the *New York Post* and *New York Times*, but quickly gained recognition and a popular following as the singular *New York Times* columnist writing on the domestic life, especially motherhood, in a weekly essay titled "Life in the 30s." Later, she brought her sensibility to bear on national affairs, as a syndicated political columnist: with "Public & Private," Quindlen became only the third woman columnist on the *Times* op-ed page (the first two women wrote about foreign affairs). She was also the first woman named deputy metropolitan editor of that newspaper.

Deeply influenced by the feminist movement and dedicated to exploring issues that reach women as well as men, she left the *Times* in 1995 to concentrate on her fiction writing. In 1999, however, she returned to the journalism world, writing a biweekly essay for *Newsweek*'s "The Last Word" column, on the magazine's final page.

A self-proclaimed liberal, feminist, and Catholic, Quindlen regards the "women's" issues she has explored throughout the decades as basic human and social dilemmas. Long derided by the political right as ill-informed and irrational in her arguments, while respected as a champion of poor and minority rights by the left, Quindlen's writing has been prized for highlighting the human interest story in issues ranging from abortion to the death penalty. After the terrorist attacks of 11 September 2001, Quindlen's was a major voice in expressing what America had lost.

Today Quindlen regularly engages with thousands of American readers, in what she has spoken of as an intimate conversation, through her columns. Similarly, with their striking detail of individual experience, her novels define, illuminate, and personalize issues such as cancer care, the right to die, and domestic abuse.

LIFE AND CAREER

Catholicism and feminism both marked Quindlen's early years, and these influences have shaped her opinions as well as her life. She was born in a Philadelphia suburb on 8 July 1952 to an Irish-American father and Italian-American mother, Robert and Prudence Quindlen. Her father worked as a management consultant and her mother was a homemaker. Anna Quindlen was the eldest of five children, and an avid reader. She attended a private Catholic school for ten years and developed a great respect for the nuns who were her teachers there, whom she remembers fondly in her writings.

Both as a Catholic and a feminist, Quindlen has long been considered a spokesperson, even a watchdog, in the public eye. In a 1991 *Publishers Weekly* interview with Sybil Steinberg, Quindlen asserts her representative voice and vigilance, and she hints at the power implicit in the media to shape public opinion: Quindlen suggests that although few Catholics have stepped forward to voice public criticism of the Catholic

Church, "They ought to know that I'm speaking for the majority of Catholic women."

After Catholic school, Quindlen attended Barnard College (then the women's college of Columbia University) as an English literature major, but she left school to nurse her dying mother, and then, when Quindlen was nineteen, her young adulthood was shaken by her mother's death from cancer. Throughout her career as a journalist and novelist, Quindlen has written and spoken repeatedly of the depths to which she was struck by this loss and how it continues to impact her life. Indeed, Quindlen has ascribed her "keen sense of mortality" directly to her mother's death and has recounted how her initial fury of ambition stemmed from this experience. Furthermore, the loss has framed her view of the family structure, as witnessed in her novels, and given her personal insight into issues such as terminal illness and care, including the right to die. Her 1994 novel, *One True Thing,* draws poignantly from this care-giving experience, and her 1998 novel, *Black and Blue,* features home nursing as the protagonist's profession.

But in terms of social movements, Quindlen has referred to feminism as the most profound sociopolitical influence on her thinking and career. She has spoken of it as a "sea change" in her life. As a girl, she says, she had the choice of becoming a nun or a housewife—but in her formative years, as the feminist movement formed and thrived, more choices fell open to her, as her "birthright."

One of the hallmarks of her columns has always been the assumption of a sisterhood of women together with her gratefulness to this sisterhood. Quindlen has written that women's lives are determined by social conditions as well as character, and that while she herself was born at a time when she was lucky enough to reap the benefits of feminism, women born a few decades earlier were not. In the preface to her 1988 volume *Living Out Loud,* an essay titled "In the Beginning," she contemplates how feminism would have changed the life of her homemaker mother, confined to a time of "roles and rules".

Quindlen's journalism and fiction routinely scrutinize the changes in the social system that followed, and the changes that have yet to come—especially as reflected in the lives of women. Her pieces draw on experiences from motherhood, examine careers such as Hillary Clinton's, interview homeless mothers, and examine the public and private aspects of abortion ("Not a Womb in the House"); they are studies in the social, legal, and political repercussions on the individual.

In the *Publishers Weekly* interview with Steinberg, Quindlen commented on her role as a "fervent feminist" and, in retrospect, on the limitations of the movement. She claims the family sphere as the litmus test to gauge the effectiveness of feminism. In order for there to be genuine equality, she argues, the family dynamic—namely, the husband–wife relationship itself—must change.

Quindlen had begun working as a part-time reporter for the *New York Post* when she was eighteen; this became a full-time position by 1974, when she graduated from Barnard. Quindlen was a freshman in college when she met her husband, Gerald Krovatin, who was attending Columbia; they married in 1978. He subsequently pursued a career as a defense attorney. Her own illustrious, controversial, and award-winning career at the *New York Times* began after she was offered a job there in 1977.

Quindlen's rise at the *Times* was marked by fervent ambition and remarkable for its rapid and precocious success. In 1974, during the heyday of the women's revolution, six women filed a class-action lawsuit against the Times, demanding equal rights in hiring, pay, and promotion. Between 1974 and the year the suit was settled, 1978, Quindlen writes, women—including herself—were hired for positions in all departments.

At twenty-two, she recalls in the essay "In the Beginning," when she first expressed the wish to write her own column, her editor replied that she "hadn't lived enough to be qualified for 'living out loud.' " After a stint as a police and city hall reporter, she was offered the paper's "About New York" column on a regular basis in 1981, and in 1983, she became the first woman appointed deputy metropolitan editor at the *Times*.

When Quindlen told the *Times* that she had decided to leave her job there in order to spend more time with her firstborn son, Quin (born in 1983), the paper responded by offering her the chance to write a column from home. "Life in the 30s" soon became a nationally syndicated column, in which she reported from the domestic front as a thirty-something mother. In 1985 a second son, Christopher, was born. With "Life in the 30s," a new voice was represented on the "Home" page (also a new section, courtesy of the feminist movement) of the *New York Times* as Quindlen began her exploration of the personal yet universal experience of the family. Some of these essays were collected in *Living Out Loud*.

In 1988 the *Times* deputy publisher Arthur Sulzberger, Jr., offered her the possibility of a more political column, "Public & Private," one that would make her only the third woman columnist on the op-ed page in the history of the *New York Times* and would win her the Pulitzer Prize for Commentary in 1992. The concept behind the column was to investigate how public policy impacted individual lives and, conversely, how individual lives reflected or reacted to public policy. From these columns Quindlen assembled the 1993 collection *Thinking Out Loud*. While working on her second novel, in 1995, she finally bade her farewell to the *New York Times*, announcing her intention to devote her career to fiction writing.

In the years that followed, Quindlen went on to write highly acclaimed and best-selling novels, but she did not leave journalism for good. In 1999 she was offered a choice spot with *Newsweek*, producing a column every other week for "The Last Word," alternating with columnist George Will. Columns from both the *Times* and *Newsweek*—"Public & Private" and "The Last Word," 1993 through 2004—make up her 2004 collection of commentary, *Loud and Clear*.

Quindlen's novels usually reflect the pressures on women characters in tense domestic situations: a girl struggling through family crises in the 1960s; a young woman immersed in home care for a mother with cancer; a middle-aged woman fleeing, with her young son, from an abusive marriage—and forced to make a new home in a new place. In the 2002 novel *Blessings*, an old woman revisits her conflicted past through memory; after the miracle of a baby enters her makeshift family, she is compelled to rethink events that have shaped her present.

Quindlen has also explored the realm of nonfiction—through guides to life, or self-help books. *A Short Guide to a Happy Life* (2000) and *Being Perfect* (2005)—the second aimed particularly at women—offer pithy advice toward valuing the small things in life and learning to accept oneself. These, as well as Quindlen's collaborations with Nick Kelsh on the coffee-table photo books *Naked Babies* (1996) and *Siblings* (1998)—she provides the commentary for each—garnered pleasant but, predictably, less serious reviews. Quindlen honored her writing influences with *How Reading Changed My Life* (1998), and combined literary observations with travel writing in *Imagined London: A Tour of the World's Greatest Fictional City* (2004). As a further testament to her versatility, she is the author of two books of children's fiction, *The Tree That Came to Stay* (1992), and *Happily Ever After* (1997).

In addition to the Pulitzer, Quindlen has been awarded several honorary degrees and prizes. Among them, Columbia University honored her with its Meyer Berger prize for the best writing about New York as well as its University Medal of Excellence.

Quindlen and her husband are the parents of two sons, Quin and Christopher, and a daughter, Maria. They divide their time between homes in New York City and Cherry Valley, Pennsylvania.

"LIFE IN THE 30S"

While she is esteemed as a novelist, journalism remains at the root of Quindlen's writing career. Journalism served as the first true vehicle for Quindlen's writing: the institution in which she practiced the economy of language, ear for dialogue, and knack for striking details that have informed her fiction. Indeed, she often describes the newsroom as one of the places she feels most at home.

In the 1988 collection *Living Out Loud*, Quindlen gathered *Times* pieces from her weekly column "Life in the 30s." These popular columns, as represented in the book, concentrate especially on the home life experiences of wife and mother (although there is a section on Catholicism) and are unabashedly domestic in sphere. "Life is in the dishes," she has philosophized. Quindlen regularly quotes her two very young sons, and invites the reader into an intimate, often funny, family atmosphere within the pages—the mostly comic, at times tragic, frenzy that emerges with toddler care. In one column, the disheveled tears in the doctor's office are the mother's. These pieces had the lightning effect of legitimizing the trials of stay-at-home motherhood and, through publication at the prestigious *New York Times*, soon reached national syndication.

The essays also gleefully depict the very real pleasures of seemingly mundane experience with the author's account, for example, of enjoying Prince Andrew and Sarah Ferguson's royal wedding with peanut M & Ms. Another column humorously recounts the state of being pregnant in New York City, where Quindlen is alternately harassed about the baby's gender, ignored on the subway, and protected by a posse of other women (an example of the sisterhood of women evinced also in later, more political writings). These instances of household wit, so relevant to mothers of the last few decades, are sometimes reminiscent of the columns of the late Erma Bombeck: sharp-tongued and bombastic, not hesitating at a bit of slapstick. And friendly. It is as though the reader were across the table in a café.

Stylistically, the columns gather force as Quindlen finds her signature metaphor. Again and again, she effectively uses a specific image to encapsulate her theme. Lightning bugs, for instance, become a poignant reminder of the hot summers of childhood—like Marcel Proust's madeleine, ushering in a whole spectrum of memories. In another deadpan piece, the purchase of an air-conditioning unit turns into a bone of contention between the wife and the "the other adult in this family," as the writer incredulously suffers through an unbearably hot summer with a spouse firmly opposed to the acquisition of an effective cooling mechanism for their row house.

Quindlen's unifying, largely cheerful reflections on the trials of wifedom and motherhood placed her solidly in the mainstream, and increased her following. But a smaller number of the columns venture into the blatantly political. These early columns are notable for their firm stance on social issues and foreshadow topics in her *Newsweek* columns and her novels: homelessness, birth control, abortion, rape. Although she outspokenly places herself in the liberal camp, as a voice of the historically underrepresented, she does not always take the predictably leftist or politically correct point of view. For instance, one essay describes how, when a woman pursued by a man shows up pounding on Quindlen's door, she hesitates to allow her inside; instead she ends up enraged, not by the potential rapist or the situation, but by the strange woman herself. Thus she condemns herself as an example of the isolated self-protection of the city dweller—insulating oneself, keeping one's distance, maintaining a fierce independence at all costs. The moral foundation Quindlen lays for herself in the columns includes self-examination and honesty over mere gesture or self-congratulation.

This willingness to question herself—indeed, even on the ultracontroversial topic of abortion, is a trademark of Quindlen's. In contemplating the famous antiabortion image of a fetus in utero, with its tiny hand scratching its face, an abortion column also illustrates some of the fierce honesty that is typical of Quindlen's best work. As a mother, she includes this image to admit the depth and complexity of the issue and to openly acknowledge a never-easy ambivalence; the answer to such difficult questions is never black or white. And yet, the column does not end equivocally or ambivalently. Ultimately, whether despite or owing to the struggle of conscience, the writer does take a stand. Nearly, but admittedly not quite, hooked by the sentimental picture on the screen, Quindlen casts her vote for, she says, the "rational": the living mother's choice over the terrible pain of the unwanted child.

While the final columns in the book return to Quindlen's family, others continue to explore the world reflected in families outside her own. In interviewer mode, Quindlen visits a family-planning clinic, reporting back on the girls' casual, but telling, opinions and attitudes. In a muted but painful column, she speaks with a couple whose six-year-old son has disappeared. Two more pieces openly discuss the uncertainty surrounding AIDS infection and explore the problems inherent in the death penalty as revenge, despite Quindlen's empathy for victims' families.

Thus, despite her being one of the youngest columnists to ever work at the *Times*, a fearlessness informs Quindlen's direct language as it admits even the visceral—those emotional factors that may or may not cloud judgment. By affirming the gut reaction, then stepping back for a more rational analysis, she aims to include readers of all political persuasions.

"PUBLIC & PRIVATE"

With her column "Public & Private," launched in 1988, Quindlen presented both a stronger feminist stance and a more definitively Catholic identity, despite being appalled in many ways by the policies of her own church. Quindlen has always been intensely aware of her exceptional status in an overwhelmingly male field of columnists, and of the criticism levied against the particular, the feminine, the personal, and the anecdotal in her columns—criticism that appears through letters she receives in the mail or via email, or in the more formal criticism of the book review. (The column that drew the most mail featured her decision to refuse an amniocentesis when pregnant with her third child.) In her introduction to *Thinking Out Loud*, a selection of those columns, Quindlen contends that it appears secondary, even inferior, when she introduces doubt or the personal into her journalistic voice. At the same time, to write in this feminine or feminist vein, in political columns no less, creates a counterbalance to a long male tradition of stolid, impersonal, even formal writing—always utterly certain of itself and its opinions. Quindlen's voice, although sometimes strident, freely utilizes a more self-questioning style.

Featured on the *New York Times* op-ed page, the "Public & Private" column resembled "Life in the 30s" in that it also regularly introduced the element of human interest; thus her discussions of potentially abstract social issues such as homelessness or abortion quickly flashed to more personal accounts, of a homeless woman speaking her mind or a woman who has lost her own mother to a botched abortion, speaking about how she misses her.

Gays in the military, Rodney King, same-sex marriage, euthanasia, Anita Hill, Robert McNamara's apology for the Vietnam War—and to a lesser extent, motherhood, family, and children—all are subjects open to examination in Quindlen's more politically titled column. She spends several columns assessing the policies of George Bush and the Gulf War, and most especially, she devotes column space to the debate about abortion, which she sees as the most controversial social question of the 1990s. It is the abortion issue that, she states, most accurately reflects the two sides in the name of her column, "Public & Private." With the 1973 Supreme Court decision in *Roe vs. Wade*, she attests, the private became public; and in the early 1990s, the significance of this very public issue was evident, for example, in Supreme Court appointments that were largely based on the justices' positions on the controversy.

Some critics took umbrage with the column for its tameness or niceness, despite Quindlen's feminist stance. Susie Linfield of the *Los Angeles Times* wrote:

> In her column "Public and Private," which ran in the *New York Times* for five years and won a Pulitzer Prize, Anna Quindlen exemplified the essence of a very nice feminist. She consistently took positions that were reasonable and fair, arguing in favor of justice and equality. But hers was a feminism that was essentially safe—for cozy suburbanites, for corporate profits, for life as we know it.
> (p. E6)

Quindlen's abortion stance might not qualify as "safe." In her columns, Quindlen consistently describes herself as "an advocate of legal abortion" and expresses her frustration with "pro-life" and "pro-choice" labels, viewing them as oversimplifications and eschewing their use in her columns. Instead, cognizant of the power media attaches to labels, she refers to these two groups literally in her columns, as those for legal abortion and those against legal abortion—not merely an academic correction, but an important clarification of terms and a refusal to play the other side's word game.

The abortion columns include explicit commentary on Quindlen's own Catholicism (necessarily, as one of the issues she views as interlocked with her integral faith) and motherhood; they readily admit and examine the author's own ambivalence with the issue's massive complexity. Several pieces explore a range of related issues including Operation Rescue's male members' belief in the subjugation of women; "abortion orphans," who have lost their mothers to botched abortions; and the various views of Catholics on this topic, many of whom support the right to legal abortion.

Conservative publications, while fairly quiet regarding Quindlen's views on the family sphere, have harshly reviewed Quindlen's leftist political stances and their rationale, and readers have sometimes challenged her Catholicism. In a 1994 essay for *Commonweal*, Margaret Steinfels mirrors Quindlen's intimate tone as she critiques the columnist's latest fulmination against the Catholic Church. The church had issued a statement that Catholics for a Free Choice, a Washington, D.C., pro-choice advocacy group, was not an authentic Catholic organization, and Quindlen—as a Catholic favoring legal abortion—had blasted the statement. Steinfels counters with a criticism suggesting that Quindlen has evolved into a "predictable" newspaperwoman:

> When she wrote her weekly "In the Thirties" column, Anna Quindlen had sensible and witty views of husbands, children, and the domestic environs; the one Times voice on family life not in thrall to Anna Freud or Planned Parenthood. She subsequently moved to her present perch, "Public and Private" on the op-ed page, where her somnambulant colleagues needed a dusting up. She did the job. I came to think of Anna Quindlen as a sister mouth.

But two columns a week take their toll; a certain predictability set in. Quindlen, nonetheless, remains an influential voice who, for better or worse, shapes a portion of the public discussion about Catholicism. And when she returned to the op-ed page from a leave of absence this last fall, there was a sprinkling of new ideas, a sense of new energy, even a hint that her brand of liberalism needed a little rethinking.

But then she went and wrote one of her totally predictable columns: she attacked the Catholic bishops for drawing a line (*New York Times*, November 18, 1993). In her essay, Steinfels joins other conservative critics in charging Quindlen with ignoring inconvenient facts; Steinfels goes on to defend the Church for its carefully worded and—Steinfels feels—innocuous statement about the Catholic pro-choice group.

In another column—the piece that Quindlen chooses as the final word in the collection *Thinking Out Loud*—Quindlen returns to family, and fierce mother mode, with an essay on her third child, her then two-year-old daughter. Maria, her mother writes, is a fiery personality whom, the writer confirms, has given her mother her righteous anger back. In this final piece, Quindlen allows herself a primal, maternal, protective rage, energized by the fact that she does not want her daughter growing up in a sexist, "two—tiered" world.

LOUD AND CLEAR

Quindlen's 2004 collection of commentary, *Loud and Clear,* combines columns from *Newsweek*'s "The Last Word" with previously unpublished "Public & Private" columns and takes an interesting leap forward, presenting the reader with the voice of a now best—selling novelist and veteran columnist, a voice of utmost confidence. The expression of the ardent fighter in Quindlen remains consistent, as she noticeably repeats the word "loud" in this, her third title of commentary, intimating a deeper luminosity and confidence in the writing. The subheadings for the columns also seem weighty, encompassing basic human elements—"Heart," "Mind," "Body," "Voice," and "Soul"—for a reason that quickly becomes apparent: this is Quindlen's first collection of columns published post–11 September 2001.

Quindlen, in the book's preface, begins by introducing the largest event to shape her journalism, September 11th, and several columns dedicate themselves to observing and recording the many strata of this event, as they work to say the seemingly unsayable from that date onward.

Before the September 11th commentary (under "Soul"), Quindlen examines an array of other social and political topics, some a reprise from earlier columns. In a piece on the color line, as she terms it, the writer details instances of racial profiling (African American men) and dismisses the myth of the integrated neighborhood. Another essay advocates tighter gun control, calling attention to the "widows and wounded" doing this work. In a column about the insidiousness of tobacco, Quindlen features a former model, a longtime smoker, who now is forced speak through a hole in her throat. Quindlen's language is blunt and deliberately shocking in forcing the reader to see the link to cancer.

Quindlen also forcefully continues to criticize the Catholic Church, which had become rife with the scandal of pedophilia, for its remoteness from the reality of its parishioners' lives even before this controversy. She condemns the Church for continuing to judge families it cannot understand, creating a dangerous and unhealthy climate she deems a pathology.

In the "Heart" section, a column denounces both presidents George W. Bush and Bill Clinton for the practice of execution in their states— Bush for his 131—inmate executions and Clinton for ordering the execution of a mentally ill man. Quindlen also devotes columns to the cause of children. She advocates for hungry children and laments the sad situation in which Americans need to help, yet believe hunger does not and cannot exist in this country. In the face of the overly scheduled child of recent decades, she also yearns for the era of unscheduled time, remembering summers when there was a time for leisure and creativity at home, for playing in the street and making up the rules—rather than the organized, structured sports and classes in which the middle- and upper-class children of America now find themselves immersed.

In "Body," Quindlen returns the reader to a range of general interest topics concerning women, as well as more blatantly feminist topics. In keeping with her spokesperson status, representative of a generation, her language utilizes the first person plural to describe herself and all the women shaped and changed from what she calls the greatest social revolution in recent decades. (Conservative critics, meanwhile, have derided Quindlen for her assumption of a voice for all women.) The kaleidoscope of women's subjects include the author's homage to Jackie Kennedy on the occasion of her death; sexual assault and media hype; and the dangers that were ultimately discovered about hormone therapy for menopause.

Abortion is approached more heavy-heartedly than heavy-handedly, but in the same vein as columns in her previous collections. The quality of ironic observation remains. Quindlen does not tone down her wry, bitter observance of the "old (Congress)men" deciding on abortion law, in a piece sharply titled "Not a Womb in the House." Although she confesses herself weary of the abortion issue, Quindlen continues to argue, in the manner of someone doomed to repeat herself, that women will continue to find a way to end pregnancy, as they have done throughout history and throughout the world. And, she offers simply, the American voter can choose to make this life-threatening for her or not.

But the abortion issue seems overshadowed by the eerie outlines of the twin towers of the World Trade Center, now looming large in their absence. Almost all her writings in "Soul" struggle to comprehend the immensity of this event in the city she feels most at home, the city with which Quindlen has long been linked as a writer, through her career at the *Times*. In the face of this life-changing event, she examines its effects on her own and on the American psyche; in one piece about the immediate aftermath of September 11th, for example, she calmly explains to readers that in the new America where they find themselves, control is an illusion.

More important, the September 11th columns force her to summon a new reserve of empathy and connection. The essays do not examine foreign affairs and are largely apolitical. Bringing her sense of mortality to bear on the most public and yet intimate event of her career, Quindlen focuses instead on the personal loss to America.

In the September 11th pieces, Quindlen does what she has learned to do best; she attaches names and histories and faces to statistics, for powerful and moving results-evoking the girl with the engagement ring who was visiting the ninety-second floor, or the couple on the plane with the two-year-old girl. Quindlen meditates on the loss of innocence in America, and at the same time, by personalizing this political event, she invites the reader to regain a sense of balance and humanity in the wake of the tragedy that has passed.

As a reporter and analyst at Ground Zero, Quindlen's voice also takes on a certain largeness; just as a preacher's eulogy brings ritual comfort at a funeral service, the more communal quality of Quindlen's tone here seeks to try to make sense of the event for her readers. One stylistic trademark that emerges more sharply from these columns than from earlier ones is the potent final summing up, in which Quindlen presents the lynchpin of her argument. Quindlen is a master at the eloquent final stroke, hammering her point with a simple yet effective phrase or image. And although her words might be sometimes carried away with their own music or verge on melodrama, the columns more often than not retain a nonpartisan, secular urgency. At best, the language of the concluding remark not only crystallizes the argument but stuns.

Criticism of the essays varied. *Kirkus Reviews* offered a mixed, but generally underwhelmed reaction, objecting to Quindlen's predictable political stance:

> Light, appealing, and devoid of nutritional value, this selection of *New York Times* and *Newsweek* essays dating from the early 1990s to last year doesn't demand that readers think much. Since the author's opinions are never surprising, they eventually become background noise. This is a shame, because much of what Quindlen has to say is valuable, if shopworn. She fulminates against cigarettes, the death penalty, and the abuse of women—all worthy targets, though Quindlen's garden-variety critiques will change few minds.

THE NOVELS

As her journalism has been recognized for its truth-seeking, so has Quindlen's fiction. Critics have noted that while much of the power in Quindlen's writing derives from her eye and ear for human interest, sharpened in the newsroom, its weaknesses might also be traced to the newsy style—in particular, its lack of subtlety and surfeit of commentary. Yet the powerful contradictions that enrich the voice remain—Quindlen as ordinary activist, sentimental cynic, self-examining absolutist—contradictions that sometimes energize, sometimes unfocus, the writing. Most significantly, the fiction genre allows the author more space to examine and give human dimension to issues from her nonfiction—including cancer and elder care, domestic abuse, and child rearing—in the families she portrays. Her prose, in effect, demands that the reader recognize this human dimension at the heart of every social issue—and give full credence to it.

One theme that unites these novels is loss. Quindlen's fiction often features the loss of a family member: grandfather, father, husband, son, mother, brother. Sometimes there is a felt absence of a family member, or a distance or estrangement from a mother, father, sister, or daughter. Entrapment serves as another motif of Quindlen's novels. An illegitimate pregnancy forces marriage, before the feminist era, in two of her novels. In other novels, illness and domestic abuse present restricted domestic environments, a sense of enclosure that is nearly claustrophobic. Finally, the female protagonist of Quindlen's novels generally attains some sense of enlightenment, no matter how small.

The critical reception for Quindlen's fiction, though largely laudatory, has been mixed. Her novels have been praised for their pace, economy with language, effective characterization, and realistic dialogue, as well as their riveting stories, while criticized for their narrative structure, sentimentality, and tidy endings.

The reading public might beg to differ. The novels' consistent debuts on the New York Times best-seller lists, along with unflagging sales, indicate that the lay reader is happy with these page-turners and that essentially, they make for an immensely satisfying read.

OBJECT LESSONS

Often called a coming-of-age novel, *Object Lessons* (1991), Quindlen's first book of fiction, stands out from the novels that followed in that its protagonist, Maggie Scanlon, is a girl maturing into a woman: she is a twelve-year-old in a mixed Irish American–Italian American household during one long summer in the 1960s. Her mother, Connie—the only Italian marrying into a very Irish American family—serves as the novel's other protagonist, whose equally important search for independence and resolution—her own "growing up"—mirrors her daughter's questioning, confusion, and hope. Quindlen introduces a large and fairly complex group of characters, some more trapped than others, in Kenwood, a Westchester County suburb that borders the Bronx.

But the small fishbowl contains a very big fish. Quindlen portrays Maggie and Connie, and Connie's husband, Tom, as virtual puppets of the family's patriarch, Tom's father, John Scanlon, who controls the money and so controls the family members. The family setting is actually the extended family, the Irish clan. (Maggie's Italian grandfather, a caretaker at a cemetery in the Bronx, serves only as a quiet and somewhat frustrated counterpoint to all things Irish.) Above all, John is Maggie's gruff Irish grandfather, and she his favorite grandchild, despite the recurring racist allegations that his son has married a "guinea." Yet he acts as a scourge upon her parents. Indeed, John exacerbates the pressure on Tom and Connie's marriage by trying to control their life as fully as possible; he has arranged his son's (all his sons') job and now wishes to move Tom's rapidly growing family—the fifth baby on the way—into a new and bigger house.

For their parts, Tom and Connie work to resist John's influence. As the strange and new encroach on daughter and mother (and also on Tom, who must deal eventually with his father's death after years of dealing with his terrible power), this is represented by a housing development being built around their old house. As the frames are built, Connie befriends an old acquaintance, Joey Martinelli, a carpenter working on the development, with whom she nearly begins an affair. Meanwhile Maggie is struggling with the desertion of her best friend, Debbie Malone; with the vague absence of her mother; and with her own maturation—her first bikini, her first interest in a boy, and questions of identity.

While her mother, Connie, is figuratively playing with fire, risking her marriage through her deepening interest in Martinelli, at the same time, Maggie's friends, and sometimes Maggie—in a futile attempt to impress Debbie and win her back—resort to actually playing with fire; in fact, they are setting matches to the construction, playing an adolescent game of arson, as if to bar any changes from taking place. (The parents, as appropriate to the time period perhaps, and certainly to Maggie's psyche, are set apart from their daughter's world.)

Gradually John Scanlon's stroke, hospitalization, and death throw the family into a further tailspin as they struggle to deal with sudden weakness in a man many despised, or at least resented, for his larger-than-life quality, his massive strength. Maggie is at a loss, calling up memories of better times with her grandfather; Tom wishes to battle his mixture of feelings alone; and Connie, especially in the deathbed scene with her father-in-law, learns to accept her marriage and growing family, and says no to her flirt with infidelity. While she is pregnant for the fifth time (in a realistic nod to the Catholicism of the 1960s, Connie and Tom unsuccessfully use the rhythm method for birth control), she asserts some independence in finally learning to drive (the driving instructor being her almost-lover).

The ultimate consequences of playing with fire serve as a wake-up call to both Maggie and her mother, bringing Maggie out of her confused stupor. Although she has sensed and seen something of her mother's affair, she senses too that her mother has returned to the family. Connie, after nearly agreeing to sleep with Martinelli, finally realizes the potential damage to her marriage. She learns to value that which she has in Tom and all his extended family, and she begins to speak her mind with her sisters-in-law, with whom as the only Italian, she has always been the black sheep. The daughter and the mother notice something of their similarities and draw more closely together in a kind of silent understanding.

Quindlen's novel resonates with lyricism and captures both thought and dialogue in her characters, who are shackled by the mores of their time. But there are hints of those mores beginning to crumble, of sexual liberation, personified in the character of Helen Malone, who seems to set herself apart from the girls around her who get pregnant and marry young. Not an ideal moral character but a mysterious and beautiful girl, she moves to Manhattan, and as a sort of teenage bohemian, wears daring miniskirts and sleeps around with men. Dressed in a semi-transparent white leotard, she also sings in an experimental theater production. Her attachment to Maggie (it is hinted that they are both special) serves as an inspiration and revelation for the younger girl—a signal that she may not be destined to live a traditional married life like so many of the rest of the girls; it is good, Helen claims, to be unsure of what she will be doing in twenty years.

Object Lessons, as the title suggests, dramatizes the process of learning, and its lessons, for mother and daughter both, are about living. Ambitious in its handling of a large group of strong characters, Quindlen's novel departs from a typical girl's coming-of-age story—for instance, Carson McCullers' 1946 novel *The Member of the Wedding*—through its equally weighted observation of a mother's coming of age, in spite of a growing brood from which she feels distanced after the babyhood stage.

As with Quindlen's columns, her first novel attracted heated analysis, with critics running the gamut on their judgments, deeming the book wise or condemning it as contrived or generic. Some noted the implausibility of the ending, with its neat resolution of Connie's marital dissatisfaction and Maggie's daughterly loneliness.

ONE TRUE THING

Quindlen's second novel, published in 1994, is distinctively powerful and, despite the stoicism of the narrator, impassioned. It creates an extraordinarily intimate depiction of a woman dying of cancer and her daughter's bearing witness to that dying, as she devotes herself to her mother's care.

The depth and power of her second novel lie in the realism of the problematic mother-daughter relationship, finally uttering its mystery—how even those as intimate as family are ultimately unknowable to each other. While the novel's first part creates an atmosphere of drama and tragedy, the second part adds the element of suspense, examining the moral dilemma of the right to die. Structured as a long flashback framed by the present, *One True Thing* provokes the reader from the onset. Quindlen seems to spare the reader little in detailing her devastating account of a mother, Kate Gulden, dying at home, of cancer, at the age of forty-six. With an eye for the wrenching word or gesture, Quindlen uses deft brushstrokes of character to paint the cancer's emotional and physical progression in Kate, as she moves from wheelchair, to hospital bed, to the teary-eyed humiliation of diapers.

Quindlen captures this quiet disintegration with an aloof, sometimes shocking clarity. Some details capture Kate's shining spirit, as on the night Ellen and her father wheel her smiling, triumphant homemaker mother to see what she knows to be her last Christmas market, and to decorate her last tree there. The beauty of the tradition, and of her last giant Christmas tree lit for all to see and admire in the public square, prove her final victory before the sickness dominates her life. This is a woman for whom home, husband, and her "babies" have been everything, a complete vocation. Indeed, Ellen painstakingly enumerates the pillows she has embroidered, the chairs she has refinished, the cribs she has stenciled.

By the end she is querulous with the need for more morphine, reduced to a "half life," aghast at the indignity. Unable anymore to feed herself, to move from her bed in the living room, Kate begs to be released, and, after an intense and moving night with her daughter, and then husband, takes a last, rattling breath.

Yet above all, Kate Gulden emerges as a heroic character, uncomplaining, bright with "feverish gaiety," even as the flame begins to go out. For Ellen, she also appears much more intelligent, courageous, and wise than her daughter ever would have expected or imagined, intimating knowledge of her husband's affairs, and, at the end, apparently deciding to take her own life, and death, in her hands.

Quindlen portrays the college-age daughter, Ellen Gulden, as a piece of work herself. An ambitious New Yorker, never having identified with or connected much with her mother, she engages in a mostly silent, hostile struggle with her philandering, and largely absent, professor father, George, who extensively and studiously avoids the reality of his wife Kate's terminal illness. This is the parent with whom she wholly identifies and has always striven to please. When she is not lashing out in anger, she is simply consumed with her mother's care. Immersed in the family triangle, Ellen does connect at least somewhat with her mother, especially when they form their own book club (books, it turns out, her mother has already read), before the cancer has really taken its toll. Her anger and coldness, however, continue to break against those around her, and in part 2 of the novel they return, only to fuel the townspeople's accusations of her as she is tried for the death of her mother from a mysterious overdose of morphine.

The second part of the story has been viewed by many critics as a distracting subplot less believable or essential than the mother-daughter relationship of the first. It unfolds the mystery of that release from pain—as the daughter, with the rabid media at her heels, is blamed for her mother's death by euthanasia. Hardened and silent, the daughter takes refuge in a former teacher's house and, from an unexpressed but fierce devotion to her father, takes the rap for what she believes her father did to her mother (she sees him spoon-feeding her mother shortly before her mother's death). But they never speak about it. A trial is held in the small town. Ellen, though seen as cold and heartless by others, is found innocent, but the silence—and misunderstanding—between herself and her father continues. Her mother's death, in effect, creates a rift between them neither can cross.

For Ellen, in muted grief for her mother, believing in her father's guilt, a chance reconciliation with the father brings the ironic twist of the epilogue. At the end Quindlen's novel is many things: a medical journal, a coming-of-age story, an ultimately ambiguous whodunit. But on its most basic level, the novel explores the family and the mystery of how we can be so strange and so familiar to each other at once—how we can know and yet not know the other at all.

The narrator is forced, at the end, to acknowledge how deeply she and her father have each shaped her mother into their own ideal image. (Indeed, Kate comes close to fulfilling her husband's ideal when she essentially admits to her furious, frustrated daughter Ellen that she has known about her husband's infidelity all along, but has decided to accept a compromise in her marriage rather than confront her husband.)

Despite her brusqueness, for Ellen, years later, as an adolescent psychiatrist, the aching loss of her mother continues, whether for a false or real maternal image. For as she states in the novel, the mother is more than love; she is everything.

Frederick Busch, in the *New York Times Book Review*, criticizes the flatness and inconsistency of the narrative voice as having no resonance, but points to Kate Gulden as the most realized character in the novel, despite its "stylistic lapses." He sums up what he sees as *One True Thing*'s strengths and limitations:

> We are united by our difficulty in finding a language for mourning, whether we seek it to comfort others or ourselves, or to assuage our need to make a reckoning with the dead. In all of this, we seek to say the unsayable, and that is as good a definition of literary art as I know.
>
> Anna Quindlen's second novel will be sought out by a lot of readers and will keep them involved. It

will speak for the experience of many of us, but not on the deepest level. It will provoke some tears, some nods of recognition and some smiles. It will, at times, feel like a good conversation about daughters and parents. But it will not offer a way of saying what had seemed unsayable to and about and for the dead.

(p. 11)

Meryl Streep, William Hurt, and Renee Zellweiger starred in a 1998 screen adaptation of *One True Thing*.

BLACK AND BLUE

Quindlen's highly acclaimed 1998 novel *Black and Blue* creates its own sense of intimate, yet nightmarish family atmosphere. Fran Benedetto's marriage and family has disintegrated, after she finally acts to escape the physical abuse she has suffered at the hands of her police-officer husband, Bobby. According to the rules of their protection program, the mother and her ten-year-old son Robert must take on false identities, leaving their home in Brooklyn to begin their lives again anonymously in a small town in Florida. *Black and Blue* presents an environment of loss and subsequent entrapment, but also duty—this time, a mother's sense of duty toward her son. Indeed, her son is the force that drives Franny to flee to survive.

Again, Quindlen does not paint her characters black or white. Fran loves her husband and openly remembers their sexual chemistry as well as his sweetness to their son, at the same time as she remembers his repeated degradation of her, his fist striking her face, or the mark of his fingertips like a tattoo on her upper arm.

The characters are lost at first in the alien Florida setting, as they make a new home in a strange apartment; the novel is filled with flashbacks, sometimes exploring Bobby's past, sometimes attesting to Fran's deep pain as her son overhears the violence in his home. Soon a pattern begins to emerge in their new life; but there remains for Fran the loneliness of their new, box-like environs; the pain she surmises from Robert's silence; and always the overriding fear that her husband will come looking for them.

Still, for Fran, these aches are preferable to exposing her son to his father's violence against her, always compounded with lies that her bruises are from her clumsiness, because of yet another accident.

Under the rules of the protection program that has placed her in Florida, which she discovered through her work in Brooklyn as an emergency room nurse (where she is witness to other victims of domestic abuse), she must have no communication with anyone from her past life, including her sister. Thus Robert undergoes his own terrible, silent pain, separated from his father, whom he loves. He is unable to reconcile his ideal image of his father with that of a wife beater.

Just as Fran had lied in the emergency room at work about the injuries to her face and other disfigurations, she must now lie to her closest friend in Florida about her name, her home, and her past. Her old identity is replaced—she is now known as Beth Crenshaw, as she ventures into her new job as a home health aide. Eventually, as she slowly builds a life, barely surviving the holidays, she meets others who are also withholding secrets and bearing losses. Mrs. Levitt, whose dying husband she nurses, turns out to be a concentration camp survivor who shows Fran her tattoo. Cindy Roerbacker, her closest friend, turns out to have had a twin sister killed in an accident as a child, of whom she never speaks.

The love interest is Mike Riordan, her son's coach, who is less tough than her husband, Bobby, but perhaps less sexually attractive to Fran as well. However, Mike's safety and kindness provide a needed refuge, especially as complications again thwart the possible happy ending of the novel; for Fran's greatest fear materializes when her husband, now seemingly monstrous, appears in the story for the first time. Until this point, aside from the flashbacks, her husband is present only in the mirrored fragments of Fran's memory, he has little substance. Like a horrible yet omnipotent apparition, Officer Bobby Benedetto seemingly effortlessly (with the aid of police devices) locates his family, breaks in, strikes out in his now-seething anger once again, and spirits their son away. For Fran, the developments of a new marriage and a new baby daughter never compensate for the shocking and profound loss—as the epilogue has it, for years, maybe forever—of her (now teenage) son, Robert. Quindlen breaks off the novel with this unresolved loss—but leaving the reader with Fran's limbo—like state, her endless suffering and waiting, is in keeping with the story's realism.

Black and Blue's power lies in its tragedy, but also in its hope. The hopefulness of Fran's getaway, her respite with her son before her husband's discovery of their whereabouts, and the gradual exorcism of Fran's fear help build in her a new, stronger identity. No longer a victim, she makes a wiser choice in her mate. Hopefulness is also borne in Fran's refusal to lie to her son anymore—when she confronts the truth with him, however brutal.

An Oprah's Book Club choice, *Black and Blue* attracted a range of criticism; many readers found themselves fascinated with the story and approved of the author's realistic choice to deprive Fran of her son at the end. Some critics, nevertheless, found the novel predictable, unrealistic, and too easily resolved, and were disappointed with the glib characterization.

Two critical pieces on this novel work to typify Quindlen criticism in general. They express reservations and, at the same time, grant the author the journalistic strengths in her fiction. In "From Discord, a Wife Makes a Nice New Life—Too Nice,", Susie Linfield of the Los Angeles Times describes flaws in the characterization of this "gripping" story:

> Quindlen's telling of this tale is expertly paced and frequently gripping. Still, there is something too pat, too glib, too predictable, too, well, nice about *Black and Blue*...
>
> In Fran, Quindlen has created a character who is perceptive, decent and consistently sympathetic. Maybe too much so: While Fran is allowed a dollop of anger, even rage, we never fully believe that this is a woman who has been vilely degraded, a woman whose body has been smashed and whose soul has been betrayed. Quindlen seems afraid to present us with a battered woman whom we might not like at every turn ...
>
> Not surprisingly, everyone Fran meets in Florida is awfully nice. There's her new best friend, Cindy Roerbacker, who cheerfully dispenses advice on makeup and romance. There's Mike Riordan, who falls in love with Fran; he coaches the soccer team and adores kids. There's old Mrs. Levitt, cranky but kind, who's placidly philosophic despite the concentration-camp numbers tattooed on her arm: "Ah, what are you going to do?" she asks. What, indeed? Apparently, when bad things happen to good people, the good people remain essentially unchanged.
> (p. E6)

Linfield finds the character of the son, Robert, the most affecting in the novel, noting the true-to-life, spooky self-possessed quality of a boy who has seen too much.

Frank L. Fennell's review of the same novel in *America* argues that Quindlen is still learning her craft. He calls the book "riveting," yet notes the flatness of the male characters (Bobby and Mike Riordan) and the novel's lack of texture:

> Quindlen's greatest asset is the skill she brings with her from her days as a Times essay writer: the ability to hold up for our examination a deeply serious moral issue. *Black and Blue* is, if nothing else, a searing indictment of the violence men inflict upon women. While Quindlen depicts little that is new, she does incorporate much of what we have come to know about spousal abuse ... More importantly, she makes us share the pain, feel the fear and care about Fran's and Robert's fates ...
>
> If *Black and Blue* shares its strongest feature with the essay, therein also lies its greatest weakness as a novel. Quindlen can dramatize spousal abuse very well, but, as a work of fiction, *Black and Blue* lacks the rich texture found in the very best examples of the genre ...
>
> In short, Quindlen has not yet gained full control of the novelist's craft. Her male characters, for example, have nothing of Fran's complexity or her mixture of hurt, tenderness, humor and budding self-confidence ... still, Anna Quindlen has sought out the qualities of novels that often matter most to people: the ability to hold up important issues to the light of public scrutiny and dramatize and humanize them—and ultimately even to galvanize them. She has welded them to the qualities that

characterized her best newspaper columns. *Black and Blue* makes for a riveting read.
(pp. 25–26)

BLESSINGS

While her earlier novels explore a woman's struggle and basic triumph in maintaining her own integrity amid traumatic circumstances, Quindlen's fourth novel, *Blessings*, which appeared in 2002, marks a departure for its author. With less tension and more sentiment than her other novels, the story focuses on two protagonists: Charles "Skip" Cuddy, a caretaker, and the elderly Lydia Blessing, whose property he looks after. The property, also named "Blessings," anchors the novel as the place Lydia has resided for decades. Much of the plot unfolds around the handyman's work, and his and Lydia's shared love of the place—evident in his hard labor and devotion to the orchard, pond, and flowers, all that needs to be fixed in the environment.

The trauma, certainly the dramatic impetus, of the tale is a baby left in the garage of Lydia Blessing's old house. Cuddy, a working-class, unassuming, and decent young man (who has refused to take part in some small-time robberies his friends have committed) embraces and takes on the care of the baby, whom he names Faith. (This nod to spirituality, combined with the book's title, might have been managed with more subtlety.) Quindlen convincingly conveys his delight as well as fatigue with his new charge—something he can call his own, and love—as he carries the baby under his jacket while working and administers to its every need.

Eventually, Cuddy must confide in the old woman, who in her gruff way takes to the baby girl as well. The maid's daughter is also let in on the secret. Slowly the baby captures the hearts of the three who protect her, boast about her, and furtively plan her future.

In part, the story examines the final chapter of a woman's life, and the silences of that life. Most of her friends and family dead, with only her servants for company, and distant from her own sixty-something daughter, Meredith, Lydia (now in her eighties) is lonely without realizing it. Memories play an increasingly larger role in her days. And so the baby becomes a springboard for Lydia's memories about her own young adulthood, her own marriage and baby. She flashes back to New York City, where she used to live—to her own affair with a married man, and her illegitimate pregnancy, and then her strange brief marriage—her own decades—long secret.

Her husband was a friend, her brother's friend, who agrees to a marriage of convenience with Lydia before he is killed in the war. Forced to leave New York City and return to her parents' rural residence, she spends the rest of her days there, basically ostracized from New York society after the illegitimate birth. In her memories, Lydia also meditates on the secret of her mother's Jewish heritage, a loss of identity for Lydia, and the reason for her brother's suicide.

But, like the insistent truths of Lydia's memories, the truth about the baby must come to light. Because of Lydia's wrongful accusation of Cuddy in a robbery attempt of her own house, the police are called and the baby discovered and taken. Finally the original young teenage mother comes to claim the baby with her parents. And so, despite Cuddy's impulse to run away with the child, the baby is returned by the state to the reluctant teenage mother and heartlessly removed from the "mother" who has stayed up nights for the infant, memorizing her every gesture and movement of her face.

Lydia dies peacefully and gracefully after coming to terms with most of her memories, never having achieved authentic connection or communication with her distant daughter, but gaining some redemption nevertheless. She still maintains the same gruff persona up to her death, moved as she has been by Faith. Yet she has accepted her past; she is enlightened and comes to peace with her brother's suicide. In a dramatic subplot, Lydia gradually learns that her brother Sunny, who committed suicide as a young man, was not only homosexual but in love with the male friend she herself married; this she gathers near the end of the novel, decades after her brief marriage, when she discovers a photo in his wallet, in the pocket of the jacket Sunny was wearing when he killed himself.

In a kind of epilogue, Lydia's will leaves the handyman mysterious boxes in the garage, which turn out to be full of old money—literally thousands of dollars her father had mailed her decades ago. Although criticized for its melodrama, simplicity, and sentimentality, especially in comparison to Quindlen's other, more matter-of-fact revelations of real-life hells, the story raises important questions about the definition of, and claims inherent in, motherhood. Other themes include the role, and entrapment, of class—as well as the roles of the past, and memory, in our lives.

In a typical divergence of critical opinion, *Publishers Weekly* called *Blessings* "immensely appealing."

In her most recent novel, *Rise and Shine*, Quindlen tackles another question of truth-telling, or the quest for what is "real." She examines the lives of two sisters in their forties, in New York City, and the gap between their working worlds: one reflecting gossip and celebrity, the other reflecting sometimes—hopeless poverty. Unexpectedly, the successful older sister, Meghan Fitzmaurice, a famous morning-show personality, has the world fall out from underneath her when she unwittingly mumbles obscenities on the air; she takes a Jamaican sabbatical to reassess her life. Meanwhile, her younger sister, Bridget, a social worker, describes the crises she helps manage, of the mainly African-American individuals striving to get by day to day, moving from one grim place to another. Quindlen particularly hones in on the sisters' complex roles within their relationship, cemented since both their parents died and left them orphans. The novel ends with a tragic blow to the family.

NONFICTION BOOKS

Alongside her successful journalism and fiction, Quindlen has also experimented with other, popular forms of writing. *A Short Guide to a Happy Life,* published in 2000, might be considered a self-help book, or a guide to life. Addressed directly to the reader, this slim book offers funny, warm advice from Quindlen. Thoughtful black-and-white images of people not wasting their minutes and years but engaged in the small but valuable moments of life, as well as attractive nature photos, accompany the book.

Quindlen still speaks plainly and directly to the life and death matters, the crucial.

Being Perfect proves a more interesting specimen of the self-help genre, targeting women and their concrete academic, career, and maternal goals. Its urging is more specific than the subject matter of the first book. It serves as an older, wiser woman's reassurance toward the young that they need to follow their hearts and dreams and not expect perfection from themselves. Quindlen also gives space in her small book to voicing the wondrous changes the feminist revolution has wrought in her lifetime, enabling women today, whether or not they know they benefit from their pioneer foremothers, to pursue any career goals they desire, without giving this freedom a second thought.

The large photo-filled volumes *Naked Babies* (1996) and *Siblings* (1998), collaborations with Nick Kelsh, celebrate, respectively, the bodies of babies in multiple ways and metaphors and the sibling relationships of childhood. The first volume has been the more popular, capitalizing on the infinite magnetism of the baby for the parent or parent-to-be or grandparent, and magnifying all the luscious parts of the baby in sensuous detail, often comparing the baby's body or the baby's purity to an element of nature.

The books are attractively photographed and modern in design. Their maternal appeal, as with the self-help books, targets the general reader, and further popularized Quindlen within a general readership. The tone is musing, and the style of the commentary, while reaching for a range of images, is notable for its radiant wholesomeness and sometimes self-conscious whimsicality—some critics would argue, sentimentality. It might also be argued that this is the nature of the genre.

LITERARY CRITICISM AND TRAVEL WRITING

In *How Reading Changed My Life* (1998), Quindlen joined economists and former presidents in contributing to the Ballantine Books series Library of Contemporary Thought, designed to tackle today's issues. Quindlen's volume is a veritable ode to books, the work of a self-confessed bookworm expounding on the love of literature and offering a vindication of the popularity of the book versus the computer, against those who have—prematurely, it seems—pronounced the book's extinction. The writing includes many insights on the appeal of the act of reading, as well as the irreplaceable feel and pleasure of physical book itself.

Quindlen begins with the description of her own love affair with books, beginning with an adamantly bookish childhood within a suburban neighborhood unsympathetic, and even hostile, toward the child reader. She is led to peruse the small library in her Catholic school. There, once she had exhausted the librarian's supply, she was—to her delight—permitted to check out other, older volumes in the library basement.

Her feelings of isolation, she states, were moot; little did she realize that all around the world there were others like her, curled up in chairs or beds, entering this dream state or private chamber, away from the crowded house. Through the wonder and immortality of a book, Quindlen reminds us, the reader may relive a story whenever he likes.

In detailing her devotion to the sacred task of reading, Quindlen names a number of books of all tastes, from John Galsworthy's *Forsyte Saga* to *Portnoy's Complaint* by Philip Roth to *Bleak House* by Charles Dickens, claiming that a writer's influences, if truly confessed, are often not the most highbrow books, but rather the lowbrow and middlebrow. According to Quindlen's experience, the reading fever seems to begin and stay rooted in childhood; thus the odd book may remain beloved to the reader whether or not it is approved by public taste, the academy, or the canon. Quindlen's voice in *How Reading Changed My Life* is emphatically anti-elitist; she expresses irritation with former professors who turned down their noses on the popular (such as Dickens), and conversely, she defends the modern-day book club—often made up of women—as choosing a fair proportion of literary classics to discuss.

Reading's appeal, Quindlen ascribes to many possible things: the yearning to experience something other than the familiar; escape; sedition (reading the forbidden); and emotional connection to a book's characters, or even to other readers. She ends her reflection with an entertaining collection of reading lists, including "Ten Books That Will Help a Teenager Feel More Human."

Quindlen makes further literary observations in her contribution to a National Geographic series that connects writers with world cities. Quindlen explores the popular genre of travel writing, combined with her own reflections, in *Imagined London: A Tour of the World's Greatest Fictional City* (2004). As its title suggests, the book views the city in the present and, simultaneously, through the examination of selected British texts taking place in historic London. Her forays also include several pilgrimages to authors' homes; sometimes Quindlen shifts between past and present on the same page, stepping backward in time to observe a great writer's residence and neighborhood, then flashing forward to a present-day exchange with an immigrant taxi driver.

Many of the books extolled in *Imagined London* are the life influences of *How Reading Changed My Life*, and with the sometimes over-referenced aid of Peter Ackroyd's 2000 tome, *London: The Biography*, the novelist covers landmarks and offers up curious historical-literary facts, past and present, famous and esoteric. Quindlen concentrates on the literature as a literature of place, both middlebrow and highbrow; she lets the still life of the writer's place resurrect the author. Fittingly, Quindlen even brings her beloved Dickens to life as she beholds his house and desk; in lively fashion she explains some of his personal history and writing habits, even his second "celebrity" marriage to a young actress.

Altogether the author's tone is of wide-eyed awe at the mystical city, as appropriate to its place in her imagination as the dreamlike setting for so many adored books.

CONCLUSION

As a Pulitzer Prize–winning commentator on both family issues and national affairs, Quindlen has spent a career studying the impact of the sociopolitical on the family or the individual. A tireless voice for the oppressed and particularly for women, in her journalism and fiction she continues to insist on the individual, lived experience as crucial to the national debate.

Quindlen has always included the experience of the "historically underrepresented" in her writing—of women and of minorities, such as the immigrant and gay population. Since September 2001, she has also given a human face to the victims of the World Trade Center attack and has comforted an America in mourning. At the same time, Quindlen remains a political watchdog, reminding readers that dissent is a necessary American freedom.

Selected Bibliography

WORKS OF ANNA QUINDLEN

NONFICTION
Living Out Loud. New York: Random House, 1988.
Thinking Out Loud: On the Personal, the Political, the Public, and the Private. New York: Random House, 1994.
Naked Babies. With Nick Kelsh. New York: Penguin, 1996.
Siblings. With Nick Kelsh. New York: Penguin, 1998.
How Reading Changed My Life. New York: Ballantine, 1998.
A Short Guide to a Happy Life. New York: Random House, 2000.
Loud and Clear. New York: Random House, 2004.
Imagined London: A Tour of the World's Greatest Fictional City. Washington, D.C.: National Geographic, 2004.
Being Perfect. New York: Random House, 2005.

FICTION
Object Lessons. New York: Random House, 1991.
The Tree That Came to Stay. New York: Crown, 1992.
One True Thing. New York: Random House, 1995.
Happily Ever After. New York: Viking, 1997.
Black and Blue. New York: Random House, 1998.
Blessings. New York: Random House, 2002.
Rise and Shine. New York: Random House, 2006.

BIOGRAPHICAL AND CRITICAL STUDIES

ARTICLES AND REVIEWS
Busch, Frederick. "A Death in the Family." *New York Times Book Review,* 11 September 1994, p. 11.

Fenichel, Marilyn. "Spokeswoman for Our Time." *Psychology Today,* April 1989. p. 71.

Fennell, Frank L. Review of *Black and Blue. America,* 6 June 1998, pp. 25–26.

Harris, Michael. "All in the Family." *Los Angeles* Times Book Review, 22 September 2002, p. 13.

Kirkus Reviews. Review of *Blessings. Kirkus Reviews,* 1 September 2002, p. 1258.

———. Review of *Loud and Clear. Kirkus Reviews,* 1 February 2004, p. 121.

Lehrman, Karen. "She the People." *New Republic,* 10 June 1991, pp. 38–41.

Linfield, Susie. "From Discord, a Wife Makes a Nice New Life—Too Nice." *Los Angeles Times,* 4 March 1998, p. E6.

McDaniel, Maude. "Anna Quindlen Writes a Wise Coming-of-Age Novel." *Chicago Tribune Books,* 21 April 1991, p. 6.

McMichael, Barbara Lloyd. "*Blessings* Sews up Faith, Hope." *Seattle Times,* 6 October 2002, p. L10.

Publishers Weekly. Review of *Blessings. Publishers Weekly,* 26 August 2002, p. 41.

Schwartz, Lynne Sharon. "Books of the Times: A Domestic Angel's Messy Death." *New York Times,* 14 September 1994, p. C17.

See, Carolyn. "A Lesson in Dying." *Washington Post,* 23 September 1994, p. F1.

Steinfels, Margaret O'Brien. "Drawing Lines: Quindlen, Kissling and Us." *Commonweal,* 14 January 1994, pp. 5–6.

Tyler, Anne. "Tribal Rites in Westchester." *New York Times Book Review,* 14 April 1991, p. 7

INTERVIEWS
Campbell, Kim. "Speaking Freely About Her Latest Novel." *Christian Science Monitor,* 11 February 1995, p. 15.

Gardner, Marilyn. "Columnist Anna Quindlen." *Christian Science Monitor,* 13 October 1988. pp. 21–22.

Santora, Alexander M. "Anna Quindlen: From the '60s to the '90s." *Commonweal,* 14 February 1992, pp. 9–13.

Steinberg, Sybil. "Anna Quindlen." *Publishers Weekly,* 15 March 1991, pp. 40–41.

JOANNA SCOTT
(1960—)

D. Quentin Miller

DARIEN, CONNECTICUT, AN affluent suburb of New York City, seems an unlikely birthplace for a novelist whose settings include a nineteenth-century slave ship, early-twentieth-century Vienna, and the Italian island of Elba, but a writer with Joanna Scott's imagination might have grown up anywhere. Scott repeatedly surprises her readers through the breadth of her vision. Born on June 22, 1960, Scott has published seven novels and two collections of short stories in the two decades since her debut in 1987. Each work is a radical departure from the others in terms of style, setting, and subject matter, yet Scott's fiction is marked by a number of recurrent motifs that give her impressive oeuvre considerable unity. Among these motifs are the costs of obsessive ambition, the power of the imagination to shape reality, the limitations of trust, and the vitality of storytelling. Most prominent is an intense examination of history, or the ghosts of the past, along with a belief that art has the power to reanimate the past or even to bring the dead to life again through storytelling. Although she is reticent about revealing details of her upbringing, Scott revealed to this author in a telephone interview that she worked at a "very young age in hospitals and on an ambulance" which gave her "an early confrontation with some of the realities" of life and death she addresses in her fiction.

Scott did not venture far from her hometown to pursue her higher education: she earned her B.A. degree at Trinity College in Hartford and an M.A. degree from Brown University in nearby Rhode Island. Since 1988 she has been Roswell Smith Burrows Professor of English at the University of Rochester in upstate New York, working alongside her husband, the poet and critic James Longenbach. She has received a number of prestigious awards, including a MacArthur fellowship, a Guggenheim fellowship, and a Lannan Literary Award. She has also been a finalist for both the Pulitzer Prize and the PEN/Faulkner Award.

Among the most respected writers of literary fiction of her generation, Scott has impressed critics with her virtuosity and with her confidence as an author of historical fiction. Given her tireless experimentation and her interest in ambiguity and eccentric vision, it is difficult to associate her with any group of writers or single literary tradition. Her attention to history and to the importance of storytelling certainly place her in the neighborhood of Toni Morrison and Richard Powers. She has cited John "Jack" Hawkes as a powerful influence, both as her teacher at Brown and as a model for her own work, and she and Maureen Howard share their work with one another at early stages of composition. Critics have described her as postmodern, and she has written appreciations of Thomas Pynchon and William Gass, yet her material generally does not shade toward the absurdist humor of the fiction of Pynchon, John Barth, Philip Roth, E. L. Doctorow, or Don DeLillo. Though difficult to categorize, Scott is clearly part of a tradition of great American novelists whose subject is history itself, viewed as a montage of close shots rather than as a sweeping panorama.

DAMAGED BOYS AND MEN: THE FIRST THREE NOVELS

From the beginning of her career it was clear that Scott would not be the kind of novelist to begin with a bildungsroman and experiment with divergent topics and characters afterward. Her first three novels are set in an undetermined rural present, on a nineteenth-century slave ship, and in early-twentieth-century Austria. Her early protagonists could be described as anything from eccentric to grotesque, and they are all male. Equally striking is her command of narrative voice in these works: whether she is narrating from the point of view of a teenage son of a slave ship owner or a peasant girl in twentieth-century Austria, Scott gives the impression that she has been there. This quality is rare in a seasoned author. It is extraordinary in a beginning writer.

Scott's first novel, *Fading, My Parmacheene Belle* (1987), marked her arrival on the literary scene as a writer of tremendous imaginative power. From the title on, the novel's unique voice is noteworthy. The narrator, a paranoid septuagenarian who reveals his name as Clarion in the book's final pages, tells his story as though he and the reader were in collusion: "I will tell you exactly how it was," he begins, and he uses the phrase "I tell you" throughout the novel, as though to establish a deep bond between teller and reader. The novel's central theme is the difficult necessity of companionship, so the emphasis on the bond between narrator and audience is fitting.

The narrator sees the world in terms of archetypes and fishing metaphors, and his unusual voice draws from his unusual perspective. At first the reader is likely to feel disoriented, as though the novel takes place in an ancient setting, but it is gradually clear that the narrator is of our world, though very much in a world of his own. His resistance to the contemporary world is strong: it is only through details that he reluctantly reveals, like his ownership of a Buick Skylark or his companion's penchant for smoking marijuana (which he calls "hemp") that we are conscious of contemporary society. His tendency is to withhold these details just as he withholds his own name and the names of others. He bluntly renames the characters who surround him in archetypal terms: the Wife, the Idiot (his mentally handicapped son), and the Mermaiden (a young drifter girl who becomes his traveling companion). Characters who do have names have unlikely ones: Gibble (his knowledgeable best friend), Magrass (a woman he fancies, after the death of his wife of fifty-three years, as a replacement), and Fyfe (a hunter and fisherman). If there is anything consistent about his behavior, it is his abuse of the characters he encounters; and yet he feels a certain tenderness or obligation to each of them that enables the reader to feel some sympathy for this largely unsympathetic narrator.

When "the Wife" dies Clarion is set adrift in a poisoned landscape: as a freshwater fisherman, that most solitary of pastimes, he has lived his life in deliberate refuge from the contemporary world. His isolation and paranoia are set loose, forcing him to confront his existence as more than animal survival. He positions himself as a kind of latter-day Henry David Thoreau at times; he says, "If we had an appetite for worms or midges or water striders there would be food abundant for us, the day has brought in spring and the insects are congregating in celebration, in the creek beds the catfish will be crawling out of the mud and in beeches the yellow warbler is caroling. Surrounding me there is renewal but I have no place here." The reason he feels he has no place is partly because he has equated his deceased wife with home and partly because he feels that the landscape is tainted by radioactivity:

> There is no treachery in the world that escapes my insight now. I see through the electricity poles disguised as trees, I see through the traitors disguised as friends and the idiots disguised as sons, I trust neither wind nor light. The country surrounding me is polluted with deception and I have only the company of a strumpet for support; we can find no refuge in these hills, no one to trust, so we must journey far, we must lose ourselves inside a city, for there is nothing left in the wilds.

His sense that the landscape is tainted is directly tied to his misanthropy, and his journey holds the possibility that he will be able to restore some of his faith in humanity, to get him to feel love for his late wife and for his son and to trust the "traitors" and "strumpets" surrounding him.

His paranoia is fueled by his rejection of those closest to him: after the Wife dies he becomes suspicious that his son, "the Idiot," is actually Gibble's son. He attacks the Idiot with a chair and flees, thinking he has killed the boy. For the remainder of the novel he travels, mostly with the Mermaiden, in refuge from the authorities and in pursuit, he eventually decides, of the Wife's childhood home by the sea. He concludes that the lack of affection the Wife displayed toward him throughout her life had something to do with her nostalgia for this home. The journey is carnivalesque. The Mermaiden is a hybrid of circus contortionist and prostitute, and the characters they encounter are cast as sideshow freaks. His lack of faith in humanity, especially in women, is originally directed toward the Mermaiden. Soon after meeting her, he confides, "I tell you women are false," echoing his descriptions of the Wife in the early chapters. Yet he later softens: "Another female I have trusted, and another female has abandoned me. I should never have been swayed by that girl's cajoling, I should have made an early departure and purged her from my heart, but now I have an obligation to watch over her, she is my responsibility however wayward she be, I must ignore her tendencies and defend her as if she were pure, untainted." She thus creates in him the role he should have assumed with his wife and son, and their journey together presents the possibility of renewal.

Whether or not he achieves this renewal is a question for the individual reader. As a paranoid elderly widower disgusted both with himself and with humanity, he does not invite the reader's sympathy, and his awkward phrasing does not help his case. Yet his misogyny and misanthropy fade as the novel continues: he seems to grow to love his wife over the course of the novel, and he returns to find his neglected son alive and in need of him at the novel's conclusion. He realizes that his son "need not be alone if he would only turn" to face his father in the final sentence (p. 262). This gradual change in the narrator, which includes his reconciliation with Gibble (whom he thinks has been controlling him throughout the narrative), is brought about through the suicide of the Mermaiden, whom he has also called Little Death. The deaths of both women can be regarded as sacrifices for his own enduring sense of life and its meaning. But the dominant note of the novel, which reads like a cross between Samuel Beckett and Cormac McCarthy, is far bleaker than that assessment would suggest. It takes a certain commitment on the reader's part to endure such sustained philosophical angst and quirky narration, and Scott seems altogether conscious of the demands she is making on the reader. Clarion describes the speech of Magrass this way:

> What with her broken language and her fanciful subjects she is lucky to find an audience like me who knows that we who have ears should attend to speech however foreign it sounds to us, for sometimes there is wit and contrast to enjoy, other times it is ribaldry stringing sentences together, and the wary audience will improve with experience, his ears will become attuned.

This relationship between teller and audience parallels his own relationship with the reader: his repeated phrase "I tell you" insists on the importance of storytelling in a decaying world.

Scott's second novel, *The Closest Possible Union* (1988), also reaches for a unique narrative voice, this time in the person of a fourteen-year-old boy on a slaving ship in the mid-nineteenth century. The world of this novel is also morally debased, and the narrator again seems to have little control over it. If Scott suggests a modern Thoreau in her first novel, she evokes the darker vision of Herman Melville in her second. The novel immediately recalls "Benito Cereno," Melville's classic tale of an inscrutable slave ship told from the point of view of a naive captain. *The Closest Possible Union* is narrated by a similarly naive adolescent boy named Tom, whose journey on the slave ship yields to a deeper journey into the self than Melville's Amasa Delano ever imagined. The novel is extraordinary for its clear-eyed view of human power relationships. The theme again involves human trust and the tenuous separation between the human world and the natural world.

The Closest Possible Union is also extraordinary in its willingness to deepen the discourse on a subject that had been seemingly resolved by the end of the twentieth century: the moral depravity of slavery. For Scott, slave ownership represents the most evident form of the human capacity for brutality and is thus the illustration of the intersection of the human and the animal in human nature. Before the reader is even introduced to the reality of this slave ship, power relationships are reinforced through sexual control, verbal regulation, and rituals. The sailors on the ship, for instance, take a sailor named Peter Gray on deck for "a happening" and force him to choose between "baptism," being dunked repeatedly over the side of the ship, and "communion," being force-fed cockroaches. This public exhibit of cruelty is in response to Peter's refusal to submit to extortion. Tom witnesses the poor sailor's force-feeding and admits, "Though he looked as pathetic as anyone I'd ever seen, I still didn't pity him." The event foreshadows a similar incident much later in the novel when the sailors force Tom down on deck and smear his face with pig excrement before shaving him, another mock ritual, in response to his pride.

Tom's inability to feel pity for another human frames his response to the slaves below decks. The reader is likely to forgive Tom some of his transgressions because of his age, but the fact remains that he is implicated in the traffic of slaves, and his naïveté is only a partial excuse. His father is the owner of this slave ship, and he expects special treatment as a result. The captain acts as a substitute father figure throughout the narrative, an agent of raw power who often protects Tom but sometimes deliberately humiliates him. Tom discovers over the course of the journey that the captain and the other major characters are all using him in one way or another and that his identity is determined not by him but by the powerful adults who surround him. In one revealing passage, he realizes, "My education has consisted of nothing but calculated insults. According to them, my destiny has already been determined, I'm bound to fall. They have portioned out my identity, fracturing me into separate Toms." This fragmentation makes it impossible for Tom to know himself, which makes it impossible for him to have any real effect on those desperate souls being transported into slavery.

Much of Tom's miseducation is brought about by the slave ship's tendency to obscure clarity: "Nothing is what it seems," he laments. Peter Gray, the sailor who was forced to eat insects, is really a woman in disguise who becomes the captain's concubine and also Tom's seductress, although neither the captain nor Tom is initially aware of her real reason for being on the ship: to find her lost half-brother Quince, who has apparently become a brutal African warlord. She tells Tom this story in such a way that he participates in its narration and becomes directly involved in it and even becomes the brutal Quince himself. He realizes that there is "no end" to the story; as Peter Gray says, "the story goes in circles." The story becomes vivid for Tom and invades his reality. When he witnesses a light-skinned slave being murdered and thrown overboard, he is certain that it is Quince, but by the end of the novel he is unsure whether or not Quince ever existed. Moral certitude is impossible when reality is so unstable.

Questions of morality are also at the heart of Scott's third novel, *Arrogance* (1990), a historical novel about the life of the Austrian artist Egon Schiele who died in the flu pandemic of 1918 following a sensational indecency trial. Scott toys with conventions of both biography and the historical novel by narrating through multiple voices and using multiple sources, knitting together official perspectives with highly private insights. What emerges is a portrait of the artist as complex and disturbing as his own portraits were. As with Scott's first two novels, the reader comes away disoriented and unsettled, unable to fully condemn Schiele (as his society did) or to love him (as only he did).

In addition to rejecting the biographical narrative convention of a single voice, *Arrogance* refutes traditional rules of chronology. The novel moves not only between voices and narrative points of view but back and forth across time. Egon's childhood is considered in the same detail as his period of incarceration or his artistic development alongside his lover Vallie Neuzil. The novel's movement across time denies privilege to any single event: the artist's life is infinitely more complex than a traditional chronological structure could depict. The reader is likely to feel somewhat dizzy, a reaction the viewer of Schiele's work might also experience after a prolonged gaze.

Egon Schiele was part of the Neuekunstgruppe, a branch of "new artists" including Gustav Klimt who led a revolt against Vienna's established art world. As with many modern artists, this group wanted to shock the art world and its patrons; as he emerges in Scott's novel, Egon is a rebel even within this group of rebels: "Egon is alone in his determination to offend the people, believing it to be the artist's rightful purpose to deflate the lies of ornament and sentimentality." His aesthetic philosophy is developed and restated in different ways throughout the book, but it is connected in some way to his relationship with his father, a drunken laborer who has no use for Egon's artistic pursuits. When Adolf Schiele discovers his son's self-portraits, he attacks Egon and burns the portraits, to the distress of Egon's sister Gerti, who rescues one of the portraits and delivers it to him later that night. Egon burns that surviving portrait too, "marveling at the fluid orange ridge moving unevenly in the dark toward the center of his face." He develops a lifelong fascination with orange and gold hues because of their association with fire and its power to destroy art: "Gold—and every other pigment with yellow as its root—was an unnatural color, the color created when light strikes something limpid, something dying."

His father's act of burning Egon's self-portraits induces another unusual reaction: "As his father mixed the ashes of the last drawing with the stove cinders Egon felt an odd triumph, a smug, private, pleasurable surge of pride." Adolf Schiele's act of immolation foreshadows the actions of the judge in Egon's indecency trial who also publicly burns Egon's work: "The bottom of the paper arched away from the match, fire crept along its edge. Egon Schiele's eyelids drooped in sulky resistance, but his lips curled as the paper burned until he looked quite pleased, his self-possession fueled by the flame." In these passages the disapproval of an older male figure who represents the tastes of mainstream society appears to be more powerful than the artist, just as fire is more powerful than paper. Yet Egon is pleased, even proud (a condition that develops into the "arrogance" of the title), presumably because his art is powerful enough to summon such a destructive reaction; he proclaims, "Men who lack any power of invention are the ones who condemn the inventors.... They tell us that we are unscrupulous and vulgar. They call us aesthetes, hedonists, decadents, perverts!"

If there is something heroic in Egon's willingness to use art to critique the bourgeoisie and to gain power, the reader can also find ample evidence that he is a pervert, that his creative impulses cross the line into pornography. Even his mother has little sympathy for him; she says, "all the thoughts that a young man should learn to keep to himself were displayed in his offensive pictures." He is a dangerous man, not necessarily because he corrupts innocent children but because he has never believed they are sexually innocent to begin with: "Egon understood enough about children to recognize the strength and legitimacy of their sexual desires.... He knows that children are dangerous; he knows as well that they should have no place in his art. Their soft lines and dimpled flesh, so seductive; their impish, upturned noses, so charming, so dishonest." He claims to use children as models because they inspire him; he is especially inspired by his sister Gerti who "undressed willingly, scrambling out of her pleated skirt and blouse and standing obediently in some awkward position, her arms raised, one foot pressed against the opposite knee at a right angle, or perhaps on her hands and knees, wagging her little bottom at him." This behavior leads to an incestuous event between them and accounts to some degree for Egon's sexual confusion thereafter. His sexual relationship with his sister causes him to contemplate suicide, but he backs away from these feelings of despair, calling them "merely an experiment—an artist should toy with the most dangerous taboos but he must never let himself be distracted from his work.... no one, not even his sister, should be allowed to distract him from his work. He would never touch Gerti again." His discovery that the production of art is superior to indulging in such "taboos" as incest and suicide exacts a price in society to which Egon seems oblivious: he does not focus on the victims of his behavior, only on himself as victim.

Egon is deeply in touch with society's taboos; he violates them in order to comfort himself in such a hostile world but also to inspire his art, believing and wanting to show in his art that "pleasure has nothing to do with reproduction." In his mind, pleasure in fact has much to do with destruction, which explains his fascination with death imagery in his art. He has a homosexual encounter with a mute peasant boy and is relieved that the boy cannot tell anyone about it, yet he denies the fact that falling asleep in the boy's arms afterward is one of the most life-affirming moments he has known. In addition, his desire for his sister even leads to a necrophilia fantasy about her. It is finally his obsession with death rather than with the bodies of children that gets him in legal trouble. The girl whose father presses charges against Egon is the narrator of the first chapter of each of the book's sections; she is motivated by revenge against Egon not because of any sexual violation but because he has drawn a grotesque vision of her in a coffin and thus reminded her of her own death. When the judge burns this portrait at the trial, the girl explains her reaction to the complex interplay between being re-created in Egon's portrait as a corpse and watching this portrait destroyed. The destruction of her monstrous portrait should be a resurrection, but to her it has the opposite effect: "So the sacrifice pleased all—the judge, the prosecutor, the public, the criminal—all except me, the girl in the coffin... . And had I lost? In a sense, I had watched myself die." Egon's real "crime" is that his art reminds his viewers of their death. Yet art can only produce anger by showcasing this fact: the destruction of art turns the viewer into a witness of death.

OBSESSION AND OTHER ANTIDOTES: THE SHORT STORIES

If the protagonists of Scott's first three novels are eccentric it is because their interests are acutely intense. Passion developing into obsession is perhaps the dominant motif of these novels and especially of Scott's fourth book, the short story collection *Various Antidotes* (1994). Scott's own obsession with somewhat less-than-famous historical figures is evident in this collection, as is the development of the theme of obsession as something that both provides meaning and potentially damages those surrounding the obsessed individual, like Clarion in *Fading, My Parmacheene Belle,* Tom's father in *The Closest Possible Union,* and especially Egon Schiele in *Arrogance.*

The first half-dozen stories in this eleven-story collection are especially illustrative of these themes. "Concerning Mold upon the Skin, Etc." is a portrait of Anton van Leeuwenhoek, the so-called "mad lens-grinder of Delft," who discovers microscopic life after inventing an early microscope. Like Egon Schiele, he favors the mysteries of his calling over the harmony of his family, and he also feels isolated even from his milieu. In order to elicit a tear from his daughter he kisses her with incestuous passion, then he catches her teardrop and puts it under a microscope in order to examine the life that lives in it. Like Schiele, his calling derives from his sense that he is gifted with special insight: he "had made visible the unimaginable." His impulse is essentially creative—"there was hardly a difference between discovering life and creating it" (p. 11)—but the fact that this discovery comes at the cost of his daughter's sorrow reinforces the theme that the creative spirit is potentially destructive.

The microscope van Leeuwenhoek invents in the first story provides deep background for the second, "Bees Bees Bees," because it gave rise to "the controversy over the source of life." The story's title itself refers to an obsession: "Bees bees bees, that's all he could talk about." Francis Huber, the blind Swiss beekeeper, allows his interest in bees to turn into a "mania," or a "system in his head." The story moves between Francis' life and the knowledge about bee societies that he has discovered. Essentially bee societies are characterized by the extreme attention most members pay to one creature—the queen. Francis is able to live in harmony with bees rather than with people because he has become so obsessed with knowledge that he overlooks the main lesson bees illustrate, that society amounts to mutual dependence. He neglects his nurse, who has loved him magnanimously, and as a result he breaks an implicit pact. The ironic ending has Francis dying at the hands of his bees; so thoroughly has he entered the world of insects that the townspeople assume the bees are punishing him for betraying bee society, not because he has neglected his own species.

The next few stories in the collection also end with pain and death after characters try to improve upon something: the human body in "Nowhere," a perfect sauce in "The Marvelous Sauce," the mysteries of birth in "Chloroform Jags," or charity in "Dorothea Dix, Samaritan." Scott begins to explore female experience in these stories. By the end of the collection, in stories like "You Must Relax!" and "Convicta et Combusta," women have become historical victims, perceived as witches merely for having some kind of power.

OF TAXIDERMY AND SOCIAL CLASS: THE MANIKIN

Women are again compared to witches in a climactic scene in Scott's fourth novel, *The Manikin* (1996) when Hal Craxton is set upon by his new wife (whom he has just beaten), his former housekeeper (to whom he had proposed months earlier), and his former housekeeper's daughter, who is the erstwhile lover of his new wife. All three of them have been victims of the impotent power of this dilettante, and they are described as "Three powerful sisters" after they nearly tear him to pieces. Women have been victimized by male power in all of Scott's first three novels, but in this novel they take a stand. By the end of the novel Peg Griswood is allowed to narrate the story which has been hers, in many ways, throughout the novel. This gender shift marks a clear departure for this phase of Scott's oeuvre.

The Manikin was nominated for a Pulitzer Prize, and Scott received a MacArthur fellowship to write it. It is a historical novel that self-consciously meditates on history and even on the preservation of history in the form of natural history museums. The title refers to the substance used to re-create the skeletons of stuffed animals in taxidermy, and more directly, "the Manikin" is the name given to the manor owned by Henry Craxton Senior, a magnate who owned the largest taxidermy supply shop of its kind. The house is in many ways the protagonist of the novel: locals believe it is haunted, and the way the dead exert power over the living is one of the novel's central concerns. *The Manikin* and the collection of taxidermy it contains are like Egon Schiele's art: a complex and macabre dance between living and dead forces. Scott's own art is in many ways an attempt to give life to the past through narratives about historical figures, and yet this novel shows the futility of any attempts to make life permanent.

Unlike the biography-in-novel-form of *Arrogance,* though, the vivid historical details of *The Manikin* are entirely products of Scott's imagination. The narrator disrupts her own historical display occasionally, commenting on the artificiality of a natural history museum, or any museum:

> Come with me and discover up close the wonders that await you in the wild. Look carefully, check under logs, below the ice, at the tops of trees. Can you find one bullfrog? Two turtles? Ten dragonflies? Now press the button on your left and listen. No, you're not hearing a thumb rubbing against the side of an inflated balloon—that's the leopard frog croaking, and if you press the next button you'll hear the northern cricket frog, which sounds quite like two steel marbles clacking together... . Here is nature in all its infinite and yet predictable variation, with time suspended by the able hand of man.

Taxidermy and its display are attempts to give order to nature and, in a sense, to insist that humans have power over nature. The novel consistently pits the urge to classify against nature's own tremendous, anarchic power. The struggle is ongoing: the Manikin still stands at the end of the book, and it still contains a few of the stuffed animals that once comprised its famous collection, but it has fallen to ruin, neglected by its inhabitants, and nature has gradually begun to reclaim it.

The characters in *The Manikin* represent similar forces: the monied Craxtons attempt to control their unruly servants. In the first half of the book the widow Mrs. Mary Craxton presides over the house with great haughtiness and fussiness. Her demands give her primary housekeeper Ellen Griswood a reason for being: Ellen is, in her daughter's view, "a working animal—does what is expected, no surprises.... She is a dumb, domesticated brute, no self separate from her role as housekeeper, while Peg is as untamed as the Craxton cougar. This absolute distinction between them is somewhat exaggerated, attributable largely to Peg's immaturity, but there is some truth to the observation that Ellen has been deprived of her wildness by her domestic role. Wildness is a dangerous if creative force in the book, though: Peg's own wildness causes her to place herself in a situation of great danger when she impulsively runs away from home and is raped. The typical response to a wild animal in this novel is to kill and stuff it. After all, domesticity may be dull, but it is safe.

The moral complexity of the book is directly tied to a hunting accident: Junket, the groundskeeper's son, shoots a snowy owl, a rare arctic bird, before he has identified his target. The bird has talismanic qualities. Peg immediately thinks that its role is to "warn a person of approaching death." According to some legends it is an "interlocutor between hell and earth." Immediately after Junket shoots the bird Peg instinctively proclaims him a "stupid, stupid boy" and thus seals his fate: he will never be anything more. The bird becomes the obsession of Boggio, the resident taxidermist, who stuffs it with care and precision and looks to it as his life's masterpiece. It is also believed to harbor the soul of Mary Craxton once she has died, and her son Hal looks upon it with dread as a result and fantasizes about having his dead mother stuffed.

The snowy owl is described in the opening pages of the novel before any human characters have been introduced. The novel's tragic strains are thus partially accounted for by the central tragedy of Junket shooting the owl, as unintentional as Oedipus killing his father. This act sets in motion the central debates of the novel: Why does one creature have power over another? Is the human attempt to understand nature through preservation and classification immoral? Is wildness a more potent force than domesticity? In casting herself as a wild animal and her mother as a domestic brute, Peg has attempted to name them and place them into a hierarchy, yet this is precisely what robs humanity of its power. Boggio, the mad fool who acts as an ironic anchor to these forces in the book, embodies the contradictions of the natural world in contact with mankind: "If Boggio is mad, then he caught his madness from the natural world. Mad nature, rabid, vicious. It has passed its frenzy to mankind.... In the form of the single animal rests the wildness that will undo mankind. Expose it, represent the living animal exactly, capture all its virulent madness, and perhaps the madness can be resisted."

The Manikin's climactic scene occurs when the characters at the Manikin seem to have given in to madness. After sending the depraved Hal Craxton away, the servants take over the house and turn it into a kind of commune. Anarchy rules; the repressed Ellen Griswood makes peace with her daughter and makes love with the groundskeeper. Peg and the other members of the younger generation drop their verbal inhibitions and hurl curses at each other. These scenes are characterized by bliss and harmony: the "nearly self-sufficient" residents of the Manikin say grace before every meal, thanking the Lord "for gardens, for orchards, for pure springs, for evergreen hedges and sunsets, for the night breeze that pushes the curtains up against the ceiling, for our food, and for our loved ones." It is as though the absence of hierarchy, of servant and employer, has promoted a pastoral existence apart from society's judgments. Sylva, the cook who says grace every night, is black, and when the outside world eventually hears about the servants living communally at the Manikin, her race becomes an issue, where it was never even mentioned during this period of happiness.

The return of Hal Craxton in the midst of a bacchanalian party puts an abrupt end to this blissful state, and the Manikin's residents scatter. Peg returns to it years later with a mature perspective that allows her to understand why she transgressed the "complicated rules of servitude" and "endless restrictions" of her youth. Like the snowy owl, humans yearn for absolute grace and freedom, and yet like the bee societies described in "Bees Bees Bees," our identities are often dictated by our sense of duty and our potentially tragic way of organizing ourselves hierarchically.

RACE, SACRIFICE, ADOPTION: MAKE BELIEVE

American social hierarchy is often based on a poisoned intertwining of race and class, and in an interview about writing her fifth novel, *Make Believe* (2000), Scott points out that she has written about race before: "Because it's our country's concern, it's my concern as a writer." Indeed, race is a peripheral concern in all of her novels except *Arrogance* and central to *The Closest Possible Union*. It is only one of the central concerns in *Make Believe*. The reader can recognize a number of Scott's recurrent concerns, including the fate of damaged boys, the importance of imaginative storytelling, the destructive, violent toll megalomaniac men exact from their female partners, the complex interplay between life and death, and the relationship between sacrifice and love. The real departure in *Make Believe* is Scott's temporary resistance to the historical novel; in the same interview she says, "I wanted to push myself away from what had, in a sense, become a crutch for me, the crutch of history, the crutch of fact."

Make Believe is the story of four-year-old Kamon Michael Templin, nicknamed "Bo" by his mother because of his hobo-like tendency to wander, both mentally and physically. Bo is the child of unmarried parents, a black father who dies before he is born and a white mother who dies in a car accident when Bo is four. Their races become especially important after their deaths, as both sets of grandparents reveal their racial biases while fighting over custody of the child. Given these biases, the relationship between Bo's parents, Kamon and Jenny, is perhaps motivated by race in the first place: both are rebelling to some extent against the race-based biases of their communities. Despite this motivation, their relationship develops into pure, almost idealized love, heightening the tragedy of Kamon's senseless death at the hands of petty thieves and Jenny's death in a car crash.

Like *The Manikin*, *Make Believe* is not organized around a single protagonist, and like *Arrogance* the plot moves back and forth across time to develop Kamon and Jenny before their deaths. From its title on, the novel has certain fairy tale qualities, centering around an idyllic romance, but it is a nightmarish version of a fairy tale. The background of Jenny's youth, for instance, is described in the three-part structure common to fairy tales, but the organizing principle of her childhood story is the three times her father loses his job for drunkenness. During the first of these three episodes her father is looking for gold, as one might in a fairy tale; Jenny thinks he has found it when he presses a stone into her hand, but the stone is actually nothing more than an ordinary piece of slate, though she later discovers that it contains a finely etched fossil. This rock becomes a talisman of good luck for Jenny. In a passage deeply laden with irony, Jenny's mother, Marge, mourning her daughter's death, finds the rock and uses it as a wishing stone, casting it into a lake and wishing that her grandson Bo would learn to love her. The act forecasts her own bad luck late in the novel when Marge plummets into a thawing lake trying to save Bo.

Marge's belief in and misunderstanding of luck frames one of the novel's central themes: the forces of fate in dialogue with the shaping powers of the imagination. Bo gets his imaginative power from his mother and from his paternal grandfather, both of whom trust that his child's mind can handle stories. As a result, "Bo knew the difference between magic and reality." His penchant for hearing made-up stories and for making up stories of his own serves as a survival mechanism when his life gets difficult, which it always does. For instance, he sees a glimmer of his mother's face in his grandmother's, "which caused him to suppose that the truth must have been the opposite of what he'd been told, and his mama would be coming back to pick him up and bring him home. He wanted to believe this version rather than the other." This unrealistic desire for life to conform to fantasy is both protective and dangerous, as it was for Peg in *The Manikin*: both of these characters wander from their safe homes into a dangerous world. The difference between them is that Bo is ultimately more powerful than Peg, partly because he is a child and warrants the protection of strangers.

Another difference between these two characters is that Bo, being a child, only wants to hear stories with happy endings and constructs the narrative of his life accordingly. He is imperiled by Eddie, his mother's stepfather, whose religious mania causes him to see Bo as the devil. Eddie's hatred of Bo is a dangerous force, and Bo is aware that he must combat it. He therefore creates an imaginary universe that accords him power, with Eddie as his absolute enemy. As in a myth, the animosity between them is absolute: "In Bo's make-believe, Marge didn't exist. Only Eddie existed, and Bo with a subtle effort tried to provoke the great battle between them that would lead to Eddie's absence." The battle takes place in reality when Bo spits in Eddie's face and Eddie hurls him across the room, but the aftermath of the battle reveals how Bo's penchant for stories allows him to survive:

> He could be, couldn't he, someone in someone else's story? And maybe in that story he died and became an angel. So what if angels aren't really true? It was only a story, one version out of many, a catastrophe loaded with meaning by the author of the tale.... It could be that he was a dead child crumpled on the dining room floor, and Eddie Gantz was guilty, the end. A dead, not-knowing child, and Marge was still bending over him, begging him to come back to life, but he refused, the end. It could be that he was a story in the newspaper, nothing more. But who wants to hear that kind of story?

Through her interpretation of storytelling, Scott underscores here the importance of choice. The cruel whims of fate take the lives of Jenny and Kamon, but for the living, choice is crucial. Sam, Bo's paternal grandfather, who has established in the boy the magic of storytelling, chides his wife for "wanting to tell a different sort of story, the fact kind, the kind I can't tinker with." In its preference for "stories that can be tinkered with" over "fact stories," *Make Believe* reinforces Scott's conviction that art is a force that rivals the power of death.

As in *Arrogance* and *The Manikin*, this novel has the ability to give life to dead characters, to animate the dead as Marge is animated after her death in the nearly frozen lake, and to give them voices and personalities. In a lengthy lyrical passage following her death, Marge's story is told as it would have been told had she been encouraged to pass it along to her surviving daughter Ann. This section is narrated in the second person, causing the reader to fully empathize with the deceased Marge: "Listen, Marge: your daughter Ann wants to know why you are gone. She wants to know what you would have done differently in life if you'd had a second chance." This passage contrasts with the narrative of the moments just before Kamon's death, which is written as though it were a police blotter, chronicling Kamon's actions minute by minute. The two narrative styles reveal the interplay between magic and realism in the book: death is not final in either case but can be thought of as a borderland between the two. In fact, as Bo is positioned between death and life in the book's opening pages, he feels he is "sinking into the realm of the unimaginable," that is, a world where neither choice nor the imagination holds any sway. His survival from this "world of strangers ... the bottom of the sea" enables him to draw on some deep reserve in his brain. Not his memory (which he continually resists), but something even more primal: a world of dreams that is made from the very reality it resists.

EXILE AND ELBA:
TOURMALINE *AND* LIBERATION

Dreams and memory are at the core of *Tourmaline* (2002) and *Liberation* (2005), both set mainly on the Italian island of Elba. In these two novels Scott makes clear that her central themes have always involved the relationship between perspective, memory, and imagination, and the way stories are generated from this relationship. Both novels cover the same historical period, the immediate aftermath of World War II regarded from the perspective of the present. Yet Elba as a setting allows for a deep consideration of history: in *Tourmaline* this depth is evident in the early pages in which the geological history of the island is provided. Scott tells the story of Murray Murdoch, his wife, Claire, and their four sons against this deep background, inviting the reader to contemplate forces of change and stability. The Murdochs have moved to Elba to follow Murray's ill-conceived plan to get rich through mining the island for its semi-precious natural resources, such as *tourmaline*.

Scott again plays with conventions of multiple narrators in *Tourmaline*. Ollie, the youngest of the four Murdoch boys, is the narrator throughout most of the book, but occasionally Claire is given a narrative voice and even speaks directly to him and to the way he is constructing the tale: "Ollie, forgive me for saying so, but I wonder why you haven't learned from past mistakes. Your penchant for melodrama." To some degree these narrative correctives undermine Ollie's project, but at the same time they force him (and the reader) to consider the very nature of storytelling as it is defined in *Make Believe:* as a combination of fact and imagination. During another interruption Claire asks Ollie, "Where are you getting your information? How do you know so much? ... What do you know, and what are you making up as you go along? I can't discern the difference anymore." The "difference" is especially important in this novel because its central crisis involves the disappearance of Adriana Nardi, a native Elban whom Murray had tried to seduce just before she vanished.

The mystery of Adriana's whereabouts consumes the island and makes the Murdochs pariahs. The scandal is filtered through the perspective of an aging British historian named Francis Cape, who is writing a history of Napoleon. Francis was clearly in love with Adriana and jealous of Murray's affection for her. His presence in the novel connects historical truth with a more immediate truth: "The truth, Francis Cape would have said, is a sequence of names and dates arranged as verifiable facts. The truth is a fingerprint left behind by a thief or a document signed by a king. The truth is something you see with your own eyes and remember forever." This simple definition is immediately complicated in *Tourmaline* by the multiple narrative perspectives which tend to challenge the reliability of memory. Beyond that, though, truth described in terms of legality (facts, physical evidence, witness and testimony) is only part of the story. Legends, in many ways, form truths that we live by. Ollie writes: "Catch a falling star and it will turn to blue tourmaline in your hands. This is true. If my father were here, I'd ask for clarification. What is true, Dad? He'd say, everything I tell you. He knew about falling stars turning into tourmaline because he saw it happen." As a witness, Murray is unreliable for a number of obvious reasons, especially his weakness for alcohol and his tendency to romanticize life to the point that he uproots his family and moves abroad in pursuit of semiprecious stones. And yet, until his lessons are proven false, they are true.

Ollie's relationship with his deeply flawed father is testimony to the notion that family is as important as official history, the "sequence of names and dates" that Francis Cape seeks. Murray's drunkenness, his attraction to a woman who is not his wife, and his failure to prosper are obviously negative traits from his son's perspective, and yet Ollie forgives his father and is curious enough about him to re-create his life. He even begins a direct dialogue with his father late in the book, telling Murray to regard the description of himself as a wandering drunk as just "a little game I'm playing here on the page." The novel in some ways pays homage to a man who is basically ordinary in his failings:

> My tendency for exaggeration [is] a gift from my father. He was like so many others—men and women who, in resigning themselves to their fate, must forfeit their spirited ingenuity and become ordinary. Not even madness to enliven their story. They are the ones left out of history, the explorers, inventors, artists, teachers, doctors, electricians, ophthalmologists, chimney sweeps and plumbers, bus drivers and farmers and lab assistants, etcetera, etcetera, who set out to accomplish something extraordinary, and after a series of setbacks just gave up.

With an extraordinary figure from history like Napoleon lurking in the shadows of Elba, Ollie is sensitive to the forces that affect fate. An ordinary man like Murray is made extraordinary through his naive dream to get rich from the natural resources available on Elba. Dreaming amounts to the resistance to one's fate; in a scintillating passage Ollie defines dreams as "stories we tell ourselves when we are alone."

The connection between dreaming and storytelling forms the basis for this narrative, not unlike Bo's flights of fancy in *Make Believe*. Ollie's mother, looking back on the events of their time in exile, observes, "We need the mingling of minds in order to know what is real. A story becomes true with recognition." This observation develops the idea that dreams are stories people tell themselves when they are alone: storytelling is communal and based on remembered facts as well as the speculations we must attempt in order to make sense of a narrative, just as we must revise our dreams when we tell them to others. The most valuable lessons Ollie takes away from his father's story are not universal truths about desire, loss, or failure but rather narrative truths supplied by his mother; she says, "For you, Ollie, Elba has stood in your memory as the paradise you lost because your father bungled the situation. But I'll tell you, I was relieved to leave that island behind and to have made it home, our family intact, across the ocean and into a house with a washing machine and drier and a fenced yard." Her desire for a commonplace existence is a counterpoint to Ollie's fanciful imagination: their journey to Europe is described almost mythically, and he believes that he and his brothers have a nearly magical ability to communicate in a hybrid language, or sometimes even without language. This dichotomy forms the central irony of the story: the significance of events shifts with perspective, and the artist is occasionally called back to reality from the near-chaos of his imagination. This same pattern can be observed in *Arrogance* when Egon's mother is permitted to speak, in *The Manikin* when Peg's perspective is weighed against her mother's, and in *Make Believe* when Bo must come to terms with the actual deaths of his mother and grandmother.

The relationship between knowledge and assumption within the context of storytelling is a theme Scott explores even more explicitly in *Liberation*. Until this point in her career, Scott's novels were remarkably heterogeneous in terms of setting and character, but *Liberation* revisits the setting of *Tourmaline*—Elba just after World War II—and even returns to the character of Adriana Nardi. Adriana's role in the earlier novel was to disappear and thus to become the object of fierce speculation. In *Liberation* she is the protagonist and the speculator who tries to fill in the details of her own story insofar as it connects to the narrative of a Senegalese soldier named Amdu Diop, who participated in complex ways in the liberation of Elba at the end of the war and also in the formation of Adriana's own story.

Liberation bridges the recent past with the historical past more self-consciously than *Tourmaline* does. There are two distinct story lines: the ten-year-old Adriana's life at the end of the war and the seventy-year-old Adriana's life in contemporary New Jersey. The elderly Adriana, often referred to by her married name (Mrs. Rundel), is having difficulty breathing as she rides a commuter rail to Penn Station. She is suffering from a blocked artery and is unable to communicate with her fellow riders to make them understand the seriousness of her situation. Scott intersperses this narrative with Adriana's story in 1944—from hiding in a cabinet to avoid German soldiers, to her discovery of Amdu in the family's boathouse, to Amdu's disappearance from her life as the African soldiers return to their homeland.

The novel culminates with a group of Fascists demolishing one of the Africans' ships, and although Adriana does not know for certain whether Amdu is on the ship, she feels certain that he is. Their relationship is based on intuition more than on conventional communication. They speak to each other in broken French, and their discussions are further hampered by Amdu's status as an African (discriminated against by native Elbans), as a soldier (known on the island for brutality, especially where young girls are concerned), and as an exile (driven into hiding by his own high moral principles). Underscoring the theme of failed communication, the final pages of the novel are preoccupied with the existence of a letter Amdu wrote asking Adriana's mother for Adriana's hand in marriage once she reaches womanhood. Adriana relies heavily on this letter to make sense of her narrative, but she has never seen the letter and does not even know if it ever existed. As a young woman she attempts to research Senegal with the desperate hope of discovering Amdu's fate. This research contrasts with her purer, if misguided, version of knowledge at a younger age: "When she was a young girl, she couldn't adequately appreciate the fact that what she called knowledge was based in large part on assumption. But then, one by one, so many of her assumptions proved wrong." Like Ollie in *Tourmaline,* these assumptions—whether wrong or right—are necessary to produce a unified story of one's life.

The theme of creating a self-narrative is as prominent in this novel as it is in all of Scott's previous novels. It could be said that the enduring theme of her work is the way attempts to create stories about oneself form the cornerstone of identity. *Liberation* re-creates Amdu and Adriana's story from both of their perspectives, which are brought together, surprisingly and violently, in the context of the war. Foreshadowing Adriana's adult conviction "that she will always, everywhere, be perceived as a foreigner," Amdu's narrative begins with his understanding of how his identity changes within the context of his relocation in Elba: "Where had he arrived, and where was here in relation to there? Here wasn't clay baked underfoot and coated with dust. There wasn't terraced with vineyards and olive groves.... There he had talent for everything. Here if they caught him they would kill him slowly.... Whatever story was told about him, he could tell a better one." Amdu's conclusion is that one's fate is determined by one's self-narrative. Like Bo in *Make Believe,* his self-stories are complex and imaginative: "In the future of this story, he would play lovely music on a piano, and a boy whose name he didn't know would listen through an open window of the lycée. Many years later the boy would remember Amdu's music at a moment of indecision. The memory would cause him to choose the path leading to happiness instead of sorrow." This particular iteration of Amdu's self-narrative reveals his essential empathy for others: his generosity of spirit and pureness of thought coupled with his pacifism make him the noblest character in the book.

Yet he doubts his own goodness because he fails to act when a group of his fellow soldiers rapes and murders an Elban girl, Sofia Canuti. His witnessing of this act causes the soldiers to threaten him, which precipitates his exile. Even though he knows "himself to be a good man" he is haunted by guilt:

> by running away from the place where a girl had been murdered, [he] had forfeited the one meaningful gift he could have offered the people of this island—the gift of testimony. Here he had kept his mouth shut. Here he had persuaded himself that with enough faith and the proper magical incantation conceived as prayer, he could revive everything that had been lost. And here he had come to his senses and understood that some forms of suffering cannot be rectified with a miracle.

This perspective had been with him throughout his exile from his fellow soldiers, and its theme is reinforced through the story of Adriana's Uncle Mario, who is a silent witness to the discussions of the Fascists who demolish the Africans' boat.

Before Amdu arrives at his final assessment of his identity "here" on Elba, he pursues the story of his life that enables him to continue forward, and to bond with Adriana, whom he had initially dismissed as a spoiled "princess." At the age of thirteen Amdu, who had "been encouraged by his mother through his early childhood to fashion faith into a belief that had practical uses," prays to God that the fish his uncle caught and kept in a hot truck for seven hours would not spoil, and his prayers are heard: "This was when Amdu first became aware of his potential holiness." Following the horror of the rape and murder he witnesses, Amdu relies on his belief in himself as a miracle worker to ensure that his life/narrative continues forward. His first "miracle" is to prevent an egg that Adriana has dropped from cracking:

> Amdu sensed the future in an instant. The girl would collapse in tears, blaming herself for the loss, then blaming him, demanding that Amdu

match her unhappiness with his own. As Amdu blinked, he told himself that the egg must not crack. Unhappiness must be avoided. Closing his eyes to the egg plunging toward the cobble, he murmured a prayer for it to survive intact. With absolute faith, he requested the exchange of what would happen with what should happen—life instead of death—a request as sensible as it was impossible or, perhaps, as possible as it was ridiculous.

Both Amdu and Adriana believe that he performs some sort of miracle that day, altering the laws of physics to prevent the unhappiness associated with death.

Amdu performs a second miracle after a group of Elban boys are torturing him by throwing rocks at him. When Pippa, Adriana's favorite dog, attacks one of the boys, Amdu "felt a sudden urge to prove that he could act heroically." As is often the case in wartime, heroism is associated with murder: in order to save the boy who had just been tormenting him, Amdu kills the dog. Surprised and ashamed by what he has done, Amdu, who believes that his purpose is "to work the works of God," promises to trade his abilities to work miracles for the rest of his life if God enables him to bring the dog back to life, which he does. By performing this miracle, "he had relinquished all claim to his magnificent potential.... He was through with his good work before he'd properly begun." Amdu has thus altered his story of his own life, and thus his fate. He also relinquishes his ability to "tell a better story" of his life than others tell: the boys he saved report only his brutality against the dog, not their own brutality, and he is ultimately associated with the soldiers who raped Sofia Canuti. He has lost his status as the moral, if cowardly, resister to the corrupt status quo of wartime.

Adriana is alone in her understanding of Amdu's special status. They have shared the experience of exile, of being completely cut off from their communities, and thus they develop a richer understanding of storytelling and its ability to transcend the seemingly absolute barrier between life and death. This notion accounts for the fact that the elderly Adriana doesn't die on the commuter train: as long as she continues to believe in the story of her future—that her husband will arrive in her hospital room and kiss her—it will be true.

Scott's absolute faith in narrative to shape the events of history as well as individual lives is what makes her one of the most substantial fiction writers of her generation. Her ability to resist the trends and market forces of the contemporary literary marketplace is testimony to her belief in fiction as a pure and vital art. In a 1998 essay in *Salon* she defended her belief in fiction as a form that should be allowed to flourish according to the author's imagination:

> The fake, the invented, the celebration of the unreal—these are among the finest joys of fiction. To demand "truth" from imaginative writing is to keep the balloons from soaring in the air... . We must keep the dreams, the flagrant inventions, the weird, strange, lyrical flights of fiction. We must keep the art as expansive as possible and allow the inspired writers ... to wander where they will.

No matter where her fiction wanders, it is clear that Scott will be counted among the most "inspired" writers of her time.

Selected Bibliography

WORKS OF JOANNA SCOTT

NOVELS
Fading, My Parmacheene Belle. New York: Henry Holt, 1987.
The Closest Possible Union. New York: Ticknor and Fields, 1988.
Arrogance. New York: Linden Press/Simon & Schuster, 1990.
The Manikin. New York: Henry Holt, 1996.
Make Believe. Boston: Little, Brown, 2000.
Tourmaline. Boston: Little, Brown, 2002.
Liberation. New York: Little, Brown, 2005.

SHORT STORY COLLECTIONS
Various Antidotes. New York: Henry Holt, 1994.
Everybody Loves Somebody. Boston: Little, Brown, 2006.

ESSAYS
"Yip." *Conjunctions* 28: 37–45 (spring 1997).
"Public Notice." *Conjunctions* 30:297–306 (spring 1998).
"Male Writers Vs. Female Writers: Beyond the Preconceptions." *Salon* (http://www.salon.com/media/1998/07/02media.html). July 2, 1998.

"The Leaps and Bounds of Conjunctions." *Review of Contemporary Fiction* 20, no. 1:126–132 (spring 2000).

"The Usefulness of Ugliness." *Conjunctions* 37:331–341 (fall 2001).

"Sebald Crawling." *Salmagundi* 135–136:243–254 (summer–fall 2002).

"On William Gaddis." *Conjunctions* 41: 393–394 (fall 2003).

"The Nature of Refuge." *Salmagundi* 143:167–171 (summer 2004).

"In a Glance." *Conjunctions* 46: 16–28 (fall 2006).

"Heaven and Hell." *Conjunctions* 47 (fall 2006).

CRITICAL AND BIOGRAPHICAL STUDIES

Rabinowitz, Paula. "Pulp Theory: On Literary History." *Poetics/Politics: Radical Aesthetics for the Classroom.* Edited by Amitava Kumar. New York: St. Martin's, 1999. Pp. 83–100.

Schechner, Mark. "Until the Music Stops: Women Novelists in a Post-Feminist Age." *Salmagundi* 113:220–238 (winter 1997).

Tissut, Anne-Laure. "Wonder-Working 'Antidotes': The Storyteller's Paraphernalia." *Revue française d'études américaines* 94:85–90 (December 2002).

GAY TALESE

(1932—)

Susan Butterworth

GAY TALESE IS a writer who is dedicated to the art and craft of nonfiction. He has made a significant contribution to the genre in American writing known as New Journalism, literary journalism, or creative nonfiction. He is respected for his thorough research and his artistic use of the techniques of fiction—especially setting, dialogue, and the use of varied and intimate points of view—in nonfiction writing. The threads of several recurrent themes and interests run through his work: an interest in the unknown and obscure and in failure; an ability to discover the extraordinary in the ordinary subject or to present the extraordinary subject from an unusual point of view; an interest in sportswriting and in Italian American subjects; a thread of intergenerational and father-son relationships; and of allowing a series of individual scenes and stories to illuminate larger themes.

Talese takes time with his subjects. His seductiveness as an interviewer is an important part of his gift. He is an easy man to like: well dressed, well mannered, respectful, sincerely interested, curious, and a good listener. He is easy to trust; people are willing to reveal their secrets and stories in response to his questions. He collects stories that are difficult to obtain, on hidden or risky subjects, the kind of stories that have been kept secret or fictionalized in the past. He is determined to use real names, to write accurate nonfiction, and to elevate nonfiction to a genre that is as respected as fiction. His genius is in taking so much time with his carefully gathered material and in knowing his subject so well that he writes from the inside out. Once he is thoroughly immersed in his subject he writes carefully, choosing the correct words for his precise, respectful tone and the correct transitions to weave together the threads of many stories coherently, artfully, without confusing the reader.

THE TAILOR'S SON

Gay Talese, named for his Italian grandfather Gaetano, was born February 7, 1932, in Ocean City, New Jersey. His Italian American background and his upbringing in Ocean City would be lifelong influences on his writing as well as his character. His father, Joseph Talese, had emigrated from Calabria in southern Italy as a young man of seventeen in the early 1920s. Joseph had apprenticed as a tailor in his hometown while still a young child and later continued to learn his trade from a cousin in Paris before emigrating to the United States and opening a tailoring business in Ocean City. He married Catherine DiPaola, whose family was also from Maida, his native village in Calabria. The couple became established in Ocean City, a sober, correct, and conservative town on an island near Atlantic City. Catherine's dress boutique joined Joseph's tailoring and dry-cleaning business in their building on the main street of town. Talese and his sister, Marian, four years younger, grew up in the apartment above the business, helping in the shop.

In *Unto the Sons* (1992), his book about his father's immigration from Italy, Talese describes his childhood as a lonely one, the life of an outsider, a minority within a minority, a Catholic in a Protestant community, an Italian among Irish Catholics at his parochial school. His father was a foreigner, marked by his accent and his tailored suits. While he was a respected businessman in the community, his position was tenuous, especially during the years of World War II when the United States and Italy were at war. Talese has written movingly of his father's anguish as the United States dropped bombs on southern Italy, where his mother and brothers still lived.

199

Yet his family did not fit the image of the typical Italian American home either. His mother was not the stereotypical Italian mama presiding over a kitchen and large family. Rather she was a businesswoman, ahead of her time, preoccupied with the shop. The elder Taleses were compatible and close, rarely out of each other's sight. Talese has written that he sometimes felt like an outsider in the family as well, an intruder on the devotion of his parents for each other. Thus he grew up a quiet, shy boy, well dressed and polite but always with a sense of being an outsider, observing from the background.

Talese attributes much of his success as an interviewer to his upbringing in the store. His well-tailored, well-mannered parents were liked by their customers and treated them with respect. His mother became a confidante to the women who tried on dresses in her boutique. Observing her, he learned to listen, to ask the right questions, to wait for the story to emerge. He would always identify with and be interested in the outsider, the unnoticed, and look for the extraordinary story hidden beneath the ordinary surface. Many of the subjects of his later profiles and books would be Italian Americans, and themes of fathers and sons would appear throughout his work.

THE YOUNG SPORTSWRITER

Shy and curious, the young Talese blossomed as a sportswriter for the high school newspaper. His high school teams were rarely winners, so he learned to write about losing. Riding the team bus to games, he found that he could befriend the athletes, that they would trust him with their stories. Even in high school Talese found his voice writing about the obscure, the losers. The role of curious observer and sympathetic reporter agreed with him. Talese became the high school correspondent for his hometown weekly, the *Ocean City Sentinel-Ledger,* and for the daily *Atlantic City Press.*

A mediocre student, Talese was nevertheless determined to go to college rather than follow his father into the tailoring business. He graduated from high school in 1949 and was rejected from a dozen colleges in the New Jersey, Pennsylvania, and New York area. Fortunately a customer of his father's was an alumnus of the University of Alabama and recommended Talese to the dean. Talese was accepted and enrolled at the University of Alabama. A northerner in a southern setting, Talese was still an outsider.

Majoring in journalism, Talese became sports editor of the college weekly and campus correspondent for the *Birmingham Post-Herald.* His interest in the unusual subject began to appear in articles about the benchwarmers, the athlete whose play lost the game, the locker-room attendant. At the same time, young Talese was reading fiction, the works of John O'Hara and Irwin Shaw, and beginning to experiment with narrative technique and point of view in his journalism.

After graduation from the University of Alabama in 1953 Talese found a job at the *New York Times,* where he worked as a news assistant during the summer and fall of 1953. During the Korean conflict all male students at the University of Alabama were enrolled in the Reserve Officers' Training Corps (ROTC), and Talese was commissioned in the army in 1954. He left the *Times* for Fort Knox and a tour of duty in Germany but returned to the *Times* after his military service as a reporter in the sports department.

Admiring the way a good fiction writer like O'Hara could weave together facts with the sensory details of the setting, dialogue, and imagery to give a feeling of immediacy and being present at the scene, Talese realized that he could meet the *New York Times*'s demanding standards of accuracy as well as use the techniques of fiction to make each sports article an example of fine writing craft.

These strict standards of nonfiction combined with a fictional approach to the art and craft of writing would become Talese trademarks. While a sportswriter for the *Times* he showed the special interest in writing about boxers that would last throughout his career. Talese befriended the prizefighter Floyd Patterson, sometimes joining him in his hotel room after the fight, developing the in-depth relationship that would allow him to write more than thirty articles about Patterson for the *Times*.

The *New York Times* was a venerable institution, considered America's "paper of record," known for its strictly factual, complete, and well-balanced reporting. Reportorial standards were high, and several of the paper's older writers were considered the preeminent figures of the day in journalism and nonfiction writing. However, by the late 1950s and early 1960s, the years that Talese was writing for the *Times*, print journalism was facing challenges from television. Americans were beginning to get their news and information from a medium even more ephemeral than the daily newspaper. Television was fast, first with the breaking news, and visual. Turner Catledge, managing editor of the *Times*, let it be known that he was looking for livelier, spicier writing. So in 1958 Talese was transferred from the sports desk to the news desk to be a part of this new emphasis on writing as well as reporting.

On June 10, 1959, Talese was married to Nan Ahearn, an editor at Random House. They had been dating for two years when she flew to Rome to join him after he had finished an assignment for the *New York Times Magazine* on the Via Veneto, where the director Federico Fellini was filming *La Dolce Vita*. Nan told her parents she was going to Rome to marry Talese, who was unaware that this was her intention. The convent-educated young editor contacted Talese's parents and arrived in Rome with his baptismal certificate and a plan to be married at the church of Trinità dei Monti. Talese agreed, and when they discovered that the marriage at Trinità dei Monti was impossible, they were married by an Italian magistrate in a civil ceremony in an ornate Roman municipal building. One of Talese's most admired authors, Irwin Shaw, to whom he had been introduced years earlier, was in Rome having a drink at the bar of the hotel where the young couple was drinking champagne on the eve of the ceremony. Shaw become the impromptu best man and gave the newlyweds a festive wedding party on the Via Veneto, attended by many involved in the filming of *La Dolce Vita*—a scene worthy of a Talese story, but this time he was a participant rather than an observer.

The couple moved into a brownstone on the Upper East Side of Manhattan, where they still live, gradually acquiring more space in the building until they had the opportunity to buy it. The Taleses have two daughters, Pamela Frances, born in 1964, and Catherine Gay, born in 1967. After the birth of their second daughter they bought a second home near the beach and his parents in Ocean City. Throughout their two-career marriage Nan Talese has worked as an editor, eventually becoming a senior vice president at Doubleday and issuing books under her own imprint.

THE ESQUIRE PROFILES

Talese rewrote his news articles up until minutes before each deadline, determined to get each word and transition right, with an eye to chronicling contemporary events as a record for future historians. He chafed under the restrictions of time and space as well as editorial constraints on style and material at the daily *Times*. He needed to write for a less perishable, ephemeral medium than a daily newspaper. In addition to his reporting for the *Times*, Talese began to freelance for the monthly *Esquire* magazine, which allowed him the opportunity to gather material over a period of time as well as freedom to write longer, more in-depth articles about riskier subjects. More space allowed him to develop more points of view, to use to better advantage the literary elements of setting, dialogue, and character development over time.

Writing for a monthly rather than a daily deadline, Talese was able to devote more time to research and interviewing. Talese is a listener, an observer, a practitioner of what he calls "the fine art of hanging out." He prefers to conduct his interviews face to face, without a tape recorder, certainly not over the telephone. He takes notes on small pieces of shirt cardboard that he keeps in his front pocket, but he is gathering visual details of the subject and the atmosphere even more than he is gathering his subject's words. He wants to see people in their environment. Talese gathers such an abundance of material that much of it never makes it into an article or book, but this thoroughness gives him the ability to write about his subject from an intimate point of view. Talese tries to stay with his subject until he can understand what the subject is thinking and to return often enough to observe some significant change over time.

Some of the early *Esquire* articles, first collected as *The Overreachers* in 1965 and reissued as *Fame and Obscurity* (1970) and again in *The Gay Talese Reader* (2003), reveal the subjects and themes that would preoccupy Talese for the rest of his career as he followed his subjects, described them in ordinary situations, and talked to the people around them. In "The Loser," Talese writes intimately about the boxer Floyd Patterson, with whom he spent a great deal of time. The opening scene, set in an abandoned clubhouse, evokes a mood of melancholy, of past glory, of an athlete trying to rebuild his fading career. The reader is introduced to interior monologue, to Patterson's thoughts in response to the Talese curiosity.

In "Joe Louis: The King as a Middle-Aged Man," Talese follows the prizefighter Joe Louis at age fifty, another portrait of a sports figure past his prime. This piece, which appeared in *Esquire* in 1962, caused the writer Tom Wolfe to coin the term "New Journalism," meaning a form of nonfiction that creates a mood using techniques similar to short-story writing—scene setting, intimate detail, interior monologue—combined with accurate journalistic reporting. A profile of the stage director Joshua Logan illustrates Talese's use of scenes and of using serendipitously observed material. The article includes a revealing argument between Logan and his leading lady, which offers a different perspective and possibly more insight into his subject than a traditional interview. "The Ethnics of Frank Costello" reveals Talese's interest in Italian American subjects and in the attitudes of southern Italians toward the underworld.

Talese had come to New York City as a small-town boy from southern New Jersey. He approached city life with fresh eyes, and years later he wrote an essay called "When I Was Twenty-five." His sense of wonder and his wanderings around the city gave him material for many articles and essays. "New York Is a City of Things Unnoticed," Talese's first essay for *Esquire* in 1960, became the opening chapter of his first book. *New York: A Serendipiter's Journey* (1961) is a short book illustrated with photographs, based on his keen sense of observation and his delight in everyday people and scenes, focusing on obscure neighborhoods and people, much of the material gathered while on assignment for the *Times*.

This same intense curiosity about the city, ability to find an unusual angle, and interest in unnoticed people led to Talese's next book, *The Bridge* (1964). He observed the building of the Verrazano-Narrows Bridge between Brooklyn and Staten Island and the way it changed once isolated neighborhoods. He hung around the construction sites, observing, waiting, and getting to know people. His commitment to detailed, meticulous research and reporting is evident in this elegant slim volume, illustrated with photographs and drawings, which focuses on the lives of the steelworkers working on the bridge, the unnoticed, unchronicled "boomers." A photo of a steelworker hanging from the skeleton of the unfinished bridge is a haunting visual image for the book.

These two early books are rooted in Talese's sense of place, of setting. The New York Times Building on West Forty-third Street in Manhattan would be the stage from which the action of his first best-seller, *The Kingdom and the Power* (1969), would unfold.

BEST-SELLERS

In 1965 Talese left his job at the *New York Times* to concentrate on writing more in-depth magazine articles and to write longer, book-length nonfiction than he had previously attempted. The years at the *Times* would continue to influence Talese in his strict insistence on verifiable facts and the use of real names in his nonfiction, no matter how risky or intimate the subject. But leaving the newspaper gave him the time necessary for carrying out his research, for exploring his subjects in width and depth, and for crafting long works of well-researched, beautifully-written nonfiction.

His first long project was about what he knew best, the *New York Times*. Talese had previously written some articles about the *Times* for *Esquire* and felt that the subject was worthy of more in-depth treatment. Talese's genius for interviewing and observation served him well. The behind-the-scenes portrait of the workings of the institution is told as a series of stories about people, a series of interlocking profiles. With the voices and points of view of dozens of characters available as raw material, he was able to weave a tale of the venerable institution through the detailed stories of the men who worked and wrote there. In two and a half years of interviews Talese was able to learn what the paper's publishers and editors and reporters felt and thought as events unfolded.

The Kingdom and the Power is Talese's first intergenerational saga, depicting the Ochs/Sulzberger dynasty that controls the family-run newspaper. The book centers around a time of change in an institution that had been stable and conservative for more than half a century, changes that coincided with the time that Talese worked for the paper, and ends with the upheavals of 1968 at the newspaper and in the country, the passing of the old order into the new. The book's revelations are groundbreaking, revealing an alliance between the government and the media and raising questions of objectivity. The detailed motivations of individuals at the *New York Times* suggest some larger implications about how public opinion is shaped. Events as reported by the *Times,* with its reputation for thorough and strictly factual reporting, were widely regarded as truth by the public. Talese suggests that there is no objective truth in journalism; rather, the choices made by reporters and editors influence the way people think.

Not only is the material dense and detailed, but the care taken with the writing is evident. Each word is precise; the commentary is clear, lucid, and intelligent, with layers of information carefully and artfully arranged. The result is crisp and three-dimensional-constructed, like sculpture or architecture. The book's setting, the New York Times Building, ties together the dozens of characters in one place. Talese's intimate point of view, his instinct for material, his attention to style, and his incisive commentary on power and politics was an immediate success. *The Kingdom and the Power* was a surprise hit with the public, a national best-seller, and the first of a wave of nonfiction books about journalism and the media.

Talese was working on several projects simultaneously at this time and was beginning to be financially successful. He was able to buy, and later to beautifully restore, the brownstone on the Upper East Side where he and his family had been renting, with the money he began to make with the success of *The Kingdom and the Power.*

In the late 1960s, while researching and writing *The Kingdom and the Power,* he was also shadowing the underworld figure Salvatore (Bill) Bonanno for a book about the inner life of a Mafia crime family. At the same time, he continued to write profiles for *Esquire*. A second collection of short works was published as *Fame and Obscurity: Portraits by Gay Talese* (1970). While several of the profiles contained in the earlier collection were reprinted, along with the short works *New York: A Serendipiter's Journey* and *The Bridge,* the new collection contained the profiles "Frank Sinatra Has a Cold," a portrait of the famous singer from an unusual and original point of view, and "The Silent Season of a Hero," a portrait of Joe DiMaggio in his later years, which are among Talese's best writing.

Typical of Talese's work, both of these profiles are written as a series of scenes. "Frank Sinatra Has a Cold" opens in a club in Beverly Hills and describes the fifty-year-old Sinatra on a bad day: the singer has a cold. Talese was not able to interview the celebrity, so he interviewed the people around him and observed Sinatra's behavior in several situations in Beverly Hills, Las Vegas, and New York. The resulting profile presents Sinatra from a singular point of view, as a father, a son, and a friend as well as a demanding, sometimes petulant and quarrelsome entertainer.

"The Silent Season of a Hero" depicts the retired Yankees baseball player Joe DiMaggio as a man who is determined to protect his private life and the memory of his former wife Marilyn

Monroe. The opening of the essay is set at DiMaggio's Restaurant in San Francisco, and subsequent scenes describe the great hitter and those around him on the golf course, at Mickey Mantle Day in Yankee Stadium, and at spring training in Florida. The Sicilian background of both DiMaggio and Sinatra is mentioned as an influence on their personalities. "The Silent Season of a Hero" was later anthologized in the 1999 volume *The Best American Sports Writing of the Century.*

In the author's note at the beginning of *Fame and Obscurity,* Talese discusses his work as New Journalism, defending the form, asserting that while it reads like fiction it should be strictly based on reliable reportage, which demands an imaginative approach and observation over time, leading to insights into the subject's mind. Talese was aware that the success of his method depended on his skill as an interviewer. This depth and insight cannot be as fully accomplished in magazine writing, he notes, as in an extended work of nonfiction like his recent *The Kingdom and the Power* or his upcoming book on three generations of an Italian American family, *Honor Thy Father* (1971), because it takes more time and space: both *The Kingdom and the Power* and *Honor Thy Father* are over five hundred pages long.

Taking time with his subject became another Talese trademark. After leaving the *Times,* Talese was able to spend months, even years, with his subjects. He spent much time in the mid-1960s into the 1970s living in hotels, traveling, and researching in California—in Beverly Hills for the Sinatra profile, San Francisco for the DiMaggio piece, living with the Bonanno family in San Jose researching *Honor Thy Father,* and later spending two months at the Sandstone commune in Topanga Canyon researching *Thy Neighbor's Wife* (1980).

Honor Thy Father, Talese's book about the Bonanno crime family, took over five years to research and write. As a reporter for the *Times* in 1965 Talese first saw Bill Bonanno at a federal courthouse in Manhattan where he was testifying about the disappearance of his father, Joe Bonanno, head of one of the New York crime families. His curiosity was aroused. Bill Bonanno was a young Italian American man like himself but one who had followed a different path. Talese's own father had resented the Mafia stereotype which tainted respectable Italian American citizens like himself. Now Talese would explore the forbidden subject.

Talese became friendly and intimate with Bill Bonanno, spending time with him in New York, having dinner with both wives and sets of children present, and spending much of one winter and spring at the Bonanno home in San Jose, California, with Bill's wife, children, bodyguards, and associates. Talese traveled to Sicily to visit the Bonanno family village. Scenes and settings took shape. He approached his story of a Mafia family's rise and fall as an intergenerational history and ultimately described the fall and exile of the Bonanno family as the weakening of ethnic traditions.

Honor Thy Father is framed by scenes that depict the once powerful Bonanno family in retreat and decline. The book opens with head of the family, Joseph Bonanno, being abducted at gunpoint by a rival crime boss, and the family in hiding. The final words of the book are "Salvatore Bonanno has surrendered," as Bill gives himself up to a federal marshal. *Honor Thy Father* is about the exile of the Bonannos to Tucson and San Jose and about the intimate life of the family in the larger context of the Sicilian culture that fostered organized crime.

Gaining the trust of the subject in this case meant gaining the trust of the entire family: Bill Bonanno's wife, sister, children, and bodyguards. Talese spent years shadowing the Bonannos, following their fortunes when Bill was in hiding or in jail, observing changes over time, until he knew his subject from the inside out. Talese learned what it was like to think and feel as Bill Bonanno. What is it like to spend most of your adult life in hiding or in jail? What is it like to be the wife or the child of a criminal? His ability to gain the trust of Bill Bonanno and his household is a testament to his skill as an interviewer, and the choice of exploring organized crime from such an intimate perspective represents his riskiest and most dramatic subject up to that time. Yet

Talese's tone is not sensational; rather, it is understated and respectful. The focus is on the cultural aspects of Mafia life and the effects of the organized-crime lifestyle on Bill Bonanno's psyche and on his family.

Talese's tolerant and nonjudgmental approach to underworld crime figures as ordinary people in extraordinary circumstances was not always appreciated by the critics, although it does reflect the underlying consciousness of many Sicilians and southern Italians. In a culture where centuries of hostile invaders made many laws for their own convenience, there was no social stigma attached to breaking the law. In spite of such criticism, *Honor Thy Father* was another popular bestseller. The respectful tone, intimate details of family life, and carefully written scenes reveal more about the Mafia than any previous nonfiction. Talese cared about his subjects, and they trusted him enough to break the Mafia "code of silence." Talese was able to establish trust funds for the education of his daughters, and for the education of Bill Bonanno's four children, with the proceeds from the book.

Now with two full-length nonfiction bestsellers behind him, Talese was offered a contract and advance from Doubleday for his next book. The subject of *Thy Neighbor's Wife* (1980), the American sexual revolution, would be broader and even riskier and more controversial than the underworld he revealed in *Honor Thy Father*. The trust required to allow his subjects to break the code of silence surrounding sexuality and to allow him to use their real names and describe their deepest sexual fantasies in print challenged his persuasiveness as an interviewer. Talese continued to be adamant about his standards of nonfiction. If a subject asked that his real name not be used, Talese did not wish to talk to him. Always, while his writing style was novelistic his research standards were strictly reportorial and factual.

While researching *Thy Neighbor's Wife,* Talese managed two massage parlors in New York City and lived at the free-love commune Sandstone, which would become the stage on which the tale unfolds. He conducted hundreds of interviews and researched such diverse stories as the life of Hugh Hefner and origins of *Playboy* magazine, the background and history of censorship and sex laws in the United States, and the lives of nude models and a couple, the Bullaros, who became involved in free love and open marriage.

The way was not always smooth, and the book took years to complete. At first Talese had planned to focus on the story of a college-educated masseuse and one of her clients. The couple fell in love, married, and then declined to allow Talese to use their story. After being exceedingly candid about their sexual experiences and involvement in Sandstone, the Bullaros changed their minds about being part of the book. Their story was pivotal; they were the "everyman" thread of the book, the typical American couple who became part of the sexual revolution. Talese flew to Los Angeles and convinced them that their story was honest and important, one that needed to be told. Their particular and intimate story, in Talese's hands, is connected to a universal theme, a larger significance. His handling of sensitive material is so accurate, nonjudgmental, and respectful that none of his subjects have ever been angry with him for what he has published.

Talese has said that he enjoys research and reporting but finds the writing a slow and difficult task. Years of research yield a vast amount of material, of which perhaps only 20 percent will be used in the subsequent book. Years of gathering material and hours behind the typewriter may leave him without a word of his book written, not yet sure of how to begin, how to organize the material, or how to offer new insights. Weaving the threads of many stories together in a clear and seamless manner is a challenge to the writer's craft, one that takes as much time as Talese's careful research. The description in *Thy Neighbor's Wife* is graphic, but never crude. Talese's talent is for the precise word. Even the most intimate details are presented with his characteristic factual and formal tone.

Talese was attacked, sometimes personally, for the subject matter of *Thy Neighbor's Wife* and for his research methods, his participation in the world of massage parlors and the life of the nudist free-love retreat at Sandstone. His transparency, his relentless openness about his reporting methods, sources, and experiences, had repercussions for his family. His wife felt that her privacy had been invaded to an intolerable extent. His marriage was strained, as were the social sensibilities of his parents in conservative Ocean City. This was a book that people covered in brown paper when they carried it on the train. It was, however, another extraordinary best-seller, earning millions of dollars in sales and movie rights.

Deeply interested in the radical changes in attitude toward sexuality in the 1960s, he wrote the book partly in reaction to his strict and sexually repressive upbringing in the conservative town of Ocean City, where the nuns at his parochial school had counseled their students to sleep with their arms crossed, hands on shoulders, to discourage masturbation. In the final chapter of *Thy Neighbor's Wife,* Talese abandons the voice of the invisible narrator for the first time and writes about himself in the third person. In the closing scene, set in a nudist colony close to Ocean City, he is nude on the beach, showing himself to the anchored yachts belonging to the voyeurs of his hometown.

His immigrant father had worked hard for acceptance in the community, becoming president of the Rotary Club, a golfer, a member of the country club. Now the son had openly challenged the conventional standards of morality. His book was criticized by the local Ocean City newspaper, and his father was slighted on the golf course. Talese offered to sell his summer home in Ocean City to save his parents further embarrassment. Having revealed himself, the quiet, well-behaved boy confronted his own conservative, repressive past. The stage was set for his next book.

There is a gap of over ten years between *Thy Neighbor's Wife* and his next full-length work. Wanting to return to an Italian American subject, Talese considered revisiting Frank Sinatra or Joe DiMaggio as subjects. Struggling with a direction for a new book, he invested some time researching Lee Iacocca and the Chrysler Corporation before deciding to write a more autobiographical book, a book that would include himself as a character.

Unto the Sons (1992), his most complex work, would take five years to research and five more to write. Talese would depart for the first time from strict reportorial writing. He writes about his boyhood in the first person, entering the realm of memoir, including more interior, reflective writing than in any previous work.

Unto the Sons begins where *Thy Neighbor's Wife* leaves off, on the beach in Ocean City. *Unto the Sons* is his father's story, the story of life in southern Italy, immigration to America, and integration into the life of Ocean City. The book spans two continents and hundreds of years of history but is centered in his parents' shop in Ocean City and framed with his father's conflicting loyalties as an Italian American during the invasion of Italy in 1944. The larger history of southern Italy in entwined with the intergenerational story of Talese's family, always returning to the shop in Ocean City and to Joseph's struggle for assimilation.

His most novelistic work, *Unto the Sons* contains some beautiful descriptive writing. Talese traveled to Italy and Paris while researching the book and was fortunate to have the diary of his father's cousin, a tailor in Paris, as a source. Thanks to Talese's trademark fictional techniques of scene setting and exploration of characters, and to his weaving together of the various threads of the story with careful transitions, the reader is able to clearly understand the complicated history of southern Italy and the causes and motivation for the major wave of Italian immigration in the early twentieth century.

With *Unto the Sons,* Talese set himself the most difficult and complex writing task of his career. The subject was vaster and the time needed for research was greater than any project he had undertaken so far. Much of the research had to be done in Italy, and at the same time the writing task, combining elements of novelistic, reportorial, and first-person memoir styles, was an artistic and technical challenge. To understand the immigrant, the reader needs to understand where he has come from. As Talese clarifies history, he also clarifies cultural traits. The book achieves a universal significance beyond the memoir, moving from the intimate first-person voice of the opening—a particular family history—to the dramatic final scene, where Talese writes the ending of his story in the third person, shedding light on the larger Italian American experience.

Talese has noted that silence is a habit with southern Italians. The code of silence applies not only to the underworld but also to the past. With *Unto the Sons,* Talese broke another barrier of silence. But the book came at a cost. Writing about his own past was technically and psychologically difficult, and always a perfectionist, he demanded a higher level of writing from himself.

Sometimes called "the Italian *Roots,*" *Unto the Sons* was highly acclaimed when it was published in 1992 and became Talese's fourth best-seller. Once again he had conceived and successfully completed a book that was pioneering in its subject matter as well as superbly crafted. Sections of the book, including the moving first and last chapters, have been anthologized in collections of Italian-American writing and as fine examples of American autobiography.

Joseph Talese died in 1993, having lived to see the completion and publication of *Unto the Sons.* The elder Taleses had been married and lived in Ocean City for over sixty years. Talese would continue to divide his time between New York and Ocean City, even to the point of having duplicate offices and sets of clothes in his two homes. With or without his wife and daughters, Talese would regularly commute to Ocean City to visit his mother and take her to restaurants and casinos for the rest of her life.

A WRITER'S LIFE

Unto the Sons was conceived as the first book in a three-volume series. In 1992 Talese signed a contract with a six-figure advance from Knopf for the sequel, which would be due in 1995. The sequel would be the writer's own story, the story of the immigrant's son growing up as an outsider in mid- and late-twentieth-century America. The manuscripts for both *Unto the Sons* and *Thy Neighbor's Wife* had been delivered to the publisher four or five years late, partly due to his long research process and partly due to his complex subject matter and demanding standards for his writing. He had struggled with beginning *Thy Neighbor's Wife* and struggled with moving through *Unto the Sons.* Although he is a disciplined worker while writing, his daily output is small, as he slowly assembles each sentence and paragraph until it meets his standards for good prose. His new book project presented the extra difficulty of requiring him to write about himself as the main character, a task that was contrary to the journalistic instincts of the former *New York Times* reporter.

In 1993 Talese accepted an assignment as a contributor to *The New Yorker* magazine. He hoped that the shorter deadlines at the weekly periodical would give him the satisfaction of completing articles such as those he had written for *Esquire* in earlier years. Reflecting his interest in American sexuality and in risky and unusual subjects, he spent six months in 1993–1994 pursuing a story about the notorious Bobbitt case, in which a wife had cut off her husband's penis. Once written, however, the story was rejected by *New Yorker* editor Tina Brown. Magazine publishing had changed since the 1960s. Talese found that he had less freedom in choosing his subjects and also that production costs had limited the space available for the lengthy in-depth articles that he preferred to write.

A piece entitled *"Ali in Havana,"* which appeared in *Esquire* in 1996, was the only long new piece by Gay Talese to appear in the period of more than ten years between *Unto the Sons* and its sequel. This essay, which was selected for the anthology *The Best American Essays 1997,* skillfully exemplifies some of the qualities that by this time had become identified with Talese's work. Talese returns to writing about sports from an unusual angle. The subject, Muhammad Ali, is a former champion prizefighter, fifty-four years old, retired for fifteen years, and suffering from Parkinson's disease. The opening establishes the setting, Havana, Cuba; the first scene is a negotiation for black market Cuban cigars. Talese describes the people around Ali and then moves to the central scene, a meeting between Fidel Castro and Ali. The conversation is rather strained. The writing is understated; the extraordinary situation is presented by focusing on the ordinariness of the two celebrated, aging men.

Working with Barbara Lounsberry, a professor of English and journalism at the University of Northern Iowa, Talese coedited an anthology of nonfiction, a college text called *Writing Creative Nonfiction: The Literature of Reality* (1996). His introduction, titled "Origins of a Nonfiction Writer," is something of a manifesto of his beginnings and his writing philosophy. Selections from his own work appear in the anthology, illustrating the elements of writing literary nonfiction. The section on reporting includes a chapter of *The Bridge;* the profile of Floyd Patterson called "The Loser" illustrates the technique of writing interior monologue; and the final chapter of *Unto the Sons* appears as an illustration of the principle that a larger, universal significance needs to be present in personal memoir writing. Talese's methods and ideas have become part of the accepted pedagogy of nonfiction writing.

A collection of Talese's shorter works had not appeared since 1970. Thirty years later he was the successful and well-known author of four best-sellers and a model for writers of literary nonfiction. A new collection, *The Gay Talese Reader: Portraits & Encounters* (2003), included several of the previously collected and now classic profiles along with some newer material: "Ali in Havana," "Origins of a Nonfiction Writer," and the selection from *Unto the Sons* called "The Brave Tailors of Maida," which had earlier appeared in *Esquire* and then in the anthology *Best American Essays 1989.*

The long-awaited sequel to *Unto the Sons* was finished in 2005 and appeared as *A Writer's Life* (2006). Talese's most autobiographical work, *A Writer's Life* is a book about craft; its structure is the story of his struggle to write the book. He reveals his methods while tying together several stories to which he has committed hours and years of research but which have not come to fruition as books. Once again the structure is complex, as he weaves his background and his methods into his stories. Each story reveals something about his writing process as well as something about Talese's collection of interests and obsessions.

Talese's writing career began with sports, and in the opening scene of *A Writer's Life* we find the writer at home, struggling with his book and watching sports on television. During a slow-moving Yankees game he changes the channel to the final game of the 1999 women's World Cup soccer tournament. The scoreless game between the United States and China moves into the deciding penalty-kick stage, and one of the Chinese women, Liu Ying, misses her all-important kick. China loses the game and the title. The sportswriter in him is awakened. Here is a loser whose story he cannot get out of his mind, and soon he is on an airplane flying to China in pursuit of Liu Ying's story. The tale of his extraordinary persistence in tracking down this young woman and her story is one of the threads of his revealing book.

Another thread—the most autobiographical in the book—is a memoir of his experiences in Alabama. From a discussion of his college years he moves to his coverage of the civil rights demonstrations in Selma, which he reported for the *New York Times* in 1965, and his return twenty-five years later on freelance assignment for the same paper to cover the silver anniversary of the event. He approaches the political event as the story of individuals both black and white, sheriffs, politicians, and lawyers, reflecting his interest in people and his skills as an interviewer. Again his gift for gaining entry into private lives and his interest in the ordinary, personal angle is evident as he focuses a story about twenty-five years of change in race relations on an interracial wedding in Selma to which he manages to obtain an invitation.

A third thread is the story of John and Lorena Bobbitt. In 1993 Lorena Bobbitt cut off her husband's penis while he slept, claiming that he had committed "marital sexual abuse." Talese flew to Manassas, Virginia, to observe the court hearings and trials and interview dozens of people involved with the Bobbitts and the case. Reminiscent of his approach in *Thy Neighbor's Wife,* he re-creates and describes the sensational event graphically but carefully and respectfully. He becomes intimately acquainted with John

Bobbitt, an ordinary man, an inarticulate ex-marine.

In an interview with the journalist and editor Robert Boynton, Talese later described the level of trust he had received from John Bobbitt. In an extraordinary scene retold in Boynton's book *The New New Journalism*, Bobbitt and his urologist watch a pornographic movie in Talese's hotel room in order to test the function of Bobbitt's reattached penis. Talese staged the scene of the female urologist holding the erect penis and talking about its blood flow, seeing himself as the director of a visual story. Talese's purpose in including the detailed account of his pursuit of the Bobbitt story is not only to illustrate his commitment to research and his ability to obtain his subject's trust, but also to illustrate that his interest in failure extends even to his own failure, as this story in which he has invested so much time is rejected by his editor at *The New Yorker*.

And Talese writes about restaurants. He tells the reader that he loves restaurants, has loved them since childhood in Ocean City. He and his family have always relaxed in restaurants. His father became more communicative and animated away from the store; his beautiful, well-dressed mother enjoyed being seen in restaurants. Talese enjoys interviewing in restaurants. He gets away from the solitary work of writing in restaurants. He has more than once contemplated writing a restaurant story. A book idea that Talese spent years researching but never got into print is the story he calls "The Building," about a building on East Sixty-third Street that houses a series of restaurants that fail. Completing the circle back to his first book and "New York Is a City of Things Unnoticed," this story had been in the back of his mind for years. He considered the building as the setting for the stalled sequel to *Unto the Sons,* the book that is years behind schedule, the book that he is now struggling to write.

And writing is a struggle, he tells us in *A Writer's Life*. Every morning while he is writing, he arrives at his desk at 8 A.M. and works for four hours, breaks for lunch and an afternoon walk, and returns to his desk for another four hours. A disciplined worker, he has duplicate desks and workrooms at his homes in New York and New Jersey, where he is surrounded by panels of Styrofoam on which he pins his notes and organizes his intricate constructs of interlocking stories. In spite of experimenting with computer word processing, his most serious writing is done in pencil on yellow lined pads, word by word, sentence by sentence, lingering over each sentence until it is as perfect as he can make it. It is a tedious, slow, demanding process.

A Writer's Life ends where it began: with Liu Ying, the Chinese soccer player. Talese leaves a note for his wife and flies to Beijing, where he persists for five months until he finally is able to interview the soccer player and her mother. The book is rambling and circular but fascinating and worthwhile for its stories as well as what it reveals about Talese's methods and craft. *A Writer's Life* illustrates the fact that Talese is a perfectionist who is not willing to publish anything that doesn't meet his standards and who has experienced failure as well as success. *A Writer's Life* was completed in 2005, ten years after the original publisher's due date. Catherine Talese, the writer's mother, who had inspired his dedication to interviewing, died on August 11, 2005, at age ninety-eight, days after the completion of the manuscript.

Unto the Sons and *A Writer's Life* are the first two books in a planned three-book autobiographical series. In his mid-seventies, Talese is vigorous and youthful, and pursuing ideas for his next book. He has spoken of following each of these long and complex books with a shorter book about the groundskeepers at Yankee Stadium, which would be consistent with his interests in sports, New York, and telling the stories of the unknown and obscure. But, he says, he doesn't find this subject risky enough. Instead he is organizing material for a book tentatively called *A Writer's Marriage*. Would this be sufficiently interesting to the reader, worth expending the necessary time, worth revealing such personal material? Considering the amount of time he and his wife have spent apart pursuing their two visible and successful careers in their nearly fifty years of marriage, and especially in view of his highly publicized and criticized research method for *Thy Neighbor's Wife,* surely this subject will be of more than passing interest to Talese's readers.

THE ART OF NONFICTION

Gay Talese has specialized in widening the subject matter of nonfiction, in breaking ground, in exposing to the air of books in print subjects traditionally hidden. He has written in *The Kingdom and the Power* about what goes on behind the scenes in American media; he has penetrated the Mafia code of silence in *Honor Thy Father,* broken the silence surrounding sexual behavior in *Thy Neighbor's Wife,* given voice to the reticent Italian-American writer in *Unto the Sons,* and exposed a writer's struggles in *A Writer's Life. A Writer's Marriage* would break the code of silence once more.

In writing about his own marriage Talese would be exploring in reportorial nonfiction an intimate subject that has traditionally been the material of either fiction or confessional memoir writing. This is exactly what he has sought to do: to develop a genre of nonfiction that is intimate and personal without being confessional, a genre that has no appropriate label on the shelves of bookstores. Talese is a teller of stories, true stories with real names, not a writer of memoir.

Talese has been hailed a founder of New Journalism, defined as reportorially based, narrative-driven long-form nonfiction. His immersion-research technique, spending months and years observing and living with (and as one of) his subjects broke ground for a new generation of journalists, anthropologists, and academics who would immerse themselves in the worlds of their subjects in order to write from the inside out. Jon Krakauer's *Into Thin Air* (1997), Barbara Ehrenreich's *Nickel and Dimed: On (Not) Getting By in America* (2001), and Michael Lewis' *Moneyball: The Art of Winning an Unfair Game* (2003) are examples of an increasingly popular trend in nonfiction writing for narration from an insider's point of view. Gay Talese's devotion to research and experiments with point of view in nonfiction have influenced the rise of nonfiction as a genre.

Talese's work goes beyond using the techniques of fiction to explore nonfiction subjects in depth. His purpose is to use intimate detail, language, and form to raise nonfiction to the level of art equally deserving of the respect given to fiction or poetry. He is a reporter who is reaching for art and respect for his genre, who combines extraordinary journalistic reporting with the mood and intimacy of fiction, who strives to present reality in a way that is factual, multifaceted, evocative, and beautiful. Talese is a storyteller, but a teller of stories that are true and accurate and completely nonfictional. Unlike *The Kingdom and the Power, Honor Thy Father,* and *Thy Neighbor's Wife,* Talese's last two books do not have an index. Why? Because there are no indexes in fiction. In fiction the reader is invited to read the entire story, not to reference unconnected facts. Talese's tales are complex. He moves around in time, from past to present and back again. The connections are essential. A creative arrangement of the material, careful organization, and clear transitions are as fundamental to the craft as the tone and mood of scenes, the intimate moments and interior monologues of characters, and the impeccable accumulation of background material. Talese proves the point that nonfiction as literary work is as beautiful, precise, and demanding a craft as fiction. Formerly the realm of fiction, detailed and intimate stories about ordinary people in extraordinary situations, or extraordinary people in ordinary situations, become in Gay Talese's hands a vital literary nonfiction, the literature of reality.

Selected Bibliography

WORKS OF GAY TALESE

NONFICTION
New York: A Serendipiter's Journey. New York: Harper & Row, 1961.
The Bridge. New York: Harper & Row, 1964.
The Overreachers. New York: Harper & Row, 1965.
The Kingdom and the Power. New York: World, 1969.

Fame and Obscurity: Portraits by Gay Talese. New York: World, 1970.

Honor Thy Father. New York: World, 1971.

Thy Neighbor's Wife. Garden City, N.Y.: Doubleday, 1980.

Unto the Sons. New York: Knopf, 1992.

Writing Creative Nonfiction: The Literature of Reality. With Barbara Lounsberry. New York: HarperCollins, 1996.

The Gay Talese Reader: Portraits & Encounters. Introduction by Barbara Lounsberry. New York: Walker, 2003.

A Writer's Life. New York: Knopf, 2006.

CRITICAL AND BIOGRAPHICAL STUDIES

Aste, Mario. "Talese's *Unto the Sons:* An Inward Journey to Italian/American Roots." *Canadian Journal of Italian Studies* 19, no. 53:150–163 (1996).

Boynton, Robert S. *The New New Journalism: Conversations with America's Best Nonfiction Writers on Their Craft.* New York: Vintage, 2005.

Gambino, Richard. "The Need to Reframe Talese's Question." *Italian Americana* 12, no. 1:30–37 (fall-winter 1993).

Gioia, Dana. "Low Visibility: Thoughts on Italian American Writers." *Italian Americana* 12, no. 1:7–15 (fall-winter 1993).

Lounsberry, Barbara. "Gay Talese's *Fathers and Sons.*" In her *The Art of Fact: Contemporary Artists of Nonfiction.* New York: Greenwood, 1990.

———. "Gay Talese and the Fine Art of Hanging Out." *Creative Nonfiction* 16:121–134 (2001).

———. "Bridging the Silence: Gay Talese's Uncomfortable Journey." *Lit: Literature Interpretation Theory* 14, no. 1:37–62 (January-March 2003).

———. Introduction to *The Gay Talese Reader: Portraits & Encounters.* New York: Walker, 2003.

SCOTT TUROW
(1949—)

Nancy L. Bunge

SCOTT TUROW HAS spent his entire career writing best-sellers, which invites the assumption that market calculations shape his choices. But he seems determined to realize as many of his abilities, emotions, and values as possible, and this requires an honesty about who he is and what he wants incompatible with merchandizing himself. Because Turow insists on accepting himself as he is, even though many critics have proclaimed that he produces literature, not genre fiction, Turow happily sees himself as a mystery writer.

Throughout his career Scott Turow has manifested loyalty not only to his own insights and intuitions but also to his wife, Annette; to his family; to his editor, Jonathan Galassi; to his agent, Gail Hochman; to his publisher, Farrar, Straus and Giroux; to his law firm, Sonnenschein Nath & Rosenthal; to the law, to the city of Chicago; and to his fans.

Scott Turow accepts himself, but that does not mean he rests in self-satisfaction. Instead he engages in lifelong learning: practicing law in new contexts, writing fresh books and moving into the political arena, acting as president of the Authors Guild, serving on the Illinois Executive Ethics Committee, chairing the Illinois State Appellate Defender's Commission, and accepting a position on the commission appointed by George Ryan, then governor of Illinois, to reconsider the death penalty in Illinois. Turow has even begun to sing in public, performing "Take Me Out to the Ball Game" during the seventh-inning stretch at a Chicago Cubs game and appearing with the Rock Bottom Remainders, the group of author-musicians that includes Stephen King and Amy Tan.

Scott Turow was born April 12, 1949, in Chicago, the son of David D. Turow, an obstetrician-gynecologist, and Rita Turow, who produced children's books, a nonfiction book, and longed to build a writing career. He grew up in a predominantly Jewish neighborhood on the north side of Chicago and relished trips with friends into Chicago's Loop, where he encountered the complications of city life. When his family moved to the elegant suburb of Winnetka on Chicago's north shore, the thirteen-year-old Turow, who felt more at home in his old neighborhood, took his Chicago accent with him.

His parents wanted him to become a doctor, like his father, so when Turow announced his intention of becoming a writer, his mother pointed out that he could practice medicine *and* write, like William Carlos Williams and Anton Chekhov. Turow rebuffed this suggestion, determined to live a completely literary life. He began this project early, writing for the newspaper at New Trier High School, eventually becoming its editor. At Amherst College he majored in English so he could spend as much time as possible reading and writing. Although he claims his obsession with his own work made him an indifferent student, he graduated with high honors, while also managing to publish two stories in the *Transatlantic Review*.

After graduation in 1970 he headed for the Creative Writing Program at Stanford University with Annette Weisberg, an artist he had met on a blind date while home from college on Christmas break; they married in April 1971. One of only two Mirrielees fellows in the Stanford Creative Writing Program, Turow, after graduating in 1972, taught at Stanford as an E. H. Jones Lecturer from 1972 to 1975. He had produced a book manuscript, "The Ways Things Are," but it failed to find a publisher. The University of Rochester offered Turow a teaching job, but he decided to attend law school instead because in the course of working on his manuscript he had familiarized himself with the law, and it fascinated him. He had taken the law aptitude test—he thought as a joke—and scored near the ninety-ninth percentile. So he applied to law schools and found himself debating whether to attend Yale or Harvard. He settled on Harvard because living in Boston would afford Annette more possibilities than New Haven and because of Harvard's prestige and power. Because Turow had protested the war in Vietnam so vehemently at Amherst that he lost his student deferment (but then got a permanent deferment because of blood problems), had vowed not to return to Chicago because of its treatment of protestors at the 1968 Democratic Convention, and had devoted his life to art, he considered going to Harvard Law School a way for him to confront "the enemy."

He wrote to his literary agent, explaining his law school plans, and happened to suggest that someone should write a book about attending law school. To his amazement he found a contract to write a book about his first year at Harvard Law School in his mailbox one day when he returned home from Stanford. So, after renouncing the writing life, Turow received a book contract. He wrote the memoir, *One L* (1977), the summer after his first year at Harvard, using a journal he kept.

ONE L

"The enemy" Turow confronted at Harvard Law included those who aggrandize themselves at others' expense. Turow's primary example is Professor Perini (Turow uses pseudonyms to protect privacy), who delights in using the Socratic method to humiliate students. When Perini first goes on the attack against a fellow student, Karlin, Turow finds his classmates' reactions disturbing.

Later, after Perini treats a classmate particularly harshly, Turow joins other students in signing a letter protesting his behavior. But still Turow admires Perini, especially after Turow's failure to work hard on a brief results in his doing a job so poorly that it shames him. On the other hand, he feels Perini had been "cruel" and wonders if his legal education has so undermined his common sense that he can no longer respond appropriately to bad behavior.

After Turow's ambivalence about law school hurts his performance on both the brief and a practice exam, he decides he must give himself over to law school, allowing it to change him. He does well on his two midyear exams and also when Professor Perini calls on him. But after surviving Professor Perini's interrogation, his attitude toward Perini changes again. He finds it despicable that Perini humiliates students who struggle with the law Perini has studied for thirty years. When Perini conducts a job search in the classroom, subjecting six candidates to public questioning, he appalls Turow. When his classmates rise to give Perini a standing ovation at the final class meeting, Turow stays seated.

Although the competitiveness pervading Harvard Law both offends and infects Turow, he enjoys the kind of thinking taking place there. When he debated going to law school he concluded that he would deny part of himself if he did not. This intuition proves true. Harvard Law often feels like home. A class where the professor displays the law's complexity by setting out one alternative version of it after another so fascinates Turow that he cannot sit still. Although the ruthlessness and the arrogance he finds at Harvard disturb him, Turow enjoys the pressure to do as well as he can.

In the afterword to the 1988 edition of *One L*, written eleven years after its first publication, Turow pleads for a legal education that places the law in a broader human context, one that would produce less division in students like himself who love learning about the law but fear that the competitiveness pervading law school will alienate them from their innate sense of decency. In this hope he was joined by one of *One L*'s fans, Supreme Court Justice Harry Blackmun.

PRESUMED INNOCENT

Appearing almost ten years after *One L*, *Presumed Innocent* (1987) enjoyed enormous success even before its publication date. Turow had sold the book at auction to Farrar, Straus and Giroux for $200,000 after turning down an offer from another press for $250,000. Turow credits Farrar, Straus and Giroux's literary reputation for his choice but admits gratitude also played a role: Turow's editor there, Jon Galassi, was an early admirer of Turow's work; the only editor to send Turow a personal letter rather than a form letter rejecting the novel he wrote his freshman year of college was from Farrar, Straus and Giroux, and the only encouraging letter he received when he submitted "The Way Things Are" to twenty-three presses came from Robert Giroux. Turow has stayed with the press and repeatedly commented that given its generous treatment of him, leaving would certify him an ungrateful fool.

Sydney Pollak bought the film rights to *Presumed Innocent* for a million dollars; the Literary Guild selected it and paperback bids began at $670,000. Turow credits Gail Hochman, his agent, for this promising beginning, while she argues that Turow had produced a terrific book that emerged authentically from his experiences and concerns. Reviews validated the prepublication excitement: *Presumed Innocent* was widely seen as compelling and well written. All this success made Scott Turow cry as he recognized how badly he had wanted it when younger; by the time it arrived he worried about it disrupting the rhythm of his life, especially fearing that it would intrude upon his relationship with his wife, Annette, and their three children, Rachel, Gabriel, and Eve.

Although interviewers sometimes ask if Turow attended Harvard Law because he planned to write legal thrillers—a genre many credit him with establishing—in fact, as he wrote *Presumed Innocent* he saw himself as a lawyer and squeezed his writing into the corners of that busy life, most famously by writing in spiral notebooks while commuting to work at the Chicago U.S. Attorney's office.

As an honors graduate of Harvard Law he could have found more remunerative work, but the political corruption in his hometown bothered him, so he could not refuse the chance to help remedy it. Similarly, since *One L* had done well he could have written another memoir, but he had a deeper need to write fiction than to take a safe path toward profitable publication. Just as he took the legal job that made sense to him and wrote what he needed to write, not what the market would welcome, he allowed his intuitive sense of appropriateness to guide the writing of *Presumed Innocent* until he collected 150 manuscript pages that had, as far as he could tell, no coherence. Writing down whatever resonates with him until the fragments begin to come together is a "method" that has persisted throughout his career.

Turow says that *Presumed Innocent* grew from his experiences working in the Suffolk County District Attorney's office while he attended Harvard Law School. In Boston, as in *Presumed Innocent,* a former member of his staff ran for election against a veteran prosecutor. He got many specifics for Carolyn Polhemus' murder from the first jury trial he witnessed, one concerning the murder of a prostitute. He put the sections he had written aside for two years to think about the plot, often while gardening, and returned to a novella he had started earlier called "Cut Up in Pieces."

He eventually sent "Cut Up in Pieces" to Gail Hochman and then returned to *Presumed Innocent*. When Hochman called to tell Turow that "Cut Up in Pieces" interested Jon Galassi, then an editor at Random House, *Presumed Innocent* was absorbing Turow too intensely for him to turn away from it. For one thing, he enjoyed writing in his own voice rather than working to achieve a literary voice; for another, its subject matter correlated more closely with the concerns central to the rest of his life. So he continued to produce pieces of *Presumed Innocent* until he took a three-week leave from the U.S. Attorney's office to write essays about criminal justice. After the first week he found himself writing the ending of *Presumed Innocent*. Then he returned to work, and as he lay awake early one morning worrying yet again about his responsibilities at the office, his wife Annette urged him to quit his job and finish *Presumed Innocent,* encouraging him to spend their savings if necessary. He wrote the final manuscript during three months between leaving the U.S. Attorney's Office and joining the Chicago law firm of Sonnenschein Nath & Rosenthal, carefully leaving time at the end of this break to paint his porch, so that no matter what happened with the manuscript he would not have wasted the summer.

When asked to identify the book that changed his life, Turow picks Alexandre Dumas's *The Count of Monte Cristo,* which absorbed him during a bout with measles at age ten; Turow confesses that he still loves complicated plots, and not surprisingly, *Presumed Innocent* has one, as does every novel Turow has published.

The book's central character, Rusty Sabich, is a prosecutor as Turow was, and Turow reports that he gave Rusty his voice rather than that of the hard-boiled investigator who usually tells such stories. While detectives in murder mysteries typically stay in charge, Turow points out that Rusty loses control, becoming the accused. Turow also notes with pleasure that rather than leaving a gap between the primary character's personal life and the crime, *Presumed Innocent* integrates the two. Sensitive, out-of-control investigators and links between the novel's events and its characters' emotional lives also recur in Turow's subsequent fiction. In order to persuasively show how their feelings influence events, Turow consistently draws rich characters rather than the stock figures that often populate genre fiction.

In discussing *Presumed Innocent,* Turow first articulates his view that mysteries, unlike trials, expose the truth; in *Presumed Innocent,* for instance, the reader learns what happens even though the jury and the trial's spectators never do. All the same, the judicial process arrives at the right conclusion, finding Rusty innocent. Turow sees this as accurate since the judicial process does not produce a complete version of reality but usually culminates in an appropriate verdict. Since he tried to make the novel as true to the realities of a trial as possible, it pleases him to discover that audiences, rather than finding these authentic details tedious, relish them. This concern with accuracy persists in Turow's subsequent books. When a novel's events take him away from familiar territory, he does research.

Although Rusty Sabich has Turow's voice, unlike his creator, Rusty has little interest in actively attempting to understand or shape his life. He knows, for instance, that his marriage deadens him, but he "deals" with this problem by ignoring it.

He has an affair with a colleague, Carolyn Polhemus, attracted initially by her rapport with an abused child; her allure makes sense because both Carolyn and Rusty come from troubled families. But Rusty has no awareness of what pulls him, nor does he attempt to achieve it: he simply gives in to his yearning for something, anything to fill the emptiness of his life, no matter how destructive.

After Rusty realizes that his wife murdered Carolyn and framed him, Barbara's move to Detroit disappoints him because he had hoped they could work things out; after all, she obviously cares for him. As the novel ends, Rusty comforts himself by seeing his attraction to Carolyn as evidence of idealism, not emptiness.

A few critics have complained about the negative portrayal of the women in this book: after all, Barbara is a depressed murderess and Carolyn a controlling slut. But it seems difficult to claim that Turow makes them look more psychologically bankrupt than Rusty, or even more ethically defective: after all, Rusty, a prosecutor who knows that his wife killed someone he supposedly cares for, does nothing about it. Close relationships with psychologically healthy people of any gender rest beyond Rusty Sabich's capabilities.

THE BURDEN OF PROOF

The Burden of Proof (1990) manifests consistent characteristics of Turow's work: complex plot, compelling characters, and realistic detail. Turow also composed much of this novel while commuting (a practice he has continued), but after trying six cases in four or five months in 1988 he asked the other partners in his law firm for permission to cut down his hours. They agreed, so by the end of 1988 he was spending more time writing at home, and by 1989 he had started writing a complete draft. Presumably because he was spending less time on legal work than he had while writing *Presumed Innocent, The Burden of Proof* appeared three years after *Presumed Innocent,* establishing a pattern that has persisted: a new novel every three years.

As *The Burden of Proof* opens, Sandy Stern, the adept courtroom performer who successfully defended Rusty Sabich in *Presumed Innocent,* arrives home and discovers that his fifty-two-year-old wife, Clara, has committed suicide; shortly thereafter he learns she had herpes. At the same time, his troublesome brother-in-law, Dixon Hartnell, needs Sandy's help yet again, this time to answer accusations about commodity trading. When he wrote *The Burden of Proof,* Turow was by now a defense lawyer who had handled cases involving commodities trading, so once again his protagonist shares his calling.

The Burden of Proof introduces some new patterns for Turow. It takes place, like *Presumed Innocent* and like all the novels that follow, in Kindle County, a place resembling Cook County, where Turow just happens to live and work, but Turow enjoys leaving it imaginative territory. He also begins to repeat characters, not using the same protagonist in the tradition of detective fiction but often bringing a relatively minor character from an earlier book to the forefront of a later book and taking a closer look. The protagonist of *The Burden of Proof,* Sandy Stern, appeared in all of Turow's earlier books. He is described briefly in *One L* as an almost compulsively conscientious student. In *Presumed Innocent* he acquires an Argentinean background and Spanish first name, Alejandro, and saves Rusty from prosecution. As *The Burden of Proof* opens, his apparently well-composed life blows up, and the book traces his attempt to find his balance. After readers watch Stern from a distance during two books, Turow exposes his intimate thoughts.

Turow had also given his readers entry to Rusty's "thinking," showing Rusty feeling an impulse and then following it. Sandy Stern also indulges in emotionally driven behavior, falling into bed with various women who cross his path after his wife's death. While Rusty accepts this impulsive life, Sandy questions himself, laughs at himself, and apologizes to a woman he makes a pass at inappropriately; in sum, Sandy reflects on his life and takes responsibility for what he does with it. Rusty does not see the fact that his wife had murdered his lover and tried to frame him for the crime as an impediment to continuing their marriage, but when Sandy's wife dies he realizes that she had mediated his relationship to his children and so whatever bond he'd had with them has weakened. Unlike Rusty, when his wife "leaves," Sandy accepts that the terms on which he has conducted his life have fundamentally changed.

Since Sandy has a more complicated awareness than Rusty, the characters in *The Burden of Proof* have more dimension than those in *Presumed Innocent.* Rusty, for instance, has little interest in exploring his wife's motivation, so *Presumed Innocent* presents Barbara as someone who kills Carolyn because she's miserable. On the other hand, stunned to learn that his perception of his wife had been so skewered, Sandy Stern spends a great deal of time trying to understand what went on behind her orderly facade and stumbles on a number of insights, all of which he handles compassionately.

He suddenly realizes that as she killed herself, she drowned out the sound of the car's engine by playing a Mozart cassette, allowing her to rest in the illusion of perfection at the end.

Because Sandy, unlike Rusty, faces reality, he starts to build a new life after his wife's death. He suddenly finds himself attracted to many women, so when he falls into a relationship with an old friend, Helen Dudak, Stern suspects himself of desperation. But Sandy realizes that he truly loves her.

Although the novel was widely praised, some critics accused Turow of attempting to produce literature rather than a thriller when he wrote *The Burden of Proof,* while others commended him for precisely the same reason. These comments apparently unsettled Turow, who clearly sees writing as a way to express parts of himself that would otherwise remain silent but at the same time wants his work to move others.

PLEADING GUILTY

Turow wrote *Pleading Guilty* (1993) after hitting a wall while working on what would become his subsequent book, *The Laws of Our Fathers*. In the Bunge interview he says the decision to write *Pleading Guilty* grew from much the same impulse as that to work on *Presumed Innocent* rather than "Cut Up in Pieces." Perhaps to ensure that the book appealed to those audience members who found *The Burden of Proof* tough going, Turow told NPR's Noah Adams that, after his wife Annette, as usual, was the manuscript's first reader, he asked "non-literary professionals." Apparently these readers liked the book, as did most critics.

Again, the central character's voice and point of view distinguish the novel: Mack Malloy, an ex-cop who now practices law, dictates events into a tape recorder as he searches for a missing law partner, Bert Kamin, and the $5.6 million Kamin apparently took with him. This narrative device gives the book a compelling flow conveyed by an accessible voice.

Mack Malloy has several selves and enjoys using them all. But having so many dimensions makes it impossible for Malloy to fit easily into any group. When he worked as a policeman, he and his partner Pigeyes functioned on different frequencies. When he practices law he has a class consciousness endemic to policemen. He therefore feels ambivalent about his law firm's culture. As a result Mack feels isolated, and he believes all people need connection.

Mack has numerous other problems: a recent divorce, a depressing son, and recurrent alcoholism, for instance. Throughout the book he thinks about stealing the money he's supposed to recover because he thinks it will liberate him; he affirms to himself, again and again, that choice shapes one's existence. The book's epigraph from Saint Augustine suggests another conclusion. After he takes the money and leaves to start again, Mack feels not elated but sad; then he realizes that he cannot escape himself. His only liberation consists of narrating his story: "I know this is the only new life I will get, that the telling is the only place where I can really reinvent myself." The process of talking about his life gives him the sense of connection he truly needs.

Unlike Turow's first two novels, *Pleading Guilty* does not coordinate the crime under investigation with a family crisis, but it does point out that all actions, no matter how apparently rational, have emotional bases. Appropriately, Mack's clever theft leaves unresolved the emotional issues that make him miserable.

THE LAWS OF OUR FATHERS

Turow worked on this book for over twenty years. In its first version he used material from "The Way Things Are," the frequently rejected manuscript he produced while in graduate school at Stanford. Then he added sections in Sonny Klonsky's voice; he had originally devoted much of *The Burden of Proof* to her until his editor persuaded him to give her a smaller role in that book. The book's narration shifts primarily between Sonny Klonsky's account of the way events unfold in December of 1996 and Seth Weissman's memories of 1969 and 1970, when Sonny and Seth lived together in California. In 1995, when they meet again in Turow's Kindle County, they rediscover their attachment to each other. Through the shifting narratives of Sonny and Seth the book weaves their history during the late 1960s and early 1970s together with their current lives. Although the book has a mystery at its core, Turow describes it as his novel about the 1960s. Turow caught the 1960s passion for change while young: in high school he participated in the civil rights movement, joining the Evanston Urban League and the NAACP Youth Board. As he aged he joined anti-Vietnam protests, campaigned for Eugene McCarthy, and resolved to go to Canada if drafted, a decision his parents supported, but then a blood condition led to his being classified 1Y.

When he moved to the San Francisco area, the epicenter of protest, he met radicals who did not shun using violence to achieve their aims. While Seth, a character Turow claims resembles him, allows himself to become involved with such types, Turow stepped back from them. *The Laws of Our Fathers* (1996) presents an ambivalent view of the 1960s, simultaneously showing the idealism motivating the protestors as well as the lunacy that beckoned in the movements they joined. When Seth gives himself over to a plot spun by Loyell Eddgar that Sonny appropriately declares insane, Seth realizes that he has betrayed himself. Also, Sonny points out that the social changes that followed in the wake of the 1960s have not all been positive. Turow sometimes reveals a similar ambivalence about what all the protests accomplished.

From their mature perspectives, Seth and Sonny see flaws in their youthful behavior and suspect that they sought primarily to escape their parents' influence. Sonny, the child of a busy communist mother, has trouble with commitment to a profession and especially to a man because her mother abandoned her so often to carry on her work. Seth, the child of Holocaust survivors, attempts to evade the impossible task of redeeming his parents' lives.

But by 1996 both Seth and Sonny have not only come to appreciate their parents' strengths, they attempt to cultivate them in themselves and pass them on to their children. And both strive to heal society, Sonny by serving as a judge and Seth by writing newspaper columns.

Although *The Laws of Our Fathers* retains its origin as a book about the 1960s, by the time Turow put it aside to write *Pleading Guilty* he realized that he wanted to write about things he had learned about people trapped in Chicago's projects from the pro bono work now central to his legal practice. To do this Turow, a privileged white, had to capture the perspective and language of an impoverished African American. Turow's book also includes a murder mystery involving a gang member from the projects called Hardcore. Turow not only makes him a complicated character, he presumes to write in Hardcore's dialect, and, to Turow's delight, it works. A number of critics have called the section of the novel where Hardcore appears the book's strongest.

Sonny Klonsky must attempt to solve the mystery since she judges the case against the defendant, Nile Eddgar, whom she also knew during the 1960s, along with his father, Loyell Eddgar, and his lawyer, Hobie Tuttle. The case involves yet another generational conflict, for Nile is accused of hiring Hardcore to kill his father, who ignored him much the same way that Sonny's mother slighted her. The trial ends because of a technicality, so Sonny never arrives at the truth; but she doesn't care. Other, more personal matters, engage her now.

Emotional realities also influence Sonny on the bench. When she feels compassion for the people who appear before her, she is her mother's daughter.

The Laws of Our Fathers persistently asserts the importance of owning the past: Seth and Sonny begin a new relationship nourished by the trust established through their shared history; Seth gives a talk at his father's funeral that shows he has come to value his father; Hobie also speaks at the funeral, dismissing the racial differences he once allowed to shatter his relationship with Seth.

Although the book has a variety of different themes, such as: the impact of historical change, the need to face and resolve psychological conflict, the importance of accepting generational differences, the burden of poverty, and the value of tradition and the law. With this novel Turow breaks new ground: shifting points of view, writing from the perspective of a woman, rendering black dialogue on the page, and putting a murder mystery in a broad context that raises questions of psychology, sociology, history, religion, and celebrates kindness and trust. Most critics commenting on the book have noted that Scott Turow stretched himself in writing it and concluded that he successfully met all the challenges he set for himself.

PERSONAL INJURIES

In *Personal Injuries* (1999), Stan Sennett, a self-righteous prosecutor in Turow's Kindle County, tells this tale when identifying the moment he knew he would become a prosecutor. Turow admits that *Personal Injuries* rests heavily on his experiences prosecuting corrupt judges as an assistant U.S. Attorney, especially in Operation Greylord where he had to persuade an attorney against whom they had evidence to help prosecute others.

Although Turow went to the U.S. Attorney's office expecting to establish moral order, he sometimes found himself awash in ethical ambiguity, particularly when trying to get someone he would eventually convict to cooperate with him. As Turow told James Buckley, Jr. for *BookPage* in 1999:

> You've pursued these people, they want to ingratiate themselves with you and get a lower sentence, you want something from them ... but you know in the end you're going to stand up in court and ask to have them sent away.... You hate their guts when you see them for what they are, but you can also become beguiled by them in a certain way. At the end of the day, you get mixed feelings about standing up and saying, "Send him to the penitentiary." Experiences like that were really the inspiration for Robbie.

Robbie Feaver, the central character in *Personal Injuries,* gets caught bribing judges. The novel's narrator, George Mason, serves as his attorney while the FBI puts a wire on him, sometimes supplementing it with video equipment, and sends him out to get judges and/or their clerks to say or do incriminating things for the record. Robbie seems a sympathetic character. He falls into bribing judges after discovering that he must to get good treatment for his clients; he cooperates with the FBI because he wants to stay out of prison and take care of his wife, Lorraine, who is dying of Lou Gerhig's disease; and he hates betraying people who have helped him. Despite his criminal behavior, Robbie is a loyal, compassionate human being. For instance, he refuses to allow Sennett to use a tape that might hurt his lifelong best friend and law partner, Mort Dinnerstein, even though it shows that friend betraying him; Robbie forgives Mort, arguing that family pressures left him no choice.

Sennett, the supposed "good guy," becomes more ruthless as the novel progresses, risking Robbie's life in the hopes of arresting his prime target, Brendan Tuohey. Finally, Sennett's determination to humiliate those he hopes to convict leads to Robbie's death: Sennett has Robbie march through a room full of people indicted as a result of Robbie's actions who have been forced to bring "gifts" they received. As Robbie walks past him, Walter Wunsch, smashes his head open with one of the golf clubs Robbie bribed him with during the investigation.

Although Robbie boasts frequently of the acting abilities he displays as he traps people, his openness distinguishes him. He manifests this quality primarily in his interactions with Evon Miller, the pseudonym of the female FBI agent assigned to watch him. Robbie has a history of affairs, which makes Evon suspicious of his kindnesses toward her until she sees his genuine love for both his wife and his mother. When Evon asks what attracts him to casual relationships with women, Robbie gives a beguiling account of the fantasy world he enters when he has sex with them. Evon finds herself impressed by his honesty. By the end of the book Evon has also achieved an admirable openness, even owning her lesbianism.

The plot meets Turow's high standards, with all kinds of twists and turns, but although the critics have generally praised it, they hover over his rich characterization of Robbie; several have called Robbie Turow's best character. Turow uses a narrator who often doesn't know what's going on to tell Robbie's story; George Mason explains that when he tells how Robbie's wife died, for instance, he guesses, as he has throughout the book. This adds a layer of ambiguity to the book: since George Mason is Robbie Feaver's lawyer, it is his job to perceive Robbie compassionately, so the reader never sees Robbie directly. The one definite truth emerging from *Personal Injuries* is that one cannot confidently judge the ethics of anyone, even someone who has bribed a judge.

REVERSIBLE ERRORS *AND* ULTIMATE PUNISHMENT: A LAWYER'S REFLECTIONS ON DEALING WITH THE DEATH PENALTY

Turow sees these books as complements, for both have their source in his 1991 decision to represent Alejandro Hernandez, who, along with Rolando Cruz, had been condemned to death, twice. When asked to review the judicial record for the case Turow agreed but doubted that he would want to represent Hernandez. After reading the documents Turow believed that he had to represent Hernandez or stop practicing law: Hernandez was, without doubt, innocent. Turow got the verdict overturned.

Turow knew that this experience would impact his fiction and sees *Reversible Errors* (2002) as the novel where this happened, although he adds that other than dealing with the acquittal of someone unjustly condemned to death, *Reversible Errors* does not reflect his experience in the Hernandez case. The prosecution of Hernandez rested on no evidence, so Turow sees the episode in black and white.

The prosecutors and investigators in *Reversible Errors* have evidence that leads them to suspect Rommy Gandolph, skillfully put in place by the policeman who committed the crime. While Hernandez continued to sit in jail even after someone with telling knowledge of the crime's specifics confessed to the rape and murder for which he had been imprisoned, discovering the murderer in *Reversible Errors* requires a long journey through yet another complicated Turowian plot.

Arthur Raven, the lawyer assigned to represent Gandolph pro bono, has had little success with women, as he frequently reminds himself, but in the process of investigating the case he meets Gillian Sullivan, one of the corrupt judges sent to jail in *Personal Injuries* and who had been the judge at Rommy Gandolph's trial. By the time *Reversible Errors* begins she has served her time and weaned herself from the heroin that made her a judge highly vulnerable to external influence. Arthur and Gillian establish a happy relationship, which educates Gillian in the power of the emotions she had disowned. She comes to see the overturning of Gandolph's conviction as a new beginning for herself as well.

So in *Reversible Errors,* although Turow's fascination with the law and courtroom drama reveal itself, the book focuses on two love relationships. Perhaps not coincidentally, Muriel and Larry, who seek control and power, lose each other and the case, while Arthur and Gillian accept their own and each other's frailties and get the verdict they wish. Turow says that he wanted emotion, not legal reasoning, to sit at the center of this book.

Turow wanted to write a story, not an exposition on capital punishment. When he produced the love stories he did not reflect on why they played such a large role in the novel, but in retrospect the reason seems clear: the book conveys the truth that despite its power, the law cannot remedy some injuries, especially not the damage done by murder.

When asked to serve on Illinois Governor Ryan's Commission on Capital Punishment in 2000, Turow confessed that he had a novel on capital punishment underway and was told that the book posed no problem, but he finished the novel before joining the panel and promised not to publish it until the commission report came out in 2002. Turow felt the two projects had entirely distinct identities, but in retrospect he believes that writing the novel may have helped him digest some issues about the death penalty.

Although Turow would certainly reject any attempts to pity him, comments of other commission members give insight into the burdens, however slight, his success imposes on him. They not only note when he uses obscure words like "hortatory" and imitate him to see if he notices, they fret about his fervent note taking. They need not have worried: Turow has only high praise for the other commission members, and *Ultimate Punishment* makes it clear he took his work there seriously. It moves gracefully and fairly through arguments pro and con for the death penalty, finally concluding that even though some cases, like that of John Wayne Gacy, who tortured thirty-three young men to death, seem to call for the death penalty, it can never be applied fairly.

ORDINARY HEROES

With *Ordinary Heroes* (2005) Turow made another leap in subject matter by writing about the Second World War. It asserts some ties to his earlier work: the central character, David Dubin, hails from Kindle County, practices law, and works for Stan Sennett; his son, Stewart Dubinsky, who constructs the book from documents, is an overweight newspaper reporter who plays minor roles in earlier Turow novels. (Stew has retrieved the original family name, Dubinsky, from the shortened "Dubin" of his father.) By the time *Ordinary Heroes* begins Stew has retired from newspaper work in hopes of producing a book. Then he stumbles upon letters his reserved father wrote during the Second World War. Stew takes up the case, persuading his father's lawyer, Bear Leach, to hand over his father's written account of his experiences during World War II. This narrative constitutes most of the novel.

Although David Dubin is a lawyer, the courtroom plays a small role in this book, but like Turow's other novels, *Ordinary Heroes* contains a mystery that keeps readers turning pages: David Dubin must find and take into custody a colorful, accomplished soldier named Robert Martin, suspected of linking up with the Russians. David repeatedly locates Martin, who always escapes, usually with Gita Lodz, a Polish woman whose attentions inspire Dubin to break with his fiancée, Grace Morton. Turow keeps the reader wondering whether Dubin will catch up with Martin, whether Martin is a traitor, and how David's relationship with Gita Lodz will end.

But the book primarily presents a segment of World War II through the eyes of a soldier who, like many American men of that time, wants to help bring down Hitler; that he is Jewish naturally intensifies this desire. Most critics believe that Turow does an excellent job of telling this story in a compelling way, even though the plot takes him far from his familiar milieu. But Turow does have a personal connection to the novel: his father, like Stew's, served in World War II and had a detachment that made him enigmatic to his son, who noted that meeting other veterans or seeing episodes from the war on television animated his father, although often producing sadness. His father served as a battlefield surgeon during the Battle of the Bulge and helped liberate the concentration camps, and Turow felt proud of his father's contribution to World War II. The author found the notion of imagining himself into his father's World War II experiences irresistible.

A few critics have complained that the imaginative basis of this narrative results in vagueness and clichés like the gallant, iconoclastic soldier and his sexy female companion. If so, this happened despite Turow's efforts to ground his narrative in reality by doing extensive research about the war; he collects his sources in a seven-page bibliography on his website with some citations referring to whole other websites. At the conclusion of *Ordinary Heroes* he also thanks individuals who shared their experiences of the war with him.

Complaints that David Dubin fails to render his experience with the detail characteristic of Turow's other work may well reflect the success of Turow's attempt to present the perspective common to soldiers in his father's generation. Indeed, the passage that several critics single out for praise, Turow's description of David Dubin and his driver, Gideon Bidwell, parachuting out of a plane, grew from a story his father told about his war experiences.

Certainly David Dubin reaches some of the same truths about war Hemingway embraces: although horrible and senseless, it exposes reality like no other experience and as a result reveals the emptiness of conventional life. But those who must endure it deaden their emotional reactions by cultivating the distance from others that frustrated both Stew Dubinsky and Scott Turow when dealing with their fathers. No wonder Turow claims that writing *Ordinary Heroes* helped him understand and accept his father. Turow not only reaches out for new subject matter in this book, he uses a fresh, distinctive style for much of it. Despite the Hemingwayesque qualities of *Ordinary Heroes,* it does not collapse into cynicism. While the three Turow books preceding *Ordinary Heroes* implied the value of love, this novel affirms it directly. As the war story ends, Gita Lodz begs Dubin, "Choose love." And he does.

LIMITATIONS

Serialized in sixteen issues of the *New York Times Magazine* starting on April 23, 2006, *Limitations* came faster than Turow's other works, perhaps in part because he apparently used some of the novella he had worked on before *Presumed Innocent*. In *Limitations* a videotape has surfaced of a group of apparently upstanding young men participating in a gang bang four years earlier; Judge Mason must decide whether or not the statute of limitations has run out for the case. If it hasn't, what does that say about his innocence? The almost invisible George Mason of *Personal Injuries* becomes a fully equipped character in *Limitations*, complete with a sense of humor. Knowing him better makes it easier to understand his fascination with Robbie Feaver, who, although guilty of criminal misconduct, treats all women, especially his wife, kindly.

Turow remarks that throughout his career, he has let his writing go until it comes together organically, but since he had a deadline for *Limitations* he plotted it more thoroughly than usual. Perhaps this helps explain why *Limitations* is vividly written with compelling movement and characters, but it does not seem to stretch the legal thriller genre any farther. *Presumed Innocent*'s Rusty Sabich even resurfaces here as the chief judge of the appellate court. So after critics proclaimed that with *Ordinary Heroes* Turow transcended the mystery, he returned to it, presumably because the move felt right to him. And why not? Authenticity has worked just fine for Scott Turow, allowing him to produce an impressive body of work both on the page and in the world.

Selected Bibliography

WORKS OF SCOTT TUROW

NOVELS AND NOVELLA

Presumed Innocent. New York: Farrar, Straus and Giroux, 1987; Warner Books, 2000.

The Burden of Proof. New York: Farrar, Straus and Giroux, 1990; Warner Books, 2000.

Pleading Guilty. New York: Farrar, Straus and Giroux, 1993; Warner Books, 1994.

The Laws of Our Fathers. New York: Farrar, Straus and Giroux, 1996; Warner Books, 1997.

Personal Injuries. New York: Farrar, Straus and Giroux, 1999; Warner Vision, 2000.

Reversible Errors. New York: Farrar, Straus and Giroux, 2002; Warner Vision, 2003.

Ordinary Heroes. New York: Farrar, Straus and Giroux, 2005.

Limitations. New York: Picador, 2006.

OTHER WORKS

One L: The Turbulent True Story of a First Year at Harvard Law School. New York: Putnam, 1977; London: Penguin, 1978; Farrar, Straus and Giroux, 1988; Warner Books, 1996. British edition as *What They Teach You at Harvard Law School.* London: Sceptre, 1988.

Ultimate Punishment: A Lawyer's Reflections on Dealing with the Death Penalty. New York: Farrar, Straus and Giroux, 2003.

AS EDITOR

Guilty as Charged: A Mystery Writers of America Anthology. Thorndike, Maine: Compass Press, 2001.

The Best American Mystery Stories 2006. Boston: Houghton Mifflin, 2006.

CRITICAL AND BIOGRAPHICAL STUDIES

Chase, Anthony. "An Obscure Scandal of Consciousness." *Yale Journal of Law & The Humanities* 1:105–28 (1988).

Kopper, Edward A., Jr. "The Influence of *Heart of Darkness* on Scott Turow's *Pleading Guilty*." *Notes on Contemporary Literature* 25:8–9 (September 1995).

Lundy, Derek. *Scott Turow: Meeting the Enemy.* Toronto: ECW Press, 1995.

MacDonald, Andrew and Gina. "Scott Turow's *Presumed Innocent*: Novel and Multifaceted Character Study Versus Tailored Courtroom Drama." In *It's a Print!: Detective Fiction from Page to Screen.* Edited by William Reynolds and Elizabeth A. Trembley. Bowling Green, Ohio: Popular, 1994. Pp. 175–193.

MacDonald, Andrew, and Gina. *Scott Turow: A Critical Companion.* Westport, Conn., 2005. (Includes bibliography, pp. 231–252.)

Sanger, Carol. "Less Than Pornography: The Power of Popular Fiction." In *Representing Women: Law, Literature, and Feminism.* Edited by Susan Sage and Zipporah Wiseman. Durham, N.C.: Duke University Press, 1994. Pp. 75–100. Reprinted from *Michigan Law Review* 87:1338–1365 (1989).

Szuberia, Guy. "Paretsky, Turow and the Importance of Symbolic Ethnicity." *Midamerica: The Yearbook of the*

Society for the Study of Midwestern Literature 18:124–135 (1991).

INTERVIEWS

Abbe, Elfrieda. "Building a Legal Thriller: Scott Turow Finds Compelling Stories in the Gray Areas Between What's Legal and What's Moral." *Writer* 188:18–22 (May 2005).

Adams, Noah. "Bestselling Novelist Scott Turow Describes Creative Process." National Public Radio's *All Things Considered,* May 28, 1993. Transcript.

Anonymous. "Scott Turow Writes Historical Fiction Inspired by Father's World War II Service." *Turkish Daily News,* November 13, 2005, n.p.

Basbanes, Nicholas A. "Scott Turow Confronts the '60s in *The Laws of Our Fathers. Telegram & Gazette* (Worcester, Mass.), November 3, 1996, p. C5.

Bonetti, Kay. "An Interview with Scott Turow." *Missouri Review* 13:103–26 (1990). Reprinted in *Conversations with American Novelists: The Best Interviews from The Missouri Review and the American Audio Prose Library.* Edited by Kay Bonetti et al. Columbia, Mo.: University of Missouri Press, 1997. Pp. 153–169.

Buckley, James, Jr. "Going Undercover in Life and Law: A Talk with Scott Turow." *Bookpage* (http://www.bookpage.com). October 1, 2001.

Bunge, Nancy. "Scott Turow." In her *Master Class: Lessons from Leading Writers.* Iowa City: University of Iowa Press, 2005. Pp. 218–227.

Cuthbertson, Julia. "Lunch with the *FT:* Scott Turow." *Financial Times,* November 20, 2002, p. 1.

Engleman, Paul, and John Rezek. "Twenty Questions: Scott Turow." *Playboy,* August 1993, p. 112.

Goldstein, William. "Scott Turow." *Publishers Weekly,* July 10, 1987, pp. 52–53.

Johnson, Steve. "Presumed Invincible." *Chicago Tribune,* February 16, 1990, section 5, pp. 1, 5.

Lambert, Pam. "Scott Turow, More than Ever, Enjoying His View." *People,* June 7, 1993, p. 30.

Libman, Norma. "Scott Turow: City Provides Inspiration for Two Careers." *Chicago Tribune Sunday Magazine,* May 2, 1993, pp. 8, 10.

Mudge, Alden. "When Characters Slip from the Confines of Plot: A Talk with Scott Turow." *Bookpage* (http://www.bookpage.com). 1999.

Nolan, Tom. "Scott Turow." *Mystery Scene* 65:68–71 (1999).

Ogle, Connie. "Author Scott Turow Has Mixed Feelings About the Ultimate Punishment." *Knight Ridder/Tribune News Service,* November 27, 2002, p. K4743.

Stille, Alexander. "Fiction Follows Life in the Novels of Turow." *National Law Review,* July 9, 1990, p. 8.

Strangenes, Sharon. "Meet Scott Turow." *Chicago Tribune,* June 10, 1987, section 7, pp. 9–12.

Van Duch, Darryl. "Scott Turow Ponders the 60s in New Book." *National Law Journal,* September 9, 1996, pp. A1, A9, A13.

Weissmann, Dan. "Scott Turow, 56, is a Partner at Sonnenschein, Nath & Rosenthal and Chairs the Illinois Executive Ethics Commission." *Crain's Chicago Business,* October 31, 2005, p. 58.

FILM AND TELEVISION PRODUCTIONS BASED ON WORKS OF SCOTT TUROW

Presumed Innocent. Screenplay by Frank Pierson and Alan J. Pakula. Directed by Alan J. Pakula. Warner Brothers, 1990.

The Burden of Proof. Teleplay by John Gay. Directed by Mike Robe. Two-part television film on ABC, 1992.

Reversible Errors. Teleplay by Alan Sharp. Directed by Mike Robe. CBS miniseries. May 23 and 25, 2004.

WILLIAM T. VOLLMANN
(1959—)

J. M. Tyree

IN 2005, WHEN his historical novel *Europe Central* won the National Book Award for fiction, William T. Vollmann went from being an oddity to a rarity in American letters. Two years before, he had been a finalist for a National Books Critics' Circle Award in general nonfiction, nominated for a seven-volume meditation on violence, *Rising Up and Rising Down*. This level of critical success in both fiction and nonfiction is unusual, and Vollmann's achievement is made all the more remarkable by the fact that at the time of this writing he remains a few years shy of fifty (he was born on July 28, 1959, in the Los Angeles area). Accounts of the 2005 National Book Award ceremony revealed a writer so astonished by winning that he had not prepared any notes beforehand for presentation.

For most of his career, including the extraordinarily rapid accumulation of fifteen books since the publication of his first novel, *You Bright and Risen Angels,* in 1987, Vollmann has been the kind of writer who seemed bound to remain a lifelong professional outsider. This reputation has been fossilized into an exotic mythology through unsatisfying analogies with Thomas Pynchon and William S. Burroughs, the writers from previous generations with whom Vollmann is most often compared. Like Burroughs, Vollmann has become notorious for a variety of extreme personal experiences—going to Afghanistan with anti-Soviet jihadis, traveling to the Magnetic North Pole, having a land mine explode under his jeep in Bosnia, smoking crack with prostitutes in San Francisco, and so forth. Some of Vollmann's fans seem trapped in a voyeuristic fascination with the author's risky adventures as much as they are compelled by his extraordinary prose. Conversely, he is viewed not with indifference or even skepticism by many of his critics but rather with the kind of aggressive hostility often reserved for American writers who pursue deliberately difficult, lengthy, or even formally experimental literary projects. Difficulty becomes pretentiousness, length becomes self-indulgence, and experimentalism becomes tedious unreadability in negative notices of a new Vollmann doorstop.

There is a standard joke among scholars of Saint Augustine that anyone who claims to have read *all* of Augustine's work is a self-confessed liar, since the magnitude of the project exceeds the bounds of sheer human endurance. It might be said, tongue in cheek, that Vollmann is the Augustine of contemporary American literature, publishing hundreds or sometimes thousands of pages per year. This makes a comprehensive study of his work a difficult task even for an enthusiast. The "belated" critic who has not been following along since the early 1990s faces an Everest of text, and even younger readers who paid attention must reevaluate works last read in college or high school. Recognizing that Vollmann's career is still at an intermediate stage, the idea of a full critical study must be postponed; the critical body of Vollmann's "reception" remains in process, and this tends to make criticism provisional and humble.

Vollmann's legendary prolixity is, by all accounts, graphomaniacal and compulsive in character. Vollmann's detractors say that he publishes too much and that what he publishes is too long by half. The effect, however, is deliberate. As Vollmann has made clear in numerous interviews, he makes a habit of negotiating reduced advances in order to preserve the length of his books for artistic reasons. There is an inside joke to this effect in his 2001 novel *Argall*.

Vollmann's prose may be influenced by the frantic but controlled model of composition associated with William Faulkner, Fyodor Dostoyevsky, or Norman Mailer more than the compact, spare, clean, elegant style that pervades contemporary American writing. Vollmann, by contrast, like his contemporary David Foster Wallace, represents an idiosyncratic and maximalist strain of writing whose baroque involutions resemble the prose of the nineteenth century or even the eighteenth more than a continuation of the dominant trends in late-twentieth-century American literature. Vollmann appears to have a rather tyrannical imp/muse sitting on his shoulder, dictating book after book and driving him on.

OVERVIEW

Considered thus far, Vollmann's work, although diverse in form and genre, has not only a thematic consistency but also a sense of Life Project about it. Vollmann appears to have glimpsed fairly early on what he wanted to do with his work and since then, with certain detours, has set about doing it. It should be noted that there are a few parallel projects into which much (but not all) of Vollmann's work can be categorized, even though the threads among them overlap and the taxonomy below is nothing more than a rough guide.

Vollmann is working on a projected series of novels called the Seven Dreams, books of "North American Landscapes" that chart the history of conflict between Native Americans and their white colonizers. These include *The Ice-Shirt* (1990), about the first contact of Norse seafarers with Newfoundland; *Fathers and Crows* (1992), about Jesuit "Black Gowns" converting Quebec to Christian territory; *Argall* (2001), a retelling of the "true story" of John Smith and Pocahontas in early Virginia; and *The Rifles* (1994), about the introduction of the repeating rifle into the Inuit culture of the Canadian Arctic. With the Seven Dreams, Vollmann has been making a daring bid to write an epic universal history of North America. These novels, written in the style of the times they evoke—*Argall,* for example, employs a typography and dense syntax meant to recall Elizabethan English—are aware of both the impossibility and the necessity of such a confrontation with the past.

Another Vollmann project is a series of books, encompassing both fiction and nonfiction as well as some gray areas in between, about prostitution and the world of the global underclass, documenting its poverty, desperation, violence, and drug addiction. These books include *Whores for Gloria* (1991), a fictional rendering of the Tenderloin slum district of San Francisco through the eyes of a Vietnam vet; *Butterfly Stories* (1993), a novel-in-stories about, among other things, sex tourism in Asia; and *The Royal Family* (2000), a novel also involved with prostitutes in San Francisco. Marginalized people are the main theme of the shorter fiction pieces and novelettes collected in *The Rainbow Stories* (1989) and many of the pieces collected in *The Atlas* (1996), a hybrid book of world travels. On a very general level, Vollmann's nonfiction often takes up extremities of geography and human behavior, whether the subject is warfare *(An Afghanistan Picture Show,* 1992) or the history of violence *(Rising Up and Rising Down,* 2003).

Vollmann has also produced an early novel, *You Bright and Risen Angels* (1987), another short-story collection, *Thirteen Stories and Thirteen Epitaphs* (1991), and a biographical science essay about Copernicus *(Uncentering the Earth,* 2006). In his largest critical success to date, the National Book Award–winning novel *Europe Central* (2005), Vollmann documents the epic clash between nazism and communism during the middle of the last century. Of course, the boundaries between Vollmann's projects are not impermeable and not everything fits neatly into one category. *Europe Central,* for example, is a historical novel like the Seven Dreams but also contains some of the most gruesome chapters in the history of human violence, which connects the book to the obsessions of his nonfiction. In fact *Europe Central* in many ways represents the culmination of the current phase of Vollmann's career, with many major reviewers arguing that it was the book he was born to write.

In his 1928 essay "Dr. Williams' Position," Ezra Pound remarked that some writers seem to require a sense of structure and order to their work, while others don't. Pound himself obviously required what he termed "major form," as did Dante. Homer, by contrast, like William Carlos Williams (Pound argued), had no interest in or use for such structural patterns and yet created something extraordinary. Vollmann is somewhat aligned with the Pound-Dante mode in his endless accumulation of details from widely separated places, times, and cultures, all of which in time becomes assimilated into a lifelong epic work that spans a huge expanse of both world history and the author's own lifetime.

A former student of comparative literature at Cornell University, Vollmann has an epic narrative sensibility combined with the mentality of an intellectually voracious encyclopedist or archivist. Very often written in different styles that pastiche, mimic, satirize, undermine, and pay homage to the historical sources in which his novels are immersed, Vollmann's fiction in some ways seems modeled on the later chapters of James Joyce's *Ulysses,* at least in the sense that the form, structure, tone, and diction are borrowed from other works rather than coming from the author's "own voice." In a somewhat similar fashion to that suggested by T. S. Eliot in his original draft of *The Waste Land,* Vollmann is out to "do the police in different voices"; in the case of *Europe Central,* for example, the mockingly ironic narrative voice is guided by the thought police of Communist Russia and Nazi Germany.

NONFICTION: AN AFGHANISTAN PICTURE SHOW *AND* RISING UP AND RISING DOWN

According to his own account of his life, Vollmann spent his first five years in a Los Angeles slum filled with reconditioned army barracks that lacked air conditioning, before moving to New Hampshire. His sister's death by drowning, described in tones of self-blame in interviews and in personally revealing sections of *The Atlas* and *An Afghanistan Picture Show,* was an early and inescapable trauma that has given rise to much uninformed speculation about the potentially self-destructive risks and dangers to which Vollmann has exposed himself as a writer over the years. Far more certain is the intellectual genesis of his literary career, as he described it in a 1993 interview with Larry McCafferty for *The Review of Contemporary Fiction:*

> When I went to Afghanistan in 1982, 1 was lured there by the thought of this unknown exotic experience—or by a whole bunch of exotic experiences. I guess what I wanted was to confront this foreign "other." Later on, I began to realize that it's pretty hard to know yourself, harder still harder to know the other, and what's hardest of all to know something that is *really* foreign. So *An Afghanistan Picture Show* ended up being basically about the unknowability of their experience. That made me want to focus my interest more on things closer to home and that was one of the connecting threads connecting the different materials in *The Rainbow Stories.* The simplest way to put it is that in *The Rainbow Stories* I wanted to understand what America is like. This fascination I have with the exotic experience was also still very much there—I wanted to look at lost souls and marginal people, with the hope that maybe by understanding them I could help them somehow, as I had done with the Afghans.
> (p. 11)

The study of America in the present led logically to the study of the past:

> The experience of writing *The Rainbow Stories* led me to realize that I still didn't really understand anything about America and that I probably never would. But it occurred to me that one way of starting to understand would be to see where we as Americans have come from and how we've changed. So it seemed like a nice idea to go back to the Indians—in fact, go back as far I could, which is to the first recorded contact between Europeans and Indians—and describe everything that's happened since then in a series of books that winds up covering roughly a thousand-year period.
> (pp. 11–12)

Although it sounds neatly simplified for public consumption, this is a fairly clear statement of artistic intentions. It also bears on one of the hallmarks of Vollmann's work (and his working method), the interrelatedness of projects that at first glance might be widely divergent in genre, sensibility, and historical setting.

The "exotic experience" Vollmann describes as his primary literary fascination is what makes much of his work seem so brave and honest to some and so tiresome and monomaniacal to others. It should not be forgotten, however, that there is a model in classic American literature for such an approach: Stephen Crane. (James Gibbons first noted the resemblance; he also compared Vollmann with later war writers like George Orwell, Ernest Hemingway, John Steinbeck, and others.) Like Crane, Vollmann writes both adventure journalism and novels. Like Crane, Vollmann is drawn to wars and conflict zones. Vollmann's series of books about prostitution have a literary precedent in Crane's *Maggie: A Girl of the Streets*. Like *The Red Badge of Courage*, Vollmann's historical novels are strongly seasoned with reality and research. Even Vollmann's tremendous output resembles the famously productive Crane's; by the time he died at age twenty-eight the latter had already published two novels and a multitude of short stories and poems as well as an immense body of journalism. It's almost as if Crane knew that his time on earth would be short—a sense one also gets reading Vollmann, who, one sometimes feels, has lived longer than he thought he might.

The kind of "creative nonfiction" that Vollmann produces as an observer—participant in war-torn countries arguably had its literary genesis in writers like Crane, although, as James Gibbons notes, George Orwell, Ernest Hemingway, and John Steinbeck did similar work—as did New Journalists like Hunter S. Thompson and Norman Mailer. Vollmann's *An Afghanistan Picture Show*, published in 1992, ten years after he flung himself into the middle of the struggle against the Soviets, has the self-mocking subtitle "How I Saved the World." In it, Vollmann dissects himself as much as the conflict, creating a ruthless examination of the entire concept of misguided altruism, and American altruism in particular-themes that recur again and again in the Seven Dreams series.

One of the more devastating critiques of the literary impulse toward "exotic experience" is delivered by Vollmann himself in *An Afghanistan Picture Show*. The author and some critics regard it as a slight work, but this judgment sells the book short; it contains invisible tangent lines to alternate paths the writer has not yet pursued. At any rate, it is an intensely personal book that reveals much about his true feelings toward his subject matter and the seemingly compulsive needs driving him toward marginal topics and dangerous situations. In that sense this early book—short, intimate, readable, grimly humorous, messy, and far less forbidding and far less encrusted in references than much of his other work—is both a good place to start reading Vollmann and a magnifying glass through which to view his career. Because of its setting the book is also very timely, and its depiction of relations between well-meaning Americans and battle-hardened Islamic warriors in cold war Pakistan and Afghanistan have aged very well.

For Vollmann, the "Young Man," going to Afghanistan was supposed to have been a mission of mercy on behalf of the Afghans fighting against Soviet occupation from their bases in Peshawar and the border regions of Pakistan. His putative goal was to produce a slide show for consumption back home, for the purposes of highlighting the plight of the Afghans and rallying support and even money for their cause. In fact, apart from one skirmish, Vollmann spends most of his time in the book fruitlessly trying to get to Afghanistan and soaking up the grimly determined desperation of Afghan exiles in Pakistani cities and refugee camps. It is worth pausing for a moment to consider the utter madness of the project.

Vollmann worked in a reinsurance firm to finance his travels. As in many of his books, he provides tangentially related interludes of memoir in the narrative—including details from childhood and a long account of a hiking trip with an older female mentor in Alaska. *An Afghanistan Picture Show* also contains excerpts of letters from literary agents and publishers giving their reasons for rejecting the book, as well as correspondence from an arms dealer and a hospitable Pakistani general who advises him about his efforts to bring attention, if not actual rocket launchers and anti-aircraft weapons, to the mujahideen. Vollmann firmly believed in the cause, and, back in the Bay Area, raised the ire of hard-line socialist groups on the Berkeley

Campus over his pro-Afghan presentations.

The narrative arc of the book follows the disillusionment of the Young Man as his naive altruism implodes under the weight of desperate historical circumstances far beyond the scope of any individual to alter. "Save Them": that was the motto of the Young Man, drawing tangents between his time among the prostitutes of San Francisco and his self-proclaimed mission to the Afghans. In the end Vollmann only slows down the band of jihadis who offer to take him over the mountains into Afghanistan, spends far more money on his own travels than he raises with his slide shows, and witnesses a brief and inconsequential firefight.

During the fighting Vollmann describes the jihadis' experience of "those endless night moments of happiness near death." While perhaps descriptively accurate of the mindset of the fanatics, the phrase is more reminiscent of Hemingway's lyrical prose from the Spanish civil war in *For Whom the Bell Tolls* than Orwell's grittier depictions of death in the mud of battle in *Homage to Catalonia*. The former is a common reaction among war correspondents addled by low-intensity combat but exceedingly rare among those who have anything more than a skimming acquaintance with massive bombing or sustained heavy-duty warfare, for it is probably thrilling to come under fire from small arms and not to die, but quite another thing to bleed from the ears during an artillery barrage. The book ultimately comes to rest intellectually in a critique of aggressive violence and an apologia for violent means in cases of self-defense. Yet it would deform the entire shape of Vollmann's later book *Rising Up and Rising Down* to say that he has the habit of romanticizing warfare. In Sarajevo during the fourteenth month of the siege by Serbian forces, Vollmann lived under mortar and sniper fire and saw the broken bodies of women and children in the Kosovo Hospital.

An Afghanistan Picture Show mocks not only the Young Man but also the resort to violence in the name of ideological progress characteristic of the Soviet regime (a resounding theme in *Europe Central*). In *Rising Up and Rising Down*, Vollmann charts the descent of dreams joined to violence. Taken more universally, and given a global scale to range among various eras and corners of the world, this statement might be considered a helpful guidepost about (or perhaps even a coda for) much of Vollmann's mature fiction, whether it depicts the murderous process of "civilizing" North America (Seven Dreams) or the abyss of clashing utopias that resulted in World War II *(Europe Central)*. Idealism, for Vollmann, is cold, abstract, and often turns violent, whereas real altruism connects, sympathizes with, and helps individuals caught up in the world's traps. That is why Vollmann, in fact a high moralist, pretends to hate the good.

Despite its extraordinary seven-volume, 3,000-plus page length in its original form of publication by McSweeney's Books, the theme of *Rising Up and Rising Down* can be summarized fairly legitimately in a phrase: the causes of violent death. Following what the author calls an "inductive" method, the book attempts a comprehensive study of the nature and history of violence, dwelling upon a multitude of individual examples and incidents, many witnessed by the author himself. As with so much of Vollmann's work, a subject that ordinarily would be considered the province of sophomoric gothic obsession or Poe-like adolescent morbidity is transformed utterly by a vast capacity for human sympathy and an unwillingness to indulge in either pedantry or sensationalism for its own sake. To the extent that it resembles any other book at all, *Rising Up and Rising Down,* a twenty-plus-year task in all, is less a treatise like Robert Burton's *Anatomy of Melancholy* than it is an act of bearing witness to human suffering, like Alexander Solzhenitsyn's *Gulag Archipelago*. An encyclopedia of pain, the project's very length is part of its effect (it is effective even in the abridgement), smothering the reader with the feeling of having witnessed the horrors depicted at one all-important remove. The end result, however, is that one feels rather fortunate to be alive at all, an odd phenomenon one often feels reading Vollmann and one that gives some sense to his otherwise baffling remark that the book is intended to comfort its readers. *Things certainly could be much worse*—thus runs one of life's saving thoughts.

WILLIAM T. VOLLMANN

The depressing conclusion of *Rising Up and Rising Down,* is "conservative" in the sense that it denies progress, and it is most certainly what the doctrinaire Marxists used to call "anti-revolutionary." One of the most remarkable, strange, shocking, idiosyncratic, and extraordinary books produced in recent memory, *Rising Up and Rising Down* mixes frontline journalism from war zones, personal meditation, and free-range philosophy in a structure designed to make its readers meditate on the question of whether, and in what circumstances, violence can be justified.

"THE 'FLOOR' OF EVIL"

Characteristically self-conscious and dubious about his own motives, Vollmann remarks in essence on his entire literary life. His interest in prostitutes as subject matter follows the same thread, because it reflects on man's—in this case the gender is not neutral or accidental—capacity for evil. It is not just that his fiction and his nonfiction are linked but that his fiction is often presented with disclaimers that indicate its sources in real-life encounters. *Whores for Gloria,* for example, is a novel presented with an appendix listing mid-1980s street prices for sex in San Francisco and "A Profile of the Tenderloin Street Prostitute" with excerpts from interviews. *The Rainbow Stories,* with its subject matter of "skinheads, x-ray patients, whores, lovers, fetishists and other lost souls," includes "A Note on the Truth of the Tales." Veracity is so important to Vollmann that he insists upon gesturing toward real life in his fiction, even in *The Royal Family,* his more hallucinatory and hyper-real prostitution novel.

This effect makes Vollmann's fiction read more often than not like creative nonfiction, and much of it is structured in a form similar to that of an essay, parable, pseudo-history, or aside. The plot of *Whores for Gloria,* for example, features a protagonist who creates an imaginary woman to love by combining and transmuting various stories told to him by street prostitutes. Manifestly the fiction becomes a double meditation on the creative process of an author who might condense various real-life persons into a fictional character. This makes the book not only a story but a story about stories and storytelling. Because of its subject matter, the book contains the additional virtue of bringing the reader always back to the real suffering of real individuals in real urban settings. The reader is thereby confronted with the same paradox facing the author, namely, that he or she is being coaxed toward a seemingly exotic and mysterious lifestyle that is in fact banal, depressing, and dangerous but also ancient and all too human.

This suggests that Vollmann's continued exploration of prostitution as a subject for fiction goes beyond a personal curiosity for "exotic experience" and is designed instead as an emblem of the human condition. The charges of prurience and anti-feminism are highly problematic and complicated; if anything, Vollmann's books make prostitution seem extraordinarily monotonous at the same time that they make prostitutes seem like real people caught in dire situations to which no one should be exposed. His characters also are not portrayed solely as victims, even though they are victimized. In fact Vollmann treats prostitutes in a similar fashion to the way in which Charles Dickens treated prisons: he visits them everywhere he goes as a barometer of the place he's in, as a reflector of how a given culture treats its most desperate people.

A revealing notion, surely, and one worth parsing, and wrestling with, because the things one learns in this fashion would seem to reinforce a generally malodorous view of human nature in general. So it is a part of life that a writer does the world a painful service to encounter and depict. A critique of Vollmann's relentless "negativity," therefore, is simultaneously wholly accurate and wholly meaningless. (As the critic Steven Moore once aptly wrote, "calling *The Royal Family* an ugly book is praise, not censure.") Vollmann's world is, strictly speaking, deformed and frankly often very flat in tone; his characters are usually bad people doing bad things. But that deformation is also the wellspring of his art, so that the subject to which he has essentially limited himself—human inhumanity—has blossomed in his work precisely because of that self-imposed limitation. This makes Vollmann a contemporary writer whose work is similar in effect to that of Poe or Baudelaire in the sense that his corrosive worldview may be unpleasant but acts as a valuable antidote to the prevailing attitudes of unremitting optimism and our cultural delusions of limitless freedom and endless potential for change.

There is a supernatural figure in Mahayana Buddhist philosophy said to be "The Regarder of the Cries of the World," an enlightened being whose occupation it is to listen very intently to the world's suffering. For Vollmann, the writer's task is clearly similar, although secular. In *An Afghanistan Picture Show,* Vollmann mocks his own personal attempts to help others, but without denying the value of altruism or asserting the meaninglessness of moral action. In his preface to *The Rainbow Stories,* he sets himself up self-mockingly as a "Recording Angel" rather than an avenging angel—in short, a person who listens rather than fights. That book also states explicitly what Vollmann is setting out to record: misery. *The Rainbow Stories,* with its color—coded titles, depicts such a world, and Vollmann insists on the reader's knowledge that he did not invent most of the suffering described in the book but instead derived it from real life. Both in his fiction and his nonfiction, as well as in the books that blur the boundaries between fact and fiction, Vollmann is getting at much the same thing, whether it is the misery of prostitution, war, personal violence, and depravity or, to invoke the often—quoted phrase from Joyce, the nightmare of history from which all are trying to awake.

SEVEN DREAMS OF NORTH AMERICAN LANDSCAPES

It is no coincidence that Vollmann's National Book Award for *Europe Central* acknowledged his accomplishment in historical fiction, since it is here that his literary interests truly coalesce and where his idiosyncrasies, and even his self—imposed limitations, work to his advantage. But Vollmann's historical fiction, at least in the ongoing epic project of the Seven Dreams of North American Landscapes, is never presented straight; the author always inserts himself into the frame of the story and is never far from the surface of the fiction, feeling free to jump backward and forward in time, describe his own travels and experiences, and interject deliberately anachronistic notes and asides. (*Argall,* for example, ostensibly set in the seventeenth century, ends with a collection of signs on the freeways of the American South.) This framing effect leaves some readers cold, but when it is successful, as in the Second Dream, *Fathers and Crows,* it creates an overwhelmingly personal and honest feeling of being immersed in two eras at the same time, sliding between the present and the past, the past and the present, until one feels that time might move in either direction. Vollmann, who for some reason signs himself as "William the Blind" when he is writing the Seven Dreams, could be called a chronicler of these *between—times.* While it would be impossible to consider each of the Dreams in detail here, it is worth exploring a few threads that interlace the series.

Vollmann's historical fiction is an act of impersonation that attempts to get at the heart of a moral episode in the past without disguising the way in which the gem is being turned to reveal a particular facet by a particular hand in the showroom of the present. In effect this makes the novels a sort of extended and wholly original personal essay. Indeed, both the First Dream, *The Ice—Shirt,* and the Second Dream, *Fathers and Crows,* start off not with their subject proper but with William the Blind, the scribe in the present, looking for clues in old books, manuscripts, stories, and myths that might help him connect with his subject matter. In *The Ice—Shirt,* William the Blind sets the scene not in the ancient Icelandic Sagas describing the first white incursions into Newfoundland but rather in a library setting in which the author has trapped himself inside the book he is reading. Vollmann, then, uses William the Blind as his own prologue. The net effect turns the Seven Dreams, with their cumbersome apparatus of notes and sources, into creative nonfiction, faithful to the historical record but novelistic in form. Vollmann calls it "Symbolic History."

WILLIAM T. VOLLMANN

Fathers and Crows, the story of the Jesuit "Black Gowns" in Canada, takes this idea even further, using its historical sources to meditate upon the book's own metafictional status. In it, William the Blind uses the *Spiritual Exercises* of Saint Ignatius of Loyola as his guidepost for writing fiction, posing as a sort of heretical latter-day Jesuit who wishes to banish the present and visualize the past, not, like the saint, to imagine the crucifixion, but instead to ascend "The Stream of Time" as a visionary experience in re-creating the adventures of the French in the New World. Vollmann becomes William the Blind, and William the Blind describes the process by which he will write his "Symbolic History," while simultaneously encouraging the reader to be wary of his own inventions and potential misapprehensions by providing notes, sources, and timetables. In *Fathers and Crows* the entire story is presented as a vision quest to recover some aspects of the past that might be of use in the present. A walk through the streets of modern-day Montreal in search of a statue of Catherine Tekakwitha, a native North American who became a saint under Jesuit instruction, becomes an odyssey through the tangle of base motives, high idealism, and almost supernatural bravery or foolhardiness that is the story of the first French encounters with Canadians.

What makes *Fathers and Crows* so remarkable is that it animates the personalities in a conflict that might be considered tragic in the sense that irreparable harm and grotesque injury and violence were unleashed by people with nobler intentions. In *Argall: The True Story of Pocahontas and Captain John Smith,* the colonists' motives appear debased; the English are essentially pirates. Of course this drop in moral temperature was ordained by the author on the first page of the First Dream, on which William the Blind expressed his plan to document the "Seven Ages of WINELAND THE GOOD." The Seven Dreams follow a structure in which: "Each Age was worse than the one before, because we thought we must amend whatever we found, nothing of what *was* being reflected in the ice-mirrors of our ideas." So while the magical realist conceit of *The Ice-Shirt* is that no frost existed in the New World until the Europeans imported it—the Norse documents concerning Vinland or Vineland describe no winters—and the central theme of *Fathers and Crows* is water in the form of Canada's rivers and the Stream of Time, the keyword of *Argall* is "ooze," the physical and moral muck of Virginia swamps and English hearts. Ice, water, mud. This Hesiod-like notion of successively degraded eras is deliberately programmatic (it also denies the great American love for Progress), although it is hardly inaccurate as far as the histories of Native Americans are concerned.

Because it was published around the same time as Thomas Pynchon's *Mason & Dixon,* critics compared Vollmann's and Pynchon's use of archaic syntax, but Steven Moore suggests that the prose of *Argall* is designed to resemble that of Robert Greene, Thomas Dekker, and Thomas Nashe, the "young turks of Shakespeare's day." The hopelessly foul and mercenary English simply are not as amazing to behold as their French counterparts in Canada, so that the book induces in the author (and ultimately in the reader) the same repulsion that it sets out of document.

Throughout the Dreams, Vollmann depicts a tremendous range of very different and complex Native American cultures without resorting to exoticism, nostalgia, or sentimentality. There is an excellence of craftsmanship in all of the Dreams and a satisfying consistency to the entire project that makes the publication of each new volume an event and the series of growing significance as an important attempt at an epic form in contemporary American literature. Vollmann's way is to try to cover everything with a strangely archaic and systematic approach, and, just as with the seven volumes of *Rising Up and Rising Down,* the mammoth and encyclopedic nature of all of his projects must be accepted as the M.O. that makes his best writing possible and gives his work its panoramic scope. It is inevitable that as time passes fewer and fewer pieces of an author's body of work are read, but, even so, it should not be forgotten that the animating vision behind Vollmann's entire oeuvre has been so remarkably sustained.

WILLIAM T. VOLLMANN

The early publication of *The Rifles*—in fact the Fifth Dream but published before the Third—and with the Fourth even now in its earliest stages, suggests that Vollmann intends his history to extend from the first European steps in North America all the way down to the present day. Like *Fathers and Crows*, *The Rifles* frames its narrative in terms of a present-day Vollmann-like searcher attempting first to retrace, and then to meld with, the past. The Fourth Dream, according to advance reports that have appeared online, will take up the story of Chief Joseph, the great Nez Perce leader known for his unforgettable "I'll fight no more forever" oration. Since the larger metanarrative of the Seven Dreams series involves the history of the clashes between Native Americans and their white colonizers since the settlement of the New World, it does seem logical that Joseph could become a central figure. His tragic heroism in attempting to save his Nez Perce people from ethnic cleansing in the 1870s is a story most American schoolchildren remember. Evicted from their homeland in the Wallowa valley of what is now Oregon, they attempted to flee to Canada to avoid being put on a reservation. During his famous "fighting retreat," Joseph was pursued by a much larger force of U.S. Army regulars under the command of the one-armed general Oliver O. Howard. Joseph and his band, including many women and children, managed to elude capture for around a thousand miles of wilderness trails, forests, and mountains through extremely shrewd tactics and maneuvers. The great tragedy of the Nez Perce was that they, among all the tribes of the West, were the most consistently friendly and accommodating allies of the whites. But Vollmann has expressed the desire to meddle with the chronology of the Chief Joseph story, so that time might be reversed and the Fourth Dream be given a happy ending.

EUROPE CENTRAL

Again and again in Vollmann's work, from *An Afghanistan Picture Show* and *Rising Up and Rising Down* to the Seven Dreams and *Europe Central*, can be found a relentless examination of the kind of fanatical idealism that turns murderous when the world fails (as it always fails) to accommodate itself with the visionary plan. In fact Vollmann's Universal History, as the main line of his work might be called, is a story of eternal return. Idealists, moralists, revolutionaries, and dogmatists set out to convert humanity to the New Man, the system fails, and anarchy is unloosed upon the world, where, as W. B. Yeats put it, the best lack all conviction and the worst are full of passionate intensity. Humanity is like a computer system with a glitch; it is always messing up, rebooting, wiping its memory, and then repeating its mistakes. For Vollmann, as is made clear in *Rising Up and Rising Down,* this is simply our nature. What sets Vollmann apart as a misanthrope is that his worldview doesn't impede his extraordinarily large capacity for compassion and sympathy for his characters, which comes out strongly in his most humane work (*The Rainbow Stories, Fathers and Crows,* and *Europe Central*), and which is repressed or underachieved in his more programmatic and stylized books *(The Ice-Shirt, The Royal Family,* and *Argall*). Moral incontinence, above all, the very human trait of recycling our errors, can inspire pity and terror, or else it can provoke the easy mockery of contempt and censure. Vollmann's best work is capable of achieving the former, which is a most rare and precious artistic effect: the tragedy of conflicted hearts caught in impossible situations.

Because we are bad (or at least very prone to being very bad), it stands to reason that human happiness depends on ignoring reality—another theme repeated countless times in Vollmann's work. A quote from Samuel Butler's *Erewhon* excerpted at the front of *Argall* could stand in as a guide to nearly everything he has written. As noted above, in *Argall,* Vollmann recasts this idea as learning to encounter the world by holding our noses.

Here is the paradox driving *Europe Central:* on one hand, an unrelenting desire to know the worst (about history and about humanity), to have one's knowledge of nazism and Stalinism unfiltered; and on the other hand, to depict, in the most humane terms, the lives of people caught up in this nightmare world without losing hold of some shred of integrity. By shutting out unpleasant information, we can be "so to speak" happy; in other words, not really happy at all. Or we can set ourselves the task of learning the worst and gathering unpleasant information, in which case the implication is that the luxury of happiness deserts us. This was surely one of the crushing truths of existing in Hitler's Germany or Stalin's Russia, and it is therefore not surprising that Vollmann depicts that world with such haunting clarity.

The smallness of one life flickers like a shadow on a grand stage of mechanized armies sweeping across a continent, almost immediately lost in the crush of momentous events. Yet that is not how it feels for one person to live, even during such a time. A passage in *Europe Central*—rightly highlighted by Esposito and other critics as a clue to Vollmann's working method—implies that it is fiction's role to seep into the cracks between the ellipses of history in order to recover what is most human.

The fiction writer makes alive those "between-times," almost raising the dead necromantically in the manner of Odysseus in order to speak with them about what remains off the record. The passage, with its characteristic flourishes—the deployment of a shifting web of similes that bombard the reader with a heightened sense of the framing artifice of narrative itself—is Vollmann in miniature.

Europe Central, like much of Vollmann's work, tends to meditate on its own construction, but somehow not in a way that seems like empty gamesmanship.

In *Europe Central*, which appeared long after this note was written, Vollmann found what many reviewers believed to be the quintessential vehicle for this technique. The book's solution to the problem of depicting individual lives immersed in an epic historical cataclysm is to use real historical figures as parables, emblematic figures of the age. Parable, by contrast, intends to evoke archetypes, symbols, and motifs without ever being easily understood. Parable, then, is a sort of living contradiction of the twin millstones of nazism and communism that grind up or grind down the characters in the novel. Parable also allows for the introduction of the more fabulous, hallucinatory, or quasi-visionary qualities of Vollmann's prose to range freely over his subjects with its usual mock-supernaturalism.

Proceeding by a series of "Pincer Movements," the structure of *Europe Central* makes twins of various emblematic historical figures, starting with Fanya Kaplan, Lenin's would—be assassin, and Lenin's wife and helpmeet, called N. K. Krupskaya by Vollmann in the Soviet style. Immediately there is something exceptional and surprising in this approach, for the early chapters of *Europe Central* are dominated by strong and complex women. A haunting chapter, "Dead Woman with Child," takes up the case of Käthe Kollwitz, the German artist whose haunting etchings, woodcuts, paintings and carvings of human suffering, stand both as a mocking denial of the rosy utopianism of the early Nazi program and as a presaging vision of things to come.

In Kollwitz's "grief for Germany" is another remarkable and recurring feature of *Europe Central* that contrasts with Vollmann's depiction of North American history: the book's emphasis on the unaccountable, ineradicable, and heartbreaking human capacity for hope even in the worst situations, even while implying in this case that hope is pointless. *Europe Central* presents a world in which the flickers of compassion and goodness cannot be eradicated any more than humanity's propensity for brutal violence. The book feels capacious as a result, large in emotional—not just historical—range.

Artists as well as soldiers pervade this audacious attempt at a latter-day *War and Peace* (although given the era in question, the result is more like "War and More War"). The stories of Stalingrad's "Last Field Marshal," Friedrich Paulus, and the SS officer who attempted to document the Holocaust, Kurt Gerstein, are told alongside those of the compromised filmmaker Roman Karmen, the poet Anna Akhmatova, and the composer Dmitri Shostakovich. Notably the novel does not finish with the end of World War II but instead traces the repercussions of the conflict deep into the private lives of those who outlived an unspeakable nightmare only to be caught up in the Stalinist web afterward. Shostakovich in particular becomes a compelling figure, dwelt on at much length by Vollmann because of his epic struggles to create truly great art under the Soviet regime. Such a thing was perhaps only possible in music, where criticism would not be explicit, and even then at an almost unbearable human cost. With the addition of a compelling lifelong love affair that Vollmann insists in his notes probably never took place, Shostakovich is ground to pieces by the mechanisms of authority while attempting to write his masterpieces. Ultimately he is publicly broken, becoming a Party member after years of cat-and-mouse and unenthusiastically spouting the official "line" by rote, but retaining till the end.

One of the central conceits of *Europe Central*, emphasized especially in the first section, "View from a Ruined Romanian Fort (1945)," is that Hitler and Stalin were rather like the interlocking heads of a single monster that set itself the task of destroying the continent together, perhaps united in this sense despite their epic death struggle. Certainly they were alike in requiring the obliteration not only of subjects but also of subjectivity. Many had to die not knowing that the projects of Hitler and Stalin would fail. They had to decide how they would comport themselves through hell, and those choices are the stuff from which Vollmann constructs the extended parables of *Europe Central,* the novel regarded by many critics as his greatest accomplishment to date.

"ABYSS-REDEMPTION" AND FINAL NOTES

Cast in terms of the eternal literary divide between foxes and hedgehogs, Vollmann is a quintessential hedgehog, having grasped one main vital subject with exceptional depth and mastery, despite the great variety and volume of his published work. That subject, as expressed in *Rising Up and Rising Down,* is "the 'floor' of evil," whether Vollmann is considering prostitution, attempting to categorize violence, or immersing himself in the fouler swamps of history. There is more to Vollmann than this, of course, but the main trajectory of his work has an unmistakably consistent feel. These books are also *Songs of Experience*, in which Vollmann pursues knowledge of the worst at the expense of contentment or even physical safety. The eternal problem, as in William Blake's original conception of innocence and experience, is that once you have seen something it is not possible to unsee it.

It remains to be discovered whether Vollmann has other phases to his literary evolution, whether he is interested in producing Dante—like *Paradiso*s or even *Purgatorio*s, or whether he will remain content to dwell among the damned, creating an endless series of *Inferno*s from their stories. Certainly the darkness of Vollmann's worldview no longer seems out of step with the actual situation of the world, as it might have done during the 1980s and 1990s. It is worth noting in passing that Vollmann's critical reception has reached its apex during a period in which murderous idealism no longer seems like a relic of the past. When Vollmann first started publishing, it was Ronald Reagan's "Morning in America," and his work might have seemed (deliberately) marginal well into the 1990s, when cultural optimism still reigned. Now his work seems to presage the age of terror in several important ways, although in fact it was simply the case that Vollmann was paying attention to things that most people would have rather ignored.

Vollmann is the deeper sort of abyss-gazer who has good reasons for exposing his negatives to the world. His odd hope that *Rising Up and Rising Down* would "comfort" his readers suggests a belief in what is called "abyss-redemption." According to Jeremy Waldron's succinct summary, "abyss-redemption" is the theory that it is better to know and confront evil than to remain unaware of its existence. Vollmann does not buy into Satan's spurious logic about humanity's ability to shun evil, of course, but he does ask the first part of the question: If evil is real, why not known? The pervasiveness of the "abyss-redemption" idea up until modern times actually suggests one way in which today we are, oddly, rather prim compared with our classical counterparts. Among Waldron's other examples: Adam Smith thought watching others suffer was a good way to learn sympathy; Edmund Burke believed that terror produced delight as long as it did not press too close; and Ralph Waldo Emerson apparently once claimed it wise to expose oneself to "the vision of violent death." Although the idea of abyss-redemption takes many forms, some more compelling than others, Vollmann's version of it is not based upon adolescent prurience or the vapid notion that we are made stronger by anything that fails to kill us. He is getting at something else: it's not so much that he believes we should look as that we have to look, or even more simply, that we *do* look.

The value of bearing witness, then, the value of knowledge, even of the worst, is self-sufficient; the persistence of evil is in itself part of an education. In this sense Vollmann is hardly an immoralist, any more than Baudelaire or Poe were when they exposed their readers to flowers of evil. Anyone who finds this kind of writing a form of literary rubbernecking and nothing more can simply close the book and be done with it. There is an argument to be had about whether writers need to travel into the most extreme places and document the worst things they can find in order to produce literature of value, but it is not an argument with Vollmann. Clearly it is necessary *for him* and not necessary for others—but it is necessary for his best work. In this sense Vollmann is deeply idiosyncratic and truly original, unlikely to spawn a school of followers, and very difficult to fit into the trends and patterns of contemporary writing. His use of self-conscious literary forms bears some resemblance to the American tradition of metafiction, but as Madison Smartt Bell notes, the comparison is dissatisfying.

There is an obvious influence from New Journalism, as Bell notes, in the observer-participant stories of Vollmann's nonfiction, relayed through the prism of an unreliable or interfering narrator. The "true life novel" or "history as a novel" approach pioneered by writers like Norman Mailer and Truman Capote seems relevant, although not overwhelmingly influential. In terms of contemporary trends, it makes the most sense to place Vollmann's work within the rise of so-called creative nonfiction. His novels are seldom far from their real-life sources, many of which are listed in notes and textual appendices to the books. As for many younger writers, research is part of Vollmann's creative process. Vollmann's phantasmagorical approach to historical fiction also bears comparison with Pynchon's *Gravity's Rainbow,* an inevitable presence in *Europe Central.* Vollmann has expressed a dislike for being compared with Pynchon, but the ultimate point might be that both writers are so brilliantly idiosyncratic that it is difficult to compare them with anyone else.

Selected Bibliography

WORKS OF WILLIAM T. VOLLMANN

Fiction and Nonfiction

You Bright and Risen Angels: A Cartoon. New York: Atheneum, 1987; New York: Penguin, 1988.

The Rainbow Stories. New York: Atheneum, 1989.

The Ice-Shirt. (Seven Dreams 1.) New York: Viking, 1990.

Thirteen Stories and Thirteen Epitaphs. New York: Pantheon, 1991, 1993; New York: Grove, 1994.

Whores for Gloria. New York: Pantheon, 1991, 1992.

An Afghanistan Picture Show: or, How I Saved the World. New York: Farrar, Straus and Giroux, 1992.

Fathers and Crows. (Seven Dreams 2.) New York: Viking, 1992; London: Andre Deutsch, 1992.

Butterfly Stories. New York: Grove, 1993.

The Rifles. (Seven Dreams 6.) New York: Viking, 1993, 1994. (*The Rifles,* although written and published prior to *Argall,* is listed as Seven Dreams 6, meaning that Vollmann skipped ahead in both composition and chronology.)

The Atlas. New York: Viking, 1996.

The Royal Family. New York: Viking, 2000.

Argall: The True Story of Pocahontas and Captain John Smith. (Seven Dreams 3.) New York: Viking, 2001; New York: Penguin, 2002.

Rising Up and Rising Down: Some Thoughts on Violence, Freedom, and Urgent Means. Abridgment. New York: Ecco Books, 2004. (The original seven-volume work was published in 2003 by McSweeney's Books. All references in the text refer to the abridged edition. *McSweeney's* magazine published early studies from the book, and McSweeney's Books assumed a risk no major publisher would have been willing to take.)

Europe Central. New York: Viking, 2005; New York: Penguin, 2006.

Uncentering the Earth: Copernicus and The Revolutions of the Heavenly Spheres. New York: Norton, 2006.

ARCHIVES

The William T. Vollmann Collection is located in the William Charvat Collection of American Fiction, Special Collections, Ohio State University Libraries, Columbus, Ohio.

CRITICAL AND BIOGRAPHICAL STUDIES

CRITICAL STUDIES AND REVIEWS

Bell, Madison Smartt, "Where an Author Might Be Standing." Younger Writers Issue. *Review of Contemporary Fiction* 13, no. 2:39–45 (summer 1993).

Esposito, Scott. "Between the Ellipses: The True Life Fiction of William T. Vollmann." Unpublished essay, 2006. (Much gratitude to Mr. Esposito for lending me his thoughtful essay; I have also benefited from his web log, Conversational Reading, and from our email exchanges, for ideas about Vollmann on several occasions.)

———. "On Vollmann and Chief Joseph." Conversational Reading (*http://esposito.typepad.com/con_read/2006/03/drink_with_voll.html*).

Gibbons, James. "Tome Improvement." *Bookforum* (*http://www.bookforum.com/archive/sum_05/gibbons.html*). Summer 2005.

Moore, Steven. Review of *The Royal Family. Rain Taxi* (*http://stevenmoore.inwriting.org/vollmannrevs1.shtml*). Fall 2000.

O'Brien, John, ed., Larry McCaffery, guest ed., and Steven Moore, senior ed. Younger Writer's Issue. *Review of Contemporary Fiction* 13, no. 2 (summer 1993).

Smith, Carlton, "Arctic Revelations: Vollmann's *Rifles* and the Frozen Landscape of the Self." Younger Writers Issue. *Review of Contemporary Fiction* 13, no. 2:53–61 (summer 1993).

Waldron, Jeremy, "Boutique Faith." *London Review of Books,* July 20, 2006, pp. 22–23. (Review of *Courting the Abyss: Free Speech and the Liberal Tradition* by John Durham Peters, University of Chicago Press, 2005. My summary of "abyss-redemption" and the examples used in the text are derived from Waldron's essay.

INTERVIEWS

"A. L. [Alexander Laurence.]" Interview with William T. Vollmann. *The Write Stuff* at ALTX.com (*http://www.altx.com/int2/william.t.vollmann.html*).)

DuShane, Tony. "An Interview with William T. Vollmann." *Bookslut* (http://www.bookslut.com/features/2005_11_006908.php). McCaffery, Larry. "An Interview with William T. Vollmann." *Review of Contemporary Fiction* 13, no. 2:9–24 (summer 1993).

ONLINE RESOURCES

The Vollmann Club Portal/Reading Group (http://www.edrants.com/wtv/). (In general, some of the best early commentators on Vollmann's work have been proprietors of websites and weblogs; the Vollmann Club also has a page of links to articles on and interviews with Vollmann that I found very useful during research. Moore, Steven. "The Metamorphoses of William the Blind: A Reviewer's Log" (*http://stevenmoore.inwriting.org/vollmannrevs1.shtml*). (Archive of Vollmann reviews.)

FRANZ WRIGHT

(1953—)

Ernest Hilbert

FRANZ WRIGHT IS renowned as an author of brooding lyric poetry focused on intense emotional and religious states. He is also known for the lurid details of his former alcoholism and troubled youth, which he frequently treats with as much humor as remorse. As with many American poets writing in the wake of confessionalism—a style pioneered by Robert Lowell and W. D. Snodgrass in the early 1960s and sustained by Sylvia Plath and Anne Sexton—events drawn from Wright's life have influenced his poetry directly, though he personally disdains classification as a "confessional" poet. Wright prefers a more humanist theory of poetry, proclaiming to Anthony Cardinale of the *Buffalo News*, "Poetry is anything but self-expression. A poem only works for me if it seems to be spoken to a person in a way that causes another person to say, 'Oh, yes, I've had that feeling.' " John Beer wrote in the *Chicago Review* that some of Wright's poems resist "the pitfalls of the confessional stance almost successfully." The emphasis in this phrase should be on the word "almost." Wright's personal afflictions and histories are never far from his poems, though they often become marginal and even invisible in his more abstract and symbolist efforts.

Wright differs from the confessional poets in many respects, not merely in his level of abstraction but in his technique. While some poets and critics insist that a veneer of formal achievement or elevated language can secure raw autobiography from the welter of sloppy or indulgent "self-expression," Wright has little need for planning in his poems. Rather than building toward the completion of a given inherited form, he conceives of each poem as an unbound, organic whole, whether molded from notes or appearing fully formed in a moment of inspiration. He has explained that he channels as much as writes his poems and that they are, when completed, transcendent works of art, divorced from specific aims or models. As he put it in an e-mail interview with Tim Willcutts in the *Oberlin Review:*

> Making a good poem, a poem that "works," that is, takes on a life of its own separate from its maker and clearly transcends mere self-expression, involves a sensation of gratitude and awe which I personally find difficult to distinguish from love. In my experience, the writing (I prefer to say the hearing) of a successful poem always involves the sensation of having been its instrument or medium.

BIOGRAPHY

The events of Wright's life have provided substantial material and are often in evidence. He was born on March 18, 1953, in Vienna, where his father, the influential poet James Wright, was writing on a Fulbright scholarship. His upbringing was bookish, after a fashion, and he remembers James walking him to school while singing "Schubert's *Die Forelle* and various German marching songs and Göethe poems."

When Franz Wright was eight years old, his father abandoned the family—an event the son has described as transformative: "My father had a big breakdown, got fired, got a Guggenheim fellowship and moved to New York; while I—aged 8—and my mother and three-year-old brother moved to San Francisco."

Wright's poetry often reveals itself in terms of his troubled life: his addictions to alcohol and drugs, his manic outbursts and his catatonic depressions, none of which he hides from interviewers. This decadent image fails to provide a full portrait of the author. As a young man he was as sober and dutiful as any other student. In

The Harder They Fall: Celebrities Tell Their Real-Life Stories of Addiction and Recovery (2005), Franz Wright made a concession to the popular press's fascination with self-destructive behavior that fuels so many talk shows, tell-all memoirs, and "behind the scenes" television exposés: "When I discovered drinking as a teenager, I was happy for the first time in my life." He attended Oberlin College, which he characterizes as a great school, where he met David Young, who would continue to support and champion Wright throughout the poet's turbulent career. Upon graduating from Oberlin in 1977, Wright realized he didn't belong in the academic world and began a peripatetic life that would continue for many years. In 1980, when Franz Wright was twenty-seven years old, his father died. He accepted a position at Emerson College, where he taught from 1984 through 1989, when he was fired for what he has described with customary sarcasm as "drinking-related activities".

Throughout this period, awards and acclaim continued to accumulate. He won grants from the Guggenheim Foundation and the National Endowment for the Arts as well the PEN/Voelcker Award for Poetry and a Whiting Fellowship. But beneath the surface of critical approval and glamour, his life had run off course and his health began to suffer.

The turning point came in 1999 when he experienced a religious awakening. His first book after recovery was *The Beforelife* (2001), nominated for the Pulitzer Prize. His next commercially issued US volume, *Walking to Martha's Vineyard* (2003), took the prize. On National Public Radio's *Weekend Edition* in April 2004 he admitted, "I cried. It was a stunning shock to me."

Because so much of his earlier work concerns loneliness, depression, and madness, his religious conversion is a crucial transformation indeed. While his later poems may appear on first blush to resemble the earlier ones, they are at root vitally different. The rhythmic and imagistic styles have remained, but the message is different: life is filled with terror and uncertainty, but there is a solution. Redemption is possible, if fraught at each step with difficulty and pain. Harvey Shepard applauded this change, explaining: "We need more than the fleeting instants of respite and hope found in Wright's earlier collections." Now married to Beth Woodcome—a former student of Wright's who is also a writer and well-regarded translator of German poetry—the poet attends Catholic Mass daily and works at the Edinburg Center for Mental Health in Lexington and as a facilitator at the Center for Grieving Children in Arlington, Massachusetts. Wright remains, for the most part, socially detached and periodically hermit-like. He travels to read several times a year and will occasionally take a short-term university teaching assignment (he taught at Brandeis in the fall of 2006), but he is absent from the retreats and conferences that dominate and, to some degree, regulate the American poetry world. He is happy with this arrangement and has become notably prolific.

STYLE AND TECHNIQUE

Nihilistic despair and grim humor characterize the poetry in the first half of Franz Wright's career, comprised mainly of four commercially published books, *The One Whose Eyes Open When You Close Your Eyes* (1982), *Entry in an Unknown Hand* (1989), *The Night World and the Word Night* (1993), and *Rorschach Test* (1995). The second phase of his career, beginning with *The Beforelife* (2001)—his first book with a major commercial (non-university) publisher—and continuing with *Walking to Martha's Vineyard* (2003) and *God's Silence* (2006), is defined by undisguised expressions of religious faith. His later devotional style mingles with the earlier characteristics of his poetry to create a strange, otherworldly type of poetry unique in American letters. While most major American poets can trace a direct lineage from an earlier school—Michael Palmer from the L=A=N=G=U=A=G=E school, Sharon Olds directly from confessionalism, Jorie Graham from the high modernism of T. S. Eliot and Wallace Stevens-Franz Wright's devotional poetry stands apart. Mary Oliver's religious verse may loosely be compared with Wright's, but Wright draws on the dark, symbolic style of early-twentieth-century European expressionists such as Georg Trakl and Paul Celan. Although Wright's poems may at times resemble in tone and appearance those of Louise Glück, another poet of spiritual longing, he differs from her in many ways. Glück tends to be very serious and guarded, even in her characters' most pleading and desperate moments. Also, her work is devoid of humor, while Wright relies on a signature brand of black humor and desolate sarcasm throughout.

In 2004 Wright remarked to Sally Heaney of the *Boston Globe,* "It sounds crazy to say I'm a poet. It's like saying I'm an ancient Greek philosopher." He is critical of the MFA culture of poetry in the United States.

Since 1999 religion has come to share the place in his life once exclusively occupied by art. He remarked in *U.S. Catholic* that "poetry was a kind of religion in and of itself for a long time. I believed in poetry. I had an almost theological conception of it. But I came to realize that was a mistake." Wright's life proved an inversion of Wallace Stevens' assertion, in his 1957 *Opus Posthumous,* that "after one has abandoned a belief in God, poetry is the essence which takes its place as life's redemption."

It is possible to place Franz Wright as part of a long lineage of Catholic poets, which extends from Dante Alighieri down through to the modernists Gerard Manley Hopkins and David Jones to Czesław Miłosz and even to younger poets like Adam Zagajewski and Marie Ponsot (Wright has read before audiences with Zagajewski and shares a publisher with Ponsot).

At one time Wright may have been considered primarily a poet of painful self-examination and meaningless suffering, but he is now deemed a religious or spiritual poet. In the *American Poetry Review,* Ira Sadoff included Wright in a broad category denoting the "spiritualization of American poetry," a group that included such dissimilar figures as Li-Young Lee, W. S. Di Piero, Jane Hirschfeld, and Jorie Graham.

Comparisons with Franz Wright's father are difficult to avoid. After the son received the Pulitzer Prize for *Walking to Martha's Vineyard,* journalists were immediately attracted to the trivia that the two—James and Franz—are the only father-son duo to have each taken home the prize. There exists an important correlation between their styles as well. Even a cursory review will reveal strong similarities between James Wright's later, spare style and Franz's. Like his father, Franz wields an array of symbols and metaphors to describe an almost pantheistic blending of the individual mind with the universe. Here is an example from James Wright's poem "Brush Fire" from his 1969 collection *Shall We Gather at the River*:

In this field,
Where the small animals ran from a brush fire,
It is a voice
In burned weeds, saying
I love you.
 (p. 156)

James Wright introduced both a stylistic and philosophical template for his son to work with, but there are differences, of course. While Franz Wright may not address human suffering in the specific social terms of his father, he nonetheless experiences a strong sense of the wholeness and concord of humanity, a trend that rises directly from his devout Catholicism.

The figure addressed by the speaker could be a stranger, or even an enemy, and the speaker's voice seems to grow softer and disappear altogether as the poem's lines diminish in length.

He told Tim Willcutts in the *Oberlin Review* interview that

my desire for many years—unconscious at first I suppose, but with growing deliberateness—was to write something so completely personal that it crossed over finally into a kind of universality, but that is just a technical way of saying my wish was to write something which spoke for some other person who had gone through some things I went through.... but was not equipped to describe them himself.

This approach can be regarded as an attempt to bear witness, in the Christian sense. In the same interview Wright discussed what he feels are the therapeutic qualities of poetry:

Poetry can be a healing force, the serious reading as well as the writing of it (and I believe the ability to read poems successfully is as much a "gift" and a spiritual discipline as the ability to write them and maybe a more desirable one, since it's clear trying to write them can drive people crazy).

He said elsewhere that poetry is "the cure" (NPR). It is clear from these statements that poetry exists, for Wright, as a force much greater than it does for most poets. It is more than diversion, craft, entertainment, career, or art. This is borne out in the extraordinary pressures he places upon both himself and the art form.

INFLUENCES AND APPROACHES TO COMPOSITION

Franz Wright has expressed belief in the artist as a vessel of greater powers. André Gide is said to have remarked, "Art is a collaboration between God and the artist, and the less the artist does, the better."

Such faith in poetry as revealed knowledge has technical implications as well. Wright's reliance on Logos owes more to Christian thought than to Heracleitus, who saw it as order in the universe, or classical rhetoricians, who view it as one of three principal modes of persuasion. To Wright, Logos explains much of his compositional style. Appearing in the King James Version of the Bible as "the Word," Logos exists beyond human time. It is anterior to human thought. The ideal, as stated in John 1:1–2, is: "In the beginning was the Word, and the Word was with God, and the Word was God. The same was in the beginning with God." For Wright, words themselves are not merely devotional in the sense that the term can describe a rhetorically crafted metaphysical poem by John Donne or George Herbert. Composition and even reading poetry are devotional acts in themselves. Mary Karr, a Catholic poet, sees Wright's work as cathartic. Wright, for his part, has asserted (in the *Arkansas Democrat-Gazette*) that writing poetry is a "moral act." In *Commonweal*, Andrew Krivak, although he was not speaking specifically about Wright, described the "synthesis between theology's 'account' of the divine and poetry's own human, yet God-like, 'making.'" Wright has written that his ideal poem is one where "the terms symbolic and literal become synonyms" *(NC1)*.

Most readers of Wright's earlier work would assume that the driving force behind the poems would be his own personal depredations, but he demurs on this point, refuting the notion that suffering contributed to the quality of his early work. This is not to suggest that the details of his addiction and broken family have not supplied subjects for his poetry—as we have seen, they most certainly have—but Wright's focus is on the *way* something is said, its intensity of feeling and inventiveness, rather than *what* exactly is said. Elsewhere Wright asserts, "only emotion endures." But must this emotion stem from extreme suffering or mental illness? *(NC1)*. Wright does see suffering as an intrinsic part of his writing: "It is a privilege to suffer, the alternative is not getting to be here" *(Oberlin Review)*.

Although many of his early poems were constructed in regular stanzas, the style that has come to dominate his poems is one of jagged sparseness on the page, as in "Lines Written in the Dark Illegible Next Day":

Apple alone in a bowl, and
Then the sense—lit
Apple
Touched
(more on this presently)
And late at night I think I'm being followed: it
    Is a bald child
In a white nightgown or wedding dress
Which drags behind him
Like the tides
 (p. 67)

The furrowed syntactical style, distinguished by serrated lineation, follows the branching channels and eddying pauses of thought, but it also illustrates a sense of loneliness and detachment so often present in the poems. Wright has been described as an minimalist by some critics, and this may be true in the strict sense of severe presentation on the page and overall caginess, particularly if compared with the garrulous anecdotalism of James Tate, the routine meditations of A. R. Ammons, or the sprawling philosophical investigations of Jorie Graham. The term "minimalist" is better suited to a poet like the objectivist George Oppen or the work of the concrete poets than to Wright, who generates dynamic, fluid presences in his poems. They are rich and deeply felt.

Wright's poems are numinous—a term coined by Rudolf Otto to indicate the "other," a path to gods, mystery, or eternity. Wright's poems sometimes scarcely afford purchase at all in the world of objects. His settings, particularly in the later poems, are fragile and unpredictable. Wright's stance is utterly contrary to the nativist American modernist credo "No ideas but in things," from William Carlos Williams' 1944 poem "A Sort of Song," a credo at the core of the objectivist school of American poetry and one that heavily influenced Allen Ginsberg and others. While Williams urged poets to cast off poetic convention and see the world in concrete, realistic terms, Wright has driven ever further inward to his own emotional and psychological nucleus, flinging off the outer world as he sees fit. The settings are mental rather than physical, existing more in memory and emotion than in the fields and shuttered rooms of the poems. The speaker of the poem, the "I," is often as irregular and mysterious as his surroundings.

THE EARTH WITHOUT YOU *(1980)* AND THE ONE WHOSE EYES OPEN WHEN YOU CLOSE YOUR EYES *(1982)*

The small, virtually unobtainable chapbook *Tapping the White Cane of Solitude* (1976) was Franz Wright's first non-magazine publication. It contains early versions of poems that were reprinted with changes in his next two books. *The Earth Without You* appeared four years later and was issued the Cleveland State University Poetry Center. It marks Wright's first commercially published book, with a price ($3.50) and an ISBN code. The book introduced Wright's terse, elegiac style.

The poems from this slim volume (thirty-six pages) were duplicated, for the most part, in the following, longer book, *The One Whose Eyes Open When You Close Your Eyes* (1982), published by Pym-Randall Press in Cambridge, Massachusetts.

One thing that is almost entirely absent from *The One Whose Eyes Open When You Close Your Eyes*, or any of his early books, is a religious sensibility, except when he turns a phrase on its head for the sake of bitter satire. Wright's early poems also display the influence of the "deep image" school of poetry, a school that, as described in the *Oxford Companion to Twentieth-Century Poetry,* has "come to be associated with certain American poets, above all Robert Bly and James Wright." There is no question that Robert Bly had an enormous influence on Franz Wright in many ways. When he was young, Wright recieved magnificent stimulation from Robert Bly. Bly's influence can be seen in a comparison between his style and that of the young Wright. In Bly's anti-Vietnam War poem "Driving Through Minnesota During the Hanoi Bombings" (*The Light Around the Body,* 1967), he deploys radical imagistic leaps:

In Asia, and you will look down in your cup
And see
Black Starfighters.
 (p. 37)

The image is intended to startle and disorient while also drawing complex and profound connections over time, space, cultures, and history. Franz Wright, a far less historical or socially activist poet than Bly, uses similar techniques in his early books.

Wright tends to use vast and cosmic images—blizzards, stars, oceans—but one resonant modern technological image that appears repeatedly in his poems is the telephone, which he has learned to use as a potent symbol of disconnection, loneliness, regret, and failure to act. Wright is fascinated with the erosion of the individual into anonymousness, the slow drive toward nothingness. In "Initial" he offers a typically beguiling scenario of a man feeling like and increasingly becoming a ghost. These poems are unsettling and memorable, and the reader begins to glimpse the self-destructive, disembodied voice that will haunt so many of Wright's poems.

FRANZ WRIGHT

ENTRY IN AN UNKNOWN HAND *(1989)*

While his father and Robert Bly exerted considerable influence on his style, it is also apparent that Wright obtained valuable tools from European poets of earlier generations. In 1984 Wright published *No Siege Is Absolute,* which consists of his "versions" or rough translations from the French poet René Char. Char aligned himself with André Breton and Paul Éluard in his early career but went on to distance himself from the surrealist movement. While little of his or anyone else's surrealism affected Wright's poetry, his symbolism most likely did.

The influence of another European poet may be felt in this collection as well. In the early 1980s Wright published two collections of translations from the early-twentieth-century German poet Rainer Maria Rilke: *The Life of Mary* in 1981 and *The Unknown Rilke* in 1983 (issued in an expanded edition in 1991). Although he did not undertake a translation of Rilke's poem *"Archaischer Torso Apollos"* (Archaic torso of Apollo), its most famous line, *"Du mußt dein Leben ändern"* (You must change your life) echoes in an epiphanic moment of Wright's poem "The Crawdad".

The note of dislocation and frustration sounded in Wright's earlier collections is struck again, more forcefully, in *Entry in an Unknown Hand.* The year it appeared, he was, according to an April 16th, 2004 New York Times article, "diagnosed with manic-depressive illness" and the poems give the impression of a man trying to disappear altogether. In "Quandary" it seems that Wright sets out to fulfill the French literary critic Roland Barthes's ideal of the "death of the author," from his 1968 essay of the same name. While Barthes argued against integrating considerations of an author's personal history or private intentions into discussions of a literary work—in other words advocating a supreme division between the author and the text—Wright uses the text itself as a mechanism for the annihilation of its own author.

Wright possesses a Borgesian attraction to the image of the blank page. In "View from an Institution," in his first full-length book, he conjures the eerie image of a useless library—"You'll notice the library's books are all blank on the inside"—and this is recapitulated in "Morning Arrives." This also owes a debt to Franz Kafka, who dealt with questions of guilt (usually a nameless, undeserved, and absurd guilt) in stories of men condemned merely for being alive (rumors to the contrary, Wright is not the namesake of Kafka; he stated in private correspondence that his parents chose the name because they were in Vienna at the time and thought it was a "quintessentially Viennese name").

THE NIGHT WORLD AND THE WORD NIGHT *(1993)*

Although there is no body of criticism for Wright's first two commercial books or his early chapbooks, Wright's third full-length book was described in the *Virginia Quarterly Review* as having a "stunning sense of isolation, loss, and grief." The images Wright uses in this book are stranger, more ambitious, but less exact, as when he describes a "Hawk in golden space" at the start of "Illegibility" or "Wolf stars" in the "Icon-yellow twilight" in "Provincetown Postcards," which concludes with a perfect emblem of loneliness.

Wright is in no way evasive about his compositional approach, which involves an involuntary reception of a poem. He acknowledges that it arrives from his own subconscious, but he hints that it may be of a more supernatural origin. He attempts to form a poetic object from pure thought.

Wright's poetry is ingeniously invested with allusions to other literary works. In "Forgotten in an Old Notebook" he employs a mirror as a symbol of self-examination and allows it to recall King Richard's soliloquy in act 4 of Shakespeare's *Richard II*—"Give me that glass, and therein will I read. No deeper wrinkles yet? Hath sorrow struck / So many blows upon this face of mine / And made no deeper wounds?"

In an earlier poem ("My Brother Takes a Hammer to the Mirror") he exploits a shattered mirror as a symbol of not only self-destruction but of a broken connection with his father. The later example is a calmer consideration of aging and change.

His examination of his agonized relationship with his father takes a more mystical turn in this collection as well. For instance, in the long poem "Winter Skyline Late," he addresses "Unfather" and asks him to "unsay me." This brings to mind William Blake's "Nobodaddy," a mocking designation of the Old Testament God of Christianity.

He confesses his inability to control his alcoholism, even if he is able to write about it. It is a terrifying, brute force, and the poem constitutes a particularly violent moment in an otherwise tranquil collection.

"Midnight Postscript" is possibly the best-known poem in the collection and also serves as the title of a separate chapbook published by Tray Full of Lab Mice Press in 1992. He attempts to explain the movement of the mind into a transcendent state, equivalent to departing the physical world altogether. The extended six-beat final line is repeated almost exactly over a decade later in Wright's poem "The Only Animal" in *Walking to Martha's Vineyard*. In the second version, the younger Wright struggles to be heard amid the later, devotional stanzas of the more mature poet, who still occasionally yearns for oblivion.

RORSCHACH TEST *(1995)* AND ILL LIT: SELECTED AND NEW POEMS *(1998)*

Rorschach Test maintains the dark broodings of Wright's first three full-length collections. The feeling of disconnection hinted at from his earliest poems becomes palpable in this collection, as when the speaker of "Voice" finds himself so isolated that he begins to address the "voice" in his mind:

In "Infant Sea Turtles," Wright describes the sea as "that vast tear we came crawling out of," and the poem replicates an image used by another poet of tragedy and pity, Wilfred Owen.

Although not written in the majestic, Georgian style of Owen, Wright's poem contains strikingly similar imagery:

Unlike Wright's dominant style, which recalls European expressionism and American deep im-age poetry, his poem "The Meeting" sounds and looks like those written by two of the more "plainspoken" American poets of the past half-century, Charles Bukowski—"starving there, sitting around the bars, / and at night walking the streets for / hours" (p. 353) in "young in New Orleans"—and popular poet Billy Collins in "Bar Time." But Wright's scenario is bleaker than either and lacks Bukowski's resilient hope or Collins' friendly wink.

The conclusion of Wright's early period is marked by the publication of *Ill-Lit: Selected & New Poems* in 1998. "Ill-Lit," the title of a short poem in *Entry in an Unknown Hand,* derives its ambiguous strength from wordplay. It conjures the sense of "poorly lit" settings filled with "illness." Brett Ralph described it in *Rain Taxi* as a "sign, its crippled shorthand a harbinger of dark happenings within. It's difficult to say Ill Lit. It demands an awkward pause (a stutter, a limp), like something's a little wrong." The last chapter of the book contains previously uncollected poems.

But the new poems also suggest attempts to overcome the pervasive isolation described in the earlier poems, as in "From a Roadside Motel," when the ubiquitous telephone rings again. For the first time in more than two decades, Wright describes a person actually speaking into a phone rather than cowering from it. *Ill-Lit: Selected and New Poems* ends with one of Wright's workhorse images, the telephone, transformed from a symbol of isolation into a tool of suicide, a gun pressed to the temple.

THE BEFORELIFE *(2001)*

The Beforelife marks the beginning of the second phase in Franz Wright's career, and it signals a recognizable turn away from the despairing autobiography of the earlier books toward a more genuinely expressionistic and religious style of poetry. It is also the basis of his breakthrough in terms of popular readership. His poems began appearing regularly in *The New Yorker,* and those poems served as the core of *The Beforelife,* his first book from a major publisher. While university presses, the standard conduit for contemporary poetry, had published his earlier books, *The Beforelife* appeared on the vaunted Knopf poetry list, which has included such poets as W. H. Auden, Sharon Olds, and Anthony Hecht. Knopf is part of the Random House Group, itself part of the German media conglomerate Bertelsmann. This provided Wright's books with a correspondingly greater representation in bookstores across the country.

In his *Oberlin Review* interview, Tim Willcutts described *The Beforelife* as a "triumph over silence," and Wright responded that its composition was a result of "supernatural intervention—quite literally, a miracle occurred. From one day to the next—from one hour to the next actually." A primary difference between his earlier poems and those in *The Beforelife* is the speed with which the latter were completed.

He admits that his editor at Knopf, Deb Garrison, was "fantastically helpful in shaping" the book.

While he has successfully faced certain monsters in his life, including himself, the persona of the violent child has not entirely disappeared from his poems. Yet Wright recognizes the danger of drawing repeatedly on distressing memories. Nonetheless, Wright ends the book on a triumphant note, a note of arrival, or, more precisely, a refusal to leave, mixing his earlier sense of ghostly detachment with a powerful sense of durability.

WALKING TO MARTHA'S VINEYARD (2003)

The title of Wright's Pulitzer Prize–winning collection *Walking to Martha's Vineyard* has been the subject of much speculation. The collection is characterized by subterranean thoughts and concentrated religious feeling of a kind not seen in anything Wright had written before.

"The Only Animal" is perhaps the best-known poem in the collection and, at nearly three pages, the collection's longest. In addition to recalling his earlier poem "Midnight Postscript" and its life "scarlessly" closing "like water,", it is possible to hear other resonances.

Stephen Burt of the *New York Times* acknowledged that Wright is one of the true contemporary masters of tone, a feature of his work that only achieved a genuinely high level of sophistication in *Walking to Martha's Vineyard*. In a tentative review in *Oberlin Alumni* magazine, David Walker lamented the public's tendency to speak of Wright's poetry largely in autobiographical terms: "it seems too easy to perpetuate Romantic mythologies of the self-regarding artist." Whatever the critics thought, *Walking to Martha's Vineyard* inaugurated Wright's role as a major presence in American poetry.

GOD'S SILENCE (2006)

God's Silence, which Wright originally planned to title "Prescience," after one of its central poems, is his longest book to date.

As with his earlier books, Wright was forced to find equilibrium between his lived experience and his radical creative transports. While it is certainly possible to identify many instances of religious or devotional verse in *The Beforelife* and *Walking to Martha's Vineyard,* it is correct in viewing *God's Silence* as a fully religious book. "The Reader" takes Wright's use of Logos, or God as the Word, to its ultimate conclusion:

The mask was gone now, burned away
(from inside)
by God's gaze
There was no
I, there
was no he—
finally
there was no text, only
what the words stood for;
and then
what all things stand for.
 (p. 44)

Some of the shorter, elegiac poems sound a note of calm long absent in Wright's work. In his poem for Donald Justice, he writes of

happinesses gone forever
The days of receiving your letter
Or amidst blowing leaves, on the quiet
streets of small Midwestern towns
late at night typewriter sounds.
 (p. 55)

In his New Year's letter, "Progress," he jokes: "Nobody has called for some time. / (I was always the death of the party)." (p. 16) Troubled thoughts of his father are also ameliorated, when he writes "White fire of winter stars— / what he's thinking at fifty / I finally know." (p. 30) "Sitting Up Late with My Father, 1977" ends with a extraordinary vision of "White distant emerald fire of winter stars." Wright also continues to trawl the past, as in "Nebraska Blizzard," when he writes

We were about to make Omaha
halfway through
the winter
Someone who is dead now
handed me a joint.
 (p. 109)

While he has accepted a highly religious tone along with his Catholicism, the ghosts of the past, of other writers, of his father, and of his younger self continue to haunt him, as he writes in "Progress": "I'm still alone with all the world's / beauty and cruelty." (p. 16)

Selected Bibliography

WORKS OF FRANZ WRIGHT

Poetry

Tapping the White Cane of Solitude. Oberlin, Ohio: Triskelion Press, 1976.

The Earth Without You. Cleveland: Cleveland State University Poetry Center, 1980.

The One Whose Eyes Open When You Close Your Eyes. Cambridge, Mass.: Pym-Randall Press, 1982.

8 Poems. New York: Dan Simko [mimeograph[, 1980.

Going North in Winter. Cullman, Ala.: Gray House Press, 1986.

Entry in an Unknown Hand. Pittsburgh: Carnegie-Mellon University Press, 1989.

And Still the Hand Will Sleep in Its Glass Ship. San Francisco: Deep Forest, 1991.

Midnight Postscript. New Hampshire: Tray Full of Lab Mice Press, 1992.

The Night World and the Word Night. Pittsburgh: Carnegie-Mellon University Press, 1993.

Rorschach Test. Pittsburgh: Carnegie-Mellon University Press, 1995.

Ill Lit: Selected and New Poems. Oberlin, Ohio: Oberlin College Press, 1998.

Knell. Minneapolis: Short Line Editions, 1999.

The Beforelife. New York: Knopf, 2001.

Hell and Other Poems. Devoran, Cornwall, U.K.: Stride, 2001.

Walking to Martha's Vineyard. New York: Knopf, 2003.

God While Creating the Birds Sees Adam in His Thoughts. Kalamazoo, Mich.: Half Moon Bay Press, 2000.

God's Silence. New York: Knopf, 2006.

Translations

Jarmila. Flies: 10 Prose Poems by Erica Pedretti. Oberlin, Ohio: Pocketpal Press 1976.

The Life of Mary (Poems by Rainer Maria Rilke). Cambridge, Mass.: Middle Earth Books, 1981.

The Unknown Rilke: Selected Poems. Oberlin, Ohio: Oberlin College Press, 1983; expanded edition, 1990.

No Siege Is Absolute: Versions of Rene Char. Providence, R.I.: Lost Roads, 1984.

Anthologized and Other Works

Collins, Billy, ed. *180 More: Extraordinary Poems for Every Day.* New York: Random House, 2005. "Publication Date."

Costanzo, Gerald, ed. *The Carnegie Mellon Anthology of Poetry.* Pittsburgh: Carnegie-Mellon University Press, 1993. "The Needle: For a Friend Who Disappeared," "Pawtucket Postcards," "Joseph Come Back as the Dusk," "Entry in an Unknown Hand."

Gammon, Catherine, and Bruce Smith, eds. *Cape Discovery: The Provincetown Fine Arts Work Center Anthology.* Lebanon, N.H.: Sheep Meadow, 1994. "The Lord's Prayer," "New Leaves Bursting Into Green Flames"

Milosz, Czeslaw, ed. *A Book of Luminous Things: An International Anthology of Poetry.* New York: Harvest, 1998. "Depiction of Childhood,"

Myers, Jack, and Roger Weingarten, eds., *New American Poets of the Nineties.* Lincoln, Mass.: Godine, 1991. "Certain Tall Buildings," "The Needle," Entry in an Unknown Hand," "Elegy: Breece D'J Pancake."

Stromberg, Gary, and Jane Merrill. *The Harder They Fall: Celebrities Tell Their Real-Life Stories of Addiction and Recovery.* Center City, Minn.: Hazelden, 2005. "Empty Stage," "The Dead Dads."

Walker, David, ed. *American Alphabets: 25 Contemporary Poets.* Oberlin, Ohio: Oberlin College Press, 2006. "Blood, Morning," "Alcohol," "Illegibility," "Loneliness," "August Insomnia," "Thoughts of a Solitary

Farmhouse," "Sunday Afternoon," "Have You Seen This Child," "Circle Drawn in Water," "Flight, Walking to Martha's Vineyard," "The Only Animal," "Sitting Up Late With my Father, 1977," "Publication Date," "Lines Written in the Dark Illegible Next Day"

Wright, Franz, "On Reality Itself." *NC1: nowCulture* (spring-summer 2002).

Zaleski, Philip, and Barry Lopez, eds. *The Best American Spiritual Writing 2005.* New York: Houghton Mifflin, 2005. "Prescience."

Zaleski, Philip, and Barry Lopez, eds. *The Best American Spiritual Writing 2005.* New York: Houghton Mifflin, 2006. "East Boston, 1996"

CRITICAL AND BIOGRAPHICAL STUDIES

ARTICLES AND REVIEWS

Beer, John. Review of *Hell. Chicago Review* 47, no. 4, and 48, no. 1 (winter 2001–spring 2002).

Beggy, Carol, and Mark Shanahan. "Large Takeout Order." *Boston Globe,* July 9, 2005.

Bonikowski, Wyatt. "There Is Nothing *but* Magic: Franz Wright on Poetry as Magical Realism." *Margin: Exploring Modern Magical Realism,* April 2006.

Brown, Laura Lynn. "Life After Life: Pulitzer Prize–Winner Franz Wright Sees Poetry as a Way of Giving Back to Creation." *Arkansas Democrat-Gazette,* April 24, 2004.

Burt, Stephen. "*Walking to Martha's Vineyard:* Poems of Self-Destruction." *New York Times,* December 21, 2003.

Cardinale, Anthony. "Poet's Struggle To Be Authentic Ranges from Despair into Hope." *Buffalo News,* September 23, 2005.

Chiasson, Dan. "The Big Three: An Exchange on This Year's Prizes." *Poetry* 185, no. 1 (October 1, 2004).

Crill, Hildred. "Franz Wright's God: A Review of *Walking to Martha's Vineyard.*" *Web Del Sol Review of Books.* Symposium on the Work of Franz Wright (http://webdelsol.com).

Filkins, Peter. Review of *The Beforelife. Partisan Review* (summer 2002).

Freeman, John. "Poet Franz Wright Delights in Discovery." *Pittsburgh Post-Gazette,* April 11, 2004.

———. "The Pleasure in Wright's Work Is His and Ours." *Cleveland Plain Dealer,* April 18, 2004.

———. "Making His Peace with God but Leaving Readers Feeling Earthbound." *Seattle Times,* March 31, 2006.

Gibson, Dobby. Review of *The Beforelife. Rain Taxi Review of Books.* Online edition. Spring 2001.

Gilbert, Sandra. "Where the Boys Are." *Poetry* 178, no. 4 (July 2001). (Omnibus review including *The Beforelife.*)

Graves, Michael. "The Abandoned Male Persona and the Mysterious Feminine in the Poetry of James Wright: A Study in the Transformation of the Self." *Psychoanalytic Review* 85, no. 6 (December 1999).

———. "Swans of the Father: A Difficult Loyalty (The Poetry of Franz Wright)." *BigCityLit,* 2001.

Guillory, Daniel. Review of *The Beforelife. Library Journal* 125, no. 20 (December 1, 2000).

Hammer, Langdon. "To Live Is to Do Evil." *New York Times,* May 14, 2006.

Heaney, Sally. "Taking Poetry into the Community Center Set Up as Alternative Venue." *Boston Globe,* October 10, 2004.

Kaminsky, Ilya. "A Note on Franz Wright's Work." *Web Del Sol Review of Books.* Symposium on the Work of Franz Wright (http://webdelsol.com).

Kirsch, Adam. "April's Verses." *New York Sun,* April 14, 2006.

Kriesel, Michael. Review of *God's Silence. Library Journal* 131, no. 6 (April 1, 2006).

Krivak, Andrew. "The Language of Redemption: The Catholic Poets Adam Zagajewski, Marie Ponsot & Lawrence Joseph." *Commonweal,* May 9, 2003.

Lambert, Gregg. " 'Shall We Gather at the River?' The Contemporary Eulogy of James Wright." *Literature & Theology: An Interdisciplinary Journal of Theory and Criticism* (summer 2000).

Lee, Felicia R. "Going Early into That Good Night." *New York Times,* April 24, 2004.

Logan, William. "Stouthearted Men: Verse Chronicle." *New Criterion,* June 2004.

Lund, Elizabeth. Review of *Walking to Martha's Vineyard. Christian Science Monitor,* April 20, 2004.

Marks, Justin. "In My Father's House There Are Many Rooms." *Web Del Sol Review of Books.* Symposium on the Work of Franz Wright (http://webdelsol.com).

———. "'You Don't Remember Me': Franz Wright's *The Night World and the Word Night* and Ralph Waldo Emerson's *Foreworld.*" *Web Del Sol Review of Books.* Symposium on the Work of Franz Wright (http://webdelsol.com).

Mehegan, David. "Out of the Darkness: After Battling Alcoholism and Mental Illness, Poet Franz Wright Has Stepped into the Light." *Boston Globe,* May 18, 2004.

Paquin, Ethan. Review of *The Beforelife. Boston Review,* April-May, 2001.

Petruccelli, Kathryn. Review of *God's Silence. Agony Column.* 2006. (http://trashtron.com/agony/)

Publishers Weekly. Review of *God's Silence,* December 22, 2005.

Quinn, Alice. "In the Beforelife." *The New Yorker.* (Interview.) (http://www.newyorker.com/online)

Ralph, Brett. Review of *Ill Lit: Selected and New Poems by Franz Wright. Rain Taxi Review of Books* 3, no. 4 (winter 1998–1999).

Rourke, Bryan. "Franz Wright Says Being a Poet Is Dangerous." *Providence Journal,* April 24, 2005.

Sadoff, Ira. "Trafficking in the Radiant: The Spiritualization of American Poetry." *American Poetry Review* 34, no. 4 (July 1, 2005).

Shepard, Harvey. "Reconciliation and Healing." *Web Del Sol Review of Books.* Symposium on the Work of Franz Wright (http://webdelsol.com).

Simon, Scott. Interview with Franz Wright. National Public Radio *Weekend Edition,* April 24, 2004.

Smith, Dinitia. "The Wright Stuff, a Family Affair." *New York Times,* April 15, 2004.

St. John, Janet. Review of *God's Silence. Booklist,* April 1, 2006.

Temelko, Mark. "Wright Words." *Anchorage Daily News,* April 2, 2006.

Virginia Quarterly Review. Review of *The Night World and the Word Night. VQR* 69, no. 4 (autumn 1993).

Walker, David. Review of *Walking to Martha's Vineyard. Oberlin Alumni Magazine* 100, no. 1 (summer 2004).

Willcutts, Tim. "Ex-Obie Wright Talks Poetry." *Oberlin Review* 129, no. 18 (March 16, 2001).

———. "Franz Wright in Conversation." *Web Del Sol Review of Books.* Symposium on the Work of Franz Wright (http://webdelsol.com).

Wright, Franz. Radio interview with the band Ill Lit. *Open Source,* July 20, 2006.

Index

Arabic numbers printed in bold-face type refer to extended treatment of a subject.

"A" (Zukofsky), **Supp. III Part 2:** 611, 612, 614, 617, 619, 620, 621, 622, 623, 624, 626, 627, 628, 629, 630, 631; **Supp. IV Part 1:** 154; **Supp. XVI:**287
Aal, Katharyn, **Supp. IV Part 1:** 332
Aaron, Daniel, **IV:** 429; **Supp. I Part 2:** 647, 650
Aaron's Rod (Lawrence), **Supp. I Part 1:** 255
Abacus (Karr), **Supp. XI: 240-242,** 248, 254
Abádi-Nagy, Zoltán, **Supp. IV Part 1:** 280, 289, 291
"Abandoned House, The" (L. Michaels), **Supp. XVI:**214
"Abandoned Newborn, The" (Olds), **Supp. X:** 207
Abbey, Edward, **Supp. VIII:** 42; **Supp. X:** 24, 29, 30, 31, 36; **Supp. XIII: 1-18; Supp. XIV:**179
Abbey's Road (Abbey), **Supp. XIII:** 12
Abbott, Edith, **Supp. I Part 1:** 5
Abbott, George, **Supp. IV Part 2:** 585
Abbott, Grace, **Supp. I Part 1:** 5
Abbott, Jack Henry, **Retro. Supp. II:** 210
Abbott, Jacob, **Supp. I Part 1:** 38, 39
Abbott, Lyman, **III:** 293
Abbott, Sean, **Retro. Supp. II:** 213
ABC of Color, An: Selections from Over a Half Century of Writings (Du Bois), **Supp. II Part 1:** 186
ABC of Reading (Pound), **III:** 468, 474-475
"Abdication, An" (Merrill), **Supp. III Part 1:** 326
Abel, Lionel, **Supp. XIII:** 98
Abel, Sam, **Supp. XIII:** 199
Abelard, Peter, **I:** 14, 22
Abeles, Sigmund, **Supp. VIII:** 272
Abercrombie, Lascelles, **III:** 471; **Retro. Supp. I:** 127, 128
Abernathy, Milton, **Supp. III Part 2:** 616
Abernon, Edgar Vincent, Viscount d', **Supp. XVI:**191

Abhau, Anna. *See* Mencken, Mrs. August (Anna Abhau)
"Ability" (Emerson), **II:** 6
Abingdon, Alexander, **Supp. XVI:**99
Abish, Walter, **Supp. V:** 44
"Abishag" (Glück), **Supp. V:** 82
"Abortion, The" (Sexton), **Supp. II Part 2:** 682
"Abortions" (Dixon), **Supp. XII:** 153
"About C. D. Wright" (Colburn), **Supp. XV:** 341
"About Hospitality" (Jewett), **Retro. Supp. II:** 131
"About Kathryn" (Dubus), **Supp. VII:** 91
"About Looking Alone at a Place: Arles" (M. F. K. Fisher), **Supp. XVII:** 89, 91
About the House (Auden), **Supp. II Part 1:** 24
About Town: "The New Yorker" and the World It Made (Yagoda), **Supp. VIII:** 151
"Above Pate Valley" (Snyder), **Supp. VIII:** 293
Above the River (Wright), **Supp. III Part 2:** 589, 606
"Abraham" (Schwartz), **Supp. II Part 2:** 663
Abraham, Nelson Algren. *See* Algren, Nelson
Abraham, Pearl, **Supp. XVII:** 49
"Abraham Davenport" (Whittier), **Supp. I Part 2:** 699
"Abraham Lincoln" (Emerson), **II:** 13
Abraham Lincoln: The Prairie Years (Sandburg), **III:** 580, 587-589, 590
Abraham Lincoln: The Prairie Years and the War Years (Sandburg), **III:** 588, 590
Abraham Lincoln: The War Years (Sandburg), **III:** 588, 589-590; **Supp. XVII:** 105
"Abraham Lincoln Walks at Midnight" (Lindsay), **Supp. I Part 2:** 390-391
"Abram Morrison" (Whittier), **Supp. I Part 2:** 699

Abramovich, Alex, **Supp. X:** 302, 309
Abrams, M. H., **Supp. XVI:**19
Abridgment of Universal Geography, An: Together with Sketches of History (Rowson), **Supp. XV:** 243
"Absalom" (Rukeyser), **Supp. VI:** 278-279
Absalom, Absalom! (Faulkner), **II:** 64, 65-67, 72, 223; **IV:** 207; **Retro. Supp. I:** 75, 81, 82, 84, 85, 86, 87, 88, 89, 90, 92, 382; **Supp. V:** 261; **Supp. X:** 51; **Supp. XIV:**12-13
"Absence of Mercy" (Stone), **Supp. V:** 295
"Absentee, The" (Levertov), **Supp. III Part 1:** 284
Absentee Ownership (Veblen), **Supp. I Part 2:** 642
"Absent-Minded Bartender" (X. J. Kennedy), **Supp. XV:** 159
"Absent Thee from Felicity Awhile" (Wylie), **Supp. I Part 2:** 727, 729
"Absolution" (Fitzgerald), **Retro. Supp. I:** 108
"Absolution" (Sobin), **Supp. XVI:**289
"Abuelita's Ache" (Mora), **Supp. XIII:** 218
Abysmal Brute, The (London), **II:** 467
"Academic Story, An" (Simpson), **Supp. IX:** 279-280
"Academic Zoo, The: Theory-in Practice" (Epstein), **Supp. XIV:**107-108, 109
"Accident" (Minot), **Supp. VI: 208-209**
"Accident, The" (Southern), **Supp. XI:** 295
"Accident, The" (Strand), **Supp. IV Part 2:** 624
Accident/A Day's News (Wolf), **Supp. IV Part 1:** 310
Accidental Tourist, The (Tyler), **Supp. IV Part 2:** 657, 668-669; **Supp. V:** 227
Accordion Crimes (Proulx), **Supp. VII:** 259-261

"Accountability" (Dunbar), **Supp. II Part 1:** 197, 204
"Account of the Method of Drawing Birds" (Audubon), **Supp. XVI:**12
"Accusation, The" (Wright), **Supp. III Part 2:** 595
"Accusation of the Inward Man, The" (Taylor), **IV:** 156
"Accusing Message from Dead Father" (Karr), **Supp. XI:** 244
Ace, Goodman, **Supp. IV Part 2:** 574
Achievement in American Poetry (Bogan), **Supp. III Part 1:** 63-64
Acker, Kathy, **Supp. XII:1-20**
Ackerman, Diane, **Supp. XIII:** 154
"Acknowledgment" (Lanier), **Supp. I Part 1:** 364
Ackroyd, Peter, **Supp. V:** 233; **Supp. XVII:** 180
"Acquaintance in the Heavens, An" (Dillard), **Supp. VI:** 34
"Acquainted with the Night" (Frost), **II:** 155; **Retro. Supp. I:** 137
Across Spoon River (Masters), **Supp. I Part 2:** 455, 457, 459, 460, 466, 474-475, 476
Across the Layers: Poems Old and New (Goldbarth), **Supp. XII:** 181, **187-189**
Across the River and into the Trees (Hemingway), **I:** 491; **II:** 255-256, 261; **Retro. Supp. I:** 172, **184-185**
"Actfive" (MacLeish), **III:** 18-19, 22
Actfive and Other Poems (MacLeish), **III:** 3, 17-19, 21
Action (Shepard), **Supp. III Part 2:** 446
Active Anthology (Pound), **Supp. III Part 2:** 617
Active Service (Crane), **I:** 409
Acton, Patricia Nassif, **Supp. X:** 233
Actual, The (Bellow), **Retro. Supp. II:** 33
"Actual Experience, Preferred Narratives" (Julier), **Supp. IV Part 1:** 211
Acuff, Roy, **Supp. V:** 335
Ada (Nabokov), **Retro. Supp. I:** 265, 266, 270, 276-277, 278, 279
"Ada" (Stein), **IV:** 43
Ada; or Ardor (Nabokov), **III:** 247
"Adagia" (Stevens), **IV:** 78, 80, 88, 92
"Adam" (Hecht), **Supp. X:** 62
"Adam" (W. C. Williams), **Retro. Supp. I:** 422, 423
"Adam and Eve" (Eugene), **Supp. X:** 204
"Adam and Eve" (Shapiro), **Supp. II Part 2:** 708, 712
"Adamantine Practice of Poetry, The" (Wright), **Supp. XV:** 341-342, 343-344
Adam Bede (Eliot), **II:** 181
Adamé, Leonard, **Supp. XIII:** 316
Adam & Eve & the City (W. C. Williams), **Retro. Supp. I:** 423
"Adamic Purity as Double Agent" (Whalen-Bridge), **Retro. Supp. II:** 211-212
Adams, Althea. *See* Thurber, Mrs. James (Althea Adams)
Adams, Annie. *See* Fields, Annie Adams
Adams, Brooks, **Supp. I Part 2:** 484
Adams, Charles, **Supp. I Part 2:** 644
Adams, Charles Francis, **I:** 1, 4; **Supp. I Part 2:** 484
Adams, Franklin P., **Supp. I Part 2:** 653; **Supp. IX:** 190; **Supp. XV:** 294, 297
Adams, Henry, **I: 1-24**, 111, 243, 258; **II:** 278, 542; **III:** 396, 504; **IV:** 191, 349; **Retro. Supp. I:** 53, 59; **Retro. Supp. II:** 207; **Supp. I Part 1:** 299-300, 301, 314; **Supp. I Part 2:** 417, 492, 543, 644; **Supp. II Part 1:** 93-94, 105; **Supp. III Part 2:** 613; **Supp. IV Part 1:** 31, 208
Adams, Henry B., **Supp. I Part 1:** 369
Adams, J. Donald, **IV:** 438
Adams, James Truslow, **Supp. I Part 2:** 481, 484, 486
Adams, John, **I:** 1; **II:** 103, 301; **III:** 17, 473; **Supp. I Part 2:** 483, 506, 507, 509, 510, 511, 517, 518, 520, 524
Adams, John Luther, **Supp. XII:** 209
Adams, John Quincy, **I:** 1, 3, 16-17; **Supp. I Part 2:** 685, 686
Adams, Léonie, **Supp. I Part 2:** 707; **Supp. V:** 79; **Supp. IX:** 229; **Supp. XVII:** 75
Adams, Luella, **Supp. I Part 2:** 652
Adams, Mrs. Henry (Marian Hooper), **I:** 1, 5, 10, 17-18
Adams, Noah, **Supp. XVII:** 218
Adams, Phoebe, **Supp. IV Part 1:** 203; **Supp. VIII:** 124
Adams, Samuel, **Supp. I Part 2:** 516, 525
Adams, Timothy Dow, **Supp. XVI:**67, 69
"Ad Castitatem" (Bogan), **Supp. III Part 1:** 50
Addams, Jane, **Supp. I Part 1: 1-26**; **Supp. XI:** 200, 202
Addams, John Huy, **Supp. I Part 1:** 2
"Addendum" (Wright), **Supp. V:** 339
Addiego, John, **Supp. XII:** 182
Adding Machine, The (Rice), **I:** 479

Adding Machine, The: Selected Essays (Burroughs), **Supp. III Part 1:** 93, 97
Addison, Joseph, **I:** 8, 105, 106-107, 108, 114, 131, 300, 304; **III:** 430
"Addressed to a Political Shrimp, or, Fly upon the Wheel" (Freneau), **Supp. II Part 1:** 267
"Address to My Soul" (Wylie), **Supp. I Part 2:** 729
"Address to the Devil" (Jarman), **Supp. XVII:** 114
Address to the Government of the United States on the Cession of Louisiana to the French, An (Brown), **Supp. I Part 1:** 146
"Address to the Scholars of New England" (Ransom), **III:** 491
"Address with Exclamation Points, A" (Simic), **Supp. VIII:** 283
"Adjutant Bird, The" (Banks), **Supp. V:** 5
Adkins, Nelson F., **II:** 20
Adler, Alfred, **I:** 248
Adler, Betty, **III:** 103
Adler, George J., **III:** 81
Adler, Renata, **Supp. X:** 171
Admiral of the Ocean Sea: A Life of Christopher Columbus (Morison), **Supp. I Part 2:** 486-488
"Admirals" (Chabon), **Supp. XI:** 72
"Admonition, An" (Brodsky), **Supp. VIII:** 33
"Adolescence" (Bidart), **Supp. XV:** 32
"Adolescence" (Dove), **Supp. IV Part 1:** 245
"Adolescence" (Olds), **Supp. X:** 211
"Adolescence II" (Dove), **Supp. IV Part 1:** 242, 244-245
Adolescent's Christmas, An: 1944 (C. Bly), **Supp. XVI:**31-32
"Adolf Eichmann" (Carruth), **Supp. XVI:**47
"Adonais" (Shelley), **II:** 516, 540
Adorno, Theodor, **Supp. I Part 2:** 645, 650; **Supp. IV Part 1:** 301
"Adrienne Rich: The Poetics of Change" (Gelpi), **Supp. I Part 2:** 554
"Adultery" (Banks), **Supp. V:** 15
"Adultery" (Dubus), **Supp. VII:** 85
Adultery and Other Choices (Dubus), **Supp. VII:** 83-85
Adulthood Rites (O. Butler), **Supp. XIII:** 63, **64-65**
Adult Life of Toulouse Lautrec by Henri Toulouse Lautrec, The (Acker), **Supp. XII:** 5, 6, **8-9**
Adventure (London), **II:** 466
Adventures in Ancient Egypt

(Goldbarth), **Supp. XII:** 191
Adventures in Value (Cummings), **I:** 430
"Adventures of a Book Reviewer" (Cowley), **Supp. II Part 1:** 137, 142
Adventures of Augie March, The (Bellow), **I:** 144, 147, 149, 150, 151, 152-153, 154, 155, 157, 158-159, 164; **Retro. Supp. II:** 19, 20, **22-23**, 24, 30; **Supp. VIII:** 234, 236-237
Adventures of a Young Man (Dos Passos), **I:** 488, 489, 492
Adventures of Captain Bonneville (Irving), **II:** 312
Adventures of Huckleberry Finn, The (Twain), **I:** 307, 506; **II:** 26, 72, 262, 266-268, 290, 418, 430; **III:** 101, 112-113, 357, 554, 558, 577; **IV:** 198, 201-204, 207; **Retro. Supp. I:** 188; **Retro. Supp. II:** 121; **Supp. I Part 1:** 247; **Supp. IV Part 1:** 247, 257; **Supp. IV Part 2:** 502; **Supp. V:** 131; **Supp. VIII:** 198; **Supp. X:** 230; **Supp. XII:** 16; **Supp. XVI:**222
Adventures of Jimmy (Broughton), **Supp. XV:** 146
Adventures of Roderick Random, The (Smollett), **I:** 134
Adventures of the Letter I (Simpson), **Supp. IX:** 266, **273-274**
Adventures of Tom Sawyer, The (Twain), **II:** 26; **III:** 223, 572, 577; **IV:** 199-200, 203, 204; **Supp. I Part 2:** 456, 470; **Supp. XVI:**66
Adventures While Preaching the Gospel of Beauty (Lindsay), **Supp. I Part 2:** 374, 376, 381, 382-384, 389, 399
Adventures with Ed (Loeffler), **Supp. XIII:** 1
Advertisements for Myself (Mailer), **III:** 27, 35-38, 41-42, 45, 46; **Retro. Supp. II:** 196, 199, 200, 202, 203, 212; **Supp. IV Part 1:** 90, 284; **Supp. XIV:**157
"Advertisements for Myself on the Way Out" (Mailer), **III:** 37
"Advice to a Prophet" (Wilbur), **Supp. III Part 2:** 555-557
Advice to a Prophet and Other Poems (Wilbur), **Supp. III Part 2:** 554-558
"Advice to a Raven in Russia" (Barlow), **Supp. II Part 1:** 65, 74, 80, 83
"Advice to Players" (Bidart), **Supp. XV:** 35
Advice to the Lovelorn (film), **Retro. Supp. II:** 328
Advice to the Privileged Orders, Part I (Barlow), **Supp. II Part 1:** 80

"Aeneas and Dido" (Brodsky), **Supp. VIII:** 24-25
"Aeneas at Washington" (Tate), **IV:** 129
Aeneid (Virgil), **I:** 396; **II:** 542; **III:** 124; **Supp. XV:** 23
Aeneus Tacticus, **I:** 136
Aerial View (Barabtarlo), **Retro. Supp. I:** 278
"Aeria the Evanescent" (Sobin), **Supp. XVI:**292
Aeschylus, **I:** 274, 433; **III:** 398; **IV:** 358, 368, 370; **Retro. Supp. I:** 65; **Supp. I Part 2:** 458, 494
Aesop, **I:** 387; **II:** 154, 169, 302; **III:** 587
Aesthetic (Croce), **III:** 610
"Aesthetics" (Mumford), **Supp. II Part 2:** 476
"Aesthetics of Silence, The" (Sontag), **Supp. III Part 2:** 459
"Aesthetics of the Shah" (Olds), **Supp. X:** 205
"Affair at Coulter's Notch, The" (Bierce), **I:** 202
Affaire de viol, Une (C. Himes). See *Case of Rape, A* (C. Himes)
"Affair of Outposts, An" (Bierce), **I:** 202
Affliction (Banks), **Supp. V:** 15, 16
Affluent Society, The (Galbraith), **Supp. I Part 2:** 648
Afghanistan Picture Show, An: or, How I Saved the World (Vollmann), **Supp. XVII:** 226, **228-229**, 233
"Aficionados, The" (Carver), **Supp. III Part 1:** 137
"Afloat" (Beattie), **Supp. V:** 29
Afloat and Ashore (Cooper), **I:** 351, 355
Africa, Its Geography, People, and Products (Du Bois), **Supp. II Part 1:** 179
Africa, Its Place in Modern History (Du Bois), **Supp. II Part 1:** 179
"Africa, to My Mother" (D. Diop), **Supp. IV Part 1:** 16
African American Writers (Smith, ed.), **Supp. XIII:** 115, 127
"African Book" (Hemingway), **II:** 259
"African Chief, The" (Bryant), **Supp. I Part 1:** 168
"African Fragment" (Brooks), **Supp. III Part 1:** 85
African Queen, The (film), **Supp. XI:** 17
"African Roots of War, The" (Du Bois), **Supp. II Part 1:** 174
African Silences (Matthiessen), **Supp. V:** 203

African Treasury, An (Hughes, ed.), **Supp. I Part 1:** 344
"Afrika Revolution" (Baraka), **Supp. II Part 1:** 53
"AFRO-AMERICAN LYRIC" (Baraka), **Supp. II Part 1:** 59
After (Bukiet), **Supp. XVII:** 43, **44-45**
After All: Last Poems (Matthews), **Supp. IX:** 155, **167-169**
After and Before the Lightning (Ortiz), **Supp. IV Part 2:** 513
"After a Party" (Salinas), **Supp. XIII:** 327
"After Apple-Picking" (Frost), **Retro. Supp. I:** 126, 128
"After Arguing against the Contention That Art Must Come from Discontent" (Stafford), **Supp. XI:** 327
After Confession: Poetry as Autobiography (Harris), **Supp. XIV:**269
After Confession: Poetry as Autobiography (K. Sontag and D. Graham), **Supp. XV:** 104
"After Disappointment" (Jarman), **Supp. XVII:** 118-119
After Experience (Snodgrass), **Supp. VI:** 314-316, 317
"After great pain, a formal feeling comes" (Dickinson), **Retro. Supp. I:** 37
"After Hearing a Waltz by Bartók" (Lowell), **II:** 522
After Henry (Didion), **Supp. IV Part 1:** 195, 196, 199, 207, 208, 211
"After Henry" (Didion), **Supp. IV Part 1:** 211
"After Holbein" (Wharton), **IV:** 325; **Retro. Supp. I:** 382
After Ikkyu and Other Poems (Harrison), **Supp. VIII:** 42
"After-Image" (Bierds), **Supp. XVII:** 31-32
"After-Image" (Caldwell), **I:** 309
After-Images: Autobiographical Sketches (Snodgrass), **Supp. VI:** 314, **319-323**, 324, 326-327
After I's (Zukofsky), **Supp. III Part 2:** 628, 629
Afterlife (Monette), **Supp. X:** 153
Afterlife (Updike), **Retro. Supp. I:** 322
Afterlife, The (Levis), **Supp. XI:** 259, **260-264**
"After Magritte" (McClatchy), **Supp. XII:** 264
"After Making Love" (Dunn), **Supp. XI:** 153
Aftermath (Longfellow), **II:** 490
"Aftermath" (Longfellow), **II:** 498
After New Formalism (A. Finch, ed.), **Supp. XVII:** 74

"Afternoon" (Ellison), **Supp. II Part 1:** 238
"Afternoon at MacDowell" (Kenyon), **Supp. VII:** 159
"Afternoon Miracle, An" (O. Henry), **Supp. II Part 1:** 390
Afternoon of a Faun (Hearon), **Supp. VIII: 63-64**
Afternoon of an Author: A Selection of Uncollected Stories and Essays (Fitzgerald), **II:** 94
"Afternoon of a Playwright" (Thurber), **Supp. I Part 2:** 620
Afternoon of the Unreal (Salinas), **Supp. XIII:** 311, **316-318**
"Afternoon with the Old Man, An" (Dubus), **Supp. VII:** 84
"After Punishment Was Done with Me" (Olds), **Supp. X:** 213
"After Reading *Barely and Widely*," (Zukofsky), **Supp. III Part 2:** 625, 631
"After Reading 'In the Clearing' for the Author, Robert Frost" (Corso), **Supp. XII:** 130
"After Reading *Mickey in the Night Kitchen* for the Third Time before Bed" (Dove), **Supp. IV Part 1:** 249
"After Reading Tu Fu, I Go Outside to the Dwarf Orchard" (Wright), **Supp. V:** 343
"After Reading Wang Wei, I Go Outside to the Full Moon" (Wright), **Supp. V:** 343
After Shocks, Near Escapes (Dobyns), **Supp. XIII: 80-82**
"After Song, An" (W. C. Williams), **Retro. Supp. I:** 413
After Strange Gods (Eliot), **I:** 588
After Such Knowledge: Memory, History, and the Legacy of the Holocaust (E. Hoffman), **Supp. XVI:**152-153, **158-161**
"After the Alphabets" (Merwin), **Supp. III Part 1:** 356
"After the Argument" (Dunn), **Supp. XI:** 149
"After the Baptism" (C. Bly), **Supp. XVI:**40
"After the Burial" (Lowell), **Supp. I Part 2:** 409
"After the Curfew" (Holmes), **Supp. I Part 1:** 308
"After the Death of John Brown" (Thoreau), **IV:** 185
"After the Denim" (Carver), **Supp. III Part 1:** 144
"After the Dentist" (Swenson), **Supp. IV Part 2:** 645
After the Fall (A. Miller), **III:** 148, 149, 156, 161, 162, 163-165, 166
"After the Fire" (Merrill), **Supp. III Part 1:** 328
"After the Flood" (Sanders), **Supp. XVI:**274-275
After the Fox (film), **Supp. IV Part 2:** 575
After the Genteel Tradition (Cowley), **Supp. II Part 1:** 143
"After the Heart's Interrogation" (Komunyakaa), **Supp. XIII:** 120
After the Lost Generation: A Critical Study of the Writers of Two Wars (Aldridge), **Supp. IV Part 2:** 680
"After the Night Office-Gethsemani Abbey" (Merton), **Supp. VIII:** 195-196
"After the Persian" (Bogan), **Supp. III Part 1:** 64
"After the Pleasure Party" (Melville), **III:** 93
"After the Resolution" (Dunn), **Supp. XI:** 151
After the Stroke (Sarton), **Supp. VIII:** 264
"After the Surprising Conversions" (Lowell), **I:** 544, 545; **II:** 550; **Retro. Supp. II:** 187
"After 37 Years My Mother Apologizes for My Childhood" (Olds), **Supp. X:** 208
Afterthoughts (L. P. Smith), **Supp. XIV:**339, 345
"Afterthoughts on the Rosenbergs" (Fiedler), **Supp. XIII:** 99
"After Twenty Years" (Rich), **Supp. I Part 2:** 559-560
"Afterwake, The" (Rich), **Supp. I Part 2:** 553
"Afterward" (Wharton), **Retro. Supp. I:** 372
"After Working Long" (Kenyon), **Supp. VII:** 170
"After Yitzl" (Goldbarth), **Supp. XII:** 186
"After You, My Dear Alphonse" (Jackson), **Supp. IX:** 119
"After Your Nap" (B. Kelly), **Supp. XVII:** 124
"Again" (Dixon), **Supp. XII:** 157
"Again, Kapowsin" (Hugo), **Supp. VI:** 141
"Against" (Goldbarth), **Supp. XII:** 193
"Against Decoration" (Karr), **Supp. XI:** 248
"Against Epiphanies" (C. Baxter), **Supp. XVII:** 20
Against Interpretation (Sontag), **Supp. III Part 2:** 451, 455; **Supp. XIV:**15
"Against Interpretation" (Sontag), **Supp. III Part 2:** 456-458, 463
"Against Modernity" (Ozick), **Supp. V:** 272
"Against Nature" (Karr), **Supp. XI:** 243
Against Nature (Updike), **Retro. Supp. I:** 323
Against the Cold (Bynner), **Supp. XV:** 51
"Against the Crusades" (Stern), **Supp. IX:** 300
Against the Current: As I Remember F. Scott Fitzgerald (Kroll Ring), **Supp. IX:** 63
Agamben, Giorgio, **Supp. XVI:**289
Agapida, Fray Antonio (pseudonym). *See* Irving, Washington
"Agassiz" (Lowell), **Supp. I Part 2:** 414, 416
Agassiz, Louis, **II:** 343; **Supp. I Part 1:** 312; **Supp. IX:** 180
Âge cassant, L' (Char; Sobin, trans.), **Supp. XVI:**282
"Aged Wino's Counsel to a Young Man on the Brink of Marriage, The" (X. J. Kennedy), **Supp. XV:** 156
Agee, Emma, **I:** 26
Agee, James, **I: 25-47,** 293; **IV:** 215; **Supp. IX:** 109; **Supp. XIV:**92; **Supp. XV:** 143
"Agent, The" (Wilbur), **Supp. III Part 2:** 557-561
Age of Anxiety, The (Auden), **Supp. II Part 1:** 2, 19, 21
"Age of Conformity, The" (Howe), **Supp. VI:** 117
Age of Grief, The: A Novella and Stories (Smiley), **Supp. VI:** 292, **299-301**
Age of Innocence, The (Wharton), **IV:** 320-322, 327-328; **Retro. Supp. I:** 372, 374, **380-381; Supp. IV Part 1:** 23
Age of Longing, The (Koestler), **I:** 258
Age of Reason, The (Paine), **Supp. I Part 2:** 503, 515-517, 520
"Age of Strolling, The" (Stern), **Supp. IX:** 297
"Ages, The" (Bryant), **Supp. I Part 1:** 152, 155, 166, 167
"Aging" (Jarrell), **II:** 388
Aging and Gender in Literature (George), **Supp. IV Part 2:** 450
"Agio Neró" (Mora), **Supp. XIII:** 224
"Agitato ma non Troppo" (Ransom), **III:** 493
"Agnes of Iowa" (Moore), **Supp. X:** 165, 178
Agnes of Sorrento (Stowe), **Supp. I Part 2:** 592, 595-596

Agnon, S. Y., **Supp. V:** 266
"Agosta the Winged Man and Rasha the Black Dove" (Dove), **Supp. IV Part 1:** 246-247
Agrarian Justice (Paine), **Supp. I Part 2:** 517-518
"Agricultural Show, The" (McKay), **Supp. X:** 139
Agrippa: A Book of the Dead (W. Gibson), **Supp. XVI:**125
Agua Fresca: An Anthology of Raza Poetry (Rodríguez, ed.), **Supp. IV Part 2:** 540
Agua Santa/Holy Water (Mora), **Supp. XIII: 222-225**
Agüero Sisters, The (García), **Supp. XI: 185-190**
Aguiar, Sarah Appleton, **Supp. XIII:** 30
Ah, Wilderness! (O'Neill), **III:** 400-401; **Supp. IV Part 2:** 587
Ah, Wilderness!: The Frontier in American Literature (Humphrey), **Supp. IX:** 104
Ahearn, Barry, **Retro. Supp. I:** 415
Ahearn, Frederick L., Jr., **Supp. XI:** 184
Ahearn, Kerry, **Supp. IV Part 2:** 604
Ahmed Arabi Pasha, **I:** 453
Ahnebrink, Lars, **III:** 328
Ah Sin (Harte), **Supp. II Part 1:** 354-355
"Ah! Sun-flower" (Blake), **III:** 19
AIDS and Its Metaphors (Sontag), **Supp. III Part 2:** 452, 466-468
Aids to Reflection (Coleridge), **II:** 10
Aiieeeee! An Anthology of Asian-American Writers (The Combined Asian Resources Project), **Supp. X:** 292
Aiken, Conrad, **I: 48-70,** 190, 211, 243; **II:** 55, 530, 542; **III:** 458, 460; **Retro. Supp. I:** 55, 56, 57, 58, 60, 62; **Supp. X:** 50, 115; **Supp. XV:** 144, 297, 298, 302, 306, 309; **Supp. XVII:** 135
"Aim Was Song, The" (Frost), **Retro. Supp. I:** 133
Ainsworth, Linda, **Supp. IV Part 1:** 274
Ainsworth, William, **III:** 423
Air-Conditioned Nightmare, The (H. Miller), **III:** 186
Airing Dirty Laundry (Reed), **Supp. X:** 241
"Air Plant, The" (Crane), **I:** 401
Air Raid: A Verse Play for Radio (MacLeish), **III:** 21
"Airs above the Ground" (Sarton), **Supp. VIII:** 261

Air Tight: A Novel of Red Russia. See We the Living (Rand)
Air Up There, The (film, Glaser), **Supp. XVII:** 9
"Airwaves" (Mason), **Supp. VIII:** 146
Airways, Inc. (Dos Passos), **I:** 482
"A is for Dining Alone" (M. F. K. Fisher), **Supp. XVII:** 86
Aitken, Robert, **Supp. I Part 2:** 504
Akhmadulina, Bella, **Supp. III Part 1:** 268
Akhmatova, Anna, **Supp. III Part 1:** 268, 269; **Supp. VIII:** 20, 21, 25, 27, 30
Akhmatova Translations, The (Kenyon), **Supp. VII:** 160
"Akhnilo" (Salter), **Supp. IX:** 260
Akins, Zoë, **Supp. XVI:**187
Aksenev, Vasily P., **Retro. Supp. I:** 278
"Al Aaraaf" (Poe), **III:** 426-427
Al Aaraaf, Tamerlane, and Minor Poems (Poe), **III:** 410
"Alain Locke: Bahá'í Philosopher" (Buck), **Supp. XIV:**199
Alain Locke: Faith and Philosophy (Buck), **Supp. XIV:**200
"Alain Locke and Cultural Pluralism" (Kallen), **Supp. XIV:**197
Alarçon, **Supp. XVII:** 74
Alarcón, Justo, **Supp. IV Part 2:** 538, 539, 540
À la Recherche du Temps Perdu (Proust), **IV:** 428
"Alarm" (X. J. Kennedy), **Supp. XV:** 163
"Alastor" (Shelley), **Supp. I Part 2:** 728
"Alatus" (Wilbur), **Supp. III Part 2:** 563
"Alba" (Creeley), **Supp. IV Part 1:** 150
Albee, Edward, **I: 71-96,** 113; **II:** 558, 591; **III:** 281, 387; **IV:** 4, 230; **Retro. Supp. II:** 104; **Supp. VIII:** 331; **Supp. XIII:** 196, 197
Albers, Joseph, **Supp. IV Part 2:** 621
Alberti, Rafael, **Supp. XV:** 75
Albright, Margery, **Supp. I Part 2:** 613
"Album, The" (Morris), **III:** 220
Alcestiad, The (Wilder), **IV:** 357, 374
"Alchemist, The" (Bogan), **Supp. III Part 1:** 50
"Alchemist in the City, The" (Hopkins), **Supp. IV Part 2:** 639
Alchymist's Journal, The (Connell), **Supp. XIV:**80
"Alcmena" (Winters), **Supp. II Part 2:** 801
Alcott, Abba. *See* Alcott, Mrs. Amos

Bronson (Abigail May)
Alcott, Amos Bronson, **II:** 7, 225; **IV:** 172, 173, 184; **Retro. Supp. I:** 217; **Supp. I Part 1:** 28, 29-32, 35, 39, 41, 45; **Supp. II Part 1:** 290; **Supp. XVI:**84, 89
Alcott, Anna. *See* Pratt, Anna
Alcott, Louisa May, **IV:** 172; **Supp. I Part 1: 28-46; Supp. IX:** 128; **Supp. XV:** 338; **Supp. XVI:**84
Alcott, May, **Supp. I Part 1:** 41
Alcott, Mrs. Amos Bronson (Abigail May), **IV:** 184; **Supp. I Part 1:** 29, 30, 31, 32, 35
Alcuin: A Dialogue (Brown), **Supp. I Part 1:** 126-127, 133
Alden, Hortense. *See* Farrell, Mrs. James T. (Hortense Alden)
Alden, John, **I:** 471; **II:** 502-503
"Alder Fork, The" (Leopold), **Supp. XIV:**186
Aldington, Mrs. Richard. *See* Doolittle, Hilda
Aldington, Perdita, **Supp. I Part 1:** 258
Aldington, Richard, **II:** 517; **III:** 458, 459, 465, 472; **Retro. Supp. I:** 63, 127; **Supp. I Part 1:** 257-262, 270
Aldo Leopold: His Life and Work (Meine), **Supp. XIV:**179
"Aldo Leopold's Intellectual Heritage" (Nash), **Supp. XIV:**191-192
Aldon, Raymond, **Supp. XV:** 297
Aldrich, Thomas Bailey, **II:** 400; **Supp. II Part 1:** 192; **Supp. XIV:**45
Aldrich, Tom, **Supp. I Part 2:** 415
Aldridge, John W., **Supp. I Part 1:** 196; **Supp. IV Part 1:** 286; **Supp. IV Part 2:** 680, 681; **Supp. VIII:** 189; **Supp. XI:** 228
Aleck Maury Sportsman (Gordon), **II:** 197, 200, 203-204
Alegría, Claribel, **Supp. IV Part 1:** 208
Aleichem, Sholom, **IV:** 3, 10; **Supp. IV Part 2:** 585
"Alert Lovers, Hidden Sides, and Ice Travelers: Notes on Poetic Form and Energy" (Dunn), **Supp. XI:** 153
"Aleš Debeljak" (Simic), **Supp. VIII:** 279
"Alex" (Oliver), **Supp. VII:** 232
Alexander, Doris, **Supp. XVII:** 99
Alexander, George, **II:** 331
Alexander, Michael, **Retro. Supp. I:** 293
"Alexander Crummell Dead" (Dunbar), **Supp. II Part 1:** 207, 208-209
Alexander's Bridge (Cather), **I:** 313,

314, 316-317, 326; **Retro. Supp. I:** 1, 6, 7, 8
Alexander the Great, **IV:** 322
"Alexandra" (Cather), **Retro. Supp. I:** 7, 9, 17
Alexandrov, V. E., **Retro. Supp. I:** 270
Algonquin Round Table, **Supp. IX:** 190, 191, 197
Algren, Nelson, **I:** 211; **Supp. V:** 4; **Supp. IX: 1-18; Supp. XII:** 126; **Supp. XIII:** 173; **Supp. XIV:** 3; **Supp. XVII:** 161
Alhambra, The (Irving), **II:** 310-311
Ali, Agha Shahid, **Supp. XVII:** 74
Alias Grace (Atwood), **Supp. XIII:** 20, **31-32**
Alice (film; Allen), **Supp. XV:** 2, 11
"Alice Doane's Appeal" (Hawthorne), **II:** 227
Alice in Wonderland (Carroll), **Supp. I Part 2:** 622
Alice's Adventures in Wonderland (Carroll), **Supp. XVI:** 261
"Alicia and I Talking on Edna's Steps" (Cisneros), **Supp. VII:** 64
"Alicia Who Sees Mice" (Cisneros), **Supp. VII:** 60
Alien 3 (screenplay, W. Gibson), **Supp. XVI:** 120, 124
"Ali in Havana" (Talese), **Supp. XVII:** 207, 208
Alison, Archibald, **Supp. I Part 1:** 151, 159
Alison's House (Glaspell), **Supp. III Part 1:** 182, 188, 189
Alive (screenplay, Shanley), **Supp. XIV:** 316
Alive and Writing: Interviews with American Authors of the 1980s (McCaffery and Gregory), **Supp. X:** 260
"Alki Beach" (Hugo), **Supp. VI:** 135
ALL: The Collected Poems, 1956-1964 (Zukofsky), **Supp. III Part 2:** 630
ALL: The Collected Short Poems, 1923-1958 (Zukofsky), **Supp. III Part 2:** 629
Alla Breve Loving (Wright), **Supp. XV:** 339, 340
"Alla Breve Loving" (Wright), **Supp. XV:** 340
"All Around the Town" (Benét), **Supp. XI:** 48, 58
All at Sea (Lardner), **II:** 427
"All Boy" (Rawlings), **Supp. X:** 222
Allegiances (Stafford), **Supp. XI: 322-323,** 329
"Allegory of the Cave" (Dunn), **Supp. XI:** 150
Allegro, Johnny (film, Tetzloff), **Supp. XVII:** 62
"Allegro, L'" (Milton), **Supp. XIV:** 8
Allen, Brooke, **Supp. VIII:** 153
Allen, Dick, **Supp. IX:** 279
Allen, Donald, **Supp. VIII:** 291; **Supp. XIII:** 112
Allen, Frank, **Supp. XI:** 126; **Supp. XII:** 186
Allen, Frederick Lewis, **Supp. I Part 2:** 655
Allen, Gay Wilson, **IV:** 352; **Supp. I Part 2:** 418
Allen, Paula Gunn. *See* Gunn Allen, Paula
Allen, Walter, **I:** 505; **III:** 352; **Supp. IV Part 2:** 685; **Supp. IX:** 231
Allen, Woody, **Supp. I Part 2:** 607, 623; **Supp. IV Part 1:** 205; **Supp. X:** 164; **Supp. XI:** 307; **Supp. XV: 1-18; Supp. XVII:** 48
"Aller et Retour" (Barnes), **Supp. III Part 1:** 36
Aller Retour New York (H. Miller), **III:** 178, 182, 183
Allessandrini, Goffredo, **Supp. IV Part 2:** 520
Alleys of Eden, The (R. O. Butler), **Supp. XII:** 62, **62-64,** 68
All God's Children Need Traveling Shoes (Angelou), **Supp. IV Part 1:** 2, 9-10, 12-13, 17
All God's Chillun Got Wings (O'Neill), **III:** 387, 391, 393-394
All Gone (Dixon), **Supp. XII:** 148, 149
"All Hallows" (Glück), **Supp. V:** 82
"All I Can Remember" (Jackson), **Supp. IX:** 115
"Alligators, The" (Updike), **IV:** 219
Allingham, John Till, **Supp. XV:** 243
"ALL IN THE STREET" (Baraka), **Supp. II Part 1:** 53
"All I Want" (Tapahonso), **Supp. IV Part 2:** 508
"All Little Colored Children Should Play the Harmonica" (Patchett), **Supp. XII:** 309
"All Mountains" (Doolittle), **Supp. I Part 1:** 271
All My Friends Are Going to Be Strangers (McMurtry), **Supp. V:** 224, 228, 229
All My Pretty Ones (Sexton), **Supp. II Part 2:** 678, 679-683
"All My Pretty Ones" (Sexton), **Supp. II Part 2:** 681-682
"All My Sad Captains" (Jewett), **Retro. Supp. II:** 134
All My Sons (A. Miller), **III:** 148, 149, 150, 151-153, 154, 155, 156, 158, 159, 160, 164, 166
"All Night, All Night" (Schwartz), **Supp. II Part 2:** 665
All Night Long (Caldwell), **I:** 297
"All Our Lost Children: Trauma and Testimony in the Performance of Childhood" (Pace), **Supp. XI:** 245
"All Out" (Hecht), **Supp. X:** 72
All Over (Albee), **I:** 91-94
"Allowance" (Minot), **Supp. VI:** 206, 207-208
"Alloy" (Rukeyser), **Supp. VI:** 279
"All Parrots Speak" (Bowles), **Supp. IV Part 1:** 89
Allport, Gordon, **II:** 363-364
All Quiet on the Western Front (Remarque), **Supp. IV Part 1:** 380, 381
"ALL REACTION IS DOOMED-!-!-!" (Baraka), **Supp. II Part 1:** 59
"All Revelation" (Frost), **II:** 160-162
All Shot Up (C. Himes), **Supp. XVI:** 143, 144
"All Souls'" (Gioia), **Supp. XV:** 117
"All Souls" (Wharton), **IV:** 315-316; **Retro. Supp. I:** 382
"All Souls' Night" (Yeats), **Supp. X:** 69
All Souls' Rising (Bell), **Supp. X:** 12, **13-16,** 17
"All-Star Literary Vaudeville" (Wilson), **IV:** 434-435
Allston, Washington, **II:** 298
All Stories Are True (Wideman), **Supp. X:** 320
"All That Is" (Wilbur), **Supp. III Part 2:** 563
"All the Bearded Irises of Life: Confessions of a Homospiritual" (Walker), **Supp. III Part 2:** 527
"All the Beautiful Are Blameless" (Wright), **Supp. III Part 2:** 597
All the Conspirators (Isherwood), **Supp. XIV:** 156, 159, 160
All the Dark and Beautiful Warriors (Hansberry), **Supp. IV Part 1:** 360, 374
All the Days and Nights: The Collected Stories (Maxwell), **Supp. VIII:** 151, 158, 169
"All the Dead Dears" (Plath), **Retro. Supp. II:** 246; **Supp. I Part 2:** 537
All the Good People I've Left Behind (Oates), **Supp. II Part 2:** 510, 522, 523
"All the Hippos Were Boiled in Their Tanks" (Burroughs and Kerouac), **Supp. III Part 1:** 94
All the King's Men (Warren), **I:** 489; **IV:** 243, 248-249, 252; **Supp. V:** 261; **Supp. VIII:** 126; **Supp. X:** 1

All the Little Live Things (Stegner), **Supp. IV Part 2:** 599, 604, 605, 606, 609-610, 611, 613
All the Pretty Horses (film), **Supp. VIII:** 175
All the Pretty Horses (McCarthy), **Supp. VIII:** 175, **182-183**, 188
All the Sad Young Men (Fitzgerald), **II:** 94; **Retro. Supp. I:** 108
"All the Time in the World" (Dubus), **Supp. VII:** 91
"All the Way to Flagstaff, Arizona" (Bausch), **Supp. VII:** 47, 49
"All This and More" (Karr), **Supp. XI:** 243
All Tomorrow's Parties (W. Gibson), **Supp. XVI:**119, 121, 123, 124, **130**
"All Too Real" (Vendler), **Supp. V:** 189
All Trivia: Triva, More Trivia, Afterthoughts, Last Words (L. P. Smith), **Supp. XIV:**339
All-True Travels and Adventures of Lidie Newton (Smiley), **Supp. VI:** 292, **305-307**
All We Need of Hell (Crews), **Supp. XI: 114**
Almack, Edward, **Supp. IV Part 2:** 435
al-Maghut, Muhammad, **Supp. XIII:** 278
"Almanac" (Swenson), **Supp. IV Part 2:** 641
Almanac of the Dead (Silko), **Supp. IV Part 2:** 558-559, 560, 561, 570-571
Almon, Bert, **Supp. IX:** 93
"Almost" (Untermeyer), **Supp. XV:** 304
Almost Revolution, The (Priaulx and Ungar), **Supp. XI:** 228
Alnilam (Dickey), **Supp. IV Part 1:** 176, 186, 188-189
"Alone" (Levine), **Supp. V:** 184, 185, 186
"Alone" (Poe), **Retro. Supp. II:** 266
"Alone" (Singer), **IV:** 15
"Alone" (Winters), **Supp. II Part 2:** 786, 811
Aloneness (Brooks), **Supp. III Part 1:** 85, 86
Alone with America (Corso), **Supp. XII:** 131
Alone with America (Howard), **Supp. IX:** 326
"Along America's Edges" (Sobin), **Supp. XVI:**288
"Along the Color Line" (Du Bois), **Supp. II Part 1:** 173
Along the Illinois (Masters), **Supp. I Part 2:** 472
"Alphabet" (Nye), **Supp. XIII:** 283
Alphabet, An (Doty), **Supp. XI:** 120
Alphabet for Gourmets, An (M. F. K. Fisher), **Supp. XVII:** 86, 87, 92
Alphabet of Grace, The (Buechner), **Supp. XII:** 52
"Alphabet of My Dead, An" (Pinsky), **Supp. VI:** 235, 250
"Alphabet of Subjects, An" (Zukofsky), **Supp. III Part 2:** 624
"Alpine Christ, The" (Jeffers), **Supp. II Part 2:** 415, 419
Alpine Christ and Other Poems, The (Jeffers), **Supp. II Part 2:** 419
"Alpine Idyll, An" (Hemingway), **II:** 249; **Retro. Supp. I:** 176
Al Que Quiere! (W. C. Williams), **Retro. Supp. I:** 414, 416, **417**, 428
Alraune (Ewers; Endore, trans.), **Supp. XVII:** 54
Alsop, Joseph, **II:** 579
"Altar, The" (Herbert), **Supp. IV Part 2:** 646
"Altar, The" (MacLeish), **III:** 4
"Altar Boy" (Fante), **Supp. XI:** 160, 164
"Altar of the Dead, The" (James), **Retro. Supp. I:** 229
"Altars in the Street, The" (Levertov), **Supp. III Part 1:** 280
Alter, Robert, **Supp. XII:** 167
Altgeld, John Peter, **Supp. I Part 2:** 382, 455
Althea (Masters), **Supp. I Part 2:** 455, 459
Altick, Richard, **Supp. I Part 2:** 423
Altieri, Charles, **Supp. VIII:** 297, 303
Altman, Robert, **Supp. IX:** 143
"Alto" (C. Frost), **Supp. XV:** 101
"Altra Ego" (Brodsky), **Supp. VIII:** 31-32
A Lume Spento (Pound), **Retro. Supp. I:** 283, 285
"Aluminum House" (F. Barthelme), **Supp. XI:** 26
Alvares, Mosseh, **Supp. V:** 11
Alvarez, A., **Supp. I Part 2:** 526, 527; **Supp. II Part 1:** 99; **Supp. IX:** 248
Alvarez, Julia, **Supp. VII: 1-21**; **Supp. XI:** 177; **Supp. XVII:** 71, 112
"Always a Rose" (L.-Y. Lee), **Supp. XV:** 215, 216
"Always in Good Humor" (Adams), **Supp. XV:** 294
Always Outnumbered, Always Outgunned (Mosley), **Supp. XIII:** 242
"Always the Stories" (Ortiz), **Supp. IV Part 2:** 499, 500, 502, 504, 512
Always the Young Strangers (Sandburg), **III:** 577-578, 579
Amadeus (Shaffer), **Supp. XIV:**330
"Amahl and the Night Visitors: A Guide to the Tenor of Love" (Moore), **Supp. X:** 167
"Am and Am Not" (Olds), **Supp. X:** 212
"Amanita, The" (Francis), **Supp. IX:** 81
Amaranth (Robinson), **III:** 509, 510, 512, 513, 522, 523
Amazing Adele, The (Barillet and Grédy; Loos, trans.), **Supp. XVI:**194
Amazing Adventures of Kavalier and Clay, The (Chabon), **Supp. XI:** 68, 76, **77-80**
Amazing Science Fiction Stories, **Supp. XVI:**121
Amazons: An Intimate Memoir by the First Woman to Play in the National Hockey League (DeLillo), **Supp. VI:** 2
Ambassador of Peace, An (Abernon), **Supp. XVI:**191
Ambassadors, The (H. James), **II:** 320, 333-334, 600; **III:** 517; **IV:** 322; **Retro. Supp. I:** 215, 218, 219, 220, 221, **232-233**
Ambelain, Robert, **Supp. I Part 1:** 260, 273, 274
Ambition: The Secret Passion (Epstein), **Supp. XIV:**113-114
"Ambition Bird, The" (Sexton), **Supp. II Part 2:** 693
Ambler, Eric, **III:** 57
Ambrose Holt and Family (Glaspell), **Supp. III Part 1:** 175, 181, 184, 187, 188
"Ambrose Seyffert" (Masters), **Supp. I Part 2:** 464
"Ambush" (Komunyakaa), **Supp. XIII:** 122
Amen Corner, The (Baldwin), **Retro. Supp. II:** 5, 7; **Supp. I Part 1:** 48, 51, 54, 55, 56
America (Benét), **Supp. XI:** 46, 47, 51
"America" (Ginsberg), **Supp. II Part 1:** 58-59, 317
"America" (song), **IV:** 410
"America, America!" (poem) (Schwartz), **Supp. II Part 2:** 665
"America, Commerce, and Freedom" (Rowson and Reinagle), **Supp. XV:** 240
"America, Seen Through Photographs, Darkly" (Sontag), **Supp. III Part 2:** 464
America: The Story of a Free People (Commager and Nevins), **I:** 253

"America! America!" (story) (Schwartz), **Supp. II Part 2:** 640, 658-659, 660

America and Americans (Steinbeck), **IV:** 52

"America and the Vidal Chronicles" (Pease), **Supp. IV Part 2:** 687

America as a Civilization (Lerner), **III:** 60

"America Independent" (Freneau), **Supp. II Part 1:** 261

America Is Worth Saving (Dreiser), **Retro. Supp. II:** 96

American, The (James), **I:** 226; **II:** 326-327, 328, 331, 334; **IV:** 318; **Retro. Supp. I:** 220, **221,** 228, 376, 381

Americana (DeLillo), **Supp. VI:** 2, **3,** 5, 6, 8, 13, 14

American Adam, The (R. W. B. Lewis), **II:** 457-458; **Supp. XIII:** 93

American Almanac (Leeds), **II:** 110

American Anthem (Doctorow and Suares), **Supp. IV Part 1:** 234

"American Apocalypse" (Gunn Allen), **Supp. IV Part 1:** 325

American Aristocracy (film), **Supp. XVI:**185-186

American Blood, (Nichols), **Supp. XIII:** 268

American Blues (T. Williams), **IV:** 381, 383

American Buffalo (Mamet), **Supp. XIV:**239, 241, 242, 244-245, 246, 254, 255

American Caravan: A Yearbook of American Literature (Mumford, ed.), **Supp. II Part 2:** 482

American Cause, The (MacLeish), **III:** 3

American Childhood, An (Dillard), **Supp. VI: 19-21,** 23, 24, 25, 26, 30, 31

"American Childhood in the Dominican Republic, An" (Alvarez), **Supp. VII:** 2, 5

American Child Supreme, An: The Education of a Liberation Ecologist (Nichols), **Supp. XIII:** 256, 257, 258, 264, 265, 266, 267, 268, 269

American Claimant, The (Twain), **IV:** 194, 198-199

American Crisis I (Paine), **Supp. I Part 2:** 508

American Crisis II (Paine), **Supp. I Part 2:** 508

American Crisis XIII (Paine), **Supp. I Part 2:** 509

"American Critic, The" (J. Spingarn), **I:** 266

American Culture, Canons, and the Case of Elizabeth Stoddard (Smith and Weinauer), **Supp. XV:** 270

American Daughter, An (Wasserstein), **Supp. XV: 330-332,** 333

American Democrat, The (Cooper), **I:** 343, 346, 347, 353

American Diary (Webb), **Supp. I Part 1:** 5

American Drama since World War II (Weales), **IV:** 385

American Dream, An (Mailer), **III:** 27, 33-34, 35, 39, 41, 43, 44; **Retro. Supp. II:** 203, **204-205**

American Dream, The (Albee), **I:** 74-76, 77, 89, 94

"American Dreams" (Simpson), **Supp. IX:** 274

American Earth (Caldwell), **I:** 290, 308

"American Emperors" (Poirier), **Supp. IV Part 2:** 690

American Exodus, An (Lange and Taylor), **I:** 293

American Experience, The (Parkes), **Supp. I Part 2:** 617-618

American Express (Corso), **Supp. XII:** 129

"American Express" (Salter), **Supp. IX:** 260-261

"American Fear of Literature, The" (Lewis), **II:** 451

American Fictions (Hardwick), **Supp. X:** 171

American Fictions, 1940-1980 (Karl), **Supp. IV Part 1:** 384

"American Financier, The" (Dreiser), **II:** 428

American Folkways (book series), **I:** 290

American Heroine: The Life and Legend of Jane Addams (Davis), **Supp. I Part 1:** 1

American Historical Novel, The (Leisy), **Supp. II Part 1:** 125

"American Horse" (Erdrich), **Supp. IV Part 1:** 333

American Humor (Rourke), **IV:** 339, 352

American Hunger (Wright), **Supp. IV Part 1:** 11

American Indian Anthology, An (Tvedten, ed.), **Supp. IV Part 2:** 505

"American Indian Women: At the Center of Indigenous Resistance in Contemporary North America" (Jaimes and Halsey), **Supp. IV Part 1:** 331

"American in England, An" (Wylie), **Supp. I Part 2:** 707

American Jitters, The: A Year of the Slump (Wilson), **IV:** 427, 428

American Journal (Hayden), **Supp. II Part 1:** 367

American Journey: The Times of Robert F. Kennedy (Plimpton, ed.), **Supp. XVI:**245

"American Land Ethic, An" (Momaday), **Supp. IV Part 2:** 488

American Landscape, The, **Supp. I Part 1:** 157

American Language, The (Mencken), **II:** 289, 430; **III:** 100, 104, 105, 108, 111, 119-120

American Language, The: Supplement One (Mencken), **III:** 111

American Language, The: Supplement Two (Mencken), **III:** 111

"American Letter" (MacLeish), **III:** 13

"American Liberty" (Freneau), **Supp. II Part 1:** 257

American Literary History (Harrison), **Supp. VIII:** 37

American Mercury, **Supp. XI:** 163, 164

American Mind, The (Commager), **Supp. I Part 2:** 650

American Moderns: Bohemian New York and the Creation of a New Century (Stansell), **Supp. XVII:** 106

American Moderns: From Rebellion to Conformity (Geismar), **Supp. IX:** 15; **Supp. XI:** 223

"American Names" (Benét), **Supp. XI:** 47

American Nature Writers (Elder, ed.), **Supp. IX:** 25

American Nature Writers (Winter), **Supp. X:** 104

American Negro, The (W. H. Thomas), **Supp. II Part 1:** 168

American Notebooks, The (Hawthorne), **II:** 226

American Novel Since World War II, The (Klein, ed.), **Supp. XI:** 233

Americano, The (film), **Supp. XVI:**185

"American Original, An: Learning from a Literary Master" (Wilkinson), **Supp. VIII:** 164, 165, 168

American Ornithology (Wilson), **Supp. XVI:**4, 6

American Pastoral (P. Roth), **Retro. Supp. II:** 279, 289, **292-293; Supp. XI:** 68

American Places (Porter, Stegner and Stegner), **Supp. IV Part 2:** 599

"American Poet" (Shapiro), **Supp. II Part 2:** 701

"American Poetry" (Simpson), **Supp. IX:** 272

American Poetry, 1922: A Miscellany (Untermeyer, ed.), **Supp. XV:** 306
"American Poetry and American Life" (Pinsky), **Supp. VI:** 239-240
American Poetry from the Beginning to Whitman (Untermeyer, ed.), **Supp. XV:** 310
American Poetry since 1900 (Untermeyer, ed.), **Supp. XV:** 306
American Poetry since 1945: A Critical Survey (Stepanchev), **Supp. XI:** 312
American Poetry since 1960 (Mesic), **Supp. IV Part 1:** 175
American Poets since World War II Dictionary of Literary Biography (Gwynn, ed.), **Supp. XV:** 343
American Primer, An (Boorstin), **I:** 253
American Primer, An (Whitman), **IV:** 348
"American Primitive" (W. J. Smith), **Supp. XIII:** 333
American Primitive: Poems (Oliver), **Supp. VII:** 234-237, 238
American Procession, An: The Major American Writers from 1830-1930—the Crucial Century (Kazin), **Supp. VIII:** 105-106, 108
American Radio Company, The (radio show, Keillor), **Supp. XVI:**176-177
"American Realist Playwrights, The" (McCarthy), **II:** 562
American Register, or General Repository of History, Politics, and Science, The (Brown, ed.), **Supp. I Part 1:** 146
American Renaissance (Matthiessen), **I:** 259-260; **III:** 310; **Supp. XIII:** 93
"American Rendezvous, An" (Beauvoir), **Supp. IX:** 4
American Scene, The (James), **II:** 336; **III:** 460; **Retro. Supp. I:** 232, 235
American Scenes (Kozlenko, ed.), **IV:** 378
"American Scholar, The" (Emerson), **I:** 239; **II:** 8, 12-13; **Retro. Supp. I:** 62, 74-75, 149, 298; **Retro. Supp. II:** 155; **Supp. I Part 2:** 420; **Supp. IX:** 227, 271; **Supp. XIV:**104
Americans in England; or, Lessons for Daughters (Rowson), **Supp. XV:** 240
"American Soldier, The" (Freneau), **Supp. II Part 1:** 269
American Songbag, The (Sandburg), **III:** 583
"American Student in Paris, An" (Farrell), **II:** 45

"American Sublime, The" (Stevens), **IV:** 74
"American Tar, The; or, The Press Gang Defeated" (Rowson and Taylor), **Supp. XV:** 238
"American Temperament, The" (Locke), **Supp. XIV:**211
American Tragedy, An (Dreiser), **I:** 497, 498, 499, 501, 502, 503, 511-515, 517, 518, 519; **III:** 251; **IV:** 35, 484; **Retro. Supp. II:** 93, 95, **104-108; Supp. XVII:** 155
"American Triptych" (Kenyon), **Supp. VII:** 165
"American Use for German Ideals" (Bourne), **I:** 228
American Village, The (Freneau), **Supp. II Part 1:** 256, 257
"American Village, The" (Freneau), **Supp. II Part 1:** 256
America's Coming-of-Age (Brooks), **I:** 228, 230, 240, 245, 258; **IV:** 427
America's Humor: From Poor Richard to Doonesbury (Blair and Hill), **Retro. Supp. II:** 286
"America's Part in World Peace" (Locke), **Supp. XIV:**208
America's Rome (Vance), **Supp. IV Part 2:** 684
America Was Promises (MacLeish), **III:** 16, 17
"Amerika" (Snyder), **Supp. VIII:** 301
Ames, Fisher, **Supp. I Part 2:** 486
Ames, Lois, **Supp. I Part 2:** 541, 547
Ames, William, **IV:** 158
Ames Stewart, Beatrice, **Supp. IX:** 200
Amichai, Yehuda, **Supp. XI:** 267
Amidon, Stephen, **Supp. XI:** 333
Amiel, Henri F., **I:** 241, 243, 250
Amis, Kingsley, **IV:** 430; **Supp. IV Part 2:** 688; **Supp. VIII:** 167; **Supp. XIII:** 93; **Supp. XV:** 117
Amis, Martin, **Retro. Supp. I:** 278
Ammons, A. R., **Supp. III Part 2:** 541; **Supp. VII: 23-38; Supp. IX:** 41, 42, 46; **Supp. XII:** 121; **Supp. XV:** 115; **Supp. XVII:** 242
Ammons, Elizabeth, **Retro. Supp. I:** 364, 369; **Retro. Supp. II:** 140
"Among Children" (Levine), **Supp. V:** 192
Among Friends (M. F. K. Fisher), **Supp. XVII:** 89, 90-91, 92
Among My Books (Lowell), **Supp. I Part 2:** 407
"Among School Children" (Yeats), **III:** 249; **Supp. IX:** 52; **Supp. XIV:**8
"Among the Hills" (Whittier), **Supp. I Part 2:** 703
Among the Isles of Shoals (Thaxter),

Supp. XIII: 152
"Among Those Present" (Benét), **Supp. XI:** 53
"Amoral Moralist" (White), **Supp. I Part 2:** 648
Amory, Cleveland, **Supp. I Part 1:** 316
Amory, Fred, **Supp. III Part 1:** 2
Amos (biblical book), **II:** 166
Amran, David, **Supp. XIV:**150
"Am Strand von Tanger" (Salter), **Supp. IX:** 257
"AMTRAK" (Baraka), **Supp. II Part 1:** 60
Amy and Isabelle (Strout), **Supp. X:** 86
Amy Lowell: Portrait of the Poet in Her Time (Gregory), **II:** 512
"Amy Lowell of Brookline, Mass." (Scott), **II:** 512
"Amy Wentworth" (Whittier), **Supp. I Part 2:** 694, 696
Anabase (Perse), **III:** 12
"Anabasis (I)" (Merwin), **Supp. III Part 1:** 342, 346
"Anabasis (II)" (Merwin), **Supp. III Part 1:** 342, 346
Anagrams: A Novel (Moore), **Supp. X:** 163, 164, 167, **169-171,** 172
Analects (Confucius), **Supp. IV Part 1:** 14
Analects, The (Pound, trans.), **III:** 472
Analogy (J. Butler), **II:** 8
"Analysis of a Theme" (Stevens), **IV:** 81
Anarchiad, The, A Poem on the Restoration of Chaos and Substantial Night, in Twenty Four Books (Barlow), **Supp. II Part 1:** 70
Anarchist Woman, An (Hapgood), **Supp. XVII:** 102-103
Anatomy Lesson, and Other Stories, The (Connell), **Supp. XIV:**84, 87, 89
"Anatomy Lesson, The" (Connell), **Supp. XIV:**84, 86, 87
Anatomy Lesson, The (P. Roth), **Retro. Supp. II:** 286, 290; **Supp. III Part 2:** 422-423, 425
"Anatomy Lesson of Dr. Nicholaas Tulp, Amsterdam, 1632, The" (Bierds), **Supp. XVII:** 27-28
Anatomy of Criticism (Frye), **Supp. XIII:** 19; **Supp. XIV:**15
Anatomy of Melancholy (Burton), **III:** 78; **Supp. XVII:** 229
Anatomy of Nonsense, The (Winters), **Supp. II Part 2:** 811, 812
Anaya, Rudolfo A., **Supp. IV Part 2:** 502; **Supp. XIII:** 213, 220

"Ancestor" (A. Finch), **Supp. XVII:** 72
Ancestors (Maxwell), **Supp. VIII:** 152, 168
"Ancestors, The" (Tate), **IV:** 128
Ancestral Voice: Conversations with N. Scott Momaday (Woodard), **Supp. IV Part 2:** 484, 485, 486, 489, 493
"Anchorage" (Harjo), **Supp. XII:** 220-221
Ancient Child, The: A Novel (Momaday), **Supp. IV Part 2:** 488, 489-491, 492, 493
"Ancient Egypt/Fannie Goldbarth" (Goldbarth), **Supp. XII:** 191-192
Ancient Evenings (Mailer), **Retro. Supp. II:** 206, 210, 213
Ancient Law, The (Glasgow), **II:** 179-180, 192
Ancient Musics (Goldbarth), **Supp. XII:** 191-192
"Ancient Semitic Rituals for the Dead" (Goldbarth), **Supp. XII:** 191-192
"Ancient World, The" (Doty), **Supp. XI:** 122
& (And) (Cummings), **I:** 429, 431, 432, 437, 445, 446, 448
Andersen, Hans Christian, **I:** 441; **Supp. I Part 2:** 622
Anderson, Charles R., **Supp. I Part 1:** 356, 360, 368, 371, 372
Anderson, Frances, **I:** 231
Anderson, Guy, **Supp. X:** 264, 265
Anderson, Henry J., **Supp. I Part 1:** 156
Anderson, Irwin M., **I:** 98-99
Anderson, Jon, **Supp. V:** 338
Anderson, Judith, **III:** 399
Anderson, Karl, **I:** 99, 103
Anderson, Margaret, **I:** 103; **III:** 471
Anderson, Margaret Bartlett, **III:** 171
Anderson, Mary Jane. *See* Lanier, Mrs. Robert Sampson (Mary Jane Anderson)
Anderson, Maxwell, **III:** 159
Anderson, Mrs. Irwin M., **I:** 98-99
Anderson, Mrs. Sherwood (Tennessee Mitchell), **I:** 100; **Supp. I Part 2:** 459, 460
Anderson, Quentin, **Retro. Supp. I:** 392
Anderson, Robert, **Supp. I Part 1:** 277; **Supp. V:** 108
Anderson, Sally, **Supp. XIII:** 95
Anderson, Sherwood, **I: 97-120,** 211, 374, 375, 384, 405, 423, 445, 480, 487, 495, 506, 518; **II:** 27, 38, 44, 55, 56, 68, 250-251, 263, 271, 289, 451, 456-457; **III:** 220, 224, 382-383, 453, 483, 545, 576, 579; **IV:** 27, 40, 46, 190, 207, 433, 451, 482; **Retro. Supp. I:** 79, 80, 177; **Supp. I Part 2:** 378, 430, 459, 472, 613; **Supp. IV Part 2:** 502; **Supp. V:** 12, 250; **Supp. VIII:** 39, 152; **Supp. IX:** 14, 309; **Supp. XI:** 159, 164; **Supp. XII:** 343; **Supp. XV:** 298; **Supp. XVI:** 17, 20; **Supp. XVII:** 105
Anderson, T. J., **Supp. XIII:** 132
Anderssen, A., **III:** 252
"And Hickman Arrives" (Ellison), **Retro. Supp. II:** 118, 126; **Supp. II Part 1:** 248
And in the Hanging Gardens (Aiken), **I:** 63
"And It Came to Pass" (Wright), **Supp. XV:** 348
And I Worked at the Writer's Trade (Cowley), **Supp. II Part 1:** 137, 139, 141, 143, 147, 148
Andorra (Cameron), **Supp. XII:** 79, 81, **88-91**
"-and Other Poets" (column; Untermeyer), **Supp. XV:** 294
"-and Other Poets" (Untermeyer), **Supp. XV:** 297
Andral, Gabriel, **Supp. I Part 1:** 302
Andre, Michael, **Supp. XII:** 117-118, 129, 132, 133-134
Andre's Mother (McNally), **Supp. XIII:** 206
Andress, Ursula, **Supp. XI:** 307
"Andrew Jackson" (Masters), **Supp. I Part 2:** 472
Andrews, Bruce, **Supp. IV Part 2:** 426
Andrews, Roy Chapman, **Supp. X:** 172
Andrews, Tom, **Supp. XI:** 317
Andrews, Wayne, **IV:** 310
Andrews, William L., **Supp. IV Part 1:** 13
Andreyev, Leonid Nikolaevich, **I:** 53; **II:** 425
Andria (Terence), **IV:** 363
"Andromache" (Dubus), **Supp. VII:** 84
"And Summer Will Not Come Again" (Plath), **Retro. Supp. II:** 242
"And That Night Clifford Died" (Levine), **Supp. V:** 195
And the Band Played On (Shilts), **Supp. X:** 145
"And the Moon Be Still as Bright" (Bradbury), **Supp. IV Part 1:** 106
"And the Sea Shall Give up Its Dead" (Wilder), **IV:** 358
And Things That Go Bump in the Night (McNally), **Supp. XIII: 196-197,** 205, 208
And to Think That I Saw It on Mulberry Street (Geisel), **Supp. XVI:** 100, 101, 104
"And *Ut Pictura Poesis* Is Her Name" (Ashbery), **Supp. III Part 1:** 19
"Anecdote and Storyteller" (Howe), **Supp. VI:** 127
"Anecdote of the Jar" (Stevens), **IV:** 83-84
"Anemone" (Rukeyser), **Supp. VI:** 281, 285
"Angel, The" (Buck), **Supp. II Part 1:** 127
"Angel and Unicorn and Butterfly" (Everwine), **Supp. XV:** 76
Angela's Ashes (McCourt), **Supp. XII: 271-279,** 283, 285
"Angel at the Grave, The" (Wharton), **IV:** 310; **Retro. Supp. I:** 365
"Angel Butcher" (Levine), **Supp. V:** 181
Angel City (Shepard), **Supp. III Part 2:** 432, 445
"Angel Is My Watermark!, The" (H. Miller), **III:** 180
Angell, Carol, **Supp. I Part 2:** 655
Angell, Katharine Sergeant. *See* White, Katharine
Angell, Roger, **Supp. I Part 2:** 655; **Supp. V:** 22; **Supp. VIII:** 139
Angel Landing (Hoffman), **Supp. X: 82-83**
"Angel Levine" (Malamud), **Supp. I Part 2:** 431, 432, 433-434, 437
Angel of Bethesda, The (Mather), **Supp. II Part 2:** 464
"Angel of the Bridge, The" (Cheever), **Supp. I Part 1:** 186-187
"Angel of the Odd, The" (Poe), **III:** 425
Angelo Herndon Jones (Hughes), **Retro. Supp. I:** 203
"Angel on the Porch, An" (Wolfe), **IV:** 451
Angelou, Maya, **Supp. IV Part 1: 1-19; Supp. XI:** 20, 245; **Supp. XIII:** 185; **Supp. XVI:** 259
"Angel Poem, The" (Stern), **Supp. IX:** 292
Angels and Earthly Creatures (Wylie), **Supp. I Part 2:** 709, 713, 724-730
Angels in America: A Gay Fantasia on National Themes (Kushner), **Supp. IX:** 131, 134, **141-146**
"Angels of the Love Affair" (Sexton), **Supp. II Part 2:** 692
"Angel Surrounded by Paysans" (Stevens), **IV:** 93
Angel That Troubled the Waters, The (Wilder), **IV:** 356, 357-358

INDEX / 261

"Anger" (Creeley), **Supp. IV Part 1:** 150-152
Anger (Sarton), **Supp. VIII: 256**
"Anger against Children" (R. Bly), **Supp. IV Part 1:** 73
Angle of Ascent (Hayden), **Supp. II Part 1:** 363, 367, 370
"Angle of Geese" (Momaday), **Supp. IV Part 2:** 485
Angle of Geese and Other Poems (Momaday), **Supp. IV Part 2:** 487, 491
Angle of Repose (Stegner), **Supp. IV Part 2:** 599, 605, 606, 610-611
"*Angle of Repose* and the Writings of Mary Hallock Foote: A Source Study" (Williams-Walsh), **Supp. IV Part 2:** 611
Anglo-Saxon Century, The (Dos Passos), **I:** 474-475, 483
Angoff, Charles, **III:** 107
"Angola Question Mark" (Hughes), **Supp. I Part 1:** 344
Angry Wife, The (Sedges), **Supp. II Part 1:** 125
"Angry Women Are Building: Issues and Struggles Facing American Indian Women Today" (Gunn Allen), **Supp. IV Part 1:** 324
"Animal, Vegetable, and Mineral" (Bogan), **Supp. III Part 1:** 66
"Animal Acts" (Simic), **Supp. VIII:** 278
Animal and Vegetable Physiology Considered with Reference to Natural Theology (Roget), **Supp. I Part 1:** 312
Animal Dreams (Kingsolver), **Supp. VII:** 199, 204-207
Animal Magnetism (Prose), **Supp. XVI:** 251, 260
"Animals, The" (Merwin), **Supp. III Part 1:** 348
"Animals Are Passing from Our Lives" (Levine), **Supp. V:** 181, 182
Animals in That Country, The (Atwood), **Supp. XIII:** 20, 33
Animals of the Soul: Sacred Animals of the Oglala Sioux (Brown), **Supp. IV Part 2:** 487
"Animals You Eat, The" (X. J. Kennedy), **Supp. XV:** 169
"Animula" (Eliot), **Retro. Supp. I:** 64
Anita Loos Rediscovered (M. A. Loos), **Supp. XVI:** 196
Ankor Wat (Ginsberg), **Supp. II Part 1:** 323
"Annabelle" (Komunyakaa), **Supp. XIII:** 117
"Annabel Lee" (Poe), **Retro. Supp. I:** 273; **Retro. Supp. II:** 266
Anna Christie (O'Neill), **III:** 386, 389, 390
Anna Karenina (Tolstoy), **I:** 10; **II:** 290; **Retro. Supp. I:** 225; **Supp. V:** 323
"*Anna Karenina*" (Trilling), **Supp. III Part 2:** 508
"Anna Who Was Mad" (Sexton), **Supp. II Part 2:** 692
"Ann Burlak" (Rukeyser), **Supp. VI:** 280
"Anne" (Davis), **Supp. XVI:** 91, 92
"Anne" (Oliver), **Supp. VII:** 232
"Anne at the Symphony" (Shields), **Supp. VII:** 310
"Anne Bradstreet's Poetic Voices" (Requa), **Supp. I Part 1:** 107
Anne Sexton: The Artist and Her Critics (McClatchy), **Supp. XII:** 253
"Ann from the Street" (Dixon), **Supp. XII:** 146-147
"Ann Garner" (Agee), **I:** 27
"Anniad, The" (Brooks), **Supp. III Part 1:** 77, 78
Annie (musical), **Supp. IV Part 2:** 577
Annie Allen (Brooks), **Supp. III Part 1:** 76-79
Annie Dillard Reader, The (Dillard), **Supp. VI:** 23
Annie Hall (film; Allen), **Supp. IV Part 1:** 205; **Supp. XV:** 1, 2, 4, 5, 6-7, 14
Annie John (Kincaid), **Supp. VII:** 184-186, 193
Annie Kilburn, a Novel (Howells), **II:** 275, 286, 287
"Annihilation" (X. J. Kennedy), **Supp. XV:** 168
Anniversary (Shields), **Supp. VII:** 320, 322, 323, 324
"Annunciation, The" (Le Sueur), **Supp. V:** 130
Ann Vickers (Lewis), **II:** 453
"A No-Account Creole, A" (Chopin), **Retro. Supp. II:** 64
"Anodyne" (Komunyakaa), **Supp. XIII:** 130
Another America/Otra America (Kingsolver), **Supp. VII:** 207-209
"Another Animal" (Swenson), **Supp. IV Part 2:** 639
Another Animal: Poems (Swenson), **Supp. IV Part 2:** 639-641, 649
Another Antigone (Gurney), **Supp. V:** 97, 98, 100, 101, 102, 105
"Another August" (Merrill), **Supp. III Part 1:** 326
"Another Beer" (Matthews), **Supp. IX:** 158

Another Country (Baldwin), **Retro. Supp. II:** 9-11, 14; **Supp. I Part 1:** 51, 52, 56-58, 63, 67, 337; **Supp. II Part 1:** 40; **Supp. VIII:** 349
"Another Language" (Jong), **Supp. V:** 131
Another Mother Tongue: Gay Words, Gay Worlds (Grahn), **Supp. IV Part 1:** 330
"Another Night in the Ruins" (Kinnell), **Supp. III Part 1:** 239, 251
"Another Old Woman" (W. C. Williams), **Retro. Supp. I:** 423
Another Part of the Forest (Hellman), **Supp. I Part 1:** 282-283, 297
Another Republic: 17 European and South American Writers (Strand, trans.), **Supp. IV Part 2:** 630
Another Roadside Attraction (Robbins), **Supp. X:** 259, 261, 262, 263, 264, 265-266, **267-269,** 274, 275, 277, 284
"Another Spring Uncovered" (Swenson), **Supp. IV Part 2:** 644
Another Thin Man (film), **Supp. IV Part 1:** 355
Another Time (Auden), **Supp. II Part 1:** 15
Another Turn of the Crank (Berry), **Supp. X:** 25, 35
"Another upon the Same" (Taylor), **IV:** 161
"Another Voice" (Wilbur), **Supp. III Part 2:** 557
"Another Wife" (Anderson), **I:** 114
Another Woman (film; Allen), **Supp. XV:** 11
Another You (Beattie), **Supp. V:** 29, 31, 33-34
Anouilh, Jean, **Supp. I Part 1:** 286-288, 297
Ansky, S., **IV:** 6
Ansky, Shloime, **Supp. IX:** 131, 138
"Answer, The" (Jeffers), **Supp. III Part 2:** 423
Answered Prayers: The Unfinished Novel (Capote), **Supp. III Part 1:** 113, 125, 131-132; **Supp. XVI:** 245
"Answering the Deer: Genocide and Continuance in the Poetry of American Indian Women" (Gunn Allen), **Supp. IV Part 1:** 322, 325
"Answer of Minerva, The: Pacifism and Resistance in Simone Weil" (Merton), **Supp. VIII:** 204
Antaeus (Wolfe), **IV:** 461
"Ante-Bellum Sermon, An" (Dunbar), **Supp. II Part 1:** 203-204
Antheil, George, **III:** 471, 472; **IV:** 404
Anthem (Rand), **Supp. IV Part 2:** 523

Anthology of Holocaust Literature (Glatstein, Knox, and Margoshes, eds.), **Supp. X:** 70
Anthology of Twentieth-Century Brazilian Poetry, An (Bishop and Brasil, eds.), **Retro. Supp. II:** 50; **Supp. I Part 1:** 94
Anthon, Kate, **I:** 452
Anthony, Andrew, **Supp. XVI:**235, 245, 246
Anthony, Saint, **III:** 395
Anthony, Susan B., **Supp. XI:** 200
"Anthropologist as Hero, The" (Sontag), **Supp. III Part 2:** 451
"Anthropology of Water, The" (Carson), **Supp. XII: 102-103**
Anthropos: The Future of Art (Cummings), **I:** 430
Antichrist (Nietzsche), **III:** 176
"Anti-Father" (Dove), **Supp. IV Part 1:** 246
"Anti-Feminist Woman, The" (Rich), **Supp. I Part 2:** 550
Antigone (Sophocles), **Supp. I Part 1:** 284; **Supp. X:** 249
Antin, David, **Supp. VIII:** 292; **Supp. XII:** 2, 8
Antin, Mary, **Supp. IX:** 227; **Supp. XVI:**148, 149
Anti-Oedipus: Capitalism and Schizophrenia (Deleuze and Guattari), **Supp. XII:** 4
Antiphon, The (Barnes), **Supp. III Part 1:** 43-44
"Antiquities" (Mather), **Supp. II Part 2:** 452
"Antiquity of Freedom, The" (Bryant), **Supp. I Part 1:** 168
"Antislavery Tocsin, An" (Douglass), **Supp. III Part 1:** 171
Antoine, Andre, **III:** 387
Antonioni, Michelangelo, **Supp. IV Part 1:** 46, 47, 48
Antony and Cleopatra (Shakespeare), **I:** 285
"Antony on Behalf of the Play" (Burke), **I:** 284
"An trentiesme de mon Eage, L'" (MacLeish), **III:** 9
"Ants" (R. Bly), **Supp. IV Part 1:** 71
Anxiety of Influence, The (Bloom), **Supp. XIII:** 46
"Any City" (Untermeyer), **Supp. XV:** 296
"Any Object" (Swenson), **Supp. IV Part 2:** 640
"Any Porch" (Parker), **Supp. IX:** 194
Anything Else (film; Allen), **Supp. XV:** 2, 11
"Anywhere Out of This World" (Baudelaire), **II:** 552
Any Woman Can't (Wasserstein), **Supp. XV:** 322
Any Woman's Blues (Jong), **Supp. V:** 115, 123, 126
Anzaldúa, Gloria, **Supp. IV Part 1:** 330; **Supp. XIII:** 223
"Aphorisms on Society" (Stevens), **Retro. Supp. I:** 303
"Apiary IX" (C. Frost), **Supp. XV:** 106
"Apisculptures" (Bierds), **Supp. XVII:** 29
Apollinaire, Guillaume, **I:** 432; **II:** 529; **III:** 196; **IV:** 80; **Retro. Supp. II:** 326; **Supp. XV:** 182
Apologies to the Iroquois (Wilson), **IV:** 429
"Apology" (C. Frost), **Supp. XV:** 103
"Apology, An" (Malamud), **Supp. I Part 2:** 435, 437
"Apology for Bad Dreams" (Jeffers), **Supp. II Part 2:** 427, 438; **Supp. XVII:** 112
"Apology for Crudity, An" (Anderson), **I:** 109
Apology for Poetry (Sidney), **Supp. II Part 1:** 105
"Apostle of the Tules, An" (Harte), **Supp. II Part 1:** 356
"Apostrophe to a Dead Friend" (Kumin), **Supp. IV Part 2:** 442, 451, 452
"Apostrophe to a Pram Rider" (White), **Supp. I Part 2:** 678
"Apostrophe to Man (on reflecting that the world is ready to go to war again)" (Millay), **III:** 127
"Apostrophe to Vincentine, The" (Stevens), **IV:** 90
"Apotheosis" (Kingsolver), **Supp. VII:** 208
"Apotheosis of Martin Luther King, The" (Hardwick), **Supp. III Part 1:** 203-204
Appalachia (Wright), **Supp. V:** 333, 345
"Appalachian Book of the Dead III" (Wright), **Supp. V:** 345
"Appeal to Progressives, An" (Wilson), **IV:** 429
Appeal to Reason (Paine), **I:** 490
Appeal to the World, An (Du Bois), **Supp. II Part 1:** 184
Appearance and Reality (Bradley), **I:** 572
"Appendix to 'The Anniad'" (Brooks), **Supp. III Part 1:** 77
Apple, Max, **Supp. VIII:** 14; **Supp. XVII:** 1-11, 49-50
Apple, Sam, **Supp. XVII:** 8
"Apple, The" (Kinnell), **Supp. III Part 1:** 250
Applebaum, Anne, **Supp. XVI:**153
Applegarth, Mabel, **II:** 465, 478
"Apple of Discord, The" (Humphrey), **Supp. IX:** 109
"Apple Peeler" (Francis), **Supp. IX:** 82
"Apple Rind" (C. Frost), **Supp. XV:** 102
Appleseed, Johnny (pseudonym). See Chapman, John (Johnny Appleseed)
Appleton, Nathan, **II:** 488
Appleton, Thomas Gold, **Supp. I Part 1:** 306; **Supp. I Part 2:** 415
"Apple Tree, The" (McCarriston), **Supp. XIV:**263, 268
"Applicant, The" (Plath), **Retro. Supp. II:** 252; **Supp. I Part 2:** 535, 544, 545
"Application, The" (Neugeboren), **Supp. XVI:**219, 220, 225
"Applications of the Doctrine" (Hass), **Supp. VI:** 100-101
Appointment, The (film), **Supp. IX:** 253
Appointment in Samarra (O'Hara), **III:** 361, 363-364, 365-367, 371, 374, 375, 383
Appreciation of Sarah Orne Jewett (Cary), **Retro. Supp. II:** 132
"Approaches, The" (Merwin), **Supp. III Part 1:** 350
"Approaching Artaud" (Sontag), **Supp. III Part 2:** 470-471
"Approaching Prayer" (Dickey), **Supp. IV Part 1:** 175
Approach to Literature, An: A Collection of Prose and Verse with Analyses and Discussions (Brooks, Warren, and Purser), **Supp. XIV:**4
"Approach to Thebes, The" (Kunitz), **Supp. III Part 1:** 265-267
Approach to Vedanta, An (Isherwood), **Supp. XIV:**157, 163, 164
"Après-midi d'un faune, L'" (Mallarmé), **III:** 8
"April" (Bierds), **Supp. XVII:** 29
"April" (Winters), **Supp. II Part 2:** 788
"April" (W. C. Williams), **Retro. Supp. I:** 422
April, Steve. See Lacy, Ed
April Galleons (Ashbery), **Supp. III Part 1:** 26
"April Galleons" (Ashbery), **Supp. III Part 1:** 26
April Hopes (Howells), **II:** 285, 289
"April Lovers" (Ransom), **III:** 489-490
"April Showers" (Wharton), **Retro.**

Supp. I: 361
"April Today Main Street" (Olson), **Supp. II Part 2:** 581
April Twilights (Cather), **I:** 313; **Retro. Supp. I:** 5
"Apt Pupil" (King), **Supp. V:** 152
Arabian Nights, **I:** 204; **II:** 8; **Supp. I Part 2:** 584, 599; **Supp. IV Part 1:** 1
"Arabic Coffee" (Nye), **Supp. XIII:** 276
"Araby" (Joyce), **I:** 174; **Supp. VIII:** 15
Aragon, Louis, **I:** 429; **III:** 471; **Retro. Supp. II:** 85, 321
Arana-Ward, Marie, **Supp. VIII:** 84
Ararat (Glück), **Supp. V:** 79, 86-87
Arbre du voyageur, L' (W. J. Smith; Haussmann, trans.), **Supp. XIII:** 347
Arbus, Diane, **Supp. XII:** 188
Arbuthnott, John (pseudonym). *See* Henry, O.
"Arc, The" (Bidart), **Supp. XV:** 25-26, 27
Archaeologist of Morning (Olson), **Supp. II Part 2:** 557
"Archaic Maker, The" (Merwin), **Supp. III Part 1:** 357
"Archaic Torso of Apollo" (Rilke), **Supp. XV:** 148
"Archaischer Torso Apollos" (Rilke), **Supp. XVII:** 244
"Archbishop, The" (Gioia), **Supp. XV:** 126, 127
Archer (television show), **Supp. IV Part 2:** 474
Archer, William, **IV:** 131; **Retro. Supp. I:** 228
Archer at Large (Macdonald), **Supp. IV Part 2:** 473
Archer in Hollywood (Macdonald), **Supp. IV Part 2:** 474
"Archetype and Signature: The Relationship of Poet and Poem" (Fiedler), **Supp. XIII:** 101
"Archibald Higbie" (Masters), **Supp. I Part 2:** 461
"Architect, The" (Bourne), **I:** 223
Arctic Dreams (Lopez), **Supp. V:** 211
Arctic Refuge: A Circle of Testimony (Haines), **Supp. XII:** 205
"Arcturus" (Connell), **Supp. XIV:** 88
Arendt, Hannah, **II:** 544; **Retro. Supp. I:** 87; **Retro. Supp. II:** 28, 117; **Supp. I Part 2:** 570; **Supp. IV Part 1:** 386; **Supp. VIII:** 98, 99, 100, 243; **Supp. XII:** 166-167
Arensberg, Walter, **IV:** 408; **Retro. Supp. I:** 416

Aren't You Happy for Me? (Bausch), **Supp. VII:** 42, 51, 54
Areopagitica (Milton), **Supp. I Part 2:** 422
"Are You a Doctor?" (Carver), **Supp. III Part 1:** 139-141
"Are You Mr. William Stafford? (Stafford), **Supp. XI:** 317
Argall: The True Story of Pocahontas and Captain John Smith (Vollmann), **Supp. XVII:** 225, 226, 231, 232, 233
"Argonauts of 49, California's Golden Age" (Harte), **Supp. II Part 1:** 353, 355
"Arguments of Everlasting" (B. Kelly), **Supp. XVII:** 129
"Arguments with the Gestapo Continued: II" (Wright), **Supp. XV:** 344
"Arguments with the Gestapo Continued: Literary Resistance" (Wright), **Supp. XV:** 344
Aria da Capo (Millay), **III:** 137-138
Ariadne's Thread: A Collection of Contemporary Women's Journals (Lifshin, ed.), **Supp. XVI:** 37-38
Ariel (Plath), **Retro. Supp. II:** 250-255; **Supp. I Part 2:** 526, 539, 541; **Supp. V:** 79
"Ariel" (Plath), **Supp. I Part 2:** 542, 546
"Ariel Poems" (Eliot), **I:** 579
"Ariosto: Critical Notice of His Life and Genius" (Hunt), **Supp. XV:** 175
Ariosto, Ludovico, **Supp. XV:** 175
Arise, Arise (Zukofsky), **Supp. III Part 2:** 619, 629
Aristides. *See* Epstein, Joseph
"Aristocracy" (Emerson), **II:** 6
Aristocracy and Justice (More), **I:** 223
Aristophanes, **I:** 436; **II:** 577; **Supp. I Part 2:** 406
Aristotle, **I:** 58, 265, 280, 527; **II:** 9, 12, 198, 536; **III:** 20, 115, 145, 157, 362, 422, 423; **IV:** 10, 18, 74-75, 89; **Supp. I Part 1:** 104, 296; **Supp. I Part 2:** 423; **Supp. IV Part 1:** 391; **Supp. IV Part 2:** 526, 530; **Supp. X:** 78; **Supp. XI:** 249; **Supp. XII:** 106; **Supp. XIV:** 242-243
Aristotle Contemplating the Bust of Homer (Rembrandt), **Supp. IV Part 1:** 390, 391
"Arkansas Traveller" (Wright), **Supp. V:** 334
"Arm, The" (X. J. Kennedy), **Supp. XV:** 169
"Armadillo, The" (Bishop), **Supp. I Part 1:** 93
Armadillo in the Grass (Hearon),

Supp. VIII: 58-59
"Armageddon" (Ransom), **III:** 489, 492
Armah, Aiy Kwei, **Supp. IV Part 1:** 373
Armies of the Night, The (Mailer), **III:** 39-40, 41, 42, 44, 45, 46; **Retro. Supp. II:** 205, 206-207, 208; **Supp. IV Part 1:** 207; **Supp. XIV:** 49, 162
"Arm in Arm" (Simpson), **Supp. IX:** 267-268
Arminius, Jacobus, **I:** 557
Armitage, Shelley, **Supp. IV Part 2:** 439
Arm of Flesh, The (Salter), **Supp. IX:** 251
"Armor" (Dickey), **Supp. IV Part 1:** 179
Armored Attack (film), **Supp. I Part 1:** 281
Arms, George W., **Supp. I Part 2:** 416-417
Armstrong, George, **Supp. I Part 2:** 386
Armstrong, Louis, **Retro. Supp. II:** 114
"'Arm the Paper Arm': Kenneth Koch's Postmodern Comedy" (Chinitz), **Supp. XV:** 180, 185
"Army" (Corso), **Supp. XII:** 117, 127
Army Brat (W. J. Smith), **Supp. XIII:** 331, 347
Arna Bontemps Langston Hughes: Letters 1925-1967 (Nichols), **Retro. Supp. I:** 194
Arner, Robert D., **Retro. Supp. II:** 62
Arnold, Edwin T., **Supp. VIII:** 189
Arnold, George W., **Supp. I Part 2:** 411
Arnold, Marilyn, **Supp. IV Part 1:** 220
Arnold, Matthew, **I:** 222, 228, 275; **II:** 20, 110, 338, 541; **III:** 604; **IV:** 349; **Retro. Supp. I:** 56, 325; **Supp. I Part 2:** 416, 417, 419, 529, 552, 602; **Supp. IX:** 298; **Supp. XIV:** 11, 335
Arnold, Thurman, **Supp. I Part 2:** 645
Aronson, Steven M. L., **Supp. V:** 4
Around about America (Caldwell), **I:** 290
"Arrangement in Black and White" (Parker), **Supp. IX:** 198
"Arrival at Santos" (Bishop), **Retro. Supp. II:** 46; **Supp. IX:** 45-46
"Arrival of the Bee Box, The" (Plath), **Retro. Supp. II:** 255
Arrivistes, The: Poem 1940-1949 (Simpson), **Supp. IX:** 265, **267-268**
Arrogance (J. Scott), **Supp. XVII: 186-188,** 189, 191, 192, 194

"Arrow" (Dove), **Supp. IV Part 1:** 250
Arrowsmith (Lewis), **I:** 362; **II:** 445-446, 449
"Arsenal at Springfield, The" (Longfellow), **Retro. Supp. II:** 168
"Arson Plus" (Hammett), **Supp. IV Part 1:** 343
"Ars Poetica" (Dove), **Supp. IV Part 1:** 250
"Ars Poetica" (Dunn), **Supp. XI:** 154
"Ars Poetica" (MacLeish), **III:** 9-10
"Ars Poetica" (X. J. Kennedy), **Supp. XV:** 154
"*Ars Poetica:* A Found Poem" (Kumin), **Supp. IV Part 2:** 455
"Ars Poetica; or, Who Lives in the Ivory Tower" (McGrath), **Supp. X:** 117
"Ars Poetica: Some Recent Criticism" (Wright), **Supp. III Part 2:** 603
"Art" (Emerson), **II:** 13
"Art and Neurosis" (Trilling), **Supp. III Part 2:** 502
Art and Technics (Mumford), **Supp. II Part 2:** 483
Art & Ardor: Essays (Ozick), **Supp. V:** 258, 272
Art as Experience (Dewey), **I:** 266
Art by Subtraction (Reid), **IV:** 41
Art de toucher le clavecin, L' (Couperin), **III:** 464
Artemis to Actaeon and Other Verse (Wharton), **Retro. Supp. I:** 372
Arte of English Poesie (Puttenham), **Supp. I Part 1:** 113
Arthur, Anthony, **Supp. IV Part 2:** 606
Arthur Mervyn; or, Memoirs of the Year 1793 (Brown), **Supp. I Part 1:** 137-140, 144
"Article of Faith" (Sobin), **Supp. XVI:**291
Articles of Light & Elation (Sobin), **Supp. XVI:**291
Articulation of Sound Forms in Time (Howe), **Supp. IV Part 2:** 419, 431-433
"Artificer" (X. J. Kennedy), **Supp. XV:** 160
"Artificial Nigger, The" (O'Connor), **III:** 343, 351, 356, 358; **Retro. Supp. II:** 229, 232
Artist, The: A Drama without Words (Mencken), **III:** 104
"Artist of the Beautiful, The" (Hawthorne), **Retro. Supp. I:** 149
Artistry of Grief (Torsney), **Retro. Supp. I:** 224
"Artists' and Models' Ball, The" (Brooks), **Supp. III Part 1:** 72
"Art of Disappearing, The" (Nye), **Supp. XIII:** 287
Art of Eating, The (M. F. K. Fisher), **Supp. XVII:** 87, 90, 91
Art of Fiction, The (Gardner), **Supp. VI:** 73
"Art of Fiction, The" (H. James), **Retro. Supp. I:** 226; **Retro. Supp. II:** 223
Art of Hunger, The (Auster), **Supp. XII:** 22
"Art of Keeping Your Mouth Shut, The" (Heller), **Supp. IV Part 1:** 383
"Art of Literature and Commonsense, The" (Nabokov), **Retro. Supp. I:** 271
Art of Living and Other Stories, The (Gardner), **Supp. VI:** 72
"Art of Love, The" (Koch), **Supp. XV:** 182
Art of Love, The (Koch), **Supp. XV:** 182
Art of Poetry, The (Koch), **Supp. XV:** 175-176, 178, 188
"Art of Poetry, The" (Koch), **Supp. XV:** 182
"Art of Poetry, The" (McClatchy), **Supp. XII:** 262
"Art of Romare Bearden, The" (Ellison), **Retro. Supp. II:** 123
"Art of Storytelling, The" (Simpson), **Supp. IX:** 277
Art of Sylvia Plath, The (Newman), **Supp. I Part 2:** 527
Art of the Moving Picture, The (Lindsay), **Supp. I Part 2:** 376, 391-392, 394; **Supp. XVI:**185
Art of the Novel (H. James), **Retro. Supp. I:** 227
"Art of Theodore Dreiser, The" (Bourne), **I:** 235
Art of the Personal Essay, The (Lopate, comp.), **Supp. XIII:** 280-281; *Supp. XVI:*266
Art of the Self, The: Essays a Propos "Steps" (Kosinski), **Supp. VII:** 222
Arts and Sciences (Goldbarth), **Supp. XII: 184-186**
"Art's Bread and Butter" (Benét), **Retro. Supp. I:** 108
Arvin, Newton, **I:** 259; **II:** 508; **Retro. Supp. I:** 19, 137
Asali, Muna, **Supp. XIII:** 121, 126
Asbury, Herbert, **Supp. IV Part 1:** 353
Ascent of F6, The (Auden), **Supp. II Part 1:** 11, 13
Ascent to Truth, The (Merton), **Supp. VIII:** 208
Asch, Nathan, **Supp. XV:** 133, 134
Asch, Sholem, **IV:** 1, 9, 11, 14; **Retro. Supp. II:** 299

Ascherson, Neal, **Supp. XII:** 167
"As Close as Breathing" (Jarman), **Supp. XVII:** 120
As Does New Hampshire and Other Poems (Sarton), **Supp. VIII:** 259
"As Evening Lays Dying" (Salinas), **Supp. XIII:** 319
"As Flowers Are" (Kunitz), **Supp. III Part 1:** 265
"Ash" (Sobin), **Supp. XVI:**284-285
Ashbery, John, **Retro. Supp. I:** 313; **Supp. I Part 1:** 96; **Supp. III Part 1: 1-29; Supp. III Part 2:** 541; **Supp. IV Part 2:** 620; **Supp. VIII:** 272; **Supp. IX:** 52; **Supp. XI:** 139; **Supp. XIII:** 85; **Supp. XV:** 176, 177, 178, 188, 250
"Ashes" (Levine), **Supp. V:** 188
Ashes: Poems Old and New (Levine), **Supp. V:** 178, 188-189
"Ashes of the Beacon" (Bierce), **I:** 209
Ashford, Margaret Mary (Daisy), **II:** 426
Ash Wednesday (Eliot), **I:** 570, 574-575, 578-579, 580, 582, 584, 585; **Retro. Supp. I:** 64
"Ash Wednesday" (Eliot), **Supp. IV Part 2:** 436
"Ash Wednesday" (Garrett), **Supp. VII:** 109-110
"Ash Wednesday" (Merton), **Supp. VIII:** 199
Asian American Authors (Hsu and Palubinskas, eds.), **Supp. X:** 292
Asian American Heritage: An Anthology of Prose and Poetry (Wand), **Supp. X:** 292
Asian Figures (Mervin), **Supp. III Part 1:** 341
Asian Journal of Thomas Merton, The (Merton), **Supp. VIII:** 196, 206, 208
"Asian Peace Offers Rejected without Publication" (R. Bly), **Supp. IV Part 1:** 61
"Asides on the Oboe" (Stevens), **Retro. Supp. I:** 305
"As I Ebb'd with the Ocean of Life" (Whitman), **IV:** 342, 345-346; **Retro. Supp. I:** 404, 405
As I Lay Dying (Faulkner), **II:** 60-61, 69, 73, 74; **IV:** 100; **Retro. Supp. I:** 75, 82, 84, 85, 86, 88, 89, 91, 92; **Supp. IV Part 1:** 47; **Supp. VIII:** 37, 178; **Supp. IX:** 99, 103, 251; **Supp. XIV:**24
"As I Lay with My Head in Your Lap, Camerado" (Whitman), **IV:** 347
Asimov, Isaac, **Supp. IV Part 1:** 116; **Supp. XVI:**122
Asinof, Eliot, **II:** 424

Asirvatham, Sandy, **Supp. XVI:**249
"As Is the Daughter, So Is Her Mother" (Patchett), **Supp. XII:** 310
"As It Was in the Beginning" (Benét), **Supp. XI:** 56
"As I Walked Out One Evening" (Auden), **Supp. II Part 1:** 13; **Supp. XV:** 126
"As I Went Down by Havre de Grace" (Wylie), **Supp. I Part 2:** 723
"Ask Me" (Stafford), **Supp. XI:** 326-327
Ask Me Tomorrow (Cozzens), **I:** 365-367, 379
Ask the Dust (Fante), **Supp. XI:** 159, 160, 166, **167-169,** 172, 173, 174
Ask Your Mama (Hughes), **Supp. I Part 1:** 339, 341-342
Ask Your Mama: 12 Moods for Jazz (Hughes), **Retro. Supp. I:** 210, 211
As Little Children (R. P. Smith), **Supp. XIV:**333
"As One Put Drunk into the Packet Boat" (Ashbery), **Supp. III Part 1:** 18
"Aspects of Robinson" (Kees), **Supp. XV:** 134
Aspects of the Novel (Forster), **Retro. Supp. I:** 232; **Supp. VIII:** 155
"Aspen and the Stream, The" (Wilbur), **Supp. III Part 2:** 555, 556
Aspern Papers, The (James), **Supp. V:** 101, 102
"Aspern Papers, The" (James), **Retro. Supp. I:** 219, 227, 228
Asphalt Georgics (Carruth), **Supp. XVI:**54
Asphalt Jungle (film, Huston), **Supp. XIII:** 174
"Asphodel" (Welty), **IV:** 265, 271
"Asphodel, That Greeny Flower" (W. C. Williams), **Retro. Supp. I:** 429
"Aspic and Buttermilk" (Olds), **Supp. X:** 213
Asquith, Herbert Henry, **Retro. Supp. I:** 59
"Ass" (Cisneros), **Supp. VII:** 67
Assante, Armand, **Supp. VIII:** 74
Assassins, The (Oates), **Supp. II Part 2:** 512, 517-519
"Assault" (Millay), **III:** 130-131
"Assemblage of Husbands and Wives, An" (Lewis), **II:** 455-456
Assembly (O'Hara), **III:** 361
Assignment, Wildlife (LaBastille), **Supp. X: 99,** 104
"Assimilation in Recent American Jewish Autobiographies" (Krupnick), **Supp. XVI:**153
Assistant, The (Malamud), **Supp. I Part 2:** 427, 428, 429, 431, 435, 441-445, 451; **Supp. XVI:**220
Assommoir, L' (Zola), **II:** 291; **III:** 318
Assorted Prose (Updike), **IV:** 215-216, 218; **Retro. Supp. I:** 317, 319, 327
Astaire, Adele, **Supp. XVI:**187
As They Were (M. F. K. Fisher), **Supp. XVII:** 88, 89, 91
Astor, Mary, **Supp. IV Part 1:** 356; **Supp. XII:** 173
Astoria, or, Anecdotes of an Enterprise beyond the Rocky Mountains (Irving), **II:** 312
"Astounding News by Electric Express via Norfolk! The Atlantic Crossed in Three Days Signal Triumph of Mr. Monck's Flying-Machine ..." (Poe), **III:** 413, 420
Astraea (Holmes), **III:** 82
Astro, Richard, **Supp. I Part 2:** 429, 445
"Astrological Fricassee" (H. Miller), **III:** 187
Astrophil and Stella (Sidney), **Supp. XIV:**128
"As Weary Pilgrim" (Bradstreet), **Supp. I Part 1:** 103, 109, 122
As We Know (Ashbery), **Supp. III Part 1:** 9, 21-25
"As We Know" (Ashbery), **Supp. III Part 1:** 21-22
Aswell, Edward C., **IV:** 458, 459, 461
"Asylum, The" (Carruth), **Supp. XVI:**48-49
"As You Like It" (Chopin), **Supp. I Part 1:** 217
As You Like It (Shakespeare), **Supp. I Part 1:** 308
"At a Bar in Charlotte Amalie" (Updike), **IV:** 214
"At a Lecture" (Brodsky), **Supp. VIII:** 33
"At a March against the Vietnam War" (R. Bly), **Supp. IV Part 1:** 61
"At a Reading" (McClatchy), **Supp. XII:** 256-257
"Atavism of John Tom Little Bear, The" (O. Henry), **Supp. II Part 1:** 410
"At Chênière Caminada" (Chopin), **Supp. I Part 1:** 220
"At Chinese Checkers" (Berryman), **I:** 182
Atchity, Kenneth John, **Supp. XI:** 227
At Eighty-Two (Sarton), **Supp. VIII:** 264
"At Every Gas Station There Are Mechanics" (Dunn), **Supp. XI:** 144
At Fault (Chopin), **Retro. Supp. II:** 57, 60, **62-63;** **Supp. I Part 1:** 207, 209-211, 220
At Heaven's Gate (Warren), **IV:** 243, 247-248, 251
Atheism Refuted: in a Discourse to Prove the Existence of God (Paine), **Supp. I Part 2:** 517
"Athénaïse" (Chopin), **Retro. Supp. II:** 66, 67; **Supp. I Part 1:** 219-220
Atherton, Gertrude, **I:** 199, 207-208
Athey, Jean L., **Supp. XI:** 184
At Home: Essays, 1982-1988 (Vidal), **Supp. IV Part 2:** 682, 687, 688
"At Home With" (column; Leland), **Supp. XV:** 69
"At Kino Viejo, Mexico" (Ríos), **Supp. IV Part 2:** 541
Atkinson, Brooks, **IV:** 288; **Supp. IV Part 2:** 683
Atlantis (Doty), **Supp. XI:** 121, **126-129**
"Atlantis" (Doty), **Supp. XI:** 127-128
Atlas, James, **Supp. V:** 233; **Supp. XV:** 25
Atlas, The (Vollmann), **Supp. XVII:** 226, 227
Atlas Shrugged (Rand), **Supp. IV Part 2:** 517, 521, 523, 524-526, 528, 531
At Liberty (T. Williams), **IV:** 378
"At Melville's Tomb" (H. Crane), **I:** 393; **Retro. Supp. II:** 76, 78, 80, 82
"At Mother Teresa's" (Nye), **Supp. XIII:** 276
At Night the Salmon Move (Carver), **Supp. III Part 1:** 142
"At North Farm" (Ashbery), **Supp. III Part 1:** 1-2
At Paradise Gate (Smiley), **Supp. VI:** 292, **293-294**
"At Paso Rojo" (Bowles), **Supp. IV Part 1:** 87
At Play in the Fields of the Lord (Matthiessen), **Supp. V:** 199, 202, 204-206, 212
"At Play in the Paradise of Bombs" (Sanders), **Supp. XVI:**272-273, 274, 277
"At Pleasure By" (Pinsky), **Supp. VI:** 245
At Risk (Hoffman), **Supp. X:** 87
"At Sea" (Hemingway), **II:** 258
"At Shaft 11" (Dunbar), **Supp. II Part 1:** 212
"At Slim's River" (Haines), **Supp. XII:** 208-209
"At St. Croix" (Dubus), **Supp. VII:** 83, 87
At Sundown (Whittier), **Supp. I Part 2:** 704
"At Sunset" (Simic), **Supp. VIII:** 282
Attebery, Brian, **Supp. IV Part 1:** 101

"At That Time, or The History of a Joke" (Paley), **Supp. VI:** 229-230
At the Back of the North Wind (Macdonald), **Supp. XIII:** 75
"At the Birth of an Age" (Jeffers), **Supp. II Part 2:** 432
"At the Bomb Testing Site" (Stafford), **Supp. XI:** 317-318, 321, 323
At the Bottom of the River (Kincaid), **Supp. VII:** 182-184, 185
"At the 'Cadian Ball" (Chopin), **Retro. Supp. II:** 64, 65, 68
"At the Chelton-Pulver Game" (Auchincloss), **Supp. IV Part 1:** 27
"At the Drugstore" (Taylor), **Supp. V:** 323
At the Edge of the Body (Jong), **Supp. V:** 115, 130
At the End of the Open Road (Simpson), **Supp. IX:** 265, 269, **271-273,** 277
At the End of This Summer: Poems 1948-1954, **Supp. XII:** 211
"At the End of War" (Eberhart), **I:** 522-523
"At the Executed Murderer's Grave" (Wright), **Supp. III Part 2:** 595, 597
"At the Fishhouses" (Bishop), **Retro. Supp. II:** 45; **Supp. I Part 1:** 90, 92
"At the Grave of My Guardian Angel: St. Louis Cemetery, New Orleans" (Levis), **Supp. XI:** 268-269
"At the Gym" (Doty), **Supp. XI:** 135
"At the Indian Store" (McCarriston), **Supp. XIV:**271
"At the Lake" (Oliver), **Supp. VII:** 244
"At the Landing" (Welty), **IV:** 265-266; **Retro. Supp. I:** 348
"At the Last" (Bynner), **Supp. XV:** 44
"At the Last Rites for Two Hot Rodders" (X. J. Kennedy), **Supp. XV:** 166
"At the Premiere" (Keillor), **Supp. XVI:**167
At the Root of Stars (Barnes), **Supp. III Part 1:** 34
"At the Slackening of the Tide" (Wright), **Supp. III Part 2:** 597
"At the Tomb of Walt Whitman" (Kunitz), **Supp. III Part 1:** 262
"At the Tourist Centre in Boston" (Atwood), **Supp. XIII:** 33
"At the Town Dump" (Kenyon), **Supp. VII:** 167
"At the Worcester Museum" (Pinsky), **Supp. VI:** 251
"Atticus Finch and the Mad Dog: Harper Lee's *To Kill a Mockingbird*" (Jones), **Supp. VIII:** 128
"Atticus Finch-Right and Wrong" (Freedman), **Supp. VIII:** 127-128
"Attic Which Is Desire, The" (W. C. Williams), **Retro. Supp. I:** 422
"At Times in Flight: A Parable" (H. Roth), **Supp. IX:** 234
Attitudes toward History (Burke), **I:** 274
Atwan, Robert, **Supp. XVI:**273, 277
"At White River" (Haines), **Supp. XII:** 208-209
Atwood, Margaret, **Supp. IV Part 1:** 252; **Supp. V:** 119; **Supp. XI:** 317; **Supp. XIII: 19-39,** 291, 306
"Atwood's Gorgon Touch" (Davey), **Supp. XIII:** 33
"Aubade" (McCarriston), **Supp. XIV:**271
"Aubade: November" (McCarriston), **Supp. XIV:**261-262
"Aubade: Opal and Silver" (Doty), **Supp. XI:** 129
"Aubade of an Early Homo Sapiens" (C. Frost), **Supp. XV:** 97-98
"Au Bal Musette" (Van Vechten), **Supp. II Part 2:** 735
Auchincloss, Hugh D., **Supp. IV Part 2:** 679
Auchincloss, Louis, **I:** 375; **III:** 66; **Retro. Supp. I:** 370, 373; **Supp. IV Part 1: 21-38**
"Auction" (Simic), **Supp. VIII:** 278
"Auction, The" (Crane), **I:** 411
"Auction Model 1934" (Z. Fitzgerald), **Supp. IX:** 61
Auden, W. H., **I:** 71, 381, 539; **II:** 367, 368, 371, 376, 586; **III:** 17, 134, 269, 271, 292, 476-477, 504, 527, 530, 542, 615; **IV:** 136, 138, 240, 430; **Retro. Supp. I:** 430; **Retro. Supp. II:** 183, 242, 244, 323; **Supp. I Part 1:** 270; **Supp. I Part 2:** 552, 610; **Supp. II Part 1: 1-28; Supp. III Part 1:** 2, 3, 14, 26, 60, 61, 64, 341; **Supp. III Part 2:** 591, 595; **Supp. IV Part 1:** 79, 84, 136, 225, 302, 313; **Supp. IV Part 2:** 440, 465; **Supp. V:** 337; **Supp. VIII:** 19, 21, 22, 23, 30, 32, 155, 190; **Supp. IX:** 94, 287, 288; **Supp. X:** 35, 57, 59, 115-116, 117, 118-119; **Supp. XI:** 243, 244; **Supp. XII:** 253, 264-265, 266, 269-270; **Supp. XIV:**156, 158, 160, 162, 163; **Supp. XV:** 74, 117-118, 139, 144, 186
"Auden's OED" (McClatchy), **Supp. XII:** 264-265
"Audition" (Alvarez), **Supp. VII:** 10
Audubon, John James, **III:** 210; **IV:** 265; **Supp. IX:** 171; **Supp. XVI:**1-14
Audubon, John Woodhouse, **Supp. XVI:**10
Audubon, Maria Rebecca, **Supp. XVI:**11
Audubon, Victor Gifford, **Supp. XVI:**10
Audubon and His Journals (M. Audubon, ed.), **Supp. XVI:**11, 12
Audubon Reader, The: The Best Writings of John James Audubon (Sanders, ed.), **Supp. XVI:**269
Auer, Jane. *See* Bowles, Jane
Auerbach, Eric, **III:** 453
Auerbach, Nina, **Supp. I Part 1:** 40
"August" (Oliver), **Supp. VII:** 235
"August" (Rich), **Supp. I Part 2:** 564
"August 1968" (Auden), **Supp. II Part 1:** 25
"August Darks, The" (Clampitt), **Supp. IX:** 43, **50-51,** 52
Augustine, Saint, **I:** 279, 290; **II:** 537; **III:** 259, 270, 292, 300; **IV:** 69, 126; **Retro. Supp. I:** 247; **Supp. VIII:** 203; **Supp. XI:** 245; **Supp. XIII:** 89
August Snow (Price), **Supp. VI:** 264
"Au Jardin" (Pound), **III:** 465-466
Aunt Carmen's Book of Practical Saints (Mora), **Supp. XIII: 227-229**
"Aunt Cynthy Dallett" (Jewett), **II:** 393
"Aunt Gladys" (Karr), **Supp. XI:** 241
"Aunt Imogen" (Robinson), **III:** 521
"Aunt Jemima of the Ocean Waves" (Hayden), **Supp. II Part 1:** 368, 379
"Aunt Jennifer's Tigers" (Rich), **Supp. XV:** 252
Aunt Jo's Scrapbooks (Alcott), **Supp. I Part 1:** 43
"Aunt Mary" (Oliver), **Supp. VII:** 232
"Aunt Mary" (Stowe), **Supp. I Part 2:** 587
"Aunt Moon's Young Man" (Hogan), **Supp. IV Part 1:** 400
"Aunt Rectita's Good Friday" (X. J. Kennedy), **Supp. XV:** 166
"Aunt Sarah" (Lowell), **II:** 554
"Aunt Sue's Stories" (Hughes), **Retro. Supp. I:** 197, 199
"Aunt Violet's Canadian Honeymoon/ 1932" (Shields), **Supp. VII:** 311
"Aunt Violet's Things" (Shields), **Supp. VII:** 311-312
"Aurelia: Moon Jellies" (Mora), **Supp. XIII:** 224
Aurora Leigh (E. Browning), **Retro. Supp. I:** 33; **Supp. XI:** 197
Aurora Means Dawn (Sanders), **Supp. XVI:**268

Auroras of Autumn, The (Stevens), **Retro. Supp. I:** 297, 300, **309-312**
"Auroras of Autumn, The" (Stevens), **Retro. Supp. I:** 311, 312; **Supp. III Part 1:** 12
Auschwitz: the Nazis and the "Final Solution" (television documentary), **Supp. XVII:** 40
Auslander, Joseph, **Supp. XIV:**120
"Auspex" (Frost), **Retro. Supp. I:** 122
"Auspex" (Lowell), **Supp. I Part 2:** 424
Austen, Jane, **I:** 130, 339, 375, 378; **II:** 272, 278, 287, 568-569, 577; **IV:** 8; **Retro. Supp. I:** 354; **Supp. I Part 1:** 267; **Supp. I Part 2:** 656, 715; **Supp. IV Part 1:** 300; **Supp. VIII:** 125, 167; **Supp. IX:** 128; **Supp. XII:** 310; **Supp. XV:** 338
Auster, Paul, **Supp. XII: 21-39; Supp. XIV:**292
Austerities (Simic), **Supp. VIII: 276-278,** 283
"Austerities" (Simic), **Supp. VIII:** 277
Austin, Mary Hunter, **Retro. Supp. I:** 7; **Supp. IV Part 2:** 503; **Supp. X:** 29; **Supp. XIII:** 154
"Authentic Unconscious, The" (Trilling), **Supp. III Part 2:** 512
Author and Agent: Eudora Welty and Diarmuid Russell (Kreyling), **Retro. Supp. I:** 342, 345, 347, 349-350
"Author at Sixty, The" (Wilson), **IV:** 426
"Author of 'Beltraffio,' The" (James), **Retro. Supp. I:** 227
"Author's House" (Fitzgerald), **Retro. Supp. I:** 98
"Author's Reflections, An: Willie Loman, Walter Younger, and He Who Must Live" (Hansberry), **Supp. IV Part 1:** 370
"Author to Her Book, The" (Bradstreet), **Supp. I Part 1:** 119; **Supp. V:** 117-118; **Supp. XV:** 125-126
"Autobiographical Note" (H. Miller), **III:** 174-175
"Autobiographical Notes" (Baldwin), **Supp. I Part 1:** 54
"Autobiographical Notes" (Holmes), **Supp. I Part 1:** 301
"Autobiographic Chapter, An" (Bourne), **I:** 236
Autobiography (Franklin), **II:** 102, 103, 108, 121-122, 302
Autobiography (James), **I:** 462
"Autobiography" (MacLeish), **III:** 20
Autobiography (Van Buren), **III:** 473
Autobiography (W. C. Williams), **Supp. I Part 1:** 254
Autobiography (Zukofsky), **Supp. III Part 2:** 627
"Autobiography in the Shape of a Book Review" (Bynner), **Supp. XV:** 40
"Autobiography of a Confluence, The" (Gunn Allen), **Supp. IV Part 1:** 321
Autobiography of Alice B. Toklas, The (Stein), **IV:** 26, 30, 35, 43; **Supp. IV Part 1:** 11, 81
Autobiography of an Ex-Colored Man, The (Johnson), **Supp. II Part 1:** 33, 194
Autobiography of a Schizophrenic Girl (Renée), **Supp. XVI:**64, 66
Autobiography of a Thief, The (Hapgood), **Supp. XVII:** 96, 101-102
Autobiography of Benjamin Franklin (Franklin), **Supp. IV Part 1:** 5
Autobiography of LeRoi Jones, The (Baraka), **Retro. Supp. I:** 411
Autobiography of Malcolm X (Little), **Supp. I Part 1:** 66; **Supp. X:** 27; **Supp. XIII:** 264
Autobiography of Mark Twain, The (Twain), **IV:** 209
Autobiography of My Mother, The (Kincaid), **Supp. VII:** 182, 188-190, 191, 192, 193
Autobiography of Red: A Novel in Verse (Carson), **Supp. XII:** 97, **106-110**
Autobiography of Upton Sinclair, The (Sinclair), **Supp. V:** 276, 282
Autobiography of W. E. B. Du Bois, The (Du Bois), **Supp. II Part 1:** 159, 186
Autobiography of William Carlos Williams, The (W. C. Williams), **Retro. Supp. I:** 51, 428
Autocrat of the Breakfast-Table, The (Holmes), **Supp. I Part 1:** 306-307
"Automatic Gate, The" (Southern), **Supp. XI:** 294
"Automotive Passacaglia" (H. Miller), **III:** 186
"Autopsy Room, The" (Carver), **Supp. III Part 1:** 137
"Auto Wreck" (Shapiro), **Supp. II Part 2:** 706
"Autre Temps" (Wharton), **IV:** 320, 324
"Autumn Afternoon" (Farrell), **II:** 45
"Autumnal" (Eberhart), **I:** 540-541
"Autumn Begins in Martins Ferry, Ohio" (Wright), **Supp. III Part 2:** 599
"Autumn Courtship, An" (Caldwell), **I:** 309
Autumn Garden, The (Hellman), **Supp. I Part 1:** 285-286, 290
"Autumn Garden, The: Mechanics and Dialectics" (Felheim), **Supp. I Part 1:** 297
"Autumn Holiday, An" (Jewett), **II:** 391; **Retro. Supp. II:** 140-141
"Autumn Musings" (Harte), **Supp. II Part 1:** 336
"Autumn Within" (Longfellow), **II:** 499
"Autumn Woods" (Bryant), **Supp. I Part 1:** 164
"Au Vieux Jardin" (Aldington), **Supp. I Part 1:** 257
"Aux Imagistes" (W. C. Williams), **Supp. I Part 1:** 266
Avakian, Aram, **Supp. XI:** 294, 295, 309
"Ave Atque Vale" (Bynner), **Supp. XV:** 49
Avedon, Richard, **Supp. I Part 1:** 58; **Supp. V:** 194; **Supp. X:** 15
Aveling, Edward, **Supp. XVI:**85
"Avenue" (Pinsky), **Supp. VI:** 248
Avenue Bearing the Initial of Christ into the New World: Poems 1946-1964 (Kinnell), **Supp. III Part 1:** 235, 239-241
"Avenue of the Americas" (Simic), **Supp. VIII:** 278
"Average Torture" (Karr), **Supp. XI:** 243
Avery, John, **Supp. I Part 1:** 153
"Avey" (Toomer), **Supp. IX:** 317
Avon's Harvest (Robinson), **III:** 510
Awake and Sing! (Odets), **Supp. II Part 2:** 530, 531, 536-538, 550; **Supp. IV Part 2:** 587
Awakening, The (Chopin), **Retro. Supp. I:** 10; **Retro. Supp. II:** 57, 59, 60, 67, **68-71,** 73; **Supp. I Part 1:** 200, 201, 202, 211, 220-225; **Supp. V:** 304; **Supp. VIII:** 198; **Supp. XII:** 170
Awful Rowing Toward God, The (Sexton), **Supp. II Part 2:** 694-696
Awiakta, Marilou, **Supp. IV Part 1:** 319, 335
Awkward Age, The (James), **II:** 332; **Retro. Supp. I:** 229, **230-231**
Axe Handles (Snyder), **Supp. VIII: 303-305**
Axel's Castle: A Study in the Imaginative Literature of 1870 to 1930 (Wilson), **I:** 185; **II:** 577; **IV:** 428, 431, 438, 439, 443; **Supp. VIII:** 101
"Ax-Helve, The" (Frost), **Retro. Supp. I:** 133

Azikewe, Nnamdi, **Supp. IV Part 1:** 361
"Aztec Angel" (Salinas), **Supp. XIII:** 314
Aztec Treasure House, The: New and Selected Essays (Connell), **Supp. XIV:** 80, 97

B

B. F.'s Daughter (Marquand), **III:** 59, 65, 68, 69
Babbitt (Lewis), **II:** 442, 443-445, 446, 447, 449; **III:** 63-64, 394; **IV:** 326
Babbitt, Irving, **I:** 247; **II:** 456; **III:** 315, 461, 613; **IV:** 439; **Retro. Supp. I:** 55; **Supp. I Part 2:** 423
Babcock, Elisha, **Supp. II Part 1:** 69
Babel, Isaac, **IV:** 1; **Supp. IX:** 260; **Supp. XII:** 308-309; **Supp. XVII:** 41
Babel, Isaak, **Supp. XIV:** 83, 84
Babel to Byzantium (Dickey), **Supp. IV Part 1:** 177, 185
Babeuf, François, **Supp. I Part 2:** 518
"Babies, The" (Strand), **Supp. IV Part 2:** 625
Babouk (Endore), **Supp. XVII:** 56-57, 61, 64
Baby, Come on Inside (Wagoner), **Supp. IX:** 335
"Baby, The" (Barthelme), **Supp. IV Part 1:** 49
Baby Doll (T. Williams), **IV:** 383, 386, 387, 389, 395
"Baby Face" (Sandburg), **III:** 584
"Babylon Revisited" (Fitzgerald), **II:** 95; **Retro. Supp. I:** 109
"Baby or the Botticelli, The" (Gass), **Supp. VI:** 92
"Baby Pictures of Famous Dictators" (Simic), **Supp. VIII:** 276
"Baby's Breath" (Bambara), **Supp. XI:** 15, 16
"Babysitter, The" (Coover), **Supp. V:** 43-44
"Baby Villon" (Levine), **Supp. V:** 182
Bacall, Lauren, **Supp. IV Part 1:** 130
"Baccalaureate" (MacLeish), **III:** 4
Bacchae, The (Euripides), **Supp. VIII:** 182
Bach, Johann Sebastian, **Supp. I Part 1:** 363; **Supp. III Part 2:** 611, 612, 619
Bachardy, Don, **Supp. XIV:** 166, 170, 172, 173
Bache, Richard, **Supp. I Part 2:** 504
Bachelard, Gaston, **Supp. XIII:** 225; **Supp. XVI:** 292
Bachelor Girls (Wasserstein), **Supp. XV:** 327-328, 332
Bachman, John, **Supp. XVI:** 10, 11

Bachmann, Ingeborg, **Supp. IV Part 1:** 310; **Supp. VIII:** 272
Bachofen, J. J., **Supp. I Part 2:** 560, 567
Back Bog Beast Bait (Shepard), **Supp. III Part 2:** 437, 438
Backbone (C. Bly), **Supp. XVI:** 34-36, 37, 40, 41
Back Country, The (Snyder), **Supp. VIII:** 296-299
"Back fom the Argentine" (Leopold), **Supp. XIV:** 186
"Background with Revolutionaries" (MacLeish), **III:** 14-15
Back in The World (Wolff), **Supp. VII:** 345
Back in the World (Wolff), **Supp. VII:** 344
"Backlash Blues, The" (Hughes), **Supp. I Part 1:** 343
"Backlash of Kindness, A" (Nye), **Supp. XIII:** 285, 286
Back to China (Fiedler), **Supp. XIII:** 102-103
Back to Methuselah (Shaw), **IV:** 64
"Backwacking: A Plea to the Senator" (Ellison), **Retro. Supp. II:** 126; **Supp. II Part 1:** 248
Backward Glance, A (Wharton), **Retro. Supp. I:** 360, 363, 366, 378, 380, 382
"Backward Glance o'er Travel'd Roads, A" (Whitman), **IV:** 348
Bacon, Francis, **II:** 1, 8, 11, 15-16, 111; **III:** 284; **Retro. Supp. I:** 247; **Supp. I Part 1:** 310; **Supp. I Part 2:** 388; **Supp. IX:** 104; **Supp. XIV:** 22, 210
Bacon, Helen, **Supp. X:** 57
Bacon, Leonard, **II:** 530
Bacon, Roger, **IV:** 69
"Bacterial War, The" (Nemerov), **III:** 272
Bad Boy Brawly Brown (Mosley), **Supp. XIII:** 237, 239, 240-241
Bad Boys (Cisneros), **Supp. VII:** 58
"Bad Dream" (Taylor), **Supp. V:** 320
Badè, William Frederic, **Supp. IX:** 178
"Bad Fisherman, The" (Wagoner), **Supp. IX:** 328
Bad for Each Other (film), **Supp. XIII:** 174
"Badger" (Clare), **II:** 387
Badger, A. G., **Supp. I Part 1:** 356
Bad Government and Silly Literature (C. Bly), **Supp. XVI:** 37, 38, 40
Badlands (film; Malick), **Supp. XV:** 351
"Bad Lay" (McCarriston), **Supp. XIV:** 267

Badley, Linda, **Supp. V:** 148
Bad Man, A (Elkin), **Supp. VI:** 47
Bad Man Ballad (Sanders), **Supp. XVI:** 268
Bad Man Blues: A Portable George Garrett (Garrett), **Supp. VII:** 111
"Bad Music, The" (Jarrell), **II:** 369
"Bad Woman, A" (Fante), **Supp. XI:** 165
Baeck, Leo, **Supp. V:** 260
Baecker, Diann L., **Supp. VIII:** 128
Baer, William, **Supp. XIII:** 112, 118, 129
Baez, Joan, **Supp. IV Part 1:** 200; **Supp. VIII:** 200, 202
Bag of Bones (King), **Supp. V:** 139, 148, 151
"Bagpipe Music" (MacNeice), **Supp. X:** 117
"Baháʼí Faith: Only Church in World That Does Not Discriminate" (Locke), **Supp. XIV:** 200
"Baháʼuʼlláh in the Garden of Ridwan" (Hayden), **Supp. II Part 1:** 370, 378
Bahr, David, **Supp. XV:** 66
"Bailbondsman, The" (Elkin), **Supp. VI:** 49, **50**, 58
Bailey, Gamaliel, **Supp. I Part 2:** 587, 590
Bailey, Peter, **Supp. XVI:** 69
Bailey, William, **Supp. IV Part 2:** 631, 634
Bailey's Café (Naylor), **Supp. VIII:** 226-228
Bailyn, Bernard, **Supp. I Part 2:** 484, 506
Bair, Deirdre, **Supp. X:** 181, 186, 187, 188, 192, 194, 195, 196, 197
Baird, Linnett, **Supp. XII:** 299
Baird, Peggy, **I:** 385, 401
Bakan, David, **I:** 59
Baker, Carlos, **II:** 259
Baker, David, **Supp. IX:** 298; **Supp. XI:** 121, 142, 153; **Supp. XII:** 175, 191-192
Baker, George Pierce, **III:** 387; **IV:** 453, 455
Baker, Gladys, **Supp. XIV:** 121
Baker, Houston A., Jr., **Retro. Supp. II:** 121; **Supp. IV Part 1:** 365; **Supp. X:** 324
Baker, Kevin, **Supp. XIV:** 96
Baker, Nicholson, **Supp. XIII:** 41-57
Baker, Robert, **Supp. XVI:** 288, 290
Bakerman, Jane S., **Supp. IV Part 2:** 468
Bakhtin, Mikhail, **Retro. Supp. II:** 273; **Supp. IV Part 1:** 301; **Supp. X:** 120, 239
Bakst, Léon, **Supp. IX:** 66

Bakunin, Mikhail Aleksandrovich, **IV:** 429
Balakian, Jan, **Supp. XV:** 327
"Balance" (Bierds), **Supp. XVII:** 31
Balbo, Ned, **Supp. XVII:** 120
Balbuena, Bernado de, **Supp. V:** 11
Balch, Emily Greene, **Supp. I Part 1:** 25
Balcony, The (Genet), **I:** 84
Bald Soprano, The (Ionesco), **I:** 74
Baldwin, David, **Supp. I Part 1:** 47, 48, 49, 50, 51, 54, 65, 66
Baldwin, James, **Retro. Supp. II:** 1-17; **Supp. I Part 1: 47-71,** 337, 341; **Supp. II Part 1:** 40; **Supp. III Part 1:** 125; **Supp. IV Part 1:** 1, 10, 11, 163, 369; **Supp. V:** 201; **Supp. VIII:** 88, 198, 235, 349; **Supp. X:** 136, 324; **Supp. XI:** 288, 294; **Supp. XIII:** 46, 111, 181, 186, 294; **Supp. XIV:**54, 71, 73, 306; **Supp. XVI:**135, 141, 143
Baldwin, Samuel, **Supp. I Part 1:** 48
Balitas, Vincent D., **Supp. XVI:**222
Balkian, Nona, **Supp. XI:** 230
Ball, Gordon, **Supp. XIV:**148
Ball, John, **Supp. XV:** 202
"Ballad: Between the Box Cars" (Warren), **IV:** 245
"Ballade" (MacLeish), **III:** 4
"Ballade at Thirty-Five" (Parker), **Supp. IX:** 192
"Ballade for the Duke of Orléans" (Wilbur), **Supp. III Part 2:** 556
"Ballade of Broken Flutes, The" (Robinson), **III:** 505
"Ballade of Meaty Inversions" (White), **Supp. I Part 2:** 676
"Ballad of Billie Potts, The" (Warren), **IV:** 241-242, 243, 253
"Ballad of Carmilhan, The" (Longfellow), **II:** 505
"ballad of chocolate Mabbie, the" (Brooks), **Supp. IV Part 1:** 15
"Ballad of Dead Ladies, The" (Villon), **Retro. Supp. I:** 286
Ballad of Dingus Magee, The (Markson), **Supp. XVII:** 139, 141
"Ballad of East and West" (Kipling), **Supp. IX:** 246
"Ballad of Jesse Neighbours, The" (Humphrey), **Supp. IX:** 100
"Ballad of Jesus of Nazareth, A" (Masters), **Supp. I Part 2:** 459
"Ballad of John Cable and Three Gentlemen" (Merwin), **Supp. III Part 1:** 342
"Ballad of Larry and Club" (Jarman), **Supp. XVII:** 115
"Ballad of Nat Turner, The" (Hayden), **Supp. II Part 1:** 378
"Ballad of Pearl May Lee, The" (Brooks), **Supp. III Part 1:** 74, 75
Ballad of Remembrance, A (Hayden), **Supp. II Part 1:** 367
"Ballad of Remembrance, A" (Hayden), **Supp. II Part 1:** 368, 372, 373
"Ballad of Ruby, The" (Sarton), **Supp. VIII:** 259-260
"Ballad of Sue Ellen Westerfield, The" (Hayden), **Supp. II Part 1:** 364
Ballad of the Brown Girl, The (Cullen), **Supp. IV Part 1:** 167, 168, 169-170, 173
"Ballad of the Brown Girl, The" (Cullen), **Supp. IV Part 1:** 168
"Ballad of the Children of the Czar, The" (Schwartz), **Supp. II Part 2:** 649
"Ballad of the Girl Whose Name Is Mud" (Hughes), **Retro. Supp. I:** 205
"Ballad of the Goodly Fere," **III:** 458
"Ballad of the Harp-Weaver" (Millay), **III:** 135
"Ballad of the Sad Cafe, The" (McCullers), **II:** 586, 587, 588, 592, 595, 596-600, 604, 605, 606
"Ballad of the Sixties" (Sarton), **Supp. VIII:** 259
"Ballad of Trees and the Master, A" (Lanier), **Supp. I Part 1:** 370
"Ballad of William Sycamore, The" (Benét), **Supp. XI:** 44, 47
Ballads and Other Poems (Longfellow), **II:** 489; **III:** 412, 422; **Retro. Supp. II:** 157, 168
Ballads for Sale (Lowell), **II:** 527
"Ballads of Lenin" (Hughes), **Supp. I Part 1:** 331
Ballantyne, Sheila, **Supp. V:** 70
Ballard, J. G., **Supp. XVI:**123, 124
Ballard, Josephine. *See* McMurtry, Josephine
"Ballena" (Mora), **Supp. XIII:** 224
"Ballet in Numbers for Mary Ellen, A" (Karr), **Supp. XI:** 241
"Ballet of a Buffoon, The" (Sexton), **Supp. II Part 2:** 693
"Ballet of the Fifth Year, The" (Schwartz), **Supp. II Part 2:** 650
"Ball Game, The" (Creeley), **Supp. IV Part 1:** 140
"Balloon Hoax, The" (Poe), **III:** 413, 420
"Balm of Recognition, The: Rectifying Wrongs through Generations" (E. Hoffman, lecture), **Supp. XVI:**155
Balo (Toomer), **Supp. III Part 2:** 484

Balsan, Consuelo, **IV:** 313-314
Balthus, **Supp. IV Part 2:** 623
Balthus Poems, The (Dobyns), **Supp. XIII:** 87
Baltimore, Lord, **I:** 132
Balzac, Honoré de, **I:** 103, 123, 339, 376, 474, 485, 499, 509, 518; **II:** 307, 322, 324, 328, 336, 337; **III:** 61, 174, 184, 320, 382; **IV:** 192; **Retro. Supp. I:** 91, 217, 218, 235; **Retro. Supp. II:** 93; **Supp. I Part 2:** 647; **Supp. XVI:**72
Bambara, Toni Cade, **Supp. XI: 1-23**
Banana Bottom (McKay), **Supp. X:** 132, **139-140**
Bananas (film; Allen), **Supp. XV:** 3, 4
Bancal, Jean, **Supp. I Part 2:** 514
Bancroft, George, **I:** 544; **Supp. I Part 2:** 479
Band of Angels (Warren), **IV:** 245, 254-255
Bang the Drum Slowly (Harris), **II:** 424-425
Banjo: A Story without a Plot (McKay), **Supp. X:** 132, **138-139**
"Banjo Song, A" (Dunbar), **Supp. II Part 1:** 197
Bankhead, Tallulah, **IV:** 357; **Supp. IV Part 2:** 574
"Banking Potatoes" (Komunyakaa), **Supp. XIII:** 126
"Bank of England Restriction, The" (Adams), **I:** 4
Banks, Joanne Trautmann, **Supp. XIII:** 297
Banks, Russell, **Supp. V: 1-19,** 227; **Supp. IX:** 153; **Supp. X:** 85; **Supp. XI:** 178; **Supp. XII:** 295, 309, 343
"Banned Poem" (Nye), **Supp. XIII:** 282
Bannon, Barbara, **Supp. XI:** 228
"Banyan" (Swenson), **Supp. IV Part 2:** 651, 652
"Baptism" (Olsen). *See* "O Yes" (Olsen)
Baptism, The (Baraka), **Supp. II Part 1:** 40, 41-42, 43
Baptism of Desire (Erdrich), **Supp. IV Part 1:** 259
"B.A.R. Man, The" (Yates), **Supp. XI:** 341
Barabtarlo, Gennady, **Retro. Supp. I:** 278
Baraka, Imamu Amiri (LeRoi Jones), **Retro. Supp. I:** 411; **Retro. Supp. II:** 280; **Supp. I Part 1:** 63; **Supp. II Part 1: 29-63,** 247, 250; **Supp. III Part 1:** 83; **Supp. IV Part 1:** 169, 244, 369; **Supp. VIII:** 295, 329, 330, 332; **Supp. X:** 324, 328;

Supp. XIII: 94; **Supp. XIV:**125, 144
"Bar at the Andover Inn, The" (Matthews), **Supp. IX:** 168
"Barbados" (Marshall), **Supp. XI:** 281
"Barbara Frietchie" (Whittier), **Supp. I Part 2:** 695-696
Barbarella (film), **Supp. XI:** 293, **307-308**
"Barbarian Status of Women, The" (Veblen), **Supp. I Part 2:** 636-637
Barbarous Coast, The (Macdonald), **Supp. IV Part 2:** 472, 474
Barbary Shore (Mailer), **III:** 27, 28, 30-31, 33, 35, 36, 40, 44; **Retro. Supp. II: 199-200,** 207; **Supp. XIV:**162
Barber, David, **Supp. IV Part 2:** 550; **Supp. XII:** 188-189
Barber, Rowland, **Supp. IV Part 2:** 581
Barber, Samuel, **Supp. IV Part 1:** 84
"Barclay of Ury" (Whittier), **Supp. I Part 2:** 693
Barcott, Bruce, **Supp. XVII:** 32
Bard of Savagery, The: Thorstein Veblen and Modern Social Theory (Diggins), **Supp. I Part 2:** 650
"Barefoot Boy, The" (Whittier), **Supp. I Part 2:** 691, 699-700
Barefoot in the Park (Simon), **Supp. IV Part 2:** 575, 578-579, 586, 590
Bare Hills, The (Winters), **Supp. II Part 2:** 786, 788
"Bare Hills, The" (Winters), **Supp. II Part 2:** 790
Barely and Widely (Zukofsky), **Supp. III Part 2:** 627, 628, 635
Barenblat, Rachel, **Supp. XIII:** 274
Barfield, Owen, **III:** 274, 279
"Bargain Lost, The" (Poe), **III:** 411
Barillas, William, **Supp. XIV:**177
Barillet, Pierre, **Supp. XVI:**194
Barker, Arthur, **Supp. XIII:** 167
Barker, Clive, **Supp. V:** 142
"Barking Man" (Bell), **Supp. X:** 9
Barking Man and Other Stories (Bell), **Supp. X:** 9
Barksdale, Richard, **Retro. Supp. I:** 202, 205; **Supp. I Part 1:** 341, 346
Barlow, Joel, **Supp. I Part 1:** 124; **Supp. I Part 2:** 511, 515, 521; **Supp. II Part 1: 65-86,** 268
Barlow, Ruth Baldwin (Mrs. Joel Barlow), **Supp. II Part 1:** 69
Barnaby Rudge (Dickens), **III:** 421
Barnard, Frederick, **Supp. I Part 2:** 684
Barnard, Rita, **Retro. Supp. II:** 324

Barn Blind (Smiley), **Supp. VI:** 292-293
"Barn Burning" (Faulkner), **II:** 72, 73; **Supp. IV Part 2:** 682
Barnes, Djuna, **Supp. III Part 1: 31-46; Supp. IV Part 1:** 79, 80; **Supp. XVI:**282
Barnett, Claudia, **Supp. XV:** 323, 330, 334
Barnett, Samuel, **Supp. I Part 1:** 2
Barnstone, Tony, **Supp. XIII:** 115, 126
Barnstone, Willis, **Supp. I Part 2:** 458
Barnum, P. T., **Supp. I Part 2:** 703
Baroja, Pío, **I:** 478
"Baroque Comment" (Bogan), **Supp. III Part 1:** 56, 58
"Baroque Sunburst, A" (Clampitt), **Supp. IX:** 49
"Baroque Wall-Fountain in the Villa Sciarra, A" (Wilbur), **Supp. III Part 2:** 553
Barr, Robert, **I:** 409, 424
Barracks Thief, The (Wolff), **Supp. VII:** 344-345
Barren Ground (Glasgow), **II:** 174, 175, 178, 179, 184-185, 186, 187, 188, 189, 191, 192, 193, 194; **Supp. X:** 228
Barrés, Auguste M., **I:** 228
Barresi, Dorothy, **Supp. XV:** 100, 102
Barrett, E. B., **Supp. XV:** 309
Barrett, Elizabeth, **Supp. IV Part 2:** 430
Barrett, George, **Supp. IX:** 250
Barrett, Ralph, **Supp. I Part 2:** 462
Barrier of a Common Language: An American Looks at Contemporary British Poetry (Gioia), **Supp. XV:** 112, **116-117**
"Barroco: An Essay" (Sobin), **Supp. XVI:**291
Barron, Jonathan, **Supp. IX:** 299
Barrow, John, **II:** 18
Barrus, Clara, **I:** 220
Barry, Iris, **Supp. XIII:** 170
Barry, Philip, **Retro. Supp. I:** 104; **Supp. IV Part 1:** 83; **Supp. V:** 95
Barstow, Elizabeth Drew. See Stoddard, Elizabeth
Bartas, Seigneur du, **IV:** 157
Barth, John, **I: 121-143; Supp. I Part 1:** 100; **Supp. III Part 1:** 217; **Supp. IV Part 1:** 48, 379; **Supp. V:** 39, 40; **Supp. IX:** 208; **Supp. X:** 263, 301, 302, 307; **Supp. XI:** 309; **Supp. XII:** 29, 289, 316; **Supp. XIII:** 41, 101, 104; **Supp. XVII:** 183
Barth, Karl, **III:** 40, 258, 291, 303,
309; **IV:** 225; **Retro. Supp. I:** 325, 326, 327
Barth, Robert C., **Supp. XV:** 169
Barthé, Richmond, **Retro. Supp. II:** 115
Barthelme, Donald, **Supp. IV Part 1: 39-58,** 227; **Supp. V:** 2, 39, 44; **Supp. VIII:** 75, 138; **Supp. X:** 263; **Supp. XI:** 25; **Supp. XII:** 29; **Supp. XIII:** 41, 46; **Supp. XVI:**206
Barthelme, Frederick, **Supp. XI: 25-41**
Barthelme, Peter, **Supp. XI:** 25
Barthelme, Steven, **Supp. XI:** 25, 27, 37
Barthes, Roland, **Supp. IV Part 1:** 39, 119, 126; **Supp. XIII:** 83; **Supp. XVI:**285, 294; **Supp. XVII:** 244
Bartholomew and the Oobleck (Geisel), **Supp. XVI:**104
"Bar Time" (B. Collins), **Supp. XVII:** 245
"Bartleby, the Scrivener; A Story of Wall-Street" (Melville), **III:** 88-89; **Retro. Supp. I:** 255
Bartleby in Manhattan and Other Essays (Hardwick), **Supp. III Part 1:** 204, 210
Bartlet, Phebe, **I:** 562
Bartlett, Lee, **Supp. VIII:** 291
Bartlett, Mary Dougherty, **Supp. IV Part 1:** 335
Barton, Bruce, **III:** 14; **Retro. Supp. I:** 179
Barton, Priscilla. *See* Morison, Mrs. Samuel Eliot (Priscilla Barton)
Barton, Ralph, **Supp. XVI:**195
Barton, Rev. William E., **Retro. Supp. I:** 179
Bartov, Omer, **Supp. XVI:**153-154
Bartram, John, **Supp. I Part 1:** 244
Bartram, William, **II:** 313; **Supp. IX:** 171; **Supp. X:** 223
Barzun, Jacques, **Supp. XIV:**54
"Basement" (Bambara), **Supp. XI:** 5
"Base of All Metaphysics, The" (Whitman), **IV:** 348
"Base Stealer, The" (Francis), **Supp. IX:** 82
Bashevis, Isaac. *See* Singer, Isaac Bashevis
Basil Stories, The (Fitzgerald), **Retro. Supp. I:** 109
Basin and Range (McPhee), **Supp. III Part 1:** 309
"Basin of Eggs, A" (Swenson), **Supp. IV Part 2:** 645
"Basket, The" (Lowell), **II:** 522
"Basketball and Beefeaters" (McPhee), **Supp. III Part 1:** 296
"Basketball and Poetry: The Two Rich-

ies" (Dunn), **Supp. XI:** 140
"Basketball Player" (L. Michaels), **Supp. XVI:**209
Baskin, Leonard, **Supp. X:** 58, 71; **Supp. XV:** 348
Bass, Rick, **Supp. XIV:**227; **Supp. XVI:15-29**
Basso, Hamilton, **Retro. Supp. I:** 80
Bastard, The (Caldwell), **I:** 291, 292, 308
"Bat, The" (Kenyon), **Supp. VII:** 168
Bataille, Georges, **Supp. VIII:** 4; **Supp. XII:** 1
"Batard" (London), **II:** 468-469
Bate, W. J., **II:** 531
Bates, Arlo, **Retro. Supp. I:** 35
Bates, Blanche, **Supp. XVI:**182
Bates, Kathy, **Supp. XIII:** 207
Bates, Lee, **Retro. Supp. II:** 46
Bates, Milton J., **Supp. XII:** 62
Bates, Sylvia Chatfield, **II:** 586
Bateson, Gregory, **Supp. XV:** 146
"Bath, The" (Carver), **Supp. III Part 1:** 144, 145
"Bath, The" (Snyder), **Supp. VIII:** 302
Bathwater Wine (Coleman), **Supp. XI:** 83, 90, **91**
"Batter my heart, three person'd God" (Donne), **Supp. I Part 2:** 726; **Supp. XVII:** 119
"Battle, The" (Simpson), **Supp. IX:** 268-269
Battlefield Where the Moon Says I Love You, The (Stanford), **Supp. XV:** 345
Battle-Ground, The (Glasgow), **II:** 175, 176, 177, 178, 193
"Battle Hymn of the Republic" (Sandburg), **III:** 585
"Battle Hymn of the Republic, The" (Howe), **III:** 505
"Battle Hymn of the Republic, The" (Updike), **Retro. Supp. I:** 324
Battle of Angels (T. Williams), **IV:** 380, 381, 383, 385, 386, 387
"Battle of Lovell's Pond, The" (Longfellow), **II:** 493
Battle of the Atlantic, The (Morison), **Supp. I Part 2:** 490
"Battle of the Baltic, The" (Campbell), **Supp. I Part 1:** 309
"Battle of the Bunker, The" (Snodgrass), **Supp. VI:** 319-320
"***Battle of the Century!!!, The***" (Goldbarth), **Supp. XII:** 193
Battle-Pieces and Aspects of the War (Melville), **II:** 538-539; **III:** 92; **IV:** 350; **Retro. Supp. I:** 257
"Battler, The" (Hemingway), **II:** 248; **Retro. Supp. I:** 175
"Baudelaire" (Schwartz), **Supp. II Part 2:** 663
Baudelaire, Charles, **I:** 58, 63, 384, 389, 420, 569; **II:** 543, 544-545, 552; **III:** 137, 141-142, 143, 409, 417, 418, 421, 428, 448, 466, 474; **IV:** 74, 79, 80, 87, 211, 286; **Retro. Supp. I:** 56, 90; **Retro. Supp. II:** 261, 262, 322, 326; **Supp. I Part 1:** 271; **Supp. III Part 1:** 4, 6, 105; **Supp. XIII:** 77, 284
Baudelaire, Charles-Pierre, **Supp. XV:** 165
Baudrillard, Jean, **Supp. IV Part 1:** 45
Bauer, Dale, **Retro. Supp. I:** 381
Bauer, Douglas, **Supp. XII:** 290
Baum, L. Frank, **Supp. I Part 2:** 621; **Supp. IV Part 1:** 101, 113; **Supp. XII:** 42
Baumann, Walter, **III:** 478
Bausch, Richard, **Supp. VII: 39-56; Supp. XVII:** 21
Bawer, Bruce, **Supp. VIII:** 153; **Supp. IX:** 135; **Supp. X:** 187
Baxter, Charles, **Supp. XII:** 22; **Supp. XIV:**89, 92; **Supp. XVII: 13-24**
Baxter, John, **Supp. XI:** 302
Baxter, Richard, **III:** 199; **IV:** 151, 153; **Supp. I Part 2:** 683
"Baxter's Procrustes" (Chesnutt), **Supp. XIV:**76
"Bay City Blues" (Chandler), **Supp. IV Part 1:** 129
Baylies, William, **Supp. I Part 1:** 153
Baym, Nina, **Supp. IV Part 2:** 463; **Supp. X:** 229; **Supp. XVI:**92
Bayou Folk (Chopin), **Retro. Supp. II: 64-65,** 73; **Supp. I Part 1:** 200, 216, 218
Baziotes, William, **Supp. XV:** 144
Beach, Anna Hampstead, **Supp. XVII:** 75
Beach, Joseph Warren, **I:** 309, 500; **II:** 27; **III:** 319
Beach, Sylvia, **IV:** 404; **Retro. Supp. I:** 109, 422
"Beach Women, The" (Pinsky), **Supp. VI:** 241
"Beaded Pear, The" (Simpson), **Supp. IX:** 276
Beagle, Peter, **Supp. X:** 24
Beam, Jeffrey, **Supp. XII:** 98
Beaman, E. O., **Supp. IV Part 2:** 604
Bean, Michael, **Supp. V:** 203
Bean, Robert Bennett, **Supp. II Part 1:** 170
Bean Eaters, The (Brooks), **Supp. III Part 1:** 79-81
Be Angry at the Sun (Jeffers), **Supp. II Part 2:** 434
"Beanstalk Country, The" (T. Williams), **IV:** 383
Bean Trees, The (Kingsolver), **Supp. VII:** 197, 199-201, 202, 207, 209
"Bear" (Hogan), **Supp. IV Part 1:** 412
Bear, The (Faulkner), **Supp. VIII:** 184
"Bear, The" (Faulkner), **II:** 71-72, 73, 228; **IV:** 203; **Supp. IV Part 2:** 434; **Supp. IX:** 95; **Supp. X:** 30; **Supp. XIV:**32
"Bear, The" (Kinnell), **Supp. III Part 1:** 244
"Bear, The" (Momaday), **Supp. IV Part 2:** 480, 487
Bear and His Daughter: Stories (Stone), **Supp. V:** 295, 308
Beard, Charles, **I:** 214; **IV:** 429; **Supp. I Part 2:** 481, 490, 492, 632, 640, 643, 647
Beard, James, **I:** 341; **Supp. XVII:** 89, 90
Beard, Mary, **Supp. I Part 2:** 481
"Bearded Oaks" (Warren), **IV:** 240
Bearden, Romare, **Retro. Supp. I:** 209; **Supp. VIII:** 337, 342
"Beard of Bees, A" (X. J. Kennedy), **Supp. XV:** 171
Beardon, Romare, **Supp. XV:** 144
Beardsley, Aubrey, **II:** 56; **IV:** 77
Beaser, Robert, **Supp. XV:** 259
"Beast" (Swenson), **Supp. IV Part 2:** 639
"Beast & Burden, The: Seven Improvisations" (Komunyakaa), **Supp. XIII:** 120, 121
Beast God Forgot to Invent, The (Harrison), **Supp. VIII:** 37, 46, **51-52**
Beast in Me, The (Thurber), **Supp. I Part 2:** 615
"Beast in the Jungle, The" (James), **I:** 570; **II:** 335; **Retro. Supp. I:** 235; **Supp. V:** 103-104
Beast in View (Rukeyser), **Supp. VI:** 272, 273, 279, 280
Beasts of Bethlehem, The (X. J. Kennedy), **Supp. XV:** 163
"Beat! Beat! Drums!" (Whitman), **III:** 585
Beat Down to Your Soul: What Was the Beat Generation? (Charters, ed.), **Supp. XIV:**152
Beaton, Cecil, **Supp. XVI:**191
"Beatrice Palmato" (Wharton), **Retro. Supp. I:** 379
Beats, The (Krim, ed.), **Supp. XV:** 338
Beattie, Ann, **Supp. V: 21-37; Supp. XI:** 26; **Supp. XII:** 80, 139, 294
Beatty, General Sam, **I:** 193
Beaty, Jerome, **Supp. IV Part 1:** 331
"Beau Monde of Mrs. Bridge, The"

(Connell), **Supp. XIV:** 88, 89
Beaumont, Francis, **Supp. I Part 2:** 422
"Beauties of Santa Cruz, The" (Freneau), **Supp. II Part 1:** 260
Beautiful and Damned, The (Fitzgerald), **II:** 88, 89-91, 93, 263; **Retro. Supp. I: 103-105,** 105, 106, 110; **Supp. IX:** 56, 57
Beautiful Changes, The (Wilbur), **Supp. III Part 2:** 544-550
"Beautiful Changes, The" (Wilbur), **Supp. III Part 2:** 549, 550
"Beautiful Child, A" (Capote), **Supp. III Part 1:** 113, 125
"Beautiful & Cruel" (Cisneros), **Supp. VII:** 63, 67
"Beautiful Woman Who Sings, The" (Gunn Allen), **Supp. IV Part 1:** 326
"Beauty" (Emerson), **II:** 2, 5
"Beauty" (Sanders), **Supp. XVI:** 277
"Beauty" (Wylie), **Supp. I Part 2:** 710
"Beauty and the Beast" (Dove), **Supp. IV Part 1:** 245
"Beauty and the Beast" (fairy tale), **IV:** 266; **Supp. X:** 88
"Beauty and the Shoe Sluts" (Karr), **Supp. XI:** 250
Beauty of the Husband, The: A Fictional Essay in Twenty-Nine Tangos (Carson), **Supp. XII: 113-114**
Beauty's Punishment (Rice), **Supp. VII:** 301
Beauty's Release: The Continued Erotic Adventures of Sleeping Beauty (Rice), **Supp. VII:** 301
Beauvoir, Simone de, **IV:** 477; **Supp. I Part 1:** 51; **Supp. III Part 1:** 200-201, 208; **Supp. IV Part 1:** 360; **Supp. IX:** 4
"Be Careful" (Zach; Everwine, trans.), **Supp. XV:** 86
Be Careful How You Live (Lacy), **Supp. XV:** 203-204
"Because I could not stop for Death-" (Dickinson), **Retro. Supp. I: 38-40,** 41, 43, 44
"Because It Happened" (Goldbarth), **Supp. XII:** 192
"Because of Libraries We Can Say These Things" (Nye), **Supp. XIII:** 283
"Because You Mentioned the Spiritual Life" (Dunn), **Supp. XI:** 154
Bech: A Book (Updike), **IV:** 214; **Retro. Supp. I:** 329, 335
Beck, Dave, **I:** 493
Beck, Jack, **Supp. IV Part 2:** 560
Becker, Carl, **Supp. I Part 2:** 492, 493
Becker, Paula. *See* Modersohn, Mrs. Otto (Paula Becker)
Beckett, Samuel, **I:** 71, 91, 142, 298, 461; **III:** 387; **IV:** 95; **Retro. Supp. I:** 206; **Supp. IV Part 1:** 297, 368-369; **Supp. IV Part 2:** 424; **Supp. V:** 23, 53; **Supp. XI:** 104; **Supp. XII:** 21, 150-151; **Supp. XIII:** 74; **Supp. XIV:** 239; **Supp. XVII:** 185
Beckett, Tom, **Supp. IV Part 2:** 419
Beckford, William, **I:** 204
Beckonings (Brooks), **Supp. III Part 1:** 85
"Becky" (Toomer), **Supp. III Part 2:** 481, 483; **Supp. IX:** 312
Becoming a Man: Half a Life Story (Monette), **Supp. X:** 146, 147, 149, 151, 152, **155-157**
"Becoming a Meadow" (Doty), **Supp. XI:** 124-125
"Becoming and Breaking: Poet and Poem" (Ríos), **Supp. IV Part 2:** 539
Becoming Canonical in American Poetry (Morris), **Retro. Supp. I:** 40
Becoming Light: New and Selected Poems (Jong), **Supp. V:** 115
Bécquer, Gustavo Adolfo, **Supp. XIII:** 312
"Bed, The" (Dixon), **Supp. XII:** 154
Beddoes, Thomas Lovell, **III:** 469; **Retro. Supp. I:** 285
Bedichek, Roy, **Supp. V:** 225
Bedient, Calvin, **Supp. IX:** 298; **Supp. XII:** 98
"Bed in the Sky, The" (Snyder), **Supp. VIII:** 300
Bednarik, Joseph, **Supp. VIII:** 39
"Bedrock" (Proulx), **Supp. VII:** 253
"Bee, The" (Lanier), **Supp. I Part 1:** 364
Beecher, Catharine, **Supp. I Part 2:** 581, 582-583, 584, 586, 588, 589, 591, 599; **Supp. X:** 103; **Supp. XI:** 193
Beecher, Charles, **Supp. I Part 2:** 588, 589
Beecher, Edward, **Supp. I Part 2:** 581, 582, 583, 584, 588, 591
Beecher, Harriet. *See* Stowe, Harriet Beecher
Beecher, Henry Ward, **II:** 275; **Supp. I Part 2:** 581; **Supp. XI:** 193
Beecher, Lyman, **Supp. I Part 2:** 580-581, 582, 583, 587, 588, 599; **Supp. XI:** 193
Beecher, Mrs. Lyman (Roxanna Foote), **Supp. I Part 2:** 580-581, 582, 588, 599
Beeching, Jack, **Supp. X:** 114, 117, 118, 123, 125, 126
"Beehive" (Toomer), **Supp. IX:** 317
"Bee Hunt, The" (Irving), **II:** 313
"Beekeeper's Daughter, The" (Plath), **Retro. Supp. II:** 246-247
"Bee Meeting, The" (Plath), **Retro. Supp. II:** 254-255
Bee Poems (Plath), **Retro. Supp. II:** 254-255
Beer, John, **Supp. XVII:** 239
Beer, Thomas, **I:** 405
Beerbohm, Max, **III:** 472; **IV:** 436; **Supp. I Part 2:** 714
"Beer in the Sergeant Major's Hat, or The Sun Also Sneezes" (Chandler), **Supp. IV Part 1:** 121
"Bees Bees Bees" (J. Scott), **Supp. XVII:** 188, 190
Beethoven, Ludwig van, **II:** 536; **III:** 118; **IV:** 274, 358; **Supp. I Part 1:** 363; **Supp. VIII:** 103
Beet Queen, The (Erdrich), **Supp. IV Part 1:** 259, 260, 264-265, 266, 273, 274, 275
Befo' de War: Echoes in Negro Dialect (Gordon), **Supp. II Part 1:** 201
"Before" (Goldbarth), **Supp. XII:** 175
"Before" (Snyder), **Supp. VIII:** 301
Before Adam (London), **II:** 466
Before Disaster (Winters), **Supp. II Part 2:** 786, 800
"Before Disaster" (Winters), **Supp. II Part 2:** 801, 815
"Before I Knocked" (D. Thomas), **III:** 534
Beforelife, The (F. Wright), **Supp. XVII:** 240, 245-246
"Before March" (MacLeish), **III:** 15
Before My Life Began (Neugeboren), **Supp. XVI: 224-225**
"Before the Altar" (Lowell), **II:** 516
"Before the Birth of one of her children" (Bradstreet), **Supp. I Part 1:** 118
"Before the Sky Darkens" (Dunn), **Supp. XI:** 155
"Begat" (Sexton), **Supp. II Part 2:** 693
Beggar on Horseback (Kaufman and Connelly), **III:** 394
"Beggar Said So, The" (Singer), **IV:** 12
Beggars in the House of Plenty (Shanley), **Supp. XIV:** 316, **327-328**
Beggar's Opera, The (Gay), **Supp. I Part 2:** 523
Begiebing, Robert, **Retro. Supp. II:** 210
Begin Again (Paley), **Supp. VI:** 221
"Beginning and the End, The" (Jeffers), **Supp. II Part 2:** 420-421, 424
"Beginning of Decadence, The" (Jeffers), **Supp. II Part 2:** 420

"Beginning of Enthusiasm, The" (Salinas), **Supp. XIII:** 327-328
Beginning of Wisdom, The (Benét), **I:** 358; **Supp. XI:** 44
Be Glad You're Neurotic (Bisch), **Supp. I Part 2:** 608
"Begotten of the Spleen" (Simic), **Supp. VIII:** 277
"Behaving Like a Jew" (Stern), **Supp. IX: 290-291**, 294
"Behavior" (Emerson), **II:** 2, 4
Behavior of Titans, The (Merton), **Supp. VIII:** 201
Behind a Mask (Alcott), **Supp. I Part 1:** 36-37, 43-44
"Behind a Wall" (Lowell), **II:** 516
Behind the Movie Camera (radio show), **Supp. XV:** 147
"Behold the Key" (Malamud), **Supp. I Part 2:** 437
Behrendt, Stephen, **Supp. X:** 204
Behrman, S. N., **Supp. V:** 95
Beidler, Peter G., **Supp. IV Part 2:** 557
Beidler, Philip D., **Supp. XII:** 69
Beige Dolorosa (Harrison), **Supp. VIII:** 40, 51
Beiles, Sinclair, **Supp. XII:** 129
Beiliss, Mendel, **Supp. I Part 2:** 427, 446, 447, 448
"Being a Constellation" (A. Finch), **Supp. XVII:** 72
"Being a Lutheran Boy-God in Minnesota" (R. Bly), **Supp. IV Part 1:** 59, 67
Being and Race (Johnson), **Supp. VI:** 193, 199
Being and Time (Heidegger), **Supp. VIII:** 9
Being Busted (Fiedler), **Supp. XIII:** 95, 102, 104
Being John Malkovich (Kaufman), **Supp. XV:** 16
Being Perfect (Quindlen), **Supp. XVII:** 167, 179
Being There (Kosinski), **Supp. VII:** 215, 216, 222-223
Beiswanger, George, **Retro. Supp. II:** 220
Belasco, David, **Supp. XVI:**182
Bel Canto (Patchett), **Supp. XII:** 307, 310, **320-322**
"Beleaguered City, The" (Longfellow), **II:** 498
Belfry of Bruges, The, and Other Poems (Longfellow), **II:** 489; **Retro. Supp. II:** 157, 168
"Belief" (Levine), **Supp. V:** 186, 190
"Beliefs of Writers, The" (Doctorow), **Supp. IV Part 1:** 235-236

Believers (C. Baxter), **Supp. XVII:** 20-21, 22
"Believers" (C. Baxter), **Supp. XVII:** 21
"Believers, The/Los Creyentes" (Kingsolver), **Supp. VII:** 208
Belinda (Rice), **Supp. VII:** 301-302
"Belinda's Petition" (Dove), **Supp. IV Part 1:** 245
"Belita" (Ríos), **Supp. IV Part 2:** 541
Belitt, Ben, **Supp. XII:** 260
Bell, Clive, **IV:** 87
Bell, Daniel, **Supp. I Part 2:** 648
Bell, George Kennedy Allen, **Retro. Supp. I:** 65
Bell, Madison Smartt, **Supp. X: 1-20; Supp. XVII:** 236
Bell, Marvin, **Supp. V:** 337, 339; **Supp. IX:** 152; **Supp. XI:** 316
Bell, Michael, **Retro. Supp. II:** 139
Bell, Pearl, **Supp. XI:** 233
Bell, Quentin, **Supp. I Part 2:** 636
Bell, Whitfield J., Jr., **II:** 123
Bellafante, Gina, **Supp. VIII:** 85
Bellamy, Edward, **II:** 276; **Supp. I Part 2:** 641; **Supp. XI:** 200, 203
Bellarosa Connection, The (Bellow), **Retro. Supp. II:** 31, 32
"Belle Dollinger" (Masters), **Supp. I Part 2:** 463
Belleforest, François de, **IV:** 370
"Belle Zoraïde, La" (Chopin), **Supp. I Part 1:** 215-216
Bell Jar, The (Plath), **Retro. Supp. II:** 242, **249-250; Supp. I Part 2:** 526, 527, 529, 531-536, 539, 540, 541, 542, 544
Belloc, Hilary, **III:** 176; **IV:** 432
Bellow, Saul, **I:** 113, 138-139, **144-166,** 375, 517; **II:** 579; **III:** 40; **IV:** 3, 19, 217, 340; **Retro. Supp. II: 19-36,** 118, 279, 307, 324; **Supp. I Part 2:** 428, 451; **Supp. II Part 1:** 109; **Supp. IV Part 1:** 30; **Supp. V:** 258; **Supp. VIII:** 98, 176, 234, 236-237, 245; **Supp. IX:** 212, 227; **Supp. XI:** 64, 233; **Supp. XII:** 159, 165, 170, 310; **Supp. XIII:** 106; **Supp. XV:** 143; **Supp. XVI:**208
Bellows, George, **Supp. XV:** 295
"Bells, The" (Poe), **III:** 593; **Retro. Supp. II:** 266; **Supp. I Part 2:** 388
"Bells, The" (Sexton), **Supp. II Part 2:** 673
"Bells for John Whiteside's Daughter" (Ransom), **III:** 490
"Bells of Lynn, The" (Longfellow), **II:** 498
"Bells of San Blas, The" (Longfellow), **II:** 490-491, 493, 498

"Bell Tower, The" (Melville), **III:** 91
"Belly, The" (Dobyns), **Supp. XIII:** 87
"Belonging Kind, The" (W. Gibson and J. Shirley), **Supp. XVI:**123
Beloved (Morrison), **Supp. III Part 1:** 364, 372-379; **Supp. IV Part 1:** 13-14; **Supp. V:** 259; **Supp. VIII:** 343; **Supp. XIII:** 60
Beloved Lady: A History of Jane Addams' Ideas on Reform and Peace (Farrell), **Supp. I Part 1:** 24
Beloved Stranger, The (Bynner), **Supp. XV:** 44, 50
Benchley, Robert, **I:** 48, 482; **II:** 435; **III:** 53; **Supp. IX:** 190, 195, 204
Benda, W. T., **Retro. Supp. I:** 13
Bend Sinister (Nabokov), **III:** 253-254; **Retro. Supp. I:** 265, 266, 270
"Beneath the Sidewalk" (Dunn), **Supp. XI:** 145
"Beneath the Smooth Skin of America" (Sanders), **Supp. XVI:**275
Benedict, Ruth, **Supp. IX:** 229
Benefactor, The (Sontag), **Supp. III Part 2:** 451, 455, 468, 469
"Benefit Performance" (Malamud), **Supp. I Part 2:** 431
Benét, Laura, **Supp. XI:** 44
Benét, Rosemary, **Supp. XI:** 44, 51
Benét, Stephen Vincent, **I:** 358; **II:** 177; **III:** 22; **IV:** 129; **Supp. XI: 43-61**
Benét, William Rose, **II:** 530; **Retro. Supp. I:** 108; **Supp. I Part 2:** 709; **Supp. XI:** 43, 44; **Supp. XIV:**119, 122, 129
Ben Franklin's Wit and Wisdom (Franklin), **II:** 111
Ben-Hur (film), **Supp. IV Part 2:** 683
Benigna Machiavelli (Gilman), **Supp. XI:** 201, 208
Benitez, R. Michael, **Retro. Supp. II:** 264
Benito Cereno (Lowell), **II:** 546; **Retro. Supp. II:** 181
"Benito Cereno" (Melville), **III:** 91; **Retro. Supp. I:** 255; **Retro. Supp. II:** 188; **Supp. XVII:** 185
Benito's Dream Bottle (Nye), **Supp. XIII:** 278
"Bênitou's Slave, The" (Chopin), **Retro. Supp. II:** 64
Benjamin, Walter, **Supp. IX:** 133; **Supp. XVI:**290, 291
Benjamin Franklin (Van Doren), **Supp. I Part 2:** 486
"Benjamin Pantier" (Masters), **Supp. I Part 2:** 461
Bennett, Anne Virginia, **II:** 184

Bennett, Arnold, **I:** 103; **II:** 337; **Supp. XVI:**190
Bennett, Elizabeth, **Supp. VIII:** 58
Bennett, Patrick, **Supp. V:** 225
Bennett, Paula, **Retro. Supp. I:** 29, 33, 42
Bennett, William, **Supp. VIII:** 245
Benson, Jackson J., **Supp. IV Part 2:** 613
Benstock, Shari, **Retro. Supp. I:** 361, 368, 371, 382
Bentham, Jeremy, **I:** 279; **Supp. I Part 2:** 635
Bentley, Eric R., **IV:** 396
Bentley, Nelson, **Supp. IX:** 324
Bentley, Richard, **III:** 79, 86
Benton, Robert, **Supp. IV Part 1:** 236
"Bent Tones" (Wright), **Supp. XV:** 346
Benveniste, Emile, **Supp. XVI:**292
Benzel, Jan, **Supp. XVI:**112
Beowulf, **Supp. II Part 1:** 6; **Supp. XVII:** 70, 73
Beran, Carol, **Supp. XIII:** 25
"Berck-Plage" (Plath), **Retro. Supp. II:** 253-254
Bercovitch, Sacvan, **Retro. Supp. I:** 408; **Retro. Supp. II:** 325, 330; **Supp. I Part 1:** 99; **Supp. I Part 2:** 659
Berdyaev, Nikolai, **I:** 494; **III:** 292
"Bereaved Apartments" (Kingsolver), **Supp. VII:** 203
"Bereavement in their death to feel" (Dickinson), **Retro. Supp. I:** 43, 44
"Berenice" (Poe), **III:** 415, 416, 425; **Retro. Supp. II:** 270
Bérénice (Racine), **II:** 573
Berenson, Bernard, **Retro. Supp. I:** 381; **Supp. IV Part 1:** 314; **Supp. XIV:**335, 336, 337; **Supp. XVII:** 99
Berg, James, **Supp. XIV:**157, 159
Berg, Stephen, **Supp. IV Part 1:** 60
Berger, Alan, **Supp. XVII:** 39
Berger, Charles, **Retro. Supp. I:** 311
Berger, John, **Supp. XVI:**284
Berger, Roger, **Supp. XIII:** 237
Berger, Thomas, **III:** 258; **Supp. XII:** 171
Bergman, Ingmar, **I:** 291; **Supp. XV:** 7, 8, 12
Bergson, Henri, **I:** 224; **II:** 163, 165, 166, 359; **III:** 8, 9, 488, 619; **IV:** 86, 122, 466, 467; **Retro. Supp. I:** 55, 57, 80; **Supp. IV Part 1:** 42
Berkeley, Anthony, **Supp. IV Part 1:** 341
Berkeley, George, **II:** 10, 349, 357, 480, 554
Berkman, Leonard, **Supp. XV:** 321

Berkowitz, Gerald, **Supp. IV Part 2:** 590
Berlin Alexanderplatz (Döblin), **Supp. XV:** 137
Berlin Stories (Isherwood), **Supp. IV Part 1:** 82; **Supp. XIV:**155, 156, 161, 162, 164, 165
Berlioz, Hector, **Supp. XV:** 33
Berlyne, Daniel E., **Supp. I Part 2:** 672
Berman, Alexander, **Supp. XVII:** 103
Bernard Clare (Farrell), **II:** 38, 39
Bernard of Clairvaux, Saint, **I:** 22; **II:** 538
Bernays, Thekla, **Retro. Supp. II:** 65
Berne, Suzanne, **Supp. XII:** 320
Berne, Victoria (pseud.). *See* Fisher, M. F. K.
Berneis, Peter, **IV:** 383
Bernhard, Brendan, **Supp. XIV:**163
Bernhardt, Sarah, **I:** 484; **Retro. Supp. I:** 377
Bernice (Glaspell), **Supp. III Part 1:** 179
"Bernice Bobs Her Hair" (Fitzgerald), **II:** 88; **Retro. Supp. I:** 103
Bernstein, Aline, **IV:** 455, 456
Bernstein, Andrea, **Supp. IX:** 146
Bernstein, Charles, **Supp. IV Part 2:** 421, 426
Bernstein, Elizabeth, **Supp. XII:** 318
Bernstein, Leonard, **I:** 28; **Supp. I Part 1:** 288, 289; **Supp. IV Part 1:** 83, 84
Bernstein, Melvin, **Supp. XIV:**41, 46
Bernstein, Michael André, **Retro. Supp. I:** 427
Bernstein, Richard, **Supp. IX:** 253, 262; **Supp. XII:** 113; **Supp. XIV:**33
Berrett, Jesse, **Supp. XIII:** 241, 242
Berrigan, Ted, **Supp. XIV:**150
"Berry" (Hughes), **Supp. I Part 1:** 329, 330
Berry, Faith, **Retro. Supp. I:** 194, 201
Berry, Walter, **IV:** 313-314, 326
Berry, Wendell, **Supp. VIII:** 304; **Supp. X: 21-39; Supp. XII:** 202; **Supp. XIII:** 1-2; **Supp. XIV:**179; **Supp. XVI:**39, 56
"Berry Feast, A" (Snyder), **Supp. VIII:** 289, 297
Berryman, John, **I: 167-189,** 405, 441-442, 521; **II:** 554; **III:** 273; **IV:** 138, 430; **Retro. Supp. I:** 430; **Retro. Supp. II:** 175, 178; **Supp. I Part 2:** 546; **Supp. II Part 1:** 109; **Supp. III Part 2:** 541, 561, 595, 596, 603; **Supp. IV Part 2:** 620, 639; **Supp. V:** 179-180, 337; **Supp. IX:** 152; **Supp. XI:** 240; **Supp. XV:** 93;

Supp. XVII: 111
Berryman, Mrs. John, **I:** 168-169
Berryman's Sonnets (Berryman), **I:** 168, 175-178
"Berry Territory" (Snyder), **Supp. VIII:** 304
Berthoff, Warner, **Supp. I Part 1:** 133
Bertolucci, Bernardo, **Supp. IV Part 1:** 94
"Bertrand Hume" (Masters), **Supp. I Part 2:** 463-464
"Best, the Most, The" (Carruth), **Supp. XVI:**59
Best American Essays 1987, The (G. Talese and R. Atwan, eds.), **Supp. XVI:**273
Best American Essays 1988, The (Dillard, ed.), **Supp. VIII:** 272
Best American Essays 1989, The (Wolff, ed.), **Supp. XVII:** 208
Best American Essays 1993, The (J. Epstein, ed.), **Supp. XVI:**275
Best American Essays 1997, The (Frazier, ed.), **Supp. VIII:** 272; **Supp. XVII:** 207
Best American Essays 1999, The (E. Hoagland and R. Atwan, eds.), **Supp. XVI:**277
Best American Essays for College Students, The (R. Atwan, ed.), **Supp. XVI:**273
Best American New Voices 2001 (C. Baxter, ed.), **Supp. XVII:** 22
Best American Poetry, The: 1988 (Ashbery, ed.), **Supp. III Part 1:** 26
Best American Short Stories, **I:**174; **II:** 587; **III:** 443; **Supp. IV Part 1:** 102, 315; **Supp. IX:** 114; **Supp. X:** 301
Best American Short Stories, 1915-1050, The, **Supp. IX:** 4
Best American Short Stories 1965, The (Foley, ed.), **Supp. XVI:**225
Best American Short Stories 1982, The (Gardner, ed.), **Supp. XVII:** 16
Best American Short Stories 1983, The (A. Tyler, ed.), **Supp. XVI:**37
Best American Short Stories 1986, The (Carver, ed.), **Supp. XVII:** 17
Best American Short Stories 1988, The (Helprin, ed.), **Supp. XVI:**16
Best American Short Stories 1989, The (Atwood, ed.), **Supp. XVII:** 18
Best American Short Stories 1991, The (Adams and Kenison, eds.), **Supp. XVI:**256
Best American Short Stories 2001, The (Kenison and Kingsover, eds.), **Supp. XVI:**24
Best American Short Stories of 1942,

The, **Supp. V:** 316
Best American Short Stories of 1944, The, **Supp. IX:** 119
Best American Short Stories of the Century (Updike, ed.), **Supp. X:** 163
Best American Short Stories of the Eighties, The (Ravenal, ed.), **Supp. IV Part 1:** 93
Best American Sports Writing of the Century, The (Halberstam, ed.), **Supp. XVII:** 204
"Best China Saucer, The" (Jewett), **Retro. Supp. II:** 145-146
Bester, Alfred, **Supp. XVI:**123
Best Hour of the Night, The (Simpson), **Supp. IX: 277-279**
Bestiaire, Le (Apollinaire), **IV:** 80
Bestiary, A (Wilbur), **Supp. III Part 2:** 552
"Bestiary for the Fingers of My Right Hand" (Simic), **Supp. VIII:** 274, 275
Best Man, The: A Play About Politics (Vidal), **Supp. IV Part 2:** 683
"Best of Everything, The" (Yates), **Supp. XI:** 341
Best of Plimpton (Plimpton), **Supp. XVI:**238, 239, 240
Best Short Plays, The (Mayorga), **IV:** 381
Best Short Stories, The (O'Brien, ed.), **I:** 289
Best Short Stories by Negro Writers, The (Hughes, ed.), **Supp. I Part 1:** 345
Best That Ever Did It, The (Lacy), **Supp. XV:** 201-202
Best Times, The: An Informal Memoir (Dos Passos), **I:** 475, 482
Best Words, Best Order: Essays on Poetry (Dobyns), **Supp. XIII:** 74, **76-78,** 87
Best Years of Our Lives, The (film; Wyler), **Supp. XV:** 195
"BETANCOURT" (Baraka), **Supp. II Part 1:** 33, 34
Bête humaine, La (Zola), **III:** 316, 318
"Bethe" (Hellman), **Supp. I Part 1:** 293
Bethea, David, **Supp. VIII:** 27
Bethel Merriday (Lewis), **II:** 455
Bethke, Bruce, **Supp. XVI:**121
Bethlehem in Broad Daylight (Doty), **Supp. XI:** 121, **122-123**
Bethune, Mary McLeod, **Retro. Supp. I:** 197; **Supp. I Part 1:** 333
Bethurum, Dorothy, **IV:** 121
"Betrayal" (Lanier), **Supp. I Part 1:** 364

"Betrothed" (Bogan), **Supp. III Part 1:** 49-51
Bettelheim, Bruno, **Supp. I Part 2:** 622; **Supp. X:** 77, 84; **Supp. XIV:**126; **Supp. XVI:**33
Better Days (Price), **Supp. VI:** 264
Better Sort, The (James), **II:** 335
"Better Things in Life, The" (Loos), **Supp. XVI:**194
Betty Leicester (Jewett), **II:** 406
Betty Leicester's Christmas (Jewett), **II:** 406; **Retro. Supp. II:** 145
Between Angels (Dunn), **Supp. XI: 149-159**
"Between Angels" (Dunn), **Supp. XI:** 150
Between Fantoine and Agapa (Pinget), **Supp. V:** 39
"Between Memory and History: A Writer's Voice" (Kreisler), **Supp. XVI:**155
"Between the Porch and the Altar" (Lowell), **II:** 540-541
"Between the World and Me" (Wright), **Supp. II Part 1:** 228
Between Time and Timbuktu (Vonnegut), **Supp. II Part 2:** 753, 759
Bevis, Howard L., **Supp. I Part 2:** 611
Bevis, John, **Supp. I Part 2:** 503
"Bewitched" (Wharton), **IV:** 316
Bewley, Marius, **I:** 336
Beyle, Marie Henri. *See* Stendhal
Beyond (Goldbarth), **Supp. XII:** 192
Beyond Black Bear Lake (LaBastille), **Supp. X:** 95, **99-102,** 108
"Beyond Charles River to the Acheron" (Lowell), **II:** 541
Beyond Criticism (Shapiro), **Supp. II Part 2:** 703, 711
Beyond Culture (Trilling), **Supp. III Part 2:** 508-512
Beyond Desire (Anderson), **I:** 111
Beyond Document: The Art of Nonfiction Film (Warren, ed.), **Supp. IV Part 2:** 434
Beyond Good and Evil (Nietzsche), **Supp. IV Part 2:** 519
"Beyond Harm" (Olds), **Supp. X:** 210
"Beyond the Alps" (Lowell), **II:** 547, 550
"Beyond the Bayou" (Chopin), **Supp. I Part 1:** 215
Beyond the Horizon (O'Neill), **III:** 389
Beyond the Hundredth Meridian: John Wesley Powell and the Second Opening of the West (Stegner), **Supp. IV Part 2:** 599, 603-604, 611
"Beyond the Kittery Bridge" (Hatlen), **Supp. V:** 138

Beyond the Law (film) (Mailer), **Retro. Supp. II:** 205
"Beyond the Sea (at the sanatorium)" (Salinas), **Supp. XIII:** 325
Beyond the Wall: Essays from the Outside (Abbey), **Supp. XIII:** 13
Beyond the Writers' Workshop: New Ways to Write Creative Nonfiction (C. Bly), **Supp. XVI:**41
Beyond Tragedy (Niebuhr), **III:** 300-303
Bezner, Kevin, **Supp. XII:** 202
Bhagavad Gita, **III:** 566; **IV:** 183
"Biafra: A People Betrayed" (Vonnegut), **Supp. II Part 2:** 760
Bianchi, Martha Dickinson, **I:** 470; **Retro. Supp. I:** 35, 37, 38
Bible, **I:** 191, 280, 414, 421, 490, 506; **II:** 6, 12, 15, 17, 108, 231, 237, 238, 252, 267, 302; **III:** 28, 199, 308-309, 341, 343, 350, 356, 402, 492, 519, 565, 577; **IV:** 11, 13, 42, 57, 60, 67, 152, 153, 154, 155, 164, 165, 296, 337, 341, 367, 369, 370, 371, 438; **Retro. Supp. I:** 91; **Supp. I Part 1:** 4, 6, 63, 101, 104, 105, 113, 193, 369; **Supp. I Part 2:** 388, 433, 494, 515, 516, 517, 583, 584, 587, 589, 653, 689, 690, 691; **Supp. IV Part 1:** 284; **Supp. VIII:** 20; **Supp. IX:** 246; **Supp. XIV:**225. *See also* names of biblical books; New Testament; Old Testament
Biblia Americana (Mather), **Supp. II Part 2:** 442
Biblical Dialogues between a Father and His Family (Rowson), **Supp. XV:** 245-246
Bibliography of the King's Book, A; or, Eikon Basilike (Almack), **Supp. IV Part 2:** 435
"Bibliography of the King's Book, A, or, Eikon Basilike" (Howe), **Supp. IV Part 2:** 435
Bickel, Freddy. *See* March, Fredric
Bidart, Frank, **Retro. Supp. II:** 48, 50, 52, 182, 183, 184; **Supp. XV: 19-37**
Bid Me to Live (Doolittle), **Supp. I Part 1:** 258, 260, 268, 269, 270
"Bien Pretty" (Cisneros), **Supp. VII:** 70
"Bienvenidos" (Mora), **Supp. XIII:** 220
Bierce, Albert, **I:** 191, 209
Bierce, Ambrose, **I:** 190-213, 419; **II:** 74, 264, 271; **IV:** 350; **Retro. Supp. II:** 72
Bierce, Day, **I:** 195, 199
Bierce, General Lucius Verus, **I:** 191
Bierce, Helen, **I:** 210

Bierce, Leigh, **I:** 195, 198, 208
Bierce, Marcus, **I:** 190, 191
Bierce, Mrs. Ambrose, **I:** 194-195, 199
Bierce, Mrs. Marcus, **I:** 190, 191
Bierds, Linda, **Supp. XVII:** 25-37
Biffle, Kent, **Supp. V:** 225
"Bi-Focal" (Stafford), **Supp. XI:** 318, 321
Big as Life (Doctorow), **Supp. IV Part 1:** 231, 234
"Big Bite" (Mailer), **Retro. Supp. II:** 204
"Big Blonde" (Parker), **Supp. IX:** 189, 192, 193, 195, 196, 203
Big Bozo, The (Glaspell), **Supp. III Part 1:** 182
Bigelow, Gordon, **Supp. X:** 222, 227, 229
Bigelow, Jacob, **Supp. I Part 1:** 302
Bigelow Papers, Second Series, The (Lowell), **Supp. I Part 2:** 406, 415-416
Bigelow Papers, The (Lowell), **Supp. I Part 2:** 406, 407, 408, 410, 411-412, 415, 417, 424
Big Fix, The (Lacy), **Supp. XV:** 204-205
Bigfoot Dreams (Prose), **Supp. XVI:** 253-254
Big Funk, The: A Casual Play (Shanley), **Supp. XIV:** 316, **327**
Big Gold Dream, The (C. Himes), **Supp. XVI:** 143, 144
"Bight, The" (Bishop), **Retro. Supp. II:** 38, 45
Big Hunger: Stories 1932-1959 (Fante), **Supp. XI:** 160
Big Knife, The (Odets), **Supp. II Part 2:** 546, 547, 548
Big Knockover, The (Hammett), **Supp. I Part 1:** 292; **Supp. IV Part 1:** 344, 345, 356
Big Laugh, The (O'Hara), **III:** 362, 373-375
Big Man (Neugeboren), **Supp. XVI:** 219, **220,** 221, 225
Big Money, The (Dos Passos), **I:** 482, 483, 486-487, 489; **Supp. I Part 2:** 646, 647
"Big Rock Candy Figgy Pudding Pitfall, The" (Didion), **Supp. IV Part 1:** 195
Big Rock Candy Mountain, The (Stegner), **Supp. IV Part 2:** 596, 597, 598, 599, 600, 603, 604, 605, 606-607, 608, 610-611
Bigsby, C. W. E. (Christopher), **Supp. IX:** 137, 140; **Supp. XV:** 332
Big Sea, The (Hughes), **Retro. Supp. I:** 195, 197, 199, 201, 204; **Supp. I Part 1:** 322, 332, 333; **Supp. II Part 1:** 233-234
Big Sky, The (Mora), **Supp. XIII:** 221
Big Sleep, The (Chandler), **Supp. IV Part 1:** 122-125, 127, 128, 134
Big Sleep, The (film), **Supp. IV Part 1:** 130
Big Sur (Kerouac), **Supp. III Part 1:** 230
Big Sur and the Oranges of Hieronymous Bosch (H. Miller), **III:** 189-190
Big Town, The (Lardner), **II:** 426, 429
"Big Two-Hearted River" (Hemingway), **II:** 249; **Retro. Supp. I:** 170-171; **Supp. IX:** 106; **Supp. XIV:** 227, 235
"Big Wind" (Roethke), **III:** 531
"Big Winner Rises Late, The" (Dunn), **Supp. XI:** 146
"Bilingual Christmas" (Mora), **Supp. XIII:** 216-217
"Bilingual Sestina" (Alvarez), **Supp. VII:** 10
"Bill" (Winters), **Supp. II Part 2:** 792
"Bill, The" (Malamud), **Supp. I Part 2:** 427, 430, 434
"Billie Holiday" (Carruth), **Supp. XVI:** 50
Billings, Gladys. *See* Brooks, Mrs. Van Wyck
Bill of Rites, a Bill of Wrongs, a Bill of Goods, A (Morris), **III:** 237
"Bill's Beans" (Nye), **Supp. XIII:** 283
"Billy" (Gordon), **Supp. IV Part 1:** 306
"Billy" (McCarriston), **Supp. XIV:** 265
Billy Bathgate (Doctorow), **Supp. IV Part 1:** 217, 219, 222, 224, 227, 229-231, 231, 232, 233, 238
Billy Bathgate (film), **Supp. IV Part 1:** 236
Billy Budd, Sailor (Melville), **III:** 40, 93-95; **IV:** 105; **Retro. Supp. I:** 249, **258-260**
Billy Phelan's Greatest Game (W. Kennedy), **Supp. VII:** 131, 132, 134, 135, 142-147, 149, 151, 153, 155
Billy the Kid, **Supp. IV Part 2:** 489, 490, 492
Biloxi Blues (Simon), **Supp. IV Part 2:** 576, 577, 584, 586-587, 590
"Bimini" (Hemingway), **II:** 258
Bingham, Anne, **Supp. XV:** 239
Bingham, Millicent Todd, **I:** 470; **Retro. Supp. I:** 36
Bingo Palace, The (Erdrich), **Supp. IV Part 1:** 259, 260, 261, 263-264, 265, 266-267, 268-269, 270, 271-273, 274, 275
"Binsey Poplars" (Hopkins), **Supp. I Part 1:** 94; **Supp. IV Part 2:** 639
Binswanger, Ludwig, **Supp. XV:** 26
Biographia Literaria (Coleridge), **II:** 10; **Retro. Supp. I:** 308
"Biography" (Francis), **Supp. IX:** 77
"Biography" (Pinsky), **Supp. VI:** 235, 236, 239, 241, **243,** 249, 250
Biography and Poetical Remains of the Late Margaret Miller Davidson (Irving), **II:** 314
"Biography in the First Person" (Dunn), **Supp. XI:** 144
"Biography of an Armenian Schoolgirl" (Nye), **Supp. XIII:** 275, 280
"Biography of a Story" (Jackson), **Supp. IX:** 113
Biondi, Joann, **Supp. XI:** 103
"Biopoetics Sketch for *Greenfield Review*" (Harjo), **Supp. XII:** 216
"Birchbrook Mill" (Whittier), **Supp. I Part 2:** 699
"Birches" (Frost), **II:** 154; **Retro. Supp. I:** 132; **Supp. XIII:** 147
Bird, Alan, **Supp. I Part 1:** 260
Bird, Gloria, **Supp. XII:** 216
Bird, Isabella, **Supp. X:** 103
Bird, Robert M., **III:** 423
"Bird, The" (Simpson), **Supp. IX:** 269-270
"Bird, the Bird, the Bird, The" (Creeley), **Supp. IV Part 1:** 149
"Bird came down the Walk, A" (Dickinson), **Retro. Supp. I:** 37
"Bird Frau, The" (Dove), **Supp. IV Part 1:** 245
"Bird in Hand" (screen story) (West and Ingster), **Retro. Supp. II:** 330
Bird Kingdom of the Mayas (LaBastille), **Supp. X:** 96
Birds and Beasts (W. J. Smith), **Supp. XIII:** 346
Bird's Nest, The (Jackson), **Supp. IX:** **124-125**
Birds of America (McCarthy), **II:** 579-583; **Supp. X:** 177
Birds of America (Moore), **Supp. X:** 163, 165, 167, 168, 171, **177-179**
Birds of America, The (Audubon), **Supp. XVI:** 5-6, 7, 9, 10, 12, 13
"Birds of Killingsworth, The" (Longfellow), **Retro. Supp. II:** 164
Birds of North America (Audubon Society), **Supp. X:** 177
"Birds of Vietnam, The" (Carruth), **Supp. XVI:** 55
"Bird-Witted" (Moore), **III:** 214
Birkerts, Sven, **Supp. IV Part 2:** 650; **Supp. V:** 212; **Supp. VIII:** 85;

Supp. X: 311
Birkhead, L. M., **III:** 116
"Birmingham Sunday" (Hughes), **Supp. I Part 1:** 343
Birnbaum, Henry, **Supp. XII:** 128
Birnbaum, Robert, **Supp. X:** 13; **Supp. XVI:** 75
Birney, James G., **Supp. I Part 2:** 587, 588
Birstein, Ann, **Supp. VIII:** 100
"Birthday, A" (Untermeyer), **Supp. XV:** 296
Birthday Basket for Tía, A (Mora), **Supp. XIII:** 221
"Birthday Cake" (Carruth), **Supp. XVI:** 59
"Birthday Cake for Lionel, A" (Wylie), **Supp. I Part 2:** 721
"Birthday Girl: 1950" (McCarriston), **Supp. XIV:** 261
"Birthday of Mrs. Pineda, The" (Ríos), **Supp. IV Part 2:** 542, 546
"Birthday Poem, A" (Hecht), **Supp. X:** 64
"Birthday Present, A" (Plath), **Supp. I Part 2:** 531
"Birthmark, The" (Ellison), **Retro. Supp. II:** 116; **Supp. II Part 1:** 237-238
"Birth-mark, The" (Hawthorne), **Retro. Supp. I:** 152
Birth-mark, The: Unsettling the Wilderness in American Literary History (Howe), **Supp. IV Part 2:** 422, 431, 434
Birth of a Nation, The (film), **Supp. I Part 1:** 66
Birth of the Poet, The (Gordon), **Supp. XII:** 7
Birth of Tragedy, The (Nietzsche), **Supp. IV Part 1:** 105, 110; **Supp. IV Part 2:** 519; **Supp. VIII:** 182
"Birth of Venus, The" (Botticelli), **IV:** 410
"Birth of Venus, The" (Rukeyser), **Supp. VI:** 281
"Birthplace Revisited" (Corso), **Supp. XII:** 123
"Birthright" (McKay), **Supp. X:** 136
Bisch, Louis E., **Supp. I Part 2:** 608
"B is for Bachelors" (M. F. K. Fisher), **Supp. XVII:** 86
Bishop, Elizabeth, **Retro. Supp. I:** 140, 296, 303; **Retro. Supp. II: 37-56,** 175, 178, 189, 233, 234, 235; **Supp. I Part 1: 72-97,** 239, 320, 326; **Supp. III Part 1:** 6, 7, 10, 18, 64, 239, 320, 326; **Supp. III Part 2:** 541, 561; **Supp. IV Part 1:** 249, 257; **Supp. IV Part 2:** 439, 626, 639, 641, 644, 647, 651, 653; **Supp. V:** 337; **Supp. IX:** 40, 41, 45, 47, 48; **Supp. X:** 58; **Supp. XI:** 123, 136; **Supp. XIII:** 115, 348; **Supp. XV:** 20-21, 100, 101, 112, 119, 249, 251; **Supp. XVII:** 36, 76
Bishop, James, Jr., **Supp. XIII:** 1, 5, 6, 7, 9, 11, 15
Bishop, John Peale, **I:** 432, 440; **II:** 81, 85, 86-87, 91, 209; **IV:** 35, 140, 427; **Retro. Supp. I:** 109; **Supp. I Part 2:** 709
Bishop, John W., **Supp. I Part 1:** 83
Bishop, Judith, **Supp. XVI:** 295
Bishop, Morris, **Supp. I Part 2:** 676
Bishop, William Thomas, **Supp. I Part 1:** 83
"Bishop Orders His Tomb at St. Praxed's Church, The" (R. Browning), **Supp. XV:** 127
"Bishop's Beggar, The" (Benét), **Supp. XI:** 56
"Bismarck" (Chapman), **Supp. XIV:** 52, 53
Bismark, Otto von, **Supp. I Part 2:** 643
"Bistro Styx, The" (Dove), **Supp. IV Part 1:** 250-251
Bitov, Andrei, **Retro. Supp. I:** 278
Bits of Gossip (Davis), **Supp. XVI:** 82-83, 84, 85, 89
"Bitter Drink, The" (Dos Passos), **Supp. I Part 2:** 647
"Bitter Farce, A" (Schwartz), **Supp. II Part 2:** 640, 657-658
"Bitter Pills for the Dark Ladies" (Jong), **Supp. V:** 118
Bitterroot (Burke), **Supp. XIV:** 34, 35
Bitter Victory (Hardy; Kinnell, trans.), **Supp. III Part 1:** 235
Bitzer, G. W. "Billy," **Supp. XVI:** 183
Bixby, Horace, **IV:** 194
Bjorkman, Frances Maule, **Supp. V:** 285
Bjorkman, Stig, **Supp. XV:** 6
Björnson, Björnstjerne, **II:** 275
Black 100, The (Salley), **Supp. XIV:** 195
Blackamerican Literature, 1760-Present (R. Miller), **Supp. X:** 324
Black American Literature Forum, **Supp. XI:** 86, 92, 93
Black and Blue (Quindlen), **Supp. XVII:** 166, **176-178**
"Black and Tan" (Bell), **Supp. X:** 9
Black Armour (Wylie), **Supp. I Part 2:** 708, 709, 712-714, 729
"Black Art" (Baraka), **Supp. II Part 1:** 49, 50-51, 59, 60
"Black Art, The" (Sexton), **Supp. II Part 2:** 682
"Black Ball, The" (Ellison), **Retro. Supp. II:** 124
Black Bart and the Sacred Hills (Wilson), **Supp. VIII:** 330, 331
Black Beetles in Amber (Bierce), **I:** 204, 209
"Blackberries" (Komunyakaa), **Supp. XIII:** 126
"Blackberry Eating" (Kinnell), **Supp. III Part 1:** 250
Blackberry Winter (Warren), **IV:** 243, 251, 252
Black Betty (Mosley), **Supp. XIII:** 237, **Supp. XIII:** 240, 243
"Black Birch in Winter, A" (Wilbur), **Supp. III Part 2:** 561
Black Boy (Wright), **IV:** 477, 478, 479, 480-482, 488, 489, 494; **Retro. Supp. II:** 117; **Supp. II Part 1:** 235-236; **Supp. IV Part 1:** 11
"Black Boys and Native Sons" (Howe), **Retro. Supp. II:** 112
Blackburn, Alex, **Supp. XIII:** 112
Blackburn, William, **IV:** 100
"Black Buttercups" (Clampitt), **Supp. IX:** 42
Black Cargo, The (Marquand), **III:** 55, 60
Black Cargoes: A History of the Atlantic Slave Trade (Cowley), **Supp. II Part 1:** 140
"Black Cat, The" (Poe), **III:** 413, 414, 415; **Retro. Supp. II:** 264, 267, 269, 270
Black Cherry Blues (Burke), **Supp. XIV:** 30
"Black Christ, The" (Cullen), **Supp. IV Part 1:** 170, 171-172
Black Christ and Other Poems, The (Cullen), **Supp. IV Part 1:** 166, 170
"Black Cottage, The" (Frost), **Retro. Supp. I:** 128
"BLACK DADA NIHILISMUS" (Baraka), **Supp. II Part 1:** 39, 41
"Black Death" (Hurston), **Supp. VI:** 153
Black Dog, Red Dog (Dobyns), **Supp. XIII:** 87, **88-89**
"Black Dog, Red Dog" (Dobyns), **Supp. XIII:** 89
"Black Earth" (Moore), **III:** 197, 212
Black Fire (Jones and Neal, eds.), **Supp. X:** 324, 328
Black Fire: An Anthology of Afro American Writing (Baraka, ed.), **Supp. II Part 1:** 53
Black Flame, The (Du Bois), **Supp. II Part 1:** 159, 185-186
Black Folk, Then and Now: An Essay

in the History and Sociology of the Negro Race (Du Bois), **Supp. II Part 1:** 159, 178, 183, 185
"Black Fox, The" (Whittier), **Supp. I Part 2:** 692
Black Freckles (Levis), **Supp. XI:** 257, 271
"Black Gang," **IV:** 406, 407
Black Genius (Mosley, ed.), **Supp. XIII:** 246
"Black Hood, The" (Francis), **Supp. IX:** 83, 91
Black House, The (Theroux), **Supp. VIII:** 319
Black Humor (Johnson), **Supp. VI:** 187, 199
Black Image in the White Mind, The (Fredrickson), **Supp. I Part 2:** 589
"Black Is My Favorite Color" (Malamud), **Supp. I Part 2:** 437
"Black Jewel, The" (Merwin), **Supp. III Part 1:** 355
Black Lamb and Grey Falcon (R. West), **Supp. XVI:**152
"Blacklegs" (B. Kelly), **Supp. XVII:** 131
Black Light (Kinnell), **Supp. III Part 1:** 235, 243
"Blacklist and the Cold War, The" (Kramer), **Supp. I Part 1:** 295
Black Literature in America (Baker), **Supp. X:** 324
Black Magic, A Pictorial History of the Negro in American Entertainment (Hughes), **Supp. I Part 1:** 345
Black Magic: Collected Poetry 1961-1967 (Baraka), **Supp. II Part 1:** 45, 49-50
"Blackmailers Don't Shoot" (Chandler), **Supp. IV Part 1:** 121-122
Black Manhattan (Johnson), **Supp. IV Part 1:** 169
Black Mass, A (Baraka), **Supp. II Part 1:** 46, 48-49, 56, 57
"Black Mesa, The" (Merrill), **Supp. III Part 1:** 328
Black Metropolis (Cayton and Drake), **IV:** 475, 486, 488
Black Misery (Hughes), **Supp. I Part 1:** 336
Blackmur, Helen Dickson (Mrs. R. P. Blackmur), **Supp. II Part 1:** 90
Blackmur, Richard P., **I:** 50, 63, 67, 280, 282, 386, 455, 472; **II:** 320, 537; **III:** 194, 208, 462, 478, 497; **Supp. II Part 1: 87-112,** 136; **Supp. II Part 2:** 543, 643; **Supp. XII:** 45
Black Music (Baraka), **Supp. II Part 1:** 47, 51

Black Nativity (Hughes), **Retro. Supp. I:** 196
Black No More (Schuyler), **Supp. XVI:**142
Black on Black: "Baby Sister" and Selected Writings (C. Himes), **Supp. XVI:**145
"Blackout" (Hay), **Supp. XIV:**121
"Black Panther" (Hughes), **Retro. Supp. I:** 211
"Black Petal" (L.-Y. Lee), **Supp. XV:** 224-225
Black Power (Wright), **IV:** 478, 488, 494
"Black Rainbow, A: Modern Afro-American Poetry" (Dove and Waniek), **Supp. IV Part 1:** 244
Black Reconstruction (Du Bois), **Supp. II Part 1:** 159, 162, 171, 182
Black Riders and Other Lines, The (Crane), **I:** 406, 419
Black Riviera, The (Jarman), **Supp. XVII:** 109, 110, **115-116**
"Black Rook in Rainy Weather" (Plath), **Supp. I Part 2:** 543, 544
Blacks (Brooks), **Supp. III Part 1:** 69, 72, 86, 87
Blacks, The (Genet), **Supp. IV Part 1:** 8
Black Skin, White Masks (Fanon), **Retro. Supp. II:** 118
Black Sleuth, The (J. Bruce), **Supp. XVI:**143
Black Spear, The (Hayden), **Supp. II Part 1:** 375
Black Spring (H. Miller), **III:** 170, 175, 178, 180-182, 183, 184; **Supp. X:** 187
"Black Stone Lying on a White Stone" (Vallejo), **Supp. XIII:** 324
Black Sun (Abbey), **Supp. XIII:** 4, **8-9,** 17
"Black Swan" (B. Kelly), **Supp. XVII:** 130-131
"Black Swan, The" (Jarrell), **II:** 382
Black Swan, The (Merrill), **Supp. III Part 1:** 319, 320
"Black Tambourine" (Crane), **I:** 387-388; **II:** 371
"Black Tuesday" (Swenson), **Supp. IV Part 2:** 646
Black Voices (Chapman), **IV:** 485
"Blackwater Mountain" (Wright), **Supp. V:** 335, 340
"Black Wedding, The" (Singer), **IV:** 12-13
Blackwell, Alice Stone, **Supp. XI:** 195, 197
Blackwell, Elizabeth, **Retro. Supp. II:** 146

Black Woman, The (Bambara, ed.), **Supp. XI:** 1
"Black Workers" (Hughes), **Retro. Supp. I:** 202
"Black Writer and the Southern Experience, The" (Walker), **Supp. III Part 2:** 521
Black Zodiac (Wright), **Supp. V:** 333, 344, 345
Blade Runner (film), **Supp. XI:** 84
Blaine, Anita McCormick, **Supp. I Part 1:** 5
Blaine, Nell, **Supp. XV:** 179
Blair, Hugh, **II:** 8, 17; **Supp. I Part 2:** 422
Blair, Robert, **Supp. I Part 1:** 150
Blair, Walter, **II:** 20; **Retro. Supp. II:** 286
Blaisdell, Gus, **Supp. XIV:**87
Blake, **Supp. XVI:**282
Blake, William, **I:** 381, 383, 389, 390, 398, 447, 476, 525, 526, 533; **II:** 321; **III:** 5, 19, 22, 195, 196, 197, 205, 485, 528, 540, 544-545, 567, 572; **IV:** 129; **Retro. Supp. II:** 76, 300; **Supp. I Part 1:** 80; **Supp. I Part 2:** 385, 514, 517, 539, 552, 708; **Supp. V:** 208, 257, 258; **Supp. VIII:** 26, 99, 103; **Supp. X:** 120; **Supp. XII:** 45; **Supp. XIV:**344; **Supp. XVII:** 119
Blakely, Barbara, **Supp. XIII:** 32
Blanc, Marie Thérèse, **Retro. Supp. II:** 135
Blanc-Bentzon, Mme. Thérèse, **II:** 405
Blanchard, Paula, **Retro. Supp. II:** 131, 133-134, 135
Blanchot, Maurice, **Supp. XVI:**288
Blancs, Les (Hansberry), **Supp. IV Part 1:** 359, 364, 365, 369, 372-374
Blancs, Les: The Collected Last Plays of Lorraine Hansberry (Nemiroff, ed.), **Supp. IV Part 1:** 365, 368, 374
"'Blandula, Tenulla, Vagula'" (Pound), **III:** 463; **Supp. V:** 336, 337, 345
Blankenship, Tom, **IV:** 193
Blanshard, Rufus A., **I:** 67
Blauvelt, William Satake, **Supp. V:** 171, 173
Blavatsky, Elena Petrovna, **III:** 176
"Blazing in Gold and Quenching in Purple" (Dickinson), **Retro. Supp. I:** 30
Bleak House (Dickens), **II:** 291; **Supp. IV Part 1:** 293
Blechman, Burt, **Supp. I Part 1:** 290
"Bleeder" (Dobyns), **Supp. XIII:** 88
"Bleeding" (Swenson), **Supp. IV Part 2:** 646-647

"Blessed Is the Man" (Moore), **III:** 215
"Blessed Man of Boston, My Grandmother's Thimble, and Fanning Island, The" (Updike), **IV:** 219
"Blessing, A" (Wright), **Supp. III Part 2:** 600, 606
Blessing on the Moon, A (Skibell), **Supp. XVII:** 48
Blessings (Quindlen), **Supp. XVII:** 167, **178-179**
"Blessing the Animals" (Komunyakaa), **Supp. XIII:** 129-130
"Blessing the Children" (Hogan), **Supp. IV Part 1:** 401
Bless Me, Ultima (Anya), **Supp. XIII:** 220
Blew, Mary Clearman, **Supp. XIV:** 227
Bligh, S. M., **I:** 226
Blind Assassin, The (Atwood), **Supp. XIII:** 20, **32**
Blind Bow-Boy, The (Van Vechten), **Supp. II Part 2:** 737, 740-742
Blind Date (Kosinski), **Supp. VII:** 215, 224-225
Blind Lion, The (Gunn Allen), **Supp. IV Part 1:** 324
"Blind Man's Holiday" (O. Henry), **Supp. II Part 1:** 401
Blind Man with a Pistol (C. Himes), **Supp. XVI:** 143, 144
Blindness and Insight (de Man), **Retro. Supp. I:** 67
"Blind Poet, The: Sidney Lanier" (Warren), **Supp. I Part 1:** 371, 373
"Blind Tom" (Davis), **Supp. XVI:** 89, 90
Blithedale Romance, The (Hawthorne), **II:** 225, 231, 239, 241-242, 271, 282, 290; **IV:** 194; **Retro. Supp. I:** 63, 149, 152, 156-157, **162-163**; **Supp. I Part 2:** 579; **Supp. II Part 1:** 280; **Supp. VIII:** 153, 201
Blitzstein, Marc, **Supp. I Part 1:** 277
Blix (Norris), **III:** 314, 322, 327, 328, 333
Blixen, Karen Denisen Baroness. *See* Dinesen, Isak
"Blizzard in Cambridge" (Lowell), **II:** 554
Blok, Aleksandr Aleksandrovich, **IV:** 443
Blonde Bait (Lacy), **Supp. XV:** 204
Blondin, Antoine, **Supp. XVI:** 230
"Blood" (Singer), **IV:** 15, 19
Blood, Tin, Straw (Olds), **Supp. X:** **212-215**
Blood and Guts in High School (Acker), **Supp. XII:** 5, 6, **11-12**
"Blood Bay, The" (Proulx), **Supp. VII:** 262-263

"Blood-Burning Moon" (Toomer), **Supp. III Part 2:** 483; **Supp. IX:** 314-315
"Bloodchild" (O. Butler), **Supp. XIII:** 61, **69-70**
Bloodchild and Other Stories (O. Butler), **Supp. XIII:** 69
"Blood Donor" (Hay), **Supp. XIV:** 121
Blood for a Stranger (Jarrell), **II:** 367, 368-369, 370-371, 375, 377
Blood Issue (Crews), **Supp. XI:** 103
Bloodlines (Wright), **Supp. V:** 332, 335, 340
Blood Meridian; or, The Evening Redness in the West (McCarthy), **Supp. VIII:** 175, 177, **180-182**, 188, 190
"Blood of the Conquistadores, The" (Alvarez), **Supp. VII:** 7
"Blood of the Lamb, The" (hymn), **Supp. I Part 2:** 385
Blood of the Martyr (Crane), **I:** 422
"Blood of the Martyrs, The" (Benét), **Supp. XI:** 56, 58
Blood of the Prophets, The (Masters), **Supp. I Part 2:** 458, 459, 461
Blood on the Forge (Attaway), **Supp. II Part 1:** 234-235
"Blood Relatives" (Apple), **Supp. XVII:** 6
"Blood Returns, The" (Kingsolver), **Supp. VII:** 209
"Bloodshed" (C. Ozick), **Supp. XVII:** 43
Bloodshed and Three Novellas (Ozick), **Supp. V:** 259-260, 261, 266-268
"Blood Stains" (Francis), **Supp. IX:** 86
Bloody Crossroads, The: Where Literature and Politics Meet (Podhoretz), **Supp. VIII:** 241-242
Bloom, Alice, **Supp. IV Part 1:** 308
Bloom, Allan, **Retro. Supp. II:** 19, 30, 31, 33-34
Bloom, Claire, **Retro. Supp. II:** 281; **Supp. IX:** 125
Bloom, Harold, **Retro. Supp. I:** 67, 193, 299; **Retro. Supp. II:** 81, 210, 262; **Supp. IV Part 2:** 620, 689; **Supp. V:** 178, 272; **Supp. VIII:** 180; **Supp. IX:** 146, 259; **Supp. XII:** 261; **Supp. XIII:** 46, 47; **Supp. XIV:** 14; **Supp. XV:** 134; **Supp. XVII:** 70, 141
Bloom, Larry, **Supp. XIII:** 133
Bloom, Leopold, **I:** 27, 150; **III:** 10
Bloom, Lynn Z., **Supp. IV Part 1:** 6
Bloomfield, Leonard, **I:** 64
Bloomingdale Papers, The (Carruth), **Supp. XVI:** 48-50
"Blossom and Fruit" (Benét), **Supp.**

XI: 52-53
Blotner, Joseph, **Retro. Supp. I:** 88
Blouin, Lenora, **Supp. VIII:** 266
Blue Angel (Prose), **Supp. XVI:** 249, 259-260
"Blue Battalions, The" (Crane), **I:** 419-420
"Bluebeard" (Barthelme), **Supp. IV Part 1:** 47
"Bluebeard" (Millay), **III:** 130
"Blueberries" (Frost), **Retro. Supp. I:** 121, 128
Blue Calhoun (Price), **Supp. VI:** 265-266
Blue City (Macdonald, under Millar), **Supp. IV Part 2:** 466-467
Blue Dahlia, The (Chandler), **Supp. IV Part 1:** 130
Blue Estuaries, The: Poems, 1923-1968 (Bogan), **Supp. III Part 1:** 48, 57, 66
Blue Hammer, The (Macdonald), **Supp. IV Part 2:** 462
"Blue Hotel, The" (Crane), **I:** 34, 415-416, 423
"Blue Hour, The" (Komunyakaa), **Supp. XIII:** 130
Blue in the Face (Auster), **Supp. XII:** 21
Blue Jay's Dance, The: A Birth Year (Erdrich), **Supp. IV Part 1:** 259-260, 265, 270, 272
"Blue Juniata" (Cowley), **Supp. II Part 1:** 144
Blue Juniata: Collected Poems (Cowley), **Supp. II Part 1:** 140
Blue Light (Mosley), **Supp. XIII:** **245-247**, 248, 249
"Blue Light Lounge Sutra for the Performance Poets at Harold Park Hotel" (Komunyakaa), **Supp. XIII:** 125
"Blue Meridian" (Toomer), **Supp. III Part 2:** 476, 487; **Supp. IX:** 320
"Blue Moles" (Plath), **Supp. I Part 2:** 539
Blue Mountain Ballads (music) (Bowles), **Supp. IV Part 1:** 84
Blue Movie (Southern), **Supp. XI:** 309
"Blue Notes" (Matthews), **Supp. IX:** 169
Blue Pastures (Oliver), **Supp. VII:** 229-230, 245
"Blueprints" (Kingsolver), **Supp. VII:** 203
Blue Rhine, Black Forest (Untermeyer), **Supp. XV:** 310
"Blue Ribbon at Amesbury, A" (Frost), **Retro. Supp. I:** 138
"Blues Ain't No Mockin Bird"

(Bambara), **Supp. XI:** 3
"Blues Chant Hoodoo Rival" (Komunyakaa), **Supp. XIII:** 117, 118
"Blues for Another Time" (Dunn), **Supp. XI:** 148
"Blues for Jimmy" (McGrath), **Supp. X:** 116
"Blues for John Coltraine, Dead at 41" (Matthews), **Supp. IX:** 157
Blues for Mister Charlie (Baldwin), **Retro. Supp. II:** 8; **Supp. I Part 1:** 48, 61-62, 63
"Blues for Warren" (McGrath), **Supp. X:** 116
Blues If You Want (Matthews), **Supp. IX:** 155, **163-165**
"Blues I'm Playing, The" (Hughes), **Retro. Supp. I:** 204
"Blue Sky, The" (Snyder), **Supp. VIII:** 306
"Blues on a Box" (Hughes), **Retro. Supp. I:** 208
"Blues People" (Ellison), **Retro. Supp. II:** 124
Blues People: Negro Music in White America (Baraka), **Retro. Supp. II:** 124; **Supp. II Part 1:** 30, 31, 33-35, 37, 41, 42, 53
Bluest Eye, The (Morrison), **Supp. III Part 1:** 362, 363-367, 379; **Supp. IV Part 1:** 2, 253; **Supp. VIII:** 213, 214, 227; **Supp. XI:** 4, 91
Bluestone, George, **Supp. IX:** 7, 15
Blue Swallows, The (Nemerov), **III:** 269, 270, 271, 274-275, 278, 284, 286-288
Blue Voyage (Aiken), **I:** 53, 56
Blum, Gustav, **Supp. XV:** 194
Blum, Morgan, **I:** 169
Blum, W. C (pseudonym). *See* Watson, James Sibley, Jr.
Blumenthal, Nathaniel. *See* Branden, Nathaniel
Blumenthal, Sidney, **Supp. VIII:** 241
Blunt, Wilfrid Scawen, **III:** 459
Bly, Carol, **Supp. XVI:31-43**
Bly, Robert, **I:** 291; **Supp. III Part 2:** 599; **Supp. IV Part 1: 59-77,** 177; **Supp. IV Part 2:** 623; **Supp. V:** 332; **Supp. VIII:** 279; **Supp. IX:** 152, 155, 265, 271, 290; **Supp. X:** 127; **Supp. XI:** 142; **Supp. XIII:** 284; **Supp. XV:** 74, 176; **Supp. XVI:**32, 36, 39, 177, 212, 230; **Supp. XVII:** 243, 244
"B Negative" (X. J. Kennedy), **Supp. XV: 156-157**
"Boarder, The" (Simpson), **Supp. IX:** 269

Boarding House Blues (Farrell), **II:** 30, 43, 45
Boas, Franz, **I:** 214; **Supp. I Part 2:** 641; **Supp. VIII:** 295; **Supp. IX:** 329; **Supp. XIV:**199, 209, 210
"Boat, The" (Oliver), **Supp. VII:** 247
"Boat, The" (Sexton), **Supp. II Part 2:** 692
Boating Party, The (Renoir), **Supp. XII:** 188
Boat of Quiet Hours, The (Kenyon), **Supp. VII:** 167-169, 171
"Boat of Quiet Hours, The" (Kenyon), **Supp. VII:** 168
"Bob and Spike" (Wolfe), **Supp. III Part 2:** 580
Bobrowski, Johannes, **Supp. XV:** 78
Bob the Gambler (F. Barthelme), **Supp. XI:** 30, 31, 32, 34-35, 36-37
Boccaccio, Giovanni, **III:** 283, 411; **IV:** 230
Bocock, Maclin, **Supp. X:** 79
Bodelson, Anders, **Supp. XVI:**33
Bodenheim, Maxwell, **II:** 42, 530; **Retro. Supp. I:** 417; **Supp. I Part 1:** 257
"Bodies" (Oates), **Supp. II Part 2:** 520
"Bodies and Souls: The Haitian Revolution and Madison Smartt Bell's *All Souls' Rising*" (Trouillot), **Supp. X:** 14
Bodies of Work: Essays (Acker), **Supp. XII:** 7
Bodily Harm (Atwood), **Supp. XIII: 25-27**
Bodley Head Jack London (London), **II:** 483
Body (Crews), **Supp. XI: 108-109**
"Body, The" (Heldreth), **Supp. V:** 151
Body and Soul (Conroy), **Supp. XVI:**63, **72-74,** 77
"Body and Soul: A Meditation" (Kumin), **Supp. IV Part 2:** 442, 452
Body and Soul: Essays on Poetry (Jarman), **Supp. XVII:** 110, **111-112**
"Body and Soul: Parts of a Life" (Jarman), **Supp. XVII:** 112, 113
Body and the Song, The (Bishop), **Retro. Supp. II:** 40
"Body Bright" (Sanders), **Supp. XVI:**276
Body of Poetry, The: Essays on Women, Form, and the Poetic Self (A. Finch), **Supp. XVII:** 69-70, **77-78**
Body of This Death: Poems (Bogan), **Supp. III Part 1:** 47, 49-52, 58
Body of Waking (Rukeyser), **Supp. VI:** 274, 281
"Body of Waking" (Rukeyser), **Supp. VI:** 279

"Body on Fire, the Soul in Flight, The" (Jarman), **Supp. XVII:** 111, 112
Body Rags (Kinnell), **Supp. III Part 1:** 235, 236, 243-245, 250, 253, 254
"Body's Curse, The" (Dobyns), **Supp. XIII:** 87
"Body's Weight, The" (Dobyns), **Supp. XIII:** 89
Body Traffic (Dobyns), **Supp. XIII:** 87, 89
"'Body with the Lamp Lit Inside, The'" (Mills), **Supp. IV Part 1:** 64
Boehm, David, **Supp. XVII:** 58
Boehme, Jakob, **I:** 10
Bogan, Louise, **I:** 169, 185; **Retro. Supp. I:** 36; **Supp. I Part 2:** 707, 726; **Supp. III Part 1: 47-68; Supp. VIII:** 171, 265; **Supp. IX:** 229; **Supp. X:** 58, 102; **Supp. XIII:** 347; **Supp. XIV:**129; **Supp. XVII:** 75
Bogan, Major Benjamin Lewis, **IV:** 120
Bogart, Humphrey, **Supp. I Part 2:** 623; **Supp. IV Part 1:** 130, 356
Bogdanovich, Peter, **Supp. V:** 226
Bogey Man, The (Plimpton), **Supp. XVI:**241
Boggs, Francis W., **Supp. XVI:**182
"Bohemian, The" (Hapgood), **Supp. XVII:** 103
"Bohemian, The" (Harte), **Supp. II Part 1:** 339
"Bohemian Girl, The" (Cather), **Retro. Supp. I:** 7
"Bohemian Hymn, The" (Emerson), **II:** 19
"Boids and Beasties" (Geisel), **Supp. XVI:**100
Boissevain, Eugen, **III:** 124
Boit, Edward, **Retro. Supp. I:** 366
Bojorquez, Jennifer, **Supp. XII:** 318
Boker, George, **Supp. XV:** 269
"Bold Words at the Bridge" (Jewett), **II:** 394
Boleslavsky, Richard, **Supp. XIV:**240, 243
Boleyn, Anne, **Supp. I Part 2:** 461
Bolick, Katie, **Supp. XVI:**167
Bolivar, Simon, **Supp. I Part 1:** 283, 284, 285
Bolton, Guy, **Supp. I Part 1:** 281
Bolts of Melody: New Poems of Emily Dickinson (Todd and Bingham, eds.), **I:** 470; **Retro. Supp. I:** 36
"Bomb" (Corso), **Supp. XII:** 117, 124, 125-126, 127
Bombeck, Erma, **Supp. XVII:** 168
Bombs Away (Steinbeck), **IV:** 51-52
"Bona and Paul" (Toomer), **Supp. IX:** 307, 318-319

Bonaparte, Marie, **III:** 418; **Retro. Supp. II:** 264, 266
"Bon-Bon" (Poe), **III:** 425
Bond, The (N. Boyce), **Supp. XVII:** 99, 100
Bondsman, The (Massinger), **Supp. XV:** 238
Bone, Robert, **Supp. IX:** 318-319; **Supp. XI:** 283
Bone by Bone (Matthiessen), **Supp. V:** 199, 212, 213, 214
Boners (Abingdon). See *Schoolboy Howlers* (Abingdon)
"Bones" (Goldbarth), **Supp. XII:** 173-174
"Bones and Jewels" (Monette), **Supp. X:** 159
"Bones and Shells" (Sanders), **Supp. XVI:** 271-272
"Bones of a House" (Cowley). See "Blue Juniata"
Bonetti, Kay, **Supp. VIII:** 47, 152, 159, 160, 165, 168, 170, 223; **Supp. XII:** 61; **Supp. XIV:** 232, 234
Bonfire of the Vanities, The (Wolfe), **Supp. III Part 2:** 584-586
Bonheur, Rosa, **Supp. XV:** 276
Bonhoeffer, Dietrich, **Supp. VIII:** 198
Boni, Charles, **Supp. XIV:** 288
Boni and Liveright, **Retro. Supp. I:** 59, 80, 178
Bonicelli, Vittorio, **Supp. XI:** 307
Bonifacius (Mather), **Supp. II Part 2:** 461, 464
Bonnefoy, Yves, **Supp. III Part 1:** 235, 243
Bonner, Robert, **Retro. Supp. I:** 246
Bonneville, Mme. Marguerite, **Supp. I Part 2:** 520, 521
Bonneville, Nicolas de, **Supp. I Part 2:** 511, 518, 519
Bonney, William. See Billy the Kid
Bontemps, Arna, **Retro. Supp. I:** 194, 196, 203; **Supp. I Part 1:** 325; **Supp. IV Part 1:** 170; **Supp. IX:** 306, 309
Book, A (Barnes), **Supp. III Part 1:** 36, 39, 44
Book about Myself, A (Dreiser), **I:** 515; **Retro. Supp. II:** 104
"Book as a Container of Consciousness, The" (Gass), **Supp. VI:** 92
Booker, Keith, **Supp. XV:** 197
"Bookies, Beware!" (Heller), **Supp. IV Part 1:** 383
Book of American Negro Poetry, The (Johnson), **Supp. IV Part 1:** 165, 166
Book of Americans, A (Benét), **Supp. XI:** 46, 47, 51

Book of Beb, The (Buechner), **Supp. XII:** 53
Book of Breeething, The (Burroughs), **Supp. III Part 1:** 97, 103
Book of Burlesques, A (Mencken), **III:** 104
Book of Common Prayer, A (Didion), **Supp. IV Part 1:** 196, 198, 203-205, 207, 208
Book of Daniel, The (Doctorow), **Supp. IV Part 1:** 218, 219, 220-222, 227, 231, 237-238, 238; **Supp. V:** 45
Book of Dreams (Kerouac), **Supp. III Part 1:** 225
"Book of Ephraim, The" (Merrill), **Supp. III Part 1:** 330-334
Book of Folly, The (Sexton), **Supp. II Part 2:** 691, 692-694
Book of Gods and Devils, The (Simic), **Supp. VIII:** 281
Book of Guys, The (Keillor), **Supp. XVI:** 177
"Book of Hours of Sister Clotilde, The" (Lowell), **II:** 522
Book of Jamaica, The (Banks), **Supp. V:** 11, 12, 16
"Book of Life" (Bidart), **Supp. XV:** 23
Book of Living Verse, The; English and American Poetry from the Thirteenth Century to the Present Day (Untermeyer, ed.), **Supp. XV:** 310
Book of Love, A (Vildrac; Bynner, trans.), **Supp. XV:** 50
Book of Lyrics (Bynner), **Supp. XV:** 51
Book of Medicines, The (Hogan), **Supp. IV Part 1:** 397, 410, 411-414
"Book of Medicines, The" (Hogan), **Supp. IV Part 1:** 412, 413
"Book of Memory, The" (Auster), **Supp. XII:** 21-22
Book of My Nights (L.-Y. Lee), **Supp. XV:** 215, **223-226**
Book of Negro Folklore, The (Hughes, ed.), **Supp. I Part 1:** 345
Book of Nightmares, The (Kinnell), **Supp. III Part 1:** 235, 236, 243, 244, 246-254
Book of Prefaces, A (Mencken), **III:** 99-100, 105
Book of Repulsive Women, The (Barnes), **Supp. III Part 1:** 33
Book of Roses, The (Parkman), **Supp. II Part 2:** 597, 598
Book of the Body, The (Bidart), **Supp. XV:** 21, **25-27**
"Book of the Dead, The" (Rukeyser), **Supp. VI:** 272, 278, 279; **Supp. XV:** 349
"Book of the Grotesque, The"
(Anderson), **I:** 106
Book of the Homeless, The (Wharton), **Retro. Supp. I:** 377
Book of the Hopi (Waters), **Supp. X:** 124
Book of Tobit (Bible), **Supp. XII:** 54
Book of Verses, A (Masters), **Supp. I Part 2:** 458
Book of Yaak, The (Bass), **Supp. XVI:** 18-19
"Book of Yolek, The" (Hecht), **Supp. X:** 69, **70-71**
"Books Considered" (Bloom), **Supp. I Part 1:** 96
Books in My Life, The (H. Miller), **II:** 176, 189
"Books/P,L,E, The" (Goldbarth), **Supp. XII:** 190
Bookviews, **Supp. XI:** 216
"Boom" (Nemerov), **III:** 278
Boom! (T. Williams), **IV:** 383
Boom Town (Wolfe), **IV:** 456
"Boom Town" (Wolfe), **IV:** 469
Boone, Daniel, **II:** 207; **III:** 444; **IV:** 192, 193
Boorstin, Daniel, **I:** 253
Booth, Charles, **Supp. I Part 1:** 13
Booth, General William, **Supp. I Part 2:** 384, 386
Booth, John Wilkes, **III:** 588
Booth, Philip, **I:** 522; **Supp. IX:** 269; **Supp. XI:** 141; **Supp. XIII:** 277; **Supp. XV:** 92
Borah, William, **III:** 475
Borden, Lizzie, **II:** 5
Borderlands/La Frontera: The New Mestiza (Anzaldúa), **Supp. XIII:** 223
Borders (Mora), **Supp. XIII:** 213, **215-217**
Border Trilogy (McCarthy), **Supp. VIII:** 175, 182
Borel, Pétrus, **III:** 320
Borges, Jorge Luis, **I:** 123, 135, 138, 140, 142; **Supp. III Part 2:** 560; **Supp. IV Part 2:** 623, 626, 630; **Supp. V:** 238; **Supp. VIII:** 15, 348, 349; **Supp. XII:** 21, 147; **Supp. XV:** 34; **Supp. XVI:** 201, 206; **Supp. XVII:** 47
"Borges and I" (Bidart), **Supp. XV:** 34, 35
"Borinken Blues" (Komunyakaa), **Supp. XIII:** 117
"Born a Square: The Westerner's Dilemma" (Stegner), **Supp. IV Part 2:** 595; **Supp. V:** 224
"Born Bad" (Cisneros), **Supp. VII:** 62
Borrowed Time: An AIDS Memoir (Monette), **Supp. X:** 145, 146, 147,

152, 154, 155
"Bosque del Apache Wildlife Refuge" (Mora), **Supp. XIII:** 218
Boss Dog, The: A Story of Provence (M. F. K. Fisher), **Supp. XVII:** 91
"Boston" (Hardwick), **Supp. III Part 1:** 201
Boston (Sinclair), **Supp. V:** 282, 288-289
Boston, B. H., **Supp. XIII:** 312
Boston Adventure (Stafford), **Retro. Supp. II:** 177, 178
"Boston Common" (Berryman), **I:** 172
"Boston Hymn" (Emerson), **II:** 13, 19
Bostonians, The (H. James), **I:** 9; **II:** 282; **IV:** 202; **Retro. Supp. I:** 216, 225
Boston Marriage (Mamet), **Supp. XIV:** 247
"Boston Nativity, The" (Lowell), **II:** 538
Boswell: A Modern Comedy (Elkin), **Supp. VI:** 42, **44-45,** 57
Boswell, James, **IV:** 431; **Supp. I Part 2:** 656
Bosworth, Patricia, **Supp. IV Part 2:** 573, 591
Botticelli (McNally), **Supp. XIII:** 197
Botticelli, Sandro, **IV:** 410; **Retro. Supp. I:** 422
"Botticellian Trees, The" (W. C. Williams), **Retro. Supp. I:** 422
"Bottle of Milk for Mother, A" (Algren), **Supp. IX:** 3
"Bottle of Perrier, A" (Wharton), **IV:** 316
"Bottles" (Kenyon), **Supp. VII:** 171
Bottom: On Shakespeare (Zukofsky), **Supp. III Part 2:** 622, 624, 625, 626, 627, 629
"Bottom Line, The" (Elkin), **Supp. VI:** 52, **53**
Boucher, Anthony, **Supp. IV Part 2:** 473; **Supp. XV:** 203, 205
Boulanger, Nadia, **Supp. IV Part 1:** 81
"Boulot and Boulette" (Chopin), **Supp. I Part 1:** 211
Boulton, Agnes, **III:** 403
Bound East for Cardiff (O'Neill), **III:** 388
"Bouquet, The" (Stevens), **IV:** 90
"Bouquet of Roses in Sunlight" (Stevens), **IV:** 93
Bourdin, Henri L., **Supp. I Part 1:** 251
Bourgeois Poet, The (Shapiro), **Supp. II Part 2:** 701, 703, 704, 713, 714-716
Bourget, James, **IV:** 319
Bourget, Paul, **II:** 325, 338; **IV:** 311, 315; **Retro. Supp. I:** 224, 359, 373

Bourjaily, Vance, **III:** 43; **Supp. IX:** 260
Bourke-White, Margaret, **I:** 290, 293, 295, 297
Bourne, Charles Rogers, **I:** 215
Bourne, Mrs. Charles Rogers, **I:** 215
Bourne, Randolph, **I: 214-238,** 243, 245, 246-247, 251, 259; **Supp. I Part 2:** 524; **Supp. XV:** 141, 298, 301
Bowden, Charles, **Supp. XIII:** 17
Bowditch, Nathaniel, **Supp. I Part 2:** 482
Bowen, Barbara, **Supp. IX:** 311
Bowen, Elizabeth, **Retro. Supp. I:** 351; **Supp. IV Part 1:** 299; **Supp. VIII:** 65, 165, 251, 265; **Supp. IX:** 128
Bowen, Francis, **Supp. I Part 2:** 413
Bowen, Louise de Koven, **Supp. I Part 1:** 5
Bowen, Michael, **Supp. VIII:** 73
Bowers, John, **Supp. XI:** 217-218
"Bowlers Anonymous" (Dobyns), **Supp. XIII:** 86
Bowles, Jane (Jane Auer), **II:** 586; **Supp. IV Part 1:** 89, 92
Bowles, Paul, **I:** 211; **II:** 586; **Supp. II Part 1:** 17; **Supp. IV Part 1: 79-99**
Bowles, Samuel, **I:** 454, 457; **Retro. Supp. I:** 30, 32, 33
"Bowl of Blood, The" (Jeffers), **Supp. II Part 2:** 434
"Bowls" (Moore), **III:** 196
Bowman, James, **I:** 193
"Bows to Drouth" (Snyder), **Supp. VIII:** 303
Box, Edgar (pseudonym). *See* Vidal, Gore
Box and Quotations from Chairman Mao Tse-tung (Albee), **I:** 89-91, 94
Box Garden, The (Shields), **Supp. VII:** 314-315, 320
"Box Seat" (Toomer), **Supp. III Part 2:** 484; **Supp. IX:** 316, 318
Boy, A (Ashbery), **Supp. III Part 1:** 5
Boyce, Horace, **II:** 136
Boyce, Neith, **Supp. XVII:** 96, 97, 98-99, 100, 106
Boyd, Brian, **Retro. Supp. I:** 270, 275
Boyd, Janet L., **Supp. X:** 229
Boyd, Nancy (pseudonym). *See* Millay, Edna St. Vincent
Boyd, Thomas, **I:** 99; **IV:** 427
Boyesen, H. H., **II:** 289
"Boyhood" (Farrell), **II:** 28
"Boy in France, A" (Salinger), **III:** 552-553
Boy in the Water (Dobyns), **Supp.**

XIII: 75, **84**
Boyle, Kay, **IV:** 404
Boyle, T. C. (Thomas Coraghessan), **Supp. VIII: 1-17**
Boyle, Thomas John. *See* Boyle, T. C.
Boynton, H. W., **Supp. IX:** 7
Boynton, Percy Holmes, **Supp. I Part 2:** 415
Boynton, Robert, **Supp. XVII:** 209
"Boy on a Train" (Ellison), **Retro. Supp. II:** 124
"Boy Riding Forward Backward" (Francis), **Supp. IX:** 82
"Boys and Girls" (Cisneros), **Supp. VII:** 59-60
Boy's Froissart, The (Lanier), **Supp. I Part 1:** 361
Boy's King Arthur, The (Lanier), **Supp. I Part 1:** 361
Boy's Mabinogion, The (Lanier), **Supp. I Part 1:** 361
"Boys of '29, The" (Holmes), **Supp. I Part 1:** 308
Boys of '76, The (Coffin), **III:** 577
Boy's Percy, The (Lanier), **Supp. I Part 1:** 361
Boy's Town (Howells), **I:** 418
Boy's Will, A (Frost), **II:** 152, 153, 155-156, 159, 164, 166; **Retro. Supp. I:** 124, 127, 128, 131; **Retro. Supp. II:** 168
"Boy Who Wrestled with Angels, The" (Hoffman), **Supp. X:** 90
"Boy with One Shoe, The" (Jewett), **Retro. Supp. II:** 132
"Brace, The" (Bausch), **Supp. VII:** 48
Bracebridge Hall, or, The Humorists (Irving), **I:** 339, 341; **II:** 308-309, 313
Bracher, Frederick, **I:** 378, 380; **Supp. I Part 1:** 185
Brackenridge, Hugh Henry, **Supp. I Part 1:** 124, 127, 145; **Supp. II Part 1:** 65
Brackett, Leigh, **Supp. IV Part 1:** 130
Bradbury, John M., **I:** 288-289; **IV:** 130, 135
Bradbury, Malcolm, **Supp. VIII:** 124
Bradbury, Ray, **Supp. I Part 2:** 621-622; **Supp. IV Part 1: 101-118;** **Supp. XVI:** 122; **Supp. XVII:** 41
Braddon, Mary E., **Supp. I Part 1:** 35, 36
Bradfield, Scott, **Supp. VIII:** 88
Bradford, Gamaliel, **I:** 248, 250
Bradford, Roark, **Retro. Supp. I:** 80
Bradford, William, **Retro. Supp. II:** 161, 162; **Supp. I Part 1:** 110, 112; **Supp. I Part 2:** 486, 494
Bradlee, Ben, **Supp. V:** 201

Bradley, Bill, **Supp. VIII:** 47
Bradley, F. H., **Retro. Supp. I:** 57, 58
Bradley, Francis Herbert, **I:** 59, 567-568, 572, 573
Bradshaw, Barbara, **Supp. XIII:** 313
Bradstreet, Anne, **I:** 178-179, 180, 181, 182, 184; **III:** 505; **Retro. Supp. I:** 40; **Supp. I Part 1: 98-123,** 300; **Supp. I Part 2:** 484, 485, 496, 546, 705; **Supp. V:** 113, 117-118; **Supp. XIII:** 152; **Supp. XIV:**128
Bradstreet, Elizabeth, **Supp. I Part 1:** 108, 122
Bradstreet, Mrs. Simon. *See* Bradstreet, Anne
Bradstreet, Simon, **I:** 178; **Supp. I Part 1:** 103, 110, 116
Brady, Alice, **III:** 399
"Bragdowdy and the Busybody, The" (Thurber), **Supp. I Part 2:** 617
"Brahma" (Emerson), **II:** 19, 20
Brahms, Johannes, **III:** 118, 448
"Braiding" (L.-Y. Lee), **Supp. XV:** 214
"Brain and the Mind, The" (James), **II:** 346
Brainard, Joe, **Supp. XV:** 33
"Brain Damage" (Barthelme), **Supp. IV Part 1:** 44
"Brain to the Heart, The" (Komunyakaa), **Supp. XIII:** 120
Braithewaite, W. S., **Retro. Supp. I:** 131
Braithwaite, William Stanley, **Supp. IX:** 309; **Supp. XV:** 296-297, 301-302, 305, 306
Brakhage, Stan, **Supp. XII:** 2
Brame, Gloria, **Supp. XV:** 113
Bramer, Monte, **Supp. X:** 152
Branch Will Not Break, The (Wright), **Supp. III Part 2:** 596, 598-601; **Supp. IV Part 1:** 60; **Supp. IX:** 159
Brancusi, Constantin, **III:** 201; **Retro. Supp. I:** 292
Brande, Dorothea, **Supp. I Part 2:** 608
Branden, Nathaniel, **Supp. IV Part 2:** 526, 528
"Brand-Name Blues" (Kaufmann), **Supp. XI:** 39
Brand New Life, A (Farrell), **II:** 46, 48
Brando, Marlon, **II:** 588; **Supp. IV Part 2:** 560
Brandon, Henry, **Supp. I Part 2:** 604, 612, 618
Brandt, Alice, **Supp. I Part 1:** 92
Brandt, Carl, **Supp. XI:** 45
Brant, Sebastian, **III:** 447, 448
Braque, Georges, **III:** 197; **Supp. IX:** 66
Brashford, Jake, **Supp. X:** 252
Brasil, Emanuel, **Supp. I Part 1:** 94

"Brasília" (Plath), **Supp. I Part 2:** 544, 545
"Brass Buttons" (McCoy), **Supp. XIII:** 161
"Brass Candlestick, The" (Francis), **Supp. IX:** 89
Brass Check, The (Sinclair), **Supp. V:** 276, 281, 282, 284-285
"Brass Ring, The" (Carver), **Supp. III Part 1:** 137
"Brass Spittoons" (Hughes), **Supp. I Part 1:** 326-327
Brats (X. J. Kennedy), **Supp. XV:** 163
Brautigan, Richard, **III:** 174; **Supp. VIII:** 42, 43; **Supp. XII:** 139; **Supp. XVI:**172
Brave Cowboy, The (Abbey), **Supp. XIII:** 4-5
Brave Men (Pyle), **Supp. XVII:** 61
Brave New World (Huxley), **II:** 454; **Supp. XIII:** 29
"Brave New World" (MacLeish), **III:** 18
Bravery of Earth, A (Eberhart), **I:** 522, 524, 525, 526, 530
"Brave Tailors of Maida, The" (Talese), **Supp. XVII:** 208
"Brave Words for a Startling Occasion" (Ellison), **Retro. Supp. II:** 118
Braving the Elements (Merrill), **Supp. III Part 1:** 320, 323, 325-327, 329
Bravo, The (Cooper), **I:** 345-346, 348
"Bravura" (Francis), **Supp. IX:** 90
Brawley, Benjamin, **Supp. I Part 1:** 327, 332
Brawne, Fanny, **I:** 284; **II:** 531
Braxton, Joanne, **Supp. IV Part 1:** 12, 15
Brazil (Bishop), **Retro. Supp. II:** 45; **Supp. I Part 1:** 92
"Brazil" (Marshall), **Supp. XI:** 281
Brazil (Updike), **Retro. Supp. I:** 329, 330, 334
"Brazil, January 1, 1502" (Bishop), **Retro. Supp. II:** 47
Braziller, George, **Supp. X:** 24
Brazzi, Rossano, **Supp. IV Part 2:** 520
"Bread" (Dickey), **Supp. IV Part 1:** 182
"Bread" (Olds), **Supp. X:** 206
"Bread Alone" (Wylie), **Supp. I Part 2:** 727
Bread in the Wilderness (Merton), **Supp. VIII:** 197, 208
Bread of Idleness, The (Masters), **Supp. I Part 2:** 460
"Bread of This World, The" (McGrath), **Supp. X:** 119, 127
Bread of Time, The (Levine), **Supp. V:** 180

Bread without Sugar (Stern), **Supp. IX: 297-298**
"Break, The" (Sexton), **Supp. II Part 2:** 689
Breakfast at Tiffany's (Capote), **Supp. III Part 1:** 113, 117, 119-121, 124, 126
Breakfast of Champions (Vonnegut), **Supp. II Part 2:** 755, 759, 769, 770, 777-778
Breaking and a Death, A (Kees), **Supp. XV:** 145
Breaking and Entering (X. J. Kennedy), **Supp. XV:** 153, **160-162**
Breaking Hard Ground (D. Hunter), **Supp. XVI:**38
Breaking Ice (McMillan, ed.), **Supp. XIII:** 182-183
Breaking Open (Rukeyser), **Supp. VI:** 274, 281
"Breaking Open" (Rukeyser), **Supp. VI:** 286
Breaking Ranks: A Political Memoir (Podhoretz), **Supp. VIII: 239-241,** 245
"Breaking the Code of Silence: Ideology and Women's Confessional Poetry" (Harris), **Supp. XIV:**269
"Breaking Up of the Winships, The" (Thurber), **Supp. I Part 2:** 616
Breast, The (P. Roth), **Retro. Supp. II:** 287-288; **Supp. III Part 2:** 416, 418
"Breast, The" (Sexton), **Supp. II Part 2:** 687
"Breasts" (Simic), **Supp. VIII:** 275
"Breath" (Levine), **Supp. V:** 185
Breathe No More, My Lady (Lacy), **Supp. XV:** 203
Breathing Lessons (Tyler), **Supp. IV Part 2:** 669-670
Breathing the Water (Levertov), **Supp. III Part 1:** 274, 283, 284
"Breath of Life, The" (C. Baxter), **Supp. XVII:** 23
Breath's Burials (Sobin), **Supp. XVI:**288-289
Breaux, Zelia, **Retro. Supp. II:** 114
Brecht, Bertolt, **I:** 60, 301; **III:** 161, 162; **IV:** 394; **Supp. I Part 1:** 292; **Supp. II Part 1:** 10, 26, 56; **Supp. IV Part 1:** 359; **Supp. IX:** 131, 133, 140; **Supp. X:** 112; **Supp. XIII:** 206, 286; **Supp. XIV:**162
Breen, Joseph I., **IV:** 390
Breit, Harvey, **I:** 433; **III:** 575; **Retro. Supp. II:** 230
Bremer, Fredrika, **Supp. I Part 1:** 407
Brendan: A Novel (Buechner), **Supp. XII:** 53

Brennan, Matthew, **Supp. XV:** 113, 125
Brent, Linda, **Supp. IV Part 1:** 12, 13
Brentano, Franz, **II:** 350; **Supp. XIV:** 198, 199
Brer Rabbit (tales), **Supp. IV Part 1:** 11, 13; **Supp. XIV:** 88
Breslin, James E. B., **Retro. Supp. I:** 430
Breslin, John B., **Supp. IV Part 1:** 308
Breslin, Paul, **Supp. VIII:** 283
Bresson, Robert, **Supp. IV Part 1:** 156
"Bresson's Movies" (Creeley), **Supp. IV Part 1:** 156-157
Breton, André, **III:** 425; **Supp. XIII:** 114; **Supp. XVII:** 244
Brett, George, **II:** 466; **Supp. V:** 286
Brevoort, Henry, **II:** 298
Brew, Kwesi, **Supp. IV Part 1:** 10, 16
Brewer, Gaylord, **Supp. XV:** 330
"Brewing of Soma, The" (Whittier), **Supp. I Part 2:** 704
Brewsie and Willie (Stein), **IV:** 27
Brewster, Martha, **Supp. I Part 1:** 114
"Brian Age 7" (Doty), **Supp. XI:** 136
"Briar Patch, The" (Warren), **IV:** 237
Briar Rose (Coover), **Supp. V:** 52
"Briar Rose (Sleeping Beauty)" (Sexton), **Supp. II Part 2:** 690
Brice, Fanny, **II:** 427
"Brick, The" (Nye), **Supp. XIII:** 276
"Bricklayer in the Snow" (Fante), **Supp. XI:** 164-165
"Brick Layer's Lunch Hour, The" (Ginsberg), **Supp. II Part 1:** 318
Brickman, Marshall, **Supp. XV:** 5
"Bricks, The" (Hogan), **Supp. IV Part 1:** 413
"Bridal Ballad, The" (Poe), **III:** 428
Bridal Dinner, The (Gurney), **Supp. V:** 109, 110
"Bride Comes to Yellow Sky, The" (Crane), **I:** 34, 415, 416, 423
"Bride in the 30's, A" (Auden), **Supp. II Part 1:** 9
Bride of Lammermoor (Scott), **II:** 291
Bride of Samoa (film), **Supp. IV Part 1:** 82
Bride of the Innisfallen, The (Welty), **IV:** 261, 275-279
"Bride of the Innisfallen, The" (Welty), **IV:** 278-279; **Retro. Supp. I:** 353
Bride of the Innisfallen, The, and Other Stories (Welty), **Retro. Supp. I:** 352-353, 355
Brides of the South Wind: Poems 1917-1922 (Jeffers), **Supp. II Part 2:** 419
Bridge, Horatio, **II:** 226
"BRIDGE, THE" (Baraka), **Supp. II Part 1:** 32, 36

Bridge, The (H. Crane), **I:** 62, 109, 266, 385, 386, 387, 395-399, 400, 402; **IV:** 123, 341, 418, 419, 420; **Retro. Supp. I:** 427; **Retro. Supp. II:** 76, 77, 81, 83, **84-87**; **Supp. V:** 342; **Supp. IX:** 306
Bridge, The (Talese), **Supp. XVII:** 202, 203, 208
Bridge at Remagen, The (film), **Supp. XI:** 343
"Bridge Burners, The" (Van Vechten), **Supp. II Part 2:** 733
Bridge of San Luis Rey, The (Wilder), **I:** 360; **IV:** 356, 357, 360-363, 365, 366
Bridge of Years, The (Sarton), **Supp. VIII:** 253
"Bridges" (Kingsolver), **Supp. VII:** 208
Bridges, Harry, **I:** 493
Bridges, Lloyd, **Supp. XV:** 202
Bridges, Robert, **II:** 537; **III:** 527; **Supp. I Part 2:** 721; **Supp. II Part 1:** 21; **Supp. XIV:** 336, 341, 342, 343
"Bridging" (Apple), **Supp. XVII:** 5
Bridgman, P. W., **I:** 278
"Bridle, The" (Carver), **Supp. III Part 1:** 138
"Brief and Blameless Outline of the Ontogeny of Crow, A" (Wright), **Supp. XV:** 347
"Brief Début of Tildy, The" (O. Henry), **Supp. II Part 1:** 408
"Brief Encounters on the Inland Waterway" (Vonnegut), **Supp. II Part 2:** 760
Briefings (Ammons), **Supp. VII:** 29
Brief Interviews with Hideous Men (Wallace), **Supp. X: 308-310**
"Brief Interviews with Hideous Men" (Wallace), **Supp. X:** 309
"Briefly It Enters, and Briefly Speaks" (Kenyon), **Supp. VII:** 174
Briffault, Robert, **Supp. I Part 2:** 560, 567
"Brigade de Cuisine" (McPhee), **Supp. III Part 1:** 307-308
Brigadier and the Golf Widow, The (Cheever), **Supp. I Part 1:** 184-185, 192
Briggs, Charles F., **Supp. I Part 2:** 411
brigham, besmilr, **Supp. XV:** 349
"Bright and Morning Star" (Wright), **IV:** 488
Bright Book of Life: American Novelists and Storytellers from Hemingway to Mailer (Kazin), **Supp. VIII:** 102, 104
Bright Center of Heaven (Maxwell), **Supp. VIII: 153-155,** 164
"Brightness from the North" (B. Kelly), **Supp. XVII:** 131
Brighton Beach Memoirs (Simon), **Supp. IV Part 2:** 576, 577, 584, 586-587, 590
Bright Procession (Sedges), **Supp. II Part 1:** 125
Bright Room Called Day, A (Kushner), **Supp. IX:** 133, **138-141,** 142
Brillat-Savarin, Jean Anthelme, **Supp. XVII:** 82, 86, 87
"Brilliance" (Doty), **Supp. XI:** 124, 128
"Brilliant Leaves" (Gordon), **II:** 199
"Brilliant Sad Sun" (W. C. Williams), **Retro. Supp. I:** 422
"Bringing Back the Trumpeter Swan" (Kumin), **Supp. IV Part 2:** 454
Bringing It All Back Home (McNally), **Supp. XIII:** 197-198
Bringing the Devil to His Knees (C. Baxter), **Supp. XVII:** 22
"Bringing the Strange Home" (Dunn), **Supp. XI:** 141
"Bring the Day!" (Roethke), **III:** 536
Brinkley, Douglas, **Supp. XIII:** 9
Brinkmeyer, Robert H., Jr., **Supp. XI:** 38
Brinnin, John Malcolm, **IV:** 26, 27, 28, 42, 46; **Supp. XV:** 139
Brissot, Jacques Pierre, **Supp. I Part 2:** 511
"Britain's Negro Problem in Sierra Leone" (Du Bois), **Supp. I Part 1:** 176
"British Guiana" (Marshall), **Supp. XI:** 281-282
"British Poets, The" (Holmes), **Supp. I Part 1:** 306
"British Prison Ship, The" (Freneau), **Supp. II Part 1:** 261
Brittan, Gordon G., Jr., **Supp. XIV:** 234
Britten, Benjamin, **II:** 586; **Supp. II Part 1:** 17; **Supp. IV Part 1:** 84
Broadwater, Bowden, **II:** 562
Broadway, Broadway (McNally). See *It's Only a Play* (McNally)
Broadway, J. William, **Supp. V:** 316
Broadway Bound (Simon), **Supp. IV Part 2:** 576, 577, 584, 586-587, 590
Broadway Danny Rose (film; Allen), **Supp. XV:** 9
"Broadway Sights" (Whitman), **IV:** 350
Broccoli, Albert R. "Cubby," **Supp. XI:** 307
Bröck, Sabine, **Supp. XI:** 275, 277, 278
Brodhead, Richard, **Retro. Supp. II:** 139; **Supp. XIV:** 61

Brodkey, Harold, **Supp. VIII:** 151; **Supp. X:** 160
Brodskii, Iosif Alexsandrovich. *See* Brodsky, Joseph
Brodsky, Joseph, **Supp. VIII: 19-35;** **Supp. X:** 65, 73; **Supp. XV:** 134, 135, 256
Brody, Alter, **Supp. XV:** 302, 307
Brodyar, Anatole, **Supp. XIV:**106
"Brokeback Mountain" (Proulx), **Supp. VII:** 264-265
"Broken Balance, The" (Jeffers), **Supp. II Part 2:** 426
"Broken Field Running" (Bambara), **Supp. XI:** 10, 11
Broken Frieze, The (Everwine), **Supp. XV:** 74, 75, 89
Broken Ground, The (Berry), **Supp. X:** 30
"Broken Home, The" (Merrill), **Supp. III Part 1:** 319, 325
"Broken Oar, The" (Longfellow), **Retro. Supp. II:** 169
"Broken Promise" (MacLeish), **III:** 15
Broken Span, The (W. C. Williams), **IV:** 419; **Retro. Supp. I:** 424
"Broken Tower, The" (H. Crane), **I:** 385, 386, 400, 401-402; **Retro. Supp. II:** 89, 90
Broken Vessels (Dubus), **Supp. VII:** 90-91; **Supp. XI:** 347
"Broken Vessels" (Dubus), **Supp. VII:** 90
"Broker" (H. Roth), **Supp. IX:** 234
Bromfield, Louis, **IV:** 380
"Brompton Cocktail" (Mamet), **Supp. XIV:**252
Bromwich, David, **Retro. Supp. I:** 305; **Supp. XII:** 162
"Broncho That Would Not Be Broken, The" (Lindsay), **Supp. I Part 2:** 383
Bronk, William, **Supp. XV:** 115
Brontë, Anne, **Supp. IV Part 2:** 430
Brontë, Branwell, **I:** 462
Brontë, Charlotte, **I:** 458; **II:** 175; **Supp. IV Part 2:** 430; **Supp. IX:** 128; **Supp. XII:** 104, 303; **Supp. XV:** 338; **Supp. XVI:**158
Brontë, Emily, **I:** 458; **Retro. Supp. I:** 43; **Supp. IV Part 2:** 430; **Supp. IX:** 128; **Supp. X:** 78, 89; **Supp. XV:** 338
"Bronze" (Francis), **Supp. IX:** 76
"Bronze" (Merrill), **Supp. III Part 1:** 336
Bronze Booklets on the History, Problems, and Cultural Contributions of the Negro series, **Supp. XIV:**202
"Bronze Buckaroo, The" (Baraka), **Supp. II Part 1:** 49

"Bronze Horses, The" (Lowell), **II:** 524
"Bronze Tablets" (Lowell), **II:** 523
Bronzeville Boys and Girls (Brooks), **Supp. III Part 1:** 79
"Bronzeville Mother Loiters in Mississippi, A. Meanwhile, a Mississippi Mother Burns Bacon" (Brooks), **Supp. III Part 1:** 80
"Brooch, The" (Singer), **IV:** 20
Brook, Peter, **Retro. Supp. II:** 182
Brooke, Rupert, **II:** 82; **III:** 3
Brook Evans (Glaspell), **Supp. III Part 1:** 182-185
"Brooking Likeness" (Glück), **Supp. V:** 85
"Brooklyn" (Marshall), **Supp. XI:** 281, 282
Brooks, Cleanth, **I:** 280, 282; **III:** 517; **IV:** 236, 279; **Retro. Supp. I:** 40, 41, 90; **Retro. Supp. II:** 235; **Supp. I Part 2:** 423; **Supp. III Part 2:** 542; **Supp. V:** 316; **Supp. IX:** 153, 155; **Supp. X:** 115, 123; **Supp. XIV:1-20**
Brooks, David, **Supp. IV Part 2:** 623, 626, 630; **Supp. VIII:** 232
Brooks, Gwendolyn, **Retro. Supp. I:** 208; **Supp. III Part 1: 69-90;** **Supp. IV Part 1:** 2, 15, 244, 251, 257; **Supp. XI:** 1, 278; **Supp. XIII:** 111, 112, 296; **Supp. XIV:**73
Brooks, Mel, **Supp. IV Part 1:** 390; **Supp. IV Part 2:** 591
Brooks, Mrs. Van Wyck (Eleanor Kenyon Stimson), **I:** 240, 245, 250, 252
Brooks, Mrs. Van Wyck (Gladys Billings), **I:** 258
Brooks, Paul, **Supp. IX:** 26, 31, 32
Brooks, Phillips, **II:** 542; **Retro. Supp. II:** 134; **Supp. XIII:** 142
Brooks, Van Wyck, **I:** 106, 117, 215, 222, 228, 230, 231, 233, 236, **239-263,** 266, 480; **II:** 30, 271, 285, 309, 337, 482; **III:** 394, 606; **IV:** 171, 312, 427, 433; **Retro. Supp. II:** 46, 137; **Supp. I Part 2:** 423, 424, 650; **Supp. II Part 1:** 137; **Supp. VIII:** 98, 101; **Supp. XIV:**11; **Supp. XV:** 298, 301
Broom of the System, The (Wallace), **Supp. X:** 301, **302-305,** 310
"Brooms" (Simic), **Supp. VIII:** 275
Brosnan, Jim, **II:** 424-425
Brother Carl (Sontag), **Supp. III Part 2:** 452
"Brother Death" (Anderson), **I:** 114
Brotherhood of the Grape, The (Fante), **Supp. XI:** 160, **171-172**

"Brothers" (Anderson), **I:** 114
Brothers, The (F. Barthelme), **Supp. XI:** 25, 28, 29, 30, 32-33
Brothers and Keepers (Wideman), **Supp. X:** 320, 321-322, 323, **325-327,** 328, 329-330, 331, 332
Brothers Ashkenazi, The (Singer), **IV:** 2
Brothers Karamazov, The (Dostoyevsky), **II:** 60; **III:** 146, 150, 283; **Supp. IX:** 102, 106; **Supp. XI:** 172; **Supp. XII:** 322
Brother to Dragons: A Tale in Verse and Voices (Warren), **IV:** 243-244, 245, 246, 251, 252, 254, 257
Broughton, James, **Supp. XV:** 146
Broughton, Rhoda, **II:** 174; **IV:** 309, 310
Broun, Heywood, **I:** 478; **II:** 417; **IV:** 432; **Supp. IX:** 190
Broussais, François, **Supp. I Part 1:** 302
Browder, Earl, **I:** 515
Brower, David, **Supp. X:** 29
Brower, Reuben, **Supp. XV:** 20
Brown, Alice, **II:** 523; **Retro. Supp. II:** 136
Brown, Andrew, **Supp. XVI:**150
Brown, Ashley, **Retro. Supp. II:** 48; **Supp. I Part 1:** 79, 80, 82, 84, 92
Brown, Charles Brockden, **I:** 54, 211, 335; **II:** 74, 267, 298; **III:** 415; **Supp. I Part 1: 124-149; Supp. II Part 1:** 65, 292
Brown, Clifford, **Supp. V:** 195
Brown, Deborah, **Supp. XVII:** 75
Brown, Dee, **Supp. IV Part 2:** 504
Brown, Elijah, **Supp. I Part 1:** 125
Brown, George Douglas, **III:** 473
Brown, Harry, **Supp. IV Part 2:** 560
Brown, Harvey, **Supp. XIV:**148
Brown, John, **II:** 13; **IV:** 125, 126, 172, 237, 249, 254; **Supp. I Part 1:** 345; **Supp. VIII:** 204
Brown, Joseph Epes, **Supp. IV Part 2:** 487
Brown, Leonard, **Supp. IX:** 117
Brown, Mary Armitt, **Supp. I Part 1:** 125
Brown, Mrs. Charles Brockden (Elizabeth Linn), **Supp. I Part 1:** 145, 146
Brown, Percy, **II:** 20
Brown, Robert E., **Supp. X:** 12
Brown, Scott, **Supp. XI:** 178
Brown, Slater, **IV:** 123; **Retro. Supp. II:** 79
Brown, Solyman, **Supp. I Part 1:** 156
Brown, Sterling, **Retro. Supp. I:** 198;

Supp. IV Part 1: 169; **Supp. XIV:**202

Brown: The Last Discovery of America (Rodriguez), **Supp. XIV:**297, 298, 300, **305-309**, 310, 311-312

Brown, Tina, **Supp. XVI:**176-177

Brown, Wesley, **Supp. V:** 6

Brown Decades, The (Mumford), **Supp. II Part 2:** 475, 478, 491-492

Brown Dog (Harrison), **Supp. VIII:** 51

Brown Dog of the Yaak: Essays on Art and Activism (Bass), **Supp. XVI:**22

"Brown Dwarf of Rügen, The" (Whittier), **Supp. I Part 2:** 696

Browne, Charles Farrar, **II:** 289; **IV:** 193, 196

Browne, Roscoe Lee, **Supp. VIII:** 345

Browne, Thomas, **II:** 15-16, 304; **III:** 77, 78, 198, 487; **IV:** 147; **Supp. IX:** 136; **Supp. XII:** 45; **Supp. XVI:**292

Browne, William, **Supp. I Part 1:** 98

Brownell, W. C., **II:** 14

Brownell, William Crary, **Retro. Supp. I:** 365, 366

Brown Girl, Brownstones (Marshall), **Supp. XI:** 275, 276, **278-280**, 282

Brownies' Book, The (Hughes), **Supp. I Part 1:** 321

Browning, Elizabeth Barrett, **I:** 458, 459; **Retro. Supp. I:** 33, 43

Browning, Robert, **I:** 50, 66, 103, 458, 460, 468; **II:** 338, 478, 522; **III:** 5, 8, 467, 469, 484, 511, 521, 524, 606, 609; **IV:** 135, 245, 366, 416; **Retro. Supp. I:** 43, 55, 217; **Retro. Supp. II:** 188, 190; **Supp. I Part 1:** 2, 6, 79, 311; **Supp. I Part 2:** 416, 468, 622; **Supp. III Part 1:** 5, 6; **Supp. IV Part 2:** 430; **Supp. X:** 65; **Supp. XV:** 92, 250, 275

Brownmiller, Susan, **Supp. X:** 252

"Brown River, Smile" (Toomer), **Supp. IV Part 1:** 16

Brownstone Eclogues and Other Poems (Aiken), **I:** 65, 67

Broyard, Anatole, **Supp. IV Part 1:** 39; **Supp. VIII:** 140; **Supp. X:** 186; **Supp. XI:** 348; **Supp. XVI:**213

Bruccoli, Matthew, **Retro. Supp. I:** 98, 102, 105, 114, 115, 359; **Supp. IV Part 2:** 468, 470

Bruce, John Edward, **Supp. XVI:**143

Bruce, Lenny, **Supp. VIII:** 198

Bruce, Virginia, **Supp. XII:** 173

Bruce-Novoa, Juan, **Supp. VIII:** 73, 74

Bruchac, Joseph, **Supp. IV Part 1:** 261, 319, 320, 321, 322, 323, 325, 328, 398, 399, 403, 408, 414; **Supp. IV Part 2:** 502, 506

Brueghel, Pieter, **I:** 174; **Supp. I Part 2:** 475

Brueghel, Pieter, the Elder, **Retro. Supp. I:** 430

Bruell, Edwin, **Supp. VIII:** 126

Brugh, Spangler Arlington. See Taylor, Robert

"Bruja: Witch" (Mora), **Supp. XIII:** 214, 220, 221, **Supp. XIII:** 222

Brulé, Claude, **Supp. XI:** 307

Brumer, Andy, **Supp. XIII:** 88

Brunner, Emil, **III:** 291, 303

"Brush Fire" (J. Wright), **Supp. XVII:** 241

Brustein, Robert, **Supp. VIII:** 331

Brutus, **IV:** 373, 374; **Supp. I Part 2:** 471

"Brutus and Antony" (Masters), **Supp. I Part 2:** 472

"Bryan, Bryan, Bryan, Bryan" (Lindsay), **Supp. I Part 2:** 394, 395, 398

Bryan, George, **Retro. Supp. II:** 76

Bryan, Sharon, **Supp. IX:** 154

Bryan, William Jennings, **I:** 483; **IV:** 124; **Supp. I Part 2:** 385, 395-396, 455, 456

Bryant, Austin, **Supp. I Part 1:** 152, 153

Bryant, Frances, **Supp. I Part 1:** 153

Bryant, Louise, **Supp. X:** 136

Bryant, Mrs. William Cullen (Frances Fairchild), **Supp. I Part 1:** 153, 169

Bryant, Peter, **Supp. I Part 1:** 150, 151, 152, 153. *See also* George, Peter

Bryant, William Cullen, **I:** 335, 458; **II:** 311; **III:** 81; **IV:** 309; **Retro. Supp. I:** 217; **Retro. Supp. II:** 155; **Supp. I Part 1: 150-173**, 312, 362; **Supp. I Part 2:** 413, 416, 420; **Supp. IV Part 1:** 165; **Supp. XIII:** 145

Bryer, Jackson R., **Supp. IV Part 2:** 575, 583, 585, 586, 589, 591; **Supp. XIII:** 200, **Supp. XIII:** 205

Bryher, Jackson R. (pseudonym). *See* Ellerman, Winifred

"Bubbs Creek Haircut" (Snyder), **Supp. VIII:** 306

Buber, Martin, **II:** 228; **III:** 45, 308, 528; **IV:** 11; **Supp. I Part 1:** 83, 88; **Supp. XVI:**291

Buccaneers, The (Wharton), **IV:** 327; **Retro. Supp. I:** 382

Buchanan Dying (Updike), **Retro. Supp. I:** 331, 335

Buchbinder, David, **Supp. XIII:** 32

Buchwald, Art, **Supp. XII:** 124-125; **Supp. XVI:**110-111

Buchwald, Emilie, **Supp. XVI:**35, 36

Buck, Dudley, **Supp. I Part 1:** 362

Buck, Gene, **II:** 427

Buck, Pearl S., **Supp. II Part 1: 113-134**; **Supp. XIV:**274

"Buckdancer's Choice" (Dickey), **Supp. IV Part 1:** 191

Buckdancer's Choice (Dickey), **Supp. IV Part 1:** 176, 177, 178, 180

Bucke, Richard Maurice, **Retro. Supp. I:** 407

"Buck Fever" (Humphrey), **Supp. IX:** 109

"Buck in the Snow, The" (Millay), **III:** 135

Buckley, Christopher, **Supp. IX:** 169; **Supp. XI:** 257, 329; **Supp. XV:** 76-77, 86

Buckley, James, Jr., **Supp. XVII:** 220

Buckminster, Joseph, **Supp. II Part 1:** 66-67, 69

Bucknell, Katherine, **Supp. XIV:**170

Bucolics (Auden), **Supp. II Part 1:** 21, 24

Budd, Louis J., **IV:** 210

Buddha, **I:** 136; **II:** 1; **III:** 173, 179, 239, 567; **Supp. I Part 1:** 363; **Supp. I Part 2:** 397

"Buddha's Last Instruction, The" (Oliver), **Supp. VII:** 239

Budding Prospects: A Pastoral (Boyle), **Supp. VIII:** 8-9

Buechner, Frederick, **III:** 310; **Supp. XII: 41-59**

Buell, Lawrence, **Supp. V:** 209; **Supp. IX:** 29; **Supp. XV:** 269, 282

"Buffalo, The" (Moore), **III:** 215

"Buffalo Bill." *See* Cody, William

Buffalo Girls (McMurtry), **Supp. V:** 229

Buffalo Girls (screenplay) (McMurtry), **Supp. V:** 232

Buffett, Jimmy, **Supp. VIII:** 42

Buffon, Comte de, **II:** 101

Buford, Fanny McConnell, **Retro. Supp. II:** 117

Bugeja, Michael, **Supp. X:** 201

Bugged for Murder (Lacy), **Supp. XV:** 205

"Buglesong" (Stegner), **Supp. IV Part 2:** 606

"Buick" (Shapiro), **Supp. II Part 2:** 705

"Builders" (Yates), **Supp. XI: 342-343**

Builders, The (Glasgow), **II:** 183-184, 193

"Builders, The" (Hay), **Supp. XIV:**125

Builders of the Bay Colony (Morison), **Supp. I Part 2:** 484-485

"Builders of the Bridge, The"

(Mumford), **Supp. II Part 2:** 475
"Building" (Snyder), **Supp. VIII:** 305
"Building, Dwelling, Thinking" (Heidegger), **Retro. Supp. II:** 87
Building a Character (Stanislavsky), **Supp. XIV:**243
"Building of the Ship, The" (Longfellow), **II:** 498; **Retro. Supp. II:** 159, 167, 168
"Build Soil" (Frost), **Retro. Supp. I:** 138, 139
"Build Soil" (Snyder), **Supp. VIII:** 304
Build-Up, The (W. C. Williams), **Retro. Supp. I:** 423
Bukiet, Melvin Jules, **Supp. XVII: 39-51**
Bukowski, Charles, **Supp. III Part 1:** 147; **Supp. XI:** 159, 161, 172, 173; **Supp. XVII:** 245
Bulgakov, Mikhail, **Supp. XIV:**97
"Bulgarian Poetess, The" (Updike), **IV:** 215, 227; **Retro. Supp. I:** 329
Bull, Ole, **II:** 504
"Bulldozer, The" (Francis), **Supp. IX:** 87
"Bullet in the Brain" (Wolff), **Supp. VII:** 342-343
Bullet Park (Cheever), **Supp. I Part 1:** 185, 187-193, 194, 195
Bullets over Broadway (film; Allen), **Supp. XV:** 12, **12-13**
Bullfight, The (Mailer), **Retro. Supp. II:** 205
Bullins, Ed, **Supp. II Part 1:** 34, 42
Bullock, Sandra, **Supp. X:** 80
"Bull-Roarer, The" (Stern), **Supp. IX:** 297
"Bully, The" (Dubus), **Supp. VII:** 84
"Bulsh" (X. J. Kennedy), **Supp. XV:** 161
Bultmann, Rudolf, **III:** 309
Bulwark, The (Dreiser), **I:** 497, 506, 516-517; **Retro. Supp. II:** 95, 96, 105, 108
Bulwer-Lytton, Edward George, **IV:** 350
"Bums in the Attic" (Cisneros), **Supp. VII:** 62
Bunche, Ralph, **Supp. I Part 1:** 343; **Supp. XIV:**202
"Bunchgrass Edge of the World, The" (Proulx), **Supp. VII:** 263
Bunge, Nancy, **Supp. XVII:** 218
"Bunner Sisters, The" (Wharton), **IV:** 317
Bunting, Basil, **Retro. Supp. I:** 422; **Supp. III Part 2:** 616, 620, 624; **Supp. XIV:**286
Buñuel, Luis, **III:** 184; **Retro. Supp. II:** 337

Bunyan, John, **I:** 445; **II:** 15, 104, 228; **IV:** 80, 84, 156, 437; **Supp. I Part 1:** 32
Burana, Lily, **Supp. XI:** 253
Burbank, Luther, **I:** 483
Burbank, Rex, **IV:** 363
Burchfield, Alice, **Supp. I Part 2:** 652, 660
Burden of Proof, The (Turow), **Supp. XVII: 216-217,** 218
Burden of Southern History, The (Woodward), **Retro. Supp. I:** 75
Burdens of Formality, The (Lea, ed.), **Supp. X:** 58
Burger, Gottfried August, **II:** 306
Burgess, Anthony, **Supp. IV Part 1:** 227; **Supp. IV Part 2:** 685; **Supp. V:** 128
Burgh, James, **Supp. I Part 2:** 522
"Burglar of Babylon, The" (Bishop), **Retro. Supp. II:** 47; **Supp. I Part 1:** 93
Burgum, E. B., **IV:** 469, 470
Buried Child (Shepard), **Supp. III Part 2:** 433, 447, 448; **Supp. XIV:**327
"Buried Lake, The" (Tate), **IV:** 136
Burke, Edmund, **I:** 9; **III:** 310; **Supp. I Part 2:** 496, 511, 512, 513, 523; **Supp. II Part 1:** 80; **Supp. XVII:** 236
Burke, James Lee, **Supp. XIV:21-38**
Burke, Kenneth, **I:** 264-287, 291; **III:** 497, 499, 546; **IV:** 123, 408; **Retro. Supp. I:** 297; **Retro. Supp. II:** 117, 120; **Supp. I Part 2:** 630; **Supp. II Part 1:** 136; **Supp. VIII:** 105; **Supp. IX:** 229; **Supp. XIV:**3
Burley, Justin, **Supp. XVI:**158
"Burly Fading One, The" (Hayden), **Supp. II Part 1:** 366
"Burned" (Levine), **Supp. V:** 186, 192
"Burned Diary, The" (Olds), **Supp. X:** 215
Burnett, Allison, **Supp. XVII:** 22
Burnett, David, **Supp. XI:** 299
Burnett, Frances Hodgson, **Supp. I Part 1:** 44
Burnett, Whit, **III:** 551; **Supp. XI:** 294
Burney, Fanny, **Supp. XV:** 232
Burnham, James, **Supp. I Part 2:** 648
Burnham, John Chynoweth, **I:** 59
"Burning, The" (Welty), **IV:** 277-278; **Retro. Supp. I:** 353
Burning Angel (Burke), **Supp. XIV:**30, 32
Burning Bright (Steinbeck), **IV:** 51, 61-62
Burning Bush (Untermeyer), **Supp. XV: 309**

"Burning Bush" (Untermeyer), **Supp. XV:** 309
Burning Bush, The (H. and G. Herczeg), **Supp. XVII:** 62
Burning Chrome (W. Gibson), **Supp. XVI:**118, 122, **128**
"Burning Chrome" (W. Gibson), **Supp. XVI:**117, 120, 123, 124, 128
Burning City (Benét), **Supp. XI:** 46, 58
Burning Daylight (London), **II:** 474, 481
Burning Down the House: Essays on Fiction (C. Baxter), **Supp. XVII:** 13, 20, 21
Burning House, The (Beattie), **Supp. V:** 29
"Burning Ladder, The" (Gioia), **Supp. XV:** 118
Burning Mystery of Anna in 1951, The (Koch), **Supp. XV:** 182-183
"Burning of Paper Instead of Children, The" (Rich), **Supp. I Part 2:** 558
Burning the Days: Recollections (Salter), **Supp. IX:** 245, 246, 248, 260, **261-262**
"Burning the Small Dead" (Snyder), **Supp. VIII:** 298
Burns, David, **III:** 165-166
Burns, Ken, **Supp. XIV:**14
Burns, Michael, **Supp. XV:** 339
Burns, Robert, **II:** 150, 306; **III:** 592; **IV:** 453; **Supp. I Part 1:** 158; **Supp. I Part 2:** 410, 455, 683, 685, 691, 692; **Supp. IX:** 173; **Supp. XII:** 171; **Supp. XIII:** 3
Burnshaw, Stanley, **Retro. Supp. I:** 298, 303; **Supp. III Part 2:** 615
"Burn the Cities" (West), **Retro. Supp. II:** 338
Burnt Norton (Eliot), **I:** 575, 580-581, 582, 584, 585; **III:** 10
"Burnt Norton" (Eliot), **Retro. Supp. I:** 66; **Supp. XV:** 216
Burnt-Out Case, A (Greene), **Supp. VIII:** 4
"Burnt-out Spa, The" (Plath), **Retro. Supp. II:** 246
Burn Witch Burn (A. Merritt), **Supp. XVII:** 58
Burr, Aaron, **I:** 7, 549, 550; **II:** 300; **IV:** 264; **Supp. I Part 2:** 461, 483
Burr: A Novel (Vidal), **Supp. IV Part 2:** 677, 682, 684, 685, 687, 688, 689, 691
Burr Oaks (Eberhart), **I:** 533, 535
Burroughs, Edgar Rice, **Supp. IV Part 1:** 101
Burroughs, John, **I:** 220, 236, 506; **IV:** 346; **Supp. IX:** 171

Burroughs, William S., **III:** 45, 174, 258; **Supp. II Part 1:** 320, 328; **Supp. III Part 1: 91-110,** 217, 226; **Supp. IV Part 1:** 79, 87, 90; **Supp. XI:** 297, 308; **Supp. XII:** 1, 3, 118, 121, 124, 129, 131, 136; **Supp. XIV:** 137, 140-141, 143-144, 150; **Supp. XVI:** 123, 135; **Supp. XVII:** 225
Burrow, Trigant, **Supp. II Part 1:** 6
Burrows, Ken, **Supp. V:** 115
Burson, Claudia, **Supp. XV:** 343
Burstein, Janet, **Supp. XVII:** 41, 44, 48
Burt, Stephen, **Supp. XV:** 341, 342, 345, 347, 351; **Supp. XVII:** 18, 246
Burt, Steve, **Supp. V:** 83
Burtis, Thomson, **Supp. XIII:** 163
Burton, Robert, **II:** 535; **III:** 77, 78; **Supp. I Part 1:** 349
Burton, William Evans, **III:** 412
"Burying Ground by the Ties" (MacLeish), **III:** 14
Bury My Heart at Wounded Knee (Brown), **Supp. IV Part 2:** 504
Bury the Dead (Shaw), **IV:** 381
"Bus Along St. Clair: December, A" (Atwood), **Supp. XIII:** 33
Busch, Frederick, **Supp. X:** 78; **Supp. XII:** 343; **Supp. XVII:** 175
Bush, Barney, **Supp. XII:** 218, 222
Bush, Douglas, **Supp. I Part 1:** 268; **Supp. XIV:** 10
"Busher Comes Back, The" (Lardner), **II:** 422
"Busher's Letters Home, A" (Lardner), **II:** 418-419, 421
"Business and Poetry" (Gioia), **Supp. XV:** 113, 115
"Business Deal" (West), **IV:** 287
"Business Man, A" (Jewett), **Retro. Supp. II:** 132
Business of Memory, The: The Art of Remembering in an Age of Forgetting (C. Baxter, ed.), **Supp. XVII:** 21
Buss, Helen M., **Supp. IV Part 1:** 12
Butcher, Margaret Just, **Supp. XIV:** 203
"Butcher, The" (Southern), **Supp. XI:** 294
"Butcher Shop" (Simic), **Supp. VIII:** 273
But Gentlemen Marry Brunettes (Loos), **Supp. XVI:** 190-191
Butler, Benjamin, **I:** 457
Butler, Dorothy. *See* Farrell, Mrs. James T. (Dorothy Butler)
Butler, Elizabeth, **Supp. I Part 1:** 260
Butler, Ethel, **Supp. XIV:** 125
Butler, Hugo, **Supp. XVII:** 63

Butler, James D., **Supp. IX:** 175
Butler, Joseph, **II:** 8, 9
Butler, Judith, **Supp. XII:** 6
Butler, Maud. *See* Falkner, Mrs. Murray C. (Maud Butler)
Butler, Nicholas Murray, **I:** 223; **Supp. I Part 1:** 23; **Supp. III Part 2:** 499
Butler, Octavia, **Supp. XIII: 59-72**
Butler, Robert Olen, **Supp. XII: 61-78,** 319
Butler, Samuel, **II:** 82, 86; **IV:** 121, 440; **Supp. VIII:** 171
Butler-Evans, Elliot, **Retro. Supp. II:** 121
"But Only Mine" (Wright), **Supp. III Part 2:** 595
Butscher, Edward, **Supp. I Part 2:** 526
Butter Battle Book, The (Geisel), **Supp. XVI:** 110
"Buttercups" (Lowell), **Retro. Supp. II:** 187
Butterfield 8 (O'Hara), **III:** 361
Butterfield, R. W., **I:** 386
Butterfield, Stephen, **Supp. IV Part 1:** 3, 11
"Butterflies Under Persimmon" (Jarman), **Supp. XVII:** 120
Butterfly (Harvey), **Supp. XIII:** 184
"Butterfly, The" (Brodksy), **Supp. VIII:** 26
"Butterfly and the Traffic Light, The" (Ozick), **Supp. V:** 263, 265
Butterfly Stories (Vollmann), **Supp. XVII:** 226
"Butterfly-toed Shoes" (Komunyakaa), **Supp. XIII:** 126
Butter Hill and Other Poems (Francis), **Supp. IX:** 88, 89
Buttons, Red, **Supp. IV Part 2:** 574
Buttrick, George, **III:** 301; **Supp. XII:** 47-48
"But What Is the Reader to Make of This?" (Ashbery), **Supp. III Part 1:** 25
Butz, Earl, **Supp. X:** 35
"Buz" (Alcott), **Supp. I Part 1:** 43
By Avon River (Doolittle), **Supp. I Part 1:** 272
"By Blue Ontario's Shore" (Whitman), **Retro. Supp. I:** 399, 400
"By Disposition of Angels" (Moore), **III:** 214
"By Earth" (Olds), **Supp. X:** 214
"By Fire" (Olds), **Supp. X:** 214
Bygones (Untermeyer), **Supp. XV:** 304, **308-309,** 312, 313
By Land and by Sea (Morison), **Supp. I Part 2:** 492
By-Line: Ernest Hemingway (Hemingway), **II:** 257-258

By Love Possessed (Cozens), **I:** 358, 365, 372-374, 375, 376, 377, 378, 379
"By Morning" (Swenson), **Supp. IV Part 2:** 642
"By Night" (Francis), **Supp. IX:** 76
Bynner, Witter, **II:** 513, 527; **Supp. XIII:** 347; **Supp. XV: 39-54**
Byrd, William, **Supp. IV Part 2:** 425
Byrne, Donn, **IV:** 67
Byron, George Gordon, Lord, **I:** 343, 568, 577; **II:** 135, 193, 296, 301, 303, 310, 315, 331, 566; **III:** 82, 137, 170, 409, 410, 412, 469; **IV:** 245, 435; **Supp. I Part 1:** 150, 312, 349; **Supp. I Part 2:** 580, 591, 683, 685, 719; **Supp. XIII:** 139; **Supp. XVI:** 188, 203, 206, 210
"Byron's Cain" (L. Michaels), **Supp. XVI:** 203
"Bystanders" (Matthews), **Supp. IX:** 160
By the Bias of Sound (Sobin), **Supp. XVI:** 281
By the North Gate (Oates), **Supp. II Part 2:** 504
"By the Waters of Babylon" (Benét), **Supp. XI:** 56, 58
By the Waters of Manhattan (Reznikoff), **Supp. XIV:** 288, 293, 294
By the Waters of Manhattan: An Annual (Reznikoff), **Supp. XIV:** 277, 280, 289
By the Waters of Manhattan: Selected Verse (Reznikoff), **Supp. XIV:** 281, 291
By the Well of Living and Seeing: New and Selected Poems 1918-1973 (Reznikoff), **Supp. XIV:** 281, 287-288, 295
By the Well of Living and Seeing and the Fifth Book of the Maccabees (Reznikoff), **Supp. XIV:** 281
By Way of Orbit (O'Neill), **III:** 405

C

"C 33" (H. Crane), **I:** 384; **Retro. Supp. II:** 76
Cabala, The (Wilder), **IV:** 356, 358-360, 369, 374
Cabaret (film), **Supp. XIV:** 155, 162
Cabaret (play), **Supp. XIV:** 162; **Supp. XVII:** 45
Cabbages and Kings (O. Henry), **Supp. II Part 1:** 394, 409
Cabell, James Branch, **II:** 42; **III:** 394; **IV:** 67, 359, 360; **Retro. Supp. I:** 80; **Supp. I Part 2:** 613, 714, 718, 721; **Supp. X:** 223
"Cabin, The" (Carver), **Supp. III Part

I: 137, 146
Cabin, The: Reminiscence and Diversions (Mamet), **Supp. XIV:** 240
Cabinet of Dr. Caligari, The (film), **Retro. Supp. I:** 268
Cable, George Washington, **II:** 289; **Retro. Supp. II:** 65; **Supp. I Part 1:** 200; **Supp. II Part 1:** 198; **Supp. XIV:** 63
Cables to the Ace; or, Familiar Liturgies of Misunderstanding (Merton), **Supp. VIII:** 208
Cabot, James, **II:** 14; **IV:** 173
Cabot, John, **Supp. I Part 2:** 496, 497
Cactus Flower (Barillet and Grédy), **Supp. XVI:** 194
"Caddy's Diary, A" (Lardner), **II:** 421-422
"Cadence" (Dubus), **Supp. VII:** 84-85
Cadieux, Isabelle, **Supp. XIII:** 127
"Cadillac Flambé" (Ellison), **Retro. Supp. II:** 119, 126; **Supp. II Part 1:** 248
Cadillac Jack (McMurtry), **Supp. V:** 225
Cadillac Jukebox (Burke), **Supp. XIV:** 32
Cadle, Dean, **Supp. I Part 2:** 429
Cady, Edwin H., **II:** 272
"Caedmon" (Garrett), **Supp. VII:** 96-97
Caesar, Julius, **II:** 12, 502, 561-562; **IV:** 372, 373
Caesar, Sid, **Supp. IV Part 2:** 574, 591
"Cafeteria, The" (Singer), **Retro. Supp. II:** 316
Cage, John, **Supp. IV Part 1:** 84; **Supp. V:** 337, 341
"Cage and the Prairie: Two Notes on Symbolism, The" (Bewley), **Supp. I Part 1:** 251
Cage of Spines, A (Swenson), **Supp. IV Part 2:** 641-642, 647
Cagney, James, **Supp. IV Part 1:** 236; **Supp. XIII:** 174
Cagney, William, **Supp. XIII:** 174
Cahalan, James, **Supp. XIII:** 1, 2, 3, 4, 12
Cahan, Abraham, **Supp. IX:** 227; **Supp. XIII:** 106
Cahill, Tim, **Supp. XIII:** 13
Cain, James M., **III:** 99; **Supp. IV Part 1:** 130; **Supp. XI:** 160; **Supp. XIII:** 159, 165
Cairns, Huntington, **III:** 103, 108, 114, 119
Cairo! Shanghai! Bombay! (Williams and Shapiro), **IV:** 380
Cake (Bynner), **Supp. XV:** 50
Cakes and Ale (Maugham), **III:** 64

Calabria, Frank, **Supp. XIII:** 164
Calamity Jane (Martha Jane Canary), **Supp. V:** 229-230; **Supp. X:** 103
"Calamus" (Whitman), **IV:** 342-343; **Retro. Supp. I:** 52, 403, 404, 407
Calasso, Roberto, **Supp. IV Part 1:** 301
Calderón, Hector, **Supp. IV Part 2:** 544
Caldwell, Christopher, **Supp. IV Part 1:** 211
Caldwell, Erskine, **I:** 97, 211, **288-311;** **IV:** 286; **Supp. IV Part 2:** 601
Caldwell, Mrs. Erskine (Helen Lannegan), **I:** 289
Caldwell, Mrs. Erskine (Margaret Bourke-White), **I:** 290, 293-295, 297
Caldwell, Mrs. Erskine (Virginia Fletcher), **I:** 290
Caldwell, Reverend Ira Sylvester, **I:** 289, 305
Caldwell, Zoe, **Supp. XIII:** 207
Caleb Williams (Godwin), **III:** 415
"Calendar" (Creeley), **Supp. IV Part 1:** 158
Calendar of Saints for Unbelievers, A (Wescott), **Supp. XIV:** 342
Calendars (A. Finch), **Supp. XVII: 76-77**
Calhoun, John C., **I:** 8; **III:** 309
"Caliban in the Coal Mines" (Untermeyer), **Supp. XV:** 296
"California" (Carruth), **Supp. XVI:** 56
"California" (Didion), **Supp. IV Part 1:** 195
"California, This Is Minnesota Speaking" (Dunn), **Supp. XI:** 146
California and Oregon Trail, The (Parkman), **Supp. I Part 2:** 486
"California Hills in August" (Gioia), **Supp. XV:** 118-119
Californians (Jeffers), **Supp. II Part 2:** 415, 418, 420
"California Oaks, The" (Winters), **Supp. II Part 2:** 798
"California Plush" (Bidart), **Supp. XV:** 23
"California Republic" (Didion), **Supp. IV Part 1:** 205
"California Requiem, A" (Gioia), **Supp. XV:** 126
California Suite (film), **Supp. IV Part 2:** 589
California Suite (Simon), **Supp. IV Part 2:** 581, 582
"Caligula" (Lowell), **II:** 554
Callahan, John F., **Retro. Supp. II:** 119, 126, 127
"Call at Corazón" (Bowles), **Supp. IV**

Part 1: 82, 87
Calle, Sophia, **Supp. XII:** 22
"Called Back" (Kazin), **Supp. VIII:** 104
Calley, Captain William, **II:** 579
Calley, John, **Supp. XI:** 305
Callicott, J. Baird, **Supp. XIV:** 184
Calligrammes (Apollinaire), **I:** 432
"Calling Jesus" (Toomer), **Supp. III Part 2:** 484
Calling Myself Home (Hogan), **Supp. IV Part 1:** 397, 399, 400, 401, 413
Call It Experience (Caldwell), **I:** 290-291, 297
"Call It Fear" (Harjo), **Supp. XII:** 220
Call It Sleep (H. Roth), **Supp. VIII:** 233; **Supp. IX:** 227, 228, **229-231;** **Supp. XIII:** 106
"Call Letters: Mrs. V. B." (Angelou), **Supp. IV Part 1:** 15
Call Me Ishmael (Olson), **Supp. II Part 2:** 556
Call Me Shakespeare (Endore), **Supp. XVII:** 65
Call of the Gospel, The (Mather), **Supp. II Part 2:** 448
Call of the Wild, The (London), **II:** 466, 470-471, 472, 481
"Call of the Wild, The" (Snyder), **Supp. VIII:** 301
"Calloway's Code" (O. Henry), **Supp. II Part 1:** 404
"Call to Arms" (Mumford), **Supp. II Part 2:** 479
Call to Arms, The (film), **Retro. Supp. I:** 325
Calmer, Ned, **Supp. XI:** 219
Calvert, George H., **Supp. I Part 1:** 361
Calverton, V. F., **Supp. VIII:** 96
Calvin, John, **II:** 342; **IV:** 160, 490
Calvino, Italo, **Supp. IV Part 2:** 623, 678
Cambridge Edition of the Works of F. Scott Fitzgerald, The (Bruccoli, ed.), **Retro. Supp. I:** 115
"Cambridge Thirty Years Ago" (Lowell), **Supp. I Part 2:** 419
Cambridge University Press, **Retro. Supp. I:** 115
"Camellia Sabina" (Moore), **III:** 208, 215
"Cameo Appearance" (Simic), **Supp. VIII:** 283
Camera Obscura (Nabokov), **III:** 255
Cameron, Elizabeth, **I:** 10, 17
Cameron, Kenneth W., **II:** 16
Cameron, Peter, **Supp. XII: 79-95**
Cameron, Sharon, **Retro. Supp. I:** 43; **Retro. Supp. II:** 40

Camerson, Don, **I:** 10, 17
Camino, Léon Felipe, **Retro. Supp. II:** 89
Camino Real (T. Williams), **IV:** 382, 385, 386, 387, 388, 391, 392, 395, 398
Camões, Luiz Vaz de, **II:** 133; **Supp. I Part 1:** 94
"Camouflaging the Chimera" (Komunyakaa), **Supp. XIII: 122-123**
Camp, James, **Supp. XV:** 165
Camp, Walter, **II:** 423
Campana, Dino, **Supp. V:** 337
Campbell, Alan, **Supp. IV Part 1:** 353; **Supp. IX:** 196, 198, 201
Campbell, Alexander, **Supp. I Part 2:** 381, 395
Campbell, Donna, **Retro. Supp. II:** 139
Campbell, Helen, **Supp. XI:** 200, 206
Campbell, James, **Supp. XII:** 127
Campbell, James Edwin, **Supp. II Part 1:** 202
Campbell, Joanna (pseud.). See Bly, Carol
Campbell, Joseph, **I:** 135; **IV:** 369, 370; **Supp. IX:** 245
Campbell, Lewis, **III:** 476
Campbell, Thomas, **II:** 8, 303, 314; **III:** 410; **Supp. I Part 1:** 309, 310
Campbell, Virginia, **Supp. XIII:** 114
Campbell (Hale), Janet, **Supp. IV Part 2:** 503
"Campers Leaving: Summer 1981" (Kenyon), **Supp. VII:** 169
"Camp Evergreen" (Kenyon), **Supp. VII:** 168
"Camping in Madera Canyon" (Swenson), **Supp. IV Part 2:** 649
Campion, Thomas, **I:** 439; **Supp. VIII:** 272
Campo, Rafael, **Supp. XVII:** 112
Camus, Albert, **I:** 53, 61, 292, 294, 494; **II:** 57, 244; **III:** 292, 306, 453; **IV:** 6, 211, 236, 442, 487; **Retro. Supp. I:** 73; **Retro. Supp. II:** 20; **Supp. I Part 2:** 621; **Supp. VIII:** 11, 195, 241; **Supp. XI:** 96; **Supp. XIII:** 74, 165, 233, 247; **Supp. XVII:** 137
Camuto, Christopher, **Supp. V:** 212-213
Canada Fragrant with Resin, **Supp. XVI:** 149
"Canadian Mosaic, The" (Beran), **Supp. XIII:** 25
"Canadians and Pottawatomies" (Sandburg), **III:** 592-593
"Can a Good Wife Be a Good Sport?" (T. Williams), **IV:** 380
"Canal, The: A Poem on the Application of Physical Science to Political Economy" (Barlow), **Supp. II Part 1:** 73
Canary, Martha Jane. See Calamity Jane (Martha Jane Canary)
"Canary for One, A" (Hemingway), **Retro. Supp. I:** 170, 189
Canary in a Cat House (Vonnegut), **Supp. II Part 2:** 758
"Canary in Bloom" (Dove), **Supp. IV Part 1:** 248
Canby, Henry Seidel, **IV:** 65, 363
"Cancer" (McClatchy), **Supp. XII:** 266
"Cancer Match, The" (Dickey), **Supp. IV Part 1:** 182
"Canción y Glosa" (Merwin), **Supp. III Part 1:** 342
Candide (Hellman), **I:** 28; **Supp. I Part 1:** 288-289, 292
Candide (Voltaire), **Supp. I Part 1:** 288-289; **Supp. XI:** 297; **Supp. XVI:** 189
Candide (Voltaire; Wilbur, trans.), **Supp. III Part 2:** 560
Candle in the Cabin, The (Lindsay), **Supp. I Part 2:** 398, 400
"Candles" (Plath), **Retro. Supp. II:** 248, 257
Candles in Babylon (Levertov), **Supp. III Part 1:** 283
Candles in the Sun (T. Williams), **IV:** 381
Candles of Your Eyes, The (Purdy), **Supp. VII:** 278
Candy (Southern), **Supp. XI:** 297, **298-299**, 305
"Candy-Man Beechum" (Caldwell), **I:** 309
Cane (Toomer), **Supp. III Part 2:** 475, 481-486, 488; **Supp. IV Part 1:** 164, 168; **Supp. IX:** 305, 306, 307, **308-320**
"Cane in the Corridor, The" (Thurber), **Supp. I Part 2:** 616
Canfield, Cass, **Supp. I Part 2:** 668
Canfield, Dorothy, **Retro. Supp. I:** 4, 11, 14, 18. See also Fisher, Dorothy Canfield
Can Grande's Castle (Lowell), **II:** 518, 524
"Canicula di Anna" (Carson), **Supp. XII: 101-102**
"Canis Major" (Frost), **Retro. Supp. I:** 137
Cannery Row (Steinbeck), **IV:** 50, 51, 64-65, 66, 68
Cannibal Galaxy, The (Ozick), **Supp. V:** 270
Cannibals and Christians (Mailer), **III:** 38-39, 40, 42; **Retro. Supp. II:** 203, 204, 205
Canning, George, **I:** 7, 8
Canning, Richard, **Supp. X:** 147
Cannon, Jimmy, **II:** 424
Cannon, Steve, **Retro. Supp. II:** 111
Cannon between My Knees, A (Gunn Allen), **Supp. IV Part 1:** 324
Canolle, Jean, **Supp. XVI:** 194
"Canonization, The" (Donne), **Supp. XIV:** 8
"Can Poetry Matter?" (Gioia), **Supp. XV:** 113, 114
Can Poetry Matter?: Essays on Poetry and American Culture (Gioia), **Supp. XV:** 112, **113-115**
"Canso" (Merwin), **Supp. III Part 1:** 344
Can Such Things Be? (Bierce), **I:** 203, 204, 205, 209
Canterbury Tales (Chaucer), **II:** 504; **III:** 411; **IV:** 65
"Canto Amor" (Berryman), **I:** 173
Canto I (Pound), **III:** 469, 470; **Retro. Supp. I:** 286
Canto II (Pound), **III:** 470
Canto III (Pound), **III:** 470
Canto IV (Pound), **III:** 470
Canto VIII (Pound), **III:** 472
Canto IX (Pound), **III:** 472
Canto X (Pound), **III:** 472
Canto XIII (Pound), **III:** 472
Canto XXXIX (Pound), **III:** 468
Canto LXV (Pound), **Retro. Supp. I:** 292
Canto LXXXI (Pound), **III:** 459; **Retro. Supp. I:** 293
Cantor, Lois, **Supp. IV Part 1:** 285
Cantos (Pound), **I:** 482; **III:** 13-14, 17, 457, 462, 463, 466, 467, 469-470, 472-473, 474, 475, 476, 492; **Retro. Supp. I:** 284, 292, **292-293**, 293, 427; **Supp. I Part 1:** 272; **Supp. II Part 1:** 5; **Supp. II Part 2:** 420, 557, 564, 644; **Supp. IV Part 1:** 153; **Supp. V:** 343, 345; **Supp. VIII:** 305; **Supp. XIV:** 55, 96; **Supp. XV:** 349
"Cantus Planis" (Pound), **III:** 466
Cantwell, Robert, **Retro. Supp. I:** 85; **Supp. VIII:** 96; **Supp. XIII:** 292
"Can You Carry Me" (O'Hara), **III:** 369
Canzoneri, Robert, **IV:** 114, 116
Canzoni (Pound), **Retro. Supp. I:** 286, 288, 413
"Cap" (Shaw), **Supp. IV Part 1:** 345
"Cape Breton" (Bishop), **Supp. I Part 1:** 92; **Supp. IX:** 45

Cape Cod (Thoreau), **II:** 540
"Cape Cod, Rome, and Jerusalem" (Chapman), **Supp. XIV:**55
Capitalism: The Unknown Ideal (Rand), **Supp. IV Part 2:** 518, 527, 531, 532
Caponi, Gena Dagel, **Supp. IV Part 1:** 95
Capote, Truman, **Supp. I Part 1:** 291, 292; **Supp. III Part 1:** 111-133; **Supp. III Part 2:** 574; **Supp. IV Part 1:** 198, 220; **Supp. VIII:** 105; **Supp. XII:** 43, 249; **Supp. XV:** 146; **Supp. XVI:**245-246; **Supp. XVII:** 236
Capouya, Emile, **Supp. I Part 1:** 50
Cappetti, Carla, **Supp. IX:** 4, 8
Capra, Frank, **Supp. XVI:**102
Capra, Fritjof, **Supp. X:** 261
Capron, Marion, **Supp. IX:** 193
"Capsule History of Conservation, A" (Stegner), **Supp. IV Part 2:** 600
"Captain Carpenter" (Ransom), **III:** 491
Captain Craig (Robinson), **III:** 508, 523; **Supp. II Part 1:** 192
"Captain Jim's Friend" (Harte), **Supp. II Part 1:** 337
"Captain Jones's Invitation" (Freneau), **Supp. II Part 1:** 261
"Captain's Son, The" (Taylor), **Supp. V:** 314, 325, 327
"Captain's Wife, The" (Salter), **Supp. IX:** 261
"Capt Christopher Levett (of York)" (Olson), **Supp. II Part 2:** 576, 577
Captive Israel (Reznikoff), **Supp. XIV:**283
"Captivity and Restoration of Mrs. Mary Rowlandson, The" (Howe), **Supp. IV Part 2:** 419, 431, 434
"Captivity of the Fly" (MacLeish), **III:** 19
"Captured Goddess, The" (Lowell), **II:** 520
Caputi, Jane, **Supp. IV Part 1:** 334, 335
Caputo, Philip, **Supp. XI:** 234
Capuzzo, Michael, **Supp. XIII:** 254
Car (Crews), **Supp. XI: 110-111**
Carabi, Angels, **Supp. VIII:** 223; **Supp. XII:** 215
"Caramels" (Zinberg), **Supp. XV:** 195
"Caravaggio: Swirl & Vortex" (Levis), **Supp. XI:** 258, 269
Caravan (Bynner), **Supp. XV:** 50
Carby, Hazel B., **Supp. IV Part 1:** 13
"Carcassonne" (Faulkner), **Retro. Supp. I:** 81
Card, Antha E., **Supp. I Part 2:** 496

Cárdenas, Lupe, **Supp. IV Part 2:** 538, 539, 540
Cardinale, Anthony, **Supp. XVII:** 239
Cardinale, Ernesto, **Supp. XII:** 225
"Cardinal Ideograms" (Swenson), **Supp. IV Part 2:** 645
"Cards" (Beattie), **Supp. V:** 31
"Career Woman" (Hay), **Supp. XIV:**131
Carefree (film, Sandrich), **Supp. XVII:** 59
"Careful" (Carver), **Supp. III Part 1:** 138
Careful and Strict Enquiry into the Modern Prevailing Notions of That Freedom of Will, Which Is Supposed to be Essential to Moral Agency, Vertue and Vice, Reward and Punishment, Praise and Blame, A (Edwards), **I:** 549, 557, 558, 562
Carel: A Poem and Pilgrimage in the Holy Land (Melville), **III:** 92-93
"Carentan O Carentan" (Simpson), **Supp. IX:** 267
Carew, Thomas, **IV:** 453
Carey, Gary, **Supp. XVI:**186
Carey, Mathew, **Supp. XV:** 238
"Car Games" (Conroy), **Supp. XVI:**72
Cargill, Oscar, **Supp. II Part 1:** 117
Caribbean as Columbus Saw It (Morison and Obregon), **Supp. I Part 2:** 488
"Caribou Kitchen" (A. Finch), **Supp. XVII:** 76-77
Caribou Rising: Defending the Porcupine Herd, Gwich-'in Culture, and the Arctic National Wildlife Refuge (Bass), **Supp. XVI:**27-28, 28
Carl, K. A., **III:** 475
"Carlos Who Died, and Left Only This, The" (Ríos), **Supp. IV Part 2:** 547
Carlotta (empress of Mexico), **Supp. I Part 2:** 457
Carl Sandburg (Golden), **III:** 579
Carlson, Susan L., **Supp. XV:** 323
Carlyle, Thomas, **I:** 103, 279; **II:** 5, 7, 11, 15-16, 17, 20, 145, 315; **III:** 82, 84, 85, 87; **IV:** 169, 182, 338, 350; **Retro. Supp. I:** 360, 408; **Supp. I Part 1:** 2, 349; **Supp. I Part 2:** 410, 422, 482, 485, 552
"Carma" (Toomer), **Supp. III Part 2:** 481-483; **Supp. IX:** 312-313
"Carmen de Boheme" (Crane), **I:** 384
Carmen Jones (film), **Supp. I Part 1:** 66
Carmina Burana, **Supp. X:** 63
Carnegie, Andrew, **I:** 483; **IV:** 192; **Supp. I Part 2:** 639, 644; **Supp. V:** 285

Carnegie, Dale, **Supp. I Part 2:** 608
"Carnegie Hall: Rescued" (Moore), **III:** 215
Carne-Ross, D. S., **Supp. I Part 1:** 268, 269
Carnes, Mark C., **Supp. X:** 14
"Carnets" poems (Sobin), **Supp. XVI:**286-287
Carnovsky, Morris, **III:** 154
"Carol for Carolyn, A" (A. Finch), **Supp. XVII:** 74, 75
Caroling Dusk: An Anthology of Verse by Negro Poets (Cullen), **Supp. IV Part 1:** 166, 169
"Carol of Occupations" (Whitman), **I:** 486
Carolyn Kizer: Perspectives on Her Life and Work (A. Finch), **Supp. XVII: 74-75**
"Carolyn Kizer and the Chain of Women" (A. Finch), **Supp. XVII:** 74-75
"Carpe Diem" (Frost), **Supp. XII:** 303
"Carpe Noctem, if You Can" (Thurber), **Supp. I Part 2:** 620
Carpenter, Dan, **Supp. V:** 250
Carpenter, David, **Supp. VIII:** 297
Carpenter, Frederic I., **II:** 20
Carpentered Hen and Other Tame Creatures, The (Updike), **IV:** 214; **Retro. Supp. I:** 320
Carpenter's Gothic (Gaddis), **Supp. IV Part 1:** 288, 289-291, 293, 294
Carr, Dennis W., **Supp. IV Part 2:** 560
Carr, Elias, **Supp. XIV:**57
Carr, Rosemary. *See* Benét, Rosemary
Carrall, Aaron, **Supp. IV Part 2:** 499
Carrel, Alexis, **IV:** 240
"Carrell/Klee/and Cosmos's Groom" (Goldbarth), **Supp. XII:** 183
"Carriage from Sweden, A" (Moore), **III:** 212
Carrie (King), **Supp. V:** 137
Carried Away (Harrison), **Supp. VIII:** 39
Carrier of Ladders (Merwin), **Supp. III Part 1:** 339, 346, 350-352, 356, 357
"Carriers of the Dream Wheel" (Momaday), **Supp. IV Part 2:** 481
Carriers of the Dream Wheel: Contemporary Native American Poetry (Niatum, ed.), **Supp. IV Part 2:** 484, 505
Carrington, Carroll, **I:** 199
"Carrion Spring" (Stegner), **Supp. IV Part 2:** 604
Carroll, Charles, **Supp. I Part 2:** 525
Carroll, Lewis, **I:** 432; **II:** 431; **III:** 181; **Supp. I Part 1:** 44; **Supp. I**

Part 2: 622, 656; **Supp. XVI:**103
"Carrots, Noses, Snow, Rose, Roses" (Gass), **Supp. VI:** 87
Carrouges, Michel, **Supp. IV Part 1:** 104
"Carrousel, The" (Rilke), **III:** 558
Carruth, Hayden, **Supp. IV Part 1:** 66; **Supp. VIII:** 39; **Supp. IX:** 291; **Supp. XIII:** 112; **Supp. XIV:**273-274; **Supp. XVI:45-61**
Carruth, Joe-Anne McLaughlin, **Supp. XVI:**47
"Carry" (Hogan), **Supp. IV Part 1:** 412
"Carrying On" (Dunn), **Supp. XI:** 145
Cars of Cuba (García), **Supp. XI:** 190
Carson, Anne, **Supp. XII: 97-116;** **Supp. XV:** 252
Carson, Johnny, **Supp. IV Part 2:** 526
Carson, Rachel, **Supp. V:** 202; **Supp. IX: 19-36; Supp. X:** 99; **Supp. XVI:**36
Carson, Tom, **Supp. XI:** 227
Cart, Michael, **Supp. X:** 12
Carter, Elliott, **Supp. III Part 1:** 21
Carter, Hodding, **Supp. XIV:**2
Carter, Jared, **Supp. XVII:** 110
Carter, Jimmy, **Supp. I Part 2:** 638; **Supp. XIV:**107
Carter, Marcia, **Supp. V:** 223
Carter, Mary, **Supp. IV Part 2:** 444
Carter, Stephen, **Supp. XI:** 220
Cartesian Sonata and Other Novellas (Gass), **Supp. VI: 92-93**
Cartier, Jacques, **Supp. I Part 2:** 496, 497
Cartier-Bresson, Henri, **Supp. VIII:** 98
"Cartographies of Silence" (Rich), **Supp. I Part 2:** 571-572
Cartwright, Louis, **Supp. XIV:**147, 149, 151
Carver, Raymond, **Supp. III Part 1: 135-151; Supp. IV Part 1:** 342; **Supp. V:** 22, 23, 220, 326; **Supp. VIII:** 15; **Supp. X:** 85, 167; **Supp. XI:** 26, 65, 116, 153; **Supp. XII:** 79, 139, 289, 294
Cary, Alice, **Retro. Supp. II:** 145; **Supp. XV:** 273
Cary, Phoebe, **Supp. XV:** 273
Cary, Richard, **Retro. Supp. II:** 132, 137
"Casabianca" (Bishop), **Retro. Supp. II:** 42; **Supp. I Part 1:** 86
Casablanca (film), **Supp. VIII:** 61; **Supp. XV:** 14
Casanova: His Known and Unknown Life (Endore), **Supp. XVII:** 54
Case of Rape, A (C. Himes), **Supp. XVI:**143

Case of the Crushed Petunias, The (T. Williams), **IV:** 381
Case of the Officers of Excise (Paine), **Supp. I Part 2:** 503-504
Casey, John, **Supp. X:** 164
Cash, Arthur, **Supp. IV Part 1:** 299
Cashman, Nellie, **Supp. X:** 103
Casiero, Robert, **Supp. XIV:**167
Casino Royale (film), **Supp. XI: 306-307**
Caskey, William, **Supp. XIV:**166
"Cask of Amontillado, The" (Poe), **II:** 475; **III:** 413; **Retro. Supp. II:** 268, 269, 270, 273
Casper, Robert N., **Supp. XV:** 339, 347
Cassada (Salter), **Supp. IX: 251-252**
Cassady, Carolyn, **Supp. XIV:**150
Cassady, Neal, **Supp. II Part 1:** 309, 311; **Supp. XIV:**137, 144
"Cassandra Southwick" (Whittier), **Supp. I Part 2:** 693
Cassell, Verlin, **Supp. XI:** 315
Cassill, R. V., **Supp. V:** 323
Cassirer, Ernst, **I:** 265; **IV:** 87, 89
Cass Timberlane (Lewis), **II:** 455-456
Cast a Cold Eye (McCarthy), **II:** 566
Castaway (Cozzens), **I:** 363, 370, 374, 375, 379
"Caste in America" (Du Bois), **Supp. II Part 1:** 169
Castiglione, Baldassare, **I:** 279; **III:** 282
"Castilian" (Wylie), **Supp. I Part 2:** 714
Castillo, Ana, **Supp. XI:** 177
"Castle in Lynn, A" (McCarriston), **Supp. XIV:**265, 268
"Castles and Distances" (Wilbur), **Supp. III Part 2:** 550
Castle Sinister (Marquand), **III:** 58
Cast of Thousands (Loos), **Supp. XVI:**192, 193, 195
Castro, Fidel, **II:** 261, 434
Cast the First Stone (C. Himes), **Supp. XVI:**135, 137-138
"Casual Incident, A" (Hemingway), **II:** 44
"Cat, The" (Matthews), **Supp. IX: 157-158**
Cat, You Better Come Home (Keillor), **Supp. XVI:**177
"Catbird Seat, The" (Thurber), **Supp. I Part 2:** 623
"Catch" (Francis), **Supp. IX:** 82
Catch-22 (Heller), **III:** 558; **Supp. IV Part 1:** 379, 380, 381-382, 383, 384-386, 387, 390, 391, 392, 393, 394; **Supp. V:** 244, 248; **Supp. XII:** 167-168
Catcher in the Rye, The (Salinger), **I:** 493; **III:** 551, 552, 553-558, 567, 571; **Retro. Supp. I:** 102; **Retro. Supp. II:** 222, 249; **Supp. I Part 2:** 535; **Supp. V:** 119; **Supp. VIII:** 242; **Supp. XI:** 65; **Supp. XVII:** 2
"Catching Frogs" (Kenyon), **Supp. VII:** 170
Catching the Mermother (A. Finch), **Supp. XVII:** 72
catechism of d neoamerican hoodoo church (Reed), **Supp. X:** 240, 241
Catered Affair, The (film), **Supp. IV Part 2:** 683
"Cathay" (Goldbarth), **Supp. XII:** 185, 186
Cathay (Pound), **II:** 527; **Retro. Supp. I:** 289
Cathedral (Carver), **Supp. III Part 1:** 144-146; **Supp. XII:** 139
"Cathedral" (Carver), **Supp. III Part 1:** 144-145
Cathedral, The (Lowell), **Supp. I Part 2:** 407, 416-417
Cather, Willa, **I: 312-334,** 405; **II:** 51, 96, 177, 404, 412; **III:** 453; **IV:** 190; **Retro. Supp. I: 1-23,** 355, 382; **Retro. Supp. II:** 71, 136; **Supp. I Part 2:** 609, 719; **Supp. IV Part 1:** 31; **Supp. VIII:** 101, 102, 263; **Supp. X:** 103; **Supp. XIII:** 253; **Supp. XIV:**112; **Supp. XV:** 40, 51; **Supp. XVI:**226
Catherine, Saint, **II:** 211
Catherine II, **Supp. I Part 2:** 433
Catholic Art and Culture (Watkin), **Retro. Supp. II:** 187
"Catholic Novelist in the Protestant South, The" (O'Connor), **Retro. Supp. II:** 223, 224
"Cathy Queen of Cats" (Cisneros), **Supp. VII:** 59
Cat Inside, The (Burroughs), **Supp. III Part 1:** 105
Cat in the Hat, The (Geisel), **Supp. XVI:**106-107, 112
Cat in the Hat Come Back, The (Geisel), **Supp. XVI:**107
"Cat in the Hat for President, The" (Coover), **Supp. V:** 44, 46-47
Cat in The Hat Songbook, The (Geisel), **Supp. XVI:**104
Cato, **II:** 114, 117
Cat on a Hot Tin Roof (T. Williams), **II:** 190; **IV:** 380, 382, 383, 386, 387, 389, 390, 391, 394, 395, 397-398
"Cat People: What Dr. Seuss Really Taught Us" (Menand), **Supp. XVI:**106
Cat's Cradle (Vonnegut), **Supp. II Part 2:** 758, 759, 767-768, 770,

771, 772; **Supp. V:** 1
Cat's Eye (Atwood), **Supp. XIII:** 29-30
"Cat's Meow, A" (Brodsky), **Supp. VIII:** 31
Cat's Quizzer, The (Geisel), **Supp. XVI:**111
"Catterskill Falls" (Bryant), **Supp. I Part 1:** 160
"Cattle Car Complex" (T. Rosenbaum), **Supp. XVII:** 48
Catullus, **Supp. XII:** 2, 13, **112**; **Supp. XV:** 23, 27, 35, 36
Catullus (Gai Catulli Veronensis Liber) (Zukofsky), **Supp. III Part 2:** 625, 627, 628, 629
"Catullus: Carmina" (Carson), **Supp. XII: 112**
"Catullus: Excrucior" (Bidart), **Supp. XV:** 32, 35
Catullus, Gaius Valerius, **I:** 381; **Supp. I Part 1:** 261; **Supp. I Part 2:** 728
"Cat Who Aspired to Higher Things, The" (X. J. Kennedy), **Supp. XV:** 163
Caudwell, Christopher, **Supp. X:** 112
"Caul, The" (Banks), **Supp. V:** 10-11
Cause for Wonder (Morris), **III:** 232-233
"Causerie" (Tate), **IV:** 129
Causes and Consequences (Chapman), **Supp. XIV:**41, 49, 51
"Causes of American Discontents before 1768, The" (Franklin), **II:** 120
Causley, Charles, **Supp. XV:** 117
Cavafy, Constantine P., **Supp. IX:** 275; **Supp. XI:** 119, 123
Cavalcade of America, The (radio program), **III:** 146
Cavalcanti (Pound, opera), **Retro. Supp. I:** 287
Cavalcanti, Guido, **I:** 579; **III:** 467; **Supp. III Part 2:** 620, 621, 622, 623
Cavalieri, Grace, **Supp. IV Part 2:** 630, 631
"Cavalry Crossing the Ford" (Whitman), **IV:** 347
"Cave, The" (Bass), **Supp. XVI:**23
Cave, The (Warren), **IV:** 255-256
Cavell, Stanley, **Retro. Supp. I:** 306-307, 309
Cavender's House (Robinson), **III:** 510
Caviare at the Funeral (Simpson), **Supp. IX:** 266, **276-277**
"Cawdor" (Jeffers), **Supp. II Part 2:** 431
Caxton, William, **III:** 486
Cayton, Horace, **IV:** 475, 488
Cazamian, Louis, **II:** 529
Celan, Paul, **Supp. X:** 149; **Supp. XII:** 21, 110-111; **Supp. XVI:**284-285, 288; **Supp. XVII:** 241
"Celebrated Jumping Frog of Calaveras County, The" (Twain), **IV:** 196
Celebrated Jumping Frog of Calaveras County, The, and Other Sketches (Twain), **IV:** 197
Celebration (Crews), **Supp. XI:** 103, **108**
Celebration at Dark (W. J. Smith), **Supp. XIII:** 332
"Celebration for June 24th" (McGrath), **Supp. X:** 116
Celebration of the Sound Through (Sobin), **Supp. XVI:**284-285
Celebrations after the Death of John Brennan (X. J. Kennedy), **Supp. XV:** 165
Celebrity (film; Allen), **Supp. XV:** 11
"Celery" (Stein), **IV:** 43
"Celestial Games" (Conroy), **Supp. XVI:**72
"Celestial Globe" (Nemerov), **III:** 288
Celestial Navigation (Tyler), **Supp. IV Part 2:** 662-663, 671
"Celestial Railroad, The" (Hawthorne), **Retro. Supp. I:** 152; **Supp. I Part 1:** 188
Celibate Season, A (Shields), **Supp. VII:** 323, 324
Cellini (Shanley), **Supp. XIV:**316, **329-330**
"Cemetery at Academy, California" (Levine), **Supp. V:** 182
Cemetery Nights (Dobyns), **Supp. XIII:** 85, 87, 89
"Censors As Critics: *To Kill a Mockingbird* As a Case Study" (May), **Supp. VIII:** 126
"Census-Taker, The" (Frost), **Retro. Supp. I:** 129
"Centaur, The" (Swenson), **Supp. IV Part 2:** 641
Centaur, The (Updike), **IV:** 214, 216, 217, 218, 219-221, 222; **Retro. Supp. I:** 318, 322, 324, 331, 336
"Centennial Meditation of Columbia, The" (Lanier), **Supp. I Part 1:** 362
Centeno, Agusto, **IV:** 375
"Centipede" (Dove), **Supp. IV Part 1:** 246
"Central Man, The" (Bloom), **Supp. IV Part 2:** 689
"Central Park" (Lowell), **II:** 552
Central Park (Wasserstein and Drattel), **Supp. XV:** 333
Central Park West (Allen), **Supp. XV:** 13
Century of Dishonor, A (Jackson), **Retro. Supp. I:** 31
"Cerebral Snapshot, The" (Theroux), **Supp. VIII:** 313
"Ceremonies" (Rukeyser), **Supp. VI:** 279
Ceremony (Silko), **Supp. IV Part 1:** 274, 333; **Supp. IV Part 2:** 557-558, 558-559, 559, 561-566, 570
Ceremony (Wilbur), **Supp. III Part 2:** 550-551
"Ceremony, The" (Harjo), **Supp. XII:** 230
"Ceremony, The-Anatomy of a Massacre" (E. Hoffman, play), **Supp. XVI:**160
Ceremony in Lone Tree (Morris), **III:** 229-230, 232, 238, 558
Ceremony of Brotherhood, A (Anaya and Ortiz, eds.), **Supp. IV Part 2:** 502
Cerf, Bennett, **III:** 405; **IV:** 288; **Retro. Supp. II:** 330; **Supp. XIII:** 172
"Certain Attention to the World, A" (Haines), **Supp. XII:** 201
Certain Distance, A (Francis), **Supp. IX:** 85
"Certain Music, A" (Rukeyser), **Supp. VI:** 273
Certain Noble Plays of Japan (Pound), **III:** 458
Certain People (Wharton), **Retro. Supp. I:** 382
"Certain Poets" (MacLeish), **III:** 4
"Certain Testimony" (Bausch), **Supp. VII:** 48
Certificate, The (Singer), **IV:** 1; **Retro. Supp. II:** 314-315
Cervantes, Lorna Dee, **Supp. IV Part 2:** 545
Cervantes, Miguel de, **I:** 130, 134; **II:** 8, 272, 273, 276, 289, 302, 310, 315; **III:** 113, 614; **IV:** 367; **Retro. Supp. I:** 91; **Supp. I Part 2:** 406; **Supp. V:** 277; **Supp. XIII:** 17
Césaire, Aimé, **Supp. X:** 132, 139; **Supp. XIII:** 114
"Cesarean" (Kenyon), **Supp. VII:** 173
Cézanne, Paul, **II:** 576; **III:** 210; **IV:** 26, 31, 407; **Supp. V:** 333, 341-342
Chabon, Michael, **Supp. XI: 63-81**; **Supp. XVI:**259
Chaboseau, Jean, **Supp. I Part 1:** 260
Chaikin, Joseph, **Supp. III Part 2:** 433, 436-437
"Chain, The" (Kumin), **Supp. IV Part 2:** 452
Chainbearer, The (Cooper), **I:** 351, 352-353
"Chain of Love, A" (Price), **Supp. VI:** **258-259**, 260
Chains of Dew (Glaspell), **Supp. III**

Part 1: 181
Challacombe, Robert Hamilton, **III:** 176
Challenge (Untermeyer), **Supp. XV:** 296, 303
"Challenge" (Untermeyer), **Supp. XV:** 296
Chalmers, George, **Supp. I Part 2:** 514, 521
"Chambered Nautilus, The" (Holmes), **Supp. I Part 1:** 254, 307, 312-313, 314
Chamberlain, John, **Supp. I Part 2:** 647; **Supp. IV Part 2:** 525
Chamberlain, Neville, **II:** 589; **Supp. I Part 2:** 664
Chamber Music (Joyce), **III:** 16
Chambers, Richard, **Supp. III Part 2:** 610, 611, 612
Chambers, Whittaker, **Supp. III Part 2:** 610; **Supp. IV Part 2:** 526; **Supp. XV:** 143
Chameleon (C. Baxter), **Supp. XVII:** 14-15
"Champ, The" (Zinberg), **Supp. XV:** 193
"Champagne Regions" (Ríos), **Supp. IV Part 2:** 553
"Champion" (Lardner), **II:** 420-421, 428, 430
Champion, Laurie, **Supp. VIII:** 128
Champollion-Figeac, Jean Jacques, **IV:** 426
"Chance" (Doolittle), **Supp. I Part 1:** 271
Chance, Frank, **II:** 418
Chance Acquaintance, A (Howells), **II:** 278
"Chanclas" (Cisneros), **Supp. VII:** 61
Chandler, Raymond, **Supp. III Part 1:** 91; **Supp. IV Part 1: 119-138,** 341, 344, 345; **Supp. IV Part 2:** 461, 464, 469, 470, 471, 472, 473; **Supp. XI:** 160, 228; **Supp. XII:** 307; **Supp. XIII:** 159, 233; **Supp. XIV:**21; **Supp. XV:** 119; **Supp. XVI:**122; **Supp. XVII:** 137
Chaney, "Professor" W. H., **II:** 463-464
Chang, Leslie C., **Supp. IV Part 1:** 72
"Change, The: Kyoto-Tokyo Express" (Ginsberg), **Supp. II Part 1:** 313, 329
Changed Man, A (Prose), **Supp. XVI:**261-262
Changeling (Middleton), **Retro. Supp. I:** 62
"Changeling, The" (Lowell), **Supp. I Part 2:** 409
"Changeling, The" (Whittier), **Supp. I Part 2:** 697
Change of World, A (Rich), **Supp. I Part 2:** 551, 552
"Changes of Mind" (Baker), **Supp. XIII:** 52
"Change the Joke and Slip the Yoke" (Ellison), **Retro. Supp. II:** 118
Changing Light at Sandover, The (Merrill), **Supp. III Part 1:** 318, 319, 323, 327, 332, 335-336; **Supp. XII:** 269-270; **Supp. XV:** 264
"Changing Same, The" (Baraka), **Supp. II Part 1:** 47, 51, 53
Changing the Bully Who Rules the World: Reading and Thinking about Ethics (C. Bly), **Supp. XVI:**32, **39-40,** 41
Chanler, Mrs. Winthrop, **I:** 22; **IV:** 325
Channing, Carol, **IV:** 357
Channing, Edward, **Supp. I Part 2:** 479-480
Channing, Edward Tyrrel, **Supp. I Part 1:** 155; **Supp. I Part 2:** 422
Channing, William Ellery, **I:** 336; **II:** 224, 495; **IV:** 172, 173, 176, 177; **Retro. Supp. I:** 54; **Supp. I Part 1:** 103; **Supp. I Part 2:** 589
Channing, William Henry, **IV:** 178; **Supp. II Part 1:** 280, 285
Chanson de Roland, La, **I:** 13
"Chanson un Peu Naïve" (Bogan), **Supp. III Part 1:** 50-51
"Chanteuse" (Doty), **Supp. XI:** 119
"Chant for May Day" (Hughes), **Supp. I Part 1:** 331
Chants (Mora), **Supp. XIII: 214-215**
Chaos (Dove), **Supp. IV Part 1:** 243
"Chaperone, The" (Van Vechten), **Supp. II Part 2:** 728
Chaplin, Charles Spencer, **I:** 27, 32, 43, 386, 447; **III:** 403; **Supp. I Part 2:** 607; **Supp. IV Part 1:** 146; **Supp. IV Part 2:** 574
"Chaplinesque" (H. Crane), **Retro. Supp. II:** 79
"Chapman" (Rukeyser), **Supp. VI:** 273
Chapman, Abraham, **IV:** 485
Chapman, George, **Supp. I Part 2:** 422
Chapman, John (Johnny Appleseed), **Supp. I Part 2:** 397
Chapman, John Jay, **IV:** 436; **Supp. XIV:39-56**
Chapman, Stephen, **Supp. XIII:** 12
Chappell, Fred, **Supp. IV Part 1:** 69; **Supp. XI:** 317
Chapters in a Mythology: The Poetry of Sylvia Plath (Kroll), **Supp. I Part 2:** 541-543
Chapters on Erie (Adams and Adams), **Supp. I Part 2:** 644
Chapter Two (Simon), **Supp. IV Part 2:** 575, 586
"Chapter VI" (Hemingway), **II:** 252
Char, René, **Supp. XVI:**282; **Supp. XVII:** 244
"Character" (Emerson), **II:** 6
"Character of Presidents, The" (Doctorow), **Supp. IV Part 1:** 224
"Character of Socrates, The" (Emerson), **II:** 8-9
Character of the Poet, The (Simpson), **Supp. IX:** 273, 275, 278
"Characters in Fiction" (McCarthy), **II:** 562
"Charades" (Moore), **Supp. X:** 178
"Charge It" (Fante), **Supp. XI:** 164-165
Charlatan, The (Singer), **IV:** 1
"Charles" (Jackson), **Supp. IX:** 125
"Charles Baxter, August Kleinzahler, Adrienne Rich: Contemporary Stevensians and the Problem of 'Other Lives' " (S. Burt), **Supp. XVII:** 18-19
Charles Goodnight: Cowman and Plainsman (Haley), **Supp. V:** 226
Charles Simic: Essays on the Poetry (Weigl), **Supp. VIII:** 269
Charles the Bold, Duke of Burgundy, **III:** 487
Charleville, Victoria Verdon, **Supp. I Part 1:** 200-201, 205, 206, 210
Charley's Aunt (B. Thomas), **II:** 138
Charlie Chan Is Dead: An Anthology of Contemporary Asian American Fiction (Hagedorn), **Supp. X:** 292
"Charlie Christian Story, The" (Ellison), **Retro. Supp. II:** 121
"Charlie Howard's Descent" (Doty), **Supp. XI:** 122
Charlotte: A Tale of Truth (Rowson), **Supp. I Part 1:** 128; **Supp. XV: 234-235,** 238. See also *Charlotte Temple* (Rowson)
Charlotte's Daughter; or, The Three Orphans (Rowson), **Supp. XV: 246**
Charlotte's Web (White), **Supp. I Part 2:** 655, 656, 658, 667, 670
Charlotte Temple (Rowson), **Supp. XV:** 229, **238-239.** See also *Charlotte: A Tale of Truth* (Rowson)
Charm, The (Creeley), **Supp. IV Part 1:** 139, 141, 144, 149-150
Charmed Life, A (McCarthy), **II:** 571-574
Charms for the Easy Life (Gibbons), **Supp. X:** 45, **47-48**
Charnel Rose, The (Aiken), **I:** 50, 57, 62
Charon's Cosmology (Simic), **Supp.**

VIII: 276-278
Charterhouse, The (Percy), **Supp. III Part 1:** 388
Charvat, William, **II:** 244
Charyn, Jerome, **Supp. XVII:** 5
Chase, Mary Ellen, **Retro. Supp. II:** 243, 245
Chase, Richard, **IV:** 202, 443; **Retro. Supp. I:** 40, 395
Chase, Salmon P., **Supp. I Part 2:** 584
Chase, Stuart, **Supp. I Part 2:** 609
Chase, The (Foote), **Supp. I Part 1:** 281
"Chaste Land, The" (Tate), **IV:** 122
Château, The (Maxwell), **Supp. VIII:** 152, 160, **165-167,** 168, 169
Chatham, Russell, **Supp. VIII:** 40
Chatterdon, The Black Death, and Meriwether Lewis (Reznikoff), **Supp. XIV:**288
Chatterton, Thomas, **Supp. I Part 1:** 349; **Supp. I Part 2:** 410, 716
Chatterton, Wayne, **Supp. IX:** 2, 4, 11-12
Chatwin, Bruce, **Supp. VIII:** 322
Chaucer, Geoffrey, **I:** 131; **II:** 11, 504, 516, 542, 543; **III:** 283, 411, 473, 492, 521; **Retro. Supp. I:** 135, 426; **Supp. I Part 1:** 356, 363; **Supp. I Part 2:** 422, 617; **Supp. V:** 259; **Supp. XII:** 197; **Supp. XVII:** 70
Chauncy, Charles, **I:** 546-547; **IV:** 147
Chavez, César, **Supp. V:** 199
Chávez, Denise, **Supp. IV Part 2:** 544; **Supp. XI:** 316
Chavez, Lydia, **Supp. VIII:** 75
Chavkin, Allan, **Supp. IV Part 1:** 259
Chavkin, Nancy Feyl, **Supp. IV Part 1:** 259
Chayefsky, Paddy, **Supp. XI:** 306
Cheang, Shu Lea, **Supp. XI:** 20
"Cheat Takes Over" (Leopold), **Supp. XIV:**189
"Cheers" (Carver), **Supp. III Part 1:** 138
Cheetham, James, **Supp. I Part 2:** 521
Cheever, Benjamin Hale, **Supp. I Part 1:** 175
Cheever, David W., **Supp. I Part 1:** 304
Cheever, Ezekiel, **Supp. I Part 1:** 174, 193
Cheever, Federico, **Supp. I Part 1:** 175
Cheever, Fred, **Supp. I Part 1:** 174
Cheever, Frederick L., **Supp. I Part 1:** 174
Cheever, John, **Retro. Supp. I:** 116, 333, 335; **Supp. I Part 1: 174-199;** **Supp. V:** 23, 95; **Supp. VIII:** 151; **Supp. IX:** 114, 208; **Supp. XI:** 65, 66, 99; **Supp. XII:** 140; **Supp. XIV:**93; **Supp. XV:** 119, 142
Cheever, Mary Liley, **Supp. I Part 1:** 174
Cheever, Mrs. John (Mary Winternitz), **Supp. I Part 1:** 175
Cheever, Susan. *See* Cowley, Susan Cheever (Susan Cheever)
Cheever Evening, A (Gurney), **Supp. V:** 95
Chekhov, Anton, **I:** 52, 90; **II:** 27, 38, 44, 49, 198, 542; **III:** 362, 467; **IV:** 17, 53, 359, 446; **Retro. Supp. I:** 5, 355; **Retro. Supp. II:** 299; **Supp. I Part 1:** 196; **Supp. II Part 1:** 6; **Supp. IV Part 2:** 585; **Supp. V:** 265; **Supp. VIII:** 153, 332; **Supp. IX:** 260, 265, 274; **Supp. XI:** 66; **Supp. XII:** 94, 307; **Supp. XIII:** 79; **Supp. XIV:**87, 242; **Supp. XV:** 320, 329
"Chekhov's Sense of Writing as Seen Through His Letters" (Dobyns), **Supp. XIII:** 77-78
"Chemin de Fer" (Bishop), **Retro. Supp. II:** 41; **Supp. I Part 1:** 80, 85, 86
Cheney, Brainard, **Retro. Supp. II:** 229
Chenzira, Ayoka, **Supp. XI:** 19
Cherkovski, Neeli, **Supp. XII:** 118, 132, 134
Chernyshevski, Nikolai, **III:** 261, 262, 263; **Retro. Supp. I:** 269
Cherokee Lottery, The: A Sequence of Poems (W. J. Smith), **Supp. XIII: 340-344**
Cherry (Karr), **Supp. XI:** 239, **251-254**
Cherry Orchard, The (Chekhov), **IV:** 359, 426; **Supp. VIII:** 153
Cheslock, Louis, **III:** 99, 118, 119
Chesnutt, Charles Waddell, **Supp. II Part 1:** 174, 193, 211; **Supp. IV Part 1:** 257; **Supp. XIV:**57-78
"Chess House, The" (Dixon), **Supp. XII:** 139
Chessman, Caryl, **Supp. I Part 2:** 446
Chester, Alfred, **Retro. Supp. II:** 111, 112; **Supp. X:** 192
Chesterfield, Lord, **II:** 36
Chesterton, Gilbert Keith, **I:** 226; **IV:** 432
Cheuse, Alan, **Supp. IV Part 2:** 570
Chevigny, Bell Gale, **Supp. XI:** 283
"Chicago" (Sandburg), **III:** 581, 592, 596; **Supp. III Part 1:** 71

Chicago (Shepard), **Supp. III Part 2:** 439
Chicago: City on the Make (Algren), **Supp. IX:** 1, 3
"*Chicago Defender* Sends a Man to Little Rock, The" (Brooks), **Supp. III Part 1:** 80-81
"Chicago Hamlet, A" (Anderson), **I:** 112
Chicago Loop (Theroux), **Supp. VIII:** 324
"Chicago Picasso, The" (Brooks), **Supp. III Part 1:** 70-71, 84
Chicago Poems (Sandburg), **III:** 579, 581-583, 586
"Chicano/Borderlands Literature and Poetry" (Ríos), **Supp. IV Part 2:** 537, 538, 542, 545
Chick, Nancy, **Supp. IV Part 1:** 1
"Chickamauga" (Bierce), **I:** 201
"Chickamauga" (Wolfe), **IV:** 460
Chickamauga (Wright), **Supp. V:** 333, 343-344
"Chickamauga" (Wright), **Supp. V:** 334
"Chiefly about War Matters" (Hawthorne), **II:** 227; **Retro. Supp. I:** 165
"Child" (Plath), **Supp. I Part 2:** 544
Child, Julia, **Supp. XVII:** 89, 90
Child, Lydia Maria, **Supp. XIII:** 141
"Child, The" (Ríos), **Supp. IV Part 2:** 543
"Child by Tiger, The" (Wolfe), **IV:** 451
"Childhood" (Wright), **Supp. V:** 341
Childhood, A: The Biography of a Place (Crews), **Supp. XI:** 102-103, 245
"Childhood, When You Are in It ..." (Kenyon), **Supp. VII:** 160, 170
"Childhood Sketch" (Wright), **Supp. III Part 2:** 589
"Child Is Born, A" (Benét), **Supp. XI:** 46
"Child Is the Meaning of This Life, The" (Schwartz), **Supp. II Part 2:** 659-660
"Childlessness" (Merrill), **Supp. III Part 1:** 323
"Childless Woman" (Plath), **Supp. I Part 2:** 544
Child-Life (Whittier and Larcom, eds.), **Supp. XIII:** 142
Child-Life in Prose (Whittier and Larcom, eds.), **Supp. XIII:** 142
Childlike Life of the Black Tarantula, The (Acker), **Supp. XII:** 4, 6, **7-8**
"Child Margaret" (Sandburg), **III:** 584
"Child of Courts, The" (Jarrell), **II:** 378, 379, 381

Child of God (McCarthy), **Supp. VIII:** 177-178
"CHILD OF THE THIRTIES" (Baraka), **Supp. II Part 1:** 60
"Child on Top of a Greenhouse" (Roethke), **III:** 531
Children (Gurney), **Supp. V:** 95, 96
"Children" (Stowe), **Supp. I Part 2:** 587
"Children, The" (Jarman), **Supp. XVII:** 116
Children, The (Wharton), **IV:** 321, 326; **Retro. Supp. I:** 381
"Children, the Sandbar, That Summer" (Rukeyser), **Supp. VI:** 274
Children and Others (Cozzens), **I:** 374
Children Is All (Purdy), **Supp. VII:** 277, 278, 282
"Children of Adam" (Whitman), **IV:** 342; **Retro. Supp. I:** 403, 405
Children of Job, The: American Second-Generation Witnesses to the Holocaust (A. Berger), **Supp. XVII:** 39
Children of Light (Stone), **Supp. V:** 304-306
Children of Light and the Children of Darkness, The (Niebuhr), **III:** 292, 306, 310
Children of the Frost (London), **II:** 469, 483
Children of the Holocaust (H. Epstein), **Supp. XVII:** 48
"Children of the Lord's Supper, The" (Tegnér), **Retro. Supp. II:** 155, 157
Children of the Market Place (Masters), **Supp. I Part 2:** 471
"Children on Their Birthdays" (Capote), **Supp. III Part 1:** 114, 115
"Children Selecting Books in a Library" (Jarrell), **II:** 371
Children's Hour, The (Hellman), **Supp. I Part 1:** 276-277, 281, 286, 297
"Children's Rhymes" (Hughes), **Supp. I Part 1:** 340
Childress, Mark, **Supp. X:** 89
Child's Garden of Verses, A (Stevenson), **Supp. IV Part 1:** 298, 314; **Supp. XIII:** 75
"Child's Reminiscence, A" (Whitman), **IV:** 344
Childwold (Oates), **Supp. II Part 2:** 519-520
Chill, The (Macdonald), **Supp. IV Part 2:** 473
Chills and Fever (Ransom), **III:** 490, 491-492, 493
Chilly Scenes of Winter (Beattie), **Supp. V:** 21, 22, 23, 24, 26, 27
Chime of Words, A: The Letters of Logan Pearsall Smith (Tribble, ed.), **Supp. XIV:**348-349
Chimera (C. Frost), **Supp. XV:** 94, 95, 100
"Chimes for Yahya" (Merrill), **Supp. III Part 1:** 329
Chin, Frank, **Supp. V:** 164, 172
"China" (Johnson), **Supp. VI:** 193-194
"Chinaman's Hat" (Kingston), **Supp. V:** 169
China Men (Kingston), **Supp. V:** 157, 158, 159, 160, 161, 164-169; **Supp. X:** 292; **Supp. XV:** 220
China Trace (Wright), **Supp. V:** 332, 340, 341, 342
Chinese Classics (Legge), **III:** 472
Chinese Materia Medica (P. Smith), **III:** 572
"Chinese Nightingale, The" (Lindsay), **Supp. I Part 2:** 392-393, 394
Chinese Nightingale and Other Poems, The (Lindsay), **Supp. I Part 2:** 392
Chinese Siamese Cat, The (Tan), **Supp. X:** 289
Chinese Translations, The (Bynner), **Supp. XV:** 47, 52
Chinitz, David, **Supp. XV:** 180, 185
"Chinoiseries" (Lowell), **II:** 524-525
Chip (Untermeyer), **Supp. XV:** 310
Chirico, Giorgio de, **Supp. III Part 1:** 14
Chirico, Miriam M., **Supp. XV:** 323
"Chiron" (Winters), **Supp. II Part 2:** 801
"Chloroform Jags" (J. Scott), **Supp. XVII:** 189
Chodorov, Jerome, **IV:** 274
"Choice, The" (Karr), **Supp. XI:** 251
"Choice of Profession, A" (Malamud), **Supp. I Part 2:** 437
Chomei, Kamo No, **IV:** 170, 171, 184
Chomsky, Noam, **Supp. IV Part 2:** 679
Choosing not Choosing (Cameron), **Retro. Supp. I:** 43
Chopin, Felix, **Supp. I Part 1:** 202
Chopin, Frédéric, **Supp. I Part 1:** 363
Chopin, Jean, **Supp. I Part 1:** 206
Chopin, Kate, **II:** 276; **Retro. Supp. I:** 10, 215; **Retro. Supp. II:** 57-74; **Supp. I Part 1:** 200-226; **Supp. V:** 304; **Supp. X:** 227
"Choral: The Pink Church" (W. C. Williams), **Retro. Supp. I:** 428
"Chord" (Merwin), **Supp. III Part 1:** 356
"Chords and Dischords" (column; Untermeyer), **Supp. XV:** 294
Choruses from Iphigenia in Aulis (Doolittle, trans.), **Supp. I Part 1:** 257, 268, 269
"Chosen Blindness" (Karr), **Supp. XI:** 251
Chosen Country (Dos Passos), **I:** 475, 490-491
Chosen Place, The Timeless People, The (Marshall), **Supp. XI:** 275, 276, **282-284**
Chosön (Lowell), **II:** 513
Choukri, Mohamed, **Supp. IV Part 1:** 92
Chovteau, Mane Thérèse, **Supp. I Part 1:** 205
Chrisman, Robert, **Supp. IV Part 1:** 1
Christabel (Coleridge), **Supp. IV Part 2:** 465
"Christ for Sale" (Lowell), **II:** 538
Christian, Graham, **Supp. XII:** 193
Christian Dictionary, A (Wilson), **IV:** 153
"Christian in World Crisis, The" (Merton), **Supp. VIII:** 203
Christianity and Power Politics (Niebuhr), **III:** 292, 303
"Christianity and the Survival of Creation" (Berry), **Supp. X:** 30
"Christian Minister, The" (Emerson), **II:** 10
Christian Philosopher, The (Mather), **Supp. II Part 2:** 463-464
Christian Realism and Practical Problems (Niebuhr), **III:** 292, 308
"Christian Roommates, The" (Updike), **IV:** 226-227; **Retro. Supp. I:** 319, 323
Christiansen, Carrie, **I:** 210
Christian's Secret of a Happy Life, The (H. W. Smith), **Supp. XIV:**333-334
Christie, Agatha, **Supp. IV Part 1:** 341; **Supp. IV Part 2:** 469
Christine (King), **Supp. V:** 139, 148
"Christ Light, The" (Chopin), **Retro. Supp. II:** 61
"Christmas 1944" (Levertov), **Supp. III Part 1:** 274
"Christmas, or the Good Fairy" (Stowe), **Supp. I Part 2:** 586
"Christmas Banquet, The" (Hawthorne), **II:** 227
Christmas Card, A (Theroux), **Supp. VIII:** 322
Christmas Carol, A (Dickens), **Retro. Supp. I:** 196; **Supp. I Part 2:** 409-410; **Supp. X:** 252, 253
"Christmas Eve at Johnson's Drugs N Goods" (Bambara), **Supp. XI:** 11-12
"Christmas Eve in the Time of War: A Capitalist Meditates by a Civil War Monument" (Lowell), **II:** 538
"Christmas Eve under Hooker's Statue"

(Lowell), **II:** 539-540
"Christmas Gift" (Warren), **IV:** 252-253
"Christmas Greeting, A" (Wright), **Supp. III Part 2:** 601
"Christmas Hymn, A" (Wilbur), **Supp. III Part 2:** 557
Christmas Memory, A (Capote), **Supp. III Part 1:** 118, 119, 129
"Christmass Poem" (West), **Retro. Supp. II:** 338
Christmas Story (Mencken), **III:** 111
"Christmas to Me" (Lee), **Supp. VIII:** 113
Christographia (Taylor), **IV:** 164-165
"*Christ on the Cross*/Nuestro Señor Crucificado" (Mora), **Supp. XIII:** 229
Christopher and His Kind: 1929-1939 (Isherwood), **Supp. XIV:**157, 163, 164, 171
"Christopher Cat" (Cullen), **Supp. IV Part 1:** 173
Christopher Columbus, Mariner (Morison), **Supp. I Part 2:** 488
Christopher Isherwood: A Critical Biography (Finney), **Supp. XIV:**158
Christophersen, Bill, **Supp. IX:** 159, 167; **Supp. XI:** 155; **Supp. XIII:** 87
"Christ's Passion" (Karr), **Supp. XI:** 251
Christus: A Mystery (Longfellow), **II:** 490, 493, 495, 505-507; **Retro. Supp. II:** 161, 165, 166
Chroma (F. Barthelme), **Supp. XI:** 30, 33, 34
"Chroma" (F. Barthelme), **Supp. XI:** 31
"Chronicle of Race Relations, A" (Du Bois), **Supp. II Part 1:** 182
Chronicle of the Conquest of Granada (Irving), **II:** 310
"Chronologues" (Goldbarth), **Supp. XII:** 183, 184
"Chrysanthemums, The" (Steinbeck), **IV:** 53
"Chrysaor" (Longfellow), **II:** 498
Chu, Louis, **Supp. X:** 291
Chuang, Hua, **Supp. X:** 291
Chuang-Tzu, **Supp. VIII:** 206
"Chunk of Amethyst, A" (R. Bly), **Supp. IV Part 1:** 72
Church, Margaret, **IV:** 466
"Church and the Fiction Writer, The" (O'Connor), **Retro. Supp. II:** 223, 233
Churchill, Charles, **Supp. XV:** 232
Churchill, Winston, **I:** 9, 490; **Supp. I Part 2:** 491

Church of Dead Girls, The (Dobyns), **Supp. XIII:** 75, **83-84**
"Church Porch, The" (Herbert), **IV:** 153
Church Psalmody, Selected from Dr. Watts and Other Authors (Mason and Greene, ed.), **I:** 458
Ciannic, Saint, **II:** 215
Ciano, Edda, **IV:** 249
Ciardi, John, **I:** 169, 179, 535; **III:** 268; **Supp. IV Part 1:** 243; **Supp. IV Part 2:** 639; **Supp. IX:** 269, 324; **Supp. XII:** 119
Cicada (Haines), **Supp. XII: 206-207**
"Cicadas" (Wilbur), **Supp. III Part 2:** 549
Cicero, **I:** 279; **II:** 8, 14-15; **III:** 23; **Supp. I Part 2:** 405
Cider House Rules, The (Irving), **Supp. VI:** 164, **173-175**
"Cigales" (Wilbur), **Supp. III Part 2:** 549
"Cigarette" (L. Michaels), **Supp. XVI:**214
Cimarron, Rose (Burke), **Supp. XIV:**22, 35
"Cimetière Marin, Le" (Valéry), **IV:** 91-92
Cimino, Michael, **Supp. X:** 126
Cincinnati Kid, The (film), **Supp. XI: 306**
"Cinderella" (Jarrell), **II:** 386
"Cinderella" (Perrault), **IV:** 266, 267
"Cinderella" (Sexton), **Supp. II Part 2:** 691
"Cinema, The" (Salter), **Supp. IX:** 257
Cinema of Tony Richardson, The: Essays and Interviews (Phillips), **Supp. XI:** 306
Cinthio, **IV:** 370
Ciolkowski, Laura, **Supp. XVI:**24
CIOPW (Cummings), **I:** 429
"Circe" (Welty), **Retro. Supp. I:** 353
Circle Game, The (Atwood), **Supp. XIII:** 20, 33
"Circle in the Fire, A" (O'Connor), **III:** 344-345, 349-350, 351, 353, 354; **Retro. Supp. II:** 229, 232
"Circle of Breath" (Stafford), **Supp. XI:** 318, 322
"Circles" (Emerson), **I:** 455, 460
"Circles" (Lowell), **II:** 554
"Circus, The" (Porter), **III:** 443, 445
"Circus Animals' Desertion" (Yeats), **I:** 389
"Circus in the Attic" (Warren), **IV:** 253
Circus in the Attic, The (Warren), **IV:** 243, 251-253
"Circus in Three Rings" (Plath), **Retro. Supp. II:** 243; **Supp. I Part 2:** 536

Circus of Needs, A (Dunn), **Supp. XI: 147-148**
"Cirque d'Hiver" (Bishop), **Supp. I Part 1:** 85
Cisneros, Sandra, **Supp. IV Part 2:** 544; **Supp. VII: 57-73**; **Supp. XI:** 177; **Supp. XVII:** 71
Cities of the Interior (Nin), **Supp. X:** 182
Cities of the Plain (McCarthy), **Supp. VIII:** 175, **186-187**
Cities of the Red Night (Burroughs), **Supp. III Part 1:** 106
"Citizen Cain" (Baraka), **Supp. II Part 1:** 49
Citizen Kane (film), **Retro. Supp. I:** 115; **Supp. V:** 251; **Supp. XI:** 169
"Citizen of the World" (Goldsmith), **II:** 299
"City" (Francis), **Supp. IX:** 87
City and the Pillar, The (Vidal), **Supp. IV Part 2:** 677, 680-681; **Supp. XIV:**170
"*City and the Pillar, The,* as Gay Fiction" (Summers), **Supp. IV Part 2:** 680-681
City Boy (L. Michaels), **Supp. XVI:**212
"City Boy" (L. Michaels), **Supp. XVI:**203-204
City in History, The (Mumford), **Supp. II Part 2:** 495
"City in the Sea, The" (Poe), **III:** 411; **Retro. Supp. II:** 274
City in Which I Love You, The (L.-Y. Lee), **Supp. XV:** 212, **215-220**
"City in Which I Love You, The" (L.-Y. Lee), **Supp. XV:** 215, **217-218**
City Life (Barthelme), **Supp. IV Part 1:** 44, 47
"City of Change, A" (Bynner), **Supp. XV:** 45
City of Glass (Auster), **Supp. XII:** 22, **24-26**
City of God, The (St. Augustine), **IV:** 126
City of the Living and Other Stories, The (Stegner), **Supp. IV Part 2:** 599, 609, 613
City of Words: American Fiction 1950-1970 (T. Tanner), **Supp. XVI:**69
City of Your Final Destination, The (Cameron), **Supp. XII:** 79, 82, **91-94**
"City on a Hill" (Lowell), **II: 552**
"City Person Encountering Nature, A" (Kingston), **Supp. V:** 170
"City Planners, The" (Atwood), **Supp. XIII:** 33

City Without Walls (Auden), **Supp. II Part 1:** 24
Civil Disobedience (Thoreau), **IV:** 185; **Supp. I Part 2:** 507
Civilization in the United States (Stearns), **I:** 245
"Civil Rights" (Lanier), **Supp. I Part 1:** 357
Cixous, Hélène, **Supp. X:** 102; **Supp. XIII:** 297; **Supp. XV:** 347
Claiborne, Craig, **Supp. XVII:** 89
Claiborne, William, **I:** 132
Claiming of Sleeping Beauty, The (Rice), **Supp. VII:** 301
Clampitt, Amy, **Supp. IX: 37-54; Supp. X:** 120; **Supp. XI:** 249; **Supp. XV:** 251, 256
Clancy's Wake, At (Crane), **I:** 422
"Clandeboye" (Leopold), **Supp. XIV:** 189
Clara Howard; or, The Enthusiasm of Love (Brown), **Supp. I Part 1:** 145
Clara's Ole Man (Bullins), **Supp. II Part 1:** 42
Clare, John, **II:** 387; **III:** 528; **Supp. XVI:** 295
Clarel: A Poem and Pilgrimage in the Holy Land (Melville), **Retro. Supp. I:** 257
Clarissa (Richardson), **II:** 111; **Supp. I Part 2:** 714; **Supp. V:** 127; **Supp. XV:** 231
Clark, Alex, **Supp. XII:** 307
Clark, Charles, **I:** 470
Clark, Eleanor. *See* Warren, Mrs. Robert Penn (Eleanor Clark)
Clark, Francis Edward, **II:** 9
Clark, Geoffrey, **Supp. XI:** 342
Clark, Harry Hayden, **Supp. I Part 2:** 423
Clark, John Bates, **Supp. I Part 2:** 633
Clark, Kenneth, **Supp. XIV:** 342, 348
Clark, Thomas, **Supp. III Part 2:** 629; **Supp. IV Part 1:** 140, 145, 147
Clark, Walter, **Supp. XI:** 315
Clark, William, **III:** 14; **IV:** 179, 283
Clark, Willis Gaylord, **Supp. I Part 2:** 684
Clarke, James Freeman, **Supp. II Part 1:** 280
Clarke, John, **Supp. IV Part 1:** 8
Clarke, John J., **III:** 356
Clarke, Samuel, **II:** 108
Clark Lectures, **Retro. Supp. I:** 65
Clash by Night (Odets), **Supp. II Part 2:** 531, 538, 544-546, 550, 551
Classical Tradition, The (Highet), **Supp. I Part 1:** 268
Classic Ballroom Dances (Simic), **Supp. VIII:** 271, **276-278,** 283

Classics and Commercials: A Literary Chronicle of the Forties (Wilson), **IV:** 433
"CLASS STRUGGLE" (Baraka), **Supp. III Part 1:** 55
"Claude Glass, The: 1890" (Bierds), **Supp. XVII:** 27
Claudel, Paul, **I:** 60
Claudelle Inglish (Caldwell), **I:** 304
Clavel, Marcel, **I:** 343
"CLAY" (Baraka), **Supp. II Part 1:** 54
Clay, Henry, **I:** 8; **Supp. I Part 2:** 684, 686
Clay's Ark (O. Butler), **Supp. XIII:** 63
Clayton, John J., **Supp. IV Part 1:** 238
"Clean, Well Lighted Place, A" (Hemingway), **Retro. Supp. I:** 181
"Clear, with Light Variable Winds" (Lowell), **II:** 522
"Clear Days" (White), **Supp. I Part 2:** 664, 665
Clearing (Berry), **Supp. X:** 22
"Clearing, A" (Simpson), **Supp. IX:** 280
"Clearing, The" (Kenyon), **Supp. VII:** 174
"Clearing the Title" (Merrill), **Supp. III Part 1:** 336
"Clearing Up the Question of Stesichoros' Blinding by Helen" (Carson), **Supp. XII:** 107-108
"Clear Morning" (Glück), **Supp. V:** 88
"Clearness" (Wilbur), **Supp. III Part 2:** 544, 550
"Clear Night" (Wright), **Supp. V:** 341
Clear Pictures: First Loves, First Guides (Price), **Supp. VI:** 253, 254, 255, 256, 265
Clear Springs (Mason), **Supp. VIII:** 134-136, 137-138, 139, 147
Cleaver, Eldridge, **Retro. Supp. II:** 12; **Supp. IV Part 1:** 206; **Supp. X:** 249
"Cleaving, The" (L.-Y. Lee), **Supp. XV:** 215, **218-220**
Cleland, John, **Supp. V:** 48, 127
Clemenceau, Georges, **I:** 490
Clemens, Jane, **I:** 247
Clemens, Mrs. Samuel Langhorne (Olivia Langdon), **I:** 197, 208, 247; **Supp. I Part 2:** 457
Clemens, Orion, **IV:** 193, 195
Clemens, Samuel Langhorne. *See* Twain, Mark
Clemens, Susie, **IV:** 208
Clementine Recognitions (novel), **Supp. IV Part 1:** 280
Clements, Colin Campbell, **Supp. XVI:** 190

Clemons, Walter, **Supp. IV Part 1:** 305, 307
Cleopatra, **III:** 44; **IV:** 373; **Supp. I Part 1:** 114
"Clepsydra" (Ashbery), **Supp. III Part 1:** 10-15
"Clerks, The" (Robinson), **III:** 517-518
Cleveland, Carol, **Supp. IX:** 120, 125
Cleveland, Ceil, **Supp. V:** 222
Cleveland, Grover, **II:** 126, 128, 129, 130, 137, 138; **Supp. I Part 2:** 486
"Clever Magician Carrying My Heart, A" (Salinas), **Supp. XIII:** 323
"Cliff, The" (C. Baxter), **Supp. XVII:** 16-17
Clifford, Craig, **Supp. IX:** 99
Clift, Montgomery, **III:** 161
Climate of Monastic Prayer, The (Merton), **Supp. VIII:** 205, 207
"Climber, The" (Mason), **Supp. VIII:** 140-141
"Climbing the Tower" (Crews), **Supp. XI:** 102
Clinton, De Witt, **I:** 338
"Clipped Wings" (H. Miller), **III:** 176-177
Clive, Robert, **Supp. I Part 2:** 505
Clock Winder, The (Tyler), **Supp. IV Part 2:** 661-662, 670
Clock Without Hands (McCullers), **II:** 587-588, 604-606
Clockwork Orange, A (Burgess), **Supp. XIII:** 29
Clorindy (Cook), **Supp. II Part 1:** 199
"Close, The" (Jarman), **Supp. XVII:** 113
"Close Calls" (Wolff), **Supp. VII:** 332-333
"Closed Book, A" (Mosley), **Supp. XIII:** 237
Close Range: Wyoming Stories (Proulx), **Supp. VII:** 261-265
Closest Possible Union, The (J. Scott), **Supp. XVII: 185-186,** 188, 191
Close the Book (Glaspell), **Supp. III Part 1:** 179
"Close the Book" (Lowell), **II:** 554
Close to Shore: A True Story of Terror in an Age of Innocence (Capuzzo), **Supp. XIII:** 254
Closet Writing & Gay Reading: The Case of Melville's Pierre (Creech), **Retro. Supp. I:** 254
Closing Circle, The (Commoner), **Supp. XIII:** 264
Closing of the American Mind, The (Bloom), **Retro. Supp. II:** 19, 30, 31
"Closing of the Rodeo, The" (W. J. Smith), **Supp. XIII:** 332

Closing Time (Heller), **Supp. IV Part 1:** 382, 386, 391-394
Closset, Marie, **Supp. VIII:** 251, 265
"Cloud, The" (Shelley), **Supp. I Part 2:** 720
"Cloud and Fame" (Berryman), **I:** 173
Cloud Forest, The: A Chronicle of the South American Wilderness (Matthiessen), **Supp. V:** 202, 204
"Cloud on the Way, The" (Bryant), **Supp. I Part 1:** 171
"Cloud River" (Wright), **Supp. V:** 341
"Clouds" (Levine), **Supp. V:** 184
Cloudsplitter (Banks), **Supp. V:** 16
"Clover" (Lanier), **Supp. I Part 1:** 362-364
Clover and Other Poems (Lanier), **Supp. I Part 1:** 362
"Clown" (Corso), **Supp. XII:** 127
Clown in the Belfry, The: Writings on Faith and Fiction (Buechner), **Supp. XII:** 53
Cluck, Julia, **Supp. I Part 2:** 728
Clum, John M., **Supp. XIII: 200,** 201, 209
Cluny, Hugo, **IV:** 290
Clurman, Harold, **I:** 93; **IV:** 381, 385
Clytus, Radiclani, **Supp. XIII:** 128, **Supp. XIII:** 129, 132
"Coal: Beginning and End" (Winters), **Supp. II Part 2:** 791
Coale, Howard, **Supp. XIII:** 15
"Coast, The" (column), **Supp. IV Part 1:** 198
"Coast Guard's Cottage, The" (Wylie), **Supp. I Part 2:** 723
Coast of Trees, A (Ammons), **Supp. VII:** 24, 34
"Coast-Range Christ, The" (Jeffers), **Supp. II Part 2:** 414, 419
"Coast-Road, The" (Jeffers), **Supp. II Part 2:** 425
"Coat, The" (Everwine), **Supp. XV:** 80
Coates, Joseph, **Supp. VIII:** 80
Coates, Robert, **I:** 54; **IV:** 298
"Coatlicue's Rules: Advice from an Aztec Goddess" (Mora), **Supp. XIII:** 223
"Coats" (Kenyon), **Supp. VII:** 172
Cobb, Lee J., **III:** 153
Cobb, Ty, **III:** 227, 229
Cobbett, William, **Supp. I Part 2:** 517; **Supp. XV:** 237
"Cobbler Keezar's Vision" (Whittier), **Supp. I Part 2:** 699
"Cobweb, The" (Carver), **Supp. III Part 1:** 148
Cobwebs From an Empty Skull (Bierce), **I:** 195
Coccimiglio, Vic, **Supp. XIII:** 114

"Cock-a-Doodle-Doo!" (Melville), **III:** 89
"Cockayne" (Emerson), **II:** 6
"Cock-Crow" (Gordon), **II:** 219
Cock Pit (Cozzens), **I:** 359, 378, 379
Cockpit (Kosinski), **Supp. XII:** 21
Cockpit: A Novel (Kosinski), **Supp. VII:** 215, 223-224, 225
"Cock Robin Takes Refuge in the Storm House" (Snodgrass), **Supp. VI:** 319
Cocktail Hour, The (Gurney), **Supp. V:** 95, 96, 100, 101, 103, 105, 108
Cocktail Hour and Two Other Plays: Another Antigone and *The Perfect Party* (Gurney), **Supp. V:** 100
Cocktail Party, The (Eliot), **I:** 571, 582-583; **III:** 21; **Retro. Supp. I:** 65; **Supp. V:** 101, 103
Cocteau, Jean, **III:** 471; **Retro. Supp. I:** 82, 378; **Supp. IV Part 1:** 82; **Supp. XVI:**135
"Coda: Wilderness Letter" (Stegner), **Supp. IV Part 2:** 595
"Code, The" (Frost), **Retro. Supp. I:** 121, 128
Codman, Florence, **Supp. II Part 1:** 92, 93
Codman, Ogden, Jr., **Retro. Supp. I:** 362, 363
Cody, William ("Buffalo Bill"), **I:** 440; **III:** 584; **Supp. V:** 230
Coffey, Michael, **Supp. V:** 243; **Supp. XV:** 65
Coffey, Warren, **III:** 358
Coffin, Charles, **III:** 577
Cogan, David J., **Supp. IV Part 1:** 362
Coghill, Nevill, **Supp. II Part 1:** 4; **Supp. XIV:**13
Cohan, George M., **II:** 427; **III:** 401
Cohen, Edward M., **Supp. XVI:**212
Cohen, Esther, **Supp. XV:** 323
Cohen, Hettie, **Supp. II Part 1:** 30
Cohen, Marty, **Supp. X:** 112
Cohen, Norman J., **Supp. IX:** 132, 143
Cohen, Rosetta, **Supp. XV:** 257
Cohen, Sarah Blacher, **Supp. V:** 273
"Coherent Decentering: Towards a New Model of the Poetic Self" (A. Finch), **Supp. XVII:** 76
"Coin" (Goldbarth), **Supp. XII:** 187
Coindreau, Maurice, **III:** 339
Coiner, Constance, **Supp. XIII:** 297, 302
Coit, Lille Hitchcock, **Supp. X:** 103
"Coitus" (Pound), **III:** 466
Colburn, Nadia Herman, **Supp. XV:** 339, 341, 347
"Cold, The" (Kenyon), **Supp. VII:** 164
"Cold, The" (Winters), **Supp. II Part 2:** 790-791, 809, 811

"Cold-blooded Creatures" (Wylie), **Supp. I Part 2:** 729
Colden, Cadwallader, **Supp. I Part 1:** 250
"Colder the Air, The" (Bishop), **Supp. I Part 1:** 86
Cold Feet (Harrison), **Supp. VIII:** 39
Cold Frame (C. Frost), **Supp. XV:** 93, 96
Cold Ground Was My Bed Last Night (Garrett), **Supp. VII:** 98
"Cold Ground Was My Bed Last Night" (Garrett), **Supp. VII:** 100
"Cold Night, The" (W. C. Williams), **Retro. Supp. I:** 418
"Cold Plunge into Skin Diving, A" (Knowles), **Supp. XII:** 241
Cold Spring, A (Bishop), **Retro. Supp. II:** 45
Cold Springs Harbor (Yates), **Supp. XI:** 348
Cold War American Poetry, **Supp. V:** 182
Cold War and the Income Tax, The (Wilson), **IV:** 430
Cole, Goody, **Supp. I Part 2:** 696-697
Cole, Lester, **Retro. Supp. II:** 329
Cole, Nat King, **Retro. Supp. I:** 334; **Supp. X:** 255
Cole, Thomas, **Supp. I Part 1:** 156, 158, 171
"Coleman" (Karr), **Supp. XI:** 244
Coleman, Wanda, **Supp. XI: 83-98**
Coleridge, Samuel Taylor, **I:** 283, 284, 447, 522; **II:** 7, 10, 11, 19, 71, 169, 273, 301, 502, 516, 549; **III:** 77, 83-84, 424, 461, 488, 523; **IV:** 74, 173, 250, 349, 453; **Retro. Supp. I:** 65, 308; **Supp. I Part 1:** 31, 311, 349; **Supp. I Part 2:** 376, 393, 422; **Supp. IV Part 2:** 422, 465; **Supp. V:** 258; **Supp. IX:** 38, 50; **Supp. XIII:** 139; **Supp. XIV:**21-22; **Supp. XV:** 250
Coles, Katharine, **Supp. IV Part 2:** 630
Colette, **Supp. VIII:** 40, 171
Colette, Sidonie-Gabrielle, **Supp. XVI:**193-194
"Coliseum, The" (Poe), **III:** 411
Collage of Dreams (Spencer), **Supp. X:** 196
"Collapse of Tomorrow, The" (Mumford), **Supp. II Part 2:** 482
"Collected by a Valetudinarian" (E. Stoddard), **Supp. XV:** 286-287
Collected Earlier Poems (Hecht), **Supp. X:** 58, 59
Collected Earlier Poems (W. C.

Williams), **Retro. Supp. I:** 414, 428
Collected Earlier Poems 1940-1960 (Levertov), **Supp. III Part 1:** 273, 275
Collected Essays (Tate), **IV:** 133-134
Collected Essays of Ralph Ellison, The (Ellison), **Retro. Supp. II:** 119
Collected Essays of Robert Creeley, The (Creeley), **Supp. IV Part 1:** 153, 154
Collected Later Poems (W. C. Williams), **Retro. Supp. I:** 428
Collected Plays (A. Miller), **III:** 158
Collected Plays, 1974-1983 (Gurney), **Supp. V:** 99
Collected Poems (Aiken), **I:** 50
Collected Poems (Burke), **I:** 269
Collected Poems (Cummings), **I:** 430, 439, 441
Collected Poems (Doolittle), **Supp. I Part 1:** 264-267, 269
Collected Poems (Frost), **Retro. Supp. I:** 136
Collected Poems (Kees; Justice, ed.), **Supp. XV:** 134
Collected Poems (Lindsay), **Supp. I Part 2:** 380, 387, 392, 396-397, 400
Collected Poems (Lowell), **Supp. XV:** 20
Collected Poems (Markson), **Supp. XVII:** 143
Collected Poems (Moore), **III:** 194, 215
Collected Poems (Price), **Supp. VI:** 267
Collected Poems (Simpson), **Supp. IX:** 279
Collected Poems (Winters), **Supp. II Part 2:** 791, 810
Collected Poems (Wright), **Supp. III Part 2:** 602
Collected Poems (W. C. Williams), **IV:** 415; **Retro. Supp. I:** 430
Collected Poems (Yeats), **Supp. XV:** 152
Collected Poems 1909-1935 (Eliot), **I:** 580; **Retro. Supp. I:** 66
Collected Poems 1909-1962 (Eliot), **I:** 583
Collected Poems 1917-1952 (MacLeish), **III:** 3, 4, 19
Collected Poems 1921-1931 (W. C. Williams), **Retro. Supp. I:** 422; **Supp. XIV:**285
Collected Poems 1930-1960 (Eberhart), **I:** 522, 525-526, 540, 541
Collected Poems, 1923-1953 (Bogan), **Supp. III Part 1:** 64
Collected Poems, 1936-1976 (Francis), **Supp. IX:** 77, 80, **87**
Collected Poems: 1939-1989 (W. J. Smith), **Supp. XIII:** 332, 340, 343, 345
Collected Poems: 1940-1978 (Shapiro), **Supp. II Part 2:** 703, 717
Collected Poems: 1951-1971 (Ammons), **Supp. VII:** 24, 26-29, 32, 33
Collected Poems: 1956-1976 (Wagoner), **Supp. IX:** 323, **328-329**
Collected Poems, The (Stevens), **III:** 273; **IV:** 75, 76, 87, 93; **Retro. Supp. I:** 296, 309
Collected Poems of Amy Clampitt, The (Clampitt), **Supp. IX:** 37, 44, 53
Collected Poems of George Garrett (Garrett), **Supp. VII:** 109
Collected Poems of Hart Crane, The (Crane), **I:** 399-402
Collected Poems of James Agee, The (Fitzgerald, ed.), **I:** 27-28
Collected Poems of James T. Farrell, The (Farrell), **II:** 45
Collected Poems of Langston Hughes, The (Rampersad and Roessel, ed.), **Retro. Supp. I:** 194, 196, 212
Collected Poems of Muriel Rukeyser, The (Rukeyser), **Supp. VI:** 274
Collected Poems of Thomas Merton, The, **Supp. VIII:** 207, 208
Collected Poetry (Auden), **Supp. II Part 1:** 18
Collected Prose (Wright), **Supp. III Part 2:** 596
Collected Prose, The (Bishop), **Retro. Supp. II:** 51
Collected Recordings (W. C. Williams), **Retro. Supp. I:** 431
Collected Shorter Poems, 1946-1991 (Carruth), **Supp. XVI:**47
Collected Short Stories, The (Wharton), **Retro. Supp. I:** 362, 363, 366
Collected Sonnets (Millay), **III:** 136-137
Collected Stories, 1939-1976 (Bowles), **Supp. IV Part 1:** 92
Collected Stories, The (Paley), **Supp. VI:** 218
Collected Stories, The (Price), **Supp. VI:** 266
Collected Stories, The (Theroux), **Supp. VIII:** 318
Collected Stories, The (Wharton), **Retro. Supp. I:** 361
Collected Stories of Eudora Welty, The (Welty), **Retro. Supp. I:** 355
Collected Stories of Isaac Bashevis Singer (Singer), **Retro. Supp. II:** **307-308**
Collected Stories of Katherine Anne Porter (Porter), **III:** 454
Collected Stories of Peter Taylor (Taylor), **Supp. V:** 314, 320, 323-324, 325, 326
Collected Stories of Richard Yates, The, **Supp. XI:** 349
Collected Stories of Wallace Stegner (Stegner), **Supp. IV Part 2:** 599, 605
Collected Stories of William Faulkner (Faulkner), **II:** 72; **Retro. Supp. I:** 75
Collected Stories of William Humphrey, The (Humphrey), **Supp. IX:** 106
Collected Works (Bierce), **I:** 204, 208-210
Collected Works of Buck Rogers in the 25th Century, The (Bradbury), **Supp. IV Part 1:** 101
Collected Writings, The (Z. Fitzgerald; Bruccoli, ed.), **Supp. IX:** 65, 68
Collecting the Animals (Everwine), **Supp. XV:** 73, 75, **78-81**, 85, 88
Collection of Epigrams, **II:** 111
Collection of Poems, on American Affairs, and a Variety of Other Subjects ... (Freneau), **Supp. II Part 1:** 274
Collection of Select Aphorisms and Maxims (Palmer), **II:** 111
"Collectors" (Carver), **Supp. III Part 1:** 141-142
Collette, **Supp. XVII:** 86
Collier, Michael, **Supp. XVII:** 23, 110
Collingwood, R. G., **I:** 278
Collins, Billy, **Supp. XI:** 143; **Supp. XIV:**123; **Supp. XVII:** 245
Collins, Doug, **Supp. V:** 5
Collins, Eddie, **II:** 416
Collins, Richard, **Supp. XI:** 171
Collins, Wilkie, **Supp. I Part 1:** 35, 36; **Supp. IV Part 1:** 341
Collins, William, **Supp. I Part 2:** 714
Collinson, Peter, **II:** 114
Collinson, Peter (pseudonym). *See* Hammett, Dashiell
Colloff, Pamela, **Supp. XIII:** 281
Colloque Sentimental (ballet), **Supp. IV Part 1:** 83
"Colloquy" (Kees), **Supp. XV:** 133
"Colloquy in Black Rock" (Lowell), **II:** 535; **Retro. Supp. II:** 178
"Colloquy of Monos and Una, The" (Poe), **III:** 412
Colonel's Dream, The (Chesnutt), **Supp. XIV:**63, 75-76
Colônia, Regina, **Retro. Supp. II:** 53
Color (Cullen), **Supp. IV Part 1:** 164, 166, 167, 168
"Color: The Unfinished Business of Democracy" (Locke), **Supp.**

XIV:202, 207
"Colorado" (Beattie), **Supp. V:** 27
Color and Democracy: Colonies and Peace (Du Bois), **Supp. II Part 1:** 184, 185
Color Curtain, The (Wright), **IV:** 478, 488
"Colored Americans" (Dunbar), **Supp. II Part 1:** 197
"Color Line, The" (Douglass), **Supp. III Part 1:** 163-165
Color Line, The (W. B. Smith), **Supp. II Part 1:** 168
Color of a Great City, The (Dreiser), **Retro. Supp. II:** 104
Color of Darkness (Purdy), **Supp. VII:** 271
Color Purple, The (Walker), **Supp. III Part 2:** 517, 518, 520, 525-529, 532-537; **Supp. VIII:** 141; **Supp. X:** 252, 330
Color Schemes (Cheang; film), **Supp. XI:** 20
"Colors of Night, The" (Momaday), **Supp. IV Part 2:** 490
"Colors without Objects" (Swenson), **Supp. IV Part 2:** 645
Colossus, The (Plath), **Retro. Supp. II:** 245-247; **Supp. I Part 2:** 529, 531, 536, 538, 540; **Supp. V:** 79; **Supp. XI:** 317
"Colossus, The" (Plath), **Retro. Supp. II:** 250
Colossus of Maroussi, The (H. Miller), **III:** 178, 185-186
"Colt, The" (Stegner), **Supp. IV Part 2:** 600
Coltelli, Laura, **Supp. IV Part 1:** 323, 330, 335, 409; **Supp. IV Part 2:** 493, 497, 559
Colter: The True Story of the Best Dog I Ever Had (Bass), **Supp. XVI:** 23
Coltrane, John, **Supp. VIII:** 197
Colum, Mary, **I:** 246, 252, 256; **Supp. I Part 2:** 708, 709
Columbiad, The (Barlow), **Supp. II Part 1:** 67, 72, 73, 74, 75-77, 79
Columbia History of the American Novel, **Supp. XV:** 270
Columbia Literary History of the United States, **Supp. XV:** 270
"Columbian Ode" (Dunbar), **Supp. II Part 1:** 199
"Columbia U Poesy Reading-1975" (Corso), **Supp. XII:** 134
Columbus, Christopher, **I:** 253; **II:** 6, 310; **III:** 8; **Supp. I Part 2:** 397, 479, 480, 483, 486-488, 491, 495, 497, 498
"Columbus to Ferdinand" (Freneau), **Supp. II Part 1:** 255
Comanche Moon (McMurtry), **Supp. V:** 232
"Come, Break With Time" (Bogan), **Supp. III Part 1:** 52
Come Along with Me (Jackson), **Supp. IX:** 117, 118, 122
Come Back, Charleston Blue (film), **Supp. XVI:** 144
Comeback, The (Gurney), **Supp. V:** 97
"Come Back to the Raft Ag'in, Huck Honey!" (Fiedler), **Supp. XIII:** 93, 96-97, 101
Come Blow Your Horn (Simon), **Supp. IV Part 2:** 574, 575, 577, 578, 586, 587, 591
"Come Dance with Me in Ireland" (Jackson), **Supp. IX:** 119
"Comedian as the Letter C, The" (Stevens), **IV:** 84-85, 88; **Retro. Supp. I:** 297, 301, 302
"Comedy Cop" (Farrell), **II:** 45
"Comedy's Greatest Era" (Agee), **I:** 31
"Come In" (Frost), **Retro. Supp. I:** 139
"Come On, Baby" (Zinberg), **Supp. XV:** 195
"Come on Back" (Gardner), **Supp. VI:** 73
"Come Out into the Sun" (Francis), **Supp. IX:** 82
Come Out into the Sun: Poems New and Selected (Francis), **Supp. IX:** 82-83
"Come out the Wilderness" (Baldwin), **Supp. I Part 1:** 63
Comer, Anjanette, **Supp. XI:** 305
Comer, Cornelia, **I:** 214
"Come Shining: The Spiritual South" (exhibition; Luster), **Supp. XV:** 350
Come with Me: Poems for a Journey (Nye), **Supp. XIII:** 279
"Comforts of Home, The" (O'Connor), **III:** 349, 351, 355; **Retro. Supp. II:** 237
Comic Artist, The (Glaspell and Matson), **Supp. III Part 1:** 182
"Comic Imagination of the Young Dickens, The" (Wright), **Supp. III Part 2:** 591
"Comic Textures and Female Communities 1937 and 1977: Clare Boothe and Wendy Wasserstein" (Carlson), **Supp. XV:** 323
Comic Tragedies (Alcott), **Supp. I Part 1:** 33
"Coming Close" (Levine), **Supp. V:** 192
Coming Forth by Day of Osiris Jones, The (Aiken), **I:** 59
"Coming Home" (Gordon), **Supp. IV Part 1:** 309
"Coming Home to Vermont" (McCarriston), **Supp. XIV:** 269
"Coming in From the Cold" (Walker), **Supp. III Part 2:** 526
Coming into Eighty (Sarton), **Supp. VIII:** 262
"Coming into Eighty" (Sarton), **Supp. VIII:** 262
Coming into the Country (McPhee), **Supp. III Part 1:** 298, 301-306, 309, 310
Coming Into Writing (Cixous), **Supp. X:** 102
Coming of Age in Mississippi (Moody), **Supp. IV Part 1:** 11
Comings Back (Goldbarth), **Supp. XII:** 180
Coming to Canada: Poems (Shields), **Supp. VII:** 311-312
"Coming to Canada—Age Twenty Two" (Shields), **Supp. VII:** 311
"Coming to the Morning" (Merwin), **Supp. III Part 1:** 356
"Coming to This" (Strand), **Supp. IV Part 2:** 627
Comiskey, Charles, **II:** 422
Commager, Henry Steele, **I:** 253; **Supp. I Part 1:** 372; **Supp. I Part 2:** 484, 647, 650
Command the Morning (Buck), **Supp. II Part 1:** 125
"Commencement Address, A" (Brodsky), **Supp. VIII:** 31
"Commencement Day Address, The" (Schwartz), **Supp. II Part 2:** 660
Commentaries (Caesar), **II:** 502, 561
"Commentary" (Auden), **Supp. II Part 1:** 13
"Comment on Curb" (Hughes), **Supp. I Part 1:** 340
"Commerce" (Nye), **Supp. XIII:** 281
Commins, Saxe, **Retro. Supp. I:** 73; **Retro. Supp. II:** 337
Commodity of Dreams & Other Stories, A (Nemerov), **III:** 268-269, 285
Common Carnage (Dobyns), **Supp. XIII:** 87
"Common Ground, A" (Levertov), **Supp. III Part 1:** 277
"Common Life, The" (Auden), **Supp. IV Part 1:** 302, 313
Common Room, A: Essays 1954-1987 (Price), **Supp. VI:** 264-265, 267
Commons, John, **Supp. I Part 2:** 645
Common Sense (Paine), **II:** 117; **Supp. I Part 1:** 231; **Supp. I Part 2:** 505, 506-508, 509, 513, 516, 517, 521

"Communication" (Dobyns), **Supp. XIII:** 91

"Communion" (Dubus), **Supp. VII:** 91

Communion (Mora), **Supp. XIII: 217-219**

Communist Manifesto, The (Marx), **II:** 463

"Community Life" (Moore), **Supp. X:** 178

"Community of Glaciers, The" (Bass), **Supp. XVI:**23

Comnes, Gregory, **Supp. IV Part 1:** 283, 284, 291

"Companions, The" (Nemerov), **III:** 269, 278, 287

Company of Poets, A (Simpson), **Supp. IX:** 265, 275

Company of Women, The (Gordon), **Supp. IV Part 1:** 302-304, 304, 306, 313

Company She Keeps, The (McCarthy), **II:** 562, 563-566

"Comparisons of Wonder" (Jarman), **Supp. XVII:** 114

Compass Flower, The (Merwin), **Supp. III Part 1:** 353, 357

"Compassionate Friendship" (Doolittle), **Supp. I Part 1:** 257, 258, 259, 260, 271

"Compatibility" (C. Frost), **Supp. XV:** 103

"Compendium" (Dove), **Supp. IV Part 1:** 248

"Complaint" (W. C. Williams), **Retro. Supp. I:** 418

"Complete Birth of the Cool, The" (Wright), **Supp. XV:** 343, 344

Complete Collected Poems of William Carlos Williams, 1906-1938, The (W. C. Williams), **Retro. Supp. I:** 424

"Complete Destruction" (W. C. Williams), **IV:** 413

"Complete Life of John Hopkins, The" (O. Henry), **Supp. II Part 1:** 405

Complete Poems (Frost), **II:** 155, 164

Complete Poems (Reznikoff), **Supp. XIV:**281

Complete Poems (Sandburg), **III:** 590-592, 594, 596

Complete Poems, The (Bishop), **Retro. Supp. II:** 49; **Supp. I Part 1:** 72, 82, 94

Complete Poems, The (Bradbury), **Supp. IV Part 1:** 105

Complete Poems, The: 1927-1979 (Bishop), **Retro. Supp. II:** 51

Complete Poems of Emily Dickinson, The (Bianchi and Hampson, eds.), **Retro. Supp. I:** 35

Complete Poems of Emily Dickinson, The (Johnson, ed.), **I:** 470

Complete Poems of Frederick Goddard Tuckerman, The (Momaday), **Supp. IV Part 2:** 480

Complete Poems of Hart Crane, **Retro. Supp. II:** 81

Complete Poems to Solve, The (Swenson), **Supp. IV Part 2:** 652

Complete Poetical Works (Hulme), **III:** 464

Complete Poetical Works (Longfellow), **Retro. Supp. II:** 154

Complete Poetical Works (Lowell), **II:** 512, 516-517

Complete Poetical Works of Amy Lowell, The, **Supp. XV:** 295-296

Complete Stories (O'Connor), **Supp. X:** 1

Complete Tragedies, The: Euripedes II, **Supp. XV:** 50

"Complete with Starry Night and Bourbon Shots" (Goldbarth), **Supp. XII:** 192-193

Complete Works of Kate Chopin, The (Seyersted, ed.), **Supp. I Part 1:** 212, 225

Complete Works of the Gawain-Poet (Gardner), **Supp. VI:** 64, 65

"Complex Histories, Contested Memories: Some Reflections on Remembering Difficult Pasts" (E. Hoffman, lecture), **Supp. XVI:**155

"Complicated Thoughts About a Small Son" (White), **Supp. I Part 2:** 678

"Compliments of the Season" (O. Henry), **Supp. II Part 1:** 392, 399

"Compline" (Auden), **Supp. II Part 1:** 23

Composition as Explanation (Stein), **IV:** 32, 33, 38

"Composition as Explanation" (Stein), **IV:** 27, 28

"Compounding of Consciousness" (James), **II:** 358-359

Comprehensive Bibliography (Hanneman), **II:** 259

Compton-Burnett, Ivy, **I:** 93; **II:** 580

"Comrade Laski, C.P.U.S.A. [0]sqb;M.L.[0]sqb;" (Didion), **Supp. IV Part 1:** 200

Comstock, Anthony, **Retro. Supp. II:** 95

Comus (Milton), **II:** 12; **Supp. I Part 2:** 622

Conan Doyle, Arthur. *See* Doyle, Arthur Conan

Conceptions of Reality in Modern American Poetry (Dembo), **Supp. I Part 1:** 272

"Concept of Character in Fiction, The" (Gass), **Supp. VI:** 85, **86**

Concept of Dread, The (Kierkegaard), **III:** 305

Concerning Children (Gilman), **Supp. XI:** 206

"Concerning Mold upon the Skin, Etc." (J. Scott), **Supp. XVII:** 188

"Concerning Necessity" (Carruth), **Supp. XVI:**57

"Concerning Some Recent Criticism of His Work" (Doty), **Supp. XI:** 131

Concerning the End for Which God Created the World (Edwards), **I:** 549, 557, 559

Concerto for Two Pianos, Winds, and Percussion (Bowles), **Supp. IV Part 1:** 83

Conchologist's First Book, The (Poe), **III:** 412

Conclusive Evidence (Nabokov), **III:** 247-250, 252

"Concord Hymn" (Emerson), **II:** 19

"Concrete Universal, The: Observations on the Understanding of Poetry" (Ransom), **III:** 480

Concurring Beasts (Dobyns), **Supp. XIII:** 76

Condensed Novels and Other Papers (Harte), **Supp. II Part 1:** 342

"Condition, The" (Karmi; Everwine, trans.), **Supp. XV:** 78

Condition of Man, The (Mumford), **Supp. II Part 2:** 483, 484, 486, 495-496, 498

"Condolence" (Parker), **Supp. IX:** 191

"Condominium, The" (Elkin), **Supp. VI:** 49, **50-51,** 55, 56

Condon, Charles R., **Supp. XIII:** 163

Condor and the Cows, The: A South American Travel Diary (Isherwood and Caskey), **Supp. XIV:**166

"Condor and the Guests, The" (Connell), **Supp. XIV:**86

Condorcet, Marquis de, **Supp. I Part 2:** 511

Conduct of Life, The (Emerson), **II:** 1-5, 8

Conduct of Life, The (Mumford), **Supp. II Part 2:** 485, 496-497

"Conductor of Nothing, The" (Levine), **Supp. V:** 189

"Conference Male, The" (Mora), **Supp. XIII:** 218

"Confessional" (Bidart), **Supp. XV:** 29-30, 31

Confession de Claude, La (Zola), **I:** 411

"Confession of a House-Breaker, The" (Jewett), **Retro. Supp. II:** 146-147

Confession of Jereboam O. Beauchamp, The (pamphlet), **IV:** 253
Confessions (Augustine), **I:** 279; **Supp. XVI:**288
Confessions (Rousseau), **I:** 226
Confessions of a Barbarian: Selections from the Journals of Edward Abbey, 1951-1989 (Abbey; Petersen, ed.), **Supp. XIII:** 2, 4
"Confessions of a Latina Author" (Mora), **Supp. XIII:** 221
Confessions of Nat Turner, The (Styron), **IV:** 98, 99, 105, 113-117; **Supp. X:** 16, 250
Confetti (Mora), **Supp. XIII:** 221
Confidence (James), **II:** 327, 328
Confidence-Man, The (Melville), **III:** 91; **Retro. Supp. I:** 255-256, 257; **Retro. Supp. II:** 121; **Supp. XIV:**49
Confidence Man, The (Van Vechten), **Supp. II Part 2:** 737
Confidential Clerk, The (Eliot), **I:** 570, 571-572, 583, 584; **Retro. Supp. I:** 65
Confident Years, 1885-1915, The (Brooks), **I:** 257, 259; **Supp. I Part 2:** 650
"Configurations" (Ammons), **Supp. VII:** 28
Confronting the Horror: The Novels of Nelson Algren (Giles), **Supp. IX:** 11, 15
Confucius, **II:** 1; **III:** 456, 475; **Supp. IV Part 1:** 14
Confusion (Cozzens), **I:** 358, 359, 377, 378
Congo (film), **Supp. IV Part 1:** 83
Congo (screenplay, Shanley), **Supp. XIV:**316
"Congo, The" (Lindsay), **Supp. I Part 2:** 388-389, 392, 395
Congo and Other Poems, The (Lindsay), **Supp. I Part 2:** 379, 382, 389, 390, 391
"Congress of the Insomniacs, The" (Simic), **Supp. VIII:** 281-282
Congreve, William, **III:** 195; **Supp. V:** 101
Coningsby (Disraeli), **II:** 127
Conjectures of a Guilty Bystander (Merton), **Supp. VIII:** 197, 206, 207
Conjugal Bliss: A Comedy of Marital Arts (Nichols), **Supp. XIII:** 269
"Conjugation of the Paramecium, The" (Rukeyser), **Supp. VI:** 271
"Conjuration" (Wilbur), **Supp. III Part 2:** 551
Conjure (Reed), **Supp. X:** 240, 242
Conjure (recording), **Supp. X:** 241
Conjure-Man Dies, The (R. Fisher), **Supp. XVI:**143
Conjure Woman, The (Chesnutt), **Supp. II Part 1:** 193; **Supp. XIV:**57, 58-61, 62, 63
Conklin, Grof, **Supp. I Part 2:** 672
Conkling, Hilda, **II:** 530
Conkling, Roscoe, **III:** 506
Conley, Robert J., **Supp. V:** 232
Conley, Susan, **Supp. XIII:** 111, 112
Connaroe, Joel, **Supp. IV Part 2:** 690
"Connecticut Lad, A" (White), **Supp. I Part 2:** 677
"Connecticut Valley" (Cowley), **Supp. II Part 1:** 141-142
Connecticut Yankee in King Arthur's Court, A (Twain), **I:** 209; **II:** 276; **IV:** 205
Connell, Evan S., **Supp. XIV:79-100**
Connell, Norreys (pseudonym). *See* O'Riordan, Conal Holmes O'Connell
Connelly, Marc, **III:** 394; **Supp. I Part 2:** 679; **Supp. IX:** 190
Connery, Thomas B., **Supp. XVII:** 106
Connoisseur, The (Connell), **Supp. XIV:**87
"Connoisseur of Chaos" (Stevens), **IV:** 89; **Retro. Supp. I:** 306
Connolly, Cyril, **Supp. XIV:**158, 343, 348
Connors, Elizabeth. *See* Lindsay, Mrs. Vachel (Elizabeth Connors)
Conover, Roger, **Supp. I Part 1:** 95
Conquering Horse (Manfred), **Supp. X:** 126
"Conqueror Worm, The" (Poe), **Retro. Supp. II:** 261
Conquest of Canaan (Dwight), **Supp. I Part 1:** 124
Conquistador (MacLeish), **III:** 2, 3, 13-14, 15
Conrad, Alfred, **Retro. Supp. II:** 245
Conrad, Alfred H., **Supp. I Part 2:** 552
Conrad, David, **Supp. I Part 2:** 552
Conrad, Jacob, **Supp. I Part 2:** 552
Conrad, Joseph, **I:** 123, 343, 394, 405, 409, 415, 421, 485, 506, 575-576, 578; **II:** 58, 73, 74, 91, 92, 144, 263, 320, 338, 595; **III:** 28, 102, 106, 328, 464, 467, 491, 512; **IV:** 476; **Retro. Supp. I:** 80, 91, 106, 108, 231, 274, 377; **Retro. Supp. II:** 222; **Supp. I Part 1:** 292; **Supp. I Part 2:** 621, 622; **Supp. IV Part 1:** 197, 341; **Supp. IV Part 2:** 680; **Supp. V:** 249, 251, 262, 298, 307, 311; **Supp. VIII:** 4, 310; **Supp. XIV:**112; **Supp. XVI:**158, 212
Conrad, Paul, **Supp. I Part 2:** 552
Conrad, Peter, **Supp. IV Part 2:** 688
"Conrad Aiken: From Savannah to Emerson" (Cowley), **Supp. II Part 1:** 43
Conroy, Frank, **Supp. VIII:** 145; **Supp. XI:** 245; **Supp. XVI:63-78**
Conscience with the Power and Cases thereof (Ames), **IV:** 158
"Conscientious Objector, The" (Shapiro), **Supp. II Part 2:** 710
"Consciousness and Dining" (Harrison), **Supp. VIII:** 46
"Conscription Camp" (Shapiro), **Supp. II Part 2:** 705
"Consejos de Nuestra Señora de Guadalupe: Counsel from the Brown Virgin" (Mora), **Supp. XIII:** 224
"Conservation Esthetic" (Leopold), **Supp. XIV:**179, 181, 186, 189-190
"Conserving Natural and Cultural Diversity: The Prose and Poetry of Pat Mora" (Murphy), **Supp. XIII:** 214
Considerable Town, A (M. F. K. Fisher), **Supp. XVII:** 90
"Considerations by the Way" (Emerson), **II:** 2, 5
Consider the Oyster (M. F. K. Fisher), **Supp. XVII:** 84, 87
Considine, Bob, **II:** 424
"Consolation" (Bausch), **Supp. VII:** 48
"Consolations" (Stafford), **Supp. XI:** 329
"Conspiracy of History, The: E. L. Doctorow's *The Book of Daniel*" (Levine), **Supp. IV Part 1:** 221
Conspiracy of Kings, The (Barlow), **Supp. II Part 1:** 80
Conspiracy of Pontiac, The (Parkman), **Supp. II Part 2:** 590, 595, 596, 599-600
Constab Ballads (McKay), **Supp. X:** 131, 133
Constance (Kenyon), **Supp. VII:** 170-172
Constancy (N. Boyce), **Supp. XVII:** 100
Construction of Boston, The (Koch), **Supp. XV:** 187
"Constructive Work" (Du Bois), **Supp. II Part 1:** 172
"Consumer's Report" (X. J. Kennedy), **Supp. XV:** 161-162
"Consumption" (Bryant), **Supp. I Part 1:** 169-170
"Contagiousness of Puerperal Fever, The" (Holmes), **Supp. I Part 1:** 303-304
"Contemplation in a World of Action" (Merton), **Supp. VIII:** 204
"Contemplation of Poussin" (Sarton),

Supp. VIII: 261
"Contemplations" (Bradstreet), **Supp. I Part 1:** 112, 113, 119-122
Contemporaries (Kazin), **Supp. VIII:** 102, **103-104**
Contemporary American Playwrights (Bigsby), **Supp. XV:** 332
Contemporary American Poetry (Poulin, ed.), **Supp. IX:** 272; **Supp. XI:** 259
"Contentment" (Holmes), **Supp. I Part 1:** 307
"Contest, The" (Paley), **Supp. VI:** 223, 230, 231
"Contest for Aaron Gold, The" (P. Roth), **Supp. III Part 2:** 403
Continental Drift (Banks), **Supp. V:** 13-14, 16, 227
Continental Op, The (Hammett), **Supp. IV Part 1:** 344
Continuity of American Poetry, The (Pearce), **Supp. I Part 1:** 111; **Supp. I Part 2:** 475
Continuous Harmony, A: Essays Cultural and Agricultural (Berry), **Supp. X:** 33
Continuous Life, The (Strand), **Supp. IV Part 2:** 630, 631-633
Contoski, Victor, **Supp. XII:** 181
"Contract" (Lardner), **II:** 432
"Contraption, The" (Swenson), **Supp. IV Part 2:** 643
"Contrariness of the Mad Farmer, The" (Berry), **Supp. X:** 35
"Contrition" (Dubus), **Supp. VII:** 84
"Control Burn" (Snyder), **Supp. VIII:** 301
"Control Is the Mainspring" (Komunyakaa), **Supp. XIII:** 122, 124
"Controlling the 'Sloppiness of Things' in Frank Conroy's *Stop-Time*" (Strychacz), **Supp. XVI:** 69-70
Control of Nature, The (McPhee), **Supp. III Part 1:** 310-313
"Conventional Wisdom, The" (Elkin), **Supp. VI: 52-53**
"Convergence" (Ammons), **Supp. VII:** 28
"Convergence of the Twain, The" (Hardy), **Supp. VIII:** 31, 32
Conversation (Aiken), **I:** 54
Conversation at Midnight (Millay), **III:** 138
"Conversation of Eiros and Charmion, The" (Poe), **III:** 412
"Conversation on Conversation" (Stowe), **Supp. I Part 2:** 587
"Conversations in Moscow" (Levertov), **Supp. III Part 1:** 282

Conversations on Some of the Old Poets (Lowell), **Supp. I Part 2:** 405
Conversations with Byron (Blessington), **Retro. Supp. II:** 58
Conversations with Eudora Welty (Prenshaw, ed.), **Retro. Supp. I:** 339, 340, 341, 342, 343, 352, 354
"Conversations with Helmholtz" (Allen), **Supp. XV:** 15
Conversations with Ishmael Reed (Dick and Singh, eds.), **Supp. X:** 244
Conversations with James Baldwin (Standley and Pratt, eds.), **Retro. Supp. II:** 6
Conversations with Richard Wilbur (Wilbur), **Supp. III Part 2:** 542-543
"Conversation with My Father, A" (Paley), **Supp. VI:** 220
"Conversion of the Jews, The" (P. Roth), **Retro. Supp. II:** 281; **Supp. III Part 2:** 404, 406
Convict, The: Stories (Burke), **Supp. XIV:** 25
"Convicta et Combusta" (J. Scott), **Supp. XVII:** 189
Conway, Jill, **Supp. I Part 1:** 19
Coode, John, **I:** 132
Cook, Bruce, **Supp. XII:** 130, 131, 133-134
Cook, Captain James, **I:** 2
Cook, Eleanor, **Retro. Supp. I:** 311
Cook, Elisha, **Supp. IV Part 1:** 356
Cook, Elizabeth Christine, **II:** 106
Cook, Mercer, **Supp. IV Part 1:** 368
Cooke, Alistair, **III:** 113, 119, 120
Cooke, Delmar G., **II:** 271
Cooke, Grace MacGowan, **Supp. V:** 285
Cooke, Philip Pendleton, **III:** 420
Cooke, Rose Terry, **II:** 401; **Retro. Supp. II:** 51, 136, 138; **Supp. XIII:** 152
"Cookie" (Taylor), **Supp. V:** 320
"Cookies, The" (Nye), **Supp. XIII:** 281
Cooking of Provincial France, The (M. F. K. Fisher), **Supp. XVII:** 89
Cook-Lynn, Elizabeth, **Supp. IV Part 1:** 325
Coolbrith, Ina, **I:** 193, 196
"Coole Park" (Yeats), **Supp. VIII:** 155, 159
"Coole Park and Ballylee" (Yeats), **Supp. VIII:** 156
Cooley, John, **Supp. V:** 214
Cooley, Peter, **Supp. XIII:** 76
Coolidge, Calvin, **I:** 498; **II:** 95; **Supp. I Part 2:** 647
Cooling Time: An American Poetry Vigil (Wright), **Supp. XV:** 353

"Cool Million, A" (screen story) (West and Ingster), **Retro. Supp. II:** 330
Cool Million, A (West), **III:** 425; **IV:** 287, 288, 297-299, 300; **Retro. Supp. II:** 321, 322-323, 328, **335-337**
"Cool Tombs" (Sandburg), **III:** 554
Coon, Ross, **IV:** 196
Cooney, Seamus, **Supp. XIV:** 289
"Coon Hunt" (White), **Supp. I Part 2:** 669
Co-op (Sinclair), **Supp. V:** 290
Cooper, Bernard, **Supp. XI:** 129
Cooper, Gary, **Supp. IV Part 2:** 524
Cooper, James Fenimore, **I:** 211, 257, **335-357**; **II:** 74, 277, 295-296, 302, 306, 309, 313, 314; **III:** 51; **IV:** 205, 333; **Retro. Supp. I:** 246; **Retro. Supp. II:** 160; **Supp. I Part 1:** 141, 155, 156, 158, 171, 372; **Supp. I Part 2:** 413, 495, 579, 585, 652, 660; **Supp. IV Part 1:** 80; **Supp. IV Part 2:** 463, 469; **Supp. V:** 209-210; **Supp. VIII:** 189; **Supp. XIV:** 227
Cooper, Jane, **Supp. XV:** 259
Cooper, Mrs. James Fenimore (Susan A. De Lancey), **I:** 338, 351, 354
Cooper, Mrs. William, **I:** 337
Cooper, Rand Richards, **Supp. XVI:** 74
Cooper, Susan Fenimore, **I:** 337, 354
Cooper, William, **I:** 337-338, 351
Coover, Robert, **Supp. IV Part 1:** 388; **Supp. V: 39-55**; **Supp. XII:** 152; **Supp. XIV:** 96; **Supp. XVII:** 6
Copacetic (Komunyakaa), **Supp. XIII:** **116-118,** 126
Cope, Wendy, **Supp. XV:** 117
Copland, Aaron, **II:** 586; **Supp. I Part 1:** 281; **Supp. III Part 2:** 619; **Supp. IV Part 1:** 79, 80-81, 84
Coplas de Don Jorge Manrique (Longfellow, trans.), **II:** 488, 492
Coppée, François Edouard Joachim, **II:** 325
Copperhead, The (Frederic), **II:** 134-135
Copper Sun (Cullen), **Supp. IV Part 1:** 167, 168
Coppola, Francis Ford, **Supp. XI:** 171, 172; **Supp. XII:** 75
Coprolites (Goldbarth), **Supp. XII:** **177-178,** 180, 183
Coral and Captive Israel (Reznikoff), **Supp. XIV:** 288
"Coral Ring, The" (Stowe), **Supp. I Part 2:** 586
"Cora Unashamed" (Hughes), **Supp. I Part 1:** 329, 330
"Corazón del Corrido" (Mora), **Supp.**

XIII: 225
Corban Ephphata (Li Lin Lee), **Supp. XV:** 225
Corbett, Gentlemen Jim, **II:** 416
Corbett, William, **Supp. XI:** 248; **Supp. XVI:** 286, 295
Corbière, Jean Antoine, **II:** 354-355, 528
Cordiall Water, A: A garland of Odd & Old Receipts to Assuage the Ills of Man and Beast (M. F. K. Fisher), **Supp. XVII:** 88, 90
Cording, Robert, **Supp. IX:** 328; **Supp. XII:** 184
Corelli, Marie, **III:** 579
Corey, Lewis, **Supp. I Part 2:** 645
"Corinna's Going a-Maying" (Herrick), **Supp. XIV:** 8, 9
"Coriolan" (Eliot), **I:** 580
"Coriolanus and His Mother" (Schwartz), **Supp. II Part 2:** 643, 644-645
"Corkscrew" (Hammett), **Supp. IV Part 1:** 345, 347
Corkum, Gerald, **I:** 37
"Corky's Brother" (Neugeboren), **Supp. XVI:** 225
Corky's Brother (Neugeboren), **Supp. XVI:** 225
Corliss, Richard, **Supp. VIII:** 73
Corman, Cid, **Supp. III Part 2:** 624, 625, 626, 627, 628; **Supp. IV Part 1:** 144; **Supp. VIII:** 292; **Supp. XV:** 74, 153
"Corn" (Lanier), **Supp. I Part 1:** 352, 353, 354, 356-361, 364, 366
Corn, Alfred, **Supp. IX:** 156; **Supp. XV:** 250
Corneille, Pierre, **Supp. I Part 2:** 716; **Supp. IX:** 131
Cornell, Esther, **I:** 231
Cornell, Katherine, **IV:** 356
"Corners" (Dunn), **Supp. XI:** 148
Cornhuskers (Sandburg), **III:** 583-585
"Corn-Planting, The" (Anderson), **I:** 114
"Corporal of Artillery" (Dubus), **Supp. VII:** 84, 85
"Corpse Plant, The" (Rich), **Supp. I Part 2:** 555
Corpus Christi (McNally), **Supp. XIII:** 205-206, 209
Corradi, Juan, **Supp. IV Part 1:** 208
"Correspondences" (Baudelaire), **I:** 63
"Corrido de Gregorio Cortez" (Mora), **Supp. XIII:** 225
"Corrigenda" (Komunyakaa), **Supp. XIII:** 115, 116
Corruption City (McCoy), **Supp. XIII:** 175

Corso, Gregory, **Supp. II Part 1:** 30; **Supp. IV Part 1:** 90; **Supp. XII:** 117-138; **Supp. XIV:** 150; **Supp. XVI:** 135
Corsons Inlet (Ammons), **Supp. VII:** 25-26, 28-29, 36
"Corsons Inlet" (Ammons), **Supp. VII:** 25-26
Cortázar, Julio, **Retro. Supp. I:** 278
"Cortège for Rosenbloom" (Stevens), **IV:** 81
Cortez, Hernando, **III:** 2
Coser, Lewis, **Supp. I Part 2:** 650
Cosgrave, Patrick, **Retro. Supp. II:** 185
Cosmic Optimism: A Study of the Interpretation of Evolution by American Poets from Emerson to Robinson (Conner), **Supp. I Part 1:** 73
Cosmological Eye, The (H. Miller), **III:** 174, 184
"Cosmological Eye, The" (H. Miller), **III:** 183
"Cosmos" (Beattie), **Supp. V:** 35
"Cost, The" (Hecht), **Supp. X:** 62-63
Costello, Bonnie, **Retro. Supp. II:** 40
Costner, Kevin, **Supp. VIII:** 45
"Cost of Living, The" (Malamud), **Supp. I Part 2:** 429, 437
Cott, Jonathan, **Supp. XVI:** 104, 106
"Cottage Street, 1953" (Wilbur), **Supp. III Part 2:** 543, 561
"Cottagette, The" (Gilman), **Supp. XI:** 207
Cotten, Joseph, **Supp. IV Part 2:** 524
Cotter, James Finn, **Supp. X:** 202
Cotton, John, **Supp. I Part 1:** 98, 101, 110, 111, 116
Cotton, Joseph, **Supp. XII:** 160
Cotton, Seaborn, **Supp. I Part 1:** 101
Cotton Comes to Harlem (C. Himes), **Supp. XVI:** 143, 144
Cotton Comes to Harlem (film, O. Davis), **Supp. XVI:** 144
"Cotton Song" (Toomer), **Supp. IX:** 312
Couch, W. T., **Supp. X:** 46
Coughlin, Ruth Pollack, **Supp. VIII:** 45
Coulette, Henri, **Supp. V:** 180; **Supp. XIII:** 312; **Supp. XV:** 74, 75
Coultrap-McQuin, Susan, **Supp. XVI:** 85, 92
"Council of State, A" (Dunbar), **Supp. II Part 1:** 211, 213
"Count Dracula" (Allen), **Supp. XV:** 15
"Countee Cullen at 'The Heights'" (Tuttleton), **Supp. IV Part 1:** 166

Counterfeiters, The (Gide), **Supp. IV Part 1:** 80; **Supp. IV Part 2:** 681
"Countering" (Ammons), **Supp. VII:** 28
Counterlife, The (P. Roth), **Retro. Supp. II:** 279, 280, 291; **Supp. III Part 2:** 424-426
Counter-Statement (Burke), **I:** 270-272; **IV:** 431
"Countess, The" (Whittier), **Supp. I Part 2:** 691, 694
Count Frontenac and New France Under Louis XIV (Parkman), **Supp. II Part 2:** 607, 609-610
"Counting Small-Boned Bodies" (R. Bly), **Supp. IV Part 1:** 62
"Counting the Children" (Gioia), **Supp. XV:** 122-123
"Counting the Mad" (Justice), **Supp. VII:** 117
Count of Monte Cristo, The (Dumas), **III:** 386, 396; **Supp. XVII:** 64, 216
"Countries We Live In, The" (Zach; Everwine, trans.), **Supp. XV:** 87
"Country Boy in Boston, The" (Howells), **II:** 255
Country By-Ways (Jewett), **II:** 402
Country Doctor, A (Jewett), **II:** 391, 392, 396, 404-405; **Retro. Supp. II:** 131, 141, 146
"Country Full of Swedes" (Caldwell), **I:** 297, 309
Country Girl, The (Odets), **Supp. II Part 2:** 546, 547, 548-549
"Country House" (Kumin), **Supp. IV Part 2:** 446
"Country Husband, The" (Cheever), **Supp. I Part 1:** 184, 189
"Country Marriage" (C. Frost), **Supp. XV:** 99
Countrymen of Bones (R. O. Butler), **Supp. XII:** 62, **65-66**
"Country Mouse, The" (Bishop), **Retro. Supp. II:** 37, 38, 51
Country Music: Selected Early Poems (Wright), **Supp. V:** 332, 335, 338, 342
Country of a Thousand Years of Peace, The (Merrill), **Supp. III Part 1:** 321, 322, 331
"Country of Elusion, The" (O. Henry), **Supp. II Part 1:** 407
Country Of Language, The (Sanders), **Supp. XVI:** 277
Country of Marriage, The (Berry), **Supp. X:** 33
Country of the Pointed Firs, The (Jewett), **II:** 392, 399, 405, 409-411; **Retro. Supp. I:** 6; **Retro. Supp. II:** 134, 136, 139, 140, 141, 145, 146,

147; **Supp. VIII:** 126; **Supp. XIII:** 152
"Country Printer, The" (Freneau), **Supp. II Part 1:** 269
"Country Wife, The" (Gioia), **Supp. XV:** 120
Count Your Bullets (film), **Supp. XVII:** 141
Count Zero (W. Gibson), **Supp. XVI:** 119, **126-127,** 129
Coup, The (Updike), **Retro. Supp. I:** 331, 334, 335
"Coup de Grâce, The" (Bierce), **I:** 202
Couperin, François, **III:** 464
"Couple, The" (Olds), **Supp. X:** 206
"Couple of Hamburgers, A" (Thurber), **Supp. I Part 2:** 616
"Couple of Nuts, A" (Z. Fitzgerald), **Supp. IX:** 58, 71, 72
Couples (Updike), **IV:** 214, 215, 216, 217, 227, 229-230; **Retro. Supp. I:** 320, 327, 330; **Supp. XII:** 296
Cournos, John, **III:** 465; **Supp. I Part 1:** 258
"Course in Creative Writing, A" (Stafford), **Supp. XI:** 327
"Course of a Particular, The" (Stevens), **Retro. Supp. I:** 312
"Coursier de Jeanne d'Arc, Le" (McCarriston), **Supp. XIV:** 267-268
Courtier, The (Castiglione), **III:** 282
"'Courtin,' The" (Lowell), **Supp. I Part 2:** 415
"Courting of Sister Wisby, The" (Jewett), **Retro. Supp. II:** 134, 135, 146
"Courting the Famous Figures at the Grotto of Improbable Thought" (B. Kelly), **Supp. XVII:** 127-128
"Courtship" (Dove), **Supp. IV Part 1:** 248
"Courtship, Diligence" (Dove), **Supp. IV Part 1:** 248
Courtship of Miles Standish, The (Longfellow), **II:** 489, 502-503; **Retro. Supp. II:** 155, **161-162,** 163, 166, 168
"Cousin Aubrey" (Taylor), **Supp. V:** 328
Cousine Bette (Balzac), **Retro. Supp. II:** 98
Couturier, Maurice, **Supp. IV Part 1:** 44
Covarrubias, Miguel, **Supp. XVI:** 187
"Covered Bridges" (Kingsolver), **Supp. VII:** 203
Cowan, Lester, **III:** 148
Cowan, Louise, **IV:** 120, 125
Coward, Noel, **Retro. Supp. I:** 65; **Supp. I Part 2:** 332; **Supp. V:** 101; **Supp. XV:** 329
"Cowardice" (Theroux), **Supp. VIII:** 313
Cowboy Mouth (Shepard), **Supp. III Part 2:** 441-442
"Cowboys" (Salter). *See* "Dirt" (Salter)
Cowboys (Shepard), **Supp. III Part 2:** 432
Cowboys #2 (Shepard), **Supp. III Part 2:** 437, 438
Cowell, Henry, **Supp. IV Part 1:** 80, 82
Cowen, Wilson Walker, **Supp. IV Part 2:** 435
Cowie, Alexander, **IV:** 70
"Cow in Apple Time, The" (Frost), **II:** 154; **Retro. Supp. I:** 131
Cowl, Jane, **IV:** 357
Cowley, Abraham, **III:** 508; **IV:** 158; **Supp. I Part 1:** 357
Cowley, Malcolm, **I:** 246, 253, 254, 255, 256, 257, 283, 385; **II:** 26, 57, 94, 456; **III:** 606; **IV:** 123; **Retro. Supp. I:** 73, 91, 97; **Retro. Supp. II:** 77, 83, 89, 221, 330; **Supp. I Part 1:** 174; **Supp. I Part 2:** 609, 610, 620, 647, 654, 678; **Supp. II Part 1:** 103, **135-156; Supp. VIII:** 96; **Supp. XV:** 142
Cowley, Marguerite Frances Baird (Mrs. Malcolm Cowley), **Supp. I Part 2:** 615; **Supp. II Part 1:** 138, 139
Cowley, Muriel Maurer (Mrs. Malcolm Cowley), **Supp. II Part 1:** 139
Cowley, Susan Cheever (Susan Cheever), **Supp. I Part 1:** 175; **Supp. IX:** 133
Cowper, William, **II:** 17, 304; **III:** 508, 511; **Supp. I Part 1:** 150, 151, 152; **Supp. I Part 2:** 539
"Cow Wandering in the Bare Field, The" (Jarrell), **II:** 371, 388
Cox, Martha Heasley, **Supp. IX:** 2, 4, 11-12
Cox, Sidney, **Retro. Supp. I:** 131
Cox, Stephen, **Supp. IV Part 2:** 523, 524
Coxey, Jacob, **II:** 464
"Coxon Fund, The" (James), **Retro. Supp. I:** 228
"Coy Mistress" (A. Finch), **Supp. XVII:** 72
Coyne, Patricia, **Supp. V:** 123
"Coyote Ortiz: *Canis latrans latrans* in the Poetry of Simon Ortiz" (P. C. Smith), **Supp. IV Part 2:** 509
Coyote's Daylight Trip (Gunn Allen), **Supp. IV Part 1:** 320, 324
Coyote Was Here (Ortiz), **Supp. IV Part 2:** 499
Cozzens, James Gould, **I: 358-380; II:** 459
Crabbe, George, **II:** 304; **III:** 469, 508, 511, 521
"Crab-Boil" (Dove), **Supp. IV Part 1:** 249
"Cracked Looking-Glass, The" (Porter), **III:** 434, 435, 446
"Cracker Chidlings" (Rawlings), **Supp. X:** 224, 228
Cracks (Purdy), **Supp. VII:** 277-278
"Crack-Up, The" (Fitzgerald), **I:** 509; **Retro. Supp. I:** 113, 114
Crack-Up, The (Fitzgerald), **II:** 80; **III:** 35, 45; **Retro. Supp. I:** 113, 115; **Supp. V:** 276; **Supp. IX:** 61
"Crack-up of American Optimism, The: Vachel Lindsay, the Dante of the Fundamentalists" (Viereck), **Supp. I Part 2:** 403
Cradle Will Rock, The (Blitzstein), **Supp. I Part 1:** 277, 278
Craft of Fiction, The (Lubbock), **I:** 504; **Supp. VIII:** 165
Craft of Peter Taylor, The (McAlexander, ed.), **Supp. V:** 314
Craig, Gordon, **III:** 394
Crain, Jane Larkin, **Supp. V:** 123; **Supp. XII:** 167, 168
Cram, Ralph Adams, **I:** 19
Cramer, Stephen, **Supp. XI:** 139
Cramer, Steven, **Supp. XV:** 26
Crandall, Reuben, **Supp. I Part 2:** 686
Crane, Agnes, **I:** 406
Crane, Edmund, **I:** 407
Crane, Hart, **I:** 61, 62, 97, 109, 116, 266, **381-404; II:** 133, 215, 306, 368, 371, 536, 542; **III:** 260, 276, 453, 485, 521; **IV:** 122, 123-124, 127, 128, 129, 135, 139, 140, 141, 341, 380, 418, 419; **Retro. Supp. I:** 427; **Retro. Supp. II: 75-91; Supp. I Part 1:** 86; **Supp. II Part 1:** 89, 152; **Supp. III Part 1:** 20, 63, 350; **Supp. V:** 342; **Supp. VIII:** 39; **Supp. IX:** 38, 229, 320; **Supp. X:** 115, 116, 120; **Supp. XI:** 123, 131; **Supp. XII:** 198; **Supp. XV:** 138
Crane, Jonathan, Jr., **I:** 407
Crane, Jonathan Townley, **I:** 406
Crane, Luther, **I:** 406
Crane, Milton, **Supp. XV:** 144
Crane, Mrs. Jonathan Townley, **I:** 406
Crane, Nellie, **I:** 407
Crane, R. S., **Supp. I Part 2:** 423
Crane, Stephen, **I:** 34, 169-170, 201, 207, 211, **405-427,** 477, 506, 519; **II:** 58, 144, 198, 262, 263, 264, 276, 289, 290, 291; **III:** 314, 317, 334,

335, 454, 505, 585; **IV:** 207, 208, 256, 350, 475; **Retro. Supp. I:** 231, 325; **Retro. Supp. II:** 97, 123; **Supp. I Part 1:** 314; **Supp. III Part 2:** 412; **Supp. IV Part 1:** 350, 380; **Supp. IV Part 2:** 680, 689, 692; **Supp. VIII:** 98, 105; **Supp. IX:** 1, 14; **Supp. X:** 223; **Supp. XI:** 95; **Supp. XII:** 50; **Supp. XIV:** 21, 50, 51, 227; **Supp. XVII:** 71, 228
Crane, William, **I:** 407
Cranford (Gaskell), **Supp. IX:** 79
Crashaw, William, **IV:** 145, 150, 151, 165
"Crash Report" (McGrath), **Supp. X:** 116
Crater, The (Cooper), **I:** 354, 355
Cratylus (Plato), **II:** 10
"Craven Street Gazette" (Franklin), **II:** 119
"Crawdad, The" (F. Wright), **Supp. XVII:** 244
Crawdad Creek (Sanders), **Supp. XVI:** 269
Crawford, Brad, **Supp. XI:** 133
Crawford, Eva, **I:** 199
Crawford, F. Marion, **III:** 320
Crawford, Joan, **Supp. I Part 1:** 67
Crawford, Kathleen, **I:** 289
"Crayon House" (Rukeyser), **Supp. VI:** 273
Crayon Miscellany, The (Irving), **II:** 312-313
"Crazy about her Shrimp" (Simic), **Supp. VIII:** 282
"Crazy Cock" (H. Miller), **III:** 177
Crazy Gypsy (Salinas), **Supp. XIII:** 311, **313-315,** 316
"Crazy Gypsy" (Salinas), **Supp. XIII:** 313-314
Crazy Horse, **Supp. IV Part 2:** 488, 489
Crazy Horse (McMurtry), **Supp. V:** 233
Crazy Horse in Stillness (Heyen), **Supp. XIII:** 344
"Crazy in the Stir" (C. Himes), **Supp. XVI:** 137
Crazy Kill, The (C. Himes), **Supp. XVI:** 143
Creating a Role (Stanislavsky), **Supp. XIV:** 243
"Creation, According to Coyote, The" (Ortiz), **Supp. IV Part 2:** 505
Creation: A Novel (Vidal), **Supp. IV Part 2:** 677, 685, 688
"Creation of Anguish" (Nemerov), **III:** 269
"Creation Story" (Gunn Allen), **Supp. IV Part 1:** 325

"Creative and Cultural Lag" (Ellison), **Retro. Supp. II:** 116; **Supp. II Part 1:** 229
Creative Criticism (Spingarn), **I:** 266
"Creative Democracy" (Locke), **Supp. XIV:** 208
Creative Present, The (Balkian and Simmons, eds.), **Supp. XI:** 230
Creatures in an Alphabet (illus. Barnes), **Supp. III Part 1:** 43
"Credences of Summer" (Stevens), **IV:** 93-94
"Credo" (Bynner), **Supp. XV:** 50
"Credo" (Du Bois), **Supp. II Part 1:** 169
"Credo" (Jeffers), **Supp. II Part 2:** 424
"Credos and Curios" (Thurber), **Supp. I Part 2:** 606, 613
Creech, James, **Retro. Supp. I:** 254
"Creed for Americans, A" (Benét), **Supp. XI:** 52
"Creed of a Beggar, The" (Lindsay), **Supp. I Part 2:** 379
Creekmore, Hubert, **II:** 586
Creeley, Robert, **Retro. Supp. I:** 411; **Supp. II Part 1:** 30; **Supp. III Part 1:** 2; **Supp. III Part 2:** 622, 626, 629; **Supp. IV Part 1: 139-161,** 322, 325; **Supp. XI:** 317; **Supp. XIII:** 104, 112; **Supp. XIV:** 150; **Supp. XVI:** 283
Creelman, James Ashmore, **Supp. XVI:** 186-187
"Cremona Violin, The" (Lowell), **II:** 523
"Crêpe de Chine" (Doty), **Supp. XI:** 128
"Cressy" (Harte), **Supp. II Part 1:** 354, 356
"Cretan Woman, The" (Jeffers), **Supp. II Part 2:** 435
Crèvecoeur, Michel-Guillaume Jean de, **I:** 229; **Supp. I Part 1: 227-252**
Crèvecoeur's Eighteenth-Century Travels in Pennsylvania and New York (Adams), **Supp. I Part 1:** 251
Crevel, René, **Supp. XIV:** 343
Crewe-Jones, Florence, **Supp. XVII:** 58
Crewe Train (Macaulay), **Supp. XII:** 88
Crews, Harry, **Supp. X:** 11, 12; **Supp. XI: 99-117,** 245
Crichton, Michael, **Supp. XIV:** 316
Crick, Philip, **Supp. XVI:** 289
"Crickets" (R. O. Butler), **Supp. XII:** 71
Criers and Kibitzers, Kibitzers and Criers (Elkin), **Supp. VI: 45-46,** 57
Crime and Punishment (Dostoyevsky),

II: 60, 130; **IV:** 484; **Supp. IV Part 2:** 525; **Supp. VIII:** 282; **Supp. XII:** 281; **Supp. XVII:** 155
Crime at Scottsboro, The (Endore), **Supp. XVII:** 59
Crimes and Misdemeanors (film; Allen), **Supp. XV:** 1, 2, **11,** 12
Crisis papers (Paine), **Supp. I Part 2:** 508-509, 510
"Criteria of Negro Arts" (Du Bois), **Supp. II Part 1:** 181
"Critiad, The" (Winters), **Supp. II Part 2:** 794, 799
Critical Anthology A (Untermeyer), **Supp. XV:** 310
Critical Essays on Charlotte Perkins Gilman (Karpinski, ed.), **Supp. XI:** 201
Critical Essays on Peter Taylor (McAlexander), **Supp. V:** 319, 320, 323-324
Critical Essays on Robert Bly (Davis), **Supp. IV Part 1:** 64, 69
Critical Essays on Wallace Stegner (Arthur), **Supp. IV Part 2:** 606
Critical Fable, A (Lowell), **II:** 511-512, 527, 529-530
Critical Guide to Leaves of Grass, A (J. Miller), **IV:** 352
Critical Response to Joan Didion, The (Felton), **Supp. IV Part 1:** 210
Critical Temper of Alain Locke, The: A Selection of His Essays on Art and Culture (Stewart, ed.), **Supp. XIV:** 196, **210-211,** 213
"Critic as Artist, The" (Wilde), **Supp. X:** 189
Criticism and Fiction (Howells), **II:** 288
Criticism and Ideology (Eagleton), **Retro. Supp. I:** 67
Criticism in the Borderlands (Calderón and Saldívar, eds.), **Supp. IV Part 2:** 544
"Critics, The" (Jong), **Supp. V:** 119
"Critics and Connoisseurs" (Moore), **III:** 209
Critic's Notebook, A (Howe), **Supp. VI:** 126-128
"Critic's Task, The" (Kazin), **Supp. VIII:** 103
"Critic Who Does Not Exist, The" (Wilson), **IV:** 431
"Critique de la Vie Quotidienne" (Barthelme), **Supp. IV Part 1:** 50
Critique of Pure Reason (Kant), **Supp. XVI:** 184
Croce, Benedetto, **I:** 58, 255, 265, 273, 281; **III:** 610
Crockett, Davy, **II:** 307; **III:** 227; **IV:**

266; **Supp. I Part 2:** 411
Crofter and the Laird, The (McPhee), **Supp. III Part 1:** 301-302, 307
Croly, Herbert, **I:** 229, 231, 235; **IV:** 436
Cromwell, Oliver, **IV:** 145, 146, 156; **Supp. I Part 1:** 111
Cronin, A. J., **Supp. XVII:** 59
Cronin, Dr. Archibald, **III:** 578
Cronin, Justin, **Supp. X:** 10
Crooke, Dr. Helkiah, **Supp. I Part 1:** 98, 104
Crooks, Alan, **Supp. V:** 226
Crooks, Robert, **Supp. XIII:** 237
"Crop, The" (O'Connor), **Retro. Supp. II:** 223-225
Crosby, Caresse, **I:** 385; **III:** 473; **Retro. Supp. II:** 85; **Supp. XII:** 198
Crosby, Harry, **I:** 385; **Retro. Supp. II:** 85
"Cross" (Hughes), **Supp. I Part 1:** 325
Crossan, John Dominic, **Supp. V:** 251
"Cross Country Snow" (Hemingway), **II:** 249
Cross Creek (Rawlings), **Supp. X:** 223, 226, 228, **231-232**, 233, 234, 235
Cross Creek Cookery (Rawlings), **Supp. X:** 233
Crossing, The (McCarthy), **Supp. VIII:** 175, **184-186**
"Crossing, The" (Swenson), **Supp. IV Part 2:** 644
"Crossing Brooklyn Ferry" (Whitman), **IV:** 333, 340, 341; **Retro. Supp. I:** 389, 396, 397, 400-401
"Crossing into Poland" (Babel), **Supp. XIV:** 84
Crossings (Chuang), **Supp. X:** 291
"Crossings" (Hogan), **Supp. IV Part 1:** 412
Crossing the Water (Plath), **Retro. Supp. II:** 248; **Supp. I Part 2:** 526, 538
Crossing to Safety (Stegner), **Supp. IV Part 2:** 599, 606, 612, 613-614
"Cross of Snow, The" (Longfellow), **II:** 490; **Retro. Supp. II:** 169-170
"Crossover" (O. Butler), **Supp. XIII:** 61
"Cross-Roads, The" (Lowell), **II:** 523
"Crossroads of the World Etc." (Merwin), **Supp. III Part 1:** 347, 348
Cross-Section (Seaver), **IV:** 485
Cross the Border, Close the Gap (Fiedler), **Supp. XIII:** 104
Cross Ties (X. J. Kennedy), **Supp. XV:** 165, **166-167**

"Cross Ties" (X. J. Kennedy), **Supp. XV:** 158
"Croup" (Karr), **Supp. XI:** 243
Crouse, Russel, **III:** 284
"Crow" (Hogan), **Supp. IV Part 1:** 405
Crow (Hughes), **Supp. XV:** 347, 348
"Crow, The" (Creeley), **Supp. IV Part 1:** 148-149
Crow and the Heart, The (Carruth), **Supp. XVI:** 47-48
"Crowded Street, The" (Bryant), **Supp. I Part 1:** 168
Crowder, A. B., **Supp. XI:** 107
"Crow Jane" (Baraka), **Supp. II Part 1:** 38
Crowninshield, Frank, **III:** 123; **Supp. IX:** 201
Crown of Columbus (Erdrich and Dorris), **Supp. IV Part 1:** 260
"Crows, The" (Bogan), **Supp. III Part 1:** 50, 51
Crucial Instances (Wharton), **Retro. Supp. I:** 365, 367
Crucible, The (A. Miller), **III:** 147, 148, 155, 156-158, 159, 166; **Supp. XIII:** 206
"Crucifix in the Filing Cabinet" (Shapiro), **Supp. II Part 2:** 712
"Crude Foyer" (Stevens), **Retro. Supp. I:** 310
"Cruel and Barbarous Treatment" (McCarthy), **II:** 562, 563
"Cruel Mother, The" (B. Kelly), **Supp. XVII:** 126
Cruise of the Dazzler, The (London), **II:** 465
Cruise of the Snark, The (London), **II:** 476-477
"Cruising with the Beach Boys" (Gioia), **Supp. XV:** 118
"'Crumbling Idols' by Hamlin Garland" (Chopin), **Supp. I Part 1:** 217
"Crusade of the Excelsior, The" (Harte), **Supp. II Part 1:** 336, 354
"Crusoe in England" (Bishop), **Retro. Supp. II:** 50; **Supp. I Part 1:** 93, 95, 96; **Supp. III Part 1:** 10, 18
Cry, the Beloved Country (Paton), **Supp. VIII:** 126
Cryer, Dan, **Supp. VIII:** 86, 88; **Supp. XII:** 164
Crying of Lot 49, The (Pynchon), **Supp. II Part 2:** 618, 619, 621, 630-633
"Crying Sisters, The" (Rand), **Supp. IV Part 2:** 524
"Crying Wolf" (C. Frost), **Supp. XV:** 101
Cryptogram, The (Mamet), **Supp.**

XIV: 240, 247, 255
"Crystal, The" (Aiken), **I:** 60
"Crystal, The" (Lanier), **Supp. I Part 1:** 364, 370
"Crystal Cage, The" (Kunitz), **Supp. III Part 1:** 258
"Crytal" (Sobin), **Supp. XVI:** 283
Cry to Heaven (Rice), **Supp. VII:** 300-301
"Cuba" (Hemingway), **II:** 258
"Cuba Libre" (Baraka), **Supp. II Part 1:** 33
Cudjoe, Selwyn, **Supp. IV Part 1:** 6
"Cudjo's Own Story of the Last American Slaver" (Hurston), **Supp. VI:** 153
Cudlipp, Thelma, **I:** 501
Cudworth, Ralph, **II:** 9, 10
"Cuentista" (Mora), **Supp. XIII:** 224
"Cuento de agua santa, Un" (Mora), **Supp. XIII:** 224
Cujo (King), **Supp. V:** 138-139, 143, 149, 152
Cukor, George, **Supp. XVI:** 192
Cullen, Countee, **Retro. Supp. I:** 207; **Retro. Supp. II:** 114; **Supp. I Part 1:** 49, 325; **Supp. III Part 1:** 73, 75, 76; **Supp. IV Part 1: 163-174;** **Supp. IX:** 306, 309; **Supp. X:** 136, 140; **Supp. XIII:** 186
"Cultivation of Christmas Trees, The" (Eliot), **I:** 579
"Cult of the Best, The" (Arnold), **I:** 223
"Cultural Exchange" (Hughes), **Supp. I Part 1:** 341
"Cultural Pluralism: A New Americanism" (Locke), **Supp. XIV:** 195
"Cultural Relativism and Ideological Peace" (Locke), **Supp. XIV:** 202, 212
"Culture" (Emerson), **III:** 2, 4
"Culture, Self, and Style" (Gass), **Supp. VI:** 88
"Culture and Religion" (Olds), **Supp. X:** 214
Culture of Cities, The (Mumford), **Supp. II Part 2:** 492, 494-495
Cummings, E. E., **I:** 44, 48, 64, 105, 176, **428-450**, 475, 477, 482, 526; **III:** 20, 196, 476; **IV:** 384, 402, 415, 427, 433; **Retro. Supp. II:** 178, 328; **Supp. I Part 2:** 622, 678; **Supp. III Part 1:** 73; **Supp. IV Part 2:** 637, 641; **Supp. IX:** 20; **Supp. XV:** 312, 338
Cummings, Robert, **Supp. IV Part 2:** 524
Cummins, James, **Supp. XVII:** 74
Cunard, Lady, **III:** 459

Cunningham, J. V., **Supp. XV:** 169
Cunningham, Merce, **Supp. IV Part 1:** 83; **Supp. XV:** 187
Cunningham, Michael, **Supp. XII:** 80; **Supp. XV: 55-71**
Cup of Gold (Steinbeck), **IV:** 51, 53, 61-64, 67
"Cupola, The" (Bogan), **Supp. III Part 1:** 53
"Curandera" (Mora), **Supp. XIII:** 214, 222
Curé de Tours, Le (Balzac), **I:** 509
Cure for Dreams, A: A Novel (Gibbons), **Supp. X: 45-47,** 48, 50
Curie, Marie, **IV:** 420, 421; **Supp. I Part 2:** 569
Curie, Pierre, **IV:** 420
Curiosa Americana (Mather), **Supp. II Part 2:** 463
Curiosities (Matthews), **Supp. IX:** 151, 152
"Curious Case of Sidd Finch, The" (Plimpton), **Supp. XVI:**244
"Curious Shifts of the Poor" (Dreiser), **Retro. Supp. II:** 97
"Currents and Counter-Currents in Medical Science" (Holmes), **Supp. I Part 1:** 305
"Curried Cow" (Bierce), **I:** 200
Curry, Professor W. C., **IV:** 122
Curse of the Jade Scorpion, The (film; Allen), **Supp. XV:** 11
Curse of the Starving Class (Shepard), **Supp. III Part 2:** 433, 447-448
Curse of the Werewolf, The (film), **Supp. XVII:** 56
"Curse on a Thief, A" (X. J. Kennedy), **Supp. XV:** 171
"Curtain, The" (Chandler), **Supp. IV Part 1:** 122
Curtain Calls: British and American Women and the Theater, 1660-1820 (Saar), **Supp. XV:** 237
Curtain of Green, A (Welty), **IV:** 261-264, 268, 283
"Curtain of Green, A" (Welty), **IV:** 263-264
Curtain of Green and Other Stories, A (Welty), **Retro. Supp. I:** 343, 344, 345, 346, 347, 355
Curtain of Trees (opera), **Supp. IV Part 2:** 552
"Curtain Raiser, A" (Stein), **IV:** 43, 44
"Curtains" (Cisneros), **Supp. VII:** 66
Curtin, John, **Supp. IX:** 184
Curtis, George William, **Supp. I Part 1:** 307
Curve (Goldbarth), **Supp. XII:** 181
Curve of Binding Energy, The (McPhee), **Supp. III Part 1:** 301

Curzon, Mary, **III:** 52
Cushing, Caleb, **Supp. I Part 2:** 684, 686
Cushman, Howard, **Supp. I Part 2:** 652
Cushman, Stephen, **Retro. Supp. I:** 430
"Custard Heart, The" (Parker), **Supp. IX:** 201
Custer, General George, **I:** 489, 491
Custer Died for Your Sins (Deloria), **Supp. IV Part 1:** 323; **Supp. IV Part 2:** 504
"Custom House, The" (Hawthorne), **II:** 223; **Retro. Supp. I:** 147-148, 157
Custom of the Country, The (Wharton), **IV:** 318; **Retro. Supp. I:** 374, **375-376**
"Cut" (Plath), **Retro. Supp. II:** 253
"Cut-Glass Bowl, The" (Fitzgerald), **II:** 88
Cutting, Bronson, **III:** 600
"Cuttings, *later*" (Roethke), **III:** 532
"Cyberpunk" (Bethke), **Supp. XVI:**121
Cyberspace trilogy (W. Gibson). *See* Sprawl trilogy (W. Gibson)
"Cycles, The" (Pinsky), **Supp. VI:** 250-252
Cynic's Word Book, The (Bierce), **I:** 197, 205, 208, 209, 210
Cynthia Ozick (Lowin), **Supp. V:** 273
Cynthia Ozick's Comic Art (Cohen), **Supp. V:** 273
Cynthia Ozick's Fiction (Kauvar), **Supp. V:** 273

D

"D. H. Lawrence" (Bynner), **Supp. XV:** 46
D. H. Lawrence: An Unprofessional Study (Nin), **Supp. X:** 182-183
D. H. Lawrence: The World of the Major Novels (Sanders), **Supp. XVI:**267
Dacey, Philip, **Supp. IV Part 1:** 70
Dacier, André, **II:** 10
"Dad" (Cullen), **Supp. IV Part 1:** 167
"Daddy" (Plath), **Retro. Supp. II:** 250-251; **Supp. I Part 2:** 529, 542, 545, 546; **Supp. II Part 2:** 688
"Daemon, The" (Bogan), **Supp. III Part 1:** 58, 61
"Daemon Lover, The" (Jackson), **Supp. IX:** 116-117
"Daffodils" (Wordsworth), **Supp. XIII:** 284
"Daffy Duck in Hollywood" (Ashbery), **Supp. III Part 1:** 18
D'Agata, John, **Supp. XII:** 97, 98
Dago Red (Fante), **Supp. XI:** 160, 169
Dahl, Roald, **Supp. IX:** 114

Dahlberg, Edward, **I:** 231; **Retro. Supp. I:** 426; **Supp. III Part 2:** 624; **Supp. XIV:**148
Dahlberg, R'lene, **Supp. XIV:**148
Daiches, David, **Retro. Supp. II:** 243; **Supp. I Part 2:** 536
Daily Horoscope (Gioia), **Supp. XV:** 112, **118-121,** 126
"Daily Horoscope" (Gioia), **Supp. XV:** 119
Daily Modernism (Podnieks), **Supp. X:** 189
Dain Curse, The (Hammett), **Supp. IV Part 1:** 348
"Daisies" (Glück), **Supp. V:** 88
"Daisy" (Oates), **Supp. II Part 2:** 523
Daisy-Head Mayzie (Geisel), **Supp. XVI:**112
Daisy Miller (H. James), **Retro. Supp. I:** 216, 220, 222, 223, 228, 231
"Daisy Miller" (H. James), **II:** 325, 326, 327, 329; **IV:** 316
Dale, Charlie, **Supp. IV Part 2:** 584
Dali, Salvador, **II:** 586; **Supp. IV Part 1:** 83; **Supp. XIII:** 317
Dalibard, Thomas-François, **II:** 117
"Dallas-Fort Worth: Redband and Mistletoe" (Clampitt), **Supp. IX:** 45
"Dalliance of Eagles, The" (Whitman), **IV:** 348
Dalva (Harrison), **Supp. VIII:** 37, 45, 46, **48-49**
Daly, Carroll John, **Supp. IV Part 1:** 343, 345
Daly, John, **II:** 25, 26
Daly, Julia Brown, **II:** 25, 26
"Dalyrimple Goes Wrong" (Fitzgerald), **II:** 88
"Dam, The" (Rukeyser), **Supp. VI:** 283
Damas, Leon, **Supp. X:** 139
Damascus Gate (Stone), **Supp. V:** 308-311
Damballah (Wideman), **Supp. X:** 319, 320, 321, 322, 323, 326, 327, 331, 333-334
Damnation of Theron Ware, The (Frederic), **II:** 140-143, 144, 146, 147; **Retro. Supp. I:** 325
"Damned Thing, The" (Bierce), **I:** 206
Damon, Matt, **Supp. VIII:** 175
Damon, S. Foster, **I:** 26; **II:** 512, 514, 515
"Damon and Vandalia" (Dove), **Supp. IV Part 1:** 252
Dana, H. W. L., **I:** 225
Dana, Richard Henry, **I:** 339, 351; **Supp. I Part 1:** 103, 154, 155; **Supp. I Part 2:** 414, 420
Dana, Richard Henry, Jr., **III:** 81

Dana, Robert, **Supp. V:** 178, 180
"Dana Gioia and Fine Press Printing" (Peich), **Supp. XV:** 117
"Dance, The" (Crane), **I:** 109
"Dance, The" (Roethke), **III:** 541
"Dance, The" (W. C. Williams), **Supp. XVII:** 113
Dance of Death, The (Auden), **Supp. II Part 1:** 10
Dance of Death, The (Bierce and Harcourt), **I:** 196
Dance of the Sleepwalkers (Calabria), **Supp. XIII:** 164
"Dance of the Solids, The" (Updike), **Retro. Supp. I:** 323
Dances with Wolves (film), **Supp. X:** 124
Dancing After Hours (Dubus), **Supp. VII:** 91
Dancing Bears, The (Merwin), **Supp. III Part 1:** 343-344
Dancing on the Stones (Nichols), **Supp. XIII:** 256, 257, 259, 267, 269
"Dancing the Jig" (Sexton), **Supp. II Part 2:** 692
Dandelion Wine (Bradbury), **Supp. IV Part 1:** 101, 109-110
Dandurand, Karen, **Retro. Supp. I:** 30
"Dandy Frightening the Squatters, The" (Twain), **IV:** 193-194
Dangerous Crossroads (film), **Supp. XIII:** 163
Dangerous Moonlight (Purdy), **Supp. VII:** 278
"Dangerous Road Before Martin Luther King" (Baldwin), **Supp. I Part 1:** 52
"Dangerous Summer, The" (Hemingway), **II:** 261
"Dangers of Authorship, The" (Blackmur), **Supp. II Part 1:** 147
Dangling Man (Bellow), **I:** 144, 145, 147, 148, 150-151, 153-154, 158, 160, 161, 162, 163; **Retro. Supp. II:** 19, 20-21, 22, 23; **Supp. VIII:** 234
Daniel (biblical book), **Supp. I Part 1:** 105
Daniel (film), **Supp. IV Part 1:** 236
Daniel, Arnaut, **III:** 467
Daniel, Robert W., **III:** 76
Daniel, Samuel, **Supp. I Part 1:** 369
Daniel Deronda (Eliot), **I:** 458
Daniels, Kate, **Supp. XVII:** 112
Danielson, Linda, **Supp. IV Part 2:** 569
D'Annunzio, Gabriele, **II:** 515
Danny and the Deep Blue Sea: An Apache Dance (Shanley), **Supp. XIV:** 315, **318-319**, 320, 321, 323, 324
Danny O'Neill pentalogy (Farrell), **II:** 35-41
Danse Macabre (King), **Supp. IV Part 1:** 102; **Supp. V:** 144
"Danse Russe" (W. C. Williams), **IV:** 412-413
"Dans le Restaurant" (Eliot), **I:** 554, 578
Dans l'ombre des cathédrales (Ambelain), **Supp. I Part 1:** 273
Dante Alighieri, **I:** 103, 136, 138, 250, 384, 433, 445; **II:** 8, 274, 278, 289, 490, 492, 493, 494, 495, 504, 508, 524, 552; **III:** 13, 77, 124, 182, 259, 278, 448, 453, 467, 533, 607, 609, 610-612, 613; **IV:** 50, 134, 137, 138, 139, 247, 437, 438; **Retro. Supp. I:** 62, 63, 64, 66, 360; **Retro. Supp. II:** 330; **Supp. I Part 1:** 256, 363; **Supp. I Part 2:** 422, 454; **Supp. III Part 2:** 611, 618, 621; **Supp. IV Part 2:** 634; **Supp. V:** 277, 283, 331, 338, 345; **Supp. VIII:** 27, 219-221; **Supp. X:** 120, 121, 125; **Supp. XII:** 98; **Supp. XV:** 254; **Supp. XVII:** 227, 241
Danziger, Adolphe, **I:** 199-200
Dar (Nabokov), **III:** 246, 255
D'Arcy, Randall, **Supp. XVII:** 76
"Dare's Gift" (Glasgow), **II:** 190
Dark Angel, The (Bolton), **Supp. I Part 1:** 281
"Dark Angel Travels With Us to Canada and Blesses Our Vacation, The" (Dunn), **Supp. XI:** 146
Dark Carnival (Bradbury), **Supp. IV Part 1:** 102
Darker (Strand), **Supp. IV Part 2:** 619, 626-628
Darker Face of the Earth, The (Dove), **Supp. IV Part 1:** 255-257
Dark Green, Bright Red (Vidal), **Supp. IV Part 2:** 677
Dark Half, The (King), **Supp. V:** 141
Dark Harbor: A Poem (Strand), **Supp. IV Part 2:** 633-634
"Dark Hills, The" (Robinson), **III:** 523
Dark Horses (X. J. Kennedy), **Supp. XV:** **167-170**
Dark Laughter (Anderson), **I:** 111, 116; **II:** 250-251
"Darkling Alphabet, A" (Snodgrass), **Supp. VI:** 323
Darkling Child (Merwin and Milroy), **Supp. III Part 1:** 346
"Darkling Summer, Ominous Dusk, Rumorous Rain" (Schwartz), **Supp. II Part 2:** 661
"Darkling Thrush" (Hardy), **Supp. IX:** 40
"Dark Men, The" (Dubus), **Supp. VII:** 86
Dark Mirrors (Sobin), **Supp. XVI:** 295
Darkness and the Light, The (Hecht), **Supp. X:** 58
"Darkness on the Edge of Town" (O'Brien), **Supp. V:** 246
Darkness under the Trees/Walking behind the Spanish (Salinas), **Supp. XIII:** 311, **319-324**
"Dark Night" (St. John of the Cross), **Supp. XV:** 30
Dark Night of the Soul, The (St. John of the Cross), **I:** 1, 585
"Dark Ones" (Dickey), **Supp. IV Part 1:** 182
Dark Princess: A Romance (Du Bois), **Supp. II Part 1:** 179, 181-182
Dark Room, The (T. Williams), **IV:** 381
"Dark Summer" (Bogan), **Supp. III Part 1:** 51, 53
Dark Summer: Poems (Bogan), **Supp. III Part 1:** 52-53, 57
"Dark Tower, The" (column), **Supp. IV Part 1:** 168, 170
Dark Tower, The: The Gunslinger (King), **Supp. V:** 152
Dark Tower IV, The: Wizard and Glass (King), **Supp. V:** 139
Dark Tunnel, The (Macdonald, under Millar), **Supp. IV Part 2:** 465, 466
"Dark TV Screen" (Simic), **Supp. VIII:** 282
"Dark Voyage, The" (McLay), **Supp. XIII:** 21
"Dark Walk, The" (Taylor), **Supp. V:** 320-321, 322, 326
Darkwater: Voices from Within the Veil (Du Bois), **Supp. II Part 1:** 178, 180, 183
Dark Waves and Light Matter (Goldbarth), **Supp. XII:** 176, 193
Dark World (Carruth), **Supp. XVI:** 55
"Darling" (Nye), **Supp. XIII:** 283-284
"Darling, The" (Chekhov), **Supp. IX:** 202
Darling-Darling (Barillet and Grédy; Loos, trans.), **Supp. XVI:** 194
Darnell, Linda, **Supp. XII:** 173
Darragh, Tina, **Supp. IV Part 2:** 427
Darreu, Robert Donaldson, **Supp. II Part 1:** 89, 98, 102
Darrow, Clarence, **Supp. I Part 1:** 5; **Supp. I Part 2:** 455
Darwin, Charles, **I:** 457; **II:** 323, 462, 481; **III:** 226, 231; **IV:** 69, 304; **Retro. Supp. I:** 254; **Retro. Supp. II:** 60, 65; **Supp. I Part 1:** 368;

Supp. IX: 180; **Supp. XI:** 203; **Supp. XVI:**13
"Darwin in 1881" (Schnackenberg), **Supp. XV:** 253, 254, 258
Daryush, Elizabeth, **Supp. V:** 180
Dash, Julie, **Supp. XI:** 17, 18, 20
Dashell, Alfred, **Supp. X:** 224
"DAS KAPITAL" (Baraka), **Supp. II Part 1:** 55
Datlow, Ellen, **Supp. XVI:**123
"Datum Centurio" (Wallace), **Supp. X:** 309
Daudet, Alphonse, **II:** 325, 338
"Daughter" (Caldwell), **I:** 309
"Daughter in the House" (X. J. Kennedy), **Supp. XV:** 160
Daughter of Earth (Smedly), **Supp. XIII:** 295
Daughter of the Snows, A (London), **II:** 465, 469-470
"Daughters" (Anderson), **I:** 114
Daughters (Marshall), **Supp. XI:** 275, 276, 277, **286-288,** 289, 290
Daughters, I Love You (Hogan), **Supp. IV Part 1:** 397, 399, 401
"Daughters of Invention" (Alvarez), **Supp. VII:** 9
Daughters of the Dust (Dash; film), **Supp. XI:** 17, 18
Daumier, Honoré, **IV:** 412
Dave, R. A., **Supp. VIII:** 126
Davenport, Abraham, **Supp. I Part 2:** 699
Davenport, Gary, **Supp. IX:** 98
Davenport, Guy, **Supp. XIV:**96
Davenport, Herbert J., **Supp. I Part 2:** 642
Davenport, James, **I:** 546
Daves, E. G., **Supp. I Part 1:** 369
Davey, Frank, **Supp. XIII:** 33
"David" (Garrett), **Supp. VII:** 109-110
"David" (Gordon), **Supp. IV Part 1:** 298-299
"David and Agnes, a Romance" (Keillor), **Supp. XVI:**175
David Copperfield (Dickens), **I:** 458; **II:** 290; **Retro. Supp. I:** 33; **Supp. XVI:**65, 72
"David Crockett's Other Life" (Nye), **Supp. XIII:** 282
Davideis (Cowley), **IV:** 158
David Harum (Westcott), **I:** 216
"David Lynch Keeps His Head" (Wallace), **Supp. X:** 314
David Show, The (Gurney), **Supp. V:** 97
Davidson, Cathy, **Supp. XV:** 238
Davidson, Donald, **I:** 294; **III:** 495, 496; **IV:** 121, 122, 124, 125, 236; **Supp. II Part 1:** 139; **Supp. XIV:**2

Davidson, John, **Retro. Supp. I:** 55
Davidson, Michael, **Supp. VIII:** 290, 293, 294, 302-303
Davidson, Sara, **Supp. IV Part 1:** 196, 198, 203
Davidsz de Heem, Jan, **Supp. XI:** 133
Davie, Donald, **III:** 478; **Supp. IV Part 2:** 474; **Supp. V:** 331; **Supp. X:** 55, 59; **Supp. XVII:** 111, 112, 121
Davies, Arthur, **III:** 273
Davies, Marion, **Supp. XVI:**186
Davies, Sir John, **III:** 541
Da Vinci, Leonardo, **I:** 274; **II:** 536; **III:** 210
Davis, Allen F., **Supp. I Part 1:** 1, 7
Davis, Allison, **Supp. I Part 1:** 327
Davis, Angela, **Supp. I Part 1:** 66; **Supp. X:** 249
Davis, Bette, **I:** 78; **Supp. I Part 1:** 67
Davis, Bill, **Supp. XIII:** 267
Davis, Christina, **Supp. XV:** 264
Davis, Donald, **Supp. XIII:** 93
Davis, Elizabeth Gould, **Supp. I Part 2:** 567
Davis, George, **II:** 586
Davis, Glover, **Supp. V:** 180, 182, 186
Davis, Jefferson, **II:** 206; **IV:** 122, 125, 126
Davis, Jordan, **Supp. XV:** 178, 181, 186, 188
Davis, Katie, **Supp. VIII:** 83
Davis, L. J., **Supp. XI:** 234
Davis, Lydia, **Supp. XII:** 24; **Supp. XVII:** 21
Davis, Miles, **Supp. XV:** 346
Davis, Ossie, Jr., **Supp. IV Part 1:** 362; **Supp. XVI:**144
Davis, Rebecca Harding, **Supp. I Part 1:** 45; **Supp. XIII:** 292, 295, 305; **Supp. XVI:**79-96
Davis, Richard Harding, **III:** 328; **Supp. II Part 1:** 393; **Supp. XVI:**85
Davis, Robert Gorham, **II:** 51; **IV:** 108
Davis, Stuart, **IV:** 409; **Supp. XV:** 295
Davis, Thulani, **Supp. XI:** 179; **Supp. XIII:** 233, 234, 239
Davis, William V., **Supp. IV Part 1:** 63, 64, 68, 69, 70
Davy's Lake (M. Finch), **Supp. XVII:** 69
Dawn (Dreiser), **I:** 498, 499, 503, 509, 515, 519
Dawn (O. Butler), **Supp. XIII:** 63, **64**
"Dawnbreaker" (Hayden), **Supp. II Part 1:** 370
"Dawn Patrol: A Review of the Literature of the Negro for 1948" (Locke), **Supp. XIV:**211
Dawn Patrol, The (film), **Supp. XIV:**81

Dawson, Edward, **IV:** 151
Dawson, Emma, **I:** 199
Dawson, Ruth, **Supp. XI:** 120
Day, Dorothy, **II:** 215; **Supp. I Part 2:** 524; **Supp. X:** 142
Day, Georgiana, **Supp. I Part 2:** 585
Dayan, Joan, **Retro. Supp. II:** 270
Day Book, A (Creeley), **Supp. IV Part 1:** 155
"Daybreak" (Kinnell), **Supp. III Part 1:** 250
"Daybreak Blues" (Kees), **Supp. XV:** 133
"Daybreak in Alabama" (Hughes), **Retro. Supp. I:** 211; **Supp. I Part 1:** 344
Day by Day (Lowell), **Retro. Supp. II:** 184, 186, 191
"Day-Care Field Trip: Aquarium" (Karr), **Supp. XI:** 243
"Day-Dream, A" (Bryant), **Supp. I Part 1:** 160
"Day for Poetry and Song, A" (Douglass), **Supp. III Part 1:** 172
Day Late and a Dollar Short, A (McMillan), **Supp. XIII:** 184, **Supp. XIII:** 185, **191-192**
"Day longs for the evening, The" (Levertov), **Supp. III Part 1:** 274
Day of a Stranger (Merton), **Supp. VIII:** 203
"Day of Days, A" (James), **II:** 322
Day of Doom (Wigglesworth), **IV:** 147, 155, 156
Day of the Body (C. Frost), **Supp. XV:** 93, **98-100,** 106
Day of the Locust, The (West), **I:** 298; **IV:** 288, 299-306; **Retro. Supp. II:** 321, 323, 324, 329, **337-338;** **Supp. II Part 2:** 626; **Supp. XI:** 296; **Supp. XII:** 173; **Supp. XIII:** 170; **Supp. XIV:**328
"Day on the Big Branch, A" (Nemerov), **III:** 275-276
"Day on the Connecticut River, A" (Merrill), **Supp. III Part 1:** 336
Day Room, The (DeLillo), **Supp. VI:** 4
"Days" (Emerson), **II:** 19, 20
Days: Tangier Journal, 1987-1989 (Bowles), **Supp. IV Part 1:** 94
"Days and Nights" (Koch), **Supp. XV:** 179, 180
"Days and Nights: A Journal" (Price), **Supp. VI:** 265
Days Before, The (Porter), **III:** 433, 453
"Days of 1935" (Merrill), **Supp. III Part 1:** 325, 328
"Days of 1964" (Merrill), **Supp. III Part 1:** 328, 352

"Days of 1971" (Merrill), **Supp. III Part 1:** 328
"Days of 1981" (Doty), **Supp. XI:** 123
"Days of 1941 and '44" (Merrill), **Supp. III Part 1:** 336
"Days of Awe: The Birth of Lucy Jane" (Wasserstein), **Supp. XV:** 332
"Days of Edward Hopper" (Haines), **Supp. XII:** 210
"Days of Heaven" (Bass), **Supp. XVI:** 20
Days of Obligation: An Argument with My Mexican Father (Rodriguez), **Supp. XIV:** 298, 300, **302-305,** 307, 310
Days of Our Lives (soap opera), **Supp. XI:** 83
Days of Our Lives Lie in Fragments: New and Old Poems (Garrett), **Supp. VII:** 109-110, 111
Days of the Phoenix (Brooks), **I:** 266
Days of Wine and Roses (J. P. Miller), **Supp. XIII:** 262
Days to Come (Hellman), **Supp. I Part 1:** 276, 277-278
Days without End (O'Neill), **III:** 385, 391, 397
"Day's Work, A" (Capote), **Supp. III Part 1:** 120
"Day's Work, A" (Porter), **III:** 443, 446
"Day the Presidential Candidate Came to Ciudad Tamaulipas, The" (Caldwell), **I:** 309
Day the World ended, The (Coover), **Supp. V:** 1
"Day with Conrad Green, A" (Lardner), **II:** 428-429, 430
"Deacon's Masterpiece, The" (Holmes), **Supp. I Part 1:** 302, 307
"Dead, The" (Joyce), **I:** 285; **III:** 343
Dead and the Living, The (Olds), **Supp. X:** 201, **204-206,** 207
"Dead Body, The" (Olds), **Supp. X:** 210
"Dead by the Side of the Road, The" (Snyder), **Supp. VIII:** 301
"Dead Doe" (B. Kelly), **Supp. XVII:** 128-129
Dead End (Kingsley), **Supp. I Part 1:** 277, 281
Dead Father, The (Barthelme), **Supp. IV Part 1:** 43, 47, 50-51
"Dead Fiddler, The" (Singer), **IV:** 20
Dead Fingers Talk (Burroughs), **Supp. III Part 1:** 103
"Dead Hand" series (Sinclair), **Supp. V:** 276, 277, 281
"Dead Languages, The" (Humphrey), **Supp. IX:** 109

Dead Lecturer, The (Baraka), **Supp. II Part 1:** 31, 33, 35-37, 49
Deadline at Dawn (Odets), **Supp. II Part 2:** 546
"Dead-Lock and Its Key, A" (E. Stoddard), **Supp. XV:** 286
"Dead Loon, The" (Bynner), **Supp. XV: 44-45**
Deadly Affair, A (Lacy), **Supp. XV:** 205-206
Deadly is the Female (film), **Supp. XVII:** 62
Dead Man's Walk (McMurtry), **Supp. V:** 231, 232
Dead Man's Walk (screenplay; McMurtry and Ossana), **Supp. V:** 231
Dead Man Walking (opera libretto, McNally), **Supp. XIII:** 207
"Dead Reckoning" (Jarman), **Supp. XVII:** 113
Dead Souls (Gogol), **I:** 296
"Dead Souls on Campus" (Kosinski), **Supp. VII:** 222
"Dead Wingman, The" (Jarrell), **II:** 374
"Dead Yellow Women" (Hammett), **Supp. IV Part 1:** 345
Dead Zone, The (King), **Supp. V:** 139, 143, 144, 148, 152
Dean, James, **I:** 493
Dean, Man Mountain, **II:** 589
Deane, Silas, **Supp. I Part 2:** 509, 524
"Dean of Men" (Taylor), **Supp. V:** 314, 323
Dean's December, The (Bellow), **Retro. Supp. II:** 30-31
"Dear Adolph" (Benét), **Supp. XI:** 46
"Dear America" (Ortiz), **Supp. IV Part 2:** 503
"Dearest M—" (Carruth), **Supp. XVI:** 59
"Dear Judas" (Jeffers), **Supp. II Part 2:** 431-432, 433
Dear Juliette (Sarton), **Supp. VIII:** 265
Dear Lovely Death (Hughes), **Retro. Supp. I:** 203; **Supp. I Part 1:** 328
"Dear Villon" (Corso), **Supp. XII:** 135
"Dear World" (Gunn Allen), **Supp. IV Part 1:** 321
Death (Allen), **Supp. XV:** 3
"Death" (Corso), **Supp. XII:** 127
"Death" (Lowell), **II:** 536
"Death" (Mailer), **III:** 38
"Death" (West), **IV:** 286
"Death" (W. C. Williams), **Retro. Supp. I:** 422
"Death and Absence" (Glück), **Supp. V:** 82
Death and Taxes (Parker), **Supp. IX:** 192

"Death and the Child" (Crane), **I:** 414
"Death as a Society Lady" (Hecht), **Supp. X:** 71-72
Death before Bedtime (Vidal, under pseudonym Box), **Supp. IV Part 2:** 682
"Death Be Not Proud" (Donne), **Supp. XVI:** 158
"Death by Water" (Eliot), **I:** 395, 578
Death Comes for the Archbishop (Cather), **I:** 314, 327, 328-330; **Retro. Supp. I:** 16-18, 21; **Supp. XIII:** 253
Death in the Afternoon (Hemingway), **II:** 253; **IV:** 35; **Retro. Supp. I:** 182; **Supp. VIII:** 182; **Supp. XVI:** 205
"Death in the Country, A" (Benét), **Supp. XI:** 53-54
Death in the Family, A (Agee), **I:** 25, 29, 42, 45
Death in the Fifth Position (Vidal, under pseudonym Box), **Supp. IV Part 2:** 682
"Death in the Woods" (Anderson), **I:** 114, 115
Death in the Woods and Other Stories (Anderson), **I:** 112, 114, 115
Death in Venice (Mann), **III:** 231; **Supp. IV Part 1:** 392; **Supp. V:** 51
"Death in Viet Nam" (Salinas), **Supp. XIII:** 315
"Death in Winter" (C. Frost), **Supp. XV:** 98
Death Is a Lonely Business (Bradbury), **Supp. IV Part 1:** 102, 103, 111-112, 115
"Death Is Not the End" (Wallace), **Supp. X:** 309
Death Kit (Sontag), **Supp. III Part 2:** 451, 468-469
Death Likes It Hot (Vidal, under pseudonym Box), **Supp. IV Part 2:** 682
"*Death*/Muerta" (Mora), **Supp. XIII:** 228
Death Notebooks, The (Sexton), **Supp. II Part 2:** 691, 694, 695
"Death of a Jazz Musician" (W. J. Smith), **Supp. XIII:** 334
Death of a Kinsman, The (Taylor), **Supp. V:** 324, 326
"Death of an Old Seaman" (Hughes), **Retro. Supp. I:** 199
"Death of a Pig" (White), **Supp. I Part 2:** 665-668
Death of a Salesman (A. Miller), **I:** 81; **III:** 148, 149, 150, 153-154, 156, 157, 158, 159, 160, 163, 164, 166; **IV:** 389; **Supp. IV Part 1:** 359; **Supp. XIV:** 102, 239, 254, 255;

Supp. XV: 205
"Death of a Soldier, The" (Stevens), **Retro. Supp. I:** 299, 312. *see also* "Lettres d'un Soldat" (Stevens)
"Death of a Soldier, The" (Wilson), **IV:** 427, 445
"Death of a Toad" (Wilbur), **Supp. III Part 2:** 550
"Death of a Traveling Salesman" (Welty), **IV:** 261; **Retro. Supp. I:** 344
"Death of a Young Son by Drowning" (Atwood), **Supp. XIII:** 33
Death of Bessie Smith, The (Albee), **I:** 76-77, 92
Death of Billy the Kid, The (Vidal), **Supp. IV Part 2:** 683
Death of Cock Robin, The (Snodgrass), **Supp. VI:** 315, **317-319**, 324
"Death of General Wolfe, The" (Paine), **Supp. I Part 2:** 504
"Death of Halpin Frayser, The" (Bierce), **I:** 205
"Death of Justina, The" (Cheever), **Supp. I Part 1:** 184-185
Death of Life, The (Barnes), **Supp. III Part 1:** 34
Death of Malcolm X, The (Baraka), **Supp. II Part 1:** 47
"Death of Marilyn Monroe, The" (Olds), **Supp. X:** 205
"Death of Me, The" (Malamud), **Supp. I Part 2:** 437
"Death of Slavery, The" (Bryant), **Supp. I Part 1:** 168-169
"Death of St. Narcissus, The" (Eliot), **Retro. Supp. I:** 291
"Death of the Ball Turret Gunner, The" (Jarrell), **II:** 369-370, 372, 374, 375, 376, 378
"Death of the Fathers, The" (Sexton), **Supp. II Part 2:** 692
"Death of the Flowers, The" (Bryant), **Supp. I Part 1:** 170
Death of the Fox (Garrett), **Supp. VII:** 99, 101-104, 108
"Death of the Hired Man, The" (Frost), **III:** 523; **Retro. Supp. I:** 121, 128; **Supp. IX:** 261
Death of the Kapowsin Tavern (Hugo), **Supp. VI:** 133-135
"Death of the Kapowsin Tavern" (Hugo), **Supp. VI:** 137, 141
"Death of the Lyric, The: The Achievement of Louis Simpson" (Jarman and McDowell), **Supp. IX:** 266, 270, 276
"Death of Venus, The" (Creeley), **Supp. IV Part 1:** 143, 144-145
"Death on All Fronts" (Ginsberg),
Supp. II Part 1: 326
"Deaths" (Dunn), **Supp. XI:** 147
"Death Sauntering About" (Hecht), **Supp. X:** 72
Deaths for the Ladies (and Other Disasters) (Mailer), **Retro. Supp. II:** 203
Death's Jest-Book (Beddoes), **Retro. Supp. I:** 285
Death Song (McGrath), **Supp. X:** 127
"Death the Carnival Barker" (Hecht), **Supp. X:** 72
"Death the Film Director" (Hecht), **Supp. X:** 72
"Death the Judge" (Hecht), **Supp. X:** 72
"Death the Mexican Revolutionary" (Hecht), **Supp. X:** 72
"Death the Oxford Don" (Hecht), **Supp. X:** 72
"Death the Painter" (Hecht), **Supp. X:** 72
Death the Proud Brother (Wolfe), **IV:** 456
"Death to Van Gogh's Ear!" (Ginsberg), **Supp. II Part 1:** 320, 322, 323
"Death Warmed Over!" (Bradbury), **Supp. IV Part 1:** 104-105, 112
Débâcle, La (Zola), **III:** 316
"Debate with the Rabbi" (Nemerov), **III:** 272
Debeljak, Aleš, **Supp. VIII:** 272
De Bellis, Jack, **Supp. I Part 1:** 366, 368, 372
DeBoer-Langworthy, Carol, **Supp. XVII:** 98, 99, 100
De Bosis, Lauro, **IV:** 372
"Debriefing" (Sontag), **Supp. III Part 2:** 468-470
Debs, Eugene, **I:** 483, 493; **III:** 580, 581; **Supp. I Part 2:** 524; **Supp. IX:** 1, 15
Debt to Pleasure, The (Lanchester), **Retro. Supp. I:** 278
Debussy, Claude, **Retro. Supp. II:** 266; **Supp. XIII:** 44
Decameron (Boccaccio), **III:** 283, 411; **Supp. IX:** 215
"Deceased" (Hughes), **Retro. Supp. I:** 208
"December" (Oliver), **Supp. VII:** 245
"December 1, 1994" (Stern), **Supp. IX:** 299
"December Eclogue" (Winters), **Supp. II Part 2:** 794
Deception (P. Roth), **Retro. Supp. II:** 291; **Supp. III Part 2:** 426-427
"Deceptions" (Dobyns), **Supp. XIII:** 77

De Chiara, Ann. *See* Malamud, Mrs. Bernard (Ann de Chiara)
De Chirico, Giorgio, **Supp. XIII:** 317
"Decided Loss, A" (Poe), **II:** 411
"Decisions to Disappear" (Dunn), **Supp. XI:** 144
"Decisive Moment, The" (Auster), **Supp. XIV:** 292
Decker, James A., **Supp. III Part 2:** 621
Declaration of Gentlemen and Merchants and Inhabitants of Boston, and the Country Adjacent, A (Mather), **Supp. II Part 2:** 450
"Declaration of Paris, The" (Adams), **I:** 4
Declaration of the Rights of Man and the Citizen, **Supp. I Part 2:** 513, 519
Declaration of Universal Peace and Liberty (Paine), **Supp. I Part 2:** 512
Decline and Fall (Waugh), **Supp. I Part 2:** 607; **Supp. XV:** 142
Decline and Fall of the English System of Finance, The (Paine), **Supp. I Part 2:** 518
Decline and Fall of the Roman Empire, The (Gibbons), **Supp. III Part 2:** 629
"Decline of Book Reviewing, The" (Hardwick), **Supp. III Part 1:** 201-202
Decline of the West, The (Spengler), **I:** 270; **IV:** 125
Deconstructing Harry (film; Allen), **Supp. XV:** 12, 13
"Décor" (X. J. Kennedy), **Supp. XV:** 171
"Decoration Day" (Jewett), **II:** 412; **Retro. Supp. II:** 138
Decoration of Houses, The (Wharton and Codman), **IV:** 308; **Retro. Supp. I:** 362, 363-364, 366
"Decoy" (Ashbery), **Supp. III Part 1:** 13-14
"De Daumier-Smith's Blue Period" (Salinger), **III:** 560-561
"Dedication and Household Map" (Erdrich), **Supp. IV Part 1:** 272
"Dedication Day" (Agee), **I:** 34
"Dedication for a Book" (Hay), **Supp. XIV:** 125
"Dedication for a Book of Criticism" (Winters), **Supp. II Part 2:** 801
"Dedication in Postscript, A" (Winters), **Supp. II Part 2:** 801
Dedications and Other Darkhorses (Komunyakaa), **Supp. XIII:** 112, **113-114**

"Dedication to Hunger" (Glück), **Supp. V:** 83

"Dedication to My Wife, A" (Eliot), **I:** 583

Dee, Ruby, **Supp. IV Part 1:** 362

Deeds of Utmost Kindness (Gander), **Supp. XV:** 340

"Deep Breath at Dawn, A" (Hecht), **Supp. X:** 58

Deeper into Movies: The Essential Kael Collection from '69 to '72 (Kael), **Supp. IX:** 253

"Deeper Wisdom, The" (Hay), **Supp. XIV:** 129

Deep Green Sea (R. O. Butler), **Supp. XII:** 62, **74**

Deephaven (Jewett), **II:** 398-399, 400, 401, 410, 411; **Retro. Supp. II:** 133, 134, 135, 136, 137, 138, 140, 141, 143, 144

"Deep Sight and Rescue Missions" (Bambara), **Supp. XI:** 18-19

Deep Sightings and Rescue Missions: Fiction, Essays, and Conversations (Bambara), **Supp. XI:** 1, 3, **14-20**

Deep Sleep, The (Morris), **III:** 224-225

Deep South (Caldwell), **I:** 305, 309, 310

Deepstep Come Shining (Wright), **Supp. XV:** 337, 341, 344, **349-350**, 351, 353

"Deep Water" (Marquand), **III:** 56

"Deep Woods" (Nemerov), **III:** 272-273, 275

"Deer at Providencia, The" (Dillard), **Supp. VI:** 28, 32

"Deer Dancer" (Harjo), **Supp. XII:** 224-225

"Deer Ghost" (Harjo), **Supp. XII:** 225

Deer Park, The (Mailer), **I:** 292; **III:** 27, 31-33, 35-36, 37, 39, 40, 42, 43, 44; **Retro. Supp. II:** 200-202, 205, 207, 211

Deer Park, The: A Play (Mailer), **Retro. Supp. II:** 205

Deer Pasture, The (Bass), **Supp. XVI:** 15, 16, 23

Deerslayer, The (Cooper), **I:** 341, 349, 350, 355; **Supp. I Part 1:** 251

"Defence of Poesy, The" (Sidney), **Supp. V:** 250

"Defence of Poetry" (Longfellow), **II:** 493-494

"Defender of the Faith" (P. Roth), **Retro. Supp. II:** 281; **Supp. III Part 2:** 404, 407, 420

"Defenestration in Prague" (Matthews), **Supp. IX:** 168

Defenestration of Prague (Howe), **Supp. IV Part 2:** 419, 426, 429-430

Defense, The (Nabokov), **III:** 251-252; **Retro. Supp. I:** 266, 268, **270-272**

"Defense of Poetry" (Francis), **Supp. IX:** 83-84

Defiant Ones, The (film), **Supp. I Part 1:** 67

"Defining the Age" (Davis), **Supp. IV Part 1:** 64

"Definition" (Ammons), **Supp. VII:** 28

Defoe, Daniel, **I:** 204; **II:** 104, 105, 159, 304-305; **III:** 113, 423; **IV:** 180; **Supp. I Part 2:** 523; **Supp. V:** 127

De Forest, John William, **II:** 275, 280, 288, 289; **IV:** 350

Degas, Brian, **Supp. XI:** 307

Degler, Carl, **Supp. I Part 2:** 496

"Degrees of Fidelity" (Dunn), **Supp. XI:** 148, 156

Deguy, Michel, **Supp. XV:** 178

De Haven, Tom, **Supp. XI:** 39; **Supp. XII:** 338-339

Deitch, Joseph, **Supp. VIII:** 125

"Dejection" (Coleridge), **II:** 97

DeJong, Constance, **Supp. XII:** 4

DeJong, David Cornel, **I:** 35

Dekker, Thomas, **Supp. XVII:** 232

de Kooning, Willem, **Supp. XII:** 198; **Supp. XV:** 177, 178

Delacroix, Henri, **I:** 227

De La Mare, Walter, **III:** 429; **Supp. II Part 1:** 4; **Supp. XVII:** 69

Delamotte, Eugenia C., **Supp. XI:** 279

De Lancey, James, **I:** 338

De Lancey, Mrs. James (Anne Heathcote), **I:** 338

De Lancey, Susan A. *See* Cooper, Mrs. James Fenimore

De Lancey, William Heathcote, **I:** 338, 353

Delano, Amasa, **III:** 90

Delattre, Roland A., **I:** 558

De Laurentiis, Dino, **Supp. XI:** 170, 307

De la Valdéne, Guy, **Supp. VIII:** 40, 42

De l'éducation d'un homme sauvage (Itard), **Supp. I Part 2:** 564

"Delft" (Goldbarth), **Supp. XII:** 189

Delft: An Essay-Poem (Goldbarth), **Supp. XII:** 187

Delicate Balance, A (Albee), **I:** 86-89, 91, 93, 94

Delicate Balance, The (Hay), **Supp. XIV:** 121, 122, 124, 129, 133-134

"Delicate Balance, The" (Hay), **Supp. XIV:** 122

"Delicate Prey, The" (Bowles), **Supp. IV Part 1:** 86

Delicate Prey and Other Stories, The (Bowles), **Supp. IV Part 1:** 86-87

Délie (Scève), **Supp. III Part 1:** 11

DeLillo, Don, **Retro. Supp. I:** 278; **Retro. Supp. II:** 279; **Supp. VI:** **1-18**; **Supp. IX:** 212; **Supp. XI:** 68; **Supp. XII:** 21, 152; **Supp. XVII:** 183

DeLisle, Anne, **Supp. VIII:** 175

Deliverance (Dickey), **Supp. IV Part 1:** 176, 186-188, 190; **Supp. X:** 30

Deliverance, The (Glasgow), **II:** 175, 176, 177-178, 181

"Delivering" (Dubus), **Supp. VII:** 87

Dell, Floyd, **I:** 103, 105; **Supp. I Part 2:** 379; **Supp. XV:** 295; **Supp. XVII:** 96

Della Francesca, Piero, **Supp. XV:** 262

"Della Primavera Trasportata al Morale" (W. C. Williams), **Retro. Supp. I:** 419, 422

DeLoria, Philip J., **Supp. XIV:** 306

Deloria, Vine, Jr., **Supp. IV Part 1:** 323; **Supp. IV Part 2:** 504

"Delta Autumn" (Faulkner), **II:** 71

"Delta Factor, The" (Percy), **Supp. III Part 1:** 386

Delta of Venus: Erotica (Nin), **Supp. X:** 192, 195

Delta Wedding (Welty), **IV:** 261, 268-271, 273, 281; **Retro. Supp. I:** 349-350, 351

Delusions (Berryman), **I:** 170

De Man, Paul, **Supp. XVII:** 70

de Man, Paul, **Retro. Supp. I:** 67

DeMarinis, Rick, **Supp. XIV:** 22

DeMars, James, **Supp. IV Part 2:** 552

Dembo, L. S., **I:** 386, 391, 396, 397, 398, 402; **III:** 478; **Supp. I Part 1:** 272; **Supp. XIV:** 277, 282, 288, 290

"Dementia Translucida" (Bierds), **Supp. XVII:** 33

Demetrakopoulous, Stephanie A., **Supp. IV Part 1:** 12

DeMille, Cecil B., **Supp. IV Part 2:** 520; **Supp. XV:** 42

Demme, Jonathan, **Supp. V:** 14

Democracy (Adams), **I:** 9-10, 20; **Supp. IV Part 1:** 208

Democracy (Didion), **Supp. IV Part 1:** 198, 208-210

"Democracy" (Lowell), **Supp. I Part 2:** 419

Democracy and Education (Dewey), **I:** 232

Democracy and Other Addresses (Lowell), **Supp. I Part 2:** 407

Democracy and Social Ethics (Addams), **Supp. I Part 1:** 8-11

Democracy in America (Tocqueville),

Retro. Supp. I: 235; Supp. XIV:306
Democratic Vistas (Whitman), IV: 333, 336, 348-349, 351, 469; Retro. Supp. I: 408; Supp. I Part 2: 456
Democritus, I: 480-481; II: 157; III: 606; Retro. Supp. I: 247
"Demon Lover, The" (Rich), Supp. I Part 2: 556
"Demonstrators, The" (Welty), IV: 280; Retro. Supp. I: 355
DeMott, Benjamin, Supp. IV Part 1: 35; Supp. V: 123; Supp. XIII: 95; Supp. XIV:106
DeMott, Robert, Supp. VIII: 40, 41
Demuth, Charles, IV: 404; Retro. Supp. I: 412, 430
"Demystified Zone" (Paley), Supp. VI: 227
Denmark Vesey (opera) (Bowles), Supp. IV Part 1: 83
Denney, Joseph Villiers, Supp. I Part 2: 605
Denney, Reuel, Supp. XII: 121
Dennie, Joseph, II: 298; Supp. I Part 1: 125
Denniston, Dorothy Hamer, Supp. XI: 276, 277
"Den of Lions" (Plath), Retro. Supp. II: 242
"Dental Assistant, The" (Simpson), Supp. IX: 280
Den Uyl, Douglas, Supp. IV Part 2: 528, 530
"Deodand, The" (Hecht), Supp. X: 65
"Departing" (Cameron), Supp. XII: 81
"Departure" (Glück), Supp. V: 89
"Departure" (Plath), Supp. I Part 2: 537
"Departure, The" (Freneau), Supp. II Part 1: 264
"Departure from Hydra, The" (Koch), Supp. XV: 180-181
Departures (Justice), Supp. VII: 124-127
Departures and Arrivals (Shields), Supp. VII: 320, 322
"Depressed by a Book of Bad Poetry, I Walk Toward an Unused Pasture and Invite the Insects to Join Me" (Wright), Supp. III Part 2: 600
"Depressed Person, The" (Wallace), Supp. X: 309
"Depression Days" (Mora), Supp. XIII: 224-225
De Puy, John, Supp. XIII: 12
D'Erasmo, Stacey, Supp. IX: 121
De Reilhe, Catherine, Supp. I Part 1: 202
De Rerum Natura (Lucretius), II: 162

"De Rerum Virtute" (Jeffers), Supp. II Part 2: 424
De Rioja, Francisco, Supp. I Part 1: 166
"Derivative Sport in Tornado Alley" (Wallace), Supp. X: 314
Derleth, August, Supp. I Part 2: 465, 472
Deronda, Daniel, II: 179
Derrida, Jacques, Supp. IV Part 1: 45; Supp. XV: 215, 224; Supp. XVI:285, 288
Deruddere, Dominique, Supp. XI: 173
Der Wilde Jäger (Bürger), II: 306
Derzhavin, Gavrila Romanovich, Supp. VIII: 27
Desai, Anita, Supp. XVI:156, 157, 158
De Santis, Christopher, Retro. Supp. I: 194
Descartes, René, I: 255; III: 618-619; IV: 133
Descendents, The (Glasgow), II: 173, 174-175, 176
Descending Figure (Glück), Supp. V: 83-84
"Descending Theology: Christ Human" (Karr), Supp. XI: 251
"Descending Theology: The Garden" (Karr), Supp. XI: 251
"Descent, The" (W. C. Williams), Retro. Supp. I: 428, 429
"Descent from the Cross" (Eliot), Retro. Supp. I: 57, 58
"Descent in the Maelström, A" (Poe), Retro. Supp. II: 274
"Descent into Proselito" (Knowles), Supp. XII: 237
"Descent into the Maelström, A" (Poe), III: 411, 414, 416, 424
Descent of Man (Boyle), Supp. VIII: 1, 12-13
"Descent of Man" (Boyle), Supp. VIII: 14
Descent of Man, The (Darwin), Supp. XIV:192
Descent of Man, The (Wharton), IV: 311; Retro. Supp. I: 367
Descent of Man and Other Stories, The (Wharton), Retro. Supp. I: 367
Descent of Winter, The (W. C. Williams), Retro. Supp. I: 419, 428
De Schloezer, Doris, III: 474
"Description" (Doty), Supp. XI: 126
"Description of the great Bones dug up at Clavarack on the Banks of Hudsons River A.D. 1705, The" (Taylor), IV: 163, 164
"Description without Place" (Stevens), Retro. Supp. I: 422

"Desert" (Hughes), Retro. Supp. I: 207
"Deserted Cabin" (Haines), Supp. XII: 203
Deserted Village, The (Goldsmith), II: 304
Desert Is My Mother, The/El desierto es mi madre (Mora), Supp. XIII: 214, 221
Desert Music, The (W. C. Williams), IV: 422; Retro. Supp. I: 428, 429
"Desert Music, The" (W. C. Williams), Retro. Supp. I: 428, 429
"Desert Places" (Frost), II: 159; Retro. Supp. I: 121, 123, 129, 138, 299; Supp. XIV:229
Desert Rose, The (McMurtry), Supp. V: 225, 231
Desert Solitaire (Abbey), Supp. X: 30; Supp. XIII: 7-8, 12; Supp. XIV:177, 179
"Design" (Frost), II: 158, 163; Retro. Supp. I: 121, 126, 138, 139; Supp. IX: 81; Supp. XVII: 132
"Designated National Park, A" (Ortiz), Supp. IV Part 2: 509
"Designs on a Point of View" (Everwine), Supp. XV: 76
Des Imagistes (Pound), II: 513; Supp. I Part 1: 257, 261, 262
"Desire" (Beattie), Supp. V: 29
Desire (Bidart), Supp. XV: 32-34, 35
"Desire" (Everwine), Supp. XV: 85
"Désirée's Baby" (Chopin), Retro. Supp. II: 64, 65; Supp. I Part 1: 213-215
Desire under the Elms (O'Neill), III: 387, 390
"Desolate Field, The" (W. C. Williams), Retro. Supp. I: 418
"Desolation, A" (Ginsberg), Supp. II Part 1: 313
Desolation Angels (Kerouac), Supp. III Part 1: 218, 225, 230
"Desolation Is a Delicate Thing" (Wylie), Supp. I Part 2: 729
Despair (Nabokov), Retro. Supp. I: 270, 274
"Despisals" (Rukeyser), Supp. VI: 282
Des Pres, Terrence, Supp. X: 113, 120, 124
"Destiny and the Lieutenant" (McCoy), Supp. XIII: 171
"Destruction of Kreshev, The" (Singer), IV: 13; Retro. Supp. II: 307
Destruction of the European Jews, The (Hilberg), Supp. V: 267
"Destruction of the Goetheanum, The" (Salter), Supp. IX: 257
"Destruction of the Long Branch, The"

(Pinsky), **Supp. VI:** 239, 240, 243-244, 245, 247, 250
Destructive Element, The (Spender), **Retro. Supp. I:** 216
"Detail & Parody for the poem 'Paterson'" (W. C. Williams), **Retro. Supp. I:** 424
Detmold, John, **Supp. I Part 2:** 670
Detour at Night (Endore), **Supp. XVII:** 64
Deuce, The (R. O. Butler), **Supp. XII:** 62, **69-70,** 72
Deus Lo Volt! (Connell), **Supp. XIV:** 80, 81, 95
Deuteronomy (biblical book), **II:** 166
Deutsch, Andre, **Supp. XI:** 297, 301
Deutsch, Babette, **Supp. I Part 1:** 328, 341
Deutsch, Michel, **Supp. IV Part 1:** 104
Deutsche, Babette, **Supp. XV:** 305
"Devaluation Blues: Ruminations on Black Families in Crisis" (Coleman), **Supp. XI:** 87
Devane, William, **Supp. XI:** 234
"Development of the Literary West" (Chopin), **Retro. Supp. II:** 72
"Development of the Modern English Novel, The" (Lanier), **Supp. I Part 1:** 370-371
DeVeriante (Herbert of Cherbury), **II:** 108
"Devil and Daniel Webster, The" (Benét), **III:** 22; **Supp. XI:** 45-46, 47, 50-51, 52
Devil and Daniel Webster and Other Writings, The (Benét), **Supp. XI:** 48
"Devil and Tom Walker, The" (Irving), **II:** 309-310
Devil At Large, The: Erica Jong on Henry Miller (Jong), **Supp. V:** 115, 131
Devil-Doll, The (film, Browning), **Supp. XVII:** 58-59
Devil Finds Work, The (Baldwin), **Retro. Supp. II:** 14; **Supp. I Part 1:** 48, 52, 66-67
Devil in a Blue Dress (Mosley), **Supp. XIII:** 237, 239
"Devil in Manuscript, The" (Hawthorne), **II:** 226; **Retro. Supp. I:** 150-151
Devil in Paradise, A (H. Miller), **III:** 190
"Devil in the Belfry, The" (Poe), **III:** 425; **Retro. Supp. II:** 273
"Devil Is a Busy Man, The" (Wallace), **Supp. X:** 309
Devil's Dictionary, The (Bierce), **I:** 196, 197, 205, 208, 209, 210
Devil's Stocking, The (Algren), **Supp. IX:** 5, 16
Devil's Tour, The (Karr), **Supp. XI:** 240, **242-244**
Devil Tree, The (Kosinski), **Supp. VII:** 215, 222, 223
"Devising" (Ammons), **Supp. VII:** 28
De Voto, Bernard, **I:** 247, 248; **II:** 446; **Supp. IV Part 2:** 599, 601
"Devout Meditation in Memory of Adolph Eichmann, A" (Merton), **Supp. VIII:** 198, 203
De Vries, Peter, **Supp. I Part 2:** 604
Dewberry, Elizabeth, **Supp. XII:** 62, 72
Dewey, John, **I:** 214, 224, 228, 232, 233, 266, 267; **II:** 20, 27, 34, 229, 361; **III:** 112, 294-295, 296, 303, 309-310, 599, 605; **IV:** 27, 429; **Supp. I Part 1:** 3, 5, 7, 10, 11, 12, 24; **Supp. I Part 2:** 493, 641, 647, 677; **Supp. V:** 290; **Supp. IX:** 179; **Supp. XIV:** 3; **Supp. XV:** 41
Dewey, Joseph, **Supp. IX:** 210
Dewey, Thomas, **IV:** 161
Dexter, Peter, **Supp. XIV:** 221
De Young, Charles, **I:** 194
Dhairyam, Sagari, **Supp. IV Part 1:** 329, 330
Dharma Bums, The (Kerouac), **Supp. III Part 1:** 230, 231; **Supp. VIII:** 289, 305
D'Houdetot, Madame, **Supp. I Part 1:** 250
"Diabetes" (Dickey), **Supp. IV Part 1:** 182
Diaghilev, Sergei, **Supp. I Part 1:** 257
Dial (publication), **I:** 58, 109, 115, 116, 215, 231, 233, 245, 261, 384, 429; **II:** 8, 430; **III:** 194, 470, 471, 485; **IV:** 122, 171, 427; **Retro. Supp. I:** 58; **Retro. Supp. II:** 78; **Supp. I Part 2:** 642, 643, 647; **Supp. II Part 1:** 168, 279, 291; **Supp. II Part 2:** 474; **Supp. III Part 2:** 611
"Dialectics of Love, The" (McGrath), **Supp. X:** 116
"Dialogue" (Rich), **Supp. I Part 2:** 560
Dialogue, A (Baldwin and Giovanni), **Supp. I Part 1:** 66
"Dialogue: William Harvey; Joan of Arc" (Goldbarth), **Supp. XII:** 178
"Dialogue Between Franklin and the Gout" (Franklin), **II:** 121
"Dialogue Between General Wolfe and General Gage in a Wood near Boston, A" (Paine), **Supp. I Part 2:** 504
"Dialogue between Old England and New" (Bradstreet), **Supp. I Part 1:** 105-106, 110-111, 116
"Dialogue between the Writer and a Maypole Dresser, A" (Taylor), **IV:** 155
Dialogues (Bush, ed.), **III:** 4
Dialogues in Limbo (Santayana), **III:** 606
"Diamond as Big as the Ritz, The" (Fitzgerald), **II:** 88-89
Diamond Cutters and Other Poems, The (Rich), **Supp. I Part 2:** 551, 552, 553
"Diamond Guitar, A" (Capote), **Supp. III Part 1:** 124
"Diana and Persis" (Alcott), **Supp. I Part 1:** 32, 41
Diaries of Charlotte Perkins Gilman (Knight, ed.), **Supp. XI:** 201
Diary of a Chambermaid, The (film; Renoir), **Supp. XVI:** 193
Diary of Anaïs Nin, The (1931-1974), **Supp. X:** 181, 185-189, 191, 192, 193, 195
Diary of a Rapist, The: A Novel (Connell), **Supp. XIV:** 80, 82, 94
Diary of a Yuppie (Auchincloss), **Supp. IV Part 1:** 31, 32-33
Diary of "Helena Morley," The (Bishop, trans.), **Retro. Supp. II:** 45, 51; **Supp. I Part 1:** 92
Díaz del Castillo, Bernál, **III:** 13, 14
Dick, Philip K., **Supp. XVI:** 123
Dickens, Charles, **I:** 152, 198, 505; **II:** 98, 179, 186, 192, 271, 273-274, 288, 290, 297, 301, 307, 316, 322, 559, 561, 563, 577, 582; **III:** 146, 247, 325, 368, 411, 421, 426, 572, 577, 613-614, 616; **IV:** 21, 192, 194, 211, 429; **Retro. Supp. I:** 33, 91, 218; **Retro. Supp. II:** 204; **Supp. I Part 1:** 13, 34, 35, 36, 41, 49; **Supp. I Part 2:** 409, 523, 579, 590, 622, 675; **Supp. IV Part 1:** 293, 300, 341; **Supp. IV Part 2:** 464; **Supp. VIII:** 180; **Supp. IX:** 246; **Supp. XI:** 277; **Supp. XII:** 335, 337; **Supp. XIII:** 233; **Supp. XV:** 62; **Supp. XVI:** 63, 65-66, 72-73, 202
Dickey, James, **I:** 29, 535; **III:** 268; **Retro. Supp. II:** 233; **Supp. III Part 1:** 354; **Supp. III Part 2:** 541, 597; **Supp. IV Part 1:** **175-194;** **Supp. V:** 333; **Supp. X:** 30; **Supp. XI:** 312, 317; **Supp. XV:** 115, 348
Dick Gibson Show, The (Elkin), **Supp. VI:** 42, **48-49**
Dickie, Margaret, **Retro. Supp. II:** 53, 84
Dickinson, Donald, **Retro. Supp. I:** 206, 212
Dickinson, Edward, **I:** 451-452, 453

Dickinson, Emily, **I:** 384, 419, 433, **451-473; II:** 272, 276, 277, 530; **III:** 19, 194, 196, 214, 493, 505, 508, 556, 572, 576; **IV:** 134, 135, 331, 444; **Retro. Supp. I: 25-50; Retro. Supp. II:** 39, 40, 43, 45, 50, 76, 134, 155, 170; **Supp. I Part 1:** 29, 79, 188, 372; **Supp. I Part 2:** 375, 546, 609, 682, 691; **Supp. II Part 1:** 4; **Supp. III Part 1:** 63; **Supp. III Part 2:** 600, 622; **Supp. IV Part 1:** 31, 257; **Supp. IV Part 2:** 434, 637, 641, 643; **Supp. V:** 79, 140, 332, 335; **Supp. VIII:** 95, 104, 106, 108, 198, 205, 272; **Supp. IX:** 37, 38, 53, 87, 90; **Supp. XII:** 226; **Supp. XIII:** 153, 339; **Supp. XIV:**45, 127-128, 133, 261, 284; **Supp. XV:** 287, 303, 309; **Supp. XVI:**288; **Supp. XVII:** 71, 73, 74, 75, 132

Dickinson, Gilbert, **I:** 469

Dickinson, Goldsworthy Lowes, **Supp. XIV:**336

Dickinson, Lavinia Norcross, **I:** 451, 453, 462, 470

Dickinson, Mrs. Edward, **I:** 451, 453

Dickinson, Mrs. William A. (Susan Gilbert), **I:** 452, 453, 456, 469, 470

Dickinson, William Austin, **I:** 451, 453, 469

Dickinson and the Strategies of Reticence (Dobson), **Retro. Supp. I:** 29, 42

Dickson, Helen. *See* Blackmur, Helen Dickson

Dickstein, Morris, **Supp. XIII:** 106

"Dick Whittington and His Cat," **Supp. I Part 2:** 656

"DICTATORSHIP OF THE PROLETARIAT, THE" (Baraka), **Supp. II Part 1:** 54

Dictionary of Literary Biography (Kibler, ed.), **Supp. IX:** 94, 109; **Supp. XI:** 297

Dictionary of Literary Biography (Knight), **Supp. XIV:**144

Dictionary of Literary Biography (Sicher, ed.), **Supp. XVII:** 41

Dictionary of Modern English Usage, A (Fowler), **Supp. I Part 2:** 660

"Dictum: For a Masque of Deluge" (Merwin), **Supp. III Part 1:** 342-343

"Didactic Poem" (Levertov), **Supp. III Part 1:** 280

Diderot, Denis, **II:** 535; **IV:** 440; **Supp. XVI:**293; **Supp. XVII:** 145

Did I Ever Tell You How Lucky You Are? (Geisel), **Supp. XVI:**109

Didion, Joan, **Retro. Supp. I:** 116; **Retro. Supp. II:** 209; **Supp. I Part 1:** 196, 197; **Supp. III Part 1:** 302; **Supp. IV Part 1: 195-216; Supp. XI:** 221; **Supp. XII:** 307

Dido, **I:** 81

"Did You Ever Dream Lucky?" (Ellison), **Supp. II Part 1:** 246

"Die-Hard, The" (Benét), **Supp. XI:** 54-55, 56

Diehl, Digby, **Supp. IV Part 1:** 204

Dien Cai Dau (Komunyakaa), **Supp. XIII:** 121, **122-124,** 125, 131, 132

"Dies Irae" (Lowell), **II:** 553

Die Zeit Ohne Beispiel, (Goebbels), **III:** 560

Difference Engine, The (W. Gibson and B. Sterling), **Supp. XVI:**121, 124, **128-129**

Different Drummer, A (Larkin; film), **Supp. XI:** 20

Different Fleshes (Goldbarth), **Supp. XII:** 181-182, 188

Different Hours (Dunn), **Supp. XI:** 139, 142, 143, 155

Different Seasons (King), **Supp. V:** 148, 152

Different Ways to Pray (Nye), **Supp. XIII:** 274, 275, 277, 285, 287

"Different Ways to Pray" (Nye), **Supp. XIII:** 275

"Difficulties of a Statesman" (Eliot), **I:** 580

"Difficulties of Modernism and the Modernism of Difficulty" (Poirier), **Supp. II Part 1:** 136

Diff'rent (O'Neill), **III:** 389

DiGaetani, John L., **Supp. XIII:** 200

"Digging" (Sanders), **Supp. XVI:**272

"Digging in the Garden of Age I Uncover a Live Root" (Swenson), **Supp. IV Part 2:** 649

Diggins, John P., **Supp. I Part 2:** 650

"Dignity of Life, The" (C. Bly), **Supp. XVI:**34, 36-37

Digregorio, Charles, **Supp. XI:** 326

"Dilemma of Determinism, The" (James), **II:** 347-348, 352

"Dilemma of the Negro Writer, The" (speech, C. Himes), **Supp. XVI:**140

"Dilettante, The" (Wharton), **IV:** 311, 313

"Dilettante, The: A Modern Type" (Dunbar), **Supp. II Part 1:** 199

Dillard, Annie, **Supp. VI: 19-39; Supp. VIII:** 272; **Supp. X:** 31; **Supp. XIII:** 154

Dillard, R. H. W., **Supp. XII:** 16

Dillman, Bradford, **III:** 403; **Supp. XII:** 241

Dillon, Brian, **Supp. X:** 209

Dillon, George, **III:** 141; **Supp. III Part 2:** 621

Dillon, Millicent, **Supp. IV Part 1:** 95

Dilsaver, Paul, **Supp. XIII:** 112

Dilthey, Wilhelm, **I:** 58

Dime-Store Alchemy: The Art of Joseph Cornell, **Supp. VIII:** 272

"Diminuendo" (Dunn), **Supp. XI:** 152-153

"Dimout in Harlem" (Hughes), **Supp. I Part 1:** 333

Dinesen, Isak, **IV:** 279; **Supp. VIII:** 171; **Supp. XVI:**250

Dining Room, The (Gurney), **Supp. V:** 105-106

"Dinner at ———, A" (O. Henry), **Supp. II Part 1:** 402

"Dinner at Sir Nigel's" (Bowles), **Supp. IV Part 1:** 94

Dinner at the Homesick Restaurant (Tyler), **Supp. IV Part 2:** 657, 667-668

"Dinner at Uncle Borris's" (Simic), **Supp. VIII:** 272

Dinner Bridge (Lardner), **II:** 435

Dinosaur Tales (Bradbury), **Supp. IV Part 1:** 103

"Diogenes Invents a Game" (Karr), **Supp. XI:** 240-241

"Diogenes Tries to Forget" (Karr), **Supp. XI:** 241

Dionysis in Doubt (Robinson), **III:** 510

Diop, Birago, **Supp. IV Part 1:** 16

Diop, David, **Supp. IV Part 1:** 16

Di Piero, W. S., **Supp. XVII:** 241

Di Prima, Diane, **Supp. III Part 1:** 30; **Supp. XIV:**125, 144, 148, 150

Direction of Poetry, The: An Anthology of Rhymed and Metered Verse Written in the English Language since 1975 (Richman, ed.), **Supp. XV:** 250, 251

Direction of Poetry, The: Rhymed and Metered Verse Written in the English Language since 1975 (Richman), **Supp. XI:** 249

"Directive" (Bishop), **Retro. Supp. II:** 42

"Directive" (Frost), **III:** 287; **Retro. Supp. I:** 140; **Supp. VIII:** 32, 33

"Dire Cure" (Matthews), **Supp. IX:** 168

"Dirge" (Dunbar), **Supp. II Part 1:** 199

"Dirge without Music" (Millay), **III:** 126

"Dirt" (Salter), **Supp. IX:** 257, 260, 261

"Dirt and Desire: Essay on the Phe-

nomenology of Female Pollution in Antiquity" (Carson), **Supp. XII:** 111
Dirty Dingus Magee (film), **Supp. XVII:** 139
"Dirty English Potatoes" (X. J. Kennedy), **Supp. XV:** 165
"Dirty Memories" (Olds), **Supp. X:** 211
Dirty Story (Shanley), **Supp. XIV:**316, 331
"Dirty Word, The" (Shapiro), **Supp. II Part 2:** 710
Disappearance of the Jews, The (Mamet), **Supp. XIV:**249-250, 250-251, 252, 254
Disappearances (Auster), **Supp. XII:** 23
"Disappearances" (Hogan), **Supp. IV Part 1:** 401
"Disappeared, The " (C. Baxter), **Supp. XVII:** 19
Disappearing Acts (McMillan), **Supp. XIII:** 182, 183, **188-189,** 192
Disappearing Ink: Poetry at the End of Print Culture (Gioia), **Supp. XV:** 112
"Disappointment, The" (Creeley), **Supp. IV Part 1:** 143
"Disappointment and Desire" (R. Bly), **Supp. IV Part 1:** 71
"Discards" (Baker), **Supp. XIII:** 53, 55-56
Discerning the Signs of the Times (Niebuhr), **III:** 300-301, 307-308
"Disciple of Bacon, The" (Epstein), **Supp. XII:** 163-164
"Discordants" (Aiken), **I:** 65
Discourse on Method (Descartes), **I:** 255
"Discourtesies" (Kirsch), **Supp. XV:** 341
"Discovering Theme and Structure in the Novel" (Schuster), **Supp. VIII:** 126
"Discovery" (Freneau), **Supp. II Part 1:** 258
"Discovery of the Madeiras, The" (Frost), **Retro. Supp. I:** 139
"Discovery of What It Means to Be an American, The" (Baldwin), **Supp. I Part 1:** 54-55
Discovery! The Search for Arabian Oil (Stegner), **Supp. IV Part 2:** 599
"Discrete Series" (Zukofsky), **Supp. III Part 2:** 616
"Discretions of Alcibiades" (Pinsky), **Supp. VI:** 241
"Disease, The" (Rukeyser), **Supp. VI:** 279
Disenchanted, The (Schulberg), **II:** 98; **Retro. Supp. I:** 113
Disenchantments: An Anthology of Modern Fairy Tale Poetry (Mieder), **Supp. XIV:**126
"Dish of Green Pears, A" (Ríos), **Supp. IV Part 2:** 552
"Disillusion and Dogma" (Untermeyer), **Supp. XV:** 306
Dismantling the Silence (Simic), **Supp. VIII: 273-274,** 275, 276
Disney, Walt, **III:** 275, 426
"Disney of My Mind" (Chabon), **Supp. XI:** 63
Dispatches (Herr), **Supp. XI:** 245
"Displaced Person, The" (O'Connor), **III:** 343-344, 350, 352, 356; **Retro. Supp. II:** 229, 232, 236
"Disposal" (Snodgrass), **Supp. VI:** 314
Dispossessed, The (Berryman), **I:** 170, 172, 173, 174, 175, 176, 178
"Disquieting Muses, The" (Plath), **Supp. I Part 2:** 538
Disraeli, Benjamin, **II:** 127
Dissent (Didion), **Supp. IV Part 1:** 208
"Dissenting Opinion on Kafka, A" (Wilson), **IV:** 437-438
Dissent in Three American Wars (Morison, Merk, and Freidel), **Supp. I Part 2:** 495
Dissertation on Liberty and Necessity, Pleasure and Pain, A (Franklin), **II:** 108
Dissertations on Government; the Affairs of the Bank: and Paper Money (Paine), **Supp. I Part 2:** 510
"Distance" (Carver), **Supp. III Part 1:** 146
"Distance" (Everwine), **Supp. XV:** 85
"Distance" (Paley), **Supp. VI:** 222
"Distance, The" (Karr), **Supp. XI:** 241
"Distance from the Sea, A" (Kees), **Supp. XV:** 147
"Distance Nowhere" (Hughes), **Retro. Supp. I:** 207
"Distant Episode, A" (Bowles), **Supp. IV Part 1:** 84-85, 86, 90
Distant Episode, A: The Selected Stories (Bowles), **Supp. IV Part 1:** 79
Distinguished Guest, The (Miller), **Supp. XII: 299-301**
Distortions (Beattie), **Supp. V:** 21, 23, 24, 25, 27
"Distrest Shepherdess, The" (Freneau), **Supp. II Part 1:** 258
District of Columbia (Dos Passos), **I:** 478, 489-490, 492
Disturber of the Peace (Manchester), **III:** 103
Disturbing the Peace (Yates), **Supp. XI:** 345, 346
"Diver, The" (Hayden), **Supp. II Part 1:** 368, 372, 373
"Divided Life of Jean Toomer, The" (Toomer), **Supp. III Part 2:** 488
Divina Commedia (Longfellow, trans.), **II:** 490, 492, 493
"Divine Collaborator" (Simic), **Supp. VIII:** 282
Divine Comedies (Merrill), **Supp. III Part 1:** 324, 329-332
Divine Comedy (Dante), **I:** 137, 265, 400, 446; **II:** 215, 335, 490, 492, 493; **III:** 13, 448, 453; **Supp. V:** 283, 331, 338, 345; **Supp. X:** 253; **Supp. XIV:**6
"Divine Image, The" (Blake), **Supp. V:** 257
Divine Pilgrim, The (Aiken), **I:** 50, 55
Divine Tragedy, The (Longfellow), **II:** 490, 500, 505, 506, 507; **Retro. Supp. II:** 165, 166
Divine Weekes and Workes (Sylvester, trans.), **Supp. I Part 1:** 104
Divine Weeks (Du Bartas), **IV:** 157-158
Diving into the Wreck: Poems 1971-1972 (Rich), **Supp. I Part 2:** 550, 559-565, 569; **Supp. XV:** 252
"Diving Past African Violets" (A. Finch), **Supp. XVII:** 72
Diving Rock on the Hudson, A (H. Roth), **Supp. IX:** 236, **237-238**
"Divinity in Its Fraying Fact, A" (Levis), **Supp. XI:** 271
"Divinity School Address" (Emerson), **II:** 12-13
"Divisions upon a Ground" (Hecht), **Supp. X:** 58
"Divorce" (Karr), **Supp. XI:** 244
Divorced in America: Marriage in an Age of Possibility (Epstein), **Supp. XIV:**113
Dix, Douglas Shields, **Supp. XII:** 14
Dixie City Jam (Burke), **Supp. XIV:**32
Dixon, Ivan, **Supp. IV Part 1:** 362
Dixon, Stephen, **Supp. XII: 139-158**
Dixon, Terrell F., **Supp. XVI:**21
Dixon, Thomas, Jr., **Supp. II Part 1:** 169, 171, 177
Djinn (Robbe-Grillet), **Supp. V:** 48
D'Lugoff, Burt, **Supp. IV Part 1:** 362, 370
Do, Lord, Remember Me (Garrett), **Supp. VII:** 98-100, 110
"Doaksology, The" (Wolfe), **IV:** 459
Dobie, J. Frank, **Supp. V:** 225; **Supp. XIII:** 227
Döblin, Alfred, **Supp. XV:** 137
Dobriansky, Lev, **Supp. I Part 2:** 648, 650

Dobson, Joanne, **Retro. Supp. I:** 29, 31, 42
Dobyns, Stephen, **Supp. XIII: 73-92**
"Docking at Palermo" (Hugo), **Supp. VI:** 137-138
"Dock Rats" (Moore), **III:** 213
"Dock-Witch, The" (Ozick), **Supp. V:** 262, 264
"Doc Mellhorn and the Pearly Gates" (Benét), **Supp. XI:** 55
"Doctor, The" (Dubus), **Supp. VII:** 80-81
"Doctor and the Doctor's Wife, The" (Hemingway), **II:** 248; **Retro. Supp. I:** 174, 175
Doctor Breen's Practice, a Novel (Howells), **I:** 282
Doctor Faustus (Mann), **III:** 283
Doctor Jazz (Carruth), **Supp. XVI:** 47, 59
"Doctor Jekyll" (Sontag), **Supp. III Part 2:** 469
"Doctor Leavis and the Moral Tradition" (Trilling), **Supp. III Part 2:** 512-513
Doctor Martino and Other Stories (Faulkner), **II:** 72; **Retro. Supp. I:** 84
"Doctor of the Heart, The" (Sexton), **Supp. II Part 2:** 692
Doctorow, E. L., **Retro. Supp. I:** 97; **Supp. III Part 2:** 590, 591; **Supp. IV Part 1: 217-240; Supp. V:** 45; **Supp. XVI:** 73; **Supp. XVII:** 183
Doctor Sax (Kerouac), **Supp. III Part 1:** 220-222, 224-227
Doctor Sleep (Bell), **Supp. X: 9-11**
"Doctors' Row" (Aiken), **I:** 67
Doctor's Son and Other Stories, The (O'Hara), **III:** 361
Doctor Stories, The (W. C. Williams), **Retro. Supp. I:** 424
"Doctor's Wife, The" (Ozick), **Supp. V:** 262, 265
Doctor Zhivago (Pasternak), **IV:** 434, 438, 443
"Documentary" (Simic), **Supp. VIII:** 282
Dodd, Elizabeth, **Supp. V:** 77
Dodd, Wayne, **Supp. IV Part 2:** 625
Dodson, Owen, **Supp. I Part 1:** 54
Dodsworth (Lewis), **II:** 442, 449-450, 453, 456
Doenitz, Karl, **Supp. I Part 2:** 491
Does Civilization Need Religion? (Niebuhr), **III:** 293-294
"Does 'Consciousness' Exist?" (James), **II:** 356
"Does Education Pay?" (Du Bois), **Supp. II Part 1:** 159

"Dog" (B. Kelly), **Supp. XVII:** 126
Dog (Shepard), **Supp. III Part 2:** 434
"Dog Act, The" (Komunyakaa), **Supp. XIII:** 114-115
"Dog and the Playlet, The" (O. Henry), **Supp. II Part 1:** 399
Dog Beneath the Skin, The (Auden), **Supp. II Part 1:** 10
"Dog Creek Mainline" (Wright), **Supp. V:** 340
"Dogfight" (W. Gibson and Swanwick), **Supp. XVI:** 128
Dog in the Manger, The (Vega; Merwin, trans.), **Supp. III Part 1:** 341, 347
Dogs Bark, but the Caravan Rolls On (Conroy), **Supp. XVI:** 63, 70, 74, **75-76**
Dogs Bark, The: Public People and Private Places (Capote), **Supp. III Part 1:** 120, 132
Dog Soldiers (Stone), **Supp. V:** 298, 299-301
"Dog Stories" (Prose), **Supp. XVI:** 256
Dog & the Fever, The (Quevedo), **Retro. Supp. I:** 423
"Dogtown Letters, The" (Jarman and R. McDowell), **Supp. XVII:** 111
"Dogwood, The" (Levertov), **Supp. III Part 1:** 276
"Dogwood Tree, The: A Boyhood" (Updike), **IV:** 218; **Retro. Supp. I:** 318, 319
Doig, Ivan, **Supp. XIV:** 227
"Doing Battle with the Wolf" (Coleman), **Supp. XI:** 87-88
Doing Literary Business: American Women Writers in the Nineteenth Century (Coultrap-McQuin), **Supp. XVI:** 85
Doings and Undoings (Podhoretz), **Supp. VIII: 236-237**
"Do-It-Yourself" (C. Baxter), **Supp. XVII:** 14-15
Dolan, Jill, **Supp. XV:** 327
"Dolce Far' Niente" (Humphrey), **Supp. IX:** 106
Dolci, Carlo, **III:** 474-475
"Dollhouse, The" (Haines), **Supp. XII:** 204
Dollmaker's Ghost, The (Levis), **Supp. XI:** 259, 260, **264-268**
Doll's House, A (Ibsen), **III:** 523; **IV:** 357; **Supp. XVI:** 182
Dolmetsch, Arnold, **III:** 464
Dolores Claiborne (King), **Supp. V:** 138, 141, 147, 148, 149-150, 152
"Dolph Heyliger" (Irving), **II:** 309
Dolphin, The (Lowell), **Retro. Supp. II:** 183, 186, 188, **190-191**; **Supp.**

XII: 253-254
"Dolphins" (Francis), **Supp. IX:** 83
Dome of Many-Coloured Class, A (Lowell), **II:** 515, 516-517
Domesday Book (Masters), **Supp. I Part 2:** 465, 466-469, 471, 473, 476
"Domestic Economy" (Gilman), **Supp. XI:** 206
"Domestic Manners" (Hardwick), **Supp. III Part 1:** 211
"Dominant White, The" (McKay), **Supp. X:** 134
Dominguez, Robert, **Supp. VIII:** 83
Dominique, Jean. *See* Closset, Marie
Donahue, Phil, **Supp. IV Part 2:** 526; **Supp. X:** 311
Doña Perfecta (Galdós), **II:** 290
Dong, Stella, **Supp. XVI:** 222
Don Juan (Byron), **Supp. XV:** 259
"DON JUAN IN HELL" (Baraka), **Supp. II Part 1:** 33
Donkey of God, The (Untermeyer), **Supp. XV:** 310
"Donna mi Prega" (Cavalcanti), **Supp. III Part 2:** 620, 621, 622
Donn-Byrne, Brian Oswald. *See* Byrne, Donn
Donne, John, **I:** 358-359, 384, 389, 522, 586; **II:** 254; **III:** 493; **IV:** 83, 88, 135, 141, 144, 145, 151, 156, 165, 331, 333; **Retro. Supp. II:** 76; **Supp. I Part 1:** 80, 364, 367; **Supp. I Part 2:** 421, 424, 467, 725, 726; **Supp. III Part 2:** 614, 619; **Supp. VIII:** 26, 33, 164; **Supp. IX:** 44; **Supp. XII:** 45, 159; **Supp. XIII:** 94, 130; **Supp. XIV:** 122; **Supp. XV:** 92, 251; **Supp. XVI:** 158, 204
Donne's Sermons: Selected Passages (L. P. Smith, ed.), **Supp. XIV:** 342
Donoghue, Denis, **I:** 537; **Supp. IV Part 1:** 39; **Supp. VIII:** 105, 189
Donohue, H. E. F., **Supp. IX:** 2, 3, 15, 16
Donovan, Josephine, **Retro. Supp. II:** 138, 139, 147
Don Quixote (Cervantes), **I:** 134; **II:** 291, 434; **III:** 113, 614; **Supp. I Part 2:** 422; **Supp. IX:** 94
Don Quixote: Which Was a Dream (Acker), **Supp. XII:** 5, **12-14**
Don't Ask (Levine), **Supp. V:** 178
Don't Ask Questions (Marquand), **III:** 58
Don't Bet on the Prince: Contemporary Feminist Fairy Tales in North America and England (Zipes), **Supp. XIV:** 126
Don't Drink the Water (Allen), **Supp. XV:** 3, 14

"Don't Shoot the Warthog" (Corso), **Supp. XII:** 123
"Don't Tell Mother" (Wasserstein), **Supp. XV:** 319
"Don't Worry About the Kids" (Neugeboren), **Supp. XVI:**226
Don't Worry About the Kids (Neugeboren), **Supp. XVI:**226
Don't You Want to Be Free? (Hughes), **Retro. Supp. I:** 203; **Supp. I Part 1:** 339
"Doodler, The" (Merrill), **Supp. III Part 1:** 321
Doolan, Moira, **Retro. Supp. II:** 247
Doolittle, Hilda (H. D.), **II:** 517, 520-521; **III:** 194, 195-196, 457, 465; **IV:** 404, 406; **Retro. Supp. I:** 288, 412, 413, 414, 415, 417; **Supp. I Part 1: 253-275; Supp. I Part 2:** 707; **Supp. III Part 1:** 48; **Supp. III Part 2:** 610; **Supp. IV Part 1:** 257; **Supp. V:** 79; **Supp. XV:** 43, 249, 301, 302; **Supp. XVII:** 77
Doolittle, Thomas, **IV:** 150
"Doomed by Our Blood to Care" (Orfalea), **Supp. XIII:** 278
"Doomsday" (Plath), **Retro. Supp. II:** 242
Doomsters, The (Macdonald), **Supp. IV Part 2:** 462, 463, 472, 473
"Door, The" (Creeley), **Supp. IV Part 1:** 145, 146, 156-157
"Door, The" (White), **Supp. I Part 2:** 651, 675-676
"Door in the Dark, The" (Frost), **II:** 156
Door in the Hive, A (Levertov), **Supp. III Part 1:** 283, 284
"Door of the Trap, The" (Anderson), **I:** 112
"Doors, Doors, Doors" (Sexton), **Supp. II Part 2:** 681
Doors, The, **Supp. X:** 186
"Doorways into the Depths" (Sanders), **Supp. XVI:**272
Doreski, William, **Retro. Supp. II:** 185
Dorfman, Ariel, **Supp. IX:** 131, 138
Dorfman, Joseph, **Supp. I Part 2:** 631, 647, 650
Dorman, Jen, **Supp. XI:** 240
Dorn, Edward, **Supp. IV Part 1:** 154
"Dorothea Dix, Samaritan" (J. Scott), **Supp. XVII:** 189
Dorr, Julia, **Supp. XV:** 286
Dorris, Michael, **Supp. IV Part 1:** 260, 272
Dos Passos, John, **I:** 99, 288, 374, 379, **474-496,** 517, 519; **II:** 74, 77, 89, 98; **III:** 2, 28, 29, 70, 172, 382-383; **IV:** 340, 427, 433; **Retro. Supp. I:** 105, 113, 187; **Retro. Supp. II:** 95, 196; **Supp. I Part 2:** 646; **Supp. III Part 1:** 104, 105; **Supp. V:** 277; **Supp. VIII:** 101, 105; **Supp. XIV:**24; **Supp. XV:** 135, 137, 182; **Supp. XVII:** 105, 107
"Dos Passos: Poet Against the World" (Cowley), **Supp. II Part 1:** 143, 145
Dostoyevsky, Fyodor, **I:** 53, 103, 211, 468; **II:** 60, 130, 275, 320, 587; **III:** 37, 61, 155, 174, 176, 188, 189, 267, 272, 283, 286, 354, 357, 358, 359, 467, 571, 572; **IV:** 1, 7, 8, 17, 21, 50, 59, 106, 110, 128, 134, 285, 289, 476, 485, 491; **Retro. Supp. II:** 20, 204, 299; **Supp. I Part 1:** 49; **Supp. I Part 2:** 445, 466; **Supp. IV Part 2:** 519, 525; **Supp. VIII:** 175; **Supp. X:** 4-5; **Supp. XI:** 161; **Supp. XII:** 322; **Supp. XVI:**63; **Supp. XVII:** 225
Doty, M. R. *See* Dawson, Ruth; Doty, Mark
Doty, Mark, **Supp. IX:** 42, 300; **Supp. XI: 119-138**
Double, The (Dostoyevsky), **Supp. IX:** 105
"Double, The" (Levis), **Supp. XI:** 260, **261-263**
Double, The (Rank), **Supp. IX:** 105
Double Agent, The (Blackmur), **Supp. II Part 1:** 90, 108, 146
Double Axe, The (Jeffers), **Supp. II Part 2:** 416, 434
Doubleday, Frank, **I:** 500, 502, 515, 517; **III:** 327
Doubleday, Mrs. Frank, **I:** 500
Double Down (F. and S. Barthelme), **Supp. XI:** 27, 34, 35, 36-38
Double Dream of Spring, The (Ashbery), **Supp. III Part 1:** 11-13
Double Fold: Libraries and the Assault on Paper (Baker), **Supp. XIII:** 52, 56
Double Game (Calle), **Supp. XII:** 22
"Double Gap, The" (Auchincloss), **Supp. IV Part 1:** 33
"Double-Headed Snake of Newbury, The" (Whittier), **Supp. I Part 2:** 698
Double Honeymoon (Connell), **Supp. XIV:**80, 87
Double Image, The (Levertov), **Supp. III Part 1:** 274, 276
"Double Image, The" (Sexton), **Supp. II Part 2:** 671, 677-678
Double Indemnity (film), **Supp. IV Part 1:** 130
"Double Limbo" (Komunyakaa), **Supp. XIII:** 132
Double Man, The (Auden), **Supp. III Part 1:** 16; **Supp. X:** 118
"Double Ode" (Rukeyser), **Supp. VI:** 282-283, 286
Double Persephone (Atwood), **Supp. XIII:** 19
Doubles in Literary Psychology (Tymms), **Supp. IX:** 105
Double Vision: American Thoughts Abroad (Knowles), **Supp. XII:** 249
"Doubt on the Great Divide" (Stafford), **Supp. XI:** 322
Dougherty, Steve, **Supp. X:** 262
Douglas, Aaron, **Supp. I Part 1:** 326
Douglas, Alfred, **Supp. X:** 151
Douglas, Ann, **Supp. XII:** 136
Douglas, Claire, **III:** 552
Douglas, George (pseudonym). *See* Brown, George Douglas
Douglas, Kirk, **Supp. XIII:** 5-6
Douglas, Lloyd, **IV:** 434
Douglas, Melvyn, **Supp. V:** 223
Douglas, Michael, **Supp. XI:** 67
Douglas, Paul, **III:** 294
Douglas, Stephen A., **III:** 577, 588-589; **Supp. I Part 2:** 456, 471
Douglas, William O., **III:** 581
Douglass, Frederick, **Supp. I Part 1:** 51, 345; **Supp. I Part 2:** 591; **Supp. II Part 1:** 157, 195, 196, 292, 378; **Supp. III Part 1: 153-174; Supp. IV Part 1:** 1, 2, 13, 15, 256; **Supp. VIII:** 202
Douglass Pilot, The (Baldwin, ed.), **Supp. I Part 1:** 49
Dove, Belle, **I:** 451
Dove, Rita, **Supp. IV Part 1: 241-258; Supp. XVII:** 71, 110
"Dover Beach" (Arnold), **Retro. Supp. I:** 325
Dow, Lorenzo, **IV:** 265
Dowd, Douglas, **Supp. I Part 2:** 645, 650
"Do We Understand Each Other?" (Ginsberg), **Supp. II Part 1:** 311
Dowie, William, **Supp. V:** 199
Do with Me What You Will (Oates), **Supp. II Part 2:** 506, 515-517
Dowling, Eddie, **IV:** 394
Down and Out (Shanley), **Supp. XIV:**317
"Down at City Hall" (Didion), **Supp. IV Part 1:** 211
"Down at the Cross" (Baldwin), **Retro. Supp. II:** 1, 2, 7, 12, 13, 15; **Supp. I Part 1:** 60, 61
"Down at the Dinghy" (Salinger), **III:** 559, 563
"Down by the Station, Early in the

Morning" (Ashbery), **Supp. III Part 1:** 25
Downhill Racer (film), **Supp. IX:** 253
"Down in Alabam" (Bierce), **I:** 193
Downing, Ben, **Supp. XII:** 175, 189, 190-191
Downing, Major Jack (pseudonym). See Smith, Seba
Down in My Heart (Stafford), **Supp. XI:** 313, 315
Down Mailer's Way (Solotaroff), **Retro. Supp. II:** 203
Down the Rabbit Hole: Adventures and Misadventures in the Realm of Children's Literature (Lanes), **Supp. XVI:**104
Down There on a Visit (Isherwood), **Supp. XIV:**159, 161, 164, **168-169,** 170, 171
Down the River (Abbey), **Supp. XIII:** 12-13
"Down the River with Henry Thoreau" (Abbey), **Supp. XIII:** 12-13
Down These Mean Streets (P. Thomas), **Supp. XIII:** 264
Down the Starry River (Purdy), **Supp. VII:** 278
"Downward Path to Wisdom, The" (Porter), **III:** 442, 443, 446
"Down Where I Am" (Hughes), **Supp. I Part 1:** 344
Dowson, Ernest C., **I:** 384
Doyle, Arthur Conan, **Retro. Supp. I:** 270; **Supp. IV Part 1:** 128, 341; **Supp. IV Part 2:** 464, 469; **Supp. XI:** 63
Doyle, C. W., **I:** 199
"Dr. Bergen's Belief" (Schwartz), **Supp. II Part 2:** 650
"Dr. Jack-o'-Lantern" (Yates), **Supp. XI:** 340-341
Dr. Jekyll and Mr. Hyde (film), **Supp. XVII:** 57
Dr. Seuss. See Geisel, Theodor Seuss (Dr. Seuss)
Dr. Seuss and Mr. Geisel (J. and N. Morgan), **Supp. XVI:**103
Dr. Seuss Goes to War: The World War II Editorial Cartoons of Theodor Seuss Geisel (Minear), **Supp. XVI:**101
Dr. Seuss's ABC (Geisel), **Supp. XVI:**99
Dr. Strangelove; or, How I Learned to Stop Worrying and Love the Bomb (film), **Supp. XI:** 293, **301-305**
"Dr. Williams' Position" (Pound), **Supp. XVII:** 226-227
"Draba" (Leopold), **Supp. XIV:**186
Drabble, Margaret, **Supp. IV Part 1:** 297, 299, 305
Drabelle, Dennis, **Supp. XIII:** 13
Drach, Ivan, **Supp. III Part 1:** 268
Dracula (film), **Supp. IV Part 1:** 104; **Supp. XVII:** 57
"Draft Horse, The" (Frost), **Retro. Supp. I:** 141
"Draft Lyrics for *Candide*" (Agee), **I:** 28
Draft of XVI Cantos, A (Pound), **III:** 472; **Retro. Supp. I:** 292
Draft of XXX Cantos, A (Pound), **III:** 196; **Retro. Supp. I:** 292
Drafts &Fragments (Pound), **Retro. Supp. I:** 293
Dragon Country (T. Williams), **IV:** 383
Dragon Seed (Buck), **Supp. II Part 1:** 124
Dragon's Teeth (Sinclair), **Supp. V:** 290
Drake, Benjamin, **Supp. I Part 2:** 584
Drake, Daniel, **Supp. I Part 2:** 584
Drake, Sir Francis, **Supp. I Part 2:** 497
Drake, St. Clair, **IV:** 475
Drake, William, **Supp. XV:** 295
Dramatic Duologues (Masters), **Supp. I Part 2:** 461
Drattel, Deborah, **Supp. XV:** 333
Drat These Brats (X. J. Kennedy), **Supp. XV:** 163
"Draught" (Cowley), **Supp. II Part 1:** 141, 142
Drayton, Michael, **IV:** 135; **Retro. Supp. II:** 76
"Dreadful Has Already Happened, The" (Strand), **Supp. IV Part 2:** 627
"Dream, A" (Ginsberg), **Supp. II Part 1:** 312
"Dream, A" (Tate), **IV:** 129
"Dream, The" (Hayden), **Supp. II Part 1:** 368, 377
Dream at the End of the World, The: Paul Bowles and the Literary Renegades in Tangier (Green), **Supp. IV Part 1:** 95
"Dream Avenue" (Simic), **Supp. VIII:** 282
"Dream Boogie" (Hughes), **Retro. Supp. I:** 208; **Supp. I Part 1:** 339-340
"Dreambook Bestiary" (Komunyakaa), **Supp. XIII:** 120
Dreamer (Johnson), **Supp. VI:** 186, **196-199**
dreamer examines his pillow, the (Shanley), **Supp. XIV:**315, **327**
"Dreamer in a Dead Language" (Paley), **Supp. VI:** 217
Dreaming in Cuban (García), **Supp. XI:** 178, **179-185,** 190
"Dreaming of Hair" (L.-Y. Lee), **Supp. XV:** 214
"Dreaming the Breasts" (Sexton), **Supp. II Part 2:** 692
"Dream Interpreted, The" (Paine), **Supp. I Part 2:** 505
Dream Jumbo (Longo), **Supp. XVI:**124
Dream Keeper, The (Hughes), **Supp. I Part 1:** 328, 332, 333, 334
Dream Keeper and Other Poems, The (Hughes), **Retro. Supp. I:** 201, 202
Dreamland (Baker), **Supp. XIV:**96
"Dream-Land" (Poe), **Retro. Supp. II:** 274
Dream Life of Balso Snell, The (West), **IV:** 286, 287, 288-290, 291, 297; **Retro. Supp. II:** 321, 322, 327, 328, **330-332**
Dream of a Common Language, The: Poems, 1974-1977 (Rich), **Supp. I Part 2:** 551, 554, 569-576
Dream of Arcadia: American Writers and Artists in Italy (Brooks), **I:** 254
Dream of Governors, A (Simpson), **Supp. IX:** 265, **269-270**
"Dream of Italy, A" (Masters), **Supp. I Part 2:** 458
"Dream of Mourning, The" (Glück), **Supp. V:** 84
"Dream of the Blacksmith's Room, A" (R. Bly), **Supp. IV Part 1:** 73
"Dream of the Cardboard Lover" (Haines), **Supp. XII:** 204
Dream of the Golden Mountains, The (Cowley), **Supp. II Part 1:** 139, 141, 142, 144
"Dream Pang, A" (Frost), **II:** 153
"Dreams About Clothes" (Merrill), **Supp. III Part 1:** 328-329
Dreams from Bunker Hill (Fante), **Supp. XI:** 160, 166, **172-173**
"Dreams of Adulthood" (Ashbery), **Supp. III Part 1:** 26
"Dreams of Glory on the Mound" (Plimpton), **Supp. XVI:**238-239
"Dreams of Math" (Kenyon), **Supp. VII:** 160-161
"Dreams of the Animals" (Atwood), **Supp. XIII:** 33
"Dream Variations" (Hughes), **Retro. Supp. I:** 198; **Supp. I Part 1:** 323
"Dream Vision" (Olsen), **Supp. XIII:** 295-296
Dream Work (Oliver), **Supp. VII:** 234-235, 236-238, 240
Dred: A Tale of the Great Dismal Swamp (Stowe), **Supp. I Part 2:** 592

Dreiser, Theodore, **I:** 59, 97, 109, 116, 355, 374, 375, 475, 482, **497-520;** **II:** 26, 27, 29, 34, 38, 44, 74, 89, 93, 180, 276, 283, 428, 444, 451, 456-457, 467-468; **III:** 40, 103, 106, 251, 314, 319, 327, 335, 453, 576, 582; **IV:** 29, 35, 40, 135, 208, 237, 475, 482, 484; **Retro. Supp. I:** 325, 376; **Retro. Supp. II: 93-110,** 114, 322; **Supp. I Part 1:** 320; **Supp. I Part 2:** 461, 468; **Supp. III Part 2:** 412; **Supp. IV Part 1:** 31, 236, 350; **Supp. IV Part 2:** 689; **Supp. V:** 113, 120; **Supp. VIII:** 98, 101, 102; **Supp. IX:** 1, 14, 15, 308; **Supp. XI:** 207; **Supp. XIV:**111; **Supp. XVII:** 95, 96-97, 105, 155

"Drenched in Light" (Hurston), **Supp. VI:** 150-151

Dresser, Paul, **Retro. Supp. II:** 94, 103

Dress Gray (Truscott), **Supp. IV Part 2:** 683

Dress Gray (teleplay), **Supp. IV Part 2:** 683

"Dressing for Dinner" (Ríos), **Supp. IV Part 2:** 548

Dressing Up for the Carnival (Shields), **Supp. VII:** 328

Drew, Bettina, **Supp. IX:** 2, 4

Drew, Elizabeth, **Retro. Supp. II:** 242, 243

Drexler, Eric, **Supp. XVI:**121

Dreyfus, Alfred, **Supp. I Part 2:** 446

Drift and Mastery (Lippmann), **I:** 222-223

"Driftwood" (C. Frost), **Supp. XV:** 106-107

"Drinker, The" (Lowell), **II:** 535, 550

"Drinking Cold Water" (Everwine), **Supp. XV:** 80-81

"Drinking from a Helmet" (Dickey), **Supp. IV Part 1:** 180

Drinking Gourd, The (Hansberry), **Supp. IV Part 1:** 359, 365-367, 374

Drinks before Dinner (Doctorow), **Supp. IV Part 1:** 231, 234-235

Drive, He Said (Larner), **Supp. XVI:**220

"Drive Home, The" (Banks), **Supp. V:** 7

"Driver" (Merrill), **Supp. III Part 1:** 331

"Driving Through Minnesota During the Hanoi Bombings" (R. Bly), **Supp. IV Part 1:** 61; **Supp. XVII:** 243

"Driving through Oregon" (Haines), **Supp. XII:** 207

"Driving toward the Lac Qui Parle River" (R. Bly), **Supp. IV Part 1:** 61

"Drone" (Coleman), **Supp. XI:** 85-86

"Drowned Man, The: Death between Two Rivers" (McGrath), **Supp. X:** 116

"Drowning 1954" (Keillor), **Supp. XVI:**172

Drowning Pool, The (film), **Supp. IV Part 2:** 474

Drowning Pool, The (Macdonald), **Supp. IV Part 2:** 470, 471

Drowning Season, The (Hoffman), **Supp. X: 82**

Drowning with Others (Dickey), **Supp. IV Part 1:** 176, 178, 179

"Drowsy Day, A" (Dunbar), **Supp. II Part 1:** 198

Drugiye Berega (Nabokov), **III:** 247-250, 252

"Drug Shop, The, or Endymion in Edmonstoun" (Benét), **Supp. XI:** 43

"Drug Store" (Shapiro), **Supp. II Part 2:** 705

"Drugstore in Winter, A" (Ozick), **Supp. V:** 272

Drukman, Steven, **Supp. XIII:** 195, 197, 202

"Drum" (Hogan), **Supp. IV Part 1:** 413

"Drum, The" (Alvarez), **Supp. VII:** 7

"Drumlin Woodchuck, A" (Frost), **II:** 159-160; **Retro. Supp. I:** 138

Drummond, William, **Supp. I Part 1:** 369

Drummond de Andrade, Carlos, **Supp. IV Part 2:** 626, 629, 630

Drum-Taps (Whitman), **IV:** 346, 347, 444; **Retro. Supp. I:** 406

"Drunken Fisherman, The" (Lowell), **II:** 534, 550

"Drunken Sisters, The" (Wilder), **IV:** 374

Drunk in the Furnace, The (Merwin), **Supp. III Part 1:** 345-346

"Drunk in the Furnace, The" (Merwin), **Supp. III Part 1:** 346

Druten, John van, **Supp. XIV:**162

Dryden, John, **II:** 111, 542, 556; **III:** 15; **IV:** 145; **Retro. Supp. I:** 56; **Supp. I Part 1:** 150; **Supp. I Part 2:** 422; **Supp. IX:** 68; **Supp. XIV:**5; **Supp. XV:** 258

Drye, Captain Frank, **Retro. Supp. II:** 115

Dry Salvages, The (Eliot), **I:** 581

"Dry Salvages, The" (Eliot), **Retro. Supp. I:** 66

"Dry September" (Faulkner), **II:** 72, 73

Dry Sun, Dry Wind (Wagoner), **Supp. IX:** 323, 324

D'Souza, Dinesh, **Supp. X:** 255

"Dual" (Goldbarth), **Supp. XII:** 188

"Dual Curriculum" (Ozick), **Supp. V:** 270

"Dualism" (Reed), **Supp. X:** 242

Duane's Depressed (McMurtry), **Supp. V:** 233

Du Bartas, Guillaume, **Supp. I Part 1:** 98, 104, 111, 118, 119

Duberman, Martin, **Supp. I Part 2:** 408, 409

"Dubin's Lives" (Malamud), **Supp. I Part 2:** 451

Dubious Honors (M. F. K. Fisher), **Supp. XVII:** 91

Dubliners (Joyce), **I:** 130, 480; **III:** 471; **Supp. VIII:** 146

"Dubliners" (J. Joyce), **Supp. XVI:**41

Du Bois, Nina Gomer (Mrs. W. E. B. Du Bois), **Supp. II Part 1:** 158; **Supp. XIV:** 200

Du Bois, Shirley Graham (Mrs. W. E. B. Du Bois), **Supp. II Part 1:** 186

Du Bois, W. E. B., **I:** 260; **Supp. I Part 1:** 5, 345; **Supp. II Part 1:** 33, 56, 61, **157-189,** 195; **Supp. IV Part 1:** 9, 164, 170, 362; **Supp. X:** 133, 134, 137, 139, 242; **Supp. XIII:** 185, Supp. XIII: 186, 233, 238, 243, 244, 247; **Supp. XIV:**54, 69, 72, 201, 202; **Supp. XVI:**135

Dubreuil, Jean, **Supp. IV Part 2:** 425

Dubus, Andre, **Supp. VII: 75-93;** **Supp. XI:** 347,**Supp. XI:** 349; **Supp. XIV:**21

Duchamp, Marcel, **IV:** 408; **Retro. Supp. I:** 416, 417, 418, 430; **Supp. IV Part 2:** 423, 424; **Supp. XII:** 124; **Supp. XV:** 157

"Duchess at Prayer, The" (Wharton), **Retro. Supp. I:** 365

Duchess of Malfi, The (Webster), **IV:** 131

Duck Soup (film), **Supp. IV Part 1:** 384

Duck Variations, The (Mamet), **Supp. XIV:**239, 240, 249

Dudley, Anne. See Bradstreet, Anne

Dudley, Joseph, **III:** 52

Dudley, Thomas, **III:** 52; **Supp. I Part 1:** 98, 99, 110, 116

"Duet, With Muffled Brake Drums" (Updike), **Retro. Supp. I:** 319

Duet for Cannibals (Sontag), **Supp. III Part 2:** 452, 456

Duffey, Bernard, **Supp. I Part 2:** 458, 471

Duffus, R. L., **Supp. I Part 2:** 650

Duffy, Martha, **Supp. IV Part 1:** 207
Duffy, William, **Supp. XVI:**32
Du Fu (Tu Fu), **Supp. XV:** 217
Dufy, Raoul, **I:** 115; **IV:** 80
Dugan, Alan, **Supp. XIII:** 76
Dugan, James, **Supp. XV:** 197
Duhamel, Marcel, **Supp. XVI:**135, 143
Dujardin, Edouard, **I:** 53
"Duke de l'Omelette, The" (Poe), **III:** 411, 425
"Duke in His Domain, The" (Capote), **Supp. III Part 1:** 113, 126
Duke of Deception, The (G. Wolff), **Supp. II Part 1:** 97; **Supp. XI:** 246
"Duke's Child, The" (Maxwell), **Supp. VIII:** 172
"Dulham Ladies, The" (Jewett), **II:** 407, 408; **Retro. Supp. II:** 143
Duluth (Vidal), **Supp. IV Part 2:** 677, 685, 689, 691-692
Dumas, Alexandre, **III:** 386; **Supp. XVII:** 64
"Dumb Oax, The" (Lewis), **Retro. Supp. I:** 170
"Dummy, The" (Sontag), **Supp. III Part 2:** 469
"Dump Ground, The" (Stegner), **Supp. IV Part 2:** 601
Dunbar, Alice Moore (Mrs. Paul Laurence Dunbar), **Supp. II Part 1:** 195, 200, 217
Dunbar, Paul Laurence, **Supp. I Part 1:** 320; **Supp. II Part 1:** 174, **191-219**; **Supp. III Part 1:** 73; **Supp. IV Part 1:** 15, 165, 170; **Supp. X:** 136; **Supp. XI:** 277; **Supp. XIII:** 111
Duncan, Harry, **Supp. XV:** 75
Duncan, Isadora, **I:** 483; **Supp. XV:** 42, 50
Duncan, Robert, **Retro. Supp. II:** 49; **Supp. III Part 2:** 625, 626, 630, 631; **Supp. VIII:** 304; **Supp. XVI:**282-283
Dunciad, The (Pope), **I:** 204
Dunford, Judith, **Supp. VIII:** 107
Dunlap, William, **Supp. I Part 1:** 126, 130, 137, 141, 145
Dunn, Stephen, **Supp. XI: 139-158**
Dunne, Finley Peter, **II:** 432
Dunne, John Gregory, **Supp. IV Part 1:** 197, 198, 201, 203, 207
"Dunnet Shepherdess, A" (Jewett), **II:** 392-393; **Retro. Supp. II:** 139
Dunning, Stephen, **Supp. XIV:**126
Dunning, William Archibald, **Supp. II Part 1:** 170; **Supp. XIV:**48
Dunnock, Mildred, **III:** 153
Dunster, Henry, **Supp. I Part 2:** 485
"Duo Tried Killing Man with Bacon" (Goldbarth), **Supp. XII:** 176
Dupee, F. W., **I:** 254; **II:** 548; **Supp. VIII:** 231; **Supp. IX:** 93, 96
DuPlessis, Rachel Blau, **Supp. IV Part 2:** 421, 426, 432; **Supp. XVI:**284
Duplicate Keys (Smiley), **Supp. VI:** 292, **294-296**
Duplications, The (Koch), **Supp. XV:** 181, 183, 186
Durable Fire, A (Sarton), **Supp. VIII:** 260
Durand, Asher, B., **Supp. I Part 1:** 156, 157
Durand, Régis, **Supp. IV Part 1:** 44
"Durango Suite" (Gunn Allen), **Supp. IV Part 1:** 326
"Durations" (Matthews), **Supp. IX:** 152-153, 154
Dürer, Albrecht, **III:** 212; **Supp. XII:** 44
"During Fever" (Lowell), **II:** 547
Durkheim, Émile, **I:** 227; **Retro. Supp. I:** 55, 57; **Supp. I Part 2:** 637, 638
Durrell, Lawrence, **III:** 184, 190; **IV:** 430; **Supp. X:** 108, 187; **Supp. XVI:**294
Dürrenmatt, Friedrich, **Supp. IV Part 2:** 683
Duse, Eleonora, **II:** 515, 528
Dusk and Other Stories (Salter), **Supp. IX: 260-261**
Dusk of Dawn: An Essay Toward an Autobiography of a Race Concept (Du Bois), **Supp. II Part 1:** 159, 183, 186
"Dusting" (Alvarez), **Supp. VII:** 4
"Dusting" (Dove), **Supp. IV Part 1:** 247, 248
"Dusting" (Schnackenberg), **Supp. XV:** 256
"Dust of Snow" (Frost), **II:** 154
Dust Tracks on a Road (Hurston), **Supp. IV Part 1:** 5, 11; **Supp. VI:** 149, 151, 158-159
"Dusty Braces" (Snyder), **Supp. VIII:** 302
Dutchman (Baraka), **Supp. II Part 1:** 38, 40, 42-44, 54, 55
"Dutch Nick Massacre, The" (Twain), **IV:** 195
"Dutch Picture, A" (Longfellow), **Retro. Supp. II:** 171
Dutton, Charles S., **Supp. VIII:** 332, 342
Dutton, Clarence Earl, **Supp. IV Part 2:** 598
Duvall, Robert, **Supp. V:** 227
"Duwamish" (Hugo), **Supp. VI:** 136
"Duwamish, Skagit, Hoh" (Hugo), **Supp. VI:** 136-137
"Duwamish No. 2" (Hugo), **Supp. VI:** 137
Duyckinck, Evert, **III:** 77, 81, 83, 85; **Retro. Supp. I:** 155, 247, 248; **Supp. I Part 1:** 122, 317
Duyckinck, George, **Supp. I Part 1:** 122
"Dvonya" (Simpson), **Supp. IX:** 274
Dwellings: A Spiritual History of the Living World (Hogan), **Supp. IV Part 1:** 397, 410, 415-416, 417
Dwight, Sereno E., **I:** 547
Dwight, Timothy, **Supp. I Part 1:** 124; **Supp. I Part 2:** 516, 580; **Supp. II Part 1:** 65, 69
Dworkin, Andrea, **Supp. XII:** 6
Dwyer, Jim, **Supp. XVI:**16, 19
Dybbuk, A, or Between Two Worlds: Dramatic Legend in Four Acts (Kushner), **Supp. IX:** 138
Dybbuk, The (Ansky), **IV:** 6
Dyer, Geoff, **Supp. X:** 169
Dyer, R. C., **Supp. XIII:** 162
Dying Animal, The (P. Roth), **Retro. Supp. II:** 288
"Dying Elm, The" (Freneau), **Supp. II Part 1:** 258
"Dying Indian, The" (Freneau), **Supp. II Part 1:** 262
"Dying Man, The" (Roethke), **III:** 540, 542, 543-545
Dylan, Bob, **Supp. VIII:** 202; **Supp. XIII:** 114, 119; **Supp. XV:** 349, 350
Dynamo (O'Neill), **III:** 396
"Dysfunctional Narratives: Or, 'Mistakes Were Made' " (C. Baxter), **Supp. XVII:** 20
"Dysfunctional Nation" (Karr), **Supp. XI:** 245
Dyson, A. E., **Retro. Supp. II:** 247
Dyson, Freeman, **Supp. XVII:** 42
E
E. E. Cummings (Marks), **I:** 438
E. E. Cummings: A Miscellany (Cummings), **I:** 429, 441
E. E. Cummings: A Miscellany, Revised (Cummings), **I:** 429
E. L. Doctorow (Harter and Thompson), **Supp. IV Part 1:** 217
E. M. Forster (Trilling), **Supp. III Part 2:** 496, 501, 504
"Each and All" (Emerson), **II:** 19
Each in His Season (Snodgrass), **Supp. VI:** 324, 327
"Each Like a Leaf" (Swenson), **Supp. IV Part 2:** 644
Eager, Allen, **Supp. XI:** 294
"Eagle, The" (Tate), **IV:** 128
"Eagle and the Mole, The" (Wylie),

Supp. I Part 2: 710, 711, 713, 714, 729
Eagle as Wide as the World, The (X. J. Kennedy), **Supp. XV:** 162, 164
"Eagle Poem" (Harjo), **Supp. XII:** 224, 226
"Eagles" (Dickey), **Supp. IV Part 1:** 186
Eagle's Mile, The (Dickey), **Supp. IV Part 1:** 178, 185-186
"Eagle That Is Forgotten, The" (Lindsay), **Supp. I Part 2:** 382, 387
Eagleton, Terry, **Retro. Supp. I:** 67
Eakin, Paul John, **Supp. VIII:** 167, 168; **Supp. XIII:** 225; **Supp. XVI:** 70
Eakins, Thomas, **Supp. XIV:** 338
Eames, Roscoe, **II:** 476
"Earl: My Life with a Louse" (Keillor), **Supp. XVI:** 176
"Earl Painter" (Banks), **Supp. V:** 14-15
"Early Adventures of Ralph Ringwood, The" (Irving), **II:** 314
Early Ayn Rand, The: A Selection of Her Unpublished Fiction (Rand), **Supp. IV Part 2:** 520
Early Dark (Price), **Supp. VI:** 262
Early Diary of Anaïs Nin, The, **Supp. X:** 184, 192
Early Elkin (Elkin), **Supp. VI:** 42-43, 45
"Early Evenin' Blues" (Hughes), **Retro. Supp. I:** 205
"Early History of a Seamstress" (Reznikoff), **Supp. XIV:** 277, 289
"Early History of a Sewing-Machine Operator" (Reznikoff), **Supp. XIV:** 277
Early History of a Sewing-Machine Operator (Reznikoff), **Supp. XIV:** 289
"Early History of a Writer" (Reznikoff), **Supp. XIV:** 278, 290
"Early in the Morning" (L.-Y. Lee), **Supp. XV:** 214
Early Lectures of Ralph Waldo Emerson, The (Emerson), **II:** 11
Early Lives of Melville, The (Sealts), **Retro. Supp. I:** 257
Early Martyr and Other Poems, An (W. C. Williams), **Retro. Supp. I:** 423
"Early Morning: Cape Cod" (Swenson), **Supp. IV Part 2:** 641
"Early Spring between Madison and Bellingham" (R. Bly), **Supp. IV Part 1:** 71
Earnhardt, Dale, **Supp. XII:** 310
Earnshaw, Doris, **Supp. IV Part 1:** 310
"Earth" (Bryant), **Supp. I Part 1:** 157, 164, 167

"Earth, The" (Sexton), **Supp. II Part 2:** 696
"Earth and Fire" (Berry), **Supp. X:** 27
Earth as Air, The: An Ars Poetica (Sobin), **Supp. XVI:** 285-286
"Earth Being" (Toomer), **Supp. IX:** 320
"Earthly Care a Heavenly Discipline" (Stowe), **Supp. I Part 2:** 586
"Earthly City of the Jews, The" (Kazin), **Retro. Supp. II:** 286
Earthly Possessions (Tyler), **Supp. IV Part 2:** 665-666, 671
Earth Power Coming (Ortiz, ed.), **Supp. IV Part 2:** 502
"Earth's Holocaust" (Hawthorne), **II:** 226, 231, 232, 242; **III:** 82; **Retro. Supp. I:** 152
Earth Without You, The (F. Wright), **Supp. XVII:** 243
East Coker (Eliot), **I:** 580, 581, 582, 585, 587
"East Coker" (Eliot), **Retro. Supp. I:** 66; **Supp. VIII:** 195, 196
"Easter" (Toomer), **Supp. III Part 2:** 486
"Easter, an Ode" (Lowell), **II:** 536
"Easter Morning" (Ammons), **Supp. VII:** 34
"Easter Morning" (Clampitt), **Supp. IX:** 45
"Easter Ode, An" (Dunbar), **Supp. II Part 1:** 196
Easter Parade, The (Yates), **Supp. XI:** 346, 349
"Easter Sunday: Recollection" (Gunn Allen), **Supp. IV Part 1:** 322
"Easter Wings" (Herbert), **Supp. IV Part 2:** 646
"East European Cooking" (Simic), **Supp. VIII:** 277
East Is East (Boyle), **Supp. VIII:** 1-3
Eastlake, William, **Supp. XIII:** 12
East Lynne (Wood), **Supp. I Part 1:** 35, 36; **Supp. I Part 2:** 459, 462; **Supp. XVI:** 182
Eastman, Elaine Goodale, **Supp. X:** 103
Eastman, Max, **Supp. III Part 2:** 620; **Supp. X:** 131, 134, 135, 137; **Supp. XV:** 295; **Supp. XVI:** 185; **Supp. XVII:** 96
East of Eden (Steinbeck), **IV:** 51, 56-57, 59
"East of the Sun and West of the Moon" (Merwin), **Supp. III Part 1:** 344
Easton, Alison, **Retro. Supp. II:** 143, 144, 145
Easton, Bret Ellis, **Supp. XI:** 65

Easton, Robert, **Supp. IV Part 2:** 461, 474
East Wind (Lowell), **II:** 527
East Wind: West Wind (Buck), **Supp. II Part 1:** 114-115
Easy Rawlins mysteries, **Supp. XIII:** 236, **237-241**, 242
Easy Rider (film), **Supp. XI:** 293, **308**, 309
Eat a Bowl of Tea (Chu), **Supp. X:** 291
"Eating " (Bass), **Supp. XVI:** 23-24
"Eating Alone" (L.-Y. Lee), **Supp. XV:** 214
Eating Naked (Dobyns), **Supp. XIII: 78-79**
"Eating Out" (L. Michaels), **Supp. XVI:** 209
"Eating Poetry" (Strand), **Supp. IV Part 2:** 626
"Eating the Whole" (C. Frost), **Supp. XV:** 101
"Eating Together" (L.-Y. Lee), **Supp. XV:** 214
"Eating with My Fingers" (C. Frost), **Supp. XV:** 97
Eaton, Edith, **Supp. X:** 291
Eaton, Peggy, **Supp. I Part 2:** 461
Eaton, Winnifred, **Supp. X:** 291
"Eatonville Anthology, The" (Hurston), **Supp. VI:** 152
"Ebb and Flow, The" (Taylor), **IV:** 161
"Ebenezer Marsh, 1725" (Schnackenberg), **Supp. XV:** 256
Eben Holden (Bacheller), **I:** 216
Eberhardt, Isabelle, **Supp. IV Part 1:** 92
Eberhart, Mrs., **I:** 521-522, 530
Eberhart, Richard, **I: 521-543; II:** 535-536; **III:** 527; **IV:** 416; **Retro. Supp. II:** 176, 178; **Supp. I Part 1:** 83; **Supp. XII:** 119
Eble, Kenneth E., **Supp. I Part 1:** 201
Eccentricities of a Nightingale (T. Williams), **IV:** 382, 385, 397, 398
Ecclesiastica Historia Integram Ecclesiae (Taylor), **IV:** 163
"Echart" (Sobin), **Supp. XVI:** 289
"Echo, The" (Bowles), **Supp. IV Part 1:** 84, 86, 87
Echoes inside the Labyrinth (McGrath), **Supp. X:** 127
Eckehart, Meister, **Supp. XV:** 225
Eckhart, Maria, **Supp. V:** 212
Eclipse (Hogan), **Supp. IV Part 1:** 397, 400, 402
Eclipse, a Nightmare (Montalembert), **Supp. XV:** 349
Eclogues (Virgil), **Supp. VIII:** 31
"Ecologue" (Ginsberg), **Supp. II Part 1:** 326

"Ecologues of These States 1969-1971" (Ginsberg), **Supp. II Part 1:** 325

"Economics of Negro Emancipation in the United States, The" (Du Bois), **Supp. II Part 1:** 174

"Economic Theory of Women's Dress, The" (Veblen), **Supp. I Part 2:** 636

Economy of the Unlost: Reading Simonides of Keos with Paul Celan (Carson), **Supp. XII:** 110-111

Ecotactics: The Sierra Club Handbook for Environmental Activists (Mitchell and Stallings, eds.), **Supp. IV Part 2:** 488

"Ecstasy" (Bierds), **Supp. XVII:** 34

"Ecstasy" (Olds), **Supp. X:** 206

"Ecstatic" (Komunyakaa), **Supp. XIII:** 131

Edda, **Supp. X:** 114

Eddy, Mary Baker, **I:** 583; **III:** 506

Edel, Leon, **I:** 20; **II:** 338-339; **Retro. Supp. I:** 218, 224, 231

Edelberg, Cynthia, **Supp. IV Part 1:** 155

"Eden and My Generation" (Levis), **Supp. XI:** 270

Edenbaum, Robert, **Supp. IV Part 1:** 352

Eden Tree (Bynner), **Supp. XV:** 42, 51

Eder, Richard, **Supp. XII:** 189; **Supp. XV:** 62, 187, 259, 261

Edgar Huntly; or, Memoirs of a Sleep-Walker (Brown), **Supp. I Part 1:** 140-144, 145

"Edge" (Plath), **Retro. Supp. II:** 256; **Supp. I Part 2:** 527, 547

Edge, Mary E., **II:** 316

"Edge of the Great Rift, The" (Theroux), **Supp. VIII:** 325

Edge of the Sea, The (Carson), **Supp. IX:** 19, 25-31, 32

Edgers, Geoff, **Supp. XV:** 113

Edgeworth, Maria, **II:** 8; **Supp. XV:** 231

Edible Woman, The (Atwood), **Supp. XIII:** 19, 20, 20-21

"Edict by the King of Prussia, An" (Franklin), **II:** 120

Edie: An American Biography (Stein), **Supp. XVI:**245

Edison, Thomas A., **I:** 483; **Supp. I Part 2:** 392

Edith Wharton (Joslin), **Retro. Supp. I:** 376

Edith Wharton: A Biography (Lewis), **Retro. Supp. I:** 362

Edith Wharton: A Woman in Her Time (Auchincloss), **Retro. Supp. I:** 370

Edith Wharton: Matters of Mind and Spirit (Singley), **Retro. Supp. I:** 373

Edith Wharton: Traveller in the Land of Letters (Goodwyn), **Retro. Supp. I:** 370

Edith Wharton's Argument with America (Ammons), **Retro. Supp. I:** 364

Edith Wharton's Brave New Politics (Bauer), **Retro. Supp. I:** 381

Edith Wharton's Letters from the Underworld (Waid), **Retro. Supp. I:** 360

"Editing and Glosses" (Reznikoff), **Supp. XIV:**283

Editing of Emily Dickinson, The (Franklin), **Retro. Supp. I:** 41

"Editor and the Schoolma'am, The" (Frederic), **II:** 130

"Editor's Easy Chair" (Howells), **II:** 276

"Editor's Study, The" (Howells), **II:** 275, 276, 285

"Editor Whedon" (Masters), **Supp. I Part 2:** 463

Edlin, Mari, **Supp. X:** 266

Edman, Irwin, **III:** 605

Edmond (Mamet), **Supp. XIV:**241, 248, 249, 250

Edmundson, Mark, **Retro. Supp. II:** 262

Edsel (Shapiro), **Supp. II Part 2:** 703, 704, 717-719

Edson, Russell, **Supp. VIII:** 279

"Educated American Woman, An" (Cheever), **Supp. I Part 1:** 194

"Education, An" (Ozick), **Supp. V:** 267

Education and Living (Bourne), **I:** 252

"Education by Poetry" (Frost), **Supp. XV:** 215

"Education of a Storyteller, The" (Bambara), **Supp. XI:** 20

Education of Black People, The (Du Bois), **Supp. II Part 1:** 186

Education of Harriet Hatfield, The (Sarton), **Supp. VIII:** 257-258

Education of Henry Adams, The (Adams), **I:** 1, 5, 6, 11, 14, 15-18, 19, 20-21, 111; **II:** 276; **III:** 504; **Retro. Supp. I:** 53, 59; **Supp. IX:** 19; **Supp. XIV:**299

*Education of H*y*m*a*n K*a*p*l*a*n, The* (Rosten), **Supp. XVII:** 9

"Education of Mingo, The" (Johnson), **Supp. VI:** 193, 194

"Education of Norman Podhoretz, The" (Goldberg), **Supp. VIII:** 238

Education of Oscar Fairfax, The (Auchincloss), **Supp. IV Part 1:** 25, 36

"Education of the Poet" (Glück), **Supp. V:** 78, 80

Education sentimentale (Flaubert), **III:** 315

"Education the Imagination" (Koch), **Supp. XV:** 175-176, 177

Edwards, Eli. *See* McKay, Claude

Edwards, Esther, **I:** 545

Edwards, John, **I:** 478

Edwards, Jonathan, **I:** **544-566**; **II:** 432; **Retro. Supp. II:** 187; **Supp. I Part 1:** 301, 302; **Supp. I Part 2:** 552, 594, 700; **Supp. IV Part 2:** 430; **Supp. VIII:** 205

Edwards, Sarah, **I:** 545

Edwards, Thomas, **Supp. XV:** 20

Edwards, Thomas R., **Supp. XVI:**207

Edwards, Timothy, **I:** 545

Edwards-Yearwood, Grace, **Supp. VIII:** 81

"Edwin Arlington Robinson" (Cowley), **Supp. II Part 1:** 144

Edwin Arlington Robinson (Winters), **Supp. II Part 2:** 812

Edwin Booth (play), **Supp. IV Part 1:** 89

"Effects of Analogy" (Stevens), **Retro. Supp. I:** 297

Effluences from the Sacred Caves; More Selected Essays and Reviews (Carruth), **Supp. XVI:**46

"Effort at Speech between Two People" (Rukeyser), **Supp. VI:** 276, 284

"Efforts of Affection" (Moore), **III:** 214

"Efforts of Affection: A Memoir of Marianne Moore" (Bishop), **Retro. Supp. II:** 52

"Egg, The" (Anderson), **I:** 113, 114

"Egg, The" (Snyder), **Supp. VIII:** 302

"Eggplant Epithalamion, The" (Jong), **Supp. V:** 119

"Eggs" (Olds), **Supp. X:** 206

"Eggshell" (Stern), **Supp. IX:** 299

Egoist, The (Meredith), **II:** 186

Egorova, Lubov, **Supp. IX:** 58

"Egotism, or the Bosom Sergent" (Hawthorne), **II:** 227, 239

"Egyptian Pulled Glass Bottle in the Shape of a Fish, An" (Moore), **III:** 195, 213

Ehrenfels, Christian von, **Supp. XIV:**198

Ehrenpreis, Irvin, **Supp. XII:** 128

Ehrenreich, Barbara, **Supp. XVII:** 210

Ehrlich, Gretel, **Supp. XIV:**227

Eichmann, Adolf, **Supp. XII:** 166

Eichmann in Jerusalem (Arendt),

Retro. Supp. II: 28; Supp. VIII: 243; Supp. XII: 166
"Eichmann in New York: The New York Intellectuals and the Hannah Arendt Controversy" (Rabinbach), Supp. XII: 166
"Eidolon" (Warren), IV: 239
Eight Cousins (Alcott), Supp. I Part 1: 29, 38, 42, 43
18 Poems from the Quechua (Strand, trans.), Supp. IV Part 2: 630
1876: A Novel (Vidal), Supp. IV Part 2: 677, 684, 688, 689, 691, 692
"18 West 11th Street" (Merrill), Supp. III Part 1: 323, 328
"Eighth Air Force" (Jarrell), II: 373-374, 377
Eight Harvard Poets, I: 429, 475
"Eighth Day, The" (Apple), Supp. XVII: 6, 50
"Eighth Ditch, The" (Baraka), Supp. II Part 1: 40
"'80s Pastoral: Frederick Barthelme's *Moon Deluxe* Ten Years On" (Peters), Supp. XI: 39
Eight Men (Wright), IV: 478, 488, 494
80 Flowers (Zukofsky), Supp. III Part 2: 631
Eikon Basilike, The, Supp. IV Part 2: 435
Eileen (Masters), Supp. I Part 2: 460
Eimi (Cummings), I: 429, 433, 434, 439-440
"Einstein" (MacLeish), III: 5, 8, 10-11, 18-19
Einstein, Albert, I: 493; III: 8, 10, 21, 161; IV: 69, 375, 410, 411, 421; Retro. Supp. I: 63; Supp. I Part 2: 609, 643; Supp. III Part 2: 621; Supp. V: 290; Supp. XII: 45
Eiseley, Loren, III: 227-228
Eisenhower, Dwight D., I: 136, 376; II: 548; III: 215; IV: 75; Supp. I Part 1: 291; Supp. III Part 2: 624; Supp. V: 45
Eisenstein, Sergei, I: 481
Eisinger, Chester E., I: 302; II: 604; Supp. IX: 15
Eisner, Douglas, Supp. X: 155
Elam, Angela, Supp. XI: 290
El Bernardo (Balbuena), Supp. V: 11
Elbert, Sarah, Supp. I Part 1: 34, 41
Elder, Donald, II: 417, 426, 435, 437; Supp. XV: 137
Elder, John, Supp. IX: 25
Elder, Lonne, III, Supp. IV Part 1: 362
Elder, Richard, Supp. XII: 172
"Elder Sister, The" (Olds), Supp. X: 205-206

Elder Statesman, The (Eliot), I: 572, 573, 583; Retro. Supp. I: 53, 65
Eldredge, Kay, Supp. IX: 254, 259
Eldridge, Florence, III: 154, 403; IV: 357
Eleanor of Aquitaine, III: 470
Eleanor of Guienne, I: 14
"Elect, The" (Taylor), Supp. V: 323
"Elections, Nicaragua, 1984" (Kingsolver), Supp. VII: 208
Elective Affinities (Goethe; Bogan and Mayer, trans.), Supp. III Part 1: 63
Electra (Euripides), III: 398
Electra (Sophocles), III: 398; IV: 370; Supp. IX: 102
"Electra on Azalea Path" (Plath), Supp. I Part 2: 538
"Electrical Storm" (Bishop), Supp. I Part 1: 93
"Electrical Storm" (Hayden), Supp. II Part 1: 370
"Electric Arrows" (Proulx), Supp. VII: 256
"Electricity Saviour" (Olds), Supp. X: 215
Electric Kool-Aid Acid Test, The (Wolfe), Supp. III Part 2: 575-577, 582-584; Supp. XI: 239
Electric Lady, The (film), Supp. XI: 309
Elegant Extracts (Knox), II: 8
Elegiac Feelings American (Corso), Supp. XII: 131-134
"Elegiac Fragments" (Everwine), Supp. XV: 89
Elegies (Rukeyser), Supp. VI: 273
"Elegies" (Rukeyser), Supp. VI: 272
"Elegies for Paradise Valley" (Hayden), Supp. II Part 1: 363
"Elegy" (Bidart), Supp. XV: 25, 29
Elegy (Levis), Supp. XI: 257, 259, 261, 271-272
"Elegy" (Merwin), Supp. III Part 1: 351
"Elegy" (Stafford), Supp. XI: 322
"Elegy" (Tate), IV: 128
"Elegy, for the U.S.N. Dirigible, Macon, An" (Winters), Supp. II Part 2: 810
"Elegy Ending in the Sound of a Skipping Rope" (Levis), Supp. XI: 271-272
"Elegy for D. H. Lawrence, An" (W. C. Williams), Retro. Supp. I: 421
"Elegy for My Father" (Strand), Supp. IV Part 2: 628
"Elegy for My Mother" (Wagoner), Supp. IX: 330
"Elegy for Redondo Beach" (Jarman), Supp. XVII: 112, 113

Elegy for September, An (Nichols), Supp. XIII: 268
"Elegy for Thelonious" (Komunyakaa), Supp. XIII: 118
"Elegy for the U.S.N. Dirigible, Macon, A" (Winters), Supp. II Part 2: 810
"Elegy for 41 Whales Beached in Florence, Oregon, June 1979" (Bierds), Supp. XVII: 27
"Elegy of Last Resort" (Nemerov), III: 271
"Elegy with a Thimbleful of Water in the Cage" (Levis), Supp. XI: 272
Elegy Written in a Country Churchyard (Gray), I: 68
"Elegy Written in a Country Churchyard" (Gray), Supp. XIV:8
"Elementary Scene, The" (Jarrell), II: 387, 388, 389
"Elements" (Frank), Supp. X: 213
Elements of Style, The (Strunk), Supp. I Part 2: 670
"Elenita, Cards, Palm, Water" (Cisneros), Supp. VII: 64
"Eleonora" (Poe), III: 412
Eleothriambos (Lee), IV: 158
"Elephants" (Moore), III: 203
"Elevator, The" (Dixon), Supp. XII: 154
"Elevator Boy" (Hughes), Retro. Supp. I: 200; Supp. I Part 1: 326
"Eleven" (Cisneros), Supp. VII: 69
Eleven Essays in the European Novel (Blackmur), Supp. II Part 1: 91, 111
Eleven Kinds of Loneliness (Yates), Supp. XI: 340-343, 349
Eleven Poems on the Same Theme (Warren), IV: 239-241
"Eleven Times a Poem" (Corso), Supp. XII: 132, 133
El Greco (Doménikos Theotokópoulos), I: 387; III: 212
"El-Hajj Malik El-Shabazz" (Hayden), Supp. II Part 1: 379
"Eli, the Fanatic" (P. Roth), Supp. III Part 2: 407-408
Eliade, Mircea, Supp. XVI:292
Eliot, Charles W., I: 5; II: 345; Supp. I Part 2: 479; Supp. IX: 94
Eliot, Charles William, Retro. Supp. I: 55
Eliot, George, I: 375, 458, 459, 461, 467; II: 179, 181, 191-192, 275, 319, 324, 338, 577; IV: 311, 322; Retro. Supp. I: 218, 220, 225; Supp. I Part 1: 370; Supp. I Part 2: 559, 579; Supp. IV Part 1: 31, 297; Supp. IV Part 2: 677; Supp.

V: 258; **Supp. IX:** 38, 43, 51; **Supp. XI:** 68; **Supp. XII:** 335; **Supp. XIV:**344
Eliot, T. S., **I:** 48, 49, 52, 59, 60, 64, 66, 68, 105, 107, 215-216, 236, 243, 256, 259, 261, 266, 384, 386, 395, 396, 399, 403, 430, 433, 441, 446, 475, 478, 479, 482, 521, 522, 527, **567-591; II:** 65, 96, 158, 168, 316, 371, 376, 386, 529, 530, 532, 537, 542, 545; **III:** 1, 4, 5, 6, 7-8, 9, 10, 11, 14, 17, 20, 21, 23, 26, 34, 174, 194, 195-196, 205-206, 220, 236, 239, 269, 270-271, 277-278, 301, 409, 428, 435, 436, 453, 456-457, 459-460, 461-462, 464, 466, 471, 476, 478, 485, 488, 492, 493, 498, 504, 509, 511, 517, 524, 527, 539, 572, 575, 586, 591, 594, 600, 613; **IV:** 27, 74, 82, 83, 95, 122, 123, 127, 129, 134, 138, 140, 141, 191, 201, 237, 331, 379, 402, 403, 418, 419, 420, 430, 431, 439, 442, 491; **Retro. Supp. I: 51-71,** 74, 80, 89, 91, 171, 198, 210, 283, 289, 290, 292, 296, 298, 299, 311, 324, 359, 411, 413, 414, 416, 417, 420, 428; **Retro. Supp. II:** 79, 178, 189, 262, 326; **Supp. I Part 1:** 257, 264, 268, 270, 274, 299; **Supp. I Part 2:** 387, 423, 455, 536, 554, 624, 659, 721; **Supp. II Part 1:** 1, 4, 8, 20, 30, 91, 98, 103, 136, 314; **Supp. XVII:** 36, 71, 75, 111, 240; **Supp. III Part 1:** 9, 10, 26, 31, 37, 41, 43, 44, 48, 62-64, 73, 91, 99-100, 105-106, 273; **Supp. III Part 2:** 541, 611, 612, 617, 624; **Supp. IV Part 1:** 40, 47, 284, 380, 404; **Supp. IV Part 2:** 436; **Supp. V:** 79, 97, 101, 338, 343, 344; **Supp. VIII:** 19, 21, 93, 102, 105, 182, 195, 205, 290, 292; **Supp. IX:** 158-159, 229; **Supp. X:** 59, 115, 119, 124, 187, 324; **Supp. XI:** 242; **Supp. XII:** 45, 159, 198, 308; **Supp. XIII:** 77, 104, 115, 332, 341-342, 344, 346; **Supp. XIV:**5, 13, 107, 287, 290, 306, 347; **Supp. XV:** 20,**Supp. XV:** 251, 51, 139, 177, 181, 186, 216, 218, 250, 258, 298, 302, 303, 306, 307; **Supp. XVI:**158-159, 204, 207, 282
Eliot's Early Years (Gordon), **Retro. Supp. I:** 55
"Elizabeth" (Longfellow), **I:** 502
"Elizabeth, 1905" (Schnackenberg), **Supp. XV:** 253, 256
Elizabeth Appleton (O'Hara), **III:** 362, 364, 375-377
"Elizabeth Bishop (1911-1979)" (Merrill), **Retro. Supp. II:** 53
"Elizabeth Bishop in Brazil" (Brown), **Supp. I Part 1:** 96
"Elizabeth Bishop's *North & South*" (Lowell), **Retro. Supp. II:** 40-41
"Elizabeth Gone" (Sexton), **Supp. II Part 2:** 674, 681
Elizabeth Stoddard and the Boundaries of Bourgeois Culture (Mahoney), **Supp. XV:** 270
Elk Heads on the Wall (Ríos), **Supp. IV Part 2:** 540
Elkin, Stanley, **Supp. VI: 41-59**
"Elk Song" (Hogan), **Supp. IV Part 1:** 406
Ella in Bloom (Hearon), **Supp. VIII: 70-71**
Elledge, Jim, **Supp. XIII:** 88
Ellen Foster: A Novel (Gibbons), **Supp. X:** 41, **42-44,** 46, 47, 49, 50
Ellen Rogers (Farrell), **II:** 42-43
"Ellen's Dream" (Gioia), **Supp. XV:** 128
"Ellen West" (Bidart), **Supp. XV: 26-27**
Eller, Ernest, **Supp. I Part 2:** 497
Ellerman, Winifred, **Supp. I Part 1:** 258-259. *See also* McAlmon, Mrs. Robert (Winifred Ellerman)
"*El libro de la sexualidad*" (Simic), **Supp. VIII:** 283
Ellington, Duke, **Retro. Supp. II:** 115; **Supp. IV Part 1:** 360; **Supp. IX:** 164
Elliot, Charles, **Supp. V:** 161
Elliot, George P., **Supp. XV:** 92
Elliott, George B., **III:** 478
"Ellipsis" (C. Frost), **Supp. XV:** 107
Ellis, Albert, **Supp. IV Part 2:** 527
Ellis, Anne, **Supp. XVI:**38
Ellis, Bret Easton, **Supp. XII:** 81
Ellis, Brett Easton, **Supp. X:** 7
Ellis, Charles, **Supp. I Part 1:** 99
Ellis, Havelock, **II:** 276
Ellis, John Harvard, **Supp. I Part 1:** 103
Ellis, Katherine, **IV:** 114
Ellison, Harlan, **Supp. XIII:** 61
Ellison, Ralph, **IV:** 250, 493; **Retro. Supp. II:** 3, **111-130; Supp. II Part 1:** 33, **221-252; Supp. IV, Part 1:** 374; **Supp. VIII:** 105, 245; **Supp. IX:** 114, 316; **Supp. X:** 324; **Supp. XI:** 18, 92, 275; **Supp. XIII:** 186, 233, 305; **Supp. XIV:**306; **Supp. XV:** 194; **Supp. XVI:**135, 139
Ellmann, Maud, **Supp. IV Part 1:** 302
Ellmann, Richard, **Supp. VIII:** 105; **Supp. XV:** 74
Ellroy, James, **Supp. XIV:**26
Elman, Richard, **Supp. V:** 40
"Elmer" (Faulkner), **Retro. Supp. I:** 79, 80
Elmer Gantry (Lewis), **I:** 26, 364; **II:** 447-449, 450, 455
Elmer the Great (Lardner), **II:** 427
"Elms" (Glück), **Supp. V:** 85
Eloges (Perse), **Supp. XIII:** 344
"Eloquence of Grief, An" (Crane), **I:** 411
"El Río Grande" (Mora), **Supp. XIII:** 224
"*El* Round up" (Alvarez), **Supp. VII:** 11
"El Salvador: Requiem and Invocation" (Levertov), **Supp. III Part 1:** 284
Elsasser, Henry, **I:** 226
"Elsa Wertman" (Masters), **Supp. I Part 2:** 462-463
Elsie John and Joey Martinez: Two Stories (Huncke), **Supp. XIV:**148
Elsie Venner (Holmes), **Supp. I Part 1:** 243, 315-316
Elton, Charles, **Supp. XIV:**192
Éluard, Paul, **III:** 528; **Supp. IV Part 1:** 80; **Supp. XVII:** 244
Elvins, Kells, **Supp. III Part 1:** 93, 101
Ely, Richard T., **Supp. I Part 1:** 5; **Supp. I Part 2:** 640, 645
"Emancipation. A Life Fable" (Chopin), **Retro. Supp. II:** 59; **Supp. I Part 1:** 207-208
"Emancipation in the British West Indies" (Emerson), **II:** 13
"Emancipation Proclamation, The" (Emerson), **II:** 13
Emanuel, James, **Supp. I Part 1:** 346
Embargo, The (Bryant), **Supp. I Part 1:** 152-153
Embarrassments (James), **Retro. Supp. I:** 229
Embezzler, The (Auchincloss), **Supp. IV Part 1:** 24, 30-31
"Embroidery, The" (C. Frost), **Supp. XV:** 97
"Emerald" (Doty), **Supp. XI:** 131
"Emerald, The" (Merrill), **Supp. III Part 1:** 328
"Emergence of Flight from Aristotle's Mud, The" (Goldbarth), **Supp. XII:** 190
"Emergency Haying" (Carruth), **Supp. XVI:**55
"Emergency Room" (Mora), **Supp. XIII:** 218
"Emerging Voices: The Teaching of Writing" (Mora), **Supp. XIII:** 220
Emerson, and Other Essays

(Chapman), **Supp. XIV:** 41-44
Emerson, Ellen, **Supp. I Part 1:** 33
Emerson, John, **Supp. XVI:** 185, 186, 190, 192
Emerson, Ralph Waldo, **I:** 98, 217, 220, 222, 224, 228, 239, 246, 251, 252, 253, 257, 260, 261, 283, 386, 397, 402, 424, 433, 444, 447, 455, 458, 460-461, 463, 464, 485, 561; **II:** 1-24, 49, 92, 127-128, 169, 170, 226, 233, 237, 273-274, 275, 278, 289, 295, 301, 313, 315, 336, 338, 344, 402, 491, 503; **III:** 53, 82, 171, 174, 260, 277, 409, 424, 428, 453, 454, 507, 576-577, 606, 614; **IV:** 60, 167, 169, 170, 171, 172, 173-174, 176, 178, 183, 186, 187, 192, 201, 202, 211, 335, 338, 340, 342, 350; **Retro. Supp. I:** 34, 53, 54, 57, 62, 74-75, 76, 125, 148-149, 152-153, 159, 217, 250, 298, 392, 400, 403; **Retro. Supp. II:** 96, 113, 135, 142, 155, 207, 262; **Supp. I Part 1:** 2, 28-29, 31, 33, 188, 299, 308-309, 317, 358, 365, 366, 368; **Supp. I Part 2:** 374, 383, 393, 407, 413, 416, 420, 422, 474, 482, 580, 582, 602, 659, 679; **Supp. II Part 1:** 280, 288; **Supp. III Part 1:** 387; **Supp. IV Part 2:** 439, 597, 619; **Supp. V:** 118; **Supp. VIII:** 42, 105, 106, 108, 198, 201, 204, 205, 292; **Supp. IX:** 38, 90, 175, 176, 181; **Supp. X:** 42, 45, 121, 223; **Supp. XI:** 203; **Supp. XIII:** 141, 145, 233, 246, **Supp. XIII:** 247; **Supp. XIV:** 41-44, 46, 54, 104, 177; **Supp. XV:** 219, 224; **Supp. XVI:** 84; **Supp. XVII:** 42, 236
"Emerson and the Essay" (Gass), **Supp. VI:** 88
"Emerson the Lecturer" (Lowell), **Supp. I Part 2:** 420, 422
Emerson-Thoreau Award, **Retro. Supp. I:** 67
Emery, Clark, **III:** 478
"Emigre in Autumn, An" (Gioia), **Supp. XV:** 120
Emily Dickinson: Woman Poet (Bennett), **Retro. Supp. I:** 42
"Emily Dickinson and Class" (Erkkila), **Retro. Supp. I:** 42-43
Emily Dickinson Editorial Collective, **Retro. Supp. I:** 47
Emily Dickinson in Southern California (X. J. Kennedy), **Supp. XV:** 164-165
Eminent Victorians (Strachey), **Supp. I Part 2:** 485

"Emma and Eginhard" (Longfellow), **III:** 505
"Emma Enters a Sentence of Elizabeth Bishop's" (Gass), **Supp. VI:** 93
Emperor Jones, The (O'Neill), **II:** 278; **III:** 391, 392
Emperor of Haiti (Hughes), **Supp. I Part 1:** 339
"Emperor of Ice Cream, The" (Stevens), **IV:** 76, 80-81
"Emperors" (Dunn), **Supp. XI:** 155
"Emperor's New Clothes, The" (Anderson), **I:** 441
"Empire" (Ford), **Supp. V:** 69
Empire: A Novel (Vidal), **Supp. IV Part 2:** 677, 684, 686, 690
"Empire Builders" (MacLeish), **III:** 14
Empire Falls (Russo), **Supp. XII:** 339-343
Empire of Summer, The (Doty), **Supp. XI:** 120
Empire of the Senseless (Acker), **Supp. XII:** 5, **6**, 14-16
"Empires" (Simic), **Supp. VIII:** 282
"Emporium" (Shapiro), **Supp. II Part 2:** 705
Empress of the Splendid Season (Hijuelos), **Supp. VIII:** 86-89
Empson, William, **I:** 522, 533; **II:** 536; **III:** 286, 497, 498, 499; **IV:** 136, 431; **Retro. Supp. I:** 263; **Retro. Supp. II:** 253; **Supp. XVI:** 190
"Empty Hills, The" (Winters), **Supp. II Part 2:** 792, 793, 796
Empty Mirror, Early Poems (Ginsberg), **Supp. II Part 1:** 308, 311, 313-314, 319, 329
"Empty Room" (Hughes), **Supp. I Part 1:** 337
"Empty Threat, An" (Frost), **II:** 159
"Encantadas, The" (Melville), **III:** 89
Enchanter, The (Nabokov), **Retro. Supp. I:** 266
"Encomium Twenty Years Later" (Tate), **I:** 381
"Encounter, The" (Pound), **III:** 466
Encounter in April (Sarton), **Supp. VIII:** 259
"Encounter in April" (Sarton), **Supp. VIII:** 259
"Encountering the Sublime" (McClatchy), **Supp. XII:** 261
"Encounter on the Seine: Black Meets Brown" (Baldwin), **Retro. Supp. II:** 2
Encounters with Chinese Writers (Dillard), **Supp. VI:** 19, 23, 31
Encounters with the Archdruid (McPhee), **Supp. III Part 1:** 292-294, 301; **Supp. X:** 30

Encyclopedia of Scotland, The (A. Finch), **Supp. XVII:** 70-71
"End, The" (Olds), **Supp. X:** 205
"Endangered Species" (Mora), **Supp. XIII:** 219-220
Endecott and the Red Cross (Lowell), **II:** 545
Endgame (Beckett), **Supp. XIII:** 196
"Endgame" (Tan), **Supp. X:** 290
"Endicott and the Red Cross" (Hawthorne), **Retro. Supp. II:** 181, 187-188
"End of Books, The" (Coover), **Supp. V:** 53
End of Education, The (Postman), **Supp. XI:** 275
"End of Season" (Warren), **IV:** 239-240
"End of Something, The" (Hemingway), **II:** 248
End of the Affair, The (Greene), **Supp. XI:** 99
End of the Age of Innocence, The (Price), **Retro. Supp. I:** 377
"End of the Line, The" (Jarrell), **III:** 527
"End of the Rainbow, The" (Jarrell), **II:** 386
End of the Road (film), **Supp. XI:** 309
End of the Road, The (Barth), **I:** 121, 122, 126-131; **Supp. XI:** 309
"End of the World, The" (Gioia), **Supp. XV:** 126
"End of the World, The" (MacLeish), **III:** 8
Endor (Nemerov), **III:** 269, 270, 279
Endore, Guy, **Supp. XVII:** 53-67
"Ends" (Dixon), **Supp. XII:** 153
End to Innocence, An: Essays on Culture and Politics (Fiedler), **Supp. XIII:** 98-99
Endure: The Diaries of Charles Walter Stetson (Stetson), **Supp. XI:** 196
"Enduring Chill, The" (O'Connor), **III:** 349, 351, 357; **Retro. Supp. II:** 236
Enduring Vision of Norman Mailer, The (Leeds), **Retro. Supp. II:** 204
Endymion (Keats), **IV:** 405; **Retro. Supp. I:** 412
End Zone (DeLillo), **Supp. VI:** 2, 3, 4, 10, 11, 12
Enemies (Hapgood and N. Boyce), **Supp. XVII:** 100
Enemies: A Love Story (Singer), **IV:** 1; **Retro. Supp. II:** 310-311
Enemy, The: Time (T. Williams), **IV:** 391
Enemy of the People, An (adapt. Miller), **III:** 154-156
"Energy Vampire" (Ginsberg), **Supp.**

II Part 1: 326
"Enforcement of the Slave Trade Laws, The" (Du Bois), **Supp. II Part 1:** 161
"Engaging the Past" (Bell), **Supp. X:** 17
Engel, Bernard F., **I:** 532
Engels, Friedrich, **IV:** 429, 443-444; **Supp. I Part 1:** 13
Engineer of Beasts, The (Sanders), **Supp. XVI:**270
Engineer of Moonlight (DeLillo), **Supp. VI:** 4
Engineers and the Price System, The (Veblen), **I:** 475-476; **Supp. I Part 2:** 638, 642, 648
Engines of Creation: the Coming Era of Nanotechnology (Drexler), **Supp. XVI:**121
"England" (Moore), **III:** 203, 207, 214
Engle, Paul, **III:** 542; **Retro. Supp. II:** 220, 221; **Supp. V:** 337; **Supp. XI:** 315; **Supp. XIII:** 76
English, Zoë, **Supp. XVI:**293
English Elegy, The: Studies in the Genre from Spenser to Yeats (Sacks), **Supp. IV Part 2:** 450
English Hours (James), **II:** 337; **Retro. Supp. I:** 235
English Language, The (L. P. Smith), **Supp. XIV:**341
Englishmen of Letters (James), **II:** 327
English Notebooks, The (Hawthorne), **II:** 226, 227-228
English Novel, The (Lanier), **Supp. I Part 1:** 371
English Poets, The: Lessing, Rousseau (Lowell), **Supp. I Part 2:** 407
English Prosody and Modern Poetry (Shapiro), **Supp. II Part 2:** 710
English Traits (Emerson), **II:** 1, 5, 6-7, 8
"English Writers on America" (Irving), **II:** 308
Engstrand, Stuart, **Supp. I Part 1:** 51
"Enoch and the Gorilla" (O'Connor), **Retro. Supp. II:** 225
Enormous Changes at the Last Minute (Paley), **Supp. VI:** 218
"Enormous Changes at the Last Minute" (Paley), **Supp. VI:** 226, 232
"Enormous Radio, The" (Cheever), **Supp. I Part 1:** 175-177, 195
Enormous Radio and Other Stories, The (Cheever), **Supp. I Part 1:** 175-177
Enormous Room, The (Cummings), **I:** 429, 434, 440, 445, 477
"Enough for a Lifetime" (Buck), **Supp. II Part 1:** 127
Enough Rope (Parker), **Supp. IX:** 189, 192
Enquiry Concerning Political Justice (Godwin), **Supp. I Part 1:** 126, 146
Entered From the Sun (Garrett), **Supp. VII:** 105-106, 107-109
"Entering the Kingdom" (Oliver), **Supp. VII:** 234
Entertaining Strangers (Gurney), **Supp. V:** 98, 99
Enter without Desire (Lacy), **Supp. XV:** 201
Entrance: Four Chicano Poets, **Supp. XIII:** 316
Entrance to Porlock, The (Buechner), **Supp. XII:** 52
Entries (Berry), **Supp. X:** 23
"Entropy" (Pynchon), **Supp. II Part 2:** 619, 621
Entry in an Unknown Hand (F. Wright), **Supp. XVII:** 240, 244, 245
Environmental Imagination, The (Buell), **Supp. V:** 209; **Supp. IX:** 29
"Envoys, The" (Merrill), **Supp. III Part 1:** 326
"Envy; or, Yiddish in America" (Ozick), **Supp. V:** 263, 265-266
"Eolian Harp, The" (Coleridge), **I:** 284
"Eototo" (Sobin), **Supp. XVI:**283-284
"Ephemera, The" (Franklin), **II:** 121
Ephesians (biblical book), **Supp. I Part 1:** 117
Epictetus, **III:** 566
"Epicurean, The" (Auchincloss), **Supp. IV Part 1:** 25
Epicurus, **I:** 59
"Epigram" (Lowell), **II:** 550
"Epilogue" (Lowell), **Retro. Supp. II:** 191
"Epimanes" (Poe), **III:** 411
"Epimetheus" (Longfellow), **II:** 494
"Epiphany" (X. J. Kennedy), **Supp. XV:** 166, 167
"Epipsychidion" (Shelley), **Supp. I Part 2:** 718
Episode in Palmetto (Caldwell), **I:** 297, 307
"Epistle" (L.-Y. Lee), **Supp. XV:** 212
Epistle to a Godson (Auden), **Supp. II Part 1:** 24
"Epistle to Be Left in the Earth" (MacLeish), **III:** 13
"Epistle to George William Curtis" (Lowell), **Supp. I Part 2:** 416
"Epistle to Léon-Paul Fargue" (MacLeish), **III:** 15
"Epitaph Ending in And, The" (Stafford), **Supp. XI:** 321-322
Epitaph for a Dead Beat (Markson), 139; **Supp. XVII: 136-138,** 141
Epitaph for a Desert Anarchist (Bishop), **Supp. XIII:** 1
Epitaph for a Tramp (Markson), **Supp. XVII:** 136, 137, 139 142
"Epitaph for Fire and Flower" (Plath), **Supp. I Part 2:** 537
"Epitaph for the Race of Man" (Millay), **III:** 127-128
"Epithalamium" (Auden), **Supp. II Part 1:** 15
"Epstein" (P. Roth), **Retro. Supp. II:** 281; **Supp. III Part 2:** 404, 406-407, 412, 422
Epstein, Helen, **Supp. XVII:** 47
Epstein, Jason, **Supp. VIII:** 233
Epstein, Joseph, **Supp. IV Part 2:** 692; **Supp. VIII:** 236, 238; **Supp. XIV:101-117; Supp. XVI:**230, 275
Epstein, Leslie, **Supp. XII: 159-174**
Epstein, Philip, **Supp. XII:** 159
"Equal in Paris" (Baldwin), **Retro. Supp. II:** 3; **Supp. I Part 1:** 52
"Equals" (Untermeyer), **Supp. XV:** 304
"Equations of the Light" (Gioia), **Supp. XV:** 125
"Equilibrists, The" (Ransom), **III:** 490, 494
"Equipment for Pennies" (H. Roth), **Supp. IX:** 233
Erasmus, Desiderius, **Supp. XV:** 258
"Erat Hora" (Pound), **III:** 463; **Retro. Supp. I:** 413
Erdrich, Louise, **Supp. IV Part 1: 259-278,** 333, 404; **Supp. X:** 290
"Erectus" (Karr), **Supp. XI:** 243
"Ere Sleep Comes Down to Soothe the Weary Eyes" (Dunbar), **Supp. II Part 1:** 199, 207-208
Erikson, Erik, **I:** 58, 214, 218
Erisman, Fred, **Supp. VIII:** 126
Erkkila, Betsy, **Retro. Supp. I:** 42
"Ernest: or Parent for a Day" (Bourne), **I:** 232
Ernst, Max, **Retro. Supp. II:** 321
"Eros" (Komunyakaa), **Supp. XIII:** 130
"Eros and Anteros" (E. Stoddard), **Supp. XV:** 283
Eros and Civilization (Marcuse), **Supp. XII:** 2
"Eros at Temple Stream" (Levertov), **Supp. III Part 1:** 278-279
Eros the Bittersweet (Carson), **Supp. XII:** 97, **98-99**
"Eros Turannos" (Robinson), **III:** 510, 512, 513-516, 517, 518

"Eroticism in Women" (Nin), **Supp. X:** 195
"Errand" (Carver), **Supp. III Part 1:** 149
Erskine, Albert, **IV:** 261; **Retro. Supp. II:** 117
Erskine, John, **I:** 223; **Supp. X:** 183; **Supp. XIV:**120
Erstein, Hap, **Supp. IV Part 2:** 589, 590
"Escape" (MacLeish), **III:** 4
Escape Artist, The (Wagoner), **Supp. IX:** 324, **334-335**
Escher, M. C., **Supp. XII:** 26; **Supp. XVI:**102
"Escudilla" (Leopold), **Supp. XIV:**188
Eshleman, Clayton, **Supp. XVI:**284
"Eskimo Love" (Apple), **Supp. XVII:** 5
Espen, Hal, **Supp. X:** 15
Espey, John, **III:** 463, 468, 478
Esposito, Scott, **Supp. XVII:** 234
Essais (Renouvier), **II:** 344-345
"Essay: The Love of Old Houses" (Doty), **Supp. XI:** 136
Essay Concerning Human Understanding, An (Locke), **I:** 554; **II:** 8, 348-349
Essay on American Poetry (Brown), **Supp. I Part 1:** 156
"Essay on Aristocracy" (Paine), **Supp. I Part 2:** 515
"Essay on Friendship, An" (McClatchy), **Supp. XII:** 258-259
"Essay on Love" (Carruth), **Supp. XVI:**56
Essay on Man (Pope), **II:** 111; **Supp. I Part 2:** 516
"Essay on Marriage" (Carruth), **Supp. XVI:**48
Essay on Our Changing Order (Veblen), **Supp. I Part 2:** 629, 642
"Essay on Poetics" (Ammons), **Supp. VII:** 29-31
Essay on Projects (Defoe), **II:** 104
"Essay on Psychiatrists" (Pinsky), **Supp. VI:** 237, 238, 241, 242, 249, 250
Essay on Rime (Shapiro), **I:** 430; **Supp. II Part 2:** 702, 703, 708-711
"Essay on Sanity" (Dunn), **Supp. XI:** 147
"Essay on the Character of Robespierre" (Paine), **Supp. I Part 2:** 515
Essay on the Chinese Written Character (Fenollosa), **III:** 474
"Essay on What I Think About Most" (Carson), **Supp. XII: 111-112**
Essays (Emerson), **II:** 1, 7, 8, 12-13, 15, 21

Essays, Speeches, and Public Letters by William Faulkner (Meriweather, ed.), **Retro. Supp. I:** 77
Essays in Anglo-Saxon Law (Adams), **I:** 5
Essays in London (James), **II:** 336
Essays in Radical Empiricism (James), **II:** 355, 356-357
Essays on Norman Mailer (Lucid), **Retro. Supp. II:** 195
Essays on the Nature and Principles of Taste (Alison), **Supp. I Part 1:** 151
Essays to Do Good (Mather), **II:** 104; **Supp. II Part 2:** 461, 467
"Essay Toward a Point of View, An" (Brooks), **I:** 244
"Essence, Absence, and Sobin's *Venus Blue*" (English), **Supp. XVI:**293
Essential Haiku, The (Hass), **Supp. VI:** 102
Essential Keats (Levine, ed.), **Supp. V:** 179
"Essential Oils-are wrung" (Dickinson), **I:** 471; **Retro. Supp. I:** 43, 46
"Essentials" (Toomer), **Supp. III Part 2:** 486
Essentials: A Philosophy of Life in Three Hundred Definitions and Aphorisms (Toomer), **Supp. III Part 2:** 486
Essentials: Definitions and Aphorisms (Toomer), **Supp. IX:** 320
"Essentials of Spontaneous Prose" (Kerouac), **Supp. III Part 1:** 227-228
"Estate Sale" (Nye), **Supp. XIII:** 283
Estess, Sybil, **Supp. IV Part 2:** 449, 452
Esther (Adams), **I:** 9-10, 20
"Esther" (Toomer), **Supp. IX:** 313-314
"Esthétique du Mal" (Stevens), **IV:** 79; **Retro. Supp. I:** 300, 311, 312
"Estoy-eh-muut and the Kunideeyahs (Arrowboy and the Destroyers)" (film), **Supp. IV Part 2:** 560
Estrada, Genaro, **Retro. Supp. II:** 89
Estray, The (Longfellow, ed.), **Retro. Supp. II:** 155
Esty, William, **III:** 358
"Etching, An" (Masters), **Supp. I Part 2:** 458
"Eternal Goodness, The" (Whittier), **Supp. I Part 2:** 704
Eternal Spring, The (N. Boyce), **Supp. XVII:** 100
"Eternity, An" (W. C. Williams), **Retro. Supp. I:** 423
"Eternity Is Now" (Roethke), **III:** 544-545

"Ethan Brand" (Hawthorne), **II:** 227
Ethan Frome (Wharton), **IV:** 316-317, 327; **Retro. Supp. I:** 372-373; **Supp. IX:** 108
Ethics (Spinoza), **IV:** 12; **Retro. Supp. II:** 300
"Ethics of Culture, The" (Locke), **Supp. XIV:**211
"Ethnics of Frank Costello, The" (Talese), **Supp. XVII:** 202
Etulain, Richard, **Supp. IV Part 2:** 597, 601, 604, 606, 607, 608, 610, 611
Euclid, **III:** 6, 620
"Euclid Alone Has Looked on Beauty Bare" (Millay), **III:** 133
Eugene, Frank, **Supp. X:** 204
Eugene Onegin (Pushkin), **III:** 246, 263
Eugene Onegin (Pushkin; Nabokov, trans.), **Retro. Supp. I:** 266, 267, 272
Eugénie, Empress, **IV:** 309
Eugénie Grandet (Balzac), **II:** 328
"Eugénie Grandet" (Barthelme), **Supp. IV Part 1:** 47
"Eulogy for Richard Hugo (1923-1982)" (Wagoner), **Supp. IX:** 330-331
"Eulogy on the Flapper" (Z. Fitzgerald), **Supp. IX:** 71
Eumenides (Aeschylus), **Retro. Supp. I:** 65
"E Unibus Pluram: Television and U.S. Fiction" (Wallace), **Supp. X:** 315-316
"Euphemisms" (Matthews), **Supp. IX: 167-168**
Eureka (Poe), **III:** 409, 424, 428-429
Eurekas (Goldbarth), **Supp. XII:** 181
Euripides, **I:** 325; **II:** 8, 282, 543; **III:** 22, 145, 398; **IV:** 370; **Supp. I Part 1:** 268, 269, 270; **Supp. I Part 2:** 482; **Supp. V:** 277
"Euripides and Professor Murray" (Eliot), **Supp. I Part 1:** 268
"Euripides-A Playwright" (West), **IV:** 286; **Retro. Supp. II:** 326
"Europe" (Ashbery), **Supp. III Part 1:** 7-10, 13, 18
European Discovery of America, The: The Northern Voyages (Morison), **Supp. I Part 2:** 496-497
European Discovery of America, The: The Southern Voyages (Morison), **Supp. I Part 2:** 497
Europeans, The (H. James), **I:** 452; **II:** 327, 328; **Retro. Supp. I:** 216, 220
Europe Central (Vollmann), **Supp.**

XVII: 225, 226, 227, 229, 231, **233-235,** 236
"Europe! Europe!" (Ginsberg), **Supp. II Part 1:** 320, 322
Europe of Trusts, The: Selected Poems (Howe), **Supp. IV Part 2:** 420, 422, 426
Europe without Baedeker (Wilson), **IV:** 429
Eurydice in the Underworld (Acker), **Supp. XII:** 7
Eustace, Saint, **II:** 215
Eustace Chisholm and the Works (Purdy), **Supp. VII:** 273-274, 279-280
"Euthanasia" (Tate), **IV:** 122
Eva-Mary (McCarriston), **Supp. XIV:**259, 260, **263-268**
"Evangeline" (Dixon), **Supp. XII:** 153
Evangeline (Longfellow), **II:** 489, 501-502; **Retro. Supp. II:** 155, **156-159,** 162, 164; **Supp. I Part 2:** 586
Evanier, David, **Supp. XVI:**212
Evans, Alice, **Supp. XVII:** 71, 72
Evans, Mary Ann. *See* Eliot, George
Evans, Oliver, **Supp. IV Part 1:** 85, 91
Evans, Sandy, **Supp. XIII:** 129
Evans, Walker, **I:** 36, 38, 293; **Retro. Supp. II:** 85
Eve (A. Finch), **Supp. XVII: 72-74**
"Eve" (W. C. Williams), **Retro. Supp. I:** 423
Even Cowgirls Get the Blues (Robbins), **Supp. X:** 259, 260, 261, 262-263, 264, 266, **269-271,** 272, 274, 277, 284; **Supp. XIII:** 11
"Evening" (Carver), **Supp. III Part 1:** 148
Evening (Minot), **Supp. VI:** 204-205, 208, **213-215**
"Evening at a Country Inn" (Kenyon), **Supp. VII:** 167
"Evening in a Sugar Orchard" (Frost), **Retro. Supp. I:** 133
"Evening in Nuevo Leon, An" (Caldwell), **I:** 309
"Evening in the Sanitarium" (Bogan), **Supp. III Part 1:** 61
"Evening of the 4th of July, The" (Kees), **Supp. XV:** 140, 142
"Evening on the Cote d'Azur" (Yates), **Supp. XI:** 349
Evening Performance, An: New and Selected Short Stories (Garrett), **Supp. VII:** 109
"Evenings at Home" (Hardwick), **Supp. III Part 1:** 195-196
"Evening's at Seven, The" (Thurber), **Supp. I Part 2:** 616

"Evening Star" (Bogan), **Supp. III Part 1:** 56
Evening Star, The (McMurtry), **Supp. V:** 230
Evening Star, The (screenplay) (McMurtry), **Supp. V:** 232
"Evening Sun" (Kenyon), **Supp. VII:** 168
Evening Sun Turned Crimson, The (Huncke), **Supp. XIV:**140, 149-150
"Evening Sun Turned Crimson, The" (Huncke), **Supp. XIV:**137-138, 139
"Evening Wind, The" (Bryant), **Supp. I Part 1:** 164
"Evening without Angels" (Stevens), **Retro. Supp. I:** 302
Evening with Richard Nixon, An (Vidal), **Supp. IV Part 2:** 683
"Even Sea, The" (Swenson), **Supp. IV Part 2:** 641
Even Stephen (Perelman and West), **Retro. Supp. II:** 328
"Event, An" (Wilbur), **Supp. III Part 2:** 547, 554
"Event, The" (Dove), **Supp. IV Part 1:** 242, 247-248
"Eventide" (Brooks), **Supp. III Part 1:** 73
"Eventide" (Purdy), **Supp. VII:** 270
"Event Itself, The" (Carruth), **Supp. XVI:**47
Eve of Saint Agnes, The (Keats), **II:** 82, 531
"Eve of St. Agnes, The" (Clampitt), **Supp. IX:** 40
"Ever a Bridegroom: Reflections on the Failure of Texas Literature" (McMurtry), **Supp. V:** 225
Everett, Alexander Hill, **Supp. I Part 1:** 152
Everlasting Story of Nory, The (Baker), **Supp. XIII:** 52, **Supp. XIII: 53-55**
Ever-Present Past, The (Hamilton), **Supp. XVI:**196
Evers, Medgar, **IV:** 280; **Retro. Supp. II:** 13; **Supp. I Part 1:** 52, 65
Everwine, Peter, **Supp. V:** 180; **Supp. XIII:** 312; **Supp. XV: 73-90**
"Everybody's Protest Novel" (Baldwin), **Retro. Supp. II:** 4; **Supp. I Part 1:** 50, 51
"Everybody's Reading Li Po' Silk-screened on a Purple T-Shirt" (Komunyakaa), **Supp. XIII:** 120
Everybody's Story: Writing by Older Minnesotans (C. Bly, ed.), **Supp. XVI:**38
"Everybody Was Very Nice" (Benét), **Supp. XI:** 53
"Every-Day Girl, A" (Jewett), **Retro.**

Supp. II: 132
"Everyday Use" (Walker), **Supp. III Part 2:** 534
"Every-Day Work" (Jewett), **Retro. Supp. II:** 132
Everyone Says I Love You (film; Allen), **Supp. XV:** 11
Every Pleasure (Goldbarth), **Supp. XII:** 181
Every Soul Is a Circus (Lindsay), **Supp. I Part 2:** 384, 394, 399
"Everything Is a Human Being" (Walker), **Supp. III Part 2:** 527
Everything Is Illuminated (Foer), **Supp. XII:** 169
"Everything Stuck to Him" (Carver), **Supp. III Part 1:** 143
Everything That Rises Must Converge (O'Connor), **III:** 339, 348-349, 350-351; **Retro. Supp. II:** 235, **236-237**
"Everything That Rises Must Converge" (O'Connor), **III:** 349, 352, 357; **Retro. Supp. II:** 236
Everything You Always Wanted to Know about Sex (film; Allen), **Supp. XV:** 4-5, 13
Eve's Diary (Twain), **IV:** 208-209
"Eve Speaks" (Untermeyer), **Supp. XV:** 300
"Eve the Fox" (Gunn Allen), **Supp. IV Part 1:** 331
"Evidence" (Harjo), **Supp. XII:** 219
Evidence of the Senses, The (Kelley), **Supp. IV Part 2:** 529
Evidence of Things Not Seen, The (Baldwin), **Retro. Supp. II:** 15
"Evil Seekers, The" (Sexton), **Supp. II Part 2:** 696
"Evolution" (Swenson), **Supp. IV Part 2:** 639
Evolving the Idol: The Poetry of Gustaf Sobin (Crick), **Supp. XVI:**289
Ewing, Jon, **Supp. X:** 253
Ewings, The (O'Hara), **III:** 383
"Examination at the Womb Door" (Hughes), **Supp. XV:** 347
"Examination of the Hero in a Time of War" (Stevens), **Retro. Supp. I:** 305-306, 308
"Excavation of Troy" (MacLeish), **III:** 18
Excellent Becomes the Permanent, The (Addams), **Supp. I Part 1:** 25
"Excelsior" (Longfellow), **Retro. Supp. II:** 169
"Excerpts from Swan Lake" (Cameron), **Supp. XII:** 80, **84**
"Excerpts from the Epistemology Workshops" (Rand), **Supp. IV Part 2:** 529

"Excess of Charity" (Wylie), **Supp. I Part 2:** 720
"Exchange, The" (Swenson), **Supp. IV Part 2:** 644
"Excitement, The " (Jarman), **Supp. XVII:** 120-121
"Exclusive" (Olds), **Supp. X:** 206
"Excrement Poem, The" (Kumin), **Supp. IV Part 2:** 448
"Excursion" (Garrett), **Supp. VII:** 100
Excursions (Thoreau), **IV:** 188
"Excursus of Reassurance in Begonia Time, An" (Carruth), **Supp. XVI:**58
Executioner's Song, The (Mailer), **Retro. Supp. II:** 108, 209
Exercises in History, Chronology, and Biography, in Question and Answer (Rowson), **Supp. XV:** 245
Ex-Friends: Falling Out with Allen Ginsberg, Lionel and Diana Trilling, Lillian Hellman, Hannah Arendt, and Norman Mailer (Podhoretz), **Supp. VIII:** 239, **242-244**
"Exhausted Bug, The" (R. Bly), **Supp. IV Part 1:** 73
"Exhortation" (Bogan), **Supp. III Part 1:** 58
"Exhortation" (McKay), **Supp. X:** 135
"Exile" (Gass), **Supp. VI:** 92
"Exile" (Oates), **Supp. II Part 2:** 523
Exile, The (Buck), **Supp. II Part 1:** 119, 131
"Exiles, The" (Bradbury), **Supp. IV Part 1:** 113
"Exiles, The" (Whittier), **Supp. I Part 2:** 692-693
Exiles and Fabrications (Scott), **II:** 512
Exile's Daughter, The (Spencer), **Supp. II Part 1:** 121
"Exile's Departure, The" (Whittier), **Supp. I Part 2:** 683
Exiles from Paradise: Zelda and Scott Fitzgerald (Mayfield), **Supp. IX:** 65
"Exile's Letter" (Karr), **Supp. XI:** 241
Exile's Return (Cowley), **Supp. III Part 1:** 136, 138, 140, 141, 144, 147, 148
"Exile's Return, The" (Lowell), **II:** 539; **Retro. Supp. II:** 187
"Existences" (Stafford), **Supp. XI:** 324
Existentialism from Dostoevsky to Sartre (W. Kaufmann), **Supp. XVII:** 137
Exit into History (Hoffman), **Supp. XVI:**148, 150, **151-153**
Exit to Eden (Rampling), **Supp. VII:** 301-302
Exley, Frederick, **Supp. XVII:** 135

Exley, Frederick, **Supp. XVI:**69
Exodus (biblical book), **IV:** 300
Exodus (Uris), **Supp. IV Part 1:** 379
"Exorcism" (Snodgrass), **Supp. VI:** 314
"Exorcism, An" (Malamud), **Supp. I Part 2:** 435
Exorcist, The (film), **Supp. I Part 1:** 66
"Expanses" (Dickey), **Supp. IV Part 1:** 186
"Ex Parte" (Lardner), **II:** 432
"Expatiation on the Combining of Weathers at Thirty-seventh and Indiana Where the Southern More or Less Crosses the Dog, The" (Carruth), **Supp. XVI:**51-52
"Expectant Father Compares His Wife to a Rabbit, An" (White), **Supp. I Part 2:** 678
"Expedition to the Pole, An" (Dillard), **Supp. VI:** 32, 34
"Expelled" (Cheever), **Supp. I Part 1:** 174, 186
Expense of Greatness, The (Blackmur), **Supp. II Part 1:** 90, 107
Expense of Vision, The (Holland), **Retro. Supp. I:** 216
"Expensive Gifts" (Miller), **Supp. XII:** 294
"Expensive Moment, The" (Paley), **Supp. VI:** 222, **227-228**, 230
Expensive People (Oates), **Supp. II Part 2:** 509, 510-511
"Experience" (Emerson), **Supp. XIV:**42
"Experience and Fiction" (Jackson), **Supp. IX:** 121
"Experience and the Objects of Knowledge in the Philosophy of F. H. Bradley" (Eliot), **I:** 572; **Retro. Supp. I:** 59
Experience of Literature, The (Trilling), **Supp. III Part 2:** 493
"Experiences and Principles of an Historian" (Morison), **Supp. I Part 2:** 492
Experimental Death Unit # 1 (Baraka), **Supp. II Part 1:** 46
"Experimental Life, The" (Bourne), **I:** 217, 220
"Experiment in Misery, An" (S. Crane), **I:** 411; **Retro. Supp. II:** 97
Experiments and Observations on Electricity (Franklin), **II:** 102, 114-115
"Expiation" (Wharton), **Retro. Supp. I:** 367
"Explaining Evil" (Gordon), **Supp. IV Part 1:** 310
"Explanation" (Stevens), **IV:** 79

Explanation of America, An (Pinsky), **Supp. VI:** 237, **241-243**
Exploding Gravy (X. J. Kennedy), **Supp. XV:** 163
"Exploit" (Wharton), **IV:** 324
"Exploration in the Great Tuolumne Cañon" (Muir), **Supp. IX:** 181
"Explorer, The" (Brooks), **Supp. III Part 1:** 79-80
"Exploring the Magalloway" (Parkman), **Supp. II Part 2:** 591
Expositor's Bible, The (G. A. Smith), **III:** 199
Expressions of Sea Level (Ammons), **Supp. VII:** 24, 28, 36
Extract from Captain Stormfield's Visit to Heaven (Twain), **IV:** 209-210
Extracts from Adam's Diary (Twain), **IV:** 208-209
"Exulting, The" (Roethke), **III:** 544
"Eye, The" (Bowles), **Supp. IV Part 1:** 93
Eye, The (Nabokov), **III:** 251
Eye-Beaters, Blood, Victory, Madness, Buckhead and Mercy, The (Dickey), **Supp. IV Part 1:** 178, 182-183
"Eye for an Eye, An" (Humphrey), **Supp. IX:** 108
"Eye in the Rock, The" (Haines), **Supp. XII:** 208, 209
"Eye-Mote, The" (Plath), **Retro. Supp. II:** 246, 247
"Eye of Paris, The" (H. Miller), **III:** 183-184
Eye of the Poet, The: Six Views of the Art and Craft of Poetry (Citino, ed.), **Supp. XIII:** 115
"Eye of the Rock, The" (Haines), **Supp. XII:** 208
"Eye of the Story, The" (Porter), **IV:** 279
Eye of the Story, The: Selected Essays and Reviews (Welty), **Retro. Supp. I:** 339, 342, 344, 345, 346, 351, 354, 355, 356
"Eyes, The" (Wharton), **IV:** 315
"Eyes like They Say the Devil Has" (Ríos), **Supp. IV Part 2:** 543, 544
Eyes of the Dragon, The (King), **Supp. V:** 139, 152
Eyes of the Heart: A Memoir of the Lost and Found (Buechner), **Supp. XII:** 53
"Eyes of Zapata" (Cisneros), **Supp. VII:** 70
"Eyes to See" (Cozzens), **I:** 374
Eye-to-Eye (Nye), **Supp. XIII:** 274
Eysturoy, Annie O., **Supp. IV Part 1:** 321, 322, 323, 328
Ezekiel (biblical book), **II:** 541

Ezekiel, Mordecai, **Supp. I Part 2:** 645
"Ezra Pound" (Bynner), **Supp. XV:** 49
"Ezra Pound: His Cantos" (Zukofsky), **Supp. III Part 2:** 612, 619, 622
Ezra Pound's Mauberley (Espey), **III:** 463
"Ezra Pound's Very Useful Labors" (Schwartz), **Supp. II Part 2:** 644

F

"F. S. F., 1896-1996, R.I.P." (Doctorow), **Retro. Supp. I:** 97
F. Scott Fitzgerald: A Critical Portrait (Piper), **Supp. IX:** 65
Faas, Ekbert, **Supp. VIII:** 292
"Fabbri Tape, The" (Auchincloss), **Supp. IV Part 1:** 21-22
Faber, Geoffrey, **Retro. Supp. I:** 63
Faber Book of Movie Verse, The (French and Wlaschin, eds.), **Supp. XVI:** 294
"Fable" (Merwin), **Supp. III Part 1:** 343
"Fable" (Wylie), **Supp. I Part 2:** 714
Fable, A (Faulkner), **II:** 55, 73; **Retro. Supp. I:** 74
"Fable, A" (Glück), **Supp. V:** 86
"Fable, The" (Winters), **Supp. II Part 2:** 792, 793, 796
Fable for Critics, A (Lowell), **Supp. I Part 2:** 406, 407-408, 409, 412-413, 416, 420, 422
"Fable of the War, A" (Nemerov), **III:** 272
Fables (Gay), **II:** 111
Fables and Distances: New and Selected Essays (Haines), **Supp. XII:** 197, 199, 207-208, 211
Fables for Our Time (Thurber), **Supp. I Part 2:** 610
Fables of Identity: Studies in Poetic Mythology (Frye), **Supp. X:** 80
Fables of La Fontaine, The (Moore), **III:** 194, 215
"Fables of Representation: Poetry of the New York School" (Hoover), **Supp. XV:** 179
"Fables of the Fallen Guy" (Rosaldo), **Supp. IV Part 2:** 544
"Fables of the Moscow Subway" (Nemerov), **III:** 271
Fabulators, The (Scholes), **Supp. V:** 40
Fabulous Small Jews (Epstein), **Supp. XIV:** 112
Face against the Glass, The (Francis), **Supp. IX:** 80-81
Face of Time, The (Farrell), **II:** 28, 34, 35, 39

Faces of Jesus, The (Buechner), **Supp. XII:** 53
Face to the Wind (film), **Supp. XVII:** 141
Fachinger, Petra, **Supp. XVI:** 153
"Facing It" (Komunyakaa), **Supp. XIII:** 117, 124, 125
"Facing West from California's Shores" (Jeffers), **Supp. II Part 2:** 437-438
"Fact in Fiction, The" (McCarthy), **II:** 562
"Facts" (Levine), **Supp. V:** 193
"Facts" (Oliver), **Supp. VII:** 231-232
"Facts" (Snyder), **Supp. VIII:** 301
"Facts, The" (Lardner), **II:** 431
Facts, The: A Novelist's Autobiography (P. Roth), **Retro. Supp. II:** 280, 291; **Supp. III Part 2:** 401, 405, 417, 426
"Facts and Traditions Respecting the Existence of Indigenous Intermittent Fever in New England" (Holmes), **Supp. I Part 1:** 303
"Facts in the Case of M. Valdemar, The" (Poe), **III:** 416
Faderman, Lillian, **Retro. Supp. II:** 135; **Supp. XIII:** 313
Fadiman, Clifton, **II:** 430, 431, 443, 591-592; **Supp. IX:** 8; **Supp. XVI:** 100, 106; **Supp. XVII:** 87, 90
Fading, My Parmacheene Belle (J. Scott), **Supp. XVII:** 184-185, 188
"Fado" (McClatchy), **Supp. XII:** 265-266
Faerie Queene, The (Spenser), **III:** 487; **IV:** 253; **Supp. XIV:** 6; **Supp. XV:** 181
Faery, Rebecca Blevins, **Retro. Supp. I:** 374
Fagan, Kathy, **Supp. V:** 180; **Supp. XV:** 73
Fahrenheit 451 (Bradbury), **Supp. IV Part 1:** 101, 102, 104, 107-109, 110, 113; **Supp. XIII:** 29
"Failure" (Gioia), **Supp. XV:** 125
"Failure" (Zach; Everwine, trans.), **Supp. XV:** 86
"Failure of David Barry, The" (Jewett), **Retro. Supp. II:** 132
Fainlight, Ruth, **Supp. XV:** 261, 264
Faint Perfume (Gale), **Supp. I Part 2:** 613
Fair, Bryan K., **Supp. VIII:** 128
Fairbanks, Douglas, **Supp. XVI:** 185, 186
Fairchild, Frances. *See* Bryant, Mrs. William Cullen (Frances Fairchild)
Fairchild, Hoxie, **Supp. XIV:** 120
Fairfield, Flora (pseudonym). *See* Alcott, Louisa May

Fairly Conventional Woman, A (Shields), **Supp. VII:** 312, 316, 318
"Fairly Sad Tale, A" (Parker), **Supp. IX:** 192
Fair Warning (R. O. Butler), **Supp. XII:** 62, **75-76**
Faith (Goldbarth), **Supp. XII:** 181, **182-183**
Faith and History (Niebuhr), **III:** 308
Faith and the Good Thing (Johnson), **Supp. VI:** 187, **188-190,** 191, 193, 194, 196
Faith for Living (Mumford), **Supp. II Part 2:** 479-480
Faithful Narrative of the Surprising Works of God in the Conversion of Many Hundred Souls in Northampton, and the Neighboring Towns and Villages of New-Hampshire in New-England, A (Edwards), **I:** 545, 562
"Faith Healer" (Komunyakaa), **Supp. XIII:** 117
"Faith in a Tree" (Paley), **Supp. VI:** 217-218, 224, 230
"Faith in Search of Understanding" (Updike), **Retro. Supp. I:** 327
"Faith of an Historian" (Morison), **Supp. I Part 2:** 492
Faker's Dozen, A (Bukiet), **Supp. XVII:** 47
Falcoff, Mark, **Supp. VIII:** 88
Falcon (Hammett), **Supp. IV Part 1:** 351
Falconer (Cheever), **Supp. I Part 1:** 176, 193-195, 196
Falconer, A. F., **Supp. XIV:** 2
"Falcon of Ser Federigo, The" (Longfellow), **II:** 505
Falk, Peter, **Supp. XI:** 174
Falkner, Dean, **II:** 55
Falkner, John, **II:** 55
Falkner, Mrs. Murray C. (Maud Butler), **II:** 55
Falkner, Murray, **II:** 55
Falkner, Murray C., **II:** 55
Falkner, William C., **II:** 55
"Fall" (Francis), **Supp. IX:** 76
"Fall 1961" (Lowell), **II:** 550
"Fall, The" (Bass), **Supp. XVI:** 25
"Fallen Western Star: The Decline of San Francisco as a Literary Region" (Gioia), **Supp. XV:** 112, **115-116**
"Fallen Western Star" Wars, The: A Debate about Literary California (Foley, ed.), **Supp. XV:** 112, 116
"Fall in Corrales" (Wilbur), **Supp. III Part 2:** 556
Falling (Dickey), **Supp. IV Part 1:** 178, 181-182

"Falling" (Dickey), **Supp. IV Part 1:** 182

"Falling Asleep over the Aeneid" (Lowell), **II:** 542; **Retro. Supp. II:** 188

Falling in Place (Beattie), **Supp. V:** 28-29

"Falling into Holes in Our Sentences" (R. Bly), **Supp. IV Part 1:** 71

"Fall Journey" (Stafford), **Supp. XI:** 322

Fall of America, The: 1965-1971 (Ginsberg), **Supp. II Part 1:** 323, 325, 327; **Supp. XV:** 264

Fall of Eve, The (Loos), **Supp. XVI:** 187

Fall of the City, The: A Verse Play for Radio (MacLeish), **III:** 20

"Fall of the House of Usher, The" (Poe), **III:** 412, 414, 415, 419; **Retro. Supp. II:** 270

Fall of the Magicians, The (Kees), **Supp. XV:** 144

Fallows, James, **Supp. VIII:** 241

Fall Quarter (Kees), **Supp. XV:** 141

Fall & Rise (Dixon), **Supp. XII:** 147-148, 148, 153, 157

"Falls, The" (Olds), **Supp. X:** 215

"Falls Fight, The" (Howe), **Supp. IV Part 2:** 431-432

Falon, Janet Ruth, **Supp. IV Part 2:** 422

"False Dawn" (Wharton), **Retro. Supp. I:** 381

"False Documents" (Doctorow), **Supp. IV Part 1:** 220, 236

"False Leads" (Komunyakaa), **Supp. XIII:** 116

Fame and Obscurity: Portraits by Gay Talese (Talese), **Supp. XVII:** 202, 203, 204

Fame & Folly: Essays (Ozick), **Supp. V:** 272

"Familiar Epistle to a Friend, A" (Lowell), **Supp. I Part 2:** 416

Familiar Territory: Observations on American Life (Epstein), **Supp. XIV:** 106

"Family" (Sanders), **Supp. XVI:** 276

"Family" (Wilson), **IV:** 426

"Family Affair, A" (Chopin), **Retro. Supp. II:** 71

Family Arsenal, The (Theroux), **Supp. VIII:** 322

Family Chronicle: An Odyssey from Russia to America (Reznikoff), **Supp. XIV:** 277, 288, 289

"Family History" (Mora), **Supp. XIII:** 217

"Family History, A" (Davis), **Supp. XVI:** 82

Family Life (Banks), **Supp. V:** 7

"Family Matters" (Alvarez), **Supp. VII:** 10

Family Moskat, The (Singer), **IV:** 1, 17, 20, 46; **Retro. Supp. II:** 304

"Family of Little Feet, The" (Cisneros), **Supp. VII:** 61

Family Party, A (O'Hara), **III:** 362

Family Pictures (Brooks), **Supp. III Part 1:** 69, 85, 86

Family Pictures (Miller), **Supp. XII:** 291, **295-297**, 299

"Family Reunion" (X. J. Kennedy), **Supp. XV:** 169

Family Reunion, The (Eliot), **I:** 570-571, 572, 581, 584, 588; **Retro. Supp. I:** 62, 65

"Family Secrets" (Kingsolver), **Supp. VII:** 208

"Family Sideshow, The" (Karr), **Supp. XI:** 245

"Family Ties" (Mora), **Supp. XIII:** 215

"Family Tree" (Komunyakaa), **Supp. XIII:** 117-118, 126

"Family Wasserstein, The" (Hoban), **Supp. XV:** 319, 325

Famous American Negroes (Hughes), **Supp. I Part 1:** 345

"Famous Gilson Bequest, The" (Bierce), **I:** 204

Famous Negro Music Makers (Hughes), **Supp. I Part 1:** 345

"Famous New York Trials" (Ellison), **Supp. II Part 1:** 230

Fanatics, The (Dunbar), **Supp. II Part 1:** 213-214

Fancher, Edwin, **Retro. Supp. II:** 202

Fancher, Lou, **Supp. XVI:** 177

"Fancy and Imagination" (Poe), **III:** 421

"Fancy Flights" (Beattie), **Supp. V:** 25

"Fancy's Show Box" (Hawthorne), **II:** 238

"Fancy Woman, The" (Taylor), **Supp. V:** 316-317, 319, 323

"Fang" (Goldbarth), **Supp. XII:** 190

Fanny: Being the True History of the Adventures of Fanny Hackabout-Jones (Jong), **Supp. V:** 115, 127

Fanny Hill (Cleland), **Supp. V:** 48, 127

Fan of Swords, The (al-Maghut), **Supp. XIII:** 278

Fanon, Frantz, **Retro. Supp. II:** 118; **Supp. X:** 131, 141

Fanshawe (Hawthorne), **II:** 223-224; **Retro. Supp. I:** 149, 151

Fan's Notes, A (Exley), **Supp. XVI:** 69

"Fantasia on 'The Nut-Brown Maid'" (Ashbery), **Supp. III Part 1:** 19

"Fantasia on the Relations between Poetry and Photography" (Strand), **Supp. IV Part 2:** 631

"Fantastic Fables" (Bierce), **I:** 209

Fante, John, **Supp. XI: 159-176**

Faraday, Michael, **I:** 480-481

Far and Away (Jarman), **Supp. XVII:** 110, 115

"Far and Away" (Jarman), **Supp. XVII:** 115

"Farewell" (Emerson), **II:** 13

Farewell, My Lovely (Chandler), **Supp. IV Part 1:** 122, 125-126, 127, 128, 130

"Farewell, My Lovely!" (White), **Supp. I Part 2:** 661-663, 665

"Farewell Performance" (Merrill), **Supp. III Part 1:** 336-337

Farewell-Sermon Preached at the First Precinct in Northampton, after the People's Publick Rejection of their Minister, A (Edwards), **I:** 548, 562

"Farewell Sweet Dust" (Wylie), **Supp. I Part 2:** 727-728

Farewell to Arms, A (Hemingway), **I:** 212, 421, 476, 477; **II:** 68-69, 248-249, 252-253, 254, 255, 262, 265; **Retro. Supp. I:** 171, 178, **180-182**, 187, 189; **Retro. Supp. II:** 108; **Supp. IV Part 1:** 380-381, 381; **Supp. VIII:** 179; **Supp. XII:** 241-242

"Farewell to Miles" (Berryman), **I:** 173

Farewell to Reform (Chamberlain), **Supp. I Part 2:** 647

Farewell to Sport (Gallico), **Supp. XVI:** 238

"Farewell to the Middle Class" (Updike), **Retro. Supp. I:** 321

Far Field, The (Roethke), **III:** 528, 529, 539, 545, 547-548

"Far Field, The" (Roethke), **III:** 537, 540

Far-Flung (Cameron), **Supp. XII:** 81

Far from the Madding Crowd (Hardy), **II:** 291

Faris, Athénaïse Charleville, **Supp. I Part 1:** 204

Farley, Abbie, **I:** 458

Farley, Harriet, **Supp. XIII:** 140

"Farm, The" (Creeley), **Supp. IV Part 1:** 155

Farmer (Harrison), **Supp. VIII:** 39, **44-45**

Farmer, Frances, **Supp. XV:** 196-197

Farmer, Richard, **Supp. XIV:** 2

"Farmer and the Fox, The" (Leopold), **Supp. XIV:** 188

"Farmers' Daughters, The" (W. C.

INDEX / 335

Williams), **Retro. Supp. I:** 423
Farmers Hotel, The (O'Hara), **III:** 361
"Farmer's Sorrow, A" (Jewett), **Retro. Supp. II:** 132
"Farmer's Wife, The" (Sexton), **Supp. II Part 2:** 676
"Farm Implements and Rutabagas in a Landscape" (Ashbery), **Supp. III Part 1:** 13
Farming: A Hand Book (Berry), **Supp. X:** 31, 35
"Farm on the Great Plains, The" (Stafford), **Supp. XI:** 322
Farnol, Jeffrey, **Supp. I Part 2:** 653
Far North (Shepard), **Supp. III Part 2:** 433, 435
"Far Northern Birch, The" (Francis), **Supp. IX:** 90
Farnsworth, Elizabeth, **Supp. XI:** 139
"Farrago" (Kees), **Supp. XV:** 145
Farrand, Max, **II:** 122
Farrar, Geraldine, **Retro. Supp. I:** 10
Farrar, John, **II:** 191; **Supp. XI:** 47
Farrell, Barry, **Supp. XIV:** 142
Farrell, James Francis, **II:** 25, 26
Farrell, James T., **I:** 97, 288, 475, 508, 517, 519; **II: 25-53,** 416, 424; **III:** 28, 114, 116, 118, 119, 317, 382; **IV:** 211, 286; **Retro. Supp. II:** 196, 327; **Supp. I Part 2:** 679; **Supp. VIII:** 96, 97; **Supp. XIV:** 3; **Supp. XV:** 141
Farrell, John, **II:** 26
Farrell, John C., **Supp. I Part 1:** 24
Farrell, Kate, **Supp. XV:** 187-188, **Supp. XV:** 190
Farrell, Kevin, **II:** 26
Farrell, Mary, **II:** 25
Farrell, Mrs. James T. (Dorothy Butler), **II:** 26
Farrell, Mrs. James T. (Hortense Alden), **II:** 26, 27, 45, 48
"Far Rockaway" (Schwartz), **Supp. II Part 2:** 649
Farrow, Mia, **Supp. XV:** 8, 10
Far Side of the Dollar, The (Macdonald), **Supp. IV Part 2:** 473
Farther Off from Heaven (Humphrey), **Supp. IX:** 93, 96, 101, **103-104,** 105, 109
Far Tortuga (Matthiessen), **Supp. V:** 201, 206-207
"Fascinating Fascism" (Sontag), **Supp. III Part 2:** 465
"Fascination of Cities, The" (Hughes), **Supp. I Part 1:** 325
Fashion, Power, Guilt and the Charity of Families (Shields), **Supp. VII:** 323
Fasman, Jonathan, **Supp. V:** 253

Fast, Howard, **Supp. I Part 1:** 295
Fast, Jonathan, **Supp. V:** 115
Fast and Loose (Wharton), **Retro. Supp. I:** 361
"Fastest Runner on Sixty-first Street, The" (Farrell), **II:** 45
"Fat" (Carver), **Supp. III Part 1:** 141
Fatal Interview (Millay), **III:** 128-129, 130
"Fatality" (Bausch), **Supp. VII:** 54
Fatal Lady (film), **Supp. XIII:** 166
"Fate" (Emerson), **II:** 2-3, 4, 16; **Supp. XIV:** 42
"Fate" (Koch), **Supp. XV:** 183
"Fate" (Mailer), **Retro. Supp. II:** 207
"Fate of Pleasure, The" (Trilling), **Supp. III Part 2:** 510
Fate of the Jury, The (Masters), **Supp. I Part 2:** 466, 468, 469
"Fat Girl, The" (Dubus), **Supp. VII:** 84, 85
"Father" (Levine), **Supp. V:** 188
"Father" (Sanders), **Supp. XVI:** 277
"Father" (Walker), **Supp. III Part 2:** 522
"Father, The" (Carver), **Supp. III Part 1:** 137, 140
Father, The (Olds), **Supp. X: 209-211**
"Father Abraham" (Faulkner), **Retro. Supp. I:** 81, 82
Fatheralong: A Meditation on Fathers and Sons, Race and Society (Wideman), **Supp. X:** 320, 332-333, 334, 335
"Father and Daughter" (Eberhart), **I:** 539
Father and Glorious Descendant (Lowe), **Supp. X:** 291
"Father and Son" (Eberhart), **I:** 539
Father and Son (Farrell), **II:** 34, 35, 290, 291
Father and Son (Gosse), **Supp. VIII:** 157
"Father and Son" (Hughes), **Retro. Supp. I:** 204; **Supp. I Part 1:** 329, 339
"Father and Son" (Kunitz), **Supp. III Part 1:** 262
"Father and Son" (Schwartz), **Supp. II Part 2:** 650
Father Bombo's Pilgrimage to Mecca (Freneau), **Supp. II Part 1:** 254
"Father Guzman" (Stern), **Supp. IX: 293,** 296
"Father out Walking on the Lawn, A" (Dove), **Supp. IV Part 1:** 246
"Fathers" (Creeley), **Supp. IV Part 1:** 157-158
Fathers, The (Tate), **IV:** 120, 127, 130, 131-133, 134, 141; **Supp. X:** 52

Fathers and Crows (Vollmann), **Supp. XVII:** 226, 231-232
"Fathers and Sons" (Hemingway), **II:** 249, 265-266; **Retro. Supp. I:** 175
"Father's Body, The" (Dickey), **Supp. IV Part 1:** 176
"Father's Story, A" (Dubus), **Supp. VII:** 88
"Father's Voice" (Stafford), **Supp. XI:** 322
"Fat Lady, The" (Carruth), **Supp. XVI:** 48
"Fat Man, Floating" (Dunn), **Supp. XI:** 144
Faulkner: A Collection of Critical Essays (Warren), **Retro. Supp. I:** 73
Faulkner, Barry, **Supp. XV:** 41
Faulkner, William, **I:** 54, 97, 99, 105, 106, 115, 117, 118, 123, 190, 204-205, 211, 288, 289, 291, 292, 297, 305, 324, 374, 378, 423, 480, 517; **II:** 28, 51, **54-76,** 131, 174, 194, 217, 223, 228, 230, 259, 301, 306, 431, 458-459, 542, 594, 606; **III:** 45, 70, 108, 164, 218, 220, 222, 236-237, 244, 292, 334, 350, 382, 418, 453, 454, 482, 483; **IV:** 2, 4, 33, 49, 97, 98, 100, 101, 120, 131, 203, 207, 211, 217, 237, 257, 260, 261, 279, 280, 352, 461, 463; **Retro. Supp. I: 73-95,** 215, 339, 347, 356, 379, 382; **Retro. Supp. II:** 19, 221, 326; **Supp. I Part 1:** 196, 197, 242, 372; **Supp. I Part 2:** 450, 621; **Supp. III Part 1:** 384-385, 396; **Supp. IV Part 1:** 47, 130, 257, 342; **Supp. IV Part 2:** 434, 463, 468, 502, 677, 682; **Supp. V:** 58, 59, 138, 210, 226, 237, 261, 262, 334-336; **Supp. VIII:** 37, 39, 40, 104, 105, 108, 175, 176, 180, 181, 183, 184, 188, 189, 215; **Supp. IX:** 20, 95; **Supp. X:** 44, 228; **Supp. XI:** 92, 247; **Supp. XII:** 16, 289, 310, 313; **Supp. XIII:** 100, 169; **Supp. XIV:** 1, 12-13, 21, 24, 93, 306; **Supp. XV:** 92, 135, 338; **Supp. XVI:** 148, 189; **Supp. XVII:** 225
Faulkner at Nagano (Jelliffe, ed.), **I:** 289; **II:** 63, 65
Faulkner-Cowley File, The: Letters and Memories 1944-1962 (Cowley, ed.), **Retro. Supp. I:** 73, 92; **Supp. II Part 1:** 140, 141
"Faun" (Plath), **Supp. I Part 2:** 537
"Fauna" (Jeffers), **Supp. II Part 2:** 415
Fauset, Jessie, **Supp. I Part 1:** 321, 325; **Supp. IV Part 1:** 164
Faust (Goethe), **I:** 396; **II:** 489; **III:**

395; **Supp. II Part 1:** 16; **Supp. IX:** 141
Faust, Clarence H., **II:** 20
Faute de l'Abbé Mouret, La (Zola), **III:** 322
Favor Island (Merwin), **Supp. III Part 1:** 346, 347
"Favrile" (Doty), **Supp. XI:** 131
Fay, Bernard, **IV:** 41
"Fear, The" (Frost), **Retro. Supp. I:** 128
"Fear & Fame" (Levine), **Supp. V:** 192
Fearful Child, The (C. Frost), **Supp. XV:** 96, 97, 106
"Fearful Child, The" (C. Frost), **Supp. XV:** 96
Fearing, Kenneth, **Supp. XV:** 138
"Fearless" (Mosley), **Supp. XIII:** 241
Fearless Jones (Mosley), **Supp. XIII: 241-242**
Fear of Fifty: A Midlife Memoir (Jong), **Supp. V:** 114, 115, 116, 131
Fear of Flying (Jong), **Supp. V:** 113, 115, 116, 119-123, 124, 129
"Feast, The" (Kinnell), **Supp. III Part 1:** 239, 250
Feast of All Saints, The (Rice), **Supp. VII:** 299-301
Feast of Love, The (C. Baxter), **Supp. XVII:** 13, 21-22
Feast of Love, The (film, R. Benton), **Supp. XVII:** 22
Feast of Snakes, A (Crews), **Supp. XI:** 102, **107-108**
"Feast of Stephen, The" (Hecht), **Supp. X:** 63-64
"Featherbed for Critics, A" (Blackmur), **Supp. II Part 1:** 93, 151
Feather Crowns (Mason), **Supp. VIII: 146-147**
"Feathers" (Carver), **Supp. III Part 1:** 145
Feathers (Van Vechten), **Supp. II Part 2:** 736, 749
"Feathers, The" (Hogan), **Supp. IV Part 1:** 416
"February" (Ellison), **Supp. II Part 1:** 229
"February: Thinking of Flowers" (Kenyon), **Supp. VII:** 171
February in Sydney (Komunyakaa), **Supp. XIII: 124-125,** 129
"February in Sydney" (Komunyakaa), **Supp. XIII:** 125
"February 14th" (Levine), **Supp. V:** 194
"Feces" (McClatchy), **Supp. XII:** 266, 267-268
Fechner, Gustav, **II:** 344, 355, 358, 359, 363

Feder, Lillian, **IV:** 136; **Supp. XVI:** 49, 50
Federal Arts Project, **Supp. III Part 2:** 618
Federigo, or, The Power of Love (Nemerov), **III:** 268, 276, 282, 283-284, 285
"Fedora" (Chopin), **Supp. I Part 1:** 220
Fedorko, Kathy A., **Retro. Supp. I:** 361, 374
"Feeling and Precision" (Moore), **III:** 206
"Feeling of Effort, The" (James), **II:** 349
"Feel Like a Bird" (Swenson), **Supp. IV Part 2:** 639
"Feel Me" (Swenson), **Supp. IV Part 2:** 647
Feeney, Mary, **Supp. IX:** 152, 154
Feinstein, Sascha, **Supp. XIII:** 125
Feldman, Charles K., **Supp. XI:** 307
Fellini, Federico, **Supp. XII:** 172; **Supp. XV:** 8
"Fellow Citizens" (Sandburg), **III:** 553
Fellows, John, **Supp. I Part 2:** 520
"Felo de Se" (Wylie), **Supp. I Part 2:** 727, 729
Felton, Sharon, **Supp. IV Part 1:** 210
"Female Author" (Plath), **Retro. Supp. II:** 243
"Female Frailty" (Freneau), **Supp. II Part 1:** 258
"Female Laughter and Comic Possibilities: *Uncommon Women and Others*" (Chirico), **Supp. XV:** 323
Female Patriot, The; or, Nature's Rights (Rowson), **Supp. XV:** 237-238
"Female Voice in *To Kill a Mockingbird*, The: Narrative Strategies in Film and Novel" (Shakelford), **Supp. VIII:** 129
"Feminine Landscape of Leslie Marmon Silko's *Ceremony*, The" (Gunn Allen), **Supp. IV Part 1:** 324
Feminism and the Politics of Literary Reputation: The Example of Erica Jong (Templin), **Supp. V:** 116
"Feminismo" (Robbins), **Supp. X:** 272
"Feminist Criticism in the Wilderness" (Showalter), **Supp. X:** 97
"Fence, The" (Oliver), **Supp. VII:** 232
"Fence Posts" (Snyder), **Supp. VIII:** 304
Fences (Wilson), **Supp. VIII:** 329, 330, 331, **334-337,** 350
Fenick, Elizabeth, **Retro. Supp. II:** 221
"Fenimore Cooper's Literary Offenses" (Twain), **IV:** 204-205
Fennell, Frank L., **Supp. XVII:** 177-178
Fenollosa, Ernest, **III:** 458, 465, 466, 474, 475, 477; **Retro. Supp. I:** 289; **Supp. IV Part 1:** 154
Fenollosa, Mrs. Ernest, **III:** 458
"Fenstad's Mother" (C. Baxter), **Supp. XVII:** 18
Fenton, Charles, **Supp. XI:** 43
Fenton, James, **Supp. XV:** 117
Ferdinand: Including "It Was" (Zukofsky), **Supp. III Part 2:** 630
"Fergus" (Bourne), **I:** 229
Ferguson, James, **Supp. I Part 2:** 503
Ferguson, Otis, **Supp. IX:** 7
Ferguson, William, **Supp. XII:** 189
Ferguson Affair, The (Macdonald), **Supp. IV Part 2:** 473
Fergusson, Francis, **I:** 265, 440; **Supp. XV:** 20
Ferlinghetti, Lawrence, **Supp. IV Part 1:** 90; **Supp. VIII:** 290, 292; **Supp. XII:** 121, 125; **Supp. XIII:** 275
Fermata, The (Baker), **Supp. XIII: 49-52,** 54
"Fern" (Toomer), **Supp. III Part 2:** 481; **Supp. IX:** 313
Fern, Fanny, **Retro. Supp. I:** 246; **Supp. V:** 122
Fernández, Enrique, **Supp. VIII:** 73
Fernandez, Ramon, **Retro. Supp. I:** 302, 303; **Supp. XVI:** 214
"Fern-Beds in Hampshire Country" (Wilbur), **Supp. III Part 2:** 558
"Fern Hill" (D. Thomas), **IV:** 93
"Fern-Life" (Larcom), **Supp. XIII:** 143
Ferragammo, Salvatore, **Supp. XVI:** 192
Ferreo, Guglielmo, **Supp. I Part 2:** 481
Fessenden, Thomas Green, **II:** 300
Fessier, Michael, **Supp. XIII:** 164
"Festival Aspect, The" (Olson), **Supp. II Part 2:** 585
"Festival of Regrets, The" (Wasserstein), **Supp. XV:** 333
Fetching the Dead (Sanders), **Supp. XVI:** 269
Fêtes galantes (Verlaine), **IV:** 79
"Fetish" (McClatchy), **Supp. XII:** 256
Fetterley, Judith, **Retro. Supp. II:** 139
"Feud" (Zinberg), **Supp. XV:** 195
"Fever" (Carver), **Supp. III Part 1:** 145
"Fever 103°" (Plath), **Supp. I Part 2:** 541
Fever: Twelve Stories (Wideman), **Supp. X:** 320

Fever Pitch (Hornby), **Supp. XII:** 286
"Few Don'ts by an Imagiste, A" (Pound), **III:** 465; **Retro. Supp. I:** 288; **Supp. I Part 1:** 261-262
"Few Stray Comments on the Cultivation of the Lyric, A" (Sobin), **Supp. XVI:**285
"Few Words of Introduction, A" (McNally), **Supp. XIII:** 198-199
Fiamengo, Janice, **Supp. XIII:** 35
Fiber (Bass), **Supp. XVI:**22
"*Fiber:* A Post-Pastoral Georgic" (Gifford), **Supp. XVI:**22
Ficke, Arthur Davison, **Supp. XIII:** 347; **Supp. XV:** 40, 42, 43, 46, 48, 49
"Fiction" (Stafford), **Supp. XI:** 327
"Fiction: A Lens on Life" (Stegner), **Supp. IV Part 2:** 595, 596, 600
Fiction and the Figures of Life (Gass), **Supp. VI:** 85
Fiction of Joseph Heller, The (Seed), **Supp. IV Part 1:** 391
Fiction of Paule Marshall, The (Denniston), **Supp. XI:** 276
Fiction of the Forties (Eisinger), **I:** 302; **II:** 604
Fictions in Autobiography: Studies in the Art of Self-Invention (Eakin), **Supp. XVI:**70
"Fiction Writer and His Country, The" (O'Connor), **III:** 342; **Retro. Supp. II:** 223, 225; **Supp. II Part 1:** 148
Fidelity (Glaspell), **Supp. III Part 1:** 177
Fiedler, Leslie A., **II:** 27; **III:** 218; **Retro. Supp. II:** 280, 324; **Supp. II Part 1:** 87; **Supp. IV Part 1:** 42, 86; **Supp. IX:** 3, 227; **Supp. X:** 80; **Supp. XIII:** 93-110; **Supp. XIV:**11
Fiedler on the Roof: Essays on Literature and Jewish Identity (Fiedler), **Supp. XIII:** 106-107
"Fie! Fie! Fi-Fi!" (Fitzgerald), **Retro. Supp. I:** 100
Field, Eugene, **Supp. II Part 1:** 197
Field, John, **IV:** 179
"Field Events" (Bass), **Supp. XVI:**19
"Field Full of Black Cats, A" (C. Frost), **Supp. XV:** 101
Field Guide, (Hass), **Supp. VI:** 97-98, **99-101,** 102, 103, 106
Field Guide to Contemporary Poetry and Poetics (Friebert and Young, eds.), **Supp. XI:** 270
"Field Guide to the Western Birds" (Stegner), **Supp. IV Part 2:** 609
Fielding, Henry, **I:** 134; **II:** 302, 304-305; **III:** 61; **Supp. I Part 2:** 421, 422, 656; **Supp. IV Part 2:** 688; **Supp. V:** 127; **Supp. IX:** 128; **Supp. XI:** 277
Fielding, Richard, **Supp. XV:** 232
"Field-larks and Blackbirds" (Lanier), **Supp. I Part 1:** 355
Field of Honor (Hay), **Supp. XIV:**120-121, 125, 130
"Field of Honor" (Hay), **Supp. XIV:**120-121, 129-130
Field of Vision, The (Morris), **III:** 226-228, 229, 232, 233, 238
"Field Report" (Corso), **Supp. XII:** 124, **136**
"Fields" (Wright), **Supp. XV:** 342
Fields, Annie Adams, **II:** 401, 402, 403-404, 406, 412; **IV:** 177; **Retro. Supp. II:** 134, 135, 142; **Supp. I Part 1:** 317; **Supp. XVI:**84, 88
Fields, James T., **II:** 274, 279, 402-403; **Retro. Supp. II:** 135; **Supp. I Part 1:** 317; **Supp. XIII:** 150; **Supp. XVI:**84, 88
Fields, Joseph, **IV:** 274
Fields, Mrs. James T., **Supp. XIV:**44, 46. *See* Fields, Annie Adams
Fields, W. C., **II:** 427; **IV:** 335
"Fields at Dusk, The" (Salter), **Supp. IX:** 260
Fields of Wonder (Hughes), **Retro. Supp. I:** 206, 207; **Supp. I Part 1:** 333-334
Fierce Invalids Home from Hot Climates (Robbins), **Supp. X:** 267, 276-277, **282-285**
Fiery Chariot, The (Hurston), **Supp. VI:** 155-156
15 Poems (Banks), **Supp. V:** 5
"Fifteenth Farewell" (Bogan), **Supp. III Part 1:** 51, 58
"Fifth Avenue, Uptown" (Baldwin), **Supp. I Part 1:** 52
"Fifth Avenue-Spring Afternoon" (Untermeyer), **Supp. XV:** 296
Fifth Book of Peace, The (Kingston), **Supp. V:** 173
Fifth Chinese Daughter (Wong), **Supp. X:** 291
Fifth Column, The (Hemingway), **II:** 254, 258; **Retro. Supp. I:** 184
"Fifth Column of the Fencerow" (Leopold), **Supp. XIV:**185
Fifth Decad of Cantos, The (Pound), **Retro. Supp. I:** 292
"Fifth Movement: *Autobiography*" (Zukofsky), **Supp. III Part 2:** 611
Fifth Sunday (Dove), **Supp. IV Part 1:** 251, 252-253
"Fifth Sunday" (Dove), **Supp. IV Part 1:** 252
Fifty Best American Short Stories (O'Brien), **III:** 56
"Fifty Dollars" (Elkin), **Supp. VI:** **43-44**
"55 Miles to the Gas Pump" (Proulx), **Supp. VII:** 264
55 Poems (Zukofsky), **Supp. III Part 2:** 611, 621
"Fifty Grand" (Hemingway), **II:** 250, 424; **Retro. Supp. I:** 177
50 Poems (Cummings), **I:** 430, 440, 442-443, 444-445, 446
"Fifty Suggestions" (Poe), **Retro. Supp. II:** 266
"52 Oswald Street" (Kinnell), **Supp. III Part 1:** 251
"Fifty Years Among the Black Folk" (Du Bois), **Supp. II Part 1:** 169
"Fifty Years of American Poetry" (Jarrell), **Retro. Supp. I:** 52
Fight, The (Mailer), **Retro. Supp. II:** 207, 208
Fight Back: For the Sake of the People, For the Sake of the Land (Ortiz), **Supp. IV Part 2:** 497, 498, 499, 503, 510-512, 514
"Fighters, The" (Zinberg), **Supp. XV:** 193
Fight for Freedom (Hughes), **Supp. I Part 1:** 345
Fightin': New and Collected Stories (Ortiz), **Supp. IV Part 2:** 513
Fighting Angel (Buck), **Supp. II Part 1:** 119, 131
Fighting France; From Dunkerque to Belfort (Wharton), **Retro. Supp. I:** 377, 378
"Figlia che Piange, La" (Eliot), **I:** 570, 584; **III:** 9
Figliola, Samantha, **Supp. V:** 143
"Figure a Poem Makes, The" (Frost), **Retro. Supp. I:** 139
"Figured Wheel, The" (Pinsky), **Supp. VI:** 243, 244, 245, 246
Figured Wheel, The: New and Collected Poems (Pinsky), **Supp. VI:** 247-248
"Figure in the Carpet, The" (James), **Retro. Supp. I:** 228, 229
"Figure in the Doorway, The" (Frost), **Retro. Supp. I:** 138
Figures from the Double World (McGrath), **Supp. X:** 118-119
"Figures in the Clock, The" (McCarthy), **II:** 561-562
Figures Made Visible in the Sadness of Time (Everwine), **Supp. XV:** 75, 88
Figures of Time (Hayden), **Supp. II Part 1:** 367
"Filling Out a Blank" (Wagoner), **Supp. IX:** 324

Fillmore, Millard, **III:** 101
Film Flam: Essays on Hollywood (McMurtry), **Supp. V:** 228
Films of Ayn Rand, The (Cox), **Supp. IV Part 2:** 524
Filo, John, **Supp. XII:** 211
Filson, John, **Retro. Supp. I:** 421
Final Beast, The (Buechner), **Supp. XII: 49-51**
"Finale" (Longfellow), **II:** 505, 506-507
"Final Fear" (Hughes), **Supp. I Part 1:** 338
Final Harvest: Emily Dickinson's Poems (Johnson, ed.), **I:** 470, 471
Final Payments (Gordon), **Supp. IV Part 1:** 297, 299, 300-302, 304, 306, 314
"Final Report, A" (Maxwell), **Supp. VIII:** 169
"Final Soliloquy of the Interior Paramour" (Stevens), **Retro. Supp. I:** 312
Final Solution, The (Reitlinger), **Supp. XII:** 161
Financier, The (Dreiser), **I:** 497, 501, 507, 509; **Retro. Supp. II:** 94, 101-102, 105
Finch, Annie, **Supp. XVII: 69-79**
Finch, Henry Leroy, **Supp. XVII:** 69
Finch, Margaret Rockwell, **Supp. XVII:** 69
Finch, Robert, **Supp. XIV:** 186-187
Find a Victim (Macdonald), **Supp. IV Part 2:** 467, 472, 473
Fin de Chéri, La (Colette; stage adaptation, Loos), **Supp. XVI:** 194
"Fin de Saison Palm Beach" (White), **Supp. I Part 2:** 673
Finding a Form (Gass), **Supp. VI:** 91-92, 93
Finding a Girl in America (Dubus), **Supp. VII:** 85-88
"Finding a Girl in America" (Dubus), **Supp. VII:** 87
"Finding Beads" (Hogan), **Supp. IV Part 1:** 400
"Finding of Zach, The" (Dunbar), **Supp. II Part 1:** 212
Findings and Keepings: Analects for an Autobiography (Mumford), **Supp. II Part 2:** 483
Finding the Center: Narrative Poetry of the Zuni Indians (Tedlock), **Supp. IV Part 2:** 509
Finding the Islands (Merwin), **Supp. III Part 1:** 353, 357
"Finding the Place: A Migrant Childhood" (Stegner), **Supp. IV Part 2:** 597

"Find the Woman" (Macdonald, under Millar), **Supp. IV Part 2:** 466
Fine, David, **Supp. XI:** 160
Fine Clothes to the Jew (Hughes), **Retro. Supp. I:** 200, 201, 203, 205; **Supp. I Part 1:** 326-328
"Fine Old Firm, A" (Jackson), **Supp. IX:** 120
Fine Preserving (Plagemann), **Supp. XVII:** 91
Fine Preserving: M. F. K. Fisher's Annotated Edition of Catherine Plagemann's Cookbook (Plagemann; M. F. K. Fisher, ed.), **Supp. XVII:** 91
Finer Grain, The (James), **II:** 335
Fine Writing (L. P. Smith), **Supp. XIV:** 347
"Finis" (X. J. Kennedy), **Supp. XV:** 169
Finished Man, The (Garrett), **Supp. VII:** 96, 97-98
Fink, Mike, **IV:** 266
Finley, John H., **II:** 418
Finn, David, **Supp. VIII:** 106-107
Finnegans Wake (Joyce), **III:** 7, 12, 14, 261; **IV:** 182, 369-370, 418, 421; **Supp. I Part 2:** 620; **Supp. II Part 1:** 2; **Supp. XIII:** 191
Finney, Brian, **Supp. XIV:** 158, 160, 161, 165, 166, 167, 169
"Finnish Rhapsody" (Ashbery), **Supp. III Part 1:** 26
Finster, Howard, **Supp. XV:** 349
Firbank, Ronald, **IV:** 77, 436
"Fire" (Hughes), **Supp. I Part 1:** 327
Fire: From "A Journal of Love," the Unexpurgated Diary of Anaïs Nin, 1934-1937, **Supp. X:** 184, 185, 189, 194, 195
"Fire and Cloud" (Wright), **IV:** 488
"Fire and Ice" (Frost), **II:** 154; **Retro. Supp. I:** 133
Fire and Ice (Stegner), **Supp. IV Part 2:** 598, 607-608
"Fire and the Cloud, The" (Hurston), **Supp. VI:** 158
"Fire and the Hearth, The" (Faulkner), **II:** 71
Firebird (Doty), **Supp. XI:** 119-120, 121, **132-133**, 134
"Firebombing, The" (Dickey), **Supp. IV Part 1:** 180-181, 187, 189-190
"Fireborn Are at Home in Fire, The" (Sandburg), **III:** 591
"Fire Chaconne" (Francis), **Supp. IX:** 87
Firecrackers (Van Vechten), **Supp. II Part 2:** 740, 742-744, 749
"Fireman, The " (Bass), **Supp. XVI:** 24

Fireman's Wife and Other Stories, The (Bausch), **Supp. VII:** 48, 54
Fire Next Time, The (Baldwin), **Retro. Supp. II:** 5, 8, 9; **Supp. I Part 1:** 48, 49, 52, 60-61
"Fire Next Time, The" (Baldwin). See "Down at the Cross" (Baldwin)
"Fire of Driftwood, The" (Longfellow), **II:** 499; **Retro. Supp. II:** 159, 168
"Fire of Life" (McCullers), **II:** 585
Fire on the Mountain (Abbey), **Supp. XIII:** 6
"Fire Poem" (Merrill), **Supp. III Part 1:** 321
"Fires" (Bass), **Supp. XVI:** 20
"Fires" (Carver), **Supp. III Part 1:** 136-139, 147
Fires: Essays, Poems, Stories (Carver), **Supp. III Part 1:** 136, 140, 142, 146-147
Fire Screen, The (Merrill), **Supp. III Part 1:** 319, 325-329
"Fire Season" (Didion), **Supp. IV Part 1:** 199
"Fire Sequence" (Winters), **Supp. II Part 2:** 791, 796, 800
Fire Sermon (Morris), **III:** 238-239
"Fire Sermon, The" (Eliot), **Retro. Supp. I:** 60-61
Fireside Travels (Lowell), **Supp. I Part 2:** 407, 419-420
Firestarter (King), **Supp. V:** 140, 141, 144; **Supp. IX:** 114
"fire the bastards" (Green), **Supp. IV Part 1:** 285
"Fire-Truck, A" (Wilbur), **Supp. III Part 2:** 556
"Fireweed" (Clampitt), **Supp. IX: 44-45**
"Firewood" (Banks), **Supp. V:** 15
"Fireworks" (Ford), **Supp. V:** 69
"Fireworks" (Shapiro), **Supp. II Part 2:** 707
Fireworks: A History and Celebration (Plimpton), **Supp. XVI:** 245
Fir-Flower Tablets (Lowell), **II:** 512, 526-527
Firkins, Oscar W., **II:** 271; **Supp. XV:** 297, 309
"Firmament, The" (Bryant), **Supp. I Part 1:** 162
Firmat, Gustavo Pérez, **Supp. VIII:** 76, 77, 79; **Supp. XI:** 184
"First American, The" (Toomer), **Supp. III Part 2:** 480, 487
"First Birth" (Olds), **Supp. X:** 212
First Book of Africa, The (Hughes), **Supp. I Part 1:** 344-345
First Book of Jazz, The (Hughes), **Supp. I Part 1:** 345

First Book of Negroes, The (Hughes), **Supp. I Part 1:** 345
First Book of Rhythms, The (Hughes), **Supp. I Part 1:** 345
First Book of the West Indies, The (Hughes), **Supp. I Part 1:** 345
Firstborn (Glück), **Supp. V:** 80, 81, 82, 84
"Firstborn" (Wright), **Supp. V:** 340
"First Chaldaic Oracle" (Carson), **Supp. XII: 111**
"First Communion" (Fante), **Supp. XI:** 160
"First Confession" (X. J. Kennedy), **Supp. XV: 154-155**
"First Day of School, The" (Gibbons), **Supp. X:** 41, 42
"First Death in Nova Scotia" (Bishop), **Supp. I Part 1:** 73
"First Formal" (Olds), **Supp. X:** 212
First Four Books of Poems, The (Glück), **Supp. V:** 81, 83
"First Grade" (Stafford), **Supp. XI:** 328
First Hand (Bierds), **Supp. XVII:** 32, 34-36
"First Hawaiian Bank" (Nye), **Supp. XIII:** 278
"First Heat" (Taylor), **Supp. V:** 323
"First Hour of the Night, The" (Bidart), **Supp. XV: 30-32**
"First Hunters and the Last, The" (Sobin), **Supp. XVI:**292
"First Job, The" (Cisneros), **Supp. VII:** 62
"1st Letter on Georges" (Olson), **Supp. II Part 2:** 578
First Light (C. Baxter), **Supp. XVII:** 15, **17-18**, 19, 22
First Light (Preston), **Supp. XVII:** 18
First Light (Wagoner), **Supp. IX:** 330
"First Love" (Welty), **IV:** 264; **Retro. Supp. I:** 347
First Love: A Lyric Sequence (Untermeyer), **Supp. XV:** 295
First Man, The (O'Neill), **III:** 390
First Manifesto (McGrath), **Supp. X:** 115
"First Meditation" (Roethke), **III:** 545-546
"First Noni Daylight, The" (Harjo), **Supp. XII:** 219
"First Passover" (Longfellow), **II:** 500-501
"First Person Female" (Harrison), **Supp. VIII:** 40, 41, 48
"First Place, The" (Wagoner), **Supp. IX:** 328
First Poems (Buechner), **Supp. XII:** 45
First Poems (Merrill), **Supp. III Part 1:** 318-321, 323
First Poems 1946-1954 (Kinnell), **Supp. III Part 1:** 235, 238-239
"First Praise" (W. C. Williams), **Retro. Supp. I:** 413
First Principles (Spencer), **Supp. I Part 1:** 368
"First Ride and First Walk" (Goldbarth), **Supp. XII:** 182-183
"First Seven Years, The" (Malamud), **Supp. I Part 2:** 431
"First Sex" (Olds), **Supp. X:** 208
"First Snow in Alsace" (Wilbur), **Supp. III Part 2:** 545, 546, 559
"First Song" (Kinnell), **Supp. III Part 1:** 239
"First Spade in the West, The" (Fiedler), **Supp. XIII:** 103
"First Steps" (McClatchy), **Supp. XII:** 256
First There Is the Need (Reznikoff), **Supp. XIV:**291
"First Things First" (Auden), **Supp. II Part 1:** 13
"First Thought, Best Thought" (Ginsberg), **Supp. II Part 1:** 327
"First Time I Saw Paris, The" (Fante), **Supp. XI:** 174
"First Travels of Max" (Ransom), **III:** 490-491
"First Tycoon of Teen, The" (Wolfe), **Supp. III Part 2:** 572
"First Views of the Enemy" (Oates), **Supp. II Part 2:** 508
"First Wife, The" (Buck), **Supp. II Part 1:** 127
First Words before Spring (Untermeyer), **Supp. XV:** 310
"First World War" (White), **Supp. I Part 2:** 665
"Fish" (F. Barthelme), **Supp. XI:** 26
"Fish" (Levis), **Supp. XI:** 259-260
Fish, Stanley, **Supp. IV Part 1:** 48; **Supp. XIV:**14, 15
"Fish, The" (Bishop), **Supp. XV:** 100, 102
"Fish, The" (Moore), **III:** 195, 197, 209, 211, 213-214
"Fish, The" (Oliver), **Supp. VII:** 236
"Fish, The/Lago Chapala" (Everwine), **Supp. XV:** 82-83
"Fish and Shadow" (Pound), **III:** 466
Fishburne, Laurence, **Supp. VIII:** 345
"Fish Cannery" (Fante), **Supp. XI:** 167
Fisher, Alexander Metcalf, **Supp. I Part 2:** 582
Fisher, Alfred, **Retro. Supp. II:** 243
Fisher, Craig, **Supp. V:** 125
Fisher, Dorothy Canfield, **Retro. Supp. I:** 21, 133; **Supp. II Part 1:** 117. *See also* Canfield, Dorothy
Fisher, M. F. K., **Supp. XVII: 81-93**
Fisher, Mary, **Supp. I Part 2:** 455
Fisher, Phillip, **Retro. Supp. I:** 39
Fisher, Rudolph, **Retro. Supp. I:** 200; **Supp. I Part 1:** 325; **Supp. X:** 139; **Supp. XVI:**143
Fisher, Vardis, **Supp. IV Part 2:** 598
Fisher King, The (Marshall), **Supp. XI:** 275-276, **288-290**
"Fisherman, The" (Merwin), **Supp. II Part 1:** 346
"Fisherman and His Wife, The" (Welty), **IV:** 266
"Fisherman from Chihuahua, The" (Connell), **Supp. XIV:**86
"Fishing" (Harjo), **Supp. XII:** 227-228
"Fish in the Stone, The" (Dove), **Supp. IV Part 1:** 245, 257
"Fish in the unruffled lakes" (Auden), **Supp. II Part 1:** 8-9
"Fish R Us" (Doty), **Supp. XI:** 135
Fisk, James, **I:** 4, 474
Fiske, John, **Supp. I Part 1:** 314; **Supp. I Part 2:** 493
"Fit Against the Country, A" (Wright), **Supp. III Part 2:** 591-592, 601
Fitch, Clyde, **Supp. IV Part 2:** 573
Fitch, Elizabeth. *See* Taylor, Mrs. Edward (Elizabeth Fitch)
Fitch, James, **IV:** 147
Fitch, Noël Riley, **Supp. X:** 186, 187
Fitts, Dudley, **I:** 169, 173; **Supp. I Part 1:** 342, 345; **Supp. XIII:** 346
FitzGerald, Edward, **Supp. I Part 2:** 416; **Supp. III Part 2:** 610
Fitzgerald, Ella, **Supp. XIII:** 132
Fitzgerald, F. Scott, **I:** 107, 117, 118, 123, 188, 221, 288, 289, 358, 367, 374-375, 382, 423, 476, 482, 487, 495, 509, 511; **II: 77-100,** 257, 263, 272, 283, 415, 416, 417-418, 420, 425, 427, 430, 431, 432, 433, 434, 436, 437, 450, 458-459, 482, 560; **III:** 2, 26, 35, 36, 37, 40, 44, 45, 69, 106, 244, 284, 334, 350-351, 453, 454, 471, 551, 552, 572; **IV:** 27, 49, 97, 101, 126, 140, 191, 222, 223, 287, 297, 427, 471; **Retro. Supp. I:** 1, 74, **97-120,** 178, 180, 186, 215, 359, 381; **Retro. Supp. II:** 257, 321, 326, 328; **Supp. I Part 1:** 196, 197; **Supp. I Part 2:** 622; **Supp. III Part 2:** 409, 411, 585; **Supp. IV Part 1:** 123, 197, 200, 203, 341; **Supp. IV Part 2:** 463, 468, 607, 689; **Supp. V:** 23, 95, 226, 251, 262, 276, 313; **Supp. VIII:** 101, 103, 106, 137; **Supp. IX:** 15,

20, 55, 57-63, 199; **Supp. X:** 225; **Supp. XI:** 65, 221, 334; **Supp. XII:** 42, 173, 295; **Supp. XIII:** 170, 263; **Supp. XV:** 135; **Supp. XVI:** 64, 75, 191, 192, 294

Fitzgerald, Robert, **I:** 27-28; **III:** 338, 348; **Retro. Supp. II:** 179, 221, 222, 223, 228, 229; **Supp. IV Part 2:** 631; **Supp. XV:** 112, 249

"Fitzgerald: The Romance of Money" (Cowley), **Supp. II Part 1:** 143

Fitzgerald, Zelda (Zelda Sayre), **I:** 482; **II:** 77, 79, 82-85, 88, 90-91, 93, 95; **Supp. IV Part 1:** 310; **Supp. IX:** 55-73; **Supp. X:** 172. *See also* Sayre, Zelda

"Fitzgerald's Tragic Sense" (Schorer), **Retro. Supp. I:** 115

Five Came Back (West), **IV:** 287

Five Corners (screenplay, Shanley), **Supp. XIV:** 316

5 Detroits (Levine), **Supp. V:** 178

"Five Dollar Guy, The" (W. C. Williams), **Retro. Supp. I:** 423

Five Easy Pieces (film), **Supp. V:** 26

"Five Elephants" (Dove), **Supp. IV Part 1:** 244-245

Five Groups of Verse (Reznikoff), **Supp. XIV:** 279, 282

500 Hundred Hats of Bartholomew Cubbins, The (Geisel), **Supp. XVI:** 100

Five Hundred Scorpions (Hearon), **Supp. VIII:** 57, 65, **66**

Five Indiscretions (Ríos), **Supp. IV Part 2:** 545-547

Five Men and Pompey (Benét), **Supp. XI:** 43, 44

Five Plays (Hughes), **Retro. Supp. I:** 197, 209

"Five Psalms" (Jarman), **Supp. XVII:** 120

Five Temperaments (Kalstone), **Retro. Supp. II:** 40

5,000 Fingers of Dr. T, The (film), **Supp. XVI:** 103

Five Young American Poets, **I:** 170; **II:** 367

Fixer, The (Malamud), **Supp. I Part 2:** 428, 435, 445, 446-448, 450, 451

Fjellestad, Danuta Zadworna, **Supp. XVI:** 150

Flaccus, Kimball, **Retro. Supp. I:** 136

Flacius, Matthias, **IV:** 163

"Flagellant's Song" (X. J. Kennedy), **Supp. XV:** 165

Flag for Sunrise, A (Stone), **Supp. V:** 301-304

Flag of Childhood, The: Poems from the Middle East (Nye, ed.), **Supp. XIII:** 280

"Flag of Summer" (Swenson), **Supp. IV Part 2:** 645

Flagons and Apples (Jeffers), **Supp. II Part 2:** 413, 414, 417-418

Flags in the Dust (Faulkner), **Retro. Supp. I:** 81, 82, 83, 86, 88

Flamel, Nicolas, **Supp. XII:** 178

Flaming Corsage, The (W. Kennedy), **Supp. VII:** 133, 153-156

Flammarion, Camille, **Supp. I Part 1:** 260

Flanagan, John T., **Supp. I Part 2:** 464, 465, 468

Flanner, Janet, **Supp. XVI:** 195

"Flannery O'Connor: Poet to the Outcast" (Sister Rose Alice), **III:** 348

Flappers and Philosophers (Fitzgerald), **II:** 88; **Retro. Supp. I:** 103; **Supp. IX:** 56

Flash and Filigree (Southern), **Supp. XI:** 295, **296-297**

"Flashcards" (Dove), **Supp. IV Part 1:** 250

Flash Fiction: Seventy-two Very Short Stories (J. Thomas, ed.), **Supp. XVI:** 268

Flatt, Lester, **Supp. V:** 335

Flaubert, Gustave, **I:** 66, 123, 130, 272, 312, 314, 315, 477, 504, 506, 513, 514; **II:** 182, 185, 194, 198-199, 205, 209, 230, 289, 311, 316, 319, 325, 337, 392, 401, 577, 594; **III:** 196, 207, 251, 315, 461, 467, 511, 564; **IV:** 4, 29, 31, 37, 40, 134, 285, 428; **Retro. Supp. I:** 5, 215, 218, 222, 225, 235, 287; **Supp. III Part 2:** 411, 412; **Supp. XI:** 334; **Supp. XIV:** 87, 336

"Flavia and Her Artists" (Cather), **Retro. Supp. I:** 5

Flavoring of New England, The (Brooks), **I:** 253, 256

Flavor of Man, The (Toomer), **Supp. III Part 2:** 487

Flaxman, Josiah, **Supp. I Part 2:** 716

"Flèche d'Or" (Merrill), **Supp. III Part 1:** 328

Flecker, James Elroy, **Supp. I Part 1:** 257

"Flee on Your Donkey" (Sexton), **Supp. II Part 2:** 683, 685

Fleming, Ian, **Supp. XI:** 307

Fleming, Rene, **Supp. XII:** 321

Fleming, Robert E., **Supp. XVII:** 155

Flesch, Rudolf, **Supp. XVI:** 105, 106

Flesh and Blood (Cunningham), **Supp. XV: 63-65**

Flesh and Blood (play; Cunnigham and Gaitens), **Supp. XV:** 65

"Fleshbody" (Ammons), **Supp. VII:** 27

Fletcher, H. D., **II:** 517, 529

Fletcher, John, **Supp. IV Part 2:** 621

Fletcher, John Gould, **I:** 243; **II:** 517, 529; **III:** 458; **Supp. I Part 1:** 263; **Supp. I Part 2:** 422; **Supp. XV:** 298, 302, 306, 307, 308

Fletcher, Phineas, **Supp. I Part 1:** 369

Fletcher, Virginia. *See* Caldwell, Mrs. Erskine (Virginia Fletcher)

Fleurs du mal, Les (Beaudelaire; Millay and Dillon, trans.), **III:** 141-142

"Flight" (Bierds), **Supp. XVII:** 36

"Flight" (Updike), **IV:** 218, 222, 224; **Retro. Supp. I:** 318

"Flight, The" (Haines), **Supp. XII:** 204-205

"Flight, The" (Roethke), **III:** 537-538

Flight among the Tombs (Hecht), **Supp. X:** 58, **71-74**

"Flight for Freedom" (McCoy), **Supp. XIII:** 170

"Flight from Byzantium" (Brodsky), **Supp. VIII:** 30-31

"Flight of Besey Lane, The" (Jewett), **Retro. Supp. II:** 139

Flight of the Rocket, The (Fitzgerald), **II:** 89

Flights of the Harvest-Mare (Bierds), **Supp. XVII:** 26-27

Flight to Canada (Reed), **Supp. X:** 240, **249-252**

Flinn, Mary, **Supp. XVII:** 110

Flint, F. S., **II:** 517; **III:** 459, 464, 465; **Retro. Supp. I:** 127; **Supp. I Part 1:** 261, 262

Flint, R. W., **Supp. XVI:** 47, 49, 57

"Flitting Flies" (X. J. Kennedy), **Supp. XV:** 166, **167**

Flivver King, The (Sinclair), **Supp. V:** 290

Floating House, The (Sanders), **Supp. XVI:** 269

Floating Light Bulb, The (Allen), **Supp. XV:** 2, 3, 13

Floating Opera, The (Barth), **I:** 121, 122-126, 127, 129, 130, 131

"Floating Poem, Unnumbered, The" (Rich), **Supp. I Part 2:** 572-573

"Floating Trees" (Wright), **Supp. XV:** 348

Flood (Matthews), **Supp. IX:** 154, **160-161**

Flood (Warren), **IV:** 252, 256-257

"Flood of Years, The" (Bryant), **Supp. I Part 1:** 159, 170, 171; **Supp. I Part 2:** 416

"Floor and the Ceiling, The" (W. J.

Smith), **Supp. XIII:** 345, 346
"Floor Plans" (Komunyakaa), **Supp. XIII:** 114
"Floral Decorations for Bananas" (Stevens), **IV:** 8
Florida (Acker), **Supp. XII:** 5
"Florida" (Bishop), **Retro. Supp. II:** 43
"Florida Road Workers" (Hughes), **Retro. Supp. I:** 203
"Florida Sunday, A" (Lanier), **Supp. I Part 1:** 364, 366
"Flossie Cabanis" (Masters), **Supp. I Part 2:** 461-462
Flow Chart (Ashbery), **Supp. VIII:** 275
"Flowchart" (Ashbery), **Supp. III Part 1:** 26
Flower, Fruit, and Thorn Pieces (Richter), **Supp. XVI:**182
Flower-de-Luce (Longfellow), **II:** 490
Flower Fables (Alcott), **Supp. I Part 1:** 33
"Flower-Fed Buffaloes, The" (Lindsay), **Supp. I Part 2:** 398
"Flower Garden" (Jackson), **Supp. IX:** 119
"Flower-gathering" (Frost), **II:** 153
Flower Herding on Mount Monadnock (Kinnell), **Supp. III Part 1:** 235, 239, 241-244
"Flower Herding on Mount Monadnock" (Kinnell), **Supp. III Part 1:** 242
"Flowering Death" (Ashbery), **Supp. III Part 1:** 22
"Flowering Dream, The" (McCullers), **II:** 591
"Flowering Judas" (Porter), **III:** 434, 435-436, 438, 441, 445, 446, 450-451
Flowering Judas and Other Stories (Porter), **III:** 433, 434
Flowering of New England, The (Brooks), **IV:** 171-172; **Supp. VIII:** 101
Flowering of the Rod (Doolittle), **Supp. I Part 1:** 272
Flowering Peach, The (Odets), **Supp. II Part 2:** 533, 547, 549-550
"Flowering Plum" (Glück), **Supp. V:** 82
"Flowers for Marjorie" (Welty), **IV:** 262
"Flowers of the Fallow" (Larcom), **Supp. XIII:** 143, 145-146
"Flowers Well if anybody" (Dickinson), **Retro. Supp. I:** 30
"Fly, The" (Kinnell), **Supp. III Part 1:** 249

"Fly, The" (Shapiro), **Supp. II Part 2:** 705
"Fly, The" (Simic), **Supp. VIII:** 278
Flye, Father James Harold, **I:** 25, 26, 35-36, 37, 42, 46; **IV:** 215
"Fly in Buttermilk, A" (Baldwin), **Retro. Supp. II:** 8
"Flying High" (Levertov), **Supp. III Part 1:** 284
"Flying Home" (Ellison), **Retro. Supp. II:** 117, **125-126**; **Supp. II Part 1:** 235, 238-239
"Flying Home" (Kinnell), **Supp. III Part 1:** 250
"Flying Home" and Other Stories (Ellison), **Retro. Supp. II:** 119, 124
"Flying Home from Utah" (Swenson), **Supp. IV Part 2:** 645
"Flying over Clouds" (Gioia), **Supp. XV:** 118
"Flying to Hanoi" (Rukeyser), **Supp. VI:** 279
Flynn, Richard, **Supp. XVII:** 115
Fly-Truffler, The (Sobin), **Supp. XVI:294-295,** 296
Foata, Anne, **Supp. XI:** 104
Focillon, Henri, **IV:** 90
Focus (A. Miller), **III:** 150-151, 156
Foer, Jonathan Safran, **Supp. XII:** 169
Foerster, Norman, **I:** 222; **Supp. I Part 2:** 423, 424; **Supp. IV Part 2:** 598
"Fog" (Sandburg), **III:** 586
"Fog Galleon" (Komunyakaa), **Supp. XIII:** 127
"Foggy Lane, The" (Simpson), **Supp. IX:** 274
Folded Leaf, The (Maxwell), **Supp. III Part 1:** 62; **Supp. VIII: 159-162**
Folding Star, The (Hollinghurst), **Supp. XIII:** 52
Foley, Jack, **Supp. X:** 125; **Supp. XV:** 112, 116; **Supp. XVII:** 77
Foley, Martha, **II:** 587; **Supp. XVI:**225
Folks from Dixie (Dunbar), **Supp. II Part 1:** 211-212
Folkways (Sumner), **III:** 102
Follain, Jean, **Supp. IX:** 152, 154
Follett, Wilson, **I:** 405; **Supp. XIII:** 173
Follower of Dusk (Salinas), **Supp. XIII:** 326
Following the Equator (Twain), **II:** 434; **IV:** 208
Folly (Minot), **Supp. VI:** 205, 208, **210-213**
Folly of Others, The (N. Boyce), **Supp. XVII:** 100
Folsom, Charles, **Supp. I Part 1:** 156
Folsom, Ed, **Retro. Supp. I:** 392
Folson, Marcia McClintock, **Retro.**

Supp. II: 139
Fonda, Henry, **Supp. I Part 1:** 67; **Supp. IV Part 1:** 236
Fonda, Jane, **III:** 284; **Supp. XI:** 307
Fonda, Peter, **Supp. VIII:** 42; **Supp. XI:** 293, 308
Foner, Eric, **Supp. I Part 2:** 523
Fong and the Indians (Theroux), **Supp. VIII:** 314, 315, **316-317**
Fontanne, Lynn, **III:** 397
Food and Drink (Untermeyer), **Supp. XV:** 310
Fool for Love (Shepard), **Supp. III Part 2:** 433, 447, 448
Fools (Simon), **Supp. IV Part 2:** 584-585
Fool's Progress, The: An Honest Novel (Abbey), **Supp. XIII:** 4, **13-15**
Foot Book, The (Geisel), **Supp. XVI:**108
Foote, Horton, **Supp. I Part 1:** 281; **Supp. VIII:** 128, 129
Foote, Mary Hallock, **Retro. Supp. II:** 72; **Supp. IV Part 2:** 611
Foote, Roxanna. *See* Beecher, Mrs. Lyman (Roxanna Foote)
Foote, Samuel, **Supp. I Part 2:** 584
Foote, Stephanie, **Retro. Supp. II:** 139
"Foot Fault" (pseudonym). *See* Thurber, James
Footing on This Earth, A (Hay), **Supp. XIV:**125, 126, 130
"Footing up a Total" (Lowell), **II:** 528
"Footnote to Howl" (Ginsberg), **Supp. II Part 1:** 316-317
"Footnote to Weather Forecasts, A" (Brodsky), **Supp. VIII:** 32
Footprints (Hearon), **Supp. VIII: 69-70**
Footprints (Levertov), **Supp. III Part 1:** 272, 281
"Footsteps of Angels" (Longfellow), **II:** 496
For a Bitter Season: New and Selected Poems (Garrett), **Supp. VII:** 99-100
"For a Dead Kitten" (Hay), **Supp. XIV:**119-120
"For a Dead Lady" (Robinson), **III:** 508, 513, 517
"For a Ghost Who Once Placed Bets in the Park" (Levis), **Supp. XI:** 265
"For a Lamb" (Eberhart), **I:** 523, 530, 531
"For All" (Snyder), **Supp. VIII:** 304
"For All Tuesday Travelers" (Cisneros), **Supp. VII:** 67-68
"For a Lost Child" (Stafford), **Supp. XI:** 329
"For a Marriage" (Bogan), **Supp. III Part 1:** 52

"For an Emigrant" (Jarrell), **II:** 371
"For Anna Akmatova" (Lowell), **II:** 544
"For Anna Mae Pictou Aquash, Whose Spirit Is Present Here and in the Dappled Stars" (Harjo), **Supp. XII:** 225
"For Anne, at a Little Distance" (Haines), **Supp. XII:** 207
"For Annie" (Poe), **III:** 427; **Retro. Supp. II:** 263
"For a Southern Man" (Cisneros), **Supp. VII:** 67
"For Bailey" (Angelou), **Supp. IV Part 1:** 15
Forbes, Malcolm, **Supp. IV Part 1:** 94
"Forbidden, The" (Glück), **Supp. XIV:** 269
"For Bill Nestrick (1940-96)" (Bidart), **Supp. XV:** 35
For Bread Alone (Choukri), **Supp. IV Part 1:** 92
Force of Spirit, The (Sanders), **Supp. XVI:** 277-278
Forché, Carolyn, **Supp. IV Part 1:** 208
Ford, Arthur, **Supp. IV Part 1:** 140
Ford, Ford Madox, **I:** 288, 405, 409, 417, 421, 423; **II:** 58, 144, 198, 257, 263, 265, 517, 536; **III:** 458, 464-465, 470-471, 472, 476; **IV:** 27, 126, 261; **Retro. Supp. I:** 127, 177, 178, 186, 231, 286-287, 418; **Supp. II Part 1:** 107; **Supp. III Part 2:** 617; **Supp. VIII:** 107; **Supp. XIV:** 3
Ford, Harrison, **Supp. VIII:** 323
Ford, Harry, **Supp. V:** 179; **Supp. XIII:** 76
Ford, Henry, **I:** 295, 480-481; **III:** 292, 293; **Supp. I Part 1:** 21; **Supp. I Part 2:** 644; **Supp. III Part 2:** 612, 613; **Supp. IV Part 1:** 223; **Supp. V:** 290
Ford, John, **Supp. I Part 2:** 422; **Supp. III Part 2:** 619
Ford, Richard, **Supp. IV Part 1:** 342; **Supp. V:** 22, **57-75**
Ford, Webster (pseudonym). *See* Masters, Edgar Lee
"Fording and Dread" (Harrison), **Supp. VIII:** 41
"Ford Madox Ford" (Lowell), **II:** 547; **Retro. Supp. II:** 188
"For Dudley" (Wilbur), **Supp. III Part 2:** 558
Fordyce, David, **II:** 113
Foregone Conclusion, A (Howells), **II:** 278-279, 282
"Foreign Affairs" (Kunitz), **Supp. III Part 1:** 265

"Foreigner, A" (Bynner), **Supp. XV:** 46
"Foreigner, The" (Jewett), **II:** 409-410; **Retro. Supp. II:** 133, 142
"Foreigners" (Jarman), **Supp. XVII:** 113
"Foreign Shores" (Salter), **Supp. IX:** 260
Forensic and the Navigators (Shepard), **Supp. III Part 2:** 439
Foreseeable Future, The (Price), **Supp. VI:** 265
Foreseeable Futures (Matthews), **Supp. IX:** 155, **163,** 169
"For Esmé with Love and Squalor" (Salinger), **III:** 560
"Forest" (Simic), **Supp. VIII:** 273
Forest, Jean-Claude, **Supp. XI:** 307
Forester's Letters (Paine), **Supp. I Part 2:** 508
"Forest Hymn, A" (Bryant), **Supp. I Part 1:** 156, 162, 163, 164, 165, 170
"Forest in the Seeds, The" (Kingsolver), **Supp. VII:** 203
Forest of the South, The (Gordon), **II:** 197
"Forest of the South, The" (Gordon), **II:** 199, 201
Forest without Leaves (Adams and Haines), **Supp. XII:** 209
"Forever and the Earth" (Bradbury), **Supp. IV Part 1:** 102
"Forever in That Year" (Carruth), **Supp. XVI:** 51
"Forever Young" (Jarman and R. McDowell), **Supp. XVII:** 111
"For Fathers of Girls" (Dunn), **Supp. XI:** 146
"For/From Lew" (Snyder), **Supp. VIII:** 303
"For Garrison Keillor, Fantasy Is a Lot More Fun then Reality" (Letofsky), **Supp. XVI:** 167
"For George Santayana" (Lowell), **II:** 547
Forgotten Helper, The: A Story for Children (Moore), **Supp. X:** 175
"Forgotten in an Old Notebook" (F. Wright), **Supp. XVII:** 244
Forgotten Village, The (Steinbeck), **IV:** 51
"For Grizzel McNaught (1709-1792)" (A. Finch), **Supp. XVII:** 72
Forgue, Guy J., **III:** 118, 119
"FOR HETTIE" (Baraka), **Supp. II Part 1:** 32
"FOR HETTIE IN HER FIFTH MONTH" (Baraka), **Supp. II Part 1:** 32, 38
"For Homer" (Corso), **Supp. XII:** 135

"For I'm the Boy" (Barthelme), **Supp. IV Part 1:** 47
"For Jessica, My Daughter" (Strand), **Supp. IV Part 2:** 629
"For John, Who Begs Me not to Enquire Further" (Sexton), **Supp. II Part 2:** 676
"For Johnny Pole on the Forgotten Beach" (Sexton), **Supp. II Part 2:** 675
"For Joy to Leave Upon" (Ortiz), **Supp. IV Part 2:** 508
"Fork" (Simic), **Supp. VIII:** 275
For Lancelot Andrewes (Eliot), **Retro. Supp. I:** 64
For Lizzie and Harriet (Lowell), **Retro. Supp. II:** 183, 186, 190
"Forlorn Hope of Sidney Lanier, The" (Leary), **Supp. I Part 1:** 373
For Love (Creeley), **Supp. IV Part 1:** 139, 140, 142-145, 147-149, 150, 154
"For Love" (Creeley), **Supp. IV Part 1:** 145
For Love (Miller), **Supp. XII:** **297-299,** 299
For Love of Imabelle (C. Himes), **Supp. XVI:** 135, 143, 144
"Formal Elegy" (Berryman), **I:** 170
Formal Feeling Comes, A (A. Finch, ed.), **Supp. XVII: 71-72**
"Formalist Criticism: Its Principles and Limits" (Burke), **I:** 282
Forman, Milos, **Supp. IV Part 1:** 236
"Form and Function of the Novel, The" (Goldbarth), **Supp. XII:** 183
"For Marse Chouchoute" (Chopin), **Retro. Supp. II:** 60
"For Mary Ann Youngren" (Bidart), **Supp. XV:** 29
"Format and Form" (A. Rich), **Supp. XVII:** 74
"Formation of a Separatist, I" (Howe), **Supp. IV Part 2:** 427
"Form Is Emptiness" (Baraka), **Supp. II Part 1:** 51
"For Mr. Death Who Stands with His Door Open" (Sexton), **Supp. II Part 2:** 695
Forms of Discovery (Winters), **Supp. II Part 2:** 812, 813
Forms of Fiction, The (Gardner and Dunlap), **Supp. VI:** 64
"For My Children" (Karr), **Supp. XI:** 254
"For My Daughter" (Kees), **Supp. XV:** 141, 147
"For My Daughter" (Olds), **Supp. X:** 206
"For My Lover, Returning to His Wife"

INDEX / 343

(Sexton), **Supp. II Part 2:** 688
"For Night to Come" (Stern), **Supp. IX:** 292
"For Once, Then, Something" (Frost), **II:** 156-157; **Retro. Supp. I:** 126, 133, 134
"For Peg: A Remnant of Song Still Distantly Sounding" (Carruth), **Supp. XVI:**54
"For Pot-Boiling" (Hay), **Supp. XIV:**128
"For Radicals" (Bourne), **I:** 221
"For Rainer Gerhardt" (Creeley), **Supp. IV Part 1:** 142-143, 147
Forrestal, James, **I:** 491; **Supp. I Part 2:** 489
"For Richard After All" (Kingsolver), **Supp. VII:** 208
"For Sacco and Vanzetti" (Kingsolver), **Supp. VII:** 208
"Forsaken Merman" (Arnold), **Supp. I Part 2:** 529
For Spacious Skies (Buck), **Supp. II Part 1:** 131
Forster, E. M., **I:** 292; **IV:** 201; **Retro. Supp. I:** 59, 232; **Supp. III Part 2:** 503; **Supp. V:** 258; **Supp. VIII:** 155, 171; **Supp. IX:** 128; **Supp. XII:** 79, 81; **Supp. XIV:**159, 160, 163; **Supp. XV:** 62; **Supp. XVI:**236
Forster, John, **II:** 315
Fort, Paul, **II:** 518, 528, 529; **Retro. Supp. I:** 55
"For the Ahkoond" (Bierce), **I:** 209
For the Century's End: Poems 1990-1999 (Haines), **Supp. XII: 211-213**
"For the Dedication of the New City Library, Boston" (Holmes), **Supp. I Part 1:** 308
"For the Fallen" (Levine), **Supp. V:** 188
For the Health of the Land: Previously Unpublished Essays and Other Writings (Leopold), **Supp. XIV:**183
"For the Last Wolverine" (Dickey), **Supp. IV Part 1:** 182
"For the Lovers of the Absolute" (Simic), **Supp. VIII:** 278-279
"For the Man Cutting the Grass" (Oliver), **Supp. VII:** 235
"For the Marriage of Faustus and Helen" (H. Crane), **I:** 395-396, 399, 402; **Retro. Supp. II:** 78-79, 82
"For the Meeting of the National Sanitary Association, 1860" (Holmes), **Supp. I Part 1:** 307
For the New Intellectual (Rand), **Supp. IV Part 2:** 521, 526-527, 527, 532
"For the New Railway Station in Rome" (Wilbur), **Supp. III Part 2:** 554
"For the Night" (Kenyon), **Supp. VII:** 163
"For Theodore Roethke: 1908-1963" (Lowell), **II:** 554
"For the Poem *Patterson*" (W. C. Williams), **Retro. Supp. I:** 424
"For the Poets of Chile" (Levine), **Supp. V:** 188
"FOR THE REVOLUTIONARY OUTBURST BY BLACK PEOPLE" (Baraka), **Supp. II Part 1:** 55
"For the Sleepless" (Dunn), **Supp. XI:** 145
For the Time Being (Auden), **Supp. II Part 1:** 2, 17, 18
For the Time Being (Dillard), **Supp. VI:** 23, 27, 29, 32, **34-35**
"For the Twentieth Century" (Bidart), **Supp. XV:** 35
For the Union Dead (Lowell), **II:** 543, 550-551, 554, 555; **Retro. Supp. II:** 181, 182, 186, 189; **Supp. X:** 53
"For the Union Dead" (Lowell), **II:** 551; **Retro. Supp. II:** 189
"For the Walking Dead" (Komunyakaa), **Supp. XIII:** 121
"For the West" (Snyder), **Supp. VIII:** 299
"For the Word Is Flesh" (Kunitz), **Supp. III Part 1:** 262-264
"Fortress, The" (Glück), **Supp. V:** 82
"Fortress, The" (Sexton), **Supp. II Part 2:** 682
Fortune, T. Thomas, **Supp. II Part 1:** 159
Fortune's Daughter (Hoffman), **Supp. X:** 77, 85
45 Mercy Street (Sexton), **Supp. II Part 2:** 694, 695, 697
Forty Poems Touching on Recent American History (Bly, ed.), **Supp. IV Part 1:** 61
42nd Parallel, The (Dos Passos), **I:** 482, 484-485
Forty Stories (Barthelme), **Supp. IV Part 1:** 47, 49, 53, 54
For Whom the Bell Tolls (Hemingway), **II:** 249, 254-255, 261; **III:** 18, 363; **Retro. Supp. I:** 115, 176-177, 178, **184,** 187; **Supp. XVII:** 229
Foscolo, Ugo, **II:** 543
Foss, Sam Walter, **Supp. II Part 1:** 197
"Fossils, The" (Kinnell), **Supp. III Part 1:** 244
Foster, Edward, **Supp. IV Part 2:** 431, 434; **Supp. XVI:**281, 293
Foster, Edward Halsey, **Supp. XII:** 120, 129, 130, 135
Foster, Emily, **II:** 309
Foster, Hannah, **Supp. XV:** 234
Foster, John Wilson, **Supp. XIII:** 32-33
Foster, Phil, **Supp. IV Part 2:** 574
Foster, Richard, **Supp. XV:** 269
Foster, Stephen, **Supp. I Part 1:** 100-101; **Supp. I Part 2:** 699
Foucault, Michel, **Supp. VIII:** 5; **Supp. XII:** 98; **Supp. XV:** 344; **Supp. XVI:**285
"Founder, The" (Stern), **Supp. IX:** 297
Founding of Harvard College, The (Morison), **Supp. I Part 2:** 485
"Fountain, The" (Bryant), **Supp. I Part 1:** 157, 165, 166, 168
Fountain, The (O'Neill), **III:** 391
Fountain and Other Poems, The (Bryant), **Supp. I Part 1:** 157
Fountainhead, The (film), **Supp. IV Part 2:** 524
Fountainhead, The (Rand), **Supp. IV Part 2:** 517, 521-523, 525, 531
Fountainhead, The: A Fiftieth Anniversary Celebration (Cox), **Supp. IV Part 2:** 523
"Fountain Piece" (Swenson), **Supp. IV Part 2:** 641
"Four Ages of Man, The" (Bradstreet), **Supp. I Part 1:** 111, 115
Four American Indian Literary Masters (Velie), **Supp. IV Part 2:** 486
"Four Beasts in One; the Homo Cameleopard" (Poe), **III:** 425
Four Black Revolutionary Plays (Baraka), **Supp. II Part 1:** 45; **Supp. VIII:** 330
"Four Brothers, The" (Sandburg), **III:** 585
Four Dogs and a Bone and the Wild Goose (Shanley), **Supp. XIV:**316, **328-329**
"Four Evangelists, The" (Komunyakaa), **Supp. XIII:** 131
"Four for Sir John Davies" (Roethke), **III:** 540, 541
"Four Girls, The" (Alvarez), **Supp. VII:** 7
4-H Club (Shepard), **Supp. III Part 2:** 439
"Four Horse Songs" (Harjo), **Supp. XII:** 220
"400-Meter Free Style" (Kumin), **Supp. IV Part 2:** 442
Fourier, Charles, **II:** 342
"Four in a Family" (Rukeyser), **Supp. VI:** 272
Four in Hand: A Quartet of Novels (Warner), **Supp. VIII:** 164

"Four Lakes' Days" (Eberhart), **I:** 525
"Four Meetings" (James), **II:** 327
Four Million, The (O. Henry), **Supp. II Part 1:** 394, 408
"Four Monarchyes" (Bradstreet), **Supp. I Part 1:** 105, 106, 116
"Four Mountain Wolves" (Silko), **Supp. IV Part 2:** 561
Four of a Kind (Marquand), **III:** 54, 55
"Four of the Horsemen (Hypertense and Stroke, Coronary Occlusion and Cerebral Insult)" (Karr), **Supp. XI:** 250
"Four Poems" (Bishop), **Supp. I Part 1:** 92
"Four Preludes on Playthings of the Wind" (Sandburg), **III:** 586
Four Quartets (Eliot), **I:** 570, 576, 580-582, 585, 587; **II:** 537; **III:** 539; **Retro. Supp. I:** 66, 67; **Supp. II Part 1:** 1; **Supp. IV Part 1:** 284; **Supp. V:** 343, 344; **Supp. VIII:** 182, 195; **Supp. XIII:** 344; **Supp. XIV:**167; **Supp. XV:** 216, 260, 266
Four Saints in Three Acts (Stein), **IV:** 30, 31, 33, 43, 44-45
"Four Seasons" (Bradstreet), **Supp. I Part 1:** 112-113
"Four Sides of One Story" (Updike), **Retro. Supp. I:** 328
"Four Skinny Trees" (Cisneros), **Supp. VII:** 64
"14: In A Dark Wood: Wood Thrushes" (Oliver), **Supp. VII:** 244
Fourteen Hundred Thousand (Shepard), **Supp. III Part 2:** 439
"14 Men Stage Head Winter 1624/ 25" (Olson), **Supp. II Part 2:** 574
Fourteen Sisters of Emilio Montez O'Brien, The (Hijuelos), **Supp. VIII: 82-85**
Fourteen Stories (Buck), **Supp. II Part 1:** 126
14 Stories (Dixon), **Supp. XII:** 141, **145-147**
"Fourteenth Ward, The" (H. Miller), **III:** 175
Fourth Book of Peace, The (Kingston), **Supp. V:** 173
"Fourth Down" (Marquand), **III:** 56
Fourth Group of Verse, A (Reznikoff), **Supp. XIV:**282, 284
"Fourth of July in Maine" (Lowell), **II:** 535, 552-553
Fourth Wall, The (Gurney), **Supp. V:** 109-110
Fowler, Douglas, **Supp. IV Part 1:** 226, 227
Fowler, Gene, **Supp. VIII:** 290

Fowler, Henry Watson, **Supp. I Part 2:** 660
Fowler, Singrid, **Supp. VIII:** 249, 258
Fowler, Virginia C., **Supp. VIII:** 224
Fox, Alan, **Supp. XIII:** 120
Fox, Dixon Ryan, **I:** 337
Fox, Joe, **Supp. IX:** 259, 261
Fox, John, **Supp. XIII:** 166
Fox, Linda C., **Supp. XIII:** 217-218
Fox, Ruth, **Supp. I Part 2:** 619
"Fox, The" (Levine), **Supp. V:** 181, 189
Fox-Genovese, Elizabeth, **Supp. IV Part 1:** 286
Fox in Socks (Geisel), **Supp. XVI:**108, 112
"Fox Night" (Jarman), **Supp. XVII:** 120
Fox of Peapack, The (White), **Supp. I Part 2:** 676, 677-678
"Fox of Peapack, The" (White), **Supp. I Part 2:** 677
Foye, Raymond, **Supp. XIV:**150
Fraenkel, Michael, **III:** 178, 183
"Fragging" (Komunyakaa), **Supp. XIII:** 123
Fragile Beauty, A: John Nichols' Milagro Country: Text and Photographs from His Life and Work (Nichols), **Supp. XIII:** 268
"Fragility" (Shields), **Supp. VII:** 318
"Fragment" (Ashbery), **Supp. III Part 1:** 11, 13, 14, 19, 20
"Fragment" (Lowell), **II:** 516
"Fragment" (Ortiz), **Supp. IV Part 2:** 507
"Fragment of a Meditation" (Tate), **IV:** 129
"Fragment of an Agon" (Eliot), **I:** 579-580
"Fragment of a Prologue" (Eliot), **I:** 579-580
"Fragment of New York, 1929" (Eberhart), **I:** 536-537
"Fragments" (Emerson), **II:** 19
"Fragments for Fall" (Salinas), **Supp. XIII:** 320-321
"Fragments of a Hologram Rose" (W. Gibson), **Supp. XVI:**122, 123, 128
"Fragments of a Liquidation" (Howe), **Supp. IV Part 2:** 426
Fragonard, Jean Honoré, **III:** 275; **IV:** 79
Fraiman, Susan, **Supp. IV Part 1:** 324
"Frame for Poetry, A" (W. J. Smith), **Supp. XIII:** 333
France, Anatole, **IV:** 444; **Supp. I Part 2:** 631; **Supp. XIV:**79
France and England in North America (Parkman), **Supp. II Part 2:** 596,

600-605, 607, 613-614
Franchere, Hoyt C., **II:** 131
Franchiser, The (Elkin), **Supp. VI: 51-52,** 58
Franciosi, Robert, **Supp. XIV:**283
Francis, Lee, **Supp. IV Part 2:** 499
Francis, Richard, **Supp. XV:** 121
Francis, Robert, **Supp. IX: 75-92**
Francis of Assisi, Saint, **III:** 543; **IV:** 69, 375, 410; **Supp. I Part 2:** 394, 397, 441, 442, 443
Franco, Francisco, **II:** 261
Franconia (Fraser), **Retro. Supp. I:** 136
"Franconia" tales (Abbott), **Supp. I Part 1:** 38
Frank, Anne, **Supp. X:** 149; **Supp. XVII:** 39
Frank, Frederick S., **Retro. Supp. II:** 273
Frank, James M., **Supp. XIV:**1
Frank, Jerome, **Supp. I Part 2:** 645
Frank, Joseph, **II:** 587
Frank, Mary, **Supp. X:** 213
Frank, Robert, **Supp. XI:** 295; **Supp. XII:** 127; **Supp. XIV:**150
Frank, Waldo, **I:** 106, 109, 117, 229, 236, 245, 259, 400; **Retro. Supp. II:** 77, 79, 83; **Supp. IX:** 308, 309, 311, 320; **Supp. XV:** 298
Frankel, Charles, **III:** 291
Frankel, Haskel, **Supp. I Part 2:** 448
Frankenberg, Lloyd, **I:** 436, 437, 445, 446; **III:** 194
Frankenheimer, John, **Supp. XI:** 343
Frankenstein (film), **Supp. IV Part 1:** 104; **Supp. XVII:** 57
Frankenstein (Gardner), **Supp. VI:** 72
Frankenstein (Shelley), **Supp. XII:** 79
Frankfurter, Felix, **I:** 489
"Frankie" (Keillor), **Supp. XVI:**167
Frankie and Johnny (film), **Supp. XIII:** 206
Frankie and Johnny in the Clair de Lune (McNally), **Supp. XIII: 200,** 201
Franklin, Benjamin, **II:** 6, 8, 92, **101-125,** 127, 295, 296, 302, 306; **III:** 74, 90; **IV:** 73, 193; **Supp. I Part 1:** 306; **Supp. I Part 2:** 411, 503, 504, 506, 507, 510, 516, 518, 522, 524, 579, 639; **Supp. VIII:** 202, 205; **Supp. XIII:** 150; **Supp. XIV:**306
Franklin, Cynthia, **Supp. IV Part 1:** 332
Franklin, R. W., **Retro. Supp. I:** 29, 41, 43, 47
Franklin, Ruth, **Supp. XVI:**160
Franklin, Sarah, **II:** 122
Franklin, Temple, **II:** 122

Franklin, William, **II:** 122; **Supp. I Part 2:** 504
Franklin Evans (Whitman), **Retro. Supp. I:** 393
"Frank O'Connor and *The New Yorker*" (Maxwell), **Supp. VIII:** 172
Franks, Lucinda, **Supp. XIII:** 12
"Frank Sinatra Has a Cold" (Talese), **Supp. XVII:** 203
"Frank Stanford of the Mulberry Family: An Arkansas Epilogue" (Wright), **Supp. XV:** 339-340
"Franny" (Salinger), **III:** 564, 565-566
Franny and Zooey (Salinger), **III:** 552, 564-567; **IV:** 216; **Supp. XIII:** 263
Franzen, Jonathan, **Retro. Supp. II:** 279
Fraser, G. S., **Supp. XII:** 128; **Supp. XIV:** 162
Fraser, Joe, **III:** 46
Fraser, Marjorie Frost, **Retro. Supp. I:** 136
Frayn, Michael, **Supp. IV Part 2:** 582
Frazee, E. S., **Supp. I Part 2:** 381
Frazee, Esther Catherine. *See* Lindsay, Mrs. Vachel Thomas (Esther Catherine Frazee)
Frazer, Sir James G., **I:** 135; **II:** 204; **III:** 6-7; **IV:** 70; **Retro. Supp. I:** 80; **Supp. I Part 1:** 18; **Supp. I Part 2:** 541
Frazier, Ian, **Supp. VIII:** 272
Freaks: Myths and Images of the Secret Self (Fiedler), **Supp. XIII:** 106, 107
"Freak Show, The" (Sexton), **Supp. II Part 2:** 695
Freddy's Book (Gardner), **Supp. VI:** 72
Frederic, Harold, **I:** 409; **II: 126-149,** 175, 276, 289; **Retro. Supp. I:** 325
"Frederick Douglass" (Dunbar), **Supp. II Part 1:** 197, 199
"Frederick Douglass" (Hayden), **Supp. II Part 1:** 363
Frederick the Great, **II:** 103; **Supp. I Part 2:** 433
Fredrickson, George M., **Supp. I Part 2:** 589
"Free" (O'Hara), **III:** 369
Free, and Other Stories (Dreiser), **Retro. Supp. II:** 104
Free Agents (Apple), **Supp. XVII:** 5-6
Free Air (Lewis), **II:** 441
Freedman, Monroe H., **Supp. VIII:** 127
Freedman, Richard, **Supp. V:** 244
"Freedom" (White), **Supp. I Part 2:** 659
"Freedom, New Hampshire" (Kinnell), **Supp. III Part 1:** 238, 239, 251

"Freedom and Discipline" (Carruth), **Supp. XVI:** 50
Freedom Is the Right to Choose: An Inquiry into the Battle for the American Future (MacLeish), **III:** 3
"Freedom's a Hard-Bought Thing" (Benét), **Supp. XI:** 47, 48
"Freedom's Plow" (Hughes), **Supp. I Part 1:** 346
"Free Fantasia: Tiger Flowers" (Hayden), **Supp. II Part 1:** 363, 366
Freeing of the Dust, The (Levertov), **Supp. III Part 1:** 281-282
"Free Lance, The" (Mencken), **III:** 104, 105
Free-Lance Pallbearers, The (Reed), **Supp. X:** 240, **242-243,** 244
Freeloaders, The (Lacy), **Supp. XV:** 204
"Free Man" (Hughes), **Supp. I Part 1:** 333
Freeman, Chris, **Supp. XIV:** 157, 159
Freeman, Douglas Southall, **Supp. I Part 2:** 486, 493
Freeman, Joseph, **II:** 26; **Supp. I Part 2:** 610
Freeman, Mary E. Wilkins, **II:** 401; **Supp. IX:** 79
Freeman, Mary Wilkins, **Retro. Supp. II:** 51, 136, 138
Freeman, Morgan, **Supp. XII:** 317
Freeman, Suzanne, **Supp. X:** 83
"Free Man's Worship, A" (Russell), **Supp. I Part 2:** 522
Freilicher, Jane, **Supp. XV:** 178
Freinman, Dorothy, **Supp. IX:** 94
Frémont, John Charles, **Supp. I Part 2:** 486
Fremont-Smith, Eliot, **Supp. XIII:** 263
Fremstad, Olive, **I:** 319; **Retro. Supp. I:** 10
French, Warren, **Supp. XII:** 118-119
French Chef, The (television program), **Supp. XVII:** 89
French Connection, The (film), **Supp. V:** 226
French Leave (X. J. Kennedy), **Supp. XV:** 165
French Poets and Novelists (James), **II:** 336; **Retro. Supp. I:** 220
"French Scarecrow, The" (Maxwell), **Supp. VIII:** 169, 170
French Ways and Their Meaning (Wharton), **IV:** 319; **Retro. Supp. I:** 378
Freneau, Eleanor Forman (Mrs. Philip Freneau), **Supp. II Part 1:** 266
Freneau, Philip M., **I:** 335; **II:** 295; **Supp. I Part 1:** 124, 125, 127, 145; **Supp. II Part 1:** 65, **253-277**

Frescoes for Mr. Rockefeller's City (MacLeish), **III:** 14-15
"Fresh Air" (Koch), **Supp. XV:** 181, 185
Fresh Air Fiend: Travel Writings, 1985-2000 (Theroux), **Supp. VIII:** 325
Fresh Brats (X. J. Kennedy), **Supp. XV:** 163
"Freshman" (Sanders), **Supp. XVI:** 277
Freud, Sigmund, **I:** 55, 58, 59, 66, 67, 135, 241, 242, 244, 247, 248, 283; **II:** 27, 370, 546-547; **III:** 134, 390, 400, 418, 488; **IV:** 7, 70, 138, 295; **Retro. Supp. I:** 80, 176, 253; **Retro. Supp. II:** 104; **Supp. I Part 1:** 13, 43, 253, 254, 259, 260, 265, 270, 315; **Supp. I Part 2:** 493, 527, 616, 643, 647, 649; **Supp. IV Part 2:** 450; **Supp. VIII:** 103, 196; **Supp. IX:** 102, 155, 161, 308; **Supp. X:** 193, 194; **Supp. XII:** 14-15; **Supp. XIII:** 75; **Supp. XIV:** 83; **Supp. XV:** 219; **Supp. XVI:** 157-158, 161, 292
Freud: The Mind of the Moralist (Sontag and Rieff), **Supp. III Part 2:** 455
"Freud: Within and Beyond Culture" (Trilling), **Supp. III Part 2:** 508
"Freud and Literature" (Trilling), **Supp. III Part 2:** 502-503
Freudian Psychology and Veblen's Social Theory, The (Schneider), **Supp. I Part 2:** 650
Freudian Wish and Its Place in Ethics, The (Holt), **I:** 59
"Freud's Room" (Ozick), **Supp. V:** 268
"Friday Morning Trial of Mrs. Solano, The" (Ríos), **Supp. IV Part 2:** 538, 548
Frieburger, William, **Supp. XIII:** 239
Friede, Donald, **Supp. XVII:** 85, 86, 87, 90
Friedenberg, Edgar Z., **Supp. VIII:** 240
Friedman, Bruce Jay, **I:** 161; **Supp. IV Part 1:** 379
Friedman, Lawrence S., **Supp. V:** 273
Friedman, Milton, **Supp. I Part 2:** 648
Friedman, Norman, **I:** 431-432, 435, 439
Friedman, Stan, **Supp. XII:** 186
Friedmann, Georges, **Supp. I Part 2:** 645
"Fried Sausage" (Simic), **Supp. VIII:** 270
Friend, Julius, **Retro. Supp. I:** 80
Friend, The (Coleridge), **II:** 10
"Friend Husband's Latest" (Sayre), **Retro. Supp. I:** 104
"Friendly Debate between a Conform-

ist and a Non-Conformist, A" (Wild), **IV:** 155
"Friendly Neighbor" (Keillor), **Supp. XVI:**172
Friend of the Earth (Boyle), **Supp. VIII:** 12, 16
"Friend of the Fourth Decade, The" (Merrill), **Supp. III Part 1:** 327
"Friends" (Beattie), **Supp. V:** 23, 27
"Friends" (Paley), **Supp. VI:** 219, 226
"Friends" (Sexton), **Supp. II Part 2:** 693
Friends: More Will and Magna Stories (Dixon), **Supp. XII:** 148, 149
Friend's Delight, The (Bierce), **I:** 195
"Friends from Philadelphia" (Updike), **Retro. Supp. I:** 319
"Friendship" (Emerson), **Supp. II Part 1:** 290
"Friends of Heraclitus, The" (Simic), **Supp. VIII:** 284
"Friends of Kafka, The" (Singer), **Retro. Supp. II:** 308
"Friends of the Family, The" (McCarthy), **II:** 566
"Friend to Alexander, A" (Thurber), **Supp. I Part 2:** 616
"Frigate Pelican, The" (Moore), **III:** 208, 210-211, 215
"Frill, The" (Buck), **Supp. XIV:**274
"Fringe, The" (Bass), **Supp. XVI:**19
Frobenius, Leo, **III:** 475; **Supp. III Part 2:** 620
Froebel, Friedrich, **Supp. XIV:**52-53
Frog (Dixon), **Supp. XII:** 151
"Frog Dances" (Dixon), **Supp. XII:** 151
"Frog Pond, The" (Kinnell), **Supp. III Part 1:** 254
"Frog Takes a Swim" (Dixon), **Supp. XII:** 152
Frohock, W. M., **I:** 34, 42
Frolic of His Own, A (Gaddis), **Supp. IV Part 1:** 279, 291, 292-294
"From a Mournful Village" (Jewett), **Retro. Supp. II:** 146
"From an Old House in America" (Rich), **Supp. I Part 2:** 551, 565-567
From Another World (Untermeyer), **Supp. XV:** 293, 303, 310-311, 313
"From a Roadside Motel" (F. Wright), **Supp. XVII:** 245
"From a Survivor" (Rich), **Supp. I Part 2:** 563
From A to Z (musical review; Allen), **Supp. XV:** 3, 13
From a Writer's Notebook (Brooks), **I:** 254
From Bauhaus to Our House (Wolfe),

Supp. III Part 2: 580, 581, 584
From Bondage (H. Roth), **Supp. IX:** 236, **238-240**
"From *Chants* to *Borders* to *Communion*" (Fox), **Supp. XIII:** 217-218
"From Chicago" (Anderson), **I:** 108-109
From Death to Morning (Wolfe), **IV:** 450, 456, 458
"From Discord, a Wife Makes a Nice New Life-Too Nice" (Linfield), **Supp. XVII:** 177
"From Feathers to Iron" (Kunitz), **Supp. III Part 1:** 261
"From Fifth Avenue Up" (Barnes), **Supp. III Part 1:** 33, 44
"From Gorbunov and Gorchakov" (Brodsky), **Supp. VIII:** 26
"From Grand Canyon to Burbank" (H. Miller), **III:** 186
"From Hell to Breakfast," **Supp. IX:** 326-327
From Here to Eternity (film), **Supp. XI:** 221
From Here to Eternity (Jones), **I:** 477; **Supp. XI:** 215, 216, 217, 218, **219-221,** 223, 224, 226, 229, 230, 231, 232, 234
From Here to Eternity (miniseries), **Supp. XI:** 234
From Jordan's Delight (Blackmur), **Supp. II Part 1:** 91
Fromm, Erich, **I:** 58; **Supp. VIII:** 196
From Morn to Midnight (Kaiser), **I:** 479
"From Native Son to Invisible Man" (Locke), **Supp. IX:** 306
"From Pico, the Women: A Life" (Creeley), **Supp. IV Part 1:** 149
From Ritual to Romance (Weston), **II:** 540; **III:** 12; **Supp. I Part 2:** 439
From Room to Room (Kenyon), **Supp. VII:** 163-165, 166, 167
"From Room to Room" (Kenyon), **Supp. VII:** 159, 163-165
From Sand Creek: Rising in this Heart Which Is Our America (Ortiz), **Supp. IV Part 2:** 512-513
"From Sea Cliff, March" (Swenson), **Supp. IV Part 2:** 649
"From the Antigone" (Yeats), **III:** 459
From the Barrio: A Chicano Anthology (Salinas and Faderman, eds.), **Supp. XIII:** 313
"From the Childhood of Jesus" (Pinsky), **Supp. VI:** 244-245, 247
"From the Corpse Woodpiles, From the Ashes" (Hayden), **Supp. II Part 1:** 370

"From the Country to the City" (Bishop), **Supp. I Part 1:** 85, 86
"From the Cupola" (Merrill), **Supp. III Part 1:** 324-325, 331
"From the Dark Side of the Earth" (Oates), **Supp. II Part 2:** 510
"From the Diary of a New York Lady" (Parker), **Supp. IX:** 201
"From the Diary of One Not Born" (Singer), **IV:** 9
"From the East, Light" (Carver), **Supp. III Part 1:** 138
From the First Nine: Poems 1946-1976 (Merrill), **Supp. III Part 1:** 336
"From the Flats" (Lanier), **Supp. I Part 1:** 364
From the Flower Courtyard (Everwine), **Supp. XV:** 75
From the Heart of Europe (Matthiessen), **III:** 310
From the Meadow: Selected and New Poems (Everwine), **Supp. XV:** 75, **88-89**
"From the Memoirs of a Private Detective" (Hammett), **Supp. IV Part 1:** 343
"From the Nursery" (Kenyon), **Supp. VII:** 171
"From the Poets in the Kitchen" (Marshall), **Supp. XI:** 277
From the Terrace (O'Hara), **III:** 362
"From the Thirties: Tillie Olsen and the Radical Tradition" (Rosenfelt), **Supp. XIII:** 296, 304
"From Trollope's Journal" (Bishop), **Retro. Supp. II:** 47
"Front, A" (Jarrell), **II:** 374
Front, The (film), **Supp. I Part 1:** 295
"Front and the Back Parts of the House, The" (Maxwell), **Supp. VIII:** 169
Frontier Eden (Bigelow), **Supp. X:** 227
"Frontiers of Culture" (Locke), **Supp. XIV:**213
"Front Lines" (Snyder), **Supp. VIII:** 301
Frost, A. B., **Retro. Supp. II:** 72
"Frost: A Dissenting Opinion" (Cowley), **Supp. II Part 1:** 143
Frost: A Time to Talk (Francis), **Supp. IX:** 76, **85-86**
Frost, Carol, **Supp. XV: 91-109**
"Frost: He Is Sometimes a Poet and Sometimes a Stump-Speaker" (News-Week), **Retro. Supp. I:** 137
Frost, Isabelle Moodie, **II:** 150, 151
Frost, Jeanie, **II:** 151
Frost, Richard, **Supp. XV:** 92
Frost, Robert, **I:** 26, 27, 60, 63, 64, 171, 229, 303, 326, 418; **II:** 55, 58,

150-172, 276, 289, 388, 391, 471, 523, 527, 529, 535; **III:** 5, 23, 67, 269, 271, 272, 275, 287, 453, 510, 523, 536, 575, 581, 591; **IV:** 140, 190, 415; **Retro. Supp. I:** 67, **121-144,** 276, 287, 292, 298, 299, 311, 413; **Retro. Supp. II:** 40, 47, 50, 146, 178, 181; **Supp. I Part 1:** 80, 242, 263, 264; **Supp. I Part 2:** 387, 461, 699; **Supp. II Part 1:** 4, 19, 26, 103; **Supp. III Part 1:** 63, 74-75, 239, 253; **Supp. III Part 2:** 546, 592, 593; **Supp. IV Part 1:** 15; **Supp. IV Part 2:** 439, 445, 447, 448, 599, 601; **Supp. VIII:** 20, 30, 32, 98, 100, 104, 259, 292; **Supp. IX:** 41, 42, 75, 76, 80, 87, 90, 266, 308; **Supp. X:** 64, 65, 66, 74, 120, 172; **Supp. XI:** 43, 123, 150, 153, 312; **Supp. XII:** 130, 241, 303, 307; **Supp. XIII:** 143, 147, 334-335; **Supp. XIV:** 42, 122, 222, 229; **Supp. XV:** 21, 51, 65, 96, 212, 215, 250, 256, 293, 296, 299, 301, 302, 306, 348; **Supp. XVII:** 36, 110, 115-116
Frost, William Prescott, **II:** 150-151
"Frost at Midnight" (Coleridge), **Supp. X:** 71
"Frost Flowers" (Kenyon), **Supp. VII:** 168
Frothingham, Nathaniel, **I:** 3
Frothingham, Octavius B., **IV:** 173
"Frozen City, The" (Nemerov), **III:** 270
"Frozen Fields, The" (Bowles), **Supp. IV Part 1:** 80
"Fruit Garden Path, The" (Lowell), **II:** 516
"Fruit of the Flower" (Cullen), **Supp. IV Part 1:** 167
Fruit of the Tree, The (Wharton), **IV:** 314-315; **Retro. Supp. I:** 367, **370-371,** 373
"Fruit of Travel Long Ago" (Melville), **III:** 93
Fruits and Vegetables (Jong), **Supp. V:** 113, 115, 117, 118, 119
Frumkes, Lewis Burke, **Supp. XII:** 335-336
Fry, Christopher, **Supp. I Part 1:** 270
Fry, Roger, **Supp. XIV:** 336
Frye, Joanne, **Supp. XIII:** 292, 296, 298, 302
Frye, Northrop, **Supp. I Part 2:** 530; **Supp. II Part 1:** 101; **Supp. X:** 80; **Supp. XIII:** 19; **Supp. XIV:** 11, 15; **Supp. XVI:** 149, 156
Fryer, Judith, **Retro. Supp. I:** 379
Fuchs, Daniel, **Supp. XIII:** 106
Fuchs, Miriam, **Supp. IV Part 1:** 284

Fuehrer Bunker, The (Snodgrass), **Supp. VI:** 314, 315-317, 319-321
Fuel (Nye), **Supp. XIII:** 277, **282-284**
"Fuel" (Nye), **Supp. XIII:** 283
Fuertes, Gloria, **Supp. V:** 178
Fugard, Athol, **Supp. VIII:** 330; **Supp. XIII:** 205
Fugitive Group, The (Cowan), **IV:** 120
Fugitive Kind, The (T. Williams), **IV:** 381, 383
Fugitives, The (group), **IV:** 122, 124, 125, 131, 237, 238
Fugitives, The: A Critical Account (Bradbury), **IV:** 130
"Fugitive Slave Law, The" (Emerson), **II:** 13
Fugitive's Return (Glaspell), **Supp. III Part 1:** 182-184
Fuller, B. A. G., **III:** 605
Fuller, Jesse "Lonecat," **Supp. XV:** 147
Fuller, Margaret, **I:** 261; **II:** 7, 276; **IV:** 172; **Retro. Supp. I:** 155-156, 163; **Retro. Supp. II:** 46; **Supp. I Part 2:** 524; **Supp. II Part 1: 279-306; Supp. IX:** 37
Fuller, Thomas, **II:** 111, 112
Fullerton Street (Wilson), **Supp. VIII:** 331
"Full Fathom Five" (Plath), **Supp. I Part 2:** 538
Full Measure: Modern Short Stories on Aging (D. Sennett, ed.), **Supp. XVI:** 37
Full Monty, The (musical, McNally), **Supp. XIII:** 207
"Full Moon" (Hayden), **Supp. II Part 1:** 370
"Full Moon: New Guinea" (Shapiro), **Supp. II Part 2:** 707
Full Moon and Other Plays (Price), **Supp. VI:** 266
"Full Moon and You're Not Here" (Cisneros), **Supp. VII:** 71-72
"Fullness of Life, The" (Wharton), **Retro. Supp. I:** 363
Full of Life (Fante), **Supp. XI:** 160
Full of Life (film), **Supp. XI:** 170
Full of Lust and Good Usage (Dunn), **Supp. XI: 145-147**
"Full Summer" (Olds), **Supp. X:** 212
Fulton, Robert, **Supp. I Part 2:** 519; **Supp. II Part 1:** 73
Function of Criticism, The (Winters), **Supp. II Part 2:** 812, 813
"Fundamentalism" (Tate), **IV:** 125
"Fundamental Project of Technology, The" (Kinnell), **Supp. III Part 1:** 253
"Funeral of Bobò, The" (Brodsky), **Supp. VIII:** 27, 28

"Funnel" (Sexton), **Supp. II Part 2:** 675
"Furious Seasons, The" (Carver), **Supp. III Part 1:** 137
Furious Seasons and Other Stories (Carver), **Supp. III Part 1:** 142, 143, 146
"Furious Versions" (L.-Y. Lee), **Supp. XV: 215-217,** 218, 220
"Furnished Room, The" (Hayden), **Supp. II Part 1:** 386-387, 394, 397, 399, 406, 408
"Furor Scribendi" (O. Butler), **Supp. XIII:** 70
Fur Person, The (Sarton), **Supp. VIII: 264-265**
Further Adventures with You (Wright), **Supp. XV:** 339, 342, **343-345**
Further Fables for Our Time (Thurber), **Supp. I Part 2:** 612
"Further in Summer than the Birds" (Dickinson), **I:** 471
Further Poems of Emily Dickinson (Bianchi and Hampson, ed.), **Retro. Supp. I:** 35
Further Range, A (Frost), **II:** 155; **Retro. Supp. I:** 132, 136, 137, 138, 139
"Fury of Aerial Bombardment, The" (Eberhart), **I:** 535-536
"Fury of Flowers and Worms, The" (Sexton), **Supp. II Part 2:** 694
"Fury of Rain Storms, The" (Sexton), **Supp. II Part 2:** 695
Fury of the Jungle (film), **Supp. XIII:** 163
Fussell, Paul, **Supp. V:** 241
"Future, if Any, of Comedy, The" (Thurber), **Supp. I Part 2:** 620
Future is Ours, Comrade, The: Conversations with the Russians (Kosinski), **Supp. VII:** 215
Futureland: Nine Stories of an Imminent World (Mosley), **Supp. XIII: 247-249**
"Future Life, The" (Bryant), **Supp. I Part 1:** 170
Future Punishment of the Wicked, The (Edwards), **I:** 546

G
G. K. the DJ (Keillor), **Supp. XVI:** 171
"Gabriel" (Rich), **Supp. I Part 2:** 557
Gabriel, Ralph H., **Supp. I Part 1:** 251
Gabriel, Trip, **Supp. V:** 212
Gabriel Conroy (Harte), **Supp. II Part 1:** 354
"Gabriel's Truth" (Kenyon), **Supp. VII:** 166
Gaddis, William, **Supp. IV Part 1: 279-296; Supp. IV Part 2:** 484;

Supp. V: 52; **Supp. IX:** 208; **Supp. X:** 301, 302
Gadiot, Pud, **Supp. XI:** 295
Gain (Powers), **Supp. IX:** 212, **220-221**
Gaines, Ernest, **Supp. X:** 250
Gaines, Ernest J., **Supp. X:** 24
Gaines, James R., **Supp. IX:** 190
Gaitens, Peter, **Supp. XV:** 65
Galamain, Ivan, **Supp. III Part 2:** 624
Galatea 2.2 (Powers), **Supp. IX:** 212, **219-220**
"Galatea Encore" (Brodsky), **Supp. VIII:** 31
Galbraith, John Kenneth, **Supp. I Part 2:** 645, 650
Galdós, Benito Pérez. *See* Pérez Galdós, Benito
Gale, Zona, **Supp. I Part 2:** 613; **Supp. VIII:** 155
"Gale in April" (Jeffers), **Supp. II Part 2:** 423
Galignani, Giovanni Antonio, **II:** 315
Galileo Galilei, **I:** 480-481; **Supp. XII:** 180; **Supp. XIII:** 75
Gallagher, Tess, **Supp. XVI:**36; **Supp. XVII:** 110
Gallant, Mavis, **Supp. VIII:** 151
Gallatin, Albert, **I:** 5
"Gallery" (Goldbarth), **Supp. XII:** 188
"Gallery of Real Creatures, A" (Thurber), **Supp. I Part 2:** 619
Gallico, Paul, **Supp. XVI:**238
Gallows Songs (Snodgrass), **Supp. VI:** 317
Gallup, Donald, **III:** 404, 478
Galsworthy, John, **III:** 70, 153, 382
Galton Case, The (Macdonald), **Supp. IV Part 2:** 463, 473, 474
"Gal Young 'Un" (Rawlings), **Supp. X:** 228
"Gambler, the Nun, and the Radio, The" (Hemingway), **II:** 250
"Gambler's Wife, The" (Dunbar), **Supp. II Part 1:** 196
Gambone, Philip, **Supp. XII:** 81
"Gambrel Roof, A" (Larcom), **Supp. XIII:** 144
"Game at Salzburg, A" (Jarrell), **II:** 384, 389
Game Management (Leopold), **Supp. XIV:**182
"Game of Catch, A" (Wilbur), **Supp. III Part 2:** 552
"Games in Frank Conroy's *Stop-Time*" (T. Adams), **Supp. XVI:**67
"Games Two" (Wilbur), **Supp. III Part 2:** 550
"Gamut, The" (Angelou), **Supp. IV Part 1:** 15

Gander, Forrest, **Supp. XV:** 339, 340, 342
Gandhi, Indira, **Supp. X:** 108
Gandhi, Mahatma, **III:** 179, 296-297; **IV:** 170, 185, 367; **Supp. VIII:** 203, 204; **Supp. X:** 27
Gandhi on Non-Violence (Merton, ed.), **Supp. VIII:** 204-205
"Gang of Mirrors, The" (Simic), **Supp. VIII:** 283
Gansevoort, Guert, **III:** 94
Gansevoort, Peter, **III:** 92
"Gap" (Bierds), **Supp. XVII:** 35-36
Garabedian, Michael, **Supp. XIII:** 115
Garbage (Ammons), **Supp. VII:** 24, 35-36
Garbage (Dixon), **Supp. XII:** 147, 148
Garbage Man, The (Dos Passos), **I:** 478, 479, 481, 493
Garber, Frederick, **Supp. IX:** 294-295
Garbo, Greta, **Supp. I Part 2:** 616
García, Cristina, **Supp. VIII:** 74; **Supp. XI:** **177-192**
"García Lorca: A Photograph of the Granada Cemetery, 1966" (Levis), **Supp. XI:** 264
García Lorca, Federico. *See* Lorca, Federico García
García Márquez, Gabriel, **Supp. V:** 244; **Supp. VIII:** 81, 82, 84, 85; **Supp. XII:** 147, 310, 316, 322; **Supp. XIII:** 226; **Supp. XVII:** 45
"Garden" (Marvell), **IV:** 161; **Supp. XVI:**204
"Garden, The" (Glück), **Supp. V:** 83
"Garden, The" (Strand), **Supp. IV Part 2:** 629
"Garden Among Tombs" (B. Kelly), **Supp. XVII:** 126
"Garden by Moonlight, The" (Lowell), **II:** 524
"Gardener Delivers a Fawn, The" (C. Frost), **Supp. XV:** 99
Gardener's Son, The (McCarthy), **Supp. VIII:** 187
"Gardenias" (Doty), **Supp. XI:** 122
"Gardenias" (Monette), **Supp. X:** 159
"Garden Lodge, The" (Cather), **I:** 316, 317
Garden of Adonis, The (Gordon), **II:** 196, 204-205, 209
Garden of Earthly Delights, A (Oates), **Supp. II Part 2:** 504, 507-509
"Garden of Eden" (Hemingway), **II:** 259
Garden of Eden, The (Hemingway), **Retro. Supp. I:** 186, **187-188**
"Garden of Flesh, Garden of Stone" (B. Kelly), **Supp. XVII:** 128
"Garden of the Moon, The" (Doty),

Supp. XI: 122
"Garden of the Trumpet Tree, The" (B. Kelly), **Supp. XVII:** 131
"Gardens, The" (Oliver), **Supp. VII:** 236
"Gardens of Mont-Saint-Michel, The" (Maxwell), **Supp. VIII:** 169
"Gardens of the Villa D'Este, The" (Hecht), **Supp. X:** 59
"Gardens of Zuñi, The" (Merwin), **Supp. III Part 1:** 351
Gardiner, Judith Kegan, **Supp. IV Part 1:** 205
Gardner, Erle Stanley, **Supp. IV Part 1:** 121, 345
Gardner, Isabella, **IV:** 127
Gardner, John, **Supp. I Part 1:** 193, 195, 196; **Supp. III Part 1:** 136, 142, 146; **Supp. VI:** **61-76**
Gardons, S. S. *See* Snodgrass, W. D.
"Gare de Lyon" (M. F. K. Fisher), **Supp. XVII:** 91
Garfield, John, **Supp. XII:** 160
Garibaldi, Giuseppe, **I:** 4; **II:** 284
Garibay, Angel M., **Supp. XV:** 77
Garland, Hamlin, **I:** 407; **II:** 276, 289; **III:** 576; **Retro. Supp. I:** 133; **Retro. Supp. II:** 72; **Supp. I Part 1:** 217; **Supp. IV Part 2:** 502
Garland Companion, The (Zverev), **Retro. Supp. I:** 278
Garments the Living Wear (Purdy), **Supp. VII:** 278-279, 280-281
Garner, Dwight, **Supp. X:** 202
Garnett, Edward, **I:** 405, 409, 417; **III:** 27
Garrett, George P., **Supp. I Part 1:** 196; **Supp. VII:** **95-113**; **Supp. X:** 3, 7; **Supp. XI:** 218
Garrigue, Jean, **Supp. XII:** 260
Garrison, Deborah, **Supp. IX:** 299
Garrison, Fielding, **III:** 105
Garrison, William Lloyd, **Supp. I Part 2:** 524, 588, 683, 685, 686, 687; **Supp. XIV:**54
"Garrison of Cape Ann, The" (Whittier), **Supp. I Part 2:** 691, 694
Garry Moore Show (television show), **Supp. IV Part 2:** 575
"Garter Motif" (White), **Supp. I Part 2:** 673
Gartner, Zsuzsi, **Supp. X:** 276
Garvey, Marcus, **Supp. III Part 1:** 175, 180; **Supp. IV Part 1:** 168; **Supp. X:** 135, 136
Gas (Kaiser), **I:** 479
Gas-House McGinty (Farrell), **II:** 41-42
Gaskell, Elizabeth, A., **Supp. I Part 2:** 580

Gasoline (Corso), **Supp. XII:** 118, **121-123,** 134
Gass, William, **Supp. XVII:** 183
Gass, William H., **Supp. V:** 44, 52, 238; **Supp. VI: 77-96; Supp. IX:** 208; **Supp. XII:** 152; **Supp. XIV:**305
Gassner, John, **IV:** 381; **Supp. I Part 1:** 284, 292
"Gas Stations" (Apple), **Supp. XVII:** 4
Gastronomical Me, The (M. F. K. Fisher), **Supp. XVII:** 84, 85, 87, 91, 92
Gates, David, **Supp. V:** 24; **Supp. XIII:** 93; **Supp. XVI:**73, 74
Gates, Elmer, **I:** 515-516
Gates, Henry Louis, **Retro. Supp. I:** 194, 195, 203; **Supp. X:** 242, 243, 245, 247
Gates, Lewis E., **III:** 315, 330
Gates, The (Rukeyser), **Supp. VI:** 271, 274, 281
"Gates, The" (Rukeyser), **Supp. VI:** 286
Gates, Tudor, **Supp. XI:** 307
Gates of Ivory, the Gates of Horn, The (McGrath), **Supp. X:** 118
Gates of Wrath, The; Rhymed Poems (Ginsberg), **Supp. II Part 1:** 311, 319
"Gathering of Dissidents, A" (Applebaum), **Supp. XVI:**153
Gathering of Fugitives, A (Trilling), **Supp. III Part 2:** 506, 512
Gathering of Zion, The: The Story of the Mormon Trail (Stegner), **Supp. IV Part 2:** 599, 602-603
Gather Together in My Name (Angelou), **Supp. IV Part 1:** 2, 3, 4-6, 11
Gathorne-Hardy, Robert, **Supp. XIV:**344, 347, 348, 349
Gaudier-Brzeska, Henri, **III:** 459, 464, 465, 477
Gauguin, Paul, **I:** 34; **IV:** 290; **Supp. IV Part 1:** 81; **Supp. XII:** 128
"Gauley Bridge" (Rukeyser), **Supp. VI:** 278
Gauss, Christian, **II:** 82; **IV:** 427, 439-440, 444
Gautier, Théophile, **II:** 543; **III:** 466, 467; **Supp. I Part 1:** 277
Gay, John, **II:** 111; **Supp. I Part 2:** 523; **Supp. XIV:**337
Gay, Peter, **I:** 560
Gay, Sydney Howard, **Supp. I Part 1:** 158
Gay, Walter, **IV:** 317
Gayatri Prayer, The, **III:** 572

"Gay Chaps at the Bar" (Brooks), **Supp. III Part 1:** 74, 75
Gaylord, Winfield R., **III:** 579-580
Gay Talese Reader, The: Portraits & Encounters (Talese), **Supp. XVII:** 202, 208
"Gazebo" (Carver), **Supp. III Part 1:** 138, 144, 145
Gazer Within, The, and Other Essays by Larry Levis, **Supp. XI:** 270
Gazzara, Ben, **Supp. VIII:** 319
Gazzo, Michael V., **III:** 155
"Geese Gone Beyond" (Snyder), **Supp. VIII:** 304
"Gegenwart" (Goethe), **Supp. II Part 1:** 26
Geisel, Theodor Seuss (Dr. Seuss), **Supp. X:** 56; **Supp. XVI:97-115**
Geismar, Maxwell, **II:** 178, 431; **III:** 71; **Supp. IX:** 15; **Supp. XI:** 223
Gelb, Arthur, **IV:** 380
Gelbart, Larry, **Supp. IV Part 2:** 591
Gelder, Robert Van, **Supp. XIII:** 166
Gelfant, Blanche, **Supp. XVII:** 161
Gelfant, Blanche H., **II:** 27, 41
Gelfman, Jean, **Supp. X:** 3
Gellhorn, Martha. *See* Hemingway, Mrs. Ernest (Martha Gellhorn)
Gelpi, Albert, **Supp. I Part 2:** 552, 554, 560
Gelpi, Barbara, **Supp. I Part 2:** 560
Gemini: an extended autobiographical statement on my first twenty-five years of being a black poet (Giovanni), **Supp. IV Part 1:** 11
"Gen" (Snyder), **Supp. VIII:** 302
"Gender Norms" (Radinovsky), **Supp. XV:** 285
"Gender of Sound, The" (Carson), **Supp. XII: 106**
"Genealogy" (Komunyakaa), **Supp. XIII:** 129
"General Aims and Theories" (Crane), **I:** 389
General Died at Dawn, The (Odets), **Supp. II Part 2:** 546
"General Gage's Confession" (Freneau), **Supp. II Part 1:** 257
"General Gage's Soliloquy" (Freneau), **Supp. II Part 1:** 257
General History of the Robberies and Murders of the Most Notorious Pyrates from Their First Rise and Settlement in the Island of New Providence to the Present Year, A (Johnson), **Supp. V:** 128
"General William Booth Enters into Heaven" (Lindsay), **Supp. I Part 2:** 374, 382, 384, 385-388, 389, 392, 399

General William Booth Enters into Heaven and Other Poems (Lindsay), **Supp. I Part 2:** 379, 381, 382, 387-388, 391
"Generations of Men, The" (Frost), **Retro. Supp. I:** 128; **Supp. XIII:** 147
Generous Man, A (Price), **Supp. VI:** 259, 260, 261
Genesis (biblical book), **I:** 279; **II:** 540; **Retro. Supp. I:** 250, 256; **Supp. XII:** 54
"Genesis" (Stegner), **Supp. IV Part 2:** 604
Genesis: Book One (Schwartz), **Supp. II Part 2:** 640, 651-655
Genet, Jean, **I:** 71, 82, 83, 84; **Supp. IV Part 1:** 8; **Supp. XI:** 308; **Supp. XII:** 1; **Supp. XIII:** 74; **Supp. XVII:** 95
"Genetic Expedition" (Dove), **Supp. IV Part 1:** 249, 257
"Genetics of Justice" (Alvarez), **Supp. VII:** 19
"Genial Host, The" (McCarthy), **II:** 564
"Genie in the Bottle, The" (Wilbur), **Supp. III Part 2:** 542
"Genius, The" (MacLeish), **III:** 19
Genius and Lust: A Journey through the Major Writings of Henry Miller (Mailer), **Retro. Supp. II:** 208
"Genius Child" (Hughes), **Retro. Supp. I:** 203
"*Genius,*" *The* (Dreiser), **I:** 497, 501, 509-511, 519; **Retro. Supp. II:** 94-95, **102-103,** 104, 105
"Genteel Tradition in American Philosophy, The" (Santayana), **I:** 222
"Gentle Communion" (Mora), **Supp. XIII:** 218-219
Gentle Crafter, The (O. Henry), **Supp. II Part 1:** 410
"Gentle Lena, The" (Stein), **IV:** 37, 40
Gentleman Caller, The (T. Williams), **IV:** 383
"Gentleman from Cracow, The" (Singer), **IV:** 9
"Gentleman of Bayou Têche, A" (Chopin), **Supp. I Part 1:** 211-212
"Gentleman of Shalott, The" (Bishop), **Supp. I Part 1:** 85, 86
Gentleman's Agreement (Hobson), **III:** 151
Gentlemen Prefer Blondes (Loos; musical adaptation), **Supp. XVI:**193
Gentlemen Prefer Blondes: The Illuminating Diary of a Professional Lady (Loos), **Supp. XVI:**181, 183, 186, **188-189**

Gentlemen Prefer "Books" (J. Yeats), **Supp. XVI:**190
Gentry, Marshall Bruce, **Supp. IV Part 1:** 236
"Genuine Man, The" (Emerson), **II:** 10
Geo-Bestiary (Harrison), **Supp. VIII:** 53
"Geode" (Frost), **II:** 161
Geographical History of America, The (Stein), **IV:** 31, 45
Geography and Plays (Stein), **IV:** 29-30, 32, 43, 44
Geography III (Bishop), **Retro. Supp. II:** 50; **Supp. I Part 1:** 72, 73, 76, 82, 93, 94, 95
Geography of a Horse Dreamer (Shepard), **Supp. III Part 2:** 432
Geography of Home, The: California's Poetry of Place (Bluckey and Young, eds.), **Supp. XIII:** 313
Geography of Lograire, The (Merton), **Supp. VIII:** 208
Geography of the Heart (Johnson), **Supp. XI:** 129
"Geometric Poem, The" (Corso), **Supp. XII:** 132, 133-134
George, Diana Hume, **Supp. IV Part 2:** 447, 449, 450
George, Henry, **II:** 276; **Supp. I Part 2:** 518
George, Jan, **Supp. IV Part 1:** 268
George, Lynell, **Supp. XIII:** 234-235, 237, 249
George, Peter, **Supp. XI:** 302, 303, 304
George and the Dragon (Shanley), **Supp. XIV:**315
George Bernard Shaw: His Plays (Mencken), **III:** 102
George Mills (Elkin), **Supp. VI: 53-54**
"George Robinson: Blues" (Rukeyser), **Supp. VI:** 279
George's Mother (Crane), **I:** 408
"George Thurston" (Bierce), **I:** 202
George Washington Crossing the Delaware (Koch), **Supp. XV:** 186
"Georgia: Invisible Empire State" (Du Bois), **Supp. II Part 1:** 179
Georgia Boy (Caldwell), **I:** 288, 305-306, 308, 309, 310
"Georgia Dusk" (Toomer), **Supp. IX:** 309
"Georgia Night" (Toomer), **Supp. III Part 2:** 481
Georgia Scenes (Longstreet), **II:** 70, 313; **Supp. I Part 1:** 352
Georgics (Virgil), **Retro. Supp. I:** 135; **Supp. XVI:**22
Georgoudaki, Ekaterini, **Supp. IV Part 1:** 12

Gerald McBoing-Boing (film), **Supp. XVI:**102
"Geraldo No Last Name" (Cisneros), **Supp. VII:** 60-61
Gerald's Game (King), **Supp. V:** 141, 148-150, 151, 152
Gerald's Party (Coover), **Supp. V:** 49-50, 51, 52
Gérando, Joseph Marie de, **II:** 10
"Geranium" (O'Connor), **Retro. Supp. II:** 221, 236
Gerber, Dan, **Supp. VIII:** 39
Gerhardt, Rainer, **Supp. IV Part 1:** 142
"German Girls! The German Girls!, The" (MacLeish), **III:** 16
"German Refugee, The" (Malamud), **Supp. I Part 2:** 436, 437
"Germany's Reichswehr" (Agee), **I:** 35
Germinal (Zola), **III:** 318, 322
Gernsback, Hugo, **Supp. IV Part 1:** 101
"Gernsback Continuum, The" (W. Gibson), **Supp. XVI:**123, 128
"Gerontion" (Eliot), **I:** 569, 574, 577, 578, 585, 588; **III:** 9, 435, 436; **Retro. Supp. I:** 290; **Supp. XV:** 341; **Supp. XVI:**158-159
Gerry, Elbridge, **Supp. I Part 2:** 486
"Gerry's Jazz" (Komunyakaa), **Supp. XIII:** 125
Gershwin, Ira, **Supp. I Part 1:** 281
"Gert" (Monette), **Supp. X:** 158
Gertrude of Stony Island Avenue (Purdy), **Supp. VII:** 281-282
Gertrude Stein (Sprigge), **IV:** 31
Gertrude Stein: A Biography of Her Work (Sutherland), **IV:** 38
"Gertrude Stein and the Geography of the Sentence" (Gass), **Supp. VI:** 87
Gesell, Silvio, **III:** 473
"Gestalt at Sixty" (Sarton), **Supp. VIII:** 260
"Gesture toward an Unfound Renaissance, A" (Stafford), **Supp. XI:** 323
Getlin, Josh, **Supp. V:** 22; **Supp. VIII:** 75, 76, 78, 79
"Getting Along" (Larcom), **Supp. XIII:** 144
"Getting Along with Nature" (Berry), **Supp. X:** 31-32
"Getting Away from Already Pretty Much Being Away from It All" (Wallace), **Supp. X:** 314-315
"Getting Born" (Shields), **Supp. VII:** 311
Getting Even (Allen), **Supp. XV:** 3, 14, 15
"Getting Lucky" (L. Michaels), **Supp. XVI:**205, 209

"Getting Out of Jail on Monday" (Wagoner), **Supp. IX:** 327
"Getting There" (Plath), **Supp. I Part 2:** 539, 542
"Getting to the Poem" (Corso), **Supp. XII:** 135
Getty, J. Paul, **Supp. X:** 108
Getty, Norris, **Supp. XV:** 136-137, 138, 139, 142, 143, 145, 146
"Gettysburg: July 1, 1863" (Kenyon), **Supp. VII:** 172
Gettysburg, Manila, Acoma (Masters), **Supp. I Part 2:** 471
Ghachem, Malick, **Supp. X:** 17
"Ghazals: Homage to Ghalib" (Rich), **Supp. I Part 2:** 557
Ghost, The (Crane), **I:** 409, 421
"Ghost Chant, et alii" (Komunyakaa), **Supp. XIII:** 114
Ghost in the Music, A (Nichols), **Supp. XIII:** 267
"Ghostlier Demarcations, Keener Sounds" (Vendler), **Supp. I Part 2:** 565
"Ghostly Father, I Confess" (McCarthy), **II:** 565-566
Ghostly Lover, The (Hardwick), **Supp. III Part 1:** 194-196, 208, 209
Ghost of Meter, The (A. Finch), **Supp. XVII:** 71, 73
"Ghost of the Buffaloes, The" (Lindsay), **Supp. I Part 2:** 393
Ghosts (Auster), **Supp. XII:** 22, **24, 26-27**
Ghosts (Ibsen), **III:** 152
Ghosts (Wharton), **IV:** 316, 327
Ghost Town (Coover), **Supp. V:** 52-53
Ghost Trio, The (Bierds), **Supp. XVII:** 29, **30**
Ghost Writer, The (P. Roth), **Retro. Supp. II:** 22, 290, 291; **Supp. III Part 2:** 420-421; **Supp. XVII:** 43
"G.I. Graves in Tuscany" (Hugo), **Supp. VI:** 138
Giachetti, Fosco, **Supp. IV Part 2:** 520
"Giacometti" (Wilbur), **Supp. III Part 2:** 551
Giacometti, Alberto, **Supp. VIII:** 168, 169
Giacomo, Padre, **II:** 278-279
Giant's House, The: A Romance (McCracken), **Supp. X:** 86
"Giant Snail" (Bishop), **Retro. Supp. II:** 49
Giant Weapon, The (Winters), **Supp. II Part 2:** 810
"Giant Woman, The" (Oates), **Supp. II Part 2:** 523
Gibbon, Edward, **I:** 4, 378; **IV:** 126; **Supp. I Part 2:** 503; **Supp. III Part**

INDEX / 351

2: 629; **Supp. XIII:** 75; **Supp. XIV:** 97
Gibbons, James, **Supp. XVII:** 228
Gibbons, Kaye, **Supp. X: 41-54; Supp. XII:** 311
Gibbons, Reginald, **Supp. X:** 113, 124, 127; **Supp. XV:** 105
Gibbons, Richard, **Supp. I Part 1:** 107
"Gibbs" (Rukeyser), **Supp. VI:** 273
Gibbs, Barbara, **Supp. IV Part 2:** 644
Gibbs, Wolcott, **Supp. I Part 2:** 604, 618; **Supp. VIII:** 151
"GIBSON" (Baraka), **Supp. II Part 1:** 54
Gibson, Charles Dana, **Supp. X:** 184
Gibson, Graeme, **Supp. XIII:** 20
Gibson, Wilfrid W., **Retro. Supp. I:** 128
Gibson, William, **Supp. XVI:117-133**
Giddins, Gary, **Supp. XIII:** 245
Gide, André, **I:** 271, 290; **II:** 581; **III:** 210; **IV:** 53, 289; **Supp. I Part 1:** 51; **Supp. IV Part 1:** 80, 284, 347; **Supp. IV Part 2:** 681, 682; **Supp. VIII:** 40; **Supp. X:** 187; **Supp. XIV:** 24, 348; **Supp. XVII:** 242
Gideon Planish (Lewis), **II:** 455
Gielgud, John, **I:** 82; **Supp. XI:** 305
Gierow, Dr. Karl Ragnar, **III:** 404
Gifford, Bill, **Supp. XI:** 38
Gifford, Terry, **Supp. XVI:22**
"Gift, The" (Creeley), **Supp. IV Part 1:** 153
"Gift, The" (Doolittle), **Supp. I Part 1:** 267
"Gift, The" (Jarman), **Supp. XVII:** 116
"Gift, The" (L.-Y. Lee), **Supp. XV:** 213, 214
Gift, The (Nabokov), **III:** 246, 255, 261-263; **Retro. Supp. I:** 264, 266, **268-270,** 273, 274-275, 278
"Gift from the City, A" (Updike), **Retro. Supp. I:** 320
"Gift of God, The" (Robinson), **III:** 512, 517, 518-521, 524
Gift of the Black Folk, The: The Negroes in the Making of America (Du Bois), **Supp. II Part 1:** 179
"Gift of the Magi, The" (O. Henry), **Supp. II Part 1:** 394, 406, 408
"Gift of the *Osuo,* The" (Johnson), **Supp. VI:** 194
"Gift of the Prodigal, The" (Taylor), **Supp. V:** 314, 326
"Gift Outright, The" (Frost), **II:** 152; **Supp. IV Part 1:** 15
Gigi (Colette; stage adaptation, Loos), **Supp. XVI:193**
"Gigolo" (Plath), **Retro. Supp. II:** 257
"Gila Bend" (Dickey), **Supp. IV Part 1:** 185-186
Gilbert, Jack, **Supp. IX:** 287
Gilbert, Peter, **Supp. IX:** 291, 300
Gilbert, Roger, **Supp. XI:** 124
Gilbert, Sandra M., **Retro. Supp. I:** 42; **Retro. Supp. II:** 324; **Supp. IX:** 66; **Supp. XV:** 270
Gilbert, Susan. *See* Dickinson, Mrs. William A.
Gilbert and Sullivan, **Supp. IV Part 1:** 389
Gil Blas (Le Sage), **II:** 290
Gilded Age, The (Twain), **III:** 504; **IV:** 198
Gilded Lapse of Time, A (Schnackenberg), **Supp. XV:** 258, **260-263**
"Gilded Lapse of Time, A" (Schnackenberg), **Supp. XV:** 257
"Gilded Six-Bits, The" (Hurston), **Supp. VI:** 154-155
Gilder, R. W., **Retro. Supp. II:** 66; **Supp. I Part 2:** 418
Gildersleeve, Basil, **Supp. I Part 1:** 369
Giles, H. A., **Retro. Supp. I:** 289
Giles, James R., **Supp. IX:** 11, 15; **Supp. XI:** 219, 223-224, 228, 234
"Giles Corey of the Salem Farms" (Longfellow), **II:** 505, 506; **Retro. Supp. II:** 166, 167
Giles Goat-Boy (Barth), **I:** 121, 122-123, 129, 130, 134, 135-138; **Supp. V:** 39
Gill, Brendan, **Supp. I Part 2:** 659, 660
Gillespie, Nick, **Supp. XIV:298**, 311
Gillette, Chester, **I:** 512
Gilligan, Carol, **Supp. XIII:** 216
Gillis, Jim, **IV:** 196
Gillis, Steve, **IV:** 195
Gilman, Charlotte Perkins, **Supp. I Part 2:** 637; **Supp. V:** 121, 284, 285; **Supp. XI: 193-211; Supp. XIII:** 295, 306; **Supp. XVI:84**
Gilman, Daniel Coit, **Supp. I Part 1:** 361, 368, 370
Gilman, Richard, **IV:** 115; **Supp. IV Part 2:** 577; **Supp. XIII:** 100
Gilmore, Eddy, **Supp. I Part 2:** 618
Gilmore, Mikal, **Supp. XVI:123**, 124
Gilpin, Charles, **III:** 392
Gilpin, Dewitt, **Supp. XV:** 197
Gilpin, Laura, **Retro. Supp. I:** 7
Gilpin, Sam, **Supp. V:** 213
Gilpin, William, **Supp. IV Part 2:** 603
"Gil's Furniture Bought & Sold" (Cisneros), **Supp. VII:** 61-62, 64
"Gimpel the Fool" (Singer), **IV:** 14; **Retro. Supp. II:** 22, 307
Gimpel the Fool and Other Stories (Singer), **IV:** 1, 7-9, 10, 12
"Gin" (Levine), **Supp. V:** 193
"Gingerbread House, The" (Coover), **Supp. V:** 42-43
Gingerbread Lady, The (Simon), **Supp. IV Part 2:** 580, 583-584, 588
Gingerich, Willard, **Supp. IV Part 2:** 510
Gingertown (McKay), **Supp. X:** 132, 139
Gingold, Hermione, **Supp. XV:** 13
Gingrich, Arnold, **Retro. Supp. I:** 113; **Supp. XVII:** 88
Ginna, Robert, **Supp. IX:** 259
Ginsberg, Allen, **I:** 183; **Retro. Supp. I:** 411, 426, 427; **Retro. Supp. II:** 280; **Supp. II Part 1:** 30, 32, 58, **307-333; Supp. III Part 1:** 2, 91, 96, 98, 100, 222, 226; **Supp. III Part 2:** 541, 627; **Supp. IV Part 1:** 79, 90, 322; **Supp. IV Part 2:** 502; **Supp. V:** 168, 336; **Supp. VIII:** 239, 242-243, 289; **Supp. IX:** 299; **Supp. X:** 120, 204; **Supp. XI:** 135, 297; **Supp. XII:** 118-119, 121-122, 124, 126, 130-131, 136, 182; **Supp. XIV:15**, 53, 54, 125, 137, 141, 142, 143-144, 148, 150, 269, 280, 283; **Supp. XV:** 134, 177, 263; **Supp. XVI:123**, 135; **Supp. XVII:** 138, 243
Gioia, Dana, **Supp. IX:** 279; **Supp. XII:** 209; **Supp. XIII:** 337; **Supp. XV: 111-131,** 251; **Supp. XVII:** 69, 72, 112
Giono, Jean, **Supp. XVI:135**
Giotto di Bondone, **Supp. I Part 2:** 438; **Supp. XI:** 126
Giovani, Regula, **Supp. XV:** 270
Giovanni, Nikki, **Supp. I Part 1:** 66; **Supp. II Part 1:** 54; **Supp. IV Part 1:** 11; **Supp. VIII:** 214
Giovanni's Room (Baldwin), **Retro. Supp. II:** 5, 6, **6-7,** 8, 10; **Supp. I Part 1:** 51, 52, 55-56, 57, 60, 63, 67; **Supp. III Part 1:** 125
Giovannitti, Arturo, **I:** 476; **Supp. XV:** 299, 301, 302, 307
"Giraffe" (Swenson), **Supp. IV Part 2:** 651
Giraldi, Giovanni Battista. *See* Cinthio
"Girl" (Kincaid), **Supp. VII:** 182-183
"Girl, The" (Olds), **Supp. X:** 207
"Girl Friend Poems" (Wright), **Supp. XV:** 349
"Girl from Lynn Bathes Horse!!" (McCarriston), **Supp. XIV:266**
"Girl from Red Lion, P.A., A" (Mencken), **III:** 111

Girl in Glass, The: Love Poems (W. J. Smith), **Supp. XIII:** 335
"Girl in the Grave, The" (McCoy), **Supp. XIII:** 170
Girl Like I, A (Loos), **Supp. XVI:**181, 183, 184, 187, 194, 196
"Girl of the Golden West" (Didion), **Supp. IV Part 1:** 195, 208, 211
Girl of the Golden West, The (Puccini), **III:** 139
"Girl on a Scaffold" (C. Frost), **Supp. XV:** 98
"Girl on the Baggage Truck, The" (O'Hara), **III:** 371-372
Girls at Play (Theroux), **Supp. VIII:** 314, 315, 316, **317**
"Girls at the Sphinx, The" (Farrell), **II:** 45
Girl Sleuth, The: A Feminist Guide (Mason), **Supp. VIII:** 133, 135, **139**, 142
"Girl's Story, A" (Bambara), **Supp. XI:** 10-11
"Girl the Prince Liked, The" (Z. Fitzgerald), **Supp. IX:** 71
Girl Who Loved Tom Gordon, The (King), **Supp. V:** 138, 152
Girl with Curious Hair (Wallace), **Supp. X:** 301, **305-308**
"Girl with Curious Hair" (Wallace), **Supp. X:** 306
"Girl with Silver Eyes, The" (Hammett), **Supp. IV Part 1:** 344, 345
"Girl with Talent, The" (Z. Fitzgerald), **Supp. IX:** 71
Girodias, Maurice, **III:** 171; **Supp. XI:** 297
Giroux, Robert, **Retro. Supp. II:** 177, 229, 235; **Supp. IV Part 1:** 280; **Supp. VIII:** 195; **Supp. XV:** 146
Gish, Dorothy, **Retro. Supp. I:** 103
Gish, Lillian, **Supp. XVI:**184
Gissing, George, **II:** 138, 144
Gittings, Robert, **II:** 531
"Given" (C. Frost), **Supp. XV:** 96
"Give Us Back Our Country" (Masters), **Supp. I Part 2:** 472
"Give Way, Ye Gates" (Roethke), **III:** 536
"Give Your Heart to the Hawks" (Jeffers), **Supp. II Part 2:** 433
"Giving Blood" (Updike), **IV:** 226; **Retro. Supp. I:** 332
Giving Good Weight (McPhee), **Supp. III Part 1:** 307
"Giving in to You" (X. J. Kennedy), **Supp. XV:** 160
"Giving Myself Up" (Strand), **Supp. IV Part 2:** 627

Glackens, William, **Retro. Supp. II:** 103
Gladden, Washington, **III:** 293; **Supp. I Part 1:** 5
Gladstone, William Ewart, **Supp. I Part 2:** 419
"Gladys Poem, The" (Alvarez), **Supp. VII:** 10
"Glance at German 'Kultur,' A" (Bourne), **I:** 228
Glance Away, A (Wideman), **Supp. X:** 320
"Glance from the Bridge, A" (Wilbur), **Supp. III Part 2:** 551
Glance toward Shakespeare, A (Chapman), **Supp. XIV:**44
Glanville-Hicks, Peggy, **Supp. IV Part 1:** 84
Glare (Ammons), **Supp. VII:** 35-36
Glasgow, Cary, **II:** 173, 182
Glasgow, Ellen, **II: 173-195; IV:** 328; **Supp. X:** 228, 234
Glasmon, Kubec, **Supp. XIII:** 166
Glaspell, Susan, **Supp. III Part 1: 175-191; Supp. X:** 46; **Supp. XVII:** 99
"Glass" (Francis), **Supp. IX:** 80
Glass, Irony, and God (Carson), **Supp. XII:** 97, **104-106**
"Glass Ark, The" (Komunyakaa), **Supp. XIII:** 129
Glass Bees, The (Jünger; Bogan and Mayer, trans.), **Supp. III Part 1:** 63
"Glass Blower of Venice" (Malamud), **Supp. I Part 2:** 450
"Glass Essay, The" (Carson), **Supp. XII:** 104-105
"Glass Face in the Rain, A: New Poems" (Stafford), **Supp. XI: 327-328**
Glass Key, The (Hammett), **Supp. IV Part 1:** 351-353
"Glass Meadows" (Bausch), **Supp. VII:** 53-54
Glass Menagerie, The (T. Williams), **I:** 81; **IV:** 378, 379, 380, 382, 383, 385, 386, 387, 388, 389, 390, 391, 392, 393-394, 395, 398; **Supp. IV Part 1:** 84
"Glass Mountain, The" (Barthelme), **Supp. IV Part 1:** 47
"Glass Tent, The" (Everwine), **Supp. XV:** 76
Glatstein, Jacob, **Supp. X:** 70
Glazer, Nathan, **Supp. VIII:** 93, 243
"Gleaners, The" (Merwin), **Supp. III Part 1:** 346
Gleanings in Europe (Cooper), **I:** 346
Gleason, Ralph J., **Supp. IX:** 16
Glenday, Michael, **Retro. Supp. II:** 210

Glengarry Glen Ross (film), **Supp. XIV:**242
Glengarry Glen Ross (Mamet), **Supp. XIV:**239, 240, 242, 245, 246, 250, 254, 255
Glimcher, Arne, **Supp. VIII:** 73
"Glimpses" (Jones), **Supp. XI:** 218
Glimpses of the Moon, The (Wharton), **II:** 189-190; **IV:** 322-323; **Retro. Supp. I:** 381
"Glimpses of Vietnamese Life" (Levertov), **Supp. III Part 1:** 282
Glisson, J. T., **Supp. X:** 234
Gloria Mundi (Frederic), **II:** 144-145
Gloria Naylor (Fowler), **Supp. VIII:** 224
Glorious Ones, The (Prose), **Supp. XVI:**251
Glory of Hera, The (Gordon), **II:** 196-197, 198, 199, 217-220
Glory of the Conquered, The (Glaspell), **Supp. III Part 1:** 176
Glossary of Literary Terms (Abrams), **Supp. XVI:**19
Glotfelty, Cheryll, **Supp. IX:** 25
Gluck, Christoph Willibald, **II:** 210, 211
Glück, Louise, **Supp. V: 77-94; Supp. VIII:** 272; **Supp. X:** 209; **Supp. XIV:**269; **Supp. XV:** 19, 252; **Supp. XVII:** 241
"Glutton, The" (Shapiro), **Supp. II Part 2:** 705
"Glutton for Punishment, A" (Yates), **Supp. XI:** 341
Gnädiges Fräulein, The (T. Williams), **IV:** 382, 395, 398
Gnomes and Occasions (Nemerov), **III:** 269
Gnomologia (Fuller), **II:** 111
"Gnothis Seauton" (Emerson), **II:** 11, 18-19
Go (Holmes), **Supp. XIV:**144
"Goal of Intellectual Men, The" (Eberhart), **I:** 529-530
Go-Between, The (Hartley), **Supp. I Part 1:** 293
Gobineau, Joseph Arthur de, **Supp. XIV:**209
God (Allen), **Supp. XV:** 3
God and the American Writer (Kazin), **Supp. VIII: 108-109**
Godard, Jean-Luc, **Supp. I Part 2:** 558
Godbey (Masters), **Supp. I Part 2:** 472
God Bless You, Mr. Rosewater (Vonnegut), **Supp. II Part 2:** 758, 767, 768-769, 771, 772
Goddess Abides, The (Buck), **Supp. II Part 1:** 129, 131-132
Gödel, Kurt, **Supp. IV Part 1:** 43

Godfather (Puzo), **Supp. IV Part 1:** 390

"God in the Doorway" (Dillard), **Supp. VI:** 28

"God is a distant-stately Lover" (Dickinson), **I:** 471

Godkin, E. L., **II:** 274

God Knows (Heller), **Supp. IV Part 1:** 386, 388-389

God Made Alaska for the Indians (Reed), **Supp. X:** 241

God of His Fathers, The (London), **II:** 469

God of Vengeance (Asch), **IV:** 11

Go Down, Moses (Faulkner), **Retro. Supp. I:** 75, 82, 85, 86, 88, 89, 90, 92

"Go Down, Moses" (Faulkner), **II:** 71-72

Go Down, Moses (Hayden), **Supp. II Part 1:** 365

Go Down, Moses and Other Stories (Faulkner), **II:** 71; **Supp. X:** 52

"Go Down Death A Funeral Sermon" (Johnson), **Supp. IV Part 1:** 7

"God Rest Ye Merry, Gentlemen" (Hemingway), **IV:** 122

Godric (Buechner), **Supp. XII:** 53

Gods, The (Goldbarth), **Supp. XII:** 189, 190

Gods Arrive, The (Wharton), **IV:** 326-327; **Retro. Supp. I:** 382

"God Save the Rights of Man" (Freneau), **Supp. II Part 1:** 268

"Gods|Children" (Swenson), **Supp. IV Part 2:** 645

"God's Christ Theory" (Carson), **Supp. XII:** 106

God's Country and My People (Morris), **III:** 238

Gods Determinations touching his Elect: and the Elects Combat in their Conversion, and Coming up to God in Christ together with the Comfortable Effects thereof (Taylor), **IV:** 155-160, 165

God-Seeker, The (Lewis), **II:** 456

God's Favorite (Simon), **Supp. IV Part 2:** 575, 586, 588, 590

God's Little Acre (Caldwell), **I:** 288, 289, 290, 297, 298-302, 305-306, 309, 310

God's Man: A Novel in Wood Cuts (Ward), **I:** 31

Gods of Winter, The (Gioia), **Supp. XV:** 112, **121-125**

"Gods of Winter, The" (Gioia), **Supp. XV:** 117

"God's Peace in November" (Jeffers), **Supp. II Part 2:** 420

God's Silence (F. Wright), **Supp. XVII:** 240, 246-247

"God Stiff" (Carson), **Supp. XII: 106**

God's Trombones (Johnson), **Supp. II Part 1:** 201

"God's Youth" (Untermeyer), **Supp. XV:** 296

"God the Father and the Empty House" (McCarriston), **Supp. XIV:**273

Godwin, William, **II:** 304; **III:** 415; **Supp. I Part 1:** 126, 146; **Supp. I Part 2:** 512, 513-514, 522, 709, 719

God without Thunder (Ransom), **III:** 495-496, 499

Goebbels, Josef, **III:** 560

Goebel, Irma, **Supp. X:** 95

Goen, C. C., **I:** 560

Goethe, Johann Wolfgang von, **I:** 181, 396, 587-588; **II:** 5, 6, 320, 344, 488, 489, 492, 502, 556; **III:** 395, 453, 607, 612, 616; **IV:** 50, 64, 173, 326; **Retro. Supp. I:** 360; **Retro. Supp. II:** 94; **Supp. I Part 2:** 423, 457; **Supp. II Part 1:** 26; **Supp. III Part 1:** 63; **Supp. IX:** 131, 308; **Supp. X:** 60; **Supp. XI:** 169

Go for the Body (Lacy), **Supp. XV:** 201, 204

Gogol, Nikolai, **I:** 296; **IV:** 1, 4; **Retro. Supp. I:** 266, 269; **Supp. VIII:** 14; **Supp. XVII:** 45

Going, William T., **Supp. VIII:** 126

Going After Cacciato (O'Brien), **Supp. V:** 237, 238, 239, 244-246, 248, 249

Going All the Way (Wakefield), **Supp. VIII:** 43

"Going Critical" (Bambara), **Supp. XI:** 14

Going Down (Markson), **Supp. XVII:** 136, 138, **139-140,** 141, 142-143, 144, 145

Going for the Rain (Ortiz), **Supp. IV Part 2:** 499, 505-508, 509, 514

"Going Home by Last Night" (Kinnell), **Supp. III Part 1:** 244

"Going Home in America" (Hardwick), **Supp. III Part 1:** 205

"Going North" (Salinas), **Supp. XIII:** 316

Going Places (L. Michaels), **Supp. XVI:**201, **203-206**

"Going Places" (L. Michaels), **Supp. XVI:**203

Going South (Lardner and Buck), **II:** 427

Going To and Fro and Walking Up and Down (Reznikoff), **Supp. XIV:**280, 282, 284, 285

Going to Meet the Man (Baldwin), **Supp. I Part 1:** 60, 62-63

"Going to Meet the Man" (Baldwin), **Retro. Supp. II:** 8, 9; **Supp. I Part 1:** 62-63

"Going to Naples" (Welty), **IV:** 278; **Retro. Supp. I:** 352, 353

"Going to Shrewsbury" (Jewett), **II:** 393

"Going to the Bakery" (Bishop), **Supp. I Part 1:** 93

Going-to-the-Stars (Lindsay), **Supp. I Part 2:** 398

Going-to-the-Sun (Lindsay), **Supp. I Part 2:** 397-398

Going to the Territory (Ellison), **Retro. Supp. II:** 119, 123-124

"Going towards Pojoaque, A December Full Moon/72" (Harjo), **Supp. XII:** 218

"Going Under" (Dubus), **Supp. VII:** 83

"Gold" (Francis), **Supp. IX:** 82

Gold (O'Neill), **III:** 391

Gold, Michael, **II:** 26; **IV:** 363, 364, 365; **Retro. Supp. II:** 323; **Supp. I Part 1:** 331; **Supp. I Part 2:** 609; **Supp. XIV:**288

Goldbarth, Albert, **Supp. XII: 175-195**

Goldbarth's Book of Occult Phenomena (Goldbarth), **Supp. XII:** 181

Goldberg, S. L., **Supp. VIII:** 238

"Gold Bug, The" (Poe), **III:** 410, 413, 419, 420

Gold Bug Variations, The (Powers), **Supp. IX:** 210, 212, **216-217,** 219

Gold Cell, The (Olds), **Supp. X:** 206-209

Gold Diggers, The (Monette), **Supp. X:** 153

Golde, Miss (Mencken's Secretary), **III:** 104, 107

Golden, Harry, **III:** 579, 581; **Supp. VIII:** 244

Golden, Mike, **Supp. XI:** 294, 295, 297, 299, 303

Golden Age, The (Gurney), **Supp. V:** 101-103

Golden Apples (Rawlings), **Supp. X:** **228-229,** 230, 234

Golden Apples, The (Welty), **IV:** 261, 271-274, 281, 293; **Retro. Supp. I:** 341, 342, 343, **350-351,** 352, 355

Golden Apples of the Sun, The (Bradbury), **Supp. IV Part 1:** 102, 103

Golden Book of Springfield, The (Lindsay), **Supp. I Part 2:** 376, 379, 395, 396

Golden Bough, The (Frazer), **II:** 204, 549; **III:** 6-7; **Supp. I Part 1:** 18; **Supp. IX:** 123; **Supp. X:** 124

Golden Bowl, The (James), **II:** 320, 333, 335; **Retro. Supp. I:** 215, 216, 218-219, 232, **234-235**, 374
Golden Boy (Odets), **Supp. II Part 2:** 538, 539, 540-541, 546, 551
Golden Calves, The (Auchincloss), **Supp. IV Part 1:** 35
Golden Day, The (Mumford), **Supp. II Part 2:** 471, 475, 477, 483, 484, 488-489, 493
Golden Fleece, The (Gurney), **Supp. V:** 97
Golden Gate, The (Seth), **Supp. XVII:** 117
Golden Grove, The: Selected Passages from the Sermons and Writings of Jeremy Taylor (L. P. Smith), **Supp. XIV:**345
"Golden Heifer, The" (Wylie), **Supp. I Part 2:** 707
"Golden Honeymoon, The" (Lardner), **II:** 429-430, 431
Golden Journey, The (W. J. Smith and Bogan, comps.), **Supp. XIII:** 347
"Golden Lads" (Marquand), **III:** 56
Golden Legend, The (Longfellow), **II:** 489, 490, 495, 505, 506, 507; **Retro. Supp. II:** 159, 165, 166
Golden Mean and Other Poems, The (Tate and Wills), **IV:** 122
"Golden Retrievals" (Doty), **Supp. XI:** 132
Golden Shakespeare, The: An Anthology (L. P. Smith), **Supp. XIV:**349
Goldensohn, Lorrie, **Retro. Supp. II:** 51
Golden State (Bidart), **Supp. XV: 21, 23-25**
"Golden State" (Bidart), **Supp. XV:** 23, 24, 25
Golden States (Cunningham), **Supp. XV: 55, 56-59,** 63
Golden Treasury of Best Songs and Lyrical Poems in the English Language (Palgrave), **Retro. Supp. I:** 124
Golden Treasury of the Best Songs and Lyrical Poems in the English Language (Palgrave), **Supp. XIV:**340
Golden Whales of California and Other Rhymes in the American Language, The (Lindsay), **Supp. I Part 2:** 394-395, 396
"Goldfish Bowl, The" (Francis), **Supp. IX:** 78
Goldin Boys, The (Epstein), **Supp. XIV:**112
Golding, Arthur, **III:** 467, 468
Golding, William, **Supp. IV Part 1:** 297

Goldini, Carlo, **II:** 274
Goldkorn Tales (Epstein), **Supp. XII: 163-164**
Goldman, Albert, **Supp. XI:** 299
Goldman, Emma, **III:** 176, 177; **Supp. I Part 2:** 524; **Supp. XVII:** 96, 103, 104
Goldman, William, **Supp. IV Part 2:** 474
"Gold Mountain Stories" project (Kingston), **Supp. V:** 164
Goldring, Douglas, **III:** 458
Goldsmith, Oliver, **II:** 273, 282, 299, 304, 308, 314, 315, 514; **Retro. Supp. I:** 335; **Supp. I Part 1:** 310; **Supp. I Part 2:** 503, 714, 716
Gold Standard and the Logic of Naturalism, The (Michaels), **Retro. Supp. I:** 369
Goldstein, Rebecca, **Supp. XVII:** 44
Goldwater, Barry, **I:** 376; **III:** 38
Goldwyn, Samuel, **Retro. Supp. II:** 199; **Supp. I Part 1:** 281
Golem, The (Leivick), **IV:** 6
"Goliardic Song" (Hecht), **Supp. X:** 63
"Go Like This" (Moore), **Supp. X:** 165
Goll, Ivan, **Supp. III Part 1:** 235, 243-244; **Supp. III Part 2:** 621
Goncharova, Natalya, **Supp. IX:** 66
Goncourt, Edmond de, **II:** 325, 328; **III:** 315, 317-318, 321; **Retro. Supp. I:** 226
Goncourt, Jules de, **II:** 328; **III:** 315, 317-318, 321
Gone Fishin' (Mosley), **Supp. XIII:** 235-236, 240
"Gone to War" (E. Stoddard), **Supp. XV:** 282
"Gone West" (Rodriguez), **Supp. XIV:**308
Gone with the Wind (film), **Retro. Supp. I:** 113
Gone with the Wind (Mitchell), **II:** 177; **Retro. Supp. I:** 340
Gongora y Argote, Luis de, **II:** 552
Gonzalez, David, **Supp. VIII:** 85
Gooch, Brad, **Supp. XII:** 121
Good, George, **Supp. XI:** 306
"Good, the Plaid, and the Ugly, The" (Wasserstein), **Supp. XV:** 327
"Good and Not So Good, The" (Dunn), **Supp. XI:** 141
"Good Anna, The" (Stein), **IV:** 37, 40, 43
Good As Gold (Heller), **Supp. IV Part 1:** 386, 388, 394
Good Boys and Dead Girls and Other Essays (Gordon), **Supp. IV Part 1:** 309-310

"Good-by and Keep Cold" (Frost), **Retro. Supp. I:** 135
"Good-bye" (Emerson), **II:** 19
"Goodbye, Christ" (Hughes), **Retro. Supp. I:** 202, 203
Goodbye, Columbus (P. Roth), **Retro. Supp. II:** 280, 281, 290; **Supp. III Part 2:** 403-406; **Supp. XIV:**112
"Goodbye, Columbus" (P. Roth), **Supp. III Part 2:** 401, 404, 408-409, 411
Goodbye, Columbus and Five Short Stories (P. Roth), **Retro. Supp. II:** 279
"Goodbye, Goldeneye" (Swenson), **Supp. IV Part 2:** 651
"Goodbye, Mr. Chipstein" (Epstein), **Supp. XIV:**103, 108
"Goodbye, My Brother" (Cheever), **Supp. I Part 1:** 175, 177, 193
"Goodbye and Good Luck" (Paley), **Supp. VI:** 219, 223
Goodbye Girl, The (film), **Supp. IV Part 2:** 589
Goodbye Girl, The (musical), **Supp. IV Part 2:** 576, 588
Goodbye Girl, The (Simon), **Supp. IV Part 2:** 575
Goodbye Look, The (Macdonald), **Supp. IV Part 2:** 473, 474
"Good-Bye My Fancy" (Whitman), **IV:** 348
"Goodbye to All That" (Didion), **Supp. IV Part 1:** 197
Goodbye to All That (Graves), **I:** 477
Goodbye to Berlin (Isherwood), **Supp. XIV:**159, 161, 162, 169
"Good-Bye to the Mezzogiorno" (Auden), **Supp. II Part 1:** 19
"Goodbye to the Poetry of Calcium" (Wright), **Supp. III Part 2:** 599
"Good Company" (Matthews), **Supp. IX:** 160
"Good Country People" (O'Connor), **III:** 343, 350, 351, 352, 358; **Retro. Supp. II:** 229, 232
Good Day to Die, A (Harrison), **Supp. VIII: 42-44,** 45, 47
Good Doctor, The (Simon), **Supp. IV Part 2:** 575, 585
Good Earth, The (Buck), **Supp. I Part 1:** 49; **Supp. II Part 1:** 115-175, 118, 125, 132
Good European, The (Blackmur), **Supp. II Part 1:** 91
Good Evening Mr. & Mrs. America, and All the Ships at Sea (Bausch), **Supp. VII:** 41, 47, 52
"Good Friday" (Jarman), **Supp. XVII:** 116
Good Gray Poet, The (O'Connor),

Retro. Supp. I: 407
Good Health and How We Won It (Sinclair), **Supp. V:** 285–286
Good Hearts (Price), **Supp. VI:** 259, 265
"Good Job Gone, A" (Hughes), **Retro. Supp. I:** 204
Good Journey, A (Ortiz), **Supp. IV Part 2:** 497, 499, 503, 505, 509-510, 514
Good Luck in Cracked Italian (Hugo), **Supp. VI:** 133, 137-138
Goodman, Allegra, **Supp. XII:** 159; **Supp. XVI:**205
Goodman, Ellen, **Supp. XVI:**103
Goodman, Jenny, **Supp. XV:** 343, 344
Goodman, Paul, **I:** 218, 261; **III:** 39; **Supp. I Part 2:** 524; **Supp. VIII:** 239-240
Goodman, Philip, **III:** 105, 108
Goodman, Walter, **Supp. IV Part 2:** 532
Good Man Is Hard to Find, A (O'Connor), **III:** 339, 343-345
"Good Man Is Hard to Find, A" (O'Connor), **III:** 339, 344, 353; **Retro. Supp. II:** 230-231
Good Man Is Hard to Find and Other Stories, A (O'Connor), **Retro. Supp. II:** 229, **230-232**
Good Morning, America (Sandburg), **III:** 592-593
"Good Morning, Major" (Marquand), **III:** 56
Good Morning, Midnight (Rhys), **Supp. III Part 1:** 43
"Good Morning, Revolution" (Hughes), **Retro. Supp. I:** 201, 203
Good Morning Revolution: Uncollected Writings of Social Protest (Hughes), **Retro. Supp. I:** 194, 201, 202, 209
Good Mother, The (Miller), **Supp. XII:** 289, **290-294,** 299, 301
Good News (Abbey), **Supp. XIII:** 11-12
"Good News from New-England" (Johnson), **Supp. I Part 1:** 115
Good News of Death and Other Poems (Simpson), **Supp. IX:** 265, **268-269**
Good Night, Willie Lee, I'll See You in the Morning (Walker), **Supp. III Part 2:** 520, 531
"Good Oak" (Leopold), **Supp. XIV:**185, 187, 191
Goodrich, Samuel G., **Supp. I Part 1:** 38
Good Scent from a Strange Mountain, A (R. O. Butler), **Supp. XII:** 62, **70-72**

Good School, A (Yates), **Supp. XI:** 334, **346-347,** 348, 349
"*Good Shepherdess, The*/La Buena Pastora" (Mora), **Supp. XIII:** 228-229
Good Will (Smiley), **Supp. VI:** 292, **299-300**
Goodwin, K. L., **III:** 478
Goodwin, Stephen, **Supp. V:** 314, 316, 322, 323, 325
"Good Word for Winter, A" (Lowell), **Supp. I Part 2:** 420
Goodwyn, Janet, **Retro. Supp. I:** 370
"Goophered Grapevine, The" (Chesnutt), **Supp. XIV:**57, **58-61**
"Goose Fish, The" (Nemerov), **III:** 272, 284
"Goose Pond" (Kunitz), **Supp. III Part 1:** 262
Goose-Step, The (Sinclair), **Supp. V:** 276
Gordimer, Nadine, **Supp. XV:** 251
Gordon, A. R., **III:** 199
Gordon, Ambrose, **Supp. XV:** 144
Gordon, Caroline, **II: 196-222,** 536, 537; **III:** 454, 482; **IV:** 123, 126-127, 139, 282; **Retro. Supp. II:** 177, 222, 229, 233, 235; **Supp. II Part 1:** 139
Gordon, Charles G., **I:** 454
Gordon, Don, **Supp. X:** 119
Gordon, Eugene, **Supp. II Part 1:** 170
Gordon, Fran, **Supp. XIII:** 111
Gordon, James Morris, **II:** 197
Gordon, Lois, **Supp. IV Part 1:** 48; **Supp. V:** 46
Gordon, Lyndall, **Retro. Supp. I:** 55
Gordon, Mary, **Supp. IV Part 1: 297-317**
Gordon, Neil, **Supp. XVI:**156
Gordon, Peter, **Supp. XII:** 3-4, 4-5, 8
Gordon, Ruth, **IV:** 357
Gore, Thomas Pryor, **Supp. IV Part 2:** 679
Gorey, Edward, **IV:** 430, 436
Gorilla, My Love (Bambara), **Supp. XI:** 1, **2-7**
"Gorilla, My Love" (Bambara), **Supp. XI:** 2, 3-4
Gorki, Maxim, **I:** 478; **II:** 49; **III:** 402; **IV:** 299; **Supp. I Part 1:** 5, 51
Gorney, Cynthia, **Supp. XVI:**112
Gorra, Michael, **Supp. V:** 71
Goslings, The (Sinclair), **Supp. V:** 276, 281
Go South to Sorrow (Rowan), **Supp. XIV:**306
Gospel According to Joe, The (Gurney), **Supp. V:** 99
"Gospel According to Saint Mark,

The" (Gordon), **Supp. IV Part 1:** 310
Gospel according to the Son (Mailer), **Retro. Supp. II:** 213
"Gospel for the Twentieth Century, The" (Locke), **Supp. XIV:**206
"Gospel of Beauty, The" (Lindsay), **Supp. I Part 2:** 380, 382, 384, 385, 391, 396
Gospel Singer, The (Crews), **Supp. XI:** 102, **109**
Gosse, Edmund, **II:** 538; **IV:** 350; **Supp. VIII:** 157
"Gossip" (Conroy), **Supp. XVI:**71-72
Gossips, Gorgons, and Crones: The Fates of the Earth (Caputi), **Supp. IV Part 1:** 335
Go Tell It on the Mountain (Baldwin), **Retro. Supp. II:** 1, 2, 3, **4-5,** 7, 14; **Supp. I Part 1:** 48, 49, 50, 51, 52, 53-54, 55, 56, 57, 59, 61, 63, 64, 67; **Supp. II Part 1:** 170
Gotera, Vince, **Supp. XIII:** 115, 116, 119, 121, 127
Gothic Revival, The: An Essay on the History of Taste (Clark), **Supp. XIV:**348
Gothic Writers (Thomson, Voller, and Frank, eds.), **Retro. Supp. II:** 273
"Go to the Devil and Shake Yourself" (song), **Supp. I Part 2:** 580
"Go to the Shine That's on a Tree" (Eberhart), **I:** 523
Go to the Widow-Maker (Jones), **Supp. XI:** 214, **225-226,** 227, 229, 233
Gottfried, Martin, **Supp. IV Part 2:** 584
Gotthelf, Allan, **Supp. IV Part 2:** 528
Gottlieb, Adolph, **Supp. XV:** 144
Gottlieb, Morton, **Supp. XVI:**196
Gottlieb, Robert, **Supp. IV Part 2:** 474
Gottschalk and the Grande Tarantelle (Brooks), **Supp. III Part 1:** 86
"Gottschalk and the Grande Tarantelle" (Brooks), **Supp. III Part 1:** 86-87
Gould (Dixon), **Supp. XII:** 152, **153**
Gould, Edward Sherman, **I:** 346
Gould, Janice, **Supp. IV Part 1:** 322, 327; **Supp. XII:** 229
Gould, Jay, **I:** 4
Gould, Joe, **Supp. XV:** 143
Gourd Dancer, The (Momaday), **Supp. IV Part 2:** 481, 487, 491, 493
Gourmont, Remy de, **I:** 270, 272; **II:** 528, 529; **III:** 457, 467-468, 477; **Retro. Supp. I:** 55
Gouverneurs de la Rosée (Roumain), **Supp. IV Part 1:** 360, 367
"Governors of Wyoming, The" (Proulx), **Supp. VII:** 264

Goyen, William, **Supp. V:** 220
Grabhorn, Janet, **Supp. XV:** 142
"Grace" (Dubus), **Supp. VII:** 91
"Grace" (Harjo), **Supp. XII:** 224
Grace Notes (Dove), **Supp. IV Part 1:** 248-250, 252
Grade, Chaim, **Supp. XVII:** 41
"Graduation" (Dubus), **Supp. VII:** 84
Grady, Henry W., **Supp. I Part 1:** 370
Graeber, Laurel, **Supp. V:** 15
Graham, Billy, **I:** 308
Graham, David, **Supp. XV:** 104
Graham, Don, **Supp. XI:** 252, 254
Graham, Jorie, **Supp. IX:** 38, 52; **Supp. X:** 73; **Supp. XII:** 209; **Supp. XIII:** 85; **Supp. XVII:** 110, 111, 133, 240, 241, 242
Graham, Martha, **Supp. XI:** 152
Graham, Maryemma, **Retro. Supp. I:** 201, 204
Graham, Nan, **Supp. XII:** 272
Graham, Sheilah, **II:** 94; **Retro. Supp. I:** 97, 113-114, 115; **Supp. IX:** 63
Graham, Shirley, **Supp. I Part 1:** 51
Graham, Stephen, **Supp. I Part 2:** 397
Graham, Tom (pseudonym). See Lewis, Sinclair
Grahn, Judy, **Supp. IV Part 1:** 325, 330
"Grain Field" (Crapsey), **Supp. XVII:** 77
Grainger, Percy, **Supp. I Part 2:** 386
Grain of Mustard Seed, A (Sarton), **Supp. VIII: 259-260,** 263
Gramar (Lowth), **II:** 8
Grammar of Motives, A (Burke), **I:** 272, 275, 276-278, 283, 284
Granados, Gabriel Bernal, **Supp. XV:** 350
Granberry, Edwin, **I:** 288
Grand Design, The (Dos Passos), **I:** 489-490
"Grande Malade, The" (Barnes), **Supp. III Part 1:** 36
"Grandfather" (Dunn), **Supp. XI:** 147
"Grandfather and Grandson" (Singer), **Retro. Supp. II:** 307
"Grandfather's Blessing" (Alvarez), **Supp. VII:** 2
"Grand Forks" (Bierds), **Supp. XVII:** 34
"Grand Forks" (Simpson), **Supp. IX:** 280-281
"Grand Inquisitor" (Dostoyevsky), **IV:** 106
Grandissimes (Cable), **II:** 291
"Grand-Master Nabokov" (Updike), **Retro. Supp. I:** 317
"Grand Miracle, The" (Karr), **Supp. XI:** 251

"Grandmother" (Gunn Allen), **Supp. IV Part 1:** 320, 325
"Grandmother in Heaven" (Levine), **Supp. V:** 186
"Grandmother of the Sun: Ritual Gynocracy in Native America" (Gunn Allen), **Supp. IV Part 1:** 328
Grandmothers of the Light: A Medicine Woman's Sourcebook (Gunn Allen, ed.), **Supp. IV Part 1:** 332, 333-334
"Grandmother Songs, The" (Hogan), **Supp. IV Part 1:** 413
"Grandpa and the Statue" (A. Miller), **III:** 147
"Grandparents" (Lowell), **II:** 550
"Grandsire Bells, The" (Bierds), **Supp. XVII:** 28-29
"Grandstand Complex, The" (McCoy), **Supp. XIII:** 166
Grange, Red, **II:** 416
Granger's Index to Poetry (anthology), **Retro. Supp. I:** 37, 39
Grant, Lee, **Supp. XIII:** 295
Grant, Madison, **Supp. II Part 1:** 170
Grant, Richard, **Supp. X:** 282
Grant, Ulysses S., **I:** 4, 15; **II:** 542; **III:** 506, 584; **IV:** 348, 446; **Supp. I Part 2:** 418
Grantwood, **Retro. Supp. I:** 416, 417
"Grapes, The" (Hecht), **Supp. X:** 65-66
"Grape Sherbet" (Dove), **Supp. IV Part 1:** 246
Grapes of Wrath, The (Steinbeck), **I:** 301; **III:** 589; **IV:** 51, 53-55, 59, 63, 65, 67, 68, 69; **Supp. V:** 290; **Supp. XI:** 169; **Supp. XIV:**181; **Supp. XV:** 351
"Grapevine, The" (Ashbery), **Supp. III Part 1:** 4
"Grass" (Sandburg), **III:** 584
Grass, Günter, **Supp. VIII:** 40
"Grasse: The Olive Trees" (Wilbur), **Supp. III Part 2:** 550
Grass Harp, The (Capote), **Supp. III Part 1:** 114-117, 123
Grass Still Grows, The (A. Miller), **III:** 146
Gratitude to Old Teachers (R. Bly), **Supp. IV Part 1:** 73
Graupner, Gottlieb, **Supp. XV:** 240, 244
"Grave, A" (Moore), **III:** 195, 202, 208, 213
Grave, The (Blair), **Supp. I Part 1:** 150
"Grave, The" (Porter), **III:** 433, 443, 445-446
"Grave, The" (Winters), **Supp. II Part 2:** 795, 796

"Graven Image" (O'Hara), **III:** 320
Grave of the Right Hand, The (Wright), **Supp. V:** 332, 338, 339
"Grave Piece" (Eberhart), **I:** 533
Graves, Billy, **Supp. I Part 2:** 607
Graves, John, **Supp. V:** 220
Graves, Morris, **Supp. X:** 264
Graves, Peter, **Supp. IV Part 2:** 474
Graves, Rean, **Supp. I Part 1:** 326
Graves, Robert, **I:** 437, 477, 523; **Supp. I Part 2:** 541; **Supp. IV Part 1:** 280, 348; **Supp. IV Part 2:** 685
Graveyard for Lunatics, A (Bradbury), **Supp. IV Part 1:** 102, 114-116
Gravity's Rainbow (Pynchon), **Supp. II Part 2:** 617, 618-619, 621-625, 627, 630, 633-636; **Supp. IV Part 1:** 279; **Supp. V:** 44; **Supp. XIV:**49; **Supp. XVII:** 236
Gray, Cecil, **Supp. I Part 1:** 258
Gray, Francine Du Plessix, **Supp. V:** 169
Gray, James, **III:** 207; **Supp. I Part 2:** 410
Gray, Jeffrey, **Supp. XV:** 27
Gray, Paul, **Supp. IV Part 1:** 305; **Supp. IV Part 2:** 639; **Supp. XVI:**74
Gray, Thomas, **I:** 68; **Supp. I Part 1:** 150; **Supp. I Part 2:** 422, 716
Gray, Thomas A., **Supp. I Part 2:** 710
"Gray Heron, The" (Kinnell), **Supp. III Part 1:** 250
"Gray Mills of Farley, The" (Jewett), **Retro. Supp. II:** 132, 144
"Gray Poem" (Everwine), **Supp. XV:** 81
Grayson, Charles, **Supp. XIII:** 171
"Gray Squirrel" (Francis), **Supp. IX:** 90
"Gray Wolf's H'ant, The" (Chesnutt), **Supp. XIV:**60
Grealy, Lucy, **Supp. XII:** 310
Greasy Lake (Boyle), **Supp. VIII: 14-15**
"Greasy Lake" (Boyle), **Supp. VIII:** 15
"Great Adventure of Max Breuck, The" (Lowell), **II:** 522
Great American Novel, The (P. Roth), **Retro. Supp. II:** 283, 288-289; **Supp. III Part 2:** 414-416
Great American Short Novels (Phillips, ed.), **Supp. VIII:** 156
Great Battles of the World (Crane), **I:** 415
"Great Carousel, The" (Untermeyer), **Supp. XV:** 296
Great Christian Doctrine of Original Sin Defended, The ... (Edwards), **I:**

549, 557, 559
Great Circle (Aiken), **I:** 53, 55, 57
"Great Class-Reunion Bazaar, The" (Theroux), **Supp. VIII:** 312
Great Day, The (Hurston), **Supp. VI:** 154
Great Days (Barthelme), **Supp. IV Part 1:** 39
Great Days, The (Dos Passos), **I:** 491
Great Digest (Pound, trans.), **III:** 472
"Great Elegy for John Donne" (Brodsky), **Supp. VIII:** 21, 23
Greater Inclination, The (Wharton), **Retro. Supp. I:** 363, **364-365**, 366
"Greater Torment, The" (Blackmur), **Supp. II Part 1:** 92
Greatest Hits 1969-1996 (Salinas), **Supp. XIII:** 311
"Greatest Thing in the World, The" (Mailer), **Retro. Supp. II:** 196
Great Expectations (Acker), **Supp. XII:** 5, **9-11**
Great Expectations (Dickens), **III:** 247; **Supp. I Part 1:** 35; **Supp. XVI:**73
"Great Expectations, No Satisfaction" (D. Gates), **Supp. XVI:**73
"Great Figure, The" (W. C. Williams), **IV:** 414
"Great Fillmore Street Buffalo Drive, The" (Momaday), **Supp. IV Part 2:** 493
Great Gatsby, The (Fitzgerald), **I:** 107, 375, 514; **II:** 77, 79, 83, 84, 85, 87, 91-93, 94, 96, 98; **III:** 244, 260, 372, 572; **IV:** 124, 297; **Retro. Supp. I:** 98, 105, **105-108**, 110, 114, 115, 335, 359; **Retro. Supp. II:** 107, 201; **Supp. II Part 2:** 626; **Supp. III Part 2:** 585; **Supp. IV Part 2:** 468, 475; **Supp. IX:** 57, 58; **Supp. X:** 175; **Supp. XI:** 65, 69, 334; **Supp. XVI:**64, 75
Great Gatsby, The (Fitzgerald) (Modern Library), **Retro. Supp. I:** 113
Great God Brown, The (O'Neill), **III:** 165, 391, 394-395
Great Goodness of Life: A Coon Show (Baraka), **Supp. II Part 1:** 47
Great Inclination, The (Wharton), **IV:** 310
"Great Infirmities" (Simic), **Supp. VIII:** 277
Great Jones Street (DeLillo), **Supp. VI:** 2, 3, 8-9, 11, 12
"Great Lawsuit, The: Man *versus* Men: Woman *versus* Women" (Fuller), **Retro. Supp. I:** 156; **Supp. II Part 1:** 292
"Great Men and Their Environment"

(James), **II:** 347
"Great Mississippi Bubble, The" (Irving), **II:** 314
Great Railway Bazaar, The: By Train through Asia (Theroux), **Supp. VIII:** 318, 319, **320-321**, 322
"Great Scott" (Conroy), **Supp. XVI:**75, 77
Great Stories of Suspense (Millar, ed.), **Supp. IV Part 2:** 474
Great Topics of the World (Goldbarth), **Supp. XII:** 187, 189, 191
Great Valley, The (Masters), **Supp. I Part 2:** 465
Great World and Timothy Colt, The (Auchincloss), **Supp. IV Part 1:** 25, 31, 32
Grédy, Jean-Pierre, **Supp. XVI:**194
"Greek Boy, The" (Bryant), **Supp. I Part 1:** 168
Greek Mind/Jewish Soul: The Conflicted Art of Cynthia Ozick (Strandberg), **Supp. V:** 273
"Greek Partisan, The" (Bryant), **Supp. I Part 1:** 168
"Greeks, The" (McCarriston), **Supp. XIV:**271
Greeley, Horace, **II:** 7; **IV:** 197, 286-287
Green, Ashbel, **Supp. IV Part 2:** 474
Green, Henry, **IV:** 279; **Retro. Supp. I:** 354; **Supp. III Part 1:** 3; **Supp. XI:** 294-295, 296, 297; **Supp. XII:** 315
Green, Jack, **Supp. IV Part 1:** 284-285
Green, Martin, **Supp. I Part 1:** 299
Green, Michelle, **Supp. IV Part 1:** 95
"Green Automobile, The" (Ginsberg), **Supp. II Part 1:** 322
Greenberg, Clement, **Supp. XV:** 141, 143, 144, 145
Greenberg, Eliezer, **Supp. I Part 2:** 432
Greenberg, Jonathan, **Supp. XII:** 285
Greenberg, Samuel, **I:** 393
Green Bough, A (Faulkner), **Retro. Supp. I:** 84
Green Centuries (Gordon), **II:** 196, 197-207, 209
"Green Crab's Shell, A" (Doty), **Supp. XI:** 126
"Green Door, The" (O. Henry), **Supp. II Part 1:** 395
Greene, A. C., **Supp. V:** 223, 225
Greene, Graham, **I:** 480; **II:** 62, 320; **III:** 57, 556; **Retro. Supp. I:** 215; **Supp. I Part 1:** 280; **Supp. IV Part 1:** 341; **Supp. V:** 298; **Supp. IX:** 261; **Supp. XI:** 99,**Supp. XI:** 104;

Supp. XIII: 233
Greene, Helga, **Supp. IV Part 1:** 134, 135
Greene, J. Lee, **Retro. Supp. II:** 121
Greene, Nathanael, **Supp. I Part 2:** 508
Greene, Richard Tobias, **III:** 76
Greene, Robert, **Supp. XVII:** 232
Green Eggs and Ham (Geisel), **Supp. XVI:**108, 109
"Greene-ing of the Portables, The" (Cowley), **Supp. II Part 1:** 140
"Greenest Continent, The" (Stevens), **Retro. Supp. I:** 304
Greenfeld, Josh, **III:** 364
Green Hills of Africa (Hemingway), **II:** 253; **Retro. Supp. I:** 182, 186
Greening of America, The (C. Reich), **Supp. XVII:** 3
"Green Lagoons, The" (Leopold), **Supp. XIV:**188
"Green Lampshade" (Simic), **Supp. VIII:** 283
Greenlanders, The (Smiley), **Supp. VI:** 292, **296-298**, 299, 305, 307
Greenlaw, Edwin A., **IV:** 453
"Greenleaf" (O'Connor), **III:** 350, 351; **Retro. Supp. II:** 233, 237
Greenman, Walter F., **I:** 217, 222
Green Memories (Mumford), **Supp. II Part 2:** 474, 475, 479, 480-481
"Green Pasture, The" (Leopold), **Supp. XIV:**184
Green Pastures, The (Connelly), **Supp. II Part 1:** 223
"Green Red Brown and White" (Swenson), **Supp. IV Part 2:** 639
"Green River" (Bryant), **Supp. I Part 1:** 155, 164
Green Shadows, White Whale (Bradbury), **Supp. IV Part 1:** 102, 103, 116
"Green Shirt, The" (Olds), **Supp. X:** 209
"Greensleeves" (Jarman), **Supp. XVII:** 113
Greenslet, Ferris, **I:** 19; **Retro. Supp. I:** 9, 10, 11, 13; **Retro. Supp. II:** 41
Greenspan, Alan, **Supp. IV Part 2:** 526
Greenstreet, Sydney, **Supp. IV Part 1:** 356
"Green Thought, A" (L. Michaels), **Supp. XVI:**204
Greenwald, Ted, **Supp. IV Part 2:** 423
Green Wall, The (Wright), **Supp. III Part 2:** 591, 593, 595
Green Wave, The (Rukeyser), **Supp. VI:** 273, 280
"Green Ways" (Kunitz), **Supp. III**

Part 1: 265
Green with Beasts (Merwin), **Supp. III Part 1:** 340, 344-346
Greenwood, Grace, **Supp. XIII:** 141
Gregerson, Linda, **Supp. IV Part 2:** 651; **Supp. X:** 204-205; **Supp. XI:** 142
"Gregorio Valdes" (Bishop), **Retro. Supp. II:** 51
Gregory, Alyse, **I:** 221, 226, 227, 231
Gregory, Horace, **II:** 512; **Supp. III Part 2:** 614, 615; **Supp. IX:** 229; **Supp. XV:** 143
Gregory, Lady Isabella Augusta, **III:** 458
Gregory, Sinda, **Supp. X:** 260, 268
Grendel (Gardner), **Supp. VI:** 63, **67,** 68, 74
Grenstone Poems (Bynner), **Supp. XV:** 44
"Gretel in Darkness" (Glück), **Supp. V:** 82
Gretta (Caldwell), **I:** 301, 302
Greuze, Jean Baptiste, **Supp. I Part 2:** 714
Grey, Zane, **Supp. XIII:** 5
Grieg, Michael, **Supp. XV:** 133, 148
Griffin, Bartholomew, **Supp. I Part 1:** 369
Griffin, John Howard, **Supp. VIII:** 208
Griffin, Merv, **Supp. IV Part 2:** 526
Griffith, Albert J., **Supp. V:** 325
Griffith, D. W., **I:** 31, 481-482; **Retro. Supp. I:** 103, 325; **Supp. XI:** 45; **Supp. XVI:** 183, 184
Griffiths, Clyde, **I:** 511
Grile, Dod (pseudonym). *See* Bierce, Ambrose
Grimm, Herman, **II:** 17
Grimm brothers, **II:** 378; **III:** 101, 491, 492; **IV:** 266; **Supp. I Part 2:** 596, 622; **Supp. X:** 78, 84, 86
Grinnell, George Bird, **Supp. XVI:** 13
Gris, Juan, **I:** 442; **Retro. Supp. I:** 430
Griswold, Rufus Wilmot, **III:** 409, 429; **Retro. Supp. II:** 261, 262; **Supp. XV:** 277, 278; **Supp. XVI:** 8, 10-11
Grogg, Sam, Jr., **Supp. IV Part 2:** 468, 471
Gromer, Crystal, **Supp. XII:** 297
Gronlund, Laurence, **II:** 276
Grooms, Red, **Supp. XV:** 178
"Groping for Trouts" (Gass), **Supp. VI:** 87
Grosholz, Emily, **Supp. XII:** 185
Gross, Terry, **Supp. XVI:** 167
"Grosse Fuge" (Doty), **Supp. XI:** 126-127
Grossman, Allen, **Retro. Supp. II:** 83
Grosz, George, **III:** 172; **IV:** 438; **Retro. Supp. II:** 321; **Supp. X:** 137
"Grotesque in Modern Fiction, The" (E. Hoffman, Ph.D. dissertation), **Supp. XVI:** 147
"Groundhog, The" (Eberhart), **I:** 523, 530-532, 533
"Ground on Which I Stand, The" (Wilson), **Supp. VIII:** 331
"Ground Swell" (Jarman), **Supp. XVII:** 118
Group, The (McCarthy), **II:** 570, 574-578
"Group of Two, A" (Jarrell), **II:** 368
Group Therapy (Hearon), **Supp. VIII: 64-65**
"Grove" (Goldbarth), **Supp. XII:** 176
Groves of Academe, The (McCarthy), **II:** 568-571
Growing into Love (X. J. Kennedy), **Supp. XV:** 153, **158-160**
Growing Pains (J. S. Untermeyer), **Supp. XV:** 303
"Growing Season, The" (Caldwell), **I:** 309
Growing Up Gay: A Literary Anthology (Singer, ed.), **Supp. IV Part 1:** 330
"Growing Up Good in Maycomb" (Shaffer), **Supp. VIII:** 128
"Grown-Up" (Jewett), **Retro. Supp. II:** 134
"Growth" (Lowell), **II:** 554
"Growth and Decay in Recent Verse" (Untermeyer), **Supp. XV:** 299
Growth of the American Republic, The (Morison and Commager), **Supp. I Part 2:** 484
"Growtown Buggle, The" (Jewett), **Retro. Supp. II:** 132
Gruenberg, Louis, **III:** 392
Grumbach, Doris, **II:** 560
"Gryphon" (C. Baxter), **Supp. XVII:** 14, 17
"Guacamaja" (Leopold), **Supp. XIV:** 188-189
Guardian Angel, The (Holmes), **Supp. I Part 1:** 315-316
Guard of Honor (Cozzens), **I:** 370-372, 375, 376-377, 378, 379
Guardsman, The (Molnar), **Supp. XVI:** 187
Guare, John, **Supp. XIII:** 196, 207
Gubar, Susan, **Retro. Supp. I:** 42; **Retro. Supp. II:** 324; **Supp. IX:** 66; **Supp. XV:** 270
Guerard, Albert, Jr., **Supp. X:** 79; **Supp. XIII:** 172
Guérin, Maurice de, **I:** 241
"Guerrilla Handbook, A" (Baraka), **Supp. II Part 1:** 36
Guess and Spell Coloring Book, The (Swenson), **Supp. IV Part 2:** 648
Guess Who's Coming to Dinner (film), **Supp. I Part 1:** 67
Guest, Judith, **Supp. XVI:** 36
Guest, Val, **Supp. XI:** 307
Guest Book (Bynner), **Supp. XV:** 51
"Guests of Mrs. Timms, The" (Jewett), **II:** 408; **Retro. Supp. II:** 135
"Guevara ...Guevara" (Salinas), **Supp. XIII:** 312-313, 315
Guevara, Martha, **Supp. VIII:** 74
Guided Tours of Hell (Prose), **Supp. XVI:** 257, 261
"Guided Tours of Hell" (Prose), **Supp. XVI:** 257
Guide for the Perplexed (Maimonides), **Supp. XVII:** 46
Guide in the Wilderness, A (Cooper), **I:** 337
"Guide to Dungeness Spit, A" (Wagoner), **Supp. IX:** 325-326, 329
Guide to Ezra Pound's Selected Cantos' (Kearns), **Retro. Supp. I:** 292
Guide to Kulchur (Pound), **III:** 475
Guide to the Ruins (Nemerov), **III:** 269, 270-271, 272
Guillén, Nicolás, **Retro. Supp. I:** 202; **Supp. I Part 1:** 345
Guillevic, Eugene, **Supp. III Part 1:** 283
"Guilty Man, The" (Kunitz), **Supp. II Part 1:** 263
Guilty of Everything: The Autobiography of Herbert Huncke (Huncke), **Supp. XIV:** 138, 140, 141, 150
Guilty Pleasures (Barthelme), **Supp. IV Part 1:** 44, 45, 53
Guinness, Alec, **Retro. Supp. I:** 65
Gulag Archipelago, The (Solzhenitsyn), **Supp. XVII:** 229
"Gulf, The" (Dunn), **Supp. XI:** 149
Gulistan (Saadi), **II:** 19
Gullible's Travels (Lardner), **II:** 426, 427
Gulliver's Travels (Swift), **I:** 209, 348, 366; **II:** 301; **Supp. I Part 2:** 656; **Supp. XI:** 209; **Supp. XVI:** 110
"Gulls" (Hayden), **Supp. II Part 1:** 367
"Gulls, The" (Nemerov), **III:** 272
"Gun, The" (Dobyns), **Supp. XIII:** 88
Günderode: A Translation from the German (Fuller), **Supp. II Part 1:** 293
Gundy, Jeff, **Supp. XI:** 315; **Supp. XVI:** 46, 265, 275
Gunn, Thom, **Supp. IX:** 269
Gunn, Thomas, **Supp. V:** 178

Gunn Allen, Paula, **Supp. IV Part 1: 319-340,** 404; **Supp. IV Part 2:** 499, 502, 557, 568; **Supp. XII:** 218
"Gunnar's Sword" (C. Bly), **Supp. XVI:**34, 35, 37, 42
"Guns as Keys; and the Great Gate Swings" (Lowell), **II:** 524
Gurdjieff, Georges, **Supp. V:** 199; **Supp. IX:** 320
Gurganus, Allan, **Supp. XII:** 308-309, 310
Gurko, Leo, **III:** 62
Gurney, A. R., **Supp. V: 95-112; Supp. IX:** 261
Gurney, Mary (Molly) Goodyear, **Supp. V:** 95
Gussow, Mel, **Supp. IX:** 93; **Supp. XII:** 325, 328, 341
Gustavus Vassa, the African (Vassa), **Supp. IV Part 1:** 11
Gusto, Thy Name Was Mrs. Hopkins: A Prose Rhapsody (Francis), **Supp. IX:** 89
Gute Mensch von Sezuan, Der (Brecht), **Supp. IX:** 138
Gutenberg, Johann, **Supp. I Part 2:** 392
Guthrie, A. B., **Supp. X:** 103
Gutman, Herbert, **Supp. I Part 1:** 47
Guttenplan, D. D., **Supp. XI:** 38
"Gutting of Couffignal, The" (Hammett), **Supp. IV Part 1:** 345
Guy Domville (James), **II:** 331; **Retro. Supp. I:** 228
"Gwendolyn" (Bishop), **Retro. Supp. II:** 51
Gypsy Ballads (Hughes, trans.), **Supp. I Part 1:** 345
Gypsy's Curse, The (Crews), **Supp. XI: 110**
"Gyroscope, The" (Rukeyser), **Supp. VI:** 271
Gysin, Brion, **Supp. XII:** 129
H
H. L. Mencken, a Portrait from Memory (Angoff), **III:** 107
H. L. Mencken: The American Scene (Cairns), **III:** 119
"H. L. Mencken Meets a Poet in the West Side Y.M.C.A." (White), **Supp. I Part 2:** 677
H. M. Pulham, Esquire (Marquand), **II:** 482-483; **III:** 58, 59, 65, 68-69
Haardt, Sara. *See* Mencken, Mrs. H. L. (Sara Haardt)
Habakkuk (biblical book), **III:** 200, 347
Habibi (Nye), **Supp. XIII:** 273, **279**
"Habit" (James), **II:** 351

Habitations of the Word (Gass), **Supp. VI:** 88
Hacker, Marilyn, **Supp. XV:** 250; **Supp. XVII:** 71, 76, 112
Hackett, David, **Supp. XII:** 236
Hadda, Janet, **Retro. Supp. II:** 317
Haeckel, Ernst Heinrich, **II:** 480
Haegert, John, **Supp. XVI:**69
Hafif, Marcia, **Supp. IV Part 2:** 423
Hagar's Daughter (P. Hopkins), **Supp. XVI:**143
Hagedorn, Jessica, **Supp. X:** 292
Hagen, Beulah, **Supp. I Part 2:** 679
Haggard, Rider, **III:** 189
Hagoromo (play), **III:** 466
Hagstrum, Jean, **Supp. XV:** 74
"Hail Mary" (Fante), **Supp. XI:** 160, 164
Haines, George, IV, **I:** 444
Haines, John, **Supp. XII: 197-214**
"Hair" (Corso), **Supp. XII:** 117, 126, 127
"Hair, The" (Carver), **Supp. III Part 1:** 137
"Haircut" (Lardner), **II:** 430, 436
"Hair Dressing" (Untermeyer), **Supp. XV:** 304, 305
Hairpiece: A Film for Nappy-Headed People (Chenzira; film), **Supp. XI:** 19-20
"Hairs" (Cisneros), **Supp. VII:** 59
Hairs/Pelitos (Cisneros), **Supp. VII:** 58
Hairy Ape, The (O'Neill), **III:** 391, 392, 393
"Haïta the Shepherd" (Bierce), **I:** 203
Haldeman, Anna, **Supp. I Part 1:** 2
Hale, Edward Everett, **Supp. I Part 2:** 584; **Supp. XI:** 193, 200
Hale, John Parker, **Supp. I Part 2:** 685
Hale, Nancy, **Supp. VIII:** 151, 171
Haley, Alex, **Supp. I Part 1:** 47, 66
Haley, J. Evetts, **Supp. V:** 226
"Half a Century Gone" (Lowell), **II:** 554
Half-a-Hundred: Tales by Great American Writers (Grayson, ed.), **Supp. XIII:** 171
Half Asleep in Frog Pajamas (Robbins), **Supp. X:** 259, **279-282**
Half Breed, The (film), **Supp. XVI:**185
Half-Century of Conflict, A (Parkman), **Supp. II Part 2:** 600, 607, 610
"Half Deity" (Moore), **III:** 210, 214, 215
"Half Hour of August" (Ríos), **Supp. IV Part 2:** 552
Half-Lives (Jong), **Supp. V:** 115, 119
Half Moon Street: Two Short Novels (Theroux), **Supp. VIII:** 322, 323

Half of Paradise (Burke), **Supp. XIV:**22, 24
Half-Past Nation Time (Johnson), **Supp. VI:** 187
"Half-Skinned Steer, The" (Proulx), **Supp. VII:** 261-262
"Half Sonnets" (Jarman), **Supp. XVII:** 115
Half Sun Half Sleep (Swenson), **Supp. IV Part 2:** 645-646
Halfway (Kumin), **Supp. IV Part 2:** 441-442
"Halfway" (Rich), **Supp. I Part 2:** 553
Halfway Home (Monette), **Supp. X:** 154
Halfway to Silence (Sarton), **Supp. VIII:** 261
Half You Don't Know, The: Selected Stories (Cameron), **Supp. XII:** 79, 80, 81
Haliburton, Thomas Chandler, **II:** 301; **IV:** 193; **Supp. I Part 2:** 411
Halifax, Lord, **II:** 111
Hall, Daniel, **Supp. XII:** 258
Hall, Donald, **I:** 567; **III:** 194; **Supp. IV Part 1:** 63, 72; **Supp. IV Part 2:** 621; **Supp. IX:** 269; **Supp. XIV:**82, 126; **Supp. XV:** 21, 153, 176; **Supp. XVI:**39, 230, 235
Hall, James, **II:** 313; **Supp. I Part 2:** 584, 585
Hall, James Baker, **Supp. X:** 24
Hall, Timothy L., **Supp. VIII:** 127, 128
Halleck, Fitz-Greene, **Supp. I Part 1:** 156, 158
"Hallelujah: A Sestina" (Francis), **Supp. IX:** 82
"Hallelujah on the Bum" (Abbey), **Supp. XIII:** 2
"Haller's Second Home" (Maxwell), **Supp. VIII:** 169
Halliday, Mark, **Supp. XV:** 19, 20, 21, 23, 25, 27, 30
Hallock, Rev. Moses, **Supp. I Part 1:** 153
Hall of Mirrors, A (Stone), **Supp. V:** 295, 296-299, 300, 301
"Hallowe'en" (Huncke), **Supp. XIV:**145
"Halloween Party, The" (Chabon), **Supp. XI:** 72
Halloween Tree, The (Bradbury), **Supp. IV Part 1:** 102, 112-113
Hallwas, John E., **Supp. I Part 2:** 454
Halpern, Daniel, **Supp. IV Part 1:** 94-95, 95
Halsey, Theresa, **Supp. IV Part 1:** 330, 331
"Halt in the Desert, A" (Brodsky), **Supp. VIII:** 24

"Halves" (Dunn), **Supp. XI:** 149
Hamburg, Victoria, **Supp. XVI:**126
Hamerik, Asger, **Supp. I Part 1:** 356
Hamill, Sam, **Supp. X:** 112, 125, 126, 127
Hamilton, Alexander, **I:** 485; **Supp. I Part 2:** 456, 483, 509
Hamilton, Alice, **Supp. I Part 1:** 5
Hamilton, David, **Supp. IX:** 296
Hamilton, Edith, **Supp. XVI:**196
Hamilton, Lady Emma, **II:** 524
Hamilton, Hamish, **Supp. I Part 2:** 617
Hamilton, Walton, **Supp. I Part 2:** 632
Hamilton Stark (Banks), **Supp. V:** 8, 9-10, 11
"Hamlen Brook" (Wilbur), **Supp. III Part 2:** 564
"Hamlet" (Laforgue), **I:** 573; **III:** 11
Hamlet (Miller and Fraenkel), **III:** 178, 183
Hamlet (Shakespeare), **I:** 53, 183, 205, 377, 586-587; **II:** 158, 531; **III:** 7, 11, 12, 183; **IV:** 116, 131, 227; **Supp. I Part 1:** 369; **Supp. I Part 2:** 422, 457, 471; **Supp. IV Part 2:** 612; **Supp. IX:** 14
Hamlet, The (Faulkner), **II:** 69-71, 73, 74; **IV:** 131; **Retro. Supp. I:** 82, 91, 92; **Supp. VIII:** 178; **Supp. IX:** 103; **Supp. XI:** 247
"Hamlet and His Problems" (Eliot), **I:** 586-587
Hamlet of A. MacLeish, The (MacLeish), **III:** 11-12, 14, 15, 18
Hamlin, Eva, **Retro. Supp. II:** 115
"Hammer" (Bidart), **Supp. XV:** 35
Hammer, Adam, **Supp. XIII:** 112
Hammer, Langdon, **Retro. Supp. II:** 45, 53; **Supp. X:** 65
"Hammer Man, The" (Bambara), **Supp. XI:** 4-5
Hammett, Dashiell, **IV:** 286; **Retro. Supp. II:** 327; **Supp. I Part 1:** 286, 289, 291, 292, 293, 294, 295; **Supp. III Part 1:** 91; **Supp. IV Part 1:** 120, 121, **341-357**; **Supp. IV Part 2:** 461, 464, 468, 469, 472, 473; **Supp. IX:** 200; **Supp. XI:** 228; **Supp. XIII:** 159; **Supp. XIV:**21; **Supp. XVII:** 137
Hammond, Karla, **Supp. IV Part 2:** 439, 442, 448, 637, 640, 644, 648
Hampl, Patricia, **Supp. IX:** 291; **Supp. XI:** 126; **Supp. XVII:** 21
Hampson, Alfred Leete, **Retro. Supp. I:** 35-36, 38
"Hamrick's Polar Bear" (Caldwell), **I:** 309-310
Hamsun, Knut, **Supp. VIII:** 40; **Supp.**

XI: 161, 167; **Supp. XII:** 21, 128
Hancock, John, **Supp. I Part 2:** 524
Hancock, Wade, **Supp. XVI:**34
Handbook of North American Indians (Sando), **Supp. IV Part 2:** 510
Handcarved Coffins: A Nonfiction Account of an American Crime (Capote), **Supp. III Part 1:** 131
Handel, Georg Friedrich, **III:** 210; **IV:** 369
"Handfasting" (Wright), **Supp. XV:** 343
"Handfuls" (Sandburg), **III:** 584
"Handle with Care" (Fitzgerald), **Retro. Supp. I:** 114
Handmaid's Tale, The (Atwood), **Supp. XIII:** 19, 20, **27-29**
"Hand of Emmagene, The" (Taylor), **Supp. V:** 314, 325-326
Hand of the Potter, The: A Tragedy in Four Acts (Dreiser), **Retro. Supp. II:** 104; **Supp. XVII:** 96
"Hands" (Anderson), **I:** 106, 107
"Hands" (Mora), **Supp. XIII:** 215
Hands of Orlac, The (M. Renard; Crewe-Jones, trans.), **Supp. XVII:** 58
Hand to Mouth (Auster), **Supp. XII:** 21
"Hand to Mouth" (Auster), **Supp. XII:** 31
Handy, Lowney, **Supp. XI:** 217, 220, 221, 225
Handy, W. C., **Supp. VIII:** 337
Handy Guide for Beggars, A (Lindsay), **Supp. I Part 2:** 376-378, 380, 382, 399
Hanging Garden, The (Wagoner), **Supp. IX: 338-339**
"Hanging Gardens of Tyburn, The" (Hecht), **Supp. X:** 58
"Hanging of the Crane, The" (Longfellow), **Retro. Supp. II:** 169, 171
Hanging On (Conroy), **Supp. XVI:**69
"Hanging Pictures in Nanny's Room" (Kenyon), **Supp. VII:** 164
"Hanging the Wash" (Alvarez), **Supp. VII:** 4
"Hangman, The" (Sexton), **Supp. II Part 2:** 680, 691
Hangover Mass (X. J. Kennedy), **Supp. XV:** 165
Hangsaman (Jackson), **Supp. IX:** 116, 123, **124**
Hanh, Thich Nhat, **Supp. V:** 199
Hanks, Lucy, **III:** 587
Hanks, Nancy. *See* Lincoln, Mrs. Thomas (Nancy Hanks)

Hanley, Lynne T., **Supp. IV Part 1:** 208
Hanna, Mark, **Supp. I Part 2:** 395
Hannah, Barry, **Supp. X:** 285
Hannah and Her Sisters (film; Allen), **Supp. XV:** 9, **10-11**
"Hannah Armstrong" (Masters), **Supp. I Part 2:** 461
"Hannah Binding Shoes" (Larcom), **Supp. XIII:** 141, 143
Hannah's House (Hearon), **Supp. VIII:** 58, **60-61**
Hanneman, Audre, **II:** 259
Hannibal Lecter, My Father (Acker), **Supp. XII:** 6
Hanoi (McCarthy), **II:** 579
Hansberry, Lorraine, **Supp. IV Part 1: 359-377**; **Supp. VIII:** 329
Hanscom, Leslie, **Supp. XI:** 229
"Hansel and Gretel" (Prose), **Supp. XVI:**256, 258
Hansen, Erik, **Supp. V:** 241
Hansen, Harry, **IV:** 366
Han-shan, **Supp. VIII:** 292
Hanson, Curtis, **Supp. XI:** 67
Han Suyin, **Supp. X:** 291
Hanzlicek, C. G., **Supp. XV:** 73
Hapgood, Hutchins, **Supp. XVII: 95-108**
Hapgoods, The: Three Earnest Brothers (Marcaccio), **Supp. XVII:** 106
"Happenings: An Art of Radical Juxtaposition" (Sontag), **Supp. III Part 2:** 456
"Happenstance" (Komunyakaa), **Supp. XIII:** 130
Happenstance (Shields), **Supp. VII:** 315-318, 320, 323, 324, 326
Happersberger, Lucien, **Supp. I Part 1:** 51
"Happiest I've Been, The" (Updike), **IV:** 219
Happily Ever After (Quindlen), **Supp. XVII:** 167
"Happiness" (Oliver), **Supp. VII:** 236
"Happiness" (Sandburg), **III:** 582-583
Happiness of Getting It Down Right, The (Steinman, ed.), **Supp. VIII:** 172
"Happy Birthday" (Bambara), **Supp. XI:** 4
Happy Birthday (Loos), **Supp. XVI:**193
Happy Birthday, Wanda June (Vonnegut), **Supp. II Part 2:** 759, 776-777
Happy Birthday of Death, The (Corso), **Supp. XII: 127-129**
Happy Childhood, A (Matthews), **Supp. IX:** 155, 160, **161-163**

Happy Days (Beckett), **Retro. Supp. I:** 206
Happy Days, 1880-1892 (Mencken), **III:** 100, 111, 120
"Happy End" (Simic), **Supp. VIII:** 276-277
"Happy Failure, The" (Melville), **III:** 90
Happy Families Are All Alike (Taylor), **Supp. V:** 322-323, 325
Happy Isles of Oceania, The: Paddling the Pacific (Theroux), **Supp. VIII:** 324
"Happy Journey to Trenton and Camden, The" (Wilder), **IV:** 366
"Happy Marriage, The" (MacLeish), **III:** 15-16
Happy Marriage and Other Poems, The (MacLeish), **III:** 4
Happy to Be Here (Keillor), **Supp. XVI:**165, 171
"Happy To Be Here" (Keillor), **Supp. XVI:**168
"Hapworth 16, 1924" (Salinger), **III:** 552, 571-572
"Harbor Lights" (Doty), **Supp. XI:** 122
Harcourt, Alfred, **II:** 191, 451-452; **III:** 587; **Retro. Supp. I:** 131; **Supp. XV:** 308
Harcourt, Brace, **Retro. Supp. I:** 83
Harcourt, T. A., **I:** 196
Hard Candy, a Book of Stories (T. Williams), **IV:** 383
"Hardcastle Crags" (Plath), **Supp. I Part 2:** 537
"Hard Daddy" (Hughes), **Retro. Supp. I:** 200
Harder They Fall, The (Schulberg), **Supp. XV:** 194, 201
Hard Facts (Baraka), **Supp. II Part 1:** 54, 55, 58
Hard Freight (Wright), **Supp. V:** 332, 339-340
Hard Hours, The (Hecht), **Supp. X:** 57, **59-62,** 63, 64
Hardie, Kier, **Supp. I Part 1:** 5
Harding, Walter, **IV:** 177, 178
Harding, Warren G., **I:** 486; **II:** 253, 433; **Supp. I Part 1:** 24
"Hard Kind of Courage, The" (Baldwin), **Supp. I Part 1:** 52
"Hard Time Keeping Up, A" (Ellison), **Retro. Supp. II:** 124
Hard Times (Dickens), **Supp. I Part 2:** 675
"Hard Times in Elfland, The" (Lanier), **Supp. I Part 1:** 365
Hardwick, Elizabeth, **II:** 543, 554, 566; **Retro. Supp. II:** 179, 180, 183, 184, 190, 221, 228-229, 245; **Supp. I Part 1:** 196; **Supp. III Part 1:** 193-215; **Supp. IV Part 1:** 299; **Supp. V,** 319; **Supp. X,** 171; **Supp. XII:** 209; **Supp. XIV:**89

"Hard Work 1956" (Dunn), **Supp. XI:** 147
Hardy, Barbara, **Supp. I Part 2:** 527
Hardy, Oliver, **Supp. I Part 2:** 607; **Supp. IV Part 2:** 574
Hardy, René, **Supp. III Part 1:** 235
Hardy, Thomas, **I:** 59, 103, 292, 317, 377; **II:** 181, 184-185, 186, 191-192, 271, 275, 372, 523, 542; **III:** 32, 453, 485, 508, 524; **IV:** 83, 135, 136; **Retro. Supp. I:** 141, 377-378; **Supp. I Part 1:** 217; **Supp. I Part 2:** 429, 512; **Supp. II Part 1:** 4, 26; **Supp. VIII:** 32; **Supp. IX:** 40, 78, 85, 108, 211; **Supp. X:** 228; **Supp. XI:** 311; **Supp. XIII:** 294, **Supp. XIII:** 130; **Supp. XIV:**24; **Supp. XV:** 170
Harjo, Joy, **Supp. IV Part 1:** 325, 404; **Supp. IV Part 2:** 499, 507; **Supp. XII: 215-234**
"Harlem" (Hughes), **Retro. Supp. I:** 194, 204; **Supp. I Part 1:** 340; **Supp. VIII:** 213
Harlem, Mecca of the New Negro (Locke), **Supp. XIV:**201
Harlem: Negro Metropolis (McKay), **Supp. X:** 132, 141, 142
"Harlem Dancer, The" (McKay), **Supp. X:** 134
Harlem Gallery (Tolson), **Retro. Supp. I:** 208, 209, 210
Harlem Glory: A Fragment of Aframerican Life (McKay), **Supp. X:** 132, **141-142**
"Harlem Runs Wild" (McKay), **Supp. X:** 140
Harlem Shadows (McKay), **Supp. X:** 131-132, 136
Harlem Underground (Lacy), **Supp. XV:** 206
"Harlequin of Dreams, The" (Lanier), **Supp. I Part 1:** 365
Harlot's Ghost (Mailer), **Retro. Supp. II:** 211-212
Harlow, Jean, **IV:** 256; **Retro. Supp. I:** 110
"Harm" (C. Frost), **Supp. XV:** 101
Harmon, William, **Retro. Supp. I:** 37; **Supp. XI:** 248
"Harmonic" (F. Barthelme), **Supp. XI:** 26
Harmonium (Stevens), **III:** 196; **IV:** 76, 77, 78, 82, 87, 89, 92; **Retro. Supp. I:** 296, 297, 299, **300-302,** 301, 302

"Harmony of the Gospels" (Taylor), **IV:** 149
Harmony of the World (C. Baxter), **Supp. XVII:** 16-17
"Harmony of the World" (C. Baxter), **Supp. XVII:** 16
Harnett, Vincent, **Supp. XV:** 198
Harper (film), **Supp. IV Part 2:** 473
Harper, Donna, **Retro. Supp. I:** 194, 195, 209
Harper, Frances E. Watkins, **Supp. II Part 1:** 201-202
Harper, Gordon Lloyd, **Retro. Supp. II:** 23
Harper, Michael, **Supp. XV:** 74
Harper, Michael S., **Retro. Supp. II:** 116, 123
Harper, William Rainey, **Supp. I Part 2:** 631
Harper's Anthology of 20th Century Native American Poetry (Niatum, ed.), **Supp. IV Part 1:** 331
"Harriet" (Lowell), **II:** 554
Harrigan, Edward, **II:** 276; **III:** 14
Harrington, Michael, **I:** 306
Harrington, Ollie, **Supp. XVI:**142-143
Harris, Celia, **Retro. Supp. I:** 9
Harris, George, **II:** 70
Harris, Joel Chandler, **III:** 338; **Supp. I Part 1:** 352; **Supp. II Part 1:** 192, 201; **Supp. XIV:**61
Harris, Judith, **Supp. XIV:**269
Harris, Julie, **II:** 587, 601; **Supp. IX:** 125
Harris, Leonard, **Supp. XIV:**196, 211-212
Harris, MacDonald, **Supp. XI:** 65
Harris, Marie, **Supp. IX:** 153
Harris, Peter, **Supp. X:** 206, 207
Harris, Susan K., **Supp. XV:** 269
Harris, Thomas, **Supp. XIV:**26
Harris, Victoria Frenkel, **Supp. IV Part 1:** 68, 69
Harrison, Colin, **Supp. XIV:**26
Harrison, Hazel, **Retro. Supp. II:** 115
Harrison, Jim, **Supp. VIII: 37-56**
Harrison, Kathryn, **Supp. X:** 191
Harrison, Ken, **Supp. IX:** 101
Harrison, Oliver (pseudonym). *See* Smith, Harrison
Harry: A Portrait (N. Boyce), **Supp. XVII:** 104
Harryhausen, Ray, **Supp. IV Part 1:** 115
Harryman, Carla, **Supp. XV:** 344
"Harry of Nothingham" (Hugo), **Supp. VI:** 146-147
"Harry's Death" (Carver), **Supp. III Part 1:** 146
"Harsh Judgment, The" (Kunitz),

Supp. III Part 1: 264
Hart, Albert Bushnell, **Supp. I Part 2:** 479, 480, 481
Hart, Bernard, **I:** 241, 242, 248-250, 256
Hart, Henry, **Retro. Supp. II:** 187; **Supp. XIV:** 97
Hart, Lorenz, **III:** 361
Hart, Moss, **Supp. IV Part 2:** 574; **Supp. XV:** 329
Hart, Pearl, **Supp. X:** 103
"Hart Crane" (Tate), **I:** 381
"Hart Crane and Poetry: A Consideration of Crane's Intense Poetics with Reference to 'The Return'" (Grossman), **Retro. Supp. II:** 83
Harte, Anna Griswold, **Supp. II Part 1:** 341
Harte, Bret, **I:** 193, 195, 203; **II:** 289; **IV:** 196; **Retro. Supp. II:** 72; **Supp. II Part 1: 335-359,** 399; **Supp. XV:** 115
Harte, Walter Blackburn, **I:** 199
Harter, Carol C., **Supp. IV Part 1:** 217
Hartley, David, **III:** 77
Hartley, L. P., **Supp. I Part 1:** 293
Hartley, Lois, **Supp. I Part 2:** 459, 464-465
Hartley, Marsden, **IV:** 409, 413; **Retro. Supp. I:** 430; **Supp. X:** 137; **Supp. XV:** 298
Hartman, Geoffrey, **Supp. IV Part 1:** 119; **Supp. XII:** 130, 253
Harum, David, **II:** 102
"Harvard" (Lowell), **II:** 554
Harvard College in the Seventeenth Century (Morison), **Supp. I Part 2:** 485
"Harvesters of Night and Water" (Hogan), **Supp. IV Part 1:** 412
"Harvest Song" (Toomer), **Supp. III Part 2:** 483
Harvill Book of 20th Century Poetry in English, **Supp. X:** 55
"Harv Is Plowing Now" (Updike), **Retro. Supp. I:** 318
Haselden, Elizabeth Lee, **Supp. VIII:** 125
Hass, Robert, **Supp. VI: 97-111; Supp. VIII:** 24, 28; **Supp. XI:** 142, 270; **Supp. XIV:** 83, 84
Hassam, Childe, **Retro. Supp. II:** 136
Hassan, Ihab, **IV:** 99-100, 115; **Supp. XI:** 221
Hasse, Henry, **Supp. IV Part 1:** 102
Hasty-Pudding, The (Barlow), **Supp. II Part 1:** 74, 77-80
Hatful of Rain, A (Gazzo), **III:** 155
Hatlen, Burton, **Supp. V:** 138, 139-140

"Hattie Bloom" (Oliver), **Supp. VII:** 232
Haunch, Paunch, and Jowl (Ornitz), **Supp. IX:** 227
"Haunted Landscape" (Ashbery), **Supp. III Part 1:** 22
"Haunted Mind" (Simic), **Supp. VIII:** 282
"Haunted Mind, The" (Hawthorne), **II:** 230-231
"Haunted Oak, The" (Dunbar), **Supp. II Part 1:** 207, 208
"Haunted Palace, The" (Poe), **III:** 421
"Haunted Valley, The" (Bierce), **I:** 200
Haunting, The (film), **Supp. IX:** 125
Haunting of Hill House, The (Jackson), **Supp. IX:** 117, 121, 126
Hauptmann, Gerhart, **III:** 472
Haussmann, Sonja, **Supp. XIII:** 331, **Supp. XIII:** 347
"Havanna vanities come to dust in Miami" (Didion), **Supp. IV Part 1:** 210
Haven, Cynthia, **Supp. XV:** 252, 264
Haven's End (Marquand), **III:** 55, 56, 63, 68
"Have You Ever Tried to Enter the Long Black Branches" (Oliver), **Supp. VII:** 247
"Having Been Interstellar" (Ammons), **Supp. VII:** 25
"Having It Out With Melancholy" (Kenyon), **Supp. VII:** 171
"Having Lost My Sons, I Confront the Wreckage of the Moon: Christmas, 1960" (Wright), **Supp. III Part 2:** 600
"Having Snow" (Schwartz), **Supp. II Part 2:** 652
Hawai'i One Summer (Kingston), **Supp. V:** 157, 160, 166, 169-170
"Hawk, The" (Francis), **Supp. IX:** 81
Hawke, David Freeman, **Supp. I Part 2:** 511, 516
Hawkes, John, **I:** 113; **Retro. Supp. II:** 234; **Supp. III Part 1:** 2; **Supp. V:** 40; **Supp. IX:** 212; **Supp. XVII:** 183
Hawkins, William, **II:** 587
Hawk in the Rain, The (Hughes), **Retro. Supp. II:** 244; **Supp. I Part 2:** 537, 540
Hawk Is Dying, The (Crews), **Supp. XI: 111**
Hawk Moon (Shepard), **Supp. III Part 2:** 445
Hawks, Howard, **Supp. IV Part 1:** 130
"Hawk's Cry in Autumn, The" (Brodsky), **Supp. VIII:** 29

"Hawk's Shadow" (Glück), **Supp. V:** 85
Hawk's Well, The (Yeats), **III:** 459-460
Hawley, Adelaide, **Supp. XIV:** 207
Hawley, Joseph, **I:** 546
Hawthorne (James), **II:** 372-378; **Retro. Supp. I:** 220, **223-224**
"Hawthorne" (Longfellow), **Retro. Supp. II:** 169
"Hawthorne" (Lowell), **II:** 550
Hawthorne, Julian, **II:** 225; **Supp. I Part 1:** 38; **Supp. XV:** 274
Hawthorne, Mrs. Nathaniel (Sophia Peabody), **II:** 224, 244; **III:** 75, 86
Hawthorne, Nathaniel, **I:** 106, 204, 211, 340, 355, 363, 384, 413, 458, 561-562; **II:** 7, 8, 40, 60, 63, 74, 89, 127-128, 138, 142, 198, **223-246,** 255, 259, 264, 267, 272, 274, 277, 281, 282, 295, 307, 309, 311, 313, 322, 324, 326, 402, 408, 446, 501, 545; **III:** 51, 81-82, 83, 84, 85, 87, 88, 91, 92, 113, 316, 359, 412, 415, 421, 438, 453, 454, 507, 565, 572; **IV:** 2, 4, 167, 172, 179, 194, 333, 345, 453; **Retro. Supp. I:** 1, 53, 59, 62, 63, 91, **145-167,** 215, 218, 220, 223, 248-249, 252, 257, 258, 330, 331, 365; **Retro. Supp. II:** 136, 142, 153, 156-157, 158, 159, 187, 221; **Supp. I Part 1:** 38, 188, 197, 317, 372; **Supp. I Part 2:** 420, 421, 545, 579, 580, 582, 587, 595, 596; **Supp. III Part 2:** 501; **Supp. IV Part 1:** 80, 127, 297; **Supp. IV Part 2:** 463, 596; **Supp. V:** 152; **Supp. VIII:** 103, 105, 108, 153, 201; **Supp. IX:** 114; **Supp. X:** 78; **Supp. XI:** 51, 78; **Supp. XII:** 26; **Supp. XIII:** 102; **Supp. XIV:** 48; **Supp. XV:** 269, 272, 282; **Supp. XVI:** 83, 84, 157; **Supp. XVII:** 42
Hawthorne, Rose, **II:** 225
Hawthorne, Una, **II:** 225
"Hawthorne and His Mosses" (Melville), **Retro. Supp. I:** 254; **Supp. XIV:** 48
"Hawthorne Aspect [of Henry James], The" (Eliot), **Retro. Supp. I:** 63
"Hawthorne in Solitude" (Cowley), **Supp. II Part 1:** 143
Hay, John, **I:** 1, 10, 12, 14-15; **Supp. I Part 1:** 352
Hay, Mrs. John, **I:** 14
Hay, Sara Henderson, **Supp. XIV:** 119-135
Hayakawa, S. I., **I:** 448; **Supp. I Part 1:** 315; **Supp. XV:** 176
Hayden, Robert, **Supp. II Part 1:** 361-

383; **Supp. IV Part 1:** 169; **Supp. XIII:** 115, 127; **Supp. XIV:**119, 123
Hayden, Sterling, **Supp. XI:** 304
Haydn, Hiram, **IV:** 100, 358
Hayduke Lives! (Abbey), **Supp. XIII:** 16
Hayek, Friedrich A. von, **Supp. IV Part 2:** 524
Hayes, Helen, **Supp. XVI:**193, 195
Hayes, Ira, **Supp. IV Part 1:** 326
Hayes, Richard, **Supp. V:** 320
Hayes, Rutherford B., **Supp. I Part 2:** 419
Haygood, Wil, **Supp. VIII:** 79
Hayne, Paul Hamilton, **Supp. I Part 1:** 352, 354, 355, 360, 372
Hayward, Florence, **Retro. Supp. II:** 65
Hayward, John, **Retro. Supp. I:** 67
Haywood, "Big" Bill, **I:** 483; **Supp. V:** 286
Hazard, Grace, **II:** 530
Hazard of Fortunes, A (Howells), **Retro. Supp. II:** 288
Hazard of New Fortunes, A (Howells), **II:** 275, 276, 286-297, 290
Hazel, Robert, **Supp. VIII:** 137, 138
Hazen, General W. B., **I:** 192, 193
Hazlitt, Henry, **Supp. IV Part 2:** 524
Hazlitt, William, **I:** 58, 378; **II:** 315
Hazmat (McClatchy), **Supp. XII:** 265-270
Hazo, Samuel, **I:** 386; **Supp. XIV:**123, 124
Hazzard, Shirley, **Supp. VIII:** 151
H.D. *See* Doolittle, Hilda
"He" (Porter), **III:** 434, 435
"Head and Shoulders" (Fitzgerald), **Retro. Supp. I:** 101
"Head-Hunter, The" (O. Henry), **Supp. II Part 1:** 403
"Headless Hawk, The" (Capote), **Supp. III Part 1:** 124
Headlines (T. Williams), **IV:** 381
Headlong Hall (Peacock), **Supp. I Part 1:** 307
Headmaster, The (McPhee), **Supp. III Part 1:** 291, 294, 298
"Head of Joaquín Murrieta, The" (Rodriguez), **Supp. XIV:**303
Headsman, The (Cooper), **I:** 345-346
"Headwaters" (Momaday), **Supp. IV Part 2:** 486
Healy, Eloise Klein, **Supp. XI:** 121, 124, 126, 127, 129, 137
Healy, Tim, **II:** 129, 137
Heaney, Sally, **Supp. XVII:** 241
Heaney, Seamus, **Retro. Supp. II:** 245; **Supp. IX:** 41, 42; **Supp. X:** 67, 122; **Supp. XI:** 249; **Supp. XV:** 256

"Heard through the Walls of the Racetrack Glen Motel" (X. J. Kennedy), **Supp. XV:** 170
Hearn, Lafcadio, **I:** 211; **II:** 311
Hearon, Shelby, **Supp. VIII: 57-72**
Hearst, Patty, **Supp. IV Part 1:** 195
Hearst, William Randolph, **I:** 198, 207, 208; **IV:** 298
Heart and Perimeter (Bierds), **Supp. XVII: 28-29**
"Heart and the Lyre, The" (Bogan), **Supp. III Part 1:** 65
"Heartbeat" (Harjo), **Supp. XII:** 221-222
Heartbreak Kid, The (film), **Supp. IV Part 2:** 575, 589
Heart for the Gods of Mexico, A (Aiken), **I:** 54
"Hear the Nightingale Sing" (Gordon), **II:** 200
Hear the Wind Blow (Sanders), **Supp. XVI:**268
Heart is a Lonely Hunter, The (McCullers), **II:** 586, 588-593, 604, 605
Heart of a Woman, The (Angelou), **Supp. IV Part 1:** 2, 5, 7-9, 9, 14, 17
Heart of Darkness (Conrad), **Retro. Supp. II:** 292; **Supp. V:** 249, 311; **Supp. VIII:** 4, 316
"Heart of Darkness" (Conrad), **I:** 575, 578; **II:** 595; **Supp. XVI:**212
Heart of Darkness (Didion), **Supp. IV Part 1:** 207
Heart of Happy Hollow, The (Dunbar), **Supp. II Part 1:** 214
Heart of Knowledge, The: American Indians on the Bomb (Gunn Allen and Caputi, eds.), **Supp. IV Part 1:** 334-335
"Heart of Knowledge, The: Nuclear Themes in Native American Thought and Literature" (Caputi), **Supp. IV Part 1:** 335
"Heart of the Park, The " (O'Connor), **Retro. Supp. II:** 225
Heart of the West (O. Henry), **Supp. II Part 1:** 410
"Hearts, The" (Pinsky), **Supp. VI:** 245-247, 248
"'Hearts and Flowers'" (MacLeish), **III:** 8
"Hearts and Heads" (Ransom), **Supp. I Part 1:** 373
"Heart's Graveyard Shift, The" (Komunyakaa), **Supp. XIII:** 120
Heart-Shape in the Dust (Hayden), **Supp. II Part 1:** 365, 366
"Heart's Needle" (Snodgrass), **Supp.**

VI: 311-313, 320
Heart's Needle (Snodgrass), **I:** 400
"Hearts of Oak" (Rowson), **Supp. XV:** 243
"Heart Songs" (Proulx), **Supp. VII:** 254
Heart Songs and Other Stories (Proulx), **Supp. VII:** 252-256, 261
Heart to Artemis, The (Bryher), **Supp. I Part 1:** 259
Heartwood (Burke), **Supp. XIV:**35
Heath Anthology of American Literature, The, **Supp. IX:** 4; **Supp. XV:** 270, 313
Heathcote, Anne. *See* De Lancey, Mrs. James
"Heathen Chinee, The" (Harte), **Supp. II Part 1:** 350-351, 352
Heathen Days, 1890-1936 (Mencken), **III:** 100, 111
Heath-Stubbs, John, **Supp. XV:** 153
Heat's On, The (C. Himes), **Supp. XVI:**143, 144
"Heaven" (Dunn), **Supp. XI:** 154
"Heaven" (Levine), **Supp. V:** 182
"Heaven" (Patchett), **Supp. XII:** 309
Heaven and Earth: A Cosmology (Goldbarth), **Supp. XII: 187**
"Heaven and Earth in Jest" (Dillard), **Supp. VI:** 24, 28
"Heaven as Anus" (Kumin), **Supp. IV Part 2:** 448
Heavenly Conversation, The (Mather), **Supp. II Part 2:** 460
"Heavenly Feast, The" (Schnackenberg), **Supp. XV:** 257, 259
Heavens (Untermeyer), **Supp. XV:** 306
Heavens and Earth (Benét), **Supp. XI:** 44
Heaven's Coast (Doty), **Supp. XI:** 119, 121, **129-130**, 134
Heaven's Prisoners (Burke), **Supp. XIV:**23, 29
"Heavy Angel, The" (Everwine), **Supp. XV:** 80
"Heavy Bear Who Goes with Me, The" (Schwartz), **Supp. II Part 2:** 646
"He Came Also Still" (Zukofsky), **Supp. III Part 2:** 612
Hecht, Anthony, **IV:** 138; **Supp. III Part 2:** 541, 561; **Supp. X: 55-75;** **Supp. XII:** 269-270; **Supp. XV:** 251, 256
Hecht, Ben, **I:** 103; **II:** 42; **Supp. I Part 2:** 646; **Supp. XI:** 307; **Supp. XIII:** 106
Hecht, S. Theodore, **Supp. III Part 2:** 614
Heckewelder, John, **II:** 503

"Hedge Island" (Lowell), **II:** 524
Hedges, William I., **II:** 311-312
"He 'Digesteth Harde Yron'" (Moore), **Supp. IV Part 2:** 454
Hedin, Robert, **Supp. XII:** 200, 202
Hedylus (Doolittle), **Supp. I Part 1:** 259, 270
"Heel & Toe To the End" (W. C. Williams), **Retro. Supp. I:** 430
Heffernan, Michael, **Supp. XII:** 177
"HEGEL" (Baraka), **Supp. II Part 1:** 53
Hegel, Georg Wilhelm Friedrich, **I:** 265; **II:** 358; **III:** 262, 308-309, 480, 481, 487, 607; **IV:** 86, 333, 453; **Supp. I Part 2:** 633, 635, 640, 645; **Supp. XVI:** 289
"Hegemony of Race, The" (Du Bois), **Supp. II Part 1:** 181
Hegger, Grace Livingston. *See* Lewis, Mrs. Sinclair (Grace Livingston Hegger)
"He Had Spent His Youth Dreaming" (Dobyns), **Supp. XIII:** 90
Heidegger, Martin, **II:** 362, 363; **III:** 292; **IV:** 491; **Retro. Supp. II:** 87; **Supp. V:** 267; **Supp. VIII:** 9; **Supp. XVI:** 283, 288
Heidenmauer, The (Cooper), **I:** 345-346
Heidi Chronicles, The (Wasserstein), **Supp. IV Part 1:** 309; **Supp. XV:** 319, **325-327**
"Height of the Ridiculous, The" (Holmes), **Supp. I Part 1:** 302
Heilbroner, Robert, **Supp. I Part 2:** 644, 648, 650
Heilbrun, Carolyn G., **Supp. IX:** 66; **Supp. XI:** 208; **Supp. XIV:** 161, 163
Heilman, Robert Bechtold, **Supp. XIV:** 11, 12
Heilpern, John, **Supp. XIV:** 242
Heim, Michael, **Supp. V:** 209
Heine, Heinrich, **II:** 272, 273, 277, 281, 282, 387, 544; **IV:** 5; **Supp. XV:** 293, 299; **Supp. XVI:** 188
Heineman, Frank, **Supp. III Part 2:** 619
Heinlein, Robert, **Supp. IV Part 1:** 102; **Supp. XVI:** 122
Heinz, Helen. *See* Tate, Mrs. Allen (Helen Heinz)
Heiress, The (film), **Retro. Supp. I:** 222
"Heirs" (Nye), **Supp. XIII:** 284
"He Is Not Worth the Trouble" (Rowson), **Supp. XV:** 240
"He Knew" (C. Himes), **Supp. XVI:** 137

"Helas" (Creeley), **Supp. IV Part 1:** 150, 158
Helburn, Theresa, **IV:** 381
Heldreth, Leonard, **Supp. V:** 151
"Helen" (Lowell), **II:** 544
"Helen: A Courtship" (Faulkner), **Retro. Supp. I:** 81
"Helen, Thy Beauty Is to Me" (Fante), **Supp. XI:** 169
"Helen I Love You" (Farrell), **II:** 28, 45
Helen in Egypt (Doolittle), **Supp. I Part 1:** 260, 272, 273, 274
Helen in Egypt (H.D.), **Supp. XV:** 264
Helen Keller: Sketch for a Portrait (Brooks), **I:** 254
"Helen of Tyre" (Longfellow), **II:** 496
Heliodora (Doolittle), **Supp. I Part 1:** 266
"Helix" (Sobin), **Supp. XVI:** 283
Hellbox (O'Hara), **III:** 361
Heller, Joseph, **III:** 2, 258; **IV:** 98; **Retro. Supp. II:** 324; **Supp. I Part 1:** 196; **Supp. IV Part 1: 379-396;** **Supp. V:** 244; **Supp. VIII:** 245; **Supp. XI:** 307; **Supp. XII:** 167-168; **Supp. XV:** 322; **Supp. XVII:** 139
Hellman, Lillian, **I:** 28; **III:** 28; **Supp. I Part 1: 276-298;** **Supp. IV Part 1:** 1, 12, 83, 353, 355, 356; **Supp. VIII:** 243; **Supp. IX:** 196, 198, 200-201, 204
Hellmann, Lillian, **Retro. Supp. II:** 327
Hello (Creeley), **Supp. IV Part 1:** 155, 157
"Hello, Hello Henry" (Kumin), **Supp. IV Part 2:** 446
"Hello, Stranger" (Capote), **Supp. III Part 1:** 120
Hello Dolly! (musical play), **IV:** 357
Hellyer, John, **Supp. I Part 2:** 468
Helm, Bob, **Supp. XV:** 147
Helmets (Dickey), **Supp. IV Part 1:** 175, 178, 180
"Helmsman, The" (Doolittle), **Supp. I Part 1:** 266
"Help" (Barth), **I:** 139
"Help Her to Believe" (Olsen). *See* "I Stand There Ironing" (Olsen)
"Helsinki Window" (Creeley), **Supp. IV Part 1:** 158
Hemenway, Robert E., **Supp. IV Part 1:** 6
Hemingway, Dr. Clarence Edwards, **II:** 248, 259
Hemingway, Ernest, **I:** 28, 64, 97, 99, 105, 107, 117, 150, 162, 190, 211, 221, 288, 289, 295, 367, 374, 378,
421, 423, 445, 476, 477, 478, 482, 484-485, 487, 488, 489, 491, 495, 504, 517; **II:** 27, 44, 51, 58, 68-69, 78, 90, 97, 127, 206, **247-270,** 289, 424, 431, 456, 457, 458-459, 482, 560, 600; **III:** 2, 18, 20, 35, 36, 37, 40, 61, 108, 220, 334, 363, 364, 382, 453, 454, 471-472, 476, 551, 575, 576, 584; **IV:** 27, 28, 33, 34, 35, 42, 49, 97, 108, 122, 126, 138, 190, 191, 201, 216, 217, 257, 297, 363, 404, 427, 433, 451; **Retro. Supp. I:** 74, 98, 108, 111, 112, 113, 115, **169-191,** 215, 292, 359, 418; **Retro. Supp. II:** 19, 24, 30, 68, 115, 123; **Supp. I Part 2:** 621, 658, 678; **Supp. II Part 1:** 221; **Supp. III Part 1:** 146; **Supp. III Part 2:** 617; **Supp. IV Part 1:** 48, 102, 123, 197, 236, 342, 343, 344, 348, 350, 352, 380-381, 383; **Supp. IV Part 2:** 463, 468, 502, 607, 679, 680, 681, 689, 692; **Supp. V:** 237, 240, 244, 250, 336; **Supp. VIII:** 40, 101, 105, 179, 182, 183, 188, 189, 196; **Supp. IX:** 16, 57, 58, 94, 106, 260, 262; **Supp. X:** 137, 167, 223, 225; **Supp. XI:** 214, 221; **Supp. XIII:** 96, 255, 270; **Supp. XIV:** 24, 83; **Supp. XV:** 69, 135; **Supp. XVI:** 203, 205-206, 208, 210, 233, 236-237, 281-282; **Supp. XVII:** 4, 105, 107, 137, 228, 229
Hemingway, Mrs. Ernest (Hadley Richardson), **II:** 257, 260, 263
Hemingway, Mrs. Ernest (Martha Gellhorn), **II:** 260
Hemingway, Mrs. Ernest (Mary Welsh), **II:** 257, 260
Hemingway, Mrs. Ernest (Pauline Pfeiffer), **II:** 260
"Hemingway: The Old Lion" (Cowley), **Supp. II Part 1:** 143
"Hemingway in Paris" (Cowley), **Supp. II Part 1:** 144
"Hemingway Story, A" (Dubus), **Supp. VII:** 91
"Hemp, The" (Benét), **Supp. XI:** 44
"Henchman, The" (Whittier), **Supp. I Part 2:** 696
Henderson, Alice Corbin, **Supp. I Part 2:** 387; **Supp. XV:** 302-303
Henderson, Darwin L., **Supp. XIII:** 213, 221-222
Henderson, Jane, **Supp. VIII:** 87
Henderson, Katherine, **Supp. IV Part 1:** 203, 207
Henderson, Linda. *See* Hogan, Linda
Henderson, Robert W., **Supp. VIII:** 124

INDEX / 365

Henderson, Stephen, **Supp. IV Part 1:** 365
Henderson, the Rain King (Bellow), **I:** 144, 147, 148, 152, 153, 154, 155, 158, 160, 161, 162-163; **Retro. Supp. II:** 19, **24-25,** 30
"Hen Flower, The" (Kinnell), **Supp. III Part 1:** 247-248
Henie, Sonja, **Supp. XII:** 165
Henle, James, **II:** 26, 30, 38, 41; **Supp. IX:** 2
Hennesy, Dale, **Supp. XV:** 5
Henri, Robert, **IV:** 411; **Supp. I Part 2:** 376
Henry, Arthur, **I:** 515; **Retro. Supp. II:** 97
Henry, DeWitt, **Supp. XI:** 342
Henry, O., **I:** 201; **III:** 5; **Supp. I Part 2:** 390, 462; **Supp. II Part 1: 385-412; Supp. XV:** 40
Henry, Robert, **Retro. Supp. II:** 103
Henry, William A., III, **Supp. IV Part 2:** 574
Henry and June (film), **Supp. X:** 186
Henry and June: From the Unexpurgated Diary of Anaïs Nin, **Supp. X:** 184, 185, 187, 194
Henry Holt and Company, **Retro. Supp. I:** 121, 131, 133, 136
Henry IV (Shakespeare), **III:** 166; **Supp. VIII:** 164
"Henry James, Jr." (Howells), **II:** 289; **Retro. Supp. I:** 220
"Henry James and the Art of Teaching" (Rowe), **Retro. Supp. I:** 216
"Henry Manley, Living Alone, Keeps Time" (Kumin), **Supp. IV Part 2:** 451
"Henry Manley Looks Back" (Kumin), **Supp. IV Part 2:** 451
"Henry Manley" poems (Kumin), **Supp. IV Part 2:** 446
Henry Miller Reader, The (Durrell, ed.), **III:** 175, 190
"Henry's Confession" (Berryman), **I:** 186
Henry VIII (Shakespeare), **Supp. IX:** 235
Henslee, **Supp. IV Part 1:** 217
Henson, Josiah, **Supp. I Part 2:** 589
Hentoff, Margot, **Supp. IV Part 1:** 205
Hentz, Caroline Lee, **Supp. I Part 2:** 584
Henze, Hans Werner, **Supp. II Part 1:** 24
"He of the Assembly" (Bowles), **Supp. IV Part 1:** 90
Hepburn, Katharine, **Supp. IX:** 189; **Supp. XI:** 17
Heraclitus, **II:** 1, 163; **IV:** 86

Herakles: A Play in Verse (MacLeish), **III:** 21, 22
Herald of the Autochthonic Spirit (Corso), **Supp. XII:** 134-136
He Ran All the Way (film), **Supp. XVII:** 63
Herberg, Will, **III:** 291
Herbert, Edward, **II:** 11
Herbert, Francis (pseudonym). See Bryant, William Cullen
Herbert, George, **II:** 12; **IV:** 141, 145, 146, 151, 153, 156, 165; **Retro. Supp. II:** 40; **Supp. I Part 1:** 80, 107, 108, 122; **Supp. IV Part 2:** 646; **Supp. XV:** 92, 212, 251
Herbert, Zbigniew, **Supp. VIII:** 20
Herbert Huncke Reader, The (Schafer, ed.), **Supp. XIV:**137, 138, 139, 140, 145, 147, 150, 151-152
Herbert of Cherbury, Lord, **II:** 108
"Herbert White" (Bidart), **Supp. XV:** 24, 27
Herbst, Josephine, **Retro. Supp. II:** 325, 328; **Supp. XIII:** 295
"Her Choice" (Larcom), **Supp. XIII:** 144
"Her Dead Brother" (Lowell), **Retro. Supp. II:** 188
"Her Dream Is of the Sea" (Ríos), **Supp. IV Part 2:** 546
"Here" (Kenyon), **Supp. VII:** 164
Here and Beyond (Wharton), **Retro. Supp. I:** 382
Here and Now (Levertov), **Supp. III Part 1:** 275, 276
"Here and There" (Wallace), **Supp. X:** 305-306
Here Comes the Mystery Man (Sanders), **Supp. XVI:**269
Heredia, Juanita, **Supp. XI:** 185, 190
Heredity and Variation (Lock), **Retro. Supp. I:** 375
Here is Your War (Pyle), **Supp. XVII:** 61
Here Let Us Feast (M. F. K. Fisher), **Supp. XVII:** 86, 87
Here Lies (Parker), **Supp. IX:** 192
Here on Earth (Hoffman), **Supp. X:** 77, 89
Heresy and the Ideal: On Contemporary Poetry (Baker), **Supp. XI:** 142
"Here to Learn" (Bowles), **Supp. IV Part 1:** 93
"Here to Yonder" (Hughes), **Retro. Supp. I:** 205
"Her Father's Letters" (Milburn), **Supp. XI:** 242
Herford, Reverend Brooke, **I:** 471
Hergesheimer, Joseph, **Supp. I Part 2:** 620; **Supp. XVI:**187

"Heritage" (Cullen), **Supp. IV Part 1:** 164-165, 168, 170, 171
"Heritage" (Hogan), **Supp. IV Part 1:** 413
"Her Kind" (Sexton), **Supp. II Part 2:** 687
Herland (Gilman), **Supp. XI:** 208-209
Herman, Florence. See Williams, Mrs. William Carlos (Florence Herman)
Herman, Jan, **Supp. XIV:**150-151
Herman, William (pseudonym). See Bierce, Ambrose
"Her Management" (Swenson), **Supp. IV Part 2:** 642
"Herman Melville" (Auden), **Supp. II Part 1:** 14
Herman Melville (Mumford), **Supp. II Part 2:** 471, 476, 489-491
"Hermes of the Ways" (Doolittle), **Supp. I Part 1:** 266
Hermetic Definition (Doolittle), **Supp. I Part 1:** 271, 272, 273, 274
"Hermitage, The" (Haines), **Supp. XII:** 205-206
Hermit and the Wild Woman, The (Wharton), **IV:** 315; **Retro. Supp. I:** 371
"Hermit and the Wild Woman, The" (Wharton), **Retro. Supp. I:** 372
"Hermit Meets the Skunk, The" (Kumin), **Supp. IV Part 2:** 447
"Hermit of Saba, The" (Freneau), **Supp. II Part 1:** 259
Hermit of 69th Street, The: The Working Papers or Norbert Kosky (Kosinski), **Supp. VII:** 215, 216, 223, 226-227
"Hermit Picks Berries, The" (Kumin), **Supp. IV Part 2:** 447
Hermit's Story, The (Bass), **Supp. XVI:**23-24
"Hermit Thrush, A" (Clampitt), **Supp. IX:** 40
Hernández, Miguel, **Supp. V:** 194; **Supp. XIII:** 315, 323
Herne, James A., **II:** 276; **Supp. II Part 1:** 198
Hernton, Calvin, **Supp. X:** 240
"Hero, The" (Moore), **III:** 200, 211, 212
Hero, The (Raglan), **I:** 135
Hérodiade (Mallarmé), **I:** 66
Herodotus, **Supp. I Part 2:** 405
Heroes, The (Ashbery), **Supp. III Part 1:** 3
Hero in America, The (Van Doren), **II:** 103
"Heroines of Nature: Four Women Respond to the American Landscape" (Norwood), **Supp. IX:** 24

"Heron, The" (Roethke), **III:** 540-541
"Her One Bad Eye" (Karr), **Supp. XI:** 244
"Her Own People" (Warren), **IV:** 253
"Her Quaint Honour" (Gordon), **II:** 196, 199, 200
Herr, Michael, **Supp. XI:** 245
Herrick, Robert, **II:** 11, 18, 444; **III:** 463, 592; **IV:** 453; **Retro. Supp. I:** 319; **Retro. Supp. II:** 101; **Supp. I Part 2:** 646; **Supp. XIII:** 334; **Supp. XIV:**8, 9; **Supp. XV:** 155
Herrmann, John, **Retro. Supp. II:** 328
Herron, George, **Supp. I Part 1:** 7
"Hers" (column, Prose), **Supp. XVI:**254
Herschel, Sir John, **Supp. I Part 1:** 314
"Her Sense of Timing" (Elkin), **Supp. VI:** 56, 58
Hersey, John, **IV:** 4; **Supp. I Part 1:** 196; **Supp. XVI:**105-106
"Her Sweet turn to leave the Homestead" (Dickinson), **Retro. Supp. I:** 44
Herzog (Bellow), **I:** 144, 147, 149, 150, 152, 153, 154, 155, 156, 157, 158, 159-160; **Retro. Supp. II:** 19, **26-27; Supp. IV Part 1:** 30
Hesford, Walter A., **Supp. XV:** 215, 217, 218
"He/She" (Dunn), **Supp. XI:** 149
"Hesitation Blues" (Hughes), **Retro. Supp. I:** 211
Hesse, Hermann, **Supp. V:** 208
"Hetch Hetchy Valley" (Muir), **Supp. IX:** 185
He Who Gets Slapped (Andreyev), **II:** 425
"He Who Spits at the Sky" (Stegner), **Supp. IV Part 2:** 605
"He Will Not Leave a Note" (Ríos), **Supp. IV Part 2:** 548
Hewitt, James, **Supp. XV:** 240
Hewlett, Maurice, **I:** 359
Heyen, William, **Supp. XIII:** 285, 344; **Supp. XV:** 212
"Hey! Hey!" (Hughes), **Supp. I Part 1:** 327-328
Hey Rub-a-Dub-Dub (Dreiser), **I:** 515; **II:** 26; **Retro. Supp. II:** 104, 105, 108
"Hey Sailor, What Ship?" (Olsen), **Supp. XIII:** 293, 294, 298, **299**
Hiawatha (Longfellow), **Supp. I Part 1:** 79; **Supp. III Part 2:** 609, 610
"Hibernaculum" (Ammons), **Supp. VII:** 26-27
Hichborn, Mrs. Philip. *See* Wylie, Elinor

Hichborn, Philip, **Supp. I Part 2:** 707, 708
"Hic Jacet" (W. C. Williams), **Retro. Supp. I:** 414
Hickok, James Butler ("Wild Bill"), **Supp. V:** 229, 230
Hicks, Granville, **I:** 254, 259, 374; **II:** 26; **III:** 342, 355, 452; **Supp. I Part 1:** 361; **Supp. I Part 2:** 609; **Supp. IV Part 1:** 22; **Supp. IV Part 2:** 526; **Supp. VIII:** 96, 124; **Supp. XII:** 250; **Supp. XIII:** 263
Hicok, Bethany, **Retro. Supp. II:** 39
"Hidden" (Nye), **Supp. XIII:** 283
"Hidden Gardens" (Capote), **Supp. III Part 1:** 125
Hidden Law, The (Hecht), **Supp. X:** 58
"Hidden Name and Complex Fate" (Ellison), **Supp. II Part 1:** 245
Hidden Wound, The (Berry), **Supp. X:** 23, 25, 26-27, 29, 34, 35
"Hide-and-Seek" (Francis), **Supp. IX:** 81
"Hiding" (Minot), **Supp. VI:** 203, 206
Hiding Place (Wideman), **Supp. X:** 320, 321, 327, 329, 331-332, 333
Hienger, Jorg, **Supp. IV Part 1:** 106
Higgins, George, **Supp. IV Part 1:** 356
Higginson, Thomas Wentworth, **I:** 451-452, 453, 454, 456, 458, 459, 463, 464, 465, 470; **Retro. Supp. I:** 26, 31, 33, 35, 39, 40; **Supp. I Part 1:** 307, 371; **Supp. IV Part 2:** 430
"High Bridge above the Tagus River at Toledo, The" (W. C. Williams), **Retro. Supp. I:** 429
"High Dive: A Variant" (Kumin), **Supp. IV Part 2:** 442
"High Diver" (Francis), **Supp. IX:** 82
"Higher Keys, The" (Merrill), **Supp. III Part 1:** 335-336
Higher Learning in America, The (Veblen), **Supp. I Part 2:** 630, 631, 641, 642
Highet, Gilbert, **Supp. I Part 1:** 268
High Noon (film), **Supp. V:** 46
"High on Sadness" (Komunyakaa), **Supp. XIII:** 114
"High School Senior" (Olds), **Supp. X:** 212
Highsmith, Patricia, **Supp. IV Part 1:** 79, 94, 132
"High Tide" (Marquand), **III:** 56
High Tide in Tucson: Essays from Now or Never (Kingsolver), **Supp. VII:** 198, 201, 209
"High-Toned Old Christian Woman, A" (Stevens), **Retro. Supp. I:** 301
"Highway, The" (Merwin), **Supp. III Part 1:** 346

"Highway 99E from Chico" (Carver), **Supp. III Part 1:** 136
High Window, The (Chandler), **Supp. IV Part 1:** 127-129, 130, 131
Hijuelos, Oscar, **Supp. IV Part 1:** 54; **Supp. VIII: 73-91**
Hike and the Aeroplane (Lewis), **II:** 440-441
Hilberg, Raul, **Supp. V:** 267
Hildebrand, Al, **III:** 118
Hiler, Hilaire, **Retro. Supp. II:** 327; **Supp. III Part 2:** 617
"Hill, A" (Hecht), **Supp. X:** 59-60, 63
Hill, Abram, **Supp. XV:** 194
Hill, Hamlin, **Retro. Supp. II:** 286
Hill, James J., **Supp. I Part 2:** 644
Hill, Joe, **I:** 493
Hill, Lee, **Supp. XI:** 293, 294, 297, 299, 301, 305, 307
Hill, Patti, **I:** 289
Hill, Peggy, **Supp. XIII:** 163
"Hill, The" (Strand), **Supp. IV Part 2:** 627
"Hill, The" (Toomer), **Supp. III Part 2:** 486
Hill, Vernon, **Supp. I Part 2:** 397
"Hillcrest" (Robinson), **III:** 504
Hill-Lubin, Mildred A., **Supp. IV Part 1:** 13
Hillman, Sidney, **Supp. I Part 1:** 5
Hillringhouse, Mark, **Supp. IX:** 286, 288, 299
Hills Beyond, The (Wolfe), **IV:** 450, 451, 460, 461
"Hills Beyond, The" (Wolfe), **IV:** 460
Hillside and Seaside in Poetry (Larcom, ed.), **Supp. XIII:** 142
"Hillside Thaw, A" (Frost), **Retro. Supp. I:** 133
"Hills Like White Elephants" (Hemingway), **Retro. Supp. I:** 170
"Hill-Top View, A" (Jeffers), **Supp. II Part 2:** 417
"Hill Wife, The" (Frost), **II:** 154; **Retro. Supp. I:** 131
Hillyer, Catherine, **Supp. XV:** 244
Hillyer, Robert, **I:** 475; **Supp. IX:** 75; **Supp. XIV:**11
Hilton, James, **Supp. XIII:** 166
"Hiltons' Holiday, The" (Jewett), **II:** 391; **Retro. Supp. II:** 134
Him (Cummings), **I:** 429, 434-435
Himes, Chester, **Retro. Supp. II:** 117; **Supp. I Part 1:** 51, 325; **Supp. XIII:** 233
Himes, Chester Bomar, **Supp. XVI:135-146**
Himes, Norman, **Supp. V:** 128
"Him with His Foot in His Mouth" (Bellow), **Retro. Supp. II:** 34

Him with His Foot in His Mouth and Other Stories (Bellow), **Retro. Supp. II:** 31
Hinchman, Sandra K., **Supp. IV Part 1:** 210
Hindemith, Paul, **IV:** 357; **Supp. IV Part 1:** 81
Hindsell, Oliver, **Supp. XIII:** 162
Hindus, Milton, **Supp. XIV:**288, 291, 292, 293
Hines, Suzanne, **Supp. XIV:**151
Hinge Picture (Howe), **Supp. IV Part 2:** 423–424
"Hinterlands" (W. Gibson), **Supp. XVI:**123, 128
"Hippies: Slouching towards Bethlehem" (Didion), **Supp. IV Part 1:** 200
Hippolytus (Euripides), **II:** 543; **Supp. I Part 1:** 270
Hippolytus Temporizes (Doolittle), **Supp. I Part 1:** 270
"Hips" (Cisneros), **Supp. VII:** 61, 62
"Hipster's Hipster" (Ginsberg), **Supp. XIV:**141
Hirsch, Edward, **Supp. XV:** 78, 225; **Supp. XVII:** 23
Hirsch, Edward D., **Supp. V:** 177; **Supp. IX:** 262; **Supp. XIV:**15
Hirsch, Sidney, **Supp. XIV:**1. See Mttron-Hirsch, Sidney
Hirschfeld, Jane, **Supp. XVII:** 241
Hirschorn, Clive, **Supp. IV Part 2:** 577, 579
Hirson, Roger, **Supp. XI:** 343
"His Bride of the Tomb" (Dunbar), **Supp. II Part 1:** 196
"His Chest of Drawers" (Anderson), **I:** 113, 114
"His Last Day" (C. Himes), **Supp. XVI:**137
"His Lover" (Dubus), **Supp. VII:** 86
"His Music" (Dunn), **Supp. XI:** 149
"His Own Key" (Ríos), **Supp. IV Part 2:** 543
His Picture in the Papers (film; Emerson), **Supp. XVI:**185
His Religion and Hers (Gilman), **Supp. XI:** 209
Hiss, Alger, **Supp. XV:** 143
"Hiss, Chambers, and the Age of Innocence" (Fiedler), **Supp. XIII:** 99
"His Shield" (Moore), **III:** 211
"His Story" (Cisneros), **Supp. VII:** 67
His Thought Made Pockets & the Plane Buckt (Berryman), **I:** 170
"His Three Women" (Gioia), **Supp. XV:** 119–120
Histoire comparée des systèmes de philosophie (Gérando), **II:** 10

Historical and Moral View of the Origin and Progress of the French Revolution (Wollstonecraft), **Supp. I Part 1:** 126
"Historical Conceptualization" (Huizinga), **I:** 255
Historical Evidence and the Reading of Seventeenth-Century Poetry (Brooks), **Supp. XIV:**11
"Historical Interpretation of Literature, The" (Wilson), **IV:** 431, 433, 445
Historical Jesus, The: The Life of a Mediterranean Jewish Peasant (Crossan), **Supp. V:** 251
"Historical Value of Crèvecoeur's *Voyage ...*," (Adams), **Supp. I Part 1:** 251
"History" (Emerson), **II:** 13, 15
"History" (Hughes), **Supp. I Part 1:** 344
History (Lowell), **Retro. Supp. II:** 183, 190
"History" (Simic), **Supp. VIII:** 279
"History, Myth, and the Western Writer" (Stegner), **Supp. IV Part 2:** 596, 601
"History among the Rocks" (Warren), **IV:** 252
History as a Literary Art (Morison), **Supp. I Part 2:** 493
"History as Fate in E. L. Doctorow's Tale of a Western Town" (Arnold), **Supp. IV Part 1:** 220
"History Is the Memory of Time" (Olson), **Supp. II Part 2:** 574
"History Lessons" (Komunyakaa), **Supp. XIII:** 126
"History of a Literary Movement" (Nemerov), **III:** 270
"History of a Literary Radical, The" (Bourne), **I:** 215, 235, 236
History of a Radical: Essays by Randolph Bourne (Brooks), **I:** 245
"History of Buttons, The" (Goldbarth), **Supp. XII:** 187
History of English Literature (Taine), **III:** 323
History of English Prosody (Saintsbury), **Supp. XV:** 181
History of Fortus, The (Emerson), **II:** 8
History of Henry Esmond, The (Thackeray), **II:** 91, 130
History of Modern Poetry, A (Perkins), **Supp. I Part 2:** 475; **Supp. XV:** 185
History of My Heart (Pinsky), **Supp. VI:** 243, 244, 245
History of New York, from the Beginning of the World to the End of the Dutch Dynasty, A (Irving), **II:** 300–

303, 304, 310
History of Pendennis, The (Thackeray), **II:** 291
"History of Red, The" (Hogan), **Supp. IV Part 1:** 411
"History of Rodney, The" (Bass), **Supp. XVI:**20
History of Roxbury Town (Ellis), **Supp. I Part 1:** 99
History of the Conquest of Mexico (Prescott), **Retro. Supp. I:** 123
History of the Conquest of Peru (Morison, ed.), **Supp. I Part 2:** 494
History of the Dividing Line betwixt Virginia and North Carolina (Byrd), **Supp. IV Part 2:** 425
History of the Life and Voyages of Christopher Columbus, A (Irving), **II:** 310, 314
History of the Navy of the United States of America (Cooper), **I:** 347
History of the Rise and Fall of the Slavepower in America (Wilson), **Supp. XIV:**48, 49
History of the United States of America during the Administrations of Thomas Jefferson and James Madison (Adams), **I:** 6-9, 10, 20, 21
History of the Work of Redemption, A (Edwards), **I:** 560
History of United States Naval Operations in World War II (Morison), **Supp. I Part 2:** 490–492
History of Womankind in Western Europe, The, **Supp. XI:** 197
"History Through a Beard" (Morison), **Supp. I Part 2:** 490
His Toy, His Dream, His Rest (Berryman), **I:** 169, 170, 183, 184–186
"His Words" (Roethke), **III:** 544
Hitchcock, Ada. *See* MacLeish, Mrs. Archibald (Ada Hitchcock)
Hitchcock, Alfred, **IV:** 357; **Supp. IV Part 1:** 132; **Supp. VIII:** 177
Hitchcock, George, **Supp. X:** 127; **Supp. XVII:** 110
"Hitch Haiku" (Snyder), **Supp. VIII:** 297
"Hitch-Hikers, The" (Welty), **IV:** 262
Hitchins, Christopher, **Supp. VIII:** 241
Hitler, Adolf, **I:** 261, 290, 492; **II:** 146, 454, 561, 565, 592; **III:** 2, 3, 110, 115, 140, 156, 246, 298, 446; **IV:** 5, 17, 18, 298, 372; **Supp. I Part 2:** 431, 436, 446, 664; **Supp. V:** 290
Hitler, Wendy, **III:** 404
Hitler Lives? (film), **Supp. XVI:**102
Hix, H. L., **Supp. XV:** 114
Hnizdovsky, Jacques, **Supp. XIII:** 346

"Hoadley's Test Case in Indiana" (Neugeboren), **Supp. XVI:**219
Hoagland, Edward, **Supp. XIV:**80; **Supp. XVI:**277
"Hoarder, The" (Sexton), **Supp. II Part 2:** 692
"Hoarfrost" (C. Baxter), **Supp. XVII:** 15
Hoban, Phoebe, **Supp. XV:** 319, 325
Hobb, Gormley, **I:** 203
Hobbes, Thomas, **I:** 277; **II:** 9, 10, 540; **III:** 306; **IV:** 88; **Supp. XII:** 33; **Supp. XIV:**5, 7
Hobson, Geary, **Supp. IV Part 1:** 321; **Supp. IV Part 2:** 502
Hobson, J. A., **I:** 232
Hobson, John A., **Supp. I Part 2:** 650
Hobson, Laura Z., **III:** 151
Hocking, Agnes, **Supp. VIII:** 251
Hocking, William Ernest, **III:** 303
Hodges, Campbell B., **Supp. XIV:**8
Hodgson, Captain Joseph, **III:** 328
Hoffa, Jimmy, **I:** 493
Hoffenberg, Mason, **Supp. XI:** 294, 297, 299, 305
Hoffer, Eric, **Supp. VIII:** 188
Hoffman, Abbie, **Supp. XIV:**150
Hoffman, Alice, **Supp. X: 77-94; Supp. XIII:** 13
Hoffman, Allen, **Supp. XVII:** 42, 44
Hoffman, Daniel, **Retro. Supp. II:** 265
Hoffman, Daniel G., **I:** 405; **II:** 307; **Supp. XI:** 152
Hoffman, Dustin, **Supp. IV Part 1:** 236
Hoffman, E. T. A., **Supp. XVI:**157
Hoffman, Eva, **Supp. XVI:147-164**
Hoffman, Frederick J., **I:** 60, 67; **II:** 443; **IV:** 113
Hoffman, Josiah Ogden, **II:** 297, 300
Hoffman, Matilda, **II:** 300, 314
Hoffman, Paul, **Supp. XV:** 141-142
Hoffman, William M., **Supp. X:** 153
Hoffmann, E. T. A., **III:** 415
Hofmann, Hans, **Supp. XV:** 144
Ho for a Hat (W. J. Smith), **Supp. XIII:** 346
Hofstadter, Richard, **Supp. VIII:** 98, 99, 108
Hogan, Linda, **Supp. IV Part 1:** 324, 325, **397-418**
Hogan, Randolph, **Supp. XVI:**252-253
Hogarth, William, **Supp. XII:** 44
Hogg, James, **I:** 53; **Supp. I Part 1:** 349; **Supp. IX:** 275
Hoggart, Richard, **Supp. XIV:**299
Hohne, Karen, **Supp. V:** 147
Hojoki (Chomei), **IV:** 170
Holbrook, David, **Supp. I Part 2:** 526-527, 546

Holcroft, Thomas, **Supp. I Part 2:** 514
Holden, Jonathan, **Supp. XI:** 143
Holden, Raymond, **Supp. XIV:**121-122
Holden, William, **Supp. XI:** 307
Hölderlin, Friedrich, **Supp. XVI:**48
"Holding On" (Levine), **Supp. V:** 184
Holding the Line: Women in the Great Arizona Mine Strike of 1983 (Kingsolver), **Supp. VII:** 197, 201-202, 204
"Holding the Mirror Up to Nature" (Nemerov), **III:** 275, 276
"Hold Me" (Levine), **Supp. V:** 186
Hold the Press (film), **Supp. XIII:** 163
Hold with the Hares (Zinberg), **Supp. XV:** 197-198, **Supp. XV:** 203
"Hole in the Floor, A" (Wilbur), **Supp. III Part 2:** 556-557
Holiday (Barry), **Retro. Supp. I:** 104
"Holiday" (Porter), **III:** 454
Holiday, Billie, **Supp. I Part 1:** 80; **Supp. IV Part 1:** 2, 7
Holinshed, Raphael, **IV:** 370
Holland, Josiah, **Supp. I Part 2:** 420
Holland, Laurence Bedwell, **Retro. Supp. I:** 216
Holland, Mrs. Theodore, **I:** 453, 455, 465
Holland, Theodore, **I:** 453
Holland, William, **IV:** 381
Hollander, John, **Supp. III Part 2:** 541; **Supp. IV Part 2:** 642; **Supp. IX:** 50, 153, 155; **Supp. XII:** 254, 255, 260; **Supp. XV:** 256; **Supp. XVII:** 112
Holley, Marietta, **Supp. XIII:** 152
Hollinghurst, Alan, **Supp. XIII:** 52
Hollis, Thomas Brand, **Supp. I Part 2:** 514
Hollow Men, The (Eliot), **I:** 574, 575, 578-579, 580, 585; **III:** 586; **Retro. Supp. I:** 63, 64
"Hollow Tree, A" (R. Bly), **Supp. IV Part 1:** 64, 66
Hollyberrys at the Shore, The, **Supp. X:** 42
"Hollywood!" (Vidal), **Supp. IV Part 2:** 688
Hollywood: American Movie-City (Rand, unauthorized), **Supp. IV Part 2:** 519
Hollywood: A Novel of America in the 1920s (Vidal), **Supp. IV Part 2:** 677, 684, 686, 688, 690, 691
Hollywood Ending (film; Allen), **Supp. XV:** 11
Hollywood on Trial (film), **Supp. I Part 1:** 295
Holmes, Abiel, **Supp. I Part 1:** 300, 301, 302, 310
Holmes, John, **I:** 169; **Supp. II Part 1:** 87; **Supp. IV Part 2:** 440-441; **Supp. XIV:**119
Holmes, John Clellon, **Supp. XII:** 118; **Supp. XIV:**144, 150
Holmes, Mrs. Abiel (Sarah Wendell), **Supp. I Part 1:** 300
Holmes, Mrs. Oliver Wendell (Amelia Jackson), **Supp. I Part 1:** 303
Holmes, Oliver Wendell, **I:** 487; **II:** 225, 273-274, 402, 403; **III:** 81-82, 590, 591-592; **IV:** 429, 436; **Retro. Supp. II:** 155; **Supp. I Part 1:** 103, 243, 254, **299-319; Supp. I Part 2:** 405, 414, 415, 420, 593, 704, 705; **Supp. XI:** 194
Holmes, Oliver Wendell, Jr., **I:** 3, 19; **Supp. IV Part 2:** 422
Holmes, Steven J., **Supp. IX:** 172, 177
Holmes, Ted, **Supp. V:** 180
Holmes, William Henry, **Supp. IV Part 2:** 603-604
Holocaust (Reznikoff), **Supp. XIV:**281, **291-293**
Holocaust in American Life, The (Novick), **Supp. XVI:**154
Holt, Edwin E., **I:** 59
Holt, Felix, **II:** 179
Holt, Henry, **II:** 348; **III:** 587
Holt, Patricia, **Supp. XIV:**89
Holtby, Winifred, **Supp. I Part 2:** 720
Holy Ghostly, The (Shepard), **Supp. III Part 2:** 437-438, 447
"Holy Innocents, The" (Lowell), **II:** 539
Holy Sonnets (Donne), **IV:** 145; **Supp. I Part 1:** 367; **Supp. III Part 2:** 619; **Supp. XIII:** 130-131
"Holy Terror, A" (Bierce), **I:** 203
"Holy Terror, The" (Maxwell), **Supp. VIII:** 169
Holy the Firm (Dillard), **Supp. VI:** 23, **29**, 30, 31, 32
Holy War, The (Bunyan), **IV:** 156
"Homage to Arthur Rimbaud" (Wright), **Supp. V:** 339
Homage to Baudelaire (Duncan, ed.), **Supp. XV:** 75
Homage to Catalonia (Orwell), **Supp. XVII:** 229
"Homage to Che Guevara" (Banks), **Supp. V:** 5
Homage to Clio (Auden), **Supp. II Part 1:** 24
"Homage to Elizabeth Bishop" (Ivask, ed.), **Supp. I Part 1:** 96
"Homage to Ezra Pound" (Wright), **Supp. V:** 339
Homage to Frank O'Hara (Ashbery),

Supp. III Part 1: 2-3
"Homage to Franz Joseph Haydn" (Hecht), **Supp. X:** 69
"Homage to Hemingway" (Bishop), **IV:** 35
Homage to Mistress Bradstreet (Berryman), **I:** 168, 169, 170-171, 172, 174, 175, 178-183, 184, 186
"Homage to Paul Cézanne" (Wright), **Supp. V:** 341-342
Homage to Sextus Propertius (Pound), **Retro. Supp. I:** 290
"Homage to Sextus Propertius" (Pound), **III:** 462, 476; **Supp. III Part 2:** 622
"Homage to Shakespeare" (Cheever), **Supp. I Part 1:** 180
"Homage to the Empress of the Blues" (Hayden), **Supp. II Part 1:** 379
"Homage to the Memory of Wallace Stevens" (Justice), **Supp. VII:** 126
Homage to Theodore Dreiser (Warren), **I:** 517
Homans, Margaret, **Supp. X:** 229
"Home" (Hughes), **Supp. I Part 1:** 329, 330
"Home" (Mora), **Supp. XIII:** 217
Home (Updike), **Retro. Supp. I:** 320
"Home, Home on the Strange" (J. D. Reed), **Supp. XVI:** 174
Home: Social Essays (Baraka), **Supp. II Part 1:** 45, 61
"Home, Sweet Home" (Fante), **Supp. XI:** 164, 165
Home, The (Gilman), **Supp. XI:** 206-207
"Home, The" (Jarman), **Supp. XVII:** 116
"Home after Three Months Away" (Lowell), **II:** 547
Home and Colonial Library (Murray), **Retro. Supp. I:** 246
Home as Found (Cooper), **I:** 348, 349, 350, 351
Home at the End of the World, A (Cunningham), **Supp. XV:** 59-62, 63
"Home Away from Home, A" (Humphrey), **Supp. IX:** 101
Home Book of Shakespeare Quotations (Stevenson), **Supp. XIV:** 120
"Home Burial" (Frost), **Retro. Supp. I:** 124, 125, 128, **129-130**; **Supp. VIII:** 31
"Home Burial" (R. Frost), **Supp. XV:** 159
Homecoming (Alvarez), **Supp. VII:** 1, 3-5, 9
"Homecoming" (Carruth), **Supp. XVI:** 55

"Homecoming" (McGrath), **Supp. X:** 116
"Homecoming, The" (Gioia), **Supp. XV:** 123, 124
Homecoming, The (Wilson), **Supp. VIII:** 330
Homecoming Game, The (Nemerov), **III:** 268, 282, 284-285
"Home during a Tropical Snowstorm I Feed My Father Lunch" (Karr), **Supp. XI:** 241-242, 248
Home Economics (Berry), **Supp. X:** 28, 31-32, 35, 36, 37
Home from the Hill (film), **Supp. IX:** 95
Home from the Hill (Humphrey), **Supp. IX:** 93, 95, **96-98**, 104, 106, 109
"Home Grown" (Vital), **Supp. XVI:** 160
"Homeland" (Merwin), **Supp. III Part 1:** 351
Homeland and Other Stories (Kingsolver), **Supp. VII:** 199, 202-204, 207
Home on the Range (Baraka), **Supp. II Part 1:** 47
Home Place, The (Morris), **III:** 221, 222, 232
Homer, **I:** 312, 433; **II:** 6, 8, 133, 302, 543, 544, 552; **III:** 14, 21, 278, 453, 457, 473, 567; **IV:** 54, 371; **Retro. Supp. I:** 59; **Supp. I Part 1:** 158, 283; **Supp. I Part 2:** 494; **Supp. X:** 36, 120, 122; **Supp. XIV:** 21; **Supp. XVII:** 70, 227
Homer, Louise, **Retro. Supp. I:** 10
"Home Range" (Leopold), **Supp. XIV:** 184, 185
"Homesick Blues" (Hughes), **Supp. I Part 1:** 327
Home to Harlem (McKay), **Supp. X:** 132, 137-138, **138-139**
Homeward Bound (Cooper), **I:** 348
"Homeward Star, The" (Palmer), **Supp. XV:** 81-82
Homewood trilogy (Wideman), **Supp. X:** 319
"Homework" (Cameron), **Supp. XII:** 80, **83**, 84
"Homily" (Tate), **IV:** 121-122
"Homme Moyen Sensuel, L'" (Pound), **III:** 462
Homme révolté, L' (Camus), **III:** 306
"Homoeopathy and Its Kindred Delusions" (Holmes), **Supp. I Part 1:** 303-304, 305
Homo Ludens (Huizinga), **II:** 416-417, 425
"Homosexual Villain, The" (Mailer), **III:** 36

"Homo Will Not Inherit" (Doty), **Supp. XI:** 128
Hone and Strong Diaries of Old Manhattan, The (Auchincloss, ed.), **Supp. IV Part 1:** 23
"Honey" (Beattie), **Supp. V:** 33
"Honey" (Wright), **Supp. III Part 2:** 589
"Honey, We'll Be Brave" (Farrell), **II:** 45
Honey and Salt (Sandburg), **III:** 594-596
"Honey and Salt" (Sandburg), **III:** 594
"Honey Babe" (Hughes), **Supp. I Part 1:** 334
"Honey Tree, The" (Oliver), **Supp. VII:** 236
Hong, Maxine. See Kingston, Maxine Hong
Hongo, Garrett, **Supp. X:** 292; **Supp. XIII:** 114; **Supp. XVII:** 112
"Honkytonk" (Shapiro), **Supp. II Part 2:** 705
"Honky Tonk in Cleveland, Ohio" (Sandburg), **III:** 585
Honorable Men (Auchincloss), **Supp. IV Part 1:** 23
Honor Thy Father (Talese), **Supp. XVII:** 204-205, 210
Hood, Tom, **I:** 195
"Hoodoo in America" (Hurston), **Supp. VI:** 153-154
"Hook" (Wright), **Supp. III Part 2:** 604
Hook, Sidney, **I:** 265; **Supp. IV Part 2:** 527; **Supp. VIII:** 96, 100; **Supp. XIV:** 3
Hooker, Adelaide. See Marquand, Mrs. John P. (Adelaide Hooker)
Hooker, Isabella Beecher, **Supp. XI:** 193
Hooker, Samuel, **IV:** 162, 165
Hooker, Thomas, **II:** 15-16; **IV:** 162
Hooper, Marian. See Adams, Mrs. Henry (Marian Hooper)
Hoosier Holiday, A (Dreiser), **Retro. Supp. II:** 104
Hoover, Herbert, **Supp. I Part 2:** 638
Hoover, J. Edgar, **Supp. XIII:** 170
Hoover, Paul, **Supp. XV:** 179
"Hope" (Jarrell), **II:** 389
"Hope" (Matthews), **Supp. IX:** 163
Hope, A. D., **Supp. XIII:** 347
Hope, Lynn, **Supp. II Part 1:** 38
"Hope Atherton's Wanderings" (Howe), **Supp. IV Part 2:** 432
Hope of Heaven (O'Hara), **III:** 361
"Hop-Frog" (Poe), **Retro. Supp. II:** 264, 268, 269
Hopkin, Pauline, **Supp. XVI:** 143

Hopkins, Anne Yale, **Supp. I Part 1:** 100, 102, 113
Hopkins, Gerard Manley, **I:** 171, 179, 397, 401, 522, 525, 533; **II:** 537; **III:** 197, 209, 523; **IV:** 129, 135, 141, 421; **Retro. Supp. II:** 40; **Supp. I Part 1:** 79, 81, 94; **Supp. III Part 2:** 551; **Supp. IV Part 1:** 178; **Supp. IV Part 2:** 637, 638, 639, 641, 643; **Supp. V:** 337; **Supp. IX:** 39, 42; **Supp. X:** 61, 115; **Supp. XIII:** 294; **Supp. XIV:83; Supp. XV:** 250, 347; **Supp. XVI:**282; **Supp. XVII:** 241
Hopkins, L. A., **I:** 502
Hopkins, Lemuel, **Supp. II Part 1:** 70
Hopkins, Miriam, **IV:** 381; **Supp. I Part 1:** 281
Hopkins, Samuel, **I:** 547, 549
Hopkins, Vivian, **II:** 20
Hopkinson, Francis, **Supp. I Part 2:** 504
Hopper (Strand), **Supp. IV Part 2:** 632
Hopper, Dennis, **Supp. XI:** 293, 308
Hopper, Edward, **IV:** 411, 413; **Supp. IV Part 2:** 619, 623, 631, 634
Hopwood, Avery, **Supp. IV Part 2:** 573
Horace, **II:** 8, 154, 169, 543, 552, 568; **III:** 15; **IV:** 89; **Supp. I Part 2:** 423; **Supp. IX:** 152; **Supp. X:** 65; **Supp. XII:** 258, 260, 262
Horae Canonicae (Auden), **Supp. II Part 1:** 21
"Horatian Ode" (Marvell), **IV:** 135
"Horatian Ode upon Cromwell's Return from Ireland" (Marvell), **Supp. XIV:**10
Horgan, Paul, **Supp. XV:** 46, 49, 52
Horkheimer, Max, **Supp. I Part 2:** 645; **Supp. IV Part 1:** 301
Horn, Dara, **Supp. XVII:** 50
Horn, Mother, **Supp. I Part 1:** 49, 54
Hornby, Nick, **Supp. XII:** 286
"Horn of Plenty" (Hughes), **Retro. Supp. I:** 210; **Supp. I Part 1:** 342
Horovitz, Israel, **Supp. XV:** 321
Horowitz, James. *See* Salter, James
Horowitz, Mark, **Supp. V:** 219, 231
"Horse, The" (Levine), **Supp. V:** 182
"Horse, The" (Wright), **Supp. III Part 2:** 592, 601
Horse Eats Hay (play), **Supp. IV Part 1:** 82
Horse Feathers (film), **Supp. IV Part 1:** 384
Horse Has Six Legs, The (Simic), **Supp. VIII:** 272
"Horselaugh on Dibber Lannon" (Fante), **Supp. XI:** 164

Horseman, Pass By (McMurtry), **Supp. V:** 220-221, 224
"Horses" (Doty), **Supp. XI:** 122
Horses and Men (Anderson), **I:** 112-113, 114
"Horses and Men in Rain" (Sandburg), **III:** 584
"Horse Show, The" (W. C. Williams), **Retro. Supp. I:** 423
Horses Make a Landscape More Beautiful (Walker), **Supp. III Part 2:** 521, 533
"Horse Thief" (Caldwell), **I:** 310
"Horsie" (Parker), **Supp. IX:** 193
Horton, Philip, **I:** 383, 386, 387, 393, 441; **Supp. XV:** 138
Horton Hatches the Egg (Geisel), **Supp. XVI:**100, 112
Horton Hears a Who! (Geisel), **Supp. XVI:**102
Hosea (biblical book), **II:** 166
Hospers, John, **Supp. IV Part 2:** 528
Hospital, Janette Turner, **Supp. IV Part 1:** 311-302
Hospital Sketches (Alcott), **Supp. I Part 1:** 34, 35
Hostages to Fortune (Humphrey), **Supp. IX:** 96, **104-106**, 109
"Hot Dog" (Stern), **Supp. IX: 298-299**
"Hotel Bar" (McClatchy), **Supp. XII:** 269
Hotel Dwellers, The (Lacy), **Supp. XV:** 205
Hotel Insomnia (Simic), **Supp. VIII:** 280, **281-282**
Hotel Lambosa and Other Stories (Koch), **Supp. XV:** 186
Hotel New Hampshire, The (Irving), **Supp. VI:** 163, 164, **172-173**, 177, 179
"Hot-Foot Hannibal" (Chesnutt), **Supp. XIV:**60
"Hot Night on Water Street" (Simpson), **Supp. IX:** 269, 270
"Hot Time, A" (Gunn Allen), **Supp. IV Part 1:** 333
Houdini, Harry, **IV:** 437
"Hound of Heaven" (Thompson), **Retro. Supp. I:** 55
"Hourglass, The" (Kees), **Supp. XV:** 147
"Hour in Chartres, An" (Bourne), **I:** 228
Hours, The (Cunningham), **Supp. XII:** 80; **Supp. XV: 65-68**
"Hours before Eternity" (Caldwell), **I:** 291
House, Bridge, Fountain, Gate (Kumin), **Supp. IV Part 2:** 448, 449, 451, 454

House, Edward, **Supp. I Part 2:** 643
"House, The" (Merrill), **Supp. III Part 1:** 323
House at Pooh Corner, The (Milne), **Supp. IX:** 189
House Behind the Cedars, The (Chesnutt), **Supp. XIV:69-71**
Houseboat Days (Ashbery), **Supp. III Part 1:** 18-20
Housebreaker of Shady Hill and Other Stories, The (Cheever), **Supp. I Part 1:** 184
"House by the Sea, The" (E. Stoddard), **Supp. XV:** 277
House by the Sea, The (Sarton), **Supp. VIII:** 264
House Divided, A (Buck), **Supp. II Part 1:** 118
"House Divided, The/La Casa Divida" (Kingsolver), **Supp. VII:** 207
"House Guest" (Bishop), **Retro. Supp. II:** 49; **Supp. I Part 1:** 93
Household Saints (film), **Supp. XVI:**256
Household Saints (Prose), **Supp. XVI:**252-253, 254, 261
"House in Athens, The" (Merrill), **Supp. III Part 1:** 323
House in the Uplands, A (Caldwell), **I:** 297, 301, 306
"House in Turk Street, The" (Hammett), **Supp. IV Part 1:** 344
"House in Winter, The" (Sarton), **Supp. VIII:** 259
"Housekeeping" (Alvarez), **Supp. VII:** 3-5, 10
"Housekeeping for Men" (Bourne), **I:** 231
House Made of Dawn (Momaday), **Supp. IV Part 1:** 274, 323, 326; **Supp. IV Part 2:** 479, 480, 481-484, 485, 486, 504, 562
Houseman, John, **Supp. IV Part 1:** 173
House of Dust, The: A Symphony (Aiken), **I:** 50
House of Earth trilogy (Buck), **Supp. II Part 1:** 118, 123
House of Five Talents, The (Auchincloss), **Supp. IV Part 1:** 21, 25-27
"House of Flowers" (Capote), **Supp. III Part 1:** 123
House of Games (Mamet), **Supp. XIV:**243
House of Houses (Mora), **Supp. XIII:** 213, 215, 218, 219, 223-224, **225-227**, 228, 229
House of Incest (Nin), **Supp. III Part 1:** 43; **Supp. X:** 187, 190, 193

House of Life, The: Rachel Carson at Work (Brooks), **Supp. IX:** 26

House of Light (Oliver), **Supp. VII:** 238-240

House of Mirth, The (Wharton), **II:** 180, 193; **IV:** 311-313, 314, 316, 318, 323, 327; **Retro. Supp. I:** 360, 366, 367, **367-370,** 373, 380

"House of Mist, The" (Rand), **Supp. IV Part 2:** 524

"House of My Own, A" (Cisneros), **Supp. VII:** 64

"House of Night, The" (Freneau), **Supp. II Part 1:** 259, 260

"House of Representatives and Me, The" (Conroy), **Supp. XVI:**75

House of the Far and Lost, The (Wolfe), **IV:** 456

"House of the Injured, The" (Haines), **Supp. XII:** 203

House of the Prophet, The (Auchincloss), **Supp. IV Part 1:** 31

House of the Seven Gables (Hawthorne), **I:** 106; **II:** 60, 224, 225, 231, 237, 239, 240-241, 243, 244; **Retro. Supp. I:** 63, 149, **160-162,** 163, 164; **Supp. I Part 2:** 579

House of the Solitary Maggot, The (Purdy), **Supp. VII:** 274-275

"House on Main Street, The" (B. Kelly), **Supp. XVII:** 127

House on Mango Street, The (Cisneros), **Supp. VII:** 58, 59-64, 65, 66, 67, 68, 72

"House on Mango Street, The" (Cisneros), **Supp. VII:** 59

House on Marshland, The (Glück), **Supp. V:** 81-83, 84

"House on the Heights, A" (Capote), **Supp. III Part 1:** 120

"House on the Hill, The" (Robinson), **III:** 505, 524

"House on 15th S.W., The" (Hugo), **Supp. VI:** 140

"Houses" (Hogan), **Supp. IV Part 1:** 402

"Houses, The" (Merwin), **Supp. III Part 1:** 354

"Houses of the Spirit" (Karr), **Supp. XI:** 250

"House Sparrows" (Hecht), **Supp. X:** 68

House That Tai Maing Built, The (Lee), **Supp. X:** 291

"House Unroofed by the Gale" (Tu Fu), **II:** 526

"House Where Mark Twain Was Born, The" (Masters), **Supp. I Part 2:** 472

"Housewife" (Sexton), **Supp. II Part 2:** 682

Housman, A. E., **III:** 15, 136, 606; **Supp. II Part 1:** 4; **Supp. IV Part 1:** 165; **Supp. XV:** 40-41

Houston Trilogy (McMurtry), **Supp. V:** 223-225

How" (Ginsberg), **Supp. XIV:**142, 143

"How" (Moore), **Supp. X:** 167

"How About This?" (Carver), **Supp. III Part 1:** 141

"How Annandale Went Out" (Robinson), **III:** 513

Howard, Ben, **Supp. XVI:**54

Howard, Gerald, **Supp. XII:** 21

Howard, Jane, **Retro. Supp. I:** 334

Howard, June, **Retro. Supp. II:** 139

Howard, Leon, **Supp. I Part 2:** 408, 422, 423

Howard, Maureen, **Supp. XII:** 285; **Supp. XVII:** 183

Howard, Richard, **Retro. Supp. II:** 43; **Supp. IV Part 2:** 624, 626, 640; **Supp. VIII:** 273; **Supp. IX:** 324, 326; **Supp. X:** 152; **Supp. XI:** 317; **Supp. XII:** 254; **Supp. XIII:** 76; **Supp. XV:** 23, 24

Howard, Vilma, **Retro. Supp. II:** 111, 112

Howards, J. Z., **Supp. VIII:** 178

Howards End (Forster), **Supp. XII:** 87

Howarth, Cora, **I:** 408, 409

Howbah Indians (Ortiz), **Supp. IV Part 2:** 513

"How Black Sees Green and Red" (McKay), **Supp. X:** 136

"How David Did Not Care" (R. Bly), **Supp. IV Part 1:** 73

Howe, E.W., **I:** 106

Howe, Florence, **Supp. XIII:** 295, 306

Howe, Harriet, **Supp. XI:** 200, 201

Howe, Irving, **IV:** 10; **Retro. Supp. I:** 369; **Retro. Supp. II:** 112, 286; **Supp. I Part 2:** 432; **Supp. II Part 1:** 99; **Supp. VI:** **113-129;** **Supp. VIII:** 93, 232; **Supp. IX:** 227; **Supp. X:** 203, 245; **Supp. XII:** 160; **Supp. XIII:** 98; **Supp. XVII:** 50

Howe, Irwing, **Supp. XIV:**103-104, 104

Howe, James Wong, **Supp. I Part 1:** 281; **Supp. V:** 223

Howe, Julia Ward, **III:** 505; **Retro. Supp. II:** 135

Howe, M. A. DeWolfe, **I:** 258; **II:** 406; **Supp. XIV:**54

Howe, Mary Manning, **Supp. IV Part 2:** 422

Howe, Samuel, **Supp. I Part 1:** 153

Howe, Susan, **Retro. Supp. I:** 33, 43; **Supp. IV Part 2: 419-438;** **Supp. XVI:**284

Howell, Chris, **Supp. XIII:** 112

Howell, James, **II:** 111

Howells: His Life and World (Brooks), **I:** 254

Howells, Margaret, **II:** 271

Howells, Mrs. William Dean (Elinor Mead), **II:** 273

Howells, William C., **II:** 273

Howells, William Dean, **I:** 109, 192, 204, 210, 211, 254, 355, 407, 411, 418, 459, 469; **II:** 127-128, 130, 131, 136, 137, 138, 140, **271-294,** 322, 331-332, 338, 397-398, 400, 415, 444, 451, 556; **III:** 51, 118, 314, 327-328, 461, 576, 607; **IV:** 192, 202, 342, 349; **Retro. Supp. I:** 220, 334, 362, 378; **Retro. Supp. II:** 93, 101, 135, 288; **Supp. I Part 1:** 306, 318, 357, 360, 368; **Supp. I Part 2:** 414, 420, 645-646; **Supp. II Part 1:** 198, 352; **Supp. IV Part 2:** 678; **Supp. VIII:** 98, 101, 102; **Supp. XI:** 198, 200; **Supp. XIV:**45-46; **Supp. XV:** 269, 274, 285, 287

Howells, Winifred, **II:** 271

"Howells as Anti-Novelist" (Updike), **Retro. Supp. I:** 334

Hower, Edward, **Supp. XII:** 330, 343

Howes, Barbara, **Supp. XIII:** 331

How Good Is David Mamet, Anyway? (Heilpern), **Supp. XIV:**242

"How I Became a Shadow" (Purdy), **Supp. VII:** 269

"How I Came to Vedanta" (Isherwood), **Supp. XIV:**164

"How I Learned to Sweep" (Alvarez), **Supp. VII:** 4

"How I Spent My Forties" (Wasserstein), **Supp. XV:** 325, 330, 332

"How It Began" (Stafford), **Supp. XI:** 327

"How It Feels to Be Colored Me" (Hurston), **Supp. VI:** 152

"How It Is" (Everwine), **Supp. XV:** 79, 86

"How I Told My Child About Race" (Brooks), **Supp. III Part 1:** 78

"How I Went to the Mines" (Harte), **Supp. II Part 1:** 336

"How I Write" (Welty), **IV:** 279, 280

"How Jonah Did Not Care" (R. Bly), **Supp. IV Part 1:** 73

Howl (Ginsberg), **Retro. Supp. I:** 426; **Supp. III Part 1:** 92; **Supp. IV Part 1:** 90; **Supp. V:** 336; **Supp. VIII:** 290; **Supp. XIV:**15, 126, 157

Howl: Original Draft Facsimile, Transcript and Variant Versions (Gimsberg), **Supp. XIV:**142

Howl and Other Poems (Ginsberg), **Supp. II Part 1:** 308, 317-318, 319; **Supp. X:** 123
Howlett, William, **Retro. Supp. I:** 17
"How Many Midnights" (Bowles), **Supp. IV Part 1:** 86-87
"How Many Nights" (Kinnell), **Supp. III Part 1:** 245-246
How Much? (Blechman), **Supp. I Part 1:** 290
"How Much Are You Worth" (Salinas), **Supp. XIII:** 325-326
"How Much Earth" (Levine), **Supp. V:** 184
How Much Earth: The Fresno Poets (Buckley, Oliveira, and Williams, eds.), **Supp. XIII:** 313
"How Not to Forget" (Bartov), **Supp. XVI:** 153-154
"How Poetry Comes to Me" (Corso), **Supp. XII:** 122
"How Poetry Comes to Me" (Snyder), **Supp. VIII:** 305
How Reading Changed My Life (Quindlen), **Supp. XVII:** 167, 179-180
"How She Came By Her Name: An Interview with Louis Massiah" (Bambara), **Supp. XI:** 20
"How Soon Hath Time" (Ransom), **IV:** 123
How Stella Got Her Groove Back (McMillan), **Supp. XIII:** 185, **190-191**
How the Alligator Missed Breakfast (Kinney), **Supp. III Part 1:** 235, 253
"How the Devil Came Down Division Street" (Algren), **Supp. IX:** 3
How the García Girls Lost Their Accents (Alvarez), **Supp. VII:** 3, 5-9, 11, 15, 17, 18
How the Grinch Stole Christmas! (Geisel), **Supp. XVI:** 102
How the Other Half Lives (Riis), **I:** 293
"How the Saint Did Not Care" (R. Bly), **Supp. IV Part 1:** 73
"How the Women Went from Dover" (Whittier), **Supp. I Part 2:** 694, 696, 697
"How To" (Carruth), **Supp. XVI:** 51
"How to Be an Other Woman" (Moore), **Supp. X:** 165, 167, 168
"How to Become a Writer" (Moore), **Supp. X:** 167, 168
"How to Be Happy: Another Memo to Myself" (Dunn), **Supp. XI:** 145
How To Cook a Wolf (M. F. K. Fisher), **Supp. XVII:** 84-85, 87
How to Develop Your Personality (Shellow), **Supp. I Part 2:** 608
How to Know God: The Yoga Aphorisms of Patanjali (Isherwood and Prabhavananda)), **Supp. XIV:** 164
"How To Like It" (Dobyns), **Supp. XIII: 85-86**
"How to Live. What to Do" (Stevens), **Retro. Supp. I:** 302
"How to Live on $36,000 a Year" (Fitzgerald), **Retro. Supp. I:** 105
"How Tom is Doin'" (Kees), **Supp. XV:** 143
How to Read (Pound), **Supp. VIII:** 291
How to Read a Novel (Gordon), **II:** 198
How to Save Your Own Life (Jong), **Supp. V:** 115, 123-125, 130
"How to Study Poetry" (Pound), **III:** 474
"How to Talk to Your Mother" (Moore), **Supp. X:** 167, 172
How to Win Friends and Influence People (Carnegie), **Supp. I Part 2:** 608
How to Worry Successfully (Seabury), **Supp. I Part 2:** 608
How to Write (Stein), **IV:** 32, 34, 35
"How to Write a Blackwood Article" (Poe), **III:** 425; **Retro. Supp. II:** 273
"How to Write a Memoir Like This" (Oates), **Supp. III Part 2:** 509
"How to Write Like Somebody Else" (Roethke), **III:** 540
How to Write Short Stories (Lardner), **II:** 430, 431
"How Vincentine Did Not Care" (R. Bly), **Supp. IV Part 1:** 73
How We Became Human: New and Selected Poems (Harjo), **Supp. XII: 230-232**
"How We Danced" (Sexton), **Supp. II Part 2:** 692
"How You Sound??" (Baraka), **Supp. II Part 1:** 30
Hoy, Philip, **Supp. X:** 56, 58
Hoyer, Linda Grace (pseudonym). See Updike, Mrs. Wesley
Hoyt, Constance, **Supp. I Part 2:** 707
Hoyt, Elinor Morton. See Wylie, Elinor
Hoyt, Henry (father), **Supp. I Part 2:** 707
Hoyt, Henry (son), **Supp. I Part 2:** 708
Hoyt, Henry Martyn, **Supp. I Part 2:** 707
Hsu, Kai-yu, **Supp. X:** 292
Hsu, Ruth Y., **Supp. XV:** 212
Hubba City (Reed), **Supp. X:** 241
Hubbard, Elbert, **I:** 98, 383
Hubbell, Jay B., **Supp. I Part 1:** 372
"Hubbub, The" (Ammons), **Supp. VII:** 35
Huber, François, **II:** 6
Huckins, Olga, **Supp. IX:** 32
Huckleberry Finn (Twain). See *Adventures of Huckleberry Finn, The* (Twain)
Hud (film), **Supp. V:** 223, 226
Hudgins, Andrew, **Supp. X:** 206; **Supp. XVII:** 111, 112
Hudson, Henry, **I:** 230
"Hudsonian Curlew, The" (Snyder), **Supp. VIII:** 302
Hudson River Bracketed (Wharton), **IV:** 326-327; **Retro. Supp. I:** 382
Huebsch, B. W., **III:** 110
Hueffer, Ford Madox, **Supp. I Part 1:** 257, 262. See also Ford, Ford Madox
Hug Dancing (Hearon), **Supp. VIII: 67-68**
Huge Season, The (Morris), **III:** 225-226, 227, 230, 232, 233, 238
Hugging the Jukebox (Nye), **Supp. XIII: 275-276**, 277
"Hugging the Jukebox" (Nye), **Supp. XIII:** 276
Hughes, Brigid, **Supp. XVI:** 247
Hughes, Carolyn, **Supp. XII:** 272, 285
Hughes, Frieda, **Supp. I Part 2:** 540, 541
Hughes, Glenn, **Supp. I Part 1:** 255
Hughes, H. Stuart, **Supp. VIII:** 240
Hughes, James Nathaniel, **Supp. I Part 1:** 321, 332
Hughes, Ken, **Supp. XI:** 307
Hughes, Langston, **Retro. Supp. I: 193-214; Retro. Supp. II:** 114, 115, 117, 120; **Supp. I Part 1: 320-348; Supp. II Part 1:** 31, 33, 61, 170, 173, 181, 227, 228, 233, 361; **Supp. III Part 1: 72-77; Supp. IV Part 1:** 15, 16, 164, 168, 169, 173, 243, 368; **Supp. VIII:** 213; **Supp. IX:** 306, 316; **Supp. X:** 131, 136, 139, 324; **Supp. XI:** 1; **Supp. XIII:** 75, 111, 132, 233; **Supp. XVI:** 135, 138
Hughes, Nicholas, **Supp. I Part 2:** 541
Hughes, Robert, **Supp. X:** 73
Hughes, Ted, **IV:** 3; **Retro. Supp. II:** 244, 245, 247, 257; **Supp. I Part 2:** 536, 537, 538, 539, 540, 541; **Supp. XV:** 117, 347, 348
Hughes, Thomas, **Supp. I Part 2:** 406
"Hugh Harper" (Bowles), **Supp. IV Part 1:** 94
Hughie (O'Neill), **III:** 385, 401, 405
Hugh Selwyn Mauberley (Pound), **I:** 66, 476; **III:** 9, 462-463, 465, 468; **Retro. Supp. I: 289-290**, 291, 299;

Supp. XIV:272
Hugo, Richard, **Supp. VI: 131-148**; **Supp. IX:** 296, 323, 324, 330; **Supp. XI:** 315, 317; **Supp. XII:** 178; **Supp. XIII:** 112, 113, 133
Hugo, Victor, **II:** 290, 490, 543; **Supp. IV Part 2:** 518; **Supp. IX:** 308
Hui-neng, **III:** 567
Huis Clos (Sartre), **Supp. IV Part 1:** 84
Huizinga, Johan, **I:** 225; **II:** 416-417, 418, 425
Hulbert, Ann, **Supp. XI:** 38-39
Hull, Lynda, **Supp. XI:** 131
Hulme, Thomas E., **I:** 68, 69, 475; **III:** 196, 209, 463-464, 465; **IV:** 122; **Supp. I Part 1:** 261, 262; **Supp. XV:** 43
Human, All Too Human (Nietzsche), **Supp. X:** 48
"Human Culture" (Emerson), **II:** 11-12
Human Factor, The (Greene), **Supp. V:** 298
"Human Figures" (Doty), **Supp. XI:** 123-124
"Human Geography" (Jarman), **Supp. XVII:** 116
"Human Immortality" (James), **II:** 353-354
"Human Life" (Emerson), **II:** 11-12
Human Rights, Human Wrongs: The Oxford Amnesty Lectures, 2001, **Supp. XVI:**155
Human Stain, The (P. Roth), **Retro. Supp. II:** 279, 289, 294-295
"Human Things" (Nemerov), **III:** 279
Human Universe (Olson), **Supp. II Part 2:** 571
"Human Universe" (Olson), **Supp. II Part 2:** 565, 567
Human Wishes (Hass), **Supp. VI:** 105-106, 107
Human Work (Gilman), **Supp. XI:** 206
Humbert, Humbert, **Supp. X:** 283
Humble Inquiry into the Rules of the Word of God, An, Concerning the Qualifications Requisite to a Complete Standing and Full Communion in the Visible Christian Church (Edwards), **I:** 548
Humboldt, Alexander von, **III:** 428
Humboldt's Gift (Bellow), **Retro. Supp. II:** 19, 28-29, 34; **Supp. XIII:** 320
Hume, David, **I:** 125; **II:** 349, 357, 480; **III:** 618
Humes, H. L. "Doc," **Supp. XI:** 294
Humes, Harold, **Supp. V:** 201; **Supp. XIV:**82
"Hummingbirds, The" (Welty), **IV:** 273

Humphrey, William, **Supp. IX: 93-112**; **Supp. XV:** 353
Humphreys, Christmas, **Supp. V:** 267
Humphreys, David, **Supp. II Part 1:** 65, 69, 70, 268
Humphreys, Josephine, **Supp. XII:** 311
Humphries, Rolfe, **III:** 124; **Retro. Supp. I:** 137
Hunchback of Notre Dame, The (film), **Supp. IV Part 1:** 101
Hunches in Bunches (Geisel), **Supp. XVI:**111
Huncke, Herbert, **Supp. XII:** 118; **Supp. XIV:137-153**
Huncke's Journal (Huncke), **Supp. XIV:**139, 144, 145, 146
Hundred Camels in the Courtyard, A (Bowles), **Supp. IV Part 1:** 90
"Hundred Collars, A" (Frost), **Retro. Supp. I:** 128; **Supp. XIII:** 147
Hundred Secret Senses, The (Tan), **Supp. X:** 289, 293, 295, 297, 298, 299
Hundred White Daffodils, A: Essays, Interviews, Newspaper Columns, and One Poem (Kenyon), **Supp. VII:** 160-162, 165, 166, 167, 174
Huneker, James, **III:** 102
Hunger (Hamsun), **Supp. XI:** 167
"Hunger" (Hogan), **Supp. IV Part 1:** 411
"Hunger ..." (Rich), **Supp. I Part 2:** 571
"Hungerfield" (Jeffers), **Supp. II Part 2:** 416-417, 436
Hungerfield and Other Poems (Jeffers), **Supp. II Part 2:** 422
Hunger of Memory: The Education of Richard Rodriguez (Rodriguez), **Supp. XIV:**297, 298, **298-302**, 310
Hungry Ghosts, The (Oates), **Supp. II Part 2:** 504, 510
Hungry Hearts (Prose), **Supp. XVI:**253
Hunnewell, Susannah, **Supp. VIII:** 83
Hunt, Harriot K., **Retro. Supp. II:** 146
Hunt, Leigh, **II:** 515-516; **Supp. XV:** 175
Hunt, Richard Morris, **IV:** 312
Hunt, Robert, **Supp. XV:** 42, 49, 52
Hunt, William, **II:** 343
"Hunter" (Bierds), **Supp. XVII:** 30
Hunter, Dianna, **Supp. XVI:**38
Hunter, Dr. Joseph, **II:** 217
Hunter, J. Paul, **Supp. IV Part 1:** 332
Hunter, Kim, **Supp. I Part 1:** 286
"Hunter of Doves" (Herbst), **Retro. Supp. II:** 325
"Hunter of the West, The" (Bryant), **Supp. I Part 1:** 155

Hunters, The (film), **Supp. IX:** 250
Hunters, The (Salter), **Supp. IX:** 246, **249-250**
Hunters and Gatherers (Prose), **Supp. XVI:**257
"Hunters in the Snow" (Brueghel), **I:** 174; **Retro. Supp. I:** 430
"Hunters in the Snow" (Wolff), **Supp. VII:** 339-340
"Hunter's Moon-Eating the Bear" (Oliver), **Supp. VII:** 234
"Hunter's Vision, The" (Bryant), **Supp. I Part 1:** 160
Hunting for Hope: A Father's Journey (Sanders), **Supp. XVI:**276-277, 278
"Hunting Is Not Those Heads on the Wall" (Baraka), **Supp. II Part 1:** 45
Huntington, Collis P., **I:** 198, 207
"Hunt in the Black Forest, The" (Jarrell), **II:** 379-380
Huntley, Jobe, **Supp. I Part 1:** 339
Hurray Home (Wideman), **Supp. X:** 320
"Hurricane, The" (Crane), **I:** 401
"Hurricane, The" (Freneau), **Supp. II Part 1:** 262
"Hurry Kane" (Lardner), **II:** 425, 426, 427
"Hurry up Please It's Time" (Sexton), **Supp. II Part 2:** 694, 695
Hurston, Zora Neale, **Retro. Supp. I:** 194, 198, 200, 201, 203; **Supp. I Part 1:** 325, 326, 332; **Supp. II Part 1:** 33; **Supp. IV Part 1:** 5, 11, 12, 164, 257; **Supp. VI: 149-161**; **Supp. VIII:** 214; **Supp. X:** 131, 139, 232, 242; **Supp. XI:** 85; **Supp. XIII:** 185, 233, 236, 295, 306
Hurt, John, **Supp. XIII:** 132
Husbands and Wives (film; Allen), **Supp. XV:** 12
Husband's Story, The (Shields), **Supp. VII:** 316. See also "Happenstance" (Shields)
Husserl, Edmund, **II:** 362, 363; **IV:** 491; **Supp. IV Part 1:** 42, 43
Hussey, Jo Ella, **Supp. XII:** 201
Hustler, The (film), **Supp. XI:** 306
Huston, John, **I:** 30, 31, 33, 35; **II:** 588; **III:** 161; **Supp. IV Part 1:** 102, 116, 355; **Supp. XI:** 307; **Supp. XIII:** 174
"Huswifery" (Taylor), **IV:** 161; **Supp. I Part 2:** 386
"Hut, The" (Sobin), **Supp. XVI:**284-285
Hutchens, John K., **Supp. IX:** 276
Hutcheson, Francis, **I:** 559
Hutchins, Patricia, **III:** 478
Hutchinson, Abigail, **I:** 562

Hutchinson, Anne, **Supp. I Part 1:** 100, 101, 113; **Supp. IV Part 2:** 434; **Supp. VIII:** 202, 205
Hutton, James, **Supp. IX:** 180
Huxley, Aldous, **II:** 454; **III:** 281, 428, 429-430; **IV:** 77, 435; **Supp. I Part 2:** 714; **Supp. XIV:** 3, 164; **Supp. XVI:** 189, 192
Huxley, Julian, **Supp. VIII:** 251; **Supp. X:** 108
Huxley, Juliette, **Supp. VIII:** 251, 265
Huxley, Thomas, **III:** 102, 108, 113, 281; **Retro. Supp. II:** 60, 65, 93
Huxley, Thomas Henry, **Supp. I Part 1:** 368
Huysmans, Joris Karl (Charles Marie Georges), **I:** 66; **III:** 315; **IV:** 286; **Retro. Supp. II:** 326
"Hwame, Koshkalaka, and the Rest: Lesbians in American Indian Cultures" (Gunn Allen), **Supp. IV Part 1:** 330
Hwang, David Henry, **Supp. X:** 292
"Hyacinth Drift" (Rawlings), **Supp. X: 226-227**
"Hydrangeas" (C. Frost), **Supp. XV:** 106
"Hydras, The" (Merwin), **Supp. III Part 1:** 349
"Hydriotaphia; or, Urne-Buriall" (Browne), **Supp. IX:** 136-137
Hydriotaphia, The; or, Death of Dr. Browne: An Epic Farce about Death and Primitive Capital Accumulation (Kushner), **Supp. IX:** 133, **136-138**
Hyman, Stanley Edgar, **I:** 129, 264, 363, 377, 379; **Retro. Supp. II:** 118; **Supp. IX:** 113, 114, 117, 118, 121, 122, 128
Hymen (Doolittle), **Supp. I Part 1:** 266
"Hymie's Bull" (Ellison), **Retro. Supp. II:** 124; **Supp. II Part 1:** 229
"Hymn Books" (Emerson), **II:** 10
"HYMN FOR LANIE POO" (Baraka), **Supp. II Part 1:** 31, 37
"Hymn from a Watermelon Pavilion" (Stevens), **IV:** 81
"Hymn of the Sea, A" (Bryant), **Supp. I Part 1:** 157, 163, 165
"Hymns of the Marshes" (Lanier), **Supp. I Part 1:** 364
"Hymn to Death" (Bryant), **Supp. I Part 1:** 169, 170
"Hymn to Earth" (Wylie), **Supp. I Part 2:** 727-729
"Hymn to the Night" (Longfellow), **Supp. I Part 2:** 409
Hynes, Jennifer, **Supp. XV:** 207
Hynes, Samuel, **Supp. XIV:** 159
Hyperion (Longfellow), **II:** 488, 489, 491-492, 496; **Retro. Supp. II:** 58, 155-156
"Hypocrite Auteur" (MacLeish), **III:** 19
"Hypocrite Swift" (Bogan), **Supp. III Part 1:** 55
"Hysteria" (Eliot), **I:** 570
I
I (Dixon), **Supp. XII:** 141, 155, **156-157**
I, etcetera (Sontag), **Supp. III Part 2:** 451-452, 469
I, Governor of California and How I Ended Poverty (Sinclair), **Supp. V:** 289
I: Six Nonlectures (Cummings), **I:** 430, 433, 434
"I, Too" (Hughes), **Retro. Supp. I:** 193, 199; **Supp. I Part 1:** 320
I Accuse! (film), **Supp. IV Part 2:** 683
"I Almost Remember" (Angelou), **Supp. IV Part 1:** 15
"'I Always Wanted You to Admire My Fasting'; or, Looking at Kafka"(P. Roth), **Retro. Supp. II:** 282
I am a Camera (Druten), **Supp. XIV:** 162
"I am a cowboy in the boat of Ra" (Reed), **Supp. X:** 242
"I Am a Dangerous Woman" (Harjo), **Supp. XII:** 216, 219
"I Am Alive" (Momaday), **Supp. IV Part 2:** 489
I Am a Sonnet (Goldbarth), **Supp. XII:** 181
"I Am a Writer of Truth" (Fante), **Supp. XI:** 167
"'I Am Cherry Alive,' the Little Girl Sang" (Schwartz), **Supp. II Part 2:** 663
"I Am Dying, Meester?" (Burroughs), **Supp. III Part 1:** 98
I Am Elijah Thrush (Purdy), **Supp. VII:** 274
"I Am in Love" (Stern), **Supp. IX:** 295
"I Am Not Flattered" (Francis), **Supp. IX:** 78
I Am! Says the Lamb (Roethke), **III:** 545
"I and My Chimney" (Melville), **III:** 91
I and Thou (Buber), **III:** 308
"I Apologize" (Komunyakaa), **Supp. XIII:** 120, **Supp. XIII:** 121
I Apologize for the Eyes in My Head (Komunyakaa), **Supp. XIII: 119-121**, 126
"I Believe I Shall Die an Impenetrable Secret": The Writings of Elizabeth Barstow Stoddard (Giovani), **Supp. XV:** 270
Ibsen, Henrik, **II:** 27, 276, 280, 291-292; **III:** 118, 145, 148, 149, 150, 151, 152, 154-155, 156, 161, 162, 165, 511, 523; **IV:** 397; **Retro. Supp. I:** 228; **Retro. Supp. II:** 94; **Supp. IV Part 2:** 522; **Supp. XIV:** 89; **Supp. XVII:** 100
"I Came Out of the Mother Naked" (R. Bly), **Supp. IV Part 1:** 62-63, 68
I Can Lick 30 Tigers Today! and Other Stories (Geisel), **Supp. XVI:** 108
"I Cannot Forget with What Fervid Devotion" (Bryant), **Supp. I Part 1:** 154
I Can Read with My Eyes Shut! (Geisel), **Supp. XVI:** 111
"I Can't Stand Your Books: A Writer Goes Home" (Gordon), **Supp. IV Part 1:** 314
"Icarium Mare" (Wilbur), **Supp. III Part 2:** 563
"Icarus in Winter" (C. Frost), **Supp. XV:** 94
Icarus's Mother (Shepard), **Supp. III Part 2:** 446
"Ice" (Bambara), **Supp. XI:** 16
"Iceberg, The" (Merwin), **Supp. III Part 1:** 345
Ice-Cream Headache, The, and Other Stories (Jones), **Supp. XI:** 215, 227
Ice Fire Water: A Leib Goldkorn Cocktail (Epstein), **Supp. XII: 164-166**
"Ice Fisherman, The" (C. Baxter), **Supp. XVII:** 15
"Ice House, The" (Gordon), **II:** 201
Iceman Cometh, The (O'Neill), **I:** 81; **III:** 151, 385, 386, 401, 402-403; **Supp. VIII:** 345; **Supp. XVI:** 193; **Supp. XVII:** 103
"Ice Palace, The" (Fitzgerald), **II:** 83, 88; **Retro. Supp. I:** 103
Ice-Shirt, The (Vollmann), **Supp. XVII:** 226, 231, 232, 233
"Ice Storm, The" (Ashbery), **Supp. III Part 1:** 26
"Ice-Storm, The" (Pinsky), **Supp. VI:** 247-248
"Ichabod" (Whittier), **Supp. I Part 2:** 687, 689-690; **Supp. XI:** 50
"Icicles" (Francis), **Supp. IX:** 83
"Icicles" (Gass), **Supp. VI:** 83
Ickes, Harold, **Supp. I Part 1:** 5
Iconographs (Swenson), **Supp. IV Part 2:** 638, 646-648, 651
"Icosaphere, The" (Moore), **III:** 213
"I Could Believe" (Levine), **Supp. V:** 189

"I Could Take" (Carruth), **Supp. XVI:**56

"I Cry, Love! Love!" (Roethke), **III:** 539-540

Ida (Stein), **IV:** 43, 45

"Idea, The" (Carver), **Supp. III Part 1:** 143

"Idea, The" (Strand), **Supp. IV Part 2:** 631

Ideal Husband (Wilde), **II:** 515

Idea of Florida in the American Literary Imagination, The (Rowe), **Supp. X:** 223

"Idea of Ice, The" (C. Baxter), **Supp. XVII:** 15

"Idea of Order at Key West, The" (Stevens), **IV:** 89-90; **Retro. Supp. I:** 302, 303, 313

Ideas of Order (Stevens), **Retro. Supp. I:** 296, 298, **302-303,** 303, 305

"Identity Theft: True Memory, False Memory, and the Holocaust" (R. Franklin), **Supp. XVI:**160

Ideograms in China (Michaux; Sobin, trans.), **Supp. XVI:**288

"Ideographs" (Olds), **Supp. X:** 205

Ides of March, The (Wilder), **IV:** 357, 372

"I Did Not Learn Their Names" (Ellison), **Retro. Supp. II:** 124

"I Died with the First Blow & Was Reborn Wrong" (Coleman), **Supp. XI:** 91

"Idiom of a Self, The" (Pinsky), **Supp. VI:** 240

"Idiot, The" (Crane), **I:** 401

Idiot, The (Dostoyevsky), **I:** 468

"Idiots First" (Malamud), **Supp. I Part 2:** 434-435, 437, 440-441

I Don't Need You Any More (A. Miller), **III:** 165

Idoru (W. Gibson), **Supp. XVI:**119, 124, **129-130**

"I Dream I'm the Death of Orpheus" (Rich), **Supp. I Part 2:** 557-558

I Dreamt I Became a Nymphomaniac! Imagining (Acker), **Supp. XII:** 4, 6, **8,** 11

Idylls of the King (Tennyson), **III:** 487; **Supp. I Part 2:** 410; **Supp. XIII:** 146

Idyl of Work, An (Larcom), **Supp. XIII:** 139, 142, 146-147, 150

"If" (Creeley), **Supp. IV Part 1:** 158

If Beale Street Could Talk (Baldwin), **Retro. Supp. II:** 13-14; **Supp. I Part 1:** 48, 59-60, 67

If Blessing Comes (Bambara), **Supp. XI:** 1

I Feel a Little Jumpy around You (Nye and Janeczko, eds.), **Supp. XIII:** 280

"I felt a Funeral, in my Brain" (Dickinson), **Retro. Supp. I:** 38

If He Hollers Let Him Go (C. Himes), **Supp. XVI:**135, 138-139, 142

"If I Could Be Like Wallace Stevens" (Stafford), **Supp. XI:** 327

"If I Could Only Live at the Pitch That Is Near Madness" (Eberhart), **I:** 523, 526-527

If I Die in a Combat Zone (O'Brien), **Supp. V:** 238, 239, 240, 245

"If I Had My Way" (Creeley), **Supp. IV Part 1:** 157

"*If I Might Be*" (Chopin), **Retro. Supp. II:** 61

"I Find the Real American Tragedy" (Dreiser), **Retro. Supp. II:** 105

If I Ran the Circus (Geisel), **Supp. XVI:**105

If I Ran the Zoo (Geisel), **Supp. XVI:**104-105

If It Die (Gide), **I:** 290

"If It Were Not for You" (Carruth), **Supp. XVI:**57

"If I Were a Man" (Gilman), **Supp. XI:** 207

"If I Were the Wind" (Leopold), **Supp. XIV:**184

If Morning Ever Comes (Tyler), **Supp. IV Part 2:** 658-659

If Mountains Die: A New Mexico Memoir (Nichols), **Supp. XIII:** 255, 257, 267

I Forgot to Go to Spain (Harrison), **Supp. VIII:** 39, **52-53**

If the River Was Whiskey (Boyle), **Supp. VIII:** 15-16

"If They Knew Yvonne" (Dubus), **Supp. VII:** 81

"If We Had Bacon" (H. Roth), **Supp. IX:** 232, 234

"If We Had Known" (Francis), **Supp. IX:** 78

"If We Must Die" (McKay), **Supp. IV Part 1:** 3; **Supp. X:** 132, 134

"If We Take All Gold" (Bogan), **Supp. III Part 1:** 52

If You Call This a Cry Song (Carruth), **Supp. XVI:**56

If You Want to Write (Ueland), **Supp. XVII:** 13

I Gaspiri (Lardner), **II:** 435

"I Gather the Limbs of Osiris" (Pound), **Retro. Supp. I:** 287

"I Give You Back" (Harjo), **Supp. XII:** 223

Ignatius of Loyola, **IV:** 151; **Supp. XI:** 162

Ignatow, David, **Supp. XIII:** 275

"Ignis Fatuus" (Tate), **IV:** 128

"I Go Back to May 1937" (Olds), **Supp. X:** 207

I Go Dreaming Serenades (Salinas), **Supp. XIII:** 316

I Got the Blues (Odets), **Supp. II Part 2:** 530

Iguana Killer, The (Ríos), **Supp. IV Part 2:** 542-544

"I Had Eight Birds Hatcht in One Nest" (Bradstreet), **Supp. I Part 1:** 102, 115, 117, 119

"I had no time to Hate" (Dickinson), **Retro. Supp. I:** 44-45, 46

I Had Trouble in Getting to Solla Sollew (Geisel), **Supp. XVI:**108, 109

"I Have a Rendezvous with Life" (Cullen), **Supp. IV Part 1:** 168

"I Have Increased Power" (Ginsberg), **Supp. II Part 1:** 313

"I Have Seen Black Hands" (Wright), **Supp. II Part 1:** 228

"I Hear an Army" (Joyce), **Supp. I Part 1:** 262

"I heard a Fly buzz when I died" (Dickinson), **Retro. Supp. I:** 38

"I Heard Immanuel Singing" (Lindsay), **Supp. I Part 2:** 379

"I Hear It Was Charged against Me" (Whitman), **IV:** 343

"I Held a Shelley Manuscript" (Corso), **Supp. XII:** 128

"I Held His Name" (Ríos), **Supp. IV Part 2:** 547

I Knew a Phoenix (Sarton), **Supp. VIII:** 249, 251-252

"I Know a Man" (Creeley), **Supp. IV Part 1:** 147-148, 149

I Know Some Things: Stories about Childhood by Contemporary Writers (Moore, ed.), **Supp. X:** 175

"I Know Why the Caged Bird Cannot Read" (Prose), **Supp. XVI:**259

I Know Why the Caged Bird Sings (Angelou), **Supp. IV Part 1:** 2-4, 5, 7, 11, 12, 13, 14, 15, 17; **Supp. XVI:**259

"Ikon: The Harrowing of Hell" (Levertov), **Supp. III Part 1:** 284

Ile (O'Neill), **III:** 388

"I Let Him Take Me" (Cisneros), **Supp. VII:** 71

Iliad (Bryant, trans.), **Supp. I Part 1:** 158

Iliad (Homer), **II:** 470; **Supp. IV Part 2:** 631; **Supp. IX:** 211; **Supp. X:** 114

Iliad (Pope, trans.), **Supp. I Part 1:** 152

Iliad, The (Homer), **Supp. XVII:** 117

"I like to see it lap the Miles" (Dickinson), **Retro. Supp. I:** 37

"I Live Up Here" (Merwin), **Supp. III Part 1:** 349

"Illegal Alien" (Mora), **Supp. XIII:** 215

"Illegal Days, The" (Paley), **Supp. VI:** 222

"Illegibility" (F. Wright), **Supp. XVII:** 244

Illig, Joyce, **Retro. Supp. II:** 20

"Illinois" (Masters), **Supp. I Part 2:** 458

"Illinois Bus Ride" (Leopold), **Supp. XIV:** 189

Illinois Poems (Masters), **Supp. I Part 2:** 472

"Illinois Village, The" (Lindsay), **Supp. I Part 2:** 381

"Ill-Lit" (F. Wright), **Supp. XVII:** 245

Ill-Lit: Selected & New Poems (F. Wright), **Supp. XVII:** 245

Illness as Metaphor (Sontag), **Supp. III Part 2:** 452, 461, 466

I'll Take My Stand ("Twelve Southerners"), **II:** 196; **III:** 496; **IV:** 125, 237; **Supp. X:** 25, 52-53; **Supp. XIV:** 3

"I'll Take You to Tennessee" (Connell), **Supp. XIV:** 82

Illumination (Frederic), **II:** 141

Illumination Night (Hoffman), **Supp. X:** 85, **86**, 88, 89

Illusion comique, L' (Corneille), **Supp. IX:** 138

"Illusion of Eternity, The" (Eberhart), **I:** 541

"Illusion of Fiction in Frank Conroy's *Stop-Time*, The" (R. Ramsey), **Supp. XVI:** 69

Illusions (Dash; film), **Supp. XI:** 20

"Illusions" (Emerson), **II:** 2, 5, 14, 16

Illustrated Man, The (Bradbury), **Supp. IV Part 1:** 102, 103, 113

Illustrations of Political Economy (Martineau), **Supp. II Part 1:** 288

"I Look at My Hand" (Swenson), **Supp. IV Part 2:** 638, 647

I Love Gootie: My Grandmother's Story (Apple), **Supp. XVII:** 9-10

I Love Myself When I Am Laughing ... : A Zora Neale Hurston Reader (Walker), **Supp. III Part 2:** 531, 532

"I'm a Fool" (Anderson), **I:** 113, 114, 116; **Supp. I Part 2:** 430

Image and Idea (Rahv), **Supp. II Part 1:** 146

Image and the Law, The (Nemerov), **III:** 268, 269-271, 272

"Images" (Hass), **Supp. VI:** 103

"Images and 'Images'" (Simic), **Supp. VIII:** 274

"Images for Godard" (Rich), **Supp. I Part 2:** 558

"Images of Walt Whitman" (Fiedler), **IV:** 352

"Imaginary Friendships of Tom McGrath, The" (Cohen), **Supp. X:** 112

"Imaginary Iceberg, The" (Bishop), **Retro. Supp. II:** 42; **Supp. I Part 1:** 86, 88

"Imaginary Jew, The" (Berryman), **I:** 174-175

Imaginary Letters (Pound), **III:** 473-474

Imaginary Paintings (C. Baxter), **Supp. XVII:** 18-19

"Imaginary Prisons" (Schnackenberg), **Supp. XV:** 257, 258

Imagination and Fancy; or, Selections from the English Poets, illustrative of those first requisites of their art; with markings of the best passages, critical notices of the writers, and an essay in answer to the question 'What is Poetry?' (Hunt), **II:** 515-516

"Imagination as Value" (Stevens), **Retro. Supp. I:** 298

"Imagination of Disaster, The" (Gordon), **Supp. IV Part 1:** 306

"Imagine a Day at the End of Your Life" (Beattie), **Supp. V:** 33

Imagined London: A Tour of the World's Greatest Fictional City (Quindlen), **Supp. XVII:** 167, 180

"Imagine Kissing Pete" (O'Hara), **III:** 372; **Supp. VIII:** 156

Imaging Robert: My Brother, Madness, and Survival (Neugeboren), **Supp. XVI:** 225, **226-229**

"Imagining How It Would Be to Be Dead" (Eberhart), **I:** 533

Imagining Los Angeles: A City in Fiction (Fine), **Supp. XI:** 160

"Imagining Their Own Hymns" (B. Kelly), **Supp. XVII:** 126-127

"Imagining the Midwest" (Sanders), **Supp. XVI:** 275-276

Imagining the Worst: Stephen King and the Representations of Women (Lant and Thompson), **Supp. V:** 141

"Imagisme" (Pound), **Retro. Supp. I:** 288

Imagistes, Des: An Anthology of the Imagists (Pound, ed.), **III:** 465, 471; **Retro. Supp. I:** 288

Imago (O. Butler), **Supp. XIII:** 63, **65-66**

"Imago" (Stevens), **IV:** 74, 89

Imagoes (Coleman), **Supp. XI:** 89-90

I Married a Communist (P. Roth), **Retro. Supp. II:** 289, 293-294

I Married an Angel (film), **Supp. XVI:** 193

"I May, I Might, I Must" (Moore), **III:** 215

"I'm Crazy" (Salinger), **III:** 553

"I'm Here" (Roethke), **III:** 547

Imitations (Lowell), **II:** 543, 544-545, 550, 555; **Retro. Supp. II:** 181, 187

"Imitations of Drowning" (Sexton), **Supp. II Part 2:** 684, 686

"Immaculate Man" (Gordon), **Supp. IV Part 1:** 311

"Immanence of Dostoevsky, The" (Bourne), **I:** 235

"Immigrants" (Mora), **Supp. XIII:** 216

"Immigrant Story, The" (Paley), **Supp. VI:** 230

Immobile Wind, The (Winters), **Supp. II Part 2:** 786

"Immobile Wind, The" (Winters), **Supp. II Part 2:** 788, 811

"Immolatus" (Komunyakaa), **Supp. XIII:** 126

"Immoral Proposition, The" (Creeley), **Supp. IV Part 1:** 144

"Immortal Autumn" (MacLeish), **III:** 13

"Immortality Ode" (Nemerov), **III:** 87

Immortality Ode (Wordsworth), **II:** 17; **Supp. I Part 2:** 673

"Immortal Woman, The" (Tate), **IV:** 130, 131, 137

"I'm Not Ready to Die Yet" (Harjo), **Supp. XII:** 231

"I'm on My Way" (Salinas), **Supp. XIII:** 320

"Impasse" (Hughes), **Supp. I Part 1:** 343

Imperative Duty, An, a Novel (Howells), **II:** 286

Imperial Eyes: Travel Writing and Transculturation (Pratt), **Retro. Supp. II:** 48

Imperial Germany and the Industrial Revolution (Veblen), **Supp. I Part 2:** 642, 643

Imperial Way, The: By Rail from Peshawar to Chittagong (Theroux), **Supp. VIII:** 323

"Implosions" (Rich), **Supp. I Part 2:** 556

"Imp of the Perverse, The" (Poe), **III:** 414-415; **Retro. Supp. II:** 267
Impolite Interviews, **Supp. XI:** 293
"Importance of Artists' Biographies, The" (Goldbarth), **Supp. XII:** 183, 184, 191
Importance of Being Earnest, The (Wilde), **Supp. XIV:**324, 339
"Important Houses, The" (Gordon), **Supp. IV Part 1:** 315
"Impossible Indispensability of the Ars Poetica, The" (Carruth), **Supp. XVI:**57
"Impossible to Tell" (Pinsky), **Supp. VI:** 247, 248
"Imposter, The" (West), **Retro. Supp. II:** 322, 327
"Impressionism and Symbolism in *Heart of Darkness*" (Watt), **Supp. VIII:** 4
"Impressions of a European Tour" (Bourne), **I:** 225
"Impressions of a Plumber" (H. Roth), **Supp. IX:** 228, 234
"Impressions of Europe, 1913-1914" (Bourne), **I:** 225
"I'm Walking behind the Spanish" (Salinas), **Supp. XIII:** 323-324
"I/Myself" (Shields), **Supp. VII:** 311
"In Absence" (Lanier), **Supp. I Part 1:** 364
"In Absentia" (Bowles), **Supp. IV Part 1:** 94
"In a Cab" (Untermeyer), **Supp. XV:** 296
Inada, Lawson Fusao, **Supp. V:** 180
"In a Dark Room, Furniture" (Nye), **Supp. XIII:** 274
"In a Dark Time" (Roethke), **III:** 539, 547, 548
"In a Disused Graveyard" (Frost), **Retro. Supp. I:** 126, 133
In a Dusty Light (Haines), **Supp. XII:** 207
"In a Garden" (Lowell), **II:** 513
"In a Hard Intellectual Light" (Eberhart), **I:** 523
"In a Hollow of the Hills" (Harte), **Supp. II Part 1:** 354
In America (Sontag), **Supp. XIV:**95-96
"In Amicitia" (Ransom), **IV:** 141
In a Narrow Grave: Essays on Texas (McMurtry), **Supp. V:** 220, 223
"Inanna" (A. Finch), **Supp. XVII:** 72
"In Another Country" (Hemingway), **I:** 484-485; **II:** 249
In April Once (Percy), **Retro. Supp. I:** 341
"In a Prominent Bar in Secaucus One Day" (X. J. Kennedy), **Supp. XV:** 154, 155-156
In A Shallow Grave (Purdy), **Supp. VII:** 272
"In a Station of the Metro" (Pound), **Retro. Supp. I:** 288; **Supp. I Part 1:** 265; **Supp. XIV:**284-285
"In a Strange Town" (Anderson), **I:** 114, 115
"In Athens Once" (Rodriguez), **Supp. XIV:**303
In Battle for Peace: The Story of My 83rd Birthday (Du Bois), **Supp. II Part 1:** 185
In Bed One Night & Other Brief Encounters (Coover), **Supp. V:** 49, 50
"In Bertram's Garden" (Justice), **Supp. VII:** 117
"In Blackwater Woods" (Oliver), **Supp. VII:** 244, 246
In Black & Whitey (Lacy), **Supp. XV:** 206-207
In Broken Country (Wagoner), **Supp. IX:** 330
"In California" (Simpson), **Supp. IX:** 271
"In Camp" (Stafford), **Supp. XI:** 329
"Incant against Suicide" (Karr), **Supp. XI:** 249
"In Celebration of My Uterus" (Sexton), **Supp. II Part 2:** 689
"Incendiary, The" (Rowson), **Supp. XV:** 234
"In Certain Places and Certain Times There Can Be More of You" (Dunn), **Supp. XI:** 144
Incest: From "A Journal of Love," the Unexpurgated Diary of Anaïs Nin, 1932-1934 (Nin), **Supp. X:** 182, 184, 185, 187, 191
"In Chandler Country" (Gioia), **Supp. XV:** 119
Inchbald, Elizabeth, **II:** 8
"In Cheever Country" (Gioia), **Supp. XV:** 119
Inchiquin, the Jesuit's Letters (Ingersoll), **I:** 344
"Incident" (Cullen), **Supp. IV Part 1:** 165, 166
Incidental Numbers (Wylie), **Supp. I Part 2:** 708
Incidentals (Sandburg), **III:** 579
Incident at Vichy (A. Miller), **III:** 165, 166
Incidents in the Life of a Slave Girl (Brent), **Supp. IV Part 1:** 13
Incidents in the Life of a Slavegirl (Jacobs), **Supp. XVI:**85
"Incipience" (Rich), **Supp. I Part 2:** 559
"In Clare" (McCarriston), **Supp. XIV:**270-271
Including Horace (Untermeyer), **Supp. XV:** 301, 303-304
In Cold Blood: A True Account of a Multiple Murder and Its Consequences (Capote), **Retro. Supp. II:** 107-108; **Supp. I Part 1:** 292; **Supp. III Part 1:** 111, 117, 119, 122, 123, 125-131; **Supp. III Part 2:** 574; **Supp. IV Part 1:** 220; **Supp. XIV:**162
In Cold Hell, in Thicket (Olson), **Supp. II Part 2:** 571
"In Cold Hell, in Thicket" (Olson), **Supp. II Part 2:** 558, 563-564, 566, 572, 580
"Incomparable Light, The" (Eberhart), **I:** 541
Incorporative Consciousness of Robert Bly, The (Harris), **Supp. IV Part 1:** 68
In Country (Mason), **Supp. VIII:** 133, **142-143,** 146
"Incredible Survival of Coyote, The" (Snyder), **Supp. VIII:** 297
"Increment" (Ammons), **Supp. VII:** 28
In Defense of Ignorance (Shapiro), **Supp. II Part 2:** 703, 704, 713-714
In Defense of Reason (Winters), **Supp. I Part 1:** 268
In Defense of Women (Mencken), **III:** 109
Independence Day (Ford), **Supp. V:** 57, 62-63, 67-68
Independence Day (film), **Supp. X:** 80
"Independent Candidate, The, a Story of Today" (Howells), **II:** 277
"Indestructible Mr. Gore, The" (Vidal), **Supp. IV Part 2:** 679
Index of American Design, **Supp. III Part 2:** 618
"India" (Rodriguez), **Supp. XIV:**302
"Indian at the Burial-Place of His Fathers, An" (Bryant), **Supp. I Part 1:** 155-156, 167-168
"Indian Burying Ground, The" (Freneau), **Supp. II Part 1:** 264, 266
"Indian Camp" (Hemingway), **II:** 247-248, 263; **Retro. Supp. I:** 174-175, 176, 177, 181; **Supp. XVI:**208
Indian Country (Matthiessen), **Supp. V:** 211
"Indian Country" (McCarriston), **Supp. XIV:**271
"Indian Country" (Simpson), **Supp. IX:** 274
Indian Earth (Bynner), **Supp. XV:** 46
"Indian Girls" (McCarriston), **Supp. XIV:**272-273

"Indian Manifesto" (Deloria), **Supp. IV Part 1:** 323
"Indian Names" (Sigourney), **Retro. Supp. II:** 47
"Indian Student, The" (Freneau), **Supp. II Part 1:** 264
"Indian Student, The" (Simpson), **Supp. IX:** 280
Indian Summer (Howells), **II:** 275, 279-281, 282
Indian Summer (Knowles), **Supp. XII:** 249, 250
"Indian Uprising, The" (Barthelme), **Supp. IV Part 1:** 44
Indifferent Children, The (Auchincloss), **Supp. IV Part 1:** 25
Indiscretions (Pound), **Retro. Supp. I:** 284
"Indispensability of the Eyes, The" (Olds), **Supp. X:** 202
"In Distrust of Merits" (Moore), **III:** 201, 214
"Individual and the State, The" (Emerson), **II:** 10
Individualism, Old and New (Dewey), **Supp. I Part 2:** 677
In Dreams Begin Responsibilities (Schwartz), **Supp. II Part 2:** 642, 645-650
"In Dreams Begin Responsibilities" (Schwartz), **Supp. II Part 2:** 641, 649, 654
In Dubious Battle (Steinbeck), **IV:** 51, 55-56, 59, 63
"In Durance" (Pound), **Retro. Supp. I:** 285
"Industry of Hard Kissing, The" (Ríos), **Supp. IV Part 2:** 547
"In Duty Bound" (Gilman), **Supp. XI:** 196-197
"I Need, I Need" (Roethke), **III:** 535-536
"I Need Help" (Stern), **Supp. IX:** 290
"Inés in the Kitchen" (García), **Supp. XI:** 190
"I never saw a Moor" (Dickinson), **Retro. Supp. I:** 37
I Never Told Anybody: Teaching Poetry Writing in a Nursing Home (Koch), **Supp. XV:** 190
"I Never Will Be Married, I'd Rather Be Excus'd" (Rowson), **Supp. XV:** 240
Inevitable Exiles (Kielsky), **Supp. V:** 273
"Inevitable Trial, The" (Holmes), **Supp. I Part 1:** 318
"Inexhaustible Hat, The" (Wagoner), **Supp. IX:** 327
"In Extremis" (Berry), **Supp. X:** 23

"Infancy" (Wilder), **IV:** 375
"Infant Boy at Midcentury" (Warren), **IV:** 244-245, 252
Infante, Guillermo Cabrera, **Retro. Supp. I:** 278
"Infant Sea Turtles" (F. Wright), **Supp. XVII:** 245
Inferno (Dante), **IV:** 139; **Supp. V:** 338; **Supp. VIII:** 219-221
Inferno of Dante, The (Pinsky), **Supp. VI:** 235, 248
"Infidelity" (Komunyakaa), **Supp. XIII:** 130
"Infiltration of the Universe" (MacLeish), **III:** 19
Infinite Jest: A Novel (Wallace), **Supp. X:** 301, 310-314
"Infinite Reason, The" (MacLeish), **III:** 19
"Infirmity" (Lowell), **II:** 554
"Infirmity" (Roethke), **III:** 548
In Five Years Time (Haines), **Supp. XII:** 206
"In Flower" (Snodgrass), **Supp. VI:** 325
"Influence of Landscape upon the Poet, The" (Eliot), **Retro. Supp. I:** 67
"In Football Season" (Updike), **IV:** 219
Informer, The (film), **Supp. III Part 2:** 619
Ingersoll, Charles J., **I:** 344
Ingersoll, Robert Green, **Supp. II Part 1:** 198
Ingraham, Lloyd, **Supp. XVI:** 184
Ingster, Boris, **Retro. Supp. II:** 330
Inhabitants, The (Morris), **III:** 221-222
"Inheritance and Invention in Li-Young Lee's Poetry" (Xiaojing), **Supp. XV:** 214
"Inheritance of Tools, The" (Sanders), **Supp. XVI:** 273
Inheritors (Glaspell), **Supp. III Part 1:** 175, 179-181, 186, 189
"In Honor of David Anderson Brooks, My Father" (Brooks), **Supp. III Part 1:** 79
"Inhumanist, The" (Jeffers), **Supp. II Part 2:** 423, 426
"In Illo Tempore" (Karr), **Supp. XI:** 242
"In Interims: Outlyer" (Harrison), **Supp. VIII:** 38
"Initial" (F. Wright), **Supp. XVII:** 243
"Injudicious Gardening" (Moore), **III:** 198
"Injustice" (Paley), **Supp. VI:** 220
Injustice Collectors, The (Auchincloss), **Supp. IV Part 1:** 25
Ink, Blood, Semen (Goldbarth), **Supp. XII:** 181, 183

Ink Truck, The (W. Kennedy), **Supp. VII:** 132, 133-138, 140, 141, 149, 152
In Life Sentences: Literary Essays (Epstein), **Supp. XIV:** 112
"In Limbo" (Wilbur), **Supp. III Part 2:** 544, 561
In Limestone Country (Sanders), **Supp. XVI:** 272
In Love and Trouble: Stories of Black Women (Walker), **Supp. III Part 2:** 520, 521, 530, 531, 532
In Mad Love and War (Harjo), **Supp. XII:** 224-226
"In Memoriam" (Emerson), **II:** 13
"In Memoriam" (Hay), **Supp. XIV:** 122, 127
"In Memoriam" (Tennyson), **Retro. Supp. I:** 325; **Supp. I Part 2:** 416
In Memoriam: 1933 (Reznikoff), **Supp. XIV:** 280, 285
In Memoriam to Identity (Acker), **Supp. XII:** 5, 16-18
"In Memory of Arthur Winslow" (Lowell), **II:** 541, 547, 550; **Retro. Supp. II:** 187
"In Memory of Congresswoman Barbara Jordan" (Pinsky), **Supp. VI:** 250
"In Memory of Joe Brainard" (Bidart), **Supp. XV:** 33
"In Memory of My Feelings" (O'Hara), **Supp. XV:** 215-216
"In Memory of W. B. Yeats" (Auden), **Supp. VIII:** 19, 30; **Supp. XI:** 243, 244
"In Memory of W. H. Auden" (Stern), **Supp. IX:** 288
"In Mercy on Broadway" (Doty), **Supp. XI:** 132
In Morocco (Wharton), **Retro. Supp. I:** 380; **Supp. IV Part 1:** 81
Inmost Leaf, The: A Selection of Essays (Kazin), **Supp. VIII:** 102, 103
In Motley (Bierce), **I:** 209
In My Father's Court (Singer), **IV:** 16-17; **Retro. Supp. II:** 301-302
"In My Life" (Dubus), **Supp. VII:** 81
Inner Landscape (Sarton), **Supp. VIII:** 259
Inner Room, The (Merrill), **Supp. III Part 1:** 336
"In Nine Sleep Valley" (Merrill), **Supp. III Part 1:** 328
Innocents, The: A Story for Lovers (Lewis), **II:** 441
Innocents Abroad, The; or, The New Pilgrim's Progress (Twain), **II:** 275, 434; **IV:** 191, 196, 197-198
Innocents at Cedro, The: A Memoir of

Thorstein Veblen and Some Others (Duffus), **Supp. I Part 2:** 650
"In Off the Cliffs of Moher" (McCarriston), **Supp. XIV:**270
In Old Plantation Days (Dunbar), **Supp. II Part 1:** 214
In Ole Virginia (Page), **Supp. II Part 1:** 201
In Orbit (Morris), **III:** 236
In Other Words (Swenson), **Supp. IV Part 2:** 650-652
In Our Terribleness (Some elements and meaning in black style) (Baraka), **Supp. II Part 1:** 52, 53
In Our Time (Hemingway), **I:** 117; **II:** 68, 247, 252, 263; **IV:** 42; **Retro. Supp. I:** 170, 173, 174, 178, 180; **Supp. IX:** 106
"In Our Time" (Wolfe), **Supp. III Part 2:** 584
"Inpatient" (Kenyon), **Supp. VII:** 169
In Pharaoh's Army: Memories of the Lost War (Wolff), **Supp. VII:** 331-334, 335, 338
"In Plaster" (Plath), **Supp. I Part 2:** 540
"In Prague, in Montmartre" (Bierds), **Supp. XVII:** 27
"In Praise of Johnny Appleseed" (Lindsay), **Supp. I Part 2:** 397
"In Praise of Limestone" (Auden), **Supp. II Part 1:** 20-21; **Supp. VIII:** 23
In Pursuit of a Vanishing Star (Sobin), **Supp. XVI:**294
In Quest of the Ordinary (Cavell), **Retro. Supp. I:** 307
Inquiry into the Nature of Peace, An (Veblen), **Supp. I Part 2:** 642
Inquisitor, The (Rowson), **Supp. XV:** **232,** 238
In Radical Pursuit (Snodgrass), **Supp. VI:** 312, 316, 318
In Reckless Ecstasy (Sandburg), **III:** 579
In Recognition of William Gaddis (Kuehl and Moore), **Supp. IV Part 1:** 279
"In Retirement" (Malamud), **Supp. I Part 2:** 437
"In Retrospect" (Angelou), **Supp. IV Part 1:** 15
In Russia (A. Miller), **III:** 165
"In Sabine" (Chopin), **Supp. I Part 1:** 213
"In School-Days" (Whittier), **Supp. I Part 2:** 699-700
"Inscription for the Entrance to a Wood" (Bryant), **Supp. I Part 1:** 154, 155, 161-162

Inscriptions, 1944-1956 (Reznikoff), **Supp. XIV:**281
In Search of Bisco (Caldwell), **I:** 296
"In Search of Our Mothers' Gardens" (Walker), **Supp. III Part 2:** 520-532, 524, 525, 527, 529, 532-533, 535, 536; **Supp. IX:** 306
"In Search of Thomas Merton" (Griffin), **Supp. VIII:** 208
"In Search of Yage" (Burroughs), **Supp. III Part 1:** 98
"Insertion of Self into a Space of Borderless Possibilities, The" (Fjellestad), **Supp. XVI:**150
"In Shadow" (Crane), **I:** 386
"In Sickness and in Health" (Auden), **Supp. II Part 1:** 15
"In Sickness and in Health" (Humphrey), **Supp. IX:** 94
Inside His Mind (A. Miller), **III:** 154
"Inside Norman Mailer" (Apple), **Supp. XVII:** 3, 4
"Insider Baseball" (Didion), **Supp. IV Part 1:** 211
Inside Sports magazine, **Supp. V:** 58, 61
"In So Many Dark Rooms" (Hogan), **Supp. IV Part 1:** 400
"Insomnia" (Bishop), **Supp. I Part 1:** 92
"Insomniac" (Plath), **Supp. I Part 2:** 539
"Inspiration for Greatness" (Caldwell), **I:** 291
"Instability of Race Types, The" (Boas), **Supp. XIV:**209
"Installation #6" (Beattie), **Supp. V:** 33
Instinct of Workmanship and the State of the Industrial Arts, The (Veblen), **Supp. I Part 2:** 642
Instincts of the Herd in Peace and War, The (Trotter), **I:** 249
Institute (Calvin), **IV:** 158, 160
"Instruction Manual, The" (Ashbery), **Supp. III Part 1:** 6-7, 10, 12
"Instructions for the Afternoon" (Gioia), **Supp. XV:** 120
"Instruction to Myself" (Brooks), **Supp. III Part 1:** 87
Instrument, The (O'Hara), **III:** 362, 364
"In Such Times, Ties Must Bind" (Nye), **Supp. XIII:** 286
"Insurance and Social Change" (Stevens), **Retro. Supp. I:** 297
Insurgent Mexico (Reed), **I:** 476
In Suspect Terrain (McPhee), **Supp. III Part 1:** 309, 310
"In Tall Grass" (Sandburg), **III:** 585

"Integer Vitae" (Horace), **Supp. XV:** 304
Intellectual History, An (Senghor), **Supp. X:** 139
"Intellectual Pre-Eminence of Jews in Modern Europe, The" (Veblen), **Supp. I Part 2:** 643-644
Intellectual Things (Kunitz), **Supp. III Part 1:** 260, 262-264
Intellectual versus the City, The (White), **I:** 258
"In Temporary Pain" (Bynner), **Supp. XV:** 41-42
Intentions (Wilde), **Retro. Supp. I:** 56
"Interest in Life, An" (Paley), **Supp. VI:** 222, 224-225
Interest of Great Britain Considered, with Regard to Her Colonies and the Acquisition of Canada and Guadeloupe, The (Franklin), **II:** 119
Interior Landscapes (Vizenor), **Supp. IV Part 1:** 262
Interiors (film; Allen), **Supp. IV Part 1:** 205; **Supp. XV:** 1, **7,** 10
Interlocking Lives (Koch), **Supp. XV:** 185
"Interlude" (A. Lowell), **Retro. Supp. II:** 46
Interlunar (Atwood), **Supp. XIII:** 35
"Intermezzo" (Schnackenberg), **Supp. XV:** 254
"In Terms of the Toenail: Fiction and the Figures of Life" (Gass), **Supp. VI:** 85
"International Episode, An" (James), **II:** 327
International Workers Order, **Retro. Supp. I:** 202
Interpretation of Christian Ethics, An (Niebuhr), **III:** 298-300, 301, 302
"Interpretation of Dreams, The" (Matthews), **Supp. IX:** 162-163
Interpretation of Music of the XVIIth and XVIIIth Centuries, The (Dolmetsch), **III:** 464
Interpretations and Forecasts: 1922-1972 (Mumford), **Supp. II Part 2:** 481
Interpretations of Poetry and Religion (Santayana), **III:** 611
Interpreters and Interpretations (Van Vechten), **Supp. II Part 2:** 729, 733-734
"Interrogate the Stones" (MacLeish), **III:** 9
Interrogations at Noon (Gioia), **Supp. XV:** 112, **125-127,** 128, 129
"Interrupted Conversation, An" (Van Vechten), **Supp. II Part 2:** 735

Intersect: Poems (Shields), **Supp. VII:** 310-311

Interstate (Dixon), **Supp. XII:** 140, 152-153, 153, 156

"Interview" (Hay), **Supp. XIV:**132

"Interview, The" (Thurber), **Supp. I Part 2:** 616

"Interview With a Lemming" (Thurber), **Supp. I Part 2:** 603

"Interview with Peter Everwine, An" (Veinberg and Buckley), **Supp. XV:** 76-77

Interview with the Vampire (Rice), **Supp. VII:** 287, 288-291, 297-298, 303

"Interview with the Vampire" (Rice), **Supp. VII:** 288

Interzone (Burroughs), **Supp. IV Part 1:** 90

"In the Absence of Bliss" (Kumin), **Supp. IV Part 2:** 453

"In the Afternoon" (Dunn), **Supp. XI:** 146

"In the Alley" (Elkin), **Supp. VI: 46-47**

In the American Grain (W. C. Williams), **Retro. Supp. I:** 420-421

In the American Tree (Silliman), **Supp. IV Part 2:** 426

In the Bar of a Tokyo Hotel (T. Williams), **IV:** 382, 386, 387, 391, 393

In the Beauty of the Lilies (Updike), **Retro. Supp. I:** 322, 325, 326, 327, 333

"In the Beeyard" (Bierds), **Supp. XVII:** 29

"In the Beginning" (Quindlen), **Supp. XVII:** 166

"In the Beginning ..." (Simic), **Supp. VIII:** 270, 271

In the Belly of the Beast: Letters from Prison (Abbott), **Retro. Supp. II:** 210

"In the Black Museum" (Nemerov), **III:** 275

"In the Bodies of Words" (Swenson), **Supp. IV Part 2:** 651

"In the Cage" (Gass), **Supp. VI:** 85

In the Cage (James), **Retro. Supp. I:** 229

"In the Cage" (James), **II:** 332; **Retro. Supp. I:** 231

"In the Cage" (Lowell), **Retro. Supp. II:** 187

"In the Cave at Lone Tree Meadow" (Haines), **Supp. XII:** 212

"In the City Ringed with Giants" (Kingsolver), **Supp. VII:** 209

"In the Clearing" (Brodsky), **Supp. VIII:** 32

In the Clearing (Frost), **II:** 153, 155, 164; **Retro. Supp. I:** 121, 122, 141

"In the Closet of the Soul" (Walker), **Supp. III Part 2:** 526

"In the Confidence of a Story-Writer" (Chopin), **Retro. Supp. II:** 66-67; **Supp. I Part 1:** 217

In the Country of Last Things (Auster), **Supp. XII:** 23, **29-30,** 31, 32

"In the Courtyard of the Isleta Missions" (R. Bly), **Supp. IV Part 1:** 71

"In the Dark" (Levine), **Supp. V:** 194

"In the Dark New England Days" (Jewett), **Retro. Supp. II:** 139

"In the Days of Prismatic Colour" (Moore), **III:** 205, 213

In the Electric Mist with Confederate Dead (Burke), **Supp. XIV:**30, 31-32

"In the Field" (Wilbur), **Supp. III Part 2:** 558

"In the First Stanza" (C. Kizer), **Supp. XVII:** 75

"In the Fleeting Hand of Time" (Corso), **Supp. XII:** 122-123

"In the Footsteps of Gutenberg" (Mencken), **III:** 101

"In the Forest" (Simpson), **Supp. IX:** 270

"In the Forties" (Lowell), **II:** 554

In the Garden of the North American Martyrs (Wolff), **Supp. VII:** 341-342

In the Garret (Van Vechten), **Supp. II Part 2:** 735

"In the Grove: The Poet at Ten" (Kenyon), **Supp. VII:** 160

"In the Hall of Mirrors" (Merrill), **Supp. III Part 1:** 322

In the Harbor (Longfellow), **II:** 491

In the Heart of the Heart of the Country (Gass), **Supp. VI: 82-83,** 84, 85, 93

In the Heat of the Night (Ball), **Supp. XV:** 202

In the Heat of the Night (film), **Supp. I Part 1:** 67

In the Hollow of His Hand (Purdy), **Supp. VII:** 278-280

In the House of Light (Everwine, trans.), **Supp. XV:** 73, 75, **76-78,** 82

In the Lake of the Woods (O'Brien), **Supp. V:** 240, 243, 250-252

"In the Last Days" (Everwine), **Supp. XV:** 88, 89

In the Loyal Mountains (Bass), **Supp. XVI:**19-20

"In the Loyal Mountains" (Bass), **Supp. XVI:**20

In the Mecca (Brooks), **Supp. III Part 1:** 74

"In the Mecca" (Brooks), **Supp. III Part 1:** 70, 83-84

In the Midst of Life (Bierce), **I:** 200-203, 204, 206, 208, 212

"In the Miro District" (Taylor), **Supp. V:** 323

In the Miro District and Other Stories (Taylor), **Supp. V:** 325-326

In the Money (W. C. Williams), **Retro. Supp. I:** 423

"In the Motel" (X. J. Kennedy), **Supp. XV:** 163

"In the Naked Bed, in Plato's Cave" (Schwartz), **Supp. II Part 2:** 646-649

In the Name of the Neither (Sobin), **Supp. XVI:**291

"In the Night" (Kincaid), **Supp. VII:** 183

In the Night Season: A Novel (Bausch), **Supp. VII:** 52-53

"In the Old Neighborhood" (Dove), **Supp. IV Part 1:** 241, 257

"In the Old World" (Oates), **Supp. II Part 2:** 503, 504

"In the Park" (Huncke), **Supp. XIV:**139

"In the Pit" (Proulx), **Supp. VII:** 255, 261

In the Presence of the Sun (Momaday), **Supp. IV Part 2:** 489, 490, 491-493, 493

"In the Quiet Night" (Li Po), **Supp. XV:** 47

"In the Realm of the Fisher King" (Didion), **Supp. IV Part 1:** 211

"In the Red Room" (Bowles), **Supp. IV Part 1:** 93

"In the Region of Ice" (Oates), **Supp. II Part 2:** 520

In the Room We Share (Simpson), **Supp. IX:** 279

"In These Dissenting Times" (Walker), **Supp. III Part 2:** 522

"In the Shadow of Gabriel, A.D.1550" (Frederic), **II:** 139

In the Spirit of Crazy Horse (Matthiessen), **Supp. V:** 211

"In the Subway" (Untermeyer), **Supp. XV:** 296

In the Summer House (Jane Bowles), **Supp. IV Part 1:** 83, 89

In the Tennessee Country (Taylor), **Supp. V:** 328

"In the Thick of Darkness" (Salinas), **Supp. XIII:** 325

"In the Time of the Blossoms" (Mervin), **Supp. III Part 1:** 352

In the Time of the Butterflies (Alvarez), **Supp. VII:** 1, 12-15, 18

"In the Tube" (Jarman), **Supp. XVII:** 121
"In the Tunnel Bone of Cambridge" (Corso), **Supp. XII:** 120-121
"In the Upper Pastures" (Kumin), **Supp. IV Part 2:** 453
In the Valley (Frederic), **II:** 133-134, 136, 137
"In the Village" (Bishop), **Retro. Supp. II:** 38; **Supp. I Part 1:** 73, 74-75, 76, 77, 78, 88
"In the Waiting Room" (Bishop), **Retro. Supp. II:** 50; **Supp. I Part 1:** 81, 94, 95; **Supp. IV Part 1:** 249
"In the Ward: The Sacred Wood" (Jarrell), **II:** 376, 377
In the Western Night: Collected Poems 1965-90 (Bidart), **Supp. XV:** 19, **30-32**
"In the White Night" (Beattie), **Supp. V:** 30-31
"In the Wind My Rescue Is" (Ammons), **Supp. VII:** 25
In the Winter of Cities (T. Williams), **IV:** 383
"In the X-Ray of the Sarcophagus of Ta-pero" (Goldbarth), **Supp. XII:** 191
"In the Yard" (Swenson), **Supp. IV Part 2:** 647
In the Zone (O'Neill), **III:** 388
In This, Our Life (film), **Supp. I Part 1:** 67
"In This Country, but in Another Language, My Aunt Refuses to Marry the Men Everyone Wants Her To" (Paley), **Supp. VI:** 225
In This Hung-up Age (Corso), **Supp. XII: 119-120,** 129
In This Our Life (Glasgow), **II:** 175, 178, 189
In This Our World (Gilman), **Supp. XI:** 196, 200, 202
"In Those Days" (Jarrell), **II:** 387-388
"In Time of War" (Auden), **Supp. II Part 1:** 8, 13
"Into Egypt" (Benét), **Supp. XI:** 56, 57-58
Intolerance (film; Griffith), **Supp. XVI:**184
"Into My Own" (Frost), **II:** 153; **Retro. Supp. I:** 127
"Into the Night Life ..." (H. Miller), **III:** 180, 184
"Into the Nowhere" (Rawlings), **Supp. X:** 220
Into the Stone (Dickey), **Supp. IV Part 1:** 178
"Into the Stone" (Dickey), **Supp. IV Part 1:** 179

Into the Stone and Other Poems (Dickey), **Supp. IV Part 1:** 176
Into Thin Air (Krakauer), **Supp. XVII:** 210
In Touch: The Letters of Paul Bowles (J. Miller, ed.), **Supp. IV Part 1:** 95
"Intoxicated, The" (Jackson), **Supp. IX:** 116
"Intrigue" (Crane), **I:** 419
"Introducing the Fathers" (Kumin), **Supp. IV Part 2:** 452
Introductio ad Prudentiam (Fuller), **II:** 111
"Introduction to a Haggadah" (Paley), **Supp. VI:** 219
Introduction to Objectivist Epistemology (Rand), **Supp. IV Part 2:** 527, 528-529
Introduction to Objectivist Epistemology 2nd ed. (Rand), **Supp. IV Part 2:** 529
Introduction to Poetry, An (Gioia and X. J. Kennedy), **Supp. XV:** 113, 153
"Introduction to Some Poems, An" (Stafford), **Supp. XI:** 311, 324
Introduction to the Geography of Iowa, The (Doty), **Supp. XI:** 120
"Introduction to the Hoh" (Hugo), **Supp. VI:** 136-137
"Introduction to *The New Writing in the USA*" (Creeley), **Supp. IV Part 1:** 153-154
"Introduction to William Blake, An" (Kazin), **Supp. VIII:** 103
Introitus (Longfellow), **II:** 505, 506-507
"Intruder, The" (Dubus), **Supp. VII:** 76-78, 91
Intruder, The (Maeterlinck), **I:** 91
Intruder in the Dust (Faulkner), **II:** 71, 72; **Supp. XVI:**148
"Invaders, The" (Haines), **Supp. XII:** 205
Invasion of Privacy: The Cross Creek Trial of Marjorie Kinnan Rawlings (Acton), **Supp. X:** 233
Inventing Memory: A Novel of Mothers and Daughters (Jong), **Supp. V:** 115, 129
Inventing the Abbotts (Miller), **Supp. XII: 294-295**
"Invention of God in a Mouthful of Milk, The" (Karr), **Supp. XI:** 250
Invention of Solitude, The (Auster), **Supp. XII:** 21-22
Inventions of the March Hare (Eliot), **Retro. Supp. I:** 55-56, 58
"Inventions of the March Hare" (Eliot), **Retro. Supp. I:** 55
"Inventory" (Parker), **Supp. IX:** 192

"Inverted Forest, The" (Salinger), **III:** 552, 572
"Investigations of a Dog" (Kafka), **IV:** 438
"Investiture, The" (Banks), **Supp. V:** 7
"Investiture at Cecconi's" (Merrill), **Supp. III Part 1:** 336
Invisible: Poems (Nye), **Supp. XIII:** 277
Invisible Company, The (Sanders), **Supp. XVI:**270-271
Invisible Man (Ellison), **IV:** 493; **Retro. Supp. II:** 3, 12, 111, 112, 113, 117, 119, **120-123,** 125; **Supp. II Part 1:** 40, 170, 221, 224, 226, 227, 230, 231-232, 235, 236, 241-245; **Supp. IX:** 306; **Supp. X:** 242; **Supp. XI:** 18, 92
Invisible Spectator, An (Sawyer-Lauçanno), **Supp. IV Part 1:** 95
Invisible Swords (Farrell), **II:** 27, 46, 48-49
Invisible Worm, The (Millar), **Supp. IV Part 2:** 465
Invitation to a Beheading (Nabokov), **III:** 252-253, 254, 257-258; **Retro. Supp. I:** 265, 270, 273
"Invitation to the Country, An" (Bryant), **Supp. I Part 1:** 160
"Invocation" (McKay), **Supp. X:** 134
"Invocation" (Untermeyer), **Supp. XV:** 296
"Invocation to Kali" (Sarton), **Supp. VIII:** 260
"Invocation to the Social Muse" (MacLeish), **III:** 15
"In Weather" (Hass), **Supp. VI: 102-103**
"In Your Fugitive Dream" (Hugo), **Supp. VI:** 143
"In Your Good Dream" (Hugo), **Supp. VI:** 143-144
"Iola, Kansas" (Clampitt), **Supp. IX: 45-46**
Ion (Doolittle, trans.), **Supp. I Part 1:** 269, 274
Ion (Plato), **I:** 523
"Ione" (Dunbar), **Supp. II Part 1:** 199
Ionesco, Eugène, **I:** 71, 74, 75, 84, 295; **II:** 435; **Supp. VIII:** 201
"I Only Am Escaped Alone to Tell Thee" (Nemerov), **III:** 272, 273-274
"I Opened All the Portals Wide" (Chopin), **Retro. Supp. II:** 71
I Ought to Be in Pictures (Simon), **Supp. IV Part 2:** 584
Iphigenia in Tauris (Euripedes), **Supp. XV:** 42, 50
I Promessi Sposi (Manzoni), **II:** 291

"Irascibles, The" (Kees), **Supp. XV:** 145-146

"I Remember" (Sexton), **Supp. II Part 2:** 680

"Irenicon" (Shapiro), **Supp. II Part 2:** 704

Irigaray, Luce, **Supp. XII:** 6

Iris (Jarman), **Supp. XVII:** 110, **116-117**

"Iris by Night" (Frost), **Retro. Supp. I:** 132

"Irises" (L.-Y. Lee), **Supp. XV:** 214-215

Irish Stories of Sarah Orne Jewett, The (Jewett), **Retro. Supp. II:** 142

Irish Triangle, An (Barnes), **Supp. III Part 1:** 34

"Iron Characters, The" (Nemerov), **III:** 279, 282

"Iron Hans" (Sexton), **Supp. II Part 2:** 691

Iron Heel, The (London), **II:** 466, 480

Iron John: A Book about Men (R. Bly), **Supp. IV Part 1:** 59, 67; **Supp. XVI:**177

"Iron Table, The" (Jane Bowles), **Supp. IV Part 1:** 82-83

"Iron Throat, The" (Olsen), **Supp. XIII:** 292, 297, 299

Ironweed (W. Kennedy), **Supp. VII:** 132, 133, 134, 135, 142, 144, 145-147, 148, 150, 153

"Irony as Art: The Short Fiction of William Humphrey" (Tebeaux), **Supp. IX:** 109

"Irony Is Not Enough: Essay on My Life as Catherine Deneuve" (Carson), **Supp. XII: 112-113**

Irony of American History, The (Niebuhr), **III:** 292, 306-307, 308

"Irrational Element in Poetry, The" (Stevens), **Retro. Supp. I:** 298, 301

"Irrevocable Diameter, An" (Paley), **Supp. VI:** 231-232

Irvine, Lorna, **Supp. XIII:** 26

Irving, Ebenezer, **II:** 296

Irving, John, **Supp. VI: 163-183**; **Supp. X:** 77, 85

Irving, John Treat, **II:** 296

Irving, Peter, **II:** 296, 297, 298, 299, 300, 303

Irving, Sir Henry, **IV:** 350

Irving, Washington, **I:** 211, 335, 336, 339, 343; **II: 295-318**, 488, 495; **III:** 113; **IV:** 309; **Retro. Supp. I:** 246; **Supp. I Part 1:** 155, 157, 158, 317; **Supp. I Part 2:** 377, 487, 585; **Supp. II Part 1:** 335; **Supp. IV Part 1:** 380

Irving, William, **II:** 296

Irving, William, Jr., **II:** 296, 297, 298, 299, 303

Irwin, Mark, **Supp. XII:** 21, 22, 24, 29

Irwin, William Henry, **Supp. II Part 1:** 192

Is 5 (Cummings), **I:** 429, 430, 434, 435, 440, 445, 446, 447

"Isaac and Abraham" (Brodsky), **Supp. VIII:** 21

"Isaac and Archibald" (Robinson), **III:** 511, 521, 523

"Isabel Sparrow" (Oliver), **Supp. VII:** 232

Isaiah (biblical book), **Supp. I Part 1:** 236; **Supp. I Part 2:** 516

"Isaiah Beethoven" (Masters), **Supp. I Part 2:** 461

"I Saw in Louisiana a Live-Oak Growing" (Whitman), **I:** 220

"I Shall Be Released" (Dylan), **Supp. XV:** 349

I Shall Spit on Your Graves (film), **Supp. I Part 1:** 67

Isherwood, Christopher, **II:** 586; **Supp. II Part 1:** 10, 11, 13; **Supp. IV Part 1:** 79, 82, 102; **Supp. XI:** 305; **Supp. XIV:155-175**; **Supp. XVI:**194

Isherwood Century, The (Berg and Freeman), **Supp. XIV:**157, 159

Isherwood's Fiction (Schwerdt), **Supp. XIV:**155

Ishiguro, Kazuo, **Supp. VIII:** 15

Ishi Means Man (Merton), **Supp. VIII:** 208

"Ishmael's Dream" (Stern), **Supp. IX:** 287

I Should Have Stayed Home (McCoy), **Supp. XIII:** 167, **168-170**, 171

"I Should Worry" (Kees), **Supp. XV:** 140

"I Sigh in the Afternoon" (Salinas), **Supp. XIII:** 318

"I Sing the Body Electric" (Whitman), **Retro. Supp. I:** 394, 395

"Isis: Dorothy Eady, 1924" (Doty), **Supp. XI:** 122

"Is It O.K. to Be a Luddite?" (Pynchon), **Supp. XVI:**128

"Is It True?" (Hughes), **Supp. I Part 1:** 342

"Island" (Hughes), **Supp. I Part 1:** 340

Island Garden, An (Thaxter), **Retro. Supp. II:** 136; **Supp. XIII:** 152

Island Holiday, An (Henry), **I:** 515

"Island of the Fay, The" (Poe), **III:** 412, 417

"Islands, The" (Hayden), **Supp. II Part 1:** 373

"Island Sheaf, An" (Doty), **Supp. XI:** 136

Islands in the Stream (Hemingway), **II:** 258; **Retro. Supp. I:** 186

Isn't It Romantic (Wasserstein), **Supp. XV:** 323-325, 327

Is Objectivism a Religion? (Ellis), **Supp. IV Part 2:** 527

"Isolation of Modern Poetry, The" (Schwartz), **Supp. II Part 2:** 644

"Israel" (Reznikoff), **Supp. XIV:**283

Israel Potter, or Fifty Years of Exile (Melville), **III:** 90

"Israfel" (Poe), **III:** 411

Is Sex Necessary? (Thurber and White), **Supp. I Part 2:** 607, 612, 614, 653

"Issues, The" (Olds), **Supp. X:** 205

"I Stand Here Ironing" (Olsen), **Supp. XIII:** 292, 294, 296, 298, 300, 305

I Stole a Million (West), **IV:** 287

"Is Verse a Dying Technique?" (Wilson), **IV:** 431

It (Creeley), **Supp. IV Part 1:** 157, 158

IT (King), **Supp. V:** 139, 140, 141, 146-147, 151, 152

"It" (Olds), **Supp. X:** 208

Italian American Reconciliation: A Folktale (Shanley), **Supp. XIV:**315, **324-326**, 328, 330

Italian Backgrounds (Wharton), **Retro. Supp. I:** 370

Italian Hours (James), **I:** 12; **II:** 337; **Retro. Supp. I:** 235

Italian Journeys (Howells), **II:** 274

"Italian Morning" (Bogan), **Supp. III Part 1:** 58

Italian Villas and Their Gardens (Wharton), **IV:** 308; **Retro. Supp. I:** 361, 367

Italie, Hillel, **Supp. XV:** 128

It All Adds Up: From the Dim Past to the Uncertain Future (Bellow), **Retro. Supp. II:** 32

"It Always Breaks Out" (Ellison), **Retro. Supp. II:** 126; **Supp. II Part 1:** 248

Itard, Jean-Marc Gaspard, **Supp. I Part 2:** 564

"I taste a liquor never brewed" (Dickinson), **Retro. Supp. I:** 30, 37

It Came from Outer Space (film), **Supp. IV Part 1:** 102

It Can't Happen Here (Lewis), **II:** 454

"It Don't Mean a Thing If It Ain't Got That Swing" (Matthews), **Supp. IX: 164-165**

I Tell You Now (Ortiz), **Supp. IV Part 2:** 500

"Ithaca" (Glück), **Supp. V:** 89

It Happened One Night (Capra), **Supp. XV:** 197

It Has Come to Pass (Farrell), **II:** 26

"I think to live May be a Bliss" (Dickinson), **Retro. Supp. I:** 44

I Thought of Daisy (Wilson), **IV:** 428, 434, 435

"Itinerary of an Obsession" (Kumin), **Supp. IV Part 2:** 450

"It Is a Strange Country" (Ellison), **Supp. II Part 1:** 238

"It Is Dangerous to Read Newspapers" (Atwood), **Supp. XIII:** 33

"It Must Be Abstract" (Stevens), **IV:** 95; **Retro. Supp. I:** 307

"It Must Change" (Stevens), **Retro. Supp. I:** 300, 307, 308

"It Must Give Pleasure" (Stevens), **Retro. Supp. I:** 307, 308, 309

"'It Out-Herods Herod. Pray You, Avoid It'" (Hecht), **Supp. X:** 62, 64

It's Loaded, Mr. Bauer (Marquand), **III:** 59

"It's Nation Time" (Baraka), **Supp. II Part 1:** 53

It's Nation Time (Baraka), **Supp. II Part 1:** 52, 53

It's Only a Play (McNally), **Supp. XIII:** 198

It Was (Zukofsky), **Supp. III Part 2:** 630

It Was the Nightingale (Ford), **III:** 470-471

"It Was When" (Snyder), **Supp. VIII:** 300

Ivanhoe (Scott), **I:** 216; **Supp. I Part 2:** 410

Ivens, Bryna, **Supp. XV:** 311, 312

Ivens, Joris, **I:** 488; **Retro. Supp. I:** 184

"Iverson Boy, The" (Simpson), **Supp. IX:** 280

"Ives" (Rukeyser), **Supp. VI:** 273, 283

Ives, George H., **Supp. I Part 1:** 153

Ivory Grin, The (Macdonald), **Supp. IV Part 2:** 471, 472

Ivory Tower, The (James), **II:** 337-338

"Ivory Tower, The: Louis Untermeyer as Critic" (Aiken), **Supp. XV:** 298

"Ivy Winding" (Ammons), **Supp. VII:** 33

"I Wandered Lonely as a Cloud" (Wordsworth), **Retro. Supp. I:** 121-122; **Supp. X:** 73; **Supp. XIV:** 184

"I want, I want" (Plath), **Retro. Supp. II:** 246

"I Wanted to Be There When My Father Died" (Olds), **Supp. X:** 210

"I Want to Be a Father Like the Men" (Cisneros), **Supp. VII:** 71

"I Want to Be Miss America" (Alvarez), **Supp. VII:** 18

"I Want to Know Why" (Anderson), **I:** 114, 115, 116; **II:** 263

"I Want You Women Up North To Know" (Olsen), **Supp. XIII:** 292, 297

"I Was Born in Lucerne" (Levine), **Supp. V:** 181, 189

"I Was Really Very Hungry" (M. F. K. Fisher), **Supp. XVII:** 91

"I Went into the Maverick Bar" (Snyder), **Supp. VIII:** 301

"I Will Lie Down" (Swenson), **Supp. IV Part 2:** 640

I Will Say Beauty (C. Frost), **Supp. XV:** 96, **105-107**

I Wonder As I Wander (Hughes), **Retro. Supp. I:** 196, 203; **Supp. I Part 1:** 329, 332-333

I Would Have Saved Them If I Could (L. Michaels), **Supp. XVI:** 203, 205, **206-210**

"Iyani: It goes this Way" (Gunn Allen), **Supp. IV Part 1:** 321

"I years had been from home" (Dickinson), **I:** 471

Iyer, Pico, **Supp. V:** 215

Izzo, David Garrett, **Supp. XIV:** 155, 156, 159, 160, 161, 163, 169, 171

J

J. B.: A Play in Verse (MacLeish), **II:** 163, 228; **III:** 3, 21-22, 23; **Supp. IV Part 2:** 586

"Jachid and Jechidah" (Singer), **IV:** 15

Jack and Jill (Alcott), **Supp. I Part 1:** 42

"Jack and the Beanstalk" (Hay), **Supp. XIV:** 124

Jack Kelso (Masters), **Supp. I Part 2:** 456, 471-472

Jacklight (Erdrich), **Supp. IV Part 1:** 259, 270

Jack London, Hemingway, and the Constitution (Doctorow), **Supp. IV Part 1:** 220, 222, 224, 232, 235

Jackpot (Caldwell), **I:** 304

"Jack Schmidt, Arts Administrator" (Keillor), **Supp. XVI:** 171

"Jack Schmidt on the Burning Sands" (Keillor), **Supp. XVI:** 171

Jackson, Amelia. *See* Holmes, Mrs. Oliver Wendell (Amelia Jackson)

Jackson, Andrew, **I:** 7, 20; **III:** 473; **IV:** 192, 248, 298, 334, 348; **Supp. I Part 2:** 456, 461, 473, 474, 493, 695

Jackson, Blyden, **Supp. I Part 1:** 337

Jackson, Charles, **Supp. I Part 1:** 303

Jackson, George, **Supp. I Part 1:** 66

Jackson, Helen Hunt, **I:** 459, 470; **Retro. Supp. I:** 26, 27, 30-31, 32, 33

Jackson, J. O., **III:** 213

Jackson, James, **Supp. I Part 1:** 302, 303

Jackson, Joe, **Supp. I Part 2:** 441

Jackson, Katherine Gauss, **Supp. VIII:** 124

Jackson, Lawrence, **Retro. Supp. II:** 113, 115

Jackson, Melanie, **Supp. X:** 166

Jackson, Michael, **Supp. VIII:** 146

Jackson, Richard, **II:** 119; **Supp. IX:** 165

Jackson, Shirley, **Supp. IX: 113-130**

Jackson, Thomas J. ("Stonewall"), **IV:** 125, 126

"Jackson Square" (Levertov), **Supp. III Part 1:** 276

Jackstraws (Simic), **Supp. VIII:** 280, 282-283

"Jackstraws" (Simic), **Supp. VIII: 283**

Jack Tier (Cooper), **I:** 354, 355

"Jacob" (Garrett), **Supp. VII:** 109-110

"Jacob" (Schwartz), **Supp. II Part 2:** 663

Jacob, Max, **Supp. XV:** 178, 182

"Jacob and the Indians" (Benét), **Supp. XI:** 47-48

Jacobs, Harriet, **Supp. XVI:** 85

Jacobs, Rita D., **Supp. XII:** 339

Jacobsen, Josephine, **Supp. XIII:** 346; **Supp. XIV:** 260

"Jacob's Ladder" (Rawlings), **Supp. X:** 224, 228

"Jacob's Ladder, The" (Levertov), **Supp. III Part 1:** 278

Jacob's Ladder, The (Levertov), **Supp. III Part 1:** 272, 276-278, 281

Jacobson, Dale, **Supp. X:** 112

Jacobson, Leslie, **Supp. XV:** 323

Jacoby, Russell, **Supp. IV Part 2:** 692

"Jacquerie, The" (Lanier), **Supp. I Part 1:** 355, 356, 360, 364, 370

Jacques le fataliste (D. Diderot), **Supp. XVII:** 145

Jade Mountain, The: A Chinese Anthology, Being Three Hundred Poems of the T'ang Dynasty (Bynner, trans.), **II:** 527; **Supp. XV:** 46, 47, 48

Jafsie and John Henry: Essays on Hollywood, Bad Boys, and Six Hours of Perfect Poker (Mamet), **Supp. XIV:** 252

Jaguar Totem (LaBastille), **Supp. X:** 99, 106, **107-109**

Jailbird (Vonnegut), **Supp. II Part 2:** 760, 779-780

Jaimes, M. Annette, **Supp. IV Part 1:** 330, 331
Jain, Manju, **Retro. Supp. I:** 53, 58
Jake's Women (Simon), **Supp. IV Part 2:** 576, 588
"Jakie's Mother" (Fante), **Supp. XI:** 164
Jakobson, Roman, **Supp. IV Part 1:** 155
"Jamaica Kincaid's New York" (Kincaid), **Supp. VII:** 181
James, A. Lloyd, **Supp. XIV:** 343
James, Alice, **I:** 454; **Retro. Supp. I:** 228, 235
James, Caryn, **Supp. X:** 302, 303
James, Etta, **Supp. X:** 242
James, Henry, **I:** 4, 5, 9, 10, 12, 15, 16, 20, 52, 93, 109, 211, 226, 228, 244, 246, 251, 255, 258, 259, 336, 363, 374, 375, 379, 384, 409, 429, 436, 439, 452, 454, 459, 461-462, 463, 464, 485, 500, 504, 513, 514, 517-518, 571; **II:** 38, 58, 60, 73, 74, 95, 138, 140, 144, 147, 196, 198, 199, 228, 230, 234, 243, 259, 267, 271, 272, 275, 276, 278, 281, 282, 283, 284, 285, 286, 287, 288, 290, 306, 309, 316, **319-341**, 398, 404, 410, 415, 427, 444, 542, 544, 547-548, 556, 600; **III:** 44, 51, 136, 194-195, 199, 206, 208, 218, 228-229, 237, 281, 319, 325, 326, 334, 409, 453, 454, 457, 460, 461, 464, 511, 522, 576, 607; **IV:** 8, 27, 34, 37, 40, 53, 58, 73, 74, 134, 168, 172, 182, 198, 202, 285, 308, 309, 310, 311, 314, 316, 317, 318, 319, 321, 322, 323, 324, 328, 347, 352, 359, 433, 439, 476; **Retro. Supp. I:** 1, 8, 53, 56, 59, 108, 112, **215-242**, 272, 283, 284, 362, 366, 367, 368, 371, 373, 374, 375, 376, 377, 378, 379; **Retro. Supp. II:** 93, 135, 136, 203, 223; **Supp. I Part 1:** 35, 38, 43; **Supp. I Part 2:** 414, 454, 608, 609, 612-613, 618, 620, 646; **Supp. II Part 1:** 94-95; **Supp. III Part 1:** 14, 200; **Supp. III Part 2:** 410, 412; **Supp. IV Part 1:** 31, 35, 80, 127, 197, 349, 353; **Supp. IV Part 2:** 613, 677, 678, 682, 689, 693; **Supp. V:** 97, 101, 103, 258, 261, 263, 313; **Supp. VIII:** 98, 102, 156, 166, 168; **Supp. IX:** 121; **Supp. XI:** 153; **Supp. XIII:** 102; **Supp. XIV:** 40, 110, 112, 335, 336, 348, 349; **Supp. XV:** 41; **Supp. XVII:** 5, 47
James, Henry (father), **II:** 7, 275, 321, 337, 342-344, 364; **IV:** 174; **Supp. I Part 1:** 300

James, Henry (nephew), **II:** 360
James, Horace, **Supp. XIV:** 57
James, William, **I:** 104, 220, 224, 227, 228, 255, 454; **II:** 20, 27, 165, 166, 276, 321, 337, **342-366**, 411; **III:** 303, 309, 509, 599, 600, 605, 606, 612; **IV:** 26, 27, 28-29, 31, 32, 34, 36, 37, 43, 46, 291, 486; **Retro. Supp. I:** 57, 216, 227, 228, 235, 295, 300, 306; **Supp. I Part 1:** 3, 7, 11, 20; **Supp. XIV:** 40, 50, 197, 199, 212, 335; **Supp. XVII:** 97
James, William (grandfather), **II:** 342
James Baldwin: The Legacy (Troupe, ed.), **Retro. Supp. II:** 15
James Baldwin-The Price of the Ticket (film), **Retro. Supp. II:** 2
James Dickey and the Politics of Canon (Suarez), **Supp. IV Part 1:** 175
"James Dickey on Yeats: An Interview" (Dickey), **Supp. IV Part 1:** 177
James Hogg: A Critical Study (Simpson), **Supp. IX:** 269, 276
James Jones: A Friendship (Morris), **Supp. XI:** 234
James Jones: An American Literary Orientalist Master (Carter), **Supp. XI:** 220
James Jones: Reveille to Taps (television documentary), **Supp. XI:** 234
"James Jones and Jack Kerouac: Novelists of Disjunction" (Stevenson), **Supp. XI:** 230
Jameson, F. R., **Supp. IV Part 1:** 119
Jameson, Sir Leander Starr, **III:** 327
James Shore's Daughter (Benét), **Supp. XI:** 48
"James Thurber" (Pollard), **Supp. I Part 2:** 468
"James Whitcomb Riley (From a Westerner's Point of View)" (Dunbar), **Supp. II Part 1:** 198
Jammes, Francis, **II:** 528; **Retro. Supp. I:** 55
Jan. 31 (Goldbarth), **Supp. XII:** 177, **178-179**, 180
"Jan, the Son of Thomas" (Sandburg), **III:** 593-594
Janeczko, Paul, **Supp. XIII:** 280
Jane Eyre (Brontë), **Supp. XVI:** 158
Janet, Pierre, **I:** 248, 249, 252; **Retro. Supp. I:** 55, 57
Jane Talbot: A Novel (Brown), **Supp. I Part 1:** 145-146
"Janet Waking" (Ransom), **III:** 490, 491
"Janice" (Jackson), **Supp. IX:** 117
Janowitz, Tama, **Supp. X:** 7
Jantz, Harold S., **Supp. I Part 1:** 112

"January" (Barthelme), **Supp. IV Part 1:** 54
January Man, The (screenplay, Shanley), **Supp. XIV:** 316
"January Thaw" (Leopold), **Supp. XIV:** 183-184
"Janus" (Beattie), **Supp. V:** 31
Janzen, Jean, **Supp. V:** 180
"Japanese Beetles" (X. J. Kennedy), **Supp. XV:** 161, 165
Japanese by Spring (Reed), **Supp. X:** 241, **253-255**
Japanese Cooking: A Simple Art (Tsuji), **Supp. XVII:** 90
"Japan's Young Dreams" (Geisel), **Supp. XVI:** 102
Jara, Victor, **Supp. IV Part 2:** 549
Jarman, Mark, **Supp. IV Part 1:** 68; **Supp. IX:** 266, 270, 276; **Supp. XII:** 209; **Supp. XV:** 251
Jarmon, Mark, **Supp. XVII: 109-122**
Jarrell, Mrs. Randall (Mary von Schrader), **II:** 368, 385
Jarrell, Randall, **I:** 167, 169, 173, 180; **II: 367-390**, 539-540; **III:** 134, 194, 213, 268, 527; **IV:** 352, 411, 422; **Retro. Supp. I:** 52, 121, 135, 140; **Retro. Supp. II:** 44, 177, 178, 182; **Supp. I Part 1:** 89; **Supp. I Part 2:** 552; **Supp. II Part 1:** 109, 135; **Supp. III Part 1:** 64; **Supp. III Part 2:** 541, 550; **Supp. IV Part 2:** 440; **Supp. V:** 315, 318, 323; **Supp. VIII:** 31, 100, 271; **Supp. IX:** 94, 268; **Supp. XI:** 311, 315; **Supp. XII:** 121, 260, 297; **Supp. XV:** 93, 153; **Supp. XVII:** 111
Jarry, Alfred, **Retro. Supp. II:** 326; **Supp. XV:** 177-178, 182, 188
Jarvis, John Wesley, **Supp. I Part 2:** 501, 520
Jaskoski, Helen, **Supp. IV Part 1:** 325
"Jasmine" (Komunyakaa), **Supp. XIII:** 132
"Jason" (Hecht), **Supp. X:** 62
"Jason" (MacLeish), **III:** 4
Jason and Medeia (Gardner), **Supp. VI:** 63, **68-69**
Jaspers, Karl, **III:** 292; **IV:** 491
Jay, William, **I:** 338
Jayber Crow (Berry), **Supp. X:** 28, 34
"Jaz Fantasia" (Sandburg), **III:** 585
"Jazz Age Clerk, A" (Farrell), **II:** 45
Jazz Country: Ralph Ellison in America (Porter), **Retro. Supp. II:** 127
"Jazzonia" (Hughes), **Supp. I Part 1:** 324
Jazz Poetry Anthology, The (Komunyakaa and Feinstein, eds.), **Supp. XIII:** 125

"Jazztet Muted" (Hughes), **Supp. I Part 1:** 342
"Jealous" (Ford), **Supp. V:** 71
Jealousies, The: A Faery Tale, by Lucy Vaughan Lloyd of China Walk, Lambeth (Keats), **Supp. XII:** 113
"Jean Harlow's Wedding Night" (Wasserstein), **Supp. XV:** 328
Jean Huguenot (Benét), **Supp. XI:** 44
"Jeff Briggs's Love Story" (Harte), **Supp. II Part 1:** 355
Jeffers, Robinson, **I:** 66; **III:** 134; **Retro. Supp. I:** 202; **Supp. II Part 2: 413-440; Supp. VIII:** 33, 292; **Supp. IX:** 77; **Supp. X:** 112; **Supp. XI:** 312; **Supp. XV:** 113, 114, 115; **Supp. XVII:** 111, 112, 117
Jeffers, Una Call Kuster (Mrs. Robinson Jeffers), **Supp. II Part 2:** 414
Jefferson, Blind Lemon, **Supp. VIII:** 349
Jefferson, Thomas, **I:** 1, 2, 5, 6-8, 14, 485; **II:** 5, 6, 34, 217, 300, 301, 437; **III:** 3, 17, 18, 294-295, 306, 310, 473, 608; **IV:** 133, 243, 249, 334, 348; **Supp. I Part 1:** 146, 152, 153, 229, 230, 234, 235; **Supp. I Part 2:** 389, 399, 456, 474, 475, 482, 507, 509, 510, 511, 516, 518-519, 520, 522; **Supp. X:** 26; **Supp. XIV:**191
Jefferson and/or Mussolini (Pound), **Retro. Supp. I:** 292
"Jefferson Davis as a Representative American" (Du Bois), **Supp. II Part 1:** 161
J-E-L-L-O (Baraka), **Supp. II Part 1:** 47
"Jelly-Bean, The" (Fitzgerald), **II:** 88
"Jellyfish, A" (Moore), **III:** 215
Jemie, Onwuchekwa, **Supp. I Part 1:** 343
Jenkins, J. L., **I:** 456
Jenkins, Kathleen, **III:** 403
Jenkins, Susan, **IV:** 123
Jenks, Deneen, **Supp. IV Part 2:** 550, 554
Jennie Gerhardt (Dreiser), **I:** 497, 499, 500, 501, 504-505, 506, 507, 519; **Retro. Supp. II:** 94, **99-101**
"Jennie M'Grew" (Masters), **Supp. I Part 1:** 468
Jennifer Lorn (Wylie), **Supp. I Part 2:** 709, 714-717, 718, 721, 724
"Jenny Garrow's Lover" (Jewett), **II:** 397
"Jerboa, The" (Moore), **III:** 203, 207, 209, 211-212
Jeremiah, **Supp. X:** 35
Jeremy's Version (Purdy), **Supp. VII:** 274

"Jericho" (Lowell), **II:** 536
"Jersey City Gendarmerie, Je T'aime" (Lardner), **II:** 433
Jersey Rain (Pinsky), **Supp. VI:** 235, **247-250**
"Jerusalem" (Nye), **Supp. XIII:** 287
Jerusalem the Golden (Reznikoff), **Supp. XIV:**280, 285, 286
Jessup, Richard, **Supp. XI:** 306
"Je Suis Perdu" (Taylor), **Supp. V:** 314, 321-322
Jesuits in North America in the Seventeenth Century, The (Parkman), **Supp. II Part 2:** 597, 603-605
Jesus, **I:** 27, 34, 68, 89, 136, 552, 560; **II:** 1, 16, 197, 198, 214, 215, 216, 218, 219, 239, 373, 377, 379, 537, 538, 539, 549, 569, 585, 591, 592; **III:** 39, 173, 179, 270, 291, 296-297, 300, 303, 305, 307, 311, 339, 340, 341, 342, 344, 345, 346, 347, 348, 352, 353, 354, 355, 436, 451, 489, 534, 564, 566, 567, 582; **IV:** 51, 69, 86, 107, 109, 117, 137, 138, 141, 144, 147, 149, 150, 151, 152, 155, 156, 157, 158, 159, 163, 164, 232, 241, 289, 293, 294, 296, 331, 364, 392, 396, 418, 430; **Supp. I Part 1:** 2, 54, 104, 107, 108, 109, 121, 267, 371; **Supp. I Part 2:** 379, 386, 458, 515, 580, 582, 583, 587, 588, 683; **Supp. V:** 280
"Jesus Asleep" (Sexton), **Supp. II Part 2:** 693
"Jesus of Nazareth, Then and Now" (Price), **Supp. VI:** 268
"Jesus Papers, The" (Sexton), **Supp. II Part 2:** 693
"Jesus Raises Up the Harlot" (Sexton), **Supp. II Part 2:** 693
Jetée, La (film), **Supp. IV Part 2:** 436
"Jeune Parque, La" (Valéry), **IV:** 92
"Jew as Writer/The Writer as Jew, The: Reflections on Literature and Identity" (Apple), **Supp. XVII:** 1, 9
"Jewbird, The" (Malamud), **Supp. I Part 2:** 435
"Jewboy, The" (P. Roth), **Supp. III Part 2:** 412
Jewett, Caroline, **II:** 396
Jewett, Dr. Theodore Herman, **II:** 396-397, 402
Jewett, Katharine, **Retro. Supp. II:** 46
Jewett, Mary, **II:** 396, 403
Jewett, Rutger, **Retro. Supp. I:** 381
Jewett, Sarah Orne, **I:** 313; **II: 391-414; Retro. Supp. I:** 6, 7, 19; **Retro. Supp. II:** 51, 52, **131-151**, 156; **Supp. I Part 2:** 495; **Supp. VIII:** 126; **Supp. IX:** 79; **Supp.**

XIII: 153
Jewett, Theodore Furber, **II:** 395
"Jew for Export, The" (Mamet), **Supp. XIV:**251-252
Jew in the American Novel, The (Fiedler), **Supp. XIII:** 106
"Jewish Graveyards, Italy" (Levine), **Supp. V:** 190
"Jewish Hunter, The" (Moore), **Supp. X:** 163, 165, **174**
Jewison, Norman, **Supp. XI:** 306; **Supp. XIV:**316
Jews of Shklov (Schneour), **IV:** 11
Jews without Money (Gold), **Supp. XIV:**288-289
JFK (film), **Supp. XIV:**48
Jig of Forslin, The: A Symphony (Aiken), **I:** 50, 51, 57, 62, 66
"Jig Tune: Not for Love" (McGrath), **Supp. X:** 116
"Jihad" (McClatchy), **Supp. XII:** 266
"Jilting of Granny Weatherall, The" (Porter), **III:** 434, 435, 438
Jim Crow's Last Stand (Hughes), **Retro. Supp. I:** 205
Jiménez, Juan Ramón, **Supp. XIII:** 315, 323
Jimmie Higgins (Sinclair), **Supp. V:** 288
"Jimmy Harlow" (X. J. Kennedy), **Supp. XV:** 170
Jimmy's Blues (Baldwin), **Retro. Supp. II:** 8, 9, 15
Jim's Book: A Collection of Poems and Short Stories (Merrill), **Supp. III Part 1:** 319
Jitney (Wilson), **Supp. VIII:** 330, 331, 351
Jitterbug Perfume (Robbins), **Supp. X:** 273, **274-276**, 279
Joachim, Harold, **Retro. Supp. I:** 58
Joan, Pope, **IV:** 165
Joanna and Ulysses (Sarton), **Supp. VIII: 254-255**
Joan of Arc, **IV:** 241; **Supp. I Part 1:** 286-288; **Supp. I Part 2:** 469
Joans, Ted, **Supp. IV Part 1:** 169
Job (biblical book), **II:** 165, 166-167, 168; **III:** 21, 199, 512; **IV:** 13, 158; **Supp. I Part 1:** 125
Job, The (Burroughs and Odier), **Supp. III Part 1:** 97, 103
Job, The: An American Novel (Lewis), **II:** 441
"Job History" (Proulx), **Supp. VII:** 262
Jobim, Antonio Carlos, **Supp. IV Part 2:** 549
"Job of the Plains, A" (Humphrey), **Supp. IX:** 101
"Jody Rolled the Bones" (Yates), **Supp.**

XI: 335, 341
"Joe" (Alvarez), **Supp. VII:** 7-8
Joe Hill: A Biographical Novel (Stegner), **Supp. IV Part 2:** 599
"Joe Louis: The King as a Middle-Aged Man" (Talese), **Supp. XVII:** 202
Joe Turner's Come and Gone (Wilson), **Supp. VIII:** 334, **337-342**, 345
Joe versus the Volcano (screenplay, Shanley), **Supp. XIV:**316
"Joey Martiney" (Huncke), **Supp. XIV:**149
Johannes in Eremo (Mather), **Supp. II Part 2:** 453
John (biblical book), **I:** 68; **Supp. XV:** 222, 224
"John" (Shields), **Supp. VII:** 310-311
"John, John Chinaman" (Buck), **Supp. II Part 1:** 128
John Addington Symonds: A Biographical Study (Brooks), **I:** 240, 241
John Barleycorn (London), **II:** 467, 481
John Brown (Du Bois), **Supp. II Part 1:** 171-172
"John Brown" (Emerson), **II:** 13
"John Brown" (Lindsay), **Supp. I Part 2:** 393
John Brown: The Making of a Martyr (Warren), **IV:** 236
John Brown's Body (Benét), **II:** 177; **Supp. XI:** 45, 46, 47, **56-57**
John Bull in America; or, The New Munchausen (Paulding), **I:** 344
"John Burke" (Olson), **Supp. II Part 2:** 579, 580
"John Burns of Gettysburg" (Harte), **Supp. II Part 1:** 343
"John Carter" (Agee), **I:** 27
"John Coltrane: Where Does Art Come From?" (Baraka), **Supp. II Part 1:** 60
John Deth: A Metaphysical Legend and Other Poems (Aiken), **I:** 61
"John Endicott" (Longfellow), **II:** 505, 506; **Retro. Supp. II:** 165-166, 167
"John Evereldown" (Robinson), **III:** 524
John Fante: Selected Letters, 1932-1981 (Cooney, ed.), **Supp. XI:** 170
John Fante Reader, The (Cooper, ed.), **Supp. XI:** 174
"John Gardner: The Writer As Teacher" (Carver), **Supp. III Part 1:** 136, 146-147
John Gaunt (Davis), **Supp. XVI:**89
John Jay Chapman and His Letters (Howe), **Supp. XIV:**54
John Keats (Lowell), **II:** 530-531

"John Kinsella's Lament for Mrs. Mary Moore" (Yeats), **Supp. XVII:** 144
"John L. Sullivan" (Lindsay), **Supp. I Part 2:** 394, 395
"John Lamar" (Davis), **Supp. XVI:**89-90
John Lane, **Retro. Supp. I:** 59
"John Marr" (Melville), **III:** 93
John Marr and Other Sailors (Melville), **III:** 93; **Retro. Supp. I:** 257
John Muir: A Reading Bibliography (Kimes and Kimes), **Supp. IX:** 178
Johnny Appleseed and Other Poems (Lindsay), **Supp. I Part 2:** 397
"Johnny Bear" (Steinbeck), **IV:** 67
"Johnny Mnemonic" (W. Gibson), **Supp. XVI:**122, 123-125, 128, 131
"Johnny Panic and the Bible of Dreams" (Plath), **Retro. Supp. II:** 245
"Johnny Ray" (Ríos), **Supp. IV Part 2:** 543
John of the Cross (Saint), **I:** 585; **Supp. IV Part 1:** 284; **Supp. XV:** 223; **Supp. XVII:** 112
John Paul Jones: A Sailor's Biography (Morison), **Supp. I Part 2:** 494-495
"John Redding Goes to Sea" (Hurston), **Supp. VI:** 150
Johns, George Sibley, **Retro. Supp. II:** 65
Johns, Orrick, **Retro. Supp. II:** 71
John Sloan: A Painter's Life (Brooks), **I:** 254
"John Smith Liberator" (Bierce), **I:** 209
Johnson, Alexandra, **Supp. X:** 86
Johnson, Alvin, **I:** 236; **Supp. XV:** 304
Johnson, Ben, **Retro. Supp. I:** 56
Johnson, Buffie, **Supp. IV Part 1:** 94
Johnson, Charles, **Supp. I Part 1:** 325; **Supp. V:** 128; **Supp. VI: 185-201**; **Supp. X:** 239; **Supp. XIII:** 182
Johnson, Charles S., **Supp. IX:** 309
Johnson, Claudia Durst, **Supp. VIII:** 126-127
Johnson, Diane, **Supp. XIII:** 127
Johnson, Dianne, **Retro. Supp. I:** 196
Johnson, Eastman, **IV:** 321
Johnson, Edward, **IV:** 157; **Supp. I Part 1:** 110, 115
Johnson, Fenton, **Supp. XI:** 129
Johnson, Georgia Douglas, **Supp. IV Part 1:** 164
Johnson, James Weldon, **Retro. Supp. II:** 114; **Supp. I Part 1:** 324, 325; **Supp. II Part 1:** 33, 194, 200, 202-203, 206-207; **Supp. III Part 1:** 73; **Supp. IV Part 1:** 7, 11, 15, 16, 164, 165, 166, 169; **Supp. X:** 42, 136, **246**
Johnson, Joyce, **Supp. XIV:**150
Johnson, Kent, **Supp. XV:** 347
Johnson, Lady Bird, **Supp. IV Part 1:** 22
Johnson, Lyndon B., **I:** 254; **II:** 553, 582; **Retro. Supp. II:** 27
Johnson, Marguerite. *See* Angelou, Maya
Johnson, Maurice, **Supp. XV:** 136, 137, 138
Johnson, Mordecai, **Supp. XIV:**202
Johnson, Nunnally, **Supp. IV Part 1:** 355
Johnson, Pamela Hansford, **IV:** 469
Johnson, Rafer, **Supp. I Part 1:** 271
Johnson, Reed, **Supp. IV Part 2:** 589
Johnson, Richard, **Supp. XIII:** 132
Johnson, Robert, **Supp. IV Part 1:** 146; **Supp. VIII:** 15, 134
Johnson, Robert K., **Supp. IV Part 2:** 573, 584
Johnson, Robert Underwood, **Supp. IX:** 182, 184, 185
Johnson, Samuel, **II:** 295; **III:** 491, 503; **IV:** 452; **Retro. Supp. I:** 56, 65; **Supp. I Part 1:** 33; **Supp. I Part 2:** 422, 498, 503, 523, 656; **Supp. IV Part 1:** 34, 124; **Supp. XI:** 209; **Supp. XII:** 159; **Supp. XIII:** 55, 347; **Supp. XVI:**204; **Supp. XVII:** 1
Johnson, Steve, **Supp. XVI:**177
Johnson, Thomas H., **I:** 470-471; **IV:** 144, 158; **Retro. Supp. I:** 26, 28, 36, 39, 40, 41, 43
Johnson, Walter, **II:** 422
Johnson, Willard "Spud," **Supp. XV:** 42, 46
"Johnson Girls, The" (Bambara), **Supp. XI:** 7
Johnsrud, Harold, **II:** 562
Johnston, Basil, **Supp. IV Part 1:** 269
Johnston, Mary, **II:** 194
Johnston, Robert M., **Supp. I Part 1:** 369
"John Sutter" (Winters), **Supp. II Part 2:** 810
John's Wife (Coover), **Supp. V:** 51-52
John the Baptist, **I:** 389; **II:** 537, 591
John XXIII, Pope, **Supp. I Part 2:** 492
Jolas, Eugène, **Retro. Supp. II:** 85, 328; **Supp. IV Part 1:** 80
Jolie Blon's Bounce (Burke), **Supp. XIV:**26, 33-34
Jolly (Mamet), **Supp. XIV:**240, 254
"Jolly Corner, The" (James), **I:** 571; **Retro. Supp. I:** 235
"Jonah" (Lowell), **II:** 536

Jonah's Gourd Vine (Hurston), **Supp. VI:** 149, 155
"Jonathan Edwards" (Holmes), **Supp. I Part 1:** 302, 315
"Jonathan Edwards in Western Massachusetts" (Lowell), **II:** 550
Jonathan Troy (Abbey), **Supp. XIII:** 4, 13
Jones, Anne, **Supp. X:** 8
Jones, Carolyn, **Supp. VIII:** 128
Jones, Chuck, **Supp. XVI:**102
Jones, David, **Supp. XVII:** 241
Jones, E. Stanley, **III:** 297
Jones, Edith Newbold. *See* Wharton, Edith
Jones, Everett LeRoi. *See* Baraka, Imamu Amiri
Jones, George Frederic, **IV:** 309
Jones, Grover, **Supp. XIII:** 166
Jones, Harry, **Supp. I Part 1:** 337
Jones, Howard Mumford, **I:** 353; **Supp. IV Part 2:** 606; **Supp. XIV:**11
Jones, James, **III:** 40; **IV:** 98; **Supp. XI:** 213-237
Jones, James Earl, **Supp. VIII:** 334; **Supp. XI:** 309
Jones, Jennifer, **Supp. IV Part 2:** 524
Jones, John Paul, **II:** 405-406; **Supp. I Part 2:** 479, 480, 494-495
Jones, LeRoi. *See* Baraka, Imamu Amiri
Jones, Louis B., **Supp. XVI:**41
Jones, Lucretia Stevens Rhinelander, **IV:** 309
Jones, Madison, **Retro. Supp. II:** 235; **Supp. X:** 1
Jones, Major (pseudonym). *See* Thompson, William T.
Jones, Malcolm, **Supp. V:** 219
Jones, Robert Edmond, **III:** 387, 391, 394, 399
Jones, Tommy Lee, **Supp. V:** 227
"Jones's Private Argyment" (Lanier), **Supp. I Part 1:** 352
"Jones's *The Thin Red Line:* The End of Innocence" (Michel-Michot), **Supp. XI:** 224-225
Jong, Allan, **Supp. V:** 115
Jong, Erica, **Supp. V:** 113-135
Jong-Fast, Molly Miranda, **Supp. V:** 115
Jonson, Ben, **I:** 58, 358; **II:** 11, 16, 17, 18, 436, 556; **III:** 3, 463, 575-576; **IV:** 395, 453; **Retro. Supp. II:** 76; **Supp. I Part 2:** 423; **Supp. IV Part 2:** 585
Jonsson, Thorsten, **Retro. Supp. I:** 73
Joplin, Janis, **Supp. IV Part 1:** 206; **Supp. XI:** 239
Joplin, Scott, **Supp. IV Part 1:** 223

Jordan, Barbara, **Supp. VIII:** 63; **Supp. XI:** 249
Jordan, June, **Supp. XII:** 217
Jordan, Marie, **Supp. XV:** 224
Jo's Boys (Alcott), **Supp. I Part 1:** 32, 35, 40-41, 42
Joseph Heller (Ruderman), **Supp. IV Part 1:** 380
"Josephine Has Her Day" (Thurber), **Supp. I Part 2:** 606
Josephine Stories, The (Fitzgerald), **Retro. Supp. I:** 109
"Joseph Martinez" (Huncke), **Supp. XIV:**149
"Joseph Pockets" (Stern), **Supp. IX:** 292
Josephson, Matthew, **I:** 259
"José's Country" (Winters), **Supp. II Part 2:** 789, 790
Joshua (biblical book), **Supp. I Part 2:** 515
Joslin, Katherine, **Retro. Supp. I:** 376
Journal (Emerson), **Supp. I Part 1:** 309
"Journal" (L. Michaels), **Supp. XVI:**213
Journal (Thoreau), **IV:** 175
Journal (Woolman), **Supp. VIII:** 202
"Journal for My Daughter" (Kunitz), **Supp. III Part 1:** 268
Journal of Arthur Stirling, The (Sinclair), **Supp. V:** 280
"Journal of a Solitary Man, The" (Hawthorne), **II:** 226
Journal of a Solitude (Sarton), **Supp. VIII:** 256, 262-263
Journal of My Other Self (Rilke), **Retro. Supp. II:** 20
Journal of the Fictive Life (Nemerov), **III:** 267, 268, 269, 272, 273, 274, 280-281, 284-285, 286, 287
Journal of the Plague Year, A (Defoe), **III:** 423
"Journal of the Year of the Ox, A" (Wright), **Supp. V:** 343
Journals (Thoreau), **Supp. I Part 1:** 299
Journals and Other Documents on the Life and Voyages of Christopher Columbus (Morison, ed.), **Supp. I Part 2:** 494
Journals of Ralph Waldo Emerson, The (Emerson), **II:** 8, 17, 21
Journals of Susanna Moodie, The: Poems (Atwood), **Supp. XIII:** 33
"Journey, A" (Wharton), **Retro. Supp. I:** 364
"Journey, The" (Winters), **Supp. II Part 2:** 795
"Journey, The" (Wright), **Supp. III Part 2:** 605-606
"Journey, The: For Jane at Thirteen" (Kumin), **Supp. IV Part 2:** 442
"Journey, the Arrival and the Dream, The" (Gioia), **Supp. XV:** 120
Journey and Other Poems, The (Winters), **Supp. II Part 2:** 786, 794, 795, 796, 799, 800, 801
Journey Around My Room: The Autobiography of Louise Bogan-A Mosaic (Bogan), **Supp. III Part 1:** 47, 48, 52, 53
Journey Down, The (Bernstein), **IV:** 455
Journey Home, The (Abbey), **Supp. XIII:** 2, 12
Journeyman (Caldwell), **I:** 297, 302-304, 307, 309
Journey of Tai-me, The (Momaday), **Supp. IV Part 2:** 485
"Journey of the Magi" (Eliot), **Retro. Supp. I:** 64
Journey to a War (Auden and Isherwood), **Supp. II Part 1:** 13; **Supp. XIV:**156, 158, 162
Journey to Love (W. C. Williams), **IV:** 422; **Retro. Supp. I:** 429
Journey to My Father; Isaac Bashevis Singer (Zamir), **Retro. Supp. II:** 317
"Journey to Nine Miles" (Walker), **Supp. III Part 2:** 527
"Journey to the Interior" (W. J. Smith), **Supp. XIII:** 339, 340
Journey with Genius: Recollections and Reflections Concerning the D. H. Lawrences (Bynner), **Supp. XV:** 46
Jowett, Benjamin, **Supp. XIV:**335
"Joy" (Moore), **Supp. X:** 174
"Joy" (Singer), **IV:** 9; **Retro. Supp. II:** 307
Joyce, Cynthia, **Supp. X:** 194, 195, 196
Joyce, James, **I:** 53, 105, 108, 130, 174, 256, 285, 377, 395, 475-476, 478, 480, 483, 576; **II:** 27, 42, 58, 73, 74, 198, 209, 264, 320, 569; **III:** 7, 16, 26-27, 45, 174, 181, 184, 261, 273, 277, 343, 396, 398, 465, 471, 474; **IV:** 32, 73, 85, 95, 103, 171, 182, 211, 286, 370, 412, 418, 419, 428, 434, 456; **Retro. Supp. I:** 59, 63, 75, 80, 89, 91, 108, 109, 127, 287, 290, 292, 334, 335, 420; **Retro. Supp. II:** 221, 326; **Supp. I Part 1:** 257, 262, 270; **Supp. I Part 2:** 437, 546, 613, 620; **Supp. II Part 1:** 136; **Supp. III Part 1:** 35, 36, 65, 225, 229; **Supp. III Part 2:** 611,

617, 618; **Supp. IV Part 1:** 40, 47, 80, 227, 300, 310; **Supp. IV Part 2:** 424, 677; **Supp. V:** 261, 331; **Supp. VIII:** 14, 40, 103; **Supp. IX:** 211, 229, 235, 308; **Supp. X:** 115, 137, 194, 324; **Supp. XI:** 66; **Supp. XII:** 139, 151, 165, 191, 289; **Supp. XIV:** 83; **Supp. XVI:** 41, 189, 282; **Supp. XVII:** 44

Joy Comes in the Morning (J. Rosen), **Supp. XVII:** 50

Joy Luck Club, The (Tan), **Supp. X:** 289, 291, 293, 294, 296, 297, 298, 299

"Joy of Sales Resistance, The" (Berry), **Supp. X:** 36

J R (Gaddis), **Supp. IV Part 1:** 279, 280, 285-289, 291, 294; **Supp. IV Part 2:** 484

"Juan's Song" (Bogan), **Supp. III Part 1:** 50

Jubilate Agno (Smart), **Supp. IV Part 2:** 626

Judah, Hettie, **Supp. XIII:** 246

Judah the Pious (Prose), **Supp. XVI:** 249, 250, 262

"Judas Maccabaeus" (Longfellow), **II:** 506; **Retro. Supp. II:** 165, 167

Judd, Sylvester, **II:** 290; **Supp. I Part 2:** 420

Judd Rankin's Daughter (Glaspell), **Supp. III Part 1:** 186-188

Jude the Obscure (Hardy), **Supp. I Part 1:** 217

"Judgement Day" (O'Connor), **III:** 349, 350; **Retro. Supp. II:** 236

Judgment Day (Farrell), **II:** 29, 31, 32, 34, 39

"Judgment of Paris, The" (Merwin), **Supp. III Part 1:** 350

Judgment of Paris, The (Vidal), **Supp. IV Part 2:** 680, 682

"Judgment of the Sage, The" (Crane), **I:** 420

Judith (Farrell), **II:** 46, 48

"Judith" (Garrett), **Supp. VII:** 109-110

"Juggernaut" (Bass), **Supp. XVI:** 16-17

"Jug of Sirup, A" (Bierce), **I:** 206

"Jugurtha" (Longfellow), **II:** 499

"Juice or Gravy" (P. Roth), **Retro. Supp. II:** 279

"Juke Box Love Song" (Hughes), **Retro. Supp. I:** 209

"Julia" (Hellman), **Supp. I Part 1:** 280, 293

"Julia Miller" (Masters), **Supp. I Part 2:** 461

Julian (Vidal), **Supp. IV Part 2:** 677, 684-685, 685, 689

Julian the Apostate, **Retro. Supp. I:** 247

"Julian Vreden" (Bowles), **Supp. IV Part 1:** 94

Julie; ou, La nouvelle Héloïse (Rousseau), **Supp. XVI:** 184

Julie and Romeo (Ray), **Supp. XII:** 308, 310

Julien, Isaac, **Supp. XI:** 19

Julier, Laura, **Supp. IV Part 1:** 211

Julip (Harrison), **Supp. VIII:** 51

Julius Caesar (Shakespeare), **I:** 284

"July Midnight" (Lowell), **II:** 521

Jumel, Madame, **Supp. I Part 2:** 461

Jumping Out of Bed (R. Bly), **Supp. IV Part 1:** 71

"Jump-Up Day" (Kingsolver), **Supp. VII:** 203

"June 1940" (Kees), **Supp. XV:** 141

"June Light" (Wilbur), **Supp. III Part 2:** 545

June Moon (Lardner and Kaufman), **II:** 427

"June Recital" (Welty), **IV:** 272-273

Juneteenth (Ellison), **Retro. Supp. II:** 119, 124, **126-128**

"Juneteenth" (Ellison), **Retro. Supp. II:** 119, 126; **Supp. II Part 1:** 248

"June the Third" (Gander), **Supp. XV:** 340

Jung, Carl, **I:** 58, 135, 241, 248, 252, 402; **III:** 400, 534, 543; **Supp. I Part 2:** 439; **Supp. IV Part 1:** 68, 69; **Supp. VIII:** 45; **Supp. X:** 193; **Supp. XV:** 214

Junger, Ernst, **Supp. III Part 1:** 63

Jungle, The (Sinclair), **III:** 580; **Supp. V:** 281-284, 285, 289

Jungle Lovers (Theroux), **Supp. VIII:** 314, 315, 316, **317**

"Junior Addict" (Hughes), **Supp. I Part 1:** 343

"Juniper" (Francis), **Supp. IX:** 79

"Junk" (Wilbur), **Supp. III Part 2:** 556

Junker, Howard, **Supp. XV:** 116

Junkie: Confessions of an Unredeemed Drug Addict (Burroughs), **Supp. III Part 1:** 92, 94-96, 101

Junky (Burroughs), **Supp. XIV:** 143

Juno and the Paycock (O'Casey), **Supp. IV Part 1:** 361

"Jupiter Doke, Brigadier General" (Bierce), **I:** 204

Jupiter Laughs (A. Cronin), **Supp. XVII:** 59

Jurgen (Cabell), **III:** 394; **IV:** 286; **Retro. Supp. I:** 80; **Supp. I Part 2:** 718

Jusserand, Jules, **II:** 338

Just above My Head (Baldwin), **Retro. Supp. II:** 14-15

"Just a Little One" (Parker), **Supp. IX:** 191

Just and the Unjust, The (Cozzens), **I:** 367-370, 372, 375, 377, 378, 379

Just an Ordinary Day (Jackson), **Supp. IX:** 120

Just Before Dark: Collected Nonfiction (Harrison), **Supp. VIII:** 41, 45, 46, 53

"Just Before the War with the Eskimos" (Salinger), **III:** 559

"Just Boys" (Farrell), **II:** 45

"Just for the Thrill: An Essay on the Difference Between Women and Men" (Carson), **Supp. XII:** 103-104

"Justice" (Hughes), **Supp. I Part 1:** 331

"Justice, A" (Faulkner), **Retro. Supp. I:** 83

Justice, Donald, **Retro. Supp. I:** 313; **Supp. III Part 2:** 541; **Supp. V:** 180, 337, 338, 341; **Supp. VII: 115-130**; **Supp. XI:** 141, 315; **Supp. XIII:** 76, 312; **Supp. XV:** 74, 93, 118, 119, 134; **Supp. XVII:** 110, 120, 246

Justice and Expediency (Whittier), **Supp. I Part 2:** 686

"Justice Denied in Massachusetts" (Millay), **III:** 140

Justice for Salcido (Endore), **Supp. XVII:** 63

Justice of Gold in the Damnation of Sinners, The (Edwards), **I:** 559

"Justice to Feminism" (Ozick), **Supp. V:** 272

"Just Like a Woman" (Dylan), **Supp. XV:** 350

"Just Like Job" (Angelou), **Supp. IV Part 1:** 15

Just Whistle: A Valentine (Wright), **Supp. XV: 346-348**

Just Wild About Harry (H. Miller), **III:** 190

Juvenal, **II:** 8, 169, 552

K

"K, The" (Olson), **Supp. II Part 2:** 558, 563, 569

Kabir, **Supp. IV Part 1:** 74

"Kabnis" (Toomer), **Supp. III Part 2:** 481, 484; **Supp. IX:** 309, 310, **319-320**

Kachel, Elsie. *See* Stevens, Mrs. Wallace (Elsie Kachel)

"Kaddish" (Ginsberg), **Supp. II Part 1:** 319, 327

Kaddish and Other Poems, 1958-1960 (Ginsberg), **Supp. II Part 1:** 309, 319-320; **Supp. XIV:** 269

Kael, Pauline, **Supp. IX:** 253; **Supp. XV:** 147, 148
Kafka, Franz, **II:** 244, 565, 569; **III:** 51, 253, 418, 566, 572; **IV:** 2, 113, 218, 437-439, 442; **Retro. Supp. II:** 20, 221, 282; **Supp. I Part 1:** 197; **Supp. III Part 1:** 105; **Supp. III Part 2:** 413; **Supp. IV Part 1:** 379; **Supp. IV Part 2:** 623; **Supp. VIII:** 14, 15, 103; **Supp. XII:** 21, 37, 98, 168; **Supp. XIII:** 305; **Supp. XVI:** 17, 201, 206, 209; **Supp. XVII:** 244
Kaganoff, Penny, **Supp. XI:** 122
Kagan's Superfecta (A. Hoffman), **Supp. XVII:** 42
Kahane, Jack, **III:** 171, 178
Kahn, Otto, **I:** 385; **IV:** 123; **Retro. Supp. II:** 81, 84, 85
Kahn, R. T., **Supp. XI:** 216
"Kai, Today" (Snyder), **Supp. VIII:** 300
Kaiser, Georg, **I:** 479
Kaiser, Henry, **Supp. I Part 2:** 644
Kakutani, Michiko, **Supp. IV Part 1:** 196, 201, 205, 211, 212; **Supp. V:** 63; **Supp. VIII:** 81, 84, 86, 88, 141; **Supp. X:** 171, 301, 302, 310, 314; **Supp. XI:** 38, 179; **Supp. XII:** 165, 171, 172, 299; **Supp. XVI:** 71; **Supp. XVII:** 6
Kalem, T. E., **Supp. IV Part 2:** 585
Kalevala (Finnish epic), **II:** 503, 504; **Retro. Supp. II:** 155
Kalevala (Lönnrot), **Retro. Supp. II:** 159, 160
Kalfus, Ken, **Supp. XVII:** 50
Kalki: A Novel (Vidal), **Supp. IV Part 2:** 677, 682, 685, 691, 692
Kallen, Horace, **I:** 229; **Supp. I Part 2:** 643; **Supp. XIV:** 195, 197, 198
Kallman, Chester, **II:** 586; **Supp. II Part 1:** 15, 17, 24, 26
"Kallundborg Church" (Whittier), **Supp. I Part 2:** 696
Kalstone, David, **Retro. Supp. II:** 40
Kamel, Rose, **Supp. XIII:** 306
Kamera Obskura (Nabokov), **III:** 255
Kamhi, Michelle Moarder, **Supp. IV Part 2:** 529, 530
Kandy-Kolored Tangerine-Flake Streamline Baby, The (Wolfe), **Supp. III Part 2:** 569, 573-576, 580, 581
Kane, Julie, **Supp. XVII:** 78
Kane, Lesley, **Supp. XIV:** 250
Kanellos, Nicolás, **Supp. VIII:** 82; **Supp. XIII:** 213
Kanin, Garson, **Supp. IV Part 2:** 574
"Kansas City Coyote" (Harjo), **Supp. XII:** 219, 222

"Kansas Emigrants, The" (Whittier), **Supp. I Part 2:** 687
Kant, Immanuel, **I:** 61, 277, 278; **II:** 10-11, 362, 480, 580-581, 582, 583; **III:** 300, 480, 481, 488, 612; **IV:** 90; **Supp. I Part 2:** 640; **Supp. IV Part 2:** 527; **Supp. XIV:** 198, 199; **Supp. XVI:** 184
Kanter, Hal, **IV:** 383
Kapital, Das (Marx), **III:** 580
Kaplan, Abraham, **I:** 277
Kaplan, Justin, **I:** 247-248; **Retro. Supp. I:** 392
Kaplan, Steven, **Supp. V:** 238, 241, 243, 248
Karate Is a Thing of the Spirit (Crews), **Supp. XI:** 112-113
Karbo, Karen, **Supp. X:** 259, 262
"Karintha" (Toomer), **Supp. IX:** 311
Karl, Frederick R., **Supp. IV Part 1:** 384
Karl Shapiro's America (film), **Supp. II Part 2:** 703
Karmi, T., **Supp. XV:** 78, 88
Karr, Mary, **Supp. XI: 239-256**; **Supp. XIII:** 285; **Supp. XV:** 223; **Supp. XVI:** 63, 70, 77; **Supp. XVII:** 242
Kasabian, Linda, **Supp. IV Part 1:** 206
Kasper, Catherine, **Supp. XVI:** 294-295
Kate Chopin (Toth), **Retro. Supp. II:** 71
Kate Chopin: A Critical Biography (Seyersted), **Retro. Supp. II:** 65; **Supp. I Part 1:** 225
Kate Chopin and Edith Wharton: An Annotated Bibliographical Guide to Secondary Sources (Springer), **Supp. I Part 1:** 225
Kate Chopin and Her Creole Stories (Rankin), **Retro. Supp. II:** 57; **Supp. I Part 1:** 200, 225
"Kate Chopin's *The Awakening* in the Perspective of Her Literary Career" (Arms), **Supp. I Part 1:** 225
Kate Vaiden (Price), **Supp. VI:** 264, 265
"Käthe Kollwitz" (Rukeyser), **Supp. VI:** 283, 284
Katherine and Jean (Rice), **Supp. VII:** 288
"Kathleen" (Whittier), **Supp. I Part 2:** 693
Kathleen and Frank: The Autobiography of a Family (Isherwood), **Supp. XIV:** 158, 171
Kathy Goes to Haiti (Acker), **Supp. XII:** 5
Katz, Alex, **Supp. XV:** 185
Katz, Jonathan, **Supp. XII:** 179
Katz, Steve, **Supp. V:** 44

Katz, Steven T., **Supp. XVI:** 154
Kauffman, Carol, **Supp. XI:** 295
Kauffmann, Stanley, **III:** 452; **Supp. I Part 2:** 391; **Supp. XVI:** 74
Kaufman, Charlie, **Supp. XV:** 16
Kaufman, George S., **II:** 427, 435, 437; **III:** 62, 71-72, 394; **Retro. Supp. II:** 327; **Supp. IV Part 2:** 574; **Supp. IX:** 190; **Supp. XV:** 329
Kaufmann, James, **Supp. XI:** 39
Kaufmann, Walter, **Supp. XVII:** 137
Kauvar, Elaine M., **Supp. V:** 273
Kavanaugh (Longfellow), **I:** 458; **II:** 489, 491; **Retro. Supp. II:** 156; **Supp. I Part 2:** 420
Kaveney, Roz, **Supp. XI:** 39
Kawabata, Yasunari, **Supp. XV:** 186
Kazan, Elia, **III:** 153, 163; **IV:** 383; **Supp. I Part 1:** 66, 295; **Supp. XVI:** 193
Kazin, Alfred, **I:** 248, 417, 419, 517; **II:** 177, 459; **IV:** 236; **Retro. Supp. II:** 206, 243, 246, 286; **Supp. I Part 1:** 195, 196, 294, 295, 296; **Supp. I Part 2:** 536, 631, 647, 650, 678, 679, 719; **Supp. II Part 1:** 143; **Supp. IV Part 1:** 200, 382; **Supp. V:** 122; **Supp. VIII: 93-111**; **Supp. IX:** 3, 227; **Supp. XIII:** 98, 106; **Supp. XIV:** 11; **Supp. XV:** 142
Keach, Stacey, **Supp. XI:** 309
Keane, Sarah, **Supp. I Part 1:** 100
Kearns, Cleo McNelly, **Retro. Supp. I:** 57
Kearns, George, **Retro. Supp. I:** 292
Keating, AnnLouise, **Supp. IV Part 1:** 330
Keaton, Buster, **I:** 31; **Supp. I Part 2:** 607; **Supp. IV Part 2:** 574
Keaton, Diane, **Supp. XV:** 5
Keats, John, **I:** 34, 103, 284, 314, 317-318, 385, 401, 448; **II:** 82, 88, 97, 214, 368, 512, 516, 530-531, 540, 593; **III:** 4, 10, 45, 122, 133-134, 179, 214, 237, 272, 275, 469, 485, 523; **IV:** 360, 405, 416; **Retro. Supp. I:** 91, 301, 313, 360, 395, 412; **Supp. I Part 1:** 82, 183, 266, 267, 312, 349, 362, 363, 365; **Supp. I Part 2:** 410, 422, 424, 539, 552, 675, 719, 720; **Supp. III Part 1:** 73; **Supp. IV Part 1:** 123, 168, 325; **Supp. IV Part 2:** 455; **Supp. VIII:** 41, 273; **Supp. IX:** 38, 39, 45; **Supp. XI:** 43, 320; **Supp. XII:** 9, 113, 255; **Supp. XIII:** 131, 281; **Supp. XIV:** 274; **Supp. XV:** 92; **Supp. XVII:** 76, 112
Keats, John (other), **Supp. IX:** 190, 195, 200

"Keela, the Outcast Indian Maiden" (Welty), **IV:** 263
Keeley, Mary Paxton, **Supp. XV:** 136
"Keen Scalpel on Racial Ills" (Bruell), **Supp. VIII:** 126
"Keep A-Inchin' Along" (Van Vechten), **Supp. III Part 2:** 744
Keeping (Goldbarth), **Supp. XII:** 179-180, 180
"Keeping Informed in D.C." (Nemerov), **III:** 287
Keeping Slug Woman Alive: A Holistic Approach to American Indian Texts (Sarris), **Supp. IV Part 1:** 329
"'Keeping Their World Large'" (Moore), **III:** 201-202
Keeping the Night (Everwine), **Supp. XV:** 75, **81-85,** 86
"Keeping Things Whole" (Strand), **Supp. IV Part 2:** 624
Keep It Simple: A Defense of the Earth (Nichols), **Supp. XIII:** 268
Kees, Weldon, **Supp. X:** 118; **Supp. XII:** 198; **Supp. XV:** 113, 114, 115, **133-149**
Keillor, Garrison, **Supp. XII:** 343; **Supp. XIII:** 274; **Supp. XVI:165-179**
Keillor, Gary Edward. *See* Keiller, Garrison
Keith, Brian, **Supp. IV Part 2:** 474
Keith, Minor C., **I:** 483
Keller, A. G., **III:** 108
Keller, Helen, **I:** 254, 258
Keller, Lynn, **Supp. IV Part 2:** 423; **Supp. V:** 78, 80
Kelley, David, **Supp. IV Part 2:** 528, 529
Kelley, Florence, **Supp. I Part 1:** 5, 7
Kellogg, Paul U., **Supp. I Part 1:** 5, 7, 12
Kellogg, Reverend Edwin H., **III:** 200
Kelly, **II:** 464
Kelly, Brigit Pegeen, **Supp. XVII: 123-134**
Kelly, Emmett, **Supp. XI:** 99, 106
Kelly, Walt, **Supp. XI:** 105
Kelly, William, **Supp. XV:** 75, 88
Kelsh, Nick, **Supp. XVII:** 167, 179
Kemble, Fanny, **Retro. Supp. I:** 228
Kemble, Gouverneur, **II:** 298
Kemble, Peter, **II:** 298
Kempton, Murray, **Supp. VIII:** 104
Kempton-Wace Letters, The (London and Strunsky), **II:** 465
Kennan, George F., **Supp. VIII:** 241
Kennedy, Albert J., **Supp. I Part 1:** 19
Kennedy, Arthur, **III:** 153
Kennedy, Burt, **Supp. IV Part 1:** 236

Kennedy, J. Gerald, **Retro. Supp. II:** 271
Kennedy, John F., **I:** 136, 170; **II:** 49, 152-153; **III:** 38, 41, 42, 234, 411, 415, 581; **IV:** 229; **Supp. I Part 1:** 291; **Supp. I Part 2:** 496; **Supp. VIII:** 98, 104, 203; **Supp. XII:** 132
Kennedy, John Pendleton, **II:** 313
Kennedy, Mrs. John F., **I:** 136
Kennedy, Robert, **Supp. V:** 291
Kennedy, Robert F., **I:** 294; **Supp. I Part 1:** 52; **Supp. XI:** 343
Kennedy, William, **Supp. VII: 131-157; Supp. XVII:** 135
Kennedy, X. J., **Supp. V:** 178, 182; **Supp. XV:** 113, **151-173**
Kenner, Hugh, **III:** 475, 478; **IV:** 412; **Supp. I Part 1:** 255; **Supp. IV Part 2:** 474; **Supp. XV:** 147
"Kenneth Koch's 'Serious Moment'" (Spurr), **Supp. XV:** 183
Kenneth Millar/Ross Macdonald: A Checklist (Bruccoli), **Supp. IV Part 2:** 464, 469, 471
Kenny, Maurice, **Supp. IV Part 2:** 502
Kent, George, **Supp. IV Part 1:** 11
Kent, Rockwell, **Supp. XV:** 41
Kenton, Maxwell. *See* Burnett, David; Hoffenberg, Mason; Southern, Terry
"Kent State, May 1970" (Haines), **Supp. XII:** 211
Kenyatta, Jomo, **Supp. X:** 135
Kenyon, Jane, **Supp. VII: 159-177; Supp. VIII:** 272
Keogh, Tom, **Supp. XVI:230**
Kepler, Johannes, **III:** 484; **IV:** 18
Keppel, Frederick P., **I:** 214
"Kéramos" (Longfellow), **II:** 494; **Retro. Supp. II:** 167, 169
Kéramos and Other Poems (Longfellow), **II:** 490
Kerim, Ussin, **Supp. IX:** 152
Kermode, Frank, **IV:** 133; **Retro. Supp. I:** 301
Kern, Jerome, **II:** 427
Kerouac, Jack, **III:** 174; **Retro. Supp. I:** 102; **Supp. II Part 1:** 31, 307, 309, 318, 328; **Supp. III Part 1:** 91-94, 96, 100, **217-234; Supp. IV Part 1:** 90, 146; **Supp. V:** 336; **Supp. VIII:** 42, 138, 289, 305; **Supp. IX:** 246; **Supp. XII:** 118, 121, 122, 123, 126, 131, 132; **Supp. XIII:** 275, 284; **Supp. XIV:137, 138, 141, 142, 143-144; Supp. XV:** 134, 221; **Supp. XVI:123; Supp. XVII:** 135, 138
Kerr, Deborah, **Supp. XI:** 307
Kerr, Orpheus C. (pseudonym). *See* Newell, Henry

Kerr, Walter, **Supp. IV Part 2:** 575, 579
Kerridge, Richard, **Supp. XVI:26**
Kesey, Ken, **III:** 558; **Supp. III Part 1:** 217; **Supp. V:** 220, 295; **Supp. X:** 24, 265; **Supp. XI:** 104
Kesten, Stephen, **Supp. XI:** 309
Ketchup (Shanley), **Supp. XIV:315**
Kevane, Bridget, **Supp. XI:** 185, 190
"Key, The" (Welty), **IV:** 262
"Keys" (Nye), **Supp. XIII:** 281
Key to Uncle Tom's Cabin, A (Stowe), **Supp. I Part 2:** 580
Key West (H. Crane), **Retro. Supp. II:** 84
"Key West" (H. Crane), **I:** 400
Key West: An Island Sheaf (Crane), **I:** 385, 399-402
Khrushchev, Nikita, **I:** 136
Kiang Kang-hu, **Supp. XV:** 45, 47
Kick for a Bite, A (Cobbett), **Supp. XV:** 237
"Kicking the Candles Out" (Jarman), **Supp. XVII:** 113
Kid, The (Aiken), **I:** 61
Kid, The (Chaplin), **I:** 386
Kidder, Tracy, **Supp. III Part 1:** 302
Kidman, Nicole, **Supp. X:** 80
"Kidnapping in the Family, A" (Fante), **Supp. XI:** 164
"Kid's Guide to Divorce, The" (Moore), **Supp. X:** 167, 172
Kidwell, Clara Sue, **Supp. IV Part 1:** 333
Kielsky, Vera Emuma, **Supp. V:** 273
Kiely, Brendan, **Supp. XVII:** 75
Kieran, John, **II:** 417
Kierkegaard, Søren Aabye, **II:** 229; **III:** 292, 305, 309, 572; **IV:** 438, 491; **Retro. Supp. I:** 326; **Retro. Supp. II:** 222; **Supp. V:** 9; **Supp. VIII:** 7-8
Kiernan, Robert F., **Supp. IV Part 2:** 684
Kieseritsky, L., **III:** 252
"Kilim" (McClatchy), **Supp. XII:** 258
"Killed at Resaca" (Bierce), **I:** 202
"Killed at the Ford" (Longfellow), **Retro. Supp. II:** 170-171
Killens, John Oliver, **Supp. IV Part 1:** 8, 369
"Killer in the Rain" (Chandler), **Supp. IV Part 1:** 122
"Killers, The" (Hemingway), **II:** 249; **Retro. Supp. I:** 188, 189
Killing Mister Watson (Matthiessen), **Supp. V:** 212, 214
"Killing of a State Cop, The" (Ortiz), **Supp. IV Part 2:** 499
Killing of Sister George, The (Marcus),

Supp. I Part 1: 277
"Killings" (Dubus), **Supp. VII:** 85-86
"Killing the Plants" (Kenyon), **Supp. VII:** 167, 168
Kilmer, Joyce, **Supp. I Part 2:** 387; **Supp. XV:** 294
Kilpatrick, James K., **Supp. X:** 145
Kilvert, Francis, **Supp. VIII:** 172
Kim (Kipling), **Supp. X:** 230
Kim, Alfred, **Supp. XI:** 140
Kimball, J. Golden, **Supp. IV Part 2:** 602
Kimbrough, Mary Craig. *See* Sinclair, Mary Craig (Mary Craig Kimbrough)
Kimes, Maymie B., **Supp. IX:** 178
Kimes, William F., **Supp. IX:** 178
"Kin" (Welty), **IV:** 277; **Retro. Supp. I:** 353
Kinard, Agnes Dodds, **Supp. XIV:**122, 123, 127
Kincaid, Jamaica, **Supp. VII: 179-196**
"Kindness" (Dunn), **Supp. XI:** 149, 150
"Kindness" (Nye), **Supp. XIII:** 285
"Kindness" (Plath), **Retro. Supp. II:** 256
Kind of Order, A Kind of Folly, A: Essays and Conversations (Kunitz), **Supp. III Part 1:** 262, 268
Kindred (O. Butler), **Supp. XIII: 59-60,** 69
"Kind Sir: These Woods" (Sexton), **Supp. II Part 2:** 673
Kinds of Love (Sarton), **Supp. VIII: 253-254,** 256
Kinfolk (Buck), **Supp. II Part 1:** 126
King, Alexander, **IV:** 287
King, Carole, **Supp. XII:** 308
King, Clarence, **I:** 1
King, Ernest, **Supp. I Part 2:** 491
King, Fisher, **II:** 425
King, Francis, **Supp. XIV:**155, 156, 166, 169
King, Grace, **Retro. Supp. II:** 136
King, Martin Luther, Jr., **Retro. Supp. II:** 12, 13
King, Michael, **Supp. XII:** 182
King, Queen, Knave (Nabokov), **III:** 251; **Retro. Supp. I:** 270
King, Starr, **Supp. II Part 1:** 341, 342
King, Stephen, **Supp. IV Part 1:** 102, 104; **Supp. IV Part 2:** 467; **Supp. V: 137-155; Supp. IX:** 114; **Supp. XIII:** 53
King, Tabitha (Mrs. Stephen King), **Supp. V:** 137
King, The (Barthelme), **Supp. IV Part 1:** 47, 52
King Coffin (Aiken), **I:** 53-54, 57

"King David" (Benét), **Supp. XI:** 44
"King David" (Reznikoff), **Supp. XIV:**283
Kingdom and the Power, The (Talese), **Supp. XVII:** 202, 203, 204, 210
Kingdom by the Sea, The: A Journey around Great Britain (Theroux), **Supp. VIII:** 323
Kingdom of Earth (T. Williams), **IV:** 382, 386, 387, 388, 391, 393, 398
"Kingdom of Earth, The" (T. Williams), **IV:** 384
Kingfisher, The (Clampitt), **Supp. IX:** 38
"Kingfishers, The" (Olson), **Supp. II Part 2:** 557, 558-563, 582
King Jasper (Robinson), **III:** 523
King Kong (film), **Supp. IV Part 1:** 104; **Supp. XVII:** 58
King Lear (Shakespeare), **I:** 538; **II:** 540, 551; **Retro. Supp. I:** 248; **Supp. IV Part 1:** 31, 36; **Supp. IX:** 14; **Supp. XI:** 172; **Supp. XV:** 349
King Leopold's Soliloquy (Twain), **IV:** 208
King My Father's Wreck, The (Simpson), **Supp. IX:** 266, 267, 270, 275, 276
King of Babylon Shall Not Come Against You, The (Garrett), **Supp. VII:** 110-111; **Supp. X:** 3
"King of Folly Island, The" (Jewett), **II:** 394; **Retro. Supp. II:** 132, 133
King of Kings (film), **Supp. IV Part 2:** 520
King of Paris (Endore), **Supp. XVII:** 64
"King of the Bingo Game" (Ellison), **Retro. Supp. II:** 117, 125; **Supp. II Part 1:** 235, 238, 240-241
"King of the Cats, The" (Benét), **Supp. XI:** 49-50
"King of the Clock Tower" (Yeats), **III:** 473
"King of the Desert, The" (O'Hara), **III:** 369
King of the Fields, The (Singer), **Retro. Supp. II:** 317
King of the Jews (Epstein), **Supp. XII:** 161, **166-170,** 172
King of the Mountain (Garrett), **Supp. VII:** 96, 97
"King of the River" (Kunitz), **Supp. III Part 1:** 263, 267-268
"King of the Sea" (Marquand), **III:** 60
"King over the Water" (Blackmur), **Supp. II Part 1:** 107
"King Pandar" (Blackmur), **Supp. II Part 1:** 92, 102

"King Pest" (Poe), **Retro. Supp. II:** 273
Kingsblood Royal (Lewis), **II:** 456
Kingsbury, John, **Supp. I Part 1:** 8
"King's Daughters, Home for Unwed Mothers, 1948" (Stanford), **Supp. XV:** 345
King's Henchman, The (Millay), **III:** 138-139
Kingsley, Sidney, **Supp. I Part 1:** 277, 281
King's Mare, The (Canolle; Loos, trans.), **Supp. XVI:**194
"King's Missive, The" (Whittier), **Supp. I Part 2:** 694
Kingsolver, Barbara, **Supp. VII: 197-214; Supp. XIII:** 16
King's Stilts, The (Geisel), **Supp. XVI:**100, 104
Kingston, Earll, **Supp. V:** 160
Kingston, Maxine Hong, **Supp. IV Part 1:** 1, 12; **Supp. V: 157-175,** 250; **Supp. X:** 291-292; **Supp. XI:** 18, 245
"King Volmer and Elsie" (Whittier), **Supp. I Part 2:** 696
Kinmont, Alexander, **Supp. I Part 2:** 588-589
Kinnaird, John, **Retro. Supp. I:** 399
Kinnell, Galway, **Supp. III Part 1: 235-256; Supp. III Part 2:** 541; **Supp. IV Part 2:** 623; **Supp. V:** 332; **Supp. VIII:** 39; **Supp. XI:** 139; **Supp. XII:** 241; **Supp. XV:** 212; **Supp. XVI:**53
Kinsey, Alfred, **IV:** 230; **Supp. XIV:**140
Kinsgton, Maxine Hong, **Supp. XV:** 220, 223
Kinzie, Mary, **Supp. XII:** 181
"Kipling" (Trilling), **Supp. III Part 2:** 495
Kipling, Rudyard, **I:** 421, 587-588; **II:** 271, 338, 404, 439; **III:** 55, 328, 508, 511, 521, 524, 579; **IV:** 429; **Supp. IV Part 2:** 603; **Supp. X:** 255
Kirby, David, **Supp. XIII:** 89
Kirkland, David, **Supp. XVI:**186
Kirkland, Jack, **I:** 297
Kirkpatrick, Jeane, **Supp. VIII:** 241
Kirkus, Virginia, **Supp. XV:** 198
Kirkwood, Cynthia A., **Supp. XI:** 177, 178, 179
Kirp, David L., **Supp. XI:** 129
Kirsch, Adam, **Supp. XV:** 251, 260, 264, 266, 341, 347, 350-351
Kirstein, Lincoln, **Supp. II Part 1:** 90, 97; **Supp. IV Part 1:** 82, 83
Kiss, The (Harrison), **Supp. X:** 191

"Kiss, The" (Sexton), **Supp. II Part 2:** 687
"Kiss Away" (C. Baxter), **Supp. XVII:** 20
Kissel, Howard, **Supp. IV Part 2:** 580
Kiss Hollywood Good-by (Loos), **Supp. XVI:**190, 195
Kissinger, Henry, **Supp. IV Part 1:** 388; **Supp. XII:** 9, 14
Kiss of the Spider Woman, the Musical (McNally), **Supp. XIII:** 207, **Supp. XIII:** 208
Kiss Tomorrow Good-bye (McCoy), **Supp. XIII:** 170, **172-173,** 174
"Kit and Caboodle" (Komunyakaa), **Supp. XIII:** 115
Kit Brandon: A Portrait (Anderson), **I:** 111
Kitchen, Judith, **Supp. IV Part 1:** 242, 245, 252; **Supp. IX:** 163; **Supp. XI:** 312, 313, 315, 317, 319, 320, 326, 329; **Supp. XV:** 215, 219
"Kitchenette" (Brooks), **Retro. Supp. I:** 208
Kitchen God's Wife, The (Tan), **Supp. X:** 289, 292, 293, 294-295, 296-297, 298-299
"Kitchen Terrarium: 1983" (McCarriston), **Supp. XIV:**270
Kit O'Brien (Masters), **Supp. I Part 2:** 471
Kittel, Frederick August. *See* Wilson, August
Kittredge, Charmian. *See* London, Mrs. Jack (Charmian Kittredge)
Kittredge, William, **Supp. VIII:** 39; **Supp. XI:** 316; **Supp. XII:** 209; **Supp. XIII:** 16
"Kitty Hawk" (Frost), **II:** 164; **Retro. Supp. I:** 124, 141
Kizer, Carolyn, **Supp. XVII:** 71, 72, 73, 74
Klein, Joe, **Supp. XII:** 67-68
Klein, Marcus, **Supp. I Part 2:** 432; **Supp. XI:** 233
Kleist, Heinrich von, **Supp. IV Part 1:** 224
Kline, Franz, **Supp. XII:** 198
Kline, George, **Supp. VIII:** 22, 28
Klinghoffer, David, **Supp. XVI:**74
Klinkowitz, Jerome, **Supp. IV Part 1:** 40; **Supp. X:** 263; **Supp. XI:** 347
Knapp, Adeline, **Supp. XI:** 200
Knapp, Friedrich, **III:** 100
Knapp, Samuel, **I:** 336
Knapp, Samuel Lorenzo, **Supp. XV:** 246
Kneel to the Rising Sun (Caldwell), **I:** 304, 309
"Knees/Dura-Europos" (Goldbarth),

Supp. XII: 185
"Knife" (Simic), **Supp. VIII:** 275
Knight, Arthur, **Supp. XIV:**144
Knight, Etheridge, **Supp. XI:** 239
"Knight in Disguise, The" (Lindsay), **Supp. I Part 2:** 390
Knightly Quest, The (T. Williams), **IV:** 383
Knight's Gambit (Faulkner), **II:** 72
Knish, Anne. *See* Ficke, Arthur Davison
"Knit One, Purl Two" (K. Snodgrass), **Supp. XVI:**42
"Knock" (Dickey), **Supp. IV Part 1:** 182
"Knocking Around" (Ashbery), **Supp. III Part 1:** 22
"Knocking on Three, Winston" (Epstein), **Supp. XIV:**109
Knock on Any Door (film, Ray), **Supp. XVII:** 150
Knock on Any Door (W. Motley), 158; **Supp. XVII: 150-155,** 159, 160
Knockout Artist, The (Crews), **Supp. XI: 113-114**
Knoll, Robert E., **Supp. XV:** 118
Knopf, Alfred A., **III:** 99, 105, 106, 107; **Retro. Supp. I:** 13, 19, 317; **Supp. I Part 1:** 324, 325, 327; **Supp. IV Part 1:** 125, 354; **Supp. XIII:** 172
Knopf, Blanche, **Supp. I Part 1:** 324, 325, 327, 328, 332, 341; **Supp. IV Part 1:** 128, 346, 348; **Supp. XIII:** 169
"Knot, The" (Rich), **Supp. I Part 2:** 555
Knotts, Kristina, **Supp. XIII:** 238
"Knowing, The" (Olds), **Supp. X:** 215
"Knowledge Forwards and Backwards" (Stern), **Supp. IX:** 296
Knowles, John, **Supp. IV Part 2:** 679; **Supp. XII: 235-250**
Knox, Frank, **Supp. I Part 2:** 488, 489
Knox, Israel, **Supp. X:** 70
Knox, Vicesimus, **II:** 8
Knoxville: Summer of 1915 (Agee), **I:** 42-46
Knudson, R. Rozanne, **Supp. IV Part 2:** 648
Ko; or, A Season on Earth (Koch), **Supp. XV:** 175, 180, 181, 183, 186
Kober, Arthur, **Supp. I Part 1:** 292
Koch, Frederick, **IV:** 453
Koch, John, **Supp. VIII:** 88
Koch, Kenneth, **Supp. XV: 175-192**
Koch, Vivienne, **III:** 194; **IV:** 136, 140; **Retro. Supp. I:** 428, 430
"Kochinnenako in Academe: Three Approaches to Interpreting a Keres

Indian Tale" (Gunn Allen), **Supp. IV Part 1:** 329
"Kodachromes of the Island" (Hayden), **Supp. II Part 1:** 367, 380
Koestler, Arthur, **I:** 258; **Supp. I Part 2:** 671
Kokkinen, Eila, **Supp. XIV:**146, 148
Kolbenheyer, Dr. Frederick, **Supp. I Part 1:** 207
Kolodny, Annette, **Supp. X:** 97, 103, 229
"Komodo" (C. Frost), **Supp. XV:** 95
Komunyakaa, Yusef, **Supp. XIII: 111-136**
Konigsberg, Allan Stewart. *See* Allen, Woody
Kon-Tiki (Heyerdahl), **II:** 477
Koopman, Harry Lyman, **Retro. Supp. I:** 40
Kooser, Ted, **Supp. XV:** 113, 115
Kootz, Samuel, **Supp. XV:** 144
Kora and Ka (Doolittle), **Supp. I Part 1:** 270
Kora in Hell (W. C. Williams), **Retro. Supp. I:** 416, **417-418,** 419, 430, 431
Korb, Rena, **Supp. XI:** 2
Korczak, Janosz, **Supp. X:** 70
Kornblatt, Joyce Reiser, **Supp. XV:** 62
Kort, Amy, **Supp. XIII:** 148
Kosinski, Jerzy, **Supp. VII: 215-228; Supp. XII:** 21
"Kostas Tympakianakis" (Merrill), **Supp. III Part 1:** 326
Koteliansky, S. S., **Supp. VIII:** 251, 265
Kowloon Tong (Theroux), **Supp. VIII:** 325
Kozlenko, William, **IV:** 378, 381
Krabbenhoft, Ken, **Supp. XVII:** 112
Kraft, James, **Supp. XV:** 40, 41, 42, 43, 52
Krakauer, Jon, **Supp. XVII:** 210
Kramer, Dale, **Supp. I Part 2:** 669
Kramer, Hilton, **III:** 537; **Supp. I Part 1:** 295, 296; **Supp. VIII:** 239; **Supp. XV:** 113
Kramer, Lawrence, **Supp. IV Part 1:** 61, 65, 66; **Supp. IX:** 291
Kramer, Peter D., **Supp. XVI:**229
Kramer, Stanley, **II:** 421, 587
Krapp's Last Tape (Beckett), **I:** 71; **III:** 387; **Retro. Supp. I:** 206
Krassner, Paul, **Supp. IV Part 1:** 385; **Supp. XI:** 293
Kreisler, Harry, **Supp. XVI:**155
Kreitman, Esther, **IV:** 2
"Kremlin of Smoke" (Schnackenberg), **Supp. XV:** 257-258
Kreymborg, Alfred, **II:** 530; **III:** 465;

IV: 76; **Retro. Supp. I:** 417; **Supp. XV:** 301, 306
Krim, Seymour, **Supp. XV:** 338; **Supp. XVI:** 217
Kristeva, Julia, **Supp. XII:** 6
Kristofferson, Kris, **Supp. XIII:** 119
Kristol, Irving, **Supp. VIII:** 93, 244; **Supp. XIII:** 98
Krivak, Andrew, **Supp. XVII:** 242
Kroll, Jack, **Supp. IV Part 2:** 590
Kroll, Judith, **Supp. I Part 2:** 541-543, 544, 546
Kroll Ring, Frances. *See* Ring, Frances Kroll
Krondorfer, Björn, **Supp. XVI:** 160
Krook, Dorothea, **Retro. Supp. II:** 243
Kropotkin, Peter, **I:** 493; **Supp. I Part 1:** 5; **Supp. IV Part 2:** 521
Kruif, Paul de, **II:** 446
Krupat, Arnold, **Supp. IV Part 2:** 500
Krupnick, Mark, **Supp. XVI:** 153
Krutch, Joseph Wood, **II:** 459; **III:** 425; **IV:** 70, 175
Kublai Khan, **III:** 395
"Kubla Khan" (Coleridge), **Supp. XIII:** 131, 283
Kubrick, Stanley, **Supp. IV Part 1:** 392; **Supp. XI:** 293, **Supp. XI:** 301, 302-303
Kuehl, John, **Supp. IV Part 1:** 279, 284, 285, 287
Kuehl, Linda, **Supp. IV Part 1:** 199
"Kugelmass Episode, The" (Allen), **Supp. XV:** 15, 16
Kukachin, Princess, **III:** 395
"Ku Klux" (Hughes), **Retro. Supp. I:** 205
Kulshrestha, Chirantan, **Retro. Supp. II:** 21
Kumin, Maxine, **Supp. IV Part 2:** 439-457; **Supp. XIII:** 294; **Supp. XVII:** 71, 75-76
Kundera, Milan, **Supp. VIII:** 241
Kunitz, Stanley, **I:** 179, 180, 181, 182, 521; **II:** 545; **Supp. III Part 1:** 257-270; **Supp. V:** 79; **Supp. XI:** 259; **Supp. XIII:** 341
Kuo, Helena, **Supp. X:** 291
Kuropatkin, General Aleksei Nikolaevich, **III:** 247-248
Kurzy of the Sea (Barnes), **Supp. III Part 1:** 34
Kushner, Tony, **Supp. IX:** 131-149
Kussy, Bella, **IV:** 468
Kuttner, Henry, **Supp. IV Part 1:** 102
Kuzma, Greg, **Supp. XV:** 118
L
LaBastille, Anne, **Supp. X:** 95-110
"Labours of Hercules, The" (Moore), **III:** 201

La Bruyère, Jean de, **I:** 58
La Bufera e Altro (Montale), **Supp. V:** 337
Labyrinth of Love (Untermeyer), **Supp. XV:** 312
Labyrinth of Solitude, The (Paz), **Supp. XIII:** 223
Lacan, Jacques, **Supp. IV Part 1:** 45; **Supp. VIII:** 5; **Supp. XII:** 98
La Casa en Mango Street (Cisneros), **Supp. VII:** 58-59
Lachaise, Gaston, **I:** 434
"Lackawanna" (Merwin), **Supp. III Part 1:** 350
Lackawanna Elegy (Goll; Kinnell, trans.), **Supp. III Part 1:** 235, 243-244
Laclède, Pierre, **Supp. I Part 1:** 205
"Lacquer Prints" (Lowell), **II:** 524-525
Lacy, Ed, **Supp. XV:** 193-210
Ladder of Years (Tyler), **Supp. IV Part 2:** 657, 671-672
Ladders to Fire (Nin), **Supp. X:** 185
"Ladies" (Coleman), **Supp. XI:** 93
Ladies Almanack (Barnes), **Supp. III Part 1:** 37-39, 42
"Ladies in Spring" (Welty), **IV:** 276-277; **Retro. Supp. I:** 353
Lady Audley's Secret (Braddon), **Supp. I Part 1:** 35, 36
"Lady Barberina" (James), **Retro. Supp. I:** 227
"Lady Bates" (Jarrell), **II:** 380-381
Lady Chatterley's Lover (Lawrence), **III:** 170; **IV:** 434; **Supp. XVI:** 267
Lady from Louisiana (film, Vorhaus), **Supp. XVII:** 59
"Lady from Redhorse, A" (Bierce), **I:** 203
Lady in Kicking Horse Reservoir, The (Hugo), **Supp. VI:** 134, 138-139
Lady in the Lake, The (Chandler), **Supp. IV Part 1:** 127, 129-130
"Lady in the Lake, The" (Chandler), **Supp. IV Part 1:** 129
Lady in the Lake, The (film), **Supp. IV Part 1:** 130
"Lady in the Pink Mustang, The" (Erdrich), **Supp. IV Part 1:** 270
"Lady Is Civilized, The" (Taylor), **Supp. V:** 315
Lady Is Cold, The (White), **Supp. I Part 2:** 653
"Lady Lazarus" (Plath), **Retro. Supp. II:** 250, 251, 255; **Supp. I Part 2:** 529, 535, 542, 545
Lady of Aroostook, The (Howells), **II:** 280
"Lady of Bayou St. John, A" (Chopin), **Retro. Supp. II:** 58

"Lady of the Lake, The" (Malamud), **Supp. I Part 2:** 437
Lady Oracle (Atwood), **Supp. XIII:** 21, 23-24
Lady Sings the Blues (film), **Supp. I Part 1:** 67
"Lady's Maid's Bell, The" (Wharton), **IV:** 316
"Lady Wentworth" (Longfellow), **II:** 505
"Lady with a Lamp" (Parker), **Supp. IX:** 193
"Lady with the Heron, The" (Merwin), **Supp. III Part 1:** 343
La Farge, John, **I:** 1, 2, 20; **II:** 322, 338; **Retro. Supp. I:** 217
La Farge, Oliver, **Supp. IV Part 2:** 503
Lafayette, Marquis de, **I:** 344, 345; **II:** 405-406; **Supp. I Part 2:** 510, 511, 683
"La Figlia che Piange" (Eliot), **Retro. Supp. I:** 63
La Follette, Robert, **I:** 483, 485, 492; **III:** 580
La Fontaine, Jean de, **II:** 154; **III:** 194; **IV:** 80
Laforgue, Jules, **I:** 386, 569, 570, 572-573, 575, 576; **II:** 528; **III:** 8, 11, 466; **IV:** 37, 79, 80, 122; **Retro. Supp. I:** 55, 56; **Supp. XIII:** 332, 335, 346; **Supp. XV:** 165
La Gallienne, Eva, **Supp. VIII:** 251
"Lager Beer" (Dunbar), **Supp. II Part 1:** 193
"La Gringuita: On Losing a Native Language" (Alvarez), **Supp. VII:** 18
Laguna Woman (Silko), **Supp. IV Part 2:** 557, 560-561
Laing, R. D., **Supp. I Part 2:** 527
La kabbale pratique (Ambelain), **Supp. I Part 1:** 273
"Lake, The" (Bradbury), **Supp. IV Part 1:** 101
Lake, The (play), **Supp. IX:** 189
Lakeboat (Mamet), **Supp. XIV:** 240-241
"Lake Chelan" (Stafford), **Supp. XI:** 321
Lake Effect Country (Ammons), **Supp. VII:** 34, 35
"Lake Isle of Innisfree" (Yeats), **Retro. Supp. I:** 413
"Lake Return" (Wright), **Supp. XV:** 345
Lake Wobegon Days (Keillor), **Supp. XVI:** 165, 166, **173-174**
Lake Wobegon Summer 1956 (Keillor), **Supp. XVI:** 178
Lalic, Ivan V., **Supp. VIII:** 272

L'Alouette (Anouilh), **Supp. I Part 1:** 286-288
Lamantia, Philip, **Supp. VIII:** 289
Lamb, Charles, **III:** 111, 207; **Supp. VIII:** 125
Lamb, Wendy, **Supp. IV Part 2:** 658
Lambardi, Marilyn May, **Retro. Supp. II:** 45-46
"Lament" (Wilbur), **Supp. III Part 2:** 550
"Lamentations" (Glück), **Supp. V:** 83, 84
"Lament for Dark Peoples" (Hughes), **Retro. Supp. I:** 199
"Lament for Saul and Jonathan" (Bradstreet), **Supp. I Part 1:** 111
"Lament-Heaven" (Doty), **Supp. XI:** 125
"Lament of a New England Mother, The" (Eberhart), **I:** 539
Laments for the Living (Parker), **Supp. IX:** 192
"Lame Shall Enter First, The" (O'Connor), **III:** 348, 351, 352, 355, 356-357, 358; **Retro. Supp. II:** 237
Lamia (Keats), **II:** 512; **III:** 523
La Motte-Fouqué, Friedrich Heinrich Karl, **III:** 77, 78
L'Amour, Louis, **Supp. XIII:** 5
Lamp for Nightfall, A (Caldwell), **I:** 297
Lamplit Answer, The (Schnackenberg), **Supp. XV:** 251, 254, **256-260**
"Lance" (Nabokov), **Retro. Supp. I:** 266
Lancelot (Percy), **Supp. III Part 1:** 384, 395-396
Lancelot (Robinson), **III:** 513, 522
Lanchester, John, **Retro. Supp. I:** 278
"Land" (Emerson), **II:** 6
"Land Aesthetic, The" (Callicott), **Supp. XIV:** 184
Landau, Deborah, **Supp. XI:** 122, 123
"Land beyond the Blow, The" (Bierce), **I:** 209
"Land Ethic, The" (Leopold), **Supp. XIV:** 179, 180, 183, 191, 192
Landfall (Wagoner), **Supp. IX:** 330
"Landing in Luck" (Faulkner), **Retro. Supp. I:** 85
"Landing on the Moon" (Swenson), **Supp. IV Part 2:** 643
"Landing Under Water, I See Roots" (A. Finch), **Supp. XVII:** 76
Landlord at Lion's Head, The (Howells), **II:** 276, 287-288
Landmarks of Healing: A Study of House Made of Dawn (Scarberry-García), **Supp. IV Part 2:** 486
Land of Little Rain, The (Dillard), **Supp. VI:** 27-28
Land of the Free U.S.A. (MacLeish), **I:** 293; **III:** 16-17
Land of Unlikeness (Lowell), **II:** 537-538, 539, 547; **Retro. Supp. II:** 177, 178, **184-185**
Landor, Walter Savage, **III:** 15, 469; **Supp. I Part 2:** 422
"Landscape" (Sarton), **Supp. VIII:** 259
"Landscape: The Eastern Shore" (Barth), **I:** 122
"Landscape as a Nude" (MacLeish), **III:** 14
Landscape at the End of the Century (Dunn), **Supp. XI:** 139, 143, **150-151**
"Landscape Chamber, The" (Jewett), **II:** 408-409
"Landscape for the Disappeared" (Komunyakaa), **Supp. XIII:** 120, 126
Landscape in American Poetry (Larcom), **Supp. XIII:** 142
"Landscape Painter, A" (James), **II:** 322; **Retro. Supp. I:** 219
"Landscape Symbolism in Kate Chopin's *At Fault*" (Arner), **Retro. Supp. II:** 62
"Landscape with Boat" (Stevens), **Retro. Supp. I:** 306
"Landscape with the Fall of Icarus" (Brueghel), **Retro. Supp. I:** 430
Land's End: A Walk through Provincetown (Cunningham), **Supp. XV:** 69
"Land Where There Is No Death, The" (Benét), **Supp. XI:** 56
Lane, Ann, **Supp. XI:** 195, 208
Lane, Cornelia. *See* Anderson, Mrs. Sherwood
Lane, Homer, **Supp. II Part 1:** 6; **Supp. XIV:** 160
Lane, Nathan, **Supp. XIII:** 207
Lane, Rose Wilder, **Supp. IV Part 2:** 524
Lanes, Selma G., **Supp. XVI:** 104, 107
Lang, Andrew, **Retro. Supp. I:** 127
Lang, Violet, **Supp. XII:** 119
Langdon, Olivia. *See* Clemens, Mrs. Samuel Langhorne (Olivia Langdon)
Lange, Carl Georg, **II:** 350
Lange, Dorothea, **I:** 293; **Supp. XIV:** 181
Langland, Joseph, **III:** 542
Langston Hughes, American Poet (Walker), **Supp. III Part 2:** 530-531
Langston Hughes: Modern Critical Views (Bloom, ed.), **Retro. Supp. I:** 193
Langston Hughes: The Poet and His Critics (Barksdale), **Retro. Supp. I:** 202
Langston Hughes and the "Chicago Defender": Essays on Race, Politics, and Culture (De Santis, ed.), **Retro. Supp. I:** 194
Langston Hughes Reader, The (Hughes), **Retro. Supp. I:** 202; **Supp. I Part 1:** 345
"Language, Visualization and the Inner Library" (Shepard), **Supp. III Part 2:** 436, 438, 449
"Language and the Writer" (Bambara), **Supp. XI:** 18
Language As Gesture (Blackmur), **Supp. II Part 1:** 108
Language as Symbolic Action (Burke), **I:** 275, 282, 285
Language Book, The (Andrews and Bernstein), **Supp. IV Part 2:** 426
Language in Thought and Action (Hayakawa), **I:** 448
"Language of Being and Dying, The" (Gass), **Supp. VI:** 91
"Language of Home, The" (Wideman), **Supp. X:** 320, 323-324
Language of Life, The (Moyers, television series), **Supp. XIII:** 274, 276
Language of the American South, The (Brooks), **Supp. XIV:** 14
"Language of the Brag, The" (Olds), **Supp. X:** 204
"Language We Know, The" (Ortiz), **Supp. IV Part 2:** 500
Lanier, Clifford, **Supp. I Part 1:** 349, 350, 353, 355, 356, 371
Lanier, James F. D., **Supp. I Part 1:** 350
Lanier, Lyle H., **Supp. X:** 25
Lanier, Mrs. Robert Sampson (Mary Jane Anderson), **Supp. I Part 1:** 349
Lanier, Mrs. Sidney (Mary Day), **Supp. I Part 1:** 351, 355, 357, 361, 362, 364, 370, 371
Lanier, Robert Sampson, **Supp. I Part 1:** 349, 351, 355, 356, 361
Lanier, Sidney, **IV:** 444; **Supp. I Part 1: 349-373**; **Supp. I Part 2:** 416; **Supp. IV Part 1:** 165
"Lanier as Poet" (Parks), **Supp. I Part 1:** 373
"Lanier's Reading" (P. Graham), **Supp. I Part 1:** 373
"Lanier's Use of Science for Poetic Imagery" (Beaver), **Supp. I Part 1:** 373
Lannegan, Helen. *See* Caldwell, Mrs. Erskine
Lannin, Paul, **II:** 427

Lanny Budd novels (Sinclair), **Supp. V:** 290
Lant, Kathleen Margaret, **Supp. V:** 141
Lanthenas, François, **Supp. I Part 2:** 515
Laotzu, **III:** 173, 189, 567; **Supp. XV:** 39, 46, 48
"Lapis Lazuli" (Yeats), **I:** 532; **III:** 40
Laplace, Pierre Simon de, **III:** 428
Lapouge, M. G., **Supp. I Part 2:** 633
Lappa, Katherine, **Supp. XV:** 176
Laqueur, Thomas, **Supp. XVI:**154
Larbaud, Valery, **IV:** 404; **Supp. XIII:** 332; **Supp. XIV:**338
Larcom, Lucy, **Retro. Supp. II:** 145; **Supp. XIII: 137-157**
Larcom's Poetical Works (Larcom), **Supp. XIII:** 142
Lardner, John, **II:** 437
Lardner, Ring, **I:** 487; **II:** 44, 91, 259, 263, **415-438**; **III:** 566, 572; **IV:** 433; **Retro. Supp. I:** 105; **Retro. Supp. II:** 222; **Supp. I Part 2:** 609; **Supp. IX:** 200; **Supp. XVI:**189
Lardner, Ring, Jr., **Supp. XI:** 306
"Lardner, Shakespeare and Chekhov" (Matthews), **II:** 430
"Large Bad Picture" (Bishop), **Retro. Supp. II:** 43; **Supp. I Part 1:** 73, 80-82, 85, 86, 89, 90
"Large Coffee" (Lardner), **II:** 437
Large Glass, or The Bride Stripped Bare by Her Bachelors, Even (Duchamp), **Supp. IV Part 2:** 423, 424
Largo (Handel), **IV:** 369
Lark, The (Hellman), **Supp. I Part 1:** 286-288, 297
Larkin, Philip, **Supp. I Part 2:** 536; **Supp. XI:** 243, 249; **Supp. XIII:** 76, 85; **Supp. XV:** 117, 251; **Supp. XVII:** 110
Larkin, Sharon Alile, **Supp. XI:** 20
Larmore, Phoebe, **Supp. X:** 266
Larner, Jeremy, **Supp. XVI:**220
La Rochefoucauld, François de, **I:** 279; **II:** 111; **Supp. XIV:**130
"La Rose des Vents" (Wilbur), **Supp. III Part 2:** 550
Larry's Party (Shields), **Supp. VII:** 324, 326-327
Larsen, Nella, **Supp. I Part 1:** 325, 326; **Supp. IV Part 1:** 164
Larson, Charles, **Supp. IV Part 1:** 331
Larson, Clinton, **Supp. XI:** 328
"Larval Stage of a Bookworm" (Mencken), **III:** 101
La Salle and the Discovery of the Great West (Parkman), **Supp. II Part 2:** 595, 598, 605-607

Lasch, Christopher, **I:** 259
Lasher (Rice), **Supp. VII:** 299-300
Lask, Thomas, **III:** 576; **Supp. XVI:**250
Laski, Harold, **Supp. I Part 2:** 632, 643
Lassalle, Ferdinand, **IV:** 429
Lasser, Louise, **Supp. XV:** 4
"Last Acts" (Olds), **Supp. X:** 210
Last Adam, The (Cozzens), **I:** 362-363, 364, 368, 375, 377, 378, 379
Last Analysis, The (Bellow), **I:** 152, 160, 161; **Retro. Supp. II:** 26
Last and Lost Poems of Delmore Schwartz (Phillips, ed.), **Supp. II Part 2:** 661, 665
Last Avant-Garde, The: The Making of the New York School of Poets (Lehman), **Supp. XV:** 178-179, 187
Last Beautiful Days of Autumn, The (Nichols), **Supp. XIII:** 254, 255, 267, 269
Last Blue (Stern), **Supp. IX: 299-300**
Last Carousel, The (Algren), **Supp. IX:** 16
"Last Child" (X. J. Kennedy), **Supp. XV:** 162, 165
"Last Day in the Field, The" (Gordon), **II:** 200
"Last Day of the Last Furlough" (Salinger), **III:** 552-553
"Last Days of Alice" (Tate), **IV:** 129
"Last Days of August, The" (Nye), **Supp. XIII:** 284
"Last Days of John Brown, The" (Thoreau), **IV:** 185
Last Days of Louisiana Red, The (Reed), **Supp. X:** 240, **248-249**
Last Decade, The (Trilling), **Supp. III Part 2:** 493, 499
"Last Demon, The" (Singer), **IV:** 15, 21
Last Exit to Brooklyn (Selby), **Supp. III Part 1:** 125
Last Flower, The (Thurber), **Supp. I Part 2:** 610
"Last Frontier" (McCarriston), **Supp. XIV:**272
Last Gentleman, The (Percy), **Supp. III Part 1:** 383-388, 392-393
"Last Good Country, The" (Hemingway), **II:** 258-259
Last Good Time, The (Bausch), **Supp. VII:** 45-46
"Last Hiding Places of Snow, The" (Kinnell), **Supp. III Part 1:** 252
"Last Hours, The" (Dunn), **Supp. XI:** 141
Last House: Reflections, Dreams, and Observations, 1943-1991 (M. F. K. Fisher), **Supp. XVII:** 92
Last Husband and Other Stories, The (Humphrey), **Supp. IX:** 94
Last Jew in America, The (Fiedler), **Supp. XIII:** 103
"Last Jew in America, The" (Fiedler), **Supp. XIII:** 103
Last Laugh, Mr. Moto (Marquand), **III:** 57
"Last Leaf, The" (Holmes), **Supp. I Part 1:** 302, 309
"Last Leaf, The" (Porter), **III:** 444
"Last Look at the Lilacs" (Stevens), **IV:** 74
Last Man, The (Kees), **Supp. XV:** 142, 143, 145
"Last May" (Dixon), **Supp. XII: 143**
"Last Mermother, The" (A. Finch), **Supp. XVII:** 72
"Last Mohican, The" (Malamud), **Supp. I Part 2:** 437-438, 450, 451
"Lastness" (Kinnell), **Supp. III Part 1:** 248-249
"Last Night" (Olds), **Supp. X:** 212
"Last Night at Tía's" (Alvarez), **Supp. VII:** 5
Last Night of Summer, The (Caldwell), **I:** 292-293
Last of Mr. Norris, The (Isherwood), **Supp. XIV:**161
"Last of the Brooding Miserables, The" (Karr), **Supp. XI:** 250
"Last of the Caddoes, The" (Humphrey), **Supp. IX:** 101
"Last of the Gold Star Mothers, The" (C. Bly), **Supp. XVI:**34, 35, 36
"Last of the Legions, The" (Benét), **Supp. XI:** 56, 57
Last of the Mohicans, The (Cooper), **I:** 341, 342, 349
Last of the Red Hot Lovers (Simon), **Supp. IV Part 2:** 575, 583, 589
"Last of the Valerii, The" (James), **II:** 327; **Retro. Supp. I:** 218
"Last One, The" (Merwin), **Supp. III Part 1:** 355
Last Picture Show, The (film), **Supp. V:** 223, 226
Last Picture Show, The (McMurtry), **Supp. V:** 220, 222-223, 233
Last Puritan, The (Santayana), **III:** 64, 600, 604, 607, 612, 615-617
"Last Ride Together, The" (Browning), **I:** 468
"Last River, The" (Kinnell), **Supp. III Part 1:** 236
Last Song, The (Harjo), **Supp. XII:** 218
"Last Song for the Mend-It Shop" (Nye), **Supp. XIII:** 283

"Last Tango in Fresno" (Salinas), **Supp. XIII:** 318
Last Tycoon, The: An Unfinished Novel (Fitzgerald), **II:** 84, 98; **Retro. Supp. I:** 109, 114, **114-115**; **Retro. Supp. II:** 337; **Supp. IV Part 1:** 203; **Supp. IX:** 63; **Supp. XII:** 173; **Supp. XIII:** 170
"Last WASP in the World, The" (Fiedler), **Supp. XIII:** 103
Last Watch of the Night: Essays Too Personal and Otherwise (Monette), **Supp. X:** 147, 148, 153, **157-159**
"Last Word, The" (column, Quindlen), **Supp. XVII:** 165, 167, 170
Last Word, The: Letters between Marcia Nardi and William Carlos Williams (O'Neil, ed.), **Retro. Supp. I:** 427
"Last Words" (Levine), **Supp. V:** 190
"Last Words" (Olds), **Supp. X:** 210
Last Worthless Evening, The (Dubus), **Supp. VII:** 87-88
"Las Vegas (What?) Las Vegas (Can't Hear You! Too Noisy) Las Vegas! ! ! !" (Wolfe), **Supp. III Part 2:** 572
"Late" (Bogan), **Supp. III Part 1:** 53
"Late Air" (Bishop), **Supp. I Part 1:** 89
"Late Autumn" (Sarton), **Supp. VIII:** 261
"Late Bronze, Early Iron: A Journey Book" (Sobin), **Supp. XVI:**290
Late Child, The (McMurtry), **Supp. V:** 231
"Late Conversation" (Doty), **Supp. XI:** 122
"Late Encounter with the Enemy, A" (O'Connor), **III:** 345; **Retro. Supp. II:** 232
Late Fire, Late Snow (Francis), **Supp. IX: 89-90**
Late George Apley, The (Marquand), **II:** 482-483; **III:** 50, 51, 52, 56-57, 58, 62-64, 65, 66
Late George Apley, The (Marquand and Kaufman), **III:** 62
"Late Hour" (Everwine), **Supp. XV:** 85
Late Hour, The (Strand), **Supp. IV Part 2:** 620, 629-630
"Lately, at Night" (Kumin), **Supp. IV Part 2:** 442
"Late Moon" (Levine), **Supp. V:** 186
"Late Night Ode" (McClatchy), **Supp. XII:** 262-263
Later (Creeley), **Supp. IV Part 1:** 153, 156, 157
Later Life (Gurney), **Supp. V:** 103, 105
La Terre (Zola), **III:** 316, 322

Later the Same Day (Paley), **Supp. VI:** 218
Late Settings (Merrill), **Supp. III Part 1:** 336
"Late Sidney Lanier, The" (Stedman), **Supp. I Part 1:** 373
"Late Snow & Lumber Strike of the Summer of Fifty-Four, The" (Snyder), **Supp. VIII:** 294
"Latest Freed Man, The" (Stevens), **Retro. Supp. I:** 306
"Latest Injury, The" (Olds), **Supp. X:** 209
Latest Literary Essays and Addresses (Lowell), **Supp. I Part 2:** 407
"Late Subterfuge" (Warren), **IV:** 257
"Late Supper, A" (Jewett), **Retro. Supp. II:** 137
"Late Victorians" (Rodriguez), **Supp. XIV:**303-304
"Late Walk, A" (Frost), **II:** 153; **Retro. Supp. I:** 127
Latham, Edyth, **I:** 289
Lathrop, George Parsons, **Supp. I Part 1:** 365
Lathrop, H. B., **Supp. III Part 2:** 612
Lathrop, Julia, **Supp. I Part 1:** 5
Latière de Trianon, La (Wekerlin), **II:** 515
"La Tigresse" (Van Vechten), **Supp. II Part 2:** 735, 738
Latimer, Hugh, **II:** 15
Latimer, Margery, **Supp. IX:** 320
La Traviata (Verdi), **III:** 139
"Latter-Day Warnings" (Holmes), **Supp. I Part 1:** 307
La Turista (Shepard), **Supp. III Part 2:** 440
Lauber, John, **Supp. XIII:** 21
Laud, Archbishop, **II:** 158
"Lauds" (Auden), **Supp. II Part 1:** 23
"Laughing Man, The" (Salinger), **III:** 559
Laughing to Keep From Crying (Hughes), **Supp. I Part 1:** 329-330
"Laughing with One Eye" (Schnackenberg), **Supp. XV:** 253
Laughlin, J. Laurence, **Supp. I Part 2:** 641
Laughlin, James, **III:** 171; **Retro. Supp. I:** 423, 424, 428, 430, 431; **Supp. VIII:** 195; **Supp. XV:** 140; **Supp. XVI:**284
Laughlin, Jay, **Supp. II Part 1:** 94
Laughter in the Dark (Nabokov), **III:** 255-258; **Retro. Supp. I:** 270
Laughter on the 23rd Floor (Simon), **Supp. IV Part 2:** 575, 576, 588, 591-592
"Launcelot" (Lewis), **II:** 439-440

"Laura Dailey's Story" (Bogan), **Supp. III Part 1:** 52
Laurel, Stan, **Supp. I Part 2:** 607; **Supp. IV Part 2:** 574
Laurel and Hardy Go to Heaven (Auster), **Supp. XII:** 21
Laurence, Dan H., **II:** 338-339
Laurens, John, **Supp. I Part 2:** 509
Lauter, Paul, **Supp. XV:** 313
Lautréamont, Comte de, **III:** 174
Law, John, **Supp. XI:** 307
Law and Order (television), **Supp. XVII:** 153
Lawd Today (Wright), **IV:** 478, 492
Law for the Lion, A (Auchincloss), **Supp. IV Part 1:** 25
"Law Lane" (Jewett), **II:** 407
"Law of Nature and the Dream of Man, The: Ruminations of the Art of Fiction" (Stegner), **Supp. IV Part 2:** 604
Lawrence, D. H., **I:** 291, 336, 377, 522, 523; **II:** 78, 84, 98, 102, 264, 517, 523, 532, 594, 595; **III:** 27, 33, 40, 44, 46, 172, 173, 174, 178, 184, 229, 261, 423, 429, 458, 546-547; **IV:** 138, 339, 342, 351, 380; **Retro. Supp. I:** 7, 18, 203, 204, 421; **Retro. Supp. II:** 68; **Supp. I Part 1:** 227, 230, 243, 255, 257, 258, 263, 329; **Supp. I Part 2:** 546, 613, 728; **Supp. II Part 1:** 1, 9, 20, 89; **Supp. IV Part 1:** 81; **Supp. VIII:** 237; **Supp. X:** 137, 193, 194; **Supp. XII:** 172; **Supp. XIV:**310; **Supp. XV:** 45, 46, 158, 254; **Supp. XVI:**267
Lawrence, Frieda, **Supp. XV:** 46
Lawrence, Rhoda, **Supp. I Part 1:** 45
Lawrence, Seymour, **Supp. IX:** 107; **Supp. XI:** 335, 346, 348
Lawrence, T. E., **Supp. XIV:**159
Lawrence of Arabia (Aldington), **Supp. I Part 1:** 259
Lawrence of Arabia (film), **Supp. I Part 1:** 67
Laws (Plato), **Supp. IV Part 1:** 391
Laws of Ice, The (Price), **Supp. VI:** 264
Laws of Our Fathers, The (Turow), **Supp. XVII:** 218-219
Lawson, John Howard, **I:** 479, 482
Lawton Girl, The (Frederic), **II:** 132-133, 144
Layachi, Larbi (Driss ben Hamed Charhadi), **Supp. IV Part 1:** 92, 93
Layard, John, **Supp. XIV:**160
Lay Down My Sword and Shield (Burke), **Supp. XIV:**22, 25, 34
"Layers, The" (Kunitz), **Supp. III Part**

I: 260, 266-267
"Layers, The: Some Notes on 'The Abduction'" (Kunitz), **Supp. III Part 1:** 266
"Lay-mans Lamentation, The" (Taylor), **IV:** 162-163
Lay of the Land, The: Metaphor as Experience and History in American Life and Letters (Kolodny), **Supp. X:** 97
"Layover" (Hass), **Supp. VI:** 109
"Lay Preacher" (Dennie), **Supp. I Part 1:** 125
Layton, Irving, **Supp. XII:** 121
Lazarillo de Tormes (Mendoza), **III:** 182
Lazar Malkin Enters Heaven (S. Stern), **Supp. XVII:** 42
Lazarus Laughed (O'Neill), **III:** 391, 395-396
Lazer, Hank, **Supp. IX:** 265
Lea, Luke, **IV:** 248
Leacock, Stephen, **Supp. IV Part 2:** 464
"LEADBELLY GIVES AN AUTOGRAPH" (Baraka), **Supp. II Part 1:** 49
Leaflets: Poems, 1965-1968 (Rich), **Supp. I Part 2:** 551, 556-557
"League of American Writers, The: Communist Organizational Activity among American Writers 1929-1942" (Wolfe), **Supp. III Part 2:** 568
League of Brightened Philistines and Other Papers, The (Farrell), **II:** 49
Leaning Forward (Paley), **Supp. VI:** 221
"Leaning Tower, The" (Porter), **III:** 442, 443, 446-447
Leaning Tower and Other Stories, The (Porter), **III:** 433, 442, 443-447
"Leap, The" (Dickey), **Supp. IV Part 1:** 182
"Leaping Up into Political Poetry" (R. Bly), **Supp. IV Part 1:** 61, 63
Leap Year (Cameron), **Supp. XII:** 79-80, 81, **85-86,** 88
Lear, Edward, **III:** 428, 536; **Supp. XVI:** 103
Lear, Linda, **Supp. IX:** 19, 22, 25, 26
Learned Ladies, The (Molière; Wilbur, trans.), **Supp. III Part 2:** 560
"Learning a Dead Language" (Merwin), **Supp. III Part 1:** 345
Learning a Trade: A Craftsman's Notebooks, 1955-1997 (Price), **Supp. VI:** 254, 255, 267
Learning to Love: Exploring Solitude and Freedom (Merton), **Supp. VIII:** 200
"Learning to Read" (Harper), **Supp. II Part 1:** 201-202
"Learning to Speak" (Everwine), **Supp. XV:** 79
Leary, Lewis, **III:** 478
Leary, Paris, **Supp. IV Part 1:** 176
Leary, Timothy, **Supp. X:** 265; **Supp. XIV:** 150
Least Heat Moon, William, **Supp. V:** 169
Leather-Stocking Tales, The (Cooper), **I:** 335
Leatherwood God, The (Howells), **II:** 276, 277, 288
"Leaves" (Updike), **Retro. Supp. I:** 323, 329, 335
Leaves and Ashes (Haines), **Supp. XII:** 206
Leaves from the Notebook of a Tamed Cynic (Niebuhr), **III:** 293
Leaves of Grass (Whitman), **II:** 8; **IV:** 331, 332, 333, 334, 335, 336, 340, 341-342, 348, 350, 405, 464; **Retro. Supp. I:** 387, 388, 389, 390, **392-395,** 406, 407, 408; **Retro. Supp. II:** 93; **Supp. I Part 1:** 365; **Supp. I Part 2:** 416, 579; **Supp. III Part 1:** 156; **Supp. V:** 170; **Supp. VIII:** 275; **Supp. IX:** 265; **Supp. X:** 120; **Supp. XIV:** 334; **Supp. XV:** 218
"Leaves of Grass" (Whitman), **IV:** 463
Leaves of Grass (1856) (Whitman), **Retro. Supp. I:** 399-402
Leaves of Grass (1860) (Whitman), **Retro. Supp. I:** 402-405
Leaves of the Tree, The (Masters), **Supp. I Part 2:** 460
"Leaving" (Hogan), **Supp. IV Part 1:** 400
"Leaving" (Wilbur), **Supp. III Part 2:** 563
"Leaving, The" (B. Kelly), **Supp. XVII:** 127, 132
Leaving a Doll's House: A Memoir (C. Bloom), **Retro. Supp. II:** 281
Leaving Another Kingdom: Selected Poems (Stern), **Supp. IX:** 296
"Leaving Brooklyn" (Neugeboren), **Supp. XVI:** 226
Leaving Cheyenne (McMurtry), **Supp. V:** 220, 221-222, 224, 229
Leaving Home (Keillor), **Supp. XVI:** 175
"Leaving the Island" (Olds), **Supp. X:** 214
"Leaving the Yellow House" (Bellow), **Retro. Supp. II:** 27, 32

"Leaving Town" (Kenyon), **Supp. VII:** 163
Leavis, F. R., **I:** 522; **III:** 462-463, 475, 478; **Retro. Supp. I:** 67; **Retro. Supp. II:** 243; **Supp. I Part 2:** 536; **Supp. VIII:** 234, 236, 245
"Leavis-Snow Controversy, The" (Trilling), **Supp. III Part 2:** 512
Leavitt, David, **Supp. VIII:** 88
Le Braz, Anatole, **Supp. XIII:** 253
Lecker, Robert, **Supp. XIII:** 21
LeClair, Thomas, **Supp. IV Part 1:** 286
LeClair, Tom, **Supp. V:** 53; **Supp. XII:** 152
Le Conte, Joseph, **II:** 479; **III:** 227-228
"Lecture, The" (Singer), **IV:** 21
"LECTURE PAST DEAD CATS" (Baraka), **Supp. II Part 1:** 52
Lectures in America (Stein), **IV:** 27, 32, 33, 35, 36, 41, 42
"Lectures on Poetry" (Bryant), **Supp. I Part 1:** 159, 161
Lectures on Rhetoric (Blair), **II:** 8
"Leda and the Swan" (Yeats), **III:** 347; **Supp. IX:** 52
Ledger (Fitzgerald), **Retro. Supp. I:** 109, 110
Lee (Masters), **Supp. I Part 2:** 471
Lee, Don, **Supp. XII:** 295; **Supp. XVII:** 13, 14, 15, 16
Lee, Don L. See Madhubuti, Haki R.
Lee, Gypsy Rose, **II:** 586; **III:** 161; **Supp. IV Part 1:** 84
Lee, Harper, **Supp. VIII: 113-131**
Lee, Harriett, **Supp. XV:** 230
Lee, James Kyun-Jin, **Supp. XV:** 213
Lee, James W., **Supp. IX:** 94, 97, 109
Lee, James Ward, **Supp. VIII:** 57
Lee, Li Lin, **Supp. XV:** 211, 212
Lee, Li-Young, **Supp. XV: 211-228;** **Supp. XVII:** 241
Lee, Robert E., **II:** 150, 206; **IV:** 126; **Supp. I Part 2:** 471, 486
Lee, Samuel, **IV:** 158
Lee, Spike, **Retro. Supp. II:** 12; **Supp. XI:** 19; **Supp. XIII:** 179, 186; **Supp. XVI:** 144
Lee, Virginia Chin-lan, **Supp. X:** 291
Leeds, Barry, **Retro. Supp. II:** 204
Leeds, Daniel, **II:** 110
Leeds, Titan, **II:** 110, 111
Leeming, David, **Retro. Supp. II:** 4, 10
"Lees of Happiness, The" (Fitzgerald), **II:** 88
Left Out in the Rain: New Poems 1947-1985 (Snyder), **Supp. VIII:** 305
"Legacy" (Dunn), **Supp. XI:** 148

"Legacy" (Komunyakaa), **Supp. XIII:** 132

"Legacy of Aldo Leopold, The" (Stegner), **Supp. XIV:** 193

Legacy of Fear, A (Farrell), **II:** 39

"Legacy of the Ancestral Arts, The" (Locke), **Supp. XIV:** 201

Legacy of the Civil War, The: Meditations on the Centennial (Warren), **IV:** 236

"Legal Alien" (Mora), **Supp. XIII:** 215

"Legal Tender Act, The" (Adams), **I:** 5

Légende de la mort, La (Le Braz), **Supp. XIII:** 253

"Legend of Duluoz, The" (Kerouac), **Supp. III Part 1:** 218, 226, 227, 229

"Legend of Lillian Hellman, The" (Kazin), **Supp. I Part 1:** 297

"Legend of Monte del Diablo, The" (Harte), **Supp. II Part 1:** 339

"Legend of Paper Plates, The" (Haines), **Supp. XII:** 204

"Legend of Sammtstadt, A" (Harte), **Supp. II Part 1:** 355

"Legend of Sleepy Hollow, The" (Irving), **II:** 306-308

Legends (Lowell), **II:** 525-526

Legends of New England (Whittier), **Supp. I Part 2:** 684, 692

Legends of the Fall (Harrison), **Supp. VIII:** 38, 39, **45-46**, 48

Legends of the West (Hall), **II:** 313

Léger, Fernand, **Retro. Supp. I:** 292

Legge, James, **III:** 472

Leggett, William, **Supp. I Part 1:** 157

"Legion, The" (Karr), **Supp. XI:** 243

Legs (W. Kennedy), **Supp. VII:** 133, 134, 138-142, 143, 151

Le Guin, Ursula K., **Supp. IV Part 1:** 333

Lehan, Richard, **Retro. Supp. II:** 104

Lehman, David, **Supp. IX:** 161; **Supp. XIII:** 130; **Supp. XV:** 178-179, 180, 187, 190

Lehmann, John, **Retro. Supp. II:** 243; **Supp. XIV:** 158, 159

Lehmann, Paul, **III:** 311

Lehmann-Haupt, Christopher, **Retro. Supp. II:** 291; **Supp. IV Part 1:** 205, 209, 306; **Supp. IX:** 95, 103; **Supp. XVI:** 73, 210, 294, 295

Leiber, Fritz, **Supp. XVI:** 123

Leibling, A. J., **Supp. XIV:** 112

Leibniz, Gottfried Wilhelm von, **II:** 103; **III:** 428

Leibowitz, Herbert A., **I:** 386; **Supp. XV:** 78

Leich, Roland, **Supp. XIV:** 123

Leithauser, Brad, **Retro. Supp. I:** 133; **Supp. XV:** 250; **Supp. XVII:** 112

Leitz, Robert, **Supp. XIV:** 62

Leivick, H., **IV:** 6

Lekachman, Robert, **Supp. I Part 2:** 648

Leland, Charles, **Supp. II Part 1:** 193

Leland, Charles Godfrey, **I:** 257

Leland, John, **Supp. XV:** 69

Lem, Stanislaw, **Supp. IV Part 1:** 103

"Le marais du cygne" (Whittier), **Supp. I Part 2:** 687

Lemay, Harding, **Supp. VIII:** 125; **Supp. IX:** 98

Lemercier, Eugène, **Retro. Supp. I:** 299

"Lemorne versus Huell" (E. Stoddard), **Supp. XV:** 270, 273, 283

Le Morte D'Arthur Notes (Gardner), **Supp. VI:** 65, 66

Lenin, V. I., **I:** 366, 439, 440; **III:** 14-15, 262, 475; **IV:** 429, 436, 443-444; **Supp. I Part 2:** 647

"Lenore" (Poe), **III:** 411

"Lenox Avenue: Midnight" (Hughes), **Retro. Supp. I:** 198

Leonard, Elmore, **Supp. IV Part 1:** 356; **Supp. X:** 5; **Supp. XIV:** 26

Leonard, John, **Supp. IV Part 1:** 24; **Supp. IV Part 2:** 474; **Supp. V:** 164, 223-224; **Supp. XI:** 13

Leonardo da Vinci, **Supp. XII:** 44

León-Portilla, Miguel, **Supp. XV:** 77

Leontiev, Constantine, **Supp. XIV:** 98

Leopard, The (Lampedusa), **Supp. XII:** 13-14

Leopardi, Giacomo, **II:** 543

"Leopard Man's Story, The" (London), **II:** 475

Leopard's Mouth Is Dry and Cold Inside, The (Levis), **Supp. XI:** 258

Leopold, Aldo, **Supp. V:** 202; **Supp. X:** 108; **Supp. XIV:** **177-194**

"Leper's Bell, the" (Komunyakaa), **Supp. XIII:** 118

Lerman, Leo, **Supp. X:** 188; **Supp. XVI:** 194

Lerner, Max, **III:** 60; **Supp. I Part 2:** 629, 630, 631, 647, 650, 654

"Lesbos" (Plath), **Retro. Supp. II:** 254

Lesesne, Teri, **Supp. XIII:** 277

LeSieg, Theo (pseud.). See Geisel, Theodor Seuss (Dr. Seuss)

Leskov, Nikolai, **IV:** 299

Leslie, Alfred, **Supp. XII:** 127

Les Misérables (Hugo), **II:** 179; **Supp. I Part 1:** 280

"Less and Less Human, O Savage Spirit" (W. Stevens), **Supp. XVI:** 64

Lesser, Wendy, **Supp. IV Part 2:** 453; **Supp. XII:** 297; **Supp. XVI:** 201

Lessing, Gotthold, **Supp. I Part 2:** 422

"Lesson, The" (Bambara), **Supp. XI:** 5-6

"Lesson, The" (Dunbar), **Supp. II Part 1:** 199

"Lesson, The" (Olsen), **Supp. XIII:** 297

"Lesson of the Master, The" (James), **Retro. Supp. I:** 227

Lesson of the Masters: An Anthology of the Novel from Cervantes to Hemingway (Cowley-Hugo, ed.), **Supp. II Part 1:** 140

"Lesson on Concealment, A" (Brown), **Supp. I Part 1:** 133

"Lessons" (Epstein), **Supp. XII:** 163

"Lessons of the Body" (Simpson), **Supp. IX:** 267

Less than One (Brodsky), **Supp. VIII:** 22, 29-31

Lester, Jerry, **Supp. IV Part 2:** 574

Lester, Ketty, **Supp. XV:** 133, 147

Le Style Apollinaire (Zukofsky), **Supp. III Part 2:** 616

Le Sueur, Meridel, **Supp. V:** 113, 130; **Supp. XII:** 217

"Let America Be America Again" (Hughes), **Retro. Supp. I:** 202; **Supp. I Part 1:** 331

Let Evening Come (Kenyon), **Supp. VII:** 160, 169-171

Lethem, Jonathan, **Supp. IX:** 122

Let It Come Down (Bowles), **Supp. IV Part 1:** 87

"Let Me Be" (Levine), **Supp. V:** 181, 189

"Let Me Begin Again" (Levine), **Supp. V:** 181, 189

"Let No Charitable Hope" (Wylie), **Supp. I Part 2:** 713-714, 729

Let No Man Write My Epitaph (film, Leacock), **Supp. XVII:** 150, 158

Let No Man Write My Epitaph (W. Motley), **Supp. XVII:** 150, **158-160**

Let Noon Be Fair (W. Motley), **Supp. XVII: 161**

Letofsky, Irv, **Supp. XVI:** 167

"Let one Eye his watches keep/While the Other Eye doth sleep" (Fletcher), **Supp. IV Part 2:** 621

Let's Balance the Books (radio show; Untermeyer), **Supp. XV:** 311

"Letter …" (Whittier), **Supp. I Part 2:** 687

"Letter, A" (Bogan), **Supp. III Part 1:** 54

"Letter, May 2, 1959" (Olson), **Supp. II Part 2:** 579, 580

"Letter, Much Too Late" (Stegner), **Supp. IV Part 2:** 613

"Letter, The" (Gioia), **Supp. XV:** 120
"Letter, The" (Malamud), **Supp. I Part 2:** 435-436
"Letter about Money, Love, or Other Comfort, If Any, The" (Warren), **IV:** 245
Letter Addressed to the People of Piedmont, on the Advantages of the French Revolution, and the Necessity of Adopting Its Principles in Italy, A (Barlow), **Supp. II Part 1:** 80, 81
"Letter for Marion, A" (McGrath), **Supp. X:** 116
"Letter from Aldermaston" (Merwin), **Supp. III Part 1:** 347
"Letter from a Region in My Mind" (Baldwin). *See* "Down at the Cross"
Letter from Li Po, A (Aiken), **I:** 68
"Letter from 'Manhattan'" (Didion), **Supp. IV Part 1:** 205
"Letter from the Country" (column, C. Bly), **Supp. XVI:**33
Letter from the End of the Twentieth Century (Harjo), **Supp. XII:** 223
"Letter from the End of the Twentieth Century" (Harjo), **Supp. XII:** 227
"Letter on Céline" (Kerouac), **Supp. III Part 1:** 232
Letters (Cato), **II:** 114
Letters (Landor), **Supp. I Part 2:** 422
Letters (White), **Supp. I Part 2:** 651, 653, 675, 680
Letters (Wolfe), **IV:** 462
Letters and Leadership (Brooks), **I:** 228, 240, 245, 246
"Letters for the Dead" (Levine), **Supp. V:** 186
Letters from an American Farmer (Crèvecoeur), **Supp. I Part 1:** 227-251
Letters from Maine (Sarton), **Supp. VIII: 261**
"Letters from Maine" (Sarton), **Supp. VIII:** 261
"Letters from My Father" (R. O. Butler), **Supp. XII:** 71
Letters from the Country (C. Bly), **Supp. XVI:33-34,** 35, 37
Letters from the Earth (Twain), **IV:** 209
Letters from the East (Bryant), **Supp. I Part 1:** 158
"Letters from the Ming Dynasty" (Brodsky), **Supp. VIII:** 28
Letters of a Traveller (Bryant), **Supp. I Part 1:** 158
Letters of a Traveller, Second Series (Bryant), **Supp. I Part 1:** 158
Letters of Emily Dickinson, The (Johnson and Ward, eds.), **I:** 470; **Retro. Supp. I:** 28
Letters of William James (Henry James, ed.), **II:** 362
Letters on Various Interesting and Important Subjects ... (Freneau), **Supp. II Part 1:** 272
Letters to a Niece (Adams), **I:** 22
Letters to a Young Poet (Rilke), **Supp. XIII:** 74; **Supp. XV:** 93
"Letters to Dead Imagists" (Sandburg), **I:** 421
"Letters Written on a Ferry While Crossing Long Island Sound" (Sexton), **Supp. II Part 2:** 683
"Letter to Abbé Raynal" (Paine), **Supp. I Part 2:** 510
Letter to a Man in the Fire: Does God Exist or Does He Care? (Price), **Supp. VI:** 267-268
"Letter to American Teachers of History, A" (Adams), **I:** 19
Letter to an Imaginary Friend (McGrath), **Supp. X:** 111, 112-113, 116, **119-125**
"Letter to a Reader" (Sanders), **Supp. XVI:**266, 267, 268, 269, 275
"Letter to a Young Contributor" (Higginson), **Retro. Supp. I:** 31
"Letter to a Young Writer" (Price), **Supp. VI:** 267
"Letter to Bell from Missoula" (Hugo), **Supp. VI:** 142-143
"Letter to E. Franklin Frazier" (Baraka), **Supp. II Part 1:** 49
"Letter to Elaine Feinstein" (Olson), **Supp. II Part 2:** 561
"Letter to Freddy" (music) (Bowles), **Supp. IV Part 1:** 82
"Letter to Garber from Skye" (Hugo), **Supp. VI:** 146
"Letter to George Washington" (Paine), **Supp. I Part 2:** 517
"Letter to His Brother" (Berryman), **I:** 172, 173
Letter to His Countrymen, A (Cooper), **I:** 346, 347, 349
"Letter to Kizer from Seattle" (Hugo), **Supp. VI:** 142
Letter to Lord Byron (Auden), **Supp. II Part 1:** 11
"Letter to Lord Byron" (Mumford), **Supp. II Part 2:** 494
"Letter to Matthews from Barton Street Flats" (Hugo), **Supp. VI:** 133
"Letter to Minnesota" (Dunn), **Supp. XI:** 146
"Letter to Mr." (Poe), **III:** 411
"Letter Too Late to Vallejo" (Salinas), **Supp. XIII:** 313, 324
"Letter to Sister Madeline from Iowa City" (Hugo), **Supp. VI:** 142-143
"Letter to Soto" (Salinas), **Supp. XIII:** 325
"Letter to the Lady of the House" (Bausch), **Supp. VII:** 48
"Letter to the Rising Generation, A" (Comer), **I:** 214
"Letter to Walt Whitman" (Doty), **Supp. XI:** 135-136
"Letter to Wendell Berry, A" (Stegner), **Supp. IV Part 2:** 600
"Letter Writer, The" (Singer), **IV:** 20-21
"Let the Air Circulate" (Clampitt), **Supp. IX:** 45
"Letting Down of the Hair, The" (Sexton), **Supp. II Part 2:** 692
Letting Go (P. Roth), **Retro. Supp. II:** 282, 283; **Supp. III Part 2:** 403, 404, 409-412
"Letting the Puma Go" (Dunn), **Supp. XI:** 149
"Lettres d'un Soldat" (Stevens), **Retro. Supp. I:** 299
Let Us Go into the Starry Night (Shanley), **Supp. XIV:**317
Let Us Now Praise Famous Men (Agee and Evans), **I:** 25, 27, 35, 36-39, 42, 45, 293
Let Your Mind Alone! (Thurber), **Supp. I Part 2:** 608
Leutze, Emanuel, **Supp. X:** 307
Levels of the Game (McPhee), **Supp. III Part 1:** 292, 294, 301
Levertov, Denise, **Retro. Supp. I:** 411; **Supp. III Part 1: 271-287; Supp. III Part 2:** 541; **Supp. IV Part 1:** 325; **Supp. VIII:** 38, 39; **Supp. XVI:**39, 40
Levi, Primo, **Supp. X:** 149; **Supp. XVII:** 48
Leviathan (Auster), **Supp. XII:** 27, **33-34**
"Leviathan" (Lowell), **II:** 537, 538
"Leviathan" (Merwin), **Supp. III Part 1:** 345
Levin, Harry, **Supp. I Part 2:** 647
Levin, Jennifer, **Supp. X:** 305
Lévinas, Emmanuel, **Supp. XVI:**290, 291
Levine, Ellen, **Supp. V:** 4; **Supp. XI:** 178
Levine, Paul, **Supp. IV Part 1:** 221, 224
Levine, Philip, **Supp. III Part 2:** 541; **Supp. V: 177-197,** 337; **Supp. IX:** 293; **Supp. XI:** 123, 257, 259, 267, 271, 315; **Supp. XIII:** 312; **Supp. XV:** 73, 74, 212
Levine, Rosalind, **Supp. XII:** 123

Levine, Sherry, **Supp. XII:** 4
Le Violde Lucréce (Obey), **IV:** 356
Levis, Larry, **Supp. V:** 180; **Supp. IX:** 299; **Supp. XI: 257-274; Supp. XIII:** 312; **Supp. XV:** 73; **Supp. XVII:** 110
Lévi-Strauss, Claude, **Supp. I Part 2:** 636; **Supp. IV Part 1:** 45; **Supp. IV Part 2:** 490
Levitation: Five Fictions (Ozick), **Supp. V:** 268-270
Levitt, Saul, **Supp. XV:** 197
Levy, Alan, **Supp. IV Part 2:** 574, 589
Levy, G. Rachel, **Supp. I Part 2:** 567
Lévy-Bruhl, Lucien, **Retro. Supp. I:** 57
Levy Mayer and the New Industrial Era (Masters), **Supp. I Part 2:** 473
Lewes, George Henry, **II:** 569
Lewin, Albert, **Supp. XIV:** 279, 293
Lewis, C. Day, **III:** 527
Lewis, Dr. Claude, **II:** 442
Lewis, Edith, **I:** 313; **Retro. Supp. I:** 19, 21, 22
Lewis, Edwin, J., **II:** 439, 442
Lewis, Jerry, **Supp. IV Part 2:** 575; **Supp. X:** 172
Lewis, John L., **I:** 493
Lewis, Lilburn, **IV:** 243
Lewis, Lorene, **Supp. IV Part 2:** 596, 597
Lewis, Lucy, **IV:** 243
Lewis, Maggie, **Supp. V:** 23
Lewis, Meriwether, **II:** 217; **III:** 14; **IV:** 179, 243, 283
Lewis, Merrill, **Supp. IV Part 2:** 596, 597
Lewis, Michael, **II:** 451, 452; **Supp. XVII:** 210
Lewis, Mrs. Sinclair (Dorothy Thompson), **II:** 449-450, 451, 453
Lewis, Mrs. Sinclair (Grace Livingston Hegger), **II:** 441
Lewis, R. W. B., **I:** 386, 561; **II:** 457-458; **Retro. Supp. I:** 362, 367; **Supp. I Part 1:** 233; **Supp. XIII:** 93
Lewis, Robert Q., **Supp. IV Part 2:** 574
Lewis, Sinclair, **I:** 116, 212, 348, 355, 362, 374, 378, 487, 495; **II:** 27, 34, 74, 79, 271, 277, 306, **439-461,** 474; **III:** 28, 40, 51, 60, 61, 63-64, 66, 70, 71, 106, 394, 462, 572, 606; **IV:** 53, 326, 366, 455, 468, 475, 482; **Retro. Supp. I:** 332; **Retro. Supp. II:** 95, 108, 197, 322; **Supp. I Part 2:** 378, 613, 709; **Supp. IV Part 2:** 678; **Supp. V:** 278; **Supp. IX:** 308; **Supp. X:** 137; **Supp. XVII:** 41

Lewis, Wyndham, **III:** 458, 462, 465, 470; **Retro. Supp. I:** 59, 170, 292; **Supp. III Part 2:** 617
Lexicon Tetraglotton (Howell), **II:** 111
"Leyenda" (Mora), **Supp. XIII:** 214
Leyte (Morison), **Supp. I Part 2:** 491
"Liar, The" (Baraka), **Supp. II Part 1:** 36
"Liars, The" (Sandburg), **III:** 586
Liars' Club, The: A Memoir (Karr), **Supp. XI:** 239, 240, 241, 242, **244-248,** 252, 254; **Supp. XVI:** 70
"Liar's Dice" (C. Frost), **Supp. XV:** 94, 107
Liar's Dice (C. Frost), **Supp. XV:** 93, 96
Liars in Love (Yates), **Supp. XI:** 348, 349
Libation Bearers, The (Aeschylus), **III:** 398; **Supp. IX:** 103
Li Bay. See Li Po
Libby, Anthony, **Supp. XIII:** 87
Libera, Padre, **II:** 278
Liberal Imagination, The (Trilling), **III:** 308; **Retro. Supp. I:** 97, 216; **Supp. II Part 1:** 146; **Supp. III Part 2:** 495, 498, 501-504
Liberation (J. Scott), **Supp. XVII:** 192, **194-196**
"Liberation" (Winters), **Supp. II Part 2:** 791
Liber Brunenesis (yearbook), **IV:** 286
Liberties, The (Howe), **Supp. IV Part 2:** 426-428, 430, 432
Liberty Jones (play), **Supp. IV Part 1:** 83
"Liberty Tree" (Paine), **Supp. I Part 2:** 505
Libra (DeLillo), **Supp. VI:** 2, **4, 5, 6, 7,** 9, 10, 12, 13, 14, 16
Library for Juana, A (Mora), **Supp. XIII:** 218
Library of America, **Retro. Supp. I:** 2
"Library of Babel, The" (J. Borges), **Supp. XVII:** 47
"Library of Law, A" (MacLeish), **III:** 4
"Library of Moloch, The" (Bukiet), **Supp. XVII:** 47, 49
"Librettos for Eros" (Gander), **Supp. XV:** 340
Lice, The (Merwin), **Supp. III Part 1:** 339, 341-342, 346, 348, 349, 355
Lichtenberg, Georg Christoph, **Supp. XIV:** 339
Lichtenstein, Roy, **Supp. I Part 2:** 665; **Supp. XV:** 186
"Liddy's Orange" (Olds), **Supp. X:** 209

Lieberman, Laurence, **Supp. XI:** 323-324
Liebestod (Wagner), **I:** 284, 395
Liebling, A. J., **IV:** 290; **Supp. VIII:** 151; **Supp. XVI:** 167
Lie Down in Darkness (Styron), **IV:** 98, 99, 100-104, 105, 111; **Supp. XI:** 343
Lie of the Mind, A (Shepard), **Supp. III Part 2:** 433, 435, 441, 447-449
"Lies" (Haines), **Supp. XII:** 204
Lies Like Truth (Clurman), **IV:** 385
Lieutenant, The (Dubus), **Supp. VII:** 78
"Life" (Wharton), **Retro. Supp. I:** 372
Life along the Passaic River (W. C. Williams), **Retro. Supp. I:** 423
Life Among the Savages (Jackson), **Supp. IX:** 115, **125**
Life and Gabriella (Glasgow), **II:** 175, 176, 182-183, 184, 189
"Life and I" (Wharton), **Retro. Supp. I:** 360, 361, 362
"Life and Letters" (Epstein), **Supp. XIV:** 104-105
Life and Letters of Harrison Gray Otis, Federalist, 1765-1848, The (Morison), **Supp. I Part 2:** 480-481
Life and Letters of Sir Henry Wotton (L. P. Smith), **Supp. XIV:** 340-341
Life and Times of Frederick Douglass, Written by Himself, The (Douglass), **Supp. III Part 1:** 155, 159-163
Life and Writings of Horace McCoy, The (Wolfson), **Supp. XIII:** 172, 174
"Life as a Visionary Spirit" (Eberhart), **I:** 540, 541
"Life at Angelo's, A" (Benét), **Supp. XI:** 53
Life at Happy Knoll (Marquand), **III:** 50, 61
Life Before Man (Atwood), **Supp. XIII: 24-25**
"Life Cycle of Common Man" (Nemerov), **III:** 278
"Lifecycle Stairmaster" (Karr), **Supp. XI:** 250
Life Estates (Hearon), **Supp. VIII: 68-69**
Life for Life's Sake (Aldington), **Supp. I Part 1:** 256
Life Full of Holes, A (Layachi), **Supp. IV Part 1:** 92
"Lifeguard" (Updike), **IV:** 226; **Retro. Supp. I:** 325
"Lifeguard, The" (Dickey), **Supp. IV Part 1:** 179-180
Life in the Clearings (Shields), **Supp. VII:** 313

"Life in the Country: A City Friend Asks, 'Is It Boring?'" (Paley), **Supp. VI:** 231

Life in the Forest (Levertov), **Supp. III Part 1:** 282-283

Life in the Iron Mills (Davis), **Supp. XIII:** 292, 295, 299, 305; **Supp. XVI:**79-82, **85-88,** 91

Life in the Iron Mills and Other Stories (T. Olson, ed.), **Supp. XVI:**83

"Life in the 30s" (column, Quindlen), **Supp. XVII:** 165, 167-169

Life in the Theatre, A (Mamet), **Supp. XIV:**241, 255

Life Is a Miracle: An Essay Against Modern Superstition (Berry), **Supp. X:** 35

"Life Is Fine" (Hughes), **Supp. I Part 1:** 334, 338

"Life Is Motion" (Stevens), **IV:** 74

Life of Albert Gallatin, The (Adams), **I:** 6, 14

Life of an Ordinary Woman, The: Anne Ellis (A. Ellis), **Supp. XVI:**38

Life of Dryden (Johnson), **Retro. Supp. II:** 223

Life of Emily Dickinson, The (Sewall), **Retro. Supp. I:** 25

Life of Forms, The (Focillon), **IV:** 90

Life of Franklin Pierce (Hawthorne), **Retro. Supp. I:** 163

Life of George Cabot Lodge, The (Adams), **I:** 21

Life of George Washington (Irving), **II:** 314, 315-316

Life of Henry James (Edel), **Retro. Supp. I:** 224

"Life of Irony, The" (Bourne), **I:** 219

"Life of Lincoln West, The" (Brooks), **Supp. III Part 1:** 86

Life of Mary, The (Rilke; F. Wright, trans.), **Supp. XVII:** 244

Life of Michelangelo (Grimm), **II:** 17

"Life of Nancy, The" (Jewett), **Retro. Supp. II:** 133, 144

Life of Oliver Goldsmith, The, with Selections from His Writings (Irving), **II:** 315

Life of Phips (Mather), **Supp. II Part 2:** 451, 452, 459

Life of Poetry, The (Rukeyser), **Supp. VI:** 271, 273, 275-276, 282, 283, 286

Life of Samuel Johnson (Boswell), **Supp. I Part 2:** 656

Life of Savage (Johnson), **Supp. I Part 2:** 523

Life of the Drama, The (Bentley), **IV:** 396

"Life of the Mind, The" (Kees), **Supp. XV:** 140

Life of the Right Reverend Joseph P. Machebeuf, The (Howlett), **Retro. Supp. I:** 17

Life of Thomas Paine, author of Rights of Men, With a Defence of his Writings (Chalmers), **Supp. I Part 2:** 514

Life of Thomas Paine, The (Cobbett), **Supp. I Part 2:** 517

"Life of Towne, The" (Carson), **Supp. XII:** **102**

"Life on Beekman Place, A" (Naylor), **Supp. VIII:** 214

"Life on the Black List" (Endore), **Supp. XVII:** 63

Life on the Hyphen: The Cuban-American Way (Firmat), **Supp. VIII:** 76; **Supp. XI:** 184

Life on the Mississippi (Twain), **I:** 209; **IV:** 198, 199; **Supp. I Part 2:** 440

"Life on the Rocks: The Galápagos" (Dillard), **Supp. VI:** 32

"Life Stories, East and West" (E. Hoffman), **Supp. XVI:**157

Life Story (Baker), **II:** 259

Life Studies (Lowell), **I:** 400; **II:** 384, 386, 543, 546-550, 551, 555; **Retro. Supp. II:** 180, 185, 186, 188, 189, 191; **Supp. I Part 2:** 543; **Supp. XI:** 240, 244, 250, 317; **Supp. XII:** 255; **Supp. XIV:**15; **Supp. XV:** 252

"Life Studies" (Lowell), **Retro. Supp. II:** 188

"Life Styles in the Golden Land" (Didion), **Supp. IV Part 1:** 200

"Life That Is, The" (Bryant), **Supp. I Part 1:** 169

"Life Work" (Stafford), **Supp. XI:** 329-330

"Life You Save May Be Your Own, The" (O'Connor), **III:** 344, 350, 354; **Retro. Supp. II:** 229, 230, 233

Lifshin, Lyn, **Supp. XVI:**37

"Lifting, The" (Olds), **Supp. X:** 210

"Ligeia" (Poe), **III:** 412, 414; **Retro. Supp. II:** 261, 270, 271, 275

Liggett, Walter W., **Supp. XIII:** 168

Light, James F., **IV:** 290; **Retro. Supp. II:** 325

Light, Kate, **Supp. XVII:** 109

Light around the Body, The (R. Bly), **Supp. IV Part 1:** 61-62, 62; **Supp. XVII:** 243

"Light Comes Brighter, The" (Roethke), **III:** 529-530

"Light from Above" (Eberhart), **I:** 541

Light in August (Faulkner), **II:** 63-64, 65, 74; **IV:** 207; **Retro. Supp. I:** 82, 84, 85, 86, 89, 92; **Supp. XIV:**12

"Light Man, A" (James), **II:** 322; **Retro. Supp. I:** 219

"Lightning" (Barthelme), **Supp. IV Part 1:** 53

"Lightning" (Bynner), **Supp. XV:** 44

"Lightning" (Oliver), **Supp. VII:** 235

"Lightning, The" (Swenson), **Supp. IV Part 2:** 645

"Lightning Rod Man, The" (Melville), **III:** 90

"Light of the World, The" (Hemingway), **II:** 249

"Lights in the Windows" (Nye), **Supp. XIII:** 280

Light Verse and Satires (Bynner), **Supp. XV:** 52

Light Years (Salter), **Supp. IX:** **257-259**

"LIKE, THIS IS WHAT I MEANT!" (Baraka), **Supp. II Part 1:** 59

"Like All the Other Nations" (Paley), **Supp. VI:** 220

"Like Decorations in a Nigger Cemetery" (Stevens), **IV:** 74, 79; **Retro. Supp. I:** 305

Like Ghosts of Eagles (Francis), **Supp. IX:** 86

"Like Life" (Moore), **Supp. X:** 163, 165, **172-173**

Like Life: Stories (Moore), **Supp. X:** 163, **171-175,** 177, 178

"Like Talk" (Mills), **Supp. XI:** 311

"Like the New Moon I Will Live My Life" (R. Bly), **Supp. IV Part 1:** 71

Li'l Abner (Capp), **IV:** 198

"Lilacs" (Lowell), **II:** 527

"Lilacs, The" (Wilbur), **Supp. III Part 2:** 557-558

"Lilacs for Ginsberg" (Stern), **Supp. IX:** 299

Liliom (Molnar), **Supp. XVI:**187

Lilith's Brood (O. Butler), **Supp. XIII:** 63

Lillabulero Press, **Supp. V:** 4, 5

Lillian Hellman (Adler), **Supp. I Part 1:** 297

Lillian Hellman (Falk), **Supp. I Part 1:** 297

Lillian Hellman: Playwright (Moody), **Supp. I Part 1:** 280

Lillo, George, **II:** 111, 112

"Lily Daw and the Three Ladies" (Welty), **IV:** 262

Lima, Agnes de, **I:** 231, 232

"Limbo: Altered States" (Karr), **Supp. XI:** 249-250

Lime Orchard Woman, The (Ríos), **Supp. IV Part 2:** 538, 547-550, 553

"Lime Orchard Woman, The" (Ríos),

Supp. IV Part 2: 548
Limitations (Turow), **Supp. XVII: 222-223**
"Limits" (Emerson), **II:** 19
Lincoln, Abraham, **I:** 1, 4, 30; **II:** 8, 13, 135, 273, 555, 576; **III:** 576, 577, 580, 584, 587-590, 591; **IV:** 192, 195, 298, 347, 350, 444; **Supp. I Part 1:** 2, 8, 26, 309, 321; **Supp. I Part 2:** 379, 380, 382, 385, 390, 397, 399, 418, 424, 454, 456, 471, 472, 473, 474, 483, 579, 687; **Supp. VIII:** 108; **Supp. IX:** 15; **Supp. XIV:** 73
Lincoln: A Novel (Vidal), **Supp. IV Part 2:** 677, 684, 685, 688, 689-690, 691, 692
Lincoln, Kenneth, **Supp. IV Part 1:** 329; **Supp. IV Part 2:** 507
Lincoln, Mrs. Thomas (Nancy Hanks), **III:** 587
Lincoln: The Man (Masters), **Supp. I Part 2:** 471, 473-474
Lincoln, Thomas, **III:** 587
"Lincoln Relics, The" (Kunitz), **Supp. III Part 1:** 269
Lindbergh, Charles A., **I:** 482
"Linden Branch, The" (MacLeish), **III:** 19, 20
Linden Hills (Naylor), **Supp. VIII:** 214, 218, **219-223**
Linderman, Lawrence, **Supp. IV Part 2:** 579, 583, 585, 589
Lindner, April, **Supp. XV:** 111, 119
Lindsay, Howard, **III:** 284
Lindsay, John, **Supp. I Part 2:** 374
Lindsay, Mrs. Vachel (Elizabeth Connors), **Supp. I Part 2:** 398, 399, 473
Lindsay, Mrs. Vachel Thomas (Esther Catherine Frazee), **Supp. I Part 2:** 374, 375, 384-385, 398
Lindsay, Olive, **Supp. I Part 2:** 374, 375, 392
Lindsay, Vachel, **I:** 384; **II:** 263, 276, 530; **III:** 5, 505; **Retro. Supp. I:** 133; **Supp. I Part 1:** 324; **Supp. I Part 2:** 374-403, 454, 473, 474; **Supp. III Part 1:** 63, 71; **Supp. XV:** 293, 297, 299, 301, 306; **Supp. XVI:** 184-185
Lindsay, Vachel Thomas, **Supp. I Part 2:** 374, 375
Lindsey, David, **Supp. XIV:** 26
"Line, The" (Olds), **Supp. X:** 206
Lineage of Ragpickers, Songpluckers, Elegiasts, and Jewelers, A (Goldbarth), **Supp. XII:** 191
"Line of Least Resistance, The" (Wharton), **Retro. Supp. I:** 366

Line Out for a Walk, A: Familiar Essays (Epstein), **Supp. XIV:** 107
"Liner Notes for the Poetically Unhep" (Hughes), **Retro. Supp. I:** 210
"Lines After Rereading T. S. Eliot" (Wright), **Supp. V:** 343
"Lines Composed a Few Miles Above Tintern Abbey" (Wordsworth), **Supp. III Part 1:** 12
"Lines for an Interment" (MacLeish), **III:** 15
"Lines for My Father" (Cullen), **Supp. IV Part 1:** 167
"Lines from Israel" (Lowell), **II:** 554
"Lines from Pietro Longhi" (Sobin), **Supp. XVI:** 289
"Lines on Revisiting the Country" (Bryant), **Supp. I Part 1:** 164
"Lines Suggested by a Tennessee Song" (Agee), **I:** 28
"Line-Storm Song, A" (Frost), **Retro. Supp. I:** 127
"Lines Written at Port Royal" (Freneau), **Supp. II Part 1:** 264
"Lines Written in an Asylum" (Carruth), **Supp. XVI:** 48
"Lines Written in Manassas," **Supp. XV:** 99-100
"Line Written in the Dark Illegible Next Day" (F. Wright), **Supp. XVII:** 242
Linfield, Susie, **Supp. XVII:** 169, 177
Lingeman, Richard, **Supp. X:** 82
Linn, Elizabeth. *See* Brown, Mrs. Charles Brockden (Elizabeth Linn)
Linn, John Blair, **Supp. I Part 1:** 145
Linnaeus, Carolus, **II:** 6; **Supp. I Part 1:** 245
"Linnets" (Levis), **Supp. XI:** 260, 261
"Linoleum Roses" (Cisneros), **Supp. VII:** 63, 66
Linotte: 1914-1920 (Nin), **Supp. X:** 193, 196, 197
Linschoten, Hans, **II:** 362, 363, 364
"Lion" (B. Kelly), **Supp. XVII:** 133
"Lion and Honeycomb" (Nemerov), **III:** 275, 278, 280
Lion and the Archer, The (Hayden), **Supp. II Part 1:** 366, 367
Lion and the Honeycomb, The (Blackmur), **Supp. II Part 1:** 91
Lion Country (Buechner), **Supp. XII:** 52, 53
Lionel Lincoln (Cooper), **I:** 339, 342
"Lion for Real, The" (Ginsberg), **Supp. II Part 1:** 320
Lionhearted, The: A Story about the Jews of Medieval England (Reznikoff), **Supp. XIV:** 280, 289
Lion in the Garden (Meriweather and Millgate), **Retro. Supp. I:** 91
"Lionizing" (Poe), **III:** 411, 425
"Lions, Harts, and Leaping Does" (Powers), **III:** 356
Lions and Shadows: An Education in the Twenties (Isherwood), **Supp. XIV:** 158, 159, 160, 162
"Lions in Sweden" (Stevens), **IV:** 79-80
Lipman, William R., **Supp. XIII:** 170
Li Po, **Supp. XI:** 241; **Supp. XII:** 218; **Supp. XV:** 47, 217
Lippmann, Walter, **I:** 48, 222-223, 225; **III:** 291, 600; **IV:** 429; **Supp. I Part 2:** 609, 643; **Supp. VIII:** 104
Lips Together, Teeth Apart (McNally), **Supp. XIII: 201-202,** 208, 209
Lipsyte, Robert, **Supp. XVI:** 220
Lipton, James, **Supp. IV Part 2:** 576, 577, 579, 583, 586, 588
Lipton, Lawrence, **Supp. IX:** 3
Lisbon Traviata, The (McNally), **Supp. XIII:** 198, **199-200,** 201, 204, 208
Lisicky, Paul, **Supp. XI:** 120, 131, 135
"Lisp, The" (Olds), **Supp. X:** 211
Listen, Ruben Fontanez (Neugeboren), **Supp. XVI: 220-221**
"Listeners, The" (de la Mare), **Supp. XVII:** 69
"Listeners and Readers: The Unforgetting of Vachel Lindsay" (Trombly), **Supp. I Part 2:** 403
"Listening" (Paley), **Supp. VI:** 218, 231, 232
"Listening" (Stafford), **Supp. XI:** 321, 322
Listening to Prozac (P. Kramer), **Supp. XVI:** 229
"Listening to the Desert" (Henderson), **Supp. XIII:** 221-222
"Listening to the Mockingbird" (Woodard), **Supp. VIII:** 128
Listening to Your Life: Daily Meditations with Frederick Buechner (Buechner), **Supp. XII:** 53
Listen to the Desert/Oye al desierto (Mora), **Supp. XIII:** 221
"Listen to the People" (Benét), **Supp. XI:** 51-52
Liston, Sonny, **III:** 38, 42
Li T'ai-po, **II:** 526
"Litany" (Ashbery), **Supp. III Part 1:** 21-22, 25, 26
"Litany" (Sandburg), **III:** 593
"Litany, The" (Gioia), **Supp. XV:** 125, 126
"Litany for Dictatorships" (Benét), **Supp. XI:** 46, 58
"Litany for Survival, A" (Lorde), **Supp. XII:** 220

"Litany of the Dark People, The" (Cullen), **Supp. IV Part 1:** 170, 171
"Litany of the Heroes" (Lindsay), **Supp. I Part 2:** 397
"Litany of Washington Street, The" (Lindsay), **Supp. I Part 2:** 376, 398-399
Literary Anthropology (Trumpener and Nyce), **Retro. Supp. I:** 380
Literary Art and Activism of Rick Bass, The (Weltzien), **Supp. XVI:**20-21
"Literary Blacks and Jews" (Ozick), **Supp. V:** 272
"Literary Career of Elizabeth Barstow Stoddard, The" (Matlack), **Supp. XV:** 269
Literary Criticism: A Short History (Brooks and Wimsatt), **Supp. XIV:**12
"Literary Criticism of Georg Lukács, The" (Sontag), **Supp. III Part 2:** 453
Literary Essays of Thomas Merton, The, **Supp. VIII:** 207
"Literary Folk As They Came and Went with Ourselves" (E. Stoddard), **Supp. XV:** 274
Literary Friends and Acquaintance (Howells), **Supp. I Part 1:** 318; **Supp. XV:** 287
"Literary Heritage of Tennyson, The" (Locke), **Supp. XIV:**197
Literary History of the United States (Spiller et al., ed.), **Supp. I Part 1:** 104; **Supp. II Part 1:** 95
"Literary Importation" (Freneau), **Supp. II Part 1:** 264
"Literary Life of America, The" (Brooks), **I:** 245
Literary Outlaw: The Life and Times of William S. Burroughs (Morgan), **Supp. XIV:**141
Literary Situation, The (Cowley), **Supp. II Part 1:** 135, 140, 144, 146, 147, 148
"Literary Worker's Polonius, The" (Wilson), **IV:** 431, 432
"Literature" (Emerson), **II:** 6
Literature (X. J. Kennedy), **Supp. XV:** 153
Literature and American Life (Boynton), **Supp. I Part 2:** 415
Literature and Life (Howells), **Supp. XIV:**45-46
Literature and Morality (Farrell), **II:** 49
"Literature and Place: Varieties of Regional Experience" (Erisman), **Supp. VIII:** 126

"Literature as a Symptom" (Warren), **IV:** 237
"Literature in Low Life" (Hapgood), **Supp. XVII:** 103
"Literature of Exhaustion, The" (Barth), **Supp. IV Part 1:** 48
"Lithuanian Nocturne" (Brodsky), **Supp. VIII:** 29
"Lit Instructor" (Stafford), **Supp. XI:** 321
Littauer, Kenneth, **Retro. Supp. I:** 114
Little Big Man (Berger), **Supp. XII:** 171
Little Big Man (film), **Supp. X:** 124
Littlebird, Harold, **Supp. IV Part 2:** 499
Littlebird, Larry, **Supp. IV Part 2:** 499, 505
Little Birds: Erotica (Nin), **Supp. X:** 192, 195
"Little Brown Baby" (Dunbar), **Supp. II Part 1:** 206
"Little Brown Jug" (Baraka), **Supp. II Part 1:** 51
"Little Clown, My Heart" (Cisneros), **Supp. VII:** 71
"Little Cosmic Dust Poem" (Haines), **Supp. XII:** 209-210
"Little Country Girl, A" (Chopin), **Retro. Supp. II:** 71
"Little Curtis" (Parker), **Supp. IX:** 193
Little Disturbances of Man, The (Paley), **Supp. VI:** 218
"Little Dog" (Hughes), **Supp. I Part 1:** 329
Little Dorrit (Dickens), **Supp. I Part 1:** 35
"Little Edward" (Stowe), **Supp. I Part 2:** 587
"Little Elegy" (X. J. Kennedy), **Supp. XV:** 155
Little Essays Drawn from the Writings of George Santayana (L. P. Smith), **Supp. XIV:**342
"Little Expressionless Animals" (Wallace), **Supp. X:** 305
"Little Fable" (Hay), **Supp. XIV:**131
Littlefield, Catherine, **Supp. IX:** 58
Little Foxes, The (Hellman), **Supp. I Part 1:** 276, 278-279, 281, 283, 297
"Little Fred, the Canal Boy" (Stowe), **Supp. I Part 2:** 587
"Little French Mary" (Jewett), **II:** 400
Little Friend, Little Friend (Jarrell), **II:** 367, 372, 375-376
"Little Gidding" (Eliot), **I:** 582, 588; **II:** 539; **Retro. Supp. I:** 66
"Little Girl, My Stringbean, My Lovely Woman" (Sexton), **Supp. II Part 2:** 686

"Little Girl, The" (Paley), **Supp. VI:** 222, **228-229**
"Little Girl Tells a Story to a Lady, A" (Barnes), **Supp. III Part 1:** 36
"Little Goose Girl, The" (Grimm), **IV:** 266
Little Ham (Hughes), **Retro. Supp. I:** 203; **Supp. I Part 1:** 328, 339
Little King, The (Bynner), **Supp. XV:** 42, 50
Little Lady of the Big House, The (London), **II:** 481-482
Little Liar, The (film; Ingraham), **Supp. XVI:**184-185
"Little Lion Face" (Swenson), **Supp. IV Part 2:** 651
"Little Lobelia's Song" (Bogan), **Supp. III Part 1:** 66
"Little Local Color, A" (Henry), **Supp. II Part 1:** 399
Little Lord Fauntleroy (Burnett), **Retro. Supp. I:** 188; **Supp. XVI:**182
"Little Lyric" (Hughes), **Supp. I Part 1:** 334
Little Man, Little Man (Baldwin), **Supp. I Part 1:** 67
"Little Man at Chehaw Station, The" (Ellison), **Retro. Supp. II:** 123
Little Me (musical), **Supp. IV Part 2:** 575
Little Men (Alcott), **Supp. I Part 1:** 32, 39, 40
"Little Morning Music, A" (Schwartz), **Supp. II Part 2:** 662-663
Little Ocean (Shepard), **Supp. III Part 2:** 447
"Little Old Girl, A" (Larcom), **Supp. XIII:** 144
"Little Old Spy" (Hughes), **Supp. I Part 1:** 329
"Little Owl Who Lives in the Orchard" (Oliver), **Supp. VII:** 239
"Little Peasant, The" (Sexton), **Supp. II Part 2:** 690
"Little Rapids, The" (Swenson), **Supp. IV Part 2:** 645
Little Regiment and Other Episodes of the American Civil War, The (Crane), **I:** 408
Little River: New and Selected Poems (McCarriston), **Supp. XIV:269-272**
"Little Road not made of Man , A" (Dickinson), **Retro. Supp. I:** 44
Little Sister, The (Chandler), **Supp. IV Part 1:** 122, 130, 131-132
"Little Sleep's-Head Sprouting Hair in the Moonlight" (Kinnell), **Supp. III Part 1:** 247
"Little Snow White" (Grimm), **IV:** 266

"Little Testament of Bernard Martin, Aet. 30" (Mumford), **Supp. II Part 2:** 472, 473, 474
"Little Things" (Olds), **Supp. X:** 208
Little Tour in France (James), **II:** 337
Little Women (Alcott), **Supp. I Part 1:** 28, 29, 32, 35, 37, 38, 39-40, 41, 43, 44; **Supp. IX:** 128
Little Yellow Dog, A (Mosley), **Supp. XIII:** 237, 241
"Liturgy and Spiritual Personalism" (Merton), **Supp. VIII:** 199
Litz, A. Walton, **Retro. Supp. I:** 306
"Liu Ch'e" (Pound), **III:** 466
"Live" (Sexton), **Supp. II Part 2:** 684, 686
Live from Baghdad (screenplay, Shanley), **Supp. XIV:**316
Live from Golgotha (Vidal), **Supp. IV Part 2:** 677, 682, 691, 692
Live Now and Pay Later (Garrett), **Supp. VII:** 111
"Live-Oak with Moss" (Whitman), **Retro. Supp. I:** 403
Live or Die (Sexton), **Supp. II Part 2:** 670, 683-687
Liveright, Horace, **Retro. Supp. I:** 80, 81, 83; **Supp. I Part 2:** 464
Lives (Plutarch), **II:** 5, 104
Lives of a Cell, The (L. Thomas), **Retro. Supp. I:** 322, 323
Lives of Distinguished American Naval Officers (Cooper), **I:** 347
"Lives of Gulls and Children, The" (Nemerov), **III:** 271, 272
Lives of the Artists (Vasari), **Supp. I Part 2:** 450
Lives of the Muses, The: Nine Women and the Artists They Inspired (Prose), **Supp. XVI:**250, 260
Lives of the Poets (Doctorow), **Supp. IV Part 1:** 234
"Lives of the Poets" (Doctorow), **Supp. IV Part 1:** 234
"Lives of the-Wha'?, The" (Goldbarth), **Supp. XII:** 191
"Living" (Wright), **Supp. XV:** 345
Living, The (Dillard), **Supp. VI:** 23
"Living at Home" (Gordon), **Supp. IV Part 1:** 311
Living by Fiction (Dillard), **Supp. VI:** 23, 31, **32,** 33
Living by the Word (Walker), **Supp. III Part 2:** 521, 522, 526, 527, 535
Living End, The (Elkin), **Supp. VI:** 54, 58
"Living in the Flatlands" (Carruth), **Supp. XVI:**54
"Living Like Weasels" (Dillard), **Supp. VI:** 26, 33

Living Novel, The (Hicks), **III:** 342
Living of Charlotte Perkins Gilman, The (Gilman), **Supp. XI:** 193, 209
Living off the Country: Essays on Poetry and Place (Haines), **Supp. XII:** 199, 203, 207
"Living on a Giant" (X. J. Kennedy), **Supp. XV:** 163
Living Out Loud (Quindlen), **Supp. XVII:** 166, **167-169**
Living Reed, The (Buck), **Supp. II Part 1:** 129-130
Livingston, Myra Cohn, **Supp. XV:** 153, 162
Living Theater, **Retro. Supp. I:** 424
"Living There" (Dickey), **Supp. IV Part 1:** 182-183
Living the Spirit: A Gay American Indian Anthology (Roscoe, ed.), **Supp. IV Part 1:** 330
"Living with a Peacock" (O'Connor), **III:** 350
"Livvie" (Welty), **IV:** 265; **Retro. Supp. I:** 348-349
"Livvie Is Back" (Welty), **Retro. Supp. I:** 351
Livy, **II:** 8
Lizzie (film), **Supp. IX:** 125
"Llantos de La Llorona: Warnings from the Wailer" (Mora), **Supp. XIII:** 217, 224
"L'Lapse" (Barthelme), **Supp. IV Part 1:** 45-47, 48
Lloyd, Henry Demarest, **Supp. I Part 1:** 5
Lloyd George, Harold, **I:** 490
"LMFBR" (Snyder), **Supp. VIII:** 302
"Loam" (Sandburg), **III:** 584-585
"Loan, The" (Malamud), **Supp. I Part 2:** 427, 428, 431, 437
Loberer, Eric, **Supp. XV:** 339
"Local" (McCarriston), **Supp. XIV:**270
Local Color (Capote), **Supp. III Part 1:** 120
"Local Color" (London), **II:** 475
"Local Family Keeps Son Happy" (Keillor), **Supp. XVI:**168, 169
Local Girls (Hoffman), **Supp. X:** 77, **90-91,** 92
"Local Girls" (Hoffman), **Supp. X:** 90
Local Men (Whitehead), **Supp. XV:** 339
Local Time (Dunn), **Supp. XI:** 143, **148-149**
Lock, Helen, **Supp. XIII:** 233, 237-238
Lock, Robert H., **IV:** 319; **Retro. Supp. I:** 375
Locke, Alain, **Retro. Supp. II:** 115; **Supp. I Part 1:** 323, 325, 341;

Supp. II Part 1: 53, 176, 182, 228, 247; **Supp. IV Part 1:** 170; **Supp. IX:** 306, 309; **Supp. X:** 134, 137, 139; **Supp. XIV:195-219**
Locke, Duane, **Supp. IX:** 273
Locke, John, **I:** 554-555, 557; **II:** 15-16, 113-114, 348-349, 480; **III:** 294-295; **IV:** 149; **Supp. I Part 1:** 130, 229, 230; **Supp. I Part 2:** 523
Locke, Sondra, **II:** 588
"Locked House, A" (Snodgrass), **Supp. VI:** 323
Locked Room, The (Auster), **Supp. XII:** 22, 24, **27-28**
Locket, The (Masters), **Supp. I Part 2:** 460
"Locksley Hall" (Tennyson), **Supp. IX:** 19
Lockwood Concern, The (O'Hara), **III:** 362, 364, 377-382
"Locus" (Ammons), **Supp. VII:** 28
"Locus" (Hayden), **Supp. II Part 1:** 361-362, 381
"Locusts, the Plaza, the Room, The" (Kees), **Supp. XV:** 141
Loden, Barbara, **III:** 163
Lodge, Henry Cabot, **I:** 11-12, 21
Lodge, Mrs. Henry Cabot, **I:** 11-12, 19
Lodge, Thomas, **IV:** 370
Loeb, Gerald, **Supp. IV Part 2:** 523
Loeb, Jacques, **I:** 513; **Retro. Supp. II:** 104; **Supp. I Part 2:** 641
Loeffler, Jack, **Supp. XIII:** 1, 3, 12, 14, 16
Lofty Dogmas (A. Finch, M. Kumin and D. Brown, eds.), **Supp. XVII:** 75-76
"Log" (Merrlll), **Supp. III Part 1:** 328
Logan, Rayford W., **Supp. II Part 1:** 171, 194; **Supp. XIV:**73
Logan, William, **Supp. X:** 201, 213; **Supp. XI:** 131, 132; **Supp. XII:** 98, 107, 113, 184; **Supp. XV:** 212, 226, 251, 257, 260-261, 262,**Supp. XV:** 263, 266
Log Book of "The Loved One," The, **Supp. XI:** 306
Logenbach, James, **Supp. XVII:** 183
"Logging and Pimping and 'Your Pal, Jim' " (Maclean), **Supp. XIV:**229
Logue, Christopher, **Supp. XIV:**82
Lohengrin (Wagner), **I:** 216
Lohrfinck, Rosalind, **III:** 107, 117
Lolita (Nabokov), **III:** 246, 247, 255, 258-261; **Retro. Supp. I:** 263, 264, 265, 266, 269, 270, **272-274,** 275; **Supp. V:** 127, 252; **Supp. VIII:** 133; **Supp. XVI:**294
"Lolita" (Parker), **Supp. IX:** 193
Lolly Dinks' Doings (E. Stoddard),

Supp. XV: 273, **Supp. XV:** 286
Lombardi, Marilyn May, **Retro. Supp. II:** 40
London, Eliza, **II:** 465
London, Jack, **I:** 209; **II:** 264, 440, 444, 451, **462-485**; **III:** 314, 580; **Supp. IV Part 1:** 236; **Supp. V:** 281; **Supp. IX:** 1, 14; **Supp. XIII:** 312; **Supp. XIV:** 227; **Supp. XV:** 115; **Supp. XVI:** 181
London, John, **II:** 464, 465
London, Mrs. Jack (Bessie Maddern), **II:** 465, 466, 473, 478
London, Mrs. Jack (Charmian Kittredge), **II:** 466, 468, 473, 476, 478, 481
London, Scott, **Supp. XIV:** 301, 307, 311
London: The Biography (Ackroyd), **Supp. XVII:** 180
London Embassy, The (Theroux), **Supp. VIII:** 323
London Fields (Amis), **Retro. Supp. I:** 278
"London Letter" (column; Eliot), **Supp. XV:** 306
London Magazine (Plath), **Supp. I Part 2:** 541
London Snow: A Christmas Story (Theroux), **Supp. VIII:** 322
London Suite (Simon), **Supp. IV Part 2:** 576, 581, 582, 588
Lonely Are the Brave (film), **Supp. XIII:** 6
"Lonely Coast, A" (Proulx), **Supp. VII:** 264
Lonely Crusade (C. Himes), **Supp. XVI:** 135, 139-140
Lonely for the Future (Farrell), **II:** 46, 47
Lonely Impulse of Delight, A (Shanley), **Supp. XIV:** 317-318
"Lonely Street, The" (W. C. Williams), **IV:** 413
"Lonely Worker, A" (Jewett), **Retro. Supp. II:** 132
Lonergan, Wayne, **Supp. I Part 1:** 51
Lonesome Dove (McMurtry), **Supp. V:** 226-228, 231, 232, 233
Lonesome Traveler (Kerouac), **Supp. III Part 1:** 219, 225
"Lonesome Whistle Blowing" (Skow), **Supp. XVI:** 174
"Lone Striker, A" (Frost), **Retro. Supp. I:** 136, 137
Long, Ada, **Supp. V:** 178
Long, Haniel, **Supp. XV:** 46, 49
Long, Huey, **I:** 489; **II:** 454; **IV:** 249; **Supp. IV Part 2:** 679; **Supp. XIV:** 14

Long, Ray, **II:** 430; **III:** 54
Long after Midnight (Bradbury), **Supp. IV Part 1:** 102
Long Ago in France: The Years in Dijon (M. F. K. Fisher), **Supp. XVII:** 91
Long and Happy Life, A (Price), **Supp. VI:** 258, **259-260**, 262, 264, 265
Long Approach, The (Kumin), **Supp. IV Part 2:** 452-453, 453
Long Christmas Dinner, The (Wilder), **IV:** 357, 365; **Supp. V:** 105
Long Christmas Dinner and Other Plays (Wilder), **IV:** 365-366
Long Day's Dying, A (Buechner), **Supp. XII:** **45-47**
Long Day's Journey into Night (O'Neill), **III:** 385, 401, 403-404; **Supp. IV Part 1:** 359; **Supp. XIV:** 327
Long Desire, A (Connell), **Supp. XIV:** 79, 80, 97
"Long Distance" (Stafford), **Supp. XI:** 329
"Long-Distance Runner, The" (Paley), **Supp. VI:** 221-222, 228, 230
Long Dream, The (Wright), **IV:** 478, 488, 494
"Long Embrace, The" (Levine), **Supp. V:** 187
"Long Enough" (Rukeyser), **Supp. VI:** 274
"Longest Night of My Life, The" (Nichols), **Supp. XIII:** 269
Longfellow, Henry Wadsworth, **I:** 458, 471; **II:** 274, 277, 295-296, 310, 313, 402, **486-510**; **III:** 269, 412, 421, 422, 577; **IV:** 309, 371; **Retro. Supp. I:** 54, 123, 150, 155, 362; **Retro. Supp. II: 153-174**; **Supp. I Part 1:** 158, 299, 306, 317, 362, 368; **Supp. I Part 2:** 405, 406, 408, 409, 414, 416, 420, 586, 587, 602, 699, 704; **Supp. II Part 1:** 291, 353; **Supp. III Part 2:** 609; **Supp. IV Part 1:** 165; **Supp. IV Part 2:** 503; **Supp. XII:** 260; **Supp. XIII:** 141; **Supp. XIV:** 120
"Long Feud" (Untermeyer), **Supp. XV:** 309
Long Feud: Selected Poems (Untermeyer), **Supp. XV:** 312
"Long Fourth, A" (Taylor), **Supp. V:** 313
Long Fourth and Other Stories, A (Taylor), **Supp. V:** 318-319
Long Gay Book, A (Stein), **IV:** 42
Long Goodbye, The (Chandler), **Supp. IV Part 1:** 120, 122, 132-134, 135

Long Goodbye, The (T. Williams), **IV:** 381
"Long Hair" (Snyder), **Supp. VIII:** 300
Longing for Home, The: Recollections and Reflections (Buechner), **Supp. XII:** 53
Longinus, Dionysius Cassius, **I:** 279
"Long-Legged House, The" (Berry), **Supp. X:** 21, 24-25, 27, 31
Long Live Man (Corso), **Supp. XII:** 129-130, 132
Long Love, The (Sedges), **Supp. II Part 1:** 125
Long Made Short (Dixon), **Supp. XII:** 152
Long March, The (Styron), **IV:** 97, 99, 104-107, 111, 113, 117
"Long Night, The" (Bambara), **Supp. XI:** 9
"Long Novel, A" (Ashbery), **Supp. III Part 1:** 6
Longo, Robert, **Supp. XVI:** 124
Long Patrol, The (Mailer), **III:** 46
"Long Point Light" (Doty), **Supp. XI:** 127
Long Road of Woman's Memory, The (Addams), **Supp. I Part 1:** 17-18
"Long Run, The" (Wharton), **IV:** 314
Long Season, The (Brosnan), **II:** 424, 425
"Long Shadow of Lincoln, The: A Litany" (Sandburg), **III:** 591, 593
Longshot O'Leary (McGrath), **Supp. X:** 117
"Long Shower, The" (Francis), **Supp. IX:** 90
"Long Stemmed Roses" (Jarman), **Supp. XVII:** 115
Longstreet, Augustus B., **II:** 70, 313; **Supp. I Part 1:** 352; **Supp. V:** 44; **Supp. X:** 227
"Long Summer" (Lowell), **II:** 553-554
"Long Term" (Dunn), **Supp. XI:** 149
Longtime Companion (film), **Supp. X:** 146, 152
Long Valley, The (Steinbeck), **IV:** 51
Long Voyage Home, The (O'Neill), **III:** 388
"Long Wail, A" (Crews), **Supp. XI:** 101
"Long Walk, The" (Bogan), **Supp. III Part 1:** 61
Long Walks and Intimate Talks (Paley), **Supp. VI:** 221
Long Way from Home, A (McKay), **Supp. X:** 132, 140
Lönnrot, Elias, **Retro. Supp. II:** 159
Looby, Christopher, **Supp. XIII:** 96
Look, Stranger! (Auden), **Supp. II**

Part 1: 11
"Look, The" (Olds), **Supp. X:** 210
Look at the Harlequins (Nabokov), **Retro. Supp. I:** 266, 270
"Look for My White Self" (Ammons), **Supp. VII:** 25
Look Homeward, Angel (Wolfe), **II:** 457; **IV:** 450, 452, 453, 454, 455-456, 461, 462, 463, 464, 468, 471; **Supp. XI:** 216
"Looking" (Sanders), **Supp. XVI:**277
"Looking a Mad Dog Dead in the Eyes" (Komunyakaa), **Supp. XIII:** 114
"Looking at Each Other" (Rukeyser), **Supp. VI:** 280, 285-286
"Looking at Kafka" (P. Roth), **Supp. III Part 2:** 402
"Looking at Women" (Sanders), **Supp. XVI:**274
"Looking Back" (Harjo), **Supp. XII:** 218
"Looking Back" (Merwin), **Supp. III Part 1:** 352
"Looking Back at Girlhood" (Jewett), **Retro. Supp. II:** 131, 133
Looking Backward (Bellamy), **II:** 276; **Supp. I Part 2:** 641; **Supp. XI:** 200
"Looking for a Ship" (McPhee), **Supp. III Part 1:** 312-313
"Looking for Dragon Smoke" (R. Bly), **Supp. IV Part 1:** 60
Looking for Holes in the Ceiling (Dunn), **Supp. XI:** 139, **143-145**
Looking for Langston (Julien; film), **Supp. XI:** 19, 20
Looking for Luck (Kumin), **Supp. IV Part 2:** 453, 454-455
"Looking for Mr. Green" (Bellow), **Retro. Supp. II:** 27
"Looking for the Buckhead Boys" (Dickey), **Supp. IV Part 1:** 182, 183
"Looking Forward to Age" (Harrison), **Supp. VIII:** 49
"Looking from Inside My Body" (R. Bly), **Supp. IV Part 1:** 71
"Looking Glass, The" (Wharton), **Retro. Supp. I:** 382
"Lookout's Journal" (Snyder), **Supp. VIII:** 291
"Looks Like They'll Never Learn" (McCoy), **Supp. XIII:** 166
"Look to Thy Heart ..." (Hay), **Supp. XIV:**130
Loon, Hendrik Willem van, **Supp. XVI:**185
Loon Lake (Doctorow), **Supp. IV Part 1:** 219, 222, 224-227, 230, 231, 232, 233

"Loon Point" (O'Brien), **Supp. V:** 237
Loos, Adolf, **Supp. XVI:**187
Loos, Anita, **Supp. XVI:181-199**
Loos, Mary Anita, **Supp. XVI:**196
Loosestrife (Dunn), **Supp. XI: 152-154**
"Loosestrife" (Dunn), **Supp. XI:** 154
"Loose Woman" (X. J. Kennedy), **Supp. XV:** 159
Loose Woman: Poems (Cisneros), **Supp. VII:** 58, 71-72
Lopate, Edward, **Supp. XVI:**266
Lopate, Philip, **Supp. XII:** 184; **Supp. XIII:** 280-281; **Supp. XVI:**230
Lopatnikoff, Nikolai, **Supp. XIV:**123
Lopez, Barry, **Supp. IV Part 1:** 416; **Supp. V:** 211; **Supp. X:** 29, 31; **Supp. XIII:** 16; **Supp. XIV:**227
Lopez, Rafael, **Supp. IV Part 2:** 602
Lorax, The (Geisel), **Supp. XVI:**109-110
Lorca, Federico García, **IV:** 380; **Supp. I Part 1:** 345; **Supp. IV Part 1:** 83; **Supp. VIII:** 38, 39; **Supp. XIII:** 315, 323, 324; **Supp. XV:** 186
Lord, Judge Otis P., **I:** 454, 457, 458, 470
Lorde, Audre, **Supp. I Part 2:** 550, 571; **Supp. IV Part 1:** 325; **Supp. XI:** 20; **Supp. XII:** 217, 220; **Supp. XIII:** 295; **Supp. XVII:** 71
Lord Jim (Conrad), **I:** 422; **II:** 26; **Retro. Supp. II:** 292; **Supp. I Part 2:** 623; **Supp. IV Part 2:** 680; **Supp. V:** 251
"Lord of Hosts" (Pinsky), **Supp. VI:** 244
Lord of the Flies (W. Golding), **Supp. XVI:**65
Lord of the Rings (Tolkien), **Supp. V:** 140
Lords of Misrule, The (X. J. Kennedy), **Supp. XV:** 154, **170-171**
Lords of the Housetops (Van Vechten), **Supp. II Part 2:** 736
Lord's Prayer, **I:** 579
Lord Timothy Dexter of Newburyport, Mass. (Marquand), **III:** 55
Lord Weary's Castle (Lowell), **II:** 538, 542-551; **Retro. Supp. II:** 178, **186-187**, 188; **Supp. XV:** 252
"Lorelei" (Plath), **Retro. Supp. II:** 246; **Supp. I Part 2:** 538
"Lorenzo" (Bynner), **Supp. XV:** 46, 50
Lorimer, George Horace, **II:** 430; **Retro. Supp. I:** 101, 113
Lorre, Peter, **Supp. IV Part 1:** 356
"Los Alamos" (Momaday), **Supp. IV Part 2:** 482
"Los Angeles, 1980" (Gunn Allen), **Supp. IV Part 1:** 325

"Los Angeles Days" (Didion), **Supp. IV Part 1:** 211
"Loser, The" (Talese), **Supp. XVII:** 202, 208
Losey, Joseph, **IV:** 383
"Losing a Language" (Merwin), **Supp. III Part 1:** 356
Losing Battles (Welty), **IV:** 261, 281-282; **Retro. Supp. I:** 341, 352, **353-354**
"Losing the Marbles" (Merrill), **Supp. III Part 1:** 337
"Losing Track of Language" (Clampitt), **Supp. IX:** 38, 40
Losses (Jarrell), **II:** 367, 372, 373-375, 376, 377, 380-381
"Losses" (Jarrell), **II:** 375-376
Lossky, N. O., **Supp. IV Part 2:** 519
"Loss of Breath" (Poe), **III:** 425-426
"Loss of My Arms and Legs, The" (Kingsolver), **Supp. VII:** 208
"Loss of the Creature, The" (Percy), **Supp. III Part 1:** 387
"Lost" (Wagoner), **Supp. IX:** 328
"Lost, The/Los Perdidos" (Kingsolver), **Supp. VII:** 208
"Lost and Found" (Levine), **Supp. V:** 188
"Lost Bodies" (Wright), **Supp. V:** 342
"Lost Boy, The" (Wolfe), **IV:** 451, 460, 466-467
"Lost Decade, The" (Fitzgerald), **II:** 98
Lost Galleon and Other Tales, The (Harte), **Supp. II Part 1:** 344
Lost Get-Back Boogie, The (Burke), **Supp. XIV:**22, 25
"Lost Girls, The" (Hogan), **Supp. IV Part 1:** 406-407
Lost Grizzlies, The: A Search for Survivors in the Wilderness of Colorado (Bass), **Supp. XVI:**25, 26
Lost Highway (film), **Supp. X:** 314
Lost Illusions (Balzac), **I:** 500
"Lost in Nostalgia: The Autobiographies of Eva Hoffman and Richard Rodriguez" (Fachinger), **Supp. XVI:**153
Lost in the Bonewheel Factory (Komunyakaa), **Supp. XIII: 114-115**, 116
Lost in the Cosmos: The Last Self-Help Book (Percy), **Supp. III Part 1:** 397
Lost in the Funhouse (Barth), **I:** 122, 135, 139; **Supp. X:** 307
"Lost in the Whichy Thicket" (Wolfe), **Supp. III Part 2:** 573, 574
Lost in Translation (E. Hoffman), **Supp. XVI:**147, **148-151**, 153, 154, 159

"Lost in Translation" (Hass), **Supp. VIII:** 28
"Lost in Translation" (Merrill), **Supp. III Part 1:** 324, 329-330
Lost in Yonkers (film), **Supp. IV Part 2:** 588
Lost in Yonkers (Simon), **Supp. IV Part 2:** 576, 577, 584, 587-588, 590-591
"Lost Jerusalem" (Untermeyer), **Supp. XV:** 307
Lost Lady, A (Cather), **I:** 323-325, 327; **Retro. Supp. I: 15-16,** 20, 21, 382
"Lost Lover, A" (Jewett), **II:** 400-401, 402; **Retro. Supp. II:** 137
"Lost Loves" (Kinnell), **Supp. III Part 1:** 237, 245
Lost Man's River (Matthiessen), **Supp. V:** 212, 213, 214, 215
"Lost on September Trail, 1967" (Ríos), **Supp. IV Part 2:** 540
Lost Puritan (Mariani), **Retro. Supp. II:** 189
Lost Roads Project, The: A Walk-In Book of Arkansas (exhibition; Wright and Luster), **Supp. XV:** 337, 348
"Lost Sailor, The" (Freneau), **Supp. II Part 1:** 264
Lost Son, The (Roethke), **III:** 529, 530-532, 533
"Lost Son, The" (Roethke), **III:** 536, 537-539, 542
"Lost Sons" (Salter), **Supp. IX:** 260
Lost Souls (Singer). *See* Meshugah (Singer)
Lost Weekend, The (Jackson), **Supp. XIII:** 262
"Lost World, A" (Ashbery), **Supp. III Part 1:** 9
Lost World, The (Chabon), **Supp. XI:** 72-73
Lost World, The (Jarrell), **II:** 367, 368, 371, 379-380, 386, 387
"Lost World, The" cycle (Chabon), **Supp. XI: 71-73**
"Lost World of Richard Yates, The: How the Great Writer of the Age of Anxiety Disappeared from Print" (O'Nan), **Supp. XI:** 348
"Lost Young Intellectual, The" (Howe), **Supp. VI:** 113, **115-116**
Lost Zoo, The: (A Rhyme for the Young, But Not Too Young) (Cullen), **Supp. IV Part 1:** 173
Loti, Pierre, **II:** 311, 325; **Supp. IV Part 1:** 81
"Lot of People Bathing in a Stream, A" (Stevens), **IV:** 93
Lotringer, Sylvère, **Supp. XII:** 4

"Lot's Wife" (Nemerov), **III:** 270
"Lottery, The" (Jackson), **Supp. IX:** 113, 114, 118, 120, **122-123**
Lottery, The; or, The Adventures of James Harris (Jackson), **Supp. IX:** 113, 115, 116, 124, 125
Lotze, Hermann, **III:** 600
Loud and Clear (Quindlen), **Supp. XVII:** 167, **170-172**
"Louie, His Cousin & His Other Cousin" (Cisneros), **Supp. VII:** 60
Louis, Joe, **II:** 589; **Supp. IV Part 1:** 360
Louis, Pierre Charles Alexandre, **Supp. I Part 1:** 302, 303
"Louisa, Please Come Home" (Jackson), **Supp. IX:** 122
Louis Lambert (Balzac), **I:** 499
"Louis Simpson and Walt Whitman: Destroying the Teacher" (Lazer), **Supp. IX:** 265
"Louis Zukofsky: *All: The Collected Short Poems, 1923-1958*" (Creeley), **Supp. IV Part 1:** 154
"Lounge" (Francis), **Supp. IX:** 83
Lounsberry, Barbara, **Supp. XVII:** 208
Lounsbury, Thomas R., **I:** 335
Louter, Jan, **Supp. XI:** 173
"Love" (Olson), **Supp. II Part 2:** 571
"Love" (Paley), **Supp. VI:** 219, 222, 230
Love, Deborah, **Supp. V:** 208, 210
Love Alone: 18 Elegies for Rog (Monette), **Supp. X:** 146, 154
Love Always (Beattie), **Supp. V:** 29, 30, 35
Love among the Cannibals (Morris), **III:** 228, 230-231
"Love Among the Ruins" (Mosley), **Supp. XIII:** 247
Love and Death (film; Allen), **Supp. XV:** 2, **5-6,** 7, 11
Love and Death in the American Novel (Fiedler), **Supp. XIII:** 93, 96, **99-101,** 104
Love and Exile (Singer), **Retro. Supp. II: 302-304,** 315
Love and Fame (Berryman), **I:** 170
Love and Friendship (Bloom), **Retro. Supp. II:** 31, 33-34
"Love and How to Cure It" (Wilder), **IV:** 365
Love and Scorn: New and Selected Poems (C. Frost), **Supp. XV:** 95, 96, 100, 103-105, 106
"Love and the Hate, The" (Jeffers), **Supp. II Part 2:** 434-435
Love and Will (Dixon), **Supp. XII:** 148, 149
Love and Work (Price), **Supp. VI:** 261

"Love Calls Us to the Things of This World" (Wilbur), **Supp. III Part 2:** 544, 552-553
Love Course, The (Gurney), **Supp. V:** 98
Loved One, The (film), **Supp. XI: 305-306,** 307
Loved One, The (Waugh), **Supp. XI:** 305
Love Expert, The (film; Kirkland), **Supp. XVI:**186
Love Feast (Buechner), **Supp. XII:** 52
"Love Fossil" (Olds), **Supp. X:** 203
Love in Buffalo (Gurney), **Supp. V:** 96
"Love-In Other Words" (Lee), **Supp. VIII:** 113
"Love in the Morning" (Dubus), **Supp. VII:** 91
Love in the Ruins: The Adventures of a Bad Catholic at a Time near the End of the World (Percy), **Supp. III Part 1:** 385, 387, 393-394, 397-398
Love in the Western World (de Rougemont), **Retro. Supp. I:** 328
"Love Is a Deep and a Dark and a Lonely" (Sandburg), **III:** 595
Lovejoy, Elijah P., **Supp. I Part 2:** 588
Lovejoy, Owen R., **Supp. I Part 1:** 8
Lovejoy, Thomas, **Supp. X:** 108
Lovelace, Richard, **II:** 590
"Love Letter (Schnackenberg), **Supp. XV:** 258-259
Love Letters (film), **Supp. IV Part 2:** 524
Love Letters (Gurney), **Supp. V:** 105, 108-109
Love Letters, The (Massie), **Supp. IV Part 2:** 524
Love Letters and Two Other Plays: The Golden Age and *What I Did Last Summer* (Gurney), **Supp. V:** 100
"Love Lies Sleeping" (Bishop), **Retro. Supp. II:** 42
Love Life (Mason), **Supp. VIII:** 145-146
"Love Life" (Mason), **Supp. VIII: 145-146**
Lovely Lady, The (Lawrence), **Retro. Supp. I:** 203
"Lovely Lady, The" (Lawrence), **Supp. I Part 1:** 329
Love Me (Keillor), **Supp. XVI:**178
Love Medicine (Erdrich), **Supp. IV Part 1:** 259, 260, 261, 263, 265, 266, 267-268, 270, 271, 274-275; **Supp. X:** 290
Love Medicine (expanded version) (Erdrich), **Supp. IV Part 1:** 263, 273, 274, 275

"Love Nest, The" (Lardner), **II:** 427, 429
Love Nest, The, and Other Stories (Lardner), **II:** 430-431, 436
Lovenheim, Barbara, **Supp. X:** 169
"Love of Elsie Barton: A Chronicle, The" (Warren), **IV:** 253
Love of Landry, The (Dunbar), **Supp. II Part 1:** 212
"Love of Morning, The" (Levertov), **Supp. III Part 1:** 284
Love of the Last Tycoon, The: A Western. See Last Tycoon, The
"Love on the Bon Dieu" (Chopin), **Supp. I Part 1:** 213
Love Poems (Sexton), **Supp. II Part 2:** 687-689
Love Poems of May Swenson, The (Swenson), **Supp. IV Part 2:** 652, 653
"Love Poet" (Agee), **I:** 28
"Love Ritual" (Mora), **Supp. XIII:** 215
Loveroot (Jong), **Supp. V:** 115, 130
"Lovers, The" (Berryman), **I:** 174
"Lovers, The" (Buck), **Supp. II Part 1:** 128
"Lover's Garden, A" (Ginsberg), **Supp. II Part 1:** 311
"Lovers of the Poor, The" (Brooks), **Supp. III Part 1:** 81, 85
Lovers Should Marry (Martin), **Supp. IV Part 1:** 351
"Lover's Song" (Yeats), **Supp. I Part 1:** 80
"Love Rushes By" (Salinas), **Supp. XIII:** 326-327
Lovesick (Stern), **Supp. IX:** 295-296
Love's Labour's Lost (Shakespeare), **III:** 263
Love's Old Sweet Song (Saroyan), **Supp. IV Part 1:** 83
"Love Song of J. Alfred Prufrock, The" (Eliot), **I:** 52, 66, 569-570; **III:** 460; **Retro. Supp. I:** 55, 56, 57, 60; **Supp. II Part 1:** 5; **Supp. XIII:** 346
"Lovesong of J. Alfred Prufrock, The" (T. S. Eliot), **Supp. XVI:**150
"Love Song of St. Sebastian" (Eliot), **Retro. Supp. I:** 57
Love's Pilgrimage (Sinclair), **Supp. V:** 286
"Love the Wild Swan" (Jeffers), **Supp. VIII:** 33
Love to Mamá: A Tribute to Mothers (Mora, ed.), **Supp. XIII:** 221
Lovett, Robert Morss, **II:** 43
"Love-Unknown" (Herbert), **Supp. I Part 1:** 80
Love! Valor! Compassion! (film), **Supp. XIII:** 206

Love! Valour! Compassion! (McNally), **Supp. XIII:** 199, **203-204**, 208, 209
"Love *versus* Law" (Stowe), **Supp. I Part 2:** 585-586
Love with a Few Hairs (Mrabet), **Supp. IV Part 1:** 92
Loving a Woman in Two Worlds (R. Bly), **Supp. IV Part 1:** 66, 67, 68-69, 71, 72
"Loving Shepherdess, The" (Jeffers), **Supp. II Part 2:** 432
"Loving the Killer" (Sexton), **Supp. II Part 2:** 688
Lovin' Molly (film), **Supp. V:** 223, 226
Lowe, John, **Supp. XIII:** 238
Lowe, Pardee, **Supp. X:** 291
Lowell, Abbott Lawrence, **I:** 487; **II:** 513; **Supp. I Part 2:** 483
Lowell, Amy, **I:** 231, 384, 405, 475, 487; **II:** 174, **511-533**, 534; **III:** 465, 581, 586; **Retro. Supp. I:** 131, 133, 288; **Retro. Supp. II:** 46, 175; **Supp. I Part 1:** 257-259, 261-263, 265, 266; **Supp. I Part 2:** 465, 466, 707, 714, 729; **Supp. XIV:**128; **Supp. XV:** 43, 293, 295, 297, 298, 299, 300, 301, 303, 306
Lowell, Blanche, **Supp. I Part 2:** 409
Lowell, Harriet, **II:** 553, 554
Lowell, James Russell, **I:** 216, 458; **II:** 273, 274, 289, 302, 320, 402, 529, 530, 532, 534, 551; **III:** 409; **IV:** 129, 171, 175, 180, 182-183, 186; **Retro. Supp. I:** 228; **Retro. Supp. II:** 155, 175, 326; **Supp. I Part 1:** 168, 299, 300, 303, 306, 311, 312, 317, 318, 362; **Supp. I Part 2:** **404-426**; **Supp. II Part 1:** 197, 291, 352; **Supp. XV:** 278, 279; **Supp. XVI:**84
Lowell, Mrs. James Russell (Maria White), **Supp. I Part 2:** 405, 406, 414, 424
Lowell, Percival, **II:** 513, 525, 534
Lowell, Robert, **I:** 172, 381, 382, 400, 442, 521, 544-545, 550; **II:** 371, 376, 377, 384, 386-387, 532, **534-557**; **III:** 39, 44, 142, 508, 527, 528-529, 606; **IV:** 120, 138, 402, 430; **Retro. Supp. I:** 67, 140, 411; **Retro. Supp. II:** 27, 40, 44, 46, 48, 50, **175-193**, 221, 228-229, 235, 245; **Supp. I Part 1:** 89; **Supp. I Part 2:** 538, 543, 554; **Supp. III Part 1:** 6, 64, 84, 138, 147, 193, 194, 197-202, 205-208; **Supp. III Part 2:** 541, 543, 555, 561, 599; **Supp. IV Part 2:** 439, 620, 637; **Supp. V:** 81, 179, 180, 315-316, 337, 344; **Supp. VIII:** 27, 100, 271; **Supp. IX:** 325; **Supp. X:** 53, 58; **Supp. XI:** 146, 240, 244, 250, 317; **Supp. XII:** 253-254, 255; **Supp. XIII:** 76; **Supp. XIV:**15, 126, 269; **Supp. XV:** 20, 22, 93, 184, 249, 251, 253, 340; **Supp. XVII:** 239
Lowell, Rose, **Supp. I Part 2:** 409
"Lowell in the Classrom" (Vendler), **Retro. Supp. II:** 191
Lowenthal, Michael, **Supp. XII:** 82
Lower Depths, The (Gorki), **III:** 402
"Lower the Standard" (Shapiro), **Supp. II Part 2:** 715
Lowes, John Livingston, **II:** 512, 516, 532; **IV:** 453, 455
Lowin, Joseph, **Supp. V:** 273
"Low-Lands" (Pynchon), **Supp. II Part 2:** 620, 624
Lowle, Percival, **Supp. I Part 2:** 404
Lownsbrough, John, **Supp. IV Part 1:** 209, 211
Lowry, Malcolm, **Supp. XVII:** 135, 136
Lowth, Richard, **II:** 8
Loy, Mina, **III:** 194
Loy, Myrna, **Supp. IV Part 1:** 355
"Loyal Woman's No, A" (Larcom), **Supp. XIII:** 142, 143-144
"Luani of the Jungle" (Hughes), **Supp. I Part 1:** 328
Lubbock, Percy, **I:** 504; **II:** 337; **IV:** 308, 314, 319, 322; **Retro. Supp. I:** 366, 367, 373; **Supp. VIII:** 165
Lubin, Isidor, **Supp. I Part 2:** 632
Lubow, Arthur, **Supp. VIII:** 310
Lucas, Victoria (pseudonym). See Plath, Sylvia
Luce, Dianne C., **Supp. VIII:** 189
Lucid, Robert F., **Retro. Supp. II:** 195, 204
"Lucid Eye in Silver Town, The" (Updike), **IV:** 218
"Lucid Walking" (A. Finch), **Supp. XVII:** 72
"Lucinda Matlock" (Masters), **Supp. I Part 2:** 461, 465
"Luck" (Dunn), **Supp. XI:** 149
Luck of Barry Lyndon, The (Thackeray), **II:** 290
"Luck of Roaring Camp, The" (Harte), **Supp. II Part 1:** 335, 344, 345-347
"Luck of the Bogans, The" (Jewett), **Retro. Supp. II:** 142
Lucky Life (Stern), **Supp. IX:** **290-291**
Lucretius, **I:** 59; **II:** 162, 163; **III:** 600, 610-611, 612; **Supp. I Part 1:** 363
Lucy (Kincaid), **Supp. VII:** 180, 185, 186, 187-188, 194
Lucy, Saint, **II:** 211
Lucy Gayheart (Cather), **I:** 331; **Retro.**

Supp. I: 19
"Lucy Tavish's Journey" (E. Stoddard), **Supp. XV:** 286
Lucy Temple (Rowson). See *Charlotte's Daughter; or, The Three Orphans*
Ludvigson, Susan, **Supp. IV Part 2:** 442, 446, 447, 448, 451
Lueders, Edward, **Supp. XVI:** 265
"Luggage" (Bidart), **Supp. XV:** 35
Luhan, Mabel Dodge, **Retro. Supp. I:** 7; **Supp. XV:** 46, 50
Lu Ji, **Supp. VIII:** 303
Luke (biblical book), **III:** 606
"Luke Havergal" (E. A. Robinson), **Supp. XVII:** 69
"Luke Havergal" (Robinson), **III:** 524
Lukeman, Gary, **Supp. XV:** 221
Luks, George, **IV:** 411; **Retro. Supp. II:** 103
"Lullaby" (Auden), **Supp. II Part 1:** 9
"Lullaby" (Bishop), **Supp. I Part 1:** 85
"Lullaby" (Everwine), **Supp. XV:** 89
"Lullaby" (Silko), **Supp. IV Part 2:** 560, 568-569
Lullaby: The Comforting of Cock Robin (Snodgrass), **Supp. VI:** 324
"Lullaby for Amy" (Jarman), **Supp. XVII:** 113, 121
"Lullaby of Cape Cod" (Brodsky), **Supp. VIII:** 27-28
Lullaby Raft (Nye), **Supp. XIII:** 278
Lullaby Raft (Nye, album), **Supp. XIII:** 274
"Lulls" (Walker), **Supp. III Part 2:** 525
"Lulu" (Wedekind), **Supp. XII:** 14
Lulu on the Bridge (film), **Supp. XII:** 21
Lulu's Library (Alcott), **Supp. I Part 1:** 43
"Lumber" (Baker), **Supp. XIII:** 55, 56
"Lumens, The" (Olds), **Supp. X:** 209
Lume Spento, A (Pound), **III:** 470
Lumet, Sidney, **Supp. IV Part 1:** 236; **Supp. IX:** 253
Luminous Debris: Reflecting on Vestige in Provence and Languedoc (Sobin), **Supp. XVI:** 291-293, 293-294
"Lumumba's Grave" (Hughes), **Supp. I Part 1:** 344
"Luna, Luna" (Mora), **Supp. XIII:** 217
Lupercal (Hughes), **Retro. Supp. II:** 245; **Supp. I Part 2:** 540
Lupton, Mary Jane, **Supp. IV Part 1:** 7
Luria, Isaac, **IV:** 7
Lurie, Alison, **Supp. X:** 166; **Supp. XVI:** 103, 111-112

Lust and Other Stories (Minot), **Supp. VI:** 205
Luster, Deborah, **Supp. XV:** 337, **Supp. XV:** 353, 348, 349, 350
Lustgarten, Edith, **III:** 107
Lustra (Pound), **Retro. Supp. I:** 289, 290
Luther, Martin, **II:** 11-12, 506; **III:** 306, 607; **IV:** 490
"Luther on Sweet Auburn" (Bambara), **Supp. XI:** 16-17
Lux, Thomas, **Supp. XI:** 270
Luxury Girl, The (McCoy), **Supp. XIII:** 163
Lyall, Sarah, **Supp. XIII:** 247
Lycidas (Milton), **II:** 540; **IV:** 347; **Retro. Supp. I:** 60; **Retro. Supp. II:** 186; **Supp. I Part 1:** 370; **Supp. IX:** 41
Lycographia (Paullini), **Supp. XVII:** 55
"Lydia and Marian" (Rowson), **Supp. XV:** 234
Lydon, Susan, **Supp. XII:** 170
Lyell, Charles, **Supp. IX:** 180
Lyell, Frank H., **Supp. VIII:** 125
Lyford, Harry, **Supp. I Part 2:** 679
"Lying" (Wilbur), **Supp. III Part 2:** 547, 562
"Lying and Looking" (Swenson), **Supp. IV Part 2:** 652
"Lying in a Hammock at William Duffy's Farm in Pine Island, Minnesota" (Wright), **Supp. III Part 2:** 589, 599, 600
"Lying in the Pollen and Water" (C. Frost), **Supp. XV:** 96
Lyles, Lois F., **Supp. XI:** 7, 8
Lyly, John, **III:** 536; **Supp. I Part 1:** 369
Lynch, Anne, **Supp. XV:** 273
Lynch, Doris, **Supp. XVI:** 294
Lynchburg (Gander), **Supp. XV:** 340
"Lynched Man, The" (Karr), **Supp. XI:** 241
Lynchers, The (Wideman), **Supp. X:** 320
"Lynching, The" (McKay), **Supp. I Part 1:** 63
"Lynching of Jube Benson, The" (Dunbar), **Supp. II Part 1:** 214
"Lynching Song" (Hughes), **Supp. I Part 1:** 331
Lynd, Staughton, **Supp. VIII:** 240
Lynn, Kenneth, **Supp. XIII:** 96-97
Lynn, Kenneth S., **Supp. XIV:** 103
Lynn, Vera, **Supp. XI:** 304
Lyon, Kate, **I:** 409; **II:** 138, 143, 144
Lyon, Thomas, **Supp. IX:** 175

"Lyonnesse" (Plath), **Supp. I Part 2:** 541
Lyons, Bonnie, **Supp. V:** 58; **Supp. VIII:** 138
Lyotard, Jean-François, **Supp. IV Part 1:** 54
Lyrical Ballads (Wordsworth), **III:** 583; **IV:** 120; **Supp. IX:** 274; **Supp. XI:** 243; **Supp. XV:** 21
Lyrics of Love and Laughter (Dunbar), **Supp. II Part 1:** 207
Lyrics of Lowly Life (Dunbar), **Supp. II Part 1:** 197, 199, 200, 207
Lyrics of the Hearthside (Dunbar), **Supp. II Part 1:** 206
Lytal, Tammy, **Supp. XI:** 102
Lytle, Andrew, **IV:** 125; **Retro. Supp. II:** 220, 221, 235; **Supp. II Part 1:** 139; **Supp. X:** 1, 25; **Supp. XI:** 101
Lytton of Knebworth. See Bulwer-Lytton, Edward George

M

"M. Degas Teaches Art & Science at Durfee Intermediate School, Detroit, 1942" (Levine), **Supp. V:** 181, 193
McAlexander, Hubert H., **Supp. V:** 314, 319, 320, 323
McAlmon, Mrs. Robert (Winifred Ellerman), **III:** 194. See also Ellerman, Winifred
McAlmon, Robert, **IV:** 404; **Retro. Supp. I:** 418, 419, 420; **Retro. Supp. II:** 328; **Supp. I Part 1:** 259; **Supp. III Part 2:** 614
McAninch, Jerry, **Supp. XI:** 297, 298
Macaulay, Catherine, **Supp. I Part 2:** 522
Macaulay, Rose, **Supp. XII:** 88; **Supp. XIV:** 348
Macaulay, Thomas, **II:** 15-16; **III:** 113, 591-592
Macauley, Robie, **Retro. Supp. II:** 228; **Supp. X:** 56
Macbeth (Shakespeare), **I:** 271; **IV:** 227; **Retro. Supp. I:** 131; **Supp. I Part 1:** 67; **Supp. I Part 2:** 457; **Supp. IV Part 1:** 87; **Supp. XIV:** 8
Macbeth (silent film), **Supp. XVI:** 184
MacBeth, George, **Retro. Supp. II:** 250
McCafferty, Larry, **Supp. XVII:** 227
McCaffery, Larry, **Supp. IV Part 1:** 217, 227, 234; **Supp. V:** 53, 238; **Supp. VIII:** 13, 14; **Supp. X:** 260, 268, 301, 303, 307; **Supp. XVI:** 117
McCarriston, Linda, **Supp. X:** 204; **Supp. XIV:** 259-275
McCarthy, Charles Joseph, Jr. See McCarthy, Cormac
McCarthy, Cormac, **Supp. VIII: 175-**

192; **Supp. XII:** 310; **Supp. XVII:** 185
McCarthy, Eugene, **Retro. Supp. II:** 182
McCarthy, Joseph, **I:** 31, 492; **II:** 562, 568; **Supp. I Part 1:** 294, 295; **Supp. I Part 2:** 444, 611, 612, 620; **Supp. XV:** 198, 311-312
McCarthy, Mary, **II: 558-584; Supp. I Part 1:** 84; **Supp. IV Part 1:** 209, 297, 310; **Supp. VIII:** 96, 99, 100; **Supp. X:** 177; **Supp. XI:** 246; **Supp. XIV:**3; **Supp. XV:** 142; **Supp. XVI:**64, 70; **Supp. XVII:** 43
McCay, Maura, **Supp. XII:** 271, 276
McClanahan, Ed, **Supp. X:** 24
McClanahan, Thomas, **Supp. XII:** 125-126
McClatchy, J. D., **Supp. XII: 253-270; Supp. XV:** 185, 257, 258
McClellan, John L., **I:** 493
McClung, Isabelle, **Retro. Supp. I:** 5
McClure, John, **Retro. Supp. I:** 80
McClure, Michael, **Supp. II Part 1:** 32; **Supp. VIII:** 289; **Supp. XVI:**283
McClure, S. S., **I:** 313; **II:** 465; **III:** 327; **Retro. Supp. I:** 5, 6, 9; **Supp. XV:** 40
McCombs, Judith, **Supp. XIII:** 33
McConagha, Alan, **Supp. XVI:**166
McConnell, Frank, **Supp. X:** 260, 274
McCorkle, Jill, **Supp. X:** 6
McCourt, Frank, **Supp. XII: 271-287**
McCoy, Horace, **Supp. XIII: 159-177**
McCracken, Elizabeth, **Supp. X:** 86; **Supp. XII:** 310, 315-316, 321
McCullers, Carson, **I:** 113, 190, 211; **II: 585-608; IV:** 282, 384, 385, 386; **Retro. Supp. II:** 324; **Supp. II Part 1:** 17; **Supp. IV Part 1:** 31, 84; **Supp. IV Part 2:** 502; **Supp. VIII:** 124; **Supp. XII:** 309; **Supp. XIV:**120; **Supp. XV:** 338
McCullers, Reeves, **III:** 585, 586, 587
McDavid, Raven I., **III:** 120; **Supp. XIV:**14
McDermott, Alice, **Supp. XII:** 311
McDermott, John J., **II:** 364
MacDiarmid, Hugh, **Supp. X:** 112
Macdonald, C. G., **Supp. XVII:** 73-74
Macdonald, Dwight, **I:** 233, 372, 379; **III:** 39; **Supp. V:** 265; **Supp. XIV:**340; **Supp. XV:** 140
McDonald, E. J., **Supp. I Part 2:** 670
Macdonald, George, **Supp. XIII:** 75
MacDonald, Jeanette, **II:** 589
Macdonald, Ross, **Supp. IV Part 1:** 116, 136; **Supp. IV Part 2: 459-477; Supp. XIII:** 233

MacDonald, Ruth K., **Supp. XVI:**102
MacDougall, Ruth Doan, **Supp. XV:** 58; **Supp. XVI:**174
MacDowell, Edward, **I:** 228; **III:** 504, 508, 524
McDowell, Frederick P. W., **II:** 194
McDowell, Mary, **Supp. I Part 1:** 5
McDowell, Robert, **Supp. IX:** 266, 270, 276, 279
McDowell, Robert, **Supp. XI:** 249
McDowell, Robert, **Supp. XVII:** 109, 110, 111
McElderry, Margaret K., **Supp. XV:** 162
McElrath, Joseph, **Supp. XIV:**62
McElroy, Joseph, **Supp. IV Part 1:** 279, 285
McEuen, Kathryn, **II:** 20
McEwen, Arthur, **I:** 206
McFarland, Ron, **Supp. IX:** 323, 327, 328, 333
McGann, Jerome, **Retro. Supp. I:** 47
MacGillivray, William, **Supp. XVI:**8
McGovern, Edythe M., **Supp. IV Part 2:** 573, 582, 585
McGovern, George, **III:** 46
MacGowan, Christopher, **Retro. Supp. I:** 430
MacGowan, Kenneth, **III:** 387, 391
McGrath, Douglas, **Supp. XV:** 12
McGrath, Joseph, **Supp. XI:** 307, 309
McGrath, Patrick, **Supp. IX:** 113
McGrath, Thomas, **Supp. X: 111-130**
"McGrath on McGrath" (McGrath), **Supp. X:** 119, 120
McGuane, Thomas, **Supp. V:** 53, 220; **Supp. VIII:** 39, 40, 42, 43
MacGuffin, The (Elkin), **Supp. VI: 55-56**
McGuiness, Daniel, **Supp. XV:** 261
Machado y Ruiz, Antonio, **Supp. XIII:** 315, 323
Machan, Tibor, **Supp. IV Part 2:** 528
Machen, Arthur, **IV:** 286
Machiavelli, Niccolò, **I:** 485
"Machine-Gun, The" (Jarrell), **II:** 371
"Machine Song" (Anderson), **I:** 114
McHugh, Vincent, **Supp. XV:** 147
McInerney, Jay, **Supp. X:** 7, 166; **Supp. XI:** 65; **Supp. XII:** 81
"Mac in Love" (Dixon), **Supp. XII:** 142
McIntire, Holly, **Supp. V:** 338
McIntosh, Maria, **Retro. Supp. I:** 246
Mack, Maynard, **Supp. XIV:**12
Mackail, John William, **Supp. I Part 1:** 268; **Supp. I Part 2:** 461
McKay, Claude, **Supp. I Part 1:** 63; **Supp. III Part 1:** 75, 76; **Supp. IV Part 1:** 3, 79, 164; **Supp. IX:** 306;

Supp. X: 131-144; Supp. XI: 91; **Supp. XVII:** 74
McKay, Donald, **Supp. I Part 2:** 482
McKee, Elizabeth, **Retro. Supp. II:** 221, 222
McKee, Ellen, **Retro. Supp. II:** 67
McKenney, Eileen, **IV:** 288; **Retro. Supp. II:** 321, 330
McKenney, Ruth, **IV:** 288; **Retro. Supp. II:** 321
MacKenzie, Agnes, **I:** 199
Mackenzie, Captain Alexander, **III:** 94
Mackenzie, Compton, **II:** 82; **Retro. Supp. I:** 100, 102
McKenzie, Geraldine, **Supp. XII:** 107
MacKenzie, Margaret, **I:** 199
McKinley, William, **I:** 474; **III:** 506; **Supp. I Part 2:** 395-396, 707
MacKinnon, Catharine, **Supp. XII:** 6
MacLachlan, Suzanne L., **Supp. XII:** 300,**Supp. XII:** 299
McLaverty, Michael, **Supp. X:** 67
McLay, Catherine, **Supp. XIII:** 21
Maclean, Alasdair, **Supp. V:** 244
Maclean, Norman, **Supp. XIV:221-237; Supp. XVI:**98
MacLeish, Archibald, **I:** 283, 293, 429; **II:** 165, 228; **III: 1-25,** 427; **Supp. I Part 1:** 261; **Supp. I Part 2:** 654; **Supp. IV Part 1:** 359; **Supp. IV Part 2:** 586; **Supp. X:** 120; **Supp. XIV:**11
MacLeish, Kenneth, **III:** 1
MacLeish, Mrs. Archibald (Ada Hitchcock), **III:** 1
McLennan, Gordon Lawson, **Supp. IX:** 89
McLeod, A. W., **Supp. I Part 1:** 257
McLuhan, Marshall, **Supp. IV Part 2:** 474
McLure, Michael, **Supp. XIV:**150
Macmahon, Arthur, **I:** 226
McMahon, Helen, **Supp. IV Part 2:** 579
McMichael, George, **Supp. VIII:** 124
McMichael, Morton, **Supp. I Part 2:** 707
McMichaels, James, **Supp. XIII:** 114
McMillan, James B., **Supp. VIII:** 124
McMillan, Terry, **Supp. XIII: 179-193**
McMullan, Jim, **Supp. XIV:**124
McMurtry, Josephine, **Supp. V:** 220
McMurtry, Larry, **Supp. V: 219-235; Supp. X:** 24; **Supp. XI:** 172
McNally, Terrence, **Supp. XIII: 195-211**
McNamer, Deirdre, **Supp. XI:** 190
McNeese, Gretchen, **Supp. V:** 123
MacNeice, Louis, **II:** 586; **III:** 527; **Supp. II Part 1:** 17, 24; **Supp. IV**

INDEX / 411

Part 2: 440; **Supp. X:** 116; **Supp. XIII:** 347
McNeil, Claudia, **Supp. IV Part 1:** 360, 362
McPhee, John, **Supp. III Part 1: 289-316; Supp. X:** 29, 30
MacPherson, Aimee Semple, **Supp. V:** 278
McPherson, Dolly, **Supp. IV Part 1:** 2, 3, 4, 6, 8, 11, 12
McPherson, James Allen, **Retro. Supp. II:** 126
Macpherson, Jay, **Supp. XIII:** 19
MacPherson, Kenneth, **Supp. I Part 1:** 259
McPhillips, Robert, **Supp. XV:** 119, 250, 251, 252, 264, 266
McQuade, Molly, **Supp. VIII:** 277, 281; **Supp. IX:** 151, 163
McQueen, Steve, **Supp. XI:** 306
Macrae, John, **I:** 252-253
McRobbie, Angela, **Supp. IV Part 2:** 691
MacShane, Frank, **Supp. IV Part 2:** 557; **Supp. XI:** 214, 216
"MacSwiggen" (Freneau), **Supp. II Part 1:** 259
McTaggart, John, **I:** 59
McTeague (Norris), **III:** 314, 315, 316-320, 322, 325, 327-328, 330, 331, 333, 335; **Retro. Supp. II:** 96; **Supp. IX:** 332
McWilliams, Carey, **Supp. XI:** 169
Madama Butterfly (Puccini), **III:** 139
"Madam and the Minister" (Hughes), **Supp. I Part 1:** 335
"Madam and the Wrong Visitor" (Hughes), **Supp. I Part 1:** 335
"Madame and Ahmad" (Bowles), **Supp. IV Part 1:** 93
"Madame Bai and the Taking of Stone Mountain" (Bambara), **Supp. XI:** 14-15
Madame Bovary (Flaubert), **II:** 185; **Retro. Supp. I:** 225; **Retro. Supp. II:** 70; **Supp. XI:** 334
"Madame Célestin's Divorce" (Chopin), **Supp. I Part 1:** 213
Madame Curie (film), **Retro. Supp. I:** 113
"Madame de Mauves" (James), **II:** 327; **Retro. Supp. I:** 218, 220
Madame de Treymes (Wharton), **IV:** 314, 323; **Retro. Supp. I:** 376
"Madam's Calling Cards" (Hughes), **Retro. Supp. I:** 206
Madden, David, **Supp. IV Part 1:** 285
Maddern, Bessie. *See* London, Mrs. Jack (Bessie Maddern)
Mad Dog Black Lady (Coleman),
Supp. XI: 85-89, 90
Mad Dog Blues (Shepard), **Supp. III Part 2:** 437, 438, 441
Maddox, Lucy, **Supp. IV Part 1:** 323, 325
Mad Ducks and Bears: Football Revisited (Plimpton), **Supp. XVI:**243
Mademoiselle Coeur-Brisé (Sibon, trans.), **IV:** 288
Mademoiselle de Maupin (Gautier), **Supp. I Part 1:** 277
"Mad Farmer, Flying the Flag of Rough Branch, Secedes from the Union, The" (Berry), **Supp. X:** 35
"Mad Farmer Manifesto, The: The First Amendment" (Berry), **Supp. X:** 35
"Mad Farmer's Love Song, The" (Berry), **Supp. X:** 35
Madheart (Baraka), **Supp. II Part 1:** 47
Madhouse, The (Farrell), **II:** 41
Madhubuti, Haki R. (Don L. Lee), **Supp. II Part 1:** 34, 247; **Supp. IV Part 1:** 244
Madison, Dolley, **II:** 303
Madison, James, **I:** 1, 2, 6-9; **II:** 301; **Supp. I Part 2:** 509, 524
"Madison Smartt Bell: *The Year of Silence*" (Garrett), **Supp. X:** 7
Mad Love (film, Freund), **Supp. XVII:** 58
"Madman, A" (Updike), **Retro. Supp. I:** 320
"Madman's Song" (Wylie), **Supp. I Part 2:** 711, 729
Madonick, Michael, **Supp. XVII:** 123
"Madonna" (Lowell), **II:** 535-536
"Madonna of the Evening Flowers" (Lowell), **II:** 524
"Madonna of the Future, The" (James), **Retro. Supp. I:** 219
"Mad Song" (Gioia), **Supp. XV:** 128
Madwoman in the Attic, The (Gilbert and Gubar), **Retro. Supp. I:** 42; **Supp. IX:** 66
"Maelzel's Chess-Player" (Poe), **III:** 419, 420
"Maestria" (Nemerov), **III:** 275, 278-279
Maeterlinck, Maurice, **I:** 91, 220
"Magazine-Writing Peter Snook" (Poe), **III:** 421
Magdeburg Centuries (Flacius), **IV:** 163
Magellan, Ferdinand, **Supp. I Part 2:** 497
Maggie: A Girl of the Streets (S. Crane), **I:** 407, 408, 410-411, 416; **IV:** 208; **Retro. Supp. II:** 97, 107; **Supp. XVII:** 228
Maggie Cassidy (Kerouac), **Supp. III Part 1:** 220-221, 225, 227, 229, 232
"Maggie of the Green Bottles" (Bambara), **Supp. XI:** 2-3
"Magi" (Plath), **Supp. I Part 2:** 544-545
"Magi, The" (Garrett), **Supp. VII:** 97
"Magic" (Porter), **III:** 434, 435
Magic Barrel, The (Malamud), **Supp. I Part 2:** 427, 428, 430-434
"Magic Barrel, The" (Malamud), **Supp. I Part 2:** 427, 428, 431, 432-433
Magic Christian, The (film), **Supp. XI:** 309
Magic Christian, The (Southern), **Supp. XI:** 297, **299-301,** 309
Magic City (Komunyakaa), **Supp. XIII: 125-127,** 128, 131
"Magic Flute, The" (Epstein), **Supp. XII:** 165
Magic Flute, The (Mozart), **III:** 164
Magician of Lublin, The (Singer), **IV:** 6, 9-10; **Retro. Supp. II: 308-309**
Magician's Assistant, The (Patchett), **Supp. XII:** 307, 310, **317-320,** 322
"Magician's Wife, The" (Gordon), **Supp. IV Part 1:** 306
Magic Journey, The (Nichols), **Supp. XIII:** 266-267
Magic Kingdom, The (Elkin), **Supp. VI:** 42, **54-55,** 56, 58
"Magic Mirror, The: A Study of the Double in Two of Doestoevsky's Novels" (Plath), **Supp. I Part 2:** 536
Magic Mountain, The (Mann), **III:** 281-282; **Supp. IV Part 2:** 522; **Supp. XII:** 321; **Supp. XVII:** 137
Magic Tower, The (Willams), **IV:** 380
Magnaghi, Ambrogio, **Supp. XVI:**286
Magnalia Christi Americana (Mather), **II:** 302; **Supp. I Part 1:** 102; **Supp. I Part 2:** 584; **Supp. II Part 2:** 441, 442, 452-455, 460, 467, 468; **Supp. IV Part 2:** 434
"Magnificent Little Gift" (Salinas), **Supp. XIII:** 318
"Magnifying Mirror" (Karr), **Supp. XI:** 240
Magpie, The (Baldwin, ed.), **Supp. I Part 1:** 49
Magpie's Shadow, The (Winters), **Supp. II Part 2:** 786, 788
"Magpie's Song" (Snyder), **Supp. VIII:** 302
Magritte, René, **Supp. IV Part 2:** 623
Mahan, Albert Thayer, **Supp. I Part 2:** 491
"Mahatma Joe" (Bass), **Supp. XVI:**19
"Mahogany Tree, The" (M. F. K.

Fisher), **Supp. XVII:** 88
Mahomet and His Successors (Irving), **II:** 314
Mahoney, Jeremiah, **IV:** 285
Mahoney, Lynn, **Supp. XV:** 270
"Maiden in a Tower" (Stegner), **Supp. IV Part 2:** 613
"Maiden Without Hands" (Sexton), **Supp. II Part 2:** 691
"Maid of St. Philippe, The" (Chopin), **Retro. Supp. II:** 63
"Maid's Shoes, The" (Malamud), **Supp. I Part 2:** 437
Mailer, Fanny, **III:** 28
Mailer, Isaac, **III:** 28
Mailer, Norman, **I:** 261, 292, 477; **III: 26-49,** 174; **IV:** 98, 216; **Retro. Supp. II:** 182, **195-217,** 279; **Supp. I Part 1:** 291, 294; **Supp. III Part 1:** 302; **Supp. IV Part 1:** 90, 198, 207, 236, 284, 381; **Supp. IV Part 2:** 689; **Supp. VIII:** 236; **Supp. XI:** 104, 218, 222, 229; **Supp. XIV:**49, 53, 54, 111, 162; **Supp. XVII:** 225, 228, 236
"Maimed Man, The" (Tate), **IV:** 136
Maimonides, Moses, **Supp. XVII:** 46-47
Main Currents in American Thought: The Colonial Mind, 1625-1800 (Parrington), **I:** 517; **Supp. I Part 2:** 484
"Maine Roustabout, A" (Eberhart), **I:** 539
"Maine Speech" (White), **Supp. I Part 2:** 669-670
Maine Woods, The (Thoreau), **IV:** 188
Mains d'Orlac, Les (M. Renard), **Supp. XVII:** 58
Main Street (Lewis), **I:** 362; **II:** 271, 440, 441-442, 447, 449, 453; **III:** 394
Maitland, Margaret Todd, **Supp. XVI:**292
"Majorat, Das" (Hoffman), **III:** 415
Major Barbara (Shaw), **III:** 69
"Major Chord, The" (Bourne), **I:** 221
Majors and Minors (Dunbar), **Supp. II Part 1:** 197, 198
"Major's Tale, The" (Bierce), **I:** 205
Make Believe (J. Scott), **Supp. XVII: 191-192,** 193, **194,** 195
Make-Believe Town: Essays and Remembrances (Mamet), **Supp. XIV:**240, 251
Make It New (Pound), **III:** 470
Makers and Finders (Brooks), **I:** 253, 254, 255, 257, 258
Makers of the Modern World (Untermeyer), **Supp. XV:** 312

"Making a Change" (Gilman), **Supp. XI:** 207
"Making a Living" (Sexton), **Supp. II Part 2:** 695
"Making Changes" (L. Michaels), **Supp. XVI:**204
"Making Do" (Hogan), **Supp. IV Part 1:** 406
Making Face, Making Soul: Haciendo Caras, Creative and Critical Perspectives by Feminists of Color (Anzaldúa, ed.), **Supp. IV Part 1:** 330
Making It (Podhoretz), **Supp. VIII:** 231, 232, 233, **237-238,** 239, 244
"Making Light of Auntie" (X. J. Kennedy), **Supp. XV:** 163
"Making of a Marginal Farm, The" (Berry), **Supp. X:** 22
Making of Americans, The (Stein), **IV:** 35, 37, 40-42, 45, 46; **Supp. III Part 1:** 37
"Making of Ashenden, The" (Elkin), **Supp. VI:** 49, 50
"Making of a Soldier USA, The" (Simpson), **Supp. IX:** 270
"Making of Garrison Keillor, The" (McConagha), **Supp. XVI:**166"
"Making of Paths, The" (Stegner), **Supp. IV Part 2:** 614
"Making of Poems, The" (W. J. Smith), **Supp. XIII:** 348
Making of the Modern Mind (Randall), **III:** 605
Making the Light Come: The Poetry of Gerald Stern (Somerville), **Supp. IX:** 296-297
"Making Up Stories" (Didion), **Supp. IV Part 1:** 196, 203, 205
Making Your Own Days: The Pleasures of Reading and Writing Poetry (Koch), **Supp. XV:** 188
Malady of the Ideal, The: Oberman, Maurice de Guérin, and Amiel (Brooks), **I:** 240, 241, 242
Malamud, Bernard, **I:** 144, 375; **II:** 424, 425; **III:** 40, 272; **IV:** 216; **Retro. Supp. II:** 22, 279, 281; **Supp. I Part 2: 427-453; Supp. IV Part 1:** 297, 382; **Supp. V:** 257, 266; **Supp. IX:** 114, 227; **Supp. XIII:** 106, 264, 265, 294; **Supp. XVI:**220
Malamud, Mrs. Bernard (Ann de Chiara), **Supp. I Part 2:** 451
Malanga, Gerard, **Supp. III Part 2:** 629
Malaquais, Jean, **Retro. Supp. II:** 199
Malatesta, Sigismondo de, **III:** 472, 473

Malcolm (Purdy), **Supp. VII:** 270-273, 277
"Malcolm Cowley and the American Writer" (Simpson), **Supp. II Part 1:** 147
Malcolm Lowry's "Volcano": Myth Symbol Meaning (Markson), **Supp. XVII:** 142, 144
"MALCOLM REMEMBERED (FEB. 77)" (Baraka), **Supp. II Part 1:** 60
Malcolm X, **Retro. Supp. II:** 12, 13; **Supp. I Part 1:** 52, 63, 65, 66; **Supp. IV Part 1:** 2, 10; **Supp. VIII:** 330, 345; **Supp. X:** 240; **Supp. XIV:**306
Malcolm X (film), **Retro. Supp. II:** 12
"Maldrove" (Jeffers), **Supp. II Part 2:** 418
Male, Roy, **II:** 239
Male Animal, The (Thurber), **Supp. I Part 2:** 605, 606, 610-611
"Malediction upon Myself" (Wylie), **Supp. I Part 2:** 722
Malefactors, The (Gordon), **II:** 186, 199, 213-216; **IV:** 139
"Malest Cornifici Tuo Catullo" (Ginsberg), **Supp. II Part 1:** 315
Malick, Terrence, **Supp. XI:** 234; **Supp. XV:** 351
Malin, Irving, **I:** 147; **Supp. XVI:**71-72
"Malinche's Tips: Pique from Mexico's Mother" (Mora), **Supp. XIII:** 223
"Mallard" (C. Frost), **Supp. XV:** 98, 99
Mallarmé, Stéphane, **I:** 66, 569; **II:** 529, 543; **III:** 8, 409, 428; **IV:** 80, 86; **Retro. Supp. I:** 56; **Supp. I Part 1:** 261; **Supp. II Part 1:** 1; **Supp. III Part 1:** 319-320; **Supp. III Part 2:** 630; **Supp. XIII:** 114; **Supp. XV:** 158; **Supp. XVI:**282, 285
Mallia, Joseph, **Supp. XII:** 26, 29, 37
Mallon, Thomas, **Supp. IV Part 1:** 200, 209
Maloff, Saul, **Supp. VIII:** 238
Malory, Thomas, **II:** 302; **III:** 486; **IV:** 50, 61; **Supp. IV Part 1:** 47
"Mal Paso Bridge" (Jeffers), **Supp. II Part 2:** 415, 420
Malraux, André, **I:** 33-34, 127, 509; **II:** 57, 376; **III:** 35, 310; **IV:** 236, 247, 434; **Retro. Supp. I:** 73; **Retro. Supp. II:** 115-116, 119; **Supp. II Part 1:** 221, 232
Maltese Falcon, The (film), **Supp. IV Part 1:** 342, 353, 355
Maltese Falcon, The (Hammett), **IV:** 286; **Supp. IV Part 1:** 345, 348-351

Mama (McMillan), **Supp. XIII:** 182, **187-188**
"Mama and Daughter" (Hughes), **Supp. I Part 1:** 334
Mama Day (Naylor), **Supp. VIII: 223-226,** 230
Mama Poc: An Ecologist's Account of the Extinction of a Species (LaBastille), **Supp. X:** 99, **104-105,** 106
Mama's Bank Account (K. Forbes), **Supp. XVII:** 9
"Mama Still Loves You" (Naylor), **Supp. VIII:** 214
Mambo Hips and Make Believe (Coleman), **Supp. XI: 94-96**
Mambo Kings, The (film), **Supp. VIII:** 73, 74
Mambo Kings Play Songs of Love, The (Hijuelos), **Supp. VIII:** 73-74, **79-82**
"Ma'me Pélagie" (Chopin), **Retro. Supp. II:** 64
Mamet, David, **Supp. XIV:239-258,** 315
"Mamie" (Sandburg), **III:** 582
Mammedaty, Novarro Scott. *See* Momaday, N. Scott
"Mammon and the Archer" (O. Henry), **Supp. II Part 1:** 394, 408
Mammonart (Sinclair), **Supp. V:** 276-277
"Mamouche" (Chopin), **Retro. Supp. II:** 66
"Man" (Corso), **Supp. XII:** 130
"Man" (Herbert), **II:** 12
"Man Against the Sky, The" (Robinson), **III:** 509, 523
"Man and a Woman Sit Near Each Other, A" (R. Bly), **Supp. IV Part 1:** 71
Man and Boy (Morris), **III:** 223, 224, 225
"Man and the Snake, The" (Bierce), **I:** 203
"Man and Woman" (Caldwell), **I:** 310
Manassas (Sinclair), **Supp. V:** 280, 281, 285
"Man Bring This Up Road" (T. Williams), **IV:** 383-384
"Man Carrying Thing" (Stevens), **IV:** 90
Manchester, William, **III:** 103
"Man Child, The" (Baldwin), **Supp. I Part 1:** 63
Man Could Stand Up, A (Ford), **I:** 423
"Mandarin's Jade" (Chandler), **Supp. IV Part 1:** 125
Mandel, Charlotte, **Supp. XVI:57**
Mandelbaum, Maurice, **I:** 61

Mandelstam, Osip, **Retro. Supp. I:** 278; **Supp. III Part 1:** 268; **Supp. VIII:** 21, 22, 23, 27; **Supp. XIII:** 77; **Supp. XV:** 254, 261, 263
"Mandelstam: The Poem as Event" (Dobyns), **Supp. XIII:** 78
"Mandolin" (Dove), **Supp. IV Part 1:** 247
"Mandoline" (Verlaine), **IV:** 79
"Man Eating" (Kenyon), **Supp. VII:** 173
"Man Feeding Pigeons" (Clampitt), **Supp. IX: 49-50,** 52
Manfred, Frederick, **Supp. X:** 126
Man From Limbo, The (Endore), **Supp. XVII:** 55
"Mango Says Goodbye Sometimes" (Cisneros), **Supp. VII:** 64
Manhattan (film; Allen), **Supp. IV Part 1:** 205; **Supp. XV:** 5, **7-8,** 13
"Manhattan: Luminism" (Doty), **Supp. XI:** 135
"Manhattan Dawn" (Justice), **Supp. VII:** 117
Manhattan Murder Mystery (film; Allen), **Supp. XV:** 5, 11
Manhattan Transfer (Dos Passos), **I:** 26, 475, 478, 479, 480, 481, 482-484, 487; **II:** 286; **Supp. I Part 1:** 57
"Mania" (Lowell), **II:** 554
"Manic in the Moon, The" (Thurber), **Supp. I Part 2:** 620
Manikin, The (J. Scott), **Supp. XVII: 189-191,** 192, 194
"Man in Black" (Plath), **Supp. I Part 2:** 538
Man in Prehistory (Chard), **Supp. XII:** 177-178
Man in the Black Coat Turns, The (R. Bly), **Supp. IV Part 1:** 66-68, 71, 73
"Man in the Brooks Brothers Shirt, The" (McCarthy), **II:** 563-564
"Man in the Drawer, The" (Malamud), **Supp. I Part 2:** 437
Man in the Flying Lawn Chair and Other Excursions and Observations, The (Plimpton), **Supp. XVI:234**
Man in the Gray Flannel Suit, The (Wilson), **Supp. IV Part 1:** 387
Man in the Middle, The (Wagoner), **Supp. IX:** 324, **332-333**
Mankiewicz, Herman, **Supp. XVI:189**
Mankiewicz, Joseph, **Retro. Supp. I:** 113
Mankowitz, Wolf, **Supp. XI:** 307
"Man Made of Words, The" (Momaday), **Supp. IV Part 2:** 481, 484-485, 486, 487, 488

Man-Made World, The (Gilman), **Supp. XI:** 207
"Man-Moth, The" (Bishop), **Retro. Supp. II:** 42; **Supp. I Part 1:** 85-87, 88
Mann, Charles, **Retro. Supp. II:** 40
Mann, Erika, **Supp. II Part 1:** 11
Mann, Seymour (Samuel Weisman), **Supp. V:** 113
Mann, Thomas, **I:** 271, 490; **II:** 42, 539; **III:** 231, 281-282, 283; **IV:** 70, 73, 85; **Supp. IV Part 1:** 392; **Supp. IV Part 2:** 522; **Supp. V:** 51; **Supp. IX:** 21; **Supp. XI:** 275; **Supp. XII:** 173, 310, 321; **Supp. XIV:87; Supp. XVII:** 137
Mannerhouse (Wolfe), **IV:** 460
Manner Music, The (Reznikoff), **Supp. XIV:293-295**
"Manners" (Bishop), **Supp. I Part 1:** 73
"Manners" (Emerson), **II:** 4, 6
"Manners, Morals, and the Novel" (Trilling), **Supp. III Part 2:** 502, 503
Mannheim, Karl, **I:** 279; **Supp. I Part 2:** 644
Manning, Frederic, **III:** 459
Manning, Robert, **Supp. IX:** 236
Mannix, Daniel P., **Supp. II Part 1:** 140
Man Nobody Knows, The (B. Barton), **Retro. Supp. I:** 179
Mano, D. Keith, **Supp. XVI:250**
Mano, Guy Levis, **Supp. XVI:282**
"Man of Letters as a Man of Business, The" (Howells), **Supp. XIV:45-46**
"Man of No Account, The" (Harte), **Supp. II Part 1:** 339
"Man of the Crowd, The" (Poe), **III:** 412, 417; **Retro. Supp. I:** 154
Man on Spikes (Asinof), **II:** 424
Man on Stage (Dixon), **Supp. XII:** 141, **154-155**
"Man on the Dump, The" (Stevens), **IV:** 74; **Retro. Supp. I:** 306
"Man on the Train, The" (Percy), **Supp. III Part 1:** 387
Manor, The (Singer), **IV:** 6, 17-19
Manrique, Jorge, **Retro. Supp. II:** 154
Mansart Builds a School (Du Bois), **Supp. II Part 1:** 185-186
Man's Fate (Malraux), **I:** 127; **Retro. Supp. II:** 121
"Man's Fate A Film Treatment of the Malraux Novel" (Agee), **I:** 33-34
Mansfield, June, **Supp. X:** 183, 194
Mansfield, Katherine, **III:** 362, 453
Mansfield, Stephanie, **Supp. IV Part 1:** 227

Man's Hope (Malraux), **IV:** 247
Mansion, The (Faulkner), **II:** 73; **Retro. Supp. I:** 74, 82
Man's Nature and His Communities (Niebuhr), **III:** 308
Manson, Charles, **Supp. IV Part 1:** 205
"Man Splitting Wood in the Daybreak, The" (Kinnell), **Supp. III Part 1:** 254
"Man's Pride" (Jeffers), **Supp. II Part 2:** 417
"Man's Story, The" (Anderson), **I:** 114
Man's Woman, A (Norris), **III:** 314, 322, 328, 329, 330, 332, 333
Man That Corrupted Hadleyburg, The (Twain), **I:** 204; **IV:** 208
"Man That Was Used Up, The" (Poe), **III:** 412, 425
"Mantis" (Zukofsky), **Supp. III Part 2:** 617
"'Mantis': An Interpretation" (Zukofsky), **Supp. III Part 2:** 617-618
Man to Send Rain Clouds, The (Rosen, ed.), **Supp. IV Part 2:** 499, 505, 513
"Man to Send Rain Clouds, The" (Silko), **Supp. IV Part 2:** 559
Mantrap (Lewis), **II:** 447
Manuductio Ad Ministerium (Mather), **Supp. II Part 2:** 465-467
"Manuelzinho" (Bishop), **Retro. Supp. II:** 47-48
Manuscript Books of Emily Dickinson, The (Franklin, ed.), **Retro. Supp. I:** 29, 41
"Man Waiting for It to Stop, A" (Dunn), **Supp. XI:** 144
"Man Who Became a Woman, The" (Anderson), **I:** 114
"Man Who Carries the Desert Around Inside Himself, The: For Wally" (Komunyakaa), **Supp. XIII:** 125
"Man Who Closed Shop, The" (Dunn), **Supp. XI:** 149
Man Who Gave Up His Name, The (Harrison), **Supp. VIII:** 45, 52
Man Who Had All the Luck, The (A. Miller), **III:** 148, 149, 164, 166
"Man Who Knew Belle Star, The" (Bausch), **Supp. VII:** 46
"Man Who Knew Coolidge, The" (Lewis), **II:** 449
Man Who Knew Coolidge, The: Being the Soul of Lowell Schmaltz, Constructive and Nordic Citizen (Lewis), **II:** 450
Man Who Lived Underground, The (Wright), **Supp. II Part 1:** 40

"Man Who Lived Underground, The" (Wright), **IV:** 479, 485-487, 492; **Retro. Supp. II:** 121
"Man Who Makes Brooms, The" (Nye), **Supp. XIII:** 276
"Man Who Studied Yoga, The" (Mailer), **III:** 35-36; **Retro. Supp. II:** 200
"Man Who Wanted to Win, The" (McCoy), **Supp. XIII:** 161
Man Who Was There, The (Morris), **III:** 220-221
"Man Who Writes Ants, The" (Merwin), **Supp. III Part 1:** 348
"Man with a Family" (Humphrey), **Supp. IX:** 94
Man without a Country, The (Hale), **I:** 488
"Man with the Blue Guitar, The" (Stevens), **I:** 266; **IV:** 85-87; **Retro. Supp. I:** **303-305,** 306, 307, 309
Man with the Blue Guitar and Other Poems, The (Stevens), **IV:** 76; **Retro. Supp. I:** 303, 422
Man with the Golden Arm, The (Algren), **Supp. V:** 4; **Supp. IX:** 1, 3, **9-11,** 14, 15
Man with the Golden Arm, The (film), **Supp. IX:** 3
"Man with the Golden Beef, The" (Podhoretz), **Supp. IX:** 3
"Man with the Hoe, The" (Markham), **Supp. XV:** 115
Manyan Letters (Olson), **Supp. II Part 2:** 571
Many Circles (Goldbarth), **Supp. XII:** 193
"Many Handles" (Sandburg), **III:** 594
"Many Happy Returns" (Auden), **Supp. II Part 1:** 15
Many Loves (W. C. Williams), **Retro. Supp. I:** 424
"Many Mansions" (H. Roth), **Supp. IX:** 233, 234
Many Marriages (Anderson), **I:** 104, 111, 113
"Many of Our Waters: Variations on a Poem by a Black Child" (Wright), **Supp. III Part 2:** 602
"Many Swans" (Lowell), **II:** 526
"Many Thousands Gone" (Baldwin), **Retro. Supp. II:** 4; **Supp. I Part 1:** 51
"Many Wagons Ago" (Ashbery), **Supp. III Part 1:** 22
"Many-Windowed House, A" (Cowley), **Supp. II Part 1:** 137
Many-Windowed House, A (Cowley), **Supp. II Part 1:** 141, 143
Mao II (DeLillo), **Supp. VI:** 2, 4, **5,** 6,
 7, 8, 9, 14, 16
"Map, The" (Bishop), **Retro. Supp. II:** 41; **Supp. I Part 1:** 72, 82, 85-88, 93
"Map, The" (Strand), **Supp. IV Part 2:** 623-624
"Maple Leaf, The" (Joplin), **Supp. IV Part 1:** 223
Map of Another Town: A Memoir of Provence (M. F. K. Fisher), **Supp. XVII:** 88, 89, 92
"Map of Montana in Italy, A" (Hugo), **Supp. VI:** 139
"Maps" (Hass), **Supp. VI:** 103-104
Mapson, Jo-Ann, **Supp. IV Part 2:** 440, 454
Map to the Next World, A: Poems and Tales (Harjo), **Supp. XII:** **228-230**
"Mara" (Jeffers), **Supp. II Part 2:** 434
Ma Rainey's Black Bottom (Wilson), **Supp. VIII:** 331, **332-334,** 346, 349, 350
Marat, Jean Paul, **IV:** 117; **Supp. I Part 2:** 514, 515, 521
"Marathon" (Glück), **Supp. V:** 85
Marble Faun, The (Faulkner), **II:** 55, 56; **Retro. Supp. I:** 79
Marble Faun, The; or, The Romance of Monte Beni (Hawthorne), **II:** 225, 239, 242-243, 290, 324; **IV:** 167; **Retro. Supp. I:** 63, 149, 163, **164-165;** **Supp. I Part 1:** 38; **Supp. I Part 2:** 421, 596; **Supp. XIII:** 102
Marbles (Brodsky), **Supp. VIII:** 26-27
Marcaccio, Michael, **Supp. XVII:** 97, 106
"March" (W. C. Williams), **Retro. Supp. I:** 418
March, Alan, **Supp. XVI:**242
March, Fredric, **III:** 154, 403; **IV:** 357; **Supp. X:** 220
Marchalonis, Shirley, **Supp. XIII:** 138, 140, 141, 143, 147-148
"Marché aux Oiseaux" (Wilbur), **Supp. III Part 2:** 550
"Märchen, The" (Jarrell), **II:** 378-379
March Hares (Frederic), **II:** 143-144
Marching Men (Anderson), **I:** 99, 101, 103-105, 111
"Marching Music" (Simic), **Supp. VIII:** 281
"Marcia" (Davis), **Supp. XVI:**91-92
Marco Millions (O'Neill), **III:** 391, 395
Marcosson, Isaac, **III:** 322
Marcus, Steven, **Retro. Supp. II:** 196, 200
Marcus Aurelius, **II:** 1; **III:** 566
Marcuse, Herbert, **Supp. I Part 2:** 645; **Supp. VIII:** 196; **Supp. XII:** 2

Mardi and a Voyage Thither (Melville), **I:** 384; **II:** 281; **III:** 77-79, 84, 87, 89; **Retro. Supp. I:** 247, 254, 256
Margaret (Judd), **II:** 290
"Margaret Fuller, 1847" (Clampitt), **Supp. IX:** 43
"Marginalia" (Wilbur), **Supp. III Part 2:** 544
Margin of Hope, A: An Intellectual Autobiography (Howe), **Supp. VI:** 113-114, 117, 125, 128
"Margins of Maycomb, The: A Rereading of *To Kill a Mockingbird*" (Phelps), **Supp. VIII:** 128
Margoshes, Samuel, **Supp. X:** 70
"Margrave" (Jeffers), **Supp. II Part 2:** 426
Margret Howth (Davis), **Supp. XVI:**81, 83, 84, **88-89**
Margret Howth: A Story of Today (J. Yellin, ed.), **Supp. XVI:**88
"Maria Concepción" (Porter), **III:** 434-435, 451
Mariani, Paul L., **Retro. Supp. I:** 412, 419; **Retro. Supp. II:** 189
Marianne Moore Reader, (Moore), **III:** 199
Marie Antoinette (film), **Retro. Supp. I:** 113
Marie Laveau (Prose), **Supp. XVI:**251
Mariella Gable, Sister, **III:** 339, 355
"Marijuana and a Pistol" (C. Himes), **Supp. XVI:**137
"Marijuana Notation" (Ginsberg), **Supp. II Part 1:** 313
Marilyn: A Biography (Mailer), **Retro. Supp. II:** 208
"Marin" (Cisneros), **Supp. VII:** 60, 61
Marin, Jay, **Retro. Supp. II:** 325
"Marina" (Eliot), **I:** 584, 585; **Retro. Supp. I:** 64
"Marine Surface, Low Overcast" (Clampitt), **Supp. IX:** 47-48
Marinetti, Tommaso, **Retro. Supp. I:** 59
Marionettes, The (Faulkner), **Retro. Supp. I:** 79
Maritain, Jacques, **I:** 402
Maritime Compact (Paine), **Supp. I Part 2:** 519
Maritime History of Massachusetts, 1783-1860, The (Morison), **Supp. I Part 2:** 481-483
Marjolin, Jean-Nicolas, **Supp. I Part 1:** 302
Marjorie Kinnan Rawlings: Sojourner at Cross Creek (Silverthorne), **Supp. X:** 220, 234
"Mark, The" (Bogan), **Supp. III Part 1:** 52

Marker, Chris, **Supp. IV Part 2:** 434, 436
"Market" (Hayden), **Supp. II Part 1:** 368, 369
Marketplace, The (Frederic), **II:** 145-146
Markham, Edwin, **I:** 199, 207; **Supp. XV:** 115
Markings (Hammarskjold), **Supp. II Part 1:** 26
Mark of the Vampire (film, Browning), **Supp. XVII:** 58
Markopoulos, Gregory, **Supp. XII:** 2
Markowick-Olczakowa, Hanna, **Supp. X:** 70
Marks, Alison, **Supp. I Part 2:** 660
Marks, Barry A., **I:** 435, 438, 442, 446
Markson, David, **Supp. XVII: 135-147**
Mark Twain in Eruption (Twain), **IV:** 209
Mark Twain's America (De Voto), **I:** 248
Mark Twain's Autobiography (Twain), **IV:** 209
Marley, Bob, **Supp. IX:** 152
Marlowe, Christopher, **I:** 68, 368, 384; **II:** 590; **III:** 259, 491; **Retro. Supp. I:** 127; **Retro. Supp. II:** 76; **Supp. I Part 2:** 422
"Marlowe Takes on the Syndicate" (Chandler), **Supp. IV Part 1:** 135
Marne, The (Wharton), **IV:** 319, 320; **Retro. Supp. I:** 378
Marquand, J. P., **I:** 362, 375; **II:** 459, 482-483; **III: 50-73,** 383; **Supp. I Part 1:** 196; **Supp. IV Part 1:** 31; **Supp. V:** 95
Marquand, John, **Supp. XI:** 301
Marquand, Mrs. John P. (Adelaide Hooker), **III:** 57, 61
Marquand, Mrs. John P. (Christina Sedgwick), **III:** 54, 57
Marquand, Philip, **III:** 52
Marquis, Don, **Supp. I Part 2:** 668
"Marriage" (Corso), **Supp. XII:** 117, 124, **127-128**
Marriage (Moore), **III:** 194
"Marriage" (Moore), **III:** 198-199, 213
"Marriage, A" (Untermeyer), **Supp. XV:** 305
Marriage A-la-Mode (Dryden), **Supp. IX:** 68
Marriage and Other Science Fiction (Goldbarth), **Supp. XII:** 189, 190
"Marriage in the Sixties, A" (Rich), **Supp. I Part 2:** 554
"Marriage of Heaven and Hell, The" (Blake), **III:** 544-545; **Supp. VIII:** 99
"Marriage of Phaedra, The" (Cather),

Retro. Supp. I: 5
Marrow of Tradition, The (Chesnutt), **Supp. XIV:**63, **71-75,** 76
Marryat, Captain Frederick, **III:** 423
"Marrying Absurd" (Didion), **Supp. IV Part 1:** 200
"Marrying Iseult?" (Updike), **Retro. Supp. I:** 329
Marrying Man (Simon), **Supp. IV Part 2:** 588
"Marrying the Hangman" (Atwood), **Supp. XIII:** 34
Marry Me: A Romance (Updike), **Retro. Supp. I:** 329, 330, 332
"Mars and Hymen" (Freneau), **Supp. II Part 1:** 258
Marsden, Dora, **III:** 471; **Retro. Supp. I:** 416
Marsena (Frederic), **II:** 135, 136-137
Marsh, Edward, **Supp. I Part 1:** 257, 263
Marsh, Fred T., **Supp. IX:** 232
Marsh, Mae, **Supp. I Part 2:** 391
Marshall, George, **III:** 3
Marshall, John, **Supp. I Part 2:** 455; **Supp. XVI:**117
Marshall, Paule, **Supp. IV Part 1:** 8, 14, 369; **Supp. XI:** 18, **275-292; Supp. XIII:** 295
Marshall, Tod, **Supp. XV:** 224; **Supp. XVII:** 25, 26, 29, 32
"Marshall Carpenter" (Masters), **Supp. I Part 2:** 463
"Marshes of Glynn, The" (Lanier), **Supp. I Part 1:** 364, 365-368, 370, 373
"'Marshes of Glynn, The': A Study in Symbolic Obscurity" (Ross), **Supp. I Part 1:** 373
Marsh Island, A (Jewett), **II:** 405; **Retro. Supp. II:** 134
"Marshland Elegy" (Leopold), **Supp. XIV:**187, 189
"Mars Is Heaven!" (Bradbury), **Supp. IV Part 1:** 103, 106
Marsman, Henrik, **Supp. IV Part 1:** 183
Marston, Ed, **Supp. IV Part 2:** 492
Marta y Maria (Valdes), **II:** 290
"Martha's Lady" (Jewett), **Retro. Supp. II:** 140, 143
Marthe, Saint, **II:** 213
Martial, **II:** 1, 169; **Supp. IX:** 152
Martian Chronicles, The (Bradbury), **Supp. IV Part 1:** 102, 103, 106-107
Martin, Benjamin, **Supp. I Part 2:** 503
Martin, Charles, **Supp. XVII:** 112
Martin, Dick, **Supp. XII:** 44
Martin, Jay, **I:** 55, 58, 60, 61, 67; **III:** 307; **Retro. Supp. II:** 326, 327,

329; **Supp. XI:** 162
Martin, John, **Supp. XI:** 172
Martin, Judith, **Supp. V:** 128
Martin, Nell, **Supp. IV Part 1:** 351, 353
Martin, Reginald, **Supp. X:** 247, 249
Martin, Stephen-Paul, **Supp. IV Part 2:** 430
Martin, Tom, **Supp. X:** 79
Martin du Gard, Roger, **Supp. I Part 1:** 51
Martineau, Harriet, **Supp. II Part 1:** 282, 288, 294
Martin Eden (London), **II:** 466, 477-481
Martinelli, Sheri, **Supp. IV Part 1:** 280
Martínez, Guillermo, **Supp. XIII:** 313
Mart'nez, Rafael, **Retro. Supp. I:** 423
Martone, John, **Supp. V:** 179
Marty (Chayefsky), **Supp. XV:** 205
"Martyr, The" (Porter), **III:** 454
Martz, Louis L., **IV:** 151, 156, 165; **Supp. I Part 1:** 107; **Supp. XIV:** 12
Marvell, Andrew, **IV:** 135, 151, 156, 161, 253; **Retro. Supp. I:** 62, 127; **Retro. Supp. II:** 186, 189; **Supp. I Part 1:** 80; **Supp. XII:** 159; **Supp. XIV:** 10; **Supp. XVI:** 204
"Marvella, for Borrowing" (Ríos), **Supp. IV Part 2:** 551
"Marvelous Sauce, The," **Supp. XVII:** 189
Marx, Eleanor, **Supp. XVI:** 85
Marx, Karl, **I:** 60, 267, 279, 283, 588; **II:** 376, 462, 463, 483, 577; **IV:** 429, 436, 443-444, 469; **Retro. Supp. I:** 254; **Supp. I Part 2:** 518, 628, 632, 633, 634, 635, 639, 643, 645, 646; **Supp. III Part 2:** 619; **Supp. IV Part 1:** 355; **Supp. VIII:** 196; **Supp. IX:** 133; **Supp. X:** 119, 134; **Supp. XIII:** 75
Marx, Leo, **Supp. I Part 1:** 233
"Marxism and Monastic Perpectives" (Merton), **Supp. VIII:** 196
Mary (Nabokov), **Retro. Supp. I:** 267-268, 270, 277
Mary; or, The Test of Honour (Rowson), **Supp. XV:** 233, 236
"Mary Karr, Mary Karr, Mary Karr, Mary Karr" (Harmon), **Supp. XI:** 248
Maryles, Daisy, **Supp. XII:** 271
Mary Magdalene, **I:** 303
"Mary O'Reilly" (Anderson), **II:** 44
"Mary Osaka , I Love You" (Fante), **Supp. XI:** 169
"Mary's Song" (Plath), **Supp. I Part 2:** 541
"Mary Winslow" (Lowell), **Retro.**

Supp. II: 187
Marzynski, Marian, **Supp. XVI:** 153
Masefield, John, **II:** 552; **III:** 523
Mask for Janus, A (Merwin), **Supp. III Part 1:** 339, 341, 342
Maslin, Janet, **Supp. XVI:** 213
Maslow, Abraham, **Supp. I Part 2:** 540
Mason, Bobbie Ann, **Supp. VIII:** 133-149; **Supp. XI:** 26; **Supp. XII:** 294, 298, 311
Mason, Charlotte, **Supp. XIV:** 201
Mason, David, **Supp. V:** 344; **Supp. XV:** 116, 251; **Supp. XVII:** 109, 110, 112, 121
Mason, Lowell, **I:** 458
Mason, Marsha, **Supp. IV Part 2:** 575, 586
Mason, Otis Tufton, **Supp. I Part 1:** 18
Mason, Walt, **Supp. XV:** 298
Mason & Dixon (Pynchon), **Supp. XVII:** 232
"Mason Jars by the Window" (Ríos), **Supp. IV Part 2:** 548
Masque of Mercy, A (Frost), **II:** 155, 165, 167-168; **Retro. Supp. I:** 131, 140
"Masque of Mummers, The" (MacLeish), **III:** 18
"Masque of Pandora, The" (Longfellow), **Retro. Supp. II:** 167
Masque of Pandora, The, and Other Poems (Longfellow), **II:** 490, 494, 506; **Retro. Supp. II:** 169
Masque of Poets, A (Lathrop, ed.), **Retro. Supp. I:** 31; **Supp. I Part 1:** 365, 368
Masque of Reason, A (Frost), **II:** 155, 162, 165-167; **Retro. Supp. I:** 131, 140; **Retro. Supp. II:** 42
"Masque of the Red Death, The" (Poe), **III:** 412, 419, 424; **Retro. Supp. II:** 262, 268-269
"Masquerade" (Banks), **Supp. V:** 7
"Massachusetts 1932" (Bowles), **Supp. IV Part 1:** 94
Massachusetts, Its Historians and Its History (Adams), **Supp. I Part 2:** 484
"Massachusetts to Virginia" (Whittier), **Supp. I Part 2:** 688-689
"Massacre and the Mastermind, The" (Bausch), **Supp. VII:** 49
"Massacre at Scio, The" (Bryant), **Supp. I Part 1:** 168
"Massacre of the Innocents, The" (Simic), **Supp. VIII:** 282
Masses and Man (Toller), **I:** 479
"Masseur de Ma Soeur, Le" (Hecht),

Supp. X: 58
Massey, Raymond, **Supp. IV Part 2:** 524
"Mass Eye and Ear: The Ward" (Karr), **Supp. XI:** 244
"Mass for the Day of St. Thomas Didymus" (Levertov), **Supp. III Part 1:** 283
Massie, Chris, **Supp. IV Part 2:** 524
Massing, Michael, **Supp. IV Part 1:** 208
Massinger, Philip, **Supp. I Part 2:** 422; **Supp. XV:** 238
Master Builder, The (Ibsen), **Supp. IV Part 2:** 522
Master Class (McNally), **Supp. XIII:** 204-205, 208
"Masterful" (Matthews), **Supp. IX:** 161-162
Mastering the Art of French Cooking (Child), **Supp. XVII:** 89
"Master Misery" (Capote), **Supp. III Part 1:** 117
Master of Dreams: A Memoir of Isaac Bashevis Singer (Telushkin), **Retro. Supp. II:** 317
"Master of Secret Revenges, The" (Gass), **Supp. VI:** 93
Master of the Crossroads (Bell), **Supp. X:** 16-17
"'Masterpiece of Filth, A': Portrait of Knoxville Forgets to Be Fair" (Howards), **Supp. VIII:** 178
Masterpieces of American Fiction, **Supp. XI:** 198
"Master Player, The" (Dunbar), **Supp. II Part 1:** 200
Masters, Edgar Lee, **I:** 106, 384, 475, 480, 518; **II:** 276, 529; **III:** 505, 576, 579; **IV:** 352; **Retro. Supp. I:** 131; **Supp. I Part 2:** 378, 386, 387, **454-478;** **Supp. III Part 1:** 63, 71, 73, 75; **Supp. IV Part 2:** 502; **Supp. IX:** 308; **Supp. XIV:** 282-283; **Supp. XV:** 256, 293, 297, 301, 306
Masters, Hardin W., **Supp. I Part 2:** 468
Masters, Hilary, **Supp. IX:** 96
Masters of Sociological Thought (Coser), **Supp. I Part 2:** 650
Masters of the Dew (Roumain), **Supp. IV Part 1:** 367
Matchmaker, The (Wilder), **IV:** 357, 369, 370, 374
Mate of the Daylight, The, and Friends Ashore (Jewett), **II:** 404; **Retro. Supp. II:** 146-147
Materassi, Mario, **Supp. IX:** 233
Mather, Cotton, **II:** 10, 104, 302, 506, 536; **III:** 442; **IV:** 144, 152-153,

157; **Supp. I Part 1:** 102, 117, 174, 271; **Supp. I Part 2:** 584, 599, 698; **Supp. II Part 2: 441-470; Supp. IV Part 2:** 430, 434
Mather, Increase, **II:** 10; **IV:** 147, 157; **Supp. I Part 1:** 100
Mathews, Cornelius, **III:** 81; **Supp. I Part 1:** 317
Mathews, Shailer, **III:** 293
"Matinees" (Merrill), **Supp. III Part 1:** 319, 327
"Matins" (C. Frost), **Supp. XV:** 105
"Matins" (Glück), **Supp. V:** 88
"Matisse: Blue Interior with Two Girls-1947" (Hecht), **Supp. X:** 73-74
Matisse, Henri, **III:** 180; **IV:** 90, 407; **Supp. I Part 2:** 619; **Supp. VIII:** 168; **Supp. IX:** 66; **Supp. X:** 73, 74
"Matisse: The Red Studio" (Snodgrass), **Supp. VI:** 316-317
Matlack, James, **Supp. XV:** 269, 271, 286
Matlock, Lucinda, **Supp. I Part 2:** 462
Matrimaniac, The (film), **Supp. XVI:**185, 186
Matrix Trilogy, The (film), **Supp. XVI:**271
Matson, Harold, **Supp. XIII:** 164, 166, 167, 169, 172
Matson, Peter, **Supp. IV Part 1:** 299
Matson, Suzanne, **Supp. VIII:** 281
Matters of Fact and Fiction: Essays 1973-1976 (Vidal), **Supp. IV Part 2:** 687
Matthew (biblical book), **IV:** 164; **Supp. XV:** 222
Matthew Arnold (Trilling), **Supp. III Part 2:** 500-501
Matthews, Jackson, **Supp. XVI:**282
Matthews, T. S., **II:** 430; **Supp. XV:** 142
Matthews, William, **Supp. V:** 4, 5; **Supp. IX: 151-170; Supp. XIII:** 112
Matthiessen, F. O., **I:** 254, 259-260, 517; **II:** 41, 554; **III:** 310, 453; **IV:** 181; **Retro. Supp. I:** 40, 217; **Retro. Supp. II:** 137; **Supp. IV Part 2:** 422; **Supp. XIII:** 93; **Supp. XIV:**3
Matthiessen, Peter, **Supp. V: 199-217,** 332; **Supp. XI:** 231, 294; **Supp. XIV:**82; **Supp. XVI:**230
Mattingly, Garrett, **Supp. IV Part 2:** 601
Mattu, Ravi, **Supp. XVI:**124
"Maud Island" (Caldwell), **I:** 310
Maud Martha (Brooks), **Supp. III Part 1:** 74, 78-79, 87; **Supp. XI:** 278
"Maud Muller" (Whittier), **Supp. I Part 2:** 698

Maugham, W. Somerset, **III:** 57, 64; **Supp. IV Part 1:** 209; **Supp. X:** 58; **Supp. XIV:**161
Maule's Curse: Seven Studies in the History of American Obscurantism (Winters), **Supp. II Part 2:** 807-808, 812
"Mau-mauing the Flak Catchers" (Wolfe), **Supp. III Part 2:** 577
Maupassant, Guy de, **I:** 309, 421; **II:** 191-192, 291, 325, 591; **IV:** 17; **Retro. Supp. II:** 65, 66, 67, 299; **Supp. I Part 1:** 207, 217, 223, 320; **Supp. XIV:**336
"Maurice Barrès and the Youth of France" (Bourne), **I:** 228
Maurier, George du, **II:** 338
Maurras, Charles, **Retro. Supp. I:** 55
Maus II: And Here My Troubles Began (A. Speigelman), **Supp. XVII:** 48
Mauve Gloves & Madmen, Clutter & Vine (Wolfe), **Supp. III Part 2:** 581
Maverick in Mauve (Auchincloss), **Supp. IV Part 1:** 26
"Mavericks, The" (play) (Auchincloss), **Supp. IV Part 1:** 34
"Mavericks, The" (story) (Auchincloss), **Supp. IV Part 1:** 32
"Max" (H. Miller), **III:** 183
Max and the White Phagocytes (H. Miller), **III:** 178, 183-184
Maximilian (emperor of Mexico), **Supp. I Part 2:** 457-458
Maximilian: A Play in Five Acts (Masters), **Supp. I Part 2:** 456, 457-458
"Maximus, to Gloucester" (Olson), **Supp. II Part 2:** 574
"Maximus, to himself" (Olson), **Supp. II Part 2:** 565, 566, 567, 569, 570, 572
Maximus Poems, The (Olson), **Retro. Supp. I:** 209; **Supp. II Part 2:** 555, 556, 563, 564-580, 584; **Supp. VIII:** 305; **Supp. XV:** 170, 264, 349; **Supp. XVI:**287
Maximus Poems 1-10, The (Olson), **Supp. II Part 2:** 571
Maximus Poems IV, V, VI (Olson), **Supp. II Part 2:** 555, 580, 582-584
Maximus Poems Volume Three, The (Olson), **Supp. II Part 2:** 555, 582, 584-585
"Maximus to Gloucester, Letter 19 (A Pastoral Letter)" (Olson), **Supp. II Part 2:** 567
"Maximus to Gloucester, Sunday July 19" (Olson), **Supp. II Part 2:** 580
"Maximus to himself June 1964" (Olson), **Supp. II Part 2:** 584

Maxwell, Glyn, **Supp. XV:** 252, 253, 260, 261, 263, 264
Maxwell, William, **Supp. I Part 1:** 175; **Supp. III Part 1:** 62; **Supp. VIII: 151-174; Supp. XVII:** 23
"May 1968" (Olds), **Supp. X:** 211-212
May, Abigail (Abba). *See* Alcott, Mrs. Amos Bronson (Abigail May)
May, Jill, **Supp. VIII:** 126
"May 24, 1980" (Brodsky), **Supp. VIII:** 28
"Mayan Warning" (Mora), **Supp. XIII:** 214
Maybe (Hellman), **Supp. IV Part 1:** 12
"Maybe" (Oliver), **Supp. VII:** 239
"Maybe, Someday" (Ritsos), **Supp. XIII:** 78
May Blossom (Belasco), **Supp. XVI:**182
"Mayday" (Faulkner), **Retro. Supp. I:** 80
"May Day" (Fitzgerald), **II:** 88-89; **Retro. Supp. I:** 103
"May Day Dancing, The" (Nemerov), **III:** 275
"May Day Sermon to the Women of Gilmer County, Georgia, by a Woman Preacher Leaving the Baptist Church" (Dickey), **Supp. IV Part 1:** 182
Mayer, Elizabeth, **Supp. II Part 1:** 16; **Supp. III Part 1:** 63
Mayer, John, **Retro. Supp. I:** 58
Mayer, Louis B., **Supp. XII:** 160
Mayes, Wendell, **Supp. IX:** 250
Mayfield, Sara, **Supp. IX:** 65
Mayflower, The (Stowe), **Supp. I Part 2:** 585, 586
Mayle, Peter, **Supp. XVI:**295
Maynard, Joyce, **Supp. V:** 23
Maynard, Tony, **Supp. I Part 1:** 65
Mayo, Robert, **III:** 478
Mayorga, Margaret, **IV:** 381
"Maypole of Merrymount, The" (Hawthorne), **II:** 229
May Sarton: Selected Letters 1916-1954, **Supp. VIII:** 265
"May Sun Sheds an Amber Light, The" (Bryant), **Supp. I Part 1:** 170
"May Swenson: The Art of Perceiving" (Stanford), **Supp. IV Part 2:** 637
"Maze" (Eberhart), **I:** 523, 525-526, 527
Mazel (R. Goldstein), **Supp. XVII:** 44
Mazurkiewicz, Margaret, **Supp. XI:** 2
Mazzini, Giuseppe, **Supp. I Part 1:** 2, 8; **Supp. II Part 1:** 299
M Butterfly (Hwang), **Supp. X:** 292

Mc. Names starting with Mc are alphabetized as if spelled Mac.
McElligot's Pool (Geisel), **Supp. XVI:**104
McLean, Carolyn (pseudo.). See Bly, Carol
"Me, Boy Scout" (Lardner), **II:** 433
Me: By Jimmy (Big Boy) Valente (Keillor), **Supp. XVI:**177
Me, Vashya! (T. Williams), **IV:** 381
Mead, Elinor. See Howells, Mrs. William Dean (Elinor Mead)
Mead, George Herbert, **II:** 27, 34; **Supp. I Part 1:** 5; **Supp. I Part 2:** 641
Mead, Margaret, **Supp. I Part 1:** 49, 52, 66; **Supp. IX:** 229
Mead, Taylor, **Supp. XV:** 187
Meade, Frank, **Retro. Supp. II:** 114
Meade, Marion, **Supp. IX:** 191, 193, 194, 195
Meadow, Lynne, **Supp. XIII:** 198
"Meadow House" (Carruth), **Supp. XVI:**48
Meadowlands (Glück), **Supp. V:** 88-90
"Mean, Mrs." (Gass), **Supp. VI:** 83
"Me and the Mule" (Hughes), **Supp. I Part 1:** 334
"Meaningless Institution, A" (Ginsberg), **Supp. II Part 1:** 313
"Meaning of a Literary Idea, The" (Trilling), **Supp. III Part 2:** 498
"Meaning of Birds, The" (C. Smith), **Supp. X:** 177
"Meaning of Death, The, An After Dinner Speech" (Tate), **IV:** 128, 129
"Meaning of Life, The" (Tate), **IV:** 137
"Meaning of Simplicity, The" (Ritsos), **Supp. XIII:** 78
Mean Spirit (Hogan), **Supp. IV Part 1:** 397, 404, 407-410, 415, 416-417
Mearns, Hughes, **III:** 220
"Measure" (Hass), **Supp. VI: 99-100,** 101
"Measuring My Blood" (Vizenor), **Supp. IV Part 1:** 262
Meatyard, Gene, **Supp. X:** 30
Mechan, Dennis B., **Supp. XVI:**267-268
Mechanic, The (Bynner and DeMille), **Supp. XV:** 42, 50
"Mechanism" (Ammons), **Supp. VII:** 28
"Mechanism in Thought and Morals" (Holmes), **Supp. I Part 1:** 314
Mecom, Mrs. Jane, **II:** 122
"Meddlesome Jack" (Caldwell), **I:** 309
Medea (Jeffers), **Supp. II Part 2:** 435
Medea and Some Poems, The (Cullen), **Supp. IV Part 1:** 169, 173

"Me Decade and the Third Great Awakening, The" (Wolfe), **Supp. III Part 2:** 581
"Médecin Malgré Lui, Le" (W. C. Williams), **IV:** 407-408
"Medfield" (Bryant), **Supp. I Part 1:** 157
Medical History of Contraception, A (Himes), **Supp. V:** 128
"Medicine Song" (Gunn Allen), **Supp. IV Part 1:** 326
Médicis, Marie de, **II:** 548
Medina (McCarthy), **II:** 579
"Meditation 1.6" (Taylor), **IV:** 165
"Meditation 1.20" (Taylor), **IV:** 165
"Meditation 2.102" (Taylor), **IV:** 150
"Meditation 2.112" (Taylor), **IV:** 165
"Meditation 20" (Taylor), **IV:** 154-155
"Meditation 40" (Second Series) (Taylor), **IV:** 147
"Meditation, A" (Eberhart), **I:** 533-535
"Meditation 2.68A" (Taylor), **IV:** 165
"Meditation at Lagunitas" (Hass), **Supp. VI:** 104-105
"Meditation at Oyster River" (Roethke), **III:** 537, 549
Meditations (Descartes), **III:** 618
"Meditations for a Savage Child" (Rich), **Supp. I Part 2:** 564-565
Meditations from a Movable Chair (Dubus), **Supp. VII:** 91
"Meditations in a Swine Yard" (Komunyakaa), **Supp. XIII:** 131
"Meditations of an Old Woman" (Roethke), **III:** 529, 540, 542, 543, 545-547, 548
Meditations on the Insatiable Soul (R. Bly), **Supp. IV Part 1:** 72-73
Meditative Poems, The (Martz), **IV:** 151
"Mediterranean, The" (Tate), **IV:** 129
"Medium of Fiction, The" (Gass), **Supp. VI:** 85-86
"Medley" (Bambara), **Supp. XI:** 9
"Medusa" (Bogan), **Supp. III Part 1:** 50, 51
Meehan, Thomas, **Supp. IV Part 2:** 577-578, 586, 590
Meek, Martha, **Supp. IV Part 2:** 439, 440, 441, 442, 445, 447, 448
Meeker, Richard K., **II:** 190
Meese, Elizabeth, **Supp. XIII:** 297
"Meeting, The" (F. Wright), **Supp. XVII:** 245
"Meeting and Greeting Area, The" (Cameron), **Supp. XII: 84-85**
Meeting by the River, A (Isherwood), **Supp. XIV:**164, **170-171,** 172
"Meeting-House Hill" (Lowell), **II:** 522, 527

"Meeting in the Kitchen, The" (Schnackenberg), **Supp. XV:** 256
"Meeting South, A" (Anderson), **I:** 115
"Meeting the Mountains" (Snyder), **Supp. VIII:** 300
Meeting Trees (Sanders), **Supp. XVI:**269
Meet Me at the Morgue (Macdonald), **Supp. IV Part 2:** 472
Mehta, Sonny, **Supp. XI:** 178
Meine, Curt, **Supp. XIV:**179
Meiners, R. K., **IV:** 136, 137, 138, 140
Meinong, Alexius, **Supp. XIV:**198, 199
Meisner, Sanford, **Supp. XIV:**240, 242
Meister, Charles W., **II:** 112
"Melancholia" (Dunbar), **Supp. II Part 1:** 194
"Melanctha" (Stein), **IV:** 30, 34, 35, 37, 38-40, 45
"Melancthon" (Moore), **III:** 212, 215
Meliboeus Hipponax (Lowell). See *Bigelow Papers, The* (Lowell)
Melinda and Melinda (Allen), **Supp. XV:** 16
Mellaart, James, **Supp. I Part 2:** 567
Mellard, James, **Supp. IV Part 1:** 387
Mellon, Andrew, **III:** 14
Melnick, Jeffrey, **Supp. X:** 252
Melnyczuk, Askold, **Supp. IV Part 1:** 70
Melodrama Play (Shepard), **Supp. III Part 2:** 440-441, 443, 445
Melodramatists, The (Nemerov), **III:** 268, 281-283, 284
Melting-Pot, The (Zangwill), **I:** 229
Melville, Allan, **III:** 74, 77
Melville, Gansevoort, **III:** 76
Melville, Herman, **I:** 104, 106, 211, 288, 340, 343, 348, 354, 355, 561-562; **II:** 27, 74, 224-225, 228, 230, 232, 236, 255, 259, 271, 272, 277, 281, 295, 307, 311, 319, 320, 321, 418, 477, 497, 539-540, 545; **III:** 29, 45, 70, **74-98,** 359, 438, 453, 454, 507, 562-563, 572, 576; **IV:** 57, 105, 194, 199, 202, 250, 309, 333, 345, 350, 380, 444, 453; **Retro. Supp. I:** 54, 91, 160, 215, 220, **243-262; Retro. Supp. II:** 76; **Supp. I Part 1:** 147, 238, 242, 249, 309, 317, 372; **Supp. I Part 2:** 383, 495, 579, 580, 582, 602; **Supp. IV Part 2:** 463, 613; **Supp. V:** 279, 281, 298, 308; **Supp. VIII:** 48, 103, 104, 105, 106, 108, 156, 175, 181, 188; **Supp. XI:** 83; **Supp. XII:** 282; **Supp. XIII:** 294, 305; **Supp. XIV:**48, 227; **Supp. XV:** 287; **Supp. XVII:** 42, 185

Melville, Maria Gansevoort, **III:** 74, 77, 85
Melville, Mrs. Herman (Elizabeth Shaw), **III:** 77, 91, 92
Melville, Thomas, **III:** 77, 79, 92; **Supp. I Part 1:** 309
Melville, Whyte, **IV:** 309
Melville Goodwin, USA (Marquand), **III:** 60, 65-66
Melville's Marginalia (Cowen), **Supp. IV Part 2:** 435
"Melville's Marginalia" (Howe), **Supp. IV Part 2:** 435
Member of the Wedding, The (McCullers), **II:** 587, 592, 600-604, 605, 606; **Supp. VIII:** 124
"Meme Ortiz" (Cisneros), **Supp. VII:** 60
Memmon (song cycle) (Bowles), **Supp. IV Part 1:** 82
Memnoch the Devil (Rice), **Supp. VII:** 289, 290, 294, 296-299
"Memoir" (Untermeyer), **II:** 516-517
"Memoir, A" (Koch), **Supp. XV:** 184
"Memoirist's Apology, A" (Karr), **Supp. XI:** 245, 246
Memoir of Mary Ann, A (O'Connor), **III:** 357
Memoir of Thomas McGrath, A (Beeching), **Supp. X:** 114, 118
Memoirs of Arii Taimai (Adams), **I:** 2-3
"Memoirs of Carwin, the Biloquist" (Brown), **Supp. I Part 1:** 132
Memoirs of Hecate County (Wilson), **IV:** 429
Memoirs of Margaret Fuller Ossoli (Fuller), **Supp. II Part 1:** 280, 283, 285
"Memoirs of Stephen Calvert" (Brown), **Supp. I Part 1:** 133, 144
Memorabilia (Xenophon), **II:** 105
Memorable Providences (Mather), **Supp. II Part 2:** 458
Memorial, The: Portrait of a Family (Isherwood), **Supp. XIV:**156, 159, 160-161
"Memorial Day" (Cameron), **Supp. XII:** 80, **82-83**
"Memorial for the City" (Auden), **Supp. II Part 1:** 20
"Memorial Rain" (MacLeish), **III:** 15
"Memorial to Ed Bland" (Brooks), **Supp. III Part 1:** 77
"Memorial Tribute" (Wilbur), **Supp. IV Part 2:** 642
"Memories" (Whittier), **Supp. I Part 2:** 699
Memories of a Catholic Girlhood (McCarthy), **II:** 560-561, 566; **Supp. XI:** 246; **Supp. XVI:**64, 70
"Memories of East Texas" (Karr), **Supp. XI:** 239
"Memories of Uncle Neddy" (Bishop), **Retro. Supp. II:** 38; **Supp. I Part 1:** 73, 93
"Memories of West Street and Lepke" (Lowell), **II:** 550
"Memory" (Epstein), **Supp. XII:** 163
"Memory" (Everwine), **Supp. XV:** 82
"Memory, A" (Welty), **IV:** 261-262; **Retro. Supp. I:** 344-345
"Memory, The" (Gioia), **Supp. XV:** 119
Memory Gardens (Creeley), **Supp. IV Part 1:** 141, 157
Memory of Murder, A (Bradbury), **Supp. IV Part 1:** 103
Memory of Old Jack, The (Berry), **Supp. X:** 34
Memory of Two Mondays, A (A. Miller), **III:** 153, 156, 158-159, 160, 166
"Memo to Non-White Peoples" (Hughes), **Retro. Supp. I:** 209
Men, Women and Ghosts (Lowell), **II:** 523-524
Menaker, Daniel, **Supp. VIII:** 151
Menand, Louis, **Supp. XIV:**40, 197; **Supp. XVI:**106, 107
Men and Angels (Gordon), **Supp. IV Part 1:** 304-305, 306, 308
Men and Brethen (Cozzens), **I:** 363-365, 368, 375, 378, 379
"Men and Women" (R. Bly), **Supp. IV Part 1:** 72
"Men at Forty" (Justice), **Supp. VII:** 126-127
Mencius (Meng-tzu), **IV:** 183
Mencken, August, **III:** 100, 108
Mencken, August, Jr., **III:** 99, 109, 118-119
Mencken, Burkhardt, **III:** 100, 108
Mencken, Charles, **III:** 99
Mencken, Gertrude, **III:** 99
Mencken, H. L., **I:** 199, 210, 212, 235, 245, 261, 405, 514, 515, 517; **II:** 25, 27, 42, 89, 90, 91, 271, 289, 430, 443, 449; **III:** **99-121**, 394, 482; **IV:** 76, 432, 440, 475, 482; **Retro. Supp. I:** 1, 101; **Retro. Supp. II:** 97, 98, 102, 265; **Supp. I Part 2:** 484, 629-630, 631, 647, 651, 653, 659, 673; **Supp. II Part 1:** 136; **Supp. IV Part 1:** 201, 314, 343; **Supp. IV Part 2:** 521, 692, 693; **Supp. XI:** 163-164, 166; **Supp. XIII:** 161; **Supp. XIV:**111; **Supp. XV:** 297, 301, 303; **Supp. XVI:**187-188, 189; **Supp. XVII:** 106
Mencken, Mrs. August (Anna Abhau), **III:** 100, 109
Mencken, Mrs. H. L. (Sara Haardt), **III:** 109, 111
"Men Deified Because of Their Cruelty" (Simic), **Supp. VIII:** 282
Mendelbaum, Paul, **Supp. V:** 159
Mendele, **IV:** 3, 10
Mendelief, Dmitri Ivanovich, **IV:** 421
Mendelsohn, Daniel, **Supp. X:** 153, 154; **Supp. XV:** 257, 258, 261, 266
"Mending Wall" (Frost), **II:** 153-154; **Retro. Supp. I:** 128, 130; **Supp. X:** 64
Men from the Boys, The (Lacy), **Supp. XV:** 202, 205
Men in the Off Hours (Carson), **Supp. XII:** **111-113**
"Men in the Storm, The" (Crane), **I:** 411
"Men Loved Wholly Beyond Wisdom" (Bogan), **Supp. III Part 1:** 50
"Men Made Out of Words" (Stevens), **IV:** 88
Men Must Act (Mumford), **Supp. II Part 2:** 479
Mennes, John, **II:** 111
Mennoti, Gian Carlo, **Supp. IV Part 1:** 84
Men of Brewster Place, The (Naylor), **Supp. VIII:** 213, **228-230**
"Men of Color, to Arms!" (Douglass), **Supp. III Part 1:** 171
Men of Good Hope: A Story of American Progressives (Aaron), **Supp. I Part 2:** 650
Mens' Club, The (film), **Supp. XVI:**212-213
Men's Club, The (L. Michaels), **Supp. XVI:**206, **210-212**
"Menstruation at Forty" (Sexton), **Supp. II Part 2:** 686
"Mental Hospital Garden, The" (W. C. Williams), **Retro. Supp. I:** 428
Mental Radio (Sinclair), **Supp. V:** 289
Mentoria; or, The Young Lady's Friend (Rowson), **Supp. XV:** **233-234,** 238
"Men We Carry in Our Minds, The" (Sanders), **Supp. XVI:**273
Men Who Made the Nation, The (Dos Passos), **I:** 485
Men Without Women (Hemingway), **II:** 249; **Retro. Supp. I:** 170, 176; **Supp. IX:** 202
"Merced" (Rich), **Supp. I Part 2:** 563
"Mercedes" (E. Stoddard), **Supp. XV:** 278
"Mercedes Hospital" (Bishop), **Retro. Supp. II:** 51
"Mercenary, A" (Ozick), **Supp. V:** 267

Merchant of Venice, The (Shakespeare), **IV:** 227; **Supp. XIV:** 325
Mercury Theatre, **Retro. Supp. I:** 65
Mercy, Pity, Peace, and Love (Ozick), **Supp. V:** 257, 258
Mercy, The (Levine), **Supp. V:** 194-195
Mercy of a Rude Stream (H. Roth), **Supp. IX:** 231, 234, **235-242**
Mercy Philbrick's Choice (Jackson), **Retro. Supp. I:** 26, 27, 33
Mercy Street (Sexton), **Supp. II Part 2:** 683, 689
Meredith, George, **II:** 175, 186; **Supp. IV Part 1:** 300
Meredith, Mary. *See* Webb, Mary
Meredith, William, **II:** 545; **Retro. Supp. II:** 181
"Merely to Know" (Rich), **Supp. I Part 2:** 554
"Mère Pochette" (Jewett), **II:** 400
"Merger II, The" (Auchincloss), **Supp. IV Part 1:** 34
"Mericans" (Cisneros), **Supp. VII:** 69
"Merida, 1969" (Matthews), **Supp. IX:** 151
"Meridian" (Clampitt), **Supp. IX: 48-49**
Meridian (Walker), **Supp. III Part 2:** 520, 524, 527, 528, 531-537
Mérimée, Prosper, **II:** 322
Meriweather, James B., **Retro. Supp. I:** 77, 91
Meriwether, James B., **Retro Supp. I:** 77, 91
"Meriwether Connection, The" (Cowley), **Supp. II Part 1:** 142
Merker, Kim K., **Supp. XI:** 261; **Supp. XV:** 75, 77
"Merlin" (Emerson), **II:** 19, 20
Merlin (Robinson), **III:** 522
"Merlin Enthralled" (Wilbur), **Supp. III Part 2:** 544, 554
"Mermother" (A. Finch), **Supp. XVII:** 72
Merril, Judith, **Supp. XVI:** 123
Merrill, Christopher, **Supp. XI:** 329
Merrill, James, **Retro. Supp. I:** 296; **Retro. Supp. II:** 53; **Supp. III Part 1: 317-338; Supp. III Part 2:** 541, 561; **Supp. IX:** 40, 42, 48, 52; **Supp. X:** 73; **Supp. XI:** 123, 131, 249; **Supp. XII:** 44, 254, 255, 256, 261-262, 269-270; **Supp. XIII:** 76, 85; **Supp. XV:** 249, 250, 253; **Supp. XVII:** 123
Merrill, Mark (pseud.). *See* Markson, David
Merrill, Robert, **Retro. Supp. II:** 201
Merrill, Ronald, **Supp. IV Part 2:** 521

Merritt, Abraham, **Supp. XVII:** 58
Merritt, Theresa, **Supp. VIII:** 332
"Merry-Go-Round" (Hughes), **Retro. Supp. I:** 194, 205; **Supp. I Part 1:** 333
Merry-Go-Round, The (Van Vechten), **Supp. II Part 2:** 734, 735
Merry Month of May, The (Jones), **Supp. XI: 227-228**
Merry Widow, The (Lehar), **III:** 183
Merton, Thomas, **III:** 357; **Supp. VIII: 193-212**
Merwin, W. S., **Supp. III Part 1: 339-360; Supp. III Part 2:** 541; **Supp. IV Part 2:** 620, 623, 626; **Supp. V:** 332; **Supp. IX:** 152, 155, 290; **Supp. XIII:** 274, 277; **Supp. XV:** 222, 342
Meryman, Richard, **Supp. IV Part 2:** 579, 583
Meshugah (Singer), **Retro. Supp. II: 315-316**
Mesic, Michael, **Supp. IV Part 1:** 175
Mesic, Penelope, **Supp. X:** 15
Message in the Bottle, The (Percy), **Supp. III Part 1:** 387-388, 393, 397
"Message in the Bottle, The" (Percy), **Supp. III Part 1:** 388
"Message of Flowers and Fire and Flowers, The" (Brooks), **Supp. III Part 1:** 69
Messengers Will Come No More, The (Fiedler), **Supp. XIII:** 103
Messerli, Douglas, **Supp. XVI:** 293
Messiah (Vidal), **Supp. IV Part 2:** 677, 680, 681-682, 685, 691, 692
"Messiah, The" (Wasserstein), **Supp. XV:** 328
Messiah of Stockholm, The (Ozick), **Supp. V:** 270-271; **Supp. XVII:** 42
Metamorphic Tradition in Modern Poetry (Quinn), **IV:** 421
Metamorphoses (Ovid), **II:** 542-543; **III:** 467, 468
Metamorphoses (Pound, trans.), **III:** 468-469
Metamorphosis (Ovid), **Supp. XV:** 33; **Supp. XVI:** 20
Metamorphosis, The (Kafka), **IV:** 438; **Retro. Supp. II:** 287-288; **Supp. VIII:** 3
"Metamorphosis and Survival" (Woodcock), **Supp. XIII:** 33
"Metaphor as Mistake" (Percy), **Supp. III Part 1:** 387-388
Metaphor & Memory: Essays (Ozick), **Supp. V:** 272
"Metaphors of a Magnifico" (Stevens), **IV:** 92
Metaphysical Club, The (Menand),

Supp. XIV: 40, 197
"Metaphysical Poets, The" (Eliot), **I:** 527, 586
"Metaphysics" (Ginsberg), **Supp. II Part 1:** 313
Metcalf, Paul, **Supp. XIV:** 96
"Meteor, The" (Bradbury), **Supp. IV Part 1:** 102
Methinks the Lady... (Endore), **Supp. XVII:** 61-62
Metress, Christopher P., **Supp. V:** 314
Metrical History of Christianity, The (Taylor), **IV:** 163
Metropolis, The (Sinclair), **Supp. V:** 285
"Metterling Lists, The" (Allen), **Supp. XV:** 15
"Metzengerstein" (Poe), **III:** 411, 417
Mew, Charlotte, **Retro. Supp. II:** 247
Mewshaw, Michael, **Supp. V:** 57; **Supp. X:** 82
"Mexico" (Lowell), **II:** 553, 554
"Mexico, Age Four" (Salinas), **Supp. XIII:** 315
Mexico City Blues (Kerouac), **Supp. III Part 1:** 225, 229
"Mexico Is a Foreign Country: Five Studies in Naturalism" (Warren), **IV:** 241, 252
"Mexico's Children" (Rodriguez), **Supp. XIV:** 302
Meyer, Donald B., **III:** 298
Meyer, Ellen Hope, **Supp. V:** 123
Meyers, Jeffrey, **Retro. Supp. I:** 124, 138; **Retro. Supp. II:** 191
Meynell, Alice, **Supp. I Part 1:** 220
Mezey, Robert, **Supp. IV Part 1:** 60; **Supp. V:** 180; **Supp. XIII:** 312; **Supp. XV:** 74
Mezzanine, The (Baker), **Supp. XIII: 41-43,** 44, 45, 48, 55
"Mezzo Cammin" (Longfellow), **II:** 490
"Mi Abuelo" (Ríos), **Supp. IV Part 2:** 541
Miami (Didion), **Supp. IV Part 1:** 199, 210
Miami and the Siege of Chicago (Mailer), **Retro. Supp. II:** 206
"Michael" (Wordsworth), **III:** 523
Michael, Magali Cornier, **Supp. XIII:** 32
"Michael Angelo: A Fragment" (Longfellow), **II:** 490, 494, 495, 506; **Retro. Supp. II:** 167
"Michael Egerton" (Price), **Supp. VI:** 257-258, 260
Michael Kohlhaas (Kleist), **Supp. IV Part 1:** 224

INDEX / 421

Michaels, Leonard, **Supp. XVI:201-215**
Michaels, Walter Benn, **Retro. Supp. I:** 115, 369, 379
Michael Scarlett (Cozens), **I:** 358-359, 378
Michaux, Henri, **Supp. XVI:**288
Michelangelo, **I:** 18; **II:** 11-12; **III:** 124; **Supp. I Part 1:** 363; **Supp. XVII:** 112
Michel-Michot, Paulette, **Supp. XI:** 224-225
Michelson, Albert, **IV:** 27
Mickelsson's Ghosts (Gardner), **Supp. VI:** 63, **73-74**
Mickiewicz, Adam, **Supp. II Part 1:** 299
Midair (Conroy), **Supp. XVI:**63, **71-72**
"Mid-Air" (Conroy), **Supp. XVI:**69, 71
Mid-American Chants (Anderson), **I:** 109, 114
"Midas" (Winters), **Supp. II Part 2:** 801
"Mid-August at Sourdough Mountain Lookout" (Snyder), **Supp. VIII:** 292-293
Midcentury (Dos Passos), **I:** 474, 475, 478, 490, 492-494; **Supp. I Part 2:** 646
Mid-Century American Poets, **III:** 532
"Mid-Day" (Doolittle), **Supp. I Part 1:** 266-267
"Middle Age" (Lowell), **II:** 550
"Middleaged Man, The" (Simpson), **Supp. IX:** 274-275
Middle Ages, The (Gurney), **Supp. V:** 96, 105, 108
Middlebrook, Diane Wood, **Supp. IV Part 2:** 444, 451
"Middle Daughter, The" (Kingsolver), **Supp. VII:** 209
Middlemarch (Eliot), **I:** 457, 459; **II:** 290, 291; **Retro. Supp. I:** 225; **Supp. I Part 1:** 174; **Supp. IX:** 43; **Supp. XI:** 68; **Supp. XII:** 335
Middle of My Tether, The: Familiar Essays (Epstein), **Supp. XIV:106-107**
"Middle of Nowhere, The" (Wagoner), **Supp. IX:** 327-328
Middle of the Journey, The (Trilling), **Supp. III Part 2:** 495, 504-506
"Middle of the Way" (Kinnell), **Supp. III Part 1:** 242
"Middle Passage" (Hayden), **Supp. II Part 1:** 363, 375-376
Middle Passage (Johnson), **Supp. VI:** **194-196,** 198, 199; **Supp. XIII:** 182
"Middle Toe of the Right Foot, The" (Bierce), **I:** 203

Middleton, Thomas, **Retro. Supp. I:** 62
Middle Years, The (James), **II:** 337-338; **Retro. Supp. I:** 235
"Middle Years, The" (James), **Retro. Supp. I:** 228, 272
"Midnight" (Dunn), **Supp. XI:** 147
"Midnight Consultations, The" (Freneau), **Supp. II Part 1:** 257
Midnight Cry, A (Mather), **Supp. II Part 2:** 460
"Midnight Gladness" (Levertov), **Supp. III Part 1:** 284-285
"Midnight Magic" (Mason), **Supp. VIII:** 146
Midnight Magic: Selected Stories of Bobbie Ann Mason (Mason), **Supp. VIII:** 148
Midnight Mass (Bowles), **Supp. IV Part 1:** 93
"Midnight Postscript" (F. Wright), **Supp. XVII:** 245, 246
"Midnight Show" (Shapiro), **Supp. II Part 2:** 705
"Midpoint" (Updike), **Retro. Supp. I:** 321, 323, 327, 330, 335
Midpoint and Other Poems (Updike), **IV:** 214
"Midrash on Happiness" (Paley), **Supp. VI:** 217
"Midsummer in the Blueberry Barrens" (Clampitt), **Supp. IX:** 40-41
"Midsummer Letter" (Carruth), **Supp. XVI:**47
Midsummer Night's Dream, A (Shakespeare), **Supp. I Part 1:** 369-370; **Supp. X:** 69
Midsummer Night's Sex Comedy, A (film; Allen), **Supp. XV:** 8
"Midwest" (Stafford), **Supp. XI:** 317
"Midwest Poetics" (C. Baxter), **Supp. XVII:** 18
Mieder, Wolfgang, **Supp. XIV:**126
Mies van der Rohe, Ludwig, **Supp. IV Part 1:** 40
Mighty Aphrodite (film; Allen), **Supp. XV:** 11
"Mighty Fortress, A" (Leopold), **Supp. XIV:**185
"Mighty Lord, The (Rowson), **Supp. XV:** 243
"Migration, The" (Tate), **IV:** 130
Mihailovitch, Bata, **Supp. VIII:** 272
Miklitsch, Robert, **Supp. IV Part 2:** 628, 629
Mila 18 (Uris), **Supp. IV Part 1:** 379
Milagro Beanfield War, The (film), **Supp. XIII:** 267
Milagro Beanfield War, The (Nichols), **Supp. XIII:** 253, **265-266**

Milburn, Michael, **Supp. XI:** 239, 242
Milch, David, **Supp. XI:** 348
Miles, Barry, **Supp. XII:** 123
Miles, Jack, **Supp. VIII:** 86
Miles, Josephine, **Supp. XIII:** 275
Miles, Julie, **I:** 199
Miles, Kitty, **I:** 199
Milestone, Lewis, **Supp. I Part 1:** 281
Miles Wallingford (Cooper). See *Afloat and Ashore* (Cooper)
Milford, Nancy, **II:** 83; **Supp. IX:** 60
Milhaud, Darius, **Supp. IV Part 1:** 81
Miligate, Michael, **IV:** 123, 130, 132
"Militant Nudes" (Hardwick), **Supp. III Part 1:** 210-211
"Milk Bottles" (Anderson), **I:** 114
Milk Train Doesn't Stop Here Anymore, The (T. Williams), **IV:** 382, 383, 384, 386, 390, 391, 392, 393, 394, 395, 398
Mill, James, **II:** 357
Mill, John Stuart, **III:** 294-295; **Supp. XI:** 196; **Supp. XIV:**22
Millar, Kenneth. See Macdonald, Ross
Millar, Margaret (Margaret Sturm), **Supp. IV Part 2:** 464, 465
Millay, Cora, **III:** 123, 133-134, 135-136
Millay, Edna St. Vincent, **I:** 482; **II:** 530; **III: 122-144; IV:** 433, 436; **Retro. Supp. II:** 48; **Supp. I Part 2:** 707, 714, 726; **Supp. IV Part 1:** 168; **Supp. IV Part 2:** 607; **Supp. V:** 113; **Supp. IX:** 20; **Supp. XIV:**120, 121, 122, 127; **Supp. XV:** 42, 46, 51, 250, 293, 307; **Supp. XVII:** 69, 75, 96
Millennium Approaches (Kushner), **Supp. IX:** 141, 142, 145
Miller, Arthur, **I:** 81, 94; **III: 145-169; Supp. IV Part 1:** 359; **Supp. IV Part 2:** 574; **Supp. VIII:** 334; **Supp. XIII:** 127; **Supp. XIV:**102, 239; **Supp. XVI:**194
Miller, Brown, **Supp. IV Part 1:** 67
Miller, Carol, **Supp. IV Part 1:** 400, 405, 409, 410, 411
Miller, Henry, **I:** 97, 157; **III:** 40, **170-192; IV:** 138; **Retro. Supp. II:** 327; **Supp. I Part 2:** 546; **Supp. V:** 119, 131; **Supp. X:** 183, 185, 187, 194, 195; **Supp. XIII:** 1, 17
Miller, Henry (actor), **Supp. XVI:**182
Miller, Herman, **Supp. I Part 2:** 614, 617
Miller, J. Hillis, **Supp. IV Part 1:** 387
Miller, James E., Jr., **IV:** 352
Miller, Jeffrey, **Supp. IV Part 1:** 95
Miller, Joaquin, **I:** 193, 195, 459; **Supp. II Part 1:** 351

Miller, John Duncan, **Supp. I Part 2:** 604
Miller, Jonathan, **Retro. Supp. II:** 181
Miller, Laura, **Supp. XIII:** 48
Miller, Marilyn, **Supp. XVI:** 187
Miller, Matt, **Supp. XV:** 211
Miller, Matthew, **Supp. XVI:** 47, 51
Miller, Mrs. Arthur (Ingeborg Morath), **III:** 162-163
Miller, Mrs. Arthur (Marilyn Monroe), **III:** 161, 162-163
Miller, Mrs. Arthur (Mary Grace Slattery), **III:** 146, 161
Miller, Orilla, **Supp. I Part 1:** 48
Miller, Perry, **I:** 546, 547, 549, 550, 560; **IV:** 186; **Supp. I Part 1:** 31, 104; **Supp. I Part 2:** 484; **Supp. IV Part 2:** 422; **Supp. VIII:** 101
Miller, R. Baxter, **Retro. Supp. I:** 195, 207
Miller, Robert Ellis, **II:** 588
Miller, Ruth, **Supp. X:** 324
Miller, Stuart, **Supp. XVI:** 242
Miller, Sue, **Supp. X:** 77, 85; **Supp. XI:** 190; **Supp. XII: 289-305**
Miller of Old Church, The (Glasgow), **II:** 175, 181
"Miller's Tale" (Chaucer), **III:** 283
Miller Williams and the Poetry of the Particular (Burns), **Supp. XV:** 339
Millett, Kate, **Supp. X:** 193, 196
Mill Hand's Lunch Bucket (Bearden), **Supp. VIII:** 337
Millier, Brett C., **Retro. Supp. II:** 39
Milligan, Bryce, **Supp. XIII:** 274, 275, 277
Millions of Strange Shadows (Hecht), **Supp. X:** 57, **62-65**
"Million Young Workmen, 1915, A" (Sandburg), **III:** 585
Millroy the Magician (Theroux), **Supp. VIII:** 325
Mills, Alice, **Supp. XIII:** 233
Mills, Benjamin Fay, **III:** 176
Mills, C. Wright, **Supp. I Part 2:** 648, 650
Mills, Florence, **Supp. I Part 1:** 322
Mills, Ralph J., Jr., **III:** 530; **Supp. IV Part 1:** 64; **Supp. XI:** 311
Mills, Tedi López, **Supp. XVI:** 281
Mills of the Kavanaughs, The (Lowell), **II:** 542-543, 546, 550; **III:** 508; **Retro. Supp. II:** 178, 179, 188
"Mills of the Kavanaughs, The" (Lowell), **II:** 542-543
Milne, A. A., **Supp. IX:** 189
Milne, A. J. M., **I:** 278
Milosz, Czeslaw, **Supp. III Part 2:** 630; **Supp. VIII:** 20, 22; **Supp. XI:**

267, 312; **Supp. XVII:** 241
Miltner, Robert, **Supp. XI:** 142
Milton, Edith, **Supp. VIII:** 79; **Supp. X:** 82
Milton, John, **I:** 6, 138, 273, 587-588; **II:** 11, 15, 113, 130, 411, 540, 542; **III:** 40, 124, 201, 225, 274, 468, 471, 486, 487, 503, 511; **IV:** 50, 82, 126, 137, 155, 157, 241, 279, 347, 422, 461, 494; **Retro. Supp. I:** 60, 67, 127, 360; **Retro. Supp. II:** 161, 295; **Supp. I Part 1:** 124, 150, 370; **Supp. I Part 2:** 412, 422, 491, 501, 522, 622, 722, 724; **Supp. IV Part 2:** 430, 634; **Supp. VIII:** 294; **Supp. X:** 22, 23, 36; **Supp. XII:** 180; **Supp. XIV:** 5, 7
Milton, John R., **Supp. IV Part 2:** 503
Milton and His Modern Critics (L. P. Smith), **Supp. XIV:** 347
"Milton by Firelight" (Snyder), **Supp. II Part 1:** 314; **Supp. VIII:** 294
"Miltonic Sonnet, A" (Wilbur), **Supp. III Part 2:** 558
Mimesis (Auerbach), **III:** 453
"Mimnermos and the Motions of Hedonism" (Carson), **Supp. XII: 99-100**
"Mimnermos Interviews, The" (Carson), **Supp. XII: 100-101**
Mims, Edwin, **Supp. I Part 1:** 362, 364, 365, 371
"Mind" (Wilbur), **Supp. III Part 2:** 554
"Mind, The" (Kinnell), **Supp. III Part 1:** 245
Mind Breaths: Poems 1972-1977 (Ginsberg), **Supp. II Part 1:** 326
Mindfield: New and Selected Poems (Corso), **Supp. XII:** 136
"Mind in the Modern World" (Trilling), **Supp. III Part 2:** 512
"Mind Is Shapely, Art Is Shapely" (Ginsberg), **Supp. II Part 1:** 327
Mindlin, Henrique, **Supp. I Part 1:** 92
Mind of My Mind (O. Butler), **Supp. XIII:** 62, 63
Mind of Primitive Man, The (Boas), **Supp. XIV:** 209
"Mind-Reader, The" (Wilbur), **Supp. III Part 2:** 561-562
Mind-Reader, The (Wilbur), **Supp. III Part 2:** 560-562
Mindwheel (Pinsky), **Supp. VI:** 235
Minear, Richard H., **Supp. XVI:** 101, 102
"Mined Country" (Wilbur), **Supp. III Part 2:** 546-548
"Mine Own John Berryman" (Levine), **Supp. V:** 179-180
Miner, Bob, **Supp. V:** 23

Miner, Earl, **III:** 466, 479
Miner, Madonne, **Supp. XIII:** 29
"Minerva Writes Poems" (Cisneros), **Supp. VII:** 63-64, 66
Mingus, Charles, **Supp. IX:** 152
"Mingus in Diaspora" (Matthews), **Supp. IX:** 166
"Mingus in Shadow" (Matthews), **Supp. IX:** 168-169
Ming Yellow (Marquand), **III:** 56
"Minimal, The" (Roethke), **III:** 531-532
Minimus Poems, The (X. J. Kennedy), **Supp. XV:** 169-170
"Mini-novela: *Rosa y sus espinas*" (Mora), **Supp. XIII:** 218
"Minions of Midas, The" (London), **II:** 474-475
Minister's Charge, The, or The Apprenticeship of Lemuel Barber (Howells), **II:** 285-286, 287
"Minister's Wooing, The" (Stowe), **Supp. I Part 2:** 592-595
Minister's Wooing, The (Stowe), **II:** 541
"Ministration of Our Departed Friends, The" (Stowe), **Supp. I Part 2:** 586-587
"Minneapolis Poem, The" (Wright), **Supp. III Part 2:** 601-602
Minnesota Grain Show, The (radio, Keillor), **Supp. XVI:** 170
"Minnesota Transcendentalist" (Peseroff), **Supp. IV Part 1:** 71
Minnie, Temple, **II:** 344
Minority Report: H. L. Mencken's Notebooks (Mencken), **III:** 112
Minor Pleasures of Life, The (Macaulay), **Supp. XIV:** 348
"Minor Poems" (Eliot), **I:** 579
"Minor Poet" (Hay), **Supp. XIV:** 127
"Minor Topics" (Howells), **II:** 274
Minot, Susan, **Supp. VI: 203-215**
"Minotaur Loves His Labyrinth, The" (Simic), **Supp. VIII:** 270, 279, 281
"Minstrel Man" (Hughes), **Supp. I Part 1:** 325
Mint (Nye), **Supp. XIII:** 277
"Minting Time" (Sarton), **Supp. VIII:** 259
Mint Snowball (Nye), **Supp. XIII:** 277-278, **284-285**
"Mint Snowball" (Nye), **Supp. XIII:** 278, 284
"Mint Snowball II" (Nye), **Supp. XIII:** 284, 285
Mintzlaff, Dorothy, **Supp. XV:** 153
Minutes to Go (Corso, Gysin, Beiles and Burroughs), **Supp. XII:** 129
Mirabell: Books of Number (Merrill),

Supp. III Part 1: 332-334
"Miracle" (Carver), **Supp. III Part 1:** 139-140
"Miracle for Breakfast, A" (Bishop), **Retro. Supp. II:** 43
"Miracle of Lava Canyon, The" (Henry), **Supp. II Part 1:** 389, 390
Miracle of Mindfulness, The: A Manual on Meditation (Thich Nhat Hanh), **Supp. V:** 199-200
Mirage (Masters), **Supp. I Part 2:** 459, 470, 471
"Mirages, The" (Hayden), **Supp. II Part 1:** 373
"Miranda" (Buck), **Supp. II Part 1:** 128
Miranda, Carmen, **Supp. XII:** 165
Miranda, Francisco de, **Supp. I Part 2:** 522
"Miranda Over the Valley" (Dubus), **Supp. VII:** 81-83
"Miriam" (Capote), **Supp. III Part 1:** 117, 120, 122
"Miriam" (Whittier), **Supp. I Part 2:** 691, 703
"Miriam Tazewell" (Ransom), **Supp. X:** 58
"Mirror" (Merrill), **Supp. III Part 1:** 322
"Mirror" (Plath), **Retro. Supp. II:** 248-249, 257
"Mirror, The" (Glück), **Supp. V:** 83
"Mirroring Evil: Nazi Images/Recent Art" (Epstein), **Supp. XII:** 166
Mirrors (Creeley), **Supp. IV Part 1:** 156
Mirrors and Windows (Nemerov), **III:** 269, 275-277
"Mirrors of Chartres Street" (Faulkner), **II:** 56
Misanthrope, The (Molière; Wilbur, trans.), **Supp. III Part 2:** 552, 560
Miscellaneous Poems (Rowson), **Supp. XV:** 243
Miscellaneous Works of Mr. Philip Freneau, Containing His Essays and Additional Poems (Freneau), **Supp. II Part 1:** 263, 264, 266
Miscellany of American Poetry, A (Untermeyer, ed.), **Supp. XV:** 305, 310
Misery (King), **Supp. V:** 140, 141, 142, 147-148, 151, 152
Mises, Ludwig von, **Supp. IV Part 2:** 524
Misfits, The (A. Miller), **III:** 147, 149, 156, 161-162, 163
"Misogamist, The" (Dubus), **Supp. VII:** 86-87
Misread City, The: New Literary Los Angeles (Gioia and Timberg, eds.), **Supp. XV:** 116
Misrepresentations Corrected, and Truth Vindicated, in a Reply to the Rev. Mr. Solomon Williams's Book (Edwards), **I:** 549
Miss Doll, Go Home (Markson), **Supp. XVII:** 138
"Miss Ella" (Z. Fitzgerald), **Supp. IX:** 57, 59, **71-72**
"Miss Emily and the Bibliographer" (Tate), **Supp. II Part 1:** 103
"Miss Furr and Miss Skeene" (Stein), **IV:** 29-30
"Missing Child" (Simic), **Supp. VIII:** 282
"Missing in Action" (Komunyakaa), **Supp. XIII:** 123, 124
Missing/Kissing: Missing Marisa, Kissing Christine (Shanley), **Supp. XIV:** 316
Missing Link (X. J. Kennedy), **Supp. XV:** 165
"Mission of Jane, The" (Wharton), **Retro. Supp. I:** 367
"Missions, The" (Rodriguez), **Supp. XIV:** 303
Mission to Moscow (film), **Supp. I Part 1:** 281
"Mississippi" (Bass), **Supp. XVI:** 17
"Mississippi" (Faulkner), **Retro. Supp. I:** 77
"Mississippi" (Simpson), **Supp. IX:** 271
"Miss Kate in H-1" (Twain), **IV:** 193
Miss Leonora When Last Seen (Taylor), **Supp. V:** 323
Miss Lonelyhearts (West), **I:** 107; **II:** 436; **III:** 357; **IV:** 287, 288, 290-297, 300, 301, 305, 306; **Retro. Supp. II:** 321, 322, 325, 328, **332-335**
Miss Mamma Aimee (Caldwell), **I:** 308, 309, 310
"Miss Mary Pask" (Wharton), **IV:** 316; **Retro. Supp. I:** 382
"Miss McEnders" (Chopin), **Retro. Supp. II:** 67
"Missoula Softball Tournament" (Hugo), **Supp. VI:** 132
Miss Ravenel's Conversion from Secession to Loyalty (De Forest), **IV:** 350
"Miss Tempy's Watchers" (Jewett), **II:** 401; **Retro. Supp. II:** 139
"Miss Terriberry to Wed in Suburbs" (Updike), **Retro. Supp. I:** 335
"Miss Urquhart's Tiara" (Jarman), **Supp. XVII:** 116
"Mist, The" (King), **Supp. V:** 144
"Mistaken Charity, A" (Freeman), **Retro. Supp. II:** 138
"Mister Brother" (Cunningham), **Supp. XV:** 68
"Mister Toussan" (Ellison), **Retro. Supp. II:** 124-125; **Supp. II Part 1:** 238
"Mistress of Sydenham Plantation, The" (Jewett), **Retro. Supp. II:** 141
Mitchell, Burroughs, **Supp. XI:** 218, 222, 227
Mitchell, Dr. S. Weir, **IV:** 310
Mitchell, Margaret, **II:** 177
Mitchell, Roger, **Supp. IV Part 1:** 70; **Supp. XV:** 213, 215
Mitchell, Tennessee. *See* Anderson, Mrs. Sherwood (Tennessee Mitchell)
Mitchell, Wesley C., **Supp. I Part 2:** 632, 643
Mitch Miller (Masters), **Supp. I Part 2:** 456, 466, 469-471, 474, 475, 476
Mitchum, Robert, **Supp. IX:** 95, 250
Mitgang, Herbert, **Supp. IV Part 1:** 220, 226, 307; **Supp. VIII:** 124
"Mixed Sequence" (Roethke), **III:** 547
Miyazawa Kenji, **Supp. VIII:** 292
Mizener, Arthur, **II:** 77, 81, 84, 94; **IV:** 132
Mizner, Addison, **Supp. XVI:** 191
Mizner, Wilson, **Supp. XVI:** 191, 195
Mladenoff, Nancy, **Supp. X:** 176
"M'liss: An Idyl of Red Mountain" (Harte), **Supp. II Part 1:** 339
"Mnemonic Devices" (Goldbarth), **Supp. XII:** 183
"Mobile in Back of the Smithsonian, The" (Swenson), **Supp. IV Part 2:** 646
Mobilio, Albert, **Supp. VIII:** 3
Moby Dick (film), **Supp. IV Part 1:** 102, 116
Moby Dick; or, The Whale (Melville), **I:** 106, 354; **II:** 33, 224-225, 236, 539-540; **III:** 28-29, 74, 75, 77, 81, 82, 83-86, 87, 89, 90, 91, 93, 94, 95, 359, 453, 556; **IV:** 57, 199, 201, 202; **Retro. Supp. I:** 160, 220, 243, 244, 248, **249-253**, 254, 256, 257, 335; **Retro. Supp. II:** 121, 186, 275; **Supp. I Part 1:** 249; **Supp. I Part 2:** 579; **Supp. IV Part 2:** 613; **Supp. V:** 281; **Supp. VIII:** 106, 188, 198
Mock, John, **Supp. XIII:** 174
"Mocking-Bird, The" (Bierce), **I:** 202
"Mock Orange" (Glück), **Supp. V:** 84-85
Modarressi, Mitra, **Supp. IV Part 2:** 657
Models of Misrepresentation: On the Fiction of E. L. Doctorow (Morris),

Supp. IV Part 1: 231
Model World and Other Stories, A (Chabon), **Supp. XI:** 66
Modern American and British Poetry (Untermeyer, ed.), **Supp. XV:** 306
Modern American Poetry (Untermeyer, ed.), **Supp. XV:** 293, 303, 306, 312
Modern American Verse (Untermeyer), **Supp. XV:** 301
Modern Brazilian Architecture (Bishop, trans.), **Supp. I Part 1:** 92
Modern British Poetry (Untermeyer, ed.), **Supp. XV:** 305, 308, 312
Modern Fiction Studies, **Supp. V:** 238
Modern Fiction Studies (Haegert), **Supp. XVI:**69
Modern Instance a Novel, A (Howells), **II:** 275, 279, 282-283, 285
Modern Library, The, **Retro. Supp. I:** 112, 113
Modern Mephistopheles, A (Alcott), **Supp. I Part 1:** 37-38
Modern Poetic Sequence, The (Rosenthal), **Supp. V:** 333
"Modern Poetry" (Crane), **I:** 390
Modern Poetry and the Tradition (Brooks), **Supp. XIV:5-7**
"Modern Race Creeds and Their Fallacies" (Locke), **Supp. XIV:**210
Modern Rhetoric, with Readings (Brooks and Warren), **Supp. XIV:**11
"Modern Sorcery" (Simic), **Supp. VIII:** 283
"Modern Times" (Zukofsky), **Supp. III Part 2:** 624
Modern Writer, The (Anderson), **I:** 117
Modersohn, Mrs. Otto (Paula Becker), **Supp. I Part 2:** 573-574
Modersohn, Otto, **Supp. I Part 2:** 573
"Modes of Being" (Levertov), **Supp. III Part 1:** 282
Modest Enquiry into the Nature and Necessity of a Paper-Currency, A (Franklin), **II:** 108-109
"Modest Proposal, A" (Swift), **I:** 295; **Retro. Supp. II:** 287
"Modest Proposal with Feline Feeling, A" (Neugeboren), **Supp. XVI:**219
"Modest Self-Tribute, A" (Wilson), **IV:** 431, 432
Moeller, Philip, **III:** 398, 399
"Moench von Berchtesgaden, Der" (Voss), **I:** 199-200
Moers, Ellen, **Retro. Supp. II:** 99
Moe's Villa and Other Stories (Purdy), **Supp. VII:** 270, 280
Mogen, David, **Supp. IV Part 1:** 106
Mohammed, **I:** 480; **II:** 1
Mohawk (Russo), **Supp. XII: 326-328**

Moir, William Wilmerding, **Supp. V:** 279
Moldaw, Carol, **Supp. XV:** 264; **Supp. XVII:** 127, 130
"Moles" (Oliver), **Supp. VII:** 235
Molesworth, Charles, **Supp. IV Part 1:** 39; **Supp. VIII:** 292, 306
Molière (Jean-Baptiste Poquelin), **III:** 113; **Supp. I Part 2:** 406; **Supp. III Part 2:** 552, 560; **Supp. IV Part 2:** 585; **Supp. V:** 101
"Molino Rojo, El" (Ríos), **Supp. IV Part 2:** 544
Moll Flanders (Defoe), **Supp. V:** 127; **Supp. XIII:** 43
"Molloch in State Street" (Whittier), **Supp. I Part 2:** 687
"Moll Pitcher" (Whittier), **Supp. I Part 2:** 684
"Molly Brant, Iroquois Matron" (Gunn Allen), **Supp. IV Part 1:** 331
Molnar, Ferenc, **Supp. XVI:**187
"Moloch" (H. Miller), **III:** 177
Momaday, N. Scott, **Supp. IV Part 1:** 274, 323, 324, 404; **Supp. IV Part 2: 479-496,** 504, 557, 562; **Supp. XII:** 209
" 'Momentary Stay against Confusion,' A: Frank Conroy's *Stop-Time*" (T. Adams), **Supp. XVI:**69
Moment of Untruth (Lacy), **Supp. XV:** 206, 207
Moments of the Italian Summer (Wright), **Supp. III Part 2:** 602
"Momus" (Robinson), **III:** 508
Monaghan, Pat, **Supp. XI:** 121
Monaghan, Patricia, **Supp. XVII:** 76, 123, 127, 129
Mona Lisa Overdrive (W. Gibson), **Supp. XVI:**119, 120, **127-128**
"Mon Ami" (Bourne), **I:** 227
Monet, Claude, **Retro. Supp. I:** 378
"Monet's 'Waterlilies'" (Hayden), **Supp. II Part 1:** 361-362
Monette, Paul, **Supp. X: 145-161**
Money (Amis), **Retro. Supp. I:** 278
"Money" (Matthews), **Supp. IX:** 166
"Money" (Nemerov), **III:** 287
Money, Money, Money (Wagoner), **Supp. IX:** 324, **333-334**
Moneyball: The Art of Winning an Unfair Game (M. Lewis), **Supp. XVII:** 210
Moneychangers, The (Sinclair), **Supp. V:** 285
Money Writes! (Sinclair), **Supp. V:** 277
Monica, Saint, **IV:** 140
Monikins, The (Cooper), **I:** 348, 354
Monk and the Hangman's Daughter, The (Bierce), **I:** 199-200, 209

"Monkey Garden, The" (Cisneros), **Supp. VII:** 63
"Monkey Puzzle, The" (Moore), **III:** 194, 207, 211
Monkeys (Minot), **Supp. VI:** 203-205, **206-210**
"Monkeys, The" (Moore), **III:** 201, 202
Monkey Wrench Gang, The (Abbey), **Supp. VIII:** 42; **Supp. XIII: 9-11,** 16
"Monk of Casal-Maggiore, The" (Longfellow), **II:** 505
"Monocle de Mon Oncle, Le" (Stevens), **IV:** 78, 84; **Retro. Supp. I:** 301; **Supp. III Part 1:** 20; **Supp. X:** 58
"Monolog from a Mattress" (Untermeyer), **Supp. XV:** 307
Monro, Harold, **III:** 465; **Retro. Supp. I:** 127; **Supp. XV:** 296
Monroe, Harriet, **I:** 235, 384, 390, 393; **III:** 458, 581, 586; **IV:** 74; **Retro. Supp. I:** 58, 131; **Retro. Supp. II:** 82, 83; **Supp. I Part 1:** 256, 257, 258, 262, 263, 267; **Supp. I Part 2:** 374, 387, 388, 464, 610, 611, 613, 614, 615, 616; **Supp. XIV:**286; **Supp. XV:** 43, 299, 302
Monroe, James, **Supp. I Part 2:** 515, 517
Monroe, Lucy, **Retro. Supp. II:** 70
Monroe, Marilyn, **III:** 161, 162-163
Monroe's Embassy; or, the Conduct of the Government in Relation to Our Claims to the Navigation of the Mississippi (Brown), **Supp. I Part 1:** 146
"Monsoon Season" (Komunyakaa), **Supp. XIII:** 122
Monsour, Leslie, **Supp. XV:** 125
"Monster, The" (Crane), **I:** 418
Monster, The, and Other Stories (Crane), **I:** 409
Montage of a Dream Deferred (Hughes), **Retro. Supp. I:** 194, **208-209**; **Supp. I Part 1:** 333, 339-341
Montagu, Ashley, **Supp. I Part 1:** 314
"Montaigne" (Emerson), **II:** 6
Montaigne, Michel de, **II:** 1, 5, 6, 8, 14-15, 16, 535; **III:** 600; **Retro. Supp. I:** 247; **Supp. XIV:**105
Montale, Eugenio, **Supp. III Part 1:** 320; **Supp. V:** 337-338; **Supp. VIII:** 30; **Supp. XV:** 112
Montalembert, Hughes de, **Supp. XV:** 349
"Montana; or the End of Jean-Jacques Rousseau" (Fiedler), **Supp. XIII: 97-98**

"Montana Memory" (Maclean), **Supp. XIV:**221
"Montana Ranch Abandoned" (Hugo), **Supp. VI:** 139
"Mont Blanc" (Shelley), **Supp. IX:** 52
Montcalm, Louis Joseph de, **Supp. I Part 2:** 498
Montcalm and Wolfe (Parkman), **Supp. II Part 2:** 596, 609, 610, 611-613
Montemarano, Nicholas, **Supp. XVI:**227
Montgomery, Benilde, **Supp. XIII:** 202
Montgomery, Robert, **Supp. I Part 2:** 611; **Supp. IV Part 1:** 130
Month of Sundays, A (Updike), **Retro. Supp. I:** 325, 327, 329, 330, 331, 333, 335
Monti, Luigi, **II:** 504
Montoya, José, **Supp. IV Part 2:** 545
"Montrachet-le-Jardin" (Stevens), **IV:** 82
Mont-Saint-Michel and Chartres (Adams), **I:** 1, 9, 12-14, 18, 19, 21; **Supp. I Part 2:** 417
Montserrat (Hellman), **Supp. I Part 1:** 283-285
Montserrat (Robles), **Supp. I Part 1:** 283-285
"Monument, The" (Bishop), **Supp. I Part 1:** 89
Monument, The (Strand), **Supp. IV Part 2:** 629, 630
"Monument in Utopia, A" (Schnackenberg), **Supp. XV:** 261, 263
"Monument Mountain" (Bryant), **Supp. I Part 1:** 156, 162
"Monument to After-Thought Unveiled, A" (Frost), **Retro. Supp. I:** 124
Moo (Smiley), **Supp. VI:** 292, **303-305**
Moods (Alcott), **Supp. I Part 1:** 33, 34-35, 43
Moody, Anne, **Supp. IV Part 1:** 11
Moody, Mrs. William Vaughn, **I:** 384; **Supp. I Part 2:** 394
Moody, Richard, **Supp. I Part 1:** 280
Moody, William Vaughn, **III:** 507; **IV:** 26
"Moon" (A. Finch), **Supp. XVII:** 77
"Moon and the Night and the Men, The" (Berryman), **I:** 172
"Moon Deluxe" (F. Barthelme), **Supp. XI:** 26, 27, 33, 36
Mooney, Tom, **I:** 505
"Moon-Face" (London), **II:** 475
Moon-Face and Other Stories (London), **II:** 483
"Moon Flock" (Dickey), **Supp. IV Part 1:** 186
Moon for the Misbegotten, A (O'Neill), **III:** 385, 401, 403, 404
Moon Is a Gong, The (Dos Passos). See *Garbage Man, The* (Dos Passos)
Moon Is Down, The (Steinbeck), **IV:** 51
Moon Lady, The (Tan), **Supp. X:** 289
"Moonlight Alert" (Winters), **Supp. II Part 2:** 801, 811, 815
"Moonlit Night" (Reznikoff), **Supp. XIV:**285-286
Moon of the Caribbees, The (O'Neill), **III:** 388
Moon Palace (Auster), **Supp. XII:** 22, 27, **30-32**
"Moonshine" (Komunyakaa), **Supp. XIII:** 127, 128
"Moon Solo" (Laforgue), **Supp. XIII:** 346
Moonstruck (screenplay, Shanley), **Supp. XIV:**315, 316, **321-324**
"Moon upon her fluent Route, The" (Dickinson), **I:** 471
Moony's Kid Don't Cry (T. Williams), **IV:** 381
Moore, Arthur, **Supp. I Part 1:** 49
Moore, Dr. Merrill, **III:** 506
Moore, George, **I:** 103
Moore, Hannah, **Supp. XV:** 231
Moore, John Milton, **III:** 193
Moore, Lorrie, **Supp. VIII:** 145; **Supp. X: 163-180**
Moore, Marianne, **I:** 58, 285, 401, 428; **III: 193-217**, 514, 592-593; **IV:** 74, 75, 76, 91, 402; **Retro. Supp. I:** 416, 417; **Retro. Supp. II:** 39, 44, 48, 50, 82, 178, 179, 243, 244; **Supp. I Part 1:** 84, 89, 255, 257; **Supp. I Part 2:** 707; **Supp. II Part 1:** 21; **Supp. III Part 1:** 58, 60, 63; **Supp. III Part 2:** 612, 626, 627; **Supp. IV Part 1:** 242, 246, 257; **Supp. IV Part 2:** 454, 640, 641; **Supp. XIV:**124, 130; **Supp. XV:** 306, 307; **Supp. XVII:** 131
Moore, Marie Lorena. See Moore, Lorrie
Moore, Mary Tyler, **Supp. V:** 107
Moore, Mary Warner, **III:** 193
Moore, Steven, **Supp. IV Part 1:** 279, 283, 284, 285, 287; **Supp. XII:** 151; **Supp. XVII:** 230, 231, 232
Moore, Sturge, **III:** 459
Moore, Thomas, **II:** 296, 299, 303; **Supp. IX:** 104; **Supp. X:** 114
Moore, Virginia, **Supp. XV:** 308
Moorehead, Caroline, **Supp. XIV:**337
Moorepack, Howard, **Supp. XV:** 199
Moos, Malcolm, **III:** 116, 119

"Moose, The" (Bishop), **Retro. Supp. II:** 50; **Supp. I Part 1:** 73, 93, 94, 95; **Supp. IX:** 45, 46
"Moose Wallow, The" (Hayden), **Supp. II Part 1:** 367
"Moquihuitzin's Answer" (Everwine), **Supp. XV:** 78
Mora, Pat, **Supp. XIII: 213-232**
"Moral Bully, The" (Holmes), **Supp. I Part 1:** 302
"Moral Character, the Practice of Law, and Legal Education" (Hall), **Supp. VIII:** 127
"Moral Equivalent for Military Service, A" (Bourne), **I:** 230
"Moral Equivalent of War, The" (James), **II:** 361; **Supp. I Part 1:** 20
"Moral Imperatives for World Order" (Locke), **Supp. XIV:**207, 213
Moralités Légendaires (Laforgue), **I:** 573
"Morality and Mercy in Vienna" (Pynchon), **Supp. II Part 2:** 620, 624
"Morality of Indian Hating, The" (Momaday), **Supp. IV Part 2:** 484
"Morality of Poetry, The" (Wright), **Supp. III Part 2:** 596-597, 599
Moral Man and Immoral Society (Niebuhr), **III:** 292, 295-297
"Morals Is Her Middle Name" (Hughes), **Supp. I Part 1:** 338
"Morals of Chess, The" (Franklin), **II:** 121
"Moral Substitute for War, A" (Addams), **Supp. I Part 1:** 20
"Moral Theology of Atticus Finch, The" (Shaffer), **Supp. VIII:** 127
"Moral Thought, A" (Freneau), **Supp. II Part 1:** 262
Moran, Thomas, **Supp. IV Part 2:** 603-604
Moran of the Lady Letty (Norris), **II:** 264; **III:** 314, 322, 327, 328, 329, 330, 331, 332, 333
Morath, Ingeborg. See Miller, Mrs. Arthur (Ingeborg Morath)
Moravia, Alberto, **I:** 301
Moré, Gonzalo, **Supp. X:** 185
More, Henry, **I:** 132
More, Paul Elmer, **I:** 223-224, 247; **Supp. I Part 2:** 423
Moreau, Gustave, **I:** 66
"More Blues and the Abstract Truth" (Wright), **Supp. XV:** 345
More Boners (Abingdon), **Supp. XVI:**99
More Conversations with Eudora Welty (Prenshaw, ed.), **Retro. Supp. I:**

340, 341, 342, 343, 344, 352, 353, 354
More Die of Heartbreak (Bellow), **Retro. Supp. II:** 31, 33, 34
"More Girl Than Boy" (Komunyakaa), **Supp. XIII:** 117
"More Light! More Light! (Hecht), **Supp. X:** 60
"Morella" (Poe), **III:** 412; **Retro. Supp. II:** 270
"More Love in the Western World" (Updike), **Retro. Supp. I:** 327-328, 329
"Morels" (W. J. Smith), **Supp. XIII: 336-339**
Moreno, Gary, **Supp. XV:** 5
"More Observations Now" (Conroy), **Supp. XVI:**75
"More of a Corpse Than a Woman" (Rukeyser), **Supp. VI:** 280
"More Pleasant Adventures" (Ashbery), **Supp. III Part 1:** 1
More Poems to Solve (Swenson), **Supp. IV Part 2:** 640, 642, 648
More Stately Mansions (O'Neill), **III:** 385, 401, 404-405
"More Than Human" (Chabon), **Supp. XI:** 71-72
More Trivia (L. P. Smith), **Supp. XIV:**339
Morgan, Edmund S., **IV:** 149; **Supp. I Part 1:** 101, 102; **Supp. I Part 2:** 484
Morgan, Edwin, **Supp. IV Part 2:** 688
Morgan, Emanuel. See Bynner, Witter
Morgan, Henry, **II:** 432; **IV:** 63
Morgan, J. P., **I:** 494; **III:** 14, 15
Morgan, Jack, **Retro. Supp. II:** 142
Morgan, Judith, **Supp. XVI:**103
Morgan, Neil, **Supp. XVI:**103
Morgan, Robert, **Supp. V:** 5
Morgan, Robin, **Supp. I Part 2:** 569
Morgan, Ted, **Supp. XIV:**141
Morgan's Passing (Tyler), **Supp. IV Part 2:** 666-667, 668, 669
Morgenthau, Hans, **III:** 291, 309
Morgesons, The (E. Stoddard), **Supp. XV:** 270, 273, 274, 278, **279-282,** 283
Morgesons and Other Writings, Published and Unpublished, The (Buell and Zagarell), **Supp. XV:** 269
Moricand, Conrad, **III:** 190
Morison, Mrs. Samuel Eliot (Elizabeth Shaw Greene), **Supp. I Part 2:** 483
Morison, Mrs. Samuel Eliot (Priscilla Barton), **Supp. I Part 2:** 493, 496, 497
Morison, Samuel Eliot, **Supp. I Part 2: 479-500**

"Morituri Salutamus" (Longfellow), **II:** 499, 500; **Retro. Supp. II:** 169; **Supp. I Part 2:** 416
"Moriturus" (Millay), **III:** 126, 131-132
Morley, Christopher, **III:** 481, 483, 484; **Supp. I Part 2:** 653; **Supp. IX:** 124
Morley, Edward, **IV:** 27
Morley, Lord John, **I:** 7
Mormon Country (Stegner), **Supp. IV Part 2:** 598, 601-602
"Morning, The" (Updike), **Retro. Supp. I:** 329
"Morning after My Death, The" (Levis), **Supp. XI:** 260, 263-264
"Morning Arrives" (F. Wright), **Supp. XVII:** 244
Morning for Flamingos, A (Burke), **Supp. XIV:**30, 31, 32
"Morning Glory" (Merrill), **Supp. III Part 1:** 337
Morning Glory, The (R. Bly), **Supp. IV Part 1:** 63-65, 66, 71
"Morning Imagination of Russia, A" (W. C. Williams), **Retro. Supp. I:** 428
Morning in Antibes (Knowles), **Supp. XII:** 249
Morning in the Burned House (Atwood), **Supp. XIII:** 20, 35
Morning Is Near Us, The (Glaspell), **Supp. III Part 1:** 184-185
Morning Noon and Night (Cozzens), **I:** 374, 375, 376, 377, 379, 380
"Morning of the Day They Did It, The" (White), **Supp. I Part 2:** 663
"Morning Prayers" (Harjo), **Supp. XII:** 231
"Morning Roll Call" (Anderson), **I:** 116
"Mornings in a New House" (Merrill), **Supp. III Part 1:** 327
Mornings Like This (Dillard), **Supp. VI:** 23, 34
"Morning Song" (Plath), **Retro. Supp. II:** 252
Morning Watch, The (Agee), **I:** 25, 39-42
"Morning with Broken Window" (Hogan), **Supp. IV Part 1:** 405
Morrell, Ottoline, **Retro. Supp. I:** 60
Morris, Bernard E., **Supp. XV:** 154, 169
Morris, Christopher D., **Supp. IV Part 1:** 231, 236
Morris, George Sylvester, **Supp. I Part 2:** 640
Morris, Gouverneur, **Supp. I Part 2:** 512, 517, 518

Morris, Lloyd, **III:** 458
Morris, Robert, **Supp. I Part 2:** 510
Morris, Timothy, **Retro. Supp. I:** 40
Morris, William, **II:** 323, 338, 523; **IV:** 349; **Supp. I Part 1:** 260, 356; **Supp. XI:** 202
Morris, Willie, **Supp. XI:** 216, 231, 234
Morris, Wright, **I:** 305; **III: 218-243,** 558, 572; **IV:** 211
Morrison, Charles Clayton, **III:** 297
Morrison, Jim, **Supp. IV Part 1:** 206
Morrison, Toni, **Retro. Supp. II:** 15, 118; **Supp. III Part 1: 361-381; Supp. IV Part 1:** 2, 13, 14, 250, 253, 257; **Supp. V:** 169, 259; **Supp. VIII:** 213, 214; **Supp. X:** 85, 239, 250, 325; **Supp. XI:** 4, 14, 20, 91; **Supp. XII:** 289, 310; **Supp. XIII:** 60, 185; **Supp. XVI:**143; **Supp. XVII:** 183
"Morro Bay" (Jeffers), **Supp. II Part 2:** 422
Morrow, W. C., **I:** 199
Morse, Jedidiah, **Supp. XV:** 243
Morse, Robert, **Supp. XI:** 305
Morse, Samuel F. B., **Supp. I Part 1:** 156
Mortal Acts, Mortal Words (Kinnell), **Supp. III Part 1:** 235, 236, 237, 249-254
Mortal Antipathy, A (Holmes), **Supp. I Part 1:** 315-316
"Mortal Enemies" (Humphrey), **Supp. IX:** 109
"Mortal Eternal" (Olds), **Supp. X:** 214
Mortal No, The (Hoffman), **IV:** 113
Morte D'Arthur, Le (Malory), **Supp. IV Part 1:** 47
Mortmere Stories, The (Isherwood and Upward), **Supp. XIV:**159
Morton, David, **Supp. IX:** 76
Morton, Jelly Roll, **Supp. X:** 242
"Mosaic of the Nativity: Serbia, Winter 1993" (Kenyon), **Supp. VII:** 173
Mosby's Memoirs and Other Stories (Bellow), **Retro. Supp. II:** 27
Moscow under Fire (Caldwell), **I:** 296
Moser, Barry, **Supp. XIV:**223
Moses (Untermeyer), **Supp. XV: 309**
Moses, Man of the Mountain (Hurston), **Supp. VI:** 149, 158, 160
"Moses on Sinai" (Untermeyer), **Supp. XV:** 300
Mosle, Sara, **Supp. XI:** 254
Mosley, Walter, **Supp. XIII: 233-252; Supp. XVI:**143
Mosquito Coast, The (film), **Supp. VIII:** 323
Mosquito Coast, The (Theroux), **Supp.**

INDEX / 427

VIII: 321, **322-323**
Mosquitos (Faulkner), **II:** 56; **Retro. Supp. I:** 79, 81
Moss, Howard, **III:** 452; **Supp. IV Part 2:** 642; **Supp. IX:** 39; **Supp. XIII:** 114; **Supp. XV:** 143, 152
Moss, Stanley, **Supp. XI:** 321
Moss, Thylias, **Supp. XI:** 248
Mosses from an Old Manse (Hawthorne), **I:** 562; **II:** 224; **III:** 82, 83; **Retro. Supp. I:** 157, 248
"Moss of His Skin" (Sexton), **Supp. II Part 2:** 676
"Most Extraordinary Case, A" (James), **II:** 322; **Retro. Supp. I:** 218
Most Likely to Succeed (Dos Passos), **I:** 491
"Most of It, The" (Frost), **Retro. Supp. I:** 121, 125, 129, 139
Motel Chronicles (Shepard), **Supp. III Part 2:** 445
"Mother" (Paley), **Supp. VI: 222-223**
"Mother" (Snyder), **Supp. VIII:** 298
Mother (Whistler), **IV:** 369
Mother, The (Buck), **Supp. II Part 1:** 118-119
"Mother and Jack and the Rain" (Sexton), **Supp. II Part 2:** 686
"Mother and Son" (Tate), **IV:** 128, 137-138
Mother Courage and Her Children (Brecht), **III:** 160; **Supp. IX:** 140; **Supp. XII:** 249
"Mother Earth: Her Whales" (Snyder), **Supp. VIII:** 302
"Motherhood" (Swenson), **Supp. IV Part 2:** 645
Mother Hubbard (Reed), **Supp. X:** 241
Mother Love (Dove), **Supp. IV Part 1:** 250-251, 254
"Mother Marie Therese" (Lowell), **Retro. Supp. II:** 188
Mother Night (Vonnegut), **Supp. II Part 2:** 757, 758, 767, 770, 771
"Mother Rosarine" (Kumin), **Supp. IV Part 2:** 442
"Mothers and Daughters in the Fiction of the New Republic" (Davidson), **Supp. XV:** 238
Mother's Recompense, The (Wharton), **IV:** 321, 324; **Retro. Supp. I:** 382
"Mother's Tale, A" (Agee), **I:** 29-30
"Mother's Things" (Creeley), **Supp. IV Part 1:** 141
"Mother's Voice" (Creeley), **Supp. IV Part 1:** 156
Mother to Daughter, Daughter to Mother (Olsen, ed.), **Supp. XIII:** 295

"Mother Tongue" (Simic), **Supp. VIII:** 283
"Mother to Son" (Hughes), **Retro. Supp. I:** 199, 203; **Supp. I Part 1:** 321-322, 323
Motherwell, Robert, **Supp. XV:** 145
"Mother Writes to the Murderer, The: A Letter" (Nye), **Supp. XIII:** 276
"Motion, The" (Olson), **Supp. II Part 2:** 571
Motion of History, The (Baraka), **Supp. II Part 1:** 55, 56
"Motive for Metaphor, The" (Stevens), **IV:** 89; **Retro. Supp. I:** 310
Motiveless Malignity (Auchincloss), **Supp. IV Part 1:** 31
Motley, John Lothrop, **Supp. I Part 1:** 299; **Supp. I Part 2:** 479
Motley, Willard, **Supp. XVII: 149-163**
"Motor Car, The" (White), **Supp. I Part 2:** 661
Motor-Flight Through France (Wharton), **I:** 12; **Retro. Supp. I:** 372
Mott, Michael, **Supp. VIII:** 204, 208
Mottetti: Poems of Love: The Motets of Eugenio Montale (Montale; Gioia, trans.), **Supp. XV:** 112, **127-128**
"Mountain, The" (Frost), **Retro. Supp. I:** 121
"Mountain Hermitage, The: Pages from a Japanese Notebook" (Passin), **Supp. XIII:** 337
Mountain Interval (Frost), **II:** 154; **Retro. Supp. I:** 131, 132, 133
"Mountain Lion" (Hogan), **Supp. IV Part 1:** 412
"Mountain Music" essays (Sanders), **Supp. XVI:**276-277
Mountainous Journey, A (Tuqan), **Supp. XIII:** 278
Mountains, The (Wolfe), **IV:** 461
Mountains and Rivers without End (Snyder), **Supp. VIII:** 295, **305-306**
"Mountains grow unnoticed, The" (Dickinson), **Retro. Supp. I:** 46
Mountains of California, The (Muir), **Supp. IX:** 183
"Mountain Whippoorwill, The" (Benét), **Supp. XI:** 44-45, 46, 47
"Mount-Joy: or Some Passages Out of the Life of a Castle-Builder" (Irving), **II:** 314
"Mount Venus" (Wright), **Supp. XV:** 346
"Mourners, The" (Malamud), **Supp. I Part 2:** 431, 435, 436-437
Mourners Below (Purdy), **Supp. VII:** 274, 280
"Mourning and Melancholia" (Freud),

Supp. IV Part 2: 450; **Supp. XVI:**161
Mourning Becomes Electra (O'Neill), **III:** 391, 394, 398-400
"Mourning Poem for the Queen of Sunday" (Hayden), **Supp. II Part 1:** 379-380
"Mouse Elegy" (Olds), **Supp. X:** 209
Mouse Is Born, A (Loos), **Supp. XVI:**193
"Mouse Roulette Wheel, The" (C. Bly), **Supp. XVI:**34
"Mouth of Brass" (Humphrey), **Supp. IX:** 101
Moveable Feast, A (Hemingway), **II:** 257; **Retro. Supp. I:** 108, 171, **186-187**
Movement, The: Documentary of a Struggle for Equality (Student Nonviolent Coordinating Committee), **Supp. IV Part 1:** 369
"Move over Macho, Here Comes Feminismo" (Robbins), **Supp. X:** 272
"Move to California, The" (Stafford), **Supp. XI:** 318, 321
"Movie" (Shapiro), **Supp. II Part 2:** 707
Movie at the End of the World, The (McGrath), **Supp. X:** 127
Moviegoer, The (Percy), **Supp. III Part 1:** 383-385, 387, 389-392, 394, 397
"Movie Magazine, The: A Low 'Slick'" (Percy), **Supp. III Part 1:** 385
Movies (Dixon), **Supp. XII:** 147
"Moving Around" (Matthews), **Supp. IX:** 155
"Moving Finger, The" (Wharton), **Retro. Supp. I:** 365
Moving On (McMurtry), **Supp. V:** 223-224
Moving Target, The (Macdonald), **Supp. IV Part 2:** 462, 463, 467, 470, 471, 473, 474
Moving Target, The (Merwin), **Supp. III Part 1:** 346, 347-348, 352, 357
"Mowbray Family, The" (Farrell and Alden), **II:** 45
"Mowing" (Frost), **II:** 169-170; **Retro. Supp. I:** 127, 128
"Moxan's Master" (Bierce), **I:** 206
Moxley, Jennifer, **Supp. XVII:** 70
Moyers, Bill, **Supp. IV Part 1:** 267; **Supp. VIII:** 331; **Supp. XI:** 126, 132; **Supp. XII:** 217; **Supp. XIII:** 274, 276; **Supp. XV:** 212
Moynihan, Daniel Patrick, **Retro. Supp. II:** 123; **Supp. VIII:** 241
"Mozart" (C. Frost), **Supp. XV:** 94
Mozart, Wolfgang Amadeus, **I:** 479,

588; **IV:** 74, 358; **Supp. IV Part 1:** 284
"Mozart and the Gray Steward" (Wilder), **IV:** 358
Mr. and Mrs. Baby and Other Stories (Strand), **Supp. IV Part 2:** 631
"Mr. and Mrs. Fix-It" (Lardner), **II:** 431
Mr. Arcularis (Aiken), **I:** 54, 56
"Mr. Big" (Allen), **Supp. XV:** 15
Mr. Bridge (Connell), **Supp. XIV:** 80, 82, 93
Mr. Brown Can Moo! Can You? (Geisel), **Supp. XVI:** 104
"Mr. Bruce" (Jewett), **II:** 397; **Retro. Supp. II:** 134, 143
"Mr. Burnshaw and the Statue" (Stevens), **Retro. Supp. I:** 298, 303
"Mr. Carson Death on His Nights Out" (McGrath), **Supp. X:** 118
Mr. Clemens and Mark Twain (Kaplan), **I:** 247-248
"Mr. Coffee and Mr. Fixit" (Carver), **Supp. III Part 1:** 145
"Mr. Cornelius Johnson, Office-Seeker" (Dunbar), **Supp. II Part 1:** 211, 213
"Mr. Costyve Duditch" (Toomer), **Supp. III Part 2:** 486
"Mr. Dajani, Calling from Jericho" (Nye), **Supp. XIII:** 286-287
"Mr. Edwards and the Spider" (Lowell), **I:** 544; **II:** 550; **Retro. Supp. II:** 187
Mr. Field's Daughter (Bausch), **Supp. VII:** 47-48, 51-52
"Mr. Flood's Party" (Robinson), **III:** 512
"Mr. Forster's Pageant" (Maxwell), **Supp. VIII:** 172
"Mr. Frost's Chickens" (Oliver), **Supp. VII:** 232-233
Mr. Hodge and Mr. Hazard (Wylie), **Supp. I Part 2:** 708, 709, 714, 721-724
"Mr. Hueffer and the Prose Tradition" (Pound), **III:** 465
Mr. Ives' Christmas (Hijuelos), **Supp. VIII: 85-86**
"Mr. Longfellow and His Boy" (Sandburg), **III:** 591
"Mr. Luna and History" (Ríos), **Supp. IV Part 2:** 551
"Mr. Mitochondria" (Stollman), **Supp. XVII:** 50
Mr. Moto Is So Sorry (Marquand), **III:** 57, 58
Mr. Norris Changes Trains (Isherwood), **Supp. XIV:** 161
"Mr. Preble Gets Rid of His Wife" (Thurber), **Supp. I Part 2:** 615

"Mr. Rolfe" (Wilson), **IV:** 436
Mr. Sammler's Planet (Bellow), **I:** 144, 147, 150, 151, 152, 158; **Retro. Supp. II:** 19, 28, 30
"Mr. Shelley Speaking" (Wylie), **Supp. I Part 2:** 719
Mr. Spaceman (R. O. Butler), **Supp. XII:** 62, **74-75**
"Mr. Thompson's Prodigal" (Harte), **Supp. II Part 1:** 354
Mr. Vertigo (Auster), **Supp. XII: 34-35,** 36
"Mr. Whittier" (Scott), **Supp. I Part 2:** 705
Mr. Wilson's War (Dos Passos), **I:** 485
Mrabet, Mohammed, **Supp. IV Part 1:** 92, 93
Mrs. Albert Grundy: Observations in Philistia (Frederic), **II:** 138-139
"Mrs. Bilingsby's Wine" (Taylor), **Supp. V:** 323
Mrs. Bridge: A Novel (Connell), **Supp. XIV:** 79, 80, 81, 82, **89-94,** 95
"Mrs. Cassidy's Last Year" (Gordon), **Supp. IV Part 1:** 306
Mrs. Dalloway (Woolf), **Supp. IV Part 1:** 299; **Supp. VIII:** 5; **Supp. XV:** 55, 65-66
"Mrs. Jellison" (Hay), **Supp. XIV:** 123
"Mrs. Krikorian" (Olds), **Supp. X:** 211
"Mrs. Maecenas" (Burke), **I:** 271
"Mrs. Mandrill" (Nemerov), **III:** 278
"Mrs. Manstey's View" (Wharton), **Retro. Supp. I:** 362, 363
"Mrs. Mobry's Reason" (Chopin), **Retro. Supp. II:** 61
Mrs. Reynolds (Stein), **IV:** 43
Mrs. Stevens Hears the Mermaids Singing (Sarton), **Supp. VIII:** 252-253, **256-257**
Mrs. Ted Bliss (Elkin), **Supp. VI:** 56, 58
"Mrs. Turner Cutting the Grass" (Shields), **Supp. VII:** 319-320
"Mrs. Walpurga" (Rukeyser), **Supp. VI:** 273
"MS. Found in a Bottle" (Poe), **III:** 411, 416; **Retro. Supp. II:** 274
"Ms. Lot" (Rukeyser), **Supp. VI:** 281
Ms. Magazine, **Supp. V:** 259
Mttron-Hirsch, Sidney, **III:** 484-485
"Muchas Gracias Por Todo" (Nye), **Supp. XIII:** 282-283
"Much Madness is divinest Sense" (Dickinson), **Retro. Supp. I:** 37-38
"Muck-A-Muck" (Harte), **Supp. II Part 1:** 342
"Mud Below, The" (Proulx), **Supp. VII:** 262
Mudge, Alden, **Supp. XIV:** 35

Mudrick, Marvin, **Retro. Supp. II:** 289
"Mud Season" (Kenyon), **Supp. VII:** 167-168
Mueller, Lisel, **Supp. I Part 1:** 83, 88; **Supp. XIV:** 268
Muggli, Mark, **Supp. IV Part 1:** 207
Muhammad, Elijah, **Supp. I Part 1:** 60
Muir, Edwin, **I:** 527; **II:** 368; **III:** 20
Muir, John, **Supp. VIII:** 296; **Supp. IX:** 33, **171-188; Supp. X:** 29; **Supp. XIV:** 177, 178, 181
Mujica, Barbara, **Supp. VIII:** 89
Mulatto (Hughes), **Retro. Supp. I:** 197, 203; **Supp. I Part 1:** 328, 339
Mulching of America, The (Crews), **Supp. XI:** 107
Muldoon, William, **I:** 500-501
Mule Bone (Hughes and Hurston), **Retro. Supp. I:** 194, 203; **Supp. VI:** 154
Mules and Men (Hurston), **Supp. VI:** 149, 153, 154, 160
Mulford, Prentice, **I:** 193
Mulligan, Robert, **Supp. VIII:** 128, 129
Mulligan Stew (Sorrentino), **Supp. XII:** 139
Mullins, Eustace, **III:** 479
Mullins, Priscilla, **II:** 502-503
"Multiplication of Wool, The" (Sanders), **Supp. XVI:** 268
Multitudes, Multitudes (Clampitt), **Supp. IX:** 39
Mumbo Jumbo (Reed), **Supp. X:** 240, 242, **245-248,** 251
Mumford, Lewis, **I:** 245, 250, 251, 252, 259, 261; **II:** 271, 473-474; **Supp. I Part 2:** 632, 638; **Supp. II Part 2: 471-501**
Mumford, Sophia Wittenberg (Mrs. Lewis Mumford), **Supp. II Part 2:** 474, 475
Mummy, The (film), **Supp. IV Part 1:** 104; **Supp. XVII:** 57
"Mundus et Infans" (Auden), **Supp. II Part 1:** 15
"Munich, 1938" (Lowell), **II:** 554
"Munich Mannequins, The" (Plath), **Retro. Supp. II:** 256
"Municipal Report, A" (Henry), **Supp. II Part 1:** 406-407
Munro, Alice, **Supp. IX:** 212; **Supp. X:** 290; **Supp. XII:** 289-290, 310
Munsey, Frank, **I:** 501
Munson, Gorham, **I:** 252, 388, 432; **Retro. Supp. II:** 77, 78, 79, 82, 83; **Supp. I Part 2:** 454
Münsterberg, Hugo, **Supp. XIV:** 197
Murakami, Haruki, **Supp. XVI:** 124

"Murano" (Doty), **Supp. XI:** 131
Murasaki, Lady, **II:** 577
Muratori, Fred, **Supp. XVI:**281
Muray, Nicholas, **Supp. I Part 2:** 708
Murder, My Sweet (film), **Supp. IV Part 1:** 130
"Murderer Guest, The" (Gordon), **Supp. IV Part 1:** 306
"Murderers" (L. Michaels), **Supp. XVI:**207-208
Murder in Mount Holly (Theroux), **Supp. VIII:** 315-316
Murder in the Cathedral (Eliot), **I:** 571, 573, 580, 581; **II:** 20; **Retro. Supp. I:** 65; **Retro. Supp. II:** 222
Murder of Lidice, The (Millay), **III:** 140
"Murders in the Rue Morgue, The" (Poe), **III:** 412, 416, 419-420; **Retro. Supp. II:** 271, 272
Murdoch, Iris, **Supp. VIII:** 167
Murnau, F. W., **Supp. XV:** 128
Murphy, Jacqueline Shea, **Retro. Supp. II:** 143
Murphy, Patrick, **Supp. XIII:** 214
Murphy, Richard, **Retro. Supp. II:** 250
Murray, Albert, **Retro. Supp. II:** 119, 120
Murray, Edward, **I:** 229
Murray, G. E., **Supp. X:** 201; **Supp. XI:** 143, 155
Murray, Gilbert, **III:** 468-469
Murray, Jan, **Supp. IV Part 2:** 574
Murray, John, **II:** 304; **III:** 76, 79; **Retro. Supp. I:** 246
Murray, Judith Sargent, **Supp. XV:** 236-237
Murray, Margaret A., **Supp. V:** 128
Murrell, John A., **IV:** 265
Mursell, James L., **Supp. I Part 2:** 608
"Muse" (Ammons), **Supp. VII:** 29
"Muse, Postmodern and Homeless, The" (Ozick), **Supp. V:** 272
"Musée des Beaux Arts" (Auden), **Retro. Supp. I:** 430; **Supp. II Part 1:** 14
"Muse of Aboutness, The" (Baker), **Supp. XVI:**288
Muses Are Heard, The (Capote), **Supp. III Part 1:** 126
"Muses of Terrence McNally, The" (Zinman), **Supp. XIII:** 207-208
"Muse's Tragedy, The" (Wharton), **Retro. Supp. I:** 364
Museum (Dove), **Supp. IV Part 1:** 245-247, 248
"Museum" (Hass), **Supp. VI:** 107
Museums and Women (Updike), **Retro. Supp. I:** 321

"Museum Vase" (Francis), **Supp. IX:** 83
"Mushrooms" (Plath), **Retro. Supp. II:** 246; **Supp. I Part 2:** 539
"Music" (Oliver), **Supp. VII:** 236
Music After the Great War (Van Vechten), **Supp. II Part 2:** 732
Music and Bad Manners (Van Vechten), **Supp. II Part 2:** 733
"Music for a Farce" (Bowles), **Supp. IV Part 1:** 83
Music for Chameleons (Capote), **Supp. III Part 1:** 120, 125-127, 131, 132
"Music for Museums?" (Van Vechten), **Supp. II Part 2:** 732
"Music for the Movies" (Van Vechten), **Supp. II Part 2:** 733
"Music from Spain" (Welty), **IV:** 272
Music Like Dirt (Bidart), **Supp. XV:** 35
"Music Like Dirt" (Bidart), **Supp. XV:** 35
Music of Chance, The (Auster), **Supp. XII:** 21, 23, **32-33**
"Music of Prose, The" (Gass), **Supp. VI:** 92
Music of Spain, The (Van Vechten), **Supp. II Part 2:** 734, 735
"Music of the Spheres" (Epstein), **Supp. XII:** 165
"Music School" (B. Kelly), **Supp. XVII:** 124
Music School, The (Updike), **IV:** 214, 215, 219, 226, 227; **Retro. Supp. I:** 320, 328, 329, 330
"Music School, The" (Updike), **Retro. Supp. I:** 326, 329, 335
"Music Swims Back to Me" (Sexton), **Supp. II Part 2:** 673
Muske, Carol, **Supp. IV Part 2:** 453-454
"Mussel Hunter at Rock Harbor" (Plath), **Supp. I Part 2:** 529, 537
Musset, Alfred de, **I:** 474; **II:** 543
Mussolini, Benito, **III:** 115, 473, 608; **IV:** 372, 373; **Supp. I Part 1:** 281, 282; **Supp. I Part 2:** 618; **Supp. V:** 290; **Supp. XVI:**191
"Mustafa Ferrari" (X. J. Kennedy), **Supp. XV:** 170-171
"Must the Novelist Crusade?" (Welty), **IV:** 280
"Mutability of Literature, The" (Irving), **II:** 308
"Mutation of the Spirit" (Corso), **Supp. XII:** 132, 133
Mute, The (McCullers), **II:** 586
Mutilated, The (T. Williams), **IV:** 382, 386, 393

Mutiny of the Elsinore, The (London), **II:** 467
"My Adventures as a Social Poet" (Hughes), **Retro. Supp. I:** 194, 207
"My Alba" (Ginsberg), **Supp. II Part 1:** 320, 321
My Alexandria (Doty), **Supp. XI:** 119, 120, 121, **123-125,** 130
My Ántonia (Cather), **I:** 321-322; **Retro. Supp. I:** 1, 3, 4, **11-13,** 14, 17, 18, 22; **Supp. IV Part 2:** 608; **Supp. XVI:**226
"My Appearance" (Wallace), **Supp. X:** 306-307
My Argument with the Gestapo: A Macaronic Journal (Merton), **Supp. VIII:** 207; **Supp. XV:** 344
"My Arkansas" (Angelou), **Supp. IV Part 1:** 15
"My Aunt" (Holmes), **Supp. I Part 1:** 302, 310
"My Beginnings" (Simpson), **Supp. IX:** 273
My Bondage and My Freedom (Douglass), **Supp. III Part 1:** 155, 173
My Brother (Kincaid), **Supp. VII:** 191-193
"My Brother Paul" (Dreiser), **Retro. Supp. II:** 94
"My Brothers the Silent" (Merwin), **Supp. III Part 1:** 349-350
"My Brother's Work" (Dunn), **Supp. XI:** 147
"My Brother Takes a Hammer to the Mirror" (F. Wright), **Supp. XVII:** 244
"My Butterfly" (Frost), **II:** 151; **Retro. Supp. I:** 124
"My Children, and a Prayer for Us" (Ortiz), **Supp. IV Part 2:** 507
"My Confession" (McCarthy), **II:** 562
"My Confessional Sestina" (Gioia), **Supp. XV:** 123
My Country and My People (Yutang), **Supp. X:** 291
"My Country 'Tis of Thee" (Reznikoff), **Supp. III Part 2:** 616
My Days of Anger (Farrell), **II:** 34, 35-36, 43
"My Dear Republican Mother" (C. Bly), **Supp. XVI:**31-32
My Death My Life by Pier Paolo Pasolini (Acker), **Supp. XII:** 7
My Dog Stupid (Fante), **Supp. XI:** 160, **170-171**
My Emily Dickinson (Howe), **Retro. Supp. I:** 33, 43; **Supp. IV Part 2:** 430-431
"My English" (Alvarez), **Supp. VII:** 2

Myers, Linda A., **Supp. IV Part 1:** 10
"My Extended Family" (Theroux), **Supp. VIII:** 311
"My Father" (L. Michaels), **Supp. XVI:** 214
"My Father" (Sterne), **IV:** 466
"My Father: October 1942" (Stafford), **Supp. XI:** 323
"My Father at Eighty-Five" (R. Bly), **Supp. IV Part 1:** 73
"My Father Is a Simple Man" (Salinas), **Supp. XIII:** 324
"My Fathers Came From Kentucky" (Lindsay), **Supp. I Part 2:** 395
"My Father's Friends" (Maxwell), **Supp. VIII:** 171
"My Father's Ghost" (Wagoner), **Supp. IX:** 330
"My Father's God" (Fante), **Supp. XI:** 160, 174
"My Father's House" (L.-Y. Lee), **Supp. XV:** 225
"My Father's Love Letters" (Komunyakaa), **Supp. XIII:** 127
"My Father Speaks to me from the Dead" (Olds), **Supp. X:** 210
"My Father's Telescope" (Dove), **Supp. IV Part 1:** 246, 248
"My Father with Cigarette Twelve Years Before the Nazis Could Break His Heart" (Levine), **Supp. V:** 194
"My Favorite Murder" (Bierce), **I:** 205
My Favorite Plant: Writers and Gardeners on the Plants They Love (Kincaid), **Supp. VII:** 193-194
"My Fifty-Plus Years Celebrate Spring" (Salinas), **Supp. XIII:** 327
"My First Book" (Harte), **Supp. II Part 1:** 343
My First Summer in the Sierra (Muir), **Supp. IX:** 172, 173, **178-181**, 183, 185; **Supp. XIV:** 177
"My Fountain Pen" (McClatchy), **Supp. XII:** 254, 260
My Friend, Henry Miller (Perlès), **III:** 189
My Friend, Julia Lathrop (Addams), **Supp. I Part 1:** 25
"My Friend, Walt Whitman" (Oliver), **Supp. VII:** 245
"My Garden Acquaintance" (Lowell), **Supp. I Part 2:** 420
My Garden [Book] (Kincaid), **Supp. VII:** 193-194
"My Grandfather" (Lowell), **II:** 554
"My Grandmother's Love Letters" (H. Crane), **Retro. Supp. II:** 78
"My Grandson, Home at Last" (Angelou), **Supp. IV Part 1:** 13
My Green Hills of Jamaica (McKay), **Supp. X:** 132, 142
My Guru and His Disciple (Isherwood), **Supp. XIV:** 157, 164, 172
My Heart's in the Highlands (Saroyan), **Supp. IV Part 1:** 83
"My High School Reunion" (Kingston), **Supp. V:** 169
"My Indigo" (L.-Y. Lee), **Supp. XV:** 214
"My Kinsman, Major Molineux" (Hawthorne), **II:** 228, 229, 237-239, 243; **Retro. Supp. I:** 153-154, 158, 160, 161; **Retro. Supp. II:** 181, 187; **Supp. XVI:** 157
My Kinsman, Major Molineux (Lowell), **II:** 545-546
"My Last Afternoon with Uncle Devereux Winslow" (Lowell), **II:** 547-548; **Retro. Supp. II:** 189
"My Last Drive" (Hardy), **Supp. VIII:** 32
"My Last Duchess" (Browning), **Supp. XV:** 121
"My Life" (Strand), **Supp. IV Part 2:** 627
My Life, Starring Dara Falcon (Beattie), **Supp. V:** 31, 34-35
My Life a Loaded Gun: Dickinson, Plath, Rich, and Female Creativity (Bennett), **Retro. Supp. I:** 29
My Life and Hard Times (Thurber), **Supp. I Part 2:** 607, 609
My Life as a Man (P. Roth), **Retro. Supp. II:** 281, 286, 289; **Supp. III Part 2:** 401, 404, 405, 417-418
"My Life as a P.I.G., or the True Adventures of Smokey the Cop" (Abbey), **Supp. XIII:** 3
"My life closed twice before its close" (Dickinson), **Retro. Supp. I:** 38
"My Life had stood a Loaded Gun" (Dickinson), **Retro. Supp. I:** 42, 43, 45, 46; **Supp. IV Part 2:** 430
My Life of Absurdity (C. Himes), **Supp. XVI:** 145
"My Life with Medicine" (Nye), **Supp. XIII:** 282
"My Life with *Playboy*" (Plimpton), **Supp. XVI:** 246
"My Life with R. H. Macy" (Jackson), **Supp. IX:** 118
"My Little Utopia" (Simic), **Supp. VIII:** 283
My Lives and How I Lost Them (Cullen), **Supp. IV Part 1:** 173
"My Lord Bag of Rice" (C. Bly), **Supp. XVI:** 40
My Lord Bag of Rice: New and Selected Stories (C. Bly), **Supp. XVI:** 41
"My Lost City" (Fitzgerald), **Retro. Supp. I:** 102
"My Lost Youth" (Longfellow), **II:** 487, 499; **Retro. Supp. II:** 168
My Love Affair with America: The Cautionary Tale of a Cheerful Conservative (Podhoretz), **Supp. VIII:** 232, 233, 237, **244-246**
"My Lover Has Dirty Fingernails" (Updike), **Retro. Supp. I:** 332, 333
"My Lucy Friend Who Smells Like Corn" (Cisneros), **Supp. VII:** 68-69
"My Mammogram" (McClatchy), **Supp. XII:** 263-264
"My Man Bovanne" (Bambara), **Supp. XI:** 2
"My Mariner" (Larcom), **Supp. XIII:** 147
My Mark Twain (Howells), **II:** 276
"My Metamorphosis" (Harte), **Supp. II Part 1:** 339
"My Moby Dick" (Humphrey), **Supp. IX:** 95
My Mortal Enemy (Cather), **I:** 327-328; **Retro. Supp. I:** 16-17; **Supp. I Part 2:** 719
My Mother: Demonology (Acker), **Supp. XII:** 6
My Mother, My Father and Me (Hellman), **Supp. I Part 1:** 290-291
"My Mother and My Sisters" (Ortiz), **Supp. IV Part 2:** 499
"My Mother Is Speaking from the Desert" (Gordon), **Supp. IV Part 1:** 309, 314
"My Mother's Goofy Song" (Fante), **Supp. XI:** 164
"My Mother's Memoirs, My Father's Lie, and Other True Stories" (Banks), **Supp. V:** 15
"My Mother's Nipples" (Hass), **Supp. VI:** 109
"My Mother's Story" (Kunitz), **Supp. III Part 1:** 259
"My Mother Then and Now" (Wasserstein), **Supp. XV:** 327
"My Mother with Purse the Summer They Murdered the Spanish Poet" (Levine), **Supp. V:** 194
My Movie Business: A Memoir (Irving), **Supp. VI:** 164
"My Name" (Cisneros), **Supp. VII:** 60
"My Negro Problem-And Ours" (Podhoretz), **Supp. VIII:** **234-236**
"My New Diet" (Karr), **Supp. XI:** 241
"My Old Man" (Hemingway), **II:** 263
My Other Life (Theroux), **Supp. VIII:** 310, 324
"My Own Story" (E. Stoddard), **Supp. XV:** 273, 279, 283

My Own True Name: New and Selected Poems for Young Adults, 1984-1999 (Mora), **Supp. XIII:** 222
"My Parents Have Come Home Laughing" (Jarman), **Supp. XVII:** 113
"My Passion for Ferries" (Whitman), **IV:** 350
"My People" (Hughes), **Retro. Supp. I:** 197; **Supp. I Part 1:** 321-322, 323
"My Philosophy" (Allen), **Supp. XV:** 15
"My Playmate" (Whittier), **Supp. I Part 2:** 699-700
"My Priests" (Monette), **Supp. X:** 159
Myra Breckinridge (Vidal), **Supp. IV Part 2:** 677, 685-686, 689, 691
"My Raptor" (A. Finch), **Supp. XVII:** 72
"My Recollections of S. B. Fairchild" (Jackson), **Supp. IX:** 118-119
"My Religion" (Carson), **Supp. XII:** 105-106
"My Road to Hell Was Paved" (Patchett), **Supp. XII:** 310-311
Myron (Vidal), **Supp. IV Part 2:** 677, 685, 686, 691
"My Roomy" (Lardner), **II:** 420, 421, 428, 430
"My Sad Self" (Ginsberg), **Supp. II Part 1:** 320
My Secret History (Theroux), **Supp. VIII:** 310, 324
"Myself" (Audubon), **Supp. XVI:**1-2, 5, 12
"My Shoes" (Simic), **Supp. VIII:** 275
"My Side of the Matter" (Capote), **Supp. III Part 1:** 114, 115
My Silk Purse and Yours: The Publishing Scene and American Literary Art (Garrett), **Supp. VII:** 111; **Supp. X:** 7
My Sister Eileen (McKenney), **IV:** 288; **Retro. Supp. II:** 321
My Sister's Hand in Mine: The Collected Works of Jane Bowles, **Supp. IV Part 1:** 82-83
"My Son" (Strand), **Supp. IV Part 2:** 629
My Son, John (film), **Supp. I Part 1:** 67
"My Son, the Murderer" (Malamud), **Supp. I Part 2:** 437
"My Son the Man" (Olds), **Supp. X:** 212
"My Speech to the Graduates" (Allen), **Supp. XV:** 16
"Mysteries of Caesar, The" (Hecht), **Supp. X:** 73
"Mysteries of Eleusis, The" (Hardwick), **Supp. III Part 1:** 195
Mysteries of Pittsburgh, The (Chabon), **Supp. XI:** 65, 68, **69-71**
"Mysterious Case of R, The" (Conroy), **Supp. XVI:**72
Mysterious Stranger, The (Twain), **IV:** 190-191, 210
Mystery, A (Shields). *See Swann* (Shields)
"Mystery, The" (Dunbar), **Supp. II Part 1:** 199, 210
"Mystery, The" (Glück), **Supp. V:** 91
Mystery and Manners (O'Connor), **Retro. Supp. II:** 230
"'Mystery Boy' Looks for Kin in Nashville" (Hayden), **Supp. II Part 1:** 366, 372
"Mystery of Coincidence, The" (Conroy), **Supp. XVI:**74
"Mystery of Heroism, A" (Crane), **I:** 414
"Mystery of Marie Rogêt, The" (Poe), **III:** 413, 419; **Retro. Supp. II:** 271
"Mystic" (Plath), **Retro. Supp. II:** 257; **Supp. I Part 2:** 539, 541
"Mystical Poet, A" (Bogan), **Retro. Supp. I:** 36
"Mystic of Sex, The-A First Look at D. H. Lawrence" (Nin), **Supp. X:** 188
"Mystic Vision in 'The Marshes of Glynn'" (Warfel), **Supp. I Part 1:** 366, 373
"Mystification" (Poe), **III:** 425
My Study Windows (Lowell), **Supp. I Part 2:** 407
"My Teacher" (Conroy), **Supp. XVI:**75
"Myth" (Rukeyser), **Supp. VI:** 281-282
Myth of Sisyphus, The (Camus), **I:** 294; **Supp. XIII:** 165
"Myth of the Isolated Artist, The" (Oates), **Supp. II Part 2:** 520
Myth of the Machine, The (Mumford), **Supp. II Part 2:** 476, 478, 482, 483, 493, 497
Mythology and the Romantic Tradition in English Poetry (Bush), **Supp. I Part 1:** 268
Myths and Texts (Snyder), **Supp. VIII:** **295-296**
"Myths of Bears, The" (Bass), **Supp. XVI:**19, 20
"My Tocaya" (Cisneros), **Supp. VII:** 69
My Uncle Dudley (Morris), **I:** 305; **III:** 219-220
"My Uncle's Favorite Coffee Shop" (Nye), **Supp. XIII:** 283
"My Weariness of Epic Proportions" (Simic), **Supp. VIII:** 276
My Wicked Wicked Ways (Cisneros), **Supp. VII:** 58, 64-68, 71
"My Wicked Wicked Ways" (Cisneros), **Supp. VII:** 58, 64-66
"My Word-house" (Mora), **Supp. XIII:** 219, 225
My Works and Days (Mumford), **Supp. II Part 2:** 475, 477, 481
My World and Welcome to It (Thurber), **Supp. I Part 2:** 610

N

Nabokov, Peter, **Supp. IV Part 2:** 490
Nabokov, Véra, **Retro. Supp. I:** 266, 270
Nabokov, Vladimir, **I:** 135; **III: 244-266,** 283, 286; **Retro. Supp. I: 263-281,** 317, 335; **Supp. I Part 1:** 196; **Supp. II Part 1:** 2; **Supp. IV Part 1:** 135; **Supp. V:** 127, 237, 251, 252, 253; **Supp. VIII:** 105, 133, 138; **Supp. IX:** 152, 212, 261; **Supp. X:** 283; **Supp. XI:** 66; **Supp. XII:** 310; **Supp. XIII:** 46, 52; **Supp. XVI:**148, 294
Nabokov's Dozen (Nabokov), **Retro. Supp. I:** 266
Nabokov's Garden: A Guide to Ada (Mason), **Supp. VIII:** 138
Naca, Kristin, **Supp. XIII:** 133
Nadeau, Robert, **Supp. X:** 261, 270
Nadel, Alan, **Supp. IV Part 1:** 209
Naipaul, V. S., **Supp. IV Part 1:** 297; **Supp. VIII:** 314; **Supp. X:** 131; **Supp. XIV:**111
Naked and the Dead, The (Mailer), **I:** 477; **III:** 26, 27, 28-30, 31, 33, 35, 36, 44; **Retro. Supp. II: 197-199;** **Supp. IV Part 1:** 381; **Supp. XI:** 218
Naked Babies (Quindlen and Kelsh), **Supp. XVII:** 167, 179
Naked in Garden Hills (Crews), **Supp. XI:** 102, **110**
Naked Lunch (Burroughs), **Supp. III Part 1:** 92-95, 97-105; **Supp. IV Part 1:** 90
"Naked Nude" (Malamud), **Supp. I Part 2:** 450
Naked Poetry (Berg and Mezey, eds.), **Supp. IV Part 1:** 60
Naked Poetry (Levine), **Supp. V:** 180
Naked Revenge (film), **Supp. XVII:** 141
Namedropping: Mostly Literary Memoirs (Coover), **Supp. V:** 40
"Name in the Papers" (Hughes), **Supp. I Part 1:** 330
Name Is Archer, The (Macdonald, under Millar), **Supp. IV Part 2:** 466

"Name Is Burroughs, The" (Burroughs), **Supp. III Part 1:** 93
Name Is Fogarty, The: Private Papers on Public Matters (Farrell), **II:** 49
"Names" (Carruth), **Supp. XVI:**54, 56
Names, The (DeLillo), **Supp. VI:** 3, 10, 13, 14
Names, The (Momaday), **Supp. IV Part 2:** 479, 480, 483, 486, 487, 488, 489
Names and Faces of Heroes, The (Price), **Supp. VI:** 258, 260
Names of the Lost, The (Levine), **Supp. V:** 177-178, 179, 187-188
"Naming for Love" (Carruth), **Supp. XVI:**48
"Naming Myself" (Kingsolver), **Supp. VII:** 208
"Naming of Names, The" (Sanders), **Supp. XVI:**268
Naming of the Beasts, The (Stern). *See Rejoicings: Selected Poems, 1966-1972* (Stern)
Nana (Zola), **III:** 321
"Nancy Culpepper" (Mason), **Supp. VIII:** 141
Nancy Drew stories, **Supp. VIII:** 133, 135, 137, 142
"Nancy Knapp" (Masters), **Supp. I Part 2:** 461
"Naomi Shihab Nye: U.S. Mideast-History a Harbinger of 9-11?" (Nye), **Supp. XIII:** 286
"Naomi Trimmer" (X. J. Kennedy), **Supp. XV:** 170
"Nap, The" (Banks), **Supp. V:** 7
"Napoleon" (Emerson), **II:** 6
Napoleon I, **I:** 6, 7, 8, 474; **II:** 5, 309, 315, 321, 523; **Supp. I Part 1:** 153; **Supp. I Part 2:** 518, 519
Narcissa and Other Fables (Auchincloss), **Supp. IV Part 1:** 21, 34
"Narcissus as Narcissus" (Tate), **IV:** 124
"Narcissus Leaves the Pool" (Epstein), **Supp. XIV:**110
Narcissus Leaves the Pool: Familiar Essays (Epstein), **Supp. XIV:**110
Nardal, Paulette, **Supp. X:** 139
Nardi, Marcia, **Retro. Supp. I:** 426, 427
Narration (Stein), **IV:** 27, 30, 32, 33, 36
Narrative of a Four Months' Residence among the Natives of a Valley of the Marquesas Islands (Melville), **III:** 76
Narrative of Arthur Gordon Pym, The (Poe), **III:** 412, 416; **Retro. Supp. II:** 265, **273-275**; **Supp. XI:** 293
Narrative of the Life of Frederick Douglass, an American Slave, Written by Himself (Douglass), **Supp. III Part 1:** 154-159, 162, 165; **Supp. IV Part 1:** 13; **Supp. VIII:** 202
"Narrativity Scenes" (Wright), **Supp. XV:** 345
Narrenschiff, Das (Brant), **III:** 447
"Narrow Fellow in the Grass, A" (Dickinson), **Retro. Supp. I:** 30, 37
Narrow Heart, A: Portrait of a Woman (Gordon), **II:** 197, 217
Narrow Rooms (Purdy), **Supp. VII:** 274
Nash, Roderick, **Supp. IX:** 185; **Supp. XIV:**191-192
Nash, Susan Smith, **Supp. XVI:**274
Nash, Thomas, **Supp. III Part 1:** 387-388
Nashe, Thomas, **I:** 358; **Supp. XVII:** 232
Nashville (film), **Supp. IX:** 143
Nason, Elias, **Supp. XV:** 242
Nasser, Gamal Abdel, **IV:** 490
Natalie Mann (Toomer), **Supp. III Part 2:** 484-486
Nathan, George Jean, **II:** 91; **III:** 103, 104, 106, 107; **IV:** 432; **Supp. IV Part 1:** 343; **Supp. IX:** 56-57; **Supp. XIII:** 161
"Nathanael West" (Herbst), **Retro. Supp. II:** 325
Nathanael West: The Art of His Life (Martin), **Retro. Supp. II:** 325
Nathan Coulter (Berry), **Supp. X:** 24, 33
"Nationalist, The" (Anderson), **I:** 115
"Nation Is Like Ourselves, The" (Baraka), **Supp. II Part 1:** 53
"Native, The" (Olds), **Supp. X:** 215
"Native American Attitudes to the Environment" (Momaday), **Supp. IV Part 2:** 481, 491
Native American Renaissance (Lincoln), **Supp. IV Part 2:** 507
Native American Testimony (Nabokov, ed.), **Supp. IV Part 2:** 490
"Native Hill, A" (Berry), **Supp. X:** 21
Native in a Strange Land: Trials & Tremors (Coleman), **Supp. XI: 84-85,** 87
Native of Winby and Other Tales, A (Jewett), **II:** 396; **Retro. Supp. II:** 138
Native Son (Wright), **IV:** 476, 477, 478, 479, 481, 482-484, 485, 487, 488, 491, 495; **Retro. Supp. II:** 107, 116; **Supp. I Part 1:** 51, 64, 67, 337; **Supp. II Part 1:** 170, 235-236; **Supp. IX:** 306; **Supp. XIV:**73; **Supp. XVII:** 155
"Native Trees" (Merwin), **Supp. III Part 1:** 355
Natorp, Paul, **Supp. XIV:**198
Natural, The (Malamud), **II:** 424, 425; **Retro. Supp. II:** 288; **Supp. I Part 2:** 438-441, 443
"Natural, The: Malamud's World Ceres" (Wasserman), **Supp. I Part 2:** 439
"Natural History" (Olds), **Supp. X:** 210
"Natural History Note" (Hay), **Supp. XIV:**124, 130
"Natural History of Some Poems, A" (Harrison), **Supp. VIII:** 53
"Natural History of the Dead" (Hemingway), **II:** 206; **Retro. Supp. I:** 176
"Naturally Superior School, A" (Knowles), **Supp. XII:** 235, 240-241
"Natural Method of Mental Philosophy" (Emerson), **II:** 14
"Natural Resources" (Rich), **Supp. I Part 2:** 575
Natural Selection (F. Barthelme), **Supp. XI:** 2, 28, 32, 33
Nature (Emerson), **I:** 463; **II:** 1, 8, 12, 16; **IV:** 171, 172-173
"Nature" (Emerson), **Retro. Supp. I:** 250; **Supp. I Part 2:** 383; **Supp. III Part 1:** 387; **Supp. IX:** 178
"Nature, Inc." (Lewis), **II:** 441
Nature: Poems Old and New (Swenson), **Supp. IV Part 2:** 652
Nature and Destiny of Man, The (Niebuhr), **III:** 292, 303-306, 310
"Nature and Life" (Emerson), **II:** 19
"Nature and Nurture: When It Comes to Twins, Sometimes It's Hard to Tell the Two Apart" (Bausch), **Supp. VII:** 40
"Nature-Metaphors" (Lanier), **Supp. I Part 1:** 352
Nature Morte (Brodsky), **Supp. VIII:** 25
Nature of Evil, The (James), **II:** 343
Nature of Peace, The (Veblen), **Supp. I Part 2:** 642
Nature of True Virtue, The (Edwards), **I:** 549, 557-558, 559
Nature's Economy: A History of Ecological Ideas (Worster), **Supp. IX:** 19
Nausea (Sartre), **Supp. VIII:** 7
"Navajo Blanket, A" (Swenson), **Supp. IV Part 2:** 649
Navarette, Don Martín de, **II:** 310

Navarro, Ramon, **Supp. IV Part 1:** 206
Navigator, The (film), **I:** 31
Naylor, Gloria, **Supp. VIII: 213-230**
Naylor, Paul Kenneth, **Supp. IV Part 2:** 420
Nazimova, **III:** 399
Neal, Larry, **Retro. Supp. II:** 112, 128; **Supp. X:** 324, 328
Neal, Lawrence P., **Supp. II Part 1:** 53
Neal, Patricia, **Supp. I Part 1:** 286; **Supp. IV Part 2:** 524; **Supp. V:** 223
Neale, Walter, **I:** 192, 208
Nearer the Moon: From "A Journal of Love," the Unexpurgated Diary of Anaïs Nin, 1937-1939, **Supp. X:** 184, 185
Near-Johannesburg Boy and Other Poems, The (Brooks), **Supp. III Part 1:** 86
Near Klamath (Carver), **Supp. III Part 1:** 137
"Near Perigord" (Pound), **Retro. Supp. I:** 289, 290
Near the Ocean (Lowell), **II:** 543, 550, 551-553, 554, 555; **Retro. Supp. II:** 182, 186, 189-190
"Near View of the High Sierra, A" (Muir), **Supp. IX:** 183
Nebeker, Helen, **Supp. IX:** 122
"Nebraska Blizzard" (F. Wright), **Supp. XVII:** 247
Necessary Angel, The (Stevens), **IV:** 76, 79, 89, 90
Necessities of Life: Poems, 1962-1965 (Rich), **Supp. I Part 2:** 553, 555
"Necrological" (Ransom), **III:** 486-489, 490, 492
Ned Christie's War (Conley), **Supp. V:** 232
"Need for a Cultural Base to Civil Rites & Bpower Mooments, The" (Baraka), **Supp. II Part 1:** 48
"Need for Christian Preaching, The" (Buechner), **Supp. XII:** 49
Needful Things (King), **Supp. V:** 139, 146
"Needle" (Simic), **Supp. VIII:** 275
"Needle Trade" (Reznikoff), **Supp. XIV:** 277, 289
"Need of Being Versed in Country Things, The" (Frost), **II:** 154; **Retro. Supp. I:** 133, 135
Neel, Philippe, **Supp. XIV:** 338
Neelakantappa, Tara, **Supp. XV:** 104-105
Neeley, Barbara, **Supp. XVI:** 143
"Negative Capability" (Komunyakaa), **Supp. XIII:** 131

Negligible Tales (Bierce), **I:** 209
"Negotiating the Darkness, Fortified by Poets' Strength" (Karr), **Supp. XI:** 254; **Supp. XIII:** 285
Negotiating with the Dead (Atwood), **Supp. XIII:** 20, 35
Negritude movement, **Supp. X:** 131, 139
"Negro" (Hughes), **Supp. I Part 1:** 321-322
Negro, The (Du Bois), **Supp. II Part 1:** 178, 179, 185
Negro, The: The Southerner's Problem (Page), **Supp. II Part 1:** 168
Negro and His Music, The (Locke), **Supp. XIV:** 202
Negro Art: Past and Present (Locke), **Supp. XIV:** 202
"Negro Artisan, The" (Du Bois), **Supp. II Part 1:** 166
"Negro Artist and the Racial Mountain, The" (Hughes), **Retro. Supp. I:** 200, 207; **Supp. I Part 1:** 323, 325; **Supp. IV Part 1:** 169
"Negro Assays the Negro Mood, A" (Baldwin), **Supp. I Part 1:** 52
"Negro Citizen, The" (Du Bois), **Supp. II Part 1:** 179
"Negro Dancers" (Hughes), **Retro. Supp. I:** 199; **Supp. I Part 1:** 324
Negroes in America, The (McKay), **Supp. X:** 132, 136
"Negroes of Farmville, Virginia, The: A Social Study" (Du Bois), **Supp. II Part 1:** 166
Negro Family, The: The Case for National Action (Moynihan), **Retro. Supp. II:** 123
"Negro Farmer, The" (Du Bois), **Supp. II Part 1:** 167
"Negro Ghetto" (Hughes), **Supp. I Part 1:** 331
Negro in America, The (Locke), **Supp. XIV:** 208
Negro in American Civilization, The (Du Bois), **Supp. II Part 1:** 179
Negro in American Culture, The (Locke and Butcher), **Supp. XIV:** 202-203
Negro in Art, The: A Pictorial Record of the Negro Artist and of the Negro Theme in Art (Locke), **Supp. XIV:** 202
"Negro in Large Cities, The" (Du Bois), **Supp. II Part 1:** 169
"Negro in Literature and Art, The" (Du Bois), **Supp. II Part 1:** 174
Negro in New York, The (Ellison), **Supp. II Part 1:** 230
"Negro in the Black Belt, The: Some Social Sketches" (Du Bois), **Supp.**

II Part 1: 166
"Negro in the Three Americas, The" (Locke), **Supp. XIV:** 211
"Negro in the Well, The" (Caldwell), **I:** 309
"Negro Love Song, A" (Dunbar), **Supp. II Part 1:** 204
"Negro Martyrs Are Needed" (C. Himes), **Supp. XVI:** 138
Negro Mother, The (Hughes), **Supp. I Part 1:** 328
Negro Mother and Other Dramatic Recitations, The (Hughes), **Retro. Supp. I:** 203
Negro Novel in America, The (Bone), **Supp. IX:** 318-319
Negro Publication Society of America, **Retro. Supp. I:** 205
"Negro Renaissance, The: Jean Toomer and the Harlem of the 1920s" (Bontemps), **Supp. IX:** 306
"Negro Schoolmaster in the New South, A" (Du Bois), **Supp. II Part 1:** 168
"Negro's Contribution to American Culture, The" (Locke), **Supp. XIV:** 210, 211
"Negro Sermon, A: Simon Legree" (Lindsay), **Supp. I Part 2:** 393
"Negro Sings of Rivers, The" (Hughes), **Supp. IV Part 1:** 16
"Negro Speaks of Rivers, The" (Hughes), **Retro. Supp. I:** 199; **Supp. I Part 1:** 321
"Negro Spirituals, The (Locke), **Supp. XIV:** 201
"Negro Takes Stock, The" (Du Bois), **Supp. II Part 1:** 180
"Negro Theatre, The" (Van Vechten), **Supp. II Part 2:** 735
"Negro Voter Sizes Up Taft, A" (Hurston), **Supp. VI:** 160
"Negro Writer and His Roots, The: Toward a New Romanticism" (Hansberry), **Supp. IV Part 1:** 364
"Negro Youth Speaks" (Locke), **Supp. XIV:** 201
"Nehemias Americanus" (Mather), **Supp. II Part 2:** 453
Nehru, Jawaharlal, **IV:** 490
"Neighbor" (Hugo), **Supp. VI:** 135-136
"Neighbors" (Carver), **Supp. III Part 1:** 135, 139, 141; **Supp. XI:** 153
"Neighbors" (Hogan), **Supp. IV Part 1:** 405
"Neighbors, The" (Hay), **Supp. XIV:** 126
"Neighbour Rosicky" (Cather), **I:** 331-332

Neil Simon (Johnson), **Supp. IV Part 2:** 573

"Neil Simon: Toward Act III?" (Walden), **Supp. IV Part 2:** 591

"Neil Simon's Jewish-Style Comedies" (Walden), **Supp. IV Part 2:** 584, 591

Neilson, Heather, **Supp. IV Part 2:** 681

Neiman, Gilbert, **Supp. XV:** 140

"Neither Out Far Nor In Deep" (Frost), **I:** 303; **Retro. Supp. I:** 121, 138

"Nellie Clark" (Masters), **Supp. I Part 2:** 461

Nelson, Alice Dunbar, **Supp. XVII:** 75

Nelson, Ernest, **I:** 388

Nelson, Howard, **Supp. IV Part 1:** 66, 68

Nelson, Lord Horatio, **II:** 524

Nelson, Marilyn, **Supp. XVII:** 74, 112

Nelson, Shirley, **Supp. XII:** 293

Nelson Algren (Cox and Chatterton), **Supp. IX:** 11-12

Nelson Algren: A Life on the Wild Side (Drew), **Supp. IX:** 2

Nemerov, David, **II:** 268

Nemerov, Howard, **III: 267-289; IV:** 137, 140; **Supp. III Part 2:** 541; **Supp. IV Part 2:** 455, 650; **Supp. IX:** 114

Nemiroff, Robert Barron, **Supp. IV Part 1:** 360, 361, 365, 369, 370, 374

Neoconservative Criticism: Norman Podhoretz, Kenneth S. Lynn, and Joseph Epstein (Winchell), **Supp. VIII:** 241; **Supp. XIV:** 103

"Neo-Hoodoo Manifesto, The" (Reed), **Supp. X:** 242

Neon Rain, The (Burke), **Supp. XIV:** 22, 24, 26-27, 28-29, 30

Neon Vernacular (Komunyakaa), **Supp. XIII:** 121, **127-128,** 131

Neon Wilderness, The (Algren), **Supp. IX:** 3, 4

Neo-Slave Narratives (Rushdy), **Supp. X:** 250

Nepantla: Essays from the Land in the Middle (Mora), **Supp. XIII:** 213, **219-221,** 227

Nephew, The (Purdy), **Supp. VII:** 271, 273, 282

"Nereids of Seriphos, The" (Clampitt), **Supp. IX:** 41

Nericcio, William, **Supp. XIV:** 304-305

Neruda, Pablo, **Supp. I Part 1:** 89; **Supp. IV Part 2:** 537; **Supp. V:** 332; **Supp. VIII:** 272, 274; **Supp. IX:** 157, 271; **Supp. X:** 112; **Supp. XI:** 191; **Supp. XII:** 217; **Supp. XIII:** 114, 315, 323

Nesbit, Edith, **Supp. VIII:** 171

Nesbitt, Robin, **Supp. VIII:** 89

Nesting Ground, The (Wagoner), **Supp. IX:** 324, **325-326**

Nest of Ninnies, A (Ashbery and Schuyler), **Supp. III Part 1:** 3; **Supp. XV:** 178

Nets to Catch the Wind (Wylie), **Supp. I Part 2:** 709, 710-712, 714

Nettleton, Asahel, **I:** 458

"Net to Snare the Moonlight, A" (Lindsay), **Supp. I Part 2:** 387

Neubauer, Carol E., **Supp. IV Part 1:** 9

Neugeboren, Jacob Mordecai. See Neugeboren, Jay

Neugeboren, Jay, **Supp. XVI:** 217-231

Neugroschel, Joachim, **Supp. IX:** 138

Neuhaus, Richard John, **Supp. VIII:** 245

Neumann, Erich, **Supp. I Part 2:** 567; **Supp. IV Part 1:** 68, 69

Neuromancer (W. Gibson), **Supp. XII:** 15; **Supp. XVI:** 117, 119-120, 122, 124, **125-126,** 127, 129, 131

Neurotica: Jewish Writers on Sex (Bukiet, ed.), **Supp. XVII:** 48

"Neurotic America and the Sex Impulse" (Dreiser), **Retro. Supp. II:** 105

Neutra, Richard, **Supp. XVI:** 192

"Never Bet the Devil Your Head" (Poe), **III:** 425; **Retro. Supp. II:** 273

Never Come Morning (Algren), **Supp. IX:** 3, **7-9**

Never in a Hurry: Essays on People and Places (Nye), **Supp. XIII:** 273, **280-282,** 286

"Never Marry a Mexican" (Cisneros), **Supp. VII:** 70

"Never Room with a Couple" (Hughes), **Supp. I Part 1:** 330

"Nevertheless" (Moore), **III:** 214

Nevins, Allan, **I:** 253; **Supp. I Part 2:** 486, 493

"Nevsky Prospekt" (Olds), **Supp. X:** 205

New Adam, The (Untermeyer), **Supp. XV:** 304, 305

New Addresses (Koch), **Supp. XV:** 177, 184

"New Age of the Rhetoricians, The" (Cowley), **Supp. II Part 1:** 135

New American Literature, The (Pattee), **II:** 456

New American Novel of Manners, The (Klinkowitz), **Supp. XI:** 347

"New American Ode, The" (Wright), **Supp. XV:** 346

New American Poetry, 1945-1960 (Allen, ed.), **Supp. XIII:** 112

New American Poetry, The (Allen, ed.), **Supp. VIII:** 291, 292

"New American Writer, A" (W. C. Williams), **Retro. Supp. II:** 335

New and Collected Poems (Reed), **Supp. X:** 241

New and Collected Poems (Wilbur), **Supp. III Part 2:** 562-564

New and Selected Poems (Nemerov), **III:** 269, 275, 277-279

New and Selected Poems (Oliver), **Supp. VII:** 240-241, 245

New and Selected Poems (Wagoner), **Supp. IX: 326-327**

New and Selected Poems (W. J. Smith), **Supp. XIII:** 332

New and Selected Poems: 1974-1994 (Dunn), **Supp. XI: 151-152**

New and Selected Things Taking Place (Swenson), **Supp. IV Part 2:** 648-650, 651

"New Art Gallery Society, The" (Wolfe), **Supp. III Part 2:** 580

"New Capitalist Tool, The" (Wasserstein), **Supp. XV:** 328

Newcomb, Ralph, **Supp. XIII:** 12

Newcomb, Robert, **II:** 111

New Conscience and an Ancient Evil, A (Addams), **Supp. I Part 1:** 14-15, 16

"New Conservatism in American Poetry, The" (Wakoski), **Supp. XVII:** 112

"New Conservatives, The: Intellectuals in Retreat" (Epstein), **Supp. XIV:** 103

New Criticism, The (Ransom), **III:** 497-498, 499, 501

"New Day, A" (Levine), **Supp. V:** 182

Newdick, Robert Spangler, **Retro. Supp. I:** 138

Newdick's Season of Frost (Newdick), **Retro. Supp. I:** 138

New Dictionary of Quotations, A (Mencken), **III:** 111

New Directions Anthology in Prose and Poetry (Laughlin, ed.), **Supp. XVI:** 284

"New Directions in Poetry" (D. Locke), **Supp. IX:** 273

"New Dog, The: Variations on a Text by Jules Laforgue" (C. Frost), **Supp. XV:** 98

Newell, Henry, **IV:** 193

"New England" (Lowell), **II:** 536

"New England" (Robinson), **III:** 510, 524

New England: Indian Summer

(Brooks), **I:** 253, 256
"New England Bachelor, A" (Eberhart), **I:** 539
"New Englander, The" (Anderson), **I:** 114
New England Girlhood, A (Larcom), **Supp. XIII:** 137, 142, 143, 144, **147-154**
New England Local Color Literature (Donovan), **Retro. Supp. II:** 138
"New England Sabbath-Day Chace, The" (Freneau), **Supp. II Part 1:** 273
New-England Tale, A (Sedgwick), **I:** 341
New England Tragedies, The (Longfellow), **II:** 490, 505, 506; **Retro. Supp. II:** 165, 167
New Era in American Poetry, The (Untermeyer, ed.), **Supp. XV:** 301, 303, 306
Newer Ideals of Peace (Addams), **Supp. I Part 1:** 11-12, 15, 16-17, 19, 20-21
New Feminist Criticism, The: Essays on Women, Literature, and Theory (Showalter), **Supp. X:** 97
"New Folsom Prison" (Matthews), **Supp. IX:** 165
New Formalism, The: A Critical Introduction (McPhillips), **Supp. XV:** 250, 251, 252, 264
New Found Land: Fourteen Poems (MacLeish), **III:** 12-13
New Hampshire: A Poem with Notes and Grace Notes (Frost), **II:** 154-155; **Retro. Supp. I:** 132, 133, 135
"New Hampshire, February" (Eberhart), **I:** 536
New Hard-Boiled Writers (Panek), **Supp. XIV:**27
New Industrial State, The (Galbraith), **Supp. I Part 2:** 648
"New Journalism, The" (Wolfe), **Supp. III Part 2:** 571
New Journalism, The (Wolfe and Johnson, eds.), **Supp. III Part 2:** 570, 579-581, 583, 586
New Left, The: The Anti-Industrial Revolution (Rand), **Supp. IV Part 2:** 527
"New Letters from Thomas Jefferson" (Stafford), **Supp. XI:** 324
New Letters on the Air: Contemporary Writers on Radio, **Supp. X:** 165, 169, 173
"New Life" (Glück), **Supp. V:** 90
New Life, A (Malamud), **Supp. I Part 2:** 429-466

"New Life, The" (Bynner), **Supp. XV:** 44
"New Life at Kyerefaso" (Sutherland), **Supp. IV Part 1:** 9
"New Light on Veblen" (Dorfman), **Supp. I Part 2:** 650
Newman, Charles, **Supp. I Part 2:** 527, 546-548
Newman, Edwin, **Supp. IV Part 2:** 526
Newman, Judie, **Supp. IV Part 1:** 304, 305
Newman, Paul, **Supp. IV Part 2:** 473, 474
New Man, The (Merton), **Supp. VIII:** 208
"New Medea, The" (Howells), **II:** 282
New Mexico trilogy (Nichols), **Supp. XIII:** 269
"New Mother" (Olds), **Supp. X:** 206
"New Mothers, The" (Shields), **Supp. VII:** 310
New Music (Price), **Supp. VI:** 264, 265
"New Mutants, The" (Fiedler), **Supp. XIII:** 104
"New Name for Some Old Ways of Thinking, A" (James), **II:** 353
New Native American Novel, The: Works in Progress (Bartlett), **Supp. IV Part 1:** 335
"New Natural History, A" (Thurber), **Supp. I Part 2:** 619
"New Negro, The" (Locke), **Supp. XIV:**201
New Negro, The (Locke, ed.), **Supp. II Part 1:** 176; **Supp. IX:** 309; **Supp. X:** 137
New Negro, The: An Interpretation (Locke, ed.), **Retro. Supp. I:** 199; **Supp. IV Part 1:** 170; **Supp. XIV:**195, 201-202
New Negro for a New Century, A (Washington, Wood, and Williams), **Supp. XIV:**201
New New Journalism, The (R. Boynton), **Supp. XVII:** 209
"New Nomads, The" (E. Hoffman), **Supp. XVI:**161
"New Orleans" (Carruth), **Supp. XVI:**50
New Orleans Sketches (Faulkner), **Retro. Supp. I:** 80
New Path to the Waterfall, A (Carver), **Supp. III Part 1:** 138-140, 147, 149
"New Poem, The" (Wright), **Supp. V:** 339, 340
"New Poems" (MacLeish), **III:** 19
"New Poems" (Oliver), **Supp. VII:** 240

New Poems 1960 (Bynner), **Supp. XV:** 51
New Poems: 1980-88 (Haines), **Supp. XII: 209-210**
New Poetry, The (Monroe and Henderson, eds.), **Supp. I Part 2:** 387
"New Poetry Handbook, The" (Strand), **Supp. IV Part 2:** 626
New Poetry of Mexico (Strand, trans.), **Supp. IV Part 2:** 630
New Poets of England and America (Hall, Pack, and Simpson, eds.), **Supp. IV Part 2:** 621
"Newport of Anchuria" (Henry), **Supp. II Part 1:** 409
New Princeton Encyclopedia of Poetry and Poetics (Preminger and Brogan, eds.), **Supp. XV:** 250
"*New Republic* Moves Uptown, The" (Cowley), **Supp. II Part 1:** 142
"New Rose Hotel" (W. Gibson), **Supp. XVI:**120, 122, 124
"News, The" (McClatchy), **Supp. XII:** 269
"New Season" (Levine), **Supp. V:** 188
New Seeds of Contemplation (Merton), **Supp. VIII:** 200, 208
News from the Glacier: Selected Poems 1960-1980 (Haines), **Supp. XII:** 207, 208-209
"News Item" (Parker), **Supp. IX:** 190
New Song, A (Hughes), **Retro. Supp. I:** 202; **Supp. I Part 1:** 328, 331-332
"New South, The" (Lanier), **Supp. I Part 1:** 352, 354, 370
Newspaper Days, 1899-1906 (Mencken), **III:** 100, 102, 120
"New Spirit, The" (Ashbery), **Supp. III Part 1:** 14, 15
New Spoon River, The (Masters), **Supp. I Part 2:** 461-465, 473
New Star Chamber and Other Essays, The (Masters), **Supp. I Part 2:** 455-456, 459
New Tales of the Vampires (Rice), **Supp. VII:** 290
New Testament, **I:** 303, 457, 458; **II:** 167; **III:** 305; **IV:** 114, 134, 152; **Retro. Supp. I:** 58, 140, 360; **Supp. I Part 1:** 104, 106; **Supp. I Part 2:** 516; **Supp. XVII:** 155. *See also* names of New Testament books
New Testament, A (Anderson), **I:** 101, 114
"New Theory of Thorstein Veblen, A" (Galbraith), **Supp. I Part 2:** 650
Newton, Benjamin Franklin, **I:** 454
Newton, Huey P., **Supp. I Part 1:** 66; **Supp. IV Part 1:** 206

Newton, Isaac, **I:** 132, 557; **II:** 6, 103, 348-349; **III:** 428; **IV:** 18, 149
Newton, Sarah Emily, **Supp. XV:** 234
"New-Wave Format, A" (Mason), **Supp. VIII:** 141, 143, 147
New West of Edward Abbey, The (Ronald), **Supp. XIII:** 4
New Wolves, The: The Return of the Mexican Wolf to the American Southwest (Bass), **Supp. XVI:**26-27
New Woman's Survival Sourcebook, The (Rennie and Grimstead, eds.), **Supp. I Part 2:** 569
New World, The (Bynner), **Supp. XV:** 41, 42
New World, The: Tales (Banks), **Supp. V:** 8, 9, 10
New World Naked, A (Mariani), **Retro. Supp. I:** 419
New Worlds of Literature (Beaty and Hunter, eds.), **Supp. IV Part 1:** 331
New World Writing (Updike), **IV:** 217
New Year Letter (Auden), **Supp. II Part 1:** 14, 16
"New Year's Day" (Wharton), **Retro. Supp. I:** 381
"New Year's Eve" (Schwartz), **Supp. II Part 2:** 640, 656-657
New Year's Eve/1929 (Farrell), **II:** 43
"New Year's Eve 1968" (Lowell), **II:** 554
"New Year's Gift, The" (Stowe), **Supp. I Part 2:** 587
"New York" (Capote), **Supp. III Part 1:** 122
"New York" (Moore), **III:** 196, 198, 202, 206
"New York 1965" (Bowles), **Supp. IV Part 1:** 94
New York: A Serendipiter's Journey (Talese), **Supp. XVII:** 202, 203
New York City Arts Project, **Supp. III Part 2:** 618
"New York City in 1979"(Acker), **Supp. XII:** 5
New York Edition, **Retro. Supp. I:** 235
"New York Edition" (James), **II:** 336, 337
"New York Gold Conspiracy, The" (Adams), **I:** 4
New York Hat, The (film; Griffith), **Supp. XVI:**183
New York Intellectuals, **Supp. VIII:** 93
"New York Intellectuals, The" (Howe), **Supp. VI:** 120
"New York Is a City of Things Unnoticed" (Talese), **Supp. XVII:** 202, 209
New York Jew (Kazin), **Supp. VIII:** 95, **97-100**
"New York Theater: Isn't It Romantic" (Wasserstein), **Supp. XV:** 320
New York Trilogy, The (Auster), **Supp. XII:** 21, **24-28**
Next (McNally), **Supp. XIII:** 197
"Next in Line, The" (Bradbury), **Supp. IV Part 1:** 102
Next Room of the Dream, The (Nemerov), **III:** 269, 275, 278, 279-280, 284
"Next Time I Crossed the Line into Oklahoma, The" (Wright), **Supp. XV:** 345
Next-to-Last Things: New Poems and Essays (Kunitz), **Supp. III Part 1:** 257-259, 261, 262, 265, 266, 268
"'Next to Reading Matter'" (Henry), **Supp. II Part 1:** 399
Nexus (H. Miller), **III:** 170, 187, 188, 189
Niatum, Duane, **Supp. IV Part 1:** 331; **Supp. IV Part 2:** 505
Nice and Noir (Schwartz), **Supp. XIV:**23
Nice Jewish Boy, The (P. Roth), **Supp. III Part 2:** 412
Nicholas II, Tsar, **Supp. I Part 2:** 447
Nichols, Charles, **Retro. Supp. I:** 194
Nichols, John Treadwell, **Supp. XIII: 253-272**
Nichols, Luther, **Supp. X:** 265
Nichols, Mike, **Supp. IV Part 1:** 234; **Supp. IV Part 2:** 577
Nicholson, Colin, **Supp. VIII:** 129
Nicholson, Harold, **Supp. XIV:**163
Nicholson, Jack, **Supp. V:** 26; **Supp. VIII:** 45; **Supp. XI:** 308
Nicholson, John, **Supp. XVI:**293
Nick Adams Stories, The (Hemingway), **II:** 258; **Retro. Supp. I:** 174
"Nick and the Candlestick" (Plath), **Supp. I Part 2:** 544
Nickel and Dimed: On (Not) Getting By in America (Ehrenreich), **Supp. XVII:** 210
Nickel Mountain: A Pastoral Novel (Gardner), **Supp. VI:** 63, 64, 68, **69**
"Nicodemus" (Keillor), **Supp. XVI:**167
Nicoll, Allardyce, **III:** 400
Nicoloff, Philip, **II:** 7
Niebuhr, Gustav, **III:** 292
Niebuhr, H. Richard, **I:** 494
Niebuhr, Lydia, **III:** 292
Niebuhr, Reinhold, **III: 290-313**; **Supp. I Part 2:** 654
Niedecker, Lorine, **Supp. III Part 2:** 616, 623; **Supp. XIV:**287
Nielsen, Ed, **Supp. IX:** 254
Nielson, Dorothy, **Supp. I Part 2:** 659
Nietzsche, Friedrich Wilhelm, **I:** 227, 283, 383, 389, 396, 397, 402, 509; **II:** 7, 20, 27, 42, 90, 145, 262, 462, 463, 577, 583, 585; **III:** 102-103, 113, 156, 176; **IV:** 286, 491; **Supp. I Part 1:** 254, 299, 320; **Supp. I Part 2:** 646; **Supp. IV Part 1:** 104, 105-106, 107, 110, 284; **Supp. IV Part 2:** 519; **Supp. V:** 277, 280; **Supp. VIII:** 11, 181, 189; **Supp. X:** 48; **Supp. XII:** 98; **Supp. XIV:**339
Niflis, N. Michael, **Supp. IV Part 1:** 175
Nigger Heaven (Van Vechten), **Supp. II Part 2:** 739, 744-746
"Nigger Jeff" (Dreiser), **Retro. Supp. II:** 97
Nigger of the "Narcissus," The (Conrad), **II:** 91; **Retro. Supp. I:** 106
"NIGGY THE HO" (Baraka), **Supp. II Part 1:** 54
"Night, Death, Mississippi" (Hayden), **Supp. II Part 1:** 369
'Night, Mother (Norman), **Supp. VIII:** 141
"Night above the Avenue" (Merwin), **Supp. III Part 1:** 355
"Night among the Horses, A" (Barnes), **Supp. III Part 1:** 33-34, 39, 44
Night at the Movies, A, or, You Must Remember This: Fictions (Coover), **Supp. V:** 50-51
"Night at the Opera, A" (Matthews), **Supp. IX:** 167
"Night before the Sentence Is Carried Out, The" (Wright), **Supp. XV:** 341
"Nightbird" (Komunyakaa), **Supp. XIII:** 132
"Night-Blooming Cereus, The" (Hayden), **Supp. II Part 1:** 367
Night-Blooming Cereus, The (Hayden), **Supp. II Part 1:** 367, 373
Night-Born, The (London), **II:** 467
"Nightbreak" (Rich), **Supp. I Part 2:** 556
Night Dance (Price), **Supp. VI:** 264
"Night Dances, The" (Plath), **Supp. I Part 2:** 544
"Night Dream, The" (MacLeish), **III:** 15
"Night Ferry" (Doty), **Supp. XI:** 124
"Nightfishing" (Schnackenberg), **Supp. XV:** 254
"Night I Met Little Floyd, The" (Wright), **Supp. XV:** 345-346
Night in Acadie, A (Chopin), **Retro. Supp. II:** 66-67, 73; **Supp. I Part 1:** 200, 219, 220, 224

"Night in Acadie, A" (Chopin), **Retro. Supp. II:** 66
"Night in June, A" (W. C. Williams), **Retro. Supp. I:** 424
"Night in New Arabia, A" (Henry), **Supp. II Part 1:** 402
Night in Question, The: Stories (Wolff), **Supp. VII:** 342-344
"Night Journey" (Roethke), **Supp. III Part 1:** 260
Night Light (Justice), **Supp. VII:** 126-127
"Nightmare" (Kumin), **Supp. IV Part 2:** 442
Nightmare Factory, The (Kumin), **Supp. IV Part 2:** 444-447, 451
"Nightmare Factory, The" (Kumin), **Supp. IV Part 2:** 445, 453
Nightmare on Main Street (Poe), **Retro. Supp. II:** 262
"Nightmare" poems (Benét), **Supp. XI:** 46, 58
"Night Mirror" (L.-Y. Lee), **Supp. XV:** 225
Night Music (Odets), **Supp. II Part 2:** 541, 543, 544
"Night of First Snow" (R. Bly), **Supp. IV Part 1:** 71
Night of January 16th (Rand), **Supp. IV Part 2:** 527
Night of the Iguana, The (T. Williams), **IV:** 382, 383, 384, 385, 386, 387, 388, 391, 392, 393, 394, 395, 397, 398
"Night of the Iguana, The" (T. Williams), **IV:** 384
"Night of the Living Beanfield: How an Unsuccessful Cult Novel Became an Unsuccessful Cult Film in Only Fourteen Years, Eleven Nervous Breakdowns, and $20 Million" (Nichols), **Supp. XIII:** 267
Night Rider (Warren), **IV:** 243, 246-247
Nights (Doolittle), **Supp. I Part 1:** 270, 271
Nights and Days (Merrill), **Supp. III Part 1:** 319, 320, 322-325
"Nights and Days" (Rich), **Supp. I Part 2:** 574
"Night's for Cryin,' The" (C. Himes), **Supp. XVI:** 137
"Night Shift" (Plath), **Supp. I Part 2:** 538
"Night-Side" (Oates), **Supp. II Part 2:** 523
Night-Side (Oates), **Supp. II Part 2:** 522
"Night Sketches: Beneath an Umbrella" (Hawthorne), **II:** 235-237, 238, 239, 242
"Night-Sweat" (Lowell), **II:** 554
"Night-Talk" (Ellison), **Retro. Supp. II:** 126; **Supp. II Part 1:** 248
Night Thoughts (Young), **III:** 415
Night Traveler, The (Oliver), **Supp. VII:** 233
"Night Watch" (Gioia), **Supp. XV:** 117
"Night Watch, The" (Wright), **Supp. V:** 339
"Night We All Had Grippe, The" (Jackson), **Supp. IX:** 118
Nightwood (Barnes), **Supp. III Part 1:** 31, 32, 35-37, 39-43
Night World and the Word Night, The (F. Wright), **Supp. XVII:** 240, 244-245
"Nihilist as Hero, The" (Lowell), **II:** 554; **Retro. Supp. II:** 190
Nijinsky, Vaslav, **Supp. XV:** 28-29
Nikolai Gogol (Nabokov), **Retro. Supp. I:** 266
Niles, Thomas, **Retro. Supp. I:** 35
Niles, Thomas, Jr., **Supp. I Part 1:** 39
Nilsson, Christine, **Supp. I Part 1:** 355
Nilsson, Harry, **Supp. XI:** 309
Nilsson, Jenny Lind, **Supp. XVI:** 177
Nimitz, Chester, **Supp. I Part 2:** 491
"Nimram" (Gardner), **Supp. VI:** 73
Nims, John Frederick, **III:** 527; **Supp. XVII:** 112
Nin, Anaïs, **III:** 182, 184, 190; **Supp. III Part 1:** 43; **Supp. IV Part 2:** 680; **Supp. X:** 181-200
"9" (Oliver), **Supp. VII:** 244
"Nine from Eight" (Lanier), **Supp. I Part 1:** 352-354
Nine Headed Dragon River: Zen Journals 1969-1982 (Matthiessen), **Supp. V:** 199
Ninemile Wolves, The (Bass), **Supp. XVI:** 24-25, 26
"Nine Nectarines" (Moore), **III:** 203, 209, 215
Nine Plays (Reznikoff), **Supp. XIV:** 288
"Nine Poems for the Unborn Child" (Rukeyser), **Supp. VI:** 280-281, 284
Nine Stories (Nabokov), **Retro. Supp. I:** 266
Nine Stories (Salinger), **III:** 552, 558-564
1984 (Orwell), **Supp. XIII:** 29
"1940" (Stafford), **Supp. XI:** 328-329
"1945-1985: Poem for the Anniversary" (Oliver), **Supp. VII:** 237
"19 Hadley Street" (Schnackenberg), **Supp. XV:** 253
19 Necromancers from Now (Reed), **Supp. X:** 240
1919 (Dos Passos), **I:** 482, 485-486, 487, 489, 490, 492
"1975" (Wright), **Supp. V:** 341
"1910" (Mora), **Supp. XIII:** 215
"1938" (Komunyakaa), **Supp. XIII:** 114
"1939" (Taylor), **Supp. V:** 316
1933 (Levine), **Supp. V:** 185-187
"1933" (Levine), **Supp. V:** 188
"Nineteenth New York, The" (Doctorow), **Supp. IV Part 1:** 232
"1929" (Auden), **Supp. II Part 1:** 6
"1926" (Kees), **Supp. XV:** 135
19 Varieties of Gazelle (Nye), **Supp. XIII:** 275, **286-288**
"19 Varieties of Gazelle" (Nye), **Supp. XIII:** 286
95 Poems (Cummings), **I:** 430, 433, 435, 439, 446, 447
"90 North" (Jarrell), **II:** 370, 371
"91 Revere Street" (Lowell), **II:** 547; **Retro. Supp. II:** 188; **Supp. XI:** 240
90 Trees (Zukofsky), **Supp. III Part 2:** 631
"Nine Years Later" (Brodsky), **Supp. VIII:** 32
"Nirvana" (Lanier), **Supp. I Part 1:** 352
Nirvana Blues, The (Nichols), **Supp. XIII:** 266, 267
Nishikigi (play), **III:** 466
Niven, David, **Supp. XI:** 307
Nixon (film), **Supp. XIV:** 48
Nixon, Richard M., **I:** 376; **III:** 38, 46; **Supp. I Part 1:** 294, 295; **Supp. V:** 45, 46, 51; **Supp. XII:** 14; **Supp. XIV:** 306
"NJ Transit" (Komunyakaa), **Supp. XIII:** 132
Nketia, J. H., **Supp. IV Part 1:** 10
Nketsia, Nana, **Supp. IV Part 1:** 2, 10
Nkize, Julius, **Supp. IV Part 1:** 361
Nkrumah, Kwame, **I:** 490, 494; **Supp. IV Part 1:** 361; **Supp. X:** 135
Noailles, Anna de, **IV:** 328
Noa Noa (Gauguin), **I:** 34
Nobel Lecture (Singer), **Retro. Supp. II:** 300
"No Better Than a 'Withered Daffodil'" (Moore), **III:** 216
Noble, David W., **Supp. I Part 2:** 650
"Noble Rider and the Sound of Words, The" (Stevens), **Retro. Supp. I:** 299
Noble Savage, The (Coover), **Supp. V:** 40
"No Bobolink reverse His Singing" (Dickinson), **Retro. Supp. I:** 45
Nobodaddy (MacLeish), **III:** 5-6, 8, 10,

11, 18, 19, 20
"Nobodaddy" (W. Blake), **Supp. XVII:** 245
"Nobody in Hollywood" (Bausch), **Supp. VII:** 54
Nobody Knows My Name (Baldwin), **Supp. XIII:** 111
"Nobody Knows My Name" (Baldwin), **Retro. Supp. II:** 8; **Supp. I Part 1:** 52
Nobody Knows My Name: More Notes of a Native Son (Baldwin), **Retro. Supp. II:** 6, 8; **Supp. I Part 1:** 47, 52, 55
"Nobody knows this little Rose" (Dickinson), **Retro. Supp. I:** 30
"Nobody Said Anything" (Carver), **Supp. III Part 1:** 141
Nobody's Fool (Russo), **Supp. XII:** 326, **331-335,** 340
"No Change of Place" (Auden), **Supp. II Part 1:** 5
"Noche Triste, La" (Frost), **Retro. Supp. I:** 123
Nock, Albert Jay, **I:** 245; **Supp. IV Part 2:** 521, 524
"No Coward Soul Is Mine" (Brontë), **I:** 458
"No Crime in the Mountains" (Chandler), **Supp. IV Part 1:** 129
"Nocturne" (Komunyakaa), **Supp. XIII:** 126
"Nocturne" (MacLeish), **III:** 8
"Nocturne in a Deserted Brickyard" (Sandburg), **III:** 586
Nocturne of Remembered Spring (Aiken), **I:** 50
No Door (Wolfe), **IV:** 451-452, 456
"No Door" (Wolfe), **IV:** 456
"No Epitaph" (Carson), **Supp. XII:** 111
No Exit (Sartre), **I:** 82, 130; **Supp. XIV:**320
No Exit (Sartre; Bowles, trans.), **Supp. IV Part 1:** 84
No Gifts from Chance (Benstock), **Retro. Supp. I:** 361
"No-Good Blues" (Komunyakaa), **Supp. XIII:** 130
No Hero (Marquand), **III:** 57
No! In Thunder (Fiedler), **Supp. XIII:** 101
"Noiseless Patient Spider" (Whitman), **III:** 555; **IV:** 348; **Supp. IV Part 1:** 325
Noises Off (Frayn), **Supp. IV Part 2:** 582
Noi vivi. See We the Living (film)
"No Lamp Has Ever Shown Us Where to Look" (MacLeish), **III:** 9
Nolan, Sidney, **Retro. Supp. II:** 189

No Laughing Matter (Heller and Vogel), **Supp. IV Part 1:** 384, 389
No Love Lost, a Romance of Travel (Howells), **II:** 277
No Man Is an Island (Merton), **Supp. VIII:** 207
No Mother to Guide Her (Loos), **Supp. XVI:**194
No Name in the Street (Baldwin), **Retro. Supp. II:** 13, 14; **Supp. I Part 1:** 47, 48, 52, 65-66, 67
No Nature: New and Selected Poems (Snyder), **Supp. VIII: 305**
Nonconformist's Memorial, The (Howe), **Supp. IV Part 2:** 434, 435-436
Nonconformity (Algren), **Supp. IX:** 15
None but the Lonely Heart (film), **Supp. II Part 2:** 546
Nones (Auden), **Supp. II Part 1:** 21
"Nones" (Auden), **Supp. II Part 1:** 22-23
None Shall Look Back (Gordon), **II:** 205-207, 208
Nonverbal Communication: Notes on the Visual Perception of Human Relations (Kees and Ruesch), **Supp. XV:** 147
"Noon" (Bryant), **Supp. I Part 1:** 157
"No One Remembers" (Levine), **Supp. V:** 187
"Noon Walk on the Asylum Lawn" (Sexton), **Supp. II Part 2:** 673
"Noon Wine" (Porter), **III:** 436, 437-438, 442, 446
"No Pain Whatsoever" (Yates), **Supp. XI:** 341
"No Place for You, My Love" (Welty), **IV:** 278, 279; **Retro. Supp. I:** 353
No Plays of Japan, The (Waley), **III:** 466
No Pockets in a Shroud (McCoy), **Supp. XIII: 166-168,** 171, 172, 173, 174
"No Poem So Fine" (Francis), **Supp. IX:** 83
Norcross, Frances, **I:** 456, 462
Norcross, Louise, **I:** 456, 462
Nordyke, Lewis, **Supp. XIII:** 5
No Relief (Dixon), **Supp. XII:** 139, **142-143**
No Resting Place (Humphrey), **Supp. IX:** 94, **106-108**
Norfolk Poems, The (Carruth), **Supp. XVI:**47, 48
Norma (Bellini), **IV:** 309
Norma Ashe (Glaspell), **Supp. III Part 1:** 175, 186-187
"Normal Motor Adjustments" (Stein and Solomons), **IV:** 26

Norman, Charles, **III:** 479
Norman, Gurney, **Supp. X:** 24
Norman, Marsha, **Supp. VIII:** 141
Norman Mailer (Poirier), **Retro. Supp. II:** 207-208
Norman Mailer: Modern Critical Views (Bloom), **Retro. Supp. II:** 205
Norman Mailer Revisited (Merrill), **Retro. Supp. II:** 201
Norna; or, The Witch's Curse (Alcott), **Supp. I Part 1:** 33
Norris, Charles, **III:** 320; **Retro. Supp. I:** 100
Norris, Frank, **I:** 211, 355, 500, 506, 517, 518, 519; **II:** 89, 264, 276, 289, 307; **III:** 227, **314-336,** 596; **IV:** 29; **Retro. Supp. I:** 100, 325; **Retro. Supp. II:** 96, 101; **Supp. III Part 2:** 412; **Supp. VIII:** 101, 102; **Supp. IX:** 14, 15; **Supp. XV:** 115
"North" (Hugo), **Supp. VI:** 135
North, Milou (pseudonym), **Supp. IV Part 1:** 260. *See also* Dorris, Michael; Erdrich, Louise
North, Sir Thomas, **IV:** 370
"North American Sequence" (Roethke), **I:** 171-172, 183; **III:** 529, 545, 547, 548
"North Beach" (Snyder), **Supp. VIII:** 289
"North Country Sketches" (McClatchy), **Supp. XII:** 256
"Northeast Playground" (Paley), **Supp. VI:** 226-227, 229
Northern Lights (O'Brien), **Supp. V:** 237, 239, 241-244, 250
"Northern Motive" (Levine), **Supp. V:** 195
Northfield Poems (Ammons), **Supp. VII:** 29
"Northhanger Ridge" (Wright), **Supp. V:** 335, 340
"North Haven" (Bishop), **Retro. Supp. II:** 50
"North Labrador" (Crane), **I:** 386
North of Boston (Frost), **II:** 152, 153-154, 527; **Retro. Supp. I:** 121, 125, 127, **128-130,** 131; **Supp. I Part 1:** 263; **Supp. XIII:** 146
North of Jamaica (Simpson), **Supp. IV Part 2:** 448; **Supp. IX:** 275, 276
North of the Danube (Caldwell), **I:** 288, 290, 293, 294, 309, 310
Northrup, Cyrus, **Supp. I Part 1:** 350
North Sea (Jarman), **Supp. XVII:** 110, 113
"North Sea Undertaker's Complaint, The" (Lowell), **II:** 550
North & South (Bishop), **Retro. Supp.**

II: 41-43; **Supp. I Part 1:** 72, 84, 85, 89
North Star, The (Hellman), **Supp. I Part 1:** 281
Northup, Solomon, **Supp. XIV:**32
"North Winter" (Carruth), **Supp. XVI:**53
Norton, Charles Eliot, **I:** 223, 568; **II:** 279, 322-323, 338; **Retro. Supp. I:** 371; **Retro. Supp. II:** 135; **Supp. I Part 1:** 103; **Supp. I Part 2:** 406, 479
Norton, Jody, **Supp. VIII:** 297
Norton, John, **Supp. I Part 1:** 99, 110, 112, 114
Norton Anthology of African American Literature, The, **Supp. X:** 325
Norton Anthology of American Literature, **Supp. X:** 325; **Supp. XV:** 270
Norton Anthology of Literature by Women (Gilbert and Gubar, eds.), **Supp. XV:** 270
Norton Anthology of Modern Poetry, The, **Supp. XI:** 259; **Supp. XV:** 258
Norton Anthology of Short Fiction, The, **Supp. IX:** 4
Norton Book of Personal Essays, The, **Supp. XIV:**105
Norton Lectures, **Retro. Supp. I:** 65
Norwood, Vera, **Supp. IX:** 24
No Safe Harbour (Porter), **III:** 447
Nosferatu: An Opera Libretto (Gioia), **Supp. XV:** 112, **128**
"Nosferatu's Serenade" (Gioia), **Supp. XV:** 128
No Siege Is Absolute (Char; version of F. Wright), **Supp. XVII:** 244
"No Snake" (A. Finch), **Supp. XVII:** 72
"No Speak English" (Cisneros), **Supp. VII:** 63
"Nostalgia of the Lakefronts" (Justice), **Supp. VII:** 118, 119, 120
"Nostalgic Mood" (Farrell), **II:** 45
No Star Is Lost (Farrell), **II:** 34, 35, 44
Nostromo (Conrad), **II:** 600; **IV:** 245
"Nosty Fright, A" (Swenson), **Supp. IV Part 2:** 651
Not about Nightingales (T. Williams), **IV:** 381
"Not a Womb in the House" (Quindlen), **Supp. XVII:** 166, 171
Not Dancing (Dunn), **Supp. XI:** 143, **148**
"Note about *Iconographs*, A" (Swenson), **Supp. IV Part 2:** 646
Notebook (Lowell), **Retro. Supp. II:** 186, 190; **Supp. V:** 343
Notebook 1967-68 (Lowell), **II:** 553-555; **Retro. Supp. II:** 182, 186, 190

Notebook of Malte Laurids Brigge, The (Rilke), **III:** 571
Notebooks (Fitzgerald), **Retro. Supp. I:** 110
"Note on Abraham Lincoln" (Vidal), **Supp. IV Part 2:** 688
"Note on Commercial Theatre" (Hughes), **Retro. Supp. I:** 207
"Note on Ezra Pound, A" (Eliot), **Retro. Supp. I:** 290
"Note on Lanier's Music, A" (P. Graham), **Supp. I Part 1:** 373
Note on Literary Criticism, A (Farrell), **II:** 26, 49
"Note on Poetry, A" (Doolittle), **Supp. I Part 1:** 254, 267-268
"Note on Realism, A" (Anderson), **I:** 110
"Note on the Limits of 'History' and the Limits of 'Criticism,' A" (Brooks), **Supp. XIV:**11
"Note on the Poetry of Love, A" (Untermeyer), **Supp. XV:** 304
"Note on the Truth of the Tales, A" (Vollmann), **Supp. XVII:** 230
"Notes" (Dove), **Supp. IV Part 1:** 246
"Notes for a Moving Picture: The House" (Agee), **I:** 33, 34
"Notes for an Autobiography" (Van Vechten), **Supp. II Part 2:** 749
"Notes for a Novel About the End of the World" (Percy), **Supp. III Part 1:** 393
"Notes for a Preface" (Sandburg), **III:** 591, 596-597
"NOTES FOR A SPEECH" (Baraka), **Supp. II Part 1:** 33
Notes for the Green Box (Duchamp), **Supp. IV Part 2:** 423
Notes from a Bottle Found on the Beach at Carmel (Connell), **Supp. XIV:**80, 87, 96, 97
Notes from a Sea Diary: Hemingway All the Way (Algren), **Supp. IX:** 16
"Notes from the Childhood and Girlhood" (Brooks), **Supp. III Part 1:** 77
"Notes from the River" (Stern), **Supp. IX:** 285, 287, 294, 295
Notes from Underground (Dostoyevsky), **III:** 571; **IV:** 485; **Retro. Supp. II:** 121
"Notes of a Faculty Wife" (Jackson), **Supp. IX:** 126
"Notes of a Native Daughter" (Didion), **Supp. IV Part 1:** 196, 197, 200, 201
Notes of a Native Son (Baldwin), **Retro. Supp. II:** 1, 2, 3, 5, 6; **Supp.**

I Part 1: 50, 52, 54; **Supp. IV Part 1:** 163
"Notes of a Native Son" (Baldwin), **Supp. I Part 1:** 50, 54
Notes of a Son and Brother (James), **II:** 337; **Retro. Supp. I:** 235
"Notes on a Departure" (Trilling), **Supp. III Part 2:** 498
"Notes on Babbitt and More" (Wilson), **IV:** 435
"Notes on Camp" (Sontag), **Supp. XIV:**167
"Notes on 'Camp'" (Sontag), **Supp. III Part 2:** 455-456
Notes on Democracy (Mencken), **III:** 104, 107-108, 109, 116, 119
"Notes on Free Verse" (Dobyns), **Supp. XIII:** 77
"Notes on 'Layover'" (Hass), **Supp. VI:** 109
Notes on Novelists (James), **II:** 336, 337; **Retro. Supp. I:** 235
"Notes on Nukes, Nookie, and Neo-Romanticism" (Robbins), **Supp. X:** 272
"Notes on Poetry" (Eberhart), **I:** 524, 527-528, 529
"Notes on the Craft of Poetry" (Strand), **Supp. IV Part 2:** 626
"Notes on the Decline of Outrage" (Dickey), **Supp. IV Part 1:** 181
"Notes on the New Formalism" (Gioia), **Supp. XV:** 113, 114-115
"Notes on the Novel-as-Autobiography" (P. Bailey), **Supp. XVI:**69
Notes on the State of Virginia (1781-1782) (Jefferson), **Supp. XIV:**191
"Notes to Be Left in a Cornerstone" (Benét), **Supp. XI:** 46, 58
"Notes toward a Supreme Fiction" (Stevens), **IV:** 87-89; **Retro. Supp. I:** 300, 306, **306-309**, 311; **Supp. I Part 1:** 80
"Notes towards a Poem That Can Never Be Written" (Atwood), **Supp. XIII:** 34-35
No Thanks (Cummings), **I:** 430, 431, 432, 436, 437, 441, 443, 446
"Nothing" (C. Frost), **Supp. XV:** 94
"Nothing Big" (Komunyakaa), **Supp. XIII:** 121
Nothing for Tigers (Carruth), **Supp. XVI:**47, 48, 50
"Nothing Gold Can Stay" (Frost), **Retro. Supp. I:** 133
"Nothing in Heaven Functions as It Ought" (X. J. Kennedy), **Supp. XV:** 158-159
Nothing Makes You Free: Writings by

Descendants of Jewish Holocaust Survivors (Bukiet, ed.), **Supp. XVII: 39-40**, 48-49
"Nothing Missing" (O'Hara), **III:** 369
Nothing Personal (Baldwin), **Supp. I Part 1:** 58, 60
"Nothing Song, The" (Snodgrass), **Supp. VI:** 326
"Nothing Stays Put" (Clampitt), **Supp. IX:** 42
"Nothing Will Yield" (Nemerov), **III:** 279
No Third Path (Kosinski), **Supp. VII:** 215
"Not Ideas About the Thing but the Thing Itself" (Stevens), **IV:** 87
Notions of the Americans: Picked up by a Travelling Bachelor (Cooper), **I:** 343-345, 346
"Not-Knowing" (Barthelme), **Supp. IV Part 1:** 48
"Not Leaving the House" (Snyder), **Supp. VIII:** 300
"'Not Marble nor the Gilded Monument'" (MacLeish), **III:** 12
Not Now But Now (M. F. K. Fisher), **Supp. XVII:** 86, 90
"Not Quite Social" (Frost), **II:** 156
"Not Sappho, Sacco" (Rukeyser), **Supp. VI:** 277
"Not Sixteen" (Anderson), **I:** 114
"Not Slightly" (Stein), **IV:** 44
Not So Deep as a Well (Parker) **Supp. IX:** 192
"Not Somewhere Else, but Here" (Rich), **Supp. I Part 2:** 552, 573
Not So Simple: The "Simple" Stories by Langston Hughes (Harper), **Retro. Supp. I:** 194, 209
Not-So-Simple Neil Simon (McGovern), **Supp. IV Part 2:** 573
"Not the Point" (Cameron), **Supp. XII:** 83
"Not They Who Soar" (Dunbar), **Supp. II Part 1:** 199
Not This Pig (Levine), **Supp. V:** 178, 181, 182-183
Not to Eat; Not for Love (Weller), **III:** 322
Not Without Laughter (Hughes), **Retro. Supp. I:** 197, 198, 201; **Supp. I Part 1:** 328, 332
Nouvelle Héloïse, La (Rousseau), **Supp. XV:** 232
Nova Express (Burroughs), **Supp. III Part 1:** 93, 103, 104
Novel, The (Bulwer), **Retro. Supp. II:** 58
"Novel as a Function of American Democracy, The" (Ellison), **Retro. Supp. II:** 124
"Novel Démeublé, The" (Cather), **Retro. Supp. I:** 15
Novel History: Historians and Novelists Confront America's Past (and Each Other) (Carnes), **Supp. X:** 14
Novella (Goethe; Bogan and Mayer, trans.), **Supp. III Part 1:** 63
Novellas and Other Writings (Wharton), **Retro. Supp. I:** 360
"Novel of the Thirties, A" (Trilling), **Supp. III Part 2:** 499
Novels and Other Writings (Bercovitch), **Retro. Supp. II:** 325
Novels and Tales of Henry James, The (James), **Retro. Supp. I:** 232
"Novel-Writing and Novel-Reading" (Howells), **II:** 276, 290
"November" (Larcom), **Supp. XIII:** 143
"November Cotton Flower" (Toomer), **Supp. IX:** 312
November Twenty Six Nineteen Sixty Three (Berry), **Supp. X:** 24
"Novices" (Moore), **III:** 200-201, 202, 213
Novick, Peter, **Supp. XVI:**154-155
"Novogodnee" ("New Year's Greetings") (Tsvetayeva), **Supp. VIII:** 30
"Novotny's Pain" (P. Roth), **Supp. III Part 2:** 403
"No Voyage" (Oliver), **Supp. VII:** 231
No Voyage and Other Poems (Oliver), **Supp. VII:** 230-231, 232
Now and Another Time (Hearon), **Supp. VIII:** 58, **61-62**
Now and Then (Buechner), **Supp. XII:** 49, 53
"Now and Then, America" (Mora), **Supp. XIII:** 217
"Nowhere" (J. Scott), **Supp. XVII:** 189
Nowhere Is a Place: Travels in Patagonia (Theroux and Chatwin), **Supp. VIII:** 322
"Now I Am Married" (Gordon), **Supp. IV Part 1:** 299
"Now I Lay Me" (Hemingway), **II:** 249; **Retro. Supp. I:** 175
"Now I Lay Me" (Olds), **Supp. X:** 208
"Now Is the Air Made of Chiming Balls" (Eberhart), **I:** 523
"No Word" (Kunitz), **Supp. III Part 1:** 263
Now Sheba Sings the Song (Angelou), **Supp. IV Part 1:** 16
"Now That We Live" (Kenyon), **Supp. VII:** 165
"Now the Servant's Name Was Malchus" (Wilder), **IV:** 358
"Now We Know" (O'Hara), **III:** 368-369
NOW with Bill Moyers (television), **Supp. XIII:** 286
Noyes, Alfred, **IV:** 434
Nuamah, Grace, **Supp. IV Part 1:** 10
"Nuances of a Theme by Williams" (Stevens), **Retro. Supp. I:** 422
Nuclear Age, The (O'Brien), **Supp. V:** 238, 243, 244, 246-248, 249, 251
"Nuclear Arms and Morality" (Sanders), **Supp. XVI:**266
Nude Croquet (Fiedler), **Supp. XIII:** 103
"Nude Descendig a Staircase" (X. J. Kennedy), **Supp. XV:** 168
"Nude Descending a Staircase" (Duchamp), **IV:** 408; **Retro. Supp. I:** 416
Nude Descending a Staircase (X. J. Kennedy), **Supp. XV:** 153, **154-157**
Nugent, Bruce, **Retro. Supp. I:** 200
Nugent, Elliot, **Supp. I Part 2:** 606, 611, 613
Nuggets and Dust (Bierce), **I:** 195
"Nullipara" (Olds), **Supp. X:** 209
Number One (Dos Passos), **I:** 489
"Numbers, Letters" (Baraka), **Supp. II Part 1:** 50
Nunc Dimittis (Brodsky), **Supp. VIII:** 25-26, 28
"Nun No More, A" (Fante), **Supp. XI:** 160
"Nun's Priest's Tale" (Chaucer), **III:** 492
Nunzio, Nanzia, **IV:** 89
Nuptial Flight, The (Masters), **Supp. I Part 2:** 460, 471
"Nuptials" (Tate), **IV:** 122
"Nurse Whitman" (Olds), **Supp. X:** 203
Nurture (Kumin), **Supp. IV Part 2:** 453-454, 455
Nussbaum, Emily, **Supp. XI:** 143
Nussbaum, Felicity A., **Supp. X:** 189
Nutcracker, The (Tchaikovsky), **Retro. Supp. I:** 196
"Nux Postcoenatica" (Holmes), **Supp. I Part 1:** 303
Nyce, James M., **Retro. Supp. I:** 380
Nye, Naomi Shihab, **Supp. XI:** 316; **Supp. XIII: 273-290**
Nyerere, Julius, **Supp. X:** 135
"Nympholepsy" (Faulkner), **Retro. Supp. I:** 81

O

"Ö" (Dove), **Supp. IV Part 1:** 245
O. Henry Biography (C. A. Smith), **Supp. II Part 1:** 395

Oak and Ivy (Dunbar), **Supp. II Part 1:** 98
Oak Openings, The (Cooper), **I:** 354, 355
Oandasan, Bill, **Supp. IV Part 2:** 499
Oasis, The (McCarthy), **II:** 566-568
Oates, Joyce Carol, **Supp. II Part 2: 503-527; Supp. IV Part 1:** 205; **Supp. IV Part 2:** 447, 689; **Supp. V:** 323; **Supp. XI:** 239; **Supp. XII:** 343; **Supp. XIII:** 306; **Supp. XIV:**26, 109
"Oath, The" (Tate), **IV:** 127
Obbligati (Hecht), **Supp. X:** 57
Ober, Harold, **Retro. Supp. I:** 101, 103, 105, 110, 113
Oberndorf, Clarence P., **Supp. I Part 1:** 315
Obey, André, **IV:** 356, 375
"Obit" (Lowell), **II:** 554
"Objective Value of a Social Settlement, The" (Addams), **Supp. I Part 1:** 4
"Objective Woman, The" (Jong), **Supp. V:** 119
Objectivist Anthology, An, **Supp. XIV:**287
"Objectivist Ethics, The" (Rand), **Supp. IV Part 2:** 530-532
"Objectivists" Anthology, An (Zukofsky), **Supp. III Part 2:** 613, 615
Object Lessons (Quindlen), **Supp. XVII: 173-174**
"Objects" (Wilbur), **Supp. III Part 2:** 545-547
Oblique Prayers (Levertov), **Supp. III Part 1:** 283
"Oblivion" (Justice), **Supp. VII:** 121
Oblivion Seekers, The (Eberhardt), **Supp. IV Part 1:** 92
"Oblong Box, The" (Poe), **III:** 416
Obregon, Maurice, **Supp. I Part 2:** 488
O'Briant, Don, **Supp. X:** 8
O'Brien, Edward, **Supp. XV:** 140
O'Brien, Edward J., **I:** 289; **III:** 56
O'Brien, Fitzjames, **I:** 211
O'Brien, Geoffrey, **Supp. IV Part 2:** 471, 473
O'Brien, John, **Supp. V:** 48, 49; **Supp. X:** 239, 244
O'Brien, Tim, **Supp. V: 237-255; Supp. XI:** 234; **Supp. XVII:** 14
"Obscene Poem, An" (Creeley), **Supp. IV Part 1:** 150
Obscure Destinies (Cather), **I:** 331-332; **Retro. Supp. I:** 19
"Observation Relative to the Intentions of the Original Founders of the Academy in Philadelphia" (Franklin), **II:** 114
"Observations" (Dillard), **Supp. VI:** 34
Observations (Moore), **III:** 194, 195-196, 197, 199, 203, 205, 215
Observations: Photographs by Richard Avedon: Comments by Truman Capote, **Supp. III Part 1:** 125-126
"Observations Now" (Conroy), **Supp. XVI:**75
O Canada: An American's Notes on Canadian Culture (Wilson), **IV:** 429-430
"O Carib Isle!" (Crane), **I:** 400-401
O'Casey, Sean, **III:** 145; **Supp. IV Part 1:** 359, 361, 364
"Occidentals" (Ford), **Supp. V:** 71-72
"Occultation of Orion, The" (Longfellow), **Retro. Supp. II:** 168
"Occurrence at Owl Creek Bridge, An" (Bierce), **I:** 200-201; **II:** 264
"Ocean 1212-W" (Plath), **Supp. I Part 2:** 528
O'Connell, Nicholas, **Supp. IX:** 323, 325, 334
O'Connor, Edward F., Jr., **III:** 337
O'Connor, Flannery, **I:** 113, 190, 211, 298; **II:** 606; **III: 337-360; IV:** 4, 217, 282; **Retro. Supp. II:** 179, **219-239,** 272, 324; **Supp. I Part 1:** 290; **Supp. III Part 1:** 146; **Supp. V:** 59, 337; **Supp. VIII:** 13, 14, 158; **Supp. X:** 1, 26, 69, 228, 290; **Supp. XI:** 104; **Supp. XIII:** 294; **Supp. XIV:**93; **Supp. XV:** 338; **Supp. XVI:**219; **Supp. XVIII:** 43, 114
O'Connor, Frank, **III:** 158; **Retro. Supp. II:** 242; **Supp. I Part 2:** 531; **Supp. VIII:** 151, 157, 165, 167, 171; **Supp. XV:** 74
O'Connor, Richard, **II:** 467
O'Connor, T. P., **II:** 129
O'Connor, William, **IV:** 346; **Retro. Supp. I:** 392, 407
O'Connor, William Van, **III:** 479; **Supp. I Part 1:** 195
"Octascope" (Beattie), **Supp. V:** 27, 28
"Octaves" (Robinson), **Supp. III Part 2:** 593
"Octet" (Wallace), **Supp. X:** 309
October (Isherwood), **Supp. XIV:**157, 164
"October" (Oliver), **Supp. VII:** 241
"October" (Swenson), **Supp. IV Part 2:** 649
"October 1913" (McCarriston), **Supp. XIV:**266
"October, 1866" (Bryant), **Supp. I Part 1:** 169
"October and November" (Lowell), **II:** 554
"October in the Railroad Earth" (Kerouac), **Supp. III Part 1:** 225, 227, 229
October Light (Gardner), **Supp. VI:** 63, **69-71,** 72
"October Maples, Portland" (Wilbur), **Supp. III Part 2:** 556
"Octopus, An" (Moore), **III:** 202, 207-208, 214
"Octopus, The" (Merrill), **Supp. III Part 1:** 321
Octopus, The (Norris), **I:** 518; **III:** 314, 316, 322-326, 327, 331-333, 334, 335
"O Daedalus, Fly Away Home" (Hayden), **Supp. II Part 1:** 377-378
"OD and Hepatitis Railroad or Bust, The" (Boyle), **Supp. VIII:** 1
Odd Couple, The (film), **Supp. IV Part 2:** 589
Odd Couple, The (Simon), **Supp. IV Part 2:** 575, 579-580, 585, 586; **Supp. XVII:** 8
Odd Couple, The (1985 version, Simon), **Supp. IV Part 2:** 580
Odd Jobs (Updike), **Retro. Supp. I:** 334
Odd Mercy (Stern), **Supp. IX: 298-299**
"Odds, The" (Hecht), **Supp. X:** 64-65
"Odds, The" (Salinas), **Supp. XIII:** 321
"Ode" (Emerson), **II:** 13
"Ode (Intimations of Immortality)" (Matthews), **Supp. IX:** 162
"Ode" (Sobin), **Supp. XVI:**284-285
"Ode" (X. J. Kennedy), **Supp. XV:** 160
"Ode: For the Budding of Islands" (Sobin), **Supp. XVI:**287
"Ode: Intimations of Immortality" (Wordsworth), **Supp. I Part 2:** 729; **Supp. III Part 1:** 12; **Supp. XIV:**8
"Ode: My 24th Year" (Ginsberg), **Supp. II Part 1:** 312
"Ode for Memorial Day" (Dunbar), **Supp. II Part 1:** 199
"Ode for the American Dead in Asia" (McGrath), **Supp. X:** 119
"Ode Inscribed to W. H. Channing" (Emerson), **Supp. XIV:**46
"Ode on a Grecian Urn" (Keats), **I:** 284; **III:** 472; **Supp. XII:** 113; **Supp. XIV:**8, 9-10; **Supp. XV:** 100
"Ode on Human Destinies" (Jeffers), **Supp. II Part 2:** 419
"Ode on Indolence" (Keats), **Supp. XII:** 113
"Ode on Melancholy" (Keats), **Retro. Supp. I:** 301

Ode Recited at the Harvard Commemoration (Lowell), **Supp. I Part 2:** 416-418, 424
"Ode Recited at the Harvard Commemoration" (Lowell), **II:** 551
"Ode Secrète" (Valéry), **III:** 609
"Odes of Estrangement" (Sobin), **Supp. XVI:** 289
"Odes to Natural Processes" (Updike), **Retro. Supp. I:** 323
"Ode to a Nightingale" (Keats), **II:** 368; **Retro. Supp. II:** 261; **Supp. IX:** 52
"Ode to Autumn" (Masters), **Supp. I Part 2:** 458
"Ode to Cervantes" (Salinas), **Supp. XIII:** 324
"Ode to Coit Tower" (Corso), **Supp. XII:** 122
"Ode to Ethiopia" (Dunbar), **Supp. II Part 1:** 199, 207, 208, 209
"Ode to Fear" (Tate), **IV:** 128
Ode to Harvard and Other Poems, An (Bynner), **Supp. XV:** 41, 44
"Ode to Meaning" (Pinsky), **Supp. VI:** **249-250,** 251
"Ode to Night" (Masters), **Supp. I Part 2:** 458
"Ode to Our Young Pro-Consuls of the Air" (Tate), **IV:** 135
"Ode to the Austrian Socialists" (Benét), **Supp. XI:** 46, 58
"Ode to the Confederate Dead" (Tate), **II:** 551; **IV:** 124, 133, 137; **Supp. X:** 52
"Ode to the Johns Hopkins University" (Lanier), **Supp. I Part 1:** 370
"Ode to the Maggot" (Komunyakaa), **Supp. XIII:** 130
"Ode to the Mexican Experience" (Salinas), **Supp. XIII:** 316-317
"Ode to the Virginian Voyage" (Drayton), **IV:** 135
"Ode to the West Wind" (Shelley), **Retro. Supp. I:** 308; **Supp. I Part 2:** 728; **Supp. IX:** 52; **Supp. XII:** 117; **Supp. XIV:** 271-272; **Supp. XV:** 221
"Ode to Walt Whitman" (Benét), **Supp. XI:** 52
Odets, Clifford, **Supp. I Part 1:** 277, 295; **Supp. I Part 2:** 679; **Supp. II Part 2: 529-554; Supp. IV Part 2:** 587; **Supp. V:** 109; **Supp. VIII:** 96
Odier, Daniel, **Supp. III Part 1:** 97
"Odi et Amo" (Catullus), **Supp. XV:** 27, 32, 35
O'Donnell, George Marion, **II:** 67
O'Donnell, Thomas F., **II:** 131
"Odor of Verbena" (Faulkner), **II:** 66

O'Doul, Lefty, **II:** 425
"Odysseus to Telemachus" (Brodsky), **Supp. VIII:** 25
Odyssey (Bryant, trans.), **Supp. I Part 1:** 158
Odyssey (Homer), **III:** 14, 470; **Retro. Supp. I:** 286, 290; **Retro. Supp. II:** 121; **Supp. I Part 1:** 185; **Supp. IV Part 2:** 631; **Supp. IX:** 211; **Supp. X:** 114; **Supp. XIV:** 191; **Supp. XVII:** 117
"Odyssey of a Wop, The" (Fante), **Supp. XI:** 164, 165
Oedipus Rex (Sophocles), **I:** 137; **III:** 145, 151, 152, 332; **Supp. I Part 2:** 428
Oedipus Tyrannus (Sophocles), **II:** 203; **Supp. XV:** 265
Oehlschlaeger, Fritz, **Supp. IX:** 123
"Of Alexander Crummell" (Du Bois), **Supp. II Part 1:** 170
O'Faoláin, Seán, **Supp. II Part 1:** 101
Of a World That Is No More (Singer), **IV:** 16
"Of Booker T. Washington and Others" (Du Bois), **Supp. II Part 1:** 168
"Of Bright & Blue Birds & the Gala Sun" (Stevens), **IV:** 93
"Of Christian Heroism" (Ozick), **Supp. V:** 272
"Of Dying Beauty" (Zukofsky), **Supp. III Part 2:** 610
"Of 'Father and Son'" (Kunitz), **Supp. III Part 1:** 262
Offenbach, Jacques, **II:** 427
"Offering for Mr. Bluehart, An" (Wright), **Supp. III Part 2:** 596, 601
"Offerings" (Mason), **Supp. VIII:** 141
"Official Piety" (Whittier), **Supp. I Part 2:** 687
"Off-Shore Pirates, The" (Fitzgerald), **II:** 88
Off the Beaten Path (Proulx), **Supp. VII:** 261
Off the Beaten Path: Stories of Place, **Supp. XVI:** 22
"Off the Cuff" (Simpson), **Supp. IX:** 278
Off the Map (Levine), **Supp. V:** 178
O'Flaherty, George, **Supp. I Part 1:** 202, 205-206
O'Flaherty, Kate. *See* Chopin, Kate
O'Flaherty, Thomas, **Supp. I Part 1:** 202, 203-204, 205
O'Flaherty, Thomas, Jr., **Supp. I Part 1:** 202
"Of Maids and Other Muses" (Alvarez), **Supp. VII:** 11
"Of Margaret" (Ransom), **III:** 491

Of Mice and Men (Steinbeck), **IV:** 51, 57-58
"Of Modern Poetry" (Stevens), **IV:** 92
Of Plymouth Plantation (Bradford), **Retro. Supp. II:** 161, 162
Of Plymouth Plantation (Morison, ed.), **Supp. I Part 2:** 494
"Ofrenda for Lobo" (Mora), **Supp. XIII:** 224
"Often" (Kenyon), **Supp. VII:** 171
"Often, in Dreams, He Moved through a City" (Dobyns), **Supp. XIII:** 90
"Of the Coming of John" (Du Bois), **Supp. II Part 1:** 170
"Of the Culture of White Folk" (Du Bois), **Supp. II Part 1:** 175
Of the Farm (Updike), **IV:** 214, 217, 223-225, 233; **Retro. Supp. I:** 318, 329, 332
"Of the Four-Winged Cherubim as Signature" (Sobin), **Supp. XVI:** 287
"Of 'The Frill'" (McCarriston), **Supp. XIV:** 274
"Of the Passing of the First-Born" (Du Bois), **Supp. II Part 1:** 170
"Of the Sorrow Songs" (Du Bois), **Supp. II Part 1:** 170
"Of the Wings of Atlanta" (Du Bois), **Supp. II Part 1:** 170
Of This Time, Of This Place (Trilling), **Supp. III Part 2:** 498, 504
Of Time and the River (Wolfe), **IV:** 450, 451, 452, 455, 456, 457, 458, 459, 462, 464-465, 467, 468, 469
Of Woman Born: Motherhood as Experience and Institution (Rich), **Supp. I Part 2:** 554, 567-569
Of Women and Their Elegance (Mailer), **Retro. Supp. II:** 209
Ogden, Archie, **Supp. XIII:** 174
Ogden, Henry, **II:** 298
Ogden, Uzal, **Supp. I Part 2:** 516
"Oh, Fairest of the Rural Maids" (Bryant), **Supp. I Part 1:** 169
"Oh, Immobility, Death's Vast Associate" (Dobyns), **Supp. XIII:** 89
"Oh, Joseph, I'm So Tired" (Yates), **Supp. XI:** 348
Oh, the Places You'll Go! (Geisel), **Supp. XVI:** 111
Oh, the Thinks You can Think! (Geisel), **Supp. XVI:** 111
"O'Halloran's Luck" (Benét), **Supp. XI:** 47
O'Hara, Frank, **Supp. XII:** 121; **Supp. XV:** 93, 176, 177, 178, 179-180, 182, 186, 187, 215-216
O'Hara, J. D., **Supp. IV Part 1:** 43; **Supp. V:** 22; **Supp. XVI:** 221
O'Hara, John, **I:** 375, 495; **II:** 444,

459; **III:** 66, **361-384; IV:** 59; **Retro. Supp. I:** 99, 112; **Supp. I Part 1:** 196; **Supp. II Part 1:** 109; **Supp. IV Part 1:** 31, 383; **Supp. IV Part 2:** 678; **Supp. V:** 95; **Supp. VIII:** 151, 156; **Supp. IX:** 208
O'Hehir, Andrew, **Supp. XII:** 280
"Ohio Pagan, An" (Anderson), **I:** 112, 113
Oh Say Can You Say? (Geisel), **Supp. XVI:**111
Oil! (Sinclair), **Supp. V:** 276, 277-279, 282, 288, 289
Oil Notes (Bass), **Supp. XVI:**17
"Oil Painting of the Artist as the Artist" (MacLeish), **III:** 14
O'Keeffe, Georgia, **Supp. IX:** 62, 66
"Oklahoma" (Levis), **Supp. XI:** 267
Oktenberg, Adrian, **Supp. XVII:** 76
"Old, Old, Old, Old Andrew Jackson" (Lindsay), **Supp. I Part 2:** 398
"Old Amusement Park, An" (Moore), **III:** 216
"Old Angel Midnight" (Kerouac), **Supp. III Part 1:** 229-230
"Old Apple Dealer, The" (Hawthorne), **II:** 227, 233-235, 237, 238
"Old Apple-Tree, The" (Dunbar), **Supp. II Part 1:** 198
"Old Army Game, The" (Garrett), **Supp. VII:** 100-101
"Old Aunt Peggy" (Chopin), **Retro. Supp. II:** 64
"Old Barn at the Bottom of the Fogs, The" (Frost), **Retro. Supp. I:** 138
Old Beauty and Others, The (Cather), **I:** 331
Old Bruin: Commodore Matthew C. Perry, 1794-1858 (Morison), **Supp. I Part 2:** 494-495
"Old Cracked Tune, An" (Kunitz), **Supp. III Part 1:** 264
Old Curiosity Shop, The (Dickens), **I:** 458; **Supp. I Part 2:** 409
Oldest Killed Lake in North America, The (Carruth), **Supp. XVI:**51
"Oldest Man, The" (M. F. K. Fisher), **Supp. XVII:** 91
"Old Farmer, The" (Jeffers), **Supp. II Part 2:** 418
Old-Fashioned Girl, An (Alcott), **Supp. I Part 1:** 29, 41, 42
"Old Father Morris" (Stowe), **Supp. I Part 2:** 586
"Old Flame, The" (Lowell), **II:** 550
"Old Florist" (Roethke), **III:** 531
"Old Folsom Prison" (Matthews), **Supp. IX:** 165
Old Forest, The (Taylor), **Supp. V:** 320, 321, 326, 327

"Old Forest, The" (Taylor), **Supp. V:** 313, 321, 323, 326
Old Forest and Other Stories (Taylor), **Supp. V:** 326
Old Friends and New (Jewett), **II:** 402; **Retro. Supp. II:** 137, 140
Old Glory, The (Lowell), **II:** 543, 545-546, 555; **Retro. Supp. II:** 188
"Old Homestead, The" (Dunbar), **Supp. II Part 1:** 198
"Old Iron" (Nye), **Supp. XIII:** 276
"Old Ironsides" (Holmes), **Supp. I Part 1:** 302
"Old Lady We Saw, An" (Shields), **Supp. VII:** 310-311
"Old Love" (Singer), **Retro. Supp. II:** 307
"Old McGrath Place, The" (McGrath), **Supp. X:** 114
"Old Maid, The" (Wharton), **Retro. Supp. I:** 381, 382
"Old Man" (Faulkner), **II:** 68, 69
Old Man and the Sea, The (Hemingway), **II:** 250, 256-257, 258, 265; **III:** 40; **Retro. Supp. I:** 180, **185,** 186
"Old Man Drunk" (Wright), **Supp. III Part 2:** 595
"Old Man Feeding Hens" (Francis), **Supp. IX:** 78
"Old Man on the Hospital Porch" (Ríos), **Supp. IV Part 2:** 546-547
Old Man Rubbing His Eyes (R. Bly), **Supp. IV Part 1:** 65
"Old Manse, The" (Hawthorne), **II:** 224
"Old Man's Winter Night, An" (Frost), **Retro. Supp. I:** 126, 131
Old Man Who Love Cheese, The (Keillor), **Supp. XVI:**177
"Old Man with a Dog" (Wright), **Supp. XV:** 346
"Old Meeting House, The" (Stowe), **Supp. I Part 2:** 586
"Old Memory, An" (Dunbar), **Supp. II Part 1:** 198
"Old Men, The" (McCarthy), **II:** 566
"Old Men Pitching Horseshoes" (X. J. Kennedy), **Supp. XV:** 166
Old Money (Wasserstein), **Supp. XV:** 333-334
"Old Morgue, The" (Prose), **Supp. XVI:**250
Old Morning Program, The (radio show, Keillor). See *Prairie Home Companion, A* (radio show, Keillor)
"Old Mortality" (Porter), **III:** 436, 438-441, 442, 445, 446
"Old Mrs. Harris" (Cather), **I:** 332; **Retro. Supp. I:** 19

Old Neighborhood, The (Mamet), **Supp. XIV:**240, 241, 242, 249-250, 251, 252, 254
Old New York (Wharton), **IV:** 322; **Retro. Supp. I:** 381
"Ol' Doc Hyar" (Campbell), **Supp. II Part 1:** 202
Old One-Two, The (Gurney), **Supp. V:** 98
"Old Order, The" (Porter), **III:** 443, 444-445, 451
"Old Osawatomie" (Sandburg), **III:** 584
Old Patagonia Express, The: By Train through the Americas (Theroux), **Supp. VIII:** 322
"Old People, The" (Faulkner), **II:** 71-72
"Old Poet Moves to a New Apartment 14 Times, The" (Zukofsky), **Supp. III Part 2:** 628
Old Possum's Book of Practical Cats (Eliot), **Supp. XIII:** 228, 344
"Old Red" (Gordon), **II:** 199, 200, 203
Old Red and Other Stories (Gordon), **II:** 157
Old Régime in Canada, The (Parkman), **Supp. II Part 2:** 600, 607, 608-609, 612
Old Religion, The (Mamet), **Supp. XIV:**253
Olds, Sharon, **Supp. X:** 201-217; **Supp. XI:** 139, 142, 244; **Supp. XII:** 229; **Supp. XIV:**265; **Supp. XVII:** 114, 240
"Old Saws" (Garrett), **Supp. VII:** 96-97
Old Testament, **I:** 109, 181, 300, 328, 401, 410, 419, 431, 457, 458; **II:** 166, 167, 219; **III:** 270, 272, 348, 390, 396; **IV:** 41, 114, 152, 309; **Retro. Supp. I:** 122, 140, 249, 311, 360; **Retro. Supp. II:** 299; **Supp. I Part 1:** 60, 104, 106, 151; **Supp. I Part 2:** 427, 515, 516; **Supp. IX:** 14. See also names of Old Testament books
"Old Things, The" (James), **Retro. Supp. I:** 229
"Old Times on the Mississippi" (Twain), **IV:** 199
Oldtown Folks (Stowe), **Supp. I Part 2:** 587, 596-598
"Old Town of Berwick, The" (Jewett), **Retro. Supp. II:** 132
"Old Trails" (Robinson), **III:** 513, 517
"Old Tyrannies" (Bourne), **I:** 233
"Old West" (Bausch), **Supp. VII:** 48
"Old Whorehouse, An" (Oliver), **Supp. VII:** 235

"Old Woman" (Pinsky), **Supp. VI:** 238
"Old Woman of Beare, The" (X. J. Kennedy), **Supp. XV:** 156
"Old Word, The" (Simic), **Supp. VIII:** 282
"Old-World Landowners" (Gogol), **Supp. XV:** 262
Oldys, Francis. *See* Chalmers, George
Oleanna (Mamet), **Supp. XIV:**239, 241, 245, 248, 250
Olendorf, Donna, **Supp. IV Part 1:** 196
"Olga Poems, The" (Levertov), **Supp. III Part 1:** 279-281
"Olive Groves of Thasos, The" (Clampitt), **Supp. IX:** 51-52
Oliver, Bill, **Supp. VIII:** 138
Oliver, Mary, **Supp. VII: 229-248; Supp. X:** 31; **Supp. XVI:**39; **Supp. XVII:** 111, 240
Oliver, Sydney, **I:** 409
Oliver Goldsmith: A Biography (Irving), **II:** 315
Oliver Twist (Dickens), **I:** 354; **Supp. IV Part 2:** 464
"Olivia" (Salinas), **Supp. XIII:** 316
Olivieri, David (pseudonym), **Retro. Supp. I:** 361. *See also* Wharton, Edith
Ollive, Samuel, **Supp. I Part 2:** 503
Olmsted, Frederick Law, **Supp. I Part 1:** 355
Olsen, Lance, **Supp. IV Part 1:** 54; **Supp. IV Part 2:** 623
Olsen, Tillie, **Supp. V:** 114, 220; **Supp. XIII: 291-309; Supp. XVI:**83, 90
Olson, Charles, **Retro. Supp. I:** 209; **Supp. II Part 1:** 30, 328; **Supp. II Part 2: 555-587; Supp. III Part 1:** 9, 271; **Supp. III Part 2:** 542, 624; **Supp. IV Part 1:** 139, 144, 146, 153, 154, 322; **Supp. IV Part 2:** 420, 421, 423, 426; **Supp. VIII:** 290, 291; **Supp. XII:** 2, 198; **Supp. XIII:** 104; **Supp. XIV:**96; **Supp. XV:** 177
Olson, Ray, **Supp. XVII:** 111, 112, 119
"Ol' Tunes, The" (Dunbar), **Supp. II Part 1:** 197
"O Lull Me, Lull Me" (Roethke), **III:** 536-537
Omar Khayyam, **Supp. I Part 1:** 363
O'Meally, Robert, **Retro. Supp. II:** 112
"Omen" (Komunyakaa), **Supp. XIII:** 126, 127
Omensetter's Luck (Gass), **Supp. VI: 80-82,** 87
Omeros (Walcott), **Supp. XV:** 264
"Ominous Baby, An" (Crane), **I:** 411

Ommateum, with Doxology (Ammons), **Supp. VII:** 24-26, 27, 28, 36
"Omnibus Jaunts and Drivers" (Whitman), **IV:** 350
Omoo: A Narrative of Adventures in the South Seas (Melville), **III:** 76-77, 79, 84; **Retro. Supp. I:** 247
O My Land, My Friends (H. Crane), **Retro. Supp. II:** 76
"On a Certain Condescension in Foreigners" (Lowell), **Supp. I Part 2:** 419
"On a Certain Engagement South of Seoul" (Carruth), **Supp. XVI:**47
"On a Child Who Lived One Minute" (X. J. Kennedy), **Supp. XV:** 152, 155
"On Acquiring Riches" (Banks), **Supp. V:** 5
On a Darkling Plain (Stegner), **Supp. IV Part 2:** 598, 607
On a Fire on the Moon (Mailer), **Retro. Supp. II:** 206
"On a Hill Far Away" (Dillard), **Supp. VI:** 28
"On a Honey Bee, Drinking from a Glass and Drowned Therein" (Freneau), **Supp. II Part 1:** 273
"On a Monument to a Pigeon" (Leopold), **Supp. XIV:**187-188
"On a Mountainside" (Wagoner), **Supp. IX:** 332
O'Nan, Stewart, **Supp. XI:** 348
"On an Old Photograph of My Son" (Carver), **Supp. III Part 1:** 140
"Onan's Soliloquy" (X. J. Kennedy), **Supp. XV:** 165
"On a Proposed Trip South" (W. C. Williams), **Retro. Supp. I:** 413
"On a Tree Fallen across the Road" (Frost), **Retro. Supp. I:** 134
"On a View of Pasadena from the Hills" (Winters), **Supp. II Part 2:** 795, 796-799, 814
"On a Visit to a Halfway House after a Long Absence" (Salinas), **Supp. XIII:** 325
"On a Windy Night" (Dixon), **Supp. XII:** 155
On Becoming a Novelist (Gardner), **Supp. VI:** 64
"On Being an American" (Toomer), **Supp. III Part 2:** 479
"On Being Asked to Write a Poem against the War in Vietnam" (Carruth), **Supp. XVI:**55-56
"On Being a Woman" (Parker), **Supp. IX:** 201
On Being Blue (Gass), **Supp. VI:** 77, 78, 86, 94; **Supp. XIV:**305

"On Being Too Inhibited" (Hay), **Supp. XIV:**130
On Beyond Zebra! (Geisel), **Supp. XVI:**105
"On Burroughs' Work" (Ginsberg), **Supp. II Part 1:** 320
Once (Walker), **Supp. III Part 2:** 519, 522, 530
Once at Antietam (Gaddis), **Supp. IV Part 1:** 285
"Once by the Pacific" (Frost), **II:** 155; **Retro. Supp. I:** 122, 137
"Once More, the Round" (Roethke), **III:** 529
Once More around the Block: Familiar Essays (Epstein), **Supp. XIV:**107
"Once More to the Lake" (White), **Supp. I Part 2:** 658, 668, 673-675
"On Certain Political Measures Proposed to Their Consideration" (Barlow), **Supp. II Part 1:** 82
"Once There Was Light" (Kenyon), **Supp. VII:** 171-172
Ondaatje, Michael, **Supp. IV Part 1:** 252
"On Dining Alone" (M. F. K. Fisher), **Supp. XVII:** 83
On Distant Ground (R. O. Butler), **Supp. XII:** 62, **66-68,** 69, 74
O'Neale, Sondra, **Supp. IV Part 1:** 2
"One A.M. with Voices" (X. J. Kennedy), **Supp. XV:** 157
"One Arm" (T. Williams), **IV:** 383
One Arm, and Other Stories (T. Williams), **IV:** 383
"One Art" (Bell), **Supp. X:** 2
One Art (Bishop), **Retro. Supp. II:** 51
"One Art" (Bishop), **Retro. Supp. II:** 50; **Supp. I Part 1:** 72, 73, 82, 93, 94-95, 96; **Supp. XV:** 126
"One Art: The Poetry of Elizabeth Bishop, 1971-1976" (Schwartz), **Supp. I Part 1:** 81
One Big Self: Prisoners of Louisiana (Wright and Luster), **Supp. XV:** 337, 344, 350, **351-353**
"One Blessing had I than the rest" (Dickinson), **Retro. Supp. I:** 45
"One Body" (Hass), **Supp. VI:** 106
One Boy's Boston, 1887-1901 (Morison), **Supp. I Part 2:** 494
"One Coat of Paint" (Ashbery), **Supp. III Part 1:** 26
"One Dash-Horses" (Crane), **I:** 416
One Day (Morris), **III:** 233-236
One Day, When I Was Lost (Baldwin), **Retro. Supp. II:** 13; **Supp. I Part 1:** 48, 66, 67
"One Dead Friend" (Kumin), **Supp. IV Part 2:** 441

One Fish Two Fish Red Fish Blue Fish (Geisel), **Supp. XVI:**108
One Flew Over the Cuckoo's Nest (Kesey), **III:** 558
One for the Rose (Levine), **Supp. V:** 178, 179, 181, 187, 189-191
"One for the Rose" (Levine), **Supp. V:** 181, 190
"One Friday Morning" (Hughes), **Supp. I Part 1:** 330
"One Holy Night" (Cisneros), **Supp. VII:** 69-70
"One Home" (Stafford), **Supp. XI:** 321
"$106,000 Blood Money" (Hammett), **Supp. IV Part 1:** 345, 346
$106,000 Blood Money (Hammett), **Supp. IV Part 1:** 345
One Hundred Days in Europe (Holmes), **Supp. I Part 1:** 317
100 Faces of Death, The, Part IV (Boyle), **Supp. VIII:** 16
158-Pound Marriage, The (Irving), **Supp. VI:** 163, 164, **167-170**
O'Neil, Elizabeth Murrie, **Retro. Supp. I:** 427
O'Neill, Brendan, **Supp. XII:** 286
O'Neill, Eugene, **I:** 66, 71, 81, 94, 393, 445; **II:** 278, 391, 427, 585; **III:** 151, 165, **385-408;** **IV:** 61, 383; **Retro. Supp. II:** 82, 104; **Supp. III Part 1:** 177-180, 189; **Supp. IV Part 1:** 359; **Supp. IV Part 2:** 587, 607; **Supp. V:** 277; **Supp. VIII:** 332, 334; **Supp. XIV:**239, 320, 328; **Supp. XVI:**193; **Supp. XVII:** 96, 99-100, 103, 105, 107
"One Is a Wanderer" (Thurber), **Supp. I Part 2:** 616
"1 January 1965" (Brodsky), **Supp. VIII:** 23-24
One L (Turow), **Supp. XVII: 214,** 215, 217
"One Last Look at the Adige: Verona in the Rain" (Wright), **Supp. III Part 2:** 603
One Life (Rukeyser), **Supp. VI:** 273, 281, 283
One Life at a Time, Please (Abbey), **Supp. XIII:** 13
One Man in His Time (Glasgow), **II:** 178, 184
"One Man's Fortunes" (Dunbar), **Supp. II Part 1:** 211, 212-213
One Man's Initiation (Dos Passos), **I:** 476-477, 479, 488
"One Man's Meat" (White), **Supp. I Part 2:** 655
One Man's Meat (White), **Supp. I Part 2:** 654, 669, 676
"One Moment on Top of the Earth" (Nye), **Supp. XIII:** 282
One More July: A Football Dialogue with Bill Curry (Plimpton), **Supp. XVI:**243
"One More Song" (Lindsay), **Supp. I Part 2:** 400-401
"One More Thing" (Carver), **Supp. III Part 1:** 138, 144
"One More Time" (Gordon), **II:** 200
One Nation (Stegner), **Supp. IV Part 2:** 599, 608
"One-Night Homecoming" (X. J. Kennedy), **Supp. XV:** 167
"ONE NIGHT STAND" (Baraka), **Supp. II Part 1:** 32
"One of Our Conquerors" (Bourne), **I:** 223
One of Ours (Cather), **I:** 322-323; **Retro. Supp. I:** 1, 3, **13-15,** 20
"One of the Missing" (Bierce), **I:** 201-202
"One of the Rooming Houses of Heaven" (Doty), **Supp. XI:** 131
"One of the Smallest" (Stern), **Supp. IX:** 299-300
"One of Us" (Fante), **Supp. XI:** 165
"One Out of Twelve: Writers Who Are Women in Our Century" (Olsen), **Supp. XIII:** 294
"One Part Humor, 2 Parts Whining" (Kakutani), **Supp. XI:** 38
"One Person" (Wylie), **Supp. I Part 2:** 709, 724-727
"One Sister have I in our house" (Dickinson), **Retro. Supp. I:** 34
"One Song, The" (Strand), **Supp. IV Part 2:** 619
"One Summer in Spain" (Coover), **Supp. V:** 40
One Thousand Avant-Garde Plays (Koch), **Supp. XV:** 187
One Time, One Place: Mississippi in the Depression, a Snapshot Album (Welty), **Retro. Supp. I:** 339, 343, 344
1 x 1 (One Times One) (Cummings), **I:** 430, 436, 438-439, 441, 446, 447, 448
"One Touch of Nature" (McCarthy), **II:** 580
One Train (Koch), **Supp. XV:** 177, 184
"One Trip Abroad" (Fitzgerald), **II:** 95
One True Thing (film), **Supp. XVII:** 176
One True Thing (Quindlen), **Supp. XVII:** 166, **174-176**
"One Way" (Creeley), **Supp. IV Part 1:** 150-151
One Way or Another (Cameron), **Supp. XII:** 81
One-Way Ticket (Hughes), **Retro. Supp. I:** 206, 207, 208; **Supp. I Part 1:** 333-334
One Way to Heaven (Cullen), **Supp. IV Part 1:** 170, 172
One Way to Spell Man (Stegner), **Supp. IV Part 2:** 595, 598, 601, 609
"One Way to Spell Man" (Stegner), **Supp. IV Part 2:** 601
One Whose Eyes Open When You Close Your Eyes, The (F. Wright), **Supp. XVII:** 240, 243
"One Who Skins Cats, The" (Gunn Allen), **Supp. IV Part 1:** 331
"One Who Went Forth to Feel Fear" (Grimms), **Supp. X:** 86
"One Winter I Devise a Plan of My Own" (Ríos), **Supp. IV Part 2:** 549
One Winter Night in August (X. J. Kennedy), **Supp. XV:** 154, 162
One Writer's Beginnings (Welty), **Retro. Supp. I:** 339, 340, 341, 343, 344, 355-356
"One Year" (Olds), **Supp. X:** 210
"On First Looking Out through Juan de la Cosa's Eyes" (Olson), **Supp. II Part 2:** 565, 566, 570, 579
"On First Opening *The Lyric Year*" (W. C. Williams), **Retro. Supp. I:** 414
"On Freedom's Ground" (Wilbur), **Supp. III Part 2:** 562
On Glory's Course (Purdy), **Supp. VII:** 275-276, 279, 280
On Grief and Reason (Brodsky), **Supp. VIII:** 31-32
"On Hearing a Symphony of Beethoven" (Millay), **III:** 132-133
"On Hearing the Airlines Will Use a Psychological Profile to Catch Potential Skyjackers" (Dunn), **Supp. XI:** 144-145
On Human Finery (Bell), **Supp. I Part 2:** 636
"On *Imagerie*: Esther Williams, 1944" (Sobin), **Supp. XVI:**294
"On Imminence: An Essay" (Sobin), **Supp. XVI:**291
On Liberty (Mill), **Supp. XI:** 196
"On Looking Alone at a Place" (M. F. K. Fisher), **Supp. XVII:** 91
"On Looking at a Copy of Alice Meynell's Poems, Given Me, Years Ago, by a Friend" (Lowell), **II:** 527-528
"On Lookout Mountain" (Hayden), **Supp. II Part 1:** 380
Only a Few of Us Left (Marquand), **III:** 55
"Only Animal, The" (F. Wright), **Supp. XVII:** 245

"Only Bar in Dixon, The" (Hugo), **Supp. VI:** 140, 141
Only Dark Spot in the Sky, The (Dove), **Supp. IV Part 1:** 244
"Only Good Indian, The" (Humphrey), **Supp. IX:** 101
Only in America (Golden), **Supp. VIII:** 244
"Only in the Dream" (Eberhart), **I:** 523
"Only Path to Tomorrow, The" (Rand), **Supp. IV Part 2:** 524
"Only Rose, The" (Jewett), **II:** 408
"Only Son of the Doctor, The" (Gordon), **Supp. IV Part 1:** 305, 306
"Only the Cat Escapes," **Supp. XII:** 150-151
"Only the Dead Know Brooklyn" (Wolfe), **IV:** 451
Only When I Laugh (Simon), **Supp. IV Part 2:** 575
On Moral Fiction (Gardner), **Supp. VI:** 61, **71,** 72, 73
"On Morality" (Didion), **Supp. IV Part 1:** 196
"On My Own" (Levine), **Supp. V:** 181, 189-190
"On My Own Work" (Wilbur), **Supp. III Part 2:** 541-542
On Native Grounds: An Interpretation of Modern American Prose Literature (Kazin), **I:** 517; **Supp. I Part 2:** 650; **Supp. VIII:** 93, 96-97, 98, **100-102**
"On Not Being a Dove" (Updike), **Retro. Supp. I:** 323
"On Open Form" (Merwin), **Supp. III Part 1:** 347-348, 353
On Photography (Sontag), **Supp. III Part 2:** 451, 458, 462-465
"On Political Poetry" (R. Bly), **Supp. IV Part 1:** 61
On Politics: A Carnival of Buncombe (Moos, ed.), **III:** 116
"On Pretentiousness" (Kushner), **Supp. IX:** 131-132
"On Quitting a Little College" (Stafford), **Supp. XI:** 321
"On Reading Eckerman's Conversations with Goethe" (Masters), **Supp. I Part 2:** 458
On Reading Shakespeare (L. P. Smith), **Supp. XIV:** 345-346
"On Reading to Oneself" (Gass), **Supp. VI:** 88, 89
On Revolution (Arendt), **Retro. Supp. I:** 87
"On Seeing Larry Rivers' *Washington Crossing the Delaware* at the Museum of Modern Art" (O'Hara), **Supp. XV:** 186
"On Seeing Red" (Walker), **Supp. III Part 2:** 527
"On Social Plays" (A. Miller), **III:** 147, 148, 159
"On Steinbeck's Story 'Flight'" (Stegner), **Supp. IV Part 2:** 596
"On Style" (Sontag), **Supp. III Part 2:** 456-459, 465-466
"On Suicide" (Hay), **Supp. XIV:** 130, 132
"On Teaching the Young Laurel to Shoot" (Bynner), **Supp. XV:** 50
"On the Antler" (Proulx), **Supp. VII:** 252-253
"On the Banks of the Wabash" (Paul Dresser), **Retro. Supp. II:** 94
"On the Beach, at Night" (Whitman), **IV:** 348
On the Boundary (Tillich), **Retro. Supp. I:** 326
"On the Building of Springfield" (Lindsay), **Supp. I Part 2:** 381
"On the Coast of Maine" (Hayden), **Supp. II Part 1:** 381
On the Contrary: Articles of Belief (McCarthy), **II:** 559, 562
"On the Death of a Friend's Child" (Lowell), **Supp. I Part 2:** 409
"On the Death of Senator Thomas J. Walsh" (Winters), **Supp. II Part 2:** 802, 806
"On the Death of Yeats" (Bogan), **Supp. III Part 1:** 59
"On the Death of Zhukov" (Brodsky), **Supp. VIII:** 27
"On the Disadvantages of Central Heating" (Clampitt), **Supp. IX:** 41, 47, 52
"On the Edge" (Levine), **Supp. V:** 181-182
On the Edge and Over (Levine), **Supp. V:** 178, 180-182, 186
On the Edge of the Great Rift: Three Novels of Africa (Theroux), **Supp. VIII:** 316
"On the Eve of the Feast of the Immaculate Conception, 1942" (Lowell), **II:** 538; **Retro. Supp. II:** 185
"On the Eyes of an SS Officer" (Wilbur), **Supp. III Part 2:** 548
"On the Fall of General Earl Cornwallis" (Freneau), **Supp. II Part 1:** 261
"On the Folly of Writing Poetry" (Freneau), **Supp. II Part 1:** 263
On the Frontier (Auden and Isherwood), **Supp. II Part 1:** 13; **Supp. XIV:** 163
On the Great Atlantic Rainway: Selected Poems, 1950-1988 (Koch), **Supp. XV:** 177
"On the Island" (Stern), **Supp. IX:** 290
"On the Late Eclipse" (Bryant), **Supp. I Part 1:** 152
On the Laws of the Poetic Art (Hecht), **Supp. X:** 58
"On the Marginal Way" (Wilbur), **Supp. III Part 2:** 558, 559
On the Mesa (Nichols), **Supp. XIII:** 268
"On the Moon and Matriarchal Consciousness" (Neumann), **Supp. IV Part 1:** 68
"On the Morning after the Sixties" (Didion), **Supp. IV Part 1:** 205, 206
On the Motion and Immobility of Douve (Bonnefoy; Kinnell, trans.), **Supp. III Part 1:** 235
"On the Murder of Lieutenant José del Castillo by the Falangist Bravo Martinez, July 12, 1936" (Levine), **Supp. V:** 187
"On the Night of a Friend's Wedding" (Robinson), **III:** 524
"On the Occasion of a Poem: Richard Hugo" (Wright), **Supp. III Part 2:** 596
On the Occasion of My Last Afternoon (Gibbons), **Supp. X:** 46, **50-53**
On the Origin of Species (Darwin), **Supp. XIV:** 192
"On the Parapet" (Tanner), **Retro. Supp. II:** 205
"On the Platform" (Nemerov), **III:** 287
On the Poetry of Philip Levine: Stranger to Nothing (Levis), **Supp. XI:** 257
"On the Powers of the Human Understanding" (Freneau), **Supp. II Part 1:** 274
On the Prejudices, Predilections, and Firm Beliefs of William Faulkner (Brooks), **Supp. XIV:** 13
"On the Pulse of Morning" (Angelou), **Supp. IV Part 1:** 15-17
"On the Railway Platform" (Jarrell), **II:** 370
"On the Rainy River" (O'Brien), **Supp. V:** 250
On the Rebound: A Story and Nine Poems (Purdy), **Supp. VII:** 276-277
"On the Religion of Nature" (Freneau), **Supp. II Part 1:** 275
"On the River" (Dunbar), **Supp. II Part 1:** 193
"On the River" (Levine), **Supp. V:** 193
On the River Styx and Other Stories (Matthiessen), **Supp. V:** 212
On the Road (Kerouac), **Retro. Supp.**

I: 102; **Supp. III Part 1:** 92, 218, 222-224, 226, 230-231; **Supp. V:** 336; **Supp. X:** 269; **Supp. XIII:** 275; **Supp. XIV:**138, 150; **Supp. XV:** 221
"On the Road Home" (Stevens), **Retro. Supp. I:** 306
On the Road with the Archangel (Buechner), **Supp. XII:** 54
On These I Stand: An Anthology of the Best Poems of Countee Cullen (Cullen), **Supp. IV Part 1:** 173
"On the Skeleton of a Hound" (Wright), **Supp. III Part 2:** 593
"On the Street: Monument" (Gunn Allen), **Supp. IV Part 1:** 326
"On the Subway" (Olds), **Supp. X:** 207
"On the System of Policy Hitherto Pursued by Their Government" (Barlow), **Supp. II Part 1:** 82
"On the Teaching of Modern Literature" (Trilling), **Supp. III Part 2:** 509-510
"On the Uniformity and Perfection of Nature" (Freneau), **Supp. II Part 1:** 275
"On the Universality and Other Attributes of the God of Nature" (Freneau), **Supp. II Part 1:** 275
"On the Use of Trisyllabic Feet in Iambic Verse" (Bryant), **Supp. I Part 1:** 156
On the Way toward a Phenomenological Psychology: The Psychology of William James (Linschoten), **II:** 362
"On the Way to Work" (Dunn), **Supp. XI:** 149-150
"On the Wide Heath" (Millay), **III:** 130
"On the Writing of Novels" (Buck), **Supp. II Part 1:** 121
On This Island (Auden), **Supp. II Part 1:** 11
"On Time" (O'Hara), **III:** 369-370
"Ontological Episode of the Asylum" (Carruth), **Supp. XVI:**48, 50
"Ontology of the Sentence, The" (Gass), **Supp. VI:** 77
"On Top" (Leopold), **Supp. XIV:**188
"On Top" (Snyder), **Supp. VIII:** 304
"On Translating Akhmatova" (Kunitz), **Supp. III Part 1:** 268
"On Waking to Old Debts" (Keillor), **Supp. XVI:**167
On William Stafford: The Worth of Local Things (Andrews, ed.), **Supp. XI:** 311, 312, 317, 321, 324, 326
"On Writing" (Carver), **Supp. III Part 1:** 142-143
"On Writing" (Nin), **Supp. X:** 182

Opatoshu, Joseph, **IV:** 9
"Open Boat, The" (Crane), **I:** 408, 415, 416-417, 423; **Retro. Supp. I:** 325; **Supp. XIV:**51
Open Boat and Other Stories (Crane), **I:** 408
Open Heart: A Patient's Story of Life-Saving Medicine and Life-Giving Friendship (Neugeboren), **Supp. XVI:**217, **229-230**
Open House (Roethke), **III:** 529-530, 540
"Open House" (Roethke), **III:** 529
"Opening, An" (Swenson), **Supp. IV Part 2:** 639
Opening of the Field, The (Duncan), **Supp. III Part 2:** 625
Opening the Hand (Merwin), **Supp. III Part 1:** 341, 353, 355
"Open Letter" (Roethke), **III:** 532, 534
"Open Letter to Surrealists Everywhere, An" (H. Miller), **III:** 184
Open Meeting, The (Gurney), **Supp. V:** 98
Open Net (Plimpton), **Supp. XVI:**241
"Open Road, The" (Dreiser), **II:** 44
Open Sea, The (Masters), **Supp. I Part 2:** 471
Open Season: Sporting Adventures (Humphrey), **Supp. IX:** 95
"Open the Gates" (Kunitz), **Supp. III Part 1:** 264-265, 267
"Opera Company, The" (Merrill), **Supp. III Part 1:** 326
"Operation, The" (Sanders), **Supp. XVI:**266
"Operation, The" (Sexton), **Supp. II Part 2:** 675, 679
Operation Shylock: A Confession (P. Roth), **Retro. Supp. II:** 279, 280, 291
Operation Sidewinder (Shepard), **Supp. III Part 2:** 434-435, 439, 446-447
Operations in North African Waters (Morison), **Supp. I Part 2:** 490
Operation Wandering Soul (Powers), **Supp. IX:** 212, **217-219**
Opffer, Emil, **Retro. Supp. II:** 80
"Opinion" (Du Bois), **Supp. II Part 1:** 173
Opinionator, The (Bierce), **I:** 209
Opinions of Oliver Allston (Brooks), **I:** 254, 255, 256
O Pioneers! (Cather), **I:** 314, 317-319, 320; **Retro. Supp. I:** 1, 5, 6, **7-9,** 10, 13, 20; **Retro. Supp. II:** 136
Oppen, George, **IV:** 415; **Supp. III Part 2:** 614, 615, 616, 626, 628; **Supp. XIV:**285, 286, 287; **Supp.**

XVI:282, 283; **Supp. XVII:** 243
Oppenheim, James, **I:** 106, 109, 239, 245; **Supp. XV:** 294, 296, 298, 299, 301, 302, 307, 313
Oppenheimer, J. Robert, **I:** 137, 492
Oppenheimer, Judy, **Supp. IX:** 115, 116, 118, 120, 126
"Opportunity for American Fiction, An" (Howells), **Supp. I Part 2:** 645-646
Opposing Self, The (Trilling), **Supp. III Part 2:** 506-507
"Opposition" (Lanier), **Supp. I Part 1:** 368, 373
Opticks: A Poem in Seven Sections (Goldbarth), **Supp. XII:** 177, **178**
"Optimist's Daughter, The" (Welty), **IV:** 280-281
Optimist's Daughter, The (Welty), **IV:** 261, 280; **Retro. Supp. I:** 339, 355
Options (O. Henry), **Supp. II Part 1:** 410
Opus Posthumous (Stevens), **IV:** 76, 78
Opus Posthumous (W. Stevens), **Supp. XVII:** 241
Oracle at Stoneleigh Court, The (Taylor), **Supp. V:** 328
Orage, Alfred, **III:** 473
Orange, Max (pseudonym). *See* Heller, Joseph
Orange Fish, The (Shields), **Supp. VII:** 318, 320, 323, 328
Oranges (McPhee), **Supp. III Part 1:** 298-299, 301, 309
"Oranging of America, The" (Apple), **Supp. XVII:** 3-4, 6
Oranging of America and Other Short Stories, The (Apple), **Supp. XVII:** 1-2, **3-4,** 7, 8
Oration Delivered at Washington, July Fourth, 1809 (Barlow), **Supp. II Part 1:** 80, 83
Orations and Addresses (Bryant), **Supp. I Part 1:** 158
Orators, The (Auden), **Supp. II Part 1:** 6, 7, 11, 18-19
Orb Weaver, The (Francis), **Supp. IX:** **81-82**
"Orchard" (Doolittle), **Supp. I Part 1:** 263-264, 265, 266
"Orchard" (Eberhart), **I:** 539
Orchard, The (B. Kelly), **Supp. XVII:** 123, 127, **130-133**
"Orchard, The" (B. Kelly), **Supp. XVII:** 133
Orchard Keeper, The (McCarthy), **Supp. VIII: 175-176**
Orchestra (Davies), **III:** 541
"Orchids" (Roethke), **III:** 530-531

"Or Consider Prometheus" (Clampitt), **Supp. IX:** 44
Ordeal of Mansart, The (Du Bois), **Supp. II Part 1:** 185-186
Ordeal of Mark Twain, The (Brooks), **I:** 240, 247, 248; **II:** 482
"Order of Insects" (Gass), **Supp. VI:** 83
Order Out of Chaos (McPherson), **Supp. IV Part 1:** 2, 12
"Ordinary Afternoon in Charlottesville, An" (Wright), **Supp. V:** 344
"Ordinary Days" (Dunn), **Supp. XI:** 151
"Ordinary Evening in New Haven, An" (Stevens), **IV:** 91-92; **Retro. Supp. I:** 297, 300, 311, 312
Ordinary Heroes (Turow), **Supp. XVII: 221-222,** 223
Ordinary Love (Smiley), **Supp. VI:** 292, **299-300**
Ordinary Love; and Good Will: Two Novellas (Smiley), **Supp. VI:** 292, **299-300**
Ordinary Miracles (Jong), **Supp. V:** 115, 130-131
"Ordinary Time: Virginia Woolf and Thucydides on War" (Carson), **Supp. XII:** 111
"Ordinary Women, The" (Stevens), **IV:** 81
Ordways, The (Humphrey), **Supp. IX:** 95, **98-100,** 109; **Supp. XV:** 353
"Oread" (Doolittle), **II:** 520-521; **Supp. I Part 1:** 265-266
Oregon Message, An (Stafford), **Supp. XI: 328-329**
Oregon Trail, The (Parkman), **II:** 312; **Supp. II Part 2:** 592, 595-596, 598, 606
Oresteia (Aeschylus), **Supp. IX:** 103
"Orestes at Tauris" (Jarrell), **II:** 376, 377
Orfalea, Gregory, **Supp. XIII:** 278
Orfeo ed Euridice (Gluck), **II:** 210, 211
Orff, Carl, **Supp. X:** 63
"Organizer's Wife, The" (Bambara), **Supp. XI:** 8-9
"Organmeister: Hasse After Marienkirche" (Bierds), **Supp. XVII:** 34
"Orgy" (Rukeyser), **Supp. VI:** 280
Orgy, The (Rukeyser), **Supp. VI:** 274, 283
"Orientation of Hope, The" (Locke), **Supp. XIV:**212-213
Orient Express (Dos Passos), **I:** 480
"Orient Express, The" (Jarrell), **II:** 382, 383-384
Origen, Adamantius, **IV:** 153
"Origin" (Harjo), **Supp. XII:** 219

Original Child Bomb: Points for Meditation to Be Scratched on the Walls of a Cave (Merton), **Supp. VIII:** 203
Original Essays on the Poetry of Anne Sexton (George), **Supp. IV Part 2:** 450
"Original Follies Girl, The" (Z. Fitzgerald), **Supp. IX:** 71
Original Light (Goldbarth), **Supp. XII:** 181, **183-184,** 188
Original of Laura, The (Nabokov), **Retro. Supp. I:** 266
"Original Sin" (Jeffers), **Supp. II Part 2:** 426
"Original Sin" (Warren), **IV:** 245
"Origin of Extermination in the Imagination, The" (Gass), **Supp. VI:** 89
Origin of Species, The (Darwin), **II:** 173, 462; **Supp. XVI:**13
Origin of the Brunists, The (Coover), **Supp. V:** 39, 41, 52
"Origins and History of Consciousness" (Rich), **Supp. I Part 2:** 570
"Origins of a Nonfiction Writer" (Talese), **Supp. XVII:** 208
"Origins of a Poem" (Levertov), **Supp. III Part 1:** 273
"Origins of the Beat Generation, The" (Kerouac), **Supp. III Part 1:** 231
Origo, Iris, **IV:** 328
"O'Riley's Late-Bloomed Little Son" (X. J. Kennedy), **Supp. XV:** 159
"Orion" (Rich), **Supp. I Part 2:** 557
O'Riordan, Conal Holmes O'Connell, **III:** 465
Orlacs Hände (film, Weine), **Supp. XVII:** 58
Orlando (V. Woolf), **Supp. XVII:** 86
Orlando (Woolf), **Supp. I Part 2:** 718; **Supp. VIII:** 263; **Supp. XII:** 9
Orlando Furioso (Ariosto), **Supp. XV:** 175
Orlovsky, Peter, **Supp. XII:** 121, 126; **Supp. XIV:**150
Ormond; or, The Secret Witness (Brown), **Supp. I Part 1:** 133-137
Ormonde, Czenzi, **Supp. IV Part 1:** 132
Ornament and Crime (Loos), **Supp. XVI:**187
Orne, Sarah. *See* Jewett, Sarah Orne
Ornithological Biography; or, An Account of the Habits of the Birds of the United States of America, and Interspersed with Delineations of American Scenery and Manners (Audubon), **7-10; Supp. XVI:**13
Ornitz, Samuel, **Supp. IX:** 227; **Supp. XIII:** 166

Orphan Angel, The (Wylie), **Supp. I Part 2:** 707, 709, 714, 717, 719-721, 722, 724
Orphan's Tale, An (Neugeboren), **Supp. XVI:**222, 223
Orpheus (Rukeyser), **Supp. VI:** 273
"Orpheus" (Winters), **Supp. II Part 2:** 801
"Orpheus (1)" (Atwood), **Supp. XIII:** 35
"Orpheus (2)" (Atwood), **Supp. XIII:** 35
"Orpheus, Eurydice, Hermes" (Rilke), **Supp. VIII:** 31, 32
"Orpheus Alone" (Strand), **Supp. IV Part 2:** 632
Orpheus Descending (T. Williams), **IV:** 380, 381, 382, 385, 386, 387, 389, 391-392, 395, 396, 398
Orr, Peter, **Supp. I Part 2:** 538, 540, 543
Ortega y Gasset, José, **I:** 218, 222; **Supp. IV Part 2:** 521
Ortiz, Simon J., **Supp. IV Part 1:** 319, 404; **Supp. IV Part 2: 497-515,** 557; **Supp. XII:** 217, 218
O'Ruddy, The (Crane), **I:** 409, 424
Orwell, George, **I:** 489; **II:** 454, 580; **Supp. I Part 2:** 523, 620; **Supp. II Part 1:** 143; **Supp. IV Part 1:** 236; **Supp. V:** 250; **Supp. VIII:** 241; **Supp. XIV:**112, 158; **Supp. XVII:** 228, 229
Osborn, Dwight, **III:** 218-219, 223
"Osborn Look, The" (Morris), **III:** 221
Osgood, Frances, **Supp. XVII:** 75
Osgood, J. R., **II:** 283
O'Shea, Kitty, **II:** 137
O'Shea, Milo, **Supp. XI:** 308
"Oshkikwe's Baby" (traditional Chippewa story), **Supp. IV Part 1:** 333
Oshogay, Delia, **Supp. IV Part 1:** 333
Ossana, Diana, **Supp. V:** 230-231, 232
Ossian, **Supp. I Part 2:** 491
Ossip, Kathleen, **Supp. X:** 201
Ostanovka v Pustyne (A halt in the wilderness) (Brodsky), **Supp. VIII:** 21
Oster, Judith, **Supp. XVI:**151
Ostriker, Alicia, **Supp. I Part 2:** 540; **Supp. IV Part 2:** 439, 447, 449; **Supp. X:** 207, 208; **Supp. XI:** 143; **Supp. XV:** 251
Ostrom, Hans, **Retro. Supp. I:** 195
Oswald, Lee Harvey, **III:** 234, 235
Oswald II (DeLillo), **Supp. VI:** 16
Oswald's Tale (Mailer), **Retro. Supp. II:** 212-213
O Taste and See (Levertov), **Supp. III**

Part 1: 278-279, 281
Othello (Shakespeare), **I:** 284-285
"Other, The" (Sexton), **Supp. II Part 2:** 692
Other America, The (Harrington), **I:** 306
Other Destinies: Understanding the American Indian Novel (Owens), **Supp. IV Part 1:** 404
"Other Frost, The" (Jarrell), **Retro. Supp. I:** 121
Other Gods: An American Legend (Buck), **Supp. II Part 1:** 123, 130-131
Other House, The (James), **Retro. Supp. I:** 229
"Other League of Nations, The" (Ríos), **Supp. IV Part 2:** 552
"Other Margaret, The" (Trilling), **Supp. III Part 2:** 504-505
"Other Miller, The" (Wolff), **Supp. VII:** 343-344
"Other Mothers" (Paley), **Supp. VI:** 225
"Other Night at Columbia, The" (Trilling), **Supp. XII:** 126
"Other Robert Frost, The" (Jarrell), **Retro. Supp. I:** 135
Others (Shields), **Supp. VII:** 310
Other Side, The (Gordon), **Supp. IV Part 1:** 299, 306, 307-309, 310-311
Other Side, The/El Otro Lado (Alvarez), **Supp. VII:** 9-12
Other Side of the River, The (Wright), **Supp. V:** 332-333, 342
"Other Side of the River, The" (Wright), **Supp. V:** 335
"Other Tradition, The" (Ashbery), **Supp. III Part 1:** 15, 18
"Other Two, The" (Wharton), **Retro. Supp. I:** 367
Other Voices, Other Rooms (Capote), **Supp. III Part 1:** 113-118, 121, 123-124
"Other War, The" (Cowley), **Supp. II Part 1:** 144
"Otherwise" (Kenyon), **Supp. VII:** 172, 174
Otherwise: New and Selected Poems (Kenyon), **Supp. VII:** 167, 172-174
Otherwise Than Being; or, Beyond Essence (Lévinas), **Supp. XVI:** 290, 291
"Other Woman, The" (Anderson), **I:** 114
Otho the Great: A Tragedy in Five Acts (Keats), **Supp. XII:** 113
Otis, Harrison Gray, **Supp. I Part 2:** 479-481, 483, 486, 488
Otis, James, **III:** 577; **Supp. I Part 2:** 486; **Supp. XV:** 229
O to Be a Dragon (Moore), **III:** 215
Otto, Rudolf, **Supp. XVII:** 243
"Ouija" (McClatchy), **Supp. XII:** 269-270
Oupensky, Peter, **Supp. XIV:** 188
Our America (Frank), **I:** 229; **Supp. IX:** 308
Our America (Michaels), **Retro. Supp. I:** 379
"Our Assistant's Column" (Twain), **IV:** 193
"Our Bourgeois Literature" (Sinclair), **Supp. V:** 281
Our Brains and What Ails Them (Gilman), **Supp. XI:** 207
Our Century (Wilder), **IV:** 374
"Our Christmas Party" (E. Stoddard), **Supp. XV:** 273, 278
Our Country (Strong), **Supp. XIV:** 64
"Our Countrymen in Chains!" (Whittier), **Supp. I Part 2:** 688
"Our Cultural Humility" (Bourne), **I:** 223, 228
Our Depleted Society (Seymour), **Supp. XIII:** 264
"Our Dust" (Wright), **Supp. XV:** 345, 346
"Our Father Who Drowns the Birds" (Kingsolver), **Supp. VII:** 208-209
"Our First House" (Kingston), **Supp. V:** 169
Our Gang (P. Roth), **Retro. Supp. II:** 287; **Supp. III Part 2:** 414; **Supp. IV Part 1:** 388
"Our Good Day" (Cisneros), **Supp. VII:** 60
Our Ground Time Here Will Be Brief (Kumin), **Supp. IV Part 2:** 450-452
Our House in the Last World (Hijuelos), **Supp. VIII:** 73, **76-79**, 87, 88
"Our Lady" (A. Finch), **Supp. XVII:** 77
"*Our Lady of the Annunciation*/Nuestra Señora de Anunciación" (Mora), **Supp. XIII:** 217, 224, 228
"Our Lady of Troy" (MacLeish), **III:** 3, 20
"Our Limitations" (Holmes), **Supp. I Part 1:** 314
"Our Martyred Soldiers" (Dunbar), **Supp. II Part 1:** 193
"Our Master" (Whittier), **Supp. I Part 2:** 704
"Our Mother Pocahontas" (Lindsay), **Supp. I Part 2:** 393
Our Mr. Wrenn: The Romantic Adventures of a Gentle Man (Lewis), **II:** 441
Our National Parks (Muir), **Supp. IX:** 181, 184
Our New York: A Personal Vision in Words and Photographs (Kazin), **Supp. VIII: 106-107**
"Our Old Aunt Who Is Now in a Retirement Home" (Shields), **Supp. VII:** 310
Our Old Home: A Series of English Sketches (Hawthorne), **II:** 225; **Retro. Supp. I:** 163
"Our Own Movie Queen" (Z. Fitzgerald), **Supp. IX:** 71
"Our River Now" (L.-Y. Lee), **Supp. XV:** 224, 225
Ourselves to Know (O'Hara), **III:** 362, 365
"Our Story Begins" (Wolff), **Supp. VII:** 345
Our Town (Wilder), **IV:** 357, 364, 365, 366, 368-369
"Our Unplanned Cities" (Bourne), **I:** 229, 230
Our Wonder World, **Retro. Supp. I:** 341
Ouspensky, P. D., **I:** 383
"Out" (Harjo), **Supp. XII:** 219
"'Out, Out'" (Frost), **Retro. Supp. I:** 131
"Outcast" (McKay), **Supp. X:** 135
"Outcasts of Poker Flats, The" (Harte), **Supp. II Part 1:** 345, 347-348
Outcroppings (Harte), **Supp. II Part 1:** 343
Out Cry (T. Williams), **IV:** 383, 393
Outcry, The (James), **Retro. Supp. I:** 235
"Outdoor Shower" (Olds), **Supp. X:** 214
Outerbridge Reach (Stone), **Supp. V:** 306-308
Outer Dark (McCarthy), **Supp. VIII: 176-177**
Outermost Dream, The: Essays and Reviews (Maxwell), **Supp. VIII: 171-172**
"Outing, The" (Baldwin), **Supp. I Part 1:** 63
"Out Like a Lamb" (Dubus), **Supp. VII:** 91
"Outline of an Autobiography" (Toomer), **Supp. III Part 2:** 478
Outlyer and Ghazals (Harrison), **Supp. VIII:** 41
"Out of Business" (Mora), **Supp. XIII:** 217
Out of My League (Plimpton), **Supp. XVI:** 233, 239
"Out of Nowhere into Nothing" (Anderson), **I:** 113

"Out of Season" (Hemingway), **II:** 263
"Out of the Cradle Endlessly Rocking" (Whitman), **IV:** 342, 343-345, 346, 351; **Retro. Supp. I:** 404, 406
"Out of the Deeps" (E. Stoddard), **Supp. XV:** 286
"Out of the Hospital and Under the Bar" (Ellison), **Retro. Supp. II:** 118-119; **Supp. II Part 1:** 246
"Out of the Rainbow End" (Sandburg), **III:** 594-595
"Out of the Sea, Early" (Swenson), **Supp. IV Part 2:** 645
"Out of the Snow" (Dubus), **Supp. VII:** 91
Out of the Stars (Purdy), **Supp. VII:** 281-282
Outre-Mer: A Pilgrimage beyond the Sea (Longfellow), **II:** 313, 491; **Retro. Supp. II:** 155, 165
"Outside" (Stafford), **Supp. XI:** 318
Outside, The (Glaspell), **Supp. III Part 1:** 179, 187
Outsider, The (Wright), **IV:** 478, 481, 488, 491-494, 495
Out West (Shanley), **Supp. XIV:**317
"Out with the Old" (Yates), **Supp. XI:** 342
"Ouzo for Robin" (Merrill), **Supp. III Part 1:** 326
"Oval Portrait, The" (Poe), **III:** 412, 415; **Retro. Supp. II:** 270
"Oven Bird, The" (Frost), **Retro. Supp. I:** 131; **Supp. XI:** 153
"Over by the River" (Maxwell), **Supp. VIII:** 169, 170
"Overgrown Pasture, The" (Lowell), **II:** 523
"Overheard through the Walls of the Invisible City" (Bidart), **Supp. XV:** 32
"Over 2,000 Illustrations and a Complete Concordance" (Bishop), **Retro. Supp. II:** 45; **Supp. I Part 1:** 90-91
"Over Kansas" (Ginsberg), **Supp. II Part 1:** 320
Overland to the Islands (Levertov), **Supp. III Part 1:** 275, 276
"Overnight Pass" (X. J. Kennedy), **Supp. XV:** 168
Overreachers, The (Talese), **Supp. XVII:** 202
"Over-Soul, The" (Emerson), **II:** 7
"Over the Hill" (Dubus), **Supp. VII:** 76, 79-80
Overtime (Gurney), **Supp. V:** 104
"Overwhelming Question, An" (Taylor), **Supp. V:** 323
Ovid, **I:** 62; **II:** 542-543; **III:** 457, 467, 468, 470; **Retro. Supp. I:** 63; **Supp.** **IV Part 2:** 634; **Supp. XII:** 264
"Ovid's Farewell" (McClatchy), **Supp. XII:** 257-258
Owen, David, **II:** 34
Owen, Maureen, **Supp. IV Part 2:** 423
Owen, Wilfred, **II:** 367, 372; **III:** 524; **Supp. X:** 146; **Supp. XVII:** 245
Owens, Hamilton, **III:** 99, 109
Owens, Louis, **Supp. IV Part 1:** 404
"O Where Are You Going?" (Auden), **Supp. X:** 116
Owl in the Attic, The (Thurber), **Supp. I Part 2:** 614
Owl in the Mask of the Dreamer, The: Collected Poems (Haines), **Supp. XII:** 211
"Owl in the Sarcophagus, The" (Stevens), **Retro. Supp. I:** 300
"Owl's Clover" (Stevens), **IV:** 75
Owl's Clover (Stevens), **Retro. Supp. I:** 298, **303-304**
Owl's Insomnia, Poems by Rafael Alberti, The (Strand, trans.), **Supp. IV Part 2:** 630
Owlstone Crown, The (X. J. Kennedy), **Supp. XV:** 162, **164**
"Owl Who Was God, The" (Thurber), **Supp. I Part 2:** 610
Owning Jolene (Hearon), **Supp. VIII:** **66-67**
Oxford Anthology of American Literature, The, **III:** 197; **Supp. I Part 1:** 254
Oxford Book of American Verse (Matthiessen, ed.), **Retro. Supp. I:** 40
Oxford Book of Children's Verse in America, The (Hall, ed.), **Supp. XIV:**126
Oxford Companion to Twentieth-Century Poetry (Hamilton, ed.), **Supp. XVII:** 243
Oxford History of the American People, The (Morison), **Supp. I Part 2:** 495-496
Oxford History of the United States, 1783-1917, The (Morison), **Supp. I Part 2:** 483-484
Oxherding Tale (Johnson), **Supp. VI:** **190-192**, 193, 194, 196
Oxley, William, **Supp. XV:** 125
"O Yes" (Olsen), **Supp. XIII:** 294, 298, **299-300**, 301
"O Youth and Beauty!" (Cheever), **Retro. Supp. I:** 335
"Oysters" (Sexton), **Supp. II Part 2:** 692
"Ozark Odes" (Wright), **Supp. XV:** 346
Ozick, Cynthia, **Supp. V: 257-274**; **Supp. VIII:** 141; **Supp. X:** 192; **Supp. XVII:** 42, 43, 49, 50
O-Zone (Theroux), **Supp. VIII:** 323-324

P

P. D. Kimerakov (Epstein), **Supp. XII:** 160, **162**
Pace, Patricia, **Supp. XI:** 245
Pacernik, Gary, **Supp. IX:** 287, 291
"Pacific Distances" (Didion), **Supp. IV Part 1:** 211
"Pacific Village" (M. F. K. Fisher), **Supp. XVII:** 83
Pack, Robert, **Supp. IV Part 2:** 621
"Packed Dirt, Churchgoing, a Dying Cat, a Traded Cat" (Updike), **IV:** 219
"Packing Mother's Things" (C. Frost), **Supp. XV:** 97
Paddock, Joe, **Supp. XVI:**36
Paddock, Nancy, **Supp. XVI:**36
Padel, Ruth, **Supp. XII:** 107
Padgett, Ron, **Supp. XV:** 190
Pafko at the Wall (DeLillo), **Supp. VI:** 4
"Pagan Prayer" (Cullen), **Supp. IV Part 1:** 170
"Pagan Rabbi, The" (Ozick), **Supp. V:** 262, 264, 265; **Supp. XVII:** 43
Pagan Rabbi and Other Stories, The (Ozick), **Supp. V:** 260, 261, 263-265
Pagan Spain (Wright), **IV:** 478, 488, 495
Page, Geraldine, **Supp. XV:** 7
Page, Kirby, **III:** 297
Page, Thomas Nelson, **II:** 174, 176, 194; **Supp. XIV:**61
Page, Walter Hines, **II:** 174, 175; **Supp. I Part 1:** 370
"Pages from Cold Point" (Bowles), **Supp. IV Part 1:** 85, 86, 87
Paid on Both Sides: A Charade (Auden), **Supp. II Part 1:** 6, 18-19
Paige, Satchel, **Supp. I Part 1:** 234
Paige, T. D. D., **III:** 475
Pain, Joseph, **Supp. I Part 2:** 502
Paine, Albert Bigelow, **I:** 249
Paine, Thomas, **I:** 490; **II:** 117, 302; **III:** 17, 148, 219; **Retro. Supp. I:** 390; **Supp. I Part 1:** 231; **Supp. I Part 2: 501-525**; **Supp. XI:** 55
"Pain has an Element of Blank" (Dickinson), **Retro. Supp. I:** 44
"Paint and Powder" (Z. Fitzgerald), **Supp. IX:** 71
Painted Bird, The (Kosinski), **Supp. VII:** 215-217, 219-221, 222, 227
Painted Desert (F. Barthelme), **Supp. XI:** 28-29, 32

Painted Dresses (Hearon), **Supp. VIII:** 63

"Painted Head" (Ransom), **III:** 491, 494; **Supp. II Part 1:** 103, 314

Painted Word, The (Wolfe), **Supp. III Part 2:** 580-581, 584; **Supp. XV:** 143

"Painter, The" (Ashbery), **Supp. III Part 1:** 5-6, 13

Painter Dreaming in the Scholar's House, The (Nemerov), **III:** 269

"Painters" (Rukeyser), **Supp. VI:** 281

"Painting a Mountain Stream" (Nemerov), **III:** 275

"Pair a Spurs" (Proulx), **Supp. VII:** 263-264

"Pair of Bright Blue Eyes, A" (Taylor), **Supp. V:** 321

"Pajamas" (Olds), **Supp. X:** 206

Pakula, Alan, **Supp. XIII:** 264

Palace at 4 A.M. (Giacometti), **Supp. VIII:** 169

"Palantine, The" (Whittier), **Supp. I Part 2:** 694, 696

Palatella, John, **Retro. Supp. II:** 48

Pale Fire (Nabokov), **III:** 244, 246, 252, 263-265; **Retro. Supp. I:** 264, 265, 266, 270, 271, 272, 276, 278, 335; **Supp. V:** 251, 253

"Pale Horse, Pale Rider" (Porter), **III:** 436, 437, 441-442, 445, 446, 449

Pale Horse, Pale Rider: Three Short Novels (Porter), **III:** 433, 436-442; **Supp. VIII:** 157

"Pale Pink Roast, The" (Paley), **Supp. VI:** 217

"Pale Rider" (B. Kelly), **Supp. XVII:** 132-133

Paley, Grace, **Supp. VI: 217-233; Supp. IX:** 212; **Supp. X:** 79, 164; **Supp. XII:** 309

Paley, William, **II:** 9

Palgrave, Francis Turner, **Retro. Supp. I:** 124; **Supp. XIV:**340

Palgrave's Golden Treasury (Palgrave), **IV:** 405

Palimpsest (Doolittle), **Supp. I Part 1:** 259, 268, 269, 270-271

Palimpsest (Vidal), **Supp. X:** 186

"Palingenesis" (Longfellow), **II:** 498

Pal Joey (O'Hara), **III:** 361, 367-368

"Pal Joey" stories (O'Hara), **III:** 361

Pallbearers Envying the One Who Rides (Dobyns), **Supp. XIII:** 89

"Palm, The" (Merwin), **Supp. III Part 1:** 355

Palmer, Charles, **II:** 111

Palmer, Elihu, **Supp. I Part 2:** 520

Palmer, George Herbert, **Supp. XIV:**197

Palmer, Michael, **Supp. IV Part 2:** 421; **Supp. XVI:**284; **Supp. XVII:** 240

Palmer, Samuel, **Supp. XV:** 81

Palmerston, Lord, **I:** 15

Palm-of-the-Hand-Stories (Kawabata), **Supp. XV:** 186

"Palo Alto: The Marshes" (Hass), **Supp. VI:** 100

Palpable God, A: Thirty Stories Translated from the Bible with an Essay on the Origins and Life of Narrative (Price), **Supp. VI:** 262, 267

Palubinskas, Helen, **Supp. X:** 292

Pamela (Richardson), **Supp. V:** 127

Pamela's First Musical (Wasserstein), **Supp. XV:** 333

Panache de bouquets (Komunyakaa; Cadieux, trans.), **Supp. XIII:** 127

Pan-African movement, **Supp. II Part 1:** 172, 175

Pandaemonium (Epstein), **Supp. XII:** 161, **172-173**

"Pandora" (Adams), **I:** 5

Pandora: New Tales of Vampires (Rice), **Supp. VII:** 295

Panek, LeRoy, **Supp. XIV:**27

"Pangolin, The" (Moore), **III:** 210

Panic: A Play in Verse (MacLeish), **III:** 2, 20

Panic in Needle Park (film), **Supp. IV Part 1:** 198

Pantagruel (Rabelais), **II:** 112

"Pantaloon in Black" (Faulkner), **II:** 71

Panther and the Lash, The (Hughes), **Retro. Supp. I:** 204, 211; **Supp. I Part 1:** 342-344, 345-346

"Panthers, The" (Southern), **Supp. XI:** 295

"Pan versus Moses" (Ozick), **Supp. V:** 262

"Paolo Castelnuovo" (Everwine), **Supp. XV:** 83-84

"Papa and Mama Dance, The" (Sexton), **Supp. II Part 2:** 688

"Papa Who Wakes Up Tired in the Dark" (Cisneros), **Supp. VII:** 62

Pape, Greg, **Supp. V:** 180; **Supp. XIII:** 312; **Supp. XV:** 73

"Paper Dolls Cut Out of a Newspaper" (Simic), **Supp. VIII:** 282

"Paper House, The" (Mailer), **III:** 42-43

Paper Lion (film, March), **Supp. XVI:**242

Paper Lion: Confessions of a Last-String Quarterback (Plimpton), **Supp. XVI:242-243**

Papernick, Jon, **Supp. XVII:** 50

Papers on Literature and Art (Fuller), **Supp. II Part 1:** 292, 299

Papini, Giovanni, **Supp. XVI:**195

Papp, Joseph, **Supp. IV Part 1:** 234

"Paprika Johnson" (Barnes), **Supp. III Part 1:** 33

"Par" (Bausch), **Supp. VII:** 54

"Parable in the Later Novels of Henry James" (Ozick), **Supp. V:** 257

"Parable of the Gift" (Glück), **Supp. V:** 89

"Parable of the Hostages" (Glück), **Supp. V:** 89

"Parable of the King" (Glück), **Supp. V:** 89

Parable of the Sower (O. Butler), **Supp. XIII: 66-67,** 69

Parable of the Talents (O. Butler), **Supp. XIII:** 61,**Supp. XIII:** 66, **67-69**

"Parable of the Trellis" (Glück), **Supp. V:** 89

Parachutes & Kisses (Jong), **Supp. V:** 115, 123, 125-126, 129

"Parade of Painters" (Swenson), **Supp. IV Part 2:** 645

"Paradigm, The" (Tate), **IV:** 128

Paradise (Barthelme), **Supp. IV Part 1:** 52

"Paradise" (Doty), **Supp. XI:** 123

Paradise Lost (Milton), **I:** 137; **II:** 168, 549; **IV:** 126; **Supp. XII:** 173, 297; **Supp. XV:** 181

Paradise Lost (Odets), **Supp. II Part 2:** 530, 531, 538-539, 550

"Paradise of Bachelors and the Tartarus of Maids, The" (Melville), **III:** 91

Paradise of Bombs, The (Sanders), **Supp. XVI:**265, 272-273

Paradise Poems (Stern), **Supp. IX: 293-294,** 295

Paradiso (Dante), **Supp. IX:** 50

"Paradoxes and Oxymorons" (Ashbery), **Supp. III Part 1:** 23-24

Paradox of Progressive Thought, The (Noble), **Supp. I Part 2:** 650

Paragon, The (Knowles), **Supp. XII:** 249

"Paragraphs" (Carruth), **Supp. XVI:**52-53

"Parameters" (Dunn), **Supp. XI:** 154

"Paraphrase" (Crane), **I:** 391-392, 393

"Pardon, The" (Wilbur), **Supp. III Part 2:** 544, 550

Paredes, Américo, **Supp. XIII:** 225

Paredes, Raymund A., **Supp. XIII:** 320, 321

"Parentage" (Stafford), **Supp. XI:** 321, 322

*Parentheses: An Autobiographical

Journey (Neugeboren), **Supp. XVI:**217, 218, 219, 221, 226
"Parents" (F. Barthelme), **Supp. XI:** 34
"Parents Taking Shape" (Karr), **Supp. XI:** 243
"Parents' Weekend: Camp Kenwood" (Kenyon), **Supp. VII:** 169
Pareto, Vilfredo, **II:** 577
Paretsky, Sara, **Supp. XIV:**26
Paretsky, Sarah, **Supp. IV Part 2:** 462
Parini, Jay, **Supp. X:** 17
"Paris" (Stern), **Supp. IX:** 300
"Paris, 7 A.M." (Bishop), **Retro. Supp. II:** 41, 42; **Supp. I Part 1:** 85, 89
Paris France (Stein), **IV:** 45
Park, Robert, **IV:** 475
"Park Bench" (Hughes), **Supp. I Part 1:** 331-332
Park City (Beattie), **Supp. V:** 24, 35-36
"Park City" (Beattie), **Supp. V:** 35
Parker, Charlie, **Supp. I Part 1:** 59; **Supp. X:** 240, 242, 246; **Supp. XIII:** 129
Parker, Dorothy, **Retro. Supp. II:** 327; **Supp. IV Part 1:** 353; **Supp. IX:** 62, 114, **189-206**; **Supp. X:** 164; **Supp. XI:** 28
Parker, Idella, **Supp. X:** 232, 234-235
Parker, Muriel, **Supp. IX:** 232
Parker, Patricia, **Supp. XV:** 242
Parker, Robert B., **Supp. IV Part 1:** 135, 136
Parker, Theodore, **Supp. I Part 1:** 38; **Supp. I Part 2:** 518
Parker, Thomas, **Supp. I Part 1:** 102
"Parker's Back" (O'Connor), **III:** 348, 352, 358
Parkes, Henry Bamford, **Supp. I Part 2:** 617
Park-Fuller, Linda, **Supp. XIII:** 297
Parkman, Francis, **II:** 278, 310, 312; **IV:** 179, 309; **Supp. I Part 2:** 420, 479, 481-482, 486, 487, 493, 498; **Supp. II Part 2: 589-616**
Parkman Reader, The (Morison, ed.), **Supp. I Part 2:** 494
Parks, Gordon, Sr., **Supp. XI:** 17
Parks, Larry, **Supp. I Part 1:** 295
Parks, Rosa, **Supp. I Part 1:** 342
"Park Street Cemetery, The" (Lowell), **II:** 537, 538
Par le Détroit (cantata) (Bowles), **Supp. IV Part 1:** 82
Parliament of Fowls, The (Chaucer), **III:** 492
Parmenides (Plato), **II:** 10
Parnassus (Emerson), **II:** 8, 18
Parnell, Charles Stewart, **II:** 129, 137
Parole (film), **Supp. XIII:** 166

Parole Fixer (film), **Supp. XIII:** 170
Parrington, Vernon Louis, **I:** 254, 517, 561; **III:** 335, 606; **IV:** 173; **Supp. I Part 2:** 484, 640
Parrish, Dillwyn, **Supp. XVII:** 83-84, 90
Parrish, Robert, **Supp. XI:** 307
"Parrot, The" (Merrill), **Supp. III Part 1:** 320
"Parsley" (Dove), **Supp. IV Part 1:** 245, 246
Parson, Annie, **Supp. I Part 2:** 655
Parsons, Elsie Clews, **I:** 231, 235
Parsons, Ian, **Supp. IX:** 95
Parsons, Louella, **Supp. XII:** 173
Parsons, Talcott, **Supp. I Part 2:** 648
Parsons, Theophilus, **II:** 396, 504; **Retro. Supp. II:** 134; **Supp. I Part 1:** 155
"Parthian Shot, The" (Hammett), **Supp. IV Part 1:** 343
Partial Payments: Essays on Writers and Their Lives (Epstein), **Supp. XIV:**111
Partial Portraits (James), **II:** 336
Parties (Van Vechten), **Supp. II Part 2:** 739, 747-749
"Parting" (Kunitz), **Supp. III Part 1:** 263
"Parting Gift" (Wylie), **Supp. I Part 2:** 714
"Parting Glass, The" (Freneau), **Supp. II Part 1:** 273
"Partings" (Hogan), **Supp. IV Part 1:** 413
Partington, Blanche, **I:** 199
Partisans (Matthiessen), **Supp. V:** 201
"Partner, The" (Roethke), **III:** 541-542
Partners, The (Auchincloss), **Supp. IV Part 1:** 31, 34
"Part of a Letter" (Wilbur), **Supp. III Part 2:** 551
Part of Speech, A (Brodsky), **Supp. VIII:** 22
"Part of the Bee's Body Embedded in the Flesh, The" (C. Frost), **Supp. XV:** 105, 107
"Part of the Story" (Dobyns), **Supp. XIII:** 79
Parton, Sara, **Retro. Supp. I:** 246
Partridge, Jeffrey F., **Supp. XV:** 219
Partridge, John, **II:** 110, 111
"Parts of a Journal" (Gordon), **Supp. IV Part 1:** 310
Parts of a World (Stevens), **Retro. Supp. I:** **305-306**, 307, 309, 313
"Party, The" (Dunbar), **Supp. II Part 1:** 198, 205-206
"Party, The" (Taylor), **Supp. V:** 315

Party at Jack's, The (Wolfe), **IV:** 451-452, 469
"Party Down at the Square, A" (Ellison), **Retro. Supp. II:** 124
Pascal, Blaise, **II:** 8, 159; **III:** 292, 301, 304, 428; **Retro. Supp. I:** 326, 330
"Paskudnyak" (Pilcer), **Supp. XVII:** 50
"Pass, The" (Neugeboren), **Supp. XVI:**225
"Passage" (Crane), **I:** 391
"Passage in the Life of Mr. John Oakhurst, A" (Harte), **Supp. II Part 1:** 353-354
"Passages" (Duncan), **Supp. XVI:**287
"Passages from a Relinquished Work" (Hawthorne), **Retro. Supp. I:** 150
Passages toward the Dark (McGrath), **Supp. X:** 126, 127
"Passage to India" (Whitman), **IV:** 348
Passage to India, A (Forster), **II:** 600
Passaro, Vince, **Supp. X:** 167, 302, 309, 310
"Passenger Pigeons" (Jeffers), **Supp. II Part 2:** 437
Passin, Herbert, **Supp. XIII:** 337
"Passing Beauty" (C. Frost), **Supp. XV:** 97
"Passing of Grandison, The" (Chesnutt), **Supp. XIV:**62, **66-69**
"Passing of Sister Barsett, The" (Jewett), **Retro. Supp. II:** 138-139, 143
"Passing Show, The" (Bierce), **I:** 208
"Passing Through" (Kunitz), **Supp. III Part 1:** 265
"Passion, The" (Barnes), **Supp. III Part 1:** 36
"Passion, The" (Merwin), **Supp. III Part 1:** 343
Passionate, Accurate Story, The: Making Your Heart's Truth into Literature (C. Bly), **Supp. XVI:41-42**
Passionate Pilgrim, A (James), **II:** 324; **Retro. Supp. I:** 219
"Passionate Pilgrim, A" (James), **II:** 322, 323-324; **Retro. Supp. I:** 218
Passion Play (Kosinski), **Supp. VII:** 215, 225-226
Passions of Uxport, The (Kumin), **Supp. IV Part 2:** 444
"Passive Resistance" (McKay), **Supp. X:** 133
Passport to the War (Kunitz), **Supp. III Part 1:** 261-264
Passwords (Stafford), **Supp. XI: 329-330**
"Past, The" (Bryant), **Supp. I Part 1:** 157, 170

Past, The (Kinnell), **Supp. III Part 1:** 235, 253-254

"Past, The" (Kinnell), **Supp. III Part 1:** 254

Past and Present (Carlyle), **Supp. I Part 2:** 410

Pasternak, Boris, **II:** 544

"Pastiches et Pistaches" (Van Vechten), **Supp. II Part 2:** 732

"Past Is the Present, The" (Moore), **III:** 199-200

"Pastoral" (Carver), **Supp. III Part 1:** 137, 146

"Pastoral" (Dove), **Supp. IV Part 1:** 249

"Pastoral Hat, A" (Stevens), **IV:** 91

"Pastor Dowe at Tacaté" (Bowles), **Supp. IV Part 1:** 87

Pastorela (ballet) (Kirstein), **Supp. IV Part 1:** 83

Pastorius, Francis Daniel, **Supp. I Part 2:** 700

"Pasture Poems" (Kumin), **Supp. IV Part 2:** 446

Pastures of Heaven, The (Steinbeck), **IV:** 51

Patchen, Kenneth, **Supp. III Part 2:** 625

Patchett, Ann, **Supp. XII: 307-324**

Pater, Walter, **I:** 51, 272, 476; **II:** 27, 338; **III:** 604; **IV:** 74; **Retro. Supp. I:** 56, 79; **Retro. Supp. II:** 326; **Supp. I Part 2:** 552; **Supp. IX:** 66

Paterna (Mather), **Supp. II Part 2:** 451

"Paterson" (Ginsberg), **Supp. II Part 1:** 314-315, 321, 329

Paterson (W. C. Williams), **I:** 62, 446; **IV:** 418-423; **Retro. Supp. I:** 209, 284, 413, 419, 421, **424-428**, 428, 429, 430; **Retro. Supp. II:** 321, 328; **Supp. II Part 2:** 557, 564, 625; **Supp. VIII:** 275, 305; **Supp. XIV:** 96; **Supp. XV:** 264, 349

Paterson, Book Five (W. C. Williams), **IV:** 422-423

Paterson, Book One (W. C. Williams), **IV:** 421-422

Paterson, Isabel, **Supp. IV Part 2:** 524

Paterson, Part Three (W. C. Williams), **IV:** 420-421

"Path, The" (Bryant), **Supp. I Part 1:** 169

Pathfinder, The (Cooper), **I:** 349, 350, 355

Pat Hobby Stories, The (Fitzgerald), **Retro. Supp. I:** 114

"Pathos of Low Life, The" (Hapgood), **Supp. XVII:** 103

"Patience of a Saint, The" (Humphrey), **Supp. IX:** 106

Patinkin, Mandy, **Supp. IV Part 1:** 236

Paton, Alan, **Supp. VIII:** 126

Patria Mia (Pound), **III:** 460-461; **Retro. Supp. I:** 284

"Patria Mia" (Pound), **Retro. Supp. I:** 284

"Patriarch, The" (Alvares), **Supp. V:** 11

Patrimony: A True Story (P. Roth), **Retro. Supp. II:** 279, 280, 291; **Supp. III Part 2:** 427

Patriot, The (Buck), **Supp. II Part 1:** 122-123

Patriot, The (Connell), **Supp. XIV:** 94-95

Patriotic Gore: Studies in the Literature of the American Civil War (Wilson), **III:** 588; **IV:** 430, 438, 443, 445-445, 446; **Supp. VIII:** 100

"Patriots, The/Los Patriotas" (Kingsolver), **Supp. VII:** 209

Patron Saint of Liars, The (Patchett), **Supp. XII:** 307, 310, **311-314**, 317

Pattee, Fred L., **II:** 456

Patten, Gilbert, **II:** 423

Patten, Simon, **Supp. I Part 2:** 640

Patternmaster (O. Butler), **Supp. XIII:** 61, 62, 63

Patternmaster Series (O. Butler), **Supp. XIII: 62-63**

Pattern Recognition (W. Gibson), **Supp. XVI:** 124, **130-131**

"Patterns" (Lowell), **II:** 524

Patterson, Floyd, **III:** 38

Patterson, William M., **Supp. I Part 1:** 265

Patton, General George, **III:** 575; **Supp. I Part 2:** 664

"Patty-Cake, Patty-Cake...A Memoir" (Apple), **Supp. XVII:** 7

Paul, Saint, **I:** 365; **II:** 15, 494; **IV:** 122, 154, 164, 335; **Retro. Supp. I:** 247; **Supp. I Part 1:** 188

Paul, Sherman, **I:** 244; **IV:** 179

"Paula Becker to Clara Westhoff" (Rich), **Supp. I Part 2:** 573-574

"Paula Gunn Allen" (Ruppert), **Supp. IV Part 1:** 321

Paul Bowles: Romantic Savage (Caponi), **Supp. IV Part 1:** 95

Paulding, James Kirke, **I:** 344; **II:** 298, 299, 303; **Supp. I Part 1:** 157

Paul Jones (Hapgood), **Supp. XVII:** 100-101

Paul Marchand, F.M.C. (Chesnutt), **Supp. XIV:** 76

"Paul Monette: The Brink of Summer's End" (film), **Supp. X:** 152

"Paul Revere" (Longfellow), **II:** 489, 501

"Paul Revere's Ride" (Longfellow), **Retro. Supp. II:** 163

"Paul's Case" (Cather), **I:** 314-315; **Retro. Supp. I:** 3, 5

Paulsen, Friedrich, **III:** 600

"Pauper Witch of Grafton, The" (Frost), **Retro. Supp. II:** 42

"Pause by the Water, A" (Merwin), **Supp. III Part 1:** 354

"Pavane for the Nursery, A" (W. J. Smith), **Supp. XIII:** 335

"Pavement, The" (Olson), **Supp. II Part 2:** 571

Pavilion of Women (Buck), **Supp. II Part 1:** 125-126

"Pawnbroker, The" (Kumin), **Supp. IV Part 2:** 442, 443-444, 451

Pawnbroker, The (Wallant), **Supp. XVI:** 220

"Paying Dues" (Bass), **Supp. XVI:** 16

Payne, Daniel, **Supp. V:** 202

Payne, John Howard, **II:** 309

Paz, Octavio, **Supp. III Part 2:** 630; **Supp. VIII:** 272; **Supp. XI:** 191; **Supp. XIII:** 223

Peabody, Elizabeth, **Retro. Supp. I:** 155-156, 225

Peabody, Francis G., **III:** 293; **Supp. I Part 1:** 5

Peabody, Josephine Preston, **III:** 507

Peaceable Kingdom, The (Prose), **Supp. XVI:** 256-257

Peace and Bread in Time of War (Addams), **Supp. I Part 1:** 21, 22-23

"Peace Between Black and White in the United States" (Locke), **Supp. XIV:** 205

Peace Breaks Out (Knowles), **Supp. XII:** 249

"Peace March, The" (Simpson), **Supp. IX:** 279

"Peace of Cities, The" (Wilbur), **Supp. III Part 2:** 545

"Peaches-Six in a Tin Box, Sarajevo" (Cisneros), **Supp. VII:** 67

Peacock, Doug, **Supp. VIII:** 38; **Supp. XIII:** 12

Peacock, Gibson, **Supp. I Part 1:** 360

Peacock, Molly, **Supp. XVII:** 74

"Peacock, The" (Merrill), **Supp. III Part 1:** 320

Peacock, Thomas Love, **Supp. I Part 1:** 307; **Supp. VIII:** 125

"Peacock Room, The" (Hayden), **Supp. II Part 1:** 374-375

Pearce, Richard, **Supp. IX:** 254

Pearce, Roy Harvey, **II:** 244; **Supp. I**

Part 1: 111, 114; **Supp. I Part 2:** 475
Pearl, The (Steinbeck), **IV:** 51, 62-63
Pearlman, Daniel, **III:** 479
Pearlman, Mickey, **Supp. XIII:** 293, 306
Pearl of Orr's Island, The (Stowe), **Supp. I Part 2:** 592-593, 595
"Pearls" (A. Finch), **Supp. XVII:** 72
Pears, Peter, **II:** 586; **Supp. IV Part 1:** 84
Pearson, Drew, **Supp. XIV:** 126
Pearson, Norman Holmes, **Supp. I Part 1:** 259, 260, 273
"Pear Tree" (C. Frost), **Supp. XV:** 105
"Peasants' Way O' Thinkin'" (McKay), **Supp. X:** 133
Pease, Donald E., **Supp. IV Part 2:** 687
Peck, Gregory, **Supp. VIII:** 128, 129; **Supp. XII:** 160, 173
Peckinpah, Sam, **Supp. XI:** 306
"Peck of Gold, A" (Frost), **II:** 155
Peculiar Treasures: A Biblical Who's Who (Buechner), **Supp. XII:** 53
"Pedal Point" (Francis), **Supp. IX:** 87
"Pedersen Kid, The" (Gass), **Supp. VI:** 83
"Pedigree, The" (Creeley), **Supp. IV Part 1:** 150
Peebles, Melvin Van, **Supp. XI:** 17; **Supp. XVI:** 144
"Peed Onk" (Moore). *See* "People Like That Are the Only People Here: Canonical Babbling in Peed Onk" (Moore)
"Peeler, The" (O'Connor), **Retro. Supp. II:** 225
Peich, Michael, **Supp. XV:** 113, 117
Peikoff, Leonard, **Supp. IV Part 2:** 520, 526, 529
Peirce, Charles Sanders, **II:** 20, 352-353; **III:** 599; **Supp. I Part 2:** 640; **Supp. III Part 2:** 626
Pelagius, **III:** 295
"Pelican, The" (Merrill), **Supp. III Part 1:** 320
"Pelican, The" (Wharton), **IV:** 310; **Retro. Supp. I:** 364
Pellacchia, Michael, **Supp. XIII:** 16
Peltier, Leonard, **Supp. V:** 212
"Pen and Paper and a Breath of Air" (Oliver), **Supp. VII:** 245
Pence, Amy, **Supp. XV:** 211, 223
"Pencil, The" (Chandler), **Supp. IV Part 1:** 135
Pencillings by the Way (Willis), **II:** 313
"Pencils" (Sandburg), **III:** 592
"Pendulum" (Bradbury and Hasse), **Supp. IV Part 1:** 102

"Penelope's Song" (Glück), **Supp. V:** 89
Penhally (Gordon), **II:** 197, 199, 201-203, 204
"Penis" (McClatchy), **Supp. XII:** 266-267
Penitent, The (Singer), **Retro. Supp. II:** 309-310, 313
Penn, Robert, **I:** 489
Penn, Sean, **Supp. XI:** 107
Penn, Thomas, **II:** 118
Penn, William, **Supp. I Part 2:** 683
"Pennsylvania Pilgrim, The" (Whittier), **Supp. I Part 2:** 700
"Pennsylvania Planter, The" (Freneau), **Supp. II Part 1:** 268
Penny, Rob, **Supp. VIII:** 330
Penrod (Tarkington), **III:** 223
"Penseroso, Il" (Milton), **Supp. XIV:** 8
Pentagon of Power, The (Mumford), **Supp. II Part 2:** 498
Pentimento (Hellman), **Supp. I Part 1:** 280, 292-294, 296; **Supp. IV Part 1:** 12; **Supp. VIII:** 243
"Peonies at Dusk" (Kenyon), **Supp. VII:** 171
People, The (Glaspell), **Supp. III Part 1:** 179
People, Yes, The (Sandburg), **III:** 575, 589, 590, 591
"PEOPLE BURNING, THE" (Baraka), **Supp. II Part 1:** 49
"People in Hell Just Want a Drink of Water" (Proulx), **Supp. VII:** 263
"People Like That Are the Only People Here: Canonical Babbling in Peed Onk" (Moore), **Supp. X:** 168, **178-179**
People Live Here: Selected Poems 1949-1983 (Simpson), **Supp. IX:** 269, 277
"People Next Door, The" (Simpson), **Supp. IX:** 279
People of the Abyss, The (London), **II:** 465-466
"People on the Roller Coaster, The" (Hardwick), **Supp. III Part 1:** 196
People Shall Continue, The (Ortiz), **Supp. IV Part 2:** 510
"People's Surroundings" (Moore), **III:** 201, 202, 203
"People v. Abe Lathan, Colored, The" (Caldwell), **I:** 309
"Peppermint Lounge Revisited, The" (Wolfe), **Supp. III Part 2:** 571
Pepys, Samuel, **Supp. I Part 2:** 653
"Perch'io non spero di tornar giammai" (Cavalcanti), **Supp. III Part 2:** 623
Percy, Thomas, **Supp. XIV:** 2
Percy, Walker, **Supp. III Part 1:** 383-400; **Supp. IV Part 1:** 297; **Supp. V:** 334; **Supp. X:** 42; **Supp. XIV:** 21
Percy, William, **Supp. V:** 334
Percy, William Alexander, **Retro. Supp. I:** 341
Peregrin, Tony, **Supp. XV:** 69
"Peregrine" (Wylie), **Supp. I Part 2:** 712-713, 714
Perelman, Bob, **Supp. XII:** 23
Perelman, S. J., **IV:** 286; **Retro. Supp. I:** 342; **Retro. Supp. II:** 321, 322, 325, 326, 327, 336; **Supp. IV Part 1:** 353; **Supp. XI:** 66
Perestroika (Kushner), **Supp. IX:** 141, 142, 145
Péret, Benjamin, **Supp. VIII:** 272
Peretz, Isaac Loeb, **IV:** 1, 3; **Retro. Supp. II:** 299
Pérez Galdós, Benito, **II:** 275
Perfect Analysis Given by a Parrot, A (T. Williams), **IV:** 395
"Perfect Day for Bananafish, A" (Salinger), **III:** 563-564, 571
Perfect Ganesh, A (McNally), **Supp. XIII: 202-203,** 208, 209
"Perfect Knight, The" (Chandler), **Supp. IV Part 1:** 120
Perfect Party, The (Gurney), **Supp. V:** 100, 105, 106-107
"Perfect Things" (F. Barthelme), **Supp. XI:** 30, 33-34
"Performance, The" (Dickey), **Supp. IV Part 1:** 178-179, 181
"Perfume" (Mora), **Supp. XIII:** 218
"Perhaps the World Ends Here" (Harjo), **Supp. XII:** 228, 231
Perhaps Women (Anderson), **I:** 114
Pericles (Shakespeare), **I:** 585; **Supp. III Part 2:** 624, 627, 629
Period of Adjustment (T. Williams), **IV:** 382, 386, 387, 388, 389, 390, 392, 393, 394, 397
"Period Pieces from the Mid-Thirties" (Agee), **I:** 28
"Periphery" (Ammons), **Supp. VII:** 28
Perkins, David, **Supp. I Part 2:** 459, 475; **Supp. XV:** 185
Perkins, Maxwell, **I:** 252, 289, 290; **II:** 87, 93, 95, 252; **IV:** 452, 455, 457, 458, 461, 462, 463, 469; **Retro. Supp. I:** 101, 105, 108, 109, 110, 113, 114, 178; **Supp. IX:** 57, 58, 60, 232; **Supp. X:** 219, 224, 225, 229, 230, 233; **Supp. XI:** 218, 227
Perlès, Alfred, **III:** 177, 183, 187, 189
Perloff, Marjorie, **Supp. I Part 2:** 539, 542; **Supp. IV Part 1:** 68; **Supp. IV Part 2:** 420, 424, 432
Permanence and Change (Burke), **I:** 274

Permanent Errors (Price), **Supp. VI:** 261
"Permanent Traits of the English National Genius" (Emerson), **II:** 18
Permit Me Voyage (Agee), **I:** 25, 27
"Perosa Canavese" (Everwine), **Supp. XV:** 84
Perrault, Charles, **IV:** 266; **Supp. I Part 2:** 622
Perrin, Noel, **Supp. XVI:**34
Perrins, Carol. See Frost, Carol
Perry, Anne, **Supp. V:** 335
Perry, Bliss, **I:** 243
Perry, Donna, **Supp. IV Part 1:** 322, 327, 335
Perry, Dr. William, **II:** 395, 396
Perry, Edgar A., **III:** 410
Perry, Lincoln, **Supp. V:** 24, 33
Perry, Matthew C., **Supp. I Part 2:** 494-495
Perry, Patsy Brewington, **Supp. I Part 1:** 66
Perry, Ralph Barton, **I:** 224; **II:** 356, 362, 364; **Supp. XIV:**197
Perse, St.-John, **III:** 12, 13, 14, 17; **Supp. III Part 1:** 14; **Supp. IV Part 1:** 82; **Supp. XIII:** 344; **Supp. XV:** 178
"Persephone in Hell" (Dove), **Supp. IV Part 1:** 250, 251
"Persimmons" (L.-Y. Lee), **Supp. XV:** 211, 213
"Persistence of Desire, The" (Updike), **IV:** 222-223, 228
"Persistence of Poetry, The" (Bynner), **Supp. XV:** 49
"Persistences" (Hecht), **Supp. X: 68-69**
Person, Place, and Thing (Shapiro), **Supp. II Part 2:** 702, 705
Personae: The Collected Poems (Pound), **Retro. Supp. I:** 285, 286; **Supp. I Part 1:** 255; **Supp. XVII:** 32
Personae of Ezra Pound (Pound), **III:** 458
"Personal" (Stern), **Supp. IX:** 299
"Personal and Occasional Pieces" (Welty), **Retro. Supp. I:** 355
"Personal and the Individual, The" (L. Michaels), **Supp. XVI:**201
Personal Injuries (Turow), **Supp. XVII: 219-220,** 221, 223
Personal Narrative (Edwards), **I:** 545, 552, 553, 561, 562; **Supp. I Part 2:** 700
Personal Recollection of Joan of Arc (Twain), **IV:** 208
"Personals" (Didion), **Supp. IV Part 1:** 200
"Personism" (O'Hara), **Supp. XV:** 181

Persons and Places (Santayana), **III:** 615
Persons in Hiding (film), **Supp. XIII:** 170
Persons in Hiding (Hoover), **Supp. XIII:** 170
Person Sitting in Darkness, A (Twain), **IV:** 208
"Perspective" (Francis), **Supp. IX:** 78
"Perspective: Anniversary D-Day" (Karr), **Supp. XI:** 241
"Perspectives: Is It Out of Control?" (Gleason), **Supp. IX:** 16
Perspectives by Incongruity (Burke), **I:** 284-285
Perspectives on Cormac McCarthy (Arnold and Luce, eds.), **Supp. VIII:** 189
Pertes et Fracas (McCoy), **Supp. XIII:** 175
"Peruvian Child" (Mora), **Supp. XIII:** 218
Peseroff, Joyce, **Supp. IV Part 1:** 71
"Peter" (Cather), **Retro. Supp. I:** 4
"Peter" (Moore), **III:** 210, 212
Peter, Saint, **III:** 341, 346; **IV:** 86, 294
Peterkin, Julia, **Supp. I Part 1:** 328
"Peter Klaus" (German tale), **II:** 306
Peter Pan (Barrie), **Supp. XV:** 319
"Peter Parley" works (Goodrich), **Supp. I Part 1:** 38
"Peter Pendulum" (Poe), **III:** 425
"Peter Quince at the Clavier" (Stevens), **IV:** 81, 82
Peter Rabbit tales, **Retro. Supp. I:** 335
Peters, Cora, **Supp. I Part 2:** 468
Peters, Jacqueline, **Supp. XII:** 225
Peters, Margot, **Supp. VIII:** 252
Peters, Robert, **Supp. XIII:** 114
Peters, S. H. (pseudonym). See Henry, O.
Peters, Timothy, **Supp. XI:** 39
"Peter's Avocado" (Rodriguez), **Supp. XIV:**308-309
Petersen, David, **Supp. XIII:** 2
Petersen, Donald, **Supp. V:** 180; **Supp. XV:** 74, 92
Peterson, Houston, **I:** 60
Peterson, Roger Tory, **Supp. V:** 202
Peterson, Virgilia, **Supp. IV Part 1:** 30
Peter Whiffle: His Life and Works (Van Vechten), **Supp. II Part 2:** 728-729, 731, 735, 738-741, 749
"Petey and Yotsee and Mario" (H. Roth), **Supp. IX:** 234
"Petition, A" (Winters), **Supp. II Part 2:** 785
"'Pet Negro' System, The" (Hurston), **Supp. VI:** 159

"Petra and Its Surroundings" (Frost), **Retro. Supp. I:** 124
Petrarch, **I:** 176; **II:** 590; **III:** 4
"Petrarch, Shakespeare, and the Blues" (C. Frost), **Supp. XV:** 92, 104, 105
"Petrified Man" (Welty), **IV:** 262; **Retro. Supp. I:** 345, 351
"Petrified Man, The" (Twain), **IV:** 195
"Petrified Woman, The" (Gordon), **II:** 199
Petronius, **III:** 174, 179
Petry, Ann, **Supp. VIII:** 214; **Supp. XI:** 6, 85
Pet Sematary (King), **Supp. V:** 138, 143, 152
Pettengill, Richard, **Supp. VIII:** 341, 345, 348
Pettingell, Phoebe, **Supp. XV:** 251, 256-257, 262
Pettis, Joyce, **Supp. XI:** 276, 277, 278, 281
Pfaelzer, Jean, **Supp. XVI:**88, 90
Pfaff, Timothy, **Supp. V:** 166
Pfeil, Fred, **Supp. XIV:**36
Pfister, Karin, **IV:** 467, 475
Phaedo (Plato), **II:** 10
Phaedra (Lowell and Barzun, trans.), **II:** 543-544
"Phantasia for Elvira Shatayev" (Rich), **Supp. I Part 2:** 570
Phantasms of War (Lowell), **II:** 512
"Phantom of the Movie Palace, The" (Coover), **Supp. V:** 50-51
Phantom Ship, The (Marryat), **Supp. XVII:** 55
"Pharaoh, The" (Kenyon), **Supp. VII:** 172
Pharr, Mary, **Supp. V:** 147
"Phases" (E. Stoddard), **Supp. XV:** 273
"Phases" (Stevens), **Retro. Supp. I:** 299
Phases of an Inferior Planet (Glasgow), **II:** 174-175
"Pheasant, The" (Carver), **Supp. III Part 1:** 146
Pheloung, Grant, **Supp. XI:** 39
Phelps, Elizabeth Stuart, **Retro. Supp. II:** 146; **Supp. XIII:** 141; **Supp. XVI:**80
Phelps, Teresa Godwin, **Supp. VIII:** 128
"Phenomena and Laws of Race Contacts, The" (Locke), **Supp. XIV:**210
"Phenomenology of Anger, The" (Rich), **Supp. I Part 2:** 562-563, 571
Phenomenology of Moral Experience, The (Mandelbaum), **I:** 61
"Phenomenology of *On Moral Fiction*" (Johnson), **Supp. VI:** 188

Phidias, **Supp. I Part 2:** 482
Philadelphia Fire (Wideman), **Supp. X:** 320, 334
Philadelphia Negro, The (Du Bois), **Supp. II Part 1:** 158, 163-164, 166
Philbrick, Thomas, **I:** 343
Philip, Jim, **Supp. XII:** 136
Philip, Prince, **Supp. X:** 108
"Philip of Pokanoket" (Irving), **II:** 303
Philippians (biblical book), **IV:** 154
"Philippine Conquest, The" (Masters), **Supp. I Part 2:** 456
"Philip Roth Reconsidered" (Howe), **Retro. Supp. II:** 286
"Philistinism and the Negro Writer" (Baraka), **Supp. II Part 1:** 39, 44
Phillips, Adam, **Supp. XII:** 97-98
Phillips, David Graham, **II:** 444; **Retro. Supp. II:** 101
Phillips, Gene D., **Supp. XI:** 306
Phillips, J. O. C., **Supp. I Part 1:** 19
Phillips, Jayne Anne, **Supp. XIV:** 21
Phillips, Robert, **Supp. XIII:** 335, 344
Phillips, Wendell, **Supp. I Part 1:** 103; **Supp. I Part 2:** 524
Phillips, Willard, **Supp. I Part 1:** 154, 155
Phillips, William, **Supp. VIII:** 156
Phillips, William L., **I:** 106
"Philosopher, The" (Farrell), **II:** 45
Philosopher of the Forest (pseudonym). *See* Freneau, Philip
Philosophes classiques, Les (Taine), **III:** 323
"Philosophical Cobbler, The" (Sanders), **Supp. XVI:** 268
"Philosophical Concepts and Practical Results" (James), **II:** 352
"Philosophical Investigation of Metaphor, A" (Gass), **Supp. VI:** 79
Philosophical Transactions (Watson), **II:** 114
"Philosophy, Or Something Like That" (P. Roth), **Supp. III Part 2:** 403
Philosophy: Who Needs It (Rand), **Supp. IV Part 2:** 517, 518, 527, 533
"Philosophy and Its Critics" (James), **II:** 360
"Philosophy and the Form of Fiction" (Gass), **Supp. VI:** 85
"Philosophy for People" (Emerson), **II:** 14
"Philosophy in Warm Weather" (Kenyon), **Supp. VII:** 168
"Philosophy Lesson" (Levine), **Supp. V:** 195
Philosophy of Alain Locke, The: Harlem Renaissance and Beyond (Harris, ed.), **Supp. XIV:** 196, 211-212
"Philosophy of Composition, The" (Poe), **III:** 416, 421; **Retro. Supp. II:** 266, 267, 271
Philosophy of Friedrich Nietzsche, The (Mencken), **III:** 102-103
"Philosophy of Handicap, A" (Bourne), **I:** 216, 218
"Philosophy of History" (Emerson), **II:** 11-12
Philosophy of Literary Form, The (Burke), **I:** 275, 281, 283, 291
Philosophy of the Human Mind, The (Stewart), **II:** 8
Philoxenes, **Supp. VIII:** 201
"Phineas" (Knowles), **Supp. XII:** 238-240
Phineas: Six Stories (Knowles), **Supp. XII:** 249
"Phocion" (Lowell), **II:** 536
Phoenix and the Turtle, The (Shakespeare), **I:** 284
"Phoenix Lyrics" (Schwartz), **Supp. II Part 2:** 665
"Phone Booths, The" (Jarman), **Supp. XVII:** 112-113
"Phony War Films" (Jones), **Supp. XI:** 217, 232
"Photograph: Migrant Worker, Parlier, California, 1967" (Levis), **Supp. XI:** 272
"Photograph of a Child on a Vermont Hillside" (Kenyon), **Supp. VII:** 168
"Photograph of My Mother as a Young Girl" (Gioia), **Supp. XV:** 119
"Photograph of the Girl" (Olds), **Supp. X:** 205
"Photograph of the Unmade Bed" (Rich), **Supp. I Part 2:** 558
Photographs (Welty), **Retro. Supp. I:** 343
"Photographs, The" (Barthelme), **Supp. IV Part 1:** 53
"Photography" (Levine), **Supp. V:** 194
Phyrrho, **Retro. Supp. I:** 247
"Physical Universe" (Simpson), **Supp. IX:** 278
"Physicist We Know, A" (Shields), **Supp. VII:** 310
"Physics and Cosmology in the Fiction of Tom Robbins" (Nadeau), **Supp. X:** 270
Physiologie du goût (Brillat-Savarin), **Supp. XVII:** 82, 86
Physiology of Taste, The; or, Meditations on Transcendent Gastronomy (Brillat-Savarin; M. F. K. Fisher, trans.), **Supp. XVII:** 86, 87, 91
"Physiology of Versification, The: Harmonies of Organic and Animal Life" (Holmes), **Supp. I Part 1:** 311
Physique de l'Amour (Gourmont), **III:** 467-468
Piaf, Edith, **Supp. IV Part 2:** 549
Piaget, Jean, **Supp. XIII:** 75
"Piano" (Lawrence), **Supp. XV:** 254
"Piano Fingers" (Mason), **Supp. VIII:** 146
Piano Lesson, The (Bearden), **Supp. VIII:** 342
Piano Lesson, The (Wilson), **Supp. VIII:** 342-345
Piatt, James, **Supp. I Part 2:** 420
Piatt, John J., **II:** 273
Piazza, Ben, **Supp. XIII:** 163
Piazza, Paul, **Supp. XIV:** 157, 160, 171
"Piazza de Spagna, Early Morning" (Wilbur), **Supp. III Part 2:** 553
Piazza Tales (Melville), **III:** 91
Picabia, Francis, **Retro. Supp. I:** 416; **Retro. Supp. II:** 331
Picasso (Stein), **IV:** 28, 32, 45
Picasso, Pablo, **I:** 429, 432, 440, 442, 445; **II:** 602; **III:** 197, 201, 470; **IV:** 26, 31, 32, 46, 87, 407, 436; **Retro. Supp. I:** 55, 63; **Supp. IV Part 1:** 81; **Supp. IX:** 66
Piccione, Anthony, **Supp. XV:** 212
"Piccola Comedia" (Wilbur), **Supp. III Part 2:** 561
Pickard, Samuel T., **Supp. I Part 2:** 682
Picked-Up Pieces (Updike), **Retro. Supp. I:** 320, 322, 323, 335
Picker, Lauren, **Supp. VIII:** 78, 83
Picker, Tobias, **Supp. XII:** 253
Pickford, Mary, **Retro. Supp. I:** 325; **Supp. I Part 2:** 391
"Picking and Choosing" (Moore), **III:** 205
Picnic Cantata (music) (Bowles), **Supp. IV Part 1:** 89
"Picnic Remembered" (Warren), **IV:** 240
Pictorial History of the Negro in America, A (Hughes), **Supp. I Part 1:** 345
"Picture, The" (Olson), **Supp. II Part 2:** 574
Picture Bride (Son), **Supp. X:** 292
"Picture I Want, The" (Olds), **Supp. X:** 209
Picture of Dorian Gray, The (Wilde), **Supp. IX:** 105
"Picture of Little J. A. in a Prospect of Flowers, A" (Ashbery), **Supp. III Part 1:** 3
Picture Palace (Theroux), **Supp. VIII:** 322

"Pictures at an Extermination" (Epstein), **Supp. XII:** 161
"Pictures from an Expedition" (Duffy), **Supp. IV Part 1:** 207
Pictures from an Institution (Jarrell), **II:** 367, 385
Pictures from Brueghel (W. C. Williams), **Retro. Supp. I:** 429-431
"Pictures from Brueghel" (W. C. Williams), **Retro. Supp. I:** 419
"Pictures of Columbus, the Genoese, The" (Freneau), **Supp. II Part 1:** 258
Pictures of Fidelman: An Exhibition (Malamud), **Supp. I Part 2:** 450-451
"Pictures of the Artist" (Malamud), **Supp. I Part 2:** 450
Pictures of the Floating World (Lowell), **II:** 521, 524-525
Pictures of Travel (Heine), **II:** 281
"Picturesque: San Cristóbal de las Casas" (Mora), **Supp. XIII:** 218
Picturesque America; or, the Land We Live In (Bryant, ed.), **Supp. I Part 1:** 158
"Picturesque Ghetto, The" (Hapgood), **Supp. XVII:** 101
Picture This (Heller), **Supp. IV Part 1:** 386, 388, 390-391
Picturing Will (Beattie), **Supp. V:** 29, 31-32, 34
"Pie" (X. J. Kennedy), **Supp. XV:** 170
"Piece, A" (Creeley), **Supp. IV Part 1:** 155, 156
"Piece of Moon, A" (Hogan), **Supp. IV Part 1:** 407
Piece of My Heart, A (Ford), **Supp. V:** 57, 58-61, 62
Piece of My Mind, A: Reflections at Sixty (Wilson), **IV:** 426, 430, 438, 441
"Piece of News, A" (Welty), **IV:** 263; **Retro. Supp. I:** 345, 346
Pieces (Creeley), **Supp. IV Part 1:** 155
Pieces and Pontifications (Mailer), **Retro. Supp. II:** 209-210
Pieces of the Frame (McPhee), **Supp. III Part 1:** 293
Pierce, Franklin, **II:** 225, 226, 227; **III:** 88; **Retro. Supp. I:** 150, 163, 164, 165
Pierce, Frederick, **Retro. Supp. I:** 136
Piercy, Josephine K., **Supp. I Part 1:** 103
"Pierian Handsprings" (column, Untermeyer), **Supp. XV:** 294
Pierpont, Claudia Roth, **Supp. X:** 192, 193, 196

Pierre: or The Ambiguities (Melville), **III:** 86-88, 89; **IV:** 194; **Retro. Supp. I:** 249, 253-254, 256; **Supp. I Part 2:** 579
Pierre et Jean (Maupassant), **I:** 421
Pierrepont, Sarah. *See* Edwards, Sarah
Pierrot qui pleure et Pierrot qui rit (Rostand), **II:** 515
Pig Cookies (Ríos), **Supp. IV Part 2:** 537, 550, 552-554
Pigeon Feathers (Updike), **IV:** 214, 218, 219, 221-223, 226
"Pigeon Feathers" (Updike), **Retro. Supp. I:** 318, 322, 323
"Pigeons" (Rilke), **II:** 544
"Pigeon Woman" (Swenson), **Supp. IV Part 2:** 644
Pigs in Heaven (Kingsolver), **Supp. VII:** 197, 199, 209-210
Pike County Ballads, The (Hay), **Supp. I Part 1:** 352
Piket, Vincent, **Supp. IV Part 1:** 24
Pilar San-Mallafre, Maria del, **Supp. V:** 40
Pilcer, Sonya, **Supp. XVII:** 50
"Pilgrim" (Freneau), **Supp. I Part 1:** 125
"Pilgrimage" (Sontag), **Supp. III Part 2:** 454-455
"Pilgrimage, The" (Maxwell), **Supp. VIII:** 169, 171
Pilgrimage of Festus, The (Aiken), **I:** 50, 55, 57
Pilgrimage of Henry James, The (Brooks), **I:** 240, 248, 250; **IV:** 433
Pilgrim at Tinker Creek (Dillard), **Supp. VI:** 22, **23-26,** 28, 29, **30-31,** 34
"Pilgrim Makers" (Lowell), **II:** 541
Pilgrim's Progress (Bunyan), **I:** 92; **II:** 15, 168, 572; **Supp. I Part 1:** 32, 38; **Supp. I Part 2:** 599
Pili's Wall (Levine), **Supp. V:** 178, 183-184
"Pillar of Fire" (Bradbury), **Supp. IV Part 1:** 113-114
Pillars of Hercules, The: A Grand Tour of the Mediterranean (Theroux), **Supp. VIII:** 325
"Pillow" (L.-Y. Lee), **Supp. XV:** 224
Pilot, The (Cooper), **I:** 335, 337, 339, 342-343, 350
"Pilot from the Carrier, A" (Jarrell), **II:** 374
"Pilots, Man Your Planes" (Jarrell), **II:** 374-375
"Pilots, The" (Levertov), **Supp. III Part 1:** 282
"Pimp's Revenge, A" (Malamud), **Supp. I Part 2:** 435, 450, 451

Pinball (Kosinski), **Supp. VII:** 215, 226
Pinchot, Gifford, **Supp. IX:** 184; **Supp. XIV:** 178
Pindar, **I:** 381; **II:** 543; **III:** 610
"Pine" (Dickey), **Supp. IV Part 1:** 183
Pine Barrens, The (McPhee), **Supp. III Part 1:** 298-301, 309
"Pineys, The" (Stern), **Supp. IX:** 288, 296
Pinget, Robert, **Supp. V:** 39
"Pink Dog" (Bishop), **Retro. Supp. II:** 48
Pinker, James B., **I:** 409; **Retro. Supp. I:** 231
Pinkerton, Jan, **Supp. V:** 323-324
"Pink Moon-The Pond" (Oliver), **Supp. VII:** 234
Pinktoes (C. Himes), **Supp. XVI:** 142
Pinocchio in Venice (Coover), **Supp. V:** 40, 51
Pinsker, Sanford, **Retro. Supp. II:** 23; **Supp. V:** 272; **Supp. IX:** 293, 327; **Supp. XI:** 251, 254, 317
Pinsky, Robert, **Retro. Supp. II:** 50; **Supp. VI: 235-251; Supp. IX:** 155, 158; **Supp. XIII:** 277, 285
Pinter, Harold, **I:** 71; **Supp. XIII:** 20, 196; **Supp. XIV:** 239; **Supp. XVI:** 207
Pinto and Sons (Epstein), **Supp. XII:** 170, **171-172**
Pioneers, The (Cooper), **I:** 336, 337, 339, 340-341, 342, 348; **II:** 313
Pioneers of France in the New World (Parkman), **Supp. III Part 2:** 599, 602
"Pioneers! O Pioneers!" (Whitman), **Retro. Supp. I:** 8
"Pioneer's Vision, The" (Larcom), **Supp. XIII:** 140
Pious and Secular America (Niebuhr), **III:** 308
Pipe Night (O'Hara), **III:** 361, 368
Piper, Dan, **Supp. IX:** 65
Pipers at the Gates of Dawn: The Wisdom of Children's Literature (Cott), **Supp. XVI:** 104
"Piper's Rocks" (Olson), **Supp. IV Part 1:** 153
"Pipistrelles" (B. Kelly), **Supp. XVII:** 129-130
Pipkin, Charles W., **Supp. XIV:** 3
Pippa Passes (Browning), **IV:** 128
Piquion, René, **Supp. I Part 1:** 346
Pirandello, Luigi, **Supp. IV Part 2:** 576, 588
Piranesi, Giovanni Battista, **Supp. XV:** 258
Pirate, The (Robbins), **Supp. XII:** 6

Pirate, The (Scott), **I:** 339
Pirates of Penzance, The (Gilbert and Sullivan), **IV:** 386
Pisan Cantos, The (Pound), **III:** 476; **Retro. Supp. I:** 140, 283, 285, 293; **Supp. III Part 1:** 63; **Supp. V:** 331, 337; **Supp. XIV:**11; **Supp. XV:** 351
Piscator, Erwin, **IV:** 394
Pissarro, Camille, **I:** 478
"Pissing off the Back of the Boat into the Nevernais Canal" (Matthews), **Supp. IX:** 160-161
Pistol, The (Jones), **Supp. XI:** 219, **223-224**, 227, 234
Pit, The (Norris), **III:** 314, 322, 326-327, 333, 334
"Pit, The" (Roethke), **III:** 538
"Pit and the Pendulum, The" (Poe), **III:** 413, 416; **Retro. Supp. II:** 264, 269-270, 273
"Pitcher" (Francis), **Supp. IX:** 82
"Pitcher, The" (Dubus), **Supp. VII:** 87
Pitchford, Nicola, **Supp. XII:** 13
"Pits, The" (D. Graham), **Supp. XI:** 252, 254
Pitt, William, **Supp. I Part 2:** 510, 518
"Pity Me" (Wylie), **Supp. I Part 2:** 729
Pity the Monsters (Williamson), **Retro. Supp. II:** 185
Pius II, Pope, **III:** 472
Pius IX, Pope, **II:** 79
"Piute Creek" (Snyder), **Supp. VIII:** 293
Pixley, Frank, **I:** 196
Pizer, Donald, **III:** 321; **Retro. Supp. II:** 100, 199
"Place at the Outskirts" (Simic), **Supp. VIII:** 282
Place Called Estherville, A (Caldwell), **I:** 297, 307
Place Called Freedom, A (Sanders), **Supp. XVI:**269
"Place in Fiction" (Welty), **IV:** 260, 279
Place of Dead Roads, The (Burroughs), **Supp. III Part 1:** 196
Place of Love, The (Shapiro), **Supp. II Part 2:** 702, 706
"Place of Poetry, The" (Stevens), **Retro. Supp. I:** 304
Place of Science in Modern Civilization and Other Essays, The (Veblen), **Supp. I Part 2:** 629, 642
"Place of Trumpets, The" (B. Kelly), **Supp. XVII:** 127
Place on Earth, A (Berry), **Supp. X:** 33-34, 36
Places Left Unfinished at the Time of Creation (Santos), **Supp. XIII:** 274
"Places to Look for Your Mind" (Moore), **Supp. X:** 174-175
"Place They'd Never Seen, A: The Theater" (Wasserstein), **Supp. XV:** 332
"Place to Live, A" (Levertov), **Supp. III Part 1:** 281
"Place to Stand, A" (Price), **Supp. VI:** 258
Place to Stand, A (Wagoner), **Supp. IX:** 324
"Place (Any Place) to Transcend All Places, A" (W. C. Williams), **Retro. Supp. I:** 422
Placi, Carlo, **IV:** 328
Plagemann, Catherine, **Supp. XVII:** 91
"Plagiarist, The" (Singer), **IV:** 19
"Plain Language from Truthful James" (Harte). *See* "Heathen Chinee, The"
"Plain Sense of Things, The" (Stevens), **Retro. Supp. I:** 298, 299, 307, 312
"Plain Song" (Carruth), **Supp. XVI:**54
Plain Song (Harrison), **Supp. VIII: 38-39**
"Plain Song for Comadre, A" (Wilbur), **Supp. III Part 2:** 554
"Plain Talk." *See Common Sense* (Paine)
Plaint of a Rose, The (Sandburg), **III:** 579
Plain Truth: Or, Serious Considerations on the Present State of the City of Philadelphia, and Province of Pennsylvania (Franklin), **II:** 117-119
Plainwater: Essays and Poetry (Carson), **Supp. XII:** 97, **99-104**
Plan B (C. Himes), **Supp. XVI:**143, 144
"Planchette" (London), **II:** 475-476
"Planetarium" (Rich), **Supp. I Part 2:** 557
Planet News: 1961-1967 (Ginsberg), **Supp. II Part 1:** 321
"Plantation a beginning, a" (Olson), **Supp. II Part 2:** 573
Plant Dreaming Deep (Sarton), **Supp. VIII:** 250, 263
Plante, David, **Supp. IV Part 1:** 310
Planting a Sequoia (Gioia), **Supp. XV:** 117
"Planting a Sequoia" (Gioia), **Supp. XV:** 111, 112, 117, **121-122**
"Plants Fed On By Fawns" (B. Kelly), **Supp. XVII:** 133
Plarr, Victor, **III:** 459, 477
Plath, James, **Retro. Supp. I:** 334
Plath, Sylvia, **Retro. Supp. II:** 181, **241-260; Supp. I Part 2: 526-549,** 554, 571; **Supp. III Part 2:** 543, 561; **Supp. IV Part 2:** 439; **Supp. V:** 79, 81, 113, 117, 118, 119, 344; **Supp. X:** 201, 202, **203**, 215; **Supp. XI:** 146, 240, 241, 317; **Supp. XII:** 217, 308; **Supp. XIII:** 35, 76, 312; **Supp. XIV:**269; **Supp. XV:** 123, 148, 184, 252, 253, 340; **Supp. XVII:** 239
Plath, Warren, **Supp. I Part 2:** 528
Plato, **I:** 224, 279, 383, 389, 485, 523; **II:** 5, 8, 10, 15, 233, 346, 391-392, 591; **III:** 115, 480, 600, 606, 609, 619-620; **IV:** 74, 140, 333, 363, 364; **Retro. Supp. I:** 247; **Retro. Supp. II:** 31; **Supp. I Part 2:** 595, 631; **Supp. IV Part 1:** 391; **Supp. IV Part 2:** 526; **Supp. X:** 78
"Plato" (Emerson), **II:** 6
"Platonic Relationship, A" (Beattie), **Supp. V:** 22
Platonic Scripts (Justice), **Supp. VII:** 115
Platonov, Dmitri, **Supp. VIII:** 30
Platt, Anthony M., **Supp. I Part 1:** 13-14
Platte River (Bass), **Supp. XVI:**19
"Platte River" (Bass), **Supp. XVI:**20
Plausible Prejudices: Essays on American Writing (Epstein), **Supp. XIV:**111
Plautus, Titus Maccius, **IV:** 155; **Supp. III Part 2:** 630
Play and Other Stories, The (Dixon), **Supp. XII:** 148, 149
Playback (Chandler), **Supp. IV Part 1:** 134-135
Playback (script) (Chandler), **Supp. IV Part 1:** 131
"Play Ball!" (Francis), **Supp. IX:** 89
Playboy of the Western World, The (Synge), **Supp. III Part 1:** 34
Play Days (Jewett), **Retro. Supp. II:** 135
Play Days: A Book of Stories for Children (Jewett), **II:** 401-402
Player Piano (Vonnegut), **Supp. II Part 2:** 756, 757, 760-765
Players (DeLillo), **Supp. VI:** 3, 6, 8, 14
"Players, The" (W. J. Smith), **Supp. XIII:** 340, 343
"Playground, The" (Bradbury), **Supp. IV Part 1:** 104
Playing in the Dark (Morrison), **Retro. Supp. II:** 118; **Supp. XIII:** 185-186
Play in Poetry (Untermeyer), **Supp. XV:** 310

"Playin with Punjab" (Bambara), **Supp. XI:** 6
Play It Again Sam (Allen), **Supp. XV:** 2, 3, 14
Play It as It Lays (Didion), **Supp. IV Part 1:** 198, 201-203, 203, 211
Play It as It Lays (film), **Supp. IV Part 1:** 198
Plays: Winesburg and Others (Anderson), **I:** 113
"Plays and Operas Too" (Whitman), **IV:** 350
Plays of Negro Life: A Source-Book of Native American Drama (Locke and Gregory), **Supp. XIV:**202
"Playthings" (Komunyakaa), **Supp. XIII:** 126
Playwright's Voice, The (Savran), **Supp. XIII:** 209; **Supp. XV:** 321
Plaza Suite (Simon), **Supp. IV Part 2:** 575, 581-582, 583, 589
Pleading Guilty (Turow), **Supp. XVII:** 218, 219
"Plea for Captain Brown, A" (Thoreau), **IV:** 185
"Please" (Komunyakaa), **Supp. XIII:** 122
"Please Don't Kill Anything" (A. Miller), **III:** 161
"Please Don't Take My Sunshine Away" (Conroy), **Supp. XVI:**69
Pleasure Dome (Frankenberg), **I:** 436
Pleasure Dome (Komunyakaa), **Supp. XIII:** 113, 121, **131-133**
Pleasure of Hope, The (Emerson), **II:** 8
"Pleasure of Ruins, The" (McClatchy), **Supp. XII:** 256
"Pleasures of Formal Poetry, The" (Bogan), **Supp. III Part 1:** 51
"Pleasures of Peace, The" (Koch), **Supp. XV:** 180
"Plea to the Protestant Churches, A" (Brooks), **Supp. XIV:**4
Plimpton, George, **Supp. IV Part 1:** 386; **Supp. V:** 201; **Supp. VIII:** 82, 157; **Supp. IX:** 256; **Supp. XI:** 294; **Supp. XIV:**82; **Supp. XVI:233-248**
Pliny the Elder, **Supp. XVI:**292
Pliny the Younger, **II:** 113
"Ploesti Isn't Long Island" (Zinberg), **Supp. XV:** 195
"Plot against the Giant, The" (Stevens), **IV:** 81
Plotinus, **Supp. XV:** 33; **Supp. XVI:**291
Plough and the Stars, The (O'Casey), **III:** 159
"Ploughing on Sunday" (Stevens), **IV:** 74

Plowing the Dark (Powers), **Supp. IX:** 212-213, **221-224**
Plumed Serpent, The (Lawrence), **Supp. XV:** 46
"Plumet Basilisk, The" (Moore), **III:** 203, 208, 215
Plumly, Stanley, **Supp. IV Part 2:** 625
Plummer, Amanda, **Supp. IV Part 1:** 236
Plunder (serial movie), **Supp. IV Part 2:** 464
Plunket, Robert, **Supp. XV:** 68
"Plunkville Patriot" (O'Henry), **Supp. II Part 1:** 389
"Pluralism and Ideological Peace" (Locke), **Supp. XIV:**202, 212
"Pluralism and Intellectual Democracy" (Locke), **Supp. XIV:**202, 208, 212
Pluralistic Universe, A (James), **II:** 342, 348, 357-358
Plutarch, **II:** 5, 8, 16, 555; **Retro. Supp. I:** 360; **Supp. XVI:**292
Plymell, Charles, **Supp. XIV:**149
Plymell, Pam, **Supp. XIV:**149
Pnin (Nabokov), **III:** 246; **Retro. Supp. I:** 263, 265, 266, 275, 335
"Po' Boy Blues" (Hughes), **Supp. I Part 1:** 327
Pocahontas, **I:** 4; **II:** 296; **III:** 584
"Pocahontas to Her English Husband, John Rolfe" (Gunn Allen), **Supp. IV Part 1:** 331
Podhoretz, Norman, **IV:** 441; **Retro. Supp. II:** 323; **Supp. IV Part 1:** 382; **Supp. VIII:** 93, **231-247**; **Supp. IX:** 3; **Supp. XIV:**103
Podnieks, Elizabeth, **Supp. X:** 189, 190, 191, 192
"Pod of the Milkweed" (Frost), **Retro. Supp. I:** 141
Poe, Edgar Allan, **I:** 48, 53, 103, 190, 194, 200, 210, 211, 261, 340, 459; **II:** 74, 77, 194, 255, 273, 295, 308, 311, 313, 421, 475, 482, 530, 595; **III:** 259, **409-432**, 485, 507, 593; **IV:** 123, 129, 133, 141, 187, 261, 345, 350, 432, 438, 439, 453; **Retro. Supp. I:** 41, 273, 365, 421; **Retro. Supp. II:** 102, 104, 160, 164, 220, **261-277**, 322; **Supp. I Part 1:** 36, 309; **Supp. I Part 2:** 376, 384, 385, 388, 393, 405, 413, 421, 474, 682; **Supp. II Part 1:** 385, 410; **Supp. III Part 2:** 544, 549-550; **Supp. IV Part 1:** 80, 81, 101, 128, 341, 349; **Supp. IV Part 2:** 464, 469; **Supp. VIII:** 105; **Supp. IX:** 115; **Supp. X:** 42, 78; **Supp. XI:** 85, 293; **Supp. XIII:** 100, 111; **Supp. XVI:**294

Poe, Edgar Allen, **Supp. XV:** 275
Poe Abroad: Influence, Reputation, Affinities (Vines), **Retro. Supp. II:** 261
"Poem" (Bishop), **Retro. Supp. II:** 40; **Supp. I Part 1:** 73, 76-79, 82, 95
"Poem" (Harrison), **Supp. VIII:** 38
"Poem" (Justice), **Supp. VII:** 125
"Poem" (Kunitz), **Supp. III Part 1:** 263
"Poem" (Wright), **Supp. III Part 2:** 590
"Poem About George Doty in the Death House, A" (Wright), **Supp. III Part 2:** 594-595, 597-598
"Poem about People" (Pinsky), **Supp. VI: 240-241,** 244, 248
"Poem as Mask, The" (Rukeyser), **Supp. VI:** 281, 285
"Poem Beginning 'The'" (Zukofsky), **Supp. III Part 2:** 610, 611, 614
"Poem Catching Up with an Idea" (Carruth), **Supp. XVI:**56
"Poem for a Birthday" (Plath), **Supp. I Part 2:** 539
"POEM FOR ANNA RUSS AND FANNY JONES, A" (Baraka), **Supp. II Part 1:** 58
"Poem for Black Hearts, A" (Baraka), **Supp. II Part 1:** 50
"Poem for D. H. Lawrence" (Creeley), **Supp. IV Part 1:** 141
"POEM FOR DEEP THINKERS, A" (Baraka), **Supp. II Part 1:** 55
"Poem for Dorothy, A" (Merwin), **Supp. III Part 1:** 342
"Poem for Hemingway and W. C. Williams" (Carver), **Supp. III Part 1:** 147
"Poem for my Son" (Kumin), **Supp. IV Part 2:** 442
"Poem for People Who Are Understandably Too Busy to Read Poetry" (Dunn), **Supp. XI:** 147
"Poem for Someone Killed in Spain, A" (Jarrell), **II:** 371
"Poem for the Blue Heron, A" (Oliver), **Supp. VII:** 235-236
"Poem for Two Voices" (Everwine), **Supp. XV:** 89
"Poem For Willie Best, A" (Baraka), **Supp. II Part 1:** 36
"Poem in Prose" (Bogan), **Supp. III Part 1:** 58
"Poem in Which I Refuse Contemplation" (Dove), **Supp. IV Part 1:** 249
"Poem Is a Walk, A" (Ammons), **Supp. VII:** 36
"Poem Like a Grenade, A" (Haines), **Supp. XII:** 204

"Poem of Flight, The" (Levine), **Supp. V:** 189
"Poem of Liberation, The" (Stern), **Supp. IX:** 292
Poem of the Cid (Merwin, trans.), **Supp. III Part 1:** 347
"Poem of the Forgotten" (Haines), **Supp. XII:** 202-203
"Poem on the Memorable Victory Obtained by the Gallant Captain Paul Jones" (Freneau), **Supp. II Part 1:** 261
"Poem out of Childhood" (Rukeyser), **Supp. VI:** 272, 277
"Poem Read at the Dinner Given to the Author by the Medical Profession" (Holmes), **Supp. I Part 1:** 310-311
Poems (Auden), **Supp. II Part 1:** 6
Poems (Berryman), **I:** 170
Poems (Bryant), **II:** 311; **Supp. I Part 1:** 155, 157
Poems (Cummings), **I:** 430, 447
Poems (Eliot), **I:** 580, 588; **IV:** 122; **Retro. Supp. I:** 59, 291
Poems (Emerson), **II:** 7, 8, 12-13, 17
Poems (E. Stoddard), **Supp. XV:** 274
Poems (Holmes), **Supp. I Part 1:** 303
Poems (Koch), **Supp. XV:** 179
Poems (Lowell), **Supp. I Part 2:** 405
Poems (Moore), **III:** 194, 205, 215
Poems (Poe), **III:** 411
Poems (Reznikoff), **Supp. XIV:** 282, 283, 284, 285
Poems (Tate), **IV:** 121
Poems (Winters), **Supp. II Part 2:** 809, 810
Poems (Wordsworth), **I:** 468
Poems (W. C. Williams), **Retro. Supp. I:** 412-413, 416, 424
Poems (W. J. Smith), **Supp. XIII:** 332
Poems 1940-1953 (Shapiro), **Supp. II Part 2:** 703, 711
Poems 1947-1954 (Kees), **Supp. XV:** 147
Poems 1957-1967 (Dickey), **Supp. IV Part 1:** 178, 181
Poems, 1909-1925 (Eliot), **Retro. Supp. I:** 64
Poems, 1924-1933 (MacLeish), **III:** 7, 15
Poems, 1943-1956 (Wilbur), **Supp. III Part 2:** 554
Poems: 1947-1957 (W. J. Smith), **Supp. XIII:** 333
Poems: North & South-A Cold Spring, (Bishop), **Supp. I Part 1:** 83, 89
Poems, The (Freneau), **Supp. II Part 1:** 263
Poems 1918-1975 : The Complete

Poems of Charles Reznikoff (Cooney, ed.), **Supp. XIV:** 289
Poems about God (Ransom), **III:** 484, 486, 491; **IV:** 121
"Poems about Painting" (Snodgrass), **Supp. VI:** 316
Poems and Essays (Ransom), **III:** 486, 490, 492
Poems and New Poems (Bogan), **Supp. III Part 1:** 60-62
"Poems and Places" (Haines), **Supp. XII:** 203
Poems and Poetry of Europe, The (Longfellow, ed.), **Retro. Supp. II:** 155
Poems by Emily Dickinson (Todd and Higginson, eds.), **I:** 469, 470; **Retro. Supp. I:** 35, 39
Poems by Emily Dickinson, Second Series (Todd and Higginson, eds.), **I:** 454; **Retro. Supp. I:** 35
Poems by Emily Dickinson, The (Bianchi and Hampson, eds.), **Retro. Supp. I:** 35
Poems by Emily Dickinson, Third Series (Todd, ed.), **Retro. Supp. I:** 35
Poems by James Russell Lowell, Second Series (Lowell), **Supp. I Part 2:** 406, 409
Poems by Sidney Lanier, (Lanier), **Supp. I Part 1:** 364
Poems from Black Africa (Hughes, ed.), **Supp. I Part 1:** 344
"Poems I Have Lost, The" (Ortiz), **Supp. IV Part 2:** 507
Poems of a Jew (Shapiro), **Supp. II Part 2:** 703, 712-713
Poems of Anna Akhmatova, The (Kunitz and Hayward, trans.), **Supp. III Part 1:** 269
Poems of Emily Dickinson, The (Bianchi and Hampson, eds.), **Retro. Supp. I:** 35
Poems of Emily Dickinson, The (Johnson, ed.), **I:** 470
Poems of François Villon (Kinnell, trans.), **Supp. III Part 1:** 235, 243, 249
"Poems of Our Climate, The" (Stevens), **Retro. Supp. I:** 313
Poems of Philip Freneau, Written Chiefly during the Late War (Freneau), **Supp. II Part 1:** 261
Poems of Places (Longfellow, ed.), **II:** 490; **Retro. Supp. II:** 155; **Supp. I Part 1:** 368
Poems of Stanley Kunitz, The (Kunitz), **Supp. III Part 1:** 258, 263, 264, 266, 268
"Poems of These States" (Ginsberg),

Supp. II Part 1: 323, 325
Poems of Two Friends (Howells and Piatt), **II:** 273, 277
"POEM SOME PEOPLE WILL HAVE TO UNDERSTAND, A" (Baraka), **Supp. II Part 1:** 49
Poems on Slavery (Longfellow), **II:** 489; **Retro. Supp. II:** 157, 168; **Supp. I Part 2:** 406
Poems on Various Subjects (Rowson), **Supp. XV:** 232
Poem Spoken at the Public Commencement at Yale College, in New Haven; September 1, 1781, A (Barlow), **Supp. II Part 1:** 67-68, 74, 75
Poems to Solve (Swenson), **Supp. IV Part 2:** 642
Poems Written and Published during the American Revolutionary War (Freneau), **Supp. II Part 1:** 273, 274
Poems Written between the Years 1768 and 1794 (Freneau), **Supp. II Part 1:** 269
"Poem That Took the Place of a Mountain" (Olson), **Supp. II Part 2:** 582
"Poem to My First Lover" (Olds), **Supp. X:** 206
"Poem to the Reader" (Olds), **Supp. X:** 213
"Poem with No Ending, A" (Levine), **Supp. V:** 186, 190
"Poem You Asked For, The" (Levis), **Supp. XI:** 259-260
Poe Poe Poe Poe Poe Poe Poe (Hoffman), **Retro. Supp. II:** 265
Poesía Náhuatl, **Supp. XV:** 77
Poésies 1917-1920 (Cocteau), **Retro. Supp. I:** 82
"Poesis: A Conceit" (Sobin), **Supp. XVI:** 288
"Poet, The" (Dunbar), **Supp. II Part 1:** 207, 209-210
"Poet, The" (Emerson), **II:** 13, 19, 20, 170
"Poet, The" (Ortiz), **Supp. IV Part 2:** 505
"Poet and His Book, The" (Millay), **III:** 126, 138
"Poet and His Public, The" (Jarrell), **Supp. I Part 1:** 96
"Poet and His Song, The" (Dunbar), **Supp. II Part 1:** 199
"Poet and the Person, The" (Kinard), **Supp. XIV:** 127
"Poet and the World, The" (Cowley), **Supp. II Part 1:** 145
"Poet as Anti-Specialist, The" (Swenson), **Supp. IV Part 2:** 638, 643

"Poet as *Curandera*" (Mora), **Supp. XIII:** 214, 220

"Poet as Hero, The: Keats in His Letters" (Trilling), **Supp. III Part 2:** 506-507

"Poet as Religious Moralist, The" (Larson), **Supp. XI:** 328

"Poet at Seven, The" (Rimbaud), **II:** 545

Poet at the Breakfast-Table, The (Holmes), **Supp. I Part 1:** 313-314

"Poète contumace, Le" (Corbiere), **II:** 384-385

"Poet for President, A" (Mora), **Supp. XIII:** 220-221

Poetic Achievement of Ezra Pound, The (Alexander), **Retro. Supp. I:** 293

Poetic Diction: A Study in Meaning (Barfield), **III:** 274, 279

"Poetic Principle, The" (Poe), **III:** 421, 426; **Retro. Supp. II:** 266

"Poetics" (Ammons), **Supp. VII:** 29-30

Poetics (Aristotle), **III:** 422; **Supp. XI:** 249; **Supp. XIII:** 75; **Supp. XIV:**243; **Supp. XV:** 265

Poetics of Space, The (Bachelard), **Supp. XIII:** 225; **Supp. XVI:**292

"Poetics of the Periphery: Literary Experimentalism in Kathy Acker's *In Memoriam to Identity*" (Acker), **Supp. XII:** 17

"Poetics of the Physical World, The" (Kinnell), **Supp. III Part 1:** 239

Poet in the World, The (Levertov), **Supp. III Part 1:** 271, 273, 278, 282

"Poet or the Growth of a Lit'ry Figure" (White), **Supp. I Part 2:** 676

Poetry (Barber), **Supp. IV Part 2:** 550

"Poetry" (Moore), **III:** 204-205, 215

"Poetry" (Nye), **Supp. XIII:** 282

"Poetry: A Metrical Essay" (Holmes), **Supp. I Part 1:** 310

"Poetry, Community and Climax" (Snyder), **Supp. VIII:** 290

"Poetry and Belief in Thomas Hardy" (Schwartz), **Supp. II Part 2:** 666

Poetry and Criticism (Nemerov, ed.), **III:** 269

"Poetry and Drama" (Eliot), **I:** 588

Poetry and Fiction: Essays (Nemerov), **III:** 269, 281

"Poetry and Place" (Berry), **Supp. X:** 22, 28, 31, 32

Poetry and Poets (Lowell), **II:** 512

"Poetry and Religion" (Jarman), **Supp. XVII:** 111

Poetry and the Age (Jarrell), **IV:** 352; **Retro. Supp. I:** 121; **Supp. II Part 1:** 135

"Poetry and the Primitive: Notes on Poetry as an Ecological Survival Technique" (Snyder), **Supp. VIII:** 291, 292, 299, 300

"Poetry and the Public World" (MacLeish), **III:** 11

Poetry and the World (Pinsky), **Supp. VI:** 236, 239, 244, 247

Poetry and Truth (Olson), **Supp. II Part 2:** 583

"Poetry As a Way of Life" (Bishop interview), **Retro. Supp. II:** 53

"Poetry as Survival" (Harrison), **Supp. VIII:** 45

Poetry for Students (Taibl), **Supp. XV:** 255

"Poetry for the Advanced" (Baraka), **Supp. II Part 1:** 58

Poetry Handbook, A (Oliver), **Supp. VII:** 229, 245

"Poetry of Barbarism, The" (Santayana), **IV:** 353

Poetry of Chaucer, The (Gardner), **Supp. VI:** 63

Poetry of Meditation, The (Martz), **IV:** 151; **Supp. I Part 1:** 107

Poetry of Mourning: The Modern Elegy from Hardy to Heaney (Ramazani), **Supp. IV Part 2:** 450

Poetry of Stephen Crane, The (Hoffman), **I:** 405

Poetry of the Negro 1746-1949, The (Hughes, ed.), **Supp. I Part 1:** 345

Poetry Reading against the Vietnam War, A (Bly and Ray, eds.), **Supp. IV Part 1:** 61, 63

"Poetry Wreck, The" (Shapiro), **Supp. II Part 2:** 717

Poetry Wreck, The: Selected Essays (Shapiro), **Supp. II Part 2:** 703, 704, 717

"Poets" (X. J. Kennedy), **Supp. XV:** 158

Poet's Alphabet, A: Reflections on the Literary Art and Vocation (Bogan), **Supp. III Part 1:** 55, 64

Poets and Poetry of America (Griswold), **Supp. XV:** 277

Poet's Choice (Engle and Langland, eds.), **III:** 277, 542

Poets of the Old Testament, The (Gordon), **III:** 199

Poets of Today (Wheelock, ed.), **Supp. IV Part 2:** 639

Poets on Poetry (Nemerov, ed.), **III:** 269

"Poet's Tact, and a Necessary Tactlessness, The" (C. Frost), **Supp. XV:** 94-95

"Poet's View, A" (Levertov), **Supp. III Part 1:** 284

"Poet's Voice, The" (Oliver), **Supp. VII:** 245

"Poet Turns on Himself, The" (Dickey), **Supp. IV Part 1:** 177, 181, 185

Poganuc People (Stowe), **Supp. I Part 2:** 581, 596, 599-600

Pogo (comic strip), **Supp. XI:** 105

Poincaré, Raymond, **IV:** 320

"Point, The" (Hayden), **Supp. II Part 1:** 373

"Point at Issue!, A" (Chopin), **Retro. Supp. II:** 61; **Supp. I Part 1:** 208

"Point of Age, A" (Berryman), **I:** 173

Point of No Return (Marquand), **III:** 56, 59-60, 65, 67, 69

Point Reyes Poems (R. Bly), **Supp. IV Part 1:** 71

Points for a Compass Rose (Connell), **Supp. XIV:**79, 80, 96

"Point Shirley" (Plath), **Supp. I Part 2:** 529, 538

Points in Time (Bowles), **Supp. IV Part 1:** 93

"Points West" (column), **Supp. IV Part 1:** 198

Poirier, Richard, **I:** 136, 239; **III:** 34; **Retro. Supp. I:** 134; **Retro. Supp. II:** 207-208; **Supp. I Part 2:** 660, 665; **Supp. IV Part 2:** 690

Poison Pen (Garrett), **Supp. VII:** 111

Poisonwood Bible, The (Kingsolver), **Supp. VII:** 197-198, 202, 210-213

Poitier, Sidney, **Supp. IV Part 1:** 360, 362

"Polar Bear" (Heller), **Supp. IV Part 1:** 383

Pole, Rupert, **Supp. X:** 185

"Pole Star" (MacLeish), **III:** 16

Po Li, **Supp. I Part 1:** 262

Police (Baraka), **Supp. II Part 1:** 47

"Police" (Corso), **Supp. XII:** 117, 127

"Police Court Saturday Morning" (X. J. Kennedy), **Supp. XV:** 170

"Police Dreams" (Bausch), **Supp. VII:** 47

Politian (Poe), **III:** 412

"Political and Practical Conceptions of Race, The" (Locke), **Supp. XIV:**209-210

Political Essays (Lowell), **Supp. I Part 2:** 407

Political Fable, A (Coover), **Supp. V:** 44, 46, 47, 49, 51

"Political Fables" (Mather), **Supp. II Part 2:** 450

"Political Interests" (Stevens), **Retro. Supp. I:** 295

"Political Litany, A" (Freneau), **Supp.**

II Part 1: 257
"Political Pastoral" (Frost), **Retro. Supp. I:** 139
"Political Poem" (Baraka), **Supp. II Part 1:** 36
Politics (Acker), **Supp. XII:** 3, 4
Politics (Macdonald), **I:** 233–234
"Politics" (Paley), **Supp. VI:** 217
"Politics, Structure, and Poetic Development" (McCombs), **Supp. XIII:** 33
"Politics and the English Language" (Orwell), **Retro. Supp. II:** 287; **Supp. I Part 2:** 620
Politics and the Novel (Howe), **Supp. VI:** 113
"Politics and the Personal Lyric in the Poetry of Joy Harjo and C. D. Wright" (Goodman), **Supp. XV:** 344
"Politics of Ethnic Authorship, The: Li-Young Lee, Emerson, and Whitman at the Banquet Table" (Partridge), **Supp. XV:** 219
"Politics of Silence, The" (Monette), **Supp. X:** 148
Politt, Katha, **Supp. XII:** 159
Polk, James, **Supp. XIII:** 20
Polk, James K., **I:** 17; **II:** 433–434
Pollack, Sydney, **Supp. XIII:** 159
"Pollen" (Nye), **Supp. XIII:** 284
Pollitt, Katha, **Supp. X:** 186, 191, 193; **Supp. XVI:** 39
Pollock, Jackson, **IV:** 411, 420; **Supp. XV:** 145, 177, 178
"Polly" (Chopin), **Retro. Supp. II:** 72
Polo, Marco, **III:** 395
Polybius, **Supp. I Part 2:** 491
"Polydore" (Chopin), **Retro. Supp. II:** 66
"Pomegranate" (Glück), **Supp. V:** 82
"Pomegranate Seed" (Wharton), **IV:** 316; **Retro. Supp. I:** 382
Ponce de Leon, Luis, **III:** 391
"Pond, The" (Nemerov), **III:** 272
"Pond at Dusk, The" (Kenyon), **Supp. VII:** 168
Ponder Heart, The (Welty), **IV:** 261, 274–275, 281; **Retro. Supp. I:** 351–352
"Ponderosa Pine" (Huncke), **Supp. XIV:** 146
Ponsot, Margaret, **Supp. XVII:** 241
"Pony" (Sanders), **Supp. XVI:** 277
Poodle Springs (Parker and Chandler), **Supp. IV Part 1:** 135
Poodle Springs Story, The (Chandler), **Supp. IV Part 1:** 135
"Pool, The" (Doolittle), **Supp. I Part 1:** 264–265
Poole, Ernest, **II:** 444

"Pool Lights" (F. Barthelme), **Supp. XI:** 25, 26–27, 36
"Pool Room in the Lions Club" (Merwin), **Supp. III Part 1:** 346
"Poor Black Fellow" (Hughes), **Retro. Supp. I:** 204
"Poor Bustard, The" (Corso), **Supp. XII:** 134
"Poor but Happy" (Mamet), **Supp. XIV:** 252, 253
Poore, Charles, **III:** 364
Poor Fool (Caldwell), **I:** 291, 292, 308
Poorhouse Fair, The (Updike), **IV:** 214, 228–229, 232; **Retro. Supp. I:** 317, 320
"Poor Joanna" (Jewett), **II:** 394
"Poor Man's Pudding and Rich Man's Crumbs" (Melville), **III:** 89–90
"Poor Richard" (James), **II:** 322
Poor Richard's Almanac (undated) (Franklin), **II:** 112
Poor Richard's Almanac for 1733 (Franklin), **II:** 108, 110
Poor Richard's Almanac for 1739 (Franklin), **II:** 112
Poor Richard's Almanac for 1758 (Franklin), **II:** 101
Poor White (Anderson), **I:** 110–111
"Poor Working Girl" (Z. Fitzgerald), **Supp. IX:** 71
Popa, Vasko, **Supp. VIII:** 272
Pope, Alexander, **I:** 198, 204; **II:** 17, 114; **III:** 263, 267, 288, 517; **IV:** 145; **Retro. Supp. I:** 335; **Supp. I Part 1:** 150, 152, 310; **Supp. I Part 2:** 407, 422, 516, 714; **Supp. II Part 1:** 70, 71; **Supp. X:** 32, 36; **Supp. XII:** 260; **Supp. XV:** 258
Pope-Hennessy, James, **Supp. XIV:** 348
"Pope's Penis, The" (Olds), **Supp. X:** 207
"Poplar, Sycamore" (Wilbur), **Supp. III Part 2:** 549
Popo and Fifina (Hughes and Bontemps), **Retro. Supp. I:** 203
"Poppies" (Oliver), **Supp. VII:** 240
"Poppies in July" (Plath), **Supp. I Part 2:** 544
"Poppies in October" (Plath), **Supp. I Part 2:** 544
"Poppycock" (Francis), **Supp. IX:** 87
"Poppy Seed" (Lowell), **II:** 523
Popular Culture (Goldbarth), **Supp. XII: 186**
Popular History of the United States (Gay), **Supp. I Part 1:** 158
"Popular Songs" (Ashbery), **Supp. III Part 1:** 6
"Populist Manifesto" (Ferlinghetti), **Supp. VIII:** 290

"Porcelain Bowl" (Glück), **Supp. V:** 83
Porcher, Frances, **Retro. Supp. II:** 71
"Porcupine, The" (Kinnell), **Supp. III Part 1:** 244
Porcupine's Kiss, The (Dobyns), **Supp. XIII: 89–90**
Porgy and Bess (film), **Supp. I Part 1:** 66
Porgy and Bess (play), **Supp. IV Part 1:** 6
"Porphyria's Lover" (Browning), **II:** 522
Portable Beat Reader, The (Charters, ed.), **Supp. XIV:** 152
Portable Blake, The (Kazin, ed.), **Supp. VIII:** 103
Portable Faulkner, The (Cowley, ed.), **II:** 57, 59; **Retro. Supp. I:** 73
Portable Paul and Jane Bowles, The (Dillon), **Supp. IV Part 1:** 95
Portable Veblen, The (Veblen), **Supp. I Part 2:** 630, 650
"Porte-Cochere" (Taylor), **Supp. V:** 320
"Porter" (Hughes), **Supp. I Part 1:** 327
Porter, Bern, **III:** 171
Porter, Cole, **Supp. IX:** 189
Porter, Eliot, **Supp. IV Part 2:** 599
Porter, Fairfield, **Supp. XV:** 178
Porter, Herman W., **Supp. I Part 1:** 49
Porter, Horace, **Retro. Supp. II:** 4, 127
Porter, Jacob, **Supp. I Part 1:** 153
Porter, Katherine Anne, **I:** 97, 385; **II:** 194, 606; **III: 433–455**, 482; **IV:** 26, 138, 246, 261, 279, 280, 282; **Retro. Supp. I:** 354; **Retro. Supp. II:** 233, 235; **Supp. IV Part 1:** 31, 310; **Supp. V:** 225; **Supp. VIII:** 156, 157; **Supp. IX:** 93, 94, 95, 98, 128; **Supp. X:** 50; **Supp. XIII:** 294; **Supp. XIV:** 3; **Supp. XV:** 338
Porter, Noah, **Supp. I Part 2:** 640
Porter, William Sydney. *See* Henry, O.
Porteus, Beilby, **Supp. I Part 1:** 150
"Portland Going Out, The" (Merwin), **Supp. III Part 1:** 345
Portnoy's Complaint (P. Roth), **Retro. Supp. II: 282–286**, 291; **Supp. III Part 2:** 401, 404, 405, 407, 412–414, 426; **Supp. V:** 119, 122; **Supp. XI:** 140; **Supp. XVII:** 8, 43
Port of Saints (Burroughs), **Supp. III Part 1:** 106
"Portrait" (Dixon), **Supp. XII:** 154
"Portrait, A" (Parker), **Supp. IX:** 192–193
"Portrait, The" (Kunitz), **Supp. III Part 1:** 263
"Portrait, The" (Wharton), **Retro.**

Supp. I: 364
"Portrait d'une Femme" (Pound), **Retro. Supp. I:** 288
Portrait in Brownstone (Auchincloss), **Supp. IV Part 1:** 21, 23, 27, 31
"Portrait in Georgia" (Toomer), **Supp. IX:** 314
"Portrait in Greys, A" (W. C. Williams), **Retro. Supp. I:** 416
"Portrait of a Girl in Glass" (T. Williams), **IV:** 383
"Portrait of a Jewelry Drummer" (Untermeyer), **Supp. XV:** 299-300
"Portrait of a Lady" (Eliot), **I:** 569, 570, 571, 584; **III:** 4; **Retro. Supp. I:** 55, 56, 62
Portrait of a Lady, The (James), **I:** 10, 258, 461-462, 464; **II:** 323, 325, 327, 328-329, 334; **Retro. Supp. I:** 215, 216, 217, 219, 220, 223, **224-225,** 232, 233, 381
"Portrait of an Artist" (P. Roth), **Supp. III Part 2:** 412
Portrait of an Eye: Three Novels (Acker), **Supp. XII:** 6, **7-9**
"Portrait of an Invisible Man" (Auster), **Supp. XII:** 21
"Portrait of a Supreme Court Judge" (Untermeyer), **Supp. XV:** 299
Portrait of Bascom Hawkes, A (Wolfe), **IV:** 451-452, 456
Portrait of Edith Wharton (Lubbock), **Retro. Supp. I:** 366
Portrait of Logan Pearsall Smith, Drawn from His Letters and Diaries, A (Russell, ed.), **Supp. XIV:** 349
Portrait of Picasso as a Young Man (Mailer), **Retro. Supp. II:** 213
"Portrait of the Artist as an Old Man, A" (Humphrey), **Supp. IX:** 109
Portrait of the Artist as a Young Man, A (Joyce), **I:** 475-476; **III:** 471, 561; **Retro. Supp. I:** 127; **Retro. Supp. II:** 4, 331; **Supp. IX:** 236; **Supp. XIII:** 53, 95
"Portrait of the Artist with Hart Crane" (Wright), **Supp. V:** 342
"Portrait of the Intellectual as a Yale Man" (McCarthy), **II:** 563, 564-565
"Portrait of the Self ... , A" (Sobin), **Supp. XVI:** 288
Portraits and Elegies (Schnackenberg), **Supp. XV:** 249, **253-256**
"Port Town" (Hughes), **Retro. Supp. I:** 199
Portuguese Voyages to America in the Fifteenth Century (Morison), **Supp. I Part 2:** 488
"Po' Sandy" (Chesnutt), **Supp. XIV:** 60

Poseidon Adventure, The (film), **Supp. XII:** 321
Poseidon Adventure, The (Gallico), **Supp. XVI:** 238
"Poseidon and Company" (Carver), **Supp. III Part 1:** 137
"Positive Obsession" (O. Butler), **Supp. XIII:** 70
Poss, Stanley, **Supp. XIV:** 166
"Possessions" (H. Crane), **I:** 392-393; **Retro. Supp. II:** 78
Possible World, A (Koch), **Supp. XV:** 184
Postal Inspector (film), **Supp. XIII:** 166
Postcards (Proulx), **Supp. VII:** 249, 256-258, 262
"Postcolonial Tale, A" (Harjo), **Supp. XII:** 227
"Posthumous Letter to Gilbert White" (Auden), **Supp. II Part 1:** 26
"Post-Larkin Triste" (Karr), **Supp. XI:** 242-243
Postlethwaite, Diana, **Supp. XII:** 317-318; **Supp. XVI:** 176
"Postlude" (W. C. Williams), **Retro. Supp. I:** 415
Postman, Neil, **Supp. XI:** 275
Postman Always Rings Twice, The (Cain), **Supp. XIII:** 165-166
Postman Always Rings Twice, The (film), **Supp. XIV:** 241
"Postmortem Guide, A" (Dunn), **Supp. XI:** 155
Postrel, Virginia, **Supp. XIV:** 298, 311
"Postscript" (Du Bois), **Supp. II Part 1:** 173
"Postscript" (Nye), **Supp. XIII:** 287
"Potato" (Wilbur), **Supp. III Part 2:** 545
"Potatoes' Dance, The" (Lindsay), **Supp. I Part 2:** 394
Pot of Earth, The (MacLeish), **III:** 5, 6-8, 10, 12, 18
"Pot Roast" (Strand), **Supp. IV Part 2:** 629
Pot Shots at Poetry (Francis), **Supp. IX:** 83-84
Potter, Beatrix, **Supp. I Part 2:** 656; **Supp. XVI:** 100
Potter, Stephen, **IV:** 430
Potter's House, The (Stegner), **Supp. IV Part 2:** 598, 606
Poulenc, Francis, **Supp. IV Part 1:** 81
Poulin, Al, Jr., **Supp. IX:** 272; **Supp. XI:** 259
Pound, Ezra, **I:** 49, 58, 60, 66, 68, 69, 105, 236, 243, 256, 384, 403, 428, 429, 475, 476, 482, 487, 521, 578; **II:** 26, 55, 168, 263, 316, 371, 376,

513, 517, 520, 526, 528, 529, 530; **III:** 2, 5, 8, 9, 13-14, 17, 174, 194, 196, 278, 430, 453, **456-479,** 492, 504, 511, 523, 524, 527, 575-576, 586, 590; **IV:** 27, 28, 407, 415, 416, 433, 446; **Retro. Supp. I:** 51, 52, 55, 58, 59, 63, 82, 89, 127, 140, 171, 177, 178, 198, 216, **283-294,** 298, 299, 359, 411, 412, 413, 414, 417, 418, 419, 420, 423, 426, 427, 430, 431; **Retro. Supp. II:** 178, 183, 189, 326; **Supp. I Part 1:** 253, 255-258, 261-268, 272, 274; **Supp. I Part 2:** 387, 721; **Supp. II Part 1:** 1, 8, 20, 30, 91, 136; **Supp. III Part 1:** 48, 63, 64, 73, 105, 146, 225, 271; **Supp. III Part 2:** 542, **609-617,** 619, 620, 622, 625, 626, 628, 631; **Supp. IV Part 1:** 153, 314; **Supp. V:** 331, 338, 340, 343, 345; **Supp. VIII:** 39, 105, 195, 205, 271, 290, 291, 292, 303; **Supp. IX:** 291; **Supp. X:** 24, 36, 112, 120, 122; **Supp. XII:** 97; **Supp. XIV:** 11, 55, 83, 272, 284, 286, 287, 347; **Supp. XV:** 20, 42, 43, 51, 93, 161, 181, 297, 298, 299, 301, 302, 306; **Supp. XVI:** 47, 282; **Supp. XVII:** 111, 226-227
Pound, Louise, **Retro. Supp. I:** 4; **Supp. XV:** 137
Pound, T. S., **I:** 428
"Pound Reweighed" (Cowley), **Supp. II Part 1:** 143
Powell, Betty, **Retro. Supp. II:** 140
Powell, Dawn, **Supp. IV Part 2:** 678, 682
Powell, Dick, **Supp. IX:** 250
Powell, John Wesley, **Supp. IV Part 2:** 598, 604, 611
Powell, Lawrence Clark, **III:** 189
Powell, William, **Supp. IV Part 1:** 355
"Power" (Corso), **Supp. XII:** 117, 126, 127, **128**
"Power" (Emerson), **II:** 2, 3
"Power" (Rich), **Supp. I Part 2:** 569
"Power and Light" (Dickey), **Supp. IV Part 1:** 182
Power and the Glory, The (Greene), **III:** 556
"Powerhouse" (Welty), **Retro. Supp. I:** 343, 346
"Power Never Dominion" (Rukeyser), **Supp. VI:** 281
"Power of Fancy, The" (Freneau), **Supp. II Part 1:** 255
Power of Myth, The (Campbell), **Supp. IX:** 245
"Power of Prayer, The" (Lanier), **Supp. I Part 1:** 357

"Power of Stories, The" (Sanders), **Supp. XVI:**278
"Power of Suggestion" (Auchincloss), **Supp. IV Part 1:** 33
Power of Sympathy, The (Brown), **Supp. II Part 1:** 74
Power Politics (Atwood), **Supp. XIII:** 20, 33-34, 35
Powers, J. F., **Supp. V:** 319; **Supp. XVII:** 43
Powers, Kim, **Supp. VIII:** 329, 340
Powers, Richard, **Supp. IX: 207-225; Supp. XVII:** 183
Powers of Attorney (Auchincloss), **Supp. IV Part 1:** 31, 32, 33
"Powers of Darkness" (Wharton), **Retro. Supp. I:** 379
Powys, John Cowper, **Supp. I Part 2:** 454, 476; **Supp. IX:** 135
Poynton, Jerome, **Supp. XIV:**147, 150
Practical Agitation (Chapman), **Supp. XIV:**41
Practical Criticism: A Study of Literary Judgment (Richards), **Supp. XIV:**3, 16
Practical Magic (film), **Supp. X:** 80
Practical Magic (Hoffman), **Supp. X:** 78, 82, **88-89**
"Practical Methods of Meditation, The" (Dawson), **IV:** 151
Practical Navigator, The (Bowditch), **Supp. I Part 2:** 482
Practice of Perspective, The (Dubreuil), **Supp. IV Part 2:** 425
Practice of Reading, The (Donoghue), **Supp. VIII:** 189
Pragmatism: A New Name for Some Old Ways of Thinking (James), **II:** 352
"Pragmatism's Conception of Truth" (James), **Supp. XIV:**40
Prague Orgy, The (P. Roth), **Retro. Supp. II:** 280
"Praire, The" (Clampitt), **Supp. IX:** 42
"Prairie" (Sandburg), **III:** 583, 584
Prairie, The (Cooper), **I:** 339, 342
"Prairie Birthday" (Leopold), **Supp. XIV:**185
Prairie Home Companion, A (Keillor, radio program), **Supp. XIII:** 274; **Supp. XVI:**169-171, 173-178
Prairie Home Morning Show, A (Keillor, radio program), **Supp. XVI:**171
"Prairie Life, A Citizen Speaks" (Dunn), **Supp. XI:** 145
"Prairies, The" (Bryant), **Supp. I Part 1:** 157, 162, 163, 166
Praise (Hass), **Supp. VI:** 104-105, 106
"Praise for an Urn" (Crane), **I:** 388

"Praise for Sick Women" (Snyder), **Supp. VIII:** 294
"Praise in Summer" (Wilbur), **Supp. III Part 2:** 546-548, 560, 562
"Praise of a Palmtree" (Levertov), **Supp. III Part 1:** 284
"Praise of the Committee" (Rukeyser), **Supp. VI:** 278
"Praises, The" (Goldbarth), **Supp. XII:** 185
"Praises, The" (Olson), **Supp. II Part 2:** 558, 560, 563, 564
Praises and Dispraises (Des Pres), **Supp. X:** 120
Praisesong for the Widow (Marshall), **Supp. IV Part 1:** 14; **Supp. XI:** 18, 276, 278, **284-286,** 287
"Praise to the End!" (Roethke), **III:** 529, 532, 539
Prajadhipok, King of Siam, **I:** 522
Prater Violet (Isherwood), **Supp. XIV:164-166,** 169-170, 171
Pratt, Anna (Anna Alcott), **Supp. I Part 1:** 33
Pratt, Louis H., **Retro. Supp. II:** 6
Pratt, Mary Louise, **Retro. Supp. II:** 48
Pratt, Parley, **Supp. IV Part 2:** 603
"Prattler" (newspaper column), **I:** 207
"Prattler, The" (Bierce), **I:** 196
"Prayer" (Gioia), **Supp. XV:** 117
"Prayer" (Olds), **Supp. X:** 204
"Prayer" (Toomer), **Supp. IX:** 318
"Prayer, A" (Kushner), **Supp. IX: 134**
"Prayer for Columbus" (Whitman), **IV:** 348
"Prayer for My Daughter" (Yeats), **II:** 598
"Prayer for My Grandfather to Our Lady, A" (Lowell), **II:** 541-542
"Prayer for my Son" (C. Frost), **Supp. XV:** 98-99
"Prayer for Our Daughters" (Jarman), **Supp. XVII:** 120
Prayer for Owen Meany, A (Irving), **Supp. VI:** 164, 165, 166, **175-176**
"PRAYER FOR SAVING" (Baraka), **Supp. II Part 1:** 52-53
"Prayer in Spring, A" (Frost), **II:** 153, 164
"Prayer on All Saint's Day" (Cowley), **Supp. II Part 1:** 138, 153
Prayers for Dark People (Du Bois), **Supp. II Part 1:** 186
"Prayer to Hermes" (Creeley), **Supp. IV Part 1:** 156, 157
"Prayer to Masks" (Senghor), **Supp. IV Part 1:** 16
"Prayer to the Child of Prague" (Salinas), **Supp. XIII:** 327

"Prayer to the Good Poet" (Wright), **Supp. III Part 2:** 603
"Prayer to the Pacific" (Silko), **Supp. IV Part 2:** 560
"Pray without Ceasing" (Emerson), **II:** 9-10
Praz, Mario, **IV:** 430
"Preacher, The" (Whittier), **Supp. I Part 2:** 698-699
Preacher and the Slave, The (Stegner), **Supp. IV Part 2:** 599, 608, 609
Precaution (Cooper), **I:** 337, 339
"Preconceptions of Economic Science, The" (Veblen), **Supp. I Part 2:** 634
Predecessors, Et Cetera (Clampitt), **Supp. IX:** 37
"Predicament, A" (Poe), **Retro. Supp. II:** 273
Predilections (Moore), **III:** 194
Prefaces and Prejudices (Mencken), **III:** 99, 104, 106, 119
Preface to a Twenty Volume Suicide Note.... (Baraka), **Supp. II Part 1:** 31, 33-34, 51, 61
"Preference" (Wylie), **Supp. I Part 2:** 713
"Prejudice against the Past, The" (Moore), **IV:** 91
Prejudices (Mencken), **Supp. I Part 2:** 630
Prejudices: A Selection (Farrell, ed.), **III:** 116
Prejudices: First Series (Mencken), **III:** 105
"Preliminary Remarks on the Poetry in the First Person" (Wright), **Supp. XV:** 339
Prelude, A: Landscapes, Characters and Conversations from the Earlier Years of My Life (Wilson), **IV:** 426, 427, 430, 434, 445
Prelude, The (Wordsworth), **III:** 528; **IV:** 331, 343; **Supp. I Part 2:** 416, 676; **Supp. XI:** 248
Prelude and Liebestod (McNally), **Supp. XIII:** 201
"Preludes" (Eliot), **I:** 573, 576, 577; **Retro. Supp. I:** 55; **Supp. IV Part 2:** 436
Preludes for Memnon (Aiken), **I:** 59, 65
Preludes from Memnon (Aiken), **Supp. X:** 50
"Prelude to an Evening" (Ransom), **III:** 491, 492-493
Prelude to Darkness (Salinas), **Supp. XIII:** 311, **318-319,** 320
"Prelude to the Present" (Mumford), **Supp. II Part 2:** 471
"Premature Burial, The" (Poe), **III:**

415, 416, 418; **Retro. Supp. II:** 270
Preminger, Otto, **Supp. IX:** 3, 9
"Premonition" (Hay), **Supp. XIV:**122
"Premonitions of the Bread Line" (Komunyakaa), **Supp. XIII:** 114, 115
Prenshaw, Peggy Whitman, **Supp. X:** 229
"Preparations" (Silko), **Supp. IV Part 2:** 560
Preparatory Meditations (Taylor), **IV:** 145, 148, 149, 150, 152, 153, 154-155, 164, 165
"Prepare" (Carruth), **Supp. XVI:**59
Prepositions: The Collected Critical Essays of Louis Zukofsky (Zukofsky), **Supp. III Part 2:** 630
Prescott, Anne, **Supp. IV Part 1:** 299
Prescott, Orville, **Supp. IV Part 2:** 680; **Supp. XI:** 340
Prescott, Peter, **Supp. X:** 83
Prescott, Peter S., **Supp. XVI:**212
Prescott, William, **Retro. Supp. I:** 123
Prescott, William Hickling, **II:** 9, 310, 313-314; **IV:** 309; **Supp. I Part 2:** 414, 479, 493, 494
"Prescription of Painful Ends" (Jeffers), **Supp. II Part 2:** 424
"Presence, The" (Gordon), **II:** 199, 200
"Presence, The" (Kumin), **Supp. IV Part 2:** 445, 455
Presence and Desire: Essays on Gender, Sexuality, Performance (Dolan), **Supp. XV:** 327
"Presence of Others, The" (Kenyon), **Supp. VII:** 164
Presences (Taylor), **Supp. V:** 325
"Present Age, The" (Emerson), **II:** 11-12
Present Danger, The: Do We Have the Will to Reverse the Decline of American Power? (Podhoretz), **Supp. VIII:** 241
Present for Young Ladies, A (Rowson), **Supp. XV:** 245
"Present Hour" (Sandburg), **III:** 593-594
Present Philosophical Tendencies (Perry), **I:** 224
"Present State of Ethical Philosophy, The" (Emerson), **II:** 9
"Present State of Poetry, The" (Schwartz), **Supp. II Part 2:** 666
"Preservation of Innocence" (Baldwin), **Supp. I Part 1:** 51
"Preserving Wildness" (Berry), **Supp. X:** 28, 29, 32
"President and Other Intellectuals, The" (Kazin), **Supp. VIII:** 104
Presidential Papers, The (Mailer), **III:**

35, 37-38, 42, 45; **Retro. Supp. II:** 203, 204, 206
"Presidents" (Merwin), **Supp. III Part 1:** 351
Presnell, Robert, Sr., **Supp. XIII:** 166
"PRES SPOKE IN A LANGUAGE" (Baraka), **Supp. II Part 1:** 60
Presumed Innocent (Turow), 217; **Supp. XVII:** 214-216, 223
"Pretext, The" (Wharton), **Retro. Supp. I:** 371
Pretty Boy Floyd (McMurtry), **Supp. V:** 231
"Pretty Girl, The" (Dubus), **Supp. VII:** 87-88
"Pretty Mouth and Green My Eyes" (Salinger), **III:** 560
"Previous Condition" (Baldwin), **Supp. I Part 1:** 51, 55, 63
"Previous Tenant, The" (Simpson), **Supp. IX:** 278-279
Priaulx, Allan, **Supp. XI:** 228
Price, Alan, **Retro. Supp. I:** 377
Price, Reynolds, **Supp. VI:** 253-270; **Supp. IX:** 256, 257
Price, Richard, **II:** 9; **Supp. I Part 2:** 522
Price, The (A. Miller), **III:** 165-166
"Price of the Harness, The" (Crane), **I:** 414
Pricksongs & Descants; Fictions (Coover), **Supp. V:** 39, 42, 43, 49, 50
"Pride" (Hughes), **Supp. I Part 1:** 331
Pride and Prejudice (Austen), **II:** 290
Prideaux, Tom, **Supp. IV Part 2:** 574, 590
"Priesthood, The" (Winters), **Supp. II Part 2:** 786
Priestly, Joseph, **Supp. I Part 2:** 522
Primary Colors, The (A. Theroux), **Supp. VIII:** 312
"Primary Ground, A" (Rich), **Supp. I Part 2:** 563
"Prime" (Auden), **Supp. II Part 1:** 22
"Primer Class" (Bishop), **Retro. Supp. II:** 38, 51
Primer for Blacks (Brooks), **Supp. III Part 1:** 85
"Primer for the Nuclear Age" (Dove), **Supp. IV Part 1:** 246
Primer of Ignorance, A (Blackmur), **Supp. II Part 1:** 91
Primitive, The (C. Himes), **Supp. XVI:**139, 141-142
"Primitive Black Man, The" (Du Bois), **Supp. II Part 1:** 176
"Primitive Like an Orb, A" (Stevens), **IV:** 89; **Retro. Supp. I:** 309
Primitive People (Prose), **Supp.**

XVI:255, 256, 257
"Primitive Singing" (Lindsay), **Supp. I Part 2:** 389-390
Primitivism and Decadence (Winters), **Supp. II Part 2:** 786, 803-807, 812
Prince, Richard, **Supp. XII:** 4
"Prince, The" (Jarrell), **II:** 379
"Prince, The" (Winters), **Supp. II Part 2:** 802
Prince and the Pauper, The (Twain), **IV:** 200-201, 206
Prince Hagen (Sinclair), **Supp. V:** 280
Prince of a Fellow, A (Hearon), **Supp. VIII:** 58, **62-63**
Princess, The (Tennyson), **Supp. I Part 2:** 410
Princess and the Goblins, The (Macdonald), **Supp. XIII:** 75
Princess Casamassima, The (James), **II:** 276, 291; **IV:** 202; **Retro. Supp. I:** 216, 221, 222, 225, **226-227**
"Princess Casamassima, The" (Trilling), **Supp. III Part 2:** 502, 503
Princess of Arcady, A (Henry), **Retro. Supp. II:** 97
"Principles" (Du Bois), **Supp. II Part 1:** 172
Principles of Literary Criticism (Richards), **I:** 274; **Supp. I Part 1:** 264; **Supp. XIV:**3
Principles of Psychology, The (James), **II:** 321, 350-352, 353, 354, 357, 362, 363-364; **IV:** 28, 29, 32, 37
Principles of Psychology, The (W. James), **Supp. XVII:** 97
Principles of Zoölogy (Agassiz), **Supp. I Part 1:** 312
Prior, Matthew, **II:** 111; **III:** 521
Prior, Sir James, **II:** 315
"Prison, The" (Malamud), **Supp. I Part 2:** 431, 437
Prisoner of Second Avenue, The (Simon), **Supp. IV Part 2:** 583, 584
Prisoner of Sex, The (Mailer), **III:** 46; **Retro. Supp. II:** 206
Prisoner of Zenda, The (film), **Supp. I Part 2:** 615
Prisoner's Dilemma (Powers), **Supp. IX:** 212, **214-216,** 221
Prison Memoirs of an Anarchist (A. Berkman), **Supp. XVII:** 103-104
Pritchard, William, **Supp. XVI:**71
Pritchard, William H., **Retro. Supp. I:** 131, 141; **Supp. IV Part 1:** 285; **Supp. IV Part 2:** 642; **Supp. XI:** 326
Pritchett, V. S., **II:** 587; **Supp. II Part 1:** 143; **Supp. VIII:** 171; **Supp. XIII:** 168

"Privatation and Publication" (Cowley), **Supp. II Part 1:** 149
Private Contentment (Price), **Supp. VI:** 263
"Private History of a Campaign That Failed" (Twain), **IV:** 195
Private Life of Axie Reed, The (Knowles), **Supp. XII:** 249
"Private Man Confronts His Vulgarities at Dawn, A" (Dunn), **Supp. XI:** 146
Private Memoirs and Confessions of a Justified Sinner, The (Hogg), **Supp. IX:** 276
"Private Property and the Common Wealth" (Berry), **Supp. X:** 25
Private Snafu series (Geisel), **Supp. XVI:** 102
"Private Theatricals" (Howells), **II:** 280
Privilege, The (Kumin), **Supp. IV Part 2:** 442-444, 451
Prize Stories 1918 : The O. Henry Awards, **Supp. XVI:** 16
"Probing the Dark" (Komunyakaa), **Supp. XIII:** 131
"Problem from Milton, A" (Wilbur), **Supp. III Part 2:** 550
"Problem of Anxiety, The" (Koch), **Supp. XV:** 183
"Problem of Being, The" (James), **II:** 360
Problem of Classification in the Theory of Value, The (Locke), **Supp. XIV:** 199
"Problem of Housing the Negro, The" (Du Bois), **Supp. II Part 1:** 168
"Problem of the Religious Novel, The" (Isherwood), **Supp. XIV:** 172
Problems and Other Stories (Updike), **Retro. Supp. I:** 322, 329
"Problem Solving" (Goldbarth), **Supp. XII:** 185
Procedures for Underground (Atwood), **Supp. XIII:** 33
"Procedures for Underground" (Atwood), **Supp. XIII:** 33
Processional (Lawson), **I:** 479
"Procession at Candlemas, A" (Clampitt), **Supp. IX:** 41
Proclus, **Retro. Supp. I:** 247
"Prodigal" (Ammons), **Supp. VII:** 29
"Prodigal, The" (Bishop), **Supp. I Part 1:** 90, 92
Prodigal Parents, The (Lewis), **II:** 454-455
"Prodigy" (Simic), **Supp. VIII:** 278
Producers, The (film, M. Brooks), **Supp. XVII:** 45
"Proem" (Crane), **I:** 397

"Proem, The: By the Carpenter" (O. Henry), **Supp. II Part 1:** 409
"Professions for Women" (Woolf), **Supp. XIII:** 305
"Professor" (Hughes), **Supp. I Part 1:** 330
"Professor, The" (Bourne), **I:** 223
Professor at the Breakfast Table, The (Holmes), **Supp. I Part 1:** 313, 316
"Professor Clark's Economics" (Veblen), **Supp. I Part 2:** 634
Professor of Desire, The (P. Roth), **Retro. Supp. II:** 288; **Supp. III Part 2:** 403, 418-420
Professor's House, The (Cather), **I:** 325-336; **Retro. Supp. I:** 16
"Professor Veblen" (Mencken), **Supp. I Part 2:** 630
Proffer, Carl R., **Supp. VIII:** 22
Profile Makers, The (Bierds), **Supp. XVII:** 29, **30-32**, 33
"Profile of the Tenderloin Street Prostitute, A" (Vollmann), **Supp. XVII:** 230
Profits of Religion, The (Sinclair), **Supp. V:** 276
"Prognosis" (Warren), **IV:** 245
"Progress" (F. Wright), **Supp. XVII:** 247
"Progress Report" (Simic), **Supp. VIII:** 278
"Project for a Trip to China" (Sontag), **Supp. II Part 2:** 454, 469
"Project for *The Ambassadors*" (James), **Retro. Supp. I:** 229
"Projection" (Nemerov), **III:** 275
"Projective Verse" (Olson), **Supp. III Part 1:** 30; **Supp. III Part 2:** 555, 556, 557, 624; **Supp. IV Part 1:** 139, 153; **Supp. VIII:** 290
"Projector, The" (Baker), **Supp. XIII:** 53, 55
Prokofiev, Sergey Sergeyevich, **Supp. IV Part 1:** 81
"Prolegomena, Section 1" (Pound), **Supp. III Part 2:** 615-616
"Prolegomena, Section 2" (Pound), **Supp. III Part 2:** 616
"Prolegomenon to a Biography of Mailer" (Lucid), **Retro. Supp. II:** 195
Proletarian Literature in the United States (Hicks), **Supp. I Part 2:** 609-610
"Prologue" (MacLeish), **III:** 8, 14
"Prologue to Our Time" (Mumford), **Supp. III Part 2:** 473
"Prometheus" (Longfellow), **II:** 494
Prometheus Bound (Lowell), **II:** 543, 544, 545, 555

Promise, The (Buck), **Supp. II Part 1:** 124
"Promise, The" (Olds), **Supp. X:** 213
Promised Land, The (M. Antin), **Supp. IX:** 227; **Supp. XVI:** 148, 149
Promised Land, The (Porter), **III:** 447
Promised Lands (Sontag), **Supp. III Part 2:** 452
Promise of American Life, The (Croly), **I:** 229
"Promise of Blue Horses, The" (Harjo), **Supp. XII:** 228
Promise of Rest, The (Price), **Supp. VI:** 262, 266
Promises (Warren), **Supp. XIV:** 15
Promises: Poems 1954-1956 (Warren), **IV:** 244-245, 249, 252
Promises, Promises (musical), **Supp. IV Part 2:** 575
"Promise This When You Be Dying" (Dickinson), **Retro. Supp. I:** 44, 46
Proof, The (Winters), **Supp. II Part 2:** 786, 791, 792-794
Proofs and Theories: Essays on Poetry (Glück), **Supp. V:** 77, 79, 92; **Supp. XIV:** 269
"Propaganda of History, The" (Du Bois), **Supp. II Part 1:** 182
Propertius, Sextus, **III:** 467; **Retro. Supp. II:** 187; **Supp. XII:** 2
Property Of: A Novel (Hoffman), **Supp. X:** 77, 79, **80-82**
"Prophecy of Samuel Sewall, The" (Whittier), **Supp. I Part 2:** 699
Propheteers, The (Apple), **Supp. XVII:** 6-7
"Prophetic Pictures, The" (Hawthorne), **II:** 227
"Proportion" (Lowell), **II:** 525
"Proposal" (Carver), **Supp. III Part 1:** 149
Proposals Relating to the Education of Youth in Pensilvania (Franklin), **II:** 113
"Proposed New Version of the Bible" (Franklin), **II:** 110
Prose, Francine, **Supp. XII:** 333; **Supp. XVI:** 249-264
"Prose for Departure" (Merrill), **Supp. III Part 1:** 336
Prose Pieces (Bynner), **Supp. XV:** 52
"Prose Poem as an Evolving Form, The" (R. Bly), **Supp. IV Part 1:** 64
"Proserpina and the Devil" (Wilder), **IV:** 358
"Prosody" (Shapiro), **Supp. II Part 2:** 710
Prospect before Us, The (Dos Passos), **I:** 491
"Prospective Immigrants Please Note"

(Rich), **Supp. I Part 2:** 555
Prospect of Peace, The (Barlow), **Supp. II Part 1:** 67, 68, 75
Prospects of Literature, The (L. P. Smith), **Supp. XIV:**343
Prospects on the Rubicon (Paine), **Supp. I Part 2:** 510-511
Prospectus of a National Institution, to Be Established in the United States (Barlow), **Supp. II Part 1:** 80, 82
Prospice (Browning), **IV:** 366
"Protestant Easter" (Sexton), **Supp. II Part 2:** 684
"Prothalamion" (Schwartz), **Supp. II Part 2:** 649, 652
"Prothalamion" (Spenser), **Retro. Supp. I:** 62
Proud, Robert, **Supp. I Part 1:** 125
"Proud Farmer, The" (Lindsay), **Supp. I Part 2:** 381
Proud Flesh (Humphrey), **Supp. IX:** 94, 95, 96, **102-103,** 104, 105, 109
"Proud Flesh" (Warren), **IV:** 243
"Proud Lady" (Wylie), **Supp. I Part 2:** 711-712
Proulx, Annie, **Supp. VII: 249-267**
Proust, Marcel, **I:** 89, 319, 327, 377, 461; **II:** 377, 514, 606; **III:** 174, 181, 184, 244-245, 259, 471; **IV:** 32, 201, 237, 301, 312, 328, 359, 428, 431, 434, 439, 443, 466, 467; **Retro. Supp. I:** 75, 89, 169, 335; **Supp. III Part 1:** 10, 12, 14, 15; **Supp. IV Part 2:** 600; **Supp. VIII:** 103; **Supp. IX:** 211; **Supp. X:** 193, 194; **Supp. XII:** 289; **Supp. XIV:**24, 83, 95; **Supp. XVI:**295
Proverbs, **Supp. X:** 45
"Proverbs" (Jarman), **Supp. XVII:** 118
"Providence" (Komunyakaa), **Supp. XIII:** 132
"Provincetown Postcards" (F. Wright), **Supp. XVII:** 244
"Provincia deserta" (Pound), **Retro. Supp. I:** 289
"Provisional Remarks on Being / A Poet / of Arkansas" (Wright), **Supp. XV:** 337
Pruette, Lorine, **Supp. IV Part 2:** 522
Prufrock and Other Observations (Eliot), **I:** 569-570, 571, 573, 574, 576-577, 583, 584, 585; **Retro. Supp. I:** 59, 62
"Prufrock's Perivigilium" (Eliot), **Retro. Supp. I:** 57
Pryor, Richard, **Supp. XIII:** 343
Pryse, Marjorie, **Retro. Supp. II:** 139, 146
"Psalm" (Ginsberg), **Supp. II Part 1:** 312

"Psalm" (Simic), **Supp. VIII:** 282
"Psalm: Our Fathers" (Merwin), **Supp. III Part 1:** 350
"Psalm and Lament" (Justice), **Supp. VII:** 116, 117-118, 120-122, 124
"Psalm of Life, A" (Longfellow), **II:** 489, 496; **Retro. Supp. II:** 164, 168, 169; **Supp. I Part 2:** 409
"Psalm of the West" (Lanier), **Supp. I Part 1:** 362, 364
Psalms (biblical book), **I:** 83; **II:** 168, 232; **Retro. Supp. I:** 62; **Supp. I Part 1:** 125
Psalms, Hymns, and Spiritual Songs of the Rev. Isaac Watts, The (Worcester, ed.), **I:** 458
Psychiatric Novels of Oliver Wendell Holmes, The (Oberndorf), **Supp. I Part 1:** 315
Psychology: Briefer Course (James), **II:** 351-352
"Psychology and Form" (Burke), **I:** 270
Psychology of Art (Malraux), **IV:** 434
Psychology of Insanity, The (Hart), **I:** 241-242, 248-250
Psychopathia Sexualis (Shanley), **Supp. XIV:**316, **329**
Psychophysiks (Fechner), **II:** 358
"Pu-239" (Kalfus), **Supp. XVII:** 50
"Publication is the Auction" (Dickinson), **Retro. Supp. I:** 31
"Public Bath, The" (Snyder), **Supp. VIII:** 298
Public Burning, The (Coover), **Supp. IV Part 1:** 388; **Supp. V:** 44, 45, 46-47, 48, 51, 52; **Supp. XVII:** 6
"Public Burning of Julius and Ethel Rosenberg, The: An Historical Romance" (Coover), **Supp. V:** 44
"Public Figure" (Hay), **Supp. XIV:**124
"Public Garden, The" (Lowell), **II:** 550
Public Good (Paine), **Supp. I Part 2:** 509-510
Public Poetry of Robert Lowell, The (Cosgrave), **Retro. Supp. II:** 185
"Public & Private" (column, Quindlen), **Supp. XVII:** 165, 167, 169-170
Public Speech: Poems (MacLeish), **III:** 15-16
Public Spirit (Savage), **II:** 111
"Puck" (Monette), **Supp. X:** 157-158
Pudd'nhead Wilson (Twain), **I:** 197
"Pudd'nhead Wilson's Calendar" (Twain), **I:** 197
"Pueblo Revolt, The" (Sando), **Supp. IV Part 2:** 510
Puella (Dickey), **Supp. IV Part 1:** 178, 185
Pulitzer, Alfred, **Retro. Supp. I:** 257

Pull Down Vanity (Fiedler), **Supp. XIII:** 103
Pullman, George, **Supp. I Part 1:** 9
"Pullman Car Hiawatha" (Wilder), **IV:** 365-366
Pull My Daisy (film), **Supp. XII:** 126-127
"Pulpit and the Pew, The" (Holmes), **Supp. I Part 1:** 302
"Pulse-Beats and Pen-Strokes" (Sandburg), **III:** 579
"Pump, The" (Humphrey), **Supp. IX:** 101
Pump House Gang, The (Wolfe), **Supp. III Part 2:** 575, 578, 580, 581
Punch, Brothers, Punch and Other Sketches (Twain), **IV:** 200
Punch: The Immortal Liar, Documents in His History (Aiken), **I:** 57, 61
Punishment Without Vengeance (Vega; Merwin, trans.), **Supp. III Part 1:** 341, 347
"Pupil" (F. Barthelme), **Supp. XI:** 26
"Pupil, The" (James), **II:** 331; **Retro. Supp. I:** 217, 219, 228
"Purchase" (Banks), **Supp. V:** 6
"Purchase of Some Golf Clubs, A" (O'Hara), **III:** 369
"Purdah" (Plath), **Supp. I Part 2:** 602
Purdy, Charles, **Supp. VIII:** 330
Purdy, James, **Supp. VII: 269-285**
Purdy, Theodore, **Supp. VIII:** 153
Pure (C. Frost), **Supp. XV:** 93, **101-102,** 104, 106
"Pure" (C. Frost), **Supp. XV:** 101-102
"Pure and the Good, The: On Baseball and Backpaking" (Maclean), **Supp. XIV:**222
"Pure Good of Theory, The" (Stevens), **Retro. Supp. I:** 310
Purgatorio (Dante), **III:** 182
Puritan Family (Morgan), **Supp. I Part 1:** 101
"Puritanical Pleasures" (Hardwick), **Supp. III Part 1:** 213-214
Puritan Origins of the American Self, The (Bercovitch), **Supp. I Part 1:** 99
Puritan Pronaos, The: Studies in the Intellectual Life of New England in the Seventeenth Century (Morison), **Supp. I Part 2:** 485
Puritans, The (P. Miller), **Supp. VIII:** 101
"Puritan's Ballad, The" (Wylie), **Supp. I Part 2:** 723
"Purloined Letter, The" (Poe), **Retro. Supp. II:** 271, 272
Purple Cane Road (Burke), **Supp. XIV:**32, 33

Purple Decades, The (Wolfe), **Supp. III Part 2:** 584
"Purple Hat, The" (Welty), **IV:** 264
Purple Rose of Cairo, The (film; Allen), **Supp. XV:** 1, **9-10,** 12, 14
Purser, John T., **Supp. XIV:** 4
"Pursuit of Happiness" (Simpson), **Supp. IX:** 279
"Pursuit of Happiness, The" (Ashbery), **Supp. III Part 1:** 23
Pursuit of the Prodigal, The (Auchincloss), **Supp. IV Part 1:** 25
Pushcart at the Curb, A (Dos Passos), **I:** 478, 479
"Pushcart Man" (Hughes), **Supp. I Part 1:** 330
Pushcart Prize, XIII, The (Ford), **Supp. V:** 58
Pushcart Prize VII, The (Hendeson, ed.), **Supp. XVII:** 16
Pushcart Prize XIV, The (Henderson, ed.), **Supp. XVII:** 18
Pushcart Prize XX, The (Henderson, ed.), **Supp. XVII:** 20
"Pushing 100" (Mora), **Supp. XIII:** 215
Pushkin, Aleksander, **III:** 246, 261, 262; **Retro. Supp. I:** 266, 269; **Supp. XVI:** 188
Pussy, King of the Pirates (Acker), **Supp. XII:** 6-7
"Pussycat and the Expert Plumber Who Was a Man, The" (A. Miller), **III:** 146-147
Pussycat Fever (Acker), **Supp. XII:** 6
Putnam, George P., **II:** 314
Putnam, Phelps, **I:** 288
Putnam, Samuel, **II:** 26; **III:** 479; **Supp. III Part 2:** 615
"Put Off the Wedding Five Times and Nobody Comes to It" (Sandburg), **III:** 586-587
Puttenham, George, **Supp. I Part 1:** 113
Puttermesser Papers, The (Ozick), **Supp. V:** 269
"Putting on *Visit to a Small Planet*" (Vidal), **Supp. IV Part 2:** 683
Put Yourself in My Shoes (Carver), **Supp. III Part 1:** 139
"Put Yourself in My Shoes" (Carver), **Supp. III Part 1:** 139, 141
Putzi, Jennifer, **Supp. XV:** 284
Puzo, Mario, **Supp. IV Part 1:** 390
"Puzzle of Modern Society, The" (Kazin), **Supp. VIII:** 103
Pygmalion (Shaw), **Supp. XII:** 14
Pyle, Ernie, **III:** 148; **Supp. V:** 240; **Supp. XVII:** 61
Pylon (Faulkner), **II:** 64-65, 73; **Retro. Supp. I:** 84, 85
Pynchon, Thomas, **III:** 258; **Retro. Supp. I:** 278; **Retro. Supp. II:** 279, 324; **Supp. II Part 2:** 557, **617-638;** **Supp. III Part 1:** 217; **Supp. IV Part 1:** 53, 279; **Supp. IV Part 2:** 570; **Supp. V:** 40, 44, 52; **Supp. VIII:** 14; **Supp. IX:** 207, 208, 212; **Supp. X:** 260, 301, 302; **Supp. XI:** 103; **Supp. XII:** 289; **Supp. XIV:** 49, 53, 54, 96; **Supp. XVI:** 123, 128; **Supp. XVII:** 183, 225, 232, 236
Pyrah, Gill, **Supp. V:** 126
"Pyramid Club, The" (Doctorow), **Supp. IV Part 1:** 234
"Pyrography" (Ashbery), **Supp. III Part 1:** 18
Pythagoras, **I:** 332
Pythagorean Silence (Howe), **Supp. IV Part 2:** 426, 428-429

Q
"Qebehseneuf" (Goldbarth), **Supp. XII:** 186
"Quai d'Orléans" (Bishop), **Supp. I Part 1:** 89
"Quail for Mr. Forester" (Humphrey), **Supp. IX:** 94
"Quail in Autumn" (W. J. Smith), **Supp. XIII:** 334-335, 339
"Quaker Graveyard in Nantucket, The" (Lowell), **II:** 54, 550; **Retro. Supp. II:** 178, 186-187
"Quake Theory" (Olds), **Supp. X:** 203
Qualey, Carlton C., **Supp. I Part 2:** 650
Quality of Hurt, The (C. Himes), **Supp. XVI:** 137, 145
"Quality of Wine" (Carruth), **Supp. XVI:** 59
"Quality Time" (Kingsolver), **Supp. VII:** 203
"Quandary" (F. Wright), **Supp. XVII:** 244
Quang-Ngau-chè, **III:** 473
Quarles, Francis, **I:** 178, 179
Quarry, The (Chesnutt), **Supp. XIV:** 76
"Quarry, The" (Nemerov), **III:** 272
Quarry, The: New Poems (Eberhart), **I:** 532, 539
Quartermain, Peter, **Supp. IV Part 2:** 423, 434
"Quaternions, The" (Bradstreet), **Supp. I Part 1:** 104-106, 114, 122
"Quatrains for Ishi" (Komunyakaa), **Supp. XIII:** 129
"Queen Elizabeth and the Blind Girl or Music for the Dead Children" (B. Kelly), **Supp. XVII:** 124, 125
"Queen of the Blues" (Brooks), **Supp. III Part 1:** 75
Queen of the Damned, The (Rice), **Supp. VII:** 290, 292-293, 297, 299
Queen of the Mob (film), **Supp. XIII:** 170
"Queens of France" (Wilder), **IV:** 365
"Queen's Twin, The" (Jewett), **Retro. Supp. II:** 138
Queen's Twin, The, and Other Stories (Jewett), **Retro. Supp. II:** 140
Queen Victoria (Strachey), **Supp. I Part 2:** 485, 494; **Supp. XIV:** 342
Queer (Burroughs), **Supp. III Part 1:** 93-102
"Queer Beer" (Hansberry), **Supp. IV Part 1:** 374
"Quelques considérations sur la méthode subjective" (James), **II:** 345-346
"Question" (Swenson), **Supp. IV Part 2:** 640
"Question and Answer" (Hughes), **Retro. Supp. I:** 211
"Questioning Faces" (Frost), **Retro. Supp. I:** 141
"Question Mark in the Circle, The" (Stegner), **Supp. IV Part 2:** 597
"Questionnaire, The" (Snodgrass), **Supp. VI:** 318
"Question of Fidelity, A" (Beauvoir), **Supp. IX:** 4
"Question of Our Speech, The" (Ozick), **Supp. V:** 272
"Question of Simone de Beauvoir, The" (Algren), **Supp. IX:** 4
Questions for Ecclesiastes (Jarman), **Supp. XVII:** 109, 110, **118-119**
"Questions of Geography" (Hollander), **Supp. I Part 1:** 96
Questions of Travel (Bishop), **Retro. Supp. II:** **46-48;** **Supp. I Part 1:** 72, 83, 92, 94
"Questions of Travel" (Bishop), **Retro. Supp. II:** 47
"Questions to Tourists Stopped by a Pineapple Field" (Merwin), **Supp. III Part 1:** 355
"Questions without Answers" (T. Williams), **IV:** 384
"Quest of the Purple-Fringed, The" (Frost), **Retro. Supp. I:** 139
Quest of the Silver Fleece, The (Du Bois), **Supp. II Part 1:** 176-178
Quevedo y Villegas, Francisco Gómez, **Retro. Supp. I:** 423
Quickly: A Column for Slow Readers (Mailer), **Retro. Supp. II:** 202
"Quies," (Pound), **Retro. Supp. I:** 413
Quiet Days in Clichy (H. Miller), **III:** 170, 178, 183-184, 187
"Quiet Desperation" (Simpson), **Supp.**

IX: 277-278
"Quiet of the Mind" (Nye), **Supp. XIII:** 284
Quindlen, Anna, **Supp. XVI:**108; **Supp. XVII: 165-181**
Quinlan, Kathleen, **Supp. X:** 80
Quinn, John, **III:** 471
Quinn, Paul, **Supp. V:** 71
Quinn, Sister M. Bernetta, **III:** 479; **IV:** 421
Quinn, Vincent, **I:** 386, 401, 402; **Supp. I Part 1:** 270
"Quinnapoxet" (Kunitz), **Supp. III Part 1:** 263
Quinn's Book (W. Kennedy), **Supp. VII:** 133, 148-150, 153
Quintero, José, **III:** 403
Quintilian, **IV:** 123
Quinzaine for This Yule, A (Pound), **Retro. Supp. I:** 285
Quite Contrary: The Mary and Newt Story (Dixon), **Supp. XII: 144,** 153
Quod Erat Demonstrandum (Stein), **IV:** 34
Quo Vadis? (Sienkiewicz), **Supp. IV Part 2:** 518; **Supp. XVI:**182

R

Raab, Max, **Supp. XI:** 309
"Rabbi, The" (Hayden), **Supp. II Part 1:** 363, 369
Rabbit, Run (Updike), **IV:** 214, 223, 230-234; **Retro. Supp. I:** 320, 325, 326, 327, 331, 333, 335; **Supp. XI:** 140; **Supp. XII:** 298; **Supp. XVI:**220
"Rabbit, The" (Barnes), **Supp. III Part 1:** 34
Rabbit at Rest (Updike), **Retro. Supp. I:** 334
Rabbit Is Rich (Updike), **Retro. Supp. I:** 334
Rabbit novels (Updike), **Supp. V:** 269
Rabbit Redux (Updike), **IV:** 214; **Retro. Supp. I:** 332, 333
Rabbit's Umbrella, The (Plimpton), **Supp. XVI:**244
"Rabbits Who Caused All the Trouble, The" (Thurber), **Supp. I Part 2:** 610
Rabelais, and His World (Bakhtin), **Retro. Supp. II:** 273
Rabelais, François, **I:** 130; **II:** 111, 112, 302, 535; **III:** 77, 78, 174, 182; **IV:** 68; **Supp. I Part 2:** 461
Rabelais and His World (Bakhtin), **Supp. X:** 120
Rabinbach, Anson, **Supp. XII:** 166
Rabinowitz, Paula, **Supp. V:** 161
"Race" (Emerson), **II:** 6
"Race Contacts and Inter-Racial Relations" (Locke), **Supp. XIV:**211

"Race Contacts and Inter-Racial Relations: A Study in the Theory and Practice of Race" (lectures, Locke), **Supp. XIV:**199, 209
Race Contacts and Interracial Relations: Lectures on the Theory and Practice of Race (Locke, Stewart, ed.), **Supp. XIV:**196, **209-210**
"'RACE LINE' IS A PRODUCT OF CAPITALISM, THE" (Baraka), **Supp. II Part 1:** 61
"Race of Life, The" (Thurber), **Supp. I Part 2:** 614
"Race Problems and Modern Society" (Toomer), **Supp. III Part 2:** 486
Race Questions, Provincialism, and Other American Problems (Royce), **Supp. XIV:**199
"Race Riot, Tulsa, 1921" (Olds), **Supp. X:** 205
Race Rock (Matthiessen), **Supp. V:** 201
"Races, The" (Lowell), **II:** 554
Rachel Carson: Witness for Nature (Lear), **Supp. IX:** 19
Rachel River (film, Smolan), **Supp. XVI:**36
"Racial Progress and Race Adjustment" (Locke), **Supp. XIV:**210
Racine, Jean Baptiste, **II:** 543, 573; **III:** 145, 151, 152, 160; **IV:** 317, 368, 370; **Supp. I Part 2:** 716
"Radical" (Moore), **III:** 211
"Radical Chic" (Wolfe), **Supp. III Part 2:** 577-578, 584, 585
Radical Chic & Mau-mauing the Flak Catchers (Wolfe), **Supp. III Part 2:** 577-578
Radical Empiricism of William James, The (Wild), **II:** 362, 363-364
Radicalism in America, The (Lasch), **I:** 259
"Radical Jewish Humanism: The Vision of E. L. Doctorow" (Clayton), **Supp. IV Part 1:** 238
"Radically Condensed History of Postindustrial Life, A" (Wallace), **Supp. X:** 309
Radinovsky, Lisa, **Supp. XV:** 284, 285
"Radio" (O'Hara), **III:** 369
Radio Days (film; Allen), **Supp. XV:** 9
"Radio Pope" (Goldbarth), **Supp. XII:** 188, 192
Raditzer (Matthiessen), **Supp. V:** 201
Radkin, Paul, **Supp. I Part 2:** 539
"Rafaela Who Drinks Coconut & Papaya Juice on Tuesdays" (Cisneros), **Supp. VII:** 63
Rafelson, Bob, **Supp. XIV:**241
Raffalovich, Marc-André, **Supp. XIV:**335

"Raft, The" (Lindsay), **Supp. I Part 2:** 393
Rag and Bone Shop of the Heart, The: Poems for Men (Bly, Hillman, and Meade, eds.), **Supp. IV Part 1:** 67
Rage in Harlem (C. Himes). See *For Love of Imabelle* (C. Himes)
Rage to Live, A (O'Hara), **III:** 361
Raglan, Lord, **I:** 135
Rago, Henry, **Supp. III Part 2:** 624, 628, 629
Ragtime (Doctorow), **Retro. Supp. II:** 108; **Supp. IV Part 1:** 217, 222-224, 231, 232, 233, 234, 237, 238; **Supp. V:** 45
"Ragtime" (Doctorow), **Supp. IV Part 1:** 234
Ragtime (film), **Supp. IV Part 1:** 236
Ragtime (musical, McNally), **Supp. XIII:** 207
Rahaim, Liz, **Supp. XVII:** 2
Rahv, Philip, **Retro. Supp. I:** 112; **Supp. II Part 1:** 136; **Supp. VIII:** 96; **Supp. IX:** 8; **Supp. XIV:**3; **Supp. XV:** 140
"Raid" (Hughes), **Retro. Supp. I:** 208
Raids on the Unspeakable (Merton), **Supp. VIII:** 201, 208
Rail, DeWayne, **Supp. XIII:** 312
"Rain and the Rhinoceros" (Merton), **Supp. VIII:** 201
Rainbow, The (Lawrence), **III:** 27
"Rainbows" (Marquand), **III:** 56
Rainbow Stories, The (Vollmann), **Supp. XVII:** 226, 227, 230, 231, 233
Rainbow Tulip, The (Mora), **Supp. XIII:** 221
"Rain Country" (Haines), **Supp. XII:** 210
"Rain-Dream, A" (Bryant), **Supp. I Part 1:** 164
Raine, Kathleen, **I:** 522, 527
"Rain Falling Now, The" (Dunn), **Supp. XI:** 147
"Rain in the Heart" (Taylor), **Supp. V:** 317, 319
Rain in the Trees, The (Merwin), **Supp. III Part 1:** 340, 342, 345, 349, 354-356
"Rainmaker, The" (Humphrey), **Supp. IX:** 101
Rainwater, Catherine, **Supp. V:** 272
"Rainy Day" (Longfellow), **II:** 498
"Rainy Day, The" (Buck), **Supp. II Part 1:** 127
"Rainy Mountain Cemetery" (Momaday), **Supp. IV Part 2:** 486
Rainy Mountain Christmas Doll (painting) (Momaday), **Supp. IV**

Part 2: 493
"Rainy Season: Sub-Tropics" (Bishop), **Supp. I Part 1:** 93
"Raise High the Roof Beam, Carpenters" (Salinger), **III:** 567-569, 571
Raise High the Roof Beam, Carpenters; and Seymour: An Introduction (Salinger), **III:** 552, 567-571, 572
Raise Race Rays Raze: Essays Since 1965 (Baraka), **Supp. II Part 1:** 47, 52, 55
Raisin (musical), **Supp. IV Part 1:** 374
Raising Demons (Jackson), **Supp. IX: 125-126**
Raisin in the Sun, A (film: Columbia Pictures), **Supp. IV Part 1:** 360, 367
Raisin in the Sun, A (Hansberry), **Supp. IV Part 1:** 359, 360, 361, 362-364; **Supp. VIII:** 343
Raisin in the Sun, A (television film: American Playhouse), **Supp. IV Part 1:** 367, 374
Raisin in the Sun, A (unproduced screenplay) (Hansberry), **Supp. IV Part 1:** 360
Rajan, R., **I:** 390
"Rake, The" (Mamet), **Supp. XIV:**240
Rake's Progress, The (opera), **Supp. II Part 1:** 24
Rakosi, Carl, **Supp. III Part 2:** 614, 615, 616, 617, 618, 621, 629; **Supp. XIV:**286, 287
Ralegh, Sir Walter, **Supp. I Part 1:** 98
Raleigh, John Henry, **IV:** 366
Ralph, Brett, **Supp. XVII:** 245
Ramakrishna, Sri, **III:** 567
Ramakrishna and His Disciples (Isherwood), **Supp. XIV:**164
Ramazani, Jahan, **Supp. IV Part 2:** 450
"Ramble of Aphasia, A" (O. Henry), **Supp. II Part 1:** 410
Ramey, Phillip, **Supp. IV Part 1:** 94
Rampersad, Arnold, **Retro. Supp. I:** 196, 200, 201, 204; **Supp. IV Part 1:** 244, 250
Rampling, Anne, **Supp. VII:** 201. *See also* Rice, Anne
Rampling, Charlotte, **Supp. IX:** 253
Ramsey, Priscilla R., **Supp. IV Part 1:** 15
Ramsey, Roger, **Supp. XVI:**69
Ramus, Petrus, **Supp. I Part 1:** 104
Rand, Ayn, **Supp. I Part 1:** 294; **Supp. IV Part 2: 517-535**
Randall, Jarrell, 1914-1965 (Lowell, Taylor, and Warren, eds.), **II:** 368, 385
Randall, John H., **III:** 605

Randolph, John, **I:** 5-6
"Range-Finding" (Frost), **Retro. Supp. I:** 131
Range of the Possible (T. Marshall), **Supp. XVII:** 36
Rangoon (F. Barthelme), **Supp. XI:** 25
Rank, Otto, **I:** 135; **Supp. IX:** 105; **Supp. X:** 183, 185, 193
Ranke, Leopold von, **Supp. I Part 2:** 492
Rankin, Daniel, **Retro. Supp. II:** 57, 72; **Supp. I Part 1:** 200, 203, 225
Ransohoff, Martin, **Supp. XI:** 305, 306
Ransom, John Crowe, **I:** 265, 301; **II:** 34, 367, 385, 389, 536-537, 542; **III:** 454, **480-502**, 549; **IV:** 121, 122, 123, 124, 125, 127, 134, 140, 141, 236, 237, 433; **Retro. Supp. I:** 90; **Retro. Supp. II:** 176, 177, 178, 183, 220, 228, 246; **Supp. I Part 1:** 80, 361; **Supp. I Part 2:** 423; **Supp. II Part 1:** 90, 91, 136, 137, 139, 318; **Supp. II Part 2:** 639; **Supp. III Part 1:** 318; **Supp. III Part 2:** 542, 591; **Supp. IV Part 1:** 217; **Supp. V:** 315, 331, 337; **Supp. X:** 25, 56, 58; **Supp. XIV:**1
"Rape" (Coleman), **Supp. XI:** 89-90
"Rape, The" (Baraka), **Supp. II Part 1:** 40
Rape of Bunny Stuntz, The (Gurney), **Supp. V:** 109
"Rape of Philomel, The" (Shapiro), **Supp. II Part 2:** 720
"Rape of the Lock, The" (Pope), **Supp. XIV:**8
Raphael, **I:** 15; **III:** 505, 521, 524; **Supp. I Part 1:** 363
"Rapist" (Dunn), **Supp. XI:** 144
Rap on Race, A (Baldwin and Mead), **Supp. I Part 1:** 66
"Rappaccini's Daughter" (Hawthorne), **II:** 229
"Rapunzel" (Sexton), **Supp. II Part 2:** 691
Rare & Endangered Species: A Novella & Short Stories (Bausch), **Supp. VII:** 51, 54
"Raree Show" (MacLeish), **III:** 9
Rascoe, Burton, **III:** 106, 115
Raskin, Jonah, **Supp. XV:** 116
"Raskolnikov" (Simic), **Supp. VIII:** 282
Rasmussen, Douglas, **Supp. IV Part 2:** 528, 530
Rasselas (Johnson), **Supp. XI:** 209
Rathmann, Andrew, **Supp. XV:** 34
"Ration" (Baraka), **Supp. II Part 1:** 50
"Rationale of Verse, The" (Poe), **III:**

427-428; **Retro. Supp. II:** 266
Ratner, Rochelle, **Supp. XV:** 105
Ratner's Star (DeLillo), **Supp. VI:** 1, 2, 3, 4, 10, 12, 14
"Rat of Faith, The" (Levine), **Supp. V:** 192
Rattigan, Terence, **III:** 152
Raugh, Joseph, **Supp. I Part 1:** 286
Rauschenberg, Robert, **Supp. XV:** 187
Rauschenbusch, Walter, **III:** 293; **Supp. I Part 1:** 7
Ravelstein (Bellow), **Retro. Supp. II:** 19, **33-34**
Raven, Simon, **Supp. XII:** 241
Raven, The (film, Friedlander), **Supp. XVII:** 58
"Raven, The" (Poe), **III:** 413, 421-422, 426; **Retro. Supp. II:** 265, 266-267; **Supp. XVII:** 58
Raven, The, and Other Poems (Poe), **III:** 413
Ravenal, Shannon, **Supp. IV Part 1:** 93
"Raven Days, The" (Lanier), **Supp. I Part 1:** 351
Ravenna, Michael. *See* Welty, Eudora
Raven's Road (Gunn Allen), **Supp. IV Part 1:** 330, 335
"Ravine, The" (Carruth), **Supp. XVI:**53
Rawlings, Marjorie Kinnan, **Supp. X: 219-237**
Rawlins, C. L., **Supp. XVII:** 72, 73
Ray, David, **Supp. IV Part 1:** 61
Ray, Jeanne Wilkinson, **Supp. XII:** 308, 310
Ray, John, **II:** 111, 112
Ray, Man, **IV:** 404; **Retro. Supp. I:** 416; **Supp. XII:** 124
Ray Bradbury Theatre, The (television show), **Supp. IV Part 1:** 103
"Razor's Edge, The" (Wasserstein), **Supp. XV:** 328
Reactionary Essays on Poetry and Ideas (Tate), **Supp. II Part 1:** 106, 146
Read, Deborah, **II:** 122
Read, Forrest, **III:** 478
Read, Herbert, **I:** 523; **II:** 372-373, 377-378; **Retro. Supp. I:** 54; **Supp. III Part 1:** 273; **Supp. III Part 2:** 624, 626
Read, William A., **Supp. XIV:**4
Reade, Charles, **Supp. I Part 2:** 580
Reader, Constant. *See* Parker, Dorothy
Reader, Dennis J., **Supp. I Part 2:** 454
"Reader, The" (F. Wright), **Supp. XVII:** 246
Reader's Block (Markson), **Supp. XVII: 143-145,** 146

Reader's Encyclopedia, The: An Encyclopedia of World Literature and the Arts (W. Benét), **Supp. XI:** 44
Reader's Guide to William Gaddis's The Recognitions, A (Moore), **Supp. IV Part 1:** 283
Reader's Map of Arkansas (Wright), **Supp. XV:** 348
"Reader's Tale, A" (Doty), **Supp. XI:** 119, 120, 128, 129
"Reading" (Auden), **Supp. VIII:** 155
"Reading Group Guide," **Supp. XI:** 244-245
"Reading Lao Tzu Again in the New Year" (Wright), **Supp. V:** 343
"Reading Late of the Death of Keats" (Kenyon), **Supp. VII:** 169
"Reading Myself" (Lowell), **II:** 555
Reading Myself and Others (P. Roth), **Retro. Supp. II:** 282; **Supp. V:** 45
"Reading *Ode to the West Wind* 25 Years Later" (McCarriston), **Supp. XIV:**271-272
"Reading of the Psalm, The" (Francis), **Supp. IX:** 79
"Reading Philosophy at Night" (Simic), **Supp. VIII:** 272
Reading Rilke: Reflections on the Problems of Translation (Gass), **Supp. VI:** 92, **93-94**
"Reading Rorty and Paul Celan One Morning in Early June" (Wright), **Supp. V:** 343
"Reading Sarcophagi: An Essay" (Sobin), **Supp. XVI:**290
"Readings of History" (Rich), **Supp. I Part 2:** 554
"Reading the Signs, Empowering the Eye" (Bambara), **Supp. XI:** 17-18
Reading the Spirit (Eberhart), **I:** 525, 527, 530
"Ready Or Not" (Baraka), **Supp. II Part 1:** 50
Reagan, Ronald, **Supp. IV Part 1:** 224-225
"Real Bowery, The" (Hapgood), **Supp. XVII:** 103
"Real Class" (Vidal), **Supp. IV Part 1:** 35
Real Cool Killers, The (C. Himes), **Supp. XVI:**143
Real Dope, The (Lardner), **II:** 422-423
"Real Estate" (Moore), **Supp. X:** 178
"Real Gone Guy, A" (McGrath), **Supp. X:** 117
"Real Horatio Alger Story, The" (Cowley), **Supp. II Part 1:** 143
"Realities" (MacLeish), **III:** 4
"Reality in America" (Trilling), **Supp. III Part 2:** 495, 502

"Reality! Reality! What Is It?" (Eberhart), **I:** 536
Reality Sandwiches, 1953-60 (Ginsberg), **Supp. II Part 1:** 315, 320
Real Life of Sebastian Knight, The (Nabokov), **III:** 246; **Retro. Supp. I:** 266, 269, 270, 274
"Really Good Jazz Piano, A" (Yates), **Supp. XI:** 342
Real Presence: A Novel (Bausch), **Supp. VII:** 42-43, 50
"Real Revolution Is Love, The" (Harjo), **Supp. XII:** 224, 225-226
"Real Thing, The" (H. James), **Retro. Supp. I:** 228; **Retro. Supp. II:** 223
"Real Two-Party System" (Vidal), **Supp. IV Part 2:** 679
Real West Marginal Way, The (Hugo), **Supp. VI:** 132, 134
"Real World around Us, The" (Carson), **Supp. IX:** 21
Reaper Essays, The (Jarman and McDowell), **Supp. IX:** 270; **Supp. XVII:** 110-111
"*Reaper* Interviews Jean Doh and Sean Dough, The" (Jarman and McDowell), **Supp. XVII:** 110
"Reapers" (Toomer), **Supp. III Part 2:** 481; **Supp. IX:** 312
"Reason and Race: A Review of the Literature of the Negro for 1946" (Locke), **Supp. XIV:**206
"Reason for Moving, A" (Strand), **Supp. IV Part 2:** 624
"Reason for Stories, The: Toward a Moral Fiction" (Stone), **Supp. V:** 298, 300
Reasons for Moving (Strand), **Supp. IV Part 2:** 624-626, 626
"Reasons for Music" (MacLeish), **III:** 19
"Reasons of the Body" (Sanders), **Supp. XVI:**274
Rebecca, or, The Fille de Chambre (Rowson), **Supp. XV:** 229, **235-236**, 238
Rebecca Harding Davis Reader, A (Pfaelzer, ed.), **Supp. XVI:**88, 90
Rebel Angels: Twenty-five Poets of the New Formalism (Jarman and Mason, eds.), **Supp. XV:** 251; **Supp. XVII:** 109, 110, 112, 121
"Rebellion" (Lowell), **Retro. Supp. II:** 187
Rebel Powers (Bausch), **Supp. VII:** 41, 45-46, 49-51
Rebel without a Cause (film), **Supp. XII:** 9
"Rebirth of God and the Death of Man,

The " (Fiedler), **Supp. XIII:** 108
Rebolledo, Tey Diana, **Supp. XIII:** 214
Recapitulation (Stegner), **Supp. IV Part 2:** 598, 600, 612-613
"Recapitulation, The" (Eberhart), **I:** 522
"Recapitulations" (Shapiro), **Supp. II Part 2:** 701, 702, 708, 710-711
"Recencies in Poetry" (Zukofsky), **Supp. III Part 2:** 615
Recent Killing, A (Baraka), **Supp. II Part 1:** 55
"Recent Negro Fiction" (Ellison), **Supp. II Part 1:** 233, 235
"Recessional" (A. Finch), **Supp. XVII:** 70-71
"Recital, The" (Ashbery), **Supp. III Part 1:** 14
"Recitative" (H. Crane), **I:** 390; **Retro. Supp. II:** 78
Reckless Eyeballing (Reed), **Supp. X:** 241
Recognitions, The (Gaddis), **Supp. IV Part 1:** 279, 280-285, 286, 287, 288, 289, 291, 292, 294
Recollections (R. H. Stoddard), **Supp. XV:** 271
Recollections of Logan Pearsall Smith: The Story of a Friendship (Gathorne-Hardy), **Supp. XIV:**344
"Reconciliation" (Whitman), **IV:** 347
"Reconstructed but Unregenerate" (Ransom), **III:** 496
"Reconstruction and Its Benefits" (Du Bois), **Supp. II Part 1:** 171
Recovering (Sarton), **Supp. VIII:** 264
Recovering the U.S. Hispanic Literary Heritage (Paredes), **Supp. XIII:** 320
"Recovery" (Dove), **Supp. IV Part 1:** 248
Rector of Justin, The (Auchincloss), **Supp. IV Part 1:** 21, 23, 27-30, 36
"RED AUTUMN" (Baraka), **Supp. II Part 1:** 55
Red Badge of Courage, The (Crane), **I:** 201, 207, 212, 405, 406, 407, 408, 412-416, 419, 421, 422, 423, 477, 506; **II:** 264; **III:** 317; **IV:** 350; **Retro. Supp. II:** 108; **Supp. IV Part 1:** 380; **Supp. XIV:**51
Red Badge of Courage, The (S. Crane), **Supp. XVII:** 228
"Redbirds" (C. Frost), **Supp. XV:** 99
"Redbreast in Tampa" (Lanier), **Supp. I Part 1:** 364
"Red Brocade" (Nye), **Supp. XIII:** 288
Redburn: His First Voyage (Melville), **III:** 79-80, 84; **Retro. Supp. I:** 245, 247-248, 249
"Red Carpet for Shelley, A" (Wylie),

Supp. I Part 2: 724
Red Channels (Harnett), **Supp. XV:** 198
"Red Clowns" (Cisneros), **Supp. VII:** 63
Red Coal, The (Stern), **Supp. IX: 291-292**
Red Coat, The (Shanley), **Supp. XIV:**316-317
"Red Cross" (Hughes), **Retro. Supp. I:** 205
Red Cross (Shepard), **Supp. III Part 2:** 440, 446
Red Death, A (Mosley), **Supp. XIII:** 237, 239, 240
"Red Deer" (C. Frost), **Supp. XV:** 101
Redding, Saunders, **Supp. I Part 1:** 332, 333
Reddings, J. Saunders, **Supp. IV Part 1:** 164
Red Dust (Levine), **Supp. V:** 178, 183-184, 188
"Red Dust" (Levine), **Supp. V:** 184
"Redemption" (Gardner), **Supp. VI:** 72
"Redeployment" (Nemerov), **III:** 267, 272
Redfield, Robert, **IV:** 475
Redford, Robert, **Supp. IX:** 253, 259; **Supp. XIII:** 267; **Supp. XIV:**223
Redgrave, Lynn, **Supp. V:** 107
Red Harvest (Hammett), **Supp. IV Part 1:** 346-348, 348; **Supp. IV Part 2:** 468
Red-Headed Woman (film), **Retro. Supp. I:** 110; **Supp. XVI:**191
"Red Horse Wind over Albuquerque" (Harjo), **Supp. XII:** 219
Red Hot Vacuum, The (Solotaroff), **Retro. Supp. II:** 281
"Red Leaves" (Faulkner), **II:** 72
"Red Meat: What Difference Did Stesichoros Make?" (Carson), **Supp. XII:** 107
"Red Pawn" (Rand), **Supp. IV Part 2:** 520
Red Pony, The (Steinbeck), **IV:** 50, 51, 58, 70
Redrawing the Boundaries (Fisher), **Retro. Supp. I:** 39
Red Robins, The (Koch), **Supp. XV:** 185-186, 187
Red Roses for Bronze (Doolittle), **Supp. I Part 1:** 253, 268, 271
Red Rover, The (Cooper), **I:** 342-343, 355
"Red Silk Stockings" (Hughes), **Retro. Supp. I:** 200
Redskins, The (Cooper), **I:** 351, 353
"Red Star, Winter Orbit" (W. Gibson and B. Sterling), **Supp. XVI:**123
Red Suitcase (Nye), **Supp. XIII:** 277, 278, 287
"Red Wheelbarrow, The" (W. C. Williams), **IV:** 411-412; **Retro. Supp. I:** 419, 430
"Red Wind" (Chandler), **Supp. IV Part 1:** 122
"Redwings" (Wright), **Supp. III Part 2:** 603
Reed, Edward Bliss, **Supp. XV:** 297, 298, 300
Reed, Ishmael, **Retro. Supp. II:** 111, 324-325; **Supp. II Part 1:** 34; **Supp. X: 239-257,** 331; **Supp. XIII:** 181, 182; **Supp. XVI:**143
Reed, J. D., **Supp. XVI:**174
Reed, John, **I:** 48, 476, 483; **Supp. X:** 136; **Supp. XV:** 295, 299; **Supp. XVII:** 96, 99, 100
Reed, Lou, **Retro. Supp. II:** 266
"Reedbeds of the Hackensack, The" (Clampitt), **Supp. IX:** 41
"Reed of Pan, A" (McCullers), **II:** 585
Reedy, Billy, **Retro. Supp. II:** 65, 67, 71, 73
Reedy, William Marion, **Supp. I Part 2:** 456, 461, 465
Reef, The (Wharton), **IV:** 317-318, 322; **Retro. Supp. I:** 372, **373-374**
Reena and Other Stories (Marshall), **Supp. XI:** 275, 277, 278
Reeve, F. D., **Supp. XV:** 344, 349
Reeve's Tale (Chaucer), **I:** 131
"Reflection from Anita Loos" (Empson), **Supp. XVI:**190
"Reflections" (Carruth), **Supp. XVI:**54
"Reflections" (Komunyakaa), **Supp. XIII:** 117
Reflections: Thinking Part I (Arendt), **Supp. I Part 2:** 570
Reflections at Fifty and Other Essays (Farrell), **II:** 49
"Reflections by a Fire" (Sarton), **Supp. VIII:** 259
Reflections in a Golden Eye (McCullers), **II:** 586, 588, 593-596, 604; **IV:** 384, 396
Reflections of a Jacobite (Auchincloss), **Supp. IV Part 1:** 31
Reflections on a Gift of Watermelon Pickle (Dunning), **Supp. XIV:**126
Reflections on Poetry and Poetics (Nemerov), **III:** 269
"Reflections on the Constitution of Nature" (Freneau), **Supp. II Part 1:** 274
"Reflections on the Death of the Reader" (Morris), **III:** 237
Reflections on the End of an Era (Niebuhr), **III:** 297-298
"Reflections on the Life and Death of Lord Clive" (Paine), **Supp. I Part 2:** 505
Reflections on the Revolution in France (Burke), **Supp. I Part 2:** 511, 512
"Reflex Action and Theism" (James), **II:** 345, 363
"Refrains/Remains/Reminders" (Goldbarth), **Supp. XII:** 180-181, 181
"Refuge" (Kingsolver), **Supp. VII:** 208
"Refuge, A" (Goldbarth), **Supp. XII:** 190
Refugee Children: Theory, Research, and Services (Ahearn and Athey, eds.), **Supp. XI:** 184
"Refugees, The" (Jarrell), **II:** 371
"Refusal" (C. Frost), **Supp. XV:** 102
Regarding Wave (Snyder), **Supp. VIII: 299-300**
Regina (Epstein), **Supp. XII: 170-171**
"Regional Literature of the South" (Rawlings), **Supp. X:** 228
"Regional Writer, The" (O'Connor), **Retro. Supp. II:** 223, 225
Régnier, Henri de, **II:** 528-529
Regulators, The (King), **Supp. V:** 141
Rehder, Robert, **Supp. IV Part 1:** 69
Reichel, Hans, **III:** 183
Reichl, Ruth, **Supp. X:** 79, 85
Reich,Tova, **Supp. XVI:**158
Reid, B. L., **II:** 41, 47
Reid, Thomas, **II:** 9; **Supp. I Part 1:** 151
Reign of Wonder, The (Tanner), **I:** 260
Rein, Yevgeny, **Supp. VIII:** 22
Reinagle, Alexander, **Supp. XV:** 238, 240
"Reincarnation" (Dickey), **Supp. IV Part 1:** 181-182
Reine des pommes, La (C. Himes). See *For Love of Imabelle* (C. Himes)
Reiner, Carl, **Supp. IV Part 2:** 591
Reinfeld, Linda, **Supp. IV Part 2:** 421
Reinhardt, Max, **Supp. XV:** 307
Reinventing the Enemy's Language: Contemporary Native Women's Writing of North America (Bird and Harjo, eds.), **Supp. XII:** 216, 217
Reisman, Jerry, **Supp. III Part 2:** 618
Reitlinger, Gerald, **Supp. XII:** 161
Reivers, The: A Reminiscence (Faulkner), **I:** 305; **II:** 57, 73; **Retro. Supp. I:** 74, 82, 91
"Rejoicings" (Stern), **Supp. IX:** 289-290
Rejoicings: Selected Poems, 1966-1972 (Stern), **Supp. IX: 289-290**
Relation of My Imprisonment, The

(Banks), **Supp. V:** 8, 12-13
"Relations between Poetry and Painting, The" (Stevens), **Retro. Supp. I:** 312
Relations of the Alabama-Georgia Dialect to the Provincial Dialects of Great Britain, The (Brooks), **Supp. XIV:**3
Relative Stranger, A (C. Baxter), **Supp. XVII:** 19, 22
"Relativity of Beauty, The" (Rawlings), **Supp. X:** 226
Relearning the Alphabet (Levertov), **Supp. III Part 1:** 280, 281
"Release" (C. Baxter), **Supp. XVII:** 15
"Release, The" (MacLeish), **III:** 16
Reles, Abe ("Kid Twist"), **Supp. IV Part 1:** 382
"Relevance of an Impossible Ethical Ideal, The" (Niebuhr), **III:** 298
"Religion" (Dunbar), **Supp. II Part 1:** 199
"Religion" (Emerson), **II:** 6
Religion of Nature Delineated, The (Wollaston), **II:** 108
Religious Rebel, A: The Letters of "H. W. S." (Mrs. Pearsall Smith) (L. P. Smith), **Supp. XIV:**349
"Reluctance" (Frost), **II:** 153
Reluctantly: Autobiographical Essays (Carruth), **Supp. XVI:**45-46, 50
Remains (Snodgrass), **Supp. VI:** 311, **313-314**
"Remains, The" (Strand), **Supp. IV Part 2:** 627
"Remarks on Color" (Wright), **Supp. XV:** 346
"Remarks on Spencer's *Definition of Mind as Correspondence*" (James), **II:** 345
Remarque, Erich Maria, **Retro. Supp. I:** 113; **Supp. IV Part 1:** 380
Rembrandt, **II:** 536; **IV:** 310; **Supp. IV Part 1:** 390, 391
"Rembrandt, The" (Wharton), **IV:** 310
"Rembrandt's Hat" (Malamud), **Supp. I Part 2:** 435, 437
Rembrandt Takes a Walk (Strand), **Supp. IV Part 2:** 631
"Rembrandt to Rembrandt" (Robinson), **III:** 521-522
Remembered Earth, The: An Anthology of Contemporary Native American Literature (Hobson, ed.), **Supp. IV Part 1:** 321
Remembered Yesterdays (Johnson), **Supp. IX:** 184
"Remembering" (Angelou), **Supp. IV Part 1:** 15

"Remembering Allen Tate" (Cowley), **Supp. II Part 1:** 153
"Remembering Barthes" (Sontag), **Supp. III Part 2:** 451, 471
"Remembering Guston" (Kunitz), **Supp. III Part 1:** 257
"Remembering James Laughlin" (Karr), **Supp. XI:** 242
Remembering Laughter (Stegner), **Supp. IV Part 2:** 598, 606, 607, 608, 611, 614
"Remembering Lobo" (Mora), **Supp. XIII:** 220, 227
"Remembering My Father" (Berry), **Supp. X:** 23
"Remembering that Island" (McGrath), **Supp. X:** 116
"Remembering the Children of Auschwitz" (McGrath), **Supp. X:** 127
"Remembering the Lost World" (Jarrell), **II:** 388
"Remembering the Sixties" (Simpson), **Supp. IX:** 279
Remember Me to Tom (T. Williams), **IV:** 379-380
"Remember the Moon Survives" (Kingsolver), **Supp. VII:** 209
Remember to Remember (H. Miller), **III:** 186
"Remembrance, A" (Gioia), **Supp. XV:** 112
Remembrance of Things Past (Proust), **Supp. IV Part 2:** 600; **Supp. XII:** 9; **Supp. XIII:** 44
Remembrance Rock (Sandburg), **III:** 590
Reminiscence, A (Ashbery), **Supp. III Part 1:** 2
Remnick, David, **Supp. XVI:**246
"Remora" (Merrill), **Supp. III Part 1:** 326
"Removal" (White), **Supp. I Part 2:** 664-665
"Removal, The" (Merwin), **Supp. III Part 1:** 350, 351
Removed from Time (Matthews and Feeney), **Supp. IX:** 154
Remsen, Ira, **Supp. I Part 1:** 369
"Rémy de Gourmont, A Distinction" (Pound), **III:** 467
"Renaissance" (Carruth), **Supp. XVI:**56
Renaissance in the South (Bradbury), **I:** 288-289
"Renaming the Kings" (Levine), **Supp. V:** 184
Renan, Joseph Ernest, **II:** 86; **IV:** 440, 444
Renard, Jules, **IV:** 79
"Renascence" (Millay), **III:** 123, 125-

126, 128; **Supp. XV:** 42
Renault, Mary, **Supp. IV Part 2:** 685
"Rendezvous, The" (Kumin), **Supp. IV Part 2:** 455
René, Norman, **Supp. X:** 146, 152
Renée (anonymous author), **Supp. XVI:**64, 66
"Renegade, The" (Jackson), **Supp. IX:** 120
Renewal of Life series (Mumford), **Supp. II Part 2:** 476, 479, 481, 482, 485, 495, 497
Renoir, Jean, **Supp. XII:** 259
Renouvrier, Charles, **II:** 344-345, 346
"Renunciation" (Banks), **Supp. V:** 10
Renza, Louis A., **Retro. Supp. II:** 142
"Repeating Dream" (Gander), **Supp. XV:** 340
Repent in Haste (Marquand), **III:** 59
Reperusals and Re-Collections (L. P. Smith), **Supp. XIV:**346-347
"Repetitive Heart, The: Eleven Poems in Imitation of the Fugue Form" (Schwartz), **Supp. II Part 2:** 645-646
"Replacing Regionalism" (Murphy), **Retro. Supp. II:** 143
Replansky, Naomi, **Supp. X:** 119
"Reply to Mr. Wordsworth" (MacLeish), **III:** 19
"Report from a Forest Logged by the Weyhaeuser Company" (Wagoner), **Supp. IX:** 328
"Report from North Vietnam" (Paley), **Supp. VI:** 227
Report from Part One (Brooks), **Supp. III Part 1:** 70, 72, 80, 82-85
Report from Part Two (Brooks), **Supp. III Part 1:** 87
Report on a Game Survey of the North Central States (Leopold), **Supp. XIV:**182
"Report on the Barnhouse Effect" (Vonnegut), **Supp. II Part 2:** 756
"Report to Crazy Horse" (Stafford), **Supp. XI:** 324-325
"Repose of Rivers" (H. Crane), **I:** 393; **Retro. Supp. II:** 78, 81
"Repossession of a Heritage, The" (Zagarell), **Supp. XV:** 270, 281
"Representation and the War for Reality" (Gass), **Supp. VI:** 88
Representative Men (Emerson), **II:** 1, 5-6, 8
"Representing Far Places" (Stafford), **Supp. XI:** 321
"REPRISE OF ONE OF A. G.'S BEST POEMS" (Baraka), **Supp. II Part 1:** 59
"Reproducing Ourselves Is All Very

Well" (E. Hoffman), **Supp. XVI:**155
Republic (Plato), **I:** 485
"Republican Manifesto, A" (Paine), **Supp. I Part 2:** 511
Republic of Love, The (Shields), **Supp. VII:** 323-324, 326, 327
"Requa" (Olsen), **Supp. XIII:** 294, **302-303**, 304
Requa, Kenneth A., **Supp. I Part 1:** 107
"Requa I" (Olsen). See "Requa" (Olsen)
"Request for Offering" (Eberhart), **I:** 526
"Requiem" (Akhmatova), **Supp. VIII:** 20
"Requiem" (LaBastille), **Supp. X:** 105
Requiem for a Nun (Faulkner), **II:** 57, 72-73
Requiem for Harlem (H. Roth), **Supp. IX:** 235, 236, **240-242**
"Rescue, The" (Updike), **IV:** 214
Rescued Year, The (Stafford), **Supp. XI: 321-322**
"Rescued Year, The" (Stafford), **Supp. XI:** 322, 323
"Rescue with Yul Brynner" (Moore), **III:** 215
"Resemblance" (Bishop), **Supp. I Part 1:** 86
"Resemblance between a Violin Case and a Coffin, A" (T. Williams), **IV:** 378-379
"Reservations" (Taylor), **Supp. V:** 323
"Reserved Memorials" (Mather), **Supp. II Part 2:** 446, 449
"Resistance to Civil Government" (Thoreau), **Supp. X:** 27, 28
Resist Much, Obey Little (Berry), **Supp. XIII:** 2
"Resolution and Independence" (Wordsworth), **Supp. XV:** 346
Resources of Hope (R. Williams), **Supp. IX:** 146
"Respectable Place, A" (O'Hara), **III:** 369
"Respectable Woman, A" (Chopin), **Retro. Supp. II:** 66
Responses (Wilbur), **Supp. III Part 2:** 541
"Response to a Rumor that the Oldest Whorehouse in Wheeling, West Virginia, Has Been Condemned" (Wright), **Supp. III Part 2:** 602
Restif de La Bretonne, Nicolas, **III:** 175
"Rest of Life, The" (Gordon), **Supp. IV Part 1:** 311
Rest of Life, The: Three Novellas (Gordon), **Supp. IV Part 1:** 310-312
Rest of the Way, The (McClatchy), **Supp. XII:** 255, **258-259**
Restoration comedy, **Supp. I Part 2:** 617
"Restraint" (F. Barthelme), **Supp. XI:** 26
"Result" (Emerson), **II:** 6
"Résumé" (Parker), **Supp. IX:** 189
Resurrection (Della Francesca), **Supp. XV:** 262
"Resurrection" (Harjo), **Supp. XII:** 224
Resurrection, The (Gardner), **Supp. VI:** 61, 63, **64-65**, 68, 69, 73, 74
"Retort" (Hay), **Supp. XIV:**133
Retour amont (Char; Sobin, trans.), **Supp. XVI:**282
Retrieval System, The (Kumin), **Supp. IV Part 2:** 449, 451, 452
"Retrievers in Translation" (Doty), **Supp. XI:** 132
"Retroduction to American History" (Tate), **IV:** 129
"Retrospects and Prospects" (Lanier), **Supp. I Part 1:** 352
"Return" (Corso), **Supp. XII:** 135
"Return" (Creeley), **Supp. IV Part 1:** 141, 145
"Return" (MacLeish), **III:** 12
"Return: An Elegy, The" (Warren), **IV:** 239
"Return: Buffalo" (Hogan), **Supp. IV Part 1:** 411
"Return, The" (Bidart), **Supp. XV:** 32-33
"Return, The" (Pound), **Retro. Supp. I:** 288
"Return, The" (Roethke), **III:** 533
"Return, The: Orihuela, 1965" (Levine), **Supp. V:** 194
"Returning" (Komunyakaa), **Supp. XIII:** 122
"Returning a Lost Child" (Glück), **Supp. V:** 81
"Returning from the Enemy" (Harjo), **Supp. XII:** 229-230
"Returning the Borrowed Road" (Komunyakaa), **Supp. XIII:** 113, 133
"Return of Alcibiade, The" (Chopin), **Retro. Supp. II:** 58, 64
Return of Ansel Gibbs, The (Buechner), **III:** 310; **Supp. XII: 48**
"Return of Eros to Academe, The" (Bukiet), **Supp. XVII:** 47
"Return of Spring" (Winters), **Supp. II Part 2:** 791
Return of the Native, The (Hardy), **II:** 184-185, 186
Return of the Vanishing American, The (Fiedler), **Supp. XIII:** 103
Return to a Place Lit by a Glass of Milk (Simic), **Supp. VIII:** 274, 276, 283
"Return to Lavinia" (Caldwell), **I:** 310
Reuben (Wideman), **Supp. X:** 320
Reuben and Rachel; or, Tales of Old Times (Rowson), **Supp. XV: 240-241**
Reunion (Mamet), **Supp. XIV:**240, 247, 254
"Reunion in Brooklyn" (H. Miller), **III:** 175, 184
Reuther brothers, **I:** 493
"Rev. Freemont Deadman" (Masters), **Supp. I Part 2:** 463
"Reveille" (Kingsolver), **Supp. VII:** 208
"Reveille" (Untermeyer), **Supp. XV:** 300
"Reveille, The" (Harte), **Supp. II Part 1:** 342-343
Revelation (biblical book), **II:** 541; **IV:** 104, 153, 154; **Supp. I Part 1:** 105, 273
"Revelation" (O'Connor), **III:** 349, 353-354; **Retro. Supp. II:** 237
"Revelation" (Warren), **III:** 490
Revenge (Harrison), **Supp. VIII:** 39, 45
"Revenge of Hamish, The" (Lanier), **Supp. I Part 1:** 365
"Revenge of Hannah Kemhuff, The" (Walker), **Supp. III Part 2:** 521
"Revenge of Rain-in-the-Face, The" (Longfellow), **Retro. Supp. II:** 170
Reverberator, The (James), **Retro. Supp. I:** 227
"Reverdure" (Berry), **Supp. X:** 22
Reverdy, Pierre, **Supp. XV:** 178, 182
"Reverend Father Gilhooley" (Farrell), **II:** 45
Reverse Transcription (Kushner), **Supp. IX:** 138
Reversible Errors (Turow), **Supp. XVII: 220-221**
Reviewer's ABC, A (Aiken), **I:** 58
Review of Contemporary Fiction, 1990 (Tabbi, ed.), **Supp. XVII:** 143
"Revolt, against the Crepuscular Spirit in Modern Poetry" (Pound), **Retro. Supp. I:** 286
Revolutionary Petunias (Walker), **Supp. III Part 2:** 520, 522, 530
Revolutionary Road (Yates), **Supp. XI:** 334, **335-340**
"Revolutionary Symbolism in America" (Burke), **I:** 272
"Revolutionary Theatre, The" (Baraka),

Supp. II Part 1: 42
Revolution in Taste, A: Studies of Dylan Thomas, Allen Ginsberg, Sylvia Plath, and Robert Lowell (Simpson), **Supp. IX:** 276
"Revolution in the Revolution in the Revolution" (Snyder), **Supp. VIII:** 300
Revon, Marcel, **II:** 525
"Rewaking, The" (W. C. Williams), **Retro. Supp. I:** 430
"Rewrite" (Dunn), **Supp. XI:** 147
Rexroth, Kenneth, **II:** 526; **Supp. II Part 1:** 307; **Supp. II Part 2:** 436; **Supp. III Part 2:** 625, 626; **Supp. IV Part 1:** 145-146; **Supp. VIII:** 289; **Supp. XIII:** 75; **Supp. XIV:** 287; **Supp. XV:** 140, 141, 146
Reynolds, Ann (pseudo.). See Bly, Carol
Reynolds, Clay, **Supp. XI:** 254
Reynolds, David, **Supp. XV:** 269
Reynolds, Quentin, **IV:** 286
Reynolds, Sir Joshua, **Supp. I Part 2:** 716
Reznikoff, Charles, **IV:** 415; **Retro. Supp. I:** 422; **Supp. III Part 2:** 615, 616, 617, 628; **Supp. XIV:277-296**
"Rhapsodist, The" (Brown), **Supp. I Part 1:** 125-126
"Rhapsody on a Windy Night" (Eliot), **Retro. Supp. I:** 55
Rhetoric of Motives, A (Burke), **I:** 272, 275, 278, 279
Rhetoric of Religion, The (Burke), **I:** 275, 279
"Rhobert" (Toomer), **Supp. IX:** 316-317
"Rhododendrons" (Levis), **Supp. XI:** 260, 263
Rhubarb Show, The (radio, Keillor), **Supp. XVI:** 178
"Rhyme of Sir Christopher, The" (Longfellow), **II:** 501
Rhymes to Be Traded for Bread (Lindsay), **Supp. I Part 2:** 380, 381-382
Rhys, Ernest, **III:** 458
Rhys, Jean, **Supp. III Part 1:** 42, 43
"Rhythm & Blues" (Baraka), **Supp. II Part 1:** 37-38
Rhythms (Reznikoff), **Supp. XIV:** 279, 282, 283
Rhythms II (Reznikoff), **Supp. XIV:** 282, 283, 284
Ribalow, Harold, **Supp. IX:** 236
Ribbentrop, Joachim von, **IV:** 249
Ribicoff, Abraham, **Supp. IX:** 33

Ricardo, David, **Supp. I Part 2:** 628, 634
Rice, Allen Thorndike, **Retro. Supp. I:** 362
Rice, Anne, **Supp. VII: 287-306**
Rice, Elmer, **I:** 479; **III:** 145, 160-161
Rice, Mrs. Grantland, **II:** 435
Rice, Philip Blair, **IV:** 141
Rice, Stan, **Supp. XII:** 2
Rice, Tom, **Supp. XIV:** 125
Rich, Adrienne, **Retro. Supp. I:** 8, 36, 42, 47, 404; **Retro. Supp. II:** 43, 191, 245; **Supp. I Part 2:** 546-547, **550-578; Supp. III Part 1:** 84, 354; **Supp. III Part 2:** 541, 599; **Supp. IV Part 1:** 257, 325; **Supp. V:** 82; **Supp. VIII:** 272; **Supp. XII:** 217, 229, 255; **Supp. XIII:** 294; **Supp. XIV:** 126, 129; **Supp. XV:** 176, 252; **Supp. XVII:** 32, 74
Rich, Arnold, **Supp. I Part 2:** 552
Rich, Frank, **Supp. IV Part 2:** 585, 586; **Supp. V:** 106
Richard Cory (Gurney), **Supp. V:** 99-100, 105
"Richard Hunt's 'Arachne'" (Hayden), **Supp. II Part 1:** 374
Richard II (Shakespeare), **Supp. XVII:** 244
Richard III (Shakespeare), **Supp. I Part 2:** 422
Richards, David, **Supp. IV Part 2:** 576
Richards, Grant, **I:** 515
Richards, I. A., **I:** 26, 273-274, 279, 522; **III:** 498; **IV:** 92; **Supp. I Part 1:** 264, 265; **Supp. I Part 2:** 647
Richards, Ivor Armonstrong, **Supp. XIV:** 2-3, 16
Richards, Laura E., **II:** 396; **III:** 505-506, 507
Richards, Leonard, **Supp. XIV:** 48
Richards, Lloyd, **Supp. IV Part 1:** 362; **Supp. VIII:** 331
Richards, Rosalind, **III:** 506
Richards, Tad, **Supp. XVII:** 77
Richardson, Alan, **III:** 295
Richardson, Dorothy, **I:** 53; **II:** 320; **Supp. III Part 1:** 65
Richardson, Helen Patges, **Retro. Supp. II:** 95
Richardson, Henry Hobson, **I:** 3, 10
Richardson, Maurice, **Supp. XII:** 241
Richardson, Samuel, **I:** 134; **II:** 104, 111, 322; **Supp. V:** 127; **Supp. IX:** 128; **Supp. XV:** 232
Richardson, Tony, **Supp. XI:** 305, 306
"Richard Wright and Recent Negro Fiction" (Ellison), **Retro. Supp. II:** 116
"Richard Wright's Blues" (Ellison),

Retro. Supp. II: 117, 124
"Richard Yates: A Requiem" (Lawrence), **Supp. XI:** 335
"Rich Boy, The" (Fitzgerald), **II:** 94; **Retro. Supp. I:** 98, 108
"Riches" (Bausch), **Supp. VII:** 54
Richler, Mordecai, **Supp. XI:** 294, 297
Richman, Robert, **Supp. XI:** 249; **Supp. XV:** 120-121, 251
Richmond (Masters), **Supp. I Part 2:** 471
Richter, Conrad, **Supp. X:** 103
Richter, Jean Paul, **II:** 489, 492; **Supp. XVI:** 182
Rick Bass (Weltzien), **Supp. XVI:** 20
Rickman, Clio, **Supp. I Part 2:** 519
Ricks, Christopher, **Retro. Supp. I:** 56
Riddel, Joseph N., **IV:** 95
"Riddle, The" (Hay), **Supp. XIV:** 130
"Riders to the Blood-Red Wrath" (Brooks), **Supp. III Part 1:** 82-83
Riders to the Sea (Synge), **III:** 157
Ridge, Lola, **Supp. IX:** 308; **Supp. XV:** 307
Riding, Alan, **Supp. XVI:** 294
Riding, Laura, **I:** 437
"Riding Out at Evening" (McCarriston), **Supp. XIV:** 262-263
Riding the Iron Rooster: By Train through China (Theroux), **Supp. VIII:** 324
Riesenberg, Felix, **I:** 360, 361
Riesman, David, **Supp. I Part 2:** 649, 650
"Rif, to Music, The" (Bowles), **Supp. IV Part 1:** 89
Riffs & Reciprocities (Dunn), **Supp. XI:** 154-155
Rifles, The (Vollmann), **Supp. XVII:** 226, 233
Riggs, Marlon, **Supp. XI:** 19
Right Madness on Skye, The (Hugo), **Supp. VI:** 145-147
Rights of Man (Paine), **Supp. I Part 2:** 508, 511, 512-514, 516, 519, 523
"Rights of Woman" (Rowson), **Supp. XV:** 243
"Rights of Women, The" (Brown). See *Alcuin: A Dialogue* (Brown)
Right Stuff, The (Wolfe), **Supp. III Part 2:** 581-584
Right Thoughts in Sad Hours (Mather), **IV:** 144
Rigney, Barbara Hill, **Supp. VIII:** 215
"Rigorists" (Moore), **III:** 198
Riis, Jacob A., **I:** 293; **Supp. I Part 1:** 13; **Supp. XVII:** 101, 106
Riley, James Whitcomb, **I:** 205; **Supp. II Part 1:** 192, 193, 196, 197
Rilke, Rainer Maria, **I:** 445, 523; **II:**

367, 381, 382-383, 389, 543, 544; **III:** 552, 558, 563, 571, 572; **IV:** 380, 443; **Retro. Supp. II:** 20, 187; **Supp. I Part 1:** 264; **Supp. I Part 2:** 573; **Supp. III Part 1:** 239, 242, 246, 283, 319-320; **Supp. IV Part 1:** 284; **Supp. V:** 208, 343; **Supp. VIII:** 30, 40; **Supp. X:** 164; **Supp. XI:** 126; **Supp. XIII:** 74, 88; **Supp. XV:** 93, 212, 222,**Supp. XV:** 223, 225; **Supp. XVI:**292; **Supp. XVII:** 244

Rilke on Love and Other Difficulties (Rilke), **Supp. X:** 164

"Rilke's Growth as a Poet" (Dobyns), **Supp. XIII:** 77

"Rimbaud" (Kerouac), **Supp. III Part 1:** 232

Rimbaud, Arthur, **I:** 381, 383, 389, 391, 526; **II:** 528, 543, 545; **III:** 23, 174, 189; **IV:** 286, 380, 443; **Retro. Supp. I:** 56; **Retro. Supp. II:** 187, 326; **Supp. III Part 1:** 14, 195; **Supp. IV Part 2:** 624; **Supp. VIII:** 39, 40; **Supp. XII:** 1, 16, 128, 255; **Supp. XIII:** 284; **Supp. XIV:**338

Rinehart, Stanley, **III:** 36

Ring, Frances Kroll, **Supp. IX:** 63, 64

Ring and the Book, The (Browning), **Supp. I Part 2:** 416, 468

Ring cycle (Wagner), **Supp. IV Part 1:** 392

Ringe, Donald, **I:** 339, 343; **Retro. Supp. II:** 270

"Ringing" (Bierds), **Supp. XVII:** 28

"Ringing the Bells" (Sexton), **Supp. II Part 2:** 672, 687

Ringle, Ken, **Supp. X:** 15

Ring of Heaven: Poems (Hongo), **Supp. X:** 292

Rink, The (musical, McNally), **Supp. XIII:** 207

Rio Lobo (film), **Supp. XVI:**246

Ríos, Alberto Alvaro, **Supp. IV Part 2: 537-556**

"Riot" (Brooks), **Supp. III Part 1:** 71, 84-85

Ripley, Ezra, **II:** 8; **IV:** 172

Rip-off Red, Girl Detective (Acker), **Supp. XII:** 3-4

Ripostes (Pound), **Retro. Supp. I:** 287-288, 413

Ripostes of Ezra Pound, The, Whereunto Are Appended the Complete Poetical Works of T. E. Hulme, with Prefatory Note (Pound), **III:** 458, 464, 465

Riprap (Snyder), **Supp. VIII: 292-294,** 295

"Riprap" (Snyder), **Supp. VIII:** 293-294

"Rip Van Winkle" (Irving), **II:** 304-306; **Supp. I Part 1:** 185

Rischin, Moses, **Supp. XVII:** 101, 103, 106

Risco-Lozado, Eliezar, **Supp. XIII:** 313

Rise and Shine (Quindlen), **Supp. XVII:** 179

Rise of David Levinsky, The (Cahan), **Supp. IX:** 227; **Supp. XIII:** 106

Rise of Silas Lapham, The (Howells), **II:** 275, 279, 283-285; **IV:** 202; **Retro. Supp. II:** 93, 101

"Rise of the Middle Class" (Banks), **Supp. V:** 10

Rising and Falling (Matthews), **Supp. IX:** 154, **160**

"Rising Daughter, The" (Olds), **Supp. X:** 204

Rising from the Plains (McPhee), **Supp. III Part 1:** 309-310

Rising Glory of America, The (Brackenridge and Freneau), **Supp. I Part 1:** 124; **Supp. II Part 1:** 67, 253, 256, 263

"Rising of the Storm, The" (Dunbar), **Supp. II Part 1:** 199

Rising Sun in the Pacific, The (Morison), **Supp. I Part 2:** 490

Rising Up and Rising Down (Vollmann), **Supp. XVII:** 225, 226, **229-230,** 232, 233, 235-236

Risk Pool, The (Russo), **Supp. XII: 328-331**

Ristovic, Aleksandar, **Supp. VIII:** 272

"Rita Dove: Identity Markers" (Vendler), **Supp. IV Part 1:** 247, 257

Ritchey, John, **Supp. XIV:**122

"Rite of Passage" (Olds), **Supp. X:** 206

"Rites and Ceremonies" (Hecht), **Supp. X:** 61

"Rites of Spring, The" (Morris), **III:** 223

Ritivoi, Andreea Deciu, **Supp. XVI:**148

Ritschl, Albrecht, **III:** 309, 604

Ritsos, Yannis, **Supp. X:** 112

"Ritsos and the Metaphysical Moment" (Dobyns), **Supp. XIII:** 78

Rittenhouse, David, **Supp. I Part 2:** 507

Rittenhouse, Jessie, **Supp. XV:** 295

"Ritual, The" (Jarman), **Supp. XVII:** 114

"Ritual and Renewal: Keres Traditions in the Short Fiction of Leslie Silko" (Ruoff), **Supp. IV Part 2:** 559

Ritz, The (film), **Supp. XIII:** 206

Ritz, The (McNally), **Supp. XIII:** 198

"Rival, The" (Plath), **Retro. Supp. II:** 254

Riven Rock (Boyle), **Supp. VIII:** 5-6

"River" (Ammons), **Supp. VII:** 28

"River, The" (O'Connor), **III:** 344, 352, 353, 354, 356; **Retro. Supp. II:** 229, 231-232

Rivera, Tomás, **Supp. XIII:** 216, 221

Riverbed (Wagoner), **Supp. IX: 327-328**

"River Driftwood" (Jewett), **Retro. Supp. II:** 132, 133, 147

"River Jordan, The" (DeLillo), **Supp. VI:** 3, 4

River King, The (Hoffman), **Supp. X:** 78, 85, 90, **91-92**

"River Merchant's Wife: A Letter, The" (Pound), **III:** 463

"River Now, The" (Hugo), **Supp. VI:** 144

"River of Rivers in Connecticut, The" (Stevens), **Retro. Supp. I:** 313

River of the Mother of God and Other Essays by Aldo Leopold, The (Leopold), **Supp. XIV:**180

"River Profile" (Auden), **Supp. II Part 1:** 26

"River Road" (Kunitz), **Supp. III Part 1:** 260

"River Runs Through It, A" (Maclean), **Supp. XIV:**222-223, **223-229,** 233, 234, 235; **Supp. XVI:**98

River Runs Through It and Other Stories, A (Maclean), **Supp. XIV:**221, 223

Rivers, Larry, **Supp. III Part 1:** 3; **Supp. XV:** 177, 178, 186

Rivers and Mountains (Ashbery), **Supp. III Part 1:** 10, 26

Riverside Drive (Simpson), **Supp. IX: 275-276**

Rivers to the Sea (Teasdale), **Supp. XV:** 295

River Styx, Ohio, and Other Poems, The (Oliver), **Supp. VII:** 231, 232

"River That Is East, The" (Kinnell), **Supp. III Part 1:** 241-242

"River Towns" (Masters), **Supp. I Part 2:** 473

Rives, Amélie, **II:** 194

Rivière, Jacques, **Retro. Supp. I:** 63

"Rivington's Last Will and Testament" (Freneau), **Supp. II Part 1:** 261

"Rivulet, The" (Bryant), **Supp. I Part 1:** 155, 162

Rix, Alice, **I:** 199

RL's Dream (Mosley), **Supp. XIII:** 234, **244-245,** 249

Roach, Max, **Supp. X:** 239
"Road, Roadsides, and the Disparate Frames of a Sequence" (Sobin), **Supp. XVI:**288
Road Between, The (Farrell), **II:** 29, 38, 39-40
"Road Between Here and There, The" (Kinnell), **Supp. III Part 1:** 254
"Road Home, The" (Hammett), **Supp. IV Part 1:** 343
Road Home, The (Harrison), **Supp. VIII:** 37, 45, 48, **49-50,** 53
Roadless Yaak, The: Reflections and Observations about One of Our Last Great Wild Places (Bass, ed.), **Supp. XVI:**23
"Road Not Taken, The" (R. Frost), **II:** 154; **Retro. Supp. I:** 131; **Supp. XI:** 150; **Supp. XV:** 127
Roadside Poems for Summer Travellers (Larcom, ed.), **Supp. XIII:** 142
Roads of Destiny (O. Henry), **Supp. II Part 1:** 410
Road through the Wall, The (Jackson), **Supp. IX:** 115, 118, 120, 123-124
"Road to Avignon, The" (Lowell), **II:** 516
"Road to Hell, The" (Fante), **Supp. XI:** 160
Road to Los Angeles, The (Fante), **Supp. XI:** 160, 166, 167, **168,** 172
Road to Many a Wonder, The (Wagoner), **Supp. IX:** 327, **336**
Road to the Temple, The (Glaspell), **Supp. III Part 1:** 175, 182, 186
Road to Wellville, The (Boyle), **Supp. VIII:** 6-8
Road to Xanadu, The (Lowes), **IV:** 453
"Roan Stallion" (Jeffers), **Supp. II Part 2:** 428-429
"Roast-beef" (Stein), **IV:** 43
Roast Leviatham (Untermeyer), **Supp. XV:** 307
"Roast Possum" (Dove), **Supp. IV Part 1:** 247, 248
Robards, Jason, Jr., **III:** 163, 403
Robb, Christina, **Supp. XV:** 251
Robbe-Grillet, Alain, **I:** 123; **IV:** 95; **Supp. IV Part 1:** 42; **Supp. V:** 47, 48
Robber Bride, The (Atwood), **Supp. XIII:** 30-31
Robber Bridegroom, The (Welty), **IV:** 261, 266-268, 271, 274; **Retro. Supp. I:** 347
Robbins, Harold, **Supp. XII:** 6
Robbins, Henry, **Supp. IV Part 1:** 198, 201, 210, 211
Robbins, Katherine Robinson, **Supp. X:** 264

Robbins, Thomas, **Supp. XV:** 271
Robbins, Tom, **Supp. IV Part 1:** 227; **Supp. VIII:** 14; **Supp. X: 259-288; Supp. XIII:** 11
"Robe, The" (Douglas), **IV:** 434
"Robert Bly" (Davis), **Supp. IV Part 1:** 70
Robert Bly (Sugg), **Supp. IV Part 1:** 68
Robert Bly: An Introduction to the Poetry (Nelson), **Supp. IV Part 1:** 66
Robert Bly: The Poet and His Critics (Davis), **Supp. IV Part 1:** 63
"Robert Bly and the Trouble with America" (Mitchell), **Supp. IV Part 1:** 70
Robert Coover: The Universal Fiction-making Process (Gordon), **Supp. V:** 46
Robert Creeley (Ford), **Supp. IV Part 1:** 140
Robert Creeley and the Genius of the American Common Place (Clark), **Supp. IV Part 1:** 140
Robert Creeley's Poetry: A Critical Introduction (Edelberg), **Supp. IV Part 1:** 155
Robert Frost (Meyers), **Retro. Supp. I:** 138
Robert Lowell (Meyers), **Retro. Supp. II:** 191
Robert Lowell: The First Twenty years (Staples), **Retro. Supp. II:** 187
Robert Lowell and the Sublime (Hart), **Retro. Supp. II:** 187
Robert Lowell's Shifting Colors (Doreski), **Retro. Supp. II:** 185
Roberts, Diane, **Supp. X:** 15
Roberts, J. M., **IV:** 454
Roberts, Leo, **II:** 449
Roberts, Margaret, **II:** 449; **IV:** 453, 454
Roberts, Matthew, **Retro. Supp. II:** 324
Roberts, Meade, **IV:** 383
Roberts, Michael, **I:** 527, 536
Roberts, Richard, **III:** 297
Roberts, Wally, **Supp. XI:** 119, 120, 126
Roberts, William, **Supp. XI:** 343
Roberts Brothers, **Retro. Supp. I:** 31, 35
Robertson, D. B., **III:** 311
Robertson, David, **Supp. VIII:** 305
Robertson, Nan, **Supp. IV Part 1:** 300
Robertson, William, **II:** 8
Robert the Devil (Merwin, trans.), **Supp. III Part 1:** 341, 346
Robeson, Paul, **III:** 392; **Supp. IV Part 1:** 360, 361; **Supp. X:** 137

Robespierre, Maximilien, **Supp. I Part 2:** 514, 515, 517
"Robinson" (Kees), **Supp. XV:** 143-144
Robinson, Christopher L., **Supp. XII:** 13, 14
Robinson, Dean, **III:** 506
Robinson, Edward, **III:** 505
Robinson, Edward G., **Supp. XI:** 306
Robinson, Edwin Arlington, **I:** 480; **II:** 388, 391, 529, 542; **III:** 5, **503-526,** 576; **Supp. I Part 2:** 699; **Supp. II Part 1:** 191; **Supp. III Part 1:** 63, 75; **Supp. III Part 2:** 592, 593; **Supp. IX:** 77, 266, 276, 308; **Supp. XV:** 256, 299, 300, 301, 306; **Supp. XVII:** 69
Robinson, Forrest G., **Supp. IV Part 2:** 597, 601, 604
Robinson, H. M., **IV:** 369, 370
Robinson, Herman, **III:** 506-507
Robinson, Jackie, **Supp. I Part 1:** 338
Robinson, James Harvey, **I:** 214; **Supp. I Part 2:** 492
Robinson, James K., **Supp. IX:** 328
Robinson, Margaret G., **Supp. IV Part 2:** 597, 601, 604
Robinson, Mary, **Supp. XI:** 26
Robinson, Sugar Ray, **Supp. IV Part 1:** 167
Robinson, Ted, **Supp. XIII:** 166
Robinson Crusoe (Defoe), **II:** 159; **III:** 113, 423; **IV:** 369; **Retro. Supp. II:** 274; **Supp. I Part 2:** 714; **Supp. IV Part 2:** 502
Robison, Mary, **Supp. V:** 22
Roblès, Emmanuel, **Supp. I Part 1:** 283
"Robstown" (Salinas), **Supp. XIII:** 315
Rochefort, Christina, **Supp. XVI:**143
Rochefoucauld, Louis Alexandre, **Supp. I Part 2:** 510
"Rock" (Nye), **Supp. XIII:** 287
Rock (Wagoner), **Supp. IX:** 324, **334,** 335
Rock, Catherine, **Supp. XII:** 17
Rock, The (Eliot), **Retro. Supp. I:** 65
Rock, The (Stevens), **Retro. Supp. I:** 309, 312
"Rock, The" (Stevens), **Retro. Supp. I:** 312
Rockaway (Shanley), **Supp. XIV:**315
"Rock Climbers, The" (Francis), **Supp. IX:** 82
Rock-Drill (Pound), **Retro. Supp. I:** 293
Rockefeller, John D., **I:** 273; **III:** 580; **Supp. I Part 2:** 486; **Supp. V:** 286
Rockefeller, Nelson, **III:** 14, 15

Rocket to the Moon (Odets), **Supp. II Part 2:** 541-543, 544
Rock Garden, The (Shepard), **Supp. III Part 2:** 432, 447
"Rocking Horse Winner, The" (Lawrence), **Supp. I Part 1:** 329
Rocking the Boat (Vidal), **Supp. IV Part 2:** 683
"Rockpile, The" (Baldwin), **Supp. I Part 1:** 63
Rock Springs (Ford), **Supp. V:** 57, 58-59, 68-69
Rocky Mountains, The: or, Scenes, Incidents, and Adventures in the Far West; Digested from the Journal of Captain E. L. E Bonneville, of the Army of the United States, and Illustrated from Various Other Sources (Irving), **II:** 312
Rodden, John, **Supp. XVI:**63, 69, 72
Roderick, David, **Supp. XV:** 223
Roderick Hudson (James), **II:** 284, 290, 324, 326, 328; **Retro. Supp. I:** 219, **220-221,** 221, 226; **Supp. IX:** 142
Rodgers, Richard, **III:** 361
Rodgers, Ronald, **Supp. IV Part 2:** 503
Rodker, John, **III:** 470
Rodman, Selden, **Supp. I Part 1:** 83; **Supp. X:** 115
"Rodrigo Returns to the Land and Linen Celebrates" (Cisneros), **Supp. VII:** 68
Rodriguez, Randy A., **Supp. XIV:**312
Rodriguez, Richard, **Supp. XIV:**297-313
Roethke, Charles, **III:** 531
Roethke, Theodore, **I:** 167, 171-172, 183, 254, 285, 521; **III:** 273, **527-550; IV:** 138, 402; **Retro. Supp. II:** 178, 181, 246; **Supp. I Part 2:** 539; **Supp. III Part 1:** 47, 54, 56, 239, 253, 260-261, 350; **Supp. IV Part 2:** 626; **Supp. IX:** 323; **Supp. XV:** 140, 145, 212
"Roger Malvin's Burial" (Hawthorne), **II:** 243; **Retro. Supp. I:** 153
Rogers, Michael, **Supp. X:** 265, 266
Rogers, Samuel, **II:** 303; **Supp. I Part 1:** 157
Rogers, Will, **I:** 261; **IV:** 388
Roger's Version (Updike), **Retro. Supp. I:** 325, 327, 330
Roget, Peter Mark, **Supp. I Part 1:** 312
"Rogue River Jet-Board Trip, Gold Beach, Oregon, July 4, 1977" (Carver), **Supp. III Part 1:** 140
"Rogue's Gallery" (McCarthy), **II:** 563

Roland de La Platière, Jean Marie, **II:** 554
Rôle du Nègre dans la culture des Amériques, La (Locke), **Supp. XIV:**202
"Role of Society in the Artist, The" (Ammons), **Supp. VII:** 34
Rolfe, Alfred, **IV:** 427
"Roll, Jordan, Roll" (spiritual), **Supp. IV Part 1:** 16
"Roll Call" (Komunyakaa), **Supp. XIII:** 123
Rolle, Esther, **Supp. IV Part 1:** 367
Rollin, Charles, **II:** 113
Rolling Stones (O. Henry), **Supp. II Part 1:** 410
Rolling Thunder Logbook (Shepard), **Supp. III Part 2:** 433
"Rolling Up" (Simpson), **Supp. IX:** 265, 274, 280
Rollins, Howard E., Jr., **Supp. IV Part 1:** 236
Rollins, Hyder E., **Supp. IV Part 1:** 168
Rollins, Sonny, **Supp. V:** 195
"Rollo" tales (Abbott), **Supp. I Part 1:** 38
"Roma I" (Wright), **Supp. V:** 338
"Roma II" (Wright), **Supp. V:** 338
Romains, Jules, **I:** 227
Román, David, **Supp. XIII:** 208
"Romance and a Reading List" (Fitzgerald), **Retro. Supp. I:** 101
Romance of a Plain Man, The (Glasgow), **II:** 175, 180-181
"Romance of Certain Old Clothes, The" (James), **II:** 322; **Retro. Supp. I:** 218
"Roman Elegies" (Brodsky), **Supp. VIII:** 29
"Roman Fever" (Wharton), **Retro. Supp. I:** 382
"Roman Fountain" (Bogan), **Supp. III Part 1:** 56
"*Romanitas* of Gore Vidal, The" (Tatum), **Supp. IV Part 2:** 684
Romaniuk, Zbigniew, **Supp. XVI:**154
Romano, John, **Supp. XV:** 253
"Roman Sarcophagus, A" (Lowell), **II:** 544
Roman Spring of Mrs. Stone, The (T. Williams), **IV:** 383, 385
"Romantic, The" (Bogan), **Supp. III Part 1:** 50
Romantic Comedians, The (Glasgow), **II:** 175, 186, 190, 194
Romantic Egoists, The (Auchincloss), **Supp. IV Part 1:** 25
Romantic Egotist, The (Fitzgerald), **II:** 82

"Romantic Egotist, The" (Fitzgerald), **Retro. Supp. I:** 100
"Romanticism and Classicism" (Hulme), **III:** 196
"Romanticism Comes Home" (Shapiro), **Supp. II Part 2:** 713
Romantic Manifesto, The: A Philosophy of Literature (Rand), **Supp. IV Part 2:** 521, 523, 527, 529-530
"Romantic Regionalism of Harper Lee, The" (Erisman), **Supp. VIII:** 126
"Rome" (W. C. Williams), **Retro. Supp. I:** 420
Rome Brothers, **Retro. Supp. I:** 393
Romeo and Juliet (Shakespeare), **Supp. V:** 252; **Supp. VIII:** 223
Romola (Eliot), **II:** 291; **IV:** 311
Romulus: A New Comedy (Vidal), **Supp. IV Part 2:** 683
Romulus der Grosse (Dürrenmatt), **Supp. IV Part 2:** 683
Ronald, Ann, **Supp. XIII:** 4, 5, 6, 7, 9, 11
"Rondel for a September Day" (White), **Supp. I Part 2:** 676
"Ron Narrative Reconstructions, The" (Coleman), **Supp. XI:** 83
Ronsard, Pierre de, **Supp. X:** 65; **Supp. XV:** 165
Rood, John, **IV:** 261
"Roof, the Steeple, and the People, The" (Ellison), **Retro. Supp. II:** 118, 126; **Supp. II Part 1:** 248
"Room" (Levertov), **Supp. III Part 1:** 282
Roomates (film, P. Yates), **Supp. XVII:** 8, 9
Roomates: My Grandfather's Story (Apple), **Supp. XVII:** 2, **7-9**
"Room at the Heart of Things, A" (Merrill), **Supp. III Part 1:** 337
Room Called Remember, A: Uncollected Pieces (Buechner), **Supp. XII:** 53
"Roomful of Hovings, A" (McPhee), **Supp. III Part 1:** 291, 294
Room of One's Own, A (Woolf), **Supp. V:** 127; **Supp. IX:** 19; **Supp. XIII:** 305
Room Rented by a Single Woman (Wright), **Supp. XV:** 340-341
Room Temperature (Baker), **Supp. XIII:** 41, **43-45,** 48, 50
Room to Swing (Lacy), **Supp. XV:** 202, 203, 205, 207
"Room Upstairs, The" (Gioia), **Supp. XV:** 120-121, 124
Roosevelt, Eleanor, **IV:** 371; **Supp. IV Part 2:** 679
Roosevelt, Franklin, **Supp. V:** 290

Roosevelt, Franklin Delano, **I:** 482, 485, 490; **II:** 553, 575; **III:** 2, 18, 69, 110, 297, 321, 376, 476, 580, 581; **Supp. I Part 2:** 488, 489, 490, 491, 645, 654, 655
Roosevelt, Kermit, **III:** 508
Roosevelt, Theodore, **I:** 14, 62; **II:** 130; **III:** 508; **IV:** 321; **Retro. Supp. I:** 377; **Supp. I Part 1:** 1, 21; **Supp. I Part 2:** 455, 456, 502, 707; **Supp. V:** 280, 282; **Supp. IX:** 184
Roosevelt After Inauguration And Other Atrocities (Burroughs), **Supp. III Part 1:** 98
"Roosters" (Bishop), **Retro. Supp. II:** 39, 43, 250; **Supp. I Part 1:** 89
Root, Abiah, **I:** 456
Root, Elihu, **Supp. IV Part 1:** 33
Root, Simeon, **I:** 548
Root, Timothy, **I:** 548
Rootabaga Stories (Sandburg), **III:** 583, 587
"Rootedness: The Ancestor as Foundation" (Morrison), **Supp. III Part 1:** 361
Roots in the Soil (film), **Supp. IV Part 1:** 83
"Rope" (Porter), **III:** 451
Rope, The (O'Neill), **III:** 388
Ropemakers of Plymouth, The (Morison), **Supp. I Part 2:** 494
"Ropes" (Nye), **Supp. XIII:** 276
"Rope's End, The" (Nemerov), **III:** 282
Roquelaure, A. N., **Supp. VII:** 301. *See also* Rice, Anne
Rorem, Ned, **Supp. IV Part 1:** 79, 84
Rorschach Test (F. Wright), **Supp. XVII:** 240, 245
"Rosa" (Ozick), **Supp. V:** 271
Rosa, Rodrigo Rey, **Supp. IV Part 1:** 92
Rosaldo, Renato, **Supp. IV Part 2:** 544
"Rosalia" (Simic), **Supp. VIII:** 278
Roscoe, Will, **Supp. IV Part 1:** 330
"Rose" (Dubus), **Supp. VII:** 88
Rose (L.-Y. Lee), **Supp. XV:** 211, **212-215,** 218
Rose, Alice, Sister, **III:** 348
Rose, Mickey, **Supp. XV:** 3
Rose, Philip, **Supp. IV Part 1:** 362
"Rose, The" (Roethke), **III:** 537
"Rose, The" (W. C. Williams), **Retro. Supp. I:** 419
Rose, Where Did You Get That Red?: Teaching Great Poetry to Children (Koch), **Supp. XV:** 189
"Rose for Emily, A" (Faulkner), **II:** 72; **Supp. IX:** 96

Rose in Bloom (Alcott), **Supp. I Part 1:** 42
"Rose-Johnny" (Kingsolver), **Supp. VII:** 203
Rose Madder (King), **Supp. V:** 141, 148, 150, 152
"Rose-Morals" (Lanier), **Supp. I Part 1:** 364
Rosen, Jonathan, **Supp. XVII:** 50
Rosen, Kenneth, **Supp. IV Part 2:** 499, 505, 513
Rosen, Norma, **Supp. XVII:** 49, 50
Rosenbaum, Alissa Zinovievna. *See* Rand, Ayn
Rosenbaum, Thane, **Supp. XVII:** 48
Rosenberg, Bernard, **Supp. I Part 2:** 650
Rosenberg, Harold, **Supp. XV:** 143
Rosenberg, Julius and Ethel, **Supp. I Part 1:** 295; **Supp. I Part 2:** 532; **Supp. V:** 45
Rosenberg, Liz, **Supp. XV:** 251
Rosenbloom, Joel, **Supp. IV Part 2:** 527
Rosenfeld, Alvin H., **Supp. I Part 1:** 120
Rosenfeld, Isaac, **Supp. XII:** 160
Rosenfeld, Paul, **I:** 116, 117, 231, 245
Rosenfelt, Deborah, **Supp. XIII:** 296, 304
Rosenfield, Isaac, **IV:** 3
Rosenthal, Ira, **Supp. XIV:** 146-147
Rosenthal, Lois, **Supp. VIII:** 258
Rosenthal, M. L., **II:** 550; **III:** 276, 479; **Supp. V:** 333
Rosenthal, Peggy, **Supp. XVII:** 119
"Rose Pogonias" (Frost), **Retro. Supp. I:** 127
"Rose Red and Snow White" (Grimms), **Supp. X:** 82
"Roses" (Conroy), **Supp. XVI:** 72
"Roses" (Dove), **Supp. IV Part 1:** 246
"Roses and Skulls" (Goldbarth), **Supp. XII:** 192
"Roses for Lubbock" (Nye), **Supp. XIII:** 281
"Roses Only" (Moore), **III:** 195, 198, 200, 202, 215
Rose Tattoo, The (T. Williams), **IV:** 382, 383, 387, 388, 389, 392-393, 394, 397, 398
"Rosewood, Ohio" (Matthews), **Supp. IX:** 160
Rosinante to the Road Again (Dos Passos), **I:** 478
Roskies, David, **Supp. XVII:** 39, 44, 49-50
Roskolenko, Harry, **Supp. XV:** 179
Rosmersholm (Ibsen), **III:** 152
Rosmond, Babette, **II:** 432

Ross, Eleanor. *See* Taylor, Eleanor Ross
Ross, Harold, **Supp. I Part 1:** 174; **Supp. I Part 2:** 607, 617, 653, 654, 655, 660; **Supp. VIII:** 151, 170; **Supp. IX:** 190
Ross, Herbert, **Supp. XV:** 2
Ross, John F., **II:** 110
Ross, Lillilan, **Retro. Supp. II:** 198
Ross, Mitchell S., **Supp. IV Part 2:** 692; **Supp. X:** 260
Rossen, Robert, **Supp. XI:** 306
Rosset, Barney, **III:** 171
Rossetti, Christina, **Supp. XIV:** 128
Rossetti, Dante Gabriel, **I:** 433; **II:** 323; **Retro. Supp. I:** 128, 286; **Supp. I Part 2:** 552
Rossetti, William Michael, **Retro. Supp. I:** 407
Rossini, Clare, **Supp. XVII:** 111
Rosskam, Edwin, **IV:** 477
Ross Macdonald (Bruccoli), **Supp. IV Part 2:** 468, 470
Rostand, Edmond, **II:** 515; **Supp. IV Part 2:** 518
Rosten, Leo, **Supp. XVII:** 9
Rosy Crucifixion, The (H. Miller), **III:** 170, 187, 188-189, 190
Rote Walker, The (Jarman), **Supp. XVII:** 110, **113-115**
Roth, Henry, **Supp. IV Part 1:** 314; **Supp. VIII:** 233; **Supp. IX:** 227-243; **Supp. XIII:** 106
Roth, Philip, **I:** 144, 161; **II:** 591; **Retro. Supp. II:** 22, **279-297;** **Supp. I Part 1:** 186, 192; **Supp. I Part 2:** 431, 441, 443; **Supp. II Part 1:** 99; **Supp. III Part 2: 401-429;** **Supp. IV Part 1:** 236, 379, 388; **Supp. V:** 45, 119, 122, 257, 258; **Supp. VIII:** 88, 236, 245; **Supp. IX:** 227; **Supp. XI:** 64, 68, 99, 140; **Supp. XII:** 190, 310; **Supp. XIV:** 79, 93, 111, 112; **Supp. XVI:** 206; **Supp. XVII:** 43, 48, 183
Roth, Rita, **Supp. XVI:** 112
Roth, William, **Supp. XV:** 142
Rothenberg, Jerome, **Supp. VIII:** 292; **Supp. XII:** 3
Rothermere, Lady Mary, **Retro. Supp. I:** 63
Rothko, Mark, **Supp. XV:** 144
Rothstein, Mervyn, **Supp. VIII:** 142
"Rouge High" (Hughes), **Supp. I Part 1:** 330
Rougemont, Denis de, **II:** 586; **IV:** 216; **Retro. Supp. I:** 328, 329, 330, 331
Roughing It (Twain), **II:** 312; **IV:** 195, 197, 198

Roughing It in the Bush (Shields), **Supp. VII:** 313
"Rough Outline" (Simic), **Supp. VIII:** 276
Rougon-Macquart, Les (Zola), **II:** 175-176
Roumain, Jacques, **Retro. Supp. I:** 202; **Supp. IV Part 1:** 360, 367
"Round, The" (Kunitz), **Supp. III Part 1:** 268
"Round Trip" (Dunn), **Supp. XI:** 148-149
Round Up (Lardner), **II:** 426, 430, 431
Rourke, Constance, **I:** 258; **IV:** 339, 352
Rourke, Milton, **Retro. Supp. II:** 89
Rousseau, Jean-Jacques, **I:** 226; **II:** 8, 343; **III:** 170, 178, 259; **IV:** 80, 173, 440; **Supp. I Part 1:** 126; **Supp. I Part 2:** 637, 659; **Supp. IV Part 1:** 171; **Supp. XI:** 245; **Supp. XVI:**292
Roussel, Raymond, **Supp. III Part 1:** 6, 7, 10, 15, 16, 21; **Supp. XV:** 182
"Routes" (Everwine), **Supp. XV:** 82
"Route Six" (Kunitz), **Supp. III Part 1:** 258
Route Two (Erdrich and Dorris), **Supp. IV Part 1:** 260
"Routine Things Around the House, The" (Dunn), **Supp. XI:** 148
Rover Boys (Winfield), **III:** 146
Rovit, Earl, **IV:** 102
Rowan, Carl T., **Supp. XIV:**306
Rowe, Anne E., **Supp. X:** 223
Rowe, John Carlos, **Retro. Supp. I:** 216
"Rowing" (Sexton), **Supp. II Part 2:** 696
"Rowing Endeth, The" (Sexton), **Supp. II Part 2:** 696
Rowlandson, Mary, **Supp. IV Part 2:** 430, 431
"Rows of Cold Trees, The" (Winters), **Supp. II Part 2:** 790-791, 800
Rowson, Susanna, **Supp. I Part 1:** 128; **Supp. XV: 229-248**
Roxanna Slade (Price), **Supp. VI:** 267
Roxie Hart (Watkins), **Supp. XVI:**188
Royal Family, The (Vollmann), **Supp. XVII:** 226, 230, 233
"Royal Palm" (Crane), **I:** 401
Royce, Josiah, **I:** 443; **III:** 303, 600; **IV:** 26; **Retro. Supp. I:** 57; **Supp. XIV:**197, 199; **Supp. XVII:** 97
Royster, Sarah Elmira, **III:** 410, 429
Royte, Elizabeth, **Supp. XV:** 59
Różewicz, Tadeusz, **Supp. X:** 60
Ruas, Charles, **Supp. IV Part 1:** 383
Rubáiyát (Khayyám), **I:** 568
Rubáiyát of Omar Khayyam (Fitzgerald), **Supp. I Part 2:** 416; **Supp. III Part 2:** 610; **Supp. XV:** 156
"Rubber Life" (Prose), **Supp. XVI:**256
Rub from Snub, A (Swanwick), **Supp. XV:** 237
Rubin, Louis, **Supp. I Part 2:** 672, 673, 679; **Supp. X:** 42
Rubin, Louis D., Jr., **IV:** 116, 462-463
Rubin, Stan, **Supp. XIV:**307, 310
Rubin, Stan Sanvel, **Supp. IV Part 1:** 242, 245, 252
"Ruby Brown" (Hughes), **Supp. I Part 1:** 327
"Ruby Daggett" (Eberhart), **I:** 539
Rucker, Rudy, **Supp. X:** 302
Rudd, Hughes, **Supp. XII:** 141
"Rude Awakening, A" (Chopin), **Retro. Supp. II:** 64
Rudens (Plautus), **Supp. III Part 2:** 630
Ruderman, Judith, **Supp. IV Part 1:** 380
Rudge, Olga, **Supp. V:** 338
Rudikoff, Sonya, **Supp. XIV:**113
Rueckert, William, **I:** 264
Ruesch, Jurgen, **Supp. XV:** 147
Rugby Chapel (Arnold), **Supp. I Part 2:** 416
"Rugby Road" (Garrett), **Supp. VII:** 100
Ruining the New Road (Matthews), **Supp. IX:** 154, **155-157**
"Ruins of Italica, The" (Bryant, trans.), **Supp. I Part 1:** 166
Rukeyser, Muriel, **Retro. Supp. II:** 48; **Supp. VI: 271-289; Supp. XV:** 349; **Supp. XVII:** 74
"Rule of Phase Applied to History, The" (Adams), **I:** 19
Rule of the Bone (Banks), **Supp. V:** 16
"Rules by Which a Great Empire May Be Reduced to a Small One" (Franklin), **II:** 120
Rules For the Dance: A Handbook for Reading and Writing Metrical Verse (Oliver), **Supp. VII:** 229, 247
Rules of the Game, The (film), **Supp. XII:** 259
Rulfo, Juan, **Supp. IV Part 2:** 549
Rumba (film, Gering), **Supp. XVII:** 57
Rumbaut, Rubén, **Supp. XI:** 184
Rumens, Carol, **Supp. XI:** 14; **Supp. XVI:**212
Rumkowski, Chaim, **Supp. XII:** 168
Rummel, Mary Kay, **Supp. XIII:** 280
"Rumor and a Ladder" (Bowles), **Supp. IV Part 1:** 93
Rumors (Simon), **Supp. IV Part 2:** 582-583, 591
Rumpelstiltskin (Gardner), **Supp. VI:** 72
"Rumpelstiltskin" (Grimm), **IV:** 266
"Rumpelstiltskin" (Sexton), **Supp. II Part 2:** 690
"Runagate Runagate" (Hayden), **Supp. II Part 1:** 377
"Runes" (Nemerov), **III:** 267, 277-278
Run Man Run (C. Himes), **Supp. XVI:**142, 143
"Running" (Wilbur), **Supp. III Part 2:** 558-559
Running Dog (DeLillo), **Supp. VI:** 3, 6, 8, 14
"Running in Church" (A. Finch), **Supp. XVII:** 72
"Running the Table" Conroy), **Supp. XVI:**75
"Run of Bad Luck, A" (Proulx), **Supp. VII:** 253-254
Run of Jacks, A (Hugo), **Supp. VI:** 131, 133, 134, 135, 136
Run River (Didion), **Supp. IV Part 1:** 197, 199-200, 201
Ruoff, A. LaVonne Brown, **Supp. IV Part 1:** 324, 327; **Supp. IV Part 2:** 559
Rupert, Jim, **Supp. XII:** 215
Ruppert, James, **Supp. IV Part 1:** 321
Rural Hours (Cooper), **Supp. XIII:** 152
"Rural Route" (Wright), **Supp. V:** 340
"Rural South, The" (Du Bois), **Supp. II Part 1:** 174
Rush, Benjamin, **Supp. I Part 2:** 505, 507
Rushdie, Salman, **Supp. IV Part 1:** 234, 297
Rushdy, Ashraf, **Supp. X:** 250
Rushing, Jimmy, **Retro. Supp. II:** 113
Rusk, Dean, **II:** 579
Ruskin, John, **II:** 323, 338; **IV:** 349; **Retro. Supp. I:** 56, 360; **Supp. I Part 1:** 2, 10, 87, 349; **Supp. I Part 2:** 410
Russell, Ada Dwyer, **II:** 513, 527
Russell, Bertrand, **II:** 27; **III:** 605, 606; **Retro. Supp. I:** 57, 58, 59, 60; **Supp. I Part 2:** 522; **Supp. V:** 290; **Supp. XII:** 45; **Supp. XIV:**337
Russell, Diarmuid, **Retro. Supp. I:** 342, 345, 346-347, 349-350
Russell, George, **Retro. Supp. I:** 342
Russell, Herb, **Supp. I Part 2:** 465-466
Russell, John, **Supp. XIV:**344, 347, 348
Russell, Peter, **III:** 479
Russell, Richard, **Supp. XI:** 102
Russell, Sue, **Supp. IV Part 2:** 653

Russert, Tim, **Supp. XII:** 272
Russia at War (Caldwell), **I:** 296
Russian Journal, A (Steinbeck), **IV:** 52, 63
Russo, Richard, **Supp. XI:** 349; **Supp. XII: 325-344**
"Rusty Autumn" (Swenson), **Supp. IV Part 2:** 640
Rutabaga-Roo: I've Got a Song and It's for You (Nye, album), **Supp. XIII:** 274
Ruth (biblical book), **Supp. I Part 2:** 516
Ruth, George Herman ("Babe"), **II:** 423; **Supp. I Part 2:** 438, 440
Ruth Hall (Fern), **Supp. V:** 122
Rutledge, Ann, **III:** 588; **Supp. I Part 2:** 471
Ruwe, Donelle R., **Supp. XII:** 215
Ryder (Barnes), **Supp. III Part 1:** 31, 36-38, 42, 43
"Ryder" (Rukeyser), **Supp. VI:** 273, 283
Rymer, Thomas, **IV:** 122
S
S-1 (Baraka), **Supp. II Part 1:** 55, 57
S. (Updike), **Retro. Supp. I:** 330, 331, 332, 333
Saadi, **II:** 19
Saar, Doreen Alvarez, **Supp. XV:** 237
"Sabbath, The" (Stowe), **Supp. I Part 2:** 587
"Sabbath Mom" (White), **Supp. I Part 2:** 671-672
Sabbaths (Berry), **Supp. X:** 31
Sabbath's Theater (P. Roth), **Retro. Supp. II:** 279, 288
Sabines, Jaime, **Supp. V:** 178
"Sabotage" (Baraka), **Supp. II Part 1:** 49, 53
Sacco, Nicola, **I:** 482, 486, 490, 494; **II:** 38-39, 426; **III:** 139-140; **Supp. I Part 2:** 446; **Supp. V:** 288-289; **Supp. IX:** 199
Sachs, Hanns, **Supp. I Part 1:** 259; **Supp. X:** 186
"Sacks" (Carver), **Supp. III Part 1:** 143-144
Sacks, Peter, **Supp. IV Part 2:** 450
Sackville-West, Vita, **Supp. VIII:** 263
"Sacrament of Divorce, The" (Patchett), **Supp. XII:** 309
"Sacraments" (Dubus), **Supp. VII:** 91
Sacred and Profane Memories (Van Vechten), **Supp. II Part 2:** 735, 749
"Sacred Chant for the Return of Black Spirit and Power" (Baraka), **Supp. II Part 1:** 51
"Sacred Factory, The" (Toomer), **Supp. IX:** 320

Sacred Fount, The (James), **II:** 332-333; **Retro. Supp. I:** 219, 228, 232
"Sacred Hoop, The: A Contemporary Perspective" (Gunn Allen), **Supp. IV Part 1:** 324
Sacred Hoop, The: Recovering the Feminine in American Indian Traditions (Gunn Allen), **Supp. IV Part 1:** 319, 320, 322, 324, 325, 328-330, 331, 333, 334
Sacred Journey, The (Buechner), **Supp. XII:** 42, 53
Sacred Wood, The (Eliot), **IV:** 431; **Retro. Supp. I:** 59, 60; **Supp. I Part 1:** 268; **Supp. II Part 1:** 136, 146
Sacrifice, The (Bidart), **Supp. XV:** 22, **27-30**, 35
"Sacrifice, The" (Bidart), **Supp. XV:** 29
"Sacrifice, The" (Oates), **Supp. II Part 2:** 523
Sacrilege of Alan Kent, The (Caldwell), **I:** 291-292
"Sad Brazil" (Hardwick), **Supp. III Part 1:** 210
"Sad Dust Glories" (Ginsberg), **Supp. II Part 1:** 376
Sad Dust Glories: Poems Written Work Summer in Sierra Woods (Ginsberg), **Supp. II Part 1:** 326
Sade, Marquis de, **III:** 259; **IV:** 437, 442; **Supp. XII:** 1, 14-15
Sad Flower in the Sand, A (film), **Supp. XI:** 173
Sad Heart at the Supermarket, A (Jarrell), **II:** 386
"Sadie" (Matthiessen), **Supp. V:** 201
Sadness and Happiness (Pinsky), **Supp. VI:** 235, **237-241**
"Sadness of Brothers, The" (Kinnell), **Supp. III Part 1:** 237, 251
"Sadness of Days, The" (Salinas), **Supp. XIII:** 325
Sadness of Days, The: Selected and New Poems (Salinas), **Supp. XIII:** 311, **324-326**
"Sadness of Lemons, The" (Levine), **Supp. V:** 184
Sadoff, Ira, **Supp. XVII:** 241
"Sad Rite" (Karr), **Supp. XI:** 243
"Sad Strains of a Gay Waltz" (Stevens), **Retro. Supp. I:** 302
"Safe" (Gordon), **Supp. IV Part 1:** 299, 306
"Safe in their Alabaster Chambers" (Dickinson), **Retro. Supp. I:** 30
"Safe Subjects" (Komunyakaa), **Supp. XIII:** 118
"Safeway" (F. Barthelme), **Supp. XI:**

26, 27, 36
Saffin, John, **Supp. I Part 1:** 115
Saffy, Edna, **Supp. X:** 227
"Saga of Arturo Bandini" (Fante), **Supp. XI:** 159, **166-169**
"Saga of King Olaf, The" (Longfellow), **II:** 489, 505; **Retro. Supp. II:** 154, 155, 164
"Sage of Stupidity and Wonder, The" (Goldbarth), **Supp. XII:** 191
Sahl, Mort, **II:** 435-436
"Said" (Dixon), **Supp. XII:** 149-150
"Sailing after Lunch" (Stevens), **IV:** 73
"Sailing Home from Rapallo" (Lowell), **Retro. Supp. II:** 189
Sailing through China (Theroux), **Supp. VIII:** 323
"Sailing to Byzantium" (Yeats), **III:** 263; **Supp. VIII:** 30; **Supp. X:** 74; **Supp. XI:** 281
"Sail Made of Rags, The" (Nye), **Supp. XIII:** 277
"Sailors Lost at Sea" (Shields), **Supp. VII:** 318
"St. Augustine and the Bullfights" (Porter), **III:** 454
St. Elmo (Wilson), **Retro. Supp. I:** 351-352
"St. Francis Einstein of the Daffodils" (W. C. Williams), **IV:** 409-411
"St. George, the Dragon, and the Virgin" (R. Bly), **Supp. IV Part 1:** 73
St. George and the Godfather (Mailer), **III:** 46; **Retro. Supp. II:** 206, 208
St. John, David, **Supp. V:** 180; **Supp. XI:** 270, 272; **Supp. XIII:** 312
St. John, Edward B., **Supp. IV Part 2:** 490
St. John, James Hector. *See* Crèvecoeur, Michel-Guillaume Jean de
St. Louis Woman (Bontemps and Cullen), **Supp. IV Part 1:** 170
St. Mawr (Lawrence), **II:** 595
St. Petersburg (Biely), **Supp. XII:** 13
"St. Roach" (Rukeyser), **Supp. VI:** 286
"St. Thomas Aquinas" (Simic), **Supp. VIII:** 281
"*St Anne*/Santa Ana" (Mora), **Supp. XIII:** 229
"*Saint Anthony of Padua*/San Antonio de Padua" (Mora), **Supp. XIII:** 228
Sainte-Beuve, Charles Augustin, **IV:** 432
"Saint Emmanuel the Good, Martyr" (Unamuno; Everwine, trans.), **Supp. XV:** 79
Sainte Vierge, La (Picabia), **Retro. Supp. II:** 331
Saint-Exupéry, Antoine de, **Supp. IX:** 247

Saint-Gaudens, Augustus, **I:** 18, 228; **II:** 551
Saint-Gaudens, Homer, **Supp. XV:** 41
Saint Jack (Theroux), **Supp. VIII:** 319
"Saint John and the Back-Ache" (Stevens), **Retro. Supp. I:** 310
Saint Judas (Wright), **Supp. III Part 2: 595-599**
"Saint Judas" (Wright), **Supp. III Part 2:** 598-599
Saint Maybe (Tyler), **Supp. IV Part 2:** 670-671
"Saint Nicholas" (Moore), **III:** 215
Saint-Phalle, Niki de, **Supp. XV:** 187
"Saint Robert" (Dacey), **Supp. IV Part 1:** 70
Saintsbury, George, **IV:** 440; **Supp. XV:** 181
Saints' Everlasting Rest, The (Baxter), **III:** 199; **IV:** 151, 153
Saint-Simon, Claude Henri, **Supp. I Part 2:** 648
Saks, Gene, **Supp. IV Part 2:** 577, 588
Salamun, Tomaz, **Supp. VIII:** 272
Salazar, Dixie, **Supp. V:** 180; **Supp. XV:** 73
Saldívar, José David, **Supp. IV Part 2:** 544, 545
Sale, Richard, **Supp. IV Part 1:** 379
Sale, Roger, **Supp. V:** 244
Saleh, Dennis, **Supp. V:** 182, 186
"Salem" (Lowell), **II:** 550
Salemi, Joseph, **Supp. IV Part 1:** 284
Salem's Lot (King), **Supp. V:** 139, 144, 146, 151
"Sale of the Hessians, The" (Franklin), **II:** 120
Salinas, Luis Omar, **Supp. IV Part 2:** 545; **Supp. V:** 180; **Supp. XIII: 311-330; Supp. XV:** 73
"Salinas Is on His Way" (Salinas), **Supp. XIII:** 317
"Salinas Sends Messengers to the Stars" (Salinas), **Supp. XIII:** 317
"Salinas Summering at the Caspian and Thinking of Hamlet" (Salinas), **Supp. XIII:** 320
"Salinas Wakes Early and Goes to the Park to Lecture Sparrows" (Salinas), **Supp. XIII:** 320
Salinger, Doris, **III:** 551
Salinger, J. D., **II:** 255; **III: 551-574; IV:** 190, 216, 217; **Retro. Supp. I:** 102, 116, 335; **Supp. IV Part 2:** 502; **Supp. V:** 23, 119; **Supp. VIII:** 151; **Supp. XI:** 2, 66; **Supp. XIV:**93
Salisbury, Harrison, **Supp. I Part 2:** 664
Salle, David, **Supp. XII:** 4
Salley, Columbus, **Supp. XIV:**195

"Sally" (Cisneros), **Supp. VII:** 63
"Sally's Choice" (E. Stoddard), **Supp. XV:** 282
Salmagundi; or, The Whim-Whams and Opinions of Launcelot Langstaff Esq., and Others (Irving), **II:** 299, 300, 304
Salome (Strauss), **IV:** 316
Salon (online magazine), **Supp. VIII:** 310; **Supp. X:** 202
Salt Eaters, The (Bambara), **Supp. XI:** 1, **12-14**
Salt Ecstasies, The (White), **Supp. XI:** 123
Salter, James, **Supp. IX: 245-263; Supp. XVI:**237, 247
Salter, Mary Jo, **Supp. IV Part 2:** 653; **Supp. IX:** 37, 292; **Supp. XV:** 251, 253; **Supp. XVII:** 112
Salt Garden, The (Nemerov), **III:** 269, 272-275, 277
"Salt Garden, The" (Nemerov), **III:** 267-268
Salting the Ocean (Nye, ed.), **Supp. XIII:** 280
Salt Lesson, The (C. Frost), **Supp. XV:** 92, 96
"Salt Lesson, The" (C. Frost), **Supp. XV:** 99
"Salts and Oils" (Levine), **Supp. V:** 190
Saltzman, Arthur, **Supp. XIII:** 48
Saltzman, Harry, **Supp. XI:** 307
"Salut au Monde!" (Whitman), **Retro. Supp. I:** 387, 396, 400
"Salute" (MacLeish), **III:** 13
"Salute to Mister Yates, A" (Dubus), **Supp. XI:** 347, 349
Salvador (Didion), **Supp. IV Part 1:** 198, 207-208, 210
"Salvage" (Clampitt), **Supp. IX:** 41
Samain, Albert, **II:** 528
Same Door, The (Updike), **IV:** 214, 219, 226; **Retro. Supp. I:** 320
"Same in Blues" (Hughes), **Retro. Supp. I:** 208
"Samhain" (A. Finch), **Supp. XVII:** 72
Sam Lawson's Oldtown Fireside Stories (Stowe), **Supp. I Part 2:** 587, 596, 598-599
"Sa'm Pèdi" (Bell), **Supp. X:** 17
"Sampler, A" (MacLeish), **III:** 4
Sampoli, Maria, **Supp. V:** 338
Sampson, Edward, **Supp. I Part 2:** 664, 673
Sampson, Martin, **Supp. I Part 2:** 652
Sam's Legacy (Neugeboren), **Supp. XVI:**221, 222
Samson Agonistes (Milton), **III:** 274

"Samson and Delilah" (Masters), **Supp. I Part 2:** 459
Samuel de Champlain: Father of New France (Morison), **Supp. I Part 2:** 496-497
Samuels, Charles Thomas, **Retro. Supp. I:** 334
"Samuel Sewall" (Hecht), **Supp. X:** 58
Sanborn, Franklin B., **IV:** 171, 172, 178
Sanborn, Kate, **Supp. XIII:** 152
Sanborn, Sara, **Supp. XIV:**113
Sanchez, Carol Anne, **Supp. IV Part 1:** 335
Sanchez, Carol Lee, **Supp. IV Part 2:** 499, 557
Sanchez, Sonia, **Supp. II Part 1:** 34
Sanctified Church, The (Hurston), **Supp. VI:** 150
"Sanction of the Victims, The" (Rand), **Supp. IV Part 2:** 528
Sanctuary (Faulkner), **II:** 57, 61-63, 72, 73, 74, 174; **Retro. Supp. I:** 73, 84, 86-87, 87; **Supp. I Part 2:** 614; **Supp. XII:** 16
Sanctuary (Wharton), **IV:** 311
"Sanctuary" (Wylie), **Supp. I Part 2:** 711
"Sanctuary, The" (Nemerov), **III:** 272, 274
Sand, George, **II:** 322; **Retro. Supp. I:** 235, 372; **Supp. XV:** 275
"Sandalphon" (Longfellow), **II:** 498
Sandbox, The (Albee), **I:** 74-75, 89
Sandburg, Carl, **I:** 103, 109, 384, 421; **II:** 529; **III:** 3, 20, **575-598**; **Retro. Supp. I:** 133, 194; **Supp. I Part 1:** 257, 320; **Supp. I Part 2:** 387, 389, 454, 461, 653; **Supp. III Part 1:** 63, 71, 73, 75; **Supp. IV Part 1:** 169; **Supp. IV Part 2:** 502; **Supp. IX:** 1, 15, 308; **Supp. XIII:** 274, 277; **Supp. XV:** 293, 299, 300, 301, 302, 306
Sandburg, Helga, **III:** 583
Sandburg, Janet, **III:** 583, 584
Sandburg, Margaret, **III:** 583, 584
Sandburg, Mrs. Carl (Lillian Steichen), **III:** 580
Sand County Almanac and Sketches Here and There, A (Leopold), **Supp. XIV:**177, 178, **182-192**
"Sand Dabs" (Oliver), **Supp. VII:** 245
"Sand Dunes" (Frost), **Retro. Supp. I:** 137; **Retro. Supp. II:** 41
Sander, August, **Supp. IX:** 211
Sanders, Scott Russell, **Supp. XVI:265-280**
"Sandman, The" (Barthelme), **Supp. IV Part 1:** 47

Sandman's Dust (Bukiet), **Supp. XVII:** 40, 41
Sando, Joe S., **Supp. IV Part 2:** 510
Sandoe, James, **Supp. IV Part 1:** 131; **Supp. IV Part 2:** 470
Sandoz, Mari, **Supp. XV:** 141
Sandperl, Ira, **Supp. VIII:** 200
"Sand-Quarry and Moving Figures" (Rukeyser), **Supp. VI:** 271, 278
Sand Rivers (Matthiessen), **Supp. V:** 203
"Sand Roses, The" (Hogan), **Supp. IV Part 1:** 401
Sands, Diana, **Supp. IV Part 1:** 362
Sands, Robert, **Supp. I Part 1:** 156, 157
"Sands at Seventy" (Whitman), **IV:** 348
"Sandstone Farmhouse, A" (Updike), **Retro. Supp. I:** 318
Sandy Bottom Orchestra, The (Keillor and Nilsson), **Supp. XVI:**177
Sanford, John, **IV:** 286, 287
San Francisco (film), **Supp. XVI:**181, 192
"San Francisco Blues" (Kerouac), **Supp. III Part 1:** 225
Sangamon County Peace Advocate, The (Lindsay), **Supp. I Part 2:** 379
Sanger, Margaret, **Supp. I Part 1:** 19
Sansom, William, **IV:** 279
Sans Soleil (film), **Supp. IV Part 2:** 436
"Santa" (Sexton), **Supp. II Part 2:** 693
Santa Claus: A Morality (Cummings), **I:** 430, 441
"Santa Fé Trail, The" (Lindsay), **Supp. I Part 2:** 389
"Santa Lucia" (Hass), **Supp. VI:** 105-106
"Santa Lucia II" (Hass), **Supp. VI:** 105-106
Santayana, George, **I:** 222, 224, 236, 243, 253, 460; **II:** 20, 542; **III:** 64, **599-622; IV:** 26, 339, 351, 353, 441; **Retro. Supp. I:** 55, 57, 67, 295; **Retro. Supp. II:** 179; **Supp. I Part 2:** 428; **Supp. II Part 1:** 107; **Supp. X:** 58; **Supp. XIV:**199, 335, 340, 342; **Supp. XVI:**189; **Supp. XVII:** 97, 106
Santiago, Esmeralda, **Supp. XI:** 177
"Santorini: Stopping the Leak" (Merrill), **Supp. III Part 1:** 336
Santos, John Phillip, **Supp. XIII:** 274
Santos, Sherod, **Supp. VIII:** 270
Sapir, Edward, **Supp. VIII:** 295; **Supp. XVI:**283
"Sapphics for Patience" (A. Finch), **Supp. XVII:** 72

Sapphira and the Slave Girl (Cather), **I:** 331; **Retro. Supp. I:** 2, **19-20**
Sappho, **II:** 544; **III:** 142; **Supp. I Part 1:** 261, 269; **Supp. I Part 2:** 458; **Supp. XII:** 98, 99; **Supp. XVII:** 74
"Sappho" (Wright), **Supp. III Part 2:** 595, 604
"Sarah" (Schwartz), **Supp. II Part 2:** 663
Sarah; or, The Exemplary Wife (Rowson), **Supp. XV:** 242
"Saratoga" mysteries (Dobyns), **Supp. XIII:** 79-80
Sargent, John Singer, **II:** 337, 338
Saroyan, Aram, **Supp. XV:** 182
Saroyan, William, **III:** 146-147; **IV:** 393; **Supp. I Part 2:** 679; **Supp. IV Part 1:** 83; **Supp. IV Part 2:** 502; **Supp. XIII:** 280
Sarris, Greg, **Supp. IV Part 1:** 329, 330
Sarton, George, **Supp. VIII:** 249
Sarton, May, **Supp. III Part 1:** 62, 63; **Supp. VIII: 249-268; Supp. XIII:** 296; **Supp. XVII:** 71
Sartoris (Faulkner), **II:** 55, 56-57, 58, 62; **Retro. Supp. I:** 77, 81, 82, 83, 88
Sartor Resartus (Carlyle), **II:** 26; **III:** 82
Sartre, Jean-Paul, **I:** 82, 494; **II:** 57, 244; **III:** 51, 204, 292, 453, 619; **IV:** 6, 223, 236, 477, 487, 493; **Retro. Supp. I:** 73; **Supp. I Part 1:** 51; **Supp. IV Part 1:** 42, 84; **Supp. VIII:** 11; **Supp. IX:** 4; **Supp. XIII:** 74, 171; **Supp. XIV:**24; **Supp. XVII:** 137
Sassone, Ralph, **Supp. X:** 171
Sassoon, Siegfried, **II:** 367; **Supp. XV:** 308
Satan in Goray (Singer), **IV:** 1, 6-7, 12; **Retro. Supp. II:** 303, **304-305**
Satan Says (Olds), **Supp. X:** 201, 202, **202-204,** 215
"Satan Says" (Olds), **Supp. X:** 202; **Supp. XVII:** 114
Satanstoe (Cooper), **I:** 351-352, 355
"Sather Gate Illumination" (Ginsberg), **Supp. II Part 1:** 329
"Satire as a Way of Seeing" (Dos Passos), **III:** 172
Satires of Persius, The (Merwin, trans.), **Supp. III Part 1:** 347
Satirical Rogue on Poetry, The (Francis). *See Pot Shots at Poetry* (Francis)
Satori in Paris (Kerouac), **Supp. III Part 1:** 231

"Saturday" (Salinas), **Supp. XIII:** 315
Saturday Night at the War (Shanley), **Supp. XIV:**315
"Saturday Rain" (Kees), **Supp. XV:** 136
"Saturday Route, The" (Wolfe), **Supp. III Part 2:** 580
Satyagraha (Gandhi), **IV:** 185
"Satyr's Heart, The" (B. Kelly), **Supp. XVII:** 132
Saul and Patsy (C. Baxter), **Supp. XVII: 22-23**
"Saul and Patsy" (C. Baxter), **Supp. XVII:** 17
"Saul and Patsy Are Getting Comfortable in Michigan" (C. Baxter), **Supp. XVII:** 22
"Saul and Patsy Are in Labor" (C. Baxter), **Supp. XVII:** 20, 22
"Saul and Patsy Are Pregnant" (C. Baxter), **Supp. XVII:** 22
Saunders, Richard, **II:** 110
Savage, Augusta, **Retro. Supp. II:** 115
Savage, James, **II:** 111
Savage Holiday (Wright), **IV:** 478, 488
Savage in Limbo: A Concert Play (Shanley), **Supp. XIV:**315, **319-321,** 323, 324
Savage Love (Shepard and Chaikin), **Supp. III Part 2:** 433
Savage Wilds (Reed), **Supp. X:** 241
Save Me, Joe Louis (Bell), **Supp. X:** 7, 10, **11-12**
Save Me the Waltz (Z. Fitzgerald), **II:** 95; **Retro. Supp. I:** 110; **Supp. IX:** 58, 59, 65, **66-68**
Savers, Michael, **Supp. XI:** 307
Saving Lives (Goldbarth), **Supp. XII:** 192
Saving Private Ryan (film), **Supp. V:** 249; **Supp. XI:** 234
Savings (Hogan), **Supp. IV Part 1:** 397, 404, 405, 406, 410
Savo, Jimmy, **I:** 440
Savran, David, **Supp. IX:** 145; **Supp. XIII:** 209; **Supp. XV:** 321
Sawyer-Lauçanno, Christopher, **Supp. IV Part 1:** 95
Saxon, Lyle, **Retro. Supp. I:** 80
Saye and Sele, Lord, **Supp. I Part 1:** 98
Sayer, Mandy, **Supp. XIII:** 118
Sayers, Dorothy, **Supp. IV Part 1:** 341; **Supp. IV Part 2:** 464
Sayers, Valerie, **Supp. XI:** 253
"Sayings/For Luck" (Goldbarth), **Supp. XII:** 176
Say! Is This the U.S.A.? (Caldwell), **I:** 293, 294-295, 304, 309, 310
Saylor, Bruce, **Supp. XII:** 253

Sayre, Joel, **Supp. XIII:** 166
Sayre, Nora, **Supp. XII:** 119
Sayre, Zelda, **Retro. Supp. I:** 101, 102-103, 104, 105, 108, 109, 110, 113, 114. *See also* Fitzgerald, Zelda (Zelda Sayre)
"Say Yes" (Wolff), **Supp. VII:** 344
"Scales of the Eyes, The" (Nemerov), **III:** 272, 273, 277
Scalpel (McCoy), **Supp. XIII: 174-175**
Scalpel (screen treatment, McCoy), **Supp. XIII:** 174
Scandalabra (Zelda Fitzgerald), **Supp. IX:** 60, 61, 65, 67, **68-70**
"Scandal Detectives, The" (Fitzgerald), **II:** 80-81; **Retro. Supp. I:** 99
Scarberry-García, Susan, **Supp. IV Part 2:** 486
"Scarecrow, The" (Farrell), **II:** 45
"Scarf, A" (Shields), **Supp. VII:** 328
Scarlet Letter, The (Hawthorne), **II:** 63, 223, 224, 231, 233, 239-240, 241, 243, 244, 255, 264, 286, 290, 291, 550; **Retro. Supp. I:** 63, 145, 147, 152, **157-159**, 160, 163, 165, 220, 248, 330, 335; **Retro. Supp. II:** 100; **Supp. I Part 1:** 38; **Supp. II Part 1:** 386; **Supp. VIII:** 108, 198; **Supp. XII:** 11; **Supp. XVII:** 143
Scarlet Plague, The (London), **II:** 467
Scar Lover (Crews), **Supp. XI:** 103, 107, **114-115**
"Scarred Girl, The" (Dickey), **Supp. IV Part 1:** 180
Scates, Maxine, **Supp. XIV:**264, 265, 274
"Scenario" (H. Miller), **III:** 184
"Scene" (Howells), **II:** 274
"Scene in Jerusalem, A" (Stowe), **Supp. I Part 2:** 587
"Scenes" (Shields), **Supp. VII:** 318
Scènes d'Anabase (chamber music) (Bowles), **Supp. IV Part 1:** 82
Scenes from American Life (Gurney), **Supp. V:** 95, 96, 105, 108
Scenes from Another Life (McClatchy), **Supp. XII: 255-256**
"Scenes of Childhood" (Merrill), **Supp. III Part 1:** 322, 323, 327
"Scented Herbage of My Breast" (Whitman), **IV:** 342-343
"Scent of a Woman's Ink" (Prose), **Supp. XVI:**259
"Scent of Unbought Flowers, The" (Ríos), **Supp. IV Part 2:** 547
Scepticisms (Aiken), **I:** 58
Scève, Maurice, **Supp. III Part 1:** 11
Schad, Christian, **Supp. IV Part 1:** 247
Schafer, Benjamin G., **Supp. XIV:**144

Schaller, George, **Supp. V:** 208, 210-211
Schapiro, Meyer, **II:** 30
Scharmann, Hermann Balthazar, **Supp. XII:** 41
Schary, Dore, **Supp. IV Part 1:** 365; **Supp. XIII:** 163
Schaumbergh, Count de, **II:** 120
Scheele, Roy, **Supp. XVI:**54
Scheffauer, G. H., **I:** 199
"Scheherazade" (Ashbery), **Supp. III Part 1:** 18
Scheick, William, **Supp. V:** 272
Scheler, Max, **I:** 58
Schelling, Friedrich, **Supp. I Part 2:** 422
Schenck, Joseph, **Supp. XVI:**186
Schenk, Margaret, **I:** 199
Scheponik, Peter, **Supp. X:** 210
Scherer, Loline, **Supp. XIII:** 161
Schickel, Richard, **Supp. XV:** 1
Schilder, Paul, **Supp. I Part 2:** 622
Schiller, Andrew, **II:** 20
Schiller, Frederick, **Supp. V:** 290
Schiller, Johann Christoph Friedrich von, **I:** 224; **Supp. IV Part 2:** 519; **Supp. XVI:**292
Schiller, Lawrence, **Retro. Supp. II:** 208, 212, 214
Schimmel, Harold, **Supp. V:** 336
Schlegel, Augustus Wilhelm, **III:** 422, 424
Schlegell, David von, **Supp. IV Part 2:** 423
Schleiermacher, Friedrich, **III:** 290-291, 309
Schlepping Through the Alps (S. Apple), **Supp. XVII:** 8
Schlesinger, Arthur, Jr., **III:** 291, 297-298, 309
Schmidt, Jon Zlotnik, **Supp. IV Part 1:** 2
Schmidt, Kaspar. *See* Stirner, Max
Schmidt, Michael, **Supp. X:** 55
Schmitt, Carl, **I:** 386-387
Schmitz, Neil, **Supp. X:** 243
Schnackenberg, Gjertrud, **Supp. XV: 249-268**
Schneider, Alan, **I:** 87
Schneider, Louis, **Supp. I Part 2:** 650
Schneider, Romy, **Supp. IV Part 2:** 549
Schneider, Steven, **Supp. IX:** 271, 274
Schnellock, Emil, **III:** 177
Schneour, Zalman, **IV:** 11
Schnitzler, Arthur, **Supp. XV:** 307; **Supp. XVI:**187
Schoerke, Meg, **Supp. XVII:** 110
"Scholar Gypsy, The" (Arnold), **II:** 541

"Scholastic and Bedside Teaching" (Holmes), **Supp. I Part 1:** 305
Schöler, Bo, **Supp. IV Part 1:** 399, 400, 403, 407, 409; **Supp. IV Part 2:** 499
Scholes, Robert, **Supp. V:** 40, 42
Schomburg, Arthur, **Supp. X:** 134
Schoolboy Howlers (Abingdon), **Supp. XVI:**99
Schoolcraft, Henry Rowe, **II:** 503; **Retro. Supp. II:** 160
"School Daze" (Bambara), **Supp. XI:** 19
School Daze (film), **Supp. XI:** 19, 20
"Schoolhouse" (Levis), **Supp. XI:** 258
"School of Giorgione, The" (Pater), **I:** 51
"School Play, The" (Merrill), **Supp. III Part 1:** 336
"Schooner Fairchild's Class" (Benét), **Supp. XI:** 55
Schopenhauer, Arthur, **III:** 600, 604; **IV:** 7; **Retro. Supp. I:** 256; **Retro. Supp. II:** 94; **Supp. I Part 1:** 320; **Supp. I Part 2:** 457; **Supp. X:** 187; **Supp. XVI:**184
Schorer, Mark, **II:** 28; **III:** 71; **Retro. Supp. I:** 115; **Supp. IV Part 1:** 197, 203, 211; **Supp. XVI:**206
Schott, Webster, **Supp. IX:** 257
Schotts, Jeffrey, **Supp. XII:** 193
Schrader, Mary von. *See* Jarrell, Mrs. Randall (Mary von Schrader)
Schreiner, Olive, **I:** 419; **Supp. XI:** 203
Schroeder, Eric James, **Supp. V:** 238, 244
Schubert, Bernard L., **Supp. XVII:** 58
Schubert, Franz Peter, **Supp. I Part 1:** 363
Schubnell, Matthias, **Supp. IV Part 2:** 486
Schulberg, Budd, **II:** 98; **Retro. Supp. I:** 113; **Supp. XIII:** 170; **Supp. XV:** 194
Schulz, Bruno, **Supp. IV Part 2:** 623; **Supp. XVII:** 41
Schuman, William, **Supp. XII:** 253
Schumann, Dr. Alanson Tucker, **III:** 505
Schuster, Edgar H., **Supp. VIII:** 126
Schuyler, George S., **III:** 110; **Supp. XVI:**142
Schuyler, James, **Supp. XV:** 177, 178
Schuyler, William, **Supp. I Part 1:** 211
Schwartz, Delmore, **I:** 67, 168, 188, 288; **IV:** 128, 129, 437; **Retro. Supp. II:** 29, 178; **Supp. II Part 1:** 102, 109; **Supp. II Part 2: 639-668**; **Supp. VIII:** 98; **Supp. IX:** 299;

Supp. XIII: 320; Supp. XIV:3; Supp. XV: 184
Schwartz, Leonard, Supp. XVI:289
Schwartz, Lloyd, Supp. I Part 1: 81
Schwartz, Marilyn, Supp. XII: 126, 128, 130, 132
Schwartz, Richard B., Supp. XIV:23, 27
Schweitzer, Albert, Supp. IV Part 1: 373
Schweitzer, Harold, Supp. X: 210
Schwerdt, Lisa M., Supp. XIV:155, 171
Schwitters, Kurt, III: 197; Retro. Supp. II: 322, 331, 336; Supp. IV Part 1: 79
"Science" (Jeffers), Supp. II Part 2: 426
Science and Health with Key to the Scriptures (Eddy), I: 383
"Science Favorable to Virtue" (Freneau), Supp. II Part 2: 274
Science of English Verse, The (Lanier), Supp. I Part 1: 368, 369
"Science of the Night, The" (Kunitz), Supp. III Part 1: 258, 265
Sciolino, Martina, Supp. XII: 9
"Scissors" (C. Baxter), Supp. XVII: 19
Scopes, John T., III: 105, 495
"Scorched Face, The" (Hammett), Supp. IV Part 1: 344
"Scorn" (C. Frost), Supp. XV: 105
"Scorpion, The" (Bowles), Supp. IV Part 1: 84, 86
Scorsese, Martin, Supp. IV Part 1: 356
Scott, A. O., Supp. X: 301, 302; Supp. XII: 343
Scott, Anne Firor, Supp. I Part 1: 19
Scott, Evelyn, Retro. Supp. I: 73
Scott, George C., III: 165-166; Supp. XI: 304
Scott, George Lewis, Supp. I Part 2: 503, 504
Scott, Herbert, Supp. V: 180
Scott, Howard, Supp. I Part 2: 645
Scott, Joanna, Supp. XVII: 183-197
Scott, Lizabeth, Supp. IV Part 2: 524
Scott, Lynn Orilla, Retro. Supp. II: 12
Scott, Mark, Retro. Supp. I: 127
Scott, Nathan A., Jr., II: 27
Scott, Paul, Supp. IV Part 2: 690
Scott, Ridley, Supp. XIII: 268
Scott, Sir Walter, I: 204, 339, 341, 343, 354; II: 8, 17, 18, 217, 296, 301, 303, 304, 308; III: 415, 482; IV: 204, 453; Retro. Supp. I: 99; Supp. I Part 2: 579, 580, 685, 692; Supp. IV Part 2: 690; Supp. IX: 175; Supp. X: 51, 114
Scott, Walter, Supp. XVI:7, 13
Scott, Winfield Townley, II: 512; Supp. I Part 2: 705; Supp. XV: 51
Scottsboro boys, I: 505; Supp. I Part 1: 330
Scottsboro Limited (Hughes), Retro. Supp. I: 203; Supp. I Part 1: 328, 330-331, 332
Scoundrel Time (Hellman), Supp. I Part 1: 294-297; Supp. IV Part 1: 12; Supp. VIII: 243
Scrambled Eggs Super! (Geisel), Supp. XVI:105
Scrambled Eggs & Whiskey: Poems, 1991-1995 (Carruth), Supp. XVI:47
Scratch (MacLeish), III: 22-23
"Scratch Music" (Wright), Supp. XV: 343
"Scream, The" (Lowell), II: 550
"Screamer, The" (Coleman), Supp. XI: 92-93
"Screamers, The" (Baraka), Supp. II Part 1: 38
"Screen Guide for Americans" (Rand), Supp. IV Part 2: 524
"Screeno" (Schwartz), Supp. II Part 2: 660
Screens, The (Genet), Supp. XII: 12
Scribblers on the Roof: Contemporary American Jewish Fiction (Bukiet and Roskies, eds.), Supp. XVII: 39, 49-50
Scripts for the Pageant (Merrill), Supp. III Part 1: 332, 333, 335
Scrolls from the Dead Sea, The (Wilson), IV: 429
Scruggs, Earl, Supp. V: 335
Scudder, Horace Elisha, II: 400, 401; Retro. Supp. II: 67; Supp. I Part 1: 220; Supp. I Part 2: 410, 414
Scully, James, Supp. XII: 131
"Sculpting the Whistle" (Ríos), Supp. IV Part 2: 549
"Sculptor" (Plath), Supp. I Part 2: 538
"Sculptor's Funeral, The" (Cather), I: 315-316; Retro. Supp. I: 5, 6; Supp. XV: 40
Scum (Singer), Retro. Supp. II: 316-317
Scupoli, Lorenzo, IV: 156
"Scythe Song" (Lang), Retro. Supp. I: 128
"*Se:* Hegel's Absolute and Heidegger's *Ereignis*" (Agamben), Supp. XVI:289
Sea and the Mirror, The: A Commentary on Shakespeare's "The Tempest" (Auden), Supp. II Part 1: 2, 18

Sea around Us, The (Carson), Supp. IX: 19, 23-25
Sea around Us, The (film), Supp. IX: 25
Sea Birds Are Still Alive, The (Bambara), Supp. XI: 1, 4, 7-12
"Sea Birds Are Still Alive, The" (Bambara), Supp. XI: 8
"Sea-Blue and Blood-Red" (Lowell), II: 524
Seabrook, John, Supp. VIII: 157
"Sea Burial from the Cruiser Reve" (Eberhart), I: 532-533
Seabury, David, Supp. I Part 2: 608
"Sea Calm" (Hughes), Retro. Supp. I: 199
"Sea Chanty" (Corso), Supp. XII: 118
"Sea Dream, A" (Whittier), Supp. I Part 2: 699
"Seafarer, The" (Pound, trans.), Retro. Supp. I: 287
Seagall, Harry, Supp. XIII: 166
Sea Garden (Doolittle), Supp. I Part 1: 257, 259, 266, 269, 272
Seager, Allan, IV: 305
"Seagulls and Children" (C. Frost), Supp. XV: 95
"Sea Lily" (Doolittle), Supp. I Part 1: 266
Sea Lions, The (Cooper), I: 354, 355
Sealts, Merton M., Jr., Retro. Supp. I: 257
Seaman, Donna, Supp. VIII: 86; Supp. X: 1, 4, 12, 16, 213; Supp. XV: 65
"Séance, The" (Singer), IV: 20
Séance and Other Stories, The (Singer), IV: 19-21
Sea of Cortez (Steinbeck), IV: 52, 54, 62, 69
"Sea Pieces" (Melville), III: 93
Searches and Seizures (Elkin), Supp. VI: 49
"Search for Southern Identity, The" (Woodward), Retro. Supp. I: 75
Search for the King, A: A Twelfth-Century Legend (Vidal), Supp. IV Part 2: 681
Searching for Caleb (Tyler), Supp. IV Part 2: 663-665, 671
"Searching for Poetry: Real *vs.* Fake" (B. Miller), Supp. IV Part 1: 67
Searching for Survivors (Banks), Supp. V: 7
"Searching for Survivors (I)" (Banks), Supp. V: 8
"Searching for Survivors (II)" (Banks), Supp. V: 7, 8
Searching for the Ox (Simpson), Supp. IX: 266, 274-275

"Searching for the Ox" (Simpson), **Supp. IX:** 275, 280
"Searching in the Britannia Tavern" (Wagoner), **Supp. IX:** 327
Searching Wing, The, (Hellman), **Supp. I Part 1:** 277, 278, 281-282, 283, 292, 297
"Search Party, The" (Matthews), **Supp. IX: 156**
Searle, Ronald, **Supp. I Part 2:** 604, 605
Sea Road to the Indies (Hart), **Supp. XIV:**97
"Seascape" (Bishop), **Retro. Supp. II:** 42-43
"Sea's Green Sameness, The" (Updike), **IV:** 217
Seaside and the Fireside, The (Longfellow), **II:** 489; **Retro. Supp. II:** 159, 168
Season in Hell, A (Rimbaud), **III:** 189
Seasons, The (Thomson), **II:** 304; **Supp. I Part 1:** 151
Seasons' Difference, The (Buechner), **Supp. XII: 47**
Seasons of Celebration (Merton), **Supp. VIII:** 199, 208
Seasons of the Heart: In Quest of Faith (Kinard, comp.), **Supp. XIV:**127
"Seasons of the Soul" (Tate), **IV:** 136-140
Seasons on Earth (Koch), **Supp. XV: 183-184**
"Sea Surface Full of Clouds" (Stevens), **IV:** 82
"Sea Unicorns and Land Unicorns" (Moore), **III:** 202-203
Seaver, Richard, **Supp. XI:** 301
"Seaweed" (Longfellow), **II:** 498
Sea-Wolf, The (London), **II:** 264, 466, 472-473
Sebald, W. G., **Supp. XIV:**96
Seckler, David, **Supp. I Part 2:** 650
Second American Revolution and Other Essays (1976-1982), The (Vidal), **Supp. IV Part 2:** 679, 687, 688
Secondary Colors, The (A. Theroux), **Supp. VIII:** 312
Second Chance (Auchincloss), **Supp. IV Part 1:** 33
"Second Chances" (Hugo), **Supp. VI:** 144, 145
Second Coming, The (Percy), **Supp. III Part 1:** 383, 384, 387, 388, 396-397
"Second Coming, The" (Yeats), **III:** 294; **Retro. Supp. I:** 290, 311; **Supp. VIII:** 24; **Supp. XVI:**159
Second Decade, The. See Stephen King, The Second Decade: "Danse Macabre" to "The Dark Half" (Magistrale)
Second Dune, The (Hearon), **Supp. VIII:** 58, **59-60**
Second Flowering, A: Works and Days of the Lost Generation (Cowley), **Retro. Supp. II:** 77; **Supp. II Part 1:** 135, 141, 143, 144, 147, 149
Second Growth (Stegner), **Supp. IV Part 2:** 599, 608
"Second Hour of the Night, The" (Bidart), **Supp. XV:** 32, **33-34**
Second Marriage (F. Barthelme), **Supp. XI:** 32, 33
"Second Marriage" (McCarriston), **Supp. XIV:**262
Second Nature (Hoffman), **Supp. X:** 88, 89
"2nd Air Force" (Jarrell), **II:** 375
Seconds, The (Bierds), **Supp. XVII: 33-34**
Second Set, The (Komunyakaa and Feinstein, eds.), **Supp. XIII:** 125
Second Sex, The (Beauvoir), **Supp. IV Part 1:** 360
Second Stone, The (Fiedler), **Supp. XIII:** 102
"Second Swimming, The" (Boyle), **Supp. VIII:** 13, 14
Second Tree from the Corner (White), **Supp. I Part 2:** 654
"Second Tree from the Corner" (White), **Supp. I Part 2:** 651
Second Twenty Years at Hull-House, The: September 1909 to September 1929, with a Record of a Growing World Consciousness (Addams), **Supp. I Part 1:** 24-25
Second Voyage of Columbus, The (Morison), **Supp. I Part 2:** 488
Second Words, (Atwood), **Supp. XIII:** 35
Second World, The (Blackmur), **Supp. II Part 1:** 91
Secret, The (E. Hoffman), **Supp. XVI:**151, **155-158**, 161
"Secret, The" (Levine), **Supp. V:** 195
Secret Agent, The (Conrad), **Supp. IV Part 1:** 341
Secret Agent X-9 (Hammett), **Supp. IV Part 1:** 355
"Secret Courts of Men's Hearts, The: Code and Law in Harper Lee's *To Kill a Mockingbird*" (Johnson), **Supp. VIII:** 126
"Secret Dog, The" (Cameron), **Supp. XII: 83-84**
Secret Garden, The (Burnett), **Supp. I Part 1:** 44
"Secret Gladness, A" (C. Frost), **Supp. XV:** 91
Secret Historie (J. Smith), **I:** 131
Secret History of the Dividing Line (Howe), **Supp. IV Part 2:** 424, 425-426
"Secret Integration, The" (Pynchon), **Supp. II Part 2:** 624
"Secret Life of Musical Instruments, The" (Wright), **Supp. XV:** 343
"Secret Life of Walter Mitty, The" (Thurber), **Supp. I Part 2:** 623; **Supp. XVI:**233
"Secret Lion, The" (Ríos), **Supp. IV Part 2:** 543, 544
"Secret Ocean, The" (Jarman), **Supp. XVII:** 120
Secret of Poetry, The: Essays (Jarman), **Supp. XVII:** 110, 111, 120
"Secret of the Russian Ballet, The" (Van Vechten), **Supp. II Part 2:** 732
"Secret Prune" (Ríos), **Supp. IV Part 2:** 549
Secret River, The (Rawlings), **Supp. X:** 233
Secrets and Surprises (Beattie), **Supp. V:** 23, 27, 29
Secrets from the Center of the World (Harjo), **Supp. XII: 223-224**
"Secret Sharer, The" (Conrad), **Supp. IX:** 105
"Secret Sharer, The" (J. Conrad), **Supp. XVI:**158
"Secret Society, A" (Nemerov), **III:** 282
Secrets of the Universe: Scenes from the Journey Home (Sanders), **Supp. XVI:**273-274
Secular Journal of Thomas Merton, The, **Supp. VIII:** 206
"Security" (Stafford), **Supp. XI:** 329
Sedges, John (pseudonym). *See* Buck, Pearl S.
Sedgwick, Catherine Maria, **I:** 341; **Supp. I Part 1:** 155, 157
Sedgwick, Christina. *See* Marquand, Mrs. John P. (Christina Sedgwick)
Sedgwick, Ellery, **I:** 217, 229, 231; **III:** 54-55
Sedgwick, Henry, **Supp. I Part 1:** 156
Sedgwick, Robert, **Supp. I Part 1:** 156
Sedore, Timothy, **Supp. XIV:**312
"Seduction and Betrayal" (Hardwick), **Supp. III Part 1:** 207
Seduction and Betrayal: Women and Literature (Hardwick), **Supp. III Part 1:** 194, 204, 206-208, 212, 213; **Supp. XIV:**89
Seed, David, **Supp. IV Part 1:** 391

"Seed Eaters, The" (Francis), **Supp. IX:** 82
"Seed Leaves" (Wilbur), **Supp. III Part 2:** 558
"Seeds" (Anderson), **I:** 106, 114
Seeds of Contemplation (Merton), **Supp. VIII:** 199, 200, 207, 208
Seeds of Destruction (Merton), **Supp. VIII:** 202, 203, 204, 208
"See(k)ing the Self: Mirrors and Mirroring in Bicultural Texts" (Oster), **Supp. XVI:**151
Seeing through the Sun (Hogan), **Supp. IV Part 1:** 397, 400, 401-402, 402, 413
"See in the Midst of Fair Leaves" (Moore), **III:** 215
"Seekers, The" (McGrath), **Supp. X:** 117
"Seeking a Vision of Truth, Guided by a Higher Power" (Burke), **Supp. XIV:**21, 23
"Seele im Raum" (Jarrell), **II:** 382-383
"Seele im Raum" (Rilke), **II:** 382-383
"See Naples and Die" (Hecht), **Supp. X:** 69, 70
"Seen from the 'L'" (Barnes), **Supp. III Part 1:** 33
"See the Moon?" (Barthelme), **Supp. IV Part 1:** 42, 49-50, 50
Segal, D. (pseudonym). *See* Singer, Isaac Bashevis
Segal, George, **Supp. XI:** 343
Segal, Lore, **Supp. XVI:**203
Segregation: The Inner Conflict in the South (Warren), **IV:** 237, 238, 246, 252
Seidel, Frederick, **I:** 185
Seize the Day (Bellow), **I:** 144, 147, 148, 150, 151, 152, 153, 155, 158, 162; **Retro. Supp. II:** 19, **23-24,** 27, 32, 34; **Supp. I Part 2:** 428
Selby, Hubert, **Supp. III Part 1:** 125
Selby, John, **Retro. Supp. II:** 221, 222
Selden, John, **Supp. XIV:**344
Seldes, Gilbert, **II:** 437, 445; **Retro. Supp. I:** 108
Selected Criticism: Prose, Poetry (Bogan), **Supp. III Part 1:** 64
Selected Essays (Eliot), **I:** 572
Selected Essays and Reviews (Carruth), **Supp. XVI:**46
Selected Journals and Other Writings (Audubon), **Supp. XVI:**10, 12, 13
Selected Letters (Bynner), **Supp. XV:** 52
Selected Letters (W. C. Williams), **Retro. Supp. I:** 430
Selected Letters, 1940-1956 (Kerouac), **Supp. XIV:**137, 144
Selected Letters of Robert Frost (Thompson, ed.), **Retro. Supp. I:** 125
Selected Levis, The (Levis), **Supp. XI:** 257, 272
Selected Poems (Aiken), **I:** 69
Selected Poems (Ashbery), **Supp. III Part 1:** 25-26
Selected Poems (Brodsky), **Supp. VIII:** 22
Selected Poems (Brooks), **Supp. III Part 1:** 82-83
Selected Poems (Bynner), **Supp. XV:** 51, 52
Selected Poems (Corso), **Supp. XII:** 129
Selected Poems (Dove), **Supp. IV Part 1:** 241, 243, 250
Selected Poems (Frost), **Retro. Supp. I:** 133, 136
Selected Poems (Guillevic; Levertov, trans.), **Supp. III Part 1:** 283
Selected Poems (Hayden), **Supp. II Part 1:** 363, 364, 367
Selected Poems (Hughes), **Retro. Supp. I:** 202; **Supp. I Part 1:** 341, 345, 346
Selected Poems (Hugo), **Supp. VI:** 143
Selected Poems (Jarrell), **II:** 367, 370, 371, 374, 377, 379, 380, 381, 382, 384
Selected Poems (Justice), **Supp. VII:** 115
Selected Poems (Kinnell), **Supp. III Part 1:** 235, 253
Selected Poems (Levine, 1984), **Supp. V:** 178, 179
Selected Poems (Lowell), **II:** 512, 516; **Retro. Supp. II:** 184, 186, 188, 190
Selected Poems (Merton), **Supp. VIII:** 207, 208
Selected Poems (Moore), **III:** 193, 194, 205-206, 208, 215
Selected Poems (Pound), **Retro. Supp. I:** 289, 291
Selected Poems (Ransom), **III:** 490, 492
Selected Poems (Reznikoff), **Supp. XIV:**288
Selected Poems (Rukeyser), **Supp. VI:** 274
Selected Poems (R. Bly), **Supp. IV Part 1:** 60, 62, 65, 66, 68, 69-71
Selected Poems (Sexton), **Supp. IV Part 2:** 449
Selected Poems (Strand), **Supp. IV Part 2:** 630
Selected Poems 1936-1965 (Eberhart), **I:** 541
Selected Poems 1965-1975 (Atwood), **Supp. XIII:** 32-34
Selected Poems, 1923-1943 (Warren), **IV:** 241-242, 243
Selected Poems, 1928-1958 (Kunitz), **Supp. III Part 1:** 261, 263-265
Selected Poems, 1938-1988 (McGrath), **Supp. X:** 127
Selected Poems: 1957-1987 (Snodgrass), **Supp. VI:** 314-315, 323, 324
Selected Poems, 1963-1983 (Simic), **Supp. VIII:** 275
Selected Poems II: Poems Selected and New, 1976-1986 (Atwood), **Supp. XIII:** 20, **34-35**
Selected Poems of Ezra Pound (Pound), **Supp. V:** 336
Selected Poems of Gabriela Mistral (Hughes, trans.), **Supp. I Part 1:** 345
Selected Poetry of Amiri Baraka/LeRoi Jones (Baraka), **Supp. II Part 1:** 58
Selected Poetry of Hayden Carruth, The (Carruth), **Supp. XVI:**53
Selected Stories (Dubus), **Supp. VII:** 88-89
Selected Stories of Richard Bausch, The (Bausch), **Supp. VII:** 42
Selected Translations (Snodgrass), **Supp. VI:** 318, 324, **325-326**
Selected Verse of Margaret Haskins Durber, The (Keillor), **Supp. XVI:**171
Selected Witter Bynner, The, **Supp. XV:** 52
Selected Works of Djuna Barnes, The (Barnes), **Supp. III Part 1:** 44
Selected Writings 1950-1990 (Howe), **Supp. VI:** 116-117, 118, 120
Selected Writings of John Jay Chapman, The (Barzun), **Supp. XIV:**54
Select Epigrams from the Greek Anthology (Mackail), **Supp. I Part 2:** 461
"Selene Afterwards" (MacLeish), **III:** 8
"Self" (James), **II:** 351
Self and the Dramas of History, The (Niebuhr), **III:** 308
Self-Consciousness (Updike), **Retro. Supp. I:** 318, 319, 320, 322, 323, 324
"Self-Exposed, The" (X. J. Kennedy), **Supp. XV:** 159
Self-Help: Stories (Moore), **Supp. X:** 163, 166, **167-169,** 174, 175
Self-Interviews (Dickey), **Supp. IV Part 1:** 179
"Self-Made Man, A" (Crane), **I:** 420
"Self Pity" (C. Frost), **Supp. XV:** 93, 94, 101, 102, 104

"Self-Portrait" (Creeley), **Supp. IV Part 1:** 156

"Self-Portrait" (Mumford), **Supp. II Part 2:** 471

"Self-Portrait" (Wylie), **Supp. I Part 2:** 729

Self-Portrait: Ceaselessly into the Past (Millar, ed. Sipper), **Supp. IV Part 2:** 464, 469, 472, 475

"Self-Portrait in a Convex Mirror" (Ashbery), **Supp. III Part 1:** 5, 7, 9, 16-19, 22, 24, 26

"Self-Reliance" (Emerson), **II:** 7, 15, 17; **Retro. Supp. I:** 159; **Retro. Supp. II:** 155; **Supp. X:** 42, 45

Sélincourt, Ernest de, **Supp. I Part 2:** 676

Selinger, Eric, **Supp. XVI:**47

Selinger, Eric Murphy, **Supp. XI:** 248

Sell, Henry, **Supp. XVI:**188

Sellers, Isaiah, **IV:** 194-195

Sellers, Peter, **Supp. XI:** 301, 304, 306, 307, 309

Sellers, William, **IV:** 208

Seltzer, Mark, **Retro. Supp. I:** 227

Selznick, David O., **Retro. Supp. I:** 105, 113; **Supp. IV Part 1:** 353

"Semi-Lunatics of Kilmuir, The" (Hugo), **Supp. VI:** 145

"Semiotics/The Doctor's Doll" (Goldbarth), **Supp. XII:** 183-184

Semmelweiss, Ignaz, **Supp. I Part 1:** 304

Senancour, Étienne Divert de, **I:** 241

Sendak, Maurice, **Supp. IX:** 207, 208, 213, 214; **Supp. XVI:**110

Seneca, **II:** 14-15; **III:** 77

Senghor, Leopold Sédar, **Supp. IV Part 1:** 16; **Supp. X:** 132, 139

Senier, Siobhan, **Supp. IV Part 1:** 330

"Senility" (Anderson), **I:** 114

"Senior Partner's Ethics, The" (Auchincloss), **Supp. IV Part 1:** 33

Senlin: A Biography (Aiken), **I:** 48, 49, 50, 52, 56, 57, 64

Sennett, Dorothy, **Supp. XVI:**43

Sennett, Mack, **III:** 442

"Señora X No More" (Mora), **Supp. XIII:** 218

"Señor Ong and Señor Ha" (Bowles), **Supp. IV Part 1:** 87

Sense of Beauty, The (Santayana), **III:** 600

Sense of Life in the Modern Novel, The (Mizener), **IV:** 132

"Sense of Shelter, A" (Updike), **Retro. Supp. I:** 318

"Sense of the Meeting, The" (Conroy), **Supp. XVI:**72

Sense of the Past, The (James), **II:** 337-338

"Sense of the Past, The" (Trilling), **Supp. III Part 2:** 503

"Sense of the Present, The" (Hardwick), **Supp. III Part 1:** 210

"Sense of the Sleight-of-Hand Man, The" (Stevens), **IV:** 93

"Sense of Where You Are, A" (McPhee), **Supp. III Part 1:** 291, 296-298

"Sensibility! O La!" (Roethke), **III:** 536

"Sensible Emptiness, A" (Kramer), **Supp. IV Part 1:** 61, 66

"Sensuality Plunging Barefoot Into Thorns" (Cisneros), **Supp. VII:** 68

"Sentence" (Barthelme), **Supp. IV Part 1:** 47

Sent for You Yesterday (Wideman), **Supp. X:** 320, 321

"Sentimental Education, A" (Banks), **Supp. V:** 10

"Sentimental Journey" (Oates), **Supp. II Part 2:** 522, 523

"Sentimental Journey, A" (Anderson), **I:** 114

Sentimental Journey, A (Sterne), **Supp. I Part 2:** 714

"Sentimental Journeys" (Didion), **Supp. IV Part 1:** 211

Sentimental Journey through France and Italy, A (Sterne), **Supp. XV:** 232

"Sentiment of Rationality, The" (James), **II:** 346-347

Separate Flights (Dubus), **Supp. VII:** 78-83

"Separate Flights" (Dubus), **Supp. VII:** 83

Separate Peace, A (Knowles), **Supp. IV Part 2:** 679; **Supp. XII:** 241-249

Separate Way (Reznikoff), **Supp. XIV:**280

"Separating" (Updike), **Retro. Supp. I:** 321

"Separation, The" (Kunitz), **Supp. III Part 1:** 263

"Sepia High Stepper" (Hayden), **Supp. II Part 1:** 379

September (film; Allen), **Supp. XV:** 11

"September" (Komunyakaa), **Supp. XIII:** 130

"September 1, 1939" (Auden), **Supp. II Part 1:** 13; **Supp. IV Part 1:** 225; **Supp. VIII:** 30, 32; **Supp. XV:** 117-118

September 11, 2001: American Writers Respond (Heyen), **Supp. XIII:** 285

September Song (Humphrey), **Supp. IX:** 101, 102, **108-109**

"September Twelfth, 2001" (X. J. Kennedy), **Supp. XV:** 171

"Sept Vieillards, Les" (Millay, trans.), **III:** 142

Sequel to Drum-Taps (Whitman), **Retro. Supp. I:** 406

"Sequence, Sometimes Metaphysical" (Roethke), **III:** 547, 548

Sequence of Seven Plays with a Drawing by Ron Slaughter, A (Nemerov), **III:** 269

Sequoya, Jana, **Supp. IV Part 1:** 334

Seraglio, The (Merrill), **Supp. III Part 1:** 331

Seraphita (Balzac), **I:** 499

Seraph on the Suwanee (Hurston), **Supp. VI:** 149, 159-160

Serenissima: A Novel of Venice (Jong). See *Shylock's Daughter: A Novel of Love in Venice (Serenissima)* (Jong)

Sergeant, Elizabeth Shepley, **I:** 231, 236, 312, 319, 323, 328

Sergeant Bilko (television show), **Supp. IV Part 2:** 575

"Serious Talk, A" (Carver), **Supp. III Part 1:** 138, 144

Serly, Tibor, **Supp. III Part 2:** 617, 619

"Sermon by Doctor Pep" (Bellow), **I:** 151

Sermones (Horace), **II:** 154

"Sermon for Our Maturity" (Baraka), **Supp. II Part 1:** 53

Sermons and Soda Water (O'Hara), **III:** 362, 364, 371-373, 382

"Sermons on the Warpland" (Brooks), **Supp. III Part 1:** 84

"Serpent in the Wilderness, The" (Masters), **Supp. I Part 2:** 458

Servant of the Bones (Rice), **Supp. VII:** 298, 302

"Servant to Servants, A" (Frost), **Retro. Supp. I:** 125, 128; **Supp. X:** 66

Serve It Forth (M. F. K. Fisher), **Supp. XVII:** 83, 86, 87, 89, 92

Seshachari, Neila, **Supp. V:** 22

"Session, The" (Adams), **I:** 5

"Sestina" (Bishop), **Supp. I Part 1:** 73, 88

Set-angya, **Supp. IV Part 2:** 493

Seth, Vikram, **Supp. XVII:** 117

Seth's Brother's Wife (Frederic), **II:** 131-132, 137, 144

Set This House on Fire (Styron), **IV:** 98, 99, 105, 107-113, 114, 115, 117

Setting Free the Bears (Irving), **Supp. VI:** 163, **166-167,** 169-170

Setting the Tone (Rorem), **Supp. IV Part 1:** 79

Settle, Mary Lee, **Supp. IX:** 96
Settlement Horizon, The: A National Estimate (Woods and Kennedy), **Supp. I Part 1:** 19
"Settling the Colonel's Hash" (McCarthy), **II:** 559, 562
Setzer, Helen, **Supp. IV Part 1:** 217
"Seurat's Sunday Afternoon along the Seine" (Schwartz), **Supp. II Part 2:** 663-665
Seven against Thebes (Aeschylus; Bacon and Hecht, trans.), **Supp. X:** 57
Seven Ages of Man, The (Wilder), **IV:** 357, 374-375
Seven Deadly Sins, The (Wilder), **IV:** 357, 374-375
Seven Descents of Myrtle, The (T. Williams), **IV:** 382
"Seven Fat Brides, The" (P. Abraham), **Supp. XVII:** 50
Seven Guitars (Wilson), **Supp. VIII:** 331, **348-351**
Seven Lady Godivas, The (Geisel), **Supp. XVI:** 100, 103
Seven-League Crutches, The (Jarrell), **II:** 367, 372, 381, 382, 383-384, 389
Seven Mountains of Thomas Merton, The (Mott), **Supp. VIII:** 208
Seven-Ounce Man, The (Harrison), **Supp. VIII:** 51
"Seven Places of the Mind" (Didion), **Supp. IV Part 1:** 200, 210
Seven Plays (Shepard), **Supp. III Part 2:** 434
"Seven Stanzas at Easter" (Updike), **IV:** 215
Seven Storey Mountain, The (Merton), **Supp. VIII:** 193, 195, 198, 200, 207, 208
Seventh Heaven (Hoffman), **Supp. X:** 87, 89
"Seventh of March" (Webster), **Supp. I Part 2:** 687
"7000 Romaine, Los Angeles 38" (Didion), **Supp. IV Part 1:** 200
"Seventh Street" (Toomer), **Supp. IX:** 316
Seven Types of Ambiguity (Empson), **II:** 536; **IV:** 431
77 Dream Songs (Berryman), **I:** 168, 169, 170, 171, 174, 175, 183-188
73 Poems (Cummings), **I:** 430, 431, 446, 447, 448
7 Years from Somehwere (Levine), **Supp. V:** 178, 181, 188-189
Sevier, Jack, **IV:** 378
Sévigné, Madame de, **IV:** 361
Sewall, Richard, **Retro. Supp. I:** 25
Sewall, Samuel, **IV:** 145, 146, 147, 149, 154, 164; **Supp. I Part 1:** 100, 110
Sewell, Elizabeth, **Supp. XIII:** 344
"Sex" (Carruth), **Supp. XVI:** 58
Sex, Economy, Freedom and Community (Berry), **Supp. X:** 30, 36
"Sex Camp" (Mamet), **Supp. XIV:** 240
Sex Castle, The (Lacy), **Supp. XV:** 206
Sex & Character (Weininger), **Retro. Supp. I:** 416
"Sext" (Auden), **Supp. II Part 1:** 22
Sexton, Anne, **Retro. Supp. II:** 245; **Supp. I Part 2:** 538, 543, 546; **Supp. II Part 2: 669-700; Supp. III Part 2:** 599; **Supp. IV Part 1:** 245; **Supp. IV Part 2:** 439, 440-441, 442, 444, 447, 449, 451, 620; **Supp. V:** 113, 118, 124; **Supp. X:** 201, 202, 213; **Supp. XI:** 146, 240, 317; **Supp. XII:** 217, 253, 254, 256, 260, 261; **Supp. XIII:** 35, 76, 294, 312; **Supp. XIV:** 125, 126, 132, 269; **Supp. XV:** 123, 252, 340; **Supp. XVII:** 239
Sexual Behavior in the American Male (Kinsey), **Supp. XIII:** 96-97
Sexual Perversity in Chicago (Mamet), **Supp. XIV:** 239, 240, 246-247, 249
"Sexual Revolution, The" (Dunn), **Supp. XI:** 142
Sexus (H. Miller), **III:** 170, 171, 184, 187, 188
"Sex Without Love" (Olds), **Supp. X:** 206
Seyersted, Per E., **Retro. Supp. II:** 65; **Supp. I Part 1:** 201, 204, 211, 216, 225; **Supp. IV Part 2:** 558
Seyfried, Robin, **Supp. IX:** 324
"Seymour: An Introduction" (Salinger), **III:** 569-571, 572
Seymour, Miranda, **Supp. VIII:** 167
Shacochis, Bob, **Supp. VIII:** 80
"Shadow" (Creeley), **Supp. IV Part 1:** 158
"Shadow, The" (Lowell), **II:** 522
Shadow and Act (Ellison), **Retro. Supp. II:** 119; **Supp. II Part 1:** 245-246
"Shadow and Shade" (Tate), **IV:** 128
"Shadow and the Flesh, The" (London), **II:** 475
"Shadow A Parable" (Poe), **III:** 417-418
Shadow Country (Gunn Allen), **Supp. IV Part 1:** 322, 324, 325-326
Shadow Man, The (Gordon), **Supp. IV Part 1:** 297, 298, 299, 312-314, 315
Shadow of a Dream, The, a Story (Howells), **II:** 285, 286, 290
"Shadow of the Crime, The: A Word from the Author" (Mailer), **Retro. Supp. II:** 214
Shadow on the Dial, The (Bierce), **I:** 208, 209
"Shadow Passing" (Merwin), **Supp. III Part 1:** 355
Shadowplay (C. Baxter), **Supp. XVII:** 15, 19-20
Shadows (Gardner), **Supp. VI:** 74
Shadows and Fog (film; Allen), **Supp. XV:** 11
Shadows by the Hudson (Singer), **IV:** 1
Shadows of Africa (Matthiessen), **Supp. V:** 203
Shadows on the Hudson (Singer), **Retro. Supp. II: 311-313**
Shadows on the Rock (Cather), **I:** 314, 330-331, 332; **Retro. Supp. I:** 18
Shadow Train (Ashbery), **Supp. III Part 1:** 23-24, 26
"Shad-Time" (Wilbur), **Supp. III Part 2:** 563
Shaffer, Thomas L., **Supp. VIII:** 127, 128
Shaft (Parks; film), **Supp. XI:** 17
Shaftesbury, Earl of, **I:** 559
Shahn, Ben, **Supp. X:** 24
Shakedown for Murder (Lacy), **Supp. XV:** 203
Shakelford, Dean, **Supp. VIII:** 129
Shaker, Why Don't You Sing? (Angelou), **Supp. IV Part 1:** 16
Shakespear, Mrs. Olivia, **III:** 457; **Supp. I Part 1:** 257
"Shakespeare" (Emerson), **II:** 6
Shakespeare, William, **I:** 103, 271, 272, 284-285, 358, 378, 433, 441, 458, 461, 573, 585, 586; **II:** 5, 8, 11, 18, 72, 273, 297, 302, 309, 320, 411, 494, 577, 590; **III:** 3, 11, 12, 82, 83, 91, 124, 130, 134, 145, 153, 159, 183, 210, 263, 286, 468, 473, 492, 503, 511, 567, 575-576, 577, 610, 612, 613, 615; **IV:** 11, 50, 66, 127, 132, 156, 309, 313, 362, 368, 370, 373, 453; **Retro. Supp. I:** 43, 64, 91, 248; **Retro. Supp. II:** 114, 299; **Supp. I Part 1:** 79, 150, 262, 310, 356, 363, 365, 368, 369, 370; **Supp. I Part 2:** 397, 421, 422, 470, 494, 622, 716, 720; **Supp. II Part 2:** 624, 626; **Supp. IV Part 1:** 31, 83, 87, 243; **Supp. IV Part 2:** 430, 463, 519, 688; **Supp. V:** 252, 280, 303; **Supp. VIII:** 160, 164; **Supp. IX:** 14, 133; **Supp. X:** 42, 62, 65, 78; **Supp. XII:** 54-57, 277, 281; **Supp. XIII:** 111, 115, 233; **Supp.

XIV:97, 120, 225, 245, 306; **Supp. XV:** 92
Shakespeare and His Forerunners (Lanier), **Supp. I Part 1:** 369
Shakespeare in Harlem (Hughes), **Retro. Supp. I:** 194, 202, 205, 206, 207, 208; **Supp. I Part 1:** 333, 334, 345
Shalit, Gene, **Supp. VIII:** 73
Shall We Gather at the River (Wright), **Supp. III Part 2:** 601-602; **Supp. XVII:** 241
"Shame" (Oates), **Supp. II Part 2:** 520
"Shame" (Wilbur), **Supp. III Part 2:** 556
"Shame and Forgetting in the Information Age" (C. Baxter), **Supp. XVII:** 21
"Shameful Affair, A" (Chopin), **Retro. Supp. II:** 61
Shamela (Fielding), **Supp. V:** 127
"Shampoo, The" (Bishop), **Retro. Supp. II:** 46; **Supp. I Part 1:** 92
Shange, Ntozake, **Supp. VIII:** 214; **Supp. XVII:** 70
Shank, Randy, **Supp. X:** 252
Shankaracharya, **III:** 567
Shanley, John Patrick, **Supp. XIV:315-332**
Shannon, Sandra, **Supp. VIII:** 333, 348
"Shape of Flesh and Bone, The" (MacLeish), **III:** 18-19
Shape of Me and Other Stuff, The (Geisel), **Supp. XVI:**111
Shape of the Journey, The (Harrison), **Supp. VIII:** 53
Shapes of Clay (Bierce), **I:** 208, 209
Shaping Joy, A: Studies in the Writer's Craft (Brooks), **Supp. XIV:**13
Shapiro, David, **Supp. XII:** 175, 185
Shapiro, Dorothy, **IV:** 380
Shapiro, Karl, **I:** 430, 521; **II:** 350; **III:** 527; **Supp. II Part 2: 701-724; Supp. III Part 2:** 623; **Supp. IV Part 2:** 645; **Supp. X:** 116; **Supp. XI:** 315
Shapiro, Laura, **Supp. IX:** 120
Sharif, Omar, **Supp. IX:** 253
"Shark Meat" (Snyder), **Supp. VIII:** 300
Shatayev, Elvira, **Supp. I Part 2:** 570
Shaviro, Steven, **Supp. VIII:** 189
Shaw, Colonel Robert Gould, **II:** 551
Shaw, Elizabeth. *See* Melville, Mrs. Herman (Elizabeth Shaw)
Shaw, George Bernard, **I:** 226; **II:** 82, 271, 276, 581; **III:** 69, 102, 113, 145, 155, 161, 162, 163, 373, 409; **IV:** 27, 64, 397, 432, 440; **Retro. Supp. I:** 100, 228; **Supp. IV Part 1:** 36; **Supp. IV Part 2:** 585, 683; **Supp. V:** 243-244, 290; **Supp. IX:** 68, 308; **Supp. XI:** 202; **Supp. XII:** 94; **Supp. XIV:**343; **Supp. XVII:** 100
Shaw, Irwin, **IV:** 381; **Supp. IV Part 1:** 383; **Supp. IX:** 251; **Supp. XI:** 221, 229, 231
Shaw, Joseph Thompson ("Cap"), **Supp. IV Part 1:** 121, 345, 351; **Supp. XIII:** 161
Shaw, Judge Lemuel, **III:** 77, 88, 91
Shaw, Peter, **Supp. XVI:**70
Shaw, Sarah Bryant, **Supp. I Part 1:** 169
Shaw, Wilbur, Jr., **Supp. XIII:** 162
Shawl, The (Mamet), **Supp. XIV:**245
Shawl, The (Ozick), **Supp. V:** 257, 260, 271
"Shawl, The" (Ozick), **Supp. V:** 271-272
Shawl and Prarie du Chien, The: Two Plays (Mamet), **Supp. XIV:**243-244
Shawn, William, **Supp. VIII:** 151, 170
"Shawshank Redemption, The" (King), **Supp. V:** 148
She (Haggard), **III:** 189
Shearer, Flora, **I:** 199
"Sheaves, The" (Robinson), **III:** 510, 524
"She Came and Went" (Lowell), **Supp. I Part 2:** 409
Sheed, Wilfrid, **IV:** 230; **Supp. XI:** 233
Sheeler, Charles, **IV:** 409; **Retro. Supp. I:** 430
"Sheep Child" (B. Kelly), **Supp. XVII:** 131-132
"Sheep Child, The" (Dickey), **Supp. XVII:** 131-132
Sheeper (Rosenthal), **Supp. XIV:**147
Sheffer, Jonathan, **Supp. IV Part 1:** 95
She Had Some Horses (Harjo), **Supp. XII: 220-223**, 231
"She Had Some Horses" (Harjo), **Supp. XII:** 215, 222
"Shell, The" (Humphrey), **Supp. IX:** 94
Shelley, Percy Bysshe, **I:** 18, 68, 381, 476, 522, 577; **II:** 331, 516, 535, 540; **III:** 412, 426, 469; **IV:** 139; **Retro. Supp. I:** 308, 360; **Supp. I Part 1:** 79, 311, 349; **Supp. I Part 2:** 709, 718, 719, 720, 721, 722, 724, 728; **Supp. IV Part 1:** 235; **Supp. V:** 258, 280; **Supp. IX:** 51; **Supp. XII:** 117, 132, 136-137, 263; **Supp. XIV:**271-272; **Supp. XV:** 92, 175, 182
Shellow, Sadie Myers, **Supp. I Part 2:** 608
"Shelter" (C. Baxter), **Supp. XVII:** 19
"Shelter" (Doty), **Supp. XI:** 132
Sheltered Life, The (Glasgow), **II:** 174, 175, 179, 186, 187-188
Sheltering Sky, The (Bowles), **Supp. IV Part 1:** 82, 84, 85-86, 87
Sheltering Sky, The (film), **Supp. IV Part 1:** 94, 95
Shelton, Frank, **Supp. IV Part 2:** 658
Shelton, Mrs. Sarah. *See* Royster, Sarah Elmira
Shelton, Richard, **Supp. XI:** 133; **Supp. XIII:** 7
Shenandoah (Schwartz), **Supp. II Part 2:** 640, 651-652
"Shenandoah" (Shapiro), **Supp. II Part 2:** 704
Shepard, Alice, **IV:** 287
Shepard, Harvey, **Supp. XVII:** 240
Shepard, Odell, **II:** 508; **Supp. I Part 2:** 418
Shepard, Sam, **Supp. III Part 2: 431-450**
Shepard, Thomas, **I:** 554; **IV:** 158
"Shepherd of Resumed Desire, The" (Wright), **Supp. XV:** 349
Sheppard Lee (Bird), **III:** 423
"She Remembers the Future" (Harjo), **Supp. XII:** 222
Sheridan, Richard Brinsley, **Retro. Supp. I:** 127
Sherlock, William, **IV:** 152
Sherman, Sarah Way, **Retro. Supp. II:** 145
Sherman, Stuart Pratt, **I:** 222, 246-247; **Supp. I Part 2:** 423
Sherman, Susan, **Supp. VIII:** 265
Sherman, Tom, **IV:** 446
Sherman, William T., **IV:** 445, 446
Sherwood, Robert, **II:** 435; **Supp. IX:** 190
Sherwood Anderson & Other Famous Creoles (Faulkner), **I:** 117; **II:** 56
Sherwood Anderson Reader, The (Anderson), **I:** 114, 116
Sherwood Anderson's Memoirs (Anderson), **I:** 98, 101, 102, 103, 108, 112, 116
Sherwood Anderson's Notebook (Anderson), **I:** 108, 115, 117
She Stoops to Conquer (Goldsmith), **II:** 514
Shestov, Lev, **Supp. VIII:** 20, 24
Shetley, Vernon, **Supp. IX:** 292; **Supp. XI:** 123
"She Wept, She Railed" (Kunitz), **Supp. III Part 1:** 265

"Shiddah and Kuziba" (Singer), **IV:** 13, 15
Shield of Achilles, The (Auden), **Supp. II Part 1:** 21
"Shield of Achilles, The" (Auden), **Supp. II Part 1:** 21, 25
Shields, Carol, **Supp. VII: 307-330**
Shifting Landscape: A Composite, 1925-1987 (H. Roth), **Supp. IX: 233-235**
Shifts of Being (Eberhart), **I:** 525
Shigematsu, Soiko, **Supp. III Part 1:** 353
Shihab, Aziz, **Supp. XIII:** 273
Shih-hsiang Chen, **Supp. VIII:** 303
Shiksa Goddess; or, How I Spent My Forties (Wasserstein), **Supp. XV:** 319, 320, 325, 332, 333
"Shiloh" (Mason), **Supp. VIII:** 140
Shiloh and Other Stories (Mason), **Supp. VIII:** 133, **139-141**, 143, 145
Shilts, Randy, **Supp. X:** 145
Shining, The (King), **Supp. V:** 139, 140, 141, 143-144, 146, 149, 151, 152
Shining Victory (film, Rapper), **Supp. XVII:** 60
Shinn, Everett, **Retro. Supp. II:** 103
"Ship of Death" (Lawrence), **Supp. I Part 2:** 728
Ship of Fools (Porter), **III:** 433, 447, 453, 454; **IV:** 138
Shipping News, The (Proulx), **Supp. VII:** 249, 258-259
"Ships" (O. Henry), **Supp. II Part 1:** 409
Ships Going into the Blue: Essays and Notes on Poetry (Simpson), **Supp. IX:** 275
Ship to America, A (Singer), **IV:** 1
"Shipwreck, The" (Merwin), **Supp. III Part 1:** 346
Shirley, John, **Supp. XVI:**123, 128
"Shirt" (Pinsky), **Supp. VI: 236-237,** 239, 240, 241, 245, 247
"Shirt Poem, The" (Stern), **Supp. IX:** 292
"Shiva and Parvati Hiding in the Rain" (Pinsky), **Supp. VI:** 244
Shively, Charley, **Retro. Supp. I:** 391; **Supp. XII:** 181, 182
Shock of Recognition, The (Wilson), **II:** 530
Shock of the New, The (Hughes), **Supp. X:** 73
Shoe Bird, The (Welty), **IV:** 261; **Retro. Supp. I:** 353
Shoemaker of Dreams (Ferragammo), **Supp. XVI:**192

"Shoes" (O. Henry), **Supp. II Part 1:** 409
"Shoes of Wandering, The" (Kinnell), **Supp. III Part 1:** 248
"Shooters, Inc." (Didion), **Supp. IV Part 1:** 207, 211
"Shooting, The" (Dubus), **Supp. VII:** 84, 85
"Shooting Niagara; and After?" (Carlyle), **Retro. Supp. I:** 408
"Shooting Script" (Rich), **Supp. I Part 2:** 558; **Supp. IV Part 1:** 257
Shooting Star, A (Stegner), **Supp. IV Part 2:** 599, 608-609
"Shooting Whales" (Strand), **Supp. IV Part 2:** 630
"Shopgirls" (F. Barthelme), **Supp. XI:** 26, 27, 33, 36
Shop Talk (P. Roth), **Retro. Supp. II:** 282
Shoptaw, John, **Supp. IV Part 1:** 247
Shore Acres (Herne), **Supp. II Part 1:** 198
Shorebirds of North America, The (Matthiessen), **Supp. V:** 204
"Shore House, The" (Jewett), **II:** 397
Shore Leave (Wakeman), **Supp. IX:** 247
"Shoreline Horses" (Ríos), **Supp. IV Part 2:** 553
Shores of Light, The: A Literary Chronicle of the Twenties and Thirties (Wilson), **IV:** 432, 433
Shorey, Paul, **III:** 606
Short Cuts (film), **Supp. IX:** 143
"Short End, The" (Hecht), **Supp. X:** 65
"Shorter View, The" (X. J. Kennedy), **Supp. XV:** 160, 168
Short Fiction of Norman Mailer, The (Mailer), **Retro. Supp. II:** 205
Short Friday and Other Stories (Singer), **IV:** 14-16
Short Guide to a Happy Life, A (Quindlen), **Supp. XVII:** 167, 179
"Short Happy Life of Francis Macomber, The" (Hemingway), **II:** 250, 263-264; **Retro. Supp. I:** 182; **Supp. IV Part 1:** 48; **Supp. IX:** 106
Short Night, The (Turner), **Supp. XV:** 201
Short Novels of Thomas Wolfe, The (Wolfe), **IV:** 456
Short Poems (Berryman), **I:** 170
"SHORT SPEECH TO MY FRIENDS" (Baraka), **Supp. II Part 1:** 35
Short Stories (Rawlings), **Supp. X:** 224
"Short Story, The" (Welty), **IV:** 279
Short Story Masterpieces, **Supp. IX:** 4
Short Studies of American Authors (Higginson), **I:** 455
"Short-timer's Calendar" (Komunyakaa), **Supp. XIII:** 125
Shosha (Singer), **Retro. Supp. II: 313-314**
Shostakovich, Dimitri, **IV:** 75; **Supp. VIII:** 21
"Shots" (Ozick), **Supp. V:** 268
Shotts, Jeffrey, **Supp. XV:** 103, 104
"Should Wizard Hit Mommy?" (Updike), **IV:** 221, 222, 224; **Retro. Supp. I:** 335
Shoup, Barbara, **Supp. XV:** 55, 59, 62, 69
"Shovel Man, The" (Sandburg), **III:** 553
Showalter, Elaine, **Retro. Supp. I:** 368; **Supp. IV Part 2:** 440, 441, 444; **Supp. X:** 97; **Supp. XVI:**80, 92
"Shower of Gold" (Welty), **IV:** 271-272
"Shrike and the Chipmunks, The" (Thurber), **Supp. I Part 2:** 617
Shrimp Girl (Hogarth), **Supp. XII:** 44
"Shrine and the Burning Wheel, The" (Jarman), **Supp. XVII:** 116
"Shriveled Meditation" (X. J. Kennedy), **Supp. XV:** 170
Shropshire Lad, A (Housman), **Supp. XV:** 41
"Shrouded Stranger, The" (Ginsberg), **Supp. II Part 1:** 312
"Shroud of Color, The" (Cullen), **Supp. IV Part 1:** 166, 168, 170, 171
Shtetl (film; Marzynski), **Supp. XVI:**153
Shtetl: The Life and Death of a Small Town and the World of Polish Jews (E. Hoffman), **Supp. XVI:**152, **153-155**
Shuffle (L. Michaels), **Supp. XVI:**202, 203, 213
Shuffle Along (musical), **Supp. I Part 1:** 322; **Supp. X:** 136
Shultz, George, **Supp. IV Part 1:** 234
Shurr, William, **Retro. Supp. I:** 43
Shuster, Joel, **Supp. XI:** 67
Shusterman, Richard, **Retro. Supp. I:** 53
"Shut a Final Door" (Capote), **Supp. III Part 1:** 117, 120, 124
Shut Up, He Explained (Lardner), **II:** 432
Shylock's Daughter: A Novel of Love in Venice (Serenissima) (Jong), **Supp. V:** 115, 127, 128-129
Siberian Village, The (Dove), **Supp. IV Part 1:** 255, 256

Sibley, Mulford Q., **Supp. I Part 2:** 524
"Sibling Mysteries" (Rich), **Supp. I Part 2:** 574
Siblings (Quindlen and Kelsh), **Supp. XVII:** 167, 179
Sibon, Marcelle, **IV:** 288
"Sicilian Emigrant's Song" (W. C. Williams), **Retro. Supp. I:** 413
Sicilian Miniatures (Sobin), **Supp. XVI:**288
"Sick Wife, The" (Kenyon), **Supp. VII:** 173, 174
"'Sic transit gloria mundi'" (Dickinson), **Retro. Supp. I:** 30
Sid Caesar Show (television show), **Supp. IV Part 2:** 575
Siddons, Sarah, **II:** 298
Side Effects (Allen), **Supp. XV:** 3, 14, **15-16**
Side of Paradise, This (Fitgerald), **Supp. IX:** 56
Sidnee Poet Heroical, The (Baraka), **Supp. II Part 1:** 55
Sidney, Algernon, **II:** 114
Sidney, Mary, **Supp. I Part 1:** 98
Sidney, Philip, **II:** 470; **Supp. I Part 1:** 98, 111, 117-118, 122; **Supp. I Part 2:** 658; **Supp. II Part 1:** 104-105; **Supp. V:** 250; **Supp. XII:** 264; **Supp. XIV:**128
Sidney, Sylvia, **Supp. I Part 1:** 67
Sidney Lanier: A Bibliographical and Critical Study (Starke), **Supp. I Part 1:** 371
Sidney Lanier: A Biographical and Critical Study (Starke), **Supp. I Part 1:** 371
Siegel, Barry, **Supp. XIV:**82
Siegel, Catherine, **Supp. XII:** 126
Siegel, Jerry, **Supp. XI:** 67
"Siege of London, The" (James), **Retro. Supp. I:** 227
Siegle, Robert, **Supp. XII:** 8
Sienkiewicz, Henryk, **Supp. IV Part 2:** 518; **Supp. XVI:**182
"Sierra Kid" (Levine), **Supp. V:** 180-181
Sigg, Eric, **Retro. Supp. I:** 53
"Sight" (Merwin), **Supp. III Part 1:** 356
"Sight in Camp in the Daybreak Gray and Dim, A" (Whitman), **II:** 373
Sights and Spectacles (McCarthy), **II:** 562
"Sights from a Steeple" (Hawthorne), **Retro. Supp. I:** 62
Sights Unseen (Gibbons), **Supp. X: 49-50**

"Signals" (Carver), **Supp. III Part 1:** 143
"Signature for Tempo" (MacLeish), **III:** 8-9
"Signed Confession of Crimes against the State" (Merton), **Supp. VIII:** 201
Signifying Monkey, The (Gates), **Supp. X:** 243
Signifying Monkey, The (Hughes), **Retro. Supp. I:** 195
"Signing, The (Dixon), **Supp. XII: 146**
Sign in Sidney Brustein's Window, The (Hansberry), **Supp. IV Part 1:** 359, 365, 369, 370-372
Sign of Jonas, The (Merton), **Supp. VIII:** 194-195, 195, 197, 200, 206, 207
"Sign of Saturn, The" (Olds), **Supp. X:** 206
Signs and Wonders (Bukiet), **Supp. XVII: 45-46**
Sigourney, Lydia, **Supp. I Part 2:** 684
Sikora, Malgorzata, **Retro. Supp. II:** 324
Silas Marner (Eliot), **II:** 26
Silberg, Richard, **Supp. XV:** 116
"Silence" (Moore), **III:** 212
"Silence" (Poe), **III:** 416
"Silence" (Sanders), **Supp. XVI:**278
"Silence, A" (Clampitt), **Supp. IX:** 53
"Silence-A Fable" (Poe), **III:** 416
"Silence Before Harvest, The" (Merwin), **Supp. III Part 1:** 352
Silence Dogood Papers, The (Franklin), **II:** 106-107
Silence in the Snowy Fields (R. Bly), **Supp. IV Part 1:** 60-61, 62, 63, 65, 66, 72
Silence of History, The (Farrell), **II:** 46-47
Silence Opens, A (Clampitt), **Supp. IX:** 53
Silences (Olsen), **Supp. XIII:** 293, 294, 295, 296, **304-306**
"Silences: When Writers Don't Write" (Olsen), **Supp. XIII:** 294
Silencing the Past: Power and the Production of History (Trouillot), **Supp. X:** 14
"Silent in America" (Levine), **Supp. V:** 183
Silent Life, The (Merton), **Supp. VIII:** 208
Silent Partner, The (Odets), **Supp. II Part 2:** 539
"Silent Poem" (Francis), **Supp. IX:** 86
"Silent Season of a Hero, The" (Talese), **Supp. XVII:** 203-204
"Silent Slain, The" (MacLeish), **III:** 9

"Silent Snow, Secret Snow" (Aiken), **I:** 52
Silent Spring (Carson), **Supp. V:** 202; **Supp. IX:** 19, 24, **31-34**; **Supp. XIV:**177; **Supp. XVI:**36
Silhouettes of American Life (Davis), **Supp. XVI:**85
"Silken Tent, The" (Frost), **Retro. Supp. I:** 138-139; **Supp. IV Part 2:** 448
Silko, Leslie Marmon, **Supp. IV Part 1:** 274, 319, 325, 333-334, 335, 404; **Supp. IV Part 2:** 499, 505, **557-572**; **Supp. V:** 169; **Supp. XI:** 18; **Supp. XII:** 217
Silliman, Ron, **Supp. IV Part 2:** 426; **Supp. XV:** 344; **Supp. XVII:** 70, 77
Silliman's Blog (R. Silliman), **Supp. XVII:** 70
Silman, Roberta, **Supp. X:** 6
Silverblatt, Michael, **Supp. XV:** 224
"Silver Crown, The" (Malamud), **Supp. I Part 2:** 434-435, 437; **Supp. V:** 266
"Silver Dish, The" (Bellow), **Retro. Supp. II:** 30
"Silver Filigree" (Wylie), **Supp. I Part 2:** 707
"Silver Lake" (B. Kelly), **Supp. XVII:** 130
Silvers, Phil, **Supp. IV Part 2:** 574
Silverthorne, Elizabeth, **Supp. X:** 220, 221, 222, 226, 234
"Silver To Have and to Hurl" (Didion), **Supp. IV Part 1:** 197
Simic, Charles, **Supp. V:** 5, 332; **Supp. VIII:** 39, **269-287**; **Supp. XI:** 317; **Supp. XV:** 179, 185
"Similar Cases" (Gilman), **Supp. XI:** 200, 202
Similitudes, from the Ocean and Prairie (Larcom), **Supp. XIII:** 141
Simmel, Georg, **Supp. I Part 2:** 644; **Supp. XVII:** 98
Simmons, Charles, **Supp. XI:** 230
Simmons, Maggie, **Retro. Supp. II:** 21
Simms, Michael, **Supp. XII:** 184
Simms, William Gilmore, **I:** 211
Simon, John, **Supp. IV Part 2:** 691
Simon, Neil, **Supp. IV Part 2:** 573-**594**; **Supp. XVII:** 8
"Simon Gerty" (Wylie), **Supp. I Part 2:** 713
Simonides, **Supp. XII:** 110-111
"Simon Ortiz" (Gingerich), **Supp. IV Part 2:** 510
Simon Ortiz (Wiget), **Supp. IV Part 2:** 509

Simonson, Lee, **III:** 396
"Simple Art of Murder, The" (Chandler), **Supp. IV Part 1:** 121, 341
"Simple Autumnal" (Bogan), **Supp. III Part 1:** 52-53
Simple Heart (Flaubert), **I:** 504
Simple Speaks his Mind (Hughes), **Retro. Supp. I:** 209; **Supp. I Part 1:** 337
Simple Stakes a Claim (Hughes), **Retro. Supp. I:** 209; **Supp. I Part 1:** 337
Simple's Uncle Sam (Hughes), **Retro. Supp. I:** 209; **Supp. I Part 1:** 337
Simple Takes a Wife (Hughes), **Retro. Supp. I:** 209; **Supp. I Part 1:** 337
Simple Truth, The (Hardwick), **Supp. III Part 1:** 199, 200, 208
Simple Truth, The (Levine), **Supp. V:** 178, 179, 193-194
"Simplicity" (Sanders), **Supp. XVI:**276
Simply Heavenly (Hughes), **Retro. Supp. I:** 209; **Supp. I Part 1:** 338, 339
Simpson, Louis, **Supp. III Part 2:** 541; **Supp. IV Part 2:** 448, 621; **Supp. VIII:** 39, 279; **Supp. IX:** 265-283, 290; **Supp. XI:** 317; **Supp. XII:** 130; **Supp. XIII:** 337
Simpson, Mona, **Supp. XVI:**206
"Sin" (C. Frost), **Supp. XV:** 96
Sinatra, Frank, **Supp. IX:** 3; **Supp. X:** 119; **Supp. XI:** 213
Sincere Convert, The (Shepard), **IV:** 158
Sincerely, Willis Wayde (Marquand), **III:** 61, 63, 66, 67-68, 69
Sincerity (Rowson), **Supp. XV:** 242
Sincerity and Authenticity (Trilling), **Supp. III Part 2:** 510-512
"Sincerity and Objectification: With Special Reference to the Work of Charles Reznikoff" (Zukofsky), **Supp. XIV:**286
Sinclair, Mary Craig (Mary Craig Kimbrough), **Supp. V:** 275, 286, 287
Sinclair, Upton, **II:** 34, 440, 444, 451; **III:** 580; **Retro. Supp. II:** 95; **Supp. V:** 275-293; **Supp. VIII:** 11
Sinclair Lewis: An American Life (Schorer), **II:** 459
"Singapore" (Oliver), **Supp. VII:** 239, 240
Singer, Bennett L., **Supp. IV Part 1:** 330
Singer, Beth, **Supp. XIV:**203
Singer, Isaac Bashevis, **I:** 144; **IV:** 1-24; **Retro. Supp. II:** 22, 299-320; **Supp. IX:** 114
Singer, Israel Joshua, **IV:** 2, 16, 17; **Retro. Supp. II:** 302; **Supp. XVII:** 41
Singer, Joshua, **IV:** 4
Singer, Rabbi Pinchos Menachem, **IV:** 16
Singin' and Swingin' and Gettin' Merry Like Christmas (Angelou), **Supp. IV Part 1:** 2, 5, 6-7, 9, 13, 14
"Singing & Doubling Together" (Ammons), **Supp. VII:** 34-35
Singing Jailbirds (Sinclair), **Supp. V:** 277
"Singing the Black Mother" (Lupton), **Supp. IV Part 1:** 7
Single Hound, The (Sarton), **Supp. VIII:** 251, 265
Single Hound, The: Poems of a Lifetime (Dickinson; Bianchi, ed.), **Retro. Supp. I:** 35
Single Man, A (Isherwood), **Supp. XIV:**157, 164, **169-170,** 171
"Single Sonnet" (Bogan), **Supp. III Part 1:** 56-58
Singley, Carol, **Retro. Supp. I:** 373
Singular Family, A: Rosacoke and Her Kin (Price), **Supp. VI:** 258-259, 260
"Singular First Person, The" (Sanders), **Supp. XVI:**274
Singularities (Howe), **Supp. IV Part 2:** 431
Sin in Their Blood (Lacy), **Supp. XV:** 200
"Sinister Adolescents, The" (Dos Passos), **I:** 493
Sinister Street (Mackenzie), **II:** 82
Sinners in the Hands of an Angry God (Edwards), **I:** 546, 552-553, 559, 562
Sinning with Annie, and Other Stories (Theroux), **Supp. VIII:** 318
"Sins of Kalamazoo, The" (Sandburg), **III:** 586
Sintram and His Companions (La Motte-Fouqué), **III:** 78
"Siope" (Poe), **III:** 411
"Sipapu: A Cultural Perspective" (Gunn Allen), **Supp. IV Part 1:** 323
Sipchen, Bob, **Supp. X:** 145
Sipper, Ralph B., **Supp. IV Part 2:** 475
"Sire" (Cisneros), **Supp. VII:** 62-63, 64
"Siren and Signal" (Zukofsky), **Supp. III Part 2:** 611, 612
Sirens of Titan, The (Vonnegut), **Supp. II Part 2:** 757, 758, 760, 765-767
"Sir Galahad" (Tennyson), **Supp. I Part 2:** 410
Sirin, V. (pseudonym), **Retro. Supp. I:** 266. see also Nabokov, Vladimir
Sir Vadia's Shadow: A Friendship across Five Continents (Theroux), **Supp. VIII:** 309, 314, 321, 325
"Sis" (F. Barthelme), **Supp. XI:** 26
"S is for Sad" (M. F. K. Fisher), **Supp. XVII:** 86
Sisley, Alfred, **I:** 478
Sissman, L. E., **Supp. X:** 69
"Sister" (Hughes), **Retro. Supp. I:** 208
Sister Age (M. F. K. Fisher), **Supp. XVII:** 88, 91
Sister Carrie (Dreiser), **I:** 482, 497, 499, 500, 501-502, 503-504, 505, 506, 515, 519; **III:** 327; **IV:** 208; **Retro. Supp. I:** 376; **Retro. Supp. II:** 93, **96-99**
"Sister of the Minotaur" (Stevens), **IV:** 89; **Supp. IX:** 332
"Sisters, The" (Whittier), **Supp. I Part 2:** 696
Sister's Choice (Showalter), **Retro. Supp. I:** 368
Sisters Rosensweig, The (Wasserstein), **Supp. XV:** 320, **328-330**
"Sisyphus" (Kumin), **Supp. IV Part 2:** 443, 444, 451
"Sitalkas" (Doolittle), **Supp. I Part 1:** 266
Sitney, P. Adams, **Supp. XII:** 2
Sitting Bull, **Supp. IV Part 2:** 492
Sitting In: Selected Writings on Jazz, Blues, and Related Topics (Carruth), **Supp. XVI:**46
"Sitting in a Rocking Chair Going Blind" (Komunyakaa), **Supp. XIII:** 114
"Sitting Up Late with My Father, 1977" (F. Wright), **Supp. XVII:** 247
Sitti's Secrets (Nye), **Supp. XIII:** 278
Situation Normal (A. Miller), **III:** 148, 149, 156, 164
Situation of Poetry, The: Contemporary Poetry and Its Traditions (Pinsky), **Supp. VI:** 237-238, 239, 241, 242
Sitwell, Edith, **IV:** 77; **Supp. I Part 1:** 271
"Six Brothers" (Cisneros), **Supp. VII:** 67
Six Characters in Search of an Author (Pirandello), **Supp. IV Part 2:** 576
"Six Days: Some Rememberings" (Paley), **Supp. VI:** 226
"65290" (Leopold), **Supp. XIV:**184-185
Six French Poets (Lowell), **II:** 528-529
"Six in All" (Bierds), **Supp. XVII:** 31

"Six Persons" (Baraka), **Supp. II Part 1:** 53

Six Sections from Mountains and Rivers without End (Snyder), **Supp. VIII:** 305

"Sixteen Months" (Sandburg), **III:** 584

1601, or Conversation as It Was by the Fireside in the Time of the Tudors (Twain), **IV:** 201

"Sixth-Month Song in the Foothills" (Snyder), **Supp. VIII:** 297

Sixties, The (magazine) (R. Bly), **Supp. IV Part 1:** 60; **Supp. IX:** 271

"Sixty" (Dunn), **Supp. XI:** 155

"Sixty Acres" (Carver), **Supp. III Part 1:** 141

"69 Hidebound Opinions, Propositions, and Several Asides from a Manila Folder concerning the Stuff of Poetry" (Wright), **Supp. XV:** 344-345

Sixty Stories (Barthelme), **Supp. IV Part 1:** 41, 42, 44, 47, 49, 50

63: Dream Palace (Purdy), **Supp. VII:** 270-271

"Six Variations" (Levertov), **Supp. III Part 1:** 277-278

"Six-Year-Old Boy" (Olds), **Supp. X:** 206

"Six Years Later" (Brodsky), **Supp. VIII:** 26, 28

"Size and Sheer Will" (Olds), **Supp. X:** 206

Size of Thoughts, The: Essays and Other Lumber (Baker), **Supp. XIII:** **52-53,** 55, 56

Sizwe Bansi Is Dead (Fugard), **Supp. VIII:** 330

"Skagway" (Haines), **Supp. XII:** 206

"Skaters, The" (Ashbery), **Supp. III Part 1:** 10, 12, 13, 18, 25

"Skaters, The" (Jarrell), **II:** 368-369

Skau, Michael, **Supp. XII:** 129, 130, 132, 134

Skeeters Kirby (Masters), **Supp. I Part 2:** 459, 470, 471

Skeleton Crew (King), **Supp. V:** 144

"Skeleton in Armor, The" (Longfellow), **Retro. Supp. II:** 168

"Skeleton's Cave, The" (Bryant), **Supp. I Part 1:** 157

Skelton, John, **III:** 521

Skepticisms (Aiken), **Supp. XV:** 298, 302

Sketch Book of Geoffrey Crayon, Gent., The (Irving), **II:** 295, 303, 304-308, 309, 311, 491; **Supp. I Part 1:** 155

Sketches of Art (Jameson), **Retro. Supp. II:** 58

Sketches of Eighteenth Century America (Crèvecoeur), **Supp. I Part 1:** 233, 240-241, 250, 251

"Sketches of Female Biography" (Rowson), **Supp. XV:** 245

Sketches of Switzerland (Cooper), **I:** 346

Sketches Old and New (Twain), **IV:** 198

"Sketch for a Job-Application Blank" (Harrison), **Supp. VIII:** 38

Sketch of Old England, by a New England Man (Paulding), **I:** 344

Skibell, Joseph, **Supp. XVII:** 48

"Skier and the Mountain, The" (Eberhart), **I:** 528-529

"Skin-Boats: 1830, The" (Bierds), **Supp. XVII:** 28

Skinker, Mary Scott, **Supp. IX:** 20

Skinny Island (Auchincloss), **Supp. IV Part 1:** 33

Skinny Legs and All (Robbins), **Supp. X:** 267, 273, **276-279**

Skin of Our Teeth, The (Wilder), **IV:** 357, 358, 369-372; **Supp. IV Part 2:** 586

"Skins" (Wright), **Supp. V:** 340

Skins and Bones: Poems 1979-1987 (Gunn Allen), **Supp. IV Part 1:** 321, 331

"Skipper Ireson's Ride" (Whittier), **Supp. I Part 2:** 691, 693-694

"Skirmish at Sartoris" (Faulkner), **II:** 67

Skotheim, Robert Allen, **Supp. XVII:** 104

Skow, John, **Supp. V:** 213; **Supp. XVI:** 174

"Skunk Cabbage" (Oliver), **Supp. VII:** 235, 236

"Skunk Hour" (Lowell), **II:** 548-550; **Retro. Supp. II:** 188, 189; **Supp. XIV:** 269

Sky, The Stars, The Wilderness, The (Bass), **Supp. XVI:** 19, 20

"Sky Dance" (Leopold), **Supp. XIV:** 186

"Sky Line" (Taylor), **Supp. V:** 316

"Sky Line, The" (Mumford), **Supp. II Part 2:** 475

"Skyscraper" (Sandburg), **III:** 581-582

Sky's the Limit, The: A Defense of the Earth (Nichols), **Supp. XIII:** 268

"Sky Valley Rider" (Wright), **Supp. V:** 335, 340

Sky-Walk; or the Man Unknown to Himself (Brown), **Supp. I Part 1:** 127-128

"Slang in America" (Whitman), **IV:** 348

Slapstick (Vonnegut), **Supp. II Part 2:** 753, 754, 778

Slapstick Tragedy (T. Williams), **IV:** 382, 393

Slate, Lane, **Supp. IX:** 251, 253

Slattery, Mary Grace. *See* Miller, Mrs. Arthur (Mary Grace Slattery)

"Slaughterer, The" (Singer), **IV:** 19

Slaughterhouse-Five (Vonnegut), **Supp. II Part 2:** 755, 758-759, 760, 770, 772-776; **Supp. V:** 41, 244

Slave, The (Baraka), **Supp. II Part 1:** 42, 44, 56

Slave, The: A Novel (Singer), **IV:** 13; **Retro. Supp. II:** **305-307**

"Slave Coffle" (Angelou), **Supp. IV Part 1:** 16

"Slave on the Block" (Hughes), **Supp. I Part 1:** 329

Slave Power, The: The Free North and Southern Domination, 1780-1860 (Richards), **Supp. XIV:** 48

"Slave Quarters" (Dickey), **Supp. IV Part 1:** 181

"Slave's Dream, The" (Longfellow), **Supp. I Part 2:** 409

Slave Ship: A Historical Pageant (Baraka), **Supp. II Part 1:** 47-49, 53, 56-57

"Slave-Ships, The" (Whittier), **Supp. I Part 2:** 687-688

Slaves in Algiers; or, A Struggle for Freedom (Rowson), **Supp. XV:** **236-237**

Slavs! Thinking about the Longstanding Problems of Virtue and Happiness (Kushner), **Supp. IX:** 146

Sledge, Eugene, **Supp. V:** 250

Sleek for the Long Flight (Matthews), **Supp. IX:** 154, 155, **157-158**

Sleep (Dixon), **Supp. XII:** 154

"Sleep, The" (Strand), **Supp. IV Part 2:** 627

Sleeper (film; Allen), **Supp. XV:** 5

"Sleeper, The" (Poe), **III:** 411

"Sleeper 1, The" (Hay), **Supp. XIV:** 132-133

"Sleeper 2, The" (Hay), **Supp. XIV:** 132-133

"Sleepers, The" (Whitman), **IV:** 336

"Sleepers in Jaipur" (Kenyon), **Supp. VII:** 172

Sleepers in Moon-Crowned Valleys (Purdy), **Supp. VII:** 274, 275

"Sleepers Joining Hands" (R. Bly), **Supp. IV Part 1:** 63, 73

Sleeping Beauty (Macdonald), **Supp. IV Part 2:** 474, 475

Sleeping Beauty, The (Carruth), **Supp. XVI:** 53, 57-58

"Sleeping Beauty Syndrome, The: The New Agony of Single Men"

(Wasserstein), **Supp. XV:** 328
"Sleeping Fury, The" (Bogan), **Supp. III Part 1:** 58
Sleeping Fury, The: Poems (Bogan), **Supp. III Part 1:** 55-58
Sleeping Gypsy and Other Poems, The (Garrett), **Supp. VII:** 96-98
Sleeping in the Forest (Oliver), **Supp. VII:** 233
"Sleeping in the Forest" (Oliver), **Supp. VII:** 233-234
Sleeping in the Woods (Wagoner), **Supp. IX:** 328
Sleeping on Fists (Ríos), **Supp. IV Part 2:** 540
Sleeping on the Wing: An Anthology of Modern Poetry (Koch and Farrell, eds.), **Supp. XV:** 187-188
"Sleeping Standing Up" (Bishop), **Supp. I Part 1:** 85, 89, 93
"Sleeping with Animals" (Kumin), **Supp. IV Part 2:** 454
Sleeping with One Eye Open (Strand), **Supp. IV Part 2:** 621-624, 623, 628
Sleep in Thunder (Lacy), **Supp. XV:** 206
"Sleepless, The" (L.-Y. Lee), **Supp. XV:** 224
"Sleepless at Crown Point" (Wilbur), **Supp. III Part 2:** 561
Sleepless Nights (Hardwick), **Supp. III Part 1:** 193, 208-211
Sleepy Lagoon Mystery, The (Endore), **Supp. XVII:** 60
Sleight, Ken, **Supp. XIII:** 12
Slick, Sam (pseudonym). *See* Haliburton, Thomas Chandler
"Slick Gonna Learn" (Ellison), **Retro. Supp. II:** 116; **Supp. II Part 1:** 237-238
"Slight Rebellion off Madison" (Salinger), **III:** 553
"Slight Sound at Evening, A" (White), **Supp. I Part 2:** 672
"Slim Graves Show, The" (Keillor), **Supp. XVI:** 172
"Slim Greer" series (Hayden), **Supp. II Part 1:** 369
"Slim in Hell" (Hayden), **Supp. II Part 1:** 369
"Slim Man Canyon" (Silko), **Supp. IV Part 2:** 560
"Slip, Shift, and Speed Up: The Influence of Robinson Jeffers's Narrative Syntax" (Jarman), **Supp. XVII:** 111, 112
"Slippery Fingers" (Hammett), **Supp. IV Part 1:** 343
Slipping-Down Life, A (Tyler), **Supp. IV Part 2:** 660-661

Sloan, Jacob, **IV:** 3, 6
Sloan, John, **I:** 254; **IV:** 411; **Retro. Supp. II:** 103
Sloane, John, **Supp. XV:** 295
"Slob" (Farrell), **II:** 25, 28, 31
Slocum, Joshua, **Supp. I Part 2:** 497
Slonim, Véra. *See* Nabokov, Véra
Slouching towards Bethlehem (Didion), **Supp. IV Part 1:** 196, 197, 200-201, 202, 206, 210
Slovic, Scott, **Supp. XVI:** 277
"Slow Child with a Book of Birds" (Levis), **Supp. XI:** 268
"Slow Down for Poetry" (Strand), **Supp. IV Part 2:** 620
"Slow Pacific Swell, The" (Winters), **Supp. II Part 2:** 790, 793, 795, 796, 799
Slow Parade (Kees), **Supp. XV:** 137
"Slumgullions" (Olsen), **Supp. IV Part 1:** 54
Slumgullion Stew: An Edward Abbey Reader (Abbey), **Supp. XIII:** 4
"S & M" (Komunyakaa), **Supp. XIII:** 114
"Small" (C. Frost), **Supp. XV:** 102
Small, Albion, **Supp. I Part 1:** 5
"Small, Good Thing, A" (Carver), **Supp. III Part 1:** 145, 147
Small, Miriam Rossiter, **Supp. I Part 1:** 319
Small Boy and Others, A (James), **II:** 337, 547; **Retro. Supp. I:** 235
"Small but Urgent Request to the Unknowable" (Karr), **Supp. XI:** 243
Small Ceremonies (Shields), **Supp. VII:** 312-315, 320
Small Craft Warnings (T. Williams), **IV:** 382, 383, 384, 385, 386, 387, 392, 393, 396, 398
Small Place, A (Kincaid), **Supp. VII:** 186-187, 188, 191
"Small Rain, The" (Pynchon), **Supp. II Part 2:** 620
Small Room, The (Sarton), **Supp. VIII:** 252, **255-256**
Smalls, Bob, **II:** 128
Small Time Crooks (film; Allen), **Supp. XV:** 11
Small Town, A (Hearon), **Supp. VIII: 65-66**
"Small Vases from Hebron, The" (Nye), **Supp. XIII:** 283
"Small Vision, The" (Goldbarth), **Supp. XII:** 180
"Small Voice from the Wings" (Everwine), **Supp. XV:** 76
"Small Wire" (Sexton), **Supp. II Part 2:** 696
Small Worlds (A. Hoffman), **Supp.**

XVII: 44
Smardz, Zofia, **Supp. XVI:** 155
Smart, Christopher, **III:** 534; **Supp. I Part 2:** 539; **Supp. IV Part 2:** 626
Smart, Joyce H., **Supp. XI:** 169
"Smart Cookie, A" (Cisneros), **Supp. VII:** 64
"Smashup" (Thurber), **Supp. I Part 2:** 616
Smedly, Agnes, **Supp. XIII:** 295
"Smelt Fishing" (Hayden), **Supp. II Part 1:** 367
"Smile of the Bathers, The" (Kees), **Supp. XV:** 145
"Smiles" (Dunn), **Supp. XI:** 151
Smiles, Samuel, **Supp. X:** 167
Smiley, Jane, **Supp. VI: 291-309; Supp. XII:** 73, 297; **Supp. XIII:** 127
Smith, Adam, **II:** 9; **Supp. I Part 2:** 633, 634, 639; **Supp. XVII:** 235
Smith, Annick, **Supp. XIV:** 223
Smith, Benjamin, **IV:** 148
Smith, Bernard, **I:** 260
Smith, Bessie, **Retro. Supp. I:** 343; **Supp. VIII:** 330
Smith, Charlie, **Supp. X:** 177
Smith, Dale, **Supp. XV:** 136, 138, 139
Smith, Dave, **Supp. V:** 333; **Supp. XI:** 152; **Supp. XII:** 178, 198
Smith, David, **Supp. XIII:** 246, 247
Smith, David Nichol, **Supp. XIV:** 2
Smith, Dinitia, **Supp. VIII:** 74, 82, 83
Smith, Elihu Hubbard, **Supp. I Part 1:** 126, 127, 130
Smith, George Adam, **III:** 199
Smith, Hannah Whitall, **Supp. XIV:** 333, 334, 338
Smith, Harrison, **II:** 61
Smith, Henry Nash, **IV:** 210; **Supp. I Part 1:** 233
Smith, Herbert F., **Supp. I Part 2:** 423
Smith, James, **II:** 111
Smith, Jedediah Strong, **Supp. IV Part 2:** 602
Smith, Jerome, **Supp. IV Part 1:** 369
Smith, Joe, **Supp. IV Part 2:** 584
Smith, John, **I:** 4, 131; **II:** 296
Smith, John Allyn, **I:** 168
Smith, Johnston (pseudonym). *See* Crane, Stephen
Smith, Kellogg, **Supp. I Part 2:** 660
Smith, Lamar, **II:** 585
Smith, Lee, **Supp. XII:** 311
Smith, Logan Pearsall, **Supp. XIV: 333-351**
Smith, Lula Carson. *See* McCullers, Carson
Smith, Martha Nell, **Retro. Supp. I:** 33, 43, 46, 47

Smith, Mary Rozet, **Supp. I Part 1:** 5, 22
Smith, Mrs. Lamar (Marguerite Walters), **II:** 585, 587
Smith, Oliver, **II:** 586
Smith, Patricia Clark, **Supp. IV Part 1:** 397, 398, 402, 406, 408, 410; **Supp. IV Part 2:** 509; **Supp. XII:** 218
Smith, Patrick, **Supp. VIII:** 40, 41
Smith, Patti, **Supp. XII:** 136; **Supp. XIV:**151
Smith, Porter, **III:** 572
Smith, Red, **II:** 417, 424
Smith, Robert McClure, **Supp. XV:** 270
Smith, Robert Pearsall, **Supp. XIV:**333
Smith, Seba, **Supp. I Part 2:** 411
Smith, Sidonie Ann, **Supp. IV Part 1:** 11
Smith, Stevie, **Supp. V:** 84
Smith, Sydney, **II:** 295; **Supp. XIV:**112
Smith, Thorne, **Supp. IX:** 194
Smith, Wendy, **Supp. XII:** 330, 335
Smith, Wilford Bascom "Pitchfork," **Supp. XIII:** 168
Smith, William, **II:** 114
Smith, William Gardner, **Supp. XVI:**142-143
Smith, William Jay, **Supp. XIII: 331-350**
Smoke (film), **Supp. XII:** 21
Smoke and Steel (Sandburg), **III:** 585-587, 592
"Smokers" (Wolff), **Supp. VII:** 340-341
Smokey Bites the Dust (film, C. Griffith), **Supp. XVII:** 9
"Smoking My Prayers" (Ortiz), **Supp. IV Part 2:** 503
"Smoking Room, The" (Jackson), **Supp. IX:** 116
"Smoky Gold" (Leopold), **Supp. XIV:**186
Smolan, Sandy, **Supp. XVI:**36
Smollett, Tobias G., **I:** 134, 339, 343; **II:** 304-305; **III:** 61
Smuggler's Bible, A (McElroy), **Supp. IV Part 1:** 285
Smuggler's Handbook, The (Goldbarth), **Supp. XII:** 181, 183
Smugglers of Lost Soul's Rock, The (Gardner), **Supp. VI: 70**
Smyth, Albert Henry, **II:** 123
"Snack Firm Maps New Chip Push" (Keillor), **Supp. XVI:**168, 169
"Snail, The" (Hay), **Supp. XIV:**124
"Snake, The" (Berry), **Supp. X:** 31
"Snake, The" (Crane), **I:** 420

"Snakecharmer" (Plath), **Supp. I Part 2:** 538
"Snakes, Mongooses" (Moore), **III:** 207
"Snakes of September, The" (Kunitz), **Supp. III Part 1:** 258
"Snapshot of 15th S.W., A" (Hugo), **Supp. VI:** 141
"Snapshot Rediscovered, A" (X. J. Kennedy), **Supp. XV:** 170
"Snapshots of a Daughter-in-Law" (Rich), **Supp. I Part 2:** 553-554
Snapshots of a Daughter-in-Law: Poems, 1954-1962 (Rich), **Supp. I Part 2:** 550-551, 553-554; **Supp. XII:** 255
Snaring the Flightless Birds (Bierds), **Supp. XVII:** 26
Sneetches and Other Stories, The (Geisel), **Supp. XVI:**109
"Sneeze, The" (Chekhov), **Supp. IV Part 2:** 585
Snell, Ebenezer, **Supp. I Part 1:** 151
Snell, Thomas, **Supp. I Part 1:** 153
"Snob, The" (Shapiro), **Supp. II Part 2:** 705
Snobbery: The America Version (Epstein), **Supp. XIV:**102, 114-115
Snodgrass, Kathleen, **Supp. XVI:**42
Snodgrass, W. D., **I:** 400; **Retro. Supp. II:** 179; **Supp. III Part 2:** 541; **Supp. V:** 337; **Supp. VI: 311-328; Supp. XI:** 141, 315; **Supp. XIII:** 312; **Supp. XV:** 92, 153; **Supp. XVII:** 239
"Snow" (C. Baxter), **Supp. XVII:** 19
"Snow" (Frost), **Retro. Supp. I:** 133
"Snow" (Haines), **Supp. XII:** 212
"Snow" (Sexton), **Supp. II Part 2:** 696
Snow, C. P., **Supp. I Part 2:** 536
Snow, Hank, **Supp. V:** 335
Snow: Meditations of a Cautious Man in Winter (Banks), **Supp. V:** 6
Snow Ball, The (Gurney), **Supp. V:** 99
"Snow-Bound" (Whittier), **Supp. I Part 2:** 700-703
"Snow Bound at Eagle's" (Harte), **Supp. II Part 1:** 356
"Snowflakes" (Longfellow), **II:** 498
"Snow Goose, The" (Gallico), **Supp. XVI:**238
Snow-Image and Other Twice Told Tales, The (Hawthorne), **II:** 237; **Retro. Supp. I:** 160
"Snowing in Greenwich Village" (Updike), **IV:** 226; **Retro. Supp. I:** 321
"Snow in New York" (Swenson), **Supp. IV Part 2:** 644
Snow Leopard, The (Matthiessen),

Supp. V: 199, 207-211
"Snow Man, The" (Stevens), **IV:** 82-83; **Retro. Supp. I:** 299, 300, 302, 306, 307, 312
"Snowmass Cycle, The" (Dunn), **Supp. XI:** 152
Snow Poems, The (Ammons), **Supp. VII:** 32-34
"Snows of Kilimanjaro, The" (Hemingway), **II:** 78, 257, 263, 264; **Retro. Supp. I:** 98, 182; **Supp. XII:** 249
"Snows of Studiofiftyfour, The" (Plimpton), **Supp. XVI:**245
"Snow Songs" (Snodgrass), **Supp. VI:** 324
"Snowstorm, The" (Oates), **Supp. II Part 2:** 523
"Snowstorm as It Affects the American Farmer, A" (Crèvecoeur), **Supp. I Part 1:** 251
Snow White (Barthelme), **Supp. IV Part 1:** 40, 47, 48-49, 50, 52; **Supp. V:** 39
"Snowy Mountain Song, A" (Ortiz), **Supp. IV Part 2:** 506
Snyder, Gary, **Supp. III Part 1:** 350; **Supp. IV Part 2:** 502; **Supp. V:** 168-169; **Supp. VIII:** 39, **289-307; Supp. XVI:**283
Snyder, Mike, **Supp. XIV:**36
"So-and-So Reclining on Her Couch" (Stevens), **IV:** 90
"Soapland" (Thurber), **Supp. I Part 2:** 619
Soares, Lota de Macedo, **Retro. Supp. II:** 44; **Supp. I Part 1:** 89, 94
"Sobbin' Women, The" (Benét), **Supp. XI:** 47
Sobin, Gustaf, **Supp. XVI:**281-298
Social Ethics (Gilman), **Supp. XI:** 207
"Socialism and the Negro" (McKay), **Supp. X:** 135
"Socialism of the Skin, A (Liberation, Honey!)" (Kushner), **Supp. IX:** 135
Social Thought in America: The Revolt against Formalism (White), **Supp. I Part 2:** 648, 650
"Society, Morality, and the Novel" (Ellison), **Retro. Supp. II:** 118, 123-124
"Sociological Habit Patterns in Linguistic Transmogrification" (Cowley), **Supp. II Part 1:** 143
"Sociological Poet, A" (Bourne), **I:** 228
Socrates, **I:** 136, 265; **II:** 8-9, 105, 106; **III:** 281, 419, 606; **Supp. I Part 2:** 458; **Supp. XII:** 98
Socrates Fortlow stories (Mosley), **Supp. XIII: 242-243**

So Forth (Brodsky), **Supp. VIII:** 32-33
"So Forth" (Brodsky), **Supp. VIII:** 33
Soft Machine, The (Burroughs), **Supp. III Part 1:** 93, 103, 104
"Soft Mask" (Karr), **Supp. XI:** 243
Soft Side, The (James), **II:** 335; **Retro. Supp. I:** 229
"Soft Spring Night in Shillington, A" (Updike), **Retro. Supp. I:** 318, 319
"Soft Wood" (Lowell), **II:** 550-551
"So Help Me" (Algren), **Supp. IX:** 2
Soil and Survival: Land Stewardship and the Future of American Agriculture (C. Bly, J. Paddock and N. Paddock), **Supp. XVI:** 36-37
"Soirée in Hollywood" (H. Miller), **III:** 186
Sojourner, The (Rawlings), **Supp. X:** 233-234
"Sojourn in a Whale" (Moore), **III:** 211, 213
"Sojourns" (Didion), **Supp. IV Part 1:** 205
Solanus, Jane, **Supp. XVI:** 293
Solar Storms (Hogan), **Supp. IV Part 1:** 397, 410, 414-415
"Soldier, The" (Frost), **II:** 155
"Soldier Asleep at the Tomb" (Schnackenberg), **Supp. XV:** 262-263
Soldier Blue (film), **Supp. X:** 124
"Soldier of Fortune" (Wright), **Supp. XV:** 341
"Soldier's Home" (Hemingway), **Retro. Supp. I:** 189
Soldier's Joy (Bell), **Supp. X:** 7, **7-8**, 10, 11
Soldiers of the Storm (film), **Supp. XIII:** 163
Soldiers' Pay (Faulkner), **I:** 117; **II:** 56, 68; **Retro. Supp. I:** 80, 81
"Soldier's Testament, The" (Mumford), **Supp. II Part 2:** 473
"Soliloquy: Man Talking to a Mirror" (Komunyakaa), **Supp. XIII:** 116-117
"Solitary Confinement" (X. J. Kennedy), **Supp. XV:** 157
"Solitary Pond, The" (Updike), **Retro. Supp. I:** 323
So Little Time (Marquand), **III:** 55, 59, 65, 67, 69
"Solitude" (Maupassant), **Supp. I Part 1:** 223
Solo Faces (Salter), **Supp. IX: 259-260**
Solomon, Andy, **Supp. X:** 11
Solomon, Carl, **Supp. XIV:** 143, 150
Solomon, Charles, **Supp. VIII:** 82

Solomon, Henry, Jr., **Supp. I Part 2:** 490
Solomons, Leon, **IV:** 26
So Long, See You Tomorrow (Maxwell), **Supp. VIII:** 156, 160, 162, **167-169**
So Long, See You Tomorrow (W. Maxwell), **Supp. XVII:** 23
"So Long Ago" (Bausch), **Supp. VII:** 41-42
Solotaroff, Robert, **Retro. Supp. II:** 203
Solotaroff, Theodore, **III:** 452-453; **Retro. Supp. II:** 281; **Supp. I Part 2:** 440, 445; **Supp. X:** 79; **Supp. XI:** 340; **Supp. XII:** 291
"Solstice" (Jeffers), **Supp. II Part 2:** 433, 435
"Solstice, The" (Merwin), **Supp. III Part 1:** 356
"Solus Rex" (Nabokov), **Retro. Supp. I:** 274
"Solutions" (McCarthy), **II:** 578
"Solving the Puzzle" (Dunn), **Supp. XI:** 152
Solzhenitsyn, Alexandr, **Retro. Supp. I:** 278; **Supp. VIII:** 241
"Some Afternoon" (Creeley), **Supp. IV Part 1:** 150-151
Some American People (Caldwell), **I:** 292, 294, 295, 296, 304, 309
"Some Ashes Drifting above Piedra, California" (Levis), **Supp. XI:** 264-265
"Some Aspects of the Grotesque in Southern Fiction" (O'Connor), **Retro. Supp. II:** 223, 224
"Somebody Always Grabs the Purple" (H. Roth), **Supp. IX:** 234
Somebody in Boots (Algren), **Supp. IX:** 3, **5-7**, 12
Somebody's Darling (McMurtry), **Supp. V:** 225
Some Came Running (film), **Supp. XI:** 213
Some Came Running (Jones), **Supp. XI:** 214, 215, 220, **222-223**, 226, 227, 232
Some Can Whistle (McMurtry), **Supp. V:** 229
"Some Children of the Goddess" (Mailer), **Retro. Supp. II:** 204
Someday, Maybe (Stafford), **Supp. XI: 323-325; Supp. XIII:** 281
"Some Dreamers of the Golden Dream" (Didion), **Supp. IV Part 1:** 200
"Some Foreign Letters" (Sexton), **Supp. II Part 2:** 674
"Some General Instructions" (Koch), **Supp. XV:** 182

"Some Good News" (Olson), **Supp. II Part 2:** 575, 576, 577
"Some Grass along a Ditch Bank" (Levis), **Supp. XI:** 266
"Some Greek Writings" (Corso), **Supp. XII:** 130
Some Honorable Men: Political Conventions, 1960-1972 (Mailer), **Retro. Supp. II:** 208
Some Imagist Poets (Lowell), **III:** 511, 518, 520; **Supp. I Part 1:** 257, 261
"Some keep the Sabbath going to Church" (Dickinson), **Retro. Supp. I:** 30
"Some Laughed" (L. Michaels), **Supp. XVI:** 207
"Some Like Indians Endure" (Gunn Allen), **Supp. IV Part 1:** 330
"Some Like Them Cold" (Lardner), **II:** 427-428, 430, 431; **Supp. IX:** 202
"Some Lines from Whitman" (Jarrell), **IV:** 352
"Some Matters Concerning the Occupant" (Keillor), **Supp. XVI:** 167
"Some Negatives: X. at the Chateau" (Merrill), **Supp. III Part 1:** 322
"Some Neglected Points in the Theory of Socialism" (Veblen), **Supp. I Part 2:** 635
"Some Notes for an Autobiographical Lecture" (Trilling), **Supp. III Part 2:** 493, 497, 500
"Some Notes on French Poetry" (R. Bly), **Supp. IV Part 1:** 61
"Some Notes on Miss L." (West), **IV:** 290-291, 295; **Retro. Supp. II:** 322
"Some Notes on Organic Form" (Levertov), **Supp. III Part 1:** 272, 279
"Some Notes on Teaching: Probably Spoken" (Paley), **Supp. VI:** 225
"Some Notes on the Gazer Within" (Levis), **Supp. XI:** 270
"Some Notes on Violence" (West), **IV:** 304; **Retro. Supp. II:** 322, 323
"Some Observations Now" (Conroy), **Supp. XVI:** 75
Some of the Dharma (Kerouac), **Supp. III Part 1:** 225
"Someone Is Buried" (Salinas), **Supp. XIII:** 324
"Someone Puts a Pineapple Together" (Stevens), **IV:** 90-91
"Someone's Blood" (Dove), **Supp. IV Part 1:** 245
"Someone Talking" (Harjo), **Supp. XII:** 219-220
"Someone Talking to Himself" (Wilbur), **Supp. III Part 2:** 557
"Someone to Watch Over Me" (Stern),

Supp. IX: 300
Someone to Watch Over Me: Stories (Bausch), **Supp. VII:** 53
Some People, Places, & Things That Will Not Appear in My Next Novel (Cheever), **Supp. I Part 1:** 184-185
"Some Poets' Criticism and the Age" (Yenser), **Supp. XV:** 113-114
Some Problems of Philosophy: A Beginning of an Introduction to Philosophy (James), **II:** 360-361
"Some Questions You Might Ask" (Oliver), **Supp. VII:** 238-239
"Some Remarks on Humor" (White), **Supp. I Part 2:** 672
"Some Remarks on Rhythm" (Roethke), **III:** 548-549
Somers, Fred, **I:** 196
Somerville, Jane, **Supp. IX:** 289, 296-297
"Some Secrets" (Stern), **Supp. IX:** 286, 287, 288, 289, 295
Some Sort of Epic Grandeur (Bruccoli), **Retro. Supp. I:** 115, 359
"Something" (Oliver), **Supp. VII:** 236
Something Happened (Heller), **Supp. IV Part 1:** 383, 386-388, 389, 392
"Something Happened: The Imaginary, the Symbolic, and the Discourse of the Family" (Mellard), **Supp. IV Part 1:** 387
Something in Common (Hughes), **Supp. I Part 1:** 329-330
Something Inside: Conversations with Gay Fiction Writers (Gambone), **Supp. XII:** 81
"Something New" (Stern), **Supp. IX:** 290
"Something's Going to Happen" (Zinberg), **Supp. XV:** 196
"Something Spurious from the Mindinao Deep" (Stegner), **Supp. IV Part 2:** 605
Something to Declare (Alvarez), **Supp. VII:** 1, 2, 11, 17-19
Something to Remember Me By (Bellow), **Retro. Supp. II:** 32
"Something to Remember Me By" (Bellow), **Retro. Supp. II:** 32
Something Wicked This Way Comes (Bradbury), **Supp. IV Part 1:** 101, 110-111
"Something Wild ..." (T. Williams), **IV:** 381
"Some Thoughts" (McNally), **Supp. XIII:** 207
"Some Thoughts on the Line" (Oliver), **Supp. VII:** 238
"Sometimes, Reading" (Stafford), **Supp. XI:** 314

"Sometimes I Wonder" (Hughes), **Supp. I Part 1:** 337
Sometimes Mysteriously (Salinas), **Supp. XIII:** 311, **326-328**
"Sometimes Mysteriously" (Salinas), **Supp. XIII:** 328
Some Trees (Ashbery), **Supp. III Part 1:** 3-7, 12
"Some Trees" (Ashbery), **Supp. III Part 1:** 2
"Some Views on the Reading and Writing of Short Stories" (Welty), **Retro. Supp. I:** 351
"Somewhere" (Nemerov), **III:** 279-280
"Somewhere Else" (Paley), **Supp. VI:** 227
"Somewhere in Africa" (Sexton), **Supp. II Part 2:** 684-685
"Somewhere Is Such a Kingdom" (Ransom), **III:** 492
"Somewhere near Phu Bai: (Komunyakaa), **Supp. XIII:** 123-124
"Some Words with a Mummy" (Poe), **III:** 425
"Some Yips and Barks in the Dark" (Snyder), **Supp. VIII:** 291
Sommers, Michael, **Supp. IV Part 2:** 581
Sommers, William, **I:** 387, 388
"Somnambulisma" (Stevens), **Retro. Supp. I:** 310
"So Much Summer" (Dickinson), **Retro. Supp. I:** 26, 44, 45
"So Much the Worse for Boston" (Lindsay), **Supp. I Part 2:** 398
"So Much Water So Close to Home" (Carver), **Supp. III Part 1:** 143, 146
Son, Cathy, **Supp. X:** 292
"Son, The" (Dove), **Supp. IV Part 1:** 245
"Sonata" (Schnackenberg), **Supp. XV:** 259
"Sonata for the Invisible" (Harjo), **Supp. XII:** 228
Sonata for Two Pianos (Bowles), **Supp. IV Part 1:** 83
Son at the Front, A (Wharton), **II:** 183; **IV:** 320; **Retro. Supp. I:** 378
Sondheim, Stephen, **Supp. XII:** 260; **Supp. XVI:** 194
Son Excellence Eugène Rougon (Zola), **III:** 322
"Song" (Bogan), **Supp. III Part 1:** 57
"Song" (Bryant). See "Hunter of the West, The"
Song (B. Kelly), **Supp. XVII:** 123, **127-130**
"Song" (B. Kelly), **Supp. XVII:** 127
"Song" (Dunbar), **Supp. II Part 1:** 199

"Song" (Ginsberg), **Supp. II Part 1:** 317
"Song" (Kenyon), **Supp. VII:** 169
"Song" (Rich), **Supp. I Part 2:** 560
"Song" (Wylie), **Supp. I Part 2:** 729
"Song, A" (Creeley), **Supp. IV Part 1:** 145
"Song: Enlightenment" (X. J. Kennedy), **Supp. XV:** 169
"Song: Love in Whose Rich Honor" (Rukeyser), **Supp. VI:** 285
"Song: Now That She Is Here" (Carruth), **Supp. XVI:** 59
"Song: 'Rough Winds Do Shake the Darling Buds of May'" (Simpson), **Supp. IX:** 268
"Song, The" (Gioia), **Supp. XV:** 117
Song and Idea (Eberhart), **I:** 526, 529, 533, 539
"Song for Myself and the Deer to Return On" (Harjo), **Supp. XII:** 225
"Song for My Sixtieth Year" (Carruth), **Supp. XVI:** 54
"Song for Occupations, A" (Whitman), **Retro. Supp. I:** 394
"Song for Simeon, A" (Eliot), **Retro. Supp. I:** 64
"Song for the Coming of Smallpox" (Wagoner), **Supp. IX:** 329, 330
"Song for the End of Time" (Gioia), **Supp. XV:** 126-127
"Song for the First People" (Wagoner), **Supp. IX:** 328
"Song for the Last Act" (Bogan), **Supp. III Part 1:** 64
"Song for the Middle of the Night, A" (Wright), **Supp. III Part 2:** 594
"Song for the Rainy Season" (Bishop), **Supp. I Part 1:** 93-94, 96
"Song for the Romeos, A" (Stern), **Supp. IX:** 296
"Song from a Courtyard Window" (Gioia), **Supp. XV:** 119
"Songline of Dawn" (Harjo), **Supp. XII:** 229
"Song of Advent, A" (Winters), **Supp. II Part 2:** 789
"Song of a Man Who Rushed at the Enemy" (Wagoner), **Supp. IX:** 329, 330
"Song of Courage, A" (Masters), **Supp. I Part 2:** 458
Song of God, The: Bhagavad-Gita (Isherwood and Prabhavananda, trans.), **Supp. XIV:** 156, 157, 164
Song of Hiawatha, The (Longfellow), **II:** 501, 503-504; **Retro. Supp. II:** 155, **159-161**, 162, 163
"Song of Innocence, A" (Ellison),

INDEX / 499

Retro. Supp. II: 126; **Supp. II Part 1:** 248
"Song of My Fiftieth Birthday, The" (Lindsay), **Supp. I Part 2:** 399
"Song of Myself" (Whitman), **II:** 544; **III:** 572, 584, 595; **IV:** 333, 334, 337-339, 340, 341, 342, 344, 348, 349, 351, 405; **Retro. Supp. I:** 388, 389, 395-399, 400; **Supp. V:** 122; **Supp. IX:** 131, 136, 143, 328, 331; **Supp. XIV:**139
Song of Russia (film), **Supp. I Part 1:** 281, 294
Song of Russia (film, Ratoff), **Supp. XVII:** 60-61
"Song of Self" (Huncke), **Supp. XIV:**138-139, 145
Song of Solomon (biblical book), **III:** 118; **IV:** 150
Song of Solomon (Morrison), **Supp. III Part 1:** 364, 368, 369, 372, 379
Song of Songs (biblical book), **II:** 538; **IV:** 153-154; **Supp. XV:** 221
"Song of the Answerer" (Whitman), **Retro. Supp. I:** 393, 399
"Song of the Chattahoochee, The" (Lanier), **Supp. I Part 1:** 365, 368
"Song of the Degrees, A" (Pound), **III:** 466
"Song of the Exposition" (Whitman), **IV:** 332
"Song of the Gavilan" (Leopold), **Supp. XIV:**189
"Song of the Gourd" (Wright), **Supp. XV:** 348-349
"Song of the Greek Amazon" (Bryant), **Supp. I Part 1:** 168
Song of the Lark, The (Cather), **I:** 312, 319-321, 323; **Retro. Supp. I:** 1, 3, 7, **9-11,** 13, 19, 20
"Song of the Open Road" (McGrath), **Supp. X:** 127
"Song of the Open Road" (Whitman), **IV:** 340-341; **Retro. Supp. I:** 400; **Supp. IX:** 265
"Song of the Redwood Tree" (Whitman), **IV:** 348
"Song of the Scullery" (McCarriston), **Supp. XIV:**272
"Song of the Sky Loom" (traditional Tewa poem), **Supp. IV Part 1:** 325
"Song of the Son" (Toomer), **Supp. III Part 2:** 482-483; **Supp. IX:** 313
"Song of the Sower, The" (Bryant), **Supp. I Part 1:** 169
"Song of the Stars" (Bryant), **Supp. I Part 1:** 163
"Song of the Swamp-Robin, The" (Frederic), **II:** 138
"Song of the Vermonters, The"
(Whittier), **Supp. I Part 2:** 692
"Song of Three Smiles" (Merwin), **Supp. III Part 1:** 344
"Song of Wandering Aengus, The" (Yeats), **IV:** 271; **Retro. Supp. I:** 342, 350
"Song of Welcome" (Brodsky), **Supp. VIII:** 32
"Song on Captain Barney's Victory" (Freneau), **Supp. II Part 1:** 261
"Song/Poetry and Language-Expression and Perception" (Ortiz), **Supp. IV Part 2:** 500, 508
Songs and Satires (Masters), **Supp. I Part 2:** 465-466
Songs and Sonnets (L. P. Smith), **Supp. XIV:**341
Songs and Sonnets (Masters), **Supp. I Part 2:** 455, 459, 461, 466
"Songs for a Colored Singer" (Bishop), **Supp. I Part 1:** 80, 85
Songs for a Summer's Day (A Sonnet Cycle) (MacLeish), **III:** 3
Songs for Eve (MacLeish), **III:** 3, 19
"Songs for Eve" (MacLeish), **III:** 19
"Songs for My Father" (Komunyakaa), **Supp. XIII:** 128
"Songs for Two Seasons" (C. Frost), **Supp. XV:** 95-96
Songs from This Earth on Turtle's Back: Contemporary American Indian Poetry (Bruchac, ed.), **Supp. IV Part 1:** 320, 328
"Songs of a Housewife" (Rawlings), **Supp. X:** 221-222
"Songs of Billy Bathgate, The" (Doctorow), **Supp. IV Part 1:** 230
Songs of Innocence (Blake), **Supp. I Part 2:** 708
Songs of Jamaica (McKay), **Supp. X:** 131, 133
"Songs of Maximus, The" (Olson), **Supp. II Part 2:** 567
"Songs of Parting" (Whitman), **IV:** 348
Songs of the Sierras (J. Miller), **I:** 459
Songs of Three Centuries (Whittier and Larcom, eds.), **Supp. XIII:** 142
"Song to David" (Smart), **III:** 534
"Song to No Music, A" (Brodsky), **Supp. VIII:** 26
Sonneschein, Rosa, **Retro. Supp. II:** 65
"Sonnet" (Rukeyser), **Supp. VI:** 284
"Sonnet Crown for Two Voices" (Bierds), **Supp. XVII:** 35
"Sonnets" (Carruth), **Supp. XVI:**56
"Sonnets at Christmas" (Tate), **IV:** 135
Sonnets to Orpheus (Rilke), **Supp. XV:** 222
"Sonnet-To Zante" (Poe), **III:** 421

"Sonny's Blues" (Baldwin), **Retro. Supp. II:** 7, 8, 10, 14; **Supp. I Part 1:** 58-59, 63, 67; **Supp. XI:** 288
Son of Laughter, The: A Novel (Buechner), **Supp. XII:** 54
Son of Perdition, The (Cozzens), **I:** 359-360, 377, 378, 379
Son of the Circus, A (Irving), **Supp. VI:** 165, 166, **176-179**
"Son of the Gods, A" (Bierce), **I:** 202
Son of the Morning (Oates), **Supp. II Part 2:** 518, 519, 520-522
Son of the Morning Star: Custer and the Little Bighorn (Connell), **Supp. XIV:**80, 82, 97
"Son of the Romanovs, A" (Simpson), **Supp. IX:** 273-274
Son of the Wolf, The (London), **II:** 465, 469
"Son of the Wolfman" (Chabon), **Supp. XI:** 76
"Sonrisas" (Mora), **Supp. XIII:** 216, 219
Sons (Buck), **Supp. II Part 1:** 117-118
Sons and Lovers (Lawrence), **III:** 27
Sontag, Kate, **Supp. XV:** 104
Sontag, Susan, **IV:** 13, 14; **Retro. Supp. II:** 279; **Supp. I Part 2:** 423; **Supp. III Part 2: 451-473;** **Supp. VIII:** 75; **Supp. XIV:**14, 15, 95-96, 167; **Supp. XVI:**201, 204, 206
"Soonest Mended" (Ashbery), **Supp. III Part 1:** 1, 13
"Sootfall and Fallout" (White), **Supp. I Part 2:** 671
Sophocles, **I:** 274; **II:** 291, 385, 577; **III:** 145, 151, 152, 153, 159, 398, 476, 478, 609, 613; **IV:** 291, 363, 368, 370; **Supp. I Part 1:** 153, 284; **Supp. I Part 2:** 491; **Supp. V:** 97; **Supp. VIII:** 332; **Supp. XV:** 265, 266
"Sophronsiba" (Bourne), **I:** 221
Sorcerer's Apprentice, The: Tales and Conjurations (Johnson), **Supp. VI: 192-193,** 194
"Sorcerer's Eye, The" (Nemerov), **III:** 283
Sordello (Browning), **III:** 467, 469, 470
"Sordid? Good God!" (Williams), **Retro. Supp. II:** 334
"Sorghum" (Mason), **Supp. VIII:** 146
Sorokin, Pitirim, **Supp. I Part 2:** 679
Sorrentino, Gilbert, **Retro. Supp. I:** 426; **Supp. IV Part 1:** 286; **Supp. XII:** 139
"Sorrow" (Komunyakaa), **Supp. XIII:** 119
Sorrow Dance, The (Levertov), **Supp.**

III Part 1: 279-280, 283
"Sorrowful Guest, A" (Jewett), **Retro. Supp. II:** 137
Sorrows of Fat City, The: A Selection of Literary Essays and Reviews (Garrett), **Supp. VII:** 111
Sorrows of Young Werther, The (Goethe), **Supp. XI:** 169
Sorrows of Young Werther, The (Goethe; Bogan and Mayer, trans.), **Supp. III Part 1:** 63
"Sorting Facts; or, Nineteen Ways of Looking at Marker" (Howe), **Supp. IV Part 2:** 434, 436
"Sort of Song, A" (W. C. Williams), **Supp. XVII:** 243
"S O S" (Baraka), **Supp. II Part 1:** 50
"So Sassafras" (Olson), **Supp. II Part 2:** 574
"So There" (Creeley), **Supp. IV Part 1:** 157
Sotirov, Vasil, **Supp. IX:** 152
Soto, Gary, **Supp. IV Part 2:** 545; **Supp. V:** 180; **Supp. XI:** 270; **Supp. XIII:** 313, 315, 316, 320, 323; **Supp. XV:** 73
"Soto Thinking of the Ocean" (Salinas), **Supp. XIII:** 321
"Sotto Voce" (Kunitz), **Supp. III Part 1:** 265
Sot-Weed Factor, The (Barth), **I:** 122, 123, 125, 129, 130, 131-134, 135
Soul, The (Brooks), **I:** 244
Soul and Body of John Brown, The (Rukeyser), **Supp. VI:** 273
Soul Clap Hands and Sing (Marshall), **Supp. XI:** 276, 278, **280-282**

SOUL EXPEDITIONS (SINGER). *SEE* SHOSHA (SINGER)
Soul Gone Home (Hughes), **Retro. Supp. I:** 203; **Supp. I Part 1:** 328
"Soul inside the Sentence, The" (Gass), **Supp. VI:** 88
Soul Is Here for Its Own Joy, The (Bly, ed.), **Supp. IV Part 1:** 74
Soul of Man under Socialism, The (Wilde), **Supp. IX:** 134-135
Soul of the Far East, The (Lowell), **II:** 513
Soul on Ice (Cleaver), **Retro. Supp. II:** 12, 13
"Souls Belated" (Wharton), **Retro. Supp. I:** 364
"Soul selects her own Society, The" (Dickinson), **Retro. Supp. I:** 37
Souls of Black Folk, The (Du Bois),

Supp. II Part 1: 33, 40, 160, 168-170, 176, 183; **Supp. IV Part 1:** 164; **Supp. IX:** 305, 306; **Supp. X:** 133; **Supp. XIII:** 185, 238, 243
"Sound, The" (Olds), **Supp. X:** 214
"Sound and Fury" (O. Henry), **Supp. II Part 1:** 402
Sound and the Fury, The (Faulkner), **I:** 480; **II:** 55, 57, 58-60, 73; **III:** 237; **IV:** 100, 101, 104; **Retro. Supp. I:** 73, 75, 77, 82, **83-84**, 86, 88, 89, 90, 91, 92; **Supp. VIII:** 215; **Supp. IX:** 103; **Supp. X:** 44; **Supp. XII:** 33; **Supp. XIV:**12; **Supp. XVII:** 138
"Sound Bites" (Alvarez), **Supp. VII:** 11
Sound I Listened For, The (Francis), **Supp. IX: 78-79,** 87
"Sound Mind, Sound Body" (Lowell), **II:** 554
"Sound of Distant Thunder, A" (Elkin), **Supp. VI: 42-43,** 44
"Sound of Light, The" (Merwin), **Supp. III Part 1:** 356
Sound of Mountain Water, The (Stegner), **Supp. IV Part 2:** 595, 596, 598, 600, 608
"Sound of Talking" (Purdy), **Supp. VII:** 270
Sounds of Poetry, The (Pinsky), **Supp. VI:** 236, 247, 248
Soupault, Philippe, **IV:** 288, 404; **Retro. Supp. II:** 85, 321, 324
Source (Doty), **Supp. XI:** 121, **134-137**
"Source" (Doty), **Supp. XI:** 136
"Source, The" (Olds), **Supp. X:** 211
"Source, The" (Porter), **III:** 443
Source of Light, The (Price), **Supp. VI:** 262, 266
"Sources of Soviet Conduct, The" (Kennan), **Supp. VIII:** 241
Sour Grapes (W. C. Williams), **Retro. Supp. I:** 418
"South" (Levis), **Supp. XI:** 266
"South, The" (Hughes), **Supp. I Part 1:** 321
"Southbound on the Freeway" (Swenson), **Supp. IV Part 2:** 643
South Dakota Guidebook, The (C. Baxter), **Supp. XVII:** 15
Southern, Terry, **Supp. IV Part 1:** 379; **Supp. V:** 40, 201; **Supp. XI: 293-310; Supp. XVI:**230
Southern Cross, The (Wright), **Supp. V:** 332, 342
"Southern Cross, The" (Wright), **Supp. V:** 338
"Southerner's Problem, The" (Du

Bois), **Supp. II Part 1:** 168
"Southern Girl" (Zelda Fitzgerald), **Supp. IX:** 71
"Southern Mode of the Imagination, A" (Tate), **IV:** 120
"Southern Romantic, A" (Tate), **Supp. I Part 1:** 373
Southern Terry, **Supp. XIV:**82
Southey, Robert, **II:** 304, 502; **Supp. I Part 1:** 154
South Moon Under (Rawlings), **Supp. X: 225-226,** 229, 233
South Pacific Affair (Lacy), **Supp. XV:** 206
Southpaw, The (Harris), **II:** 424-425
"South Sangamon" (Cisneros), **Supp. VII:** 66
Southwell, Robert, **IV:** 151
Southwick, Marcia, **Supp. XI:** 259
Southworth, E. D. E. N, **Retro. Supp. I:** 246
Souvenir of the Ancient World, Selected Poems of Carlos Drummond de Andrade (Strand, trans.), **Supp. IV Part 2:** 630
"Sow" (Plath), **Supp. I Part 2:** 537
Space between Our Footsteps, The: Poems and Paintings from the Middle East (Nye, ed.), **Supp. XIII:** 280
"Space Quale, The" (James), **II:** 349
"Spaces Between, The" (Kingsolver), **Supp. VII:** 209
Spackman, Peter, **Supp. XVI:**221
Spacks, Patricia, **Supp. XVI:**251
"Spain" (Auden), **Supp. II Part 1:** 12-13, 14
"Spain in Fifty-Ninth Street" (White), **Supp. I Part 2:** 677
"Spanish-American War Play" (Crane), **I:** 422
Spanish Ballads (Merwin, trans.), **Supp. III Part 1:** 347
Spanish Bayonet (Benét), **Supp. XI:** 45, 47
Spanish Earth, The (film), **Retro. Supp. I:** 184
Spanish Papers and Other Miscellanies (Irving), **II:** 314
"Spanish Revolution, The" (Bryant), **Supp. I Part 1:** 153, 168
Spanish Student, The (Longfellow), **II:** 489, 506; **Retro. Supp. II:** 165
Spanking the Maid (Coover), **Supp. V:** 47, 48, 49, 52
Spargo, John, **Supp. I Part 1:** 13
"Spark, The" (Wharton), **Retro. Supp. I:** 381
"Sparkles from the Wheel" (Whitman), **IV:** 348

Sparks, Debra, **Supp. X:** 177
Sparks, Jared, **Supp. I Part 1:** 156
"Sparrow" (Berry), **Supp. X:** 31
Sparrow, Henry, **III:** 587
Sparrow, Mrs. Henry, **III:** 587
"Sparrow's Gate, The" (B. Kelly), **Supp. XVII:** 133
Spaulding, William, **Supp. XVI:** 106
"Spawning Run, The" (Humphrey), **Supp. IX:** 95
"Speak, Gay Memory" (Kirp), **Supp. XI:** 129
Speak, Memory (Nabokov), **III:** 247-250, 252; **Retro. Supp. I:** 264, 265, 266, 267, 268, 277; **Supp. XVI:** 148
Speak, Memory (V. Nabokov), **Supp. XVII:** 47
Speaking and Language (Shapiro), **Supp. II Part 2:** 721
Speaking for Nature: How Literary Naturalists from Henry Thoreau to Rachel Carson Have Shaped America (Brooks), **Supp. IX:** 31
Speaking for Ourselves: American Ethnic Writing (Faderman and Bradshaw, eds.), **Supp. XIII:** 313
Speaking of Accidents (Everwine), **Supp. XV:** 75, 88
"Speaking of Accidents" (Everwine), **Supp. XV:** 88-89
"Speaking of Counterweights" (White), **Supp. I Part 2:** 669
Speaking of Literature and Society (Trilling), **Supp. III Part 2:** 494, 496, 499
"Speaking of Love" (Gioia), **Supp. XV:** 124-125
Speaking on Stage (Kolin and Kullman, eds.), **Supp. IX:** 145
Speaking on Stage: Interviews with Contemporary American Playwrights (Balakian), **Supp. XV:** 327
"Speaking Passions" (Kitchen), **Supp. XV:** 215
Speak What We Feel (Not What We Ought to Say): Reflections on Literature and Faith (Buechner), **Supp. XII:** 57
Spear, Roberta, **Supp. V:** 180; **Supp. XV:** 73
"Special Kind of Fantasy, A: James Dickey on the Razor's Edge" (Niflis), **Supp. IV Part 1:** 175
"Special Pleading" (Lanier), **Supp. I Part 1:** 364
"Special Problems in Teaching Leslie Marmon Silko's *Ceremony*" (Gunn Allen), **Supp. IV Part 1:** 333
Special Providence, A (Yates), **Supp. XI:** 342, **344-345**

"Special Time, a Special School, A" (Knowles), **Supp. XII:** 236
Special View of History, The (Olson), **Supp. II Part 2:** 566, 569, 572
Specimen Days (Whitman), **IV:** 338, 347, 348, 350; **Retro. Supp. I:** 408
Specimens of the American Poets, **Supp. I Part 1:** 155
"Spectacles, The" (Poe), **III:** 425
Spectator Bird, The (Stegner), **Supp. IV Part 2:** 599, 604, 606, 611-612
Spector, Robert, **Supp. XIII:** 87
Spectra: A Book of Poetic Experiments (Bynner and Ficke), **Supp. XV:** 43
"Spectre Bridegroom, The" (Irving), **II:** 304
"Spectre Pig, The" (Holmes), **Supp. I Part 1:** 302
"Speculating Woman" (X. J. Kennedy), **Supp. XV:** 168
"Speech Sounds" (O. Butler), **Supp. XIII:** 61, **70**
"Speech to a Crowd" (MacLeish), **III:** 16
"Speech to the Detractors" (MacLeish), **III:** 16
"Speech to the Young" (Brooks), **Supp. III Part 1:** 79, 86
"Speech to Those Who Say Comrade" (MacLeish), **III:** 16
Speedboat (Adler), **Supp. X:** 171
Speed of Darkness, The (Rukeyser), **Supp. VI:** 274, 281
Speed-the-Plow (Mamet), **Supp. XIV:** 241, 246, 249, 250, 251
Speilberg, Steven, **Supp. XI:** 234
"Spell" (Francis), **Supp. IX:** 87
Spelling Dictionary, A (Rowson), **Supp. XV:** 244
Spence, Thomas, **Supp. I Part 2:** 518
Spence + Lila (Mason), **Supp. VIII:** 133, **143-145**
Spencer, Edward, **Supp. I Part 1:** 357, 360
Spencer, Herbert, **I:** 515; **II:** 345, 462-463, 480, 483, 536; **III:** 102, 315; **IV:** 135; **Retro. Supp. II:** 60, 65, 93, 98; **Supp. I Part 1:** 368; **Supp. I Part 2:** 635
Spencer, Sharon, **Supp. X:** 185, 186, 195, 196
Spencer, Theodore, **I:** 433; **Supp. III Part 1:** 2
Spender, Natasha, **Supp. IV Part 1:** 119, 127, 134
Spender, Stephen, **II:** 371; **III:** 504, 527; **Retro. Supp. I:** 216; **Retro. Supp. II:** 243, 244; **Supp. I Part 2:** 536; **Supp. II Part 1:** 11; **Supp. IV Part 1:** 82, 134; **Supp. IV Part 2:** 440; **Supp. X:** 116

Spengler, Oswald, **I:** 255, 270; **II:** 7, 577; **III:** 172, 176; **Retro. Supp. II:** 324; **Supp. I Part 2:** 647
Spens, Sir Patrick, **Supp. I Part 2:** 404
Spenser, Edmund, **I:** 62; **III:** 77, 78, 89; **IV:** 155, 453; **Retro. Supp. I:** 62; **Supp. I Part 1:** 98, 152, 369; **Supp. I Part 2:** 422, 719
"Spenser's Ireland" (Moore), **III:** 211, 212
Sperry, Margaret, **Supp. IV Part 1:** 169
Sphere: The Form of a Motion (Ammons), **Supp. VII:** 24, 32, 33, 35, 36
"Sphinx" (Hayden), **Supp. II Part 1:** 373
"Spiced Plums" (Ríos), **Supp. IV Part 2:** 553
"Spider and the Ghost of the Fly, The" (Lindsay), **Supp. I Part 2:** 375
Spider Bay (Van Vechten), **Supp. II Part 2:** 746
"Spiders" (Schwartz), **Supp. II Part 2:** 665
Spider's House, The (Bowles), **Supp. IV Part 1:** 87-89, 90, 91
Spider Woman's Granddaughters: Traditional Tales and Contemporary Writing by Native American Women (Gunn Allen, ed.), **Supp. IV Part 1:** 320, 326, 332-333; **Supp. IV Part 2:** 567
Spiegelman, Art, **Supp. XVII:** 48
Spiegelman, Willard, **Supp. XI:** 126
Spillane, Mickey, **Supp. IV Part 2:** 469, 472; **Supp. XV:** 200
Spiller, Robert E., **I:** 241; **Supp. I Part 1:** 104
"Spillikins: Gregor Mendel at the Table" (Bierds), **Supp. XVII:** 34-35
Spillway (Barnes), **Supp. III Part 1:** 44
Spingarn, Amy, **Supp. I Part 1:** 325, 326
Spingarn, Joel, **I:** 266; **Supp. I Part 1:** 325
Spinoza, Baruch, **I:** 493; **II:** 590, 593; **III:** 600; **IV:** 5, 7, 11, 12, 17; **Retro. Supp. II:** 300; **Supp. I Part 1:** 274; **Supp. I Part 2:** 643; **Supp. XVI:** 184
"Spinoza of Market Street, The" (Singer), **IV:** 12-13; **Retro. Supp. II:** 307
"Spinster" (Plath), **Supp. I Part 2:** 536
"Spinster's Tale, A" (Taylor), **Supp. V:** 314-315, 316-317, 319, 323
Spiral of Memory, The: Interviews

(Coltelli, ed.), **Supp. XII:** 215
Spires, Elizabeth, **Supp. X:** 8
"Spire Song" (Bowles), **Supp. IV Part 1:** 80
Spirit and the Flesh, The: Sexual Diversity in American Indian Culture (W. L. Williams), **Supp. IV Part 1:** 330
"Spirit Birth" (Cullen), **Supp. IV Part 1:** 168
Spirit in Man, The (Jung), **Supp. IV Part 1:** 68
Spirit of Culver (West), **IV:** 287
Spirit of Labor, The (Hapgood), **Supp. XVII:** 96, 99, 101-102
Spirit of Romance, The (Pound), **III:** 470; **Retro. Supp. I:** 286
Spirit of the Ghetto, The: Studies of the Jewish Quarter of New York (Hapgood), **Supp. XVII:** 96, 101, 103, 106
Spirit of Youth and the City Streets, The (Addams), **Supp. I Part 1:** 6-7, 12-13, 16, 17, 19
"Spirits" (Bausch), **Supp. VII:** 46-47
Spirits, and Other Stories (Bausch), **Supp. VII:** 46-47, 54
"Spirit Says, You Are Nothing, The" (Levis), **Supp. XI:** 265-266
Spiritual Conflict, The (Scupoli), **IV:** 156
Spiritual Exercises, The (Loyola), **IV:** 151; **Supp. XI:** 162
"Spiritual Manifestation, A" (Whittier), **Supp. I Part 2:** 699
"Spirituals and Neo-Spirituals" (Hurston), **Supp. VI:** 152-153
Spits, Ellen Handler, **Supp. XII:** 166
"Spitzbergen Tales" (Crane), **I:** 409, 415, 423
Spitzer, Philip, **Supp. XIV:** 21
"Spleen" (Eliot), **I:** 569, 573-574
Spleen de Paris, Le (Baudelaire), **Supp. XIV:** 337
Splendid Drunken Twenties, The (Van Vechten), **Supp. II Part 2:** 739-744
"Splinters" (Bukiet), **Supp. XVII:** 47
"Splittings" (Rich), **Supp. I Part 2:** 570-571
"Splitting Wood at Six Above" (Kumin), **Supp. IV Part 2:** 449
Spofford, Harriet Prescott, **Supp. XIII:** 143
Spoils of Poynton, The (James), **I:** 463; **Retro. Supp. I:** 229-230
Spoken Page, The (Nye), **Supp. XIII:** 274
"Spokes" (Auster), **Supp. XII:** 23
Spokesmen (Whipple), **II:** 456

Spook Sonata, The (Strindberg), **III:** 387, 392
Spooky Art, The: A Book about Writing (Mailer), **Retro. Supp. II:** 214
"Spoon, The" (Simic), **Supp. VIII:** 275
Spoon River Anthology (Masters), **I:** 106; **III:** 579; **Supp. I Part 2:** 454, 455, 456, 460-465, 466, 467, 471, 472, 473, 476; **Supp. IX:** 306; **Supp. XIV:** 282-283
Sport and a Pastime, A (Salter), **Supp. IX: 254-257; Supp. XVI:** 237
Sporting Club, The (McGuane), **Supp. VIII:** 43
Sport of the Gods, The (Dunbar), **Supp. II Part 1:** 193, 200, 207, 214-217
"Sportsman Born and Bred, A" (Plimpton), **Supp. XVI:** 241
Sportsman's Sketches, A (Turgenev), **I:** 106; **IV:** 277
Sportswriter, The (Ford), **Supp. V:** 57, 58, 62-67
"Spotted Horses" (Faulkner), **IV:** 260
Sprague, Morteza, **Retro. Supp. II:** 115
Spratling, William, **II:** 56; **Retro. Supp. I:** 80
Sprawl trilogy (W. Gibson), **Supp. XVI:** 117, 122, 124
"Spray Paint King, The" (Dovc), **Supp. IV Part 1:** 252-253
Spreading Fires (Knowles), **Supp. XII:** 249
Sprigge, Elizabeth, **IV:** 31
"Spring" (Millay), **III:** 126
"Spring" (Mora), **Supp. XIII:** 217
"Spring 1967" (Carruth), **Supp. XVI:** 55
Spring and All (W. C. Williams), **Retro. Supp. I:** 412, 418, **418-420**, 427, 430, 431
"Spring and All" (W. C. Williams), **Retro. Supp. I:** 419
"Spring Break-Up" (Carruth), **Supp. XVI:** 56
"Spring Bulletin" (Allen), **Supp. XV:** 15
Springer's Progress (Markson), **Supp. XVII: 141-142,** 143, 146
"Spring Evening" (Farrell), **II:** 45
"Spring Evening" (Kenyon), **Supp. VII:** 173
"Springfield Magical" (Lindsay), **Supp. I Part 2:** 379
Spring in New Hampshire and Other Poems (McKay), **Supp. X:** 131, 135
"Spring Notes from Robin Hill" (Carruth), **Supp. XVI:** 48
"Spring Pastoral" (Wylie), **Supp. I Part 2:** 707

"Spring Pools" (Frost), **II:** 155; **Retro. Supp. I:** 137
"Spring Snow" (Matthews), **Supp. IX:** 160
"SPRING SONG" (Baraka), **Supp. II Part 1:** 60
Springsteen, Bruce, **Supp. VIII:** 143
"Spring Strains" (W. C. Williams), **Retro. Supp. I:** 416
Spring Tides (Morison), **Supp. I Part 2:** 494
Springtime and Harvest (Sinclair), **Supp. V:** 280
Spruance, Raymond, **Supp. I Part 2:** 479, 491
"Spruce Has No Taproot, The" (Clampitt), **Supp. IX:** 41-42
"Spunk" (Hurston), **Supp. VI:** 150, 151-152
Spunk: The Selected Stories (Hurston), **Supp. VI:** 150
Spurr, David, **Supp. XV:** 183
Spy, The (Cooper), **I:** 335, 336, 337, 339, 340; **Supp. I Part 1:** 155
"Spy, The" (Francis), **Supp. IX:** 81
Spy, The (Freneau), **Supp. II Part 1:** 260
Spy in the House of Love, A (Nin), **Supp. X:** 186
Squanto, **Supp. I Part 2:** 486
"Square Business" (Baraka), **Supp. II Part 1:** 49
Square Root of Wonderful, The (McCullers), **II:** 587-588
"Squash in Blossom" (Francis), **Supp. IX:** 81
"Squatter on Company Land, The" (Hugo), **Supp. VI:** 133
"Squatter's Children" (Bishop), **Retro. Supp. II:** 47
"Squeak, Memory" (Bukiet), **Supp. XVII:** 47
Squeeze Play (Auster), **Supp. XII:** 21
Squires, Radcliffe, **IV:** 127; **Supp. XV:** 118
Squirrels (Mamet), **Supp. XIV:** 240
S.S. Gliencairn (O'Neill), **III:** 387, 388, 405
S.S. San Pedro (Cozzens), **I:** 360-362, 370, 378, 379
"Ssshh" (Olds), **Supp. X:** 215
St. John, David, **Supp. XV:** 73, 253
"Stacking the Straw" (Clampitt), **Supp. IX:** 41
Stade, George, **Supp. IV Part 1:** 286
Staël, Madame de, **II:** 298
"Staff of Life, The" (H. Miller), **III:** 187
Stafford, Jean, **II:** 537; **Retro. Supp. II:** 177; **Supp. V:** 316

INDEX / 503

Stafford, William, **Supp. IV Part 1:** 72; **Supp. IV Part 2:** 642; **Supp. IX:** 273; **Supp. XI: 311-332; Supp. XIII:** 76, 274, 276, 277, 281, 283; **Supp. XIV:**119, 123
"Stage All Blood, The" (MacLeish), **III:** 18
"Staggerlee Wonders" (Baldwin), **Retro. Supp. II:** 15
Stained White Radiance, A (Burke), **Supp. XIV:**28, 31
Stalin, Joseph, **I:** 261, 490; **II:** 39, 40, 49, 564; **III:** 30, 298; **IV:** 372; **Supp. V:** 290
"Stalking the Billion-Footed Beast: A Literary Manifesto for the New Social Novel" (Wolfe), **Supp. III Part 2:** 586
Stallman, R. W., **I:** 405
Stamberg, Susan, **Supp. IV Part 1:** 201; **Supp. XII:** 193
Stamford, Anne Marie, **Supp. XII:** 162
Stanard, Mrs. Jane, **III:** 410, 413
Stand, The (King), **Supp. V:** 139, 140-141, 144-146, 148, 152
"Standard of Liberty, The" (Rowson), **Supp. XV:** 243
"Standard of Living, The" (Parker), **Supp. IX: 198-199**
Stander, Lionel, **Supp. I Part 1:** 289
"Standing and the Waiting, The" (M. F. K. Fisher), **Supp. XVII:** 83
Standing by Words (Berry), **Supp. X:** 22, 27, 28, 31, 32, 33, 35
"Standing Halfway Home" (Wagoner), **Supp. IX:** 324
Stand in the Mountains, A (Taylor), **Supp. V:** 324
Standish, Burt L. (pseudonym). *See* Patten, Gilbert
Standish, Miles, **I:** 471; **II:** 502-503
Standley, Fred L., **Retro. Supp. II:** 6
Stand Still Like the Hummingbird (H. Miller), **III:** 184
"Stand Up" (Salinas), **Supp. XIII:** 315
Stand with Me Here (Francis), **Supp. IX:** 76
Stanford, Ann, **Retro. Supp. I:** 41; **Supp. I Part 1:** 99, 100, 102, 103, 106, 108, 109, 113, 117; **Supp. IV Part 2:** 637
Stanford, Donald E., **II:** 217
Stanford, Frank, **Supp. XV:** 338, 339, 341, 342-343, 343, 345, 348, 350
Stanford, Ginny (Crouch), **Supp. XV:** 339
Stanford, Leland, **I:** 196, 198
Stanislavsky, Konstantin, **Supp. XIV:**240, 243

"Stanley Kunitz" (Oliver), **Supp. VII:** 237
Stansell, Christine, **Supp. XVII:** 106
Stanton, Frank L., **Supp. II Part 1:** 192
Stanton, Robert J., **Supp. IV Part 2:** 681
"Stanzas from the Grande Chartreuse" (Arnold), **Supp. I Part 2:** 417
Stanzas in Meditation (Stein), **Supp. III Part 1:** 13
Staples, Hugh, **Retro. Supp. II:** 187
Star, Alexander, **Supp. X:** 310
Starbuck, George, **Retro. Supp. II:** 53, 245; **Supp. I Part 2:** 538; **Supp. IV Part 2:** 440; **Supp. XIII:** 76
Star Child (Gunn Allen), **Supp. IV Part 1:** 324
Stardust Memories (film; Allen), **Supp. XV:** 1, 4, **8,** 9, 13
"Stare, The" (Updike), **Retro. Supp. I:** 329
"Starfish, The" (R. Bly), **Supp. IV Part 1:** 72
"Staring at the Sea on the Day of the Death of Another" (Swenson), **Supp. IV Part 2:** 652
Star Is Born, A (film), **Supp. IV Part 1:** 198; **Supp. IX:** 198
Stark, David, **Supp. XII:** 202
"Stark Boughs on the Family Tree" (Oliver), **Supp. VII:** 232
Starke, Aubrey Harrison, **Supp. I Part 1:** 350, 352, 356, 360, 362, 365, 370, 371
Starkey, David, **Supp. XII:** 180, 181
"Starlight" (Levine), **Supp. V:** 188
"Starlight Scope Myopia" (Komunyakaa), **Supp. XIII:** 123, 124
Starnino, Carmine, **Supp. XVII:** 74
"Star of the Nativity" (Brodsky), **Supp. VIII:** 33
Starr, Ellen Gates, **Supp. I Part 1:** 4, 5, 11
Starr, Jean. *See* Untermeyer, Jean Starr
Starr, Ringo, **Supp. XI:** 309
Star Rover, The (London), **II:** 467
"Starry Night, The" (Sexton), **Supp. II Part 2:** 681
"Stars" (Frost), **II:** 153
Stars, the Snow, the Fire, The: Twenty-five Years in the Northern Wilderness (Haines), **Supp. XII: 199-201,** 206, 209
Star Shines over Mt. Morris Park, A (H. Roth), **Supp. IX:** 227, 236, **236-237**
"Stars of the Summer Night" (Longfellow), **II:** 493

"Stars over Harlem" (Hughes), **Retro. Supp. I:** 207
"Star-Spangled" (García), **Supp. XI:** 177, 178
Star-Spangled Girl, The (Simon), **Supp. IV Part 2:** 579
"Star-Splitter, The" (Frost), **Retro. Supp. I:** 123, 133
Stars Principal (McClatchy), **Supp. XII: 256-258**
"Starting from Paumanok" (Whitman), **IV:** 333
Starting Out in the Thirties (Kazin), **Supp. VIII: 95-97**
"Starved Lovers" (MacLeish), **III:** 19
Starved Rock (Masters), **Supp. I Part 2:** 465
"Starving Again" (Moore), **Supp. X:** 163, 172, 175
"State, The" (Bourne), **I:** 233
State and Main (Mamet), **Supp. XIV:**241
"Statement: Phillipa Allen" (Rukeyser), **Supp. VI:** 283-284
"Statement of Principles" (Ransom), **III:** 496
"Statements on Poetics" (Snyder), **Supp. VIII:** 291, 292
"Statement with Rhymes" (Kees), **Supp. XV:** 139
"State of the Art, The" (Elkin), **Supp. VI:** 52
"State of the Arts, The" (Wasserstein), **Supp. XV:** 332
State of the Nation (Dos Passos), **I:** 489
"State of the Union" (Vidal), **Supp. IV Part 2:** 678
Static Element, The: Selected Poems of Natan Zach (Everwine, trans.), **Supp. XV:** 73, 75, **85-88**
"Statue, The" (Berryman), **I:** 173
"Statue and Birds" (Bogan), **Supp. III Part 1:** 50
"Statues, The" (Schwartz), **Supp. II Part 2:** 654, 659
"Status Rerum" (Pound), **Supp. I Part 1:** 257
Stavans, Ilan, **Supp. XI:** 190
"Staying Alive" (Levertov), **Supp. III Part 1:** 281
Staying Alive (Wagoner), **Supp. IX:** 324, **326**
"Staying at Ed's Place" (Swenson), **Supp. IV Part 2:** 648
Staying Put : Making a Home in a Restless World (Sanders), **Supp. XVI:**274-275
Stay Me, Oh Comfort Me: Journals and Stories, 1933-1941 (M. F. K.

Fisher), **Supp. XVII:** 92
Stayton, Richard, **Supp. IX:** 133
Steadman, Goodman, **IV:** 147
"Steak" (Snyder), **Supp. VIII:** 301
Steal Away: Selected and New Poems (Wright), **Supp. XV:** 337, 340, 348, 350-351
Stealing Beauty (Minot), **Supp. VI:** 205
Stealing Glimpses (McQuade), **Supp. IX:** 151
Stealing the Language: The Emergence of Women's Poetry in America (Ostriker), **Supp. XV:** 251
"Stealing the Thunder: Future Visions for American Indian Women, Tribes, and Literary Studies" (Gunn Allen), **Supp. IV Part 1:** 331
"Steam Shovel Cut" (Masters), **Supp. I Part 2:** 468
Stearns, Harold, **I:** 245; **Supp. XVII:** 106
Stedman, Edmund Clarence, **Supp. I Part 1:** 372; **Supp. II Part 1:** 192; **Supp. XV:** 115, 269, 273, 274, 282, 286
Steele, Max, **Supp. XIV:** 82
Steele, Sir Richard, **I:** 378; **II:** 105, 107, 300; **III:** 430
Steele, Timothy, **Supp. XV:** 251; **Supp. XVII:** 112
Steenburgen, Mary, **Supp. IV Part 1:** 236
Steeple Bush (Frost), **II:** 155; **Retro. Supp. I:** 140; **Retro. Supp. II:** 42
"Steeple-Jack, The" (Moore), **III:** 212, 213, 215
"Steerage" (Goldbarth), **Supp. XII:** 187
Steers, Nina, **Retro. Supp. II:** 25
Steffens, Lincoln, **II:** 577; **III:** 580; **Retro. Supp. I:** 202; **Retro. Supp. II:** 101; **Supp. I Part 1:** 7; **Supp. XVII:** 98, 101, 106-107
Stegner, Page, **IV:** 114, 116; **Supp. IV Part 2:** 599
Stegner, Wallace, **Supp. IV Part 2:** **595-618; Supp. V:** 220, 224, 296; **Supp. X:** 23, 24; **Supp. XIV:** 82, 193, 230, 233
"Stegner's Short Fiction" (Ahearn), **Supp. IV Part 2:** 604
Steichen, Edward, **III:** 580, 594-595
Steichen, Lillian. *See* Sandburg, Mrs. Carl (Lillian Steichen)
Steier, Rod, **Supp. VIII:** 269
Steiger, Rod, **Supp. XI:** 305
Stein, Gertrude, **I:** 103, 105, 476; **II:** 56, 251, 252, 257, 260, 262-263, 264, 289; **III:** 71, 454, 471-472, 600; **IV: 24-48,** 368, 375, 404, 415, 443, 477; **Retro. Supp. I:** 108, 170, 176, 177, 186, 418, 422; **Retro. Supp. II:** 85, 207, 326, 331; **Supp. I Part 1:** 292; **Supp. III Part 1:** 13, 37, 225, 226; **Supp. III Part 2:** 626; **Supp. IV Part 1:** 11, 79, 80, 81, 322; **Supp. IV Part 2:** 468; **Supp. V:** 53; **Supp. IX:** 55, 57, 62, 66; **Supp. XII:** 1, 139; **Supp. XIV:** 336; **Supp. XVI:** 187; **Supp. XVII:** 98, 105, 107
Stein, Jean, **Supp. XVI:** 245
Stein, Karen F., **Supp. XIII:** 29, 30
Stein, Leo, **IV:** 26; **Supp. XIV:** 336; **Supp. XV:** 298
Stein, Lorin, **Supp. XII:** 254
Steinbeck, John, **I:** 107, 288, 301, 378, 495, 519; **II:** 272; **III:** 382, 453, 454, 589; **IV: 49-72; Retro. Supp. II:** 19, 196; **Supp. IV Part 1:** 102, 225; **Supp. IV Part 2:** 502; **Supp. V:** 290, 291; **Supp. VIII:** 10; **Supp. IX:** 33, 171; **Supp. XI:** 169; **Supp. XIII:** 1, 17; **Supp. XIV:** 21, 181; **Supp. XVII:** 228
Steinbeck, Olive Hamilton, **IV:** 51
Steinberg, Saul, **Supp. VIII:** 272
Steinberg, Sybil, **Supp. XVII:** 165, 166
Steinem, Gloria, **Supp. IV Part 1:** 203
Steiner, George, **Retro. Supp. I:** 327; **Supp. IV Part 1:** 286; **Supp. XVI:** 230
Steiner, Nancy, **Supp. I Part 2:** 529
Steiner, Stan, **Supp. IV Part 2:** 505
Steinfels, Margaret, **Supp. XVII:** 170
Steinhoff, Eirik, **Supp. XVI:** 290
Steinman, Michael, **Supp. VIII:** 172
Steinmetz, Charles Proteus, **I:** 483
Steinway Quintet Plus Four, The (Epstein), **Supp. XII:** 159, **162-166**
Stekel, Wilhelm, **III:** 554
Stella (Goethe), **Supp. IX:** 133, 138
Stella (Kushner), **Supp. IX:** 133
Stella, Joseph, **I:** 387
"Stellaria" (Francis), **Supp. IX:** 83
Stelligery and Other Essays (Wendell), **Supp. I Part 2:** 414
Stendhal, **I:** 316; **III:** 465, 467; **Supp. I Part 1:** 293; **Supp. I Part 2:** 445
Stepanchev, Stephen, **Supp. XI:** 312
Stephen, Leslie, **IV:** 440
Stephen, Saint, **II:** 539; **IV:** 228
Stephen, Sir Leslie, **IV:** 440; **Supp. I Part 1:** 306
Stephen Crane (Berryman), **I:** 169-170, 405
Stephen King: The Art of Darkness (Winter), **Supp. V:** 144
Stephen King, The Second Decade: "Danse Macabre" to "The Dark Half" (Magistrale), **Supp. V:** 138, 146, 151
Stephens, Jack, **Supp. X:** 11, 14, 15, 17
Stephenson, Gregory, **Supp. XII:** 120, 123
"Stepping Out" (Dunn), **Supp. XI:** 140, 141
Steps (Kosinski), **Supp. VII:** 215, 221-222, 225
"Steps" (Nye), **Supp. XIII:** 288
Steps to the Temple (Crashaw), **IV:** 145
"Steps Toward Poverty and Death" (R. Bly), **Supp. IV Part 1:** 60
Stepto, Robert B., **Retro. Supp. II:** 116, 120, 123
Sterile Cuckoo, The (Nichols), **Supp. XIII:** 258, **259-263,** 264
Sterling, Bruce, **Supp. XVI:** 118, 121, 123, 124, 128-129
Sterling, George, **I:** 199, 207, 208, 209; **II:** 440; **Supp. V:** 286
Stern, Bernhard J., **Supp. XIV:** 202, 213
Stern, Daniel, **Supp. VIII:** 238
Stern, Frederick C., **Supp. X:** 114, 115, 117
Stern, Gerald, **Supp. IX: 285-303; Supp. XI:** 139, 267; **Supp. XV:** 211, 212
Stern, Madeleine B., **Supp. I Part 1:** 35
Stern, Maurice, **IV:** 285
Stern, Philip Van Doren, **Supp. XIII:** 164
Stern, Richard, **Retro. Supp. II:** 291
Stern, Richard G., **Retro. Supp. II:** 204
Stern, Steven, **Supp. XVII:** 42, 48, 49
"Sterne" (Schwartz), **Supp. II Part 2:** 663
Sterne, Laurence, **II:** 302, 304-305, 308; **III:** 454; **IV:** 68, 211, 465; **Supp. I Part 2:** 714; **Supp. IV Part 1:** 299; **Supp. V:** 127; **Supp. X:** 324; **Supp. XV:** 232
Sterritt, David, **Supp. IV Part 2:** 574
Stetson, Caleb, **IV:** 178
Stetson, Charles Walter, **Supp. XI:** 195, 196, 197, 202, 204, 209
Stevens, Mrs. Wallace (Elsie Kachel), **IV:** 75
Stevens, Wallace, **I:** 60, 61, 266, 273, 462, 521, 528, 540-541; **II:** 56, 57, 530, 552, 556; **III:** 19, 23, 194, 216, 270-271, 272, 278, 279, 281, 453, 463, 493, 509, 521, 523, 600, 605, 613, 614; **IV: 73-96,** 140, 141, 332,

402, 415; **Retro. Supp. I:** 67, 89, 193, 284, 288, **295-315,** 335, 403, 411, 416, 417, 422; **Retro. Supp. II:** 40, 44, 326; **Supp. I Part 1:** 80, 82, 257; **Supp. II Part 1:** 9, 18; **Supp. III Part 1:** 2, 3, 12, 20, 48, 239, 318, 319, 344; **Supp. III Part 2:** 611; **Supp. IV Part 1:** 72, 393; **Supp. IV Part 2:** 619, 620, 621, 634; **Supp. V:** 337; **Supp. VIII:** 21, 102, 195, 271, 292; **Supp. IX:** 41; **Supp. X:** 58; **Supp. XI:** 123, 191, 312; **Supp. XIII:** 44, 45; **Supp. XV:** 39, 41, 92, 115, 250, 261, 298, 302, 306, 307; **Supp. XVI:**64, 158, 202, 210, 288; **Supp. XVII:** 36, 42, 110, 129, 130, 240, 241

"Stevens and the Idea of the Hero" (Bromwich), **Retro. Supp. I:** 305
Stevenson, Adlai, **II:** 49; **III:** 581
Stevenson, Anne, **Supp. XV:** 121; **Supp. XVII:** 74
Stevenson, Burton E., **Supp. XIV:**120
Stevenson, David, **Supp. XI:** 230
Stevenson, Robert Louis, **I:** 2, 53; **II:** 283, 290, 311, 338; **III:** 328; **IV:** 183-184, 186, 187; **Retro. Supp. I:** 224, 228; **Supp. I Part 1:** 49; **Supp. II Part 1:** 404-405; **Supp. IV Part 1:** 298, 314; **Supp. VIII:** 125; **Supp. XIII:** 75; **Supp. XIV:**40; **Supp. XVII:** 69
Stevick, Robert D., **III:** 509
Stewart, Dugald, **II:** 8, 9; **Supp. I Part 1:** 151, 159; **Supp. I Part 2:** 422
Stewart, Jeffrey C., **Supp. XIV:**196, 209, 210
Stewart, Randall, **II:** 244
Stewart, Robert E., **Supp. XI:** 216
Stickeen (Muir), **Supp. IX:** 182
"Sticks and Stones" (L. Michaels), **Supp. XVI:**205
Sticks and Stones (Mumford), **Supp. II Part 2:** 475, 483, 487-488
Sticks & Stones (Matthews), **Supp. IX:** 154, 155, 157, 158
Stieglitz, Alfred, **Retro. Supp. I:** 416; **Retro. Supp. II:** 103; **Supp. VIII:** 98; **Supp. XVII:** 96
"Stigmata" (Oates), **Supp. II Part 2:** 520
Stiles, Ezra, **II:** 108, 122; **IV:** 144, 146, 148
Still, William Grant, **Retro. Supp. I:** 203
"Stillborn" (Plath), **Supp. I Part 2:** 544
"Still Here" (Hughes), **Retro. Supp. I:** 211
"Still Just Writing" (Tyler), **Supp. IV Part 2:** 658
"Still Life" (Hecht), **Supp. X:** 68
"Still Life" (Malamud), **Supp. I Part 2:** 450
"Still Life" (Sandburg), **III:** 584
"Still Life: Moonlight Striking up on a Chess-Board" (Lowell), **II:** 528
"Still Life Or" (Creeley), **Supp. IV Part 1:** 141, 150, 158
Still Life with Oysters and Lemon (Doty), **Supp. XI:** 119, 121, **133-134**
Still Life with Woodpecker (Robbins), **Supp. X:** 260, **271-274,** 282
"Still Moment, A" (Welty), **IV:** 265; **Retro. Supp. I:** 347
Stillness (Gardner), **Supp. VI:** 74
"Stillness in the Air" (Dickinson), **Supp. XV:** 261
Stillness of Dancing, The (Bierds), **Supp. XVII:** 27-28
"Still Small Voices, The" (Fante), **Supp. XI:** 164
Still Such (Salter), **Supp. IX:** 246
"Still the Place Where Creation Does Some Work on Itself" (Davis), **Supp. IV Part 1:** 68
Stimpson, Catharine R., **Supp. IV Part 2:** 686
Stimson, Eleanor Kenyon. *See* Brooks, Mrs. Van Wyck
"Stimulants, Poultices, Goads" (Wright), **Supp. XV:** 349
"Stings" (Plath), **Retro. Supp. II:** 255; **Supp. I Part 2:** 541
"Stirling Street September" (Baraka), **Supp. II Part 1:** 51
Stirner, Max, **II:** 27
"Stirrup-Cup, The" (Lanier), **Supp. I Part 1:** 364
Stitt, Peter, **Supp. IV Part 1:** 68; **Supp. IV Part 2:** 628; **Supp. IX:** 152, 163, 291, 299; **Supp. XI:** 311, 317; **Supp. XIII:** 87; **Supp. XV:** 98, 99
Stivers, Valerie, **Supp. X:** 311
Stock, Noel, **III:** 479
Stockton, Frank R., **I:** 201
Stoddard, Charles Warren, **I:** 193, 195, 196; **Supp. II Part 1:** 192, 341, 351
Stoddard, Elizabeth, **II:** 275; **Supp. XV: 269-291**
Stoddard, Richard, **Supp. I Part 1:** 372
Stoddard, Richard Henry, **Supp. XV:** 269, 271, 272, 273, 274, 278, 279, 286
Stoddard, Solomon, **I:** 545, 548; **IV:** 145, 148
Stoic, The (Dreiser), **I:** 497, 502, 508, 516; **Retro. Supp. II:** 95, 96, 101, 108

Stokes, Geoffrey, **Supp. XV:** 256
"Stolen Calf, The" (Dunbar), **Supp. II Part 1:** 196
Stolen Jew, The (Neugeboren), **Supp. XVI:222-224,** 225
Stolen Past, A (Knowles), **Supp. XII:** 249
Stollman, Aryeh Lev, **Supp. XVII:** 49
"Stone" (Ozick), **Supp. XVII:** 50
Stone, Edward, **III:** 479
Stone, I. F., **Supp. XIV:**3
Stone, Irving, **II:** 463, 466, 467
Stone, Oliver, **Supp. XIV:**48, 316
Stone, Phil, **II:** 55
Stone, Richard, **Supp. XIV:**54
Stone, Robert, **Supp. V: 295-312;** **Supp. X:** 1
Stone, Rosetta (pseud.). *See* Geisel, Theodor Seuss (Dr. Seuss)
Stone, Wilmer, **Supp. I Part 1:** 49
Stone and the Shell, The (Hay), **Supp. XIV:**122, 123, 127, 130
"Stone Bear, The" (Haines), **Supp. XII:** 206-207, 212
"Stone City" (Proulx), **Supp. VII:** 251-253
Stone Country (Sanders), **Supp. XVI:**271-272
Stone Diaries, The (Shields), **Supp. VII:** 307, 315, 324-326, 327
"Stone Dreams" (Kingsolver), **Supp. VII:** 203
Stone Harp, The (Haines), **Supp. XII:** **204,** 205, 206, 207
Stonemason, The (McCarthy), **Supp. VIII:** 175, 187
"Stones" (Kumin), **Supp. IV Part 2:** 447
"Stones, The" (Plath), **Supp. I Part 2:** 535, 539
"Stones in My Passway, Hellhounds on My Trail" (Boyle), **Supp. VIII:** 15
Stones of Florence, The (McCarthy), **II:** 562
"Stone Walls" (Sarton), **Supp. VIII:** 259
"Stop" (Wilbur), **Supp. III Part 2:** 556
"Stop Me If You've Heard This One" (Lardner), **II:** 433
Stopover: Tokyo (Marquand), **III:** 53, 57, 61, 70
Stoppard, Tom, **Retro. Supp. I:** 189
"Stopping by Woods" (Frost), **II:** 154
"Stopping by Woods on a Snowy Evening" (Frost), **Retro. Supp. I:** 129, 133, 134, 135, 139
Stopping Westward (Richards), **II:** 396
"Stop Player. Joke No. 4" (Gaddis), **Supp. IV Part 1:** 280

Stop-Time (Conroy), **Supp. XVI:63-71,** 72, 75, 76-77
Store, The (Stribling), **Supp. VIII:** 126
"*Store* and *Mockingbird*: Two Pulitzer Novels about Alabama" (Going), **Supp. VIII:** 126
Storer, Edward, **Supp. I Part 1:** 261, 262
Stories: Elizabeth Stoddard, **Supp. XV:** 270
Stories, Fables and Other Diversions (Nemerov), **III:** 268-269, 285
Stories for the Sixties (Yates, ed.), **Supp. XI:** 343
Stories from Our Living Past (Prose), **Supp. XVI:**251
Stories from the Italian Poets (Hunt), **Supp. XV:** 175
Stories from the Old Testament Retold (L. P. Smith), **Supp. XIV:**342
Stories from World Literature, **Supp. IX:** 4
"Stories in the Snow" (Leopold), **Supp. XIV:**183
Stories of an Imaginary Childhood (Bukiet), **Supp. XVII: 41-44,** 45
Stories of F. Scott Fitzgerald, The (Cowley, ed.), **Retro. Supp. I:** 115
Stories of F. Scott Fitzgerald, The (Fitzgerald), **II:** 94
Stories of Modern America, **Supp. IX:** 4
Stories of Stephen Dixon, The (Dixon), **Supp. XII:** 152
Stories of the Spanish Civil War (Hemingway), **II:** 258
Stories Revived (James), **II:** 322
Stories that Could Be True (Stafford), **Supp. XI: 325-327**
Storm, The (Buechner), **Supp. XII: 54-57**
"Storm, The" (Chopin), **Retro. Supp. II:** 60, 68; **Supp. I Part 1:** 218, 224
"Storm Fear" (Frost), **II:** 153; **Retro. Supp. I:** 127
"Storm Ship, The" (Irving), **II:** 309
"Storm Warnings" (Kingsolver), **Supp. VII:** 207-208
"Stormy Weather" (Ellison), **Supp. II Part 1:** 233
"Story" (Everwine), **Supp. XV:** 89
"Story, A" (Jarrell), **II:** 371
Story, Richard David, **Supp. IV Part 2:** 575, 588
"Story about Chicken Soup, A" (Simpson), **Supp. IX: 272-273**
"Story about the Anteater, The" (Benét), **Supp. XI:** 53
"Story About the Body, A" (Hass), **Supp. VI: 107-108**

"Story Hearer, The" (Paley), **Supp. VI:** 230, 231
"Story Hour" (Hay), **Supp. XIV:**124
"Story Hour" (Jarman), **Supp. XVII:** 116
Story Hour: A Second Look at Cinderella, Bluebeard, and Company (Hay), **Supp. XIV:**119, 124, 125, 132, 133
Story of a Country Town, The (Howe), **I:** 106
Story of a Lover, The (Hapgood), **Supp. XVII:** 99, 100, 104
Story of an American Family, The (N. Boyce), **Supp. XVII:** 97
"Story of an Hour, The" (Chopin), **Retro. Supp. II:** 72; **Supp. I Part 1:** 212-213, 216
Story of a Novel, The (Wolfe), **IV:** 456, 458
"Story of a Proverb, The" (Lanier), **Supp. I Part 1:** 365
"Story of a Proverb, The: A Fairy Tale for Grown People" (Lanier), **Supp. I Part 1:** 365
Story of a Story and Other Stories, The: A Novel (Dixon), **Supp. XII:** 155
Story of a Wonder Man, The (Lardner), **II:** 433-434
"Story of a Year, The" (James), **Retro. Supp. I:** 218
Story of G.I. Joe, The (film, Wellman), **Supp. XVII:** 61, 62
"Story of Gus, The" (A. Miller), **III:** 147-148
"Story of How a Wall Stands, A" (Ortiz), **Supp. IV Part 2:** 499, 507
Story of Mount Desert Island, Maine, The (Morison), **Supp. I Part 2:** 494
Story of My Boyhood and Youth, The (Muir), **Supp. IX: 172-174,** 176
Story of My Father, The: A Memoir (Miller), **Supp. XII:** 301
Story of O, The (Réage), **Supp. XII:** 9, 10
Story of Our Lives, The (Strand), **Supp. IV Part 2:** 620, 628-629, 629
Story of the Normans, The, Told Chiefly in Relation to Their Conquest of England (Jewett), **II:** 406
"Story of Toby, The" (Melville), **III:** 76
"Story of To-day, A" (Davis), **Supp. XVI:**88, 89. See also *Margret Howth*
Story of Utopias, The (Mumford), **Supp. II Part 2:** 475, 483-486, 495
Story of Wine in California, The (M. F. K. Fisher), **Supp. XVII:** 88

Story on Page One, The (Odets), **Supp. II Part 2:** 546
Storyteller (Silko), **Supp. IV Part 2:** 558, 559, 560, 561, **566-570**
"Storyteller" (Silko), **Supp. IV Part 2:** 569
"*Storyteller*: Grandmother Spider's Web" (Danielson), **Supp. IV Part 2:** 569
"Storyteller's Notebook, A" (Carver), **Supp. III Part 1:** 142-143
Story Teller's Story, A: The Tale of an American Writer's Journey through His Own Imaginative World and through the World of Facts ... (Anderson), **I:** 98, 101, 114, 117
"Story That Could Be True, A" (Stafford), **Supp. XI:** 326
"Stout Gentleman, The" (Irving), **II:** 309
Stover at Yale (Johnson), **III:** 321
Stowe, Calvin, **IV:** 445; **Supp. I Part 2:** 587, 588, 590, 596, 597
Stowe, Charles, **Supp. I Part 2:** 581, 582
Stowe, Eliza, **Supp. I Part 2:** 587
Stowe, Harriet Beecher, **II:** 274, 399, 403, 541; **Retro. Supp. I:** 34, 246; **Retro. Supp. II:** 4, 138, 156; **Supp. I Part 1:** 30, 206, 301; **Supp. I Part 2: 579-601; Supp. III Part 1:** 154, 168, 171; **Supp. IX:** 33; **Supp. X:** 223, 246, 249, 250; **Supp. XI:** 193; **Supp. XIII:** 141, 295; **Supp. XV:** 278; **Supp. XVI:**82, 85
Stowe, Samuel Charles, **Supp. I Part 2:** 587
Stowe, William, **Supp. IV Part 1:** 129
Strachey, Lytton, **I:** 5; **IV:** 436; **Retro. Supp. I:** 59; **Supp. I Part 2:** 485, 494; **Supp. XIV:**342; **Supp. XVI:**191
"Stradivari" (Bierds), **Supp. XVII:** 28
Straight Cut (Bell), **Supp. X:** 5, **6-7,** 10
Straight Man (Russo), **Supp. XII: 335-339,** 340
Straits: Poems (Koch), **Supp. XV:** 184
Strand, Mark, **Supp. IV Part 2: 619-636; Supp. V:** 92, 332, 337, 338, 343; **Supp. IX:** 155; **Supp. XI:** 139, 145; **Supp. XII:** 254; **Supp. XIII:** 76; **Supp. XV:** 74
Strand, Paul, **Supp. VIII:** 272
Strandberg, Victor, **Supp. V:** 273
Strange Case of Dr. Jekyll and Mr. Hyde, The (Stevenson), **II:** 290
Strange Children, The (Gordon), **II:** 196, 197, 199, 211-213
Strange Fire (Bukiet), **Supp. XVII:** 46

"Strange Fruit" (Harjo), **Supp. XII:** 224, 225
"Strange Fruit" (song), **Supp. I Part 1:** 80
Strange Interlude (O'Neill), **III:** 391, 397-398; **IV:** 61
Stranger, The (Camus), **I:** 53, 292; **Supp. VIII:** 11; **Supp. XV:** 352
"Stranger, The" (Rich), **Supp. I Part 2:** 555, 560
"Stranger, The" (Salinger), **III:** 552-553
"Stranger in My Own Life, A: Alienation in American Indian Poetry and Prose" (Gunn Allen), **Supp. IV Part 1:** 322
"Stranger in the Village" (Baldwin), **Retro. Supp. II:** 3; **Supp. I Part 1:** 54; **Supp. IV Part 1:** 10
"Stranger in Town" (Hughes), **Supp. I Part 1:** 334
"Strangers" (Howe), **Supp. VI:** 120
Strangers and Wayfarers (Jewett), **Retro. Supp. II:** 138
"Strangers from the Horizon" (Merwin), **Supp. III Part 1:** 356
Strangers on a Train (Highsmith), **Supp. IV Part 1:** 132
"Strange Story, A" (Taylor), **Supp. V:** 323
"Strange Story, A" (Wylie), **Supp. I Part 2:** 723
Strange Things (Atwood), **Supp. XIII:** 35
"Strato in Plaster" (Merrill), **Supp. III Part 1:** 328
Straus, Ralph, **Supp. XIII:** 168
Straus, Roger, **Supp. VIII:** 82; **Supp. XV:** 59
Strauss, Harold, **Supp. XV:** 137
Strauss, Johann, **I:** 66
Strauss, Richard, **IV:** 316
Strauss, Robert, **Supp. XI:** 141, 142
Stravinsky (De Schloezer), **III:** 474
Stravinsky, Igor, **Retro. Supp. I:** 378; **Supp. IV Part 1:** 81; **Supp. XI:** 133; **Supp. XV:** 265
"Stravinsky's Three Pieces 'Grotesques,' for String Quartet" (Lowell), **II:** 523
Straw, The (O'Neill), **III:** 390
"Stray Document, A" (Pound), **II:** 517
Streaks of the Tulip, The: Selected Criticism (W. J. Smith), **Supp. XIII:** 333, 334, 344, **347-348**
Streamline Your Mind (Mursell), **Supp. I Part 2:** 608
"Street, Cloud" (Ríos), **Supp. IV Part 2:** 549
Streetcar Named Desire, A (T. Williams), **IV:** 382, 383, 385, 386, 387, 389-390, 395, 398; **Supp. IV Part 1:** 359
Street in Bronzeville, A (Brooks), **Retro. Supp. I:** 208; **Supp. III Part 1:** 74-78
"Street Moths" (X. J. Kennedy), **Supp. XV:** 170
"Street Musicians" (Ashbery), **Supp. III Part 1:** 18
"Street off Sunset, A" (Jarrell), **II:** 387
"Streets" (Dixon), **Supp. XII: 145-146**
Streets in the Moon (MacLeish), **III:** 5, 8-11, 15, 19
Streets of Laredo (McMurtry), **Supp. V:** 230
"Streets of Laredo" (screenplay) (McMurtry and Ossana), **Supp. V:** 226, 230
Streets of Night (Dos Passos), **I:** 478, 479-480, 481, 488
Streitfield, David, **Supp. XIII:** 234; **Supp. XVI:** 63
Strength of Fields, The (Dickey), **Supp. IV Part 1:** 178
"Strength of Fields, The" (Dickey), **Supp. IV Part 1:** 176, 184-185
"Strength of Gideon, The" (Dunbar), **Supp. II Part 1:** 212
Strength of Gideon and Other Stories, The (Dunbar), **Supp. II Part 1:** 211, 212
"Strenuous Artistry" (Zagarell), **Supp. XV:** 281
Strether, Lambert, **II:** 313
Stribling, T. S., **Supp. VIII:** 126
Strickland, Joe (pseudonym). See Arnold, George W.
"Strictly Bucolic" (Simic), **Supp. VIII:** 278
Strictly Business (O. Henry), **Supp. II Part 1:** 410
"Strike, The" (Olsen), **Supp. XIII:** 292, 297
"Strikers" (Untermeyer), **Supp. XV:** 296
Strindberg, August, **I:** 78; **III:** 145, 165, 387, 390, 391, 392, 393; **IV:** 17; **Supp. XVII:** 100
"String, The" (Dickey), **Supp. IV Part 1:** 179
String Light (Wright), **Supp. XV: 345-346**
"Strivings of the Negro People" (Du Bois), **Supp. II Part 1:** 167
Stroby, W. C., **Supp. XIV:** 26
Strohbach, Hermann, **Supp. XI:** 242
"Stroke of Good Fortune, A" (O'Connor), **III:** 344; **Retro. Supp. II:** 229, 232

Strom, Stephen, **Supp. XII:** 223
Strong, George Templeton, **IV:** 321
Strong, Josiah, **Supp. XIV:** 64
"Strong Draughts of Their Refreshing Minds" (Dickinson), **Retro. Supp. I:** 46
Strong Opinions (Nabokov), **Retro. Supp. I:** 263, 266, 270, 276
"Strong Women" (Dorman), **Supp. XI:** 240
Strout, Elizabeth, **Supp. X:** 86
Structure of Nations and Empires, The (Niebuhr), **III:** 292, 308
"Structure of Rime, The" (Duncan), **Supp. XVI:** 287
Struggle, The (film; Griffith), **Supp. XVI:** 191
"Strumpet Song" (Plath), **Retro. Supp. II:** 246; **Supp. I Part 2:** 536
Strunk, William, **Supp. I Part 2:** 652, 662, 670, 671, 672
Strunsky, Anna, **II:** 465
"Strut for Roethke, A" (Berryman), **I:** 188
Strychacz, Thomas F., **Supp. XVI:** 69-70
Stuart, Gilbert, **I:** 16
Stuart, J. E. B., **III:** 56
Stuart, Michael, **Supp. XV:** 140
Stuart Little (White), **Supp. I Part 2:** 655-658
"Student, The" (Moore), **III:** 212, 215
"Student of Salmanaca, The" (Irving), **II:** 309
"Student's Wife, The" (Carver), **Supp. III Part 1:** 141
Studies in American Indian Literature: Critical Essays and Course Designs (Gunn Allen), **Supp. IV Part 1:** 324, 333
Studies in Classic American Literature (Lawrence), **II:** 102; **III:** 33; **IV:** 333; **Retro. Supp. I:** 421
Studies in Short Fiction (Malin), **Supp. XVI:** 71
"Studs" (Farrell), **II:** 25, 28, 31
Studs Lonigan: A Trilogy (Farrell), **II:** 25, 26, 27, 31-34, 37, 38, 41-42
"Study of Images" (Stevens), **IV:** 79
"Study of Lanier's Poems, A" (Kent), **Supp. I Part 1:** 373
Study of Milton's Prosody (Bridges), **II:** 537
"Study of the Negro Problems, The" (Du Bois), **Supp. II Part 1:** 165
Stuewe, Paul, **Supp. IV Part 1:** 68
Stuhlmann, Gunther, **Supp. X:** 182, 184, 185, 187
Stultifera Navis (Brant), **III:** 447
Sturak, John Thomas, **Supp. XIII:** 162,

163, 165, 168
Sturgis, George, **III:** 600
Sturgis, Howard, **IV:** 319; **Retro. Supp. I:** 367, 373
Sturgis, Susan, **III:** 600
Sturm, Margaret. *See* Millar, Margaret
Stuttaford, Genevieve, **Supp. IX:** 279
Stuyvesant, Peter, **II:** 301
"Style" (Nemerov), **III:** 275
Styles of Radical Will (Sontag), **Supp. III Part 2:** 451, 459, 460-463
Styne, Jule, **Supp. XVI:**193
Styron, William, **III:** 40; **IV:** 4, **97-119**, 216; **Supp. V:** 201; **Supp. IX:** 208; **Supp. X:** 15-16, 250; **Supp. XI:** 229, 231, 343; **Supp. XIV:**82; **Supp. XVI:**235-236
Suares, J. C., **Supp. IV Part 1:** 234
Suarez, Ernest, **Supp. IV Part 1:** 175; **Supp. V:** 180
"Sub, The" (Dixon), **Supp. XII:** 146
Subjection of Women, The (Mill), **Supp. XI:** 196, 203
"Subjective Necessity for Social Settlements" (Addams), **Supp. I Part 1:** 4
"Subject of Childhood, A" (Paley), **Supp. VI:** 221
"Submarginalia" (Howe), **Supp. IV Part 2:** 422
Substance and Shadow (James), **II:** 344
Subterraneans, The (Kerouac), **Supp. III Part 1:** 225, 227-231
"Subtitle" (Kees), **Supp. XV:** 139
Subtreasury of American Humor, A (White and White), **Supp. I Part 2:** 668
"Suburban Culture, Imaginative Wonder: The Fiction of Frederick Barthelme" (Brinkmeyer), **Supp. XI:** 38
Suburban Sketches (Howells), **II:** 274, 277
"Subverted Flower, The" (Frost), **Retro. Supp. I:** 139
"Subway, The" (Tate), **IV:** 128
"Subway Singer, The" (Clampitt), **Supp. IX:** 45
"Success" (Mora), **Supp. XIII:** 217
Successful Love and Other Stories (Schwartz), **Supp. II Part 2:** 661, 665
Succession, The: A Novel of Elizabeth and James (Garrett), **Supp. VII:** 104-107, 108
"Success is counted sweetest" (Dickinson), **Retro. Supp. I:** 30, 31-32, 38; **Supp. XV:** 126

Success Stories (Banks), **Supp. V:** 14-15
"Success Story" (Banks), **Supp. V:** 15
"Such Counsels You Gave to Me" (Jeffers), **Supp. II Part 2:** 433
Such Silence (Milburn), **Supp. XI:** 242
"Such Things Happen Only in Books" (Wilder), **IV:** 365
Suddenly, Last Summer (film) (Vidal), **Supp. IV Part 2:** 683
Suddenly Last Summer (T. Williams), **I:** 73; **IV:** 382, 383, 385, 386, 387, 389, 390, 391, 392, 395-396, 397, 398
Sudermann, Hermann, **I:** 66
Sugg, Richard P., **Supp. IV Part 1:** 68
"Suggestion from a Friend" (Kenyon), **Supp. VII:** 171
"Suicide" (Barnes), **Supp. III Part 1:** 33
"Suicide off Egg Rock" (Plath), **Supp. I Part 2:** 529, 538
Suicides and Jazzers (Carruth), **Supp. XVI:**46
"Suicide's Note" (Hughes), **Retro. Supp. I:** 199
"Suitable Surroundings, The" (Bierce), **I:** 203
"Suitcase, The" (Ozick), **Supp. V:** 262, 264
"Suite for Augustus, A" (Dove), **Supp. IV Part 1:** 245
"Suite for Lord Timothy Dexter" (Rukeyser), **Supp. VI:** 283, 285
"Suite from the Firebird" (Stravinsky), **Supp. XI:** 133
"Suitor, The" (Kenyon), **Supp. VII:** 164-165
Sukarno, **IV:** 490
Sukenick, Ronald, **Supp. V:** 39, 44, 46; **Supp. XII:** 139
Sula (Morrison), **Supp. III Part 1:** 362, 364, 367, 368, 379; **Supp. VIII:** 219
Sullivan, Andrew, **Supp. IX:** 135
Sullivan, Frank, **Supp. IX:** 201
Sullivan, Harry Stack, **I:** 59
Sullivan, Jack, **Supp. X:** 86; **Supp. XII:** 331
Sullivan, Noel, **Retro. Supp. I:** 202; **Supp. I Part 1:** 329, 333
Sullivan, Richard, **Supp. VIII:** 124
Sullivan, Walter, **Supp. VIII:** 168
"Sullivan County Sketches" (Crane), **I:** 407, 421
"Sumach and Goldenrod: An American Idyll" (Mumford), **Supp. II Part 2:** 475
Suma Genji (Play), **III:** 466
Sumerian Vistas (Ammons), **Supp.**

VII: 34, 35
"Summer" (Emerson), **II:** 10
Summer (Gioia), **Supp. XV:** 117
"Summer" (Lowell), **II:** 554
Summer (Wharton), **IV:** 317; **Retro. Supp. I:** 360, 367, 374, **378-379**, 382
Summer, Bob, **Supp. X:** 1, 5, 6, 42
"Summer: West Side" (Updike), **Retro. Supp. I:** 320
Summer and Smoke (T. Williams), **IV:** 382, 384, 385, 386, 387, 395, 397, 398; **Supp. IV Part 1:** 84
Summer Anniversaries, The (Justice), **Supp. VII:** 115, 117
"Summer Commentary, A" (Winters), **Supp. II Part 2:** 808
"Summer Day" (O'Hara), **III:** 369
"Summer Days, The" (Oliver), **Supp. VII:** 239
"Summer Night" (Hughes), **Supp. I Part 1:** 325
"Summer Night, A" (Auden), **Supp. II Part 1:** 8
"Summer Night-Broadway" (Untermeyer), **Supp. XV:** 296
"Summer Noon: 1941" (Winters), **Supp. II Part 2:** 811
"Summer of '82" (Merwin), **Supp. III Part 1:** 355-356
Summer on the Lakes in 1843 (Fuller), **Supp. II Part 1:** 279, 295-296
"Summer People" (Hemingway), **II:** 258-259
"Summer People, The" (Jackson), **Supp. IX:** 120
"Summer People, The" (Merrill), **Supp. III Part 1:** 325-326
"Summer Ramble, A" (Bryant), **Supp. I Part 1:** 162, 164
Summers, Claude J., **Supp. IV Part 2:** 680-681; **Supp. XIV:**161, 169
Summers, Robert, **Supp. IX:** 289
"Summer Solstice, New York City" (Olds), **Supp. X:** 207
"Summer's Reading, A" (Malamud), **Supp. I Part 2:** 430-431, 442
"Summer Storm" (Gioia), **Supp. XV:** 127
"Summer Storm" (Simpson), **Supp. IX:** 268
"'Summertime and the Living …'" (Hayden), **Supp. II Part 1:** 363, 366
Summertime Island (Caldwell), **I:** 307-308
"Summer with Tu Fu, A" (Carruth), **Supp. XVI:**55, 58
"Summit Beach, 1921" (Dove), **Supp. IV Part 1:** 249
Summoning of Stones, A (Hecht), **Supp.**

X: 57, 58, **58-59**
"Summons" (Untermeyer), **Supp. XV:** 296
Summons to Memphis, A (Taylor), **Supp. V:** 313, 314, 327
Summons to the Free, A (Benét), **Supp. XI:** 47
Sumner, Charles, **I:** 3, 15; **Supp. I Part 2:** 685, 687
Sumner, John, **Retro. Supp. II:** 95
Sumner, John B., **I:** 511
Sumner, William Graham, **III:** 102, 108; **Supp. I Part 2:** 640
"Sumptuous Destination" (Wilbur), **Supp. III Part 2:** 553
"Sun" (Moore), **III:** 215
"Sun" (Swenson), **Supp. IV Part 2:** 640
"Sun, Sea, and Sand" (Marquand), **III:** 60
Sun Also Rises, The (Hemingway), **I:** 107; **II:** 68, 90, 249, 251-252, 260, 600; **III:** 36; **IV:** 35, 297; **Retro. Supp. I:** 171, **177-180**, 181, 189; **Supp. I Part 2:** 614; **Supp. XIII:** 263
"Sun and Moon" (Kenyon), **Supp. VII:** 168
"Sun and the Still-born Stars, The" (Southern), **Supp. XI:** 295
Sun at Midnight (Soseki; Merwin and Shigematsu, trans.), **Supp. III Part 1:** 353
"Sun Crosses Heaven from West to East Bringing Samson Back to the Womb, The" (R. Bly), **Supp. IV Part 1:** 73
"Sun Dance Shield" (Momaday), **Supp. IV Part 2:** 491
Sunday, Billy, **II:** 449
"Sunday Afternoons" (Komunyakaa), **Supp. XIII:** 127
Sunday after the War (H. Miller), **III:** 184
"Sunday at Home" (Hawthorne), **II:** 231-232
"Sunday Morning" (Stevens), **II:** 552; **III:** 278, 463, 509; **IV:** 92-93; **Retro. Supp. I:** 296, 300, 301, 304, 307, 313; **Supp. XV:** 120; **Supp. XVI:**210; **Supp. XVII:** 42
"Sunday Morning Apples" (Crane), **I:** 387
"Sunday Morning Prophecy" (Hughes), **Supp. I Part 1:** 334
"Sundays" (B. Kelly), **Supp. XVII:** 124-125
"Sundays" (Salter), **Supp. IX:** 257
"Sundays, They Sleep Late" (Rukeyser), **Supp. VI:** 278

"Sundays of Satin-Legs Smith, The" (Brooks), **Supp. III Part 1:** 74, 75
"Sundays Visiting" (Ríos), **Supp. IV Part 2:** 541
Sundial, The (Jackson), **Supp. IX: 126-127**
Sundog (Harrison), **Supp. VIII:** 46-48
Sun Dogs (R. O. Butler), **Supp. XII: 64-65**
Sun Do Move, The (Hughes), **Supp. I Part 1:** 339
Sundquist, Eric, **Supp. XIV:**66, 71
"Sunfish" (C. Frost), **Supp. XV:** 100-101, 102
"Sunflower Sutra" (Ginsberg), **Supp. II Part 1:** 317, 321; **Supp. XV:** 215
Sunlight Dialogues, The (Gardner), **Supp. VI:** 63, **68,** 69, 70
"Sunlight Is Imagination" (Wilbur), **Supp. III Part 2:** 549
Sun Out: Selected Poems, 1952-1954 (Koch), **Supp. XV:** 179
"Sunrise" (Lanier), **Supp. I Part 1:** 370
"Sunrise runs for Both, The" (Dickinson), **Retro. Supp. I:** 45
Sunrise with Seamonsters: Travels and Discoveries, 1964-1984 (Theroux), **Supp. VIII:** 311, 313, 323, 325
"Sun Rising" (Donne), **Supp. VIII:** 164
"Sunset" (Ransom), **III:** 484
"Sunset from Omaha Hotel Window" (Sandburg), **III:** 584
Sunset Gun (Parker), **Supp. IX:** 192
Sunset Limited (Burke), **Supp. XIV:**32, 33
Sunset Limited (Harrison), **Supp. VIII:** 51
"Sunset Maker, The" (Justice), **Supp. VII:** 123
Sunset Maker, The: Poems, Stories, a Memoir (Justice), **Supp. VII:** 116, 118, 119, 123-124
Sunshine Boys, The (film), **Supp. IV Part 2:** 589
Sunshine Boys, The (Simon), **Supp. IV Part 2:** 575, 584-585
"Sunthin' in the Pastoral Line" (Lowell), **Supp. I Part 2:** 415-416
Sun to Sun (Hurston), **Supp. VI:** 154
Sun Tracks (Ortiz), **Supp. IV Part 2:** 499, 500
Sun Under Wood (Hass), **Supp. VI:** 103, 108-109
"Superb Lily, The" (Pinsky), **Supp. VI:** 250
"Superman Comes to the Supermarket" (Mailer), **Retro. Supp. II:** 204
"Supermarket in California, A"

(Ginsberg), **Supp. XI:** 135
"Supernatural Love" (Schnackenberg), **Supp. XV:** 257, 259-260
Supernatural Love: Poems 1976-1992 (Schnackenberg), **Supp. XV:** 253, 256, 260, 263
Suplee, Curt, **Supp. XVI:**202
"Supper After the Last, The" (Kinnell), **Supp. III Part 1:** 239
"Supposedly Fun Thing I'll Never Do Again, A" (Wallace), **Supp. X:** 315
Supposedly Fun Thing I'll Never Do Again, A: Essays and Arguments (Wallace), **Supp. X: 314-316**
Suppressed Desires (Glaspell), **Supp. III Part 1:** 178
Suppression of the African Slave Trade to the United States of America, 1638-1870 (Du Bois), **Supp. II Part 1:** 157, 162
Supreme Fiction, The (Stevens), **Supp. XVI:**158
"Supremes, The" (Jarman), **Supp. XVII:** 115
Sure Hand of God, The (Caldwell), **I:** 297, 302
"Surety and Fidelity Claims" (Stevens), **Retro. Supp. I:** 296, 309
Surface of Earth, The (Price), **Supp. VI:** 261-262
"Surfaces" (Ammons), **Supp. VII:** 36
Surfacing (Atwood), **Supp. XIII:** 20, 21, **22-23,** 24, 33, 35
"Surgeon at 2 A.M." (Plath), **Supp. I Part 2:** 545
Surmmer Knowledge (Schwartz), **Supp. II Part 2:** 662, 665
"Surprise" (Kenyon), **Supp. VII:** 173
Surprised by Sin: The Reader in Paradise Lost (Fish), **Supp. XIV:**15
"Surround, The Imagining Herself as the Environment,/She Speaks to James Wright at Sundow" (Dickey), **Supp. IV Part 1:** 185
"Survey of Literature" (Ransom), **III:** 480
"Surveyor, The" (H. Roth), **Supp. IX:** 233, 234
Survival (Atwood), **Supp. XIII:** 20, 22, 35
"Survival as Tao, Beginning at 5:00 A.M." (Carruth), **Supp. XVI:**56
Survival of the Bark Canoe, The (McPhee), **Supp. III Part 1:** 301, 302, 308, 313
Survival This Way: Interviews with American Indian Poets (Bruchac), **Supp. IV Part 2:** 506
"Surviving Love" (Berryman), **I:** 173

Survivor (O. Butler), **Supp. XIII:** 62, 63
Susan and God (film; Cukor), **Supp. XVI:**192
Susanna Moodie: Voice and Vision (Shields), **Supp. VII:** 313
Suspect in Poetry, The (Dickey), **Supp. IV Part 1:** 177
"Sustained by Fiction" (Hoffman), **Supp. X:** 90, 92
"Susto" (Ríos), **Supp. IV Part 2:** 553
Sutherland, Donald, **IV:** 38, 44; **Supp. IX:** 254
Sutherland, Efua, **Supp. IV Part 1:** 9, 16
Sutherland-Smith, James, **Supp. X:** 211, 212
Sut Lovingood's Yarns (Harris), **II:** 70
Sutton, Roger, **Supp. X:** 266
Sutton, Walter, **III:** 479
Suttree (McCarthy), **Supp. VIII: 178-180,** 189
Suvero, Mark di, **Supp. IX:** 251
Svevo, Italo, **Supp. XIV:**112
Swados, Harvey, **Supp. XI:** 222
Swallow, Alan, **Supp. X:** 112, 115, 116, 120, 123
Swallow Barn (J. P. Kennedy), **II:** 313
"Swamp Boy" (Bass), **Supp. XVI:**20
Swan, Barbara, **Supp. IV Part 2:** 447
Swan, Jon, **Supp. IV Part 1:** 176
Swan Lake (Tchaikovsky), **Supp. IX:** 51
"Swan Legs" (Stern), **Supp. IX:** 299
Swann (Shields), **Supp. VII:** 315, 318-323, 326
Swann, Brian, **Supp. IV Part 2:** 500
Swanson, Gloria, **II:** 429
Swanson, Stevenson, **Supp. XIV:**111
Swanton, John Reed, **Supp. VIII:** 295
Swanwick, John, **Supp. XV:** 237
Swanwick, Michael, **Supp. XVI:**128
"Swarm, The" (Plath), **Retro. Supp. II:** 255
"Sway" (Simpson), **Supp. IX:** 276
Sweat (Hurston), **Supp. VI:** 152
Swedenborg, Emanuel, **II:** 5, 10, 321, 342, 343-344, 396
Sweeney Agonistes (Eliot), **I:** 580; **Retro. Supp. I:** 64, 65; **Retro. Supp. II:** 247
"Sweeney Among the Nightingales" (Eliot), **III:** 4
Sweet, Blanche, **Supp. I Part 2:** 391
Sweet, Timothy, **Supp. IV Part 1:** 330
Sweet and Lowdown (film; Allen), **Supp. XV:** 11
Sweet and Sour (O'Hara), **III:** 361
Sweet Bird of Youth (T. Williams), **IV:** 382, 383, 385, 386, 387, 388, 389, 390, 391, 392, 395, 396, 398; **Supp. IV Part 1:** 84, 89
Sweet Charity (musical), **Supp. IV Part 2:** 575
Sweet Flypaper of Life, The (Hughes), **Supp. I Part 1:** 335-336
"Sweetheart of the Song Tra Bong, The" (O'Brien), **Supp. V:** 243, 249
"Sweethearts" (Ford), **Supp. V:** 69
Sweet Hereafter, The (Banks), **Supp. V:** 15-16
Sweet Machine (Doty), **Supp. XI:** 121, **131-132,** 135
Sweet Sue (Gurney), **Supp. V:** 105, 107-108
Sweet Sweetback's Baadasss Song (Peebles; film), **Supp. XI:** 17
Sweet Thursday (Steinbeck), **IV:** 50, 52, 64-65
Sweet Will (Levine), **Supp. V:** 178, 187, 189, 190
"Sweet Will" (Levine), **Supp. V:** 190
"Sweet Words on Race" (Hughes), **Retro. Supp. I:** 211
Sweezy, Paul, **Supp. I Part 2:** 645
"Swell-Looking Girl, A" (Caldwell), **I:** 310
Swenson, May, **Retro. Supp. II:** 44; **Supp. IV Part 2: 637-655**
"Swift" (Schwartz), **Supp. II Part 2:** 663
Swift, Jonathan, **I:** 125, 194, 209, 441; **II:** 110, 302, 304-305, 577; **III:** 113; **IV:** 68; **Retro. Supp. I:** 66; **Supp. I Part 2:** 406, 523, 603, 656, 665, 708, 714; **Supp. IV Part 1:** 51; **Supp. IV Part 2:** 692; **Supp. XI:** 105, 209; **Supp. XII:** 276; **Supp. XV:** 258; **Supp. XVI:**110
"Swimmer" (Francis), **Supp. IX:** 82
"Swimmer, The" (Cheever), **Supp. I Part 1:** 185, 187
"Swimmer, The" (Glück), **Supp. V:** 82
"Swimmers" (Untermeyer), **Supp. XV:** 300
"Swimmers, The" (Fitzgerald), **Retro. Supp. I:** 110, 111
"Swimmers, The" (Tate), **IV:** 136
"Swimming" (Harjo), **Supp. XII:** 218
Swinburne, Algernon C., **I:** 50, 384, 568; **II:** 3, 4, 129, 400, 524; **IV:** 135; **Retro. Supp. I:** 100; **Supp. I Part 1:** 79; **Supp. I Part 2:** 422, 552; **Supp. XIV:**120, 344
"Swinburne as Poet" (Eliot), **I:** 576
Swinger of Birches, A: A Portrait of Robert Frost (Cox), **Retro. Supp. I:** 132
"Swinging on a Birch-Tree" (Larcom), **Supp. XIII:** 147

Switch, The (Dixon), **Supp. XII:** 141
Swope, D. B., **Supp. IX:** 95
Sword Blades and Poppy Seed (Lowell), **II:** 518, 520, 522, 532
Sword of God, The: Jeanne D'Arc (Endore), **Supp. XVII:** 55
Sybil (Auchincloss), **Supp. IV Part 1:** 25
"Sycamore" (Stern), **Supp. IX:** 294
"Sycamore, The" (Moore), **III:** 216
"Sycamores, The" (Whittier), **Supp. I Part 2:** 699
Sylvester, Johnny, **Supp. I Part 2:** 438
Sylvester, Joshua, **I:** 178, 179; **II:** 18; **III:** 157; **Supp. I Part 1:** 98, 104, 114, 116
Sylvia (Gurney), **Supp. V:** 105
"Sylvia" (Larcom), **Supp. XIII:** 144
"Sylvia" (L. Michaels), **Supp. XVI:**202, 213
"Sylvia" (Stern), **Supp. IX:** 297
Sylvia: A Fictional Memoir (L. Michaels), **Supp. XVI:**202, 213
Sylvia Plath: Method and Madness (Butscher), **Supp. I Part 2:** 526
Sylvia Plath: Poetry and Existence (Holbrook), **Supp. I Part 2:** 526-527
"Sylvia's Death" (Sexton), **Supp. II Part 2:** 671, 684, 685
"Symbol and Image in the Shorter Poems of Herman Melville" (Dickey), **Supp. IV Part 1:** 176
Symbolist Movement in Literature, The (Symons), **I:** 50, 569; **Retro. Supp. I:** 55
Symonds, John Addington, **I:** 241, 242, 251, 259; **IV:** 334; **Supp. XIV:**329, 335
Symons, Arthur, **I:** 50, 569; **Retro. Supp. I:** 55
Symons, Julian, **Supp. IV Part 1:** 343, 351
"Sympathy" (Dunbar), **Supp. IV Part 1:** 15
Sympathy of Souls, A (Goldbarth), **Supp. XII:** 175, 176, **186-187**
"Symphony, The" (Lanier), **Supp. I Part 1:** 352, 360-361, 364; **Supp. I Part 2:** 416
Symposium (Plato), **Retro. Supp. II:** 31; **Supp. IV Part 1:** 391
Symposium: To Kill a Mockingbird (Alabama Law Review), **Supp. VIII:** 127, 128
Symptoms of Being 35 (Lardner), **II:** 434
Synanon (Endore), **Supp. XVII:** 65
Synanon (film, Quine), **Supp. XVII:** 65

Synanon City (Endore), **Supp. XVII:** 65
Synge, John Millington, **I:** 434; **III:** 591-592; **Supp. III Part 1:** 34; **Supp. VIII:** 155
Synthetic Philosophy (Spencer), **II:** 462-463
"Syringa" (Ashbery), **Supp. III Part 1:** 19-21, 25
"Syrinx" (Clampitt), **Supp. IX:** 53
"Syrinx" (Merrill), **Supp. III Part 1:** 328
Syrkin, Marie, **Supp. XIV:**279, 288, 291
"System, The" (Ashbery), **Supp. III Part 1:** 14, 15, 18, 21-22
System of Dante's Hell, The (Baraka), **Supp. II Part 1:** 39-41, 55
"System of Dante's Inferno, The" (Baraka), **Supp. II Part 1:** 40
"System of Doctor Tarr and Professor Fether, The" (Poe), **III:** 419, 425
System of General Geography, A (Brown), **Supp. I Part 1:** 146
Sze, Mai-mai, **Supp. X:** 291
Szentgyorgyi, Tom, **Supp. IX:** 135, 136, 140, 141-142
Szulc, Tad, **Supp. XVI:**154
Szymborka, Wislawa, **Supp. XI:** 267

T

T. S. Eliot and American Philosophy (Jain), **Retro. Supp. I:** 58
T. S. Eliot's Silent Voices (Mayer), **Retro. Supp. I:** 58
Tabios, Eileen, **Supp. XV:** 214, 225, 226
"Table of Delectable Contents, The" (Simic), **Supp. VIII:** 276
Tabloid Dreams (R. O. Butler), **Supp. XII:** 70-72, 74
Tacitus, Cornelius, **I:** 485; **II:** 113
Tadic, Novica, **Supp. VIII:** 272
Taft (Patchett), **Supp. XII:** 307, 312, 314-317
"Tag" (Hughes), **Supp. I Part 1:** 341
Taggard, Genevieve, **IV:** 436
Taggart, John, **Supp. IV Part 2:** 421
Tagore, Rabindranath, **I:** 383
"Taibele and Her Demon" (Singer), **Retro. Supp. II:** 307
Taibl, Erika, **Supp. XV:** 255
"Tailor Shop, The" (H. Miller), **III:** 175
"Tails" (Dixon), **Supp. XII:** 154
Taine, Hippolyte, **I:** 503; **II:** 271; **III:** 323; **IV:** 440, 444
"Tain't So" (Hughes), **Supp. I Part 1:** 330
Takasago (play), **III:** 466
Take Away the Darkness (Bynner), **Supp. XV:** 51
Take Me Back: A Novel (Bausch), **Supp. VII:** 41, 43-45, 46, 49
"Take My Saddle from the Wall: A Valediction" (McMurtry), **Supp. V:** 219
"'Take No for an Answer'" (Didion), **Supp. IV Part 1:** 203
"Take Pity" (Malamud), **Supp. I Part 2:** 427, 428, 435, 436, 437
"Takers, The" (Olds), **Supp. X:** 205
"Take the I Out" (Olds), **Supp. X:** 213
Take the Money and Run (film; Allen), **Supp. XV:** 3-4, 6
"Taking Away the Name of a Nephew" (Ríos), **Supp. IV Part 2:** 545-546
Taking Care of Mrs. Carroll (Monette), **Supp. X:** 153
"Taking of Captain Ball, The" (Jewett), **Retro. Supp. II:** 134
"Taking Out the Lawn Chairs" (Karr), **Supp. XI:** 241
"Taking the Bypass" (Epstein), **Supp. XIV:**110
"Taking the Bypass" (J. Epstein), **Supp. XVI:**230
"Taking the Forest" (Howe), **Supp. IV Part 2:** 433
"Taking the Lambs to Market" (Kumin), **Supp. IV Part 2:** 455
"Tale, A" (Bogan), **Supp. III Part 1:** 50, 51
Taleb-Khyar, Mohamed, **Supp. IV Part 1:** 242, 243, 244, 247, 257
"Tale of Jerusalem, A" (Poe), **III:** 411
Tale of Possessors Self-Dispossessed, A (O'Neill), **III:** 404
Tale of the Body Thief, The (Rice), **Supp. VII:** 290, 293-294, 297
Tale of Two Cities, A (film), **Supp. I Part 1:** 67
"Tale of Two Liars, A" (Singer), **IV:** 12
Tales (Baraka), **Supp. II Part 1:** 39, 55
Tales (Poe), **III:** 413
Tales and Stories for Black Folks (Bambara, ed.), **Supp. XI:** 1
Tales before Midnight (Benét), **Supp. XI:** 46, 53, 57
Talese, Gay, **Supp. XVI:**273; **Supp. XVII:** 199-211
Tales of a Traveller (Irving), **II:** 309-310
Tales of a Wayside Inn (Longfellow), **II:** 489, 490, 501, 502, 504-505; **Retro. Supp. II:** 154, 162-165
Tales of Glauber-Spa (Bryant, ed.), **Supp. I Part 1:** 157
Tales of Manhattan (Auchincloss), **Supp. IV Part 1:** 23
Tales of Men and Ghosts (Wharton), **IV:** 315; **Retro. Supp. I:** 372
Tales of Rhoda, The (Rice), **Supp. VII:** 288
Tales of Soldiers and Civilians (Bierce), **I:** 200-203, 204, 206, 208, 212
Tales of the Argonauts (Harte), **Supp. II Part 1:** 337, 348, 351
Tales of the Fish Patrol (London), **II:** 465
Tales of the Grotesque and Arabesque (Poe), **II:** 273; **III:** 412, 415; **Retro. Supp. II:** 270
Tales of the Jazz Age (Fitzgerald), **II:** 88; **Retro. Supp. I:** 105; **Supp. IX:** 57
"Talisman, A" (Moore), **III:** 195-196
Talisman, The (King), **Supp. V:** 140, 144, 152
"Talkin Bout Sonny" (Bambara), **Supp. XI:** 6-7
"Talking" (Merwin), **Supp. III Part 1:** 354
Talking All Morning (R. Bly), **Supp. IV Part 1:** 59, 60, 61, 62, 64, 65
Talking Dirty to the Gods (Komunyakaa), **Supp. XIII:** 130-131
"Talking Horse" (Malamud), **Supp. I Part 2:** 435
Talking Soft Dutch (McCarriston), **Supp. XIV:**260-263, 266, 270, 271
"Talking to Barr Creek" (Wagoner), **Supp. IX:** 328
"Talking to Sheep" (Sexton), **Supp. II Part 2:** 695
Talking to the Sun: An Illustrated Anthology of Poems for Young People (Koch and Farrell, eds.), **Supp. XV:** 188
"Talk of Heroes" (C. Bly), **Supp. XVI:**34
"Talk of the Town" (*The New Yorker* column), **IV:** 215; **Supp. IV Part 1:** 53, 54
"Talk with the Yellow Kid, A" (Bellow), **I:** 151
Tallent, Elizabeth, **Supp. IV Part 2:** 570
Tallman, Warren, **Supp. IV Part 1:** 154
TallMountain, Mary, **Supp. IV Part 1:** 324-325
Talma, Louise, **IV:** 357
Talmadge, Constance, **Supp. XVI:**186, 187, 196
Talmadge, Norma, **Supp. XVI:**186, 187, 196

Talmadge Girls, The (Loos), **Supp. XVI:**186, 196
Talmey, Allene, **Supp. IV Part 1:** 197; **Supp. XIII:** 172
Talmud, **IV:** 8, 17
Taltos: Lives of the Mayfair Witches (Rice), **Supp. VII:** 299-300
"Tamar" (Jeffers), **Supp. II Part 2:** 427-428, 436
Tamar and Other Poems (Jeffers), **Supp. II Part 2:** 416, 419
Tambourines to Glory (Hughes), **Supp. I Part 1:** 338-339
"Tame Indians" (Jewett), **Retro. Supp. II:** 141
"Tamerlane" (Poe), **III:** 426
Tamerlane and Other Poems (Poe), **III:** 410
"Tammany Man, The" (Hapgood), **Supp. XVII:** 103
"Tam O'Shanter" (Burns), **II:** 306
Tan, Amy, **Supp. X: 289-300**
Tangential Views (Bierce), **I:** 209
"Tangier 1975" (Bowles), **Supp. IV Part 1:** 94
"Tankas" (McClatchy), **Supp. XII:** 266
Tanner, Laura E., **Supp. X:** 209
Tanner, Tony, **I:** 260, 261; **Retro. Supp. II:** 205; **Supp. IV Part 1:** 285; **Supp. XVI:**65, 69
Tannhäuser (Wagner), **I:** 315
"Tan Ta Ra, Cries Mars...," (Wagoner), **Supp. IX:** 325
Tao of Physics, The (Capra), **Supp. X:** 261
Tao Teh Ching (Bynner, trans.), **Supp. XV:** 46, 47
Tapahonso, Luci, **Supp. IV Part 1:** 404; **Supp. IV Part 2:** 499, 508
Tape for the Turn of the Year (Ammons), **Supp. VII:** 31-33, 35
"Tapestry" (Ashbery), **Supp. III Part 1:** 22-23
"Tapiama" (Bowles), **Supp. IV Part 1:** 89-90
"Tapiola" (W. C. Williams), **Retro. Supp. I:** 429
Tappan, Arthur, **Supp. I Part 2:** 588
Tapping the White Cane of Solitude (F. Wright), **Supp. XVII:** 243
Taps at Reveille (Fitzgerald), **II:** 94, 96; **Retro. Supp. I:** 113
Tar: A Midwest Childhood (Anderson), **I:** 98, 115; **II:** 27
Tarantino, Quentin, **Supp. IV Part 1:** 356
Tar Baby (Morrison), **Supp. III Part 1:** 364, 369-372, 379; **Supp. IV Part 1:** 13
Tarbell, Ida, **III:** 322, 580; **Retro. Supp. II:** 101

"Target Study" (Baraka), **Supp. II Part 1:** 49-50, 54
Tarkington, Booth, **II:** 444; **III:** 70; **Retro. Supp. I:** 100; **Supp. XV:** 41
Tarpon (film), **Supp. VIII:** 42
Tarr, Rodger L., **Supp. X:** 222, 224, 226
Tartuffe (Molière; Wilbur, trans.), **Supp. III Part 2:** 560
Tarumba, Selected Poems of Jaime Sabines (Levine and Trejo, trans.), **Supp. V:** 178
"Tarzan Is an Expatriate" (Theroux), **Supp. VIII:** 313
Task, The (Cowper), **II:** 304
Tasso, Torquato, **I:** 276
Taste of Palestine, A: Menus and Memories (Shihab), **Supp. XIII:** 273
Tate, Alan, **Supp. XV:** 141
Tate, Allen, **I:** 48, 49, 50, 67, 69, 381, 382, 386, 390, 396, 397, 399, 402, 441, 468; **II:** 197-198, 367, 536, 537, 542, 551, 554; **III:** 424, 428, 454, 482, 483, 485, 493, 495, 496, 497, 499, 500, 517; **IV: 120-143,** 236, 237, 433; **Retro. Supp. I:** 37, 41, 90; **Retro. Supp. II:** 77, 79, 82, 83, 89, 176, 178, 179; **Supp. I Part 1:** 364, 371; **Supp. I Part 2:** 423; **Supp. II Part 1:** 90-91, 96, 98, 103-104, 136, 139, 144, 150, 151, 318; **Supp. II Part 2:** 643; **Supp. III Part 2:** 542; **Supp. V:** 315, 331; **Supp. X:** 1, 52; **Supp. XIV:**2
Tate, Benjamin Lewis Bogan, **IV:** 127
Tate, Greg, **Supp. XIII:** 233, 237
Tate, James, **Supp. V:** 92, 338; **Supp. VIII:** 39, 279; **Supp. XV:** 250; **Supp. XVII:** 242
Tate, John Allen, **IV:** 127
Tate, Michael Paul, **IV:** 127
Tate, Mrs. Allen (Caroline Gordon). *See* Gordon, Caroline
Tate, Mrs. Allen (Helen Heinz), **IV:** 127
Tate, Mrs. Allen (Isabella Gardner), **IV:** 127
Tate, Nancy, **II:** 197
Tattooed Countess, The (Van Vechten), **I:** 295; **Supp. II Part 2:** 726-728, 738, 742
Tattooed Feet (Nye), **Supp. XIII:** 274
"Tattoos" (McClatchy), **Supp. XII:** 266-267, 268
"Tattoos" (Wright), **Supp. V:** 335, 340
Tatum, Anna, **I:** 516
Tatum, James, **Supp. IV Part 2:** 684
Taupin, René, **II:** 528, 529; **Supp. III Part 2:** 614, 615, 617, 621

Tawney, Richard Henry, **Supp. I Part 2:** 481
Taylor, Bayard, **II:** 275; **Supp. I Part 1:** 350, 361, 362, 365, 366, 372; **Supp. XV:** 269
Taylor, Cora. *See* Howarth, Cora
Taylor, Deems, **III:** 138
Taylor, Edward, **III:** 493; **IV: 144-166; Supp. I Part 1:** 98; **Supp. I Part 2:** 375, 386, 546
Taylor, Eleanor Ross, **Supp. V:** 317, 318
Taylor, Elizabeth, **II:** 588
Taylor, Frank, **III:** 81
Taylor, Frederick Winslow, **Supp. I Part 2:** 644
Taylor, Graham, **Supp. I Part 1:** 5
Taylor, Henry, **Retro. Supp. I:** 212; **Supp. XI:** 317; **Supp. XIII:** 333
Taylor, Henry W., **IV:** 144
Taylor, Jeremy, **II:** 11; **III:** 487; **Supp. I Part 1:** 349; **Supp. XII:** 45; **Supp. XIV:**344, 345
Taylor, John, **IV:** 149
Taylor, Katherine, **Supp. VIII:** 251
Taylor, Kezia, **IV:** 148
Taylor, Mrs. Edward (Elizabeth Fitch), **IV:** 147, 165
Taylor, Mrs. Edward (Ruth Wyllys), **IV:** 148
Taylor, Nathaniel W., **Supp. I Part 2:** 580
Taylor, Paul, **I:** 293
Taylor, Peter, **Retro. Supp. II:** 179; **Supp. V: 313-329; Supp. XIV:**3
Taylor, Raynor, **Supp. XV:** 238
Taylor, Richard, **IV:** 146
Taylor, Robert, **Supp. I Part 1:** 294; **Supp. XV:** 135, 138; **Supp. XVI:**277
Taylor, Stephan, **Supp. XVI:**203
Taylor, Thomas, **II:** 10
Taylor, William, **IV:** 145-146
Taylor, Zachary, **I:** 3; **II:** 433-434
Tchelitchew, Peter, **II:** 586
Tea and Sympathy (Anderson), **Supp. I Part 1:** 277; **Supp. V:** 108
"Tea at the Palaz of Hoon" (Stevens), **Retro. Supp. I:** 300, 302, 306
"Teacher's Pet" (Thurber), **Supp. I Part 2:** 605-606
"Teaching and Story Telling" (Maclean), **Supp. XIV:**234
Teaching a Stone to Talk: Expeditions and Encounters (Dillard), **Supp. VI:** 23, 26, 28, 32, 33, 34-35
Teachings of Don B., The (Barthelme), **Supp. IV Part 1:** 53
Teale, Edwin Way, **Supp. XIII:** 7

Teall, Dorothy, **I:** 221
Team Team Team (film), **Supp. IX:** 251
"Tea on the Mountain" (Bowles), **Supp. IV Part 1:** 90
"Tea Party, The" (MacLeish), **III:** 11
"Tears, Idle Tears" (Lord Tennyson), **Supp. XIV:** 8
"Tears of the Pilgrims, The" (McClatchy), **Supp. XII:** 256
Teasdale, Sara, **Retro. Supp. I:** 133; **Supp. I Part 2:** 393, 707; **Supp. XIV:** 127; **Supp. XV:** 295, 297, 301, 305, 307, 308; **Supp. XVII:** 69, 75
Tebeaux, Elizabeth, **Supp. IX:** 109
Technics and Civilization (Mumford), **Supp. I Part 2:** 638; **Supp. II Part 2:** 479, 493, 497
Technics and Human Development (Mumford), **Supp. I Part 2:** 638; **Supp. II Part 2:** 497
"Teddy" (Salinger), **III:** 561-563, 571
"Te Deum" (Reznikoff), **Supp. XIV:** 281
Tedlock, Dennis, **Supp. IV Part 2:** 509
"Teeth Mother Naked at Last, The" (R. Bly), **Supp. IV Part 1:** 63, 68, 73
Teggart, Richard, **Supp. I Part 2:** 650
Tegnér, Esaias, **Retro. Supp. II:** 155
Teilhard de Chardin, Pierre, **Supp. I Part 1:** 314
Telephone, The (film), **Supp. XI:** 309
"Telephone Call, A" (Parker), **Supp. IX:** 202-203
"Telephone Number of the Muse, The" (Justice), **Supp. VII:** 124-125
Telephone Poles and Other Poems (Updike), **IV:** 214, 215
"Television" (Beattie), **Supp. V:** 33
Teller, Edward, **I:** 137
"Telling" (Ortiz), **Supp. IV Part 2:** 509
"Telling It in Black and White: The Importance of the Africanist Presence in *To Kill a Mockingbird*" (Baecker), **Supp. VIII:** 128
Telling Secrets (Buechner), **Supp. XII:** 53-54
Telling Stories (Didion), **Supp. IV Part 1:** 197
"Telling Stories" (Didion), **Supp. IV Part 1:** 197
"Telling the Bees" (Whittier), **Supp. I Part 2:** 694-695
Telling the Little Secrets (J. Burstein), **Supp. XVII:** 44
Telling the Truth: The Gospel as Tragedy, Comedy, and Fairy Tale (Buechner), **Supp. XII:** 53
"Tell Me" (Hughes), **Supp. VIII:** 213
Tell Me, Tell Me (Moore), **III:** 215

Tell Me Again How the White Heron Rises and Flies across the Nacreous River at Twilight toward the Distant Islands (Carruth), **Supp. XVI:** 56
Tell Me a Riddle (film), **Supp. XIII:** 295
Tell Me a Riddle (Olsen), **Supp. XIII:** 294, 296, **298-302**, 303, 305
"Tell Me a Riddle" (Olsen), **Supp. XIII:** 294, 297, 298, **300-302**, 305
Tell Me How Long the Train's Been Gone (Baldwin), **Retro. Supp. II:** 9, **11-12**, 14; **Supp. I Part 1:** 48, 52, 63-65, 67
"Tell Me My Fortune" (Epstein), **Supp. XII:** 163
Tell Me Your Answer True (Sexton), **Supp. II Part 2:** 683
Tell My Horse (Hurston), **Supp. VI:** 149, 156, 158
"Tell-Tale Heart, The" (Poe), **III:** 413, 414-415, 416; **Retro. Supp. II:** 267, 269, 270
"Tell the Women We're Going" (Carver), **Supp. III Part 1:** 138, 144
"Telluride Blues-A Hatchet Job" (Abbey), **Supp. XIII:** 10
Telushkin, Dvorah, **Retro. Supp. II:** 317
Temblor (Howe), **Supp. IV Part 2:** 431
Tempering of Eugene O'Neill, The (D. Alexander), **Supp. XVII:** 99
"Temper of Steel, The" (Jones), **Supp. XI:** 218
Tempers, The (W. C. Williams), **Retro. Supp. I:** **413-414**, 415, 416, 424
Tempest, The (Shakespeare), **I:** 394; **II:** 12; **III:** 40, 61, 263; **Retro. Supp. I:** 61; **Supp. IV Part 2:** 463; **Supp. V:** 302-303; **Supp. XII:** 54-57; **Supp. XV:** 255, 256
Temple, Minnie, **II:** 323
Temple, The (Herbert), **IV:** 145, 153
Temple, William, **III:** 303
Temple House (E. Stoddard), **Supp. XV:** 273, **284-286**
Temple of My Familiar, The (Walker), **Supp. III Part 2:** 521, 527, 529, 535, 537; **Supp. IV Part 1:** 14
"Temple of the Holy Ghost, A" (O'Connor), **III:** 344, 352; **Retro. Supp. II:** 232
Templin, Charlotte, **Supp. V:** 116
Temporary Shelter (Gordon), **Supp. IV Part 1:** 299, 305-307
"Temporary Shelter" (Gordon), **Supp. IV Part 1:** 306
Temptation Game, The (Gardner), **Supp. VI:** 72
"Temptation of St. Anthony, The"

(Barthelme), **Supp. IV Part 1:** 47
Temptations, The, **Supp. X:** 242
"Tenancy, A" (Merrill), **Supp. III Part 1:** 322, 323
Tenants, The (Malamud), **Supp. I Part 2:** 448-450
Ten Commandments (McClatchy), **Supp. XII: 262-265**
Ten Days That Shook the World (Reed), **II:** 577; **Supp. X:** 136
Tendencies in Modern American Poetry (Lowell), **II:** 529
"Tender, Hilarious Reminiscences of Life in Mythical Lake Wobegon" (MacDougall), **Supp. XVI:** 174
Tender Buttons (G. Stein), **I:** 103, 105; **IV:** 27, 42-43; **Retro. Supp. II:** 331; **Supp. XV:** 347
"Tenderfoot" (Haines), **Supp. XII:** 209
Tender Is the Night (Fitzgerald), **I:** 375; **II:** 79, 84, 91, 95-96, 97, 98, 420; **Retro. Supp. I:** 105, 108, 109, **110-112**, 114; **Supp. IX:** 59, 60, 61; **Supp. XV:** 197
"Tenderloin" (Crane), **I:** 408
"Tenderly" (Dobyns), **Supp. XIII:** 86-87
'Tender Man, A" (Bambara), **Supp. XI:** 9-10
"Tenderness" (Dunn), **Supp. XI:** 149, 150
"Tender Offer, The" (Auchincloss), **Supp. IV Part 1:** 34
"Tender Organizations, The" (C. Bly), **Supp. XVI:** 40, 42
"Tenebrae" (Komunyakaa), **Supp. XIII:** 132
"Ten Forty-Four" (Kingsolver), **Supp. VII:** 208
Ten Indians (Bell), **Supp. X:** 7, **12**
"Ten Neglected American Writers Who Deserve to Be Better Known" (Cantor), **Supp. IV Part 1:** 285
Tennent, Gilbert, **I:** 546
Tennessee Day in St. Louis (Taylor), **Supp. V:** 324
"Tennessee's Partner" (Harte), **Supp. II Part 1:** 345, 348-350
"Tennis" (Pinsky), **Supp. VI:** 241, 242
Tennis Court Oath, The (Ashbery), **Supp. III Part 1:** 7, 9, 12, 14, 26
Ten North Frederick (O'Hara), **III:** 361
Tennyson, Alfred, Lord, **I:** 587-588; **II:** 18, 82, 273, 338, 404, 439, 604; **III:** 5, 409, 469, 485, 511, 521, 523; **Retro. Supp. I:** 100, 325; **Retro. Supp. II:** 135; **Supp. I Part 1:** 349, 356; **Supp. I Part 2:** 410, 416, 552; **Supp. IX:** 19; **Supp. X:** 157; **Supp. XIII:** 111; **Supp. XIV:** 40, 120

Tennyson, Alfred Lord, **Supp. XV:** 275
"Ten O'Clock News" (Ortiz), **Supp. IV Part 2:** 503-504
Ten Poems (Dove), **Supp. IV Part 1:** 244
Ten Poems of Francis Ponge Translated by Robert Bly and Ten Poems of Robert Bly Inspired by the Poems by Francis Ponge (R. Bly), **Supp. IV Part 1:** 71
"Tension in Poetry" (Tate), **IV:** 128, 129, 135
Tenth Muse, The (Bradstreet), **Supp. I Part 1:** 102, 103, 114
"Tent on the Beach, The" (Whittier), **Supp. I Part 2:** 703
"Teodoro Luna Confesses after Years to His Brother, Anselmo the Priest, Who Is Required to Understand, But Who Understands Anyway, More Than People Think" (Ríos), **Supp. IV Part 2:** 552
Teodoro Luna's Two Kisses (Ríos), **Supp. IV Part 2:** 550-552, 553
"Tepeyac" (Cisneros), **Supp. VII:** 69
"Terce" (Auden), **Supp. II Part 1:** 22
Terence, **IV:** 155, 363; **Supp. I Part 2:** 405
Terkel, Studs, **Supp. IV Part 1:** 364
"Term" (Merwin), **Supp. III Part 1:** 356-357
"Terminal Days at Beverly Farms" (Lowell), **Retro. Supp. II:** 189
Terminating, or Sonnet LXXV, or "Lass Meine Schmerzen nicht verloren sein, or Ambivalence" (Kushner), **Supp. IX:** 132
Terminations (James), **Retro. Supp. I:** 229
"Terminus" (Emerson), **II:** 13, 19
"Terminus" (Wharton), **Retro. Supp. I:** 371
"Terms in Which I Think of Reality, The" (Ginsberg), **Supp. II Part 1:** 311
Terms of Endearment (film), **Supp. V:** 226
Terms of Endearment (McMurtry), **Supp. V:** 224-225
"Terrace, The" (Wilbur), **Supp. III Part 2:** 550
Terrarium (Sanders), **Supp. XVI:**270
"Terrence McNally" (Bryer), **Supp. XIII:** 200
"Terrence McNally" (Di Gaetani), **Supp. XIII:** 200
Terrence McNally: A Casebook (Zinman), **Supp. XIII:** 209
"Terrible Peacock, The" (Barnes), **Supp. III Part 1:** 33

Terrible Threes, The (Reed), **Supp. X:** 241, 253
Terrible Twos, The (Reed), **Supp. X:** 241, 252-253
"Terrific Mother" (Moore), **Supp. X:** 178
Territory Ahead, The (Morris), **III:** 228-229, 236
Terrorism (Wright), **Supp. XV:** 341, 342
"Terrorism" (Wright), **Supp. XV:** 341
Terry, Edward A., **II:** 128, 129
Terry, Rose, **Supp. I Part 2:** 420
Tertium Organum (Ouspensky), **I:** 383
Tess of the d'Urbervilles (Hardy), **II:** 181; **Retro. Supp. II:** 100
"Testament" (Berry), **Supp. X:** 36
"Testament" (Carruth), **Supp. XVI:**59
"Testament (Or, Homage to Walt Whitman)" (Jong), **Supp. V:** 130
"Testament: Vermeer in December" (Bierds), **Supp. XVII:** 33
"Testament of Flood" (Warren), **IV:** 253
Testament of François Villon, The (Pound, opera), **Retro. Supp. I:** 287
"Testimonia on the Question of Stesichoros' Blinding by Helen" (Carson), **Supp. XII:** 107
"Testimonies of a Roasted Chicken" (Jarman), **Supp. XVII:** 120
"Testimony" (Komunyakaa), **Supp. XIII:** 129
Testimony: The United States (1885-1890): Recitative (Reznikoff), **Supp. XIV:**279, 280, 281, 285, **289-291**
Testimony: The United States (1891-1900): Recitative (Reznikoff), **Supp. XIV:**291
"Testimony of James Apthorp, The" (Kees), **Supp. XV:** 146
Testing-Tree, The (Kunitz), **Supp. III Part 1:** 269
Testing-Tree, The (Kunitz), **Supp. III Part 1:** 260, 263, 264, 267, 268
Test of Poetry, A (Zukofsky), **Supp. III Part 2:** 618, 622
"Teutonic Scholar" (X. J. Kennedy), **Supp. XV:** 161
"Texas Moon, and Elsewhere, The" (McMurtry), **Supp. V:** 225
Texas Poets in Concert: A Quartet (Gwynn, ed.), **Supp. XIII:** 277
Texas Summer (Southern), **Supp. XI:** 309
Texasville (McMurtry), **Supp. V:** 228, 233
Thacher, Molly Day, **IV:** 381
Thackeray, William Makepeace, **I:** 194, 354; **II:** 182, 271, 282, 288, 316, 321, 322; **III:** 64, 70; **IV:** 326; **Retro. Supp. I:** 218; **Supp. I Part 1:** 307; **Supp. I Part 2:** 421, 495, 579; **Supp. IV Part 1:** 297; **Supp. IX:** 200; **Supp. XI:** 277; **Supp. XIV:**306
Thaddeus, Janice Farrar, **Supp. IV Part 1:** 299
"Thailand" (Barthelme), **Supp. IV Part 1:** 41
Thalberg, Irving, **Retro. Supp. I:** 109, 110, 114; **Supp. XVI:**191, 192
Thales, **I:** 480-481
Thalia Trilogy (McMurtry), **Supp. V:** 220-223, 234
Tham, Claire, **Supp. VIII:** 79
"Thanatopsis" (Bryant), **Supp. I Part 1:** 150, 154, 155, 170
Thanatos Syndrome, The (Percy), **Supp. III Part 1:** 385, 397-399
"Thanksgiving" (Glück), **Supp. V:** 83
"Thanksgiving, A" (Auden), **Supp. II Part 1:** 26
"Thanksgiving for a Habitat" (Auden), **Supp. II Part 1:** 24
Thanksgivings (Traherne), **Supp. XVI:**288
"Thanksgiving Spirit" (Farrell), **II:** 45
Thanksgiving Visitor, The (Capote), **Supp. III Part 1:** 116, 118, 119
Thank You, Fog (Auden), **Supp. II Part 1:** 24
"Thank You, Lord" (Angelou), **Supp. IV Part 1:** 15
Thank You, Mr. Moto (Marquand), **III:** 57, 58
Thank You and Other Poems (Koch), **Supp. XV:** 180-181
"Thank You in Arabic" (Nye), **Supp. XIII:** 273, 281
"Thar's More in the Man Than Thar Is in the Land" (Lanier), **Supp. I Part 1:** 352-353, 359-360
"That Evening Sun" (Faulkner), **II:** 72; **Retro. Supp. I:** 75, 83
That Horse (Hogan), **Supp. IV Part 1:** 397, 404, 405
"That I Had the Wings" (Ellison), **Supp. II Part 1:** 238
"That's the Place Indians Talk About" (Ortiz), **Supp. IV Part 2:** 511
"That the Soul May Wax Plump" (Swenson), **Supp. IV Part 2:** 650
"That the Universe Is Chrysalid" (Sobin), **Supp. XVI:**284
"That Tree" (Porter), **III:** 434-435, 446, 451
That Was the Week That Was (television program), **Supp. XIV:**125
"That Year" (Olds), **Supp. X:** 203

"Thaw" (C. Frost), **Supp. XV:** 93, 104, 105
Thaxter, Celia, **Retro. Supp. II:** 136, 147; **Supp. XIII:** 143, 153
Thayer, Abbott, **I:** 231
Thayer, Scofield, **I:** 231; **Retro. Supp. I:** 58
Thayer and Eldridge, **Retro. Supp. I:** 403
"Theater" (Toomer), **Supp. IX:** 309, 317-318
"Theater Chronicle" (McCarthy), **II:** 562
"Theater Problems? Call Dr. Chekhov" (Wasserstein), **Supp. XV:** 320
Theatricals (James), **Retro. Supp. I:** 228
"Theft" (Porter), **III:** 434, 435
Theft, A (Bellow), **Retro. Supp. II:** 31-32, 34
The Harder They Fall: Celebrities Tell Their Real-Life Stories of Addiction and Recovery (F. Wright), **Supp. XVII:** 240
Their Eyes Were Watching God (Hurston), **Supp. VI:** 149, 152, 156-157
Their Heads Are Green and Their Hands Are Blue: Scenes from the Non-Christian World (Bowles), **Supp. IV Part 1:** 89
"Their Losses" (Taylor), **Supp. V:** 320
Their Wedding Journey (Howells), **II:** 277-278; **Retro. Supp. I:** 334
them (Oates), **Supp. II Part 2:** 503, 511-514
Theme Is Freedom, The (Dos Passos), **I:** 488-489, 492, 494
"Theme with Variations" (Agee), **I:** 27
"Then" (Barthelme), **Supp. IV Part 1:** 48
"Then It All Came Down" (Capote), **Supp. III Part 1:** 125, 131
Theocritus, **II:** 169; **Retro. Supp. I:** 286
"Theodore the Poet" (Masters), **Supp. I Part 2:** 461
Theological Position, A (Coover), **Supp. V:** 44
Theophrastus, **I:** 58
"Theoretical and Scientific Conceptions of Race, The" (Locke), **Supp. XIV:** 209
Theory and Practice of Rivers and Other Poems, The (Harrison), **Supp. VIII:** 47, 49
Theory of Business Enterprise, The (Veblen), **Supp. I Part 2:** 638, 641, 644
Theory of Flight (Rukeyser), **Supp. VI:** 272, 275, **277-278,** 284
"Theory of Flight" (Rukeyser), **Supp. VI:** 277-278
Theory of Moral Sentiments, The (A. Smith), **Supp. I Part 2:** 634
Theory of the Leisure Class, The (Veblen), **I:** 475-476; **Supp. I Part 2:** 629, 633, 641, 645; **Supp. IV Part 1:** 22
"There" (Taylor), **Supp. V:** 323
"There Are No Such Trees in Alpine California" (Haines), **Supp. XII:** 207
"There Goes (Varoom! Varoom!) That Kandy-Kolored Tangerine-Flake Streamline Baby" (Wolfe), **Supp. III Part 2:** 569-571
"There Is a Lesson" (Olsen), **Supp. XIII:** 292, 297
"There Is Only One of Everything" (Atwood), **Supp. XIII:** 34
There Is Something Out There (McNally). See *And Things That Go Bump in the Night* (McNally)
"There's a certain Slant of light" (Dickinson), **Retro. Supp. I:** 38
There's a Wocket in My Pocket! (Geisel), **Supp. XVI:**111
Thérèse de Lisieux, Saint, **Supp. VIII:** 195
"There She Is She Is Taking Her Bath" (Anderson), **I:** 113, 114
"There Was a Child Went Forth" (Whitman), **IV:** 348
"There Was a Man, There Was a Woman" (Cisneros), **Supp. VII:** 70
"There Was an Old Woman She Had So Many Children She Didn't Know What to Do" (Cisneros), **Supp. VII:** 60
"There Was a Youth Whose Name Was Thomas Granger" (Olson), **Supp. II Part 2:** 558, 560, 563
There Were Giants in the Land (Benét), **Supp. XI:** 50
There You Are (Simpson), **Supp. IX: 279-280**
"There You Are" (Simpson), **Supp. IX:** 279
"Thermopylae" (Clampitt), **Supp. IX:** 43
Theroux, Alexander, **Supp. VIII:** 312
Theroux, Marcel, **Supp. VIII:** 325
Theroux, Paul, **Supp. V:** 122; **Supp. VIII: 309-327**
"These Are My People" (Hayden), **Supp. II Part 1:** 365
"These are the days when Birds come back" (Dickinson), **Retro. Supp. I:** 30
"These Days" (Olds), **Supp. X:** 215
"These Flames and Generosities of the Heart: Emily Dickinson and the Illogic of Sumptuary Values" (Howe), **Supp. IV Part 2:** 431
"These saw Visions" (Dickinson), **Retro. Supp. I:** 46
These Thirteen (Faulkner), **II:** 72
These Three (film), **Supp. I Part 1:** 281
These Times (Untermeyer), **Supp. XV: 299-300,** 303
"These Times" (Untermeyer), **Supp. XV:** 300
"Thessalonica: A Roman Story" (Brown), **Supp. I Part 1:** 133
Thévenaz, Paul, **Supp. XV:** 42
Thew, Harvey, **Supp. XIII:** 166
"They Ain't the Men They Used To Be" (Farrell), **II:** 45
"They Burned the Books" (Benét), **Supp. XI:** 46
They Came Like Swallows (Maxwell), **Supp. VIII: 155-159,** 168, 169
"They Can't Turn Back" (Baldwin), **Supp. I Part 1:** 52
They Do Not: The Letters of a Non-Professional Lady Arranged for Public Consumption (Clements), **Supp. XVI:**190
They Feed They Lion (Levine), **Supp. V:** 178, 179, 181, 184-185, 186
"They Feed They Lion" (Levine), **Supp. V:** 188
"They Lion Grow" (Levine), **Supp. V:** 184-185
"They're Not Your Husband" (Carver), **Supp. III Part 1:** 141, 143
They're Playing Our Song (musical), **Supp. IV Part 2:** 589
They Shall Inherit the Laughter (Jones), **Supp. XI:** 217, 218, 232
They Shoot Horses (film), **Supp. XIII:** 159
They Shoot Horses, Don't They? (McCoy), **Supp. XIII:** 159, **164-166,** 168, 171, 172, 174
"They Sing, They Sing" (Roethke), **III:** 544
They Stooped to Folly (Glasgow), **II:** 175, 186-187
They Whisper (R. O. Butler), **Supp. XII: 72-73**
Thidwick the Big-Hearted Moose (Geisel), **Supp. XVI:**104
"Thief's Philosophy of Life, The" (Hapgood), **Supp. XVII:** 103
"Thief's Wife, The" (B. Kelly), **Supp. XVII:** 125-126
"Thieves" (Yates), **Supp. XI:** 349

Thieves of Paradise (Komunyakaa), **Supp. XIII:** 113, **128-130**, 132
"Thimble, The" (Kenyon), **Supp. VII:** 164
"Thing and Its Relations, The" (James), **II:** 357
"Things" (Haines), **Supp. XII:** 207
"Things" (Kenyon), **Supp. VII:** 169
"Things, The" (Kinnell), **Supp. III Part 1:** 246
Things As They Are (Stein), **IV:** 34, 37, 40
"Things Don't Stop" (Nye), **Supp. XIII:** 287
Things Gone and Things Still Here (Bowles), **Supp. IV Part 1:** 91
"Things of August" (Stevens), **Retro. Supp. I:** 309
Things of This World (Wilbur), **Supp. III Part 2:** 552-555
Things Themselves: Essays and Scenes (Price), **Supp. VI:** 261
Things They Carried, The (O'Brien), **Supp. V:** 238, 239, 240, 243, 248-250
Things They Carried, The (T. O'Brien), **Supp. XVII:** 14
"Thing That Killed My Father Off, The" (Carver), **Supp. III Part 1:** 143
"Think about It" (Conroy), **Supp. XVI:** 75
Think Back on Us … (Cowley), **Supp. II Part 1:** 139, 140, 142
Think Fast, Mr. Moto (Marquand), **III:** 57, 58
"Thinking about Barbara Deming" (Paley), **Supp. VI:** 227
"Thinking about Being Called Simple by a Critic" (Stafford), **Supp. XI:** 328
Thinking about the Longstanding Problems of Virtue and Happiness: Essays, a Play, Two Poems, and a Prayer (Kushner), **Supp. IX:** 131, 134, 135
"Thinking about the Past" (Justice), **Supp. VII:** 123-124
"Thinking about Western Thinking" (Didion), **Supp. IV Part 1:** 204, 206
"'Thinking against Oneself': Reflections on Cioran" (Sontag), **Supp. III Part 2:** 459-460
"Thinking Back Through Our Mothers: Traditions in Canadian Women's Writing" (Shields), **Supp. VII:** 307-308
"Thinking for Berky" (Stafford), **Supp. XI:** 320
"Thinking like a Mountain" (Leopold), **Supp. XIV:** 188, 189
"Thinking of the Lost World" (Jarrell), **II:** 338-389
Thinking Out Loud (Quindlen), **Supp. XVII:** 167, **169-170**
Thin Man, The (film), **Supp. IV Part 1:** 342, 355
Thin Man, The (Hammett), **Supp. IV Part 1:** 354-355
"Thinnest Shadow, The" (Ashbery), **Supp. III Part 1:** 5
"Thin People, The" (Plath), **Supp. I Part 2:** 538, 547
Thin Red Line, The (film; Malick), **Supp. V:** 249; **Supp. XV:** 351
Thin Red Line, The (Jones), **Supp. XI:** 219, **224-225**, 229, 231, 232, 233, 234
"Thin Strips" (Sandburg), **III:** 587
"Third Avenue in Sunlight" (Hecht), **Supp. X:** 61
"Third Body, A" (R. Bly), **Supp. IV Part 1:** 71
Third Circle, The (Norris), **III:** 327
"Third Expedition, The" (Bradbury), **Supp. IV Part 1:** 103, 106
Third Generation, The (C. Himes), **Supp. XVI:** 135, **140-141**
Third Life of Grange Copeland, The (Walker), **Supp. III Part 2:** 520, 527-536
Third Mind, The (Burroughs), **Supp. XII:** 3
Third Rose, The (Brinnin), **IV:** 26
"Third Sermon on the Warpland, The" (Brooks), **Supp. III Part 1:** 85
"Third Thing That Killed My Father Off, The" (Carver), **Supp. III Part 1:** 144
Third Violet, The (Crane), **I:** 408, 417-418
Thirlwall, John C., **Retro. Supp. I:** 430
"Thirst: Introduction to Kinds of Water" (Carson), **Supp. XII:** 103
13 by Shanley (Shanley), **Supp. XIV:** 316
Thirteen Hands: A Play in Two Acts (Shields), **Supp. VII:** 322-323
Thirteen O'Clock (Benét), **Supp. XI:** 46
Thirteen Other Stories (Purdy), **Supp. VII:** 278
Thirteen Stories and Thirteen Epitaphs (Vollmann), **Supp. XVII:** 226
"Thirteenth and Pennsylvania" (Stafford), **Supp. XI:** 324
"Thirteen Ways of Looking at a Blackbird" (Stevens), **IV:** 94; **Supp. IX:** 47; **Supp. XVII:** 130
"30. Meditation. 2. Cor. 5.17. He Is a New Creature" (Taylor), **IV:** 144
30: Pieces of a Novel (Dixon), **Supp. XII:** 152, **153-154**
30/6 (poetry chapbook), **Supp. V:** 5, 6
"Thirty Bob a Week" (Davidson), **Retro. Supp. I:** 55
"Thirty Delft Tiles" (Doty), **Supp. XI:** 131
"35/10" (Olds), **Supp. X:** 206
"35,000 Feet-The Lanterns" (Goldbarth), **Supp. XII:** 182
31 Letters and 13 Dreams (Hugo), **Supp. VI:** 141-144
Thirty Poems (Bryant), **Supp. I Part 1:** 157, 158
Thirty-Six Poems (Warren), **IV:** 236, 239, 240
"33" (Alvarez), **Supp. VII:** 4
"3275" (Monette), **Supp. X:** 148, 159
Thirty Years (Marquand), **III:** 56, 60-61
Thirty Years of Treason (Bentley), **Supp. I Part 1:** 297
This, My Letter (Hay), **Supp. XIV:** 121, 122, 129, 131
"This, That & the Other" (Nemerov), **III:** 269
This Body Is Made of Camphor and Gopherwood (R. Bly), **Supp. IV Part 1:** 63-65, 66, 71
This Boy's Life: A Memoir (T. Wolff), **Supp. VII:** 334-339, 340, 343; **Supp. XI:** 246, 247
"This Bright Dream" (Benét), **Supp. XI:** 55
This Coffin Has No Handles (McGrath), **Supp. X:** 117
"This Configuration" (Ashbery), **Supp. III Part 1:** 22
"This Corruptible" (Wylie), **Supp. I Part 2:** 727, 729
"This Crutch That I Love" (Nye), **Supp. XIII:** 288
"This Gentile World" (H. Miller), **III:** 177
"This Hand" (Wylie), **Supp. I Part 2:** 713
"This Hour" (Olds), **Supp. X:** 212
"This House I Cannot Leave" (Kingsolver), **Supp. VII:** 208
This Hunger (Nin), **Supp. X:** 185
"This Is a Photograph of Me" (Atwood), **Supp. XIII:** 33
"This Is a Poem, Good Afternoon" (Keillor), **Supp. XVI:** 167
"This Is It" (Stern), **Supp. IX:** 290
"This Is Just to Say" (W. C. Williams), **Supp. XI:** 328
"This Is My Heart" (Harjo), **Supp. XII:** 230

This Is Not a Novel (Markson), **Supp. XVII:** 145-146
"This Is Not Who We Are" (Nye), **Supp. XIII:** 285, 286
"This Is What I Said" (Salinas), **Supp. XIII:** 322
This Journey (Wright), **Supp. III Part 2:** 605-606
This Man and This Woman (Farrell), **II:** 42
"This Morning" (Kenyon), **Supp. VII:** 164
"This Morning, This Evening, So Soon" (Baldwin), **Supp. I Part 1:** 63
"This Morning Again It Was in the Dusty Pines" (Oliver), **Supp. VII:** 240
This Music Crept by Me upon the Waters (MacLeish), **III:** 21
This People Israel: The Meaning of Jewish Existence (Baeck), **Supp. V:** 260
"This Personal Maze Is Not the Prize" (Selinger), **Supp. XI:** 248
"This Place in the Ways" (Rukeyser), **Supp. VI:** 273-274
This Property Is Condemned (T. Williams), **IV:** 378
This Proud Heart (Buck), **Supp. II Part 1:** 119-120
This Same Sky: A Collection of Poems from around the World (Nye, ed.), **Supp. XIII:** 280
"This Sandwich Has No Mayonnaise" (Salinger), **III:** 552-553
This Side of Paradise (Fitzgerald), **I:** 358; **II:** 77, 80, 81, 82-83, 84, 85-87, 88; **Retro. Supp. I:** 99-100, **101-102**, 103, 105, 106, 110, 111
This Singing World: An Anthology of Modern Poetry for Young People (Untermeyer, ed.), **Supp. XV:** 306
This Stubborn Self: Texas Autobiographies (Almon), **Supp. XIII:** 288
This Thing Don't Lead to Heaven (Crews), **Supp. XI:** 112
This Time: New and Selected Poems (Stern), **Supp. IX:** 290-291, **299**
"Thistle Seed in the Wind" (Francis), **Supp. IX:** 81
"Thistles in Sweden, The" (Maxwell), **Supp. VIII:** 169
"This Tokyo" (Snyder), **Supp. VIII:** 298
This Tree Will Be Here for a Thousand Years (R. Bly), **Supp. IV Part 1:** 65-66, 71, 72
This Tree Will Be Here for a Thousand Years (revised edition) (R. Bly), **Supp. IV Part 1:** 66
This Very Earth (Caldwell), **I:** 297, 302
Thoens, Karen, **Supp. V:** 147
Thomas, Brandon, **II:** 138
Thomas, D. M., **Supp. VIII:** 5
Thomas, Debra, **Supp. XIII:** 114
Thomas, Dylan, **I:** 49, 64, 382, 432, 526, 533; **III:** 21, 521, 528, 532, 534; **IV:** 89, 93, 136; **Supp. I Part 1:** 263; **Supp. III Part 1:** 42, 47; **Supp. V:** 344; **Supp. VIII:** 21; **Supp. IX:** 114; **Supp. X:** 115; **Supp. XV:** 74; **Supp. XVII:** 135
Thomas, Edward, **II:** 154; **Retro. Supp. I:** 127, 131, 132; **Supp. I Part 1:** 263; **Supp. II Part 1:** 4
Thomas, J. Parnell, **Supp. I Part 1:** 286; **Supp. XV:** 198
Thomas, James, **Supp. XVI:**268
Thomas, Lewis, **Retro. Supp. I:** 323
Thomas, William I., **Supp. I Part 2:** 641
Thomas-a-Kempis, **Retro. Supp. I:** 247
Thomas and Beulah (Dove), **Supp. IV Part 1:** 242, 247-248, 249
Thomas Aquinas (Saint), **I:** 13, 14, 265, 267; **III:** 270; **Retro. Supp. II:** 222; **Supp. IV Part 2:** 526
"Thomas at the Wheel" (Dove), **Supp. IV Part 1:** 248
"Thomas McGrath: Words for a Vanished Age" (Vinz), **Supp. X:** 117
Thomas Merton on Peace, **Supp. VIII:** 208
Thomas Merton Studies Center, The, **Supp. VIII:** 208
Thompson, Barbara, **Supp. V:** 322
Thompson, Cy, **I:** 538
Thompson, Dorothy, **II:** 449-450, 451, 453; **Supp. XV:** 307
Thompson, E. P., **Supp. X:** 112, 117
Thompson, Francis, **Retro. Supp. I:** 55
Thompson, Frank, **II:** 20
Thompson, George, **Supp. I Part 2:** 686
Thompson, Hunter S., **Supp. VIII:** 42; **Supp. XI:** 105; **Supp. XIII:** 1, 17; **Supp. XVII:** 95, 102, 228
Thompson, James R., **Supp. IV Part 1:** 217
Thompson, John, **Supp. V:** 323
Thompson, Lawrance, **II:** 508
Thompson, Lawrance Roger, **Retro. Supp. I:** 138, 141
Thompson, Morton, **Supp. XIII:** 170
Thompson, Theresa, **Supp. V:** 141
Thompson, William T., **Supp. I Part 2:** 411
Supp. IV Part 1: 66
Thomson, James, **II:** 304; **Supp. I Part 1:** 150, 151
Thomson, Virgil, **IV:** 45; **Supp. IV Part 1:** 81, 83, 84, 173; **Supp. XVI:**195
"Thoreau" (Lowell), **Supp. I Part 2:** 420, 422
Thoreau, Henry David, **I:** 98, 104, 228, 236, 257, 258, 261, 305, 433; **II:** 7, 8, 13, 17, 101, 159, 224, 273-274, 295, 312-313, 321, 457-458, 540, 546-547; **III:** 171, 174, 186-187, 189, 208, 214-215, 453, 454, 507, 577; **IV: 167-189**, 191, 341; **Retro. Supp. I:** 51, 62, 122; **Retro. Supp. II:** 13, 96, 142, 158; **Supp. I Part 1:** 29, 34, 116, 188, 299, 358; **Supp. I Part 2:** 383, 400, 420, 421, 507, 540, 579, 580, 655, 659, 660, 664, 678; **Supp. III Part 1:** 340, 353; **Supp. IV Part 1:** 236, 392, 416; **Supp. IV Part 2:** 420, 430, 433, 439, 447; **Supp. V:** 200, 208; **Supp. VIII:** 40, 42, 103, 105, 198, 201, 204, 205, 292, 303; **Supp. IX:** 25, 90, 171; **Supp. X:** 21, 27, 28-29, 101, 102; **Supp. XI:** 155; **Supp. XIII:** 1, 17; **Supp. XIV:**40, 54, 106, 177, 181
Thoreau, John, **IV:** 171, 182
Thoreau, Mrs. John, **IV:** 172
"Thorn, The" (Gordon), **Supp. IV Part 1:** 314
Thorne, Francis, **Supp. XII:** 253
"Thorn Merchant, The" (Komunyakaa), **Supp. XIII:** 119-120
Thornton, Billy Bob, **Supp. VIII:** 175
Thornton, Lionel, **III:** 291
"Thorofare" (Minot), **Supp. VI: 209-210**
"Thorow" (Howe), **Supp. IV Part 2:** 419, 420, 421, 431, 433-434
Thorp, Willard, **Supp. XIII:** 101
Thorslev, Peter L., Jr., **I:** 524
Thorstein Veblen (Dowd), **Supp. I Part 2:** 650
Thorstein Veblen (Qualey, ed.), **Supp. I Part 2:** 650
Thorstein Veblen: A Chapter in American Economic Thought (Teggart), **Supp. I Part 2:** 650
Thorstein Veblen: A Critical Interpretation (Riesman), **Supp. I Part 2:** 649, 650
Thorstein Veblen: A Critical Reappraisal (Dowd, ed.), **Supp. I Part 2:** 650
Thorstein Veblen and His America (Dorfman), **Supp. I Part 2:** 631, 650

Thorstein Veblen and the Institutionalists: A Study in the Social Philosophy of Economics (Seckler), **Supp. I Part 2:** 650
"Those before Us" (Lowell), **II:** 550
"Those Being Eaten by America" (R. Bly), **Supp. IV Part 1:** 62
Those Bones Are Not My Child (Bambara), **Supp. XI:** 1, 14, **20-22**
Those Extraordinary Twins (Twain), **IV:** 205-206
"Those Graves in Rome" (Levis), **Supp. XI:** 266
"Those of Us Who Think We Know" (Dunn), **Supp. XI:** 146
"Those Times …" (Sexton), **Supp. II Part 2:** 670, 684
"Those Various Scalpels" (Moore), **III:** 202
"Those Were the Days" (Levine), **Supp. V:** 190
"Those Who Don't" (Cisneros), **Supp. VII:** 60
"Those Who Thunder" (Hogan), **Supp. IV Part 1:** 406
"Thought, A" (Sarton), **Supp. VIII:** 262
Thought and Character of William James (Perry), **II:** 362
Thoughtbook of Francis Scott Key Fitzgerald (Fitzgerald), **Retro. Supp. I:** 99
"Thoughtful Roisterer Declines the Gambit, The" (Hecht), **Supp. X:** 63
"Thought of Heaven, The" (Stern), **Supp. IX:** 297
"Thoughts after Lambeth" (Eliot), **I:** 587; **Retro. Supp. I:** 324
Thoughts and Reflections (Lord Halifax), **II:** 111
Thoughts in Solitude (Merton), **Supp. VIII:** 207
"Thoughts on Being Bibliographed" (Wilson), **IV:** 435
"Thoughts on the Establishment of a Mint in the United States" (Paine), **Supp. I Part 2:** 512
"Thoughts on the Gifts of Art" (Kenyon), **Supp. VII:** 167
Thousand Acres, A (Smiley), **Supp. VI:** 292, **301-303**
"Thousand and Second Night, The" (Merrill), **Supp. III Part 1:** 324
"Thousand Dollar Vagrant, The" (Olsen), **Supp. XIII:** 292, 297
"Thousand Faces of Danny Torrance, The" (Figliola), **Supp. V:** 143
"Thousand Genuflections, A" (McCarriston), **Supp. XIV:**266
Thousand-Mile Walk to the Gulf, A (Muir), **Supp. IX: 177-178**
"Thou Shalt Not Steal" (McClatchy), **Supp. XII:** 264
"Thread, The" (Merwin), **Supp. III Part 1:** 351
Three (film), **Supp. IX:** 253
3-3-8 (Marquand), **III:** 58
"Three Academic Pieces" (Stevens), **IV:** 90
"Three Agee Wards, The" (Morris), **III:** 220-221
"Three American Singers" (Cather), **Retro. Supp. I:** 10
"Three Around the Old Gentleman" (Berryman), **I:** 188
"Three Avilas, The" (Jeffers), **Supp. II Part 2:** 418
Three Books of Song (Longfellow), **II:** 490
"Three Bushes" (Yeats), **Supp. I Part 1:** 80
Three Cantos (Pound), **Retro. Supp. I:** 290
Three Centuries of Harvard (Morison), **Supp. I Part 2:** 485
Three Comrades (Remarque), **Retro. Supp. I:** 113
"Three Corollaries of Cultural Relativism" (Locke), **Supp. XIV:**202
"Three-Day Blow, The" (Hemingway), **II:** 248
Three Essays on America (Brooks), **I:** 246
Three Farmers on Their Way to a Dance (Powers), **Supp. IX:** 211-212, **213-214**, 222
"Three Fates, The" (Benét), **Supp. XI:** 48-49, 50
"Three Generations of Secrets" (A. Finch), **Supp. XVII:** 73
Three Gospels (Price), **Supp. VI:** 267
"Three Kings, The: Hemingway, Faulkner, and Fitzgerald" (Ford), **Supp. V:** 59
Three Lives (Auchincloss), **Supp. IV Part 1:** 25
Three Lives (Stein), **I:** 103; **IV:** 26, 27, 31, 35, 37-41, 42, 45, 46; **Supp. IX:** 306
"THREE MOVEMENTS AND A CODA" (Baraka), **Supp. II Part 1:** 50
Three One Act Plays (Riverside Drive, Old Saybrook, and Central Park West) (Allen), **Supp. XV:** 3
Three on the Tower: The Lives and Works of Ezra Pound, T. S. Eliot, and William Carlos Williams (Simpson), **Supp. IX:** 276
Three Papers on Fiction (Welty), **IV:** 261
Three-Penny Opera (Brecht), **I:** 301; **Supp. XIV:**162
Three Philosophical Poets (Santayana), **III:** 610-612
"Three Pigs in Five Days" (Prose), **Supp. XVI:**257, 258
"Three Players of a Summer Game" (T. Williams), **IV:** 383
Three Poems (Ashbery), **Supp. III Part 1:** 2, 3, 14, 15, 18, 24-26
"Three Pokes of a Thistle" (Nye), **Supp. XIII:** 281
Three Roads, The (Macdonald, under Millar), **Supp. IV Part 2:** 466, 467
"Three Silences of Molinos, The" (Longfellow), **Retro. Supp. II:** 169
Three Sisters, The (Chekhov), **Supp. XV:** 323
"Three Sisters, The" (Cisneros), **Supp. VII:** 64
Three Soldiers (Dos Passos), **I:** 477-478, 480, 482, 488, 493-494
"Three Songs at the End of Summer" (Kenyon), **Supp. VII:** 169-170
"Three Steps to the Graveyard" (Wright), **Supp. III Part 2:** 593, 596
Three Stories and Ten Poems (Hemingway), **II:** 68, 263; **Supp. XVII:** 105
Three Taverns, The (Robinson), **III:** 510
"Three Taverns, The" (Robinson), **III:** 521, 522
Three Tenant Families (Agee), **I:** 37-38
Three Tenors, One Vehicle: A Book of Songs (X. J. Kennedy, Camp, and Waldrop), **Supp. XV:** 165
"Three Types of Poetry" (Tate), **IV:** 131
"Three Vagabonds of Trinidad" (Harte), **Supp. II Part 1:** 338
"Three Waterfalls, The" (Lanier), **Supp. I Part 1:** 350
"Three-Way Mirror" (Brooks), **Supp. III Part 1:** 69-70
"Three Women" (Plath), **Supp. I Part 2:** 539, 541, 544, 545, 546
Three Young Poets (Swallow, ed.), **Supp. X:** 116
Threnody (Emerson), **Supp. I Part 2:** 416
"Threnody" (Emerson), **II:** 7
"Threnody for a Brown Girl" (Cullen), **Supp. IV Part 1:** 166
"Threshing-Floor, The" (Baldwin), **Supp. I Part 1:** 50
Threshold (film), **Supp. IX:** 254

"Threshold" (Goldbarth), **Supp. XII:** 175

Threshold (Jackson), **Supp. IX:** 117

"Throat" (Goldbarth), **Supp. XII:** 177-178

Throne of Labdacus, The (Schnackenberg), **Supp. XV:** 260, **263-266**

Thrones (Pound), **Retro. Supp. I:** 293

Through Dooms of Love (Kumin), **Supp. IV Part 2:** 444

"Through the Black Curtain" (Kingston), **Supp. V:** 169

Through the Forest: New and Selected Poems, 1977-1987 (Wagoner), **Supp. IX: 330-331**

"Through the Hills of Spain" (Salinas), **Supp. XIII:** 315

"Through the Hole in the Mundane Millstone" (West), **Retro. Supp. II:** 321, 322

Through the Ivory Gate (Dove), **Supp. IV Part 1:** 242, 243, 251, 252, 253-254, 254

"Through the Kitchen Window, Chiapas" (Nye), **Supp. XIII:** 277

Through the Safety Net (C. Baxter), **Supp. XVII:** 17, 22

"Through the Smoke Hole" (Snyder), **Supp. VIII:** 299

Thucydides, **II:** 418; **IV:** 50; **Supp. I Part 2:** 488, 489, 492; **Supp. IV Part 1:** 391; **Supp. XIII:** 233

Thunderbolt and Lightfoot (film), **Supp. X:** 126

"Thunderhead" (MacLeish), **III:** 19

Thurber, James, **I:** 487; **II:** 432; **IV:** 396; **Supp. I Part 2: 602-627,** 653, 654, 668, 672, 673, 679; **Supp. II Part 1:** 143; **Supp. IV Part 1:** 349; **Supp. IX:** 118; **Supp. XIV:**104; **Supp. XVI:**167; **Supp. XVII:** 4

Thurber, Mrs. James (Althea Adams), **Supp. I Part 2:** 613, 615, 617

Thurber, Mrs. James (Helen Muriel Wismer), **Supp. I Part 2:** 613, 617, 618

Thurber, Robert, **Supp. I Part 2:** 613, 617

Thurber, Rosemary, **Supp. I Part 2:** 616

Thurber, William, **Supp. I Part 2:** 602

Thurber Album, The (Thurber), **Supp. I Part 2:** 611, 619

Thurber Carnival, The (Thurber), **Supp. I Part 2:** 620; **Supp. XIV:**104

Thurman, Judith, **Supp. IV Part 1:** 309

Thurman, Wallace, **Retro. Supp. I:** 200; **Supp. I Part 1:** 325, 326, 328, 332; **Supp. IV Part 1:** 164; **Supp. X:** 136, 139; **Supp. XVI:**135

"Thursday" (Millay), **III:** 129

"Thurso's Landing" (Jeffers), **Supp. II Part 2:** 433

"Thus Do I Refute Gioia" (Junker), **Supp. XV:** 116

Thus Spake Zarathustra (Nietzsche), **II:** 463; **Supp. IV Part 1:** 110; **Supp. IV Part 2:** 519

Thwaite, Lady Alicia. *See* Rawlings, Marjorie Kinnan

Thy Neighbor's Wife (Talese), **Supp. XVII:** 204, 205-206, 207, 208, 210

"Tiara" (Doty), **Supp. XI:** 122

"Tibetan Time" (Prose), **Supp. XVI:**255

Ticket for a Seamstitch, A (Harris), **II:** 424-425

Tickets for a Prayer Wheel (Dillard), **Supp. VI:** 22, 34

Ticket That Exploded, The (Burroughs), **Supp. III Part 1:** 93, 103, 104

Tickless Time (Glaspell), **Supp. III Part 1:** 179

Ticknor, George, **II:** 488; **Supp. I Part 1:** 313

"Ti Démon" (Chopin), **Supp. I Part 1:** 225

Tide of Time, The (Masters), **Supp. I Part 2:** 471

"Tide Rises, the Tide Falls, The" (Longfellow), **I:** 498

Tidyman, Ernest, **Supp. V:** 226

Tietjens, Eunice, **Supp. XV:** 47, 297

"Tiger" (Blake), **Supp. I Part 1:** 80; **Supp. VIII:** 26

Tiger (Bynner), **Supp. XV:** 42, 50

"Tiger, The" (Buechner), **Supp. XII:** 48

Tiger in the House, The (Van Vechten), **Supp. II Part 2:** 736

Tiger Joy (Benét), **Supp. XI:** 45

Tiger-Lilies (Lanier), **Supp. I Part 1:** 350-351, 357, 360, 371

Tiger Who Wore White Gloves, The: or, What You Are, You Are (Brooks), **Supp. III Part 1:** 86

Till, Emmett, **Supp. I Part 1:** 61

Tillich, Paul, **II:** 244; **III:** 291, 292, 303, 309; **IV:** 226; **Retro. Supp. I:** 325, 326, 327; **Supp. V:** 267; **Supp. XIII:** 74, 91

Tillie Olsen: A Study of the Short Fiction (Frye), **Supp. XIII:** 292, 296, 298, 299, 302

Tillman, Lynne, **Supp. XII:** 4

Tillotson, John, **II:** 114

Tillotson, Kristen, **Supp. XVII:** 23

Tillstrom, Burr, **Supp. XIV:**125

Till the Day I Die (Odets), **Supp. II Part 2:** 530, 533-536, 552

Tilton, Eleanor, **Supp. I Part 1:** 317

Timaeus (Plato), **II:** 10; **III:** 609

Timber (Jonson), **II:** 16

Timberg, Scott, **Supp. XV:** 116

Timbuktu (Auster), **Supp. XII:** 34, **35-36**

"Time" (Matthews), **Supp. IX: 165-166**

"Time" (Merrill), **Supp. III Part 1:** 325

"Time and Again" (Sanders), **Supp. XVI:**269

Time and a Place, A (Humphrey), **Supp. IX:** 95, 98, **100-102**

"Time and the Garden" (Winters), **Supp. II Part 2:** 801, 809

"Time and the Liturgy" (Merton), **Supp. VIII:** 199

Time and Tide: A Walk through Nantucket (Conroy), **Supp. XVI:**63, 71, **76-77**

"Time Exposure" (C. Baxter), **Supp. XVII:** 20-21

Time in the Rock (Aiken), **I:** 65

Time Is Noon, The (Buck), **Supp. II Part 1:** 129, 130-131

Time & Money (Matthews), **Supp. IX:** 155, **165-167**

"Time of Friendship, The" (Bowles), **Supp. IV Part 1:** 90-91

"Time of Her Time, The" (Mailer), **III:** 37, 45; **Retro. Supp. II:** 200

Time of Our Time, The (Mailer), **Retro. Supp. II:** 213-214

Time of the Assassins, The: A Study of Rimbaud (H. Miller), **III:** 189

"Time Past" (Morris), **III:** 232

"Time Present" (Morris), **III:** 232

"Times" (Beattie), **Supp. V:** 31

"Times, The" (Emerson), **II:** 11-12

Times Are Never So Bad, The (Dubus), **Supp. VII:** 87-88

Time's Arrow (Amis), **Retro. Supp. I:** 278

"Time Shall Not Die" (Chandler), **Supp. IV Part 1:** 120

Times of Melville and Whitman, The (Brooks), **I:** 257

"Timesweep" (Sandburg), **III:** 595-596

Time to Act, A (MacLeish), **III:** 3

Time to Go (Dixon), **Supp. XII:** 147

Time to Kill (film), **Supp. IV Part 1:** 130

Time to Speak, A (MacLeish), **III:** 3

Time Will Darken It (Maxwell), **Supp. VIII:** 159, **162-164,** 169

"Timing of Sin, The" (Dubus), **Supp. VII:** 91

Tim O'Brien (Herzog), **Supp. V:** 239
Timoleon (Melville), **III:** 93; **Retro. Supp. I:** 257
Timothy Dexter Revisited (Marquand), **III:** 55, 62, 63
Tin Can, The (W. J. Smith), **Supp. XIII:** 334, **Supp. XIII:** 336, 337
"Tin Can, The" (W. J. Smith), **Supp. XIII: 337-339**
Tin Can Tree, The (Tyler), **Supp. IV Part 2:** 659-660
Tinguely, Jean, **Supp. XV:** 187
Tinker, Chauncey Brewster, **Supp. XIV:**12
Tintern Abbey (Wordsworth), **Supp. I Part 2:** 673, 675
Tiny Alice (Albee), **I:** 81-86, 87, 88, 94
"Tiny Mummies! The True Story of the Ruler of 43rd Street's Land of the Walking Dead" (Wolfe), **Supp. III Part 2:** 573, 574
"Tip-Top Club, The" (Keillor), **Supp. XVI:**172
"Tired" (Hughes), **Supp. I Part 1:** 331
"Tired and Unhappy, You Think of Houses" (Schwartz), **Supp. II Part 2:** 649
"Tiresias" (Garrett), **Supp. VII:** 96-97
'Tis (McCourt), **Supp. XII:** 271, **279-286**
Tisch (Dixon), **Supp. XII:** 141, **155-156**
Titan, The (Dreiser), **I:** 497, 501, 507-508, 509, 510; **Retro. Supp. II:** 94, 101, 102
Titian, **Supp. I Part 2:** 397, 714
"Tito's Goodbye" (García), **Supp. XI:** 190
To a Blossoming Pear Tree (Wright), **Supp. III Part 2:** 602-605
"To a Blossoming Pear Tree" (Wright), **Supp. III Part 2:** 604
"To Abolish Children" (Shapiro), **Supp. II Part 2:** 717
To Abolish Children and Other Essays (Shapiro), **Supp. II Part 2:** 703
"To a Caty-Did, the Precursor of Winter" (Freneau), **Supp. II Part 1:** 274-275
"To a Chameleon" (Moore), **III:** 195, 196, 215
"To a Conscript of 1940" (Read), **II:** 372-373, 377-378
"To a Contemporary Bunk Shooter" (Sandburg), **III:** 582
"To a Cough in the Street at Midnight" (Wylie), **Supp. I Part 2:** 727, 729-730
"To a Defeated Savior" (Wright), **Supp. III Part 2:** 593-594, 596

"To a Face in the Crowd" (Warren), **IV:** 239
"To a Fish Head Found on the Beach near Malaga" (Levine), **Supp. V:** 185
"To a Friend" (Nemerov), **III:** 272
"To a Friend Whose Work Has Come to Triumph" (Sexton), **Supp. II Part 2:** 683
To a God Unknown (Steinbeck), **I:** 107; **IV:** 51, 59-60, 67
"To a Greek Marble" (Aldington), **Supp. I Part 1:** 257
"To a Locomotive in Winter" (Whitman), **IV:** 348
"To a Military Rifle" (Winters), **Supp. II Part 2:** 810, 811, 815
"To a Mouse" (Burns), **Supp. IX:** 173
"To an Athlete Dying Young" (Houseman), **Supp. XVII:** 121
"To a Negro Jazz Band in a Parisian Cabaret" (Hughes), **Supp. I Part 1:** 325
"To an Old Philosopher in Rome" (Stevens), **III:** 605; **Retro. Supp. I:** 312
"To an Old Poet in Peru" (Ginsberg), **Supp. II Part 1:** 322
"To a Now-Type Poet" (X. J. Kennedy), **Supp. XV:** 161
"To Answer Your Question" (Jarman), **Supp. XVII:** 114-115
"To Any Would-Be Terrorists" (Nye), **Supp. XIII:** 285, 286
"To a Poet" (Rich), **Supp. I Part 2:** 571
"To a Prize Bird" (Moore), **III:** 215
"To a Republican, with Mr. Paine's Rights of Man" (Freneau), **Supp. II Part 1:** 267
"To a Shade" (Yeats), **III:** 18
"To a Skylark" (Shelley), **Supp. I Part 2:** 720; **Supp. X:** 31
"Toast to Harlem, A" (Hughes), **Supp. I Part 1:** 338
"To Aunt Rose" (Ginsberg), **Supp. II Part 1:** 320
"To Autumn" (Keats), **Supp. IX:** 50
"To a Waterfowl" (Bryant), **Supp. I Part 1:** 154, 155, 162, 171
"To a Young Poet" (X. J. Kennedy), **Supp. XV:** 161
"To a Young Writer" (Stegner), **Supp. X:** 24
Tobacco Road (Caldwell), **I:** 288, 289, 290, 295-296, 297, 298, 302, 307, 309, 310; **IV:** 198
"To Be a Monstrous Clever Fellow" (Fante), **Supp. XI:** 167
To Bedlam and Part Way Back (Sexton), **Retro. Supp. II:** 245; **Supp. II Part 2:** 672-678; **Supp. IV Part 2:** 441; **Supp. XI:** 317
"To Beethoven" (Lanier), **Supp. I Part 1:** 364
To Begin Again: Stories and Memoirs, 1908-1929 (M. F. K. Fisher), **Supp. XVII:** 92
Tobey, Mark, **Supp. X:** 264
To Be Young, Gifted, and Black: Lorraine Hansberry in Her Own Words (Nemiroff), **Supp. IV Part 1:** 372, 374
"To Big Mary from an Ex-Catholic" (Mora), **Supp. XIII:** 217, 224, 228
"Tobin's Palm" (O. Henry), **Supp. II Part 1:** 408; **Supp. XV:** 40
Tobit (apocryphal book), **I:** 89
"To Build a Fire" (London), **II:** 468
Toby Tyler; or, Ten Weeks with a Circus (Otis), **III:** 577
"To Change in a Good Way" (Ortiz), **Supp. IV Part 2:** 511
"To Charlotte Cushman" (Lanier), **Supp. I Part 1:** 364
"To Cole, the Painter, Departing for Europe" (Bryant), **Supp. I Part 1:** 157, 161
Tocqueville, Alexis de, **III:** 261; **IV:** 349; **Retro. Supp. I:** 235; **Supp. I Part 1:** 137; **Supp. I Part 2:** 659, 660; **Supp. II Part 1:** 281, 282, 284; **Supp. XIV:**306, 312
"To Crispin O'Conner" (Freneau), **Supp. II Part 1:** 268
"To Da-Duh, In Memoriam" (Marshall), **Supp. XI:** 276
"TODAY" (Baraka), **Supp. II Part 1:** 55
"Today" (Ginsberg), **Supp. II Part 1:** 328
"Today Is a Good Day To Die" (Bell), **Supp. X:** 7
Todd, Mabel Loomis, **I:** 454, 470; **Retro. Supp. I:** 33, 34, 35, 39, 47
"To Death" (Levertov), **Supp. III Part 1:** 274
"To Delmore Schwartz" (Lowell), **II:** 547; **Retro. Supp. II:** 188
"to disembark" (Brooks), **Supp. III Part 1:** 86
"To Dorothy on Her Exclusion from The Guinness Book of Records" (X. J. Kennedy), **Supp. XV:** 166
"To Dr. Thomas Shearer" (Lanier), **Supp. I Part 1:** 370
"To E. T." (Frost), **Retro. Supp. I:** 132
"To Earthward" (Frost), **II:** 154
"To Edwin V. McKenzie" (Winters), **Supp. II Part 2:** 801

"To Eleonora Duse" (Lowell), **II:** 528
"To Elizabeth Ward Perkins" (Lowell), **II:** 516
"To Elsie" (W. C. Williams), **Retro. Supp. I:** 419
"To Emily Dickinson" (H. Crane), **Retro. Supp. II:** 76
To Feel These Things (L. Michaels), **Supp. XVI:**205, **213-214**
"To Feel These Things" (L. Michaels), **Supp. XVI:**214
Toffler, Alvin, **Supp. IV Part 2:** 517
"To Fill" (Moore), **Supp. X:** 168, 169
"To Gabriela, a Young Writer" (Mora), **Supp. XIII:** 220
To Have and Have Not (film), **Supp. XV:** 347
To Have and Have Not (Hemingway), **I:** 31; **II:** 253-254, 264; **Retro. Supp. I:** 182, **183**, 187
"To Helen" (Poe), **III:** 410, 411, 427; **Retro. Supp. II:** 102
"To Hell With Dying" (Walker), **Supp. III Part 2:** 523
"To His Father" (Jeffers), **Supp. II Part 2:** 415
Toilet, The (Baraka), **Supp. II Part 1:** 37, 40-42
"To James Russell Lowell" (Holmes), **Supp. I Part 1:** 311
To Jerusalem and Back (Bellow), **Retro. Supp. II:** 29
"To Jesus on His Birthday" (Millay), **III:** 136-137
"To John Keats" (Lowell), **II:** 516
"To Judge Faolain, Dead Long Enough: A Summons" (McCarriston), **Supp. XIV:**264-265
"To Justify My Singing" (Wright), **Supp. III Part 2:** 590
"To Kill a Deer" (C. Frost), **Supp. XV:** 102
To Kill a Mockingbird (film), **Supp. VIII:** 128-129
To Kill a Mockingbird (Lee), **Supp. VIII: 113-129; Supp. XVI:**259
"*To Kill a Mockingbird*: Harper Lee's Tragic Vision" (Dave), **Supp. VIII:** 126
To Kill a Mockingbird: Threatening Boundaries (Johnson), **Supp. VIII:** 126
Toklas, Alice B., **IV:** 27; **Supp. IV Part 1:** 81, 91; **Supp. XVI:**187
"Tokyo Story" (Wasserstein), **Supp. XV:** 328
"To Light" (Hogan), **Supp. IV Part 1:** 402
"To Live and Diet" (Wasserstein), **Supp. XV:** 328

Tolkien, J. R. R., **Supp. V:** 140
Tolkin, Michael, **Supp. XI:** 160
Toller, Ernst, **I:** 479
"To Lose the Earth" (Sexton), **Supp. II Part 2:** 684, 685
Tolson, Melvin, **Retro. Supp. I:** 208, 209, 210
Tolstoy, Leo, **I:** 6, 7, 58, 103, 312, 376; **II:** 191-192, 205, 271, 272, 275, 276, 281, 285, 286, 320, 407, 542, 559, 570, 579, 606; **III:** 37, 45, 61, 323, 467, 572; **IV:** 17, 21, 170, 285; **Retro. Supp. I:** 91, 225; **Retro. Supp. II:** 299; **Supp. I Part 1:** 2, 3, 6, 20; **Supp. IV Part 1:** 392; **Supp. V:** 277, 323; **Supp. IX:** 246; **Supp. XI:** 68; **Supp. XII:** 310, 322; **Supp. XIV:**87, 97, 98
"To Lu Chi" (Nemerov), **III:** 275
Tom (Cummings), **I:** 430
"Tom" (Oliver), **Supp. VII:** 232
"Tom, Tom, the Piper's Son" (Ransom), **Supp. X:** 58
"To M, with a Rose" (Lanier), **Supp. I Part 1:** 364
To Make a Prairie (Kumin), **Supp. IV Part 2:** 440, 441
"To Make Words Disappear" (Simpson), **Supp. IX:** 265-266
Tomás and the Library Lady (Mora), **Supp. XIII:** 216, 221
"Tomatoes" (Francis), **Supp. IX:** 82
"Tom Brown at Fisk" (Du Bois), **Supp. II Part 1:** 160
Tom Brown's School Days (Hughes), **Supp. I Part 2:** 406
"Tomb Stone" (Dickey), **Supp. IV Part 1:** 185
Tomcat in Love (O'Brien), **Supp. V:** 238, 240, 243, 252-254
"Tomcat's Wife, The" (C. Bly), **Supp. XVI:**40
Tomcat's Wife and Other Stories, The (C. Bly), **Supp. XVI:**40-41
"Tom Fool at Jamaica" (Moore), **III:** 215
To Mix with Time (Swenson), **Supp. IV Part 2:** 637, 643-645, 645
Tom Jones (Fielding), **I:** 131; **Supp. V:** 127
Tomlinson, Charles, **Supp. XVI:**284
Tommy Gallagher's Crusade (Farrell), **II:** 44
Tommyknockers, The (King), **Supp. V:** 139, 144
"Tommy's Burglar" (Henry), **Supp. II Part 1:** 399, 401
Tomo Cheeki (pseudonym). See Freneau, Philip
Tomorrow is Another Day (film, Feist),

Supp. XVII: 62
"Tomorrow the Moon" (Dos Passos), **I:** 493
"Tom Outland's Story" (Cather), **I:** 325-326
Tompkins, Jane, **Supp. XVI:**89
Tompson, Benjamin, **Supp. I Part 1:** 110, 111
Tom Sawyer (musical) (Gurney), **Supp. V:** 96
Tom Sawyer (Twain). See *Adventures of Tom Sawyer, The* (Twain)
Tom Sawyer Abroad (Twain), **II:** 482; **IV:** 19, 204
Tom Sawyer Detective (Twain), **IV:** 204
"Tom's Husband" (Jewett), **Retro. Supp. II:** 132, 141
Tom Swift (Stratemeyer), **III:** 146
"Tom Wolfe's Guide to Etiquette" (Wolfe), **Supp. III Part 2:** 578
"To My Brother Killed: Haumont Wood: October, 1918" (Bogan), **Supp. III Part 1:** 58
"To My Class, on Certain Fruits and Flowers Sent Me in Sickness" (Lanier), **Supp. I Part 1:** 370
"To My Father's Ghost" (Everwine), **Supp. XV:** 76
"To My Ghost Reflected in the Auxvasse River" (Levis), **Supp. XI:** 265
"To My Greek" (Merrill), **Supp. III Part 1:** 326
"To My Mother" (Berry), **Supp. X:** 23
"To My Small Son, at the Photographer's" (Hay), **Supp. XIV:**121
"To My Small Son, on Certain Occasions" (Hay), **Supp. XIV:**121
"To Name is to Possess" (Kincaid), **Supp. VII:** 194
Tone, Aileen, **I:** 21-22
"Tongue Is, The" (Komunyakaa), **Supp. XIII:** 113
"Tongue of the Jews" (Bukiet), **Supp. XVII:** 47
Tongues (Shepard and Chaikin), **Supp. III Part 2:** 433
Tongues of Angels, The (Price), **Supp. VI:** 265
Tongues Untied (Riggs; film), **Supp. XI:** 19, 20
"Tonight" (Lowell), **II:** 538
Tonight Is the Night of the Prom (Jarman), **Supp. XVII:** 110, **112-113**
"Tonight Is the Night of the Prom" (Jarman), **Supp. XVII:** 113
Tony Kushner in Conversation (Vorlicky, ed.), **Supp. IX:** 132
"Too Anxious for Rivers" (Frost), **II:** 162

"Too Blue" (Hughes), **Retro. Supp. I:** 207

"Too Damn Close: Thresholds and Their Maintenance in Rick Bass's Work" (Kerridge), **Supp. XVI:** 26

"Too Early" (Leopold), **Supp. XIV:** 186

"Too Early Spring" (Benét), **Supp. XI:** 53

"Too Far from Home" (Bowles), **Supp. IV Part 1:** 94-95

Too Far from Home: Selected Writings of Paul Bowles (Halpern, ed.), **Supp. IV Part 1:** 94, 95

Too Far to Go: The Maples Stories (Updike), **Retro. Supp. I:** 321

"Too Good To Be True": The Life and Art of Leslie Fiedler (Winchell), **Supp. XIII:** 94, 98, 99, 101

Toohey, John Peter, **Supp. IX:** 190

Toolan, David, **Supp. IV Part 1:** 308

Too Late (Dixon), **Supp. XII:** 143-144

"Too-Late Born, The" (Hemingway), **III:** 9

Toole, John Kennedy, **Supp. XIV:** 21

Toomer, Jean, **Retro. Supp. II:** 79; **Supp. I Part 1:** 325, 332; **Supp. III Part 2: 475-491; Supp. IV Part 1:** 16, 164, 168; **Supp. IX: 305-322; Supp. XIII:** 305

Toomer, Nathan Eugene Pinchback. *See* Toomer, Jean

Too Much Johnson (film), **Supp. IV Part 1:** 83

"To One Who Said Me Nay" (Cullen), **Supp. IV Part 1:** 166

"Tooth, The" (Jackson), **Supp. IX:** 122

Tooth of Crime, The (Shepard), **Supp. III Part 2:** 432, 441-445, 447

"Too Young" (O'Hara), **III:** 369

"To P. L., 1916-1937" (Levine), **Supp. V:** 185

"Top Israeli Official Hints at 'Shared' Jerusalem" (Nye), **Supp. XIII:** 287

"To Please a Shadow" (Brodsky), **Supp. VIII:** 30

"Top of the Hill" (Jewett), **II:** 406

"Topography" (Olds), **Supp. X:** 208

Topper (T. Smith), **Supp. IX:** 194

Torah, **IV:** 19

"Torquemada" (Bukiet), **Supp. XVII:** 44

"Torquemada" (Longfellow), **II:** 505; **Retro. Supp. II:** 164

Torrence, Ridgely, **III:** 507

Torrent and the Night Before, The (Robinson), **III:** 504

Torrents of Spring, The (Hemingway), **I:** 117; **II:** 250-251

Torres, Héctor A., **Supp. XIII:** 225

Torres, Louis, **Supp. IV Part 2:** 529, 530

Torsney, Cheryl, **Retro. Supp. I:** 224

Tortilla Curtain, The (Boyle), **Supp. VIII:** 9-10

Tortilla Flat (Steinbeck), **IV:** 50, 51, 61, 64

Tory Lover, The (Jewett), **II:** 406; **Retro. Supp. II:** 144-145

"Toscana" (Dixon), **Supp. XII:** 154

"To Sir Toby" (Freneau), **Supp. II Part 1:** 269

"To Sophy, Expectant" (Mumford), **Supp. II Part 2:** 475

"To Speak of Woe That Is in Marriage" (Lowell), **II:** 550

"To Statecraft Embalmed" (Moore), **III:** 197

To Stay Alive (Levertov), **Supp. III Part 1:** 280-282

"Total Eclipse" (Dillard), **Supp. VI:** 28

Toth, Emily, **Retro. Supp. II:** 71

Toth, Susan Allan, **Retro. Supp. II:** 138

"To the Americans of the United States" (Freneau), **Supp. II Part 1:** 271

"To the Apennines" (Bryant), **Supp. I Part 1:** 157, 164

"To the Bleeding Hearts Association of American Novelists" (Nemerov), **III:** 281

"To the Botequim & Back" (Bishop), **Retro. Supp. II:** 51

To the Bright and Shining Sun (Burke), **Supp. XIV:** 22, 25

"To the Citizens of the United States" (Paine), **Supp. I Part 2:** 519-520

"To the Dandelion" (Lowell), **Supp. I Part 2:** 424

"To the End" (Haines), **Supp. XII:** 212-213

To the Ends of the Earth: The Selected Travels of Paul Theroux, **Supp. VIII:** 324

To the Finland Station: A Study in the Writing and Acting of History (Wilson), **IV:** 429, 436, 443-444, 446

"To the Governor & Legislature of Massachusetts" (Nemerov), **III:** 287

To the Green Man (Jarman), **Supp. XVII:** 110, 120-121

"To the Holy Spirit" (Winters), **Supp. II Part 2:** 810

"To the Keeper of the King's Water Works" (Freneau), **Supp. II Part 1:** 269

"To the Lacedemonians" (Tate), **IV:** 134

"To the Laodiceans" (Jarrell), **Retro. Supp. I:** 121, 140

To the Lighthouse (Woolf), **I:** 309; **II:** 600; **Retro. Supp. II:** 337; **Supp. VIII:** 155

"To the Man on Trail" (London), **II:** 466

"To the Memory of the Brave Americans Under General Greene" (Freneau), **Supp. II Part 1:** 262, 274

"To the Muse" (Wright), **Supp. III Part 2:** 601

"To the Nazi Leaders" (Hay), **Supp. XIV:** 121

"To the New World" (Jarrell), **II:** 371

"To the One of Fictive Music" (Stevens), **IV:** 89; **Retro. Supp. I:** 297, 300

"To the One Upstairs" (Simic), **Supp. VIII:** 283

"To the Peoples of the World" (Du Bois), **Supp. II Part 1:** 172

To the Place of Trumpets (B. Kelly), 132; **Supp. XVII:** 123-127

"To the Pliocene Skull" (Harte), **Supp. II Part 1:** 343-344

"To the Reader" (Baudelaire), **II:** 544-545

"To The Reader" (Jarman), **Supp. XVII:** 115

"To the Reader" (Levertov), **Supp. III Part 1:** 277

"To the River Arve" (Bryant), **Supp. I Part 1:** 163

"To the Snake" (Levertov), **Supp. III Part 1:** 277

"To the Stone-Cutters" (Jeffers), **Supp. II Part 2:** 420

"To the Unseeable Animal" (Berry), **Supp. X:** 31

"To the Western World" (Simpson), **Supp. IX:** 269, 270

To the White Sea (Dickey), **Supp. IV Part 1:** 186, 190-191

"To the Young Who Want to Die" (Brooks), **Supp. III Part 1:** 85-86

"To Tlaoc of the Rain" (Everwine), **Supp. XV:** 77

"To Train a Writer" (Bierce), **I:** 199

"Touch, The" (Sexton), **Supp. II Part 2:** 687

Touch and Go (M. F. K. Fisher and D. Parrish), **Supp. XVII:** 84

"Touching the Tree" (Merwin), **Supp. III Part 1:** 355

Touching the World (Eakin), **Supp. VIII:** 167

Touch of Danger, A (Jones), **Supp. XI:** 226, **228-229**
Touch of the Poet, A (O'Neill), **III:** 385, 401, 404
Touchstone, The (Wharton), **Retro. Supp. I:** 365
"Touch-up Man" (Komunyakaa), **Supp. XIII:** 119
Tough Guys Don't Dance (Mailer), **Retro. Supp. II:** 211
Toulet, Paul Jean, **IV:** 79
Tour (McNally), **Supp. XIII:** 197
"Tour 5" (Hayden), **Supp. II Part 1:** 381
To Urania (Brodsky), **Supp. VIII:** 22, 28-29
Tourgée, Albion W., **Supp. XIV:**63
"Tour Guide" (Komunyakaa), **Supp. XIII:** 114
"Tourist Death" (MacLeish), **III:** 12
Tourmaline (J. Scott), **Supp. XVII:** **192-194,** 195
Tour of Duty (Dos Passos), **I:** 489
Touron the Prairies, A (Irving), **II:** 312-313
Tovey, Donald Francis, **Supp. XIV:**336
To Walk a Crooked Mile (McGrath), **Supp. X:** 117
Toward a New Synthesis (Begiebing), **Retro. Supp. II:** 210
"Toward Nightfall" (Simic), **Supp. VIII:** 277
Towards a Better Life (Burke), **I:** 270
"Towards a Chicano Poetics: The Making of the Chicano Subject, 1969-1982" (Saldívar), **Supp. IV Part 2:** 544
Towards an Enduring Peace (Bourne), **I:** 232
Toward the Blanched Alphabets (Sobin), **Supp. XVI:**290
Toward the Gulf (Masters), **Supp. I Part 2:** 465-466
"Toward the Solstice" (Rich), **Supp. I Part 2:** 575-576
Toward Wholeness in Paule Marshall's Fiction (Pettis), **Supp. XI:** 276
"Tower" (Merwin), **Supp. III Part 1:** 343
"Tower Beyond Tragedy, The" (Jeffers), **Supp. II Part 2:** 429-430
Tower of Ivory (MacLeish), **III:** 3-4
Towers, Robert, **Supp. IX:** 259; **Supp. XVI:**211
"To What Red Hell" (C. Himes), **Supp. XVI:**137
"To Whistler, American" (Pound), **III:** 465-466
"To Wine" (Bogan), **Supp. III Part 1:** 57, 58

Town, The (Faulkner), **II:** 57, 73; **Retro. Supp. I:** 74, 82
Town and the City, The (Kerouac), **Supp. III Part 1:** 222-224; **Supp. XIV:**143
"Town Crier" (Bierce), **I:** 193, 194, 195, 196
"Town Crier Exclusive, Confessions of a Princess Manqué: 'How Royals Found Me "Unsuitable" to Marry Their Larry'" (Elkin), **Supp. VI:** 56
Town Down the River, The (Robinson), **III:** 508
"Town Dump, The" (Nemerov), **III:** 272, 275, 281
Towne, Robert, **Supp. XI:** 159, 172, 174
"Townhouse Interior with Cat" (Clampitt), **Supp. IX:** 40
"Townies" (Dubus), **Supp. VII:** 86
"Town of the Sound of a Twig Breaking" (Carson), **Supp. XII:** **102**
"Town Poor, The" (Jewett), **Retro. Supp. II:** 138, 139, 143
Townsend, Alison, **Supp. XIII:** 222
Townsend, Ann, **Supp. V:** 77
"Towns in Colour" (Lowell), **II:** 523-524
Townsman, The (Sedges), **Supp. II Part 1:** 124-125
"To World War Two" (Koch), **Supp. XV:** 184
Toys in a Field (Komunyakaa), **Supp. XIII:** 121-122
"Toys in a Field" (Komunyakaa), **Supp. XIII:** 122
Toys in the Attic (Hellman), **Supp. I Part 1:** 289-290
Tracer (F. Barthelme), **Supp. XI:** 31-32, 33
Traces of Thomas Hariot, The (Rukeyser), **Supp. VI:** 273, 274, 283
"Tracing Life with a Finger" (Caldwell), **I:** 291
Tracker (Wagoner), **Supp. IX:** 329, **336-337**
"Tracking" (Wagoner), **Supp. IX:** 329
"Track Meet, The" (Schwartz), **Supp. II Part 2:** 665
Tracks (Erdrich), **Supp. IV Part 1:** 259, 262-263, 269, 272, 273-274, 274, 275
"Tract" (W. C. Williams), **Retro. Supp. I:** 414
"Tract against Communism, A" (Twelve Southerners), **IV:** 125, 237
Tractatus (Wittgenstein), **Supp. XVII:** 143
Tracy, Lee, **IV:** 287, 288

Tracy, Steven, **Retro. Supp. I:** 195
"Trade, The" (Levine), **Supp. V:** 193
Trading Twelves (Callahan and Murray, eds.), **Retro. Supp. II:** 119
"Tradition and Industrialization" (Wright), **IV:** 489-490
"Tradition and Mythology: Signatures of Landscape in Chicana Poetry" (Rebolledo), **Supp. XIII:** 214
"Tradition and the Individual Talent" (Eliot), **I:** 441, 574, 585; **Retro. Supp. I:** 59, 286
Tragedies, Life and Letters of James Gates Percival (Swinburne), **Supp. I Part 2:** 422
Tragedy of Don Ippolito, The (Howells), **II:** 279
"Tragedy of Error, A" (James), **II:** 322; **Retro. Supp. I:** 218
Tragedy of Pudd'nhead Wilson, The (Twain), **IV:** 206-207
Tragic America (Dreiser), **Retro. Supp. II:** 95
"Tragic Dialogue" (Wylie), **Supp. I Part 2:** 724
Tragic Ground (Caldwell), **I:** 297, 306
Tragic Muse, The (James), **Retro. Supp. I:** 227
Traherne, Thomas, **IV:** 151; **Supp. III Part 1:** 14; **Supp. V:** 208; **Supp. XV:** 212; **Supp. XVI:**282, 288, 295
"Trail, The" (W. J. Smith), **Supp. XIII:** 342
Trailerpark (Banks), **Supp. V:** 12
"Trailing Arbutus, The" (Whittier), **Supp. I Part 2:** 691
Trail of the Lonesome Pine, The (Fox), **Supp. XIII:** 166
"Train, The" (O'Connor), **Retro. Supp. II:** 225
"Train Rising Out of the Sea" (Ashbery), **Supp. III Part 1:** 22
"Trains" (Banks), **Supp. V:** 8
"Train Tune" (Bogan), **Supp. III Part 1:** 64
"Traits of Indian Character" (Irving), **II:** 303
Trakl, Georg, **Supp. XVII:** 241
Tramp Abroad, A (Twain), **IV:** 200
Tramping With a Poet in the Rockies (S. Graham), **Supp. I Part 2:** 397
Tramp's Excuse, The (Lindsay), **Supp. I Part 2:** 379, 380, 382
"Transatlantic" (Toomer), **Supp. III Part 2:** 486
Transatlantic Sketches (James), **II:** 324; **Retro. Supp. I:** 219
"Transcendental Etude" (Rich), **Supp. I Part 2:** 576
"Transcontinental Highway" (Cowley),

Supp. II Part 1: 141
"Transducer" (Ammons), **Supp. VII:** 28
"Transfiguration" (Jarman), **Supp. XVII:** 118, 119
"Transfigured Bird" (Merrill), **Supp. III Part 1:** 320-321
"Transformations" (Harjo), **Supp. XII:** 226
Transformations (Sexton), **Supp. II Part 2:** 689-691; **Supp. IV Part 2:** 447; **Supp. XIV:** 125
Transforming Madness: New Lives for People Living with Mental Illness (Neugeboren), **Supp. XVI:** 229
"Transit" (Conroy), **Supp. XVI:** 72
Transit to Narcissus, A (Mailer), **Retro. Supp. II:** 196
"Translation and Transposition" (Carne-Ross), **Supp. I Part 1:** 268-269
"Translation of a Fragment of Simonides" (Bryant), **Supp. I Part 1:** 153, 155
"Translations" (Rich), **Supp. I Part 2:** 563
Translations of Ezra Pound, The (Kenner, ed.), **III:** 463
Translations of the Gospel Back into Tongues (Wright), **Supp. XV:** 342-343, 346
"Trans-National America" (Bourne), **I:** 229, 230
"Transparency" (X. J. Kennedy), **Supp. XV:** 159-160
Transparent Itineraries: 1983 (Sobin), **Supp. XVI:** 287
Transparent Itineraries: 1984 (Sobin), **Supp. XVI:** 287
Transparent Itineraries: 1992 (Sobin), **Supp. XVI:** 289
"Transparent Itineraries" poems (Sobin), **Supp. XVI:** 290
Transparent Man, The (Hecht), **Supp. X:** 57, **69-71**
"Transparent Man, The" (Hecht), **Supp. X:** 69-70
Transparent Things (Nabokov), **Retro. Supp. I:** 266, 270, 277
"Transport" (Simic), **Supp. VIII:** 282
Transport to Summer (Stevens), **IV:** 76, 93; **Retro. Supp. I:** 309-312
Tranströmer, Thomas, **Supp. IV Part 2:** 648
"Traps for the Unwary" (Bourne), **I:** 235
Trash Trilogy (McMurtry), **Supp. V:** 225-226, 231
Traubel, Horace, **IV:** 350
"Travel: After a Death" (Kenyon), **Supp. VII:** 169
Travel Alarm (Nye), **Supp. XIII:** 277
"Traveler, The" (Haines), **Supp. XII:** 203-204, 210
"Traveler, The" (Stegner), **Supp. IV Part 2:** 605
Traveler at Forty, A (Dreiser), **I:** 515
Traveler from Altruria, a Romance A, (Howells), **II:** 285, 287
Traveler's Tree, The: New and Selected Poems (W. J. Smith), **Supp. XIII:** 332, 347
"Traveling" (Paley), **Supp. VI:** 230
"Traveling Light" (Wagoner), **Supp. IX:** 329
"Traveling Onion, The" (Nye), **Supp. XIII:** 276
Traveling through the Dark (Stafford), **Supp. XI:** 311, 316, **318-321**
"Traveling through the Dark" (Stafford), **Supp. XI:** 318-320, 321, 323, 329
Travelling in Amherst: A Poet's Journal, 1931-1954, **Supp. IX: 88-89**
Travels in Alaska (Muir), **Supp. IX:** 182, 185-186
"Travels in Georgia" (McPhee), **Supp. III Part 1:** 293-294
"Travels in North America" (Kees), **Supp. XV:** 133-134
Travels in the Congo (Gide), **III:** 210
"Travels in the South" (Ortiz), **Supp. IV Part 2:** 506
Travels with Charley (Steinbeck), **IV:** 52
"Travel Writing: Why I Bother" (Theroux), **Supp. VIII:** 310
Travis, Merle, **Supp. V:** 335
Travisano, Thomas, **Retro. Supp. II:** 40
Treasure Hunt (Buechner), **Supp. XII:** 52
Treasure Island (Stevenson), **Supp. X:** 230
"Treasure of the Redwoods, A" (Harte), **Supp. II Part 1:** 337
Treasury of Art Masterpieces, A: From the Renaissance to the Present Day (Craven), **Supp. XII:** 44
Treasury of English Aphorisms, A (L. P. Smith), **Supp. XIV:** 344
Treasury of English Prose, A (L. P. Smith, ed.), **Supp. XIV:** 341
Treasury of the Theatre, A (Gassner), **Supp. I Part 1:** 292
Treasury of Yiddish Stories, A (Howe and Greenberg, eds.), **Supp. I Part 2:** 432
Treat 'Em Rough (Lardner), **II:** 422-423
Treatise Concerning Religious Affections (Edwards), **I:** 547, 552, 554, 555, 557, 558, 560, 562
Treatise Concerning the Lord's Supper (Doolittle), **IV:** 150
"Treatise on Poetry" (Milosz), **Supp. VIII:** 20
Treatise on Right and Wrong, A (Mencken), **III:** 110, 119
"Treatise on Tales of Horror, A" (Wilson), **IV:** 438
Treatise on the Gods, A (Mencken), **III:** 108-109, 119
"Treatment" (Wright), **Supp. XV:** 343
Trece poetas del mundo azteca (León-Portilla), **Supp. XV:** 77
Tre Croce (Tozzi), **Supp. III Part 2:** 616
"Tree, a Rock, a Cloud, A" (McCullers), **II:** 587
"Tree, The" (Pound), **Retro. Supp. I:** 286; **Supp. I Part 1:** 255
"Tree, the Bird, The" (Roethke), **III:** 548
"Tree at My Window" (Frost), **II:** 155
Tree Grows in Brooklyn, A (B. Smith), **Supp. XVII:** 9
Tree Grows in Brooklyn, A (film; Kazan), **Supp. XVI:** 193
"Tree House at Night, The" (Dickey), **Supp. IV Part 1:** 179
Tree Is Older Than You Are, The (Nye, ed.), **Supp. XIII:** 280
"Tree of Laughing Bells, The" (Lindsay), **Supp. I Part 2:** 376
"Tree of Night, A" (Capote), **Supp. III Part 1:** 114, 120
Tree of Night and Other Stories, A (Capote), **Supp. III Part 1:** 114
"Trees, The" (Rich), **Supp. I Part 2:** 555
"Trees Listening to Bach" (Merrill), **Supp. III Part 1:** 336
Tree That Came to Stay, The (Quindlen), **Supp. XVII:** 167
Tree Where Man Was Born, The (Matthiessen), **Supp. V:** 199, 203, 204
Trejo, Ernesto, **Supp. V:** 178, 180; **Supp. XIII:** 313, 316; **Supp. XV:** 73
Trelawny, Edward John, **Supp. I Part 2:** 721
"Trellis for R., A" (Swenson), **Supp. IV Part 2:** 647
Tremblay, Bill, **Supp. XIII:** 112
Tremble (Wright), **Supp. XV:** 348-349
"Trespass" (Frost), **Retro. Supp. I:** 139
"Tretitoli, Where the Bomb Group

Was" (Hugo), **Supp. VI:** 138
Trevelyan, Robert C., **Supp. XIV:**334
Trevor-Roper, Hugh, **Supp. XIV:**348
Trial, The (Kafka), **IV:** 113; **Retro. Supp. II:** 20
"Trial, The" (Rukeyser), **Supp. VI:** 278
"Trial by Existence, The" (Frost), **II:** 166
Trial of a Poet, The (Shapiro), **Supp. II Part 2:** 710
Trial of the Hawk, The: A Comedy of the Seriousness of Life (Lewis), **II:** 441
Trials of the Human Heart (Rowson), **Supp. XV:** 237, 239
Tribal Secrets: Recovering American Indian Intellectual Traditions (Warrior), **Supp. IV Part 1:** 329
"Tribute" (A. Finch), **Supp. XVII:** 72, 73-74
"Tribute (To My Mother)" (Cullen), **Supp. IV Part 1:** 166
"Tribute, A" (Easton), **Supp. IV Part 2:** 461
"Tribute, The" (Doolittle), **Supp. I Part 1:** 267
Tribute to Freud (Doolittle), **Supp. I Part 1:** 253, 254, 258, 259, 260, 268
Tribute to the Angels (Doolittle), **Supp. I Part 1:** 272
"Trick on the World, A" (Ríos), **Supp. IV Part 2:** 553
"Tricks" (Olds), **Supp. X:** 203-204
"Trick Scenery" (F. Barthelme), **Supp. XI:** 26
Trifler, The (Masters), **Supp. I Part 2:** 459-460
Trifles (Glaspell), **Supp. III Part 1:** 175, 178, 179, 182, 186, 187; **Supp. X:** 46
Trifonov, Iurii V., **Retro. Supp. I:** 278
Triggering Town, The: Lectures and Essays on Poetry and Writing (Hugo), **Supp. VI:** 133, 140
Trilling, Diana, **II:** 587, 600; **Supp. I Part 1:** 297; **Supp. XII:** 126
Trilling, Lionel, **I:** 48; **II:** 579; **III:** 308, 310, 319, 327; **IV:** 201, 211; **Retro. Supp. I:** 19, 97, 121, 216, 227; **Supp. III Part 2: 493-515**; **Supp. V:** 259; **Supp. VIII:** 93, 98, 190, 231, 236, 243; **Supp. IX:** 266, 287; **Supp. XIII:** 100-101; **Supp. XIV:**280, 288-289; **Supp. XV:** 20, 140, 152
Trilogy (Doolittle), **Supp. I Part 1:** 271, 272
Trilogy of Desire (Dreiser), **I:** 497,

508; **Retro. Supp. II:** 94, 96, **101-102**
Trimberger, Ellen Kay, **Supp. XVII:** 96, 106
Trimmed Lamp, The (O. Henry), **Supp. II Part 1:** 410
"Trinc" (McGrath), **Supp. X:** 127
Trio (Baker), **Supp. I Part 1:** 277
"*Trip*" (F. Barthelme), **Supp. XI:** 26
Triple Thinkers, The: Ten Essays on Literature (Wilson), **IV:** 428, 431; **Supp. II Part 1:** 146
"Triplex" (Doolittle), **Supp. I Part 1:** 271
Tripmaster Monkey: His Fake Book (Kingston), **Supp. V:** 157, 158, 169, 170-173
"Trip to Hanoi" (Sontag), **Supp. III Part 2:** 460-462
Trip to Parnassus, A; or, The Judgement of Apollo on Dramatic Authors and Performers (Rowson), **Supp. XV: 232-233**
"Triptych" (Eberhart), **I:** 522, 539
Tristan and Iseult, **Retro. Supp. I:** 328, 329, 330, 331
Tristessa (Kerouac), **Supp. III Part 1:** 225, 227, 229
Tristram (Robinson), **III:** 521, 522, 523
Tristram Shandy (Sterne), **I:** 299; **IV:** 465-466; **Supp. V:** 127
"Triumphal March" (Eliot), **I:** 580; **III:** 17; **Retro. Supp. I:** 64
Triumph of Achilles, The (Glück), **Supp. V:** 79, 84-86, 92
"Triumph of a Modern, The, or, Send for the Lawyer" (Anderson), **I:** 113, 114
"Triumph of the Egg, The" (Anderson), **I:** 113
Triumph of the Egg, The: A Book of Impressions from American Life in Tales and Poems (Anderson), **I:** 112, 114
Triumph of the Spider Monkey, The (Oates), **Supp. II Part 2:** 522
Triumphs of the Reformed Religion in America (Mather), **Supp. II Part 2:** 453
Trivia; or, the Art of Walking the Streets of London (Gay), **Supp. XIV:**337
Trivia: Printed from the Papers of Anthony Woodhouse, Esq. (L. P. Smith), **Supp. XIV:**336, **337-340**
Trivial Breath (Wylie), **Supp. I Part 2:** 709, 722-724
Trocchi, Alexander, **Supp. XI:** 294, 295, 301

Troilus and Criseyde (Chaucer), **Retro. Supp. I:** 426
Trois contes (Flaubert), **IV:** 31, 37
Trojan Horse, The: A Play (MacLeish), **III:** 21
"Trojan Women, The" (Maxwell), **Supp. VIII:** 169
Troll Garden, The (Cather), **I:** 313, 314-316, 322; **Retro. Supp. I:** 5, 6, 8, 14
"Trolling for Blues" (Wilbur), **Supp. III Part 2:** 563-564
Trollope, Anthony, **I:** 10, 375; **II:** 192, 237; **III:** 51, 70, 281, 382; **Retro. Supp. I:** 361
Trombly, Albert Edmund, **Supp. I Part 2:** 403
"Troop Train" (Shapiro), **Supp. II Part 2:** 707
"Tropes of the Text" (Gass), **Supp. VI:** 88
Tropic of Cancer (H. Miller), **III:** 170, 171, 174, 177, 178-180, 181, 182, 183, 187, 190; **Supp. V:** 119; **Supp. X:** 187
Tropic of Capricorn (H. Miller), **III:** 170, 176-177, 178, 182, 183, 184, 187, 188-189, 190
Trotsky, Leon, **I:** 366; **II:** 562, 564; **IV:** 429
Trotter, W., **I:** 249
Troubled Island (opera; Hughes and Still), **Retro. Supp. I:** 203
Troubled Lovers in History (Goldbarth), **Supp. XII:** 176, **192-193**
Trouble Follows Me (Macdonald, under Millar), **Supp. IV Part 2:** 466
Trouble in July (Caldwell), **I:** 297, 304-305, 306, 309
Trouble Island (Hughes), **Supp. I Part 1:** 328
"Trouble of Marcie Flint, The" (Cheever), **Supp. I Part 1:** 186
Trouble with Francis, The: An Autobiography (Francis), **Supp. IX:** 76, 77, 82, **84-85**
Trouble with God, The (Francis), **Supp. IX:** 88
"Trouble with the Stars and Stripes" (Nye), **Supp. XIII:** 277
Trouillot, Michel-Rolphe, **Supp. X:** 14-15
Troupe, Quincy, **Retro. Supp. II:** 15, 111; **Supp. X:** 242
"Trout" (Hugo), **Supp. VI:** 135
Trout Fishing in America (Brautigan), **Supp. VIII:** 43
"Trouvée" (Bishop), **Retro. Supp. II:** 49

"Truce of the Bishop, The" (Frederic), **II:** 139-140
"Truck Stop: Minnesota" (Dunn), **Supp. XI:** 145-146
True and False: Heresy and Common Sense for the Actor (Mamet), **Supp. XIV:** 241, 243
Trueblood, Valerie, **Supp. XIII:** 306
True Confessions (Dunne), **Supp. IV Part 1:** 198
True Confessions (film), **Supp. IV Part 1:** 198
True History of the Conquest of New Spain, The (Castillo), **III:** 13
True Intellectual System of the Universe, The (Cuddleworth), **II:** 10
"True Love" (Olds), **Supp. X:** 212
Trueman, Matthew (pseudonym). *See* Lowell, James Russell
"True Morality" (Bell), **Supp. X:** 13
True Stories (Atwood), **Supp. XIII:** 34-35
"True Stories" (Atwood), **Supp. XIII:** 34
"True Stories of Bitches" (Mamet), **Supp. XIV:** 246, 252
"Truest Sport, The: Jousting with Sam and Charlie" (Wolfe), **Supp. III Part 2:** 581-582
"True Vine" (Wylie), **Supp. I Part 2:** 723
True West (Shepard), **Supp. III Part 2:** 433, 441, 445, 447, 448
Truman, Harry, **III:** 3
Truman Capote: In Which Various Friends, Enemies, Acquaintances, and Detractors Recall His Turbulent Career (Plimpton), **Supp. XVI:** 245
Truman Show, The (film), **Supp. XVI:** 271
Trumbo, Dalton, **Supp. I Part 1:** 295; **Supp. XIII:** 6; **Supp. XVII:** 63
Trumbull, John, **Supp. II Part 1:** 65, 69, 70, 268
Trump, Donald, **Supp. IV Part 1:** 393
Trumpener, Katie, **Retro. Supp. I:** 380
"Trumpet Player" (Hughes), **Supp. I Part 1:** 333
Trumpet Shall Sound, The (Wilder), **IV:** 356
"Truro Bear, The" (Oliver), **Supp. VII:** 234
Truscott, Lucian K., **Supp. IV Part 2:** 683
Trust (Ozick), **Supp. V:** 257-258, 259, 260-263, 270, 272
Trust Me (Updike), **Retro. Supp. I:** 322
"Trust Yourself" (Emerson), **II:** 10
"Truth" (Emerson), **II:** 6

"Truth, The" (Jarrell), **II:** 381-382
"Truth about God, The" (Carson), **Supp. XII:** 105-106
"Truthful James" (Harte), **IV:** 196
"Truth Is, The" (Hogan), **Supp. IV Part 1:** 401-402
"Truth Is Forced, The" (Swenson), **Supp. IV Part 2:** 652
"Truth of the Matter, The" (Nemerov), **III:** 270
Truth Serum (Cooper), **Supp. XI:** 129
"Truth the Dead Know, The" (Sexton), **Supp. II Part 2:** 681
Trying to Save Piggy Sneed (Irving), **Supp. VI:** 19-165
"Trying to Talk with a Man" (Rich), **Supp. I Part 2:** 559
"Tryptich I" (Bell), **Supp. X:** 7
"Tryst, The" (Wharton), **Retro. Supp. I:** 378
"Try the Girl" (Chandler), **Supp. IV Part 1:** 125
"Ts'ai Chih" (Pound), **III:** 466
Tsuji, Shizuo, **Supp. XVII:** 90
Tsvetayeva, Marina, **Supp. VIII:** 30
"T-2 Tanker Blues" (Snyder), **Supp. VIII:** 294
"Tuberoses" (E. Stoddard), **Supp. XV:** 282
Tuckerman, Frederick Goddard, **IV:** 144
"Tuesday, November 5th, 1940" (Benét), **Supp. XI:** 46, 52
"Tuesday April 25th 1966" (Olson), **Supp. II Part 2:** 585
"Tuesday Night at the Savoy Ballroom" (Komunyakaa), **Supp. XIII:** 132
Tuffield, Aviva, **Supp. XVI:** 147, 148
"Tuft of Flowers, The" (Frost), **II:** 153; **Retro. Supp. I:** 126, 127
Tufts, James Hayden, **Supp. I Part 2:** 632
Tu Fu, **II:** 526; **Supp. XV:** 47
Tu Fu (Ayscough), **II:** 527
Tugwell, Rexford Guy, **Supp. I Part 2:** 645
"Tulip" (Hammett), **Supp. IV Part 1:** 356
"Tulip Man, The" (McCarriston), **Supp. XIV:** 261
"Tulips" (Nye), **Supp. XIII:** 281
"Tulips" (Plath), **Retro. Supp. II:** 252-253; **Supp. I Part 2:** 540, 542, 544
"Tulips" (Snodgrass), **Supp. VI:** 325
Tulips and Chimneys (Cummings), **I:** 436, 437, 440, 445, 447
Tully, Jim, **III:** 103, 109
Tumble Tower (Modarressi and Tyler), **Supp. IV Part 2:** 657
"Tuned in Late One Night" (Stafford),

Supp. XI: 327-328
Tunnel, The (Gass), **Supp. V:** 44; **Supp. VI:** 89-91, 94
"Tunnel, The" (Strand), **Supp. IV Part 2:** 622
"Tunnels" (Komunyakaa), **Supp. XIII:** 123
Tuqan, Fadwa, **Supp. XIII:** 278
Tura, Cosimo, **III:** 474-475
Turandot and Other Poems (Ashbery), **Supp. III Part 1:** 3
Turco, Lewis, **Supp. XV:** 118
Turgenev, Ivan Sergeevich, **I:** 106; **II:** 263, 271, 275, 280, 281, 288, 319, 320, 324-325, 338, 407; **III:** 461; **IV:** 17, 277; **Retro. Supp. I:** 215, 222; **Supp. VIII:** 167
Turgot, Anne Robert Jacques, **II:** 103; **Supp. I Part 1:** 250
"Turkey and Bones and Eating and We Liked It" (Stein), **IV:** 44
Turman, Glynn, **Supp. IV Part 1:** 362
Turnbull, Dr. George, **II:** 113
Turnbull, Lawrence, **Supp. I Part 1:** 352
"Turned" (Gilman), **Supp. XI:** 207
Turner, Addie, **IV:** 123
Turner, Darwin, **Supp. I Part 1:** 339; **Supp. IV Part 1:** 165
Turner, Frederick Jackson, **Supp. I Part 2:** 480, 481, 632, 640; **Supp. IV Part 2:** 596
Turner, Nat, **IV:** 113-114, 115, 116, 117
Turner, Patricia, **Supp. XIII:** 237
Turner, Russell. *See* Lacy, Ed
Turner, Victor, **Supp. IV Part 1:** 304
"Turning Away Variations on Estrangement" (Dickey), **Supp. IV Part 1:** 183
Turning Point, The (McCoy), **Supp. XIII:** 175
"Turning Thirty, I Contemplate Students Bicycling Home" (Dove), **Supp. IV Part 1:** 250
Turning Wind, A (Rukeyser), **Supp. VI:** 272-273, 279-280
Turn of the Screw, The (H. James), **Retro. Supp. I:** 219, 231; **Supp. IV Part 2:** 682
"Turn of the Screw, The" (H. James), **II:** 331-332; **Retro. Supp. I:** 228, 229, 231, 232; **Supp. XVII:** 143
Turns and Movies and Other Tales in Verse (Aiken), **I:** 65
"Turn with the Sun, A" (Knowles), **Supp. XII:** 237-238
Turow, Scott, **Supp. V:** 220; **Supp. XVII:** 213-224
Turrinus, Lucius Mamilius, **IV:** 373

"Turtle" (Hogan), **Supp. IV Part 1:** 401
Turtle, Swan (Doty), **Supp. XI: 121-122**
"Turtle, Swan" (Doty), **Supp. XI:** 121-122
Turtle Island (Snyder), **Supp. VIII: 300-303**
Turtle Moon (Hoffman), **Supp. X:** 77, **87-88,** 89
"Turtle Shrine near Chittagong, The" (Nye), **Supp. XIII:** 277
Turturro, John, **Supp. XI:** 174
Tuscan Cities (Howells), **II:** 280
Tuskegee movement, **Supp. II Part 1:** 169, 172
Tuten, Frederic, **Supp. VIII:** 75, 76; **Supp. XIII:** 237, 249
Tuthill, Louisa Cavolne, **Supp. I Part 2:** 684
"Tutored Child, The" (Kunitz), **Supp. III Part 1:** 264
Tuttleton, James W., **Supp. IV Part 1:** 166, 168
"T.V.A." (Agee), **I:** 35
Tvedten, Brother Benet, **Supp. IV Part 2:** 505
"TV Men" (Carson), **Supp. XII: 105,** 112
Twain, Mark, **I:** 57, 103, 107, 109, 190, 192, 193, 195, 197, 203, 209, 245, 246, 247-250, 255, 256, 257, 260, 261, 292, 342, 418, 469, 485; **II:** 70, 140, 259, 262, 266-268, 271, 272, 274-275, 276, 277, 280, 285-286, 287, 288, 289, 301, 304, 306, 307, 312, 415, 432, 434, 436, 446, 457, 467, 475, 476, 482; **III:** 65, 101, 102, 112-113, 114, 220, 347, 357, 409, 453, 454, 504, 507, 554, 558, 572, 575, 576; **IV: 190-213,** 333, 349, 451; **Retro. Supp. I:** 169, 194, 195; **Retro. Supp. II:** 123; **Supp. I Part 1:** 37, 39, 44, 247, 251, 313, 317; **Supp. I Part 2:** 377, 385, 393, 410, 455, 456, 457, 473, 475, 579, 602, 604, 618, 629, 651, 660; **Supp. II Part 1:** 193, 344, 354, 385; **Supp. IV Part 1:** 386, 388; **Supp. IV Part 2:** 463, 468, 603, 607, 693; **Supp. V:** 44, 113, 131; **Supp. VIII:** 40, 189; **Supp. IX:** 14, 171; **Supp. X:** 51, 227; **Supp. XII:** 343; **Supp. XIII:** 1, 17; **Supp. XV:** 41; **Supp. XVI:**66, 208
"Twa Sisters, The" (ballad), **Supp. I Part 2:** 696
Twelfth Night (Shakespeare), **Supp. IV Part 1:** 83; **Supp. IX:** 14
Twelve Men (Dreiser), **Retro. Supp. II:** 94, 104
Twelve Moons (Oliver), **Supp. VII:** 231, 233-236, 238, 240
"12 O'Clock News" (Bishop), **Retro. Supp. II:** 48
Twelve Southerners, **IV:** 125; **Supp. X:** 25
Twelve Years a Slave (Northup), **Supp. XIV:**32
Twentieth Century Authors, **I:** 376, 527
"Twentieth Century Fiction and the Black Mask of Humanity" (Ellison), **Retro. Supp. II:** 118
Twentieth Century Pleasures (Hass), **Supp. VI:** 103, 106, 109
"28" (Levine), **Supp. V:** 187, 191
"Twenty-Four Poems" (Schwartz), **Supp. II Part 2:** 646, 649
"2433 Agnes, First Home, Last House in Missoula" (Hugo), **Supp. VI:** 139-140
"Twenty Hill Hollow" (Muir), **Supp. IX:** 178
"Twenty Minutes" (Salter), **Supp. IX:** 260
"Twenty-One Love Poems" (Rich), **Supp. I Part 2:** 572-573
"Twenty-One Poems" (MacLeish), **III:** 19
Twenty Poems (Haines), **Supp. XII:** 204, **205-206**
Twenty Poems of Anna Akhmatova (Kenyon), **Supp. VII:** 165-166
Twenty Questions: (Posed by Poems) (McClatchy), **Supp. XII:** 254, **259-262**
27 Wagons Full of Cotton and Other One-Act Plays (T. Williams), **IV:** 381, 383
Twenty Thousand Leagues under the Sea (Verne), **I:** 480; **Supp. XI:** 63
"Twenty Years Ago" (Lindsay), **Supp. I Part 2:** 384, 399
Twenty Years at Hull-House (Addams), **Supp. I Part 1:** 3, 4, 11, 16
Twice over Lightly: New York Ten and Now (Hayes and Loos), **Supp. XVI:**195
Twice-Told Tales (Hawthorne), **I:** 354; **II:** 224; **III:** 412, 421; **Retro. Supp. I:** 154-155, 160
Twichell, Chase, **Supp. V:** 16; **Supp. XVII:** 110, 112
Twilight (Frost), **II:** 151
"Twilight's Last Gleaming" (Burroughs and Elvins), **Supp. III Part 1:** 93, 94, 101
Twilight Sleep (Wharton), **IV:** 320-322, 324-325, 327, 328; **Retro. Supp. I:** 381
"Twin, The" (Olds), **Supp. X:** 207
"Twin Beds in Rome" (Updike), **Retro. Supp. I:** 332
"Twins of Table Mountain, The" (Harte), **Supp. II Part 1:** 355
"Twist, The" (Olson), **Supp. II Part 2:** 570
Two: Gertrude Stein and Her Brother (Stein), **IV:** 43
Two Admirals, The (Cooper), **I:** 350
Two against One (F. Barthelme), **Supp. XI:** 32, 33, 36
"Two Boys" (Moore), **Supp. X:** 173
"Two Brothers, The" (Jewett), **Retro. Supp. II:** 132
Two-Character Play, The (T. Williams), **IV:** 382, 386, 393, 398
Two Citizens (Wright), **Supp. III Part 2:** 602-604
"Two Deer" (Bass), **Supp. XVI:**24
"Two Domains, The" (Goldbarth), **Supp. XII:** 192
"Two Environments, The" (Trilling), **Supp. III Part 2:** 510
"Two-Fisted Self Pity" (Broyard), **Supp. XI:** 348
Two for Texas (Burke), **Supp. XIV:**25, 34
"Two Friends" (Cather), **I:** 332
"Two Gardens in Linndale" (Robinson), **III:** 508
Two Gentlemen in Bonds (Ransom), **III:** 491-492
"Two Ghosts" (Francis), **Supp. IX:** 87
"Two Hangovers" (Wright), **Supp. III Part 2:** 596
Two-Headed Poems (Atwood), **Supp. XIII:** 34
Two Hot to Handle (Lacy), **Supp. XV:** 206
Two Hours to Doom (Bryant), **Supp. XI:** 302
"Two Kitchens in Provence" (M. F. K. Fisher), **Supp. XVII:** 88, 91
"Two Ladies in Retirement" (Taylor), **Supp. V:** 320
Two Letters to the Citizens of the United States, and One to General Washington (Barlow), **Supp. II Part 1:** 80
"Two Lives, The" (Hogan), **Supp. IV Part 1:** 400, 402, 403, 406, 411
Two Long Poems (Stern), **Supp. IX:** 296
"Two Lovers and a Beachcomber by the Real Sea" (Plath), **Supp. I Part 2:** 536
Two Men (E. Stoddard), **Supp. XV:** 272, 273, **283-284**

"Two Men" (McClatchy)", **Supp. XII:** 269

Two Men of Sandy Bar (Harte), **Supp. II Part 1:** 354

Twomey, Jay, **Supp. XVII:** 111

"Two Moods of Love" (Cullen), **Supp. IV Part 1:** 166

"Two Morning Monologues" (Bellow), **I:** 150; **Retro. Supp. II:** 20

Two-Ocean War, The (Morison), **Supp. I Part 2:** 491

"Two of Hearts" (Hogan), **Supp. IV Part 1:** 410

"Two on a Party" (T. Williams), **IV:** 388

"Two Pendants: For the Ears" (W. C. Williams), **Retro. Supp. I:** 423

"Two Poems of Going Home" (Dickey), **Supp. IV Part 1:** 182-183

"Two Portraits" (Chopin), **Supp. I Part 1:** 218

"Two Presences, The" (R. Bly), **Supp. IV Part 1:** 65

"Two Rivers" (Stegner), **Supp. IV Part 2:** 605

Tworkov, Jack, **Supp. XII:** 198

"Two Scenes" (Ashbery), **Supp. III Part 1:** 4

Two Serious Ladies (Jane Bowles), **Supp. IV Part 1:** 82

"Two Silences" (Carruth), **Supp. XVI:**55

"Two Sisters" (Farrell), **II:** 45

Two Sisters: A Memoir in the Form of a Novel (Vidal), **Supp. IV Part 2:** 679

"Two Sisters of Persephone" (Plath), **Retro. Supp. II:** 246

"Two Songs on the Economy of Abundance" (Agee), **I:** 28

"Two Tales of Clumsy" (Schnackenberg), **Supp. XV:** 258

"Two Temples, The" (Melville), **III:** 89-90

Two Thousand Seasons (Armah), **Supp. IV Part 1:** 373

Two Towns in Provence (M. F. K. Fisher), **Supp. XVII:** 91

Two Trains Running (Wilson), **Supp. VIII:** 345-348

"Two Tramps in Mudtime" (Frost), **II:** 164; **Retro. Supp. I:** 137; **Supp. IX:** 261

"Two Views of a Cadaver Room" (Plath), **Supp. I Part 2:** 538

"Two Villages" (Paley), **Supp. VI:** 227

"Two Voices in a Meadow" (Wilbur), **Supp. III Part 2:** 555

"Two Witches" (Frost), **Retro. Supp. I:** 135

"Two Words" (Francis), **Supp. IX:** 81

Two Years before the Mast (Dana), **I:** 351

"Tyger, The" (Blake), **Supp. XVII:** 128

Tyler, Anne, **Supp. IV Part 2: 657-675; Supp. V:** 227, 326; **Supp. VIII:** 141; **Supp. X:** 1, 77, 83, 85; **Supp. XII:** 307; **Supp. XVI:**37

Tyler, Royall, **I:** 344; **Retro. Supp. I:** 377

Tymms, Ralph, **Supp. IX:** 105

Tyndale, William, **II:** 15

Tyndall, John, **Retro. Supp. II:** 93

Typee: A Peep at Polynesian Life (Melville), **III:** 75-77, 79, 84; **Retro. Supp. I:** 245-246, 249, 252, 256

Types From City Streets (Hapgood), **Supp. XVII:** 103

Typewriter Town (W. J. Smith), **Supp. XIII:** 332

"Typhus" (Simpson), **Supp. IX:** 277

Tyranny of the Normal (Fiedler), **Supp. XIII: 107-108**

"Tyranny of the Normal" (Fiedler), **Supp. XIII:** 107-108

"Tyrant of Syracuse" (MacLeish), **III:** 20

"Tyrian Businesses" (Olson), **Supp. II Part 2:** 567, 568, 569

Tytell, John, **Supp. XIV:**140

Tzara, Tristan, **Supp. III Part 1:** 104, 105

U

U and I (Baker), **Supp. XIII: 45-47,** 48, 52, 55

Überdie Seelenfrage (Fechner), **II:** 358

Ubu Roi (Jarry), **Supp. XV:** 178, 186

Ueland, Brenda, **Supp. XVII:** 13

"Ulalume" (Poe), **III:** 427; **Retro. Supp. II:** 264, 266

Ulin, David, **Supp. XIII:** 244; **Supp. XVI:**74

Ullman, Leslie, **Supp. IV Part 2:** 550

Ultimate Good Luck, The (Ford), **Supp. V:** 57, 61-62

Ultimate Punishment: A Lawyer's Reflections on Dealing with the Death Penalty (Turow), **Supp. XVII:** 220-221

Ultima Thule (Longfellow), **II:** 490; **Retro. Supp. II:** 169

"Ultima Thule" (Nabokov), **Retro. Supp. I:** 274

Ultramarine (Carver), **Supp. III Part 1:** 137, 138, 147, 148

Ulysses (Joyce), **I:** 395, 475-476, 478, 479, 481; **II:** 42, 264, 542; **III:** 170, 398; **IV:** 103, 418, 428, 455; **Retro. Supp. I:** 59, 63, 290, 291; **Retro. Supp. II:** 121; **Supp. I Part 1:** 57; **Supp. III Part 2:** 618, 619; **Supp. IV Part 1:** 285; **Supp. IV Part 2:** 424; **Supp. V:** 261; **Supp. IX:** 102; **Supp. X:** 114; **Supp. XIII:** 43, 191; **Supp. XV:** 305; **Supp. XVII:** 140, 227

"*Ulysses*, Order and Myth" (Eliot), **Retro. Supp. I:** 63

Unaccountable Worth of the World, The (Price), **Supp. VI:** 267

Unamuno y Jugo, Miguel de, **III:** 310; **Supp. XV:** 79

"Unattached Smile, The" (Crews), **Supp. XI:** 101

"Unbelievable Thing Usually Goes to the Heart of the Story, The: Magic Realism in the Fiction of Rick Bass" (Dwyer), **Supp. XVI:**16

"Unbeliever, The" (Bishop), **Retro. Supp. II:** 43

"Unborn Song" (Rukeyser), **Supp. VI:** 274

Unbought Spirit: A John Jay Chapman Reader (Stone, ed.), **Supp. XIV:**54

Uncalled, The (Dunbar), **Supp. II Part 1:** 200, 211, 212

Uncentering the Earth: Copernicus and The Revolutions of the Heavenly Spheres (Vollmann), **Supp. XVII:** 226

Uncertain Certainty, The: Interviews, Essays, and Notes on Poetry (Simic), **Supp. VIII:** 270, 273, 274

Uncertainty and Plenitude: Five Contemporary Poets (Stitt), **Supp. IX:** 299

"Uncle" (Levine), **Supp. V:** 186

"Uncle Christmas" (Ríos), **Supp. IV Part 2:** 552

"Uncle Jim's Baptist Revival Hymn" (Lanier and Lanier), **Supp. I Part 1:** 353

"Uncle Lot" (Stowe), **Supp. I Part 2:** 585-586

Uncle Remus Tales (Harris), **Supp. II Part 1:** 201

Uncle Tom's Cabin (Stowe), **II:** 291; **Supp. I Part 1:** 49; **Supp. I Part 2:** 410, 579, 582, 589-592; **Supp. II Part 1:** 170; **Supp. III Part 1:** 154, 171; **Supp. IX:** 19; **Supp. X:** 246, 249, 250; **Supp. XIII:** 95; **Supp. XVI:**82, 85, 88

Uncle Tom's Children (Wright), **IV:** 476, 478, 488; **Supp. II Part 1:** 228, 235

"Uncle Wiggily in Connecticut" (Salinger), **III:** 559-560, 563

"Unclouded Day, The" (Proulx), **Supp.**

VII: 254-255
"Uncommon Visage" (Brodsky), **Supp. VIII:** 31
"Uncommon Woman: An Interview with Wendy Wasserstein" (Cohen), **Supp. XV:** 323
Uncommon Women and Others (Wasserstein), **Supp. XV:** 320-321, **322-323**
Uncompromising Fictions of Cynthia Ozick (Pinsker), **Supp. V:** 272
"Unconscious Came a Beauty" (Swenson), **Supp. IV Part 2:** 646
"Uncreation, The" (Pinsky), **Supp. VI:** 245
"Undead, The" (Wilbur), **Supp. III Part 2:** 556
"Undefeated, The" (Hemingway), **II:** 250; **Retro. Supp. I:** 180
Under a Glass Bell (Nin), **Supp. X:** 186
"Under Ben Bulben" (Yeats), **Supp. V:** 220
Undercliff: Poems 1946-1953 (Eberhart), **I:** 528, 536-537
Under Cover (Goldbarth), **Supp. XII:** 177, 180, 193
Undercover Doctor (film), **Supp. XIII:** 170
"Under Cygnus" (Wilbur), **Supp. III Part 2:** 558
"Under Forty" (Trilling), **Supp. III Part 2:** 494
Underground Man, The (film), **Supp. IV Part 2:** 474
Underground Man, The (Macdonald), **Supp. IV Part 2:** 474, 475
"Under Libra: Weights and Measures" (Merrill), **Supp. III Part 1:** 328
Under Milk Wood (D. Thomas), **III:** 21
"Undersea" (Carson), **Supp. IX:** 21
Understanding Cynthia Ozick (Friedman), **Supp. V:** 273
Understanding Drama (Brooks and Heilman), **Supp. XIV:** 12
Understanding E. L. Doctorow (Fowler), **Supp. IV Part 1:** 226
Understanding Fiction (Brooks and Warren), **IV:** 279; **Supp. XIV:** 11
Understanding Flannery O'Connor (Whitt), **Retro. Supp. II:** 226
Understanding Nicholson Baker (Saltzman), **Supp. XIII:** 48
Understanding Poetry: An Anthology for College Students (Brooks and Warren), **IV:** 236; **Retro. Supp. I:** 40, 41; **Supp. XIV:** 4-5
Understanding Tim O'Brien (Kaplan), **Supp. V:** 241

Understanding To Kill a Mockingbird: A Student Casebook to Issues, Sources, and Documents (Johnson), **Supp. VIII:** 127
Undertaker's Garland, The (Wilson and Bishop), **IV:** 427
"Under the Cedarcroft Chestnut" (Lanier), **Supp. I Part 1:** 364
"Under the Harbour Bridge" (Komunyakaa), **Supp. XIII:** 125
"Under the Influence" (Sanders), **Supp. XVI:** 274, 277
Under the Lilacs (Alcott), **Supp. I Part 1:** 42-43, 44
"Under the Maud Moon" (Kinnell), **Supp. III Part 1:** 246-247
Under the Mountain Wall: A Chronicle of Two Seasons in the Stone Age (Matthiessen), **Supp. V:** 202
"Under the Rose" (Pynchon), **Supp. II Part 2:** 620
Under the Sea-Wind: A Naturalist's Picture of Ocean Life (Carson), **Supp. IX:** 19, **22-23**
Under the Sign of Saturn (Sontag), **Supp. III Part 2:** 451, 452, 458, 470-471
"Under the Sign of Saturn" (Sontag), **Supp. III Part 2:** 470
"Under the Sky" (Bowles), **Supp. IV Part 1:** 87
Under the Volcano (M. Lowry), **Supp. XVII:** 135, 139, 140
"Under the Willows" (Lowell), **Supp. I Part 2:** 416
Under the Willows and Other Poems (Lowell), **Supp. I Part 2:** 424
Underwood, Wilbur, **Retro. Supp. II:** 79
Underworld (DeLillo), **Supp. VI:** 2, 4-5, 6-7, 8, 9, 10, 11, **13-15; Supp. XI:** 68
Undine (La Motte-Fouqué), **II:** 212; **III:** 78
Undiscovered Country, The (Howells), **II:** 282
"Undressing, The" (C. Frost), **Supp. XV:** 98
Uneasy Chair, The (Stegner), **Supp. IV Part 2:** 599
"Unemployed, Disabled, and Insane, The" (Haines), **Supp. XII:** 211-212
Unending Blues (Simic), **Supp. VIII:** **278-279**
"Unexpressed" (Dunbar), **Supp. II Part 1:** 199
"Unfinished Bronx, The" (Paley), **Supp. VI:** 228
"Unfinished Poems" (Eliot), **I:** 579

"Unfinished Song" (C. Frost), **Supp. XV:** 97
Unfinished Woman, An (Hellman), **Supp. I Part 1:** 292, 293, 294; **Supp. IV Part 1:** 12, 353-354; **Supp. IX:** 196, 200-201
Unforeseen Wilderness, The: An Essay on Kentucky's Red River Gorge (Berry), **Supp. X:** 28, 29, 30, 36
Unforgotten Years (L. P. Smith), **Supp. XIV:** 333, 334, 335, 336, 347
"Unfortunate Coincidence" (Parker), **Supp. IX:** 190
Unframed Originals (Merwin), **Supp. III Part 1:** 341
Ungar, Sanford, **Supp. XI:** 228
Ungaretti, Giuseppe, **Supp. V:** 337
Unguided Tour (Sontag), **Supp. III Part 2:** 452
"Unheimliche, Das" (The Uncanny) (Freud), **Supp. XVI:** 157-158
Unholy Sonnets (Jarman), **Supp. XVII:** 109, 110, **119-120**
"Unholy Sonnets" (Jarman), **Supp. XVII:** 118, 119-120
"Unidentified Flying Object" (Hayden), **Supp. II Part 1:** 368
"Unifying Principle, The" (Ammons), **Supp. VII:** 28
"Union" (Hughes), **Supp. I Part 1:** 331
"Union Street: San Francisco, Summer 1975" (Carver), **Supp. III Part 1:** 138
United States Army in World War II (Morison), **Supp. I Part 2:** 490
United States Constitution, **I:** 6, 283
United States Essays, 1951-1991 (Vidal), **Supp. IV Part 2:** 678, 687
United States of Poetry, The (television series), **Supp. XIII:** 274
"Unity through Diversity" (Locke), **Supp. XIV:** 212, 213
Universal Baseball Asociation, Inc., J. Henry Waugh, Prop., The (Coover), **Supp. V:** 39, 41-42, 44, 46
Universal Passion (Young), **III:** 111
"Universe of Death, The" (H. Miller), **III:** 184
Universe of Time, A (Anderson), **II:** 27, 28, 45, 46, 48, 49
"Universities" (Emerson), **II:** 6
"Universities: A Mirage? " (Mora), **Supp. XIII:** 219
"University" (Shapiro), **Supp. II Part 2:** 704-705, 717
"University Avenue" (Mora), **Supp. XIII:** 216
"University Days" (Thurber), **Supp. I Part 2:** 605

"University Hospital, Boston" (Oliver), **Supp. VII:** 235
"Unknowable, The" (Levine), **Supp. V:** 195
"Unknown Girl in the Maternity Ward" (Sexton), **Supp. II Part 2:** 676
"Unknown Love, The" (Chandler), **Supp. IV Part 1:** 120
Unknown Rilke, The (Rilke; F. Wright, trans.), **Supp. XVII:** 244
"Unknown War, The" (Sandburg), **III:** 594
Unleashed (anthology), **Supp. XI:** 132
"Unlighted Lamps" (Anderson), **I:** 112
Unloved Wife, The (Alcott), **Supp. I Part 1:** 33
Unmarried Woman, An (film), **Supp. IV Part 1:** 303
"Unnatural Mother, The" (Gilman), **Supp. XI:** 207
"Unnatural State of the Unicorn" (Komunyakaa), **Supp. XIII:** 119
"Unparalleled Adventure of One Hans Pfaall, The" (Poe), **III:** 424
Unprecedented Era, The (Goebbels), **III:** 560
"Unprofitable Servant, The" (O. Henry), **Supp. II Part 1:** 403
Unpublished Poems of Emily Dickinson (Bianchi and Hampson, ed.), **Retro. Supp. I:** 35
Unpunished (Gilman), **Supp. XI:** 208
"Unreal City" (Eliot), **Supp. XV:** 218
"Unreasoning Heart" (Untermeyer), **Supp. XV:** 309
"Unsaid (Gioia), **Supp. XV:** 129
"Unseen, The" (Pinsky), **Supp. VI:** 243-244
"Unseen, The" (Singer), **Retro. Supp. II:** 307
Unseen Hand, The (Shepard), **Supp. III Part 2:** 439, 445-446
Unselected Poems (Levine), **Supp. V:** 179
Unsettling of America, The: Culture and Agriculture (Berry), **Supp. X:** 22, 26, 29, 32, 33, 35; **Supp. XIV:** 177, 179
Unspeakable Gentleman, The (Marquand), **III:** 53-54, 60, 63
Unspeakable Practices, Unnatural Acts (Barthelme), **Supp. IV Part 1:** 39
"Unspeakable Things Unspoken: The Afro-American Presence in American Literature" (Morrison), **Supp. III Part 1:** 375, 377-379
"Untelling, The" (Strand), **Supp. IV Part 2:** 629
Unterecker, John, **I:** 386
Untermeyer, Jean Starr, **II:** 530; **Supp. XV:** 294, 295, 303, 307, 308, 310
Untermeyer, Louis, **II:** 516-517, 530, 532; **III:** 268; **Retro. Supp. I:** 124, 133, 136; **Supp. III Part 1:** 2; **Supp. IX:** 76; **Supp. XIV:** 119, 123; **Supp. XV:** 293-318
Untimely Papers (Bourne), **I:** 218, 233
"Untitled" (C. Frost), **Supp. XV:** 103
"Untitled Blues" (Komunyakaa), **Supp. XIII:** 117
Unto the Sons (Talese), **Supp. XVII:** 199-200, **206-207**, 208, 209, 210
"Untrustworthy Speaker, The" (Glück), **Supp. V:** 86
"Unused" (Anderson), **I:** 112, 113
Unvanquished, The (Faulkner), **II:** 55, 67-68, 71; **Retro. Supp. I:** 84; **Supp. I Part 2:** 450
"Unvexed Isles, The" (Warren), **IV:** 253
"Unwedded" (Larcom), **Supp. XIII:** 144
"Unweepables, The" (Karr), **Supp. XI:** 243
"Unwelcome Guest, An" (Papernick), **Supp. XVII:** 50
Unwelcome Words (Bowles), **Supp. IV Part 1:** 93, 94
"Unwelcome Words" (Bowles), **Supp. IV Part 1:** 94, 95
Unwin, T. Fisher, **Supp. XI:** 202
"Unwithered Garland, The" (Kunitz), **Supp. III Part 1:** 265
Unwobbling Pivot, The (Pound, trans.), **III:** 472
"Unwritten, The" (Merwin), **Supp. III Part 1:** 352
"Unwritten Law" (Glück), **Supp. V:** 91
Up (Sukenick), **Supp. V:** 39
Up Above the World (Bowles), **Supp. IV Part 1:** 82, 91, 92
"Up and Down" (Merrill), **Supp. III Part 1:** 328
Upanishads, **IV:** 183
Up Country: Poems of New England (Kumin), **Supp. IV Part 2:** 446, 447-448, 453
"Update" (Dunn), **Supp. XI:** 150-151
Updike, John, **I:** 54; **III:** 572; **IV: 214-235**; **Retro. Supp. I:** 116, **317-338**; **Retro. Supp. II:** 213, 279, 280; **Supp. I Part 1:** 186, 196; **Supp. IV Part 2:** 657; **Supp. V:** 23, 43, 95, 119; **Supp. VIII:** 151, 167, 236; **Supp. IX:** 208; **Supp. XI:** 65, 66, 99, 140; **Supp. XII:** 140, 296, 298, 310; **Supp. XIII:** 45-46, 47, 52; **Supp. XIV:** 79, 93, 111; **Supp. XVI:** 205, 207, 220
Updike, Mrs. Wesley, **IV:** 218, 220

Up from Slavery (Washington), **Supp. II Part 1:** 169; **Supp. IX:** 19
Upham, Thomas Goggswell, **II:** 487
"Upholsterers, The" (Lardner), **II:** 435
"Up in Michigan" (Hemingway), **II:** 263
Upjohn, Richard, **IV:** 312
"Upon a Spider Catching a Fly" (Taylor), **IV:** 161
"Upon a Wasp Child with Cold" (Taylor), **IV:** 161
"Upon Meeting Don L. Lee, in a Dream" (Dove), **Supp. IV Part 1:** 244
"Upon My Dear and Loving Husband His Going into England, Jan. 16, 1661" (Bradstreet), **Supp. I Part 1:** 110
"Upon Returning to the Country Road" (Lindsay), **Supp. I Part 2:** 382
"Upon the Burning of Our House, July 10th, 1666" (Bradstreet), **Supp. I Part 1:** 107-108, 122
"Upon the Sweeping Flood" (Taylor), **IV:** 161
"Upon Wedlock, and Death of Children" (Taylor), **IV:** 144, 147, 161
"Upset, An" (Merrill), **Supp. III Part 1:** 336
Upstairs and Downstairs (Vonnegut), **Supp. II Part 2:** 757
Upstate (Wilson), **IV:** 447
Upton, Lee, **Supp. X:** 209
"Upturned Face" (Crane), **I:** 423
Upward, Allen, **Supp. I Part 1:** 262
Upward, Edward, **Supp. XIV:** 159, 160
"Upward Moon and the Downward Moon, The" (R. Bly), **Supp. IV Part 1:** 71
Urania: A Rhymed Lesson (Holmes), **Supp. I Part 1:** 300
"Urban Convalescence, An" (Merrill), **Supp. III Part 1:** 322-324
"Urban Renewal" (Komunyakaa), **Supp. XIII:** 113
Urdang, Constance, **Supp. XV:** 74
"Urganda and Fatima" (Rowson), **Supp. XV:** 234
Urial Accosta: A Play (Reznikoff), **Supp. XIV:** 282, 288
Urich, Robert, **Supp. V:** 228
"Uriel" (Emerson), **II:** 19
Uris, Leon, **Supp. IV Part 1:** 285, 379
Uroff, Margaret D., **Supp. I Part 2:** 542
"Us" (Sexton), **Supp. II Part 2:** 687
U.S. 1 (Rukeyser), **Supp. VI:** 272, 278, 283, 285
"U.S. Commercial Orchid, The" (Agee), **I:** 35

U.S.A. (Dos Passos), **I**: 379, 475, 478, 482-488, 489, 490, 491, 492, 493, 494, 495; **Retro. Supp. II**: 197; **Supp. I Part 2**: 646; **Supp. III Part 1**: 104, 105; **Supp. XIV**:24
"U.S.A. School of Writing, The" (Bishop), **Retro. Supp. II**: 43
"Used-Boy Raisers, The" (Paley), **Supp. VI**: 218, 228
"Used Cars on Oahu" (Nye), **Supp. XIII**: 282
"Used Side of the Sofa, The" (Ríos), **Supp. IV Part 2**: 551
Use of Fire, The (Price), **Supp. VI**: 265
"Use of Force, The" (W. C. Williams), **Retro. Supp. I**: 424
Use of Poetry and the Use of Criticism, The (Eliot), **Retro. Supp. I**: 65
Uses of Enchantment, The: The Meaning and Importance of Fairy Tales (Bettelheim), **Supp. XIV**:126
Uses of Enchantment, The: The Meaning and Importance of Fairy Tales (Bettleheim), **Supp. X**: 77
"Uses of Hell, The" (E. Hoffman), **Supp. XVI**:154
"Uses of Hell, The: An Exchange"(Novick, Katz, and Szulc), **Supp. XVI**:154
Uses of Literacy, The (Hoggart), **Supp. XIV**:299
"Uses of Poetry, The" (W. C. Williams), **Retro. Supp. I**: 412
"Uses of the Blues, The" (Baldwin), **Retro. Supp. II**: 8
"USFS 1919: The Ranger, the Cook, and a Hole in the Sky" (Maclean), **Supp. XIV**:230, 234
Ushant: An Essay (Aiken), **I**: 49, 54, 55, 56, 57
"Usher 11" (Bradbury), **Supp. I Part 2**: 622
"Using Parrots to Kill Mockingbirds: Yet Another Racial Prosecution and Wrongful Conviction in Maycomb" (Fair), **Supp. VIII**: 128
Usual Star, The (Doolittle), **Supp. I Part 1**: 270
"Usurpation (Other People's Stories)" (Ozick), **Supp. V**: 268, 271
Utopia 14 (Vonnegut), **Supp. II Part 2**: 757

V

V. (Pynchon), **Supp. II Part 2**: 618, 620-622, 627-630; **Supp. IV Part 1**: 279
V. S. Naipaul: An Introduction to His Work (Theroux), **Supp. VIII**: 314, 318
"V. S. Pritchett's Apprenticeship" (Maxwell), **Supp. VIII**: 172
"V. V." (Alcott), **Supp. I Part 1**: 37
"Vacation" (Stafford), **Supp. XI**: 321, 322
"Vacation Trip" (Stafford), **Supp. XI**: 322
Vachel Lindsay: A Poet in America (Masters), **Supp. I Part 2**: 473, 474
"Vachel Lindsay: The Midwest as Utopia" (Whitney), **Supp. I Part 2**: 403
"Vachel Lindsay Writes to Floyd Dell" (Tanselle), **Supp. I Part 2**: 403
"Vacillation" (Yeats), **Supp. XV**: 253
Vadim, Roger, **Supp. XI**: 293, 307
"Vag" (Dos Passos), **I**: 487-488
Valentine, Jean, **Supp. V**: 92
Valentine, Saint, **IV**: 396
Valentino, Rudolph, **I**: 483
Valéry, Paul, **II**: 543, 544; **III**: 279, 409, 428, 609; **IV**: 79, 91, 92, 428, 443; **Retro. Supp. II**: 187
"Valhalla" (Francis), **Supp. IX**: 77
Valhalla and Other Poems (Francis), **Supp. IX**: 76
Validity in Interpretation (Hirsch), **Supp. XIV**:15
Valitsky, Ken, **Supp. XII**: 7
Vallejo, César, **Supp. V**: 332; **Supp. IX**: 271; **Supp. XIII**: 114, 315, 323
"Valley, The" (Bass), **Supp. XVI**:20, 22
Valley Between, The (Marshall), **Supp. XI**: 278
Valley of Decision, The (Wharton), **IV**: 311, 315; **Retro. Supp. I**: 365-367
Valley of the Moon, The (London), **II**: 467, 481
"Valley of Unrest, The" (Poe), **III**: 411
Valli, Alida, **Supp. IV Part 2**: 520
"Valor" (Bausch), **Supp. VII**: 54
Valparaiso (DeLillo), **Supp. VI**: 4, 12
"Value of a Place, The" (Bass), **Supp. XVI**:18
"Values and Fictions" (Toomer), **Supp. III Part 2**: 485-486
"Values and Imperatives" (Locke), **Supp. XIV**:199, 202, 212
Values of Veblen, The: A Critical Appraisal (Rosenberg), **Supp. I Part 2**: 650
"Vampire" (Karr), **Supp. XI**: 241
Vampire Armand, The (Rice), **Supp. VII**: 290, 294-295
Vampire Chronicles, The (Rice), **Supp. VII**: 290
Vampire Lestat, The (Rice), **Supp. VII**: 290-292, 298, 299
Van Buren, Martin, **II**: 134, 312; **III**: 473

Vande Kieft, Ruth M., **IV**: 260
Vanderbilt, Cornelius, **III**: 14
Van Dine, S. S., **Supp. IV Part 1**: 341
Van Doren, Carl, **I**: 252-253, 423; **II**: 103, 111, 112; **Supp. I Part 2**: 474, 486, 707, 709, 717, 718, 727; **Supp. II Part 1**: 395; **Supp. VIII**: 96-97
Van Doren, Mark, **I**: 168; **III**: 4, 23, 589; **Supp. I Part 2**: 604; **Supp. III Part 2**: 626; **Supp. VIII**: 231; **Supp. IX**: 266, 268; **Supp. XV**: 152, 305, 307
Vandover and the Brute (Norris), **III**: 314, 315, 316, 320-322, 328, 333, 334
Van Duyn, Mona, **Supp. IX**: 269
Van Dyke, Annette, **Supp. IV Part 1**: 327
Van Dyke, Henry, **I**: 223; **II**: 456
Van Gogh, Vincent, **I**: 27; **IV**: 290; **Supp. I Part 2**: 451; **Supp. IV Part 1**: 284
Van Gogh's Room at Arles (Elkin), **Supp. VI**: 56
"Vanisher, The" (Whittier), **Supp. I Part 2**: 691
Vanishing Point (Markson), **Supp. XVII**: 135, 137, 138, 145-146
"Vanishing Red, The" (Frost), **Retro. Supp. II**: 47
"Vanity" (B. Diop), **Supp. IV Part 1**: 16
Vanity Fair (Thackeray), **I**: 354; **II**: 91; **III**: 70; **Supp. IX**: 200
"Vanity of All Wordly Things, The" (Bradstreet), **Supp. I Part 1**: 102, 119
Vanity of Duluoz (Kerouac), **Supp. III Part 1**: 221, 222
"Vanity of Existence, The" (Freneau), **Supp. II Part 1**: 262
Van Matre, Lynn, **Supp. V**: 126
Vann, Barbara, **Supp. XV**: 187
Vanquished, The (Faulkner), **I**: 205
Van Rensselaer, Stephen, **I**: 351
Van Vechten, Carl, **I**: 295; **IV**: 76; **Supp. I Part 1**: 324, 327, 332; **Supp. I Part 2**: 715; **Supp. II Part 2**: 725-751; **Supp. X**: 247; **Supp. XVI**:135; **Supp. XVII**: 96, 97, 101, 104
Vanzetti, Bartolomeo, **I**: 482, 486, 490, 494; **II**: 38-39, 426; **III**: 139-140; **Supp. I Part 2**: 446, 610, 611; **Supp. V**: 288-289; **Supp. IX**: 199
"Vapor Trail Reflected in the Frog Pond" (Kinnell), **Supp. III Part 1**: 242-243
"Vapor Trails" (Snyder), **Supp. VIII**: 298

"Variation: Ode to Fear" (Warren), **IV:** 241
"Variation on a Sentence" (Bogan), **Supp. III Part 1:** 60
"Variation on Gaining a Son" (Dove), **Supp. IV Part 1:** 248
"Variation on Pain" (Dove), **Supp. IV Part 1:** 248
"Variations: The air is sweetest that a thistle guards" (Merrill), **Supp. III Part 1:** 321
"Variations: White Stag, Black Bear" (Merrill), **Supp. III Part 1:** 321
"Varick Street" (Bishop), **Supp. I Part 1:** 90, 92
Varieties of Metaphysical Poetry, The (Eliot), **Retro. Supp. I:** 65
Varieties of Religious Experience, The (William James), **II:** 344, 353, 354, 359-360, 362; **IV:** 28, 291; **Supp. IX:** 19
Variety (film), **Supp. XII:** 7
Variorum (Whitman), **Retro. Supp. I:** 406
Various Antidotes (J. Scott), **Supp. XVII: 188-189**
Various Miracles (Shields), **Supp. VII:** 318-320, 323, 324
"Various Miracles" (Shields), **Supp. VII:** 318-319, 324
Various Poems (Zach), **Supp. XV:** 86
"Various Tourists" (Connell), **Supp. XIV:** 79
"Varmint Question, The" (Leopold), **Supp. XIV:** 180-181
Vasari, Giorgio, **Supp. I Part 2:** 450; **Supp. III Part 1:** 5
Vasquez, Robert, **Supp. V:** 180
Vassall Morton (Parkman), **Supp. II Part 2:** 595, 597-598
Vasse, W. W., **III:** 478
Vaudeville for a Princess (Schwartz), **Supp. II Part 2:** 661-662
Vaughan, Henry, **IV:** 151; **Supp. XV:** 251
Vaughn, Robert, **Supp. XI:** 343
"Vaunting Oak" (Ransom), **III:** 490
Vazirani, Reetika, **Supp. XIII:** 133
Veblen (Hobson), **Supp. I Part 2:** 650
Veblen, Andrew, **Supp. I Part 2:** 640
Veblen, Mrs. Thorstein (Ellen Rolfe), **Supp. I Part 2:** 641
Veblen, Oswald, **Supp. I Part 2:** 640
Veblen, Thorstein, **I:** 104, 283, 475-476, 483, 498, 511; **II:** 27, 272, 276, 287; **Supp. I Part 2: 628-650**; **Supp. IV Part 1:** 22
Veblenism: A New Critique (Dobriansky), **Supp. I Part 2:** 648, 650

"Veblen's Attack on Culture" (Adorno), **Supp. I Part 2:** 650
Vechten, Carl Van, **Retro. Supp. I:** 199
Vedanta for Modern Man (Isherwood, ed.), **Supp. XIV:** 164
Vedanta for the Western World (Isherwood, ed.), **Supp. XIV:** 164
Vedas, **IV:** 183
Vega, Janine Pommy, **Supp. XIV:** 148
Vega, Lope de, **Retro. Supp. I:** 285; **Supp. III Part 1:** 341, 347
Vegetable, The (Fitzgerald), **Retro. Supp. I:** 105; **Supp. IX:** 57
Vegetable, The, or From President to Postman (Fitzgerald), **II:** 91
"Vegetable Love" (Apple), **Supp. XVII:** 4
Veinberg, Jon, **Supp. V:** 180; **Supp. XIII:** 313; **Supp. XV:** 76-77, 86
Vein of Iron (Glasgow), **II:** 175, 186, 188-189, 191, 192, 194
Vein of Riches, A (Knowles), **Supp. XII:** 249
Velie, Alan R., **Supp. IV Part 2:** 486
Velocities: New and Selected Poems, 1966-1992 (Dobyns), **Supp. XIII:** 86-87, 87, 88
"Velorio" (Cisneros), **Supp. VII:** 66
"Velvet Shoes" (Wylie), **Supp. I Part 2:** 711, 714
Venant, Elizabeth, **Supp. XI:** 343
Vencloca, Thomas, **Supp. VIII:** 29
Vendler, Helen H., **Retro. Supp. I:** 297; **Retro. Supp. II:** 184, 191; **Supp. I Part 1:** 77, 78, 92, 95; **Supp. I Part 2:** 565; **Supp. IV Part 1:** 245, 247, 249, 254, 257; **Supp. IV Part 2:** 448; **Supp. V:** 78, 82, 189, 343; **Supp. XII:** 187, 189; **Supp. XV:** 20, 184
"Venetian Blind, The" (Jarrell), **II:** 382-383
Venetian Glass Nephew, The (Wylie), **Supp. I Part 2:** 707, 709, 714, 717-719, 721, 724
Venetian Life (Howells), **II:** 274, 277, 279
Venetian Vespers, The (Hecht), **Supp. X:** 57, **65-69**
"Venetian Vespers, The" (Hecht), **Supp. X:** 65, **66-67**
Venice Observed (McCarthy), **II:** 562
Ventadorn, Bernard de, **Supp. IV Part 1:** 146
"Ventriloquists' Conversations" (Gentry), **Supp. IV Part 1:** 236
"Venus, Cupid, Folly and Time" (Taylor), **Supp. V:** 322-323
Venus and Adonis (film), **Supp. IV Part 1:** 82

Venus and Don Juan (C. Frost), **Supp. XV:** 93, **102-103**, 104, 107
"Venus and Don Juan" (C. Frost), **Supp. XV:** 103
Venus Blue (Sobin), **Supp. XVI:** 293-294, 294
Venus in Sparta (Auchincloss), **Supp. IV Part 1:** 25
"Venus's-flytraps" (Komunyakaa), **Supp. XIII:** 126, 127
"Veracruz" (Hayden), **Supp. II Part 1:** 371, 373
Verga, Giovanni, **II:** 271, 275
Verghese, Abraham, **Supp. X:** 160
Verhaeren, Emile, **I:** 476; **II:** 528, 529
Verlaine, Paul, **II:** 529, 543; **III:** 466; **IV:** 79, 80, 86, 286; **Retro. Supp. I:** 56, 62; **Retro. Supp. II:** 326
"Vermeer" (Nemerov), **III:** 275, 278, 280
Vermeer, Jan, **Retro. Supp. I:** 335
"Vermont" (Carruth), **Supp. XVI:** 54
Vermont Notebook, The (Ashbery), **Supp. III Part 1:** 1
"Vernal Ague, The" (Freneau), **Supp. II Part 1:** 258
Verne, Jules, **I:** 480; **Retro. Supp. I:** 270; **Supp. XI:** 63
Vernon, John, **Supp. X:** 15
Verplanck, Gulian C., **Supp. I Part 1:** 155, 156, 157, 158
Verrazano, Giovanni da, **Supp. I Part 2:** 496, 497
Verse (Zawacki), **Supp. VIII:** 272
"Verse for Urania" (Merrill), **Supp. III Part 1:** 329, 330
Verses (Wharton), **Retro. Supp. I:** 362
Verses, Printed for Her Friends (Jewett), **II:** 406
"Verses for Children" (Lowell), **II:** 516
"Verses Made at Sea in a Heavy Gale" (Freneau), **Supp. II Part 1:** 262
"Verses on the Death of T. S. Eliot" (Brodsky), **Supp. VIII:** 19
"Version of a Fragment of Simonides" (Bryant), **Supp. I Part 1:** 153, 155
Verulam, Baron. *See* Bacon, Francis
Very, Jones, **III:** 507
"Very Hot Sun in Bermuda, The" (Jackson), **Supp. IX:** 126
Very Old Bones (W. Kennedy), **Supp. VII:** 133, 148, 150-153
"Very Proper Gander, The" (Thurber), **Supp. I Part 2:** 610
"Very Short Story, A" (Hemingway), **II:** 252; **Retro. Supp. I:** 173
"Vesalius in Zante" (Wharton), **Retro. Supp. I:** 372
Vesey, Denmark, **Supp. I Part 2:** 592
Vesey, Desmond, **Supp. XIV:** 162

"Vespers" (Auden), **Supp. II Part 1:** 23
"Vespers" (Glück), **Supp. V:** 88
Vestal Lady on Brattle, The (Corso), **Supp. XII:** 119, **120-121**, 134
Vested Interests and the Common Man, The (Veblen), **Supp. I Part 2:** 642
"Vesuvius at Home" (Rich), **Retro. Supp. I:** 42
"Veteran, The" (Crane), **I:** 413
"Veterans' Cemetery" (Gioia), **Supp. XV:** 117
"Veteran Sirens" (Robinson), **III:** 512, 524
"Veterinarian" (X. J. Kennedy), **Supp. XV:** 168
"Vetiver" (Ashbery), **Supp. III Part 1:** 26
"Via Dieppe-Newhaven" (H. Miller), **III:** 183
"Via Negativa" (Salter), **Supp. IX:** 257
Vicar of Wakefield, The (Goldsmith), **I:** 216
Vicious Circle, The (film, Wilder), **Supp. XVII:** 62
"Vicissitudes of the Avant-Garde, The" (Gass), **Supp. VI:** 91
Victim, The (Bellow), **I:** 144, 145, 147, 149, 150, 151, 152, 153, 155, 156, 158, 159, 164; **IV:** 19; **Retro. Supp. II:** 21, 22, 34
"Victor" (Mumford), **Supp. II Part 2:** 476
Victoria (Rowson), **Supp. XV:** 231
Victorian in the Modern World, A (Hapgood), **Supp. XVII:** 95, 97, 100, 101, 103, 105, 106
"Victories" (Untermeyer), **Supp. XV:** 300
"Victory at Sea" (television series), **Supp. I Part 2:** 490
"Victory comes late" (Dickinson), **Retro. Supp. I:** 45
"Victory of the Moon, The" (Crane), **I:** 420
Vidal, Gore, **II:** 587; **IV:** 383; **Supp. IV Part 1:** 22, 35, 92, 95, 198; **Supp. IV Part 2: 677-696; Supp. IX:** 96; **Supp. X:** 186, 195; **Supp. XIV:**156, 170, 338
Viebahn, Fred, **Supp. IV Part 1:** 248
Viera, Joseph M., **Supp. XI:** 178, 186
Viereck, Peter, **Supp. I Part 2:** 403
Viertel, Berthold, **Supp. XIV:**165
Viertel, Salka, **Supp. XVI:**192
Viet Journal (Jones), **Supp. XI: 230-231**
Vietnam (McCarthy), **II:** 578-579
"Vietnam in Me, The" (O'Brien), **Supp. V:** 241, 252

Vie unanime, La (Romains), **I:** 227
"View, The" (Roussel), **Supp. III Part 1:** 15, 16, 21
View from 80, The (Cowley), **Supp. II Part 1:** 141, 144, 153
"View from an Institution" (F. Wright), **Supp. XVII:** 244
View from the Bridge, A (A. Miller), **III:** 147, 148, 156, 158, 159-160
View of My Own, A: Essays in Literature and Society (Hardwick), **Supp. III Part 1:** 194, 200
"View of the Capital from the Library of Congress" (Bishop), **Retro. Supp. II:** 45
View of the Soil and Climate of the United States, A (Brown, trans.), **Supp. I Part 1:** 146
"View of the Woods, A" (O'Connor), **III:** 349, 351, 358; **Retro. Supp. II:** 237
"Views of the Mysterious Hill: The Appearance of Parnassus in American Poetry" (Strand), **Supp. IV Part 2:** 631
"Vigil" (Karr), **Supp. XI:** 241
"Vigil, The" (Dante), **III:** 542
Vigny, Alfred Victor de, **II:** 543
Vildrac, Charles, **Supp. XV:** 50
Vile Bodies (Waugh), **Supp. I Part 2:** 607
"Village Blacksmith, The" (Longfellow), **Retro. Supp. II:** 167, 168; **Supp. I Part 2:** 409
Village Hymns, a Supplement to Dr. Watts's Psalms and Hymns (Nettleton), **I:** 458
"Village Improvement Parade, The" (Lindsay), **Supp. I Part 2:** 388, 389
Village Magazine, The (Lindsay), **Supp. I Part 2:** 379-380, 382
Village Virus, The (Lewis), **II:** 440
"Villanelle at Sundown" (Justice), **Supp. VII:** 119, 122-123
"Villanelle of Change" (Robinson), **III:** 524
Villard, Oswald, **Supp. I Part 1:** 332
"Villa Selene" (Simpson), **Supp. IX:** 279
Villon, François, **II:** 544; **III:** 9, 174, 592; **Retro. Supp. I:** 286; **Supp. I Part 1:** 261; **Supp. III Part 1:** 235, 243, 249, 253; **Supp. III Part 2:** 560; **Supp. IX:** 116
"Villonaud for This Yule" (Pound), **Retro. Supp. I:** 286
Vindication of the Rights of Woman (Wollstonecraft), **Supp. I Part 1:** 126; **Supp. XI:** 203

Vines, Lois Davis, **Retro. Supp. II:** 261
"Vintage Thunderbird, A" (Beattie), **Supp. V:** 27
Vinz, Mark, **Supp. X:** 117
Violence (Bausch), **Supp. VII:** 48-49, 54
Violent Bear It Away, The (O'Connor), **III:** 339, 345-348, 350, 351, 354, 355, 356, 357; **Retro. Supp. II:** 233, **234-236**
"Violent Vet, The" (O'Brien), **Supp. V:** 238
Violin (Rice), **Supp. VII:** 302
Viorst, Judith, **Supp. X:** 153
Viper Run (Karr), **Supp. XI: 248-251**
Virgil, **I:** 312, 322, 587; **II:** 133, 542; **IV:** 137, 359; **Retro. Supp. I:** 135; **Supp. I Part 1:** 153; **Supp. I Part 2:** 494; **Supp. IV Part 2:** 631
"Virgin and the Dynamo" (Adams), **III:** 396
"Virgin Carrying a Lantern, The" (Stevens), **IV:** 80
Virginia (Glasgow), **II:** 175, 178, 181-182, 193, 194
"Virginia" (Lindsay), **Supp. I Part 2:** 398
"Virginia Britannia" (Moore), **III:** 198, 208-209
"Virginians Are Coming Again, The" (Lindsay), **Supp. I Part 2:** 399
"Virgin Violeta" (Porter), **III:** 454
"Virility" (Ozick), **Supp. V:** 262, 265
Virtual Light (W. Gibson), **Supp. XVI:**124, **129**, 130
Virtue of Selfishness, The: A New Concept of Egoism (Rand), **Supp. IV Part 2:** 527, 530-532
"Virtuoso" (Francis), **Supp. IX:** 82
Virtuous Woman, A (Gibbons), **Supp. X: 44-45**, 46, 50
Visconti, Luchino, **Supp. V:** 51
Visible Saints: The History of a Puritan Idea (Morgan), **IV:** 149
"Vision, A" (Olds), **Supp. X:** 214
"Vision, A" (Winters), **Supp. II Part 2:** 785, 795
"Vision and Prayer" (D. Thomas), **I:** 432
"Visionary, The" (Poe), **III:** 411
Visionary Farms, The (Eberhart), **I:** 537-539
Visioning, The (Glaspell), **Supp. III Part 1:** 175-177, 180, 187, 188
Vision in Spring (Faulkner), **Retro. Supp. I:** 79
Vision of Columbus (Barlow), **Supp. I Part 1:** 124; **Supp. II Part 1:** 67, 68, 70-75, 77, 79

Vision of Sir Launfal, The (Lowell), **Supp. I Part 1:** 311; **Supp. I Part 2:** 406, 409, 410
"Vision of the World, A" (Cheever), **Supp. I Part 1:** 182, 192
Visions of Cody (Kerouac), **Supp. III Part 1:** 225-227
Visions of Gerard (Kerouac), **Supp. III Part 1:** 219-222, 225, 227, 229
"Visions of the Daughters of Albion" (Blake), **III:** 540
"Visit" (Ammons), **Supp. VII:** 28-29
"Visit, The" (Kenyon), **Supp. VII:** 169
"Visitant, The" (Dunn), **Supp. XI:** 147
"Visitation, The/La Visitación" (Mora), **Supp. XIII:** 217, 224, 228
"Visit Home, A" (Stafford), **Supp. XI:** 318
Visit in 2001, The (musical, McNally), **Supp. XIII:** 207
"Visiting My Own House in Iowa City" (Stern), **Supp. IX:** 300
"Visit of Charity, A" (Welty), **IV:** 262
"Visitors" (Salinas), **Supp. XIII:** 318
"Visitors, The/Los Visitantes" (Kingsolver), **Supp. VII:** 208
"Visits to St. Elizabeths" (Bishop), **Retro. Supp. II:** 47
"Visit to a Small Planet" (teleplay) (Vidal), **Supp. IV Part 2:** 682
Visit to a Small Planet: A Comedy Akin to Vaudeville (Vidal), **Supp. IV Part 2:** 682-683
"Visit to Avoyelles, A" (Chopin), **Supp. I Part 1:** 213
"Vissi d'Arte" (Moore), **Supp. X:** 173-174
Vistas of History (Morison), **Supp. I Part 2:** 492
"Vita" (Stafford), **Supp. XI:** 330
Vital, David, **Supp. XVI:** 160
Vital Provisions (Price), **Supp. VI:** 262-263
"Vitamins" (Carver), **Supp. III Part 1:** 138
Vita Nova (Glück), **Supp. V:** 90-92
Vitruvius, **Supp. XVI:** 292
Vittorio, the Vampire (Rice), **Supp. VII:** 295-296
Viudas (Dorfman), **Supp. IX:** 138
"Viva Vargas!" (Allen), **Supp. XV:** 15
Viviparous Quadrupeds of North America, The (Audubon and Bachman), **Supp. XVI:** 10
Vizenor, Gerald, **Supp. IV Part 1:** 260, 262, 329, 404; **Supp. IV Part 2:** 502
Vladimir Nabokov: The American Years (Nabokov), **Retro. Supp. I:** 275
Vlag, Piet, **Supp. XV:** 295

"Vlemk, the Box Painter" (Gardner), **Supp. VI:** 73
"V-Letter" (Shapiro), **Supp. II Part 2:** 707
V-Letter and Other Poems (Shapiro), **Supp. II Part 2:** 702, 706
"Vocabulary of Dearness" (Nye), **Supp. XIII:** 284
"Vocation" (Stafford), **Supp. XI:** 312, 321
Vocation and a Voice, A (Chopin), **Retro. Supp. II:** 67, 72
"Vocation and a Voice, A" (Chopin), **Retro. Supp. II:** 72; **Supp. I Part 1:** 200, 220, 224, 225
Vogel, David, **Supp. XV:** 88
Vogel, Speed, **Supp. IV Part 1:** 390
"Voice" (F. Wright), **Supp. XVII:** 245
"Voice, The" (Dunn), **Supp. XI:** 152
Voiced Connections of James Dickey, The (Dickey), **Supp. IV Part 1:** 177
"Voice from the Woods, A" (Humphrey), **Supp. IX:** 101
"Voice from Under the Table, A" (Wilbur), **Supp. III Part 2:** 553, 554
Voice of Reason, The: Essays in Objectivist Thought (Rand), **Supp. IV Part 2:** 527, 528, 532
"Voice of Rock, The" (Ginsberg), **Supp. II Part 1:** 313
Voice of the Butterfly, The (Nichols), **Supp. XIII:** 270
Voice of the City, The (O. Henry), **Supp. II Part 1:** 410
"Voice of the Mountain, The" (Crane), **I:** 420
Voice of the Negro (Barber), **Supp. II Part 1:** 168
Voice of the People, The (Glasgow), **II:** 175, 176
Voice of the Turtle: American Indian Literature 1900-1970 (Gunn Allen, ed.), **Supp. IV Part 1:** 332, 334
Voices from the Moon (Dubus), **Supp. VII:** 88-89
"Voices from the Other World" (Merrill), **Supp. III Part 1:** 331
Voices in the House (Sedges), **Supp. II Part 1:** 125
Voices of the Night (Longfellow), **II:** 489, 493; **Retro. Supp. II:** 154, 157, 168
"Voices of Village Square, The" (Wolfe), **Supp. III Part 2:** 571-572
Voice That Is Great within Us, The (Caruth, ed.), **Supp. XIII:** 112
Voigt, Ellen Bryan, **Supp. XIII:** 76
Volkening, Henry, **Retro. Supp. II:** 117; **Supp. XV:** 142

Vollmann, William T., **Supp. XIV:** 96; **Supp. XVII: 225-237**
Volney, Constantin François de Chasseboeuf, **Supp. I Part 1:** 146
Voltaire, **I:** 194; **II:** 86, 103, 449; **III:** 420; **IV:** 18; **Retro. Supp. II:** 94; **Supp. I Part 1:** 288-289; **Supp. I Part 2:** 669, 717; **Supp. XV:** 258
Voltaire! Voltaire! (Endore), **Supp. XVII:** 65
Volunteers, The (Rowson and Reinagle), **Supp. XV:** 238
Vonnegut, Kurt, **Retro. Supp. I:** 170; **Supp. II Part 2:** 557, 689, **753-784;** **Supp. IV Part 1:** 227, 392; **Supp. V:** 40, 42, 237, 244, 296; **Supp. X:** 260; **Supp. XI:** 104; **Supp. XII:** 139, 141
Vonnegut, Kurt, Jr., **Supp. XVII:** 41, 135
"Voracities and Verities" (Moore), **III:** 214
Vore, Nellie, **I:** 199
Vorlicky, Robert, **Supp. IX:** 132, 135, 136, 141, 144, 147
Vorse, Mary Heaton, **Supp. XVII:** 99
"Vorticism" (Pound), **Retro. Supp. I:** 288
Voss, Richard, **I:** 199-200
"Vow, The" (Hecht), **Supp. X:** 64
"Vowels 2" (Baraka), **Supp. II Part 1:** 51
Vow of Conversation, A: Journal, 1964-1965 (Merton), **Supp. VIII:** 206
Vox (Baker), **Supp. XIII: 47-49,** 50, 52, 53
"Voyage" (MacLeish), **III:** 15
"Voyage, The" (Irving), **II:** 304
Voyage, The, and Other Versions of Poems by Baudelaire (Lowell), **Retro. Supp. II:** 187
Voyage dans la Haute Pennsylvanie et dans l'état de New-York (Crèvecoeur), **Supp. I Part 1:** 250-251
Voyage of the Beagle (Darwin), **Supp. IX:** 211
Voyage Out, The (Woolf), **Supp. XV:** 65
"Voyager, The" (Everwine), **Supp. XV:** 75
"Voyages" (H. Crane), **I:** 393-395; **Retro. Supp. II:** 78, 80, 81
"Voyages" (Levine), **Supp. V:** 190
Voyages and Discoveries of the Companions of Columbus (Irving), **II:** 310
Voyage to Pagany, A (W. C. Williams), **IV:** 404; **Retro. Supp. I:** 418-419, **420-421,** 423

Voyaging Portraits (Sobin), **Supp. XVI:** 282, 287
"Voyeur, The" (Gioia), **Supp. XV:** 125
Voznesensky, Andrei, **II:** 553; **Supp. III Part 1:** 268; **Supp. III Part 2:** 560
Vrbovska, Anca, **Supp. IV Part 2:** 639
"Vulgarity in Literature" (Huxley), **III:** 429-430
"Vultures" (Oliver), **Supp. VII:** 235
W
W (Viva) (Cummings), **I:** 429, 433, 434, 436, 443, 444, 447
"W. D. Sees Himself Animated" (Snodgrass), **Supp. VI:** 327
"W. D. Sits in Kafka's Chair and Is Interrogated Concerning the Assumed Death of Cock Robin" (Snodgrass), **Supp. VI:** 319
"W. D. Tries to Warn Cock Robin" (Snodgrass), **Supp. VI:** 319
Wabash (R. O. Butler), **Supp. XII:** 61, **68-69**
Wade, Grace, **I:** 216
"Wading at Wellfleet" (Bishop), **Retro. Supp. II:** 42, 43; **Supp. I Part 1:** 80, 85, 86
Wadsworth, Charles, **I:** 454, 470; **Retro. Supp. I:** 32, 33
Wagenknecht, Edward, **II:** 508; **Supp. I Part 2:** 408, 584; **Supp. IV Part 2:** 681
"Wages of Poetry, The" (Wright), **Supp. XV:** 337
Wagner, Jean, **Supp. I Part 1:** 341, 346; **Supp. IV Part 1:** 165, 167, 171
Wagner, Richard, **I:** 284, 395; **II:** 425; **III:** 396, 507; **Supp. IV Part 1:** 392
Wagner, Robert, **Supp. IX:** 250
"Wagnerians, The" (Auchincloss), **Supp. IV Part 1:** 23
"Wagner Matinee, A" (Cather), **I:** 315-316; **Retro. Supp. I:** 5, 8
Wagoner, David, **Supp. IX:** 323-340; **Supp. XII:** 178
Waid, Candace, **Retro. Supp. I:** 360, 372, 373
Waif, The (Longfellow, ed.), **Retro. Supp. II:** 155
"Waif of the Plains, A" (Harte), **Supp. II Part 1:** 354
Wain, John, **Supp. XIV:** 166
"Wait" (Kinnell), **Supp. III Part 1:** 250
"Waiting" (Dubus), **Supp. VII:** 87
"Waiting" (W. C. Williams), **Retro. Supp. I:** 418
"Waiting, The" (L.-Y. Lee), **Supp. XV:** 218

"Waiting, The" (Olds), **Supp. X:** 209
"Waiting between the Trees" (Tan), **Supp. X:** 290
"Waiting by the Gate" (Bryant), **Supp. I Part 1:** 171
Waiting for God (Weil), **I:** 298
Waiting for Godot (Beckett), **I:** 78, 91, 298; **Supp. IV Part 1:** 368-369
Waiting for Lefty (Odets), **Supp. I Part 1:** 277; **Supp. II Part 2:** 529, 530-533, 540; **Supp. V:** 109
Waiting for the End of the World (Bell), **Supp. X:** **4-5**, 11
Waiting for the Verdict (Davis), **Supp. XVI:** 85, 89, 90
"Waiting in a Rain Forest" (Wagoner), **Supp. IX:** 329
Waiting Room, The (Kees), **Supp. XV:** 133, 148
Waiting to Exhale (McMillan), **Supp. XIII:** 184, 185, **189-190**, 191
"Waiting to Freeze" (Banks), **Supp. V:** 5, 6
Waiting to Freeze: Poems (Banks), **Supp. V:** 6, 8
Waits, Tom, **Supp. VIII:** 12
Wait until Spring, Bandini (Fante), **Supp. XI:** 160, 161, 164, 165, **166-167**
Wait until Spring, Bandini (film), **Supp. XI:** 173
"Wake, The" (Dove), **Supp. IV Part 1:** 250
"Wakefield" (Hawthorne), **Retro. Supp. I:** 154, 159
Wakefield, Dan, **Supp. VIII:** 43; **Supp. XVI:** 220
Wakefield, Richard, **Supp. IX:** 323
"Wake Island" (Rukeyser), **Supp. VI:** 273
Wakeman, Frederic, **Supp. IX:** 247
Wake Up and Live! (Brande), **Supp. I Part 2:** 608
"Waking" (C. Frost), **Supp. XV:** 93
Waking, The (Roethke), **III:** 541
"Waking Early Sunday Morning" (Lowell), **II:** 552; **Retro. Supp. II:** 190
"Waking in the Blue" (Lowell), **II:** 547; **Retro. Supp. II:** 180
"Waking in the Dark" (Rich), **Supp. I Part 2:** 559
"Waking Up the Rake" (Hogan), **Supp. IV Part 1:** 415-416, 416
Wakoski, Diane, **Supp. V:** 79; **Supp. XII:** 184; **Supp. XV:** 252; **Supp. XVII:** 112
Walcott, Charles C., **II:** 49
Walcott, Derek, **Supp. VIII:** 28; **Supp. X:** 122, 131; **Supp. XV:** 256

Walcott, Jersey Joe, **Supp. V:** 182
Wald, Alan, **Supp. XV:** 202
Wald, Lillian, **Supp. I Part 1:** 12
Walden (Thoreau), **Supp. XIV:** 177, 227; **Supp. XV:** 275
Walden, Daniel, **Supp. IV Part 2:** 584, 591; **Supp. V:** 272
Walden; or, Life in the Woods (Thoreau), **I:** 219, 305; **II:** 8, 142, 159, 312-313, 458; **IV:** 168, 169, 170, 176, 177-178, 179-182, 183, 187; **Retro. Supp. I:** 62; **Supp. I Part 2:** 579, 655, 664, 672; **Supp. VIII:** 296; **Supp. X:** 27, 101; **Supp. XIII:** 152
Waldman, Anne, **Supp. XIV:** 150
Waldmeir, Joseph, **III:** 45
Waldmeir, Joseph J., **Supp. I Part 2:** 476
Waldo (Theroux), **Supp. VIII:** 313, 314, **314-315**
Waldron, Jeremy, **Supp. XVII:** 235
Waldrop, Keith, **Supp. XV:** 153, 165
Waley, Arthur, **II:** 526; **III:** 466; **Supp. V:** 340
"Walk, A" (Snyder), **Supp. VIII:** 297
"Walk at Sunset, A" (Bryant), **Supp. I Part 1:** 155
"Walk before Mass, A" (Agee), **I:** 28-29
Walker, Alice, **Retro. Supp. I:** 215; **Supp. I Part 2:** 550; **Supp. III Part 2:** 488, **517-540**; **Supp. IV Part 1:** 14; **Supp. VIII:** 141, 214; **Supp. IX:** 306, 311; **Supp. X:** 85, 228, 252, 325, 330; **Supp. XIII:** 179, 185, 291, 295; **Supp. XVI:** 39
Walker, Cheryl, **Supp. XI:** 145
Walker, David, **Supp. V:** 189; **Supp. XVII:** 246
Walker, Franklin D., **III:** 321
Walker, Gue, **Supp. XII:** 207
Walker, Marianne, **Supp. VIII:** 139
Walker, Obadiah, **II:** 113
Walker, Scott, **Supp. XV:** 92
Walker in the City, A (Kazin), **Supp. VIII:** **93-95**, 99
Walk Hard (Blum and Hill), **Supp. XV:** 194
Walk Hard-Talk Loud (Zinberg), **Supp. XV:** 194, 202
"Walking" (Hogan), **Supp. IV Part 1:** 416
"Walking" (Thoreau), **Supp. IV Part 1:** 416; **Supp. IX:** 178
"Walking Along in Winter" (Kenyon), **Supp. VII:** 167
"Walking around the Block with a Three-Year-Old" (Wagoner), **Supp. IX:** 331-332

"Walking Backwards into the Future" (R. Williams), **Supp. IX:** 146
Walking Down the Stairs: Selections from Interviews (Kinnell), **Supp. III Part 1:** 235, 249
"Walking Home" (Schnackenberg). See "Laughing with One Eye" (Schnackenberg)
"Walking Home at Night" (Ginsberg), **Supp. II Part 1:** 313
Walking Light (Dunn), **Supp. XI:** 140, 141, 153
"Walking Man of Rodin, The" (Sandburg), **III:** 583
"Walking Sticks and Paperweights and Water Marks" (Moore), **III:** 215
Walking Tall (Dunn), **Supp. XI:** 140
Walking the Black Cat (Simic), **Supp. VIII:** 280, **282-284**
Walking to Martha's Vineyard (F. Wright), **Supp. XVII:** 240, 241, 245, 246
Walking to Sleep (Wilbur), **Supp. III Part 2:** 557-560
"Walking to Sleep" (Wilbur), **Supp. III Part 2:** 544, 557, 559, 561, 562
Walkin' the Dog (Mosley), **Supp. XIII:** 242
"Walk in the Moonlight, A" (Anderson), **I:** 114
Walk on the Wild Side, A (Algren), **Supp. V:** 4; **Supp. IX:** 3, **12-13**, 14
"Walks in Rome" (Merrill), **Supp. III Part 1:** 337
Walk with Tom Jefferson, A (Levine), **Supp. V:** 179, 187, 190-191
"Wall, The" (Brooks), **Supp. III Part 1:** 70, 71, 84
Wall, The (Hersey), **IV:** 4
"Wall, The" (Roethke), **III:** 544
"Wall, The" (Sexton), **Supp. II Part 2:** 696
Wallace, David Foster, **Retro. Supp. II:** 279; **Supp. X: 301-318**; **Supp. XVII:** 226
Wallace, Henry, **I:** 489; **III:** 111, 475; **Supp. I Part 1:** 286; **Supp. I Part 2:** 645
Wallace, Mike, **Supp. IV Part 1:** 364; **Supp. IV Part 2:** 526
Wallace Stevens (Kermode), **Retro. Supp. I:** 301
Wallace Stevens: The Poems of our Climate (Bloom), **Retro. Supp. I:** 299
Wallace Stevens: Words Chosen out of Desire (Stevens), **Retro. Supp. I:** 297
Wallach, Eli, **III:** 161

Wallant, Edward Lewis, **Supp. XVI:** 220
Wallas, Graham, **Supp. I Part 2:** 643
"Walled City" (Oates), **Supp. II Part 2:** 524
Wallenstein, Anna. See Weinstein, Mrs. Max (Anna Wallenstein)
Waller, Edmund, **III:** 463
Waller, Fats, **IV:** 263
Walling, William English, **Supp. I Part 2:** 645; **Supp. XV:** 295
Walls Do Not Fall, The (Doolittle), **Supp. I Part 1:** 271, 272
"Wall Songs" (Hogan), **Supp. IV Part 1:** 413
Wall Writing (Auster), **Supp. XII:** 23-24
Walpole, Horace, **I:** 203; **Supp. I Part 2:** 410, 714
Walpole, Hugh, **Retro. Supp. I:** 231
Walpole, Robert, **IV:** 145
Walsh, David M., **Supp. XV:** 5
Walsh, Ed, **II:** 424
Walsh, George, **Supp. IV Part 2:** 528
Walsh, Raoul, **Supp. XIII:** 174
Walsh, Richard J., **Supp. II Part 1:** 119, 130
Walsh, William, **Supp. IV Part 1:** 242, 243, 246, 248, 252, 254, 257
"Walt and Will" (Apple), **Supp. XVII:** 6
Walter, Eugene, **Supp. XVI:** 230
Walter, Joyce, **Supp. XV:** 121
Walter Benjamin at the Dairy Queen: Reflections at Sixty and Beyond (McMurtry), **Supp. V:** 232
Walters, Barbara, **Supp. XIV:** 125
Walters, Marguerite. See Smith, Mrs. Lamar (Marguerite Walters)
"Walter T. Carriman" (O'Hara), **III:** 368
Walton, Izaak, **Supp. I Part 2:** 422
"Walt Whitman" (Masters), **Supp. I Part 2:** 458
"Walt Whitman at Bear Mountain" (Simpson), **Supp. IX:** 265
Walt Whitman Bathing (Wagoner), **Supp. IX: 331-332**
Walt Whitman Handbook (Allen), **IV:** 352
Walt Whitman Reconsidered (Chase), **IV:** 352
"Waltz, The" (Parker), **Supp. IX:** 204
"Waltzer in the House, The" (Kunitz), **Supp. III Part 1:** 258
Walzer, Kevin, **Supp. XII:** 202; **Supp. XV:** 118
Wambaugh, Joseph, **Supp. X:** 5
Wampeters, Foma, & Granfalloons (Vonnegut), **Supp. II Part 2:** 758,
759-760, 776, 779
Wand, David Hsin-fu, **Supp. X:** 292
"Wanderer, The" (W. C. Williams), **Retro. Supp. I:** 414, 421
"Wanderers, The" (Welty), **IV:** 273-274
"Wandering Jew, The" (Robinson), **III:** 505, 516-517
Wanderings of Oisin (Yeats), **Supp. I Part 1:** 79
Wang, Dorothy, **Supp. X:** 289
Wang Wei, **Supp. XV:** 47
Waniek, Marilyn Nelson, **Supp. IV Part 1:** 244
"Wan Lee, the Pagan" (Harte), **Supp. II Part 1:** 351
"Want, The" (Olds), **Supp. X:** 210
Want Bone, The (Pinsky), **Supp. VI:** 236-237, 244-245, 247
"Wanted: An Ontological Critic" (Ransom), **III:** 498
"Wanting to Die" (Sexton), **Supp. II Part 2:** 684, 686; **Supp. XIV:** 132
"Wants" (Paley), **Supp. VI:** 219
Waples, Dorothy, **I:** 348
Wapshot Chronicle, The (Cheever), **Supp. I Part 1:** 174, 177-180, 181, 196
Wapshot Scandal, The (Cheever), **Supp. I Part 1:** 180-184, 187, 191, 196
"War" (Kingston), **Supp. V:** 169
"War" (Simic), **Supp. VIII:** 282
"War, Response, and Contradiction" (Burke), **I:** 283
"War and Peace" (Sanders), **Supp. XVI:** 277
War and Peace (Tolstoy), **I:** 6, 7; **II:** 191, 205, 291; **IV:** 446; **Supp. V:** 277; **Supp. XI:** 68; **Supp. XIV:** 97
War and War (F. Barthelme), **Supp. XI:** 25
"War Between Men and Women, The" (Thurber), **Supp. I Part 2:** 615
War Bulletins (Lindsay), **Supp. I Part 2:** 378-379
Ward, Aileen, **II:** 531
Ward, Artemus (pseudonym). See Browne, Charles Farrar
Ward, Douglas Turner, **Supp. IV Part 1:** 362
Ward, Henry, **Supp. I Part 2:** 588
Ward, Leo R., **Supp. VIII:** 124
Ward, Lester F., **Supp. I Part 2:** 640; **Supp. XI:** 202, 203
Ward, Lynn, **I:** 31
Ward, Mrs. Humphry, **II:** 338
Ward, Nathaniel, **Supp. I Part 1:** 99, 102, 111, 116
Ward, Theodora, **I:** 470; **Retro. Supp. I:** 28

Ward, William Hayes, **Supp. I Part 1:** 371
"War Debt, A" (Jewett), **Retro. Supp. II:** 138, 141
"War Diary" (N. Boyce), **Supp. XVII:** 104
"War Diary, A" (Bourne), **I:** 229
War Dispatches of Stephen Crane, The (Crane), **I:** 422
"Ward Line, The" (Morris), **III:** 220
Warfel, Harry R., **Supp. I Part 1:** 366
War Games (Morris), **III:** 238
War in Heaven, The (Shepard and Chaikin), **Supp. III Part 2:** 433
War Is Kind (Crane), **I:** 409; **III:** 585
"War Is Kind" (Crane), **I:** 419
Warlock (Harrison), **Supp. VIII:** 45, **46**
Warm as Wool (Sanders), **Supp. XVI:** 269
Warner, Charles Dudley, **II:** 405; **IV:** 198
Warner, Jack, **Supp. XII:** 160-161
Warner, John R., **III:** 193
Warner, Oliver, **I:** 548
Warner, Susan, **Retro. Supp. I:** 246; **Supp. XV:** 275
Warner, Sylvia Townsend, **Supp. VIII:** 151, 155, 164, 171
Warner, W. Lloyd, **III:** 60
"Warning" (Hughes), **Supp. I Part 1:** 343
"Warning" (Pound), **III:** 474
"Warning, The" (Creeley), **Supp. IV Part 1:** 150
"Warning, The" (Longfellow), **II:** 498
Warning Hill (Marquand), **III:** 55-56, 60, 68
"War of Eyes, A" (Coleman), **Supp. XI:** 93-94
War of Eyes and Other Stories, A (Coleman), **Supp. XI:** 91-92
War of the Classes (London), **II:** 466
"War of the Wall, The" (Bambara), **Supp. XI:** 15-16
"War of Vaslav Nijinsky, The" (Bidart), **Supp. XV:** 21-22, **27-29**
"War Poems" (Sandburg), **III:** 581
Warren, Austin, **I:** 265, 268, 271; **Supp. I Part 2:** 423
Warren, Earl, **III:** 581
Warren, Gabriel, **IV:** 244
Warren, Mercy Otis, **Supp. XV:** 230
Warren, Mrs. Robert Penn (Eleanor Clark), **IV:** 244
Warren, Robert Penn, **I:** 190, 211, 517; **II:** 57, 217, 228, 253; **III:** 134, 310, 382-383, 454, 482, 485, 490, 496, 497; **IV:** 121, 122, 123, 125, 126, **236-259**, 261, 262, 279, 340-341,

458; **Retro. Supp. I:** 40, 41, 73, 90; **Retro. Supp. II:** 220, 235; **Supp. I Part 1:** 359, 371; **Supp. I Part 2:** 386, 423; **Supp. II Part 1:** 139; **Supp. III Part 2:** 542; **Supp. V:** 261, 316, 318, 319, 333; **Supp. VIII:** 126, 176; **Supp. IX:** 257; **Supp. X:** 1, 25, 26; **Supp. XI:** 315; **Supp. XII:** 254, 255; **Supp. XIV:** 1, 2, 3, 4, 11, 14, 15
Warren, Rosanna, **IV:** 244; **Supp. XV:** 251, 261, 262, 263
Warrington Poems, The (Ríos), **Supp. IV Part 2:** 540
Warrior, Robert Allen, **Supp. IV Part 1:** 329
"Warrior, The" (Gunn Allen), **Supp. IV Part 1:** 326
"Warrior: 5th Grade" (Olds), **Supp. X:** 214
"Warrior Road" (Harjo), **Supp. XII:** 217
Warshavsky, Isaac (pseudonym). *See* Singer, Isaac Bashevis
Warshow, Robert, **Supp. I Part 1:** 51
Wars I Have Seen (Stein), **IV:** 27, 36, 477
Wartime (Fussell), **Supp. V:** 241
"War Widow, The" (Frederic), **II:** 135-136
"Was" (Creeley), **Supp. IV Part 1:** 155
"Was" (Faulkner), **II:** 71
"Wash" (Faulkner), **II:** 72
Wash, Richard, **Supp. XII:** 14
"Washed in the Rain" (Fante), **Supp. XI:** 165
Washington, Booker T., **Supp. I Part 2:** 393; **Supp. II Part 1:** 157, 160, 167, 168, 171, 225; **Supp. XIV:** 198, 199, 201
Washington, D.C. (Vidal), **Supp. IV Part 2:** 677, 684, 686-687, 690
Washington, George, **I:** 453; **II:** 313-314; **Supp. I Part 2:** 399, 485, 508, 509, 511, 513, 517, 518, 520, 599
Washington Crossing the Delaware (Rivers), **Supp. XV:** 186
Washington Post Book World (Lesser), **Supp. IV Part 2:** 453; **Supp. VIII:** 80, 84, 241; **Supp. X:** 282
Washington Square (James), **II:** 327, 328; **Retro. Supp. I:** 215, 220, **222-223**
"Washington Square, 1946" (Ozick), **Supp. V:** 272
Washington Square Ensemble, The (Bell), **Supp. X:** 1, **3-4**
"Was Lowell an Historical Critic?" (Altick), **Supp. I Part 2:** 423

Wasserman, Earl R., **Supp. I Part 2:** 439, 440
Wasserman, Jakob, **Supp. I Part 2:** 669
Wasserstein, Wendy, **Supp. IV Part 1:** 309; **Supp. XV: 319-336**
Wasson, Ben, **Retro. Supp. I:** 79, 83
"Waste Carpet, The" (Matthews), **Supp. IX: 158-159**
Waste Land, The (Eliot), **I:** 107, 266, 298, 395, 396, 482, 570-571, 572, 574-575, 577-578, 580, 581, 584, 585, 586, 587; **III:** 6-8, 12, 196, 277-278, 453, 471, 492, 586; **IV:** 122, 123, 124, 140, 418, 419, 420; **Retro. Supp. I:** 51, 60, **60-62**, 63, 64, 66, 210, 290, 291, 299, 311, 420, 427; **Retro. Supp. II:** 85, 121, 190; **Supp. I Part 1:** 272; **Supp. I Part 2:** 439, 455, 614; **Supp. II Part 1:** 4, 5, 11, 96; **Supp. III Part 1:** 9, 10, 41, 63, 105; **Supp. IV Part 1:** 47, 284; **Supp. V:** 338; **Supp. IX:** 158, 305; **Supp. X:** 125; **Supp. XIII:** 341-342, 344, 346; **Supp. XIV:** 6, 284; **Supp. XV:** 21, 181, 261, 306; **Supp. XVI:** 204; **Supp. XVII:** 140-141, 144, 227
"Waste Land, The": A Facsimile and Transcript of the Original Drafts Including the Annotations of Ezra Pound (Eliot, ed.), **Retro. Supp. I:** 58
Waste Land and Other Poems, The (Eliot), **Supp. XV:** 305
Wat, Alexander, **Supp. XVI:** 155, 161
Watch, The (Bass), **Supp. XVI: 16-17**
"Watch, The, -" (Bass), **Supp. XVI:** 17
Watch and Ward (James), **II:** 323; **Retro. Supp. I:** 218, **219**, 220
"Watcher, The" (R. Bly), **Supp. IV Part 1:** 71
"Watcher by the Dead, A" (Bierce), **I:** 203
Watchfires (Auchincloss), **Supp. IV Part 1:** 23
"Watching Crow, Looking toward the Manzano Mountains" (Harjo), **Supp. XII:** 219
"Watching the Oregon Whale" (A. Finch), **Supp. XVII:** 77
"Watching the Sunset" (Coleman), **Supp. XI:** 92
Watch on the Rhine (Hellman), **Supp. I Part 1:** 276, 278, 279-281, 283-284; **Supp. IV Part 1:** 83
"Water" (Emerson), **II:** 19
"Water" (Komunyakaa), **Supp. XIII:** 132
"Water" (Lowell), **II:** 550

"Waterbird" (Swenson), **Supp. IV Part 2:** 651
"Water Borders" (Dillard), **Supp. VI:** 27
"Water Buffalo" (Komunyakaa), **Supp. XIII:** 122
"Watercolor of Grantchester Meadows" (Plath), **Supp. I Part 2:** 537
"Waterfall, The" (Clampitt), **Supp. IX:** 44
"Water Hose Is on Fire, The" (Simic), **Supp. XV:** 185
Waterhouse, Keith, **Supp. VIII:** 124
"Waterlily Fire" (Rukeyser), **Supp. VI:** 285, 286
Waterlily Fire: Poems 1935-1962 (Rukeyser), **Supp. VI:** 274, 283, 285
Watermark (Brodsky), **Supp. VIII:** 29
Water-Method Man, The (Irving), **Supp. VI:** 163, **167-179**, 180
Water Music (Boyle), **Supp. VIII:** 1, 3-5, 8, 14
"Water Music for the Progress of Love in a Life-Raft Down the Sammamish Slough" (Wagoner), **Supp. IX:** 326
"Water People" (Burke), **Supp. XIV:** 21
"Water Picture" (Swenson), **Supp. IV Part 2:** 641
"Water Rising" (Hogan), **Supp. IV Part 1:** 400
Waters, Ethel, **II:** 587
Waters, Frank, **Supp. X:** 124
Waters, Muddy, **Supp. VIII:** 345
"Watershed" (Kingsolver), **Supp. VII:** 208
"Watershed" (Warren), **IV:** 239
"Watershed, The" (Auden), **Supp. II Part 1:** 5
Waters of Siloe, The (Merton), **Supp. VIII:** 196, 208
Waterston, Sam, **Supp. IX:** 253
Water Street (Merrill), **Supp. III Part 1:** 321-323
"Water Walker" (Wilbur), **Supp. III Part 2:** 548, 560
Water-Witch, The (Cooper), **I:** 342-343
Waterworks, The (Doctorow), **Supp. IV Part 1:** 218, 222, 223, 231-233, 234
"Water Works, The" (Doctorow), **Supp. IV Part 1:** 234
Watkin, E. I., **Retro. Supp. II:** 187
Watkins, Floyd C., **IV:** 452
Watkins, James T., **I:** 193, 194
Watkins, Maureen, **Supp. XVI:** 188
Watkins, Mel, **Supp. X:** 330; **Supp. XIII:** 246
Watrous, Peter, **Supp. VIII:** 79
Watson, Burton, **Supp. XV:** 47

Watson, J. B., **II:** 361
Watson, James Sibley, Jr., **I:** 261
Watson, Richard, **Supp. I Part 2:** 516, 517
Watson, William, **II:** 114
Watt, Ian, **Supp. VIII:** 4
Watteau, Jean Antoine, **III:** 275; **IV:** 79
Watts, Emily Stipes, **Supp. I Part 1:** 115
Waugh, Evelyn, **I:** 480; **III:** 281; **Supp. I Part 2:** 607; **Supp. IV Part 2:** 688; **Supp. XI:** 305, 306
"Wave" (Snyder), **Supp. VIII:** 299
Wave, A (Ashbery), **Supp. III Part 1:** 1, 4, 24-26
"Wave, A" (Ashbery), **Supp. III Part 1:** 9, 19, 24-25
"Wave, The" (MacLeish), **III:** 19
"Wave, The" (Untermeyer), **Supp. XV:** 300
"Waxwings" (Francis), **Supp. IX:** 82
Way, The (Steiner and Witt, eds.), **Supp. IV Part 2:** 505
"Way Down, The" (Kunitz), **Supp. III Part 1:** 263
"Way It Is, The" (Ellison), **Supp. II Part 1:** 245
"Way It Is, The" (Jones), **Supp. XI:** 229
Way It Is, The (Stafford), **Supp. XIII:** 274
"Way It Is, The" (Strand), **Supp. IV Part 2:** 627
"Wayland" (Sanders), **Supp. XVI:** 275
Wayne, John, **Supp. IV Part 1:** 200
Way of Chuang-Tzu, The (Merton), **Supp. VIII:** 208
"Way of Exchange in James Dickey's Poetry, The" (Weatherby), **Supp. IV Part 1:** 175
Way of Life According to Laotzu, The (Bynner), **Supp. XV:** 46, 48
Way Out, A (Frost), **Retro. Supp. I:** 133
Wayside Motor Inn, The (Gurney), **Supp. V:** 96, 105, 109
Ways of the Hour, The (Cooper), **I:** 354
Ways of White Folks, The (Hughes), **Retro. Supp. I:** 203, 204; **Supp. I Part 1:** 329, 330, 332
Way Some People Die, The (Macdonald), **Supp. IV Part 2:** 470, 471, 472, 474
Way Some People Live, The (Cheever), **Supp. I Part 1:** 175
"Way the Cards Fall, The" (Komunyakaa), **Supp. XIII:** 117
"Way Things Are, The" (Turow, unpub.), **Supp. XVII:** 215, 218

Way to Rainy Mountain, The (Momaday), **Supp. IV Part 2:** 485-486, 487-489, 491, 493
Way to Wealth, The (Franklin), **II:** 101-102, 110
Wayward and the Seeking, The: A Collection of Writings by Jean Toomer (Toomer), **Supp. III Part 2:** 478-481, 484, 487
Wayward Bus, The (Steinbeck), **IV:** 51, 64-65
"Way We Live Now, The" (Sontag), **Supp. III Part 2:** 467-468
"Way You'll Never Be, A" (Hemingway), **II:** 249
Weaks, Mary Louise, **Supp. X:** 5
Weales, Gerald, **II:** 602
"Wealth," from *Conduct of Life, The* (Emerson), **II:** 2, 3-4
"Wealth," from *English Traits* (Emerson), **II:** 6
Wealth of Nations, The (A. Smith), **II:** 109
"We Are Looking at You, Agnes" (Caldwell), **I:** 309
We Are Still Married: Stories and Letters (Keillor), **Supp. XVI:** 176, 177
"We Are the Crazy Lady and Other Feisty Feminist Fables" (Ozick), **Supp. V:** 259
Weary Blues, The (Hughes), **Retro. Supp. I:** 195, 197, 198, 199, 200, 203, 205; **Supp. I Part 1:** 325
"Weary Blues, The" (Hughes), **Retro. Supp. I:** 198, 199; **Supp. I Part 1:** 324, 325
"Weary Kingdom" (Irving), **Supp. VI:** 163
Weasels and Wisemen: Ethics and Ethnicity in the Work of David Mamet (Kane), **Supp. XIV:** 250
Weatherby, H. L., **Supp. IV Part 1:** 175
"Weathering Out" (Dove), **Supp. IV Part 1:** 248
"Weather Within, The" (M. F. K. Fisher), **Supp. XVII:** 88, 91
Weaver, Harriet, **III:** 471
Weaver, Mike, **Retro. Supp. I:** 430
Weaver, Will, **Supp. XVI:** 39
"Weaving" (Larcom), **Supp. XIII:** 142, **Supp. XIII:** 144-145, 150, 151
"Web" (Oliver), **Supp. VII:** 236
Web and the Rock, The (Wolfe), **IV:** 451, 455, 457, 459-460, 462, 464, 467, 468
Webb, Beatrice, **Supp. I Part 1:** 5
Webb, Mary, **I:** 226
Webb, Sidney, **Supp. I Part 1:** 5
Webb, W. P., **Supp. V:** 225

Weber, Brom, **I:** 383, 386
Weber, Carl, **Supp. IX:** 133, 138, 141
Weber, Max, **I:** 498; **Supp. I Part 2:** 637, 648
Weber, Sarah, **Supp. I Part 1:** 2
Web of Earth, The (Wolfe), **IV:** 451-452, 456, 458, 464, 465
"Web of Life, The" (Nemerov), **III:** 282
Webster, Brenda, **Supp. XVI:**157, 161
Webster, Daniel, **II:** 5, 9; **Supp. I Part 2:** 659, 687, 689, 690
Webster, John, **I:** 384; **Supp. I Part 2:** 422
Webster, Noah, **Supp. I Part 2:** 660; **Supp. II Part 1:** 77
Wector, Dixon, **II:** 103
"Wedding, The" (Everwine), **Supp. XV:** 83
"Wedding Cake" (Nye), **Supp. XIII:** 283
"Wedding in Brownsville, A" (Singer), **IV:** 15
Wedding in Hell, A (Simic), **Supp. VIII:** 280, **282**
"Wedding of the Rose and Lotus, The" (Lindsay), **Supp. I Part 2:** 387
"Wedding Supper, The" (Rowson), **Supp. XV:** 243
"Wedding Toast, A" (Wilbur), **Supp. III Part 2:** 561
Wedekind, Frank, **III:** 398
Wedge, The (W. C. Williams), **Retro. Supp. I:** 424
"Wednesday at the Waldorf" (Swenson), **Supp. IV Part 2:** 647
"We Don't Live Here Anymore" (Dubus), **Supp. VII:** 78-79, 85
"Weed" (McCarriston), **Supp. XIV:**259, 273
"Weed, The" (Bishop), **Supp. I Part 1:** 80, 88-89
"Weeds, The" (McCarthy), **II:** 566
"Weekend" (Beattie), **Supp. V:** 27
Weekend, The (Cameron), **Supp. XII:** 80, 81, **86-88**
"Weekend at Ellerslie, A" (Wilson), **IV:** 431
Weekend Edition (National Public Radio), **Supp. IX:** 299; **Supp. XVII:** 240, 242
Week on the Concord and Merrimack Rivers, A (Thoreau), **IV:** 168, 169, 177, 182-183; **Supp. I Part 2:** 420; **Supp. XIV:**227
Weeks, Edward, **III:** 64
Weeks, Jerome, **Supp. VIII:** 76
"Weeping Burgher" (Stevens), **IV:** 77
"Weeping Women" (Levertov), **Supp. III Part 1:** 282

We Fished All Night (W. Motley), **Supp. XVII: 155-158,** 159, 160
We Fly Away (Francis), **Supp. IX: 79-80,** 84
We Have Always Lived in the Castle (Jackson), **Supp. IX:** 121, 126, **127-128**
"We Have Our Arts So We Won't Die of Truth" (Bradbury), **Supp. IV Part 1:** 105
Weich, Dave, **Supp. XII:** 321
"Weight" (Wideman), **Supp. X:** 321
"Weights" (C. Baxter), **Supp. XVII:** 16
Weigl, Bruce, **Supp. VIII:** 269, 274; **Supp. XV:** 342
Weil, Dorothy, **Supp. XV:** 231
Weil, Robert, **Supp. IX:** 236
Weil, Simone, **I:** 298; **Supp. XV:** 259
Weiland (C. B. Brown), **Supp. XIII:** 100
Weinauer, Ellen, **Supp. XV:** 270, 284
Weinberger, Eliot, **Supp. IV Part 1:** 66; **Supp. VIII:** 290, 292; **Supp. XVI:**284
Weininger, Otto, **Retro. Supp. I:** 416
Weinreb, Mindy, **Supp. X:** 24
Weinreich, Regina, **Supp. XIV:**22
Weinstein, Hinda, **IV:** 285
Weinstein, Max, **IV:** 285
Weinstein, Mrs. Max (Anna Wallenstein), **IV:** 285, 287
Weinstein, Nathan. *See* West, Nathanael
Weisheit, Rabbi, **IV:** 76
Weismuller, Johnny, **Supp. X:** 264
Weiss, David, **Supp. XVI:**55
Weiss, Peter, **IV:** 117
Weiss, Theodore, **Supp. IV Part 2:** 440; **Supp. IX:** 96
Weist, Dianne, **Supp. X:** 80
Weithas, Art, **Supp. XI:** 231
Welch, James, **Supp. IV Part 1:** 404; **Supp. IV Part 2:** 503, 513, 557, 562
Welch, Lew, **Supp. V:** 170; **Supp. VIII:** 303
"Welcome from War" (Rukeyser), **Supp. VI:** 286
"Welcome Morning" (Sexton), **Supp. II Part 2:** 696
"Welcome the Wrath" (Kunitz), **Supp. III Part 1:** 261
Welcome to Hard Times (Doctorow), **Supp. IV Part 1:** 218, 219-220, 222, 224, 230, 238
Welcome to Hard Times (film), **Supp. IV Part 1:** 236
Welcome to Our City (Wolfe), **IV:** 461
Welcome to the Monkey House (Vonnegut), **Supp. II Part 2:** 758
Welcome to the Moon (Shanley), **Supp. XIV:**318
Welcome to the Moon and Other Plays (Shanley), **Supp. XIV:**315, **316-319**
Weld, Theodore, **Supp. I Part 2:** 587, 588
Weld, Tuesday, **Supp. XI:** 306
Welded (O'Neill), **III:** 390
"Well, The" (Momaday), **Supp. IV Part 2:** 483
"Well Dressed Man with a Beard, The" (Stevens), **Retro. Supp. I:** 297
Wellek, René, **I:** 253, 261, 282; **II:** 320; **Supp. XIV:**12, 14
Weller, George, **III:** 322
Welles, Gideon, **Supp. I Part 2:** 484
Welles, Orson, **IV:** 476; **Supp. I Part 1:** 67; **Supp. IV Part 1:** 82, 83; **Supp. V:** 251; **Supp. VIII:** 46; **Supp. XI:** 169, 307
"Wellfleet Whale, The" (Kunitz), **Supp. III Part 1:** 263, 269
Wellfleet Whale and Companion Poems, The (Kunitz), **Supp. III Part 1:** 263
Wellman, Flora, **II:** 463-464, 465
"Well Rising, The" (Stafford), **Supp. XI:** 318
Wells, H. G., **I:** 103, 226, 241, 243, 253, 405, 409, 415; **II:** 82, 144, 276, 337, 338, 458; **III:** 456; **IV:** 340, 455; **Retro. Supp. I:** 100, 228, 231; **Supp. XVI:**190
Wellspring, The (Olds), **Supp. X: 211-212**
Well Wrought Urn, The: Studies in the Structure of Poetry (Brooks), **Supp. XIV:**1, **8-9,** 14, 15, 16
Welsh, Mary. *See* Hemingway, Mrs. Ernest (Mary Welsh)
Welty, Eudora, **II:** 194, 217, 606; **IV: 260-284; Retro. Supp. I:** 339-358; **Retro. Supp. II:** 235; **Supp. IV Part 2:** 474; **Supp. V:** 59, 315, 336; **Supp. VIII:** 94, 151, 171; **Supp. X:** 42, 290; **Supp. XII:** 310, 322; **Supp. XIV:**3; **Supp. XV:** 338
Weltzien, O. Alan, **Supp. XVI:**20-21, 28
"We miss Her, not because We see-" (Dickinson), **Retro. Supp. I:** 46
We Must Dance My Darlings (Trilling), **Supp. I Part 1:** 297
Wendell, Barrett, **III:** 507; **Supp. I Part 2:** 414; **Supp. XIV:**197
Wendell, Sarah. *See* Holmes, Mrs. Abiel (Sarah Wendell)
Wendy Wasserstein: A Casebook (Barnett), **Supp. XV:** 323, 330

"Wendy Wasserstein's Three Sisters: Squandered Privilege" (Brewer), **Supp. XV:** 330
Wept of Wish-ton-Wish, The (Cooper), **I:** 339, 342, 350
Werbe, Peter, **Supp. XIII:** 236
"We Real Cool" (Brooks), **Supp. III Part 1:** 80
We're Back! A Dinosaur's Story (screenplay, Shanley), **Supp. XIV:** 316
"We're Friends Again" (O'Hara), **III:** 372-373
"Were the Whole Realm of Nature Mine" (Watts), **I:** 458
Werewolf (M. Sommers), **Supp. XVII:** 55
Were-Wolf, The (C. Housman), **Supp. XVII:** 55
Werewolf of Paris, The (Endore), **Supp. XVII:** 55-56
Werewolves in Their Youth (Chabon), **Supp. XI:** 66, **76-77**
Werlock, Abby, **Supp. XIII:** 293
Werthman, Michael, **Supp. V:** 115
"Wer-Trout, The" (Proulx), **Supp. VII:** 255-256
Wescott, Glenway, **I:** 288; **II:** 85; **III:** 448, 454; **Supp. VIII:** 156; **Supp. XIV:** 342; **Supp. XVI:** 195
"We Shall All Be Born Again But We Shall Not All Be Saved" (Matthews), **Supp. IX:** 162
West, Anthony, **Supp. IV Part 1:** 284
West, Benjamin, **Supp. I Part 2:** 511
West, Dorothy, **Supp. XIII:** 295
West, James, **II:** 562
West, Nathanael, **I:** 97, 107, 190, 211, 298; **II:** 436; **III:** 357, 425; **IV: 285-307; Retro. Supp. II: 321-341; Supp. IV Part 1:** 203; **Supp. VIII:** 97; **Supp. XI:** 85, 105, 159, 296; **Supp. XII:** 173, 310; **Supp. XIII:** 106, 170
West, Ray, **Supp. XV:** 142
West, Rebecca, **II:** 412, 445; **Supp. XVI:** 152, 153
Westall, Julia Elizabeth. *See* Wolfe, Mrs. William Oliver (Julia Elizabeth Westall)
"We Stand United" (Benét), **Supp. XI:** 46
"West Authentic, The: Willa Cather" (Stegner), **Supp. IV Part 2:** 608
"West Coast, The: Region with a View" (Stegner), **Supp. IV Part 2:** 608-609
Westcott, Edward N., **II:** 102
"Western Association of Writers" (Chopin), **Supp. I Part 1:** 217

"Western Ballad, A" (Ginsberg), **Supp. II Part 1:** 311
Western Borders, The (Howe), **Supp. IV Part 2:** 424-425
Western Canon: The Books and Schools of the Ages (Bloom), **Supp. IX:** 146
Western Lands, The (Burroughs), **Supp. III Part 1:** 106
Western Star (Benét), **Supp. XI:** 46, 47, 57
"Westland" (C. Baxter), **Supp. XVII:** 18, 19
"West Marginal Way" (Hugo), **Supp. VI:** 131, 135
West of Yesterday, East of Summer: New and Selected Poems, 1973-1993 (Monette), **Supp. X:** 159
West of Your City (Stafford), **Supp. XI:** 316, **317-318**, 321, 322
Weston, Jessie L., **II:** 540; **III:** 12; **Supp. I Part 2:** 438
"West Real" (Ríos), **Supp. IV Part 2:** 539, 540
"West-running Brook" (Frost), **II:** 150, 162-164
West-running Brook (Frost), **II:** 155; **Retro. Supp. I:** 136, 137
"West Wall" (Merwin), **Supp. III Part 1:** 355
"Westward Beach, A" (Jeffers), **Supp. II Part 2:** 418
Westward Ho (Harrison), **Supp. VIII:** 51, **52**
Westward the Course of Empire (Leutze), **Supp. X:** 307
"Westward the Course of Empire Takes Its Way" (Wallace), **Supp. X: 307-308**
"West Wind" (Oliver), **Supp. VII:** 246
West Wind: Poems and Prose Poems (Oliver), **Supp. VII:** 243, 246-248
"West Wind, The" (Bryant), **Supp. I Part 1:** 155
"Wet Casements" (Ashbery), **Supp. III Part 1:** 18-20
We the Living (film), **Supp. IV Part 2:** 520
We the Living (Rand), **Supp. IV Part 2:** 520-521
Wet Parade (Sinclair), **Supp. V:** 289
"We've Adjusted Too Well" (O'Brien), **Supp. V:** 247
Wevill, David, **Retro. Supp. II:** 247, 249
"We Wear the Mask" (Dunbar), **Supp. II Part 1:** 199, 207, 209-210
Weybright, Victor, **Supp. XIII:** 172
Weyden, Rogier van der, **Supp. IV Part 1:** 284
Whalen, Marcella, **Supp. I Part 1:** 49

Whalen, Philip, **Supp. VIII:** 289
Whalen-Bridge, John, **Retro. Supp. II:** 211-212
"Whales off Wales, The" (X. J. Kennedy), **Supp. XV:** 163
"Whales Weep Not!" (D. H. Lawrence), **Supp. XVII:** 77
Wharton, Edith, **I:** 12, 375; **II:** 96, 180, 183, 186, 189-190, 193, 283, 338, 444, 451; **III:** 69, 175, 576; **IV:** 8, 53, 58, **308-330; Retro. Supp. I:** 108, 232, **359-385; Supp. IV Part 1:** 23, 31, 35, 36, 80, 81, 310; **Supp. IX:** 57; **Supp. XII:** 308; **Supp. XIV:** 337, 347; **Supp. XVI:** 189
Wharton, Edward Robbins, **IV:** 310, 313-314, 319
"What" (Dunn), **Supp. XI:** 144
What a Kingdom It Was (Kinnell), **Supp. III Part 1:** 235, 238, 239
"What America Would Be Like without Blacks" (Ellison), **Retro. Supp. II:** 123
What Are Masterpieces (Stein), **IV:** 30-31
What Are Years (Moore), **III:** 208-209, 210, 215
"What Are Years?" (Moore), **III:** 211, 213
What a Way to Go (Morris), **III:** 230-232
"What a Wonder among the Instruments Is the Walloping Trombone!" (Carruth), **Supp. XVI:** 51
"What Became of the Flappers?" (Zelda Fitzgerald), **Supp. IX:** 71
"What Can I Tell My Bones?" (Roethke), **III:** 546, 549
"What Child Is This?" (Jarman), **Supp. XVII:** 113-114, 115
"What Do We Have Here" (Carson), **Supp. XII:** 101
"What Do We See" (Rukeyser), **Supp. VI:** 282
What Do Women Want? Bread Roses Sex Power (Jong), **Supp. V:** 115, 117, 129, 130
"What Do You Do in San Francisco?" (Carver), **Supp. III Part 1:** 143
What D'Ya Know for Sure (Zinberg), **Supp. XV:** 196
Whatever Happened to Gloomy Gus of the Chicago Bears? (Coover), **Supp. V:** 51, 52
Whatever Happened to Jacy Farrow? (Cleveland), **Supp. V:** 222
"What Every Boy Should Know" (Maxwell), **Supp. VIII:** 169
"What Feels Like the World" (Bausch), **Supp. VII:** 46

"What Fort Sumter Did for Me" (E. Stoddard), **Supp. XV:** 282
"What God Is Like to Him I Serve" (Bradstreet), **Supp. I Part 1:** 106-107
"What Happened Here Before" (Snyder), **Supp. VIII:** 302
What Have I Ever Lost by Dying? (R. Bly), **Supp. IV Part 1:** 71-72
What Have You Lost? (Nye, ed.), **Supp. XIII:** 280
"What I Believe" (Mumford), **Supp. II Part 2:** 479
"What I Call What They Call Onanism" (Goldbarth), **Supp. XII:** 175
What I Did Last Summer (Gurney), **Supp. V:** 96, 100, 107, 108
"What if God" (Olds), **Supp. X:** 208
"What I Have to Defend, What I Can't Bear Losing" (Stern), **Supp. IX:** 286, 287, 288, 298
"What I Know about Being a Playwright" (McNally), **Supp. XIII:** 195, 207
"What I Mean" (Ortiz), **Supp. IV Part 2:** 497
"What Is an Emotion" (James), **II:** 350
What Is Art? (Tolstoy), **I:** 58
"What Is Civilization? Africa's Answer" (Du Bois), **Supp. II Part 1:** 176
"What Is College For?" (Bourne), **I:** 216
"What Is Exploitation?" (Bourne), **I:** 216
What Is Found There: Notebooks on Poetry and Politics (A. Rich), **Supp. XVII:** 74
"What Is It?" (Carver), **Supp. III Part 1:** 139
What Is Man? (Twain), **II:** 434; **IV:** 209
"What Is Poetry" (Ashbery), **Supp. III Part 1:** 19
"What Is Seized" (Moore), **Supp. X:** 164, 168, 169, 172, 175
"What Is the Earth?" (Olds), **Supp. X:** 213
"What Is This Poet" (Stern), **Supp. IX:** 295
"What I Think" (Hogan), **Supp. IV Part 1:** 406
What Maisie Knew (James), **II:** 332; **Retro. Supp. I:** 229, **230**
What Makes Sammy Run? (Schulberg), **Supp. XIII:** 170
What Moon Drove Me to This? (Harjo), **Supp. XII: 218-220**
"What Must" (MacLeish), **III:** 18

"What Sally Said" (Cisneros), **Supp. VII:** 63
"What's Happening in America" (Sontag), **Supp. III Part 2:** 460-461
"What's in Alaska?" (Carver), **Supp. III Part 1:** 141, 143
What's New, Pussycat? (film; Allen), **Supp. XI:** 307; **Supp. XV:** 1, 2, 14
"What's New in American and Canadian Poetry" (R. Bly), **Supp. IV Part 1:** 67
What's O'Clock (Lowell), **II:** 511, 527, 528
What's Up, Tiger Lily? (film; Allen), **Supp. XV:** 2, **3**
"What the Arts Need Now" (Baraka), **Supp. II Part 1:** 47
"What the Brand New Freeway Won't Go By" (Hugo), **Supp. VI:** 132-133
"What the Gypsies Told My Grandmother While She Was Still a Young Girl" (Simic), **Supp. VIII:** 283
"What the Prose Poem Carries with It" (R. Bly), **Supp. IV Part 1:** 64
"What They Wanted" (Dunn), **Supp. XI:** 151
What Thou Lovest Well (Hugo), **Supp. VI:** 140, 141
"What Thou Lovest Well Remains American" (Hugo), **Supp. VI:** 140, 141
What Time Collects (Farrell), **II:** 46, 47-48
What to Do? (Chernyshevsky), **Retro. Supp. I:** 269
What Use Are Flowers? (Hansberry), **Supp. IV Part 1:** 359, 368-369, 374
What Was Literature? (Fiedler), **Supp. XIII:** 96-97, **105-106**
What Was Mine (Beattie), **Supp. V:** 33, 35
What Was the Relationship of the Lone Ranger to the Means of Production? (Baraka), **Supp. II Part 1:** 58
"What We Came Through" (Goldbarth), **Supp. XII:** 179-180
What We Talk About When We Talk About Love (Carver), **Supp. III Part 1:** 142-146
What We Talk about When We Talk about Love (Carver), **Supp. XII:** 139
"What Why When How Who" (Pinsky), **Supp. VI:** 244
What Will Suffice: Contemporary American Poets on the Art of Poetry (Buckley and Young, eds.), **Supp. XIII:** 313
What Work Is (Levine), **Supp. V:** 181, 187, 192-193

"What You Hear from Em" (Taylor), **Supp. V:** 314, 320, 324
"What You Want" (O. Henry), **Supp. II Part 1:** 402
Wheatley, Phyllis, **Supp. XVII:** 74-75
Wheatly, Phyllis, **Supp. XIII:** 111
Wheeler, David, **Supp. XVI:**277
Wheeler, John, **II:** 433
Wheeler, Monroe, **Supp. XV:** 295
Wheelock, John Hall, **IV:** 461; **Supp. IX:** 268; **Supp. XIV:**120; **Supp. XV:** 301
Wheel of Life, The (Glasgow), **II:** 176, 178, 179, 183
Wheelwright, Philip, **Supp. XV:** 20
"When" (Olds), **Supp. X:** 207
When Boyhood Dreams Come True (Farrell), **II:** 45
"When Death Came April Twelve 1945" (Sandburg), **III:** 591, 593
"When Death Comes" (Oliver), **Supp. VII:** 241
"When De Co'n Pone's Hot" (Dunbar), **Supp. II Part 1:** 202-203
"When God First Said" (Zach; Everwine trans.), **Supp. XV:** 87
"When Grandma Died-1942" (Shields), **Supp. VII:** 311
"When Howitzers Began" (Carruth), **Supp. XVI:**55
"When I Buy Pictures" (Moore), **III:** 205
"When I Came from Colchis" (Merwin), **Supp. III Part 1:** 343
"When I Left Business for Literature" (Anderson), **I:** 101
"When in Rome-Apologia" (Komunyakaa), **Supp. XIII:** 120
"When It Comes" (Olds), **Supp. X:** 213
"When I Was Seventeen" (Kincaid), **Supp. VII:** 181
"When I Was Twenty-five" (Talese), **Supp. XVII:** 202
When Knighthood Was in Flower (Major), **III:** 320
"[0]sqb;When[0]sqb; Let by rain" (Taylor), **IV:** 160-161
"When Lilacs Last in the Dooryard Bloom'd" (Whitman), **IV:** 347-348, 351; **Retro. Supp. I:** 406; **Supp. IV Part 1:** 16; **Supp. XV:** 215
"When Malindy Sings" (Dunbar), **Supp. II Part 1:** 200, 204-205
When Peoples Meet: A Study of Race and Culture (Locke and Stern), **Supp. XIV:**202, 213
When She Was Good (P. Roth), **Retro. Supp. II:** 282, 283, 284; **Supp. III Part 2:** 403, 405, 410-413

"When Sue Wears Red" (Hughes), **Retro. Supp. I:** 195, 204
"When the Dead Ask My Father about Me" (Olds), **Supp. X:** 210
"When the Frost Is on the Punkin" (Riley), **Supp. II Part 1:** 202
When the Jack Hollers (Hughes), **Retro. Supp. I:** 203; **Supp. I Part 1:** 328
"When the Last Riders" (Zach; Everwine, trans.), **Supp. XV:** 75, 86
"When the Light Gets Green" (Warren), **IV:** 252
"When the Peace Corps Was Young" (Theroux), **Supp. VIII:** 314
When the Sun Tries to Go On (Koch), **Supp. XV:** 185
"When the Sun Tries to Go On" (Koch), **Supp. XV:** 179, 180
"When the World Ended as We Knew It" (Harjo), **Supp. XII:** 231
When Time Was Born (Farrell), **II:** 46, 47
"When We Dead Awaken: Writing as Re-Vision" (Rich), **Supp. I Part 2:** 552-553, 560
"When We Gonna Rise" (Baraka), **Supp. II Part 1:** 48
"When We Have To" (Salinas), **Supp. XIII:** 322-323
"WHEN WE'LL WORSHIP JESUS" (Baraka), **Supp. II Part 1:** 54
"When we speak of God, is it God we speak of?" (J. Logan), **Supp. XVII:** 113
"When Women Throw Down Bundles: Strong Women Make Strong Nations" (Gunn Allen), **Supp. IV Part 1:** 328
"'When You Finally See Them': The Unconquered Eye in *To Kill a Mockingbird*" (Champion), **Supp. VIII:** 128
"When You Lie Down, the Sea Stands Up" (Swenson), **Supp. IV Part 2:** 643
Where Does One Go When There's No Place Left to Go? (Crews), **Supp. XI:** 103
"Where Go the Boats" (R. Stevenson), **Supp. XVII:** 69
"Where I Come from Is Like This" (Gunn Allen), **Supp. IV Part 1:** 319
"Where I'm Calling From" (Carver), **Supp. III Part 1:** 145
Where I'm Calling From: New and Selected Stories (Carver), **Supp. III Part 1:** 138, 148
"Where I Ought to Be" (Erdrich), **Supp. IV Part 1:** 265

Where Is My Wandering Boy Tonight? (Wagoner), **Supp. IX:** 335-336
"Where Is the Island?" (Francis), **Supp. IX:** 78
"Where Is the Voice Coming From?" (Welty), **IV:** 280; **Retro. Supp. I:** 355
Where Joy Resides (Isherwood), **Supp. XIV:**156
"Where Knock Is Open Wide" (Roethke), **III:** 533-535
"Where My Sympathy Lies" (H. Roth), **Supp. IX:** 234
Where's My Money? (Shanley), **Supp. XIV:**316, 328, **330-331**
Where the Bluebird Sings to the Lemonade Springs (Stegner), **Supp. IV Part 2:** 596, 597, 598, 600, 604, 606, 613
Where the Cross Is Made (O'Neill), **III:** 388, 391
Where the Sea Used to Be (Bass), **Supp. XVI:**21
"Where the Sea Used to Be" (Bass), **Supp. XVI:**20, 21
"*Where the Sea Used to Be:* Rick Bass and the Novel of Ecological Education" (Dixon), **Supp. XVI:**21
"Where the Soft Air Lives" (Nye), **Supp. XIII:** 275
Where the Twilight Never Ends (Haines), **Supp. XII:** 211
Where the Wild Things Are (Sendak), **Supp. IX:** 207
"Wherever Home Is" (Wright), **Supp. III Part 2:** 605, 606
Where Water Comes Together With Other Water (Carver), **Supp. III Part 1:** 147, 148
"Where We Crashed" (Hugo), **Supp. VI:** 138
"Where You Are" (Doty), **Supp. XI:** 131
Where You'll Find Me, and Other Stories (Beattie), **Supp. V:** 30-31
Whicher, Stephen, **II:** 20
"Which Is More Than I Can Say for Some People" (Moore), **Supp. X:** 177, 178
Which Ones Are the Enemy? (Garrett), **Supp. VII:** 98
"Which Theatre Is the Absurd One?" (Albee), **I:** 71
"Which Way to the Future?" (Rehder), **Supp. IV Part 1:** 69
While I Was Gone (Miller), **Supp. XII:** 290, **301-303**
"While Seated in a Plane" (Swenson), **Supp. IV Part 2:** 645
While the Messiah Tarries (Bukiet),
Supp. XVII: 43, **46-47**
Whilomville Stories (Crane), **I:** 414
"Whip, The" (Robinson), **III:** 513
Whipple, Thomas K., **II:** 456, 458; **IV:** 427
"Whippoorwill, The" (Francis), **Supp. IX:** 90
"Whip-poor-will, The" (Thurber), **Supp. I Part 2:** 616
Whirlpool (film, Preminger), **Supp. XVII:** 62
"Whispering Gallery, The" (Komunyakaa), **Supp. XIII:** 132
"Whispering Leaves" (Glasgow), **II:** 190
Whispering to Fool the Wind (Ríos), **Supp. IV Part 2:** 540-541, 544, 545
"Whispers in the Next Room" (Simic), **Supp. VIII:** 278
"Whispers of Heavenly Death" (Whitman), **IV:** 348
"Whispers of Immortality" (Eliot), **Supp. XI:** 242
Whistle (Jones), **Supp. XI:** 219, 224, **231-234**
"Whistle, The" (Franklin), **II:** 121
"Whistle, The" (Komunyakaa), **Supp. XIII:** 111, 126
"Whistle, The" (Welty), **IV:** 262
Whistler, James, **I:** 484; **III:** 461, 465, 466; **IV:** 77, 369
Whistler, James Abbott McNeill, **Supp. XIV:**335-336
"Whistling Dick's Christmas Stocking" (O. Henry), **Supp. II Part 1:** 390, 392
Whistling in the Dark (Garrett), **Supp. VII:** 111
Whistling in the Dark: True Stories and Other Fables (Garrett), **Supp. VII:** 95
Whitcher, Frances Miriam Berry, **Supp. XIII:** 152
"White" (Simic), **Supp. VIII: 275-276**
White, Barbara, **Retro. Supp. I:** 379
White, E. B., **Retro. Supp. I:** 335; **Supp. I Part 2:** 602, 607, 608, 612, 619, 620, **651-681**; **Supp. II Part 1:** 143; **Supp. VIII:** 171; **Supp. IX:** 20, 32; **Supp. XVI:**167
White, Elizabeth Wade, **Supp. I Part 1:** 100, 103, 111
White, Henry Kirke, **Supp. I Part 1:** 150
White, James L., **Supp. XI:** 123
White, Joel, **Supp. I Part 2:** 654, 678
White, Katharine. (Katharine Sergeant Angell), **Supp. I Part 2:** 610, 653, 655, 656, 669; **Supp. VIII:** 151, 171
White, Lillian, **Supp. I Part 2:** 651

White, Lucia, **I:** 258
White, Maria. *See* Lowell, Mrs. James Russell (Maria White)
White, Morton, **I:** 258; **Supp. I Part 2:** 647, 648, 650
White, Roberta, **Supp. XII:** 293
White, Stanford, **Supp. IV Part 1:** 223
White, Stanley, **Supp. I Part 2:** 651, 655
White, T. H., **III:** 522
White, T. W., **III:** 411, 415
White, Walter, **Supp. I Part 1:** 345
White, William, **Retro. Supp. II:** 326
White, William A., **I:** 252
White Album, The (Didion), **Supp. IV Part 1:** 198, 202, 205-207, 210
"White Album, The" (Didion), **Supp. IV Part 1:** 205, 206
"White Angel" (Cunningham), **Supp. XV:** 59
"White Apache" (Markson), **Supp. XVII:** 136
White Buildings (H. Crane), **I:** 385, 386, 390-395, 400; **Retro. Supp. II:** 77-78, **80-81,** 82, 83, 85
White Butterfly (Mosley), **Supp. XIII:** 237, 238, 240
White Center (Hugo), **Supp. VI:** 144-145
"White Center" (Hugo), **Supp. VI:** 144, 146
Whited, Stephen, **Supp. XI:** 135
White Deer, The (Thurber), **Supp. I Part 2:** 606
White Doves at Morning (Burke), **Supp. XIV:** 22-23, 32, 35-36
"White Eagle, The" (Chopin), **Retro. Supp. II:** 72
White Fang (London), **II:** 471-472, 481
Whitefield, George, **I:** 546
White-Footed Deer and Other Poems (Bryant), **Supp. I Part 1:** 157
White Goddess, The (Graves), **Supp. IV Part 1:** 280
White-Haired Lover (Shapiro), **Supp. II Part 2:** 703, 717
Whitehead, Alfred North, **III:** 605, 619, 620; **IV:** 88; **Supp. I Part 2:** 554, 647
Whitehead, Colson, **Supp. XIII:** 233, 241
Whitehead, James, **Supp. XV:** 339
Whitehead, Margaret, **IV:** 114, 115, 116
Whitehead, Mrs. Catherine, **IV:** 116
White Heat (Walsh), **Supp. XIII:** 174
"White Heron, A" (Jewett), **II:** 409; **Retro. Supp. II:** 17
White Heron and Other Stories, A (Jewett), **II:** 396

White Horses (Hoffman), **Supp. X:** 83-85, 90, 92
White House Diary, A (Lady Bird Johnson), **Supp. IV Part 1:** 22
White Jacket; or, The World in a Man-of-War (Melville), **III:** 80, 81, 84, 94; **Retro Supp. I:** 248, 249, 254
White Lantern, The (Connell), **Supp. XIV:** 97
"White Lights, The" (Robinson), **III:** 524
"White Lilies, The" (Glück), **Supp. V:** 88
White Man, Listen! (Wright), **IV:** 478, 488, 489, 494
"White Mulberry Tree, The" (Cather), **I:** 319; **Retro. Supp. I:** 7, 9, 17
White Mule (W. C. Williams), **Retro. Supp. I:** 423
"White Negro, The" (Mailer), **III:** 36-37; **Retro. Supp. II:** 202
"Whiteness of the Whale, The" (Melville), **III:** 84, 86
"White Night" (Oliver), **Supp. VII:** 236
"White Nights" (Auster), **Supp. XII:** 23-24
White Noise (DeLillo), **Supp. VI:** 1, 3-4, 5-7, 10, 11-12, 16
White Oxen and Other Stories, The (Burke), **I:** 269, 271
White Paper on Contemporary American Poetry (McClatchy), **Supp. XII:** 253, **259-260**
"White Pine" (Oliver), **Supp. VII:** 244
White Pine: Poems and Prose Poems (Oliver), **Supp. VII:** 243-246
"White Silence, The" (London), **II:** 468
"White Silk" (Nye), **Supp. XIII:** 275
"White Snake, The" (Sexton), **Supp. II Part 2:** 691
"White Spot" (Anderson), **I:** 116
"White-Tailed Hornet, The" (Frost), **Retro. Supp. I:** 138
Whitfield, Raoul, **Supp. IV Part 1:** 345
Whitlock, Brand, **II:** 276
Whitman (Masters), **Supp. I Part 2:** 473, 475, 476
Whitman, George, **IV:** 346, 350
Whitman, Sarah Wyman, **Retro. Supp. II:** 136
"Whitman: The Poet and the Mask" (Cowley), **Supp. II Part 1:** 143
Whitman, Walt, **I:** 61, 68, 98, 103, 104, 109, 219, 220, 227, 228, 242, 246, 250, 251, 260, 261, 285, 381, 384, 386, 396, 397, 398, 402, 419, 430, 459, 460, 483, 485, 486, 577; **II:** 7, 8, 18, 127, 140, 273-274, 275, 289, 295, 301, 320, 321, 373, 445, 446, 451, 457, 494, 529, 530, 552; **III:** 171, 175, 177, 181-182, 189, 203, 234, 260, 426, 430, 453, 454, 461, 505, 507-508, 511, 528, 548, 552, 555, 559, 567, 572, 576, 577, 579, 584, 585, 595, 606, 609; **IV:** 74, 169, 191, 192, 202, **331-354,** 405, 409, 416, 444, 450-451, 457, 463, 464, 469, 470, 471; **Retro. Supp. I:** 8, 52, 194, 254, 283, 284, 333, **387-410,** 412, 417, 427; **Retro. Supp. II:** 40, 76, 93, 99, 155, 156, 158, 170, 262; **Supp. I Part 1:** 6, 79, 167, 311, 314, 325, 365, 368, 372; **Supp. I Part 2:** 374, 384, 385, 387, 389, 391, 393, 399, 416, 436, 455, 456, 458, 473, 474, 475, 525, 540, 579, 580, 582, 682, 691; **Supp. III Part 1:** 6, 20, 156, 239-241, 253, 340; **Supp. III Part 2:** 596; **Supp. IV Part 1:** 16, 169, 325; **Supp. IV Part 2:** 597, 625; **Supp. V:** 113, 118, 122, 130, 170, 178, 183, 277, 279, 332; **Supp. VIII:** 42, 95, 105, 126, 198, 202, 269; **Supp. IX:** 8, 9, 15, 38, 41, 44, 48, 53, 131, 292, 298, 299, 308, 320; **Supp. X:** 36, 112, 203, 204; **Supp. XI:** 83, 123, 132, 135, 203, 321; **Supp. XII:** 132, 185, 190, 256; **Supp. XIII:** 1, 77, 115, 153, 221, 304, 335; **Supp. XIV:** 89, 312, 334, 335, 338; **Supp. XV:** 41, 93, 181, 183, 212, 213, 218, 250, 275, 301, 302, 303, 309, 352; **Supp. XVI:** 209; **Supp. XVII:** 42, 71, 112, 133
Whitmarsh, Jason, **Supp. VIII:** 283
Whitmer, Peter, **Supp. X:** 264, 265
Whitney, Blair, **Supp. I Part 2:** 403
Whitney, Josiah, **Supp. IX:** 180, 181
Whitt, Margaret Earley, **Retro. Supp. II:** 226
Whittemore, Reed, **III:** 268; **Supp. XI:** 315
Whittier, Elizabeth, **Supp. I Part 2:** 700, 701, 703; **Supp. XIII:** 141, 142
Whittier, John Greenleaf, **I:** 216; **II:** 275; **III:** 52; **Retro. Supp. I:** 54; **Retro. Supp. II:** 155, 163, 169; **Supp. I Part 1:** 168, 299, 313, 317, 372; **Supp. I Part 2:** 420, 602, **682-707; Supp. VIII:** 202, 204; **Supp. XI:** 50; **Supp. XIII:** 140, 145; **Supp. XV:** 246
Whittier, Mary, **Supp. I Part 2:** 683
"Whittier Birthday Speech" (Twain), **Supp. I Part 1:** 313
"Who" (Kenyon), **Supp. VII:** 174

"Who" (Sobin), **Supp. XVI:**284-285
"Who Am I-Who I Am" (Corso), **Supp. XII:** 134
"Who Be Kind To" (Ginsberg), **Supp. II Part 1:** 323
"Whoever Was Using This Bed" (Carver), **Supp. III Part 1:** 148
"Whoever You Are Holding Me Now in Hand" (Whitman), **IV:** 342; **Retro. Supp. I:** 52
Who Gathered and Whispered behind Me (Goldbarth), **Supp. XII:** 181, 182
"Who in One Lifetime" (Rukeyser), **Supp. VI:** 276, 279
Who Is Witter Bynner? (Kraft), **Supp. XV:** 40, 52
"Who Is Your Mother? Red Roots of White Feminism" (Gunn Allen), **Supp. IV Part 1:** 329
Whole Hog (Wagoner), **Supp. IX: 337-338**
"Whole Mess...Almost, The" (Corso), **Supp. XII:** 135
"Whole Moisty Night, The" (R. Bly), **Supp. IV Part 1:** 69
Whole New Life, A (Price), **Supp. VI:** 265, **266,** 267
"Whole Self, The" (Nye), **Supp. XIII:** 275
"Whole Soul, The" (Levine), **Supp. V:** 192
"Whole Story, The" (Strand), **Supp. IV Part 2:** 622
Whole Town's Talking, The (Loos), **Supp. XVI:**187
"Whole World Knows, The" (Welty), **IV:** 272; **Retro. Supp. I:** 343
Who'll Stop the Rain (film), **Supp. V:** 301
Who Lost an American? (Algren), **Supp. IX: 15-16**
Who Owns America? (symposium), **Supp. XIV:**4
"Who Puts Together" (Hogan), **Supp. IV Part 1:** 403, 405, 412-413
"Whore of Mensa, The" (Allen), **Supp. XV:** 15
Whores for Gloria (Vollmann), **Supp. XVII:** 226, 230
Whorf, Benjamin Lee, **Supp. XVI:**283
Who's Afraid of Virginia Woolf? (Albee), **I:** 71, 77-81, 83, 85, 86, 87, 94; **IV:** 230
Who Shall Be the Sun? Poems Based on the Lore, Legends, and Myths of the Northwest Coast and Plateau Indians (Wagoner), **Supp. IX:** 328, **329-330,** 337
"Whosis Kid, The" (Hammett), **Supp. IV Part 1:** 344
"Who Sit Watch in Daylight" (Wright), **Supp. XV:** 342
"Who's Passing for Who?" (Hughes), **Supp. I Part 1:** 330
"Who Speak on the Page?" (Sanders), **Supp. XVI:**278
Who Will Run the Frog Hospital?: A Novel (Moore), **Supp. X:** 163, 165, 169, **175-177**
Why Are We in Vietnam? (Mailer), **III:** 27, 29, 30, 33, 34-35, 39, 42, 44; **Retro. Supp. II:** 205-206
"Why Did the Balinese Chicken Cross the Road?" (Walker), **Supp. III Part 2:** 527
"Why Do the Heathens Rage?" (O'Connor), **III:** 351
"Why Do You Write About Russia?" (Simpson), **Supp. IX:** 277
"Why I Am a Danger to the Public" (Kingsolver), **Supp. VII:** 204
Why I Am Not a Christian (Russell), **Supp. I Part 2:** 522
"Why I Entered the Gurdjieff Work" (Toomer), **Supp. III Part 2:** 481
"Why I Like Laurel" (Patchett), **Supp. XII:** 309
"Why I Live at the P.O." (Welty), **IV:** 262; **Retro. Supp. I:** 345
"Why Is Economics Not an Evolutionary Science?" (Veblen), **Supp. I Part 2:** 634
"Why I Write" (Didion), **Supp. IV Part 1:** 201, 203
Why Johnny Can't Read: And What You Can Do About It (Flesch), **Supp. XVI:**105
"Why Negro Women Leave Home" (Brooks), **Supp. III Part 1:** 75
"Why the Little Frenchman Wears His Hand in a Sling" (Poe), **III:** 425
Why We Behave Like Microbe Hunters (Thurber), **Supp. I Part 2:** 606
Why We Were in Vietnam (Podhoretz), **Supp. VIII:** 241
"Why Write?" (Updike), **Retro. Supp. I:** 317
"Wichita Vortex Sutra" (Ginsberg), **Supp. II Part 1:** 319, 321, 323-325, 327
Wickes, George, **Supp. XIV:**165
Wickford Point (Marquand), **III:** 50, 58, 64-65, 69
Wicks, Robert Russell, **Supp. XII:** 49
Wide, Wide World, The (Warner), **Supp. XV:** 275
"Wide Empty Landscape with a Death in the Foreground" (Momaday), **Supp. IV Part 2:** 492
Wideman, John Edgar, **Retro. Supp. II:** 123; **Supp. X:** 239, 250, **319-336; Supp. XI:** 245; **Supp. XIII:** 247
"Wide Net, The" (Welty), **IV:** 266
Wide Net and Other Stories, The (Welty), **IV:** 261, 264-266, 271; **Retro. Supp. I: 347-349,** 352, 355
Widening Spell of the Leaves, The (Levis), **Supp. XI:** 258, 259, 261, **268-269,** 271
"Wide Prospect, The" (Jarrell), **II:** 376-377
Widow for One Year, A (Irving), **Supp. VI:** 165, **179-181**
Widows of Thornton, The (Taylor), **Supp. V:** 320, 321
Wieland; or, The Transformation. An American Tale (Brown), **Supp. I Part 1:** 128-132, 133, 137, 140
Wiene, Robert, **Retro. Supp. I:** 268
Wiener, John, **Supp. IV Part 1:** 153
Wieners, John, **Supp. II Part 1:** 32
Wiesel, Elie, **Supp. XVII:** 47, 48, 49
Wiest, Dianne, **Supp. XV:** 12
"Wife, Forty-five, Remembers Love, A" (Shields), **Supp. VII:** 310
"Wifebeater, The" (Sexton), **Supp. II Part 2:** 693
"Wife for Dino Rossi, A" (Fante), **Supp. XI:** 165
"Wife of His Youth, The" (Chesnutt), **Supp. XIV:**63-66
Wife of His Youth and Other Stories of the Color Line, The (Chesnutt), **Supp. XIV:**62, 63
"Wife of Jesus Speaks, The" (Karr), **Supp. XI:** 250-251
"Wife of Nashville, A" (Taylor), **Supp. V:** 320
"Wife's Story, The" (Davis), **Supp. XVI:**85, 91, 92-93
Wife's Story, The (Shields), **Supp. VII:** 316. See also Happenstance
"Wife-Wooing" (Updike), **IV:** 226
Wigan, Gareth, **Supp. XI:** 306
Wiget, Andrew, **Supp. IV Part 2:** 509
Wigglesworth, Michael, **IV:** 147, 156; **Supp. I Part 1:** 110, 111
Wilbur, Richard, **III:** 527; **Retro. Supp. II:** 50; **Supp. III Part 1:** 64; **Supp. III Part 2: 541-565; Supp. IV Part 2:** 626, 634, 642; **Supp. V:** 337; **Supp. VIII:** 28; **Supp. X:** 58, 120; **Supp. XII:** 258; **Supp. XIII:** 76, 336; **Supp. XV:** 51, 251, 256; **Supp. XVII:** 26
Wilcocks, Alexander, **Supp. I Part 1:** 125

Wilcox, Ella Wheeler, **Supp. II Part 1:** 197
Wild 90 (film) (Mailer), **Retro. Supp. II:** 205
Wild, John, **II:** 362, 363-364
Wild, Peter, **Supp. V:** 5
Wild, Robert, **IV:** 155
"Wild, The" (Berry), **Supp. X:** 30
Wild and Woolly (film), **Supp. XVI:**185
Wild Boy of Aveyron, The (Itard). *See* De l'éducation d'un homme sauvage
Wild Boys, The: A Book of the Dead (Burroughs), **Supp. III Part 1:** 106-107
Wilde, Oscar, **I:** 50, 66, 381, 384; **II:** 515; **IV:** 77, 350; **Retro. Supp. I:** 56, 102, 227; **Retro. Supp. II:** 76, 326; **Supp. IV Part 2:** 578, 679, 683; **Supp. V:** 106, 283; **Supp. IX:** 65, 66, 68, 189, 192; **Supp. X:** 148, 151, 188-189; **Supp. XIV:**324, 334; **Supp. XV:** 350
Wilder, Amos Parker, **IV:** 356
Wilder, Billy, **Supp. IV Part 1:** 130; **Supp. XI:** 307
Wilder, Isabel, **IV:** 357, 366, 375
Wilder, Mrs. Amos Parker (Isabella Thornton Niven), **IV:** 356
Wilder, Thornton, **I:** 360, 482; **IV: 355-377,** 431; **Retro. Supp. I:** 109, 359; **Supp. I Part 2:** 609; **Supp. IV Part 2:** 586; **Supp. V:** 105; **Supp. IX:** 140; **Supp. XII:** 236-237
"Wilderness" (Leopold), **Supp. XIV:**190
"Wilderness" (Sandburg), **III:** 584, 595
Wilderness (Warren), **IV:** 256
"Wilderness, The" (Merwin), **Supp. III Part 1:** 340, 345
"Wilderness, The" (Robinson), **III:** 524
Wilderness of Vision, The: On the Poetry of John Haines (Bezner and Walzer, eds.), **Supp. XII:** 202
Wilderness Plots: Tales about the Settlement of the American Land (Sanders), **Supp. XVI:**267-268, 269
Wilderness World of Anne LaBastille, The (LaBastille), **Supp. X: 105,** 106
Wild Flag, The (White), **Supp. I Part 2:** 654
"Wildflower, The" (W. C. Williams), **Retro. Supp. I:** 420
"Wild Flowers" (Caldwell), **I:** 310
"Wildflowers" (Minot), **Supp. VI:** 208
"Wild Geese" (Oliver), **Supp. VII:** 237
"Wild Honey Suckle, The" (Freneau), **Supp. II Part 1:** 253, 264, 266
Wild in the Country (Odets), **Supp. II Part 2:** 546
Wild Iris, The (Glück), **Supp. V:** 79, 87-89, 91
Wildlife (Ford), **Supp. V:** 57, 69-71
Wildlife in America (Matthiessen), **Supp. V:** 199, 201, 204
"Wildlife in American Culture" (Leopold), **Supp. XIV:**190, 191
"Wildness" (Sanders), **Supp. XVI:**276
Wild Old Wicked Man, The (MacLeish), **III:** 3, 20
Wild Palms, The (Faulkner), **II:** 68-69; **Retro. Supp. I:** 85
"Wild Palms, The" (Faulkner), **II:** 68
"Wild Peaches" (Wylie), **Supp. I Part 2:** 707, 712
Wild Roses of Cape Ann and Other Poems (Larcom), **Supp. XIII:** 142, 147
Wild Seed (O. Butler), **Supp. XIII:** 62, 63
"Wild Swans at Coole, The " (W. B. Yeats), **Supp. XVI:**48
"Wild Swans at Norfolk, The" (Carruth), **Supp. XVI:**48
Wild to the Heart (Bass), **Supp. XVI:**16
"Wild Turkeys: Dignity of the Damned" (B. Kelly), **Supp. XVII:** 129
"Wildwest" (MacLeish), **III:** 14
Wiley, Craig, **Supp. VIII:** 313
Wilhelm Meister (Goethe), **II:** 291
Wilkes, John, **Supp. I Part 2:** 503, 519, 522
Wilkie, Curtis, **Supp. V:** 11
Wilkins, Roy, **Supp. I Part 1:** 345
Wilkinson, Alec, **Supp. VIII:** 164, 168, 171
Wilkinson, Max, **Supp. IX:** 251
Willard, Samuel, **IV:** 150
Willard Gibbs (Rukeyser), **Supp. VI:** 273, 283, 284
Willcutts, Tim, **Supp. XVII:** 239, 241, 246
Willett, Ralph, **Supp. XIV:**27
Willey, Basil, **Retro. Supp. II:** 243
William Carlos Williams (Koch), **Retro. Supp. I:** 428
William Carlos Williams: An American Artist (Breslin), **Retro. Supp. I:** 430
William Carlos Williams: The American Background (Weaver), **Retro. Supp. I:** 430
William Carlos Williams and Alterity (Ahearn), **Retro. Supp. I:** 415
William Carlos Williams and the Meanings of Measure (Cushman), **Retro. Supp. I:** 430
William Faulkner: A Critical Study (Howe), **Supp. VI:** 119-120, 125
William Faulkner: Early Prose and Poetry (Faulkner), **Retro. Supp. I:** 80
William Faulkner: First Encounters (Brooks), **Supp. XIV:**13
"William Faulkner: The Stillness of *Light in August*" (Kazin), **Supp. VIII:** 104
William Faulkner: The Yoknapatawpha Country (Brooks), **Supp. XIV:**12-13, 16
William Faulkner: Toward Yoknapatawpha and Beyond (Brooks), **Supp. XIV:**13
"William Faulkner's Legend of the South" (Cowley), **Supp. II Part 1:** 143
"William Humphrey, 73, Writer of Novels about Rural Texas" (Gussow), **Supp. IX:** 93
William Humphrey. Boise State University Western Writers Series (Winchell), **Supp. IX:** 109
William Humphrey, Destroyer of Myths (Almon), **Supp. IX:** 93
William Humphrey. Southwestern Series (Lee), **Supp. IX:** 109
"William Humphrey Remembered" (Masters), **Supp. IX:** 96
"William Ireland's Confession" (A. Miller), **III:** 147-148
William James and Phenomenology: A Study of the "Principles of Psychology" (Wilshire), **II:** 362
William Lloyd Garrison (Chapman), **Supp. XIV:**46-51, 52, 53, 55
William Maxwell Portrait, A: Memories and Appreciations (C. Baxter, Collier, and Hirsch, eds.), **Supp. XVII:** 23
Williams, Annie Laurie, **Supp. IX:** 93
Williams, C. K., **Supp. XIII:** 114; **Supp. XVII:** 112
Williams, Cecil, **II:** 508
Williams, Charles, **Supp. II Part 1:** 15, 16
Williams, Dakin, **IV:** 379
Williams, David Reichard, **Supp. XIII:** 162
Williams, Edward, **IV:** 404
Williams, Edwina Dakin, **IV:** 379
Williams, Esther, **Supp. XII:** 165
Williams, Fannie Barrier, **Supp. XIV:**201
Williams, George, **Supp. V:** 220
Williams, Horace, **IV:** 453
Williams, Joan, **Supp. IX:** 95
Williams, John A., **Supp. XVI:**143
Williams, John Sharp, **IV:** 378
Williams, Lyle, **Supp. XIV:**22
Williams, Michael, **Supp. V:** 286
Williams, Miller, **Supp. XIV:**126;

Supp. XV: 339
Williams, Mrs. William Carlos (Florence Herman), **IV:** 404
Williams, Paul, **IV:** 404
Williams, Raymond, **Supp. IX:** 146
Williams, Roger, **Supp. I Part 2:** 699
Williams, Rose, **IV:** 379
Williams, Sherley Anne, **Supp. V:** 180
Williams, Solomon, **I:** 549
Williams, Stanley T., **II:** 301, 316; **Supp. I Part 1:** 251
Williams, Stephen, **IV:** 148
Williams, Ted, **IV:** 216; **Supp. IX:** 162
Williams, Tennessee, **I:** 73, 81, 113, 211; **II:** 190, 194; **III:** 145, 147; **IV:** 4, **378-401; Supp. I Part 1:** 290, 291; **Supp. IV Part 1:** 79, 83, 84, 359; **Supp. IV Part 2:** 574, 682; **Supp. IX:** 133; **Supp. XI:** 103; **Supp. XIII:** 331; **Supp. XIV:**250, 315; **Supp. XVI:**194
Williams, Terry Tempest, **Supp. XIII:** 16
Williams, Walter L., **Supp. IV Part 1:** 330, 331
Williams, William, **IV:** 404, 405
Williams, William Carlos, **I:** 61, 62, 229, 255, 256, 261, 285, 428, 438, 446, 539; **II:** 133, 536, 542, 543, 544, 545; **III:** 194, 196, 198, 214, 269, 409, 453, 457, 458, 464, 465, 591; **IV:** 30, 74, 75, 76, 94, 95, 286, 287, **402-425; Retro. Supp. I:** 51, 52, 62, 209, 284, 285, 288, 296, 298, **411-433; Retro. Supp. II:** 178, 181, 189, 250, 321, 322, 326, 327, 328, 334, 335; **Supp. I Part 1:** 254, 255, 259, 266; **Supp. II Part 1:** 9, 30, 308, 318; **Supp. II Part 2:** 421, 443; **Supp. III Part 1:** 9, 147, 239, 271, 275, 276, 278, 350; **Supp. III Part 2:** 542, 610, 613, 614, 615, 616, 617, 621, 622, 626, 628; **Supp. IV Part 1:** 151, 153, 246, 325; **Supp. V:** 180, 337; **Supp. VIII:** 195, 269, 272, 277, 292; **Supp. IX:** 38, 268, 291; **Supp. X:** 112, 120, 204; **Supp. XI:** 311, 328; **Supp. XII:** 198; **Supp. XIII:** 77, 90, 335; **Supp. XIV:**280, 284, 285, 293; **Supp. XV:** 42, 51, 182, 250, 306, 307; **Supp. XVI:**48, 282; **Supp. XVII:** 36, 113, 227, 243
Williams, Wirt, **Supp. XIV:**24
Williamson, Alan, **Retro. Supp. II:** 185
William Styron's Nat Turner: Ten Black Writers Respond (Clarke, ed.), **IV:** 115
Williams-Walsh, Mary Ellen, **Supp. IV Part 2:** 611
William the Conqueror, **Supp. I Part 2:** 507
William Wetmore Story and His Friends (James), **Retro. Supp. I:** 235
William Wilson (Gardner), **Supp. VI:** 72
"William Wilson" (Poe), **II:** 475; **III:** 410, 412; **Retro. Supp. II:** 269; **Supp. IX:** 105
"Willie" (Angelou), **Supp. IV Part 1:** 15
Willie Masters' Lonesome Wife (Gass), **Supp. VI:** 77, **84-85, 86-87**
"Willing" (Moore), **Supp. X:** 178
Willis, Bruce, **Supp. IV Part 1:** 236
Willis, Gordon, **Supp. XV:** 7
Willis, Mary Hard, **Supp. V:** 290-291
Willis, Nathaniel Parker, **II:** 313; **Supp. I Part 2:** 405
Williwaw (Vidal), **Supp. IV Part 2:** 677, 680, 681
"Willow Woman" (Francis), **Supp. IX:** 78
Wills, Garry, **Supp. I Part 1:** 294; **Supp. IV Part 1:** 355
Wills, Ridley, **IV:** 122
Wills, Ross B., **Supp. XI:** 169
"Will to Believe, The" (James), **II:** 352; **Supp. XIV:**50
Will to Believe, The, and Other Essays in Popular Philosophy (James), **II:** 356; **IV:** 28
Will to Change, The: Poems, 1968-1970 (Rich), **Supp. I Part 2:** 551, 557-559
"Will We Plug Chips into Our Brains?" (W. Gibson), **Supp. XVI:**117-118
"Will You Please Be Quiet, Please?" (Carver), **Supp. III Part 1:** 137, 141
Will You Please Be Quiet, Please? (Carver), **Supp. III Part 1:** 138, 140, 144
"Will You Tell Me?" (Barthelme), **Supp. IV Part 1:** 42, 47
Wilsdorf, Anne, **Supp. XVI:**177
Wilshire, Bruce, **II:** 362, 364
Wilshire, Gaylord, **Supp. V:** 280
Wilson, Adrian, **Supp. XV:** 147
Wilson, Alexander, **Supp. XVI:**4, 6
Wilson, Angus, **IV:** 430, 435
Wilson, August, **Supp. VIII:** 329-353
Wilson, Augusta Jane Evans, **Retro. Supp. I:** 351
Wilson, E. O., **Supp. X:** 35
Wilson, Earl, **Supp. X:** 264
Wilson, Edmund, **I:** 67, 185, 236, 247, 260, 434, 482; **II:** 79, 80, 81, 86, 87, 91, 97, 98, 146, 276, 430, 530, 562, 587; **III:** 588; **IV:** 308, 310, 426-449; **Retro. Supp. I:** 1, 97, 100, 101, 103, 104, 105, 115, 274; **Retro. Supp. II:** 321, 327, 329; **Supp. I Part 1:** 372; **Supp. I Part 2:** 407, 646, 678, 709; **Supp. II Part 1:** 19, 90, 106, 136, 137, 143; **Supp. III Part 2:** 612; **Supp. IV Part 2:** 693; **Supp. VIII:** 93, 95, 96, 97, 98-99, 100, 101, 103, 105, 162; **Supp. IX:** 55, 65, 190; **Supp. X:** 186; **Supp. XI:** 160; **Supp. XIII:** 170; **Supp. XIV:**338; **Supp. XV:** 142, 308; **Supp. XVI:**194
Wilson, Edmund (father), **IV:** 441
Wilson, Henry, **Supp. XIV:**48
Wilson, Reuel, **II:** 562
Wilson, Robert, **Supp. XI:** 144
Wilson, Sloan, **Supp. IV Part 1:** 387
Wilson, Thomas, **IV:** 153
Wilson, Victoria, **Supp. X:** 166
Wilson, Woodrow, **I:** 245, 246, 490; **II:** 183, 253; **III:** 105, 581; **Supp. I Part 1:** 21; **Supp. I Part 2:** 474, 643; **Supp. V:** 288
Wilton, David, **IV:** 147
Wiman, Christian, **Supp. XV:** 251, 253, 264; **Supp. XVII:** 74
Wimberly, Lowry, **Supp. XV:** 136, 137
Wimsatt, William K., **Supp. XIV:**12
Winchell, Mark, **Supp. VIII:** 176, 189
Winchell, Mark Royden, **Supp. VIII:** 241; **Supp. IX:** 97, 98, 109; **Supp. XIII:** 94, 98, 99, 101; **Supp. XIV:**103, 106, 111
Winckelmann, Johann Joachim, **Supp. XII:** 178
Wind, Sand, and Stars (Saint-Exupéry), **Supp. IX:** 247
Wind Chrysalid's Rattle (Sobin), **Supp. XVI:**283
"Windfall" (B. Kelly), **Supp. XVII:** 132
Windham, Donald, **IV:** 382
"Windhover" (Hopkins), **I:** 397; **II:** 539; **Supp. IX:** 43
Winding Stair and Other Poems, The (Yeats), **Supp. XV:** 253
"Winding Street, The" (Petry), **Supp. XI:** 6
"Window" (Pinsky), **Supp. VI:** 237, 247
Windows (Creeley), **Supp. IV Part 1:** 157, 158
"Windows" (Jarrell), **II:** 388, 389
"Window Seat, A" (Goldbarth), **Supp. XII:** 185
Wind Remains, The (opera) (Bowles), **Supp. IV Part 1:** 83
"Winds, The" (Welty), **IV:** 265; **Retro. Supp. I:** 348, 350

"Wind up Sushi" (Goldbarth), **Supp. XII:** 186-187
"Windy Day at the Reservoir, A" (Beattie), **Supp. V:** 33
Windy McPherson's Son (Anderson), **I:** 101, 102-103, 105, 111
"Wine" (Carver), **Supp. III Part 1:** 138
"Wine Menagerie, The" (H. Crane), **I:** 389, 391; **Retro. Supp. II:** 82
Wine of the Puritans, The: A Study of Present-Day America (Brooks), **I:** 240
"Wine of Wizardry, A" (Sterling), **I:** 208
Winer, Linda, **Supp. IV Part 2:** 580; **Supp. XV:** 332
Winesburg, Ohio: A Group of Tales of Ohio Small Town Life (Anderson), **I:** 97, 102, 103, 104, 105-108; **III:** 112, 113, 114, 116, 224, 579; **Supp. V:** 12; **Supp. IX:** 306, 308; **Supp. XI:** 164; **Supp. XVI:** 17
Wing-and-Wing, The (Cooper), **I:** 350, 355
Winged Seed, The: A Remembrance (L.-Y. Lee), **Supp. XV:** 211, **220-223**
Winged Words: American Indian Writers Speak (Coltelli), **Supp. IV Part 2:** 493, 497
"Wingfield" (Wolff), **Supp. VII:** 341-342
"Wings, The" (Doty), **Supp. XI:** 124
Wings of the Dove, The (James), **I:** 436; **II:** 320, 323, 333, 334-335; **Retro. Supp. I:** 215, 216, 217, 232, **233-234; Supp. II Part 1:** 94-95; **Supp. IV Part 1:** 349
Winner Take Nothing (Hemingway), **II:** 249; **Retro. Supp. I:** 170, 175, 176, 181
"Winnie" (Brooks), **Supp. III Part 1:** 86
Winokur, Maxine. See Kumin, Maxine
Winslow, Devereux, **II:** 547
Winslow, Harriet, **II:** 552-553
Winslow, Ola Elizabeth, **I:** 547
Winslow, Warren, **II:** 540
Winston, Andrew, **Supp. XII:** 189
Winston, Michael R., **Supp. XIV:** 197
Winter, Douglas, **Supp. V:** 144
Winter, Johnny and Edgar, **Supp. V:** 334
Winter, Kate, **Supp. X:** 104
Winter: Notes from Montana (Bass), **Supp. XVI:** 17-18
"Winter Branch, A" (Irving), **Supp. VI:** 163

"Winter Burial, A" (Clampitt), **Supp. IX:** 48
Winter Carnival (film), **Retro. Supp. I:** 113
"Winter Daybreak at Vence, A" (Wright), **Supp. III Part 1:** 249-250
Winter Diary, A (Van Doren), **I:** 168
"Winter Dreams" (Fitzgerald), **II:** 80, 94; **Retro. Supp. I:** 108
"Winter Drive, A" (Jewett), **Retro. Supp. II:** 147
"Winter Eden, A" (Frost), **Retro. Supp. I:** 137
"Winter Father, The" (Dubus), **Supp. VII:** 83, 87
Winter Hours: Prose, Prose Poems, and Poems (Oliver), **Supp. VII:** 230, 247
"Winter in Dunbarton" (Lowell), **II:** 547; **Retro. Supp. II:** 187
"Wintering" (Plath), **Retro. Supp. II:** 255
Winter Insomnia (Carver), **Supp. III Part 1:** 138
Winter in the Blood (Welch), **Supp. IV Part 2:** 562
"Winter Landscape" (Berryman), **I:** 174; **Retro. Supp. I:** 430
Winter Lightning (Nemerov), **III:** 269
Winter News (Haines), **Supp. XII:** 199, **201-204,** 207-208, 208
Winternitz, Mary. See Cheever, Mrs. John (Mary Winternitz)
Winter of Our Discontent, The (Steinbeck), **IV:** 52, 65-66, 68
"Winter on Earth" (Toomer), **Supp. III Part 2:** 486
"Winter Piece, A" (Bryant), **Supp. I Part 1:** 150, 155
"Winter Rains, Cataluña" (Levine), **Supp. V:** 182
"Winter Remembered" (Ransom), **III:** 492-493
Winterrowd, Prudence, **I:** 217, 224
Winters, Jonathan, **Supp. XI:** 305
Winters, Yvor, **I:** 59, 63, 386, 393, 397, 398, 402, 471; **III:** 194, 498; **IV:** 153; **Retro. Supp. II:** 76, 77, 78, 82, 83, 85, 89; **Supp. I Part 1:** 268; **Supp. II Part 2:** 416, 666, **785-816; Supp. IV Part 2:** 480; **Supp. V:** 180, 191-192; **Supp. XIV:** 287; **Supp. XV:** 74, 341
"Winter Scenes" (Bryant). See "Winter Piece, A"
Winterset (Anderson), **III:** 159
"Winter Skyline Late" (F. Wright), **Supp. XVII:** 245
"Winter Sleep" (Wylie), **Supp. I Part 2:** 711, 729

Winter's Tale, The (Shakespeare), **Supp. XIII:** 219
Winter Stars (Levis), **Supp. XI:** 259, **266-268**
"Winter Stars" (Levis), **Supp. XI:** 267-268
"Winter Stop-Over" (Everwine), **Supp. XV:** 76
Winter Stop-Over (Everwine), **Supp. XV:** 74, 76
"Winter Swan" (Bogan), **Supp. III Part 1:** 52
Winter Thunder (X. J. Kennedy), **Supp. XV:** 167
"Winter Thunder" (X. J. Kennedy), **Supp. XV:** 169
Winter Trees (Plath), **Retro. Supp. II:** 257; **Supp. I Part 2:** 526, 539, 541
"Winter Weather Advisory" (Ashbery), **Supp. III Part 1:** 26
"Winter without Snow, The" (C. Frost), **Supp. XV:** 96, 105-106
"Winter Words" (Levine), **Supp. V:** 192
Winthrop, John, **Supp. I Part 1:** 99, 100, 101, 102, 105; **Supp. I Part 2:** 484, 485
Winthrop Covenant, The (Auchincloss), **Supp. IV Part 1:** 23
Wirt, William, **I:** 232
Wirth, Louis, **IV:** 475
"Wisdom Cometh with the Years" (Cullen), **Supp. IV Part 1:** 166
Wisdom of the Desert, The: Sayings from the Desert Fathers of the Fourth Century (Merton), **Supp. VIII:** 201
Wisdom of the Heart, The (H. Miller), **III:** 178, 184
Wise Blood (O'Connor), **III:** 337, 338, 339-343, 344, 345, 346, 350, 354, 356, 357; **Retro. Supp. II:** 219, 221, 222, 223, **225-228**
Wise Men, The (Price), **Supp. VI:** 254
"Wiser Than a God" (Chopin), **Retro. Supp. II:** 61; **Supp. I Part 1:** 208
Wishes, Lies, and Dreams: Teaching Children to Write Poetry (Koch), **Supp. XV:** 176, 189
"Wish for a Young Wife" (Roethke), **III:** 548
Wishful Thinking: A Theological ABC (Buechner), **Supp. XII:** 53
Wishing Tree, The: Christopher Isherwood on Mystical Religion (Adjemian, ed.), **Supp. XIV:** 164, 173
Wismer, Helen Muriel. See Thurber, Mrs. James (Helen Muriel Wismer)
Wisse, Ruth, **Supp. XII:** 167, 168

Wister, Owen, **I:** 62; **Retro. Supp. II:** 72; **Supp. XIV:** 39
"Witchbird" (Bambara), **Supp. XI:** 11
"Witch Burning" (Plath), **Supp. I Part 2:** 539
Witchcraft of Salem Village, The (Jackson), **Supp. IX:** 121
"Witch Doctor" (Hayden), **Supp. II Part 1:** 368, 380
Witches of Eastwick, The (Updike), **Retro. Supp. I:** 330, 331
Witching Hour, The (Rice), **Supp. VII:** 299-300
"Witch of Coös, The" (Frost), **II:** 154-155; **Retro. Supp. I:** 135; **Retro. Supp. II:** 42
"Witch of Owl Mountain Springs, The: An Account of Her Remarkable Powers" (Taylor), **Supp. V:** 328
"Witch of Wenham, The" (Whittier), **Supp. I Part 2:** 694, 696
Witek, Terri, **Supp. XVII:** 117
"With a Little Help from My Friends" (Kushner), **Supp. IX:** 131
With Bold Knife and Fork (M. F. K. Fisher), **Supp. XVII:** 89, 91
"With Che at Kitty Hawk" (Banks), **Supp. V:** 6
"With Che at the Plaza" (Banks), **Supp. V:** 7
"With Che in New Hampshire" (Banks), **Supp. V:** 6
"Withdrawal Symptoms" (Mora), **Supp. XIII:** 216
"Withered Skins of Berries" (Toomer), **Supp. III Part 2:** 485; **Supp. IX:** 320
Withers, Harry Clay, **Supp. XIII:** 161
Witherspoon, John, **Supp. I Part 2:** 504
With Eyes at the Back of Our Heads (Levertov), **Supp. III Part 1:** 276-277
With Her in Ourland (Gilman), **Supp. XI:** 208-209
With His Pistol in His Hand (Paredes), **Supp. XIII:** 225
"Within the Words: An Apprenticeship" (Haines), **Supp. XII:** 197
"With Kit, Age 7, at the Beach" (Stafford), **Supp. XI:** 323
"With Mercy for the Greedy" (Sexton), **Supp. II Part 2:** 680
With My Trousers Rolled (Epstein), **Supp. XIV:** 101, 105
Without a Hero (Boyle), **Supp. VIII:** 16
Without Feathers (Allen), **Supp. XV:** 3, 14, 15
Without Stopping (Bowles), **Supp. IV Part 1:** 79, 81, 85, 90, 91, 92
"Without Tradition and within Reason: Judge Horton and Atticus Finch in Court" (Johnson), **Supp. VIII:** 127
With Shuddering Fall (Oates), **Supp. II Part 2:** 504-506
"With the Dog at Sunrise" (Kenyon), **Supp. VII:** 170
With the Empress Dowager of China (Carl), **III:** 475
"With the Horse in the Winter Pasture" (McCarriston), **Supp. XIV:** 262
With the Old Breed: At Peleliu and Okinawa (Sledge), **Supp. V:** 249-250
"With the Violin" (Chopin), **Retro. Supp. II:** 61
"Witness" (Clampitt), **Supp. IX:** 42-43, 45, 46
"Witness" (Dubus), **Supp. VII:** 89
"Witness" (Harjo), **Supp. XII:** 227-228
Witness (McNally), **Supp. XIII:** 197
"Witness, The" (Porter), **III:** 443-444
"Witness for Poetry, A" (Stafford), **Supp. XI:** 324
"Witness for the Defense" (Hay), **Supp. XIV:** 124
"Witnessing My Father's Will" (Karr), **Supp. XI:** 241
"Witnessing to a Shared World" (Sanders), **Supp. XVI:** 278
Witness to the Times! (McGrath), **Supp. X:** 118
Witness Tree, A (Frost), **II:** 155; **Retro. Supp. I:** 122, 137, 139
Wit's End: Days and Nights of the Algonquin Round Table (Gaines), **Supp. IX:** 190
Wits Recreations (Mennes and Smith), **II:** 111
Witt, Shirley Hill, **Supp. IV Part 2:** 505
Wittels, Anne F., **Supp. XV:** 59
Wittenberg, Judith Bryant, **Retro. Supp. II:** 146
Wittgenstein, Ludwig, **Retro. Supp. I:** 53; **Supp. III Part 2:** 626-627; **Supp. X:** 304; **Supp. XII:** 21; **Supp. XV:** 344, 346
Wittgensteins' Mistress (Markson), **Supp. XVII:** 135, 142, 143, 145
Wittliff, William, **Supp. V:** 227
"Witty War, A" (Simpson), **Supp. IX:** 268
"Wives and Mistresses" (Hardwick), **Supp. III Part 1:** 211-212
Wizard of Loneliness, The (Nichols), **Supp. XIII:** 259, 263, 264
Wizard of Oz, The (Baum), **Supp. IV Part 1:** 113
Wizard of Oz, The (film), **Supp. X:** 172, 214
Wizard's Tide, The: A Story (Buechner), **Supp. XII:** 54
"WLT (The Edgar Era)" (Keillor), **Supp. XVI:** 172
WLT: A Radio Romance (Keillor), **Supp. XVI:** 176
Wobegon Boy (Keillor), **Supp. XVI:** 177
Wodehouse, P. G., **Supp. IX:** 195
Woiwode, Larry, **Supp. VIII:** 151; **Supp. XVI:** 206
Wojahn, David, **Supp. IX:** 161, 292, 293
Wolcott, James, **Supp. IX:** 259
Wolf: A False Memoir (Harrison), **Supp. VIII:** 40, **41-42,** 45
Wolf, Christa, **Supp. IV Part 1:** 310, 314
Wolf, Daniel, **Retro. Supp. II:** 202
Wolfe, Ben, **IV:** 454
Wolfe, Gregory, **Supp. XIV:** 307
Wolfe, James, **Supp. I Part 2:** 498
Wolfe, Linnie, **Supp. IX:** 176
Wolfe, Mabel, **IV:** 454
Wolfe, Mrs. William Oliver (Julia Elizabeth Westall), **IV:** 454
Wolfe, Thomas, **I:** 288, 289, 374, 478, 495; **II:** 457; **III:** 40, 108, 278, 334, 482; **IV:** 52, 97, 357, **450-473**; **Retro. Supp. I:** 382; **Supp. I Part 1:** 29; **Supp. IV Part 1:** 101; **Supp. IX:** 229; **Supp. X:** 225; **Supp. XI:** 213, 216, 217, 218; **Supp. XIII:** 17; **Supp. XIV:** 122
Wolfe, Tom, **Supp. III Part 2: 567-588**; **Supp. IV Part 1:** 35, 198; **Supp. V:** 296; **Supp. X:** 264; **Supp. XI:** 239; **Supp. XV:** 143; **Supp. XVII:** 202
Wolfe, William Oliver, **IV:** 454
"Wolfe Homo Scribens" (Cowley), **Supp. II Part 1:** 144
Wolfert's Roost (Irving), **II:** 314
Wolff, Cynthia Griffin, **Retro. Supp. I:** 379; **Supp. IV Part 1:** 203
Wolff, Donald, **Supp. XIII:** 316, 317, 326
Wolff, Geoffrey, **Supp. II Part 1:** 97; **Supp. XI:** 239, 245, 246
Wolff, Tobias, **Retro. Supp. I:** 190; **Supp. V:** 22; **Supp. VII: 331-346**; **Supp. X:** 1; **Supp. XI:** 26, 239, 245, 246, 247; **Supp. XV:** 223; **Supp. XVI:** 39, 41, 63, 70, 77
Wolfson, P. J., **Supp. XIII:** 172
"Wolf Town" (Carson), **Supp. XII: 102**
Wolf Willow: A History, a Story, and a Memory of the Last Plains Frontier

(Stegner), **Supp. IV Part 2:** 595, 596, 597, 598, 599, 600, 601, 604, 606, 611, 613, 614
Wolitzer, Hilma, **Supp. XV:** 55
Wolitzer, Meg, **Supp. XV:** 65
Wollaston, William, **II:** 108
Wollstonecraft, Mary, **Supp. I Part 1:** 126; **Supp. I Part 2:** 512, 554
"Woman" (Bogan), **Supp. X:** 102
"Woman, I Got the Blues" (Komunyakaa), **Supp. XIII:** 117
"Woman, Why Are You Weeping?" (Kenyon), **Supp. VII:** 174-175
"Woman, Young and Old, A" (Paley), **Supp. VI:** 222, 225
Woman Aroused, The (Lacy), **Supp. XV:** 199-200
Woman at the Washington Zoo, The (Jarrell), **II:** 367, 386, 387, 389
"Woman Dead in Her Forties, A" (Rich), **Supp. I Part 2:** 574-575
"Woman Hanging from the Thirteenth Floor Window, The" (Harjo), **Supp. XII:** 216, 221
"Woman Hollering Creek" (Cisneros), **Supp. VII:** 70
Woman Hollering Creek and Other Stories (Cisneros), **Supp. VII:** 58, 68-70
"Womanhood" (Brooks), **Supp. III Part 1:** 77
"Woman in Rain" (X. J. Kennedy), **Supp. XV:** 168
Woman in the Dark (Hammett), **Supp. IV Part 1:** 343
"Woman in the House, A" (Caldwell), **I:** 310
Woman in the Nineteenth Century (Fuller), **Retro. Supp. I:** 156; **Supp. II Part 1:** 279, 292, 294-296; **Supp. XI:** 197, 203
Woman in White, The (Collins), **Supp. I Part 1:** 35, 36
"Womanizer, The" (Ford), **Supp. V:** 71, 72
"Woman Like Yourself, A" (C. Frost), **Supp. XV:** 107
Woman Lit by Fireflies, The (Harrison), **Supp. VIII: 50-51**
"Woman Loses Cookie Bake-Off, Sets Self on Fire" (R. O. Butler), **Supp. XII:** 72
Woman of Andros, The (Wilder), **IV:** 356, 363-364, 367, 368, 374
Woman of Means, A (Taylor), **Supp. V:** 319-320
Woman on the Edge of Time (Piercy), **Supp. XIII:** 29
Woman on the Porch, The (Gordon), **II:** 199, 209-211

"Woman on the Stair, The" (MacLeish), **III:** 15-16
"Woman's Dream, A" (E. Stoddard), **Supp. XV:** 278
"Woman's Heartlessness" (Thaxter), **Retro. Supp. II:** 147
Woman's Honor (Glaspell), **Supp. III Part 1:** 179
"Woman Singing" (Ortiz), **Supp. IV Part 2:** 513
Woman's Share in Primitive Culture (Mason), **Supp. I Part 1:** 18
"Woman Struck by Car Turns into Nymphomaniac" (R. O. Butler), **Supp. XII:** 72
"Woman's Work" (Alvarez), **Supp. VII:** 4
"Woman Uses Glass Eye to Spy on Philandering Husband" (R. O. Butler), **Supp. XII:** 70, 72
Woman Warrior (Kingston), **Supp. IV Part 1:** 12; **Supp. V:** 157, 158, 159, 160-164, 166, 169; **Supp. X:** 291-292; **Supp. XIV:**162
Woman Warrior, The (Kingston), **Supp. XV:** 220
Woman Who Fell from the Sky, The (Harjo), **Supp. XII: 226-228**
"Woman Who Fell From the Sky, The" (Iroquois creation story), **Supp. IV Part 1:** 327
Woman Who Owned the Shadows, The (Gunn Allen), **Supp. IV Part 1:** 320, 322, 326, 327-328
Woman Within, The (Glasgow), **II:** 183, 190-191
"Womanwork" (Gunn Allen), **Supp. IV Part 1:** 326
Women (Bukowski), **Supp. XI:** 172
"Women" (Didion), **Supp. IV Part 1:** 205
"Women" (Swenson), **Supp. IV Part 2:** 647
Women, The (film), **Retro. Supp. I:** 113
Women, The (film; Cukor), **Supp. XVI:**181, 192
"Women and Children First" (Prose), **Supp. XVI:**254
Women and Children First: Stories (Prose), **Supp. XVI:**254
Women and Economics (Gilman), **Supp. I Part 2:** 637; **Supp. V:** 284; **Supp. XI:** 200, 203-204, 206
Women and Thomas Harrow (Marquand), **III:** 50, 61, 62, 66, 68, 69-70, 71
Women and Vodka (Markson as Merrill, ed.), **Supp. XVII:** 136
Women and Wilderness (LaBastille),

Supp. X: 97, **102-104**
"Women as They Are" (Rowson), **Supp. XV:** 243
Women at Point Sur, The (Jeffers), **Supp. II Part 2:** 430-431
Women in Love (Lawrence), **III:** 27, 34
Women of Brewster Place, The: A Novel in Seven Stories (Naylor), **Supp. VIII:** 213, **214-218**
Women of Manhattan: An Upper West Side Story (Shanley), **Supp. XIV:**315, **326-327**
"Women of My Color" (Coleman), **Supp. XI:** 88-89
Women of Trachis (Pound, trans.), **III:** 476
Women on the Wall, The (Stegner), **Supp. IV Part 2:** 599, 605, 606
Women Poets in English (Stanford, ed.), **Retro. Supp. I:** 41
"Women Reformers and American Culture, 1870-1930" (Conway), **Supp. I Part 1:** 19
"Women's Movement, The" (Didion), **Supp. IV Part 1:** 206
"Women Waiting" (Shields), **Supp. VII:** 320
"Women We Love Whom We Never See Again" (R. Bly), **Supp. IV Part 1:** 66
"Women We Never See Again" (R. Bly), **Supp. IV Part 1:** 66
Women with Men (Ford), **Supp. V:** 57, 71-72
"Wonder" (Olds), **Supp. X:** 210
Wonder Boys (Chabon), **Supp. XI:** 67, **73-75**,**Supp. XI:** 78; **Supp. XVI:**259
Wonder Boys (film), **Supp. XI:** 67
Wonderful O, The (Thurber), **Supp. I Part 2:** 612
"Wonderful Old Gentleman, The" (Parker), **Supp. IX:** 197
"Wonderful Pen, The" (Swenson), **Supp. IV Part 2:** 650
Wonderful Words, Silent Truth: Essays on Poetry and a Memoir (Simic), **Supp. VIII:** 270
Wonderland (Oates), **Supp. II Part 2:** 511, 512, 514-515
Wonders Hidden (Sanders), **Supp. XVI:**269
Wonders of the Invisible World, The (Mather), **Supp. II Part 2:** 456-459, 460, 467
Wonder-Working Providence (Johnson), **IV:** 157
Wong, Hertha, **Supp. IV Part 1:** 275
Wong, Jade Snow, **Supp. X:** 291

Wong, Nellie, **Supp. XVII:** 72
Wong, Shawn, **Supp. XV:** 221
"Wood" (Nye), **Supp. XIII:** 276
Wood, Audrey, **IV:** 381
Wood, Charles Erskine Scott, **Supp. XV:** 301
Wood, Clement, **Supp. XV:** 298
Wood, Clement Biddle, **Supp. XI:** 307
Wood, James, **Supp. XIV:**95-96
Wood, Mabel, **I:** 199
Wood, Michael, **Supp. IV Part 2:** 691
Wood, Mrs. Henry, **Supp. I Part 1:** 35
Wood, Norman Barton, **Supp. XIV:**201
Wood, Susan, **Supp. XVI:**123
Woodard, Calvin, **Supp. VIII:** 128
Woodard, Charles L., **Supp. IV Part 2:** 484, 493
Woodard, Deborah, **Supp. XIII:** 114
Woodberry, George Edward, **III:** 508
Woodbridge, Frederick, **I:** 217, 224
Woodbridge, John, **Supp. I Part 1:** 101, 102, 114
"Wood-Choppers, The" (Chopin), **Retro. Supp. II:** 72
Woodcock, George, **Supp. XIII:** 33
Woodcome, Beth, **Supp. XVII:** 240
"Wood Dove at Sandy Spring, The" (MacLeish), **III:** 19
"Wooden Spring" (Rukeyser), **Supp. VI:** 285
"Wooden Umbrella, The" (Porter), **IV:** 26
"Woodnotes" (Emerson), **II:** 7, 19
"Wood-Pile, The" (Frost), **Retro. Supp. I:** 128; **Supp. IV Part 2:** 445
Woodrow, James, **Supp. I Part 1:** 349, 366
"Woods, Books, and Truant Officers, The" (Maclean), **Supp. XIV:**221, 225
Woods, Robert A., **Supp. I Part 1:** 19
Woods, The (Mamet), **Supp. XIV:**241, 254-255
Woodswoman (LaBastille), **Supp. X:** 95, **96-99**, 108
Woodswoman III: Book Three of the Woodswoman's Adventures (LaBastille), **Supp. X:** 95, **106-107**
"Wood Thrush" (Kenyon), **Supp. VII:** 172
Woodward, C. Vann, **IV:** 114, 470-471; **Retro. Supp. I:** 75, 76
"Wooing the Inanimate" (Brodsky), **Supp. VIII:** 32
Woolcott, Alexander, **Supp. IX:** 197
Wooley, Bryan, **Supp. V:** 225
Woolf, Leonard, **Supp. IX:** 95
Woolf, Virginia, **I:** 53, 79, 112, 309; **II:** 320, 415; **IV:** 59; **Retro. Supp. I:** 59, 75, 170, 215, 291, 359; **Supp. I Part 2:** 553, 714, 718; **Supp. IV Part 1:** 299; **Supp. V:** 127; **Supp. VIII:** 5, 155, 251, 252, 263, 265; **Supp. IX:** 66, 109; **Supp. XI:** 134, 193; **Supp. XII:** 81, 98, 289; **Supp. XIII:** 305; **Supp. XIV:**341-342, 342, 343, 346, 348; **Supp. XV:** 55, 65
Woollcott, Alexander, **IV:** 432; **Retro. Supp. II:** 327; **Supp. I Part 2:** 664; **Supp. IX:** 190, 194
Woollstonecraft, Mary, **Supp. XVI:**184
"Woolly Mammoth" (X. J. Kennedy), **Supp. XV:** 163-164
Woolman, John, **Supp. VIII:** 202, 204, 205
Woolson, Constance Fenimore, **Retro. Supp. I:** 224, 228
Worcester, Samuel, **I:** 458
Word and Idioms: Studies in the English Language (L. P. Smith), **Supp. XIV:**343
Word of God and the Word of Man, The (Barth), **Retro. Supp. I:** 327
"Word out of the Sea, A" (Whitman), **IV:** 344
Words (Creeley), **Supp. IV Part 1:** 139, 150-153, 154, 155, 158
"Words" (Creeley), **Supp. IV Part 1:** 152
"Words" (Gioia), **Supp. XV:** 125
"Words" (Merwin), **Supp. III Part 1:** 352
"Words" (Plath), **Supp. I Part 2:** 547
"Words" (Shields), **Supp. VII:** 323
"Words, The" (Wagoner), **Supp. IX:** 326
"Words above a Narrow Entrance" (Wagoner), **Supp. IX:** 325
"Words for a Bike-Racing, Osprey-Chasing Wine-Drunk Squaw Man" (Gunn Allen), **Supp. IV Part 1:** 325
Words for Dr. Y (Sexton), **Supp. II Part 2:** 698
"Words for Hart Crane" (Lowell), **I:** 381; **II:** 547; **Retro. Supp. II:** 188
"Words for Maria" (Merrill), **Supp. III Part 1:** 327
"Words for the Unknown Makers" (Kunitz), **Supp. III Part 1:** 264
Words for the Wind (Roethke), **III:** 529, 533, 541, 543, 545
"Words for the Wind" (Roethke), **III:** 542-543
Words in the Mourning Time (Hayden), **Supp. II Part 1:** 361, 366, 367
"Words in the Mourning Time" (Hayden), **Supp. II Part 1:** 370-371
"Words into Fiction" (Welty), **IV:** 279
"Words Like Freedom" (Hughes), **Retro. Supp. I:** 207
"Words of a Young Girl" (Lowell), **II:** 554
Words under the Words: Selected Poems (Nye), **Supp. XIII:** 277
Wordsworth, Dorothy, **Supp. IX:** 38
Wordsworth, William, **I:** 283, 522, 524, 525, 588; **II:** 7, 11, 17, 18, 97, 169, 273, 303, 304, 532, 549, 552; **III:** 219, 263, 277, 278, 511, 521, 523, 528, 583; **IV:** 120, 331, 343, 453, 465; **Retro. Supp. I:** 121, 196; **Supp. I Part 1:** 150, 151, 154, 161, 163, 312, 313, 349, 365; **Supp. I Part 2:** 375, 409, 416, 422, 607, 621, 622, 673, 674, 675, 676, 677, 710-711, 729; **Supp. II Part 1:** 4; **Supp. III Part 1:** 12, 15, 73, 279; **Supp. IV Part 2:** 597, 601; **Supp. V:** 258; **Supp. VIII:** 273; **Supp. IX:** 38, 41, 265, 274; **Supp. X:** 22, 23, 65, 120; **Supp. XI:** 248, 251, 312; **Supp. XIII:** 214; **Supp. XIV:**184; **Supp. XV:** 93, 250
Work (Alcott), **Supp. I Part 1:** 32-33, 42
Work (Dixon), **Supp. XII:** 141, **143**
"Work" (Oliver), **Supp. VII:** 243
Work and Love (Dunn), **Supp. XI: 147-148**
"Worker" (Coleman), **Supp. XI:** 89
Working Class Movement in America, The (E. Marx and E. Aveling), **Supp. XVI:**85
Working Papers: Selected Essays and Reviews (Carruth), **Supp. XVI:**46
"Working the Landscape" (Dunn), **Supp. XI:** 151
Workin' on the Chain Gang: Shaking Off the Dead Hand of History (Mosley), **Supp. XIII:** 247, 248
"Work Notes '66" (Baraka), **Supp. II Part 1:** 47
Work of Art (Lewis), **II:** 453-454
"Work of Shading, The" (Simic), **Supp. VIII:** 277-278
Work of Stephen Crane, The (Follett, ed.), **I:** 405
"Work on Red Mountain, The" (Harte), **Supp. II Part 1:** 339
Works of Love, The (Morris), **III:** 223-224, 225, 233
Works of Witter Bynner, The (Kraft, ed.), **Supp. XV:** 52
"World, The" (Simic), **Supp. VIII:** 282
World According to Garp, The (Irving), **Supp. VI:** 163, 164, **170-173**, 181
World and Africa, The: An Inquiry into the Part Which Africa Has Played in World History (Du Bois), **Supp.**

II Part 1: 184-185
"World and All Its Teeth, The" (Nye), **Supp. XIII:** 282
"World and the Door, The" (O. Henry), **Supp. II Part 1:** 402
"World and the Jug, The" (Ellison), **Retro. Supp. II:** 112, 119, 123
"World as We Know It, The" (Barresi), **Supp. XV:** 100
World Authors 1950-1970, **Supp. XIII:** 102
World Below, The (Miller), **Supp. XII: 303-304**
World Below the Window, The: Poems 1937-1997 (W. J. Smith), **Supp. XIII:** 332, 340, 345
World Doesn't End, The (Simic), **Supp. VIII:** 272, **279-280**
World Elsewhere, A: The Place of Style in American Literature (Poirier), **I:** 239
"World Ends Here, The" (Harjo), **Supp. XII:** 227-228
World Enough and Time (Warren), **IV:** 243, 253-254
"World I Live In, The" (T. Williams), **IV:** 388
World I Never Made, A (Farrell), **II:** 34, 35, 424
World in the Attic, The (Morris), **III:** 222-223, 224
World in the Evening, The (Isherwood), **Supp. XIV:** 157, 164, 165, **166-167,** 170
World Is a Wedding, The (Schwartz), **Supp. II Part 2:** 643, 654-660
"World Is a Wedding, The" (Schwartz), **Supp. II Part 2:** 655-656, 657
"World Is Too Much with Us, The" (Wordsworth), **Supp. I Part 1:** 312
Worldly Hopes (Ammons), **Supp. VII:** 34
Worldly Philosophers, The (Heilbroner), **Supp. I Part 2:** 644, 650
World of Apples, The (Cheever), **Supp. I Part 1:** 191, 193
World of David Wagoner, The (McFarland), **Supp. IX:** 323
"World of Easy Rawlins, The" (Mosley), **Supp. XIII:** 234, 236
World of Gwendolyn Brooks, The (Brooks), **Supp. III Part 1:** 83, 84
World of H. G. Wells, The (Brooks), **I:** 240, 241, 242
World of Light, A: Portraits and Celebrations (Sarton), **Supp. III Part 1:** 62; **Supp. VIII:** 249, 253, 262
World of Our Fathers: The Journey of the Eastern European Jews to America and the Life They Found and Made (Howe), **Supp. VI:** 113, 114, 116, 118, 119, **120-125; Supp. XIV:** 104
"World of Pure Experience, A" (James), **II:** 356-357
World of Raymond Chandler, The (Spender), **Supp. IV Part 1:** 119
World of Sex, The (H. Miller), **III:** 170, 178, 187
"World of the Perfect Tear, The" (McGrath), **Supp. X:** 116, 118
World of the Ten Thousand Things, The: Selected Poems (Wright), **Supp. V:** 333
"World of Tomorrow, The" (White), **Supp. I Part 2:** 663
World of Washington Irving, The (Brooks), **I:** 256-257
World Over, The (Wharton), **Retro. Supp. I:** 382
"Worlds" (Goldbarth), **Supp. XII:** 183, 189
World's Body, The (Ransom), **III:** 497, 499; **Supp. II Part 1:** 146
World's End (Boyle), **Supp. VIII: 11-12**
World's End and Other Stories (Theroux), **Supp. VIII:** 322
"World's Fair" (Berryman), **I:** 173
World's Fair (Doctorow), **Supp. IV Part 1:** 217, 224, 227-229, 234, 236-237
World's Fair, The (Fitzgerald), **II:** 93
Worlds of Color (Du Bois), **Supp. II Part 1:** 185-186
"Worlds of Color" (Du Bois), **Supp. II Part 1:** 175
World So Wide (Lewis), **II:** 456
"World's Worst Boyfriends, The" (Wasserstein), **Supp. XV:** 328
"World-Telegram" (Berryman), **I:** 173
World to Come, The (D. Horn), **Supp. XVII:** 50
World View on Race and Democracy: A Study Guide in Human Group Relations (Locke), **Supp. XIV:** 205, 206
World within the Word, The (Gass), **Supp. VI:** 77
"World Without Objects Is a Sensible Place, A" (Wilbur), **Supp. III Part 2:** 550
"World Without Rodrigo, The" (Cisneros), **Supp. VII:** 68
"Worm Moon" (Oliver), **Supp. VII:** 234
"Worn Path, A" (Welty), **IV:** 262; **Retro. Supp. I:** 345-346
"Worsening Situation" (Ashbery), **Supp. III Part 1:** 17-18
"Worship" (Emerson), **II:** 2, 4-5
"Worship and Church Bells" (Paine), **Supp. I Part 2:** 521
Worster, Donald, **Supp. IX:** 19
Worthington, Marjorie, **Supp. XII:** 13
Wouldn't Take Nothing for My Journey Now (Angelou), **Supp. IV Part 1:** 10, 12, 14, 15, 16
Wound and the Bow, The: Seven Studies in Literature (Wilson), **IV:** 429
Wounds in the Rain (Crane), **I:** 409, 414, 423
Woven Stone (Ortiz), **Supp. IV Part 2:** 501, 514
Woven Stories (Ortiz), **Supp. IV Part 2:** 503
"Wraith, The" (Roethke), **III:** 542
"Wrath of God, The" (Fante), **Supp. XI:** 160, 164
"Wreath for a Bridal" (Plath), **Supp. I Part 2:** 537
Wreath for Garibaldi and Other Stories, A (Garrett), **Supp. VII:** 99-101
"Wreath of Women" (Rukeyser), **Supp. VI:** 280
Wreckage of Agathon, The (Gardner), **Supp. VI:** 63, **65-66**
Wrecking Crew (Levis), **Supp. XI: 259-260**
"Wreck of Rivermouth, The" (Whittier), **Supp. I Part 2:** 694, 696-697
"Wreck of the Deutschland" (Hopkins), **Supp. X:** 61
"Wreck of the Hesperus, The" (Longfellow), **Retro. Supp. II:** 168, 169
Wrestler's Cruel Study, The (Dobyns), **Supp. XIII: 82-83**
"Wrestler with Sharks, A" (Yates), **Supp. XI:** 341
Wright, Bernie, **I:** 191, 193
Wright, C. D. (Carolyn Doris), **Supp. XV: 337-355**
Wright, Charles, **Supp. V:** 92, **331-346; Supp. VIII:** 272; **Supp. XIII:** 114; **Supp. XVII:** 71
Wright, Chauncey, **II:** 344
Wright, Frank Lloyd, **I:** 104, 483
Wright, Franz, **Supp. XVII: 239-249**
Wright, George, **III:** 479
Wright, Harold Bell, **II:** 467-468
Wright, Holly, **Supp. VIII:** 272
Wright, James, **I:** 291; **Supp. III Part 1:** 249; **Supp. III Part 2:** 541, **589-607; Supp. IV Part 1:** 60, 72; **Supp. IV Part 2:** 557, 558, 561, 566, 571, 623; **Supp. V:** 332; **Supp. IX:** 152, 155, 159, 265, 271, 290, 293, 296;

Supp. X: 69, 127; **Supp. XI:** 150; **Supp. XII:** 217; **Supp. XIII:** 76; **Supp. XV:** 79, 93, 212; **Supp. XVII:** 239, 241, 243, 244
Wright, Mrs. Richard (Ellen Poplar), **IV:** 476
Wright, Nathalia, **IV:** 155
Wright, Philip Green, **III:** 578, 579, 580
Wright, Richard, **II:** 586; **IV:** 40, **474-497**; **Retro. Supp. II:** 4, 111, 116, 120; **Supp. I Part 1:** 51, 52, 64, 332, 337; **Supp. II Part 1:** 17, 40, 221, 228, 235, 250; **Supp. IV Part 1:** 1, 11, 84, 374; **Supp. VIII:** 88; **Supp. IX:** 316; **Supp. X:** 131, 245, 254; **Supp. XI:** 85; **Supp. XII:** 316; **Supp. XIII:** 46, 233; **Supp. XIV:**73; **Supp. XVI:**135, 139, 141, 143
Wright, Sarah, **Supp. IV Part 1:** 8; **Supp. XIII:** 295
Wright, William, **Retro. Supp. II:** 76, 77
"Writer" (Sanders), **Supp. XVI:**277
"Writer, The" (Wilbur), **Supp. III Part 2:** 561, 562
"Writer as Alaskan, The" (Haines), **Supp. XII:** 199
Writer in America, The (Brooks), **I:** 253, 254, 257
Writer in America, The (Stegner), **Supp. IV Part 2:** 597, 599, 607
"Writers" (Lowell), **II:** 554
Writer's Almanac, The (Keillor, radio program), **Supp. XIII:** 274; **Supp. XVI:**178
Writer's America, A: Landscape in Literature (Kazin), **Supp. VIII:** 106
Writer's Capital, A (Auchincloss), **Supp. IV Part 1:** 21, 23, 24, 31
"Writer's Credo, A" (Abbey), **Supp. XIII:** 1, 17
Writer's Eye, A: Collected Book Reviews (Welty), **Retro. Supp. I:** 339, 354, 356
Writers in Revolt (Southern, Seaver, and Trocchi, eds.), **Supp. XI:** 301
Writer's Life, A (Talese), **Supp. XVII:** 208-209, 210
Writer's Notebook, A (Maugham), **Supp. X:** 58
Writers on America (U.S. Department of State, ed.), **Supp. XIII:** 288
Writers on the Left (Aaron), **IV:** 429; **Supp. II Part 1:** 137
Writers on Writing (Prose), **Supp. XVI:**259
"Writer's Prologue to a Play in Verse" (W. C. Williams), **Retro. Supp. I:** 424

"Writer's Quest for a Parnassus, A" (T. Williams), **IV:** 392
Writers' Workshop (University of Iowa), **Supp. V:** 42
"Writers Workshop, The" (Conroy), **Supp. XVI:**76
"Writing" (Nemerov), **III:** 275
"Writing About the Universe" (Mosley), **Supp. XIII:** 247
"Writing American Fiction" (P. Roth), **Retro. Supp. II:** 279; **Supp. I Part 1:** 192; **Supp. I Part 2:** 431; **Supp. III Part 2:** 414, 420, 421; **Supp. V:** 45
"Writing and a Life Lived Well" (Patchett), **Supp. XII:** 308
Writing a Woman's Life (Heilbrun), **Supp. IX:** 66
Writing Chicago: Modernism, Ethnography, and the Novel (Cappetti), **Supp. IX:** 4, 8
Writing Creative Nonfiction: The Literature of Reality (Talese and Lounsberry, eds.), **Supp. XVII:** 208
Writing from the Center (Sanders), **Supp. XVI:**266, 275-276
"Writing from the Inside Out: Style Is Not the Frosting; It's the Cake" (Robbins), **Supp. X:** 266
"Writing here last autumn of my hopes of seeing a hoopoe" (Updike), **Retro. Supp. I:** 335
Writing in Restaurants (Mamet), **Supp. XIV:**246
"Writing Lesson, The" (Gordon), **Supp. IV Part 1:** 306
Writing Life, The (Dillard), **Supp. VI:** 23, 31
"Writing of Apollinaire, The" (Zukofsky), **Supp. III Part 2:** 616, 617
"Writing of *Fearless Jones*, The" (Mosley), **Supp. XIII:** 242
Writing on the Wall, The, and Literary Essays (McCarthy), **II:** 579
Writings to an Unfinished Accompaniment (Merwin), **Supp. III Part 1:** 352
"Writing the Universe-Mind" (Tabios), **Supp. XV:** 225
Writing the World (Stafford), **Supp. XI:** 314
"Writing to Save Our Lives" (Milligan), **Supp. XIII:** 274
Writin' Is Fightin' (Reed), **Supp. X:** 241
"Writ on the Eve of My 32nd Birthday" (Corso), **Supp. XII:** 129-130
"Written History as an Act of Faith" (Beard), **Supp. I Part 2:** 492

"Wrong Notes" (S. Kauffmann), **Supp. XVI:**74
"Wrought Figure" (McCarriston), **Supp. XIV:**272
"Wunderkind" (McCullers), **II:** 585
Wunderlich, Mark, **Supp. XI:** 119, 132
Wundt, Wilhelm, **II:** 345
Wurster, William Wilson, **Supp. IV Part 1:** 197
WUSA (film), **Supp. V:** 301
Wuthering Heights (E. Brontë), **Supp. V:** 305; **Supp. X:** 89
WWII (Jones), **Supp. XI:** 219, 231
Wyandotté (Cooper), **I:** 350, 355
Wyatt, Robert B., **Supp. V:** 14
Wyatt, Thomas, **Supp. I Part 1:** 369
Wycherly Woman, The (Macdonald), **Supp. IV Part 2:** 473
Wydra, Ewa. *See* Hoffman, Eva
Wyler, William, **Supp. XV:** 195
Wylie, Elinor, **IV:** 436; **Supp. I Part 2: 707-730**; **Supp. III Part 1:** 2, 63, 318-319; **Supp. XI:** 44; **Supp. XIV:**127; **Supp. XV:** 307
Wylie, Horace, **Supp. I Part 2:** 708, 709
Wylie, Philip, **III:** 223
Wyllys, Ruth. *See* Taylor, Mrs. Edward (Ruth Wyllys)
"Wyoming Valley Tales" (Crane), **I:** 409
Wyzewa, Théodore de, **Supp. XIV:**336

X
Xaipe (Cummings), **I:** 430, 432-433, 447
Xenogenesis trilogy (O. Butler), **Supp. XIII: 63-66,** 69
Xenophon, **II:** 105
X Factor, The: A Quest for Excellence" (Plimpton), **Supp. XVI:**241
X Files (television series), **Supp. XVI:**125
Xiaojing, Zhou, **Supp. XV:** 214
Xingu and Other Stories (Wharton), **IV:** 314, 320; **Retro. Supp. I:** 378
Xionia (Wright), **Supp. V:** 333
XLI Poems (Cummings), **I:** 429, 432, 440, 443

Y
Yacoubi, Ahmed, **Supp. IV Part 1:** 88, 92, 93
Yage Letters, The (Burroughs), **Supp. III Part 1:** 94, 98, 100
Yagoda, Ben, **Supp. VIII:** 151
Yamamoto, Isoroku, **Supp. I Part 2:** 491
Yankee City (Warner), **III:** 60
Yankee Clipper (ballet) (Kirstein), **Supp. IV Part 1:** 82

Yankee in Canada, A (Thoreau), **IV:** 188

Yankey in London (Tyler), **I:** 344

"Yánnina" (Merrill), **Supp. III Part 1:** 329

"Yanosz Korczak's Last Walk" (Markowick-Olczakova), **Supp. X:** 70

Yarboro, Chelsea Quinn, **Supp. V:** 147

Yardley, Jonathan, **Supp. V:** 326; **Supp. XI:** 67

"Yard Sale" (Kenyon), **Supp. VII:** 169

Yates, Richard, **Supp. XI: 333-350**

"Year, The" (Sandburg), **III:** 584

"Year Between, The" (Neugeboren), **Supp. XVI:**226

Year in Provence, A (Mayle), **Supp. XVI:**295

Yearling, The (Rawlings), **Supp. X:** 219, **230-231**, 233, 234

Year of Happy, A (Goldbarth), **Supp. XII:** 180

"Year of Mourning, The" (Jeffers), **Supp. II Part 2:** 415

Year of Silence, The (Bell), **Supp. X:** 1, **5-6**, 7

"Year of the Double Spring, The" (Swenson), **Supp. IV Part 2:** 647

Year's Best Science Fiction, The (Merril, ed.), **Supp. XVI:**123

Year's Life, A (Lowell), **Supp. I Part 2:** 405

"Years of Birth" (Cowley), **Supp. II Part 1:** 149

Years of My Youth (Howells), **II:** 276

"Years of Wonder" (White), **Supp. I Part 2:** 652, 653

Years With Ross, The (Thurber), **Supp. I Part 2:** 619

Yeats, Jack, **Supp. XVI:**190

Yeats, John Butler, **III:** 458

Yeats, William Butler, **I:** 69, 172, 384, 389, 403, 434, 478, 494, 532; **II:** 168-169, 566, 598; **III:** 4, 5, 8, 18, 19, 20, 23, 29, 40, 205, 249, 269, 270-271, 272, 278, 279, 294, 347, 409, 457, 458-460, 472, 473, 476-477, 521, 523, 524, 527, 528, 533, 540, 541, 542, 543-544, 591-592; **IV:** 89, 93, 121, 126, 136, 140, 271, 394, 404; **Retro. Supp. I:** 59, 66, 127, 141, 270, 283, 285, 286, 288, 290, 311, 342, 350, 378, 413; **Retro. Supp. II:** 185, 331; **Supp. I Part 1:** 79, 80, 254, 257, 262; **Supp. I Part 2:** 388, 389; **Supp. II Part 1:** 1, 4, 9, 20, 26, 361; **Supp. III Part 1:** 59, 63, 236, 238, 253; **Supp. IV Part 1:** 81; **Supp. IV Part 2:** 634; **Supp. V:** 220; **Supp. VIII:** 19, 21, 30, 155, 156, 190, 239, 262, 292; **Supp. IX:** 43, 119; **Supp. X:** 35, 58, 119, 120; **Supp. XI:** 140; **Supp. XII:** 132, 198, 217, 266; **Supp. XIII:** 77, **Supp. XIII:** 87; **Supp. XIV:**7; **Supp. XV:** 36, 41, 181, 186; **Supp. XVI:**47-48, 159; **Supp. XVII:** 36

Yellin, Jean Fagan, **Supp. XVI:**88, 89

Yellow Back Radio Broke-Down (Reed), **Supp. X:** 240, 242, **243-245**

"Yellow Dog Café" (Komunyakaa), **Supp. XIII:** 126

"Yellow Girl" (Caldwell), **I:** 310

Yellow Glove (Nye), **Supp. XIII:** 275, **276-277**

"Yellow Glove" (Nye), **Supp. XIII:** 276

"Yellow Gown, The" (Anderson), **I:** 114

Yellow House on the Corner, The (Dove), **Supp. IV Part 1:** 244, 245, 246, 254

"Yellow Raft, The" (Connell), **Supp. XIV:**85-86

"Yellow River" (Tate), **IV:** 141

"Yellow Violet, The" (Bryant), **Supp. I Part 1:** 154, 155

"Yellow Wallpaper, The" (Gilman), **Supp. XI: 198-199**, 207; **Supp. XVI:**84

"Yellow Woman" (Keres stories), **Supp. IV Part 1:** 327

"Yellow Woman" (Silko), **Supp. IV Part 2:** 567-568

Yelverton, Theresa, **Supp. IX:** 181

Yenser, Stephen, **Supp. X:** 207, 208; **Supp. XV:** 113-114

"Yentl the Yeshiva Boy" (Singer), **IV:** 15, 20

Yerkes, Charles E., **I:** 507, 512

Yerma (opera) (Bowles), **Supp. IV Part 1:** 89

Yertle the Turtle and Other Stories (Geisel), **Supp. XVI:**109

"Yes" (Stafford), **Supp. XI:** 329

Yes, Mrs. Williams (W. C. Williams), **Retro. Supp. I:** 423

Yes, Yes, No, No (Kushner), **Supp. IX:** 133

"Yes and It's Hopeless" (Ginsberg), **Supp. II Part 1:** 326

Yesenin, Sergey, **Supp. VIII:** 40

"Yes! No!" (Oliver), **Supp. VII:** 243-244

Yesterday and Today: A Comparative Anthology of Poetry (Untermeyer, ed.), **Supp. XV:** 309

Yesterday's Self: Nostalgia and the Immigrant Identity (Ritivoi), **Supp. XVI:**148

Yesterday Will Make You Cry (C. Himes), **Supp. XVI:**137

"Yet Another Example of the Porousness of Certain Borders" (Wallace), **Supp. X:** 309

"Yet Do I Marvel" (Cullen), **Supp. IV Part 1:** 165, 169

Yet Other Waters (Farrell), **II:** 29, 38, 39, 40

Yevtushenko, Yevgeny, **Supp. III Part 1:** 268

Yezzi, David, **Supp. XII:** 193

Yizkor Book, **Supp. XVI:**154

Y no se lo trago la tierra (And the Earth Did Not Cover Him) (Rivera), **Supp. XIII:** 216

¡Yo! (Alvarez), **Supp. VII:** 1, 15-17

"Yogurt of Vasirin Kefirovsky, The" (Apple), **Supp. XVII:** 3, 4

Yohannan, J. D., **II:** 20

"Yoke, The" (Bidart), **Supp. XV:** 33

Yonge, Charlotte, **II:** 174

"Yonnondio" (Whitman), **Supp. XIII:** 304

Yonnondio: From the Thirties (Olsen), **Supp. XIII:** 295, 295, **Supp. XIII:** 292, 296, **303-304**, 305

"Yore" (Nemerov), **III:** 283

"York Beach" (Toomer), **Supp. III Part 2:** 486

Yorke, Dorothy, **Supp. I Part 1:** 258

Yorke, Henry Vincent. *See* Green, Henry

"York Garrison, 1640" (Jewett), **Retro. Supp. II:** 141

Yosemite, The (Muir), **Supp. IX:** 185

"Yosemite Glaciers: Ice Streams of the Great Valley" (Muir), **Supp. IX:** 181

Yoshe Kalb (Singer), **IV:** 2

"You, Andrew Marvell" (MacLeish), **III:** 12-13

"You, Dr. Martin" (Sexton), **Supp. II Part 2:** 673

You, Emperors, and Others: Poems 1957-1960 (Warren), **IV:** 245

"You, Genoese Mariner" (Merwin), **Supp. III Part 1:** 343

"You All Know the Story of the Other Woman" (Sexton), **Supp. II Part 2:** 688

You Are Happy (Atwood), **Supp. XIII:** 34

"You Are Happy" (Atwood), **Supp. XIII:** 34

"You Are in Bear Country" (Kumin), **Supp. IV Part 2:** 453, 455

"You Are Not I" (Bowles), **Supp. IV Part 1:** 87

"You Begin" (Atwood), **Supp. XIII:** 34
You Bright and Risen Angels (Vollmann), **Supp. XVII:** 225, 226
"You Bring Out the Mexican in Me" (Cisneros), **Supp. VII:** 71
You Came Along (film), **Supp. IV Part 2:** 524
"You Can Go Home Again" (TallMountain), **Supp. IV Part 1:** 324-325
"You Can Have It" (Levine), **Supp. V:** 188-189
You Can't Go Home Again (Wolfe), **IV:** 450, 451, 454, 456, 460, 462, 468, 469, 470
You Can't Keep a Good Woman Down (Walker), **Supp. III Part 2:** 520, 525, 531
You Can't Take It with You (Kaufman and Hart), **Supp. XIV:** 327
"You Can't Tell a Man by the Song He Sings" (P. Roth), **Supp. III Part 2:** 406
"You Don't Know What Love Is" (Carver), **Supp. III Part 1:** 147
"You Have Left Your Lotus Pods on the Bus" (Bowles), **Supp. IV Part 1:** 91
You Have Seen Their Faces (Caldwell), **I:** 290, 293-294, 295, 304, 309
You Know Me, Al: A Busher's Letters (Lardner), **Supp. XVI:** 189
You Know Me Al (comic strip), **II:** 423
You Know Me Al (Lardner), **II:** 26, 415, 419, 422, 431
"You Know What" (Beattie), **Supp. V:** 33
"You Know Who You Are" (Nye), **Supp. XIII:** 275
You Might As Well Live: The Life and Times of Dorothy Parker (Keats), **Supp. IX:** 190
"You Must Relax!" (J. Scott), **Supp. XVII:** 189
You Must Revise Your Life (Stafford), **Supp. XI:** 312-313, 313-314, 315
"Young" (Sexton), **Supp. II Part 2:** 680
Young, Al, **Supp. X:** 240
Young, Art, **IV:** 436
Young, Brigham, **Supp. IV Part 2:** 603
Young, Edward, **II:** 111; **III:** 415, 503
Young, Gary, **Supp. XV:** 88
Young, Mary, **Supp. XIII:** 236, 238, 239, 240
Young, Philip, **II:** 306; **Retro. Supp. I:** 172

Young Adventure (Benét), **Supp. XI:** 44
"Young America" (Brooks), **Supp. XV:** 298
"Young Child and His Pregnant Mother, A" (Schwartz), **Supp. II Part 2:** 650
Young Christian, The (Abbott), **Supp. I Part 1:** 38
"Young Dr. Gosse" (Chopin), **Supp. I Part 1:** 211, 216
Younger Choir, The (anthology), **Supp. XV:** 294
Younger Quire, The (Untermeyer), **Supp. XV:** 294, 297
"Young Folks, The" (Salinger), **III:** 551
Young Folk's Cyclopaedia of Persons and Places (Champlin), **III:** 577
"Young Goodman Brown" (Hawthorne), **II:** 229; **Retro. Supp. I:** 151-152, 153, 154; **Supp. XI:** 51; **Supp. XIV:** 48, 50
Young Harvard: First Poems of Witter Bynner (Bynner), **Supp. XV:** 41
Young Hearts Crying (Yates), **Supp. XI:** 348
"Young Housewife, The" (W. C. Williams), **Retro. Supp. I:** 415
Young Immigrants, The (Lardner), **II:** 426
"Young Lady's Friend, The: Verses, Addressed to a Young Lady, on Her Leaving School" (Rowson), **Supp. XV:** 234
Young Lonigan: A Boyhood in Chicago Streets (Farrell), **II:** 31, 41
Young Manhood of Studs Lonigan, The (Farrell), **II:** 31, 34
Young Men and Fire (Maclean), **Supp. XIV:** 221, **231-233**
Young People's Pride (Benét), **Supp. XI:** 44
Young Poet's Primer (Brooks), **Supp. III Part 1:** 86
Youngren, J. Alan, **Supp. XVI:** 174
"Young Sammy's First Wild Oats" (Santayana), **III:** 607, 615
"Young Sor Juana, The" (Mora), **Supp. XIII:** 218
"Your Death" (Dove), **Supp. IV Part 1:** 250
You're Only Old Once! (Geisel), **Supp. XVI:** 111
"You're Ugly, Too" (Moore), **Supp. X:** 171
"Your Face on the Dog's Neck" (Sexton), **Supp. II Part 2:** 686
Your Job in Germany (film, Capra), **Supp. XVI:** 102

Your Job in Japan (film, Capra), **Supp. XVI:** 102
"Your Life" (Stafford), **Supp. XI:** 329
"Your Mother's Eyes" (Kingsolver), **Supp. VII:** 209
"You Take a Train through a Foreign Country" (Dobyns), **Supp. XIII:** 90
"Youth" (Hughes), **Supp. I Part 1:** 321
"Youth" (Huncke), **Supp. XIV:** 145
Youth and Life (Bourne), **I:** 217-222, 232
Youth and the Bright Medusa (Cather), **I:** 322; **Retro. Supp. I:** 14
"Youthful Religious Experiences" (Corso), **Supp. XII:** 117
Youth of Parnassus, and Other Stories, The (L. P. Smith), **Supp. XIV:** 336
Youth's First Steps in Geography (Rowson), **Supp. XV:** 243
You Touched Me! (Williams and Windham), **IV:** 382, 385, 387, 390, 392-393
"You Touch Me" (X. J. Kennedy), **Supp. XV:** 166
Yurka, Blanche, **Supp. I Part 1:** 67
Yutang, Adet, **Supp. X:** 291
Yutang, Anor, **Supp. X:** 291
Yutang, Lin, **Supp. X:** 291; **Supp. XVI:** 190
Yutang, Mei-mei, **Supp. X:** 291
Yvernelle: A Legend of Feudal France (Norris), **III:** 314
Y & X (Olson), **Supp. II Part 2:** 556

Z

Zabel, Morton Dauwen, **II:** 431; **III:** 194, 215; **Supp. I Part 2:** 721
Zach, Natan, **Supp. XV:** 75, 82, 85
Zagajewski, Adam, **Supp. XVII:** 241
Zagarell, Sandra, **Supp. XV:** 269, 270, 278, 281, 282
Zagarell, Sandra A., **Retro. Supp. II:** 140, 143
"Zagrowsky Tells" (Paley), **Supp. VI:** 229
Zakrzewska, Marie, **Retro. Supp. II:** 146
Zaleski, Jeff, **Supp. XI:** 143
Zall, Paul, **Supp. XIV:** 156
Zaltzberg, Charlotte, **Supp. IV Part 1:** 374
"Zambesi and Ranee" (Swenson), **Supp. IV Part 2:** 647
Zamir, Israel, **Retro. Supp. II:** 303, 317
Zamora, Bernice, **Supp. IV Part 2:** 545
Zamoyski, Adam, **Supp. XV:** 257
Zangwill, Israel, **I:** 229
Zanita: A Tale of the Yosemite (Yelverton), **Supp. IX:** 181

Zanuck, Darryl F., **Supp. XI:** 170; **Supp. XII:** 165
Zapata, Emiliano, **Supp. XIII:** 324
"Zapatos" (Boyle), **Supp. VIII:** 15
Zapruder, Matthew, **Supp. XVI:** 55
Zarathustra, **III:** 602
Zawacki, Andrew, **Supp. VIII:** 272
"Zaydee" (Levine), **Supp. V:** 186
Zebra-Striped Hearse, The (Macdonald), **Supp. IV Part 2:** 473
Zechariah (biblical book), **IV:** 152
Zeidner, Lisa, **Supp. IV Part 2:** 453
"Zeitl and Rickel" (Singer), **IV:** 20
Zeke and Ned (McMurtry and Ossana), **Supp. V:** 232
Zeke Proctor, Cherokee Outlaw (Conley), **Supp. V:** 232
Zelda: A Biography (Milford), **Supp. IX:** 60
"Zelda and Scott: The Beautiful and Damned" (National Portrait Gallery exhibit), **Supp. IX:** 65
Zelig (film; Allen), **Supp. XV:** 4, 6, 8-9
Zen and the Birds of Appetite (Merton), **Supp. VIII:** 205-206, 208
Zend-Avesta (Fechner), **II:** 358
Zeno, **Retro. Supp. I:** 247
Zero db and Other Stories (Bell), **Supp. X:** 1, 5, 6
"Zeus over Redeye" (Hayden), **Supp. II Part 1:** 380
Zevi, Sabbatai, **IV:** 6

Ziegfeld, Florenz, **II:** 427-428
Zigrosser, Carl, **I:** 226, 228, 231
Zimmerman, Paul D., **Supp. IV Part 2:** 583, 589, 590
Zinberg, Leonard S. See Lacy, Ed
Zinman, Toby Silverman, **Supp. XIII:** 207-208, 209
Zinn, Howard, **Supp. V:** 289
Zinsser, Hans, **I:** 251, 385
Zip: A Novel of the Left and Right (Apple), **Supp. XVII:** 4-5
Zipes, Jack, **Supp. XIV:** 126
"Zipper, The" (L. Michaels), **Supp. XVI:** 214
"Zizi's Lament" (Corso), **Supp. XII:** 123
Zodiac, The (Dickey), **Supp. IV Part 1:** 178, 183-184, 185
Zola, Émile, **I:** 211, 411, 474, 500, 502, 518; **II:** 174, 175-176, 182, 194, 275, 276, 281, 282, 319, 325, 337, 338; **III:** 315, 316, 317-318, 319-320, 321, 322, 323, 393, 511, 583; **IV:** 326; **Retro. Supp. I:** 226, 235; **Retro. Supp. II:** 93; **Supp. I Part 1:** 207; **Supp. II Part 1:** 117
Zolotow, Maurice, **III:** 161
"Zone" (Bogan), **Supp. III Part 1:** 60-61
Zone Journals (Wright), **Supp. V:** 332-333, 342-343
"Zooey" (Salinger), **III:** 564-565, 566, 567, 569, 572

"Zoo Revisited" (White), **Supp. I Part 2:** 654
Zoo Story, The (Albee), **I:** 71, 72-74, 75, 77, 84, 93, 94; **III:** 281
Zorach, William, **I:** 260
Zuccotti, Susan, **Supp. XVI:** 154
Zuckerman Bound: A Trilogy and Epilogue (P. Roth), **Supp. III Part 2:** 423
Zuckerman Unbound (P. Roth), **Retro. Supp. II:** 283; **Supp. III Part 2:** 421-422
Zueblin, Charles, **Supp. I Part 1:** 5
Zuger, Abigail, **Supp. X:** 160
Zukofsky, Celia (Mrs. Louis), **Supp. III Part 2:** 619-621, 623, 625, 626-629, 631
Zukofsky, Louis, **IV:** 415; **Retro. Supp. I:** 422; **Supp. III Part 2:** **619-636**; **Supp. IV Part 1:** 154; **Supp. XIV:** 279, 282, 285, 286-287
Zukofsky, Paul, **Supp. III Part 2:** 622, 623-626, 627, 628
Zuleika Dobson (Beerbohm), **Supp. I Part 2:** 714
"Zuni Potter: Drawing the Heartline" (Bierds), **Supp. XVII:** 26
Zverev, Aleksei, **Retro. Supp. I:** 278
Zwinger, Ann, **Supp. X:** 29
Zyda, Joan, **Retro. Supp. II:** 52

A Complete Listing of Authors in *American Writers*

Abbey, Edward   Supp. XIII
Acker, Kathy   Supp. XII
Adams, Henry   Vol. I
Addams, Jane   Supp. I
Agee, James   Vol. I
Aiken, Conrad   Vol. I
Albee, Edward   Vol. I
Alcott, Louisa May   Supp. I
Algren, Nelson   Supp. IX
Allen, Woody   Supp. XV
Alvarez, Julia   Supp. VII
Ammons, A. R.   Supp. VII
Anderson, Sherwood   Vol. I
Angelou, Maya   Supp. IV
Apple, Max   Supp. XVII
Ashbery, John   Supp. III
Atwood, Margaret   Supp. XIII
Auchincloss, Louis   Supp. IV
Auden, W. H.   Supp. II
Audubon, John James   Supp. XVI
Auster, Paul   Supp. XII
Baker, Nicholson   Supp. XIII
Baldwin, James   Supp. I
Baldwin, James   Retro. Supp. II
Bambara, Toni Cade   Supp. XI
Banks, Russell   Supp. V
Baraka, Amiri   Supp. II
Barlow, Joel   Supp. II
Barnes, Djuna   Supp. III
Barth, John   Vol. I
Barthelme, Donald   Supp. IV
Barthelme, Frederick   Supp. XI
Bass, Rick   Supp. XVI
Bausch, Richard   Supp. VII
Baxter, Charles   Supp. XVII
Beattie, Ann   Supp. V

Bell, Madison Smartt   Supp. X
Bellow, Saul   Vol. I
Bellow, Saul   Retro. Supp. II
Benét, Stephen Vincent   Supp. XI
Berry, Wendell   Supp. X
Berryman, John   Vol. I
Bidart, Frank   Supp. XV
Bierce, Ambrose   Vol. I
Bierds, Linda   Supp. XVII
Bishop, Elizabeth   Supp. I
Bishop, Elizabeth   Retro. Supp. II
Blackmur, R. P.   Supp. II
Bly, Carol   Supp. XVI
Bly, Robert   Supp. IV
Bogan, Louise   Supp. III
Bourne, Randolph   Vol. I
Bowles, Paul   Supp. IV
Boyle, T. C.   Supp. VIII
Bradbury, Ray   Supp. IV
Bradstreet, Anne   Supp. I
Brodsky, Joseph   Supp. VIII
Brooks, Cleanth   Supp. XIV
Brooks, Gwendolyn   Supp. III
Brooks, Van Wyck   Vol. I
Brown, Charles Brockden   Supp. I
Bryant, William Cullen   Supp. I
Buck, Pearl S.   Supp. II
Buechner, Frederick   Supp. XII
Bukiet, Melvin Jules   Supp. XVII
Burke, James Lee   Supp. XIV
Burke, Kenneth   Vol. I
Burroughs, William S.   Supp. III
Butler, Octavia   Supp. XIII
Butler, Robert Olen   Supp. XII
Bynner, Witter   Supp. XV
Caldwell, Erskine   Vol. I
Cameron, Peter   Supp. XII

557

Capote, Truman   Supp. III
Carruth, Hayden   Supp. XVI
Carson, Anne   Supp. XII
Carson, Rachel   Supp. IX
Carver, Raymond   Supp. III
Cather, Willa   Vol. I
Cather, Willa   Retro. Supp. I
Chabon, Michael   Supp. XI
Chandler, Raymond   Supp. IV
Chapman, John Jay   Supp. XIV
Cheever, John   Supp. I
Chesnutt, Charles W.   Supp. XIV
Chopin, Kate   Supp. I
Chopin, Kate   Retro. Supp. II
Cisneros, Sandra   Supp. VII
Clampitt, Amy   Supp. IX
Coleman, Wanda   Supp. XI
Connell, Evan S.   Supp. XIV
Conroy, Frank   Supp. XVI
Cooper, James Fenimore   Vol. I
Coover, Robert   Supp. V
Corso, Gregory   Supp. XII
Cowley, Malcolm   Supp. II
Cozzens, James Gould   Vol. I
Crane, Hart   Vol. I
Crane, Hart   Retro. Supp. II
Crane, Stephen   Vol. I
Creeley, Robert   Supp. IV
Crèvecoeur, Michel-Guillaume Jean de   Supp. I
Crews, Harry   Supp. XI
Cullen, Countee   Supp. IV
Cummings, E. E.   Vol. I
Cunningham, Michael   Supp. XV
Davis, Rebecca Harding   Supp. XVI
DeLillo, Don   Supp. VI
Dickey, James   Supp. IV
Dickinson, Emily   Vol. I
Dickinson, Emily   Retro. Supp. I
Didion, Joan   Supp. IV
Dillard, Annie   Supp. VI
Dixon, Stephen   Supp. XII
Dobyns, Stephen   Supp. XIII
Doctorow, E. L.   Supp. IV

Doolittle, Hilda (H.D.)   Supp. I
Dos Passos, John   Vol. I
Doty, Mark   Supp. XI
Douglass, Frederick   Supp. III
Dove, Rita   Supp. IV
Dreiser, Theodore   Vol. I
Dreiser, Theodore   Retro. Supp. II
Du Bois, W. E. B.   Supp. II
Dubus, Andre   Supp. VII
Dunbar, Paul Laurence   Supp. II
Dunn, Stephen   Supp. XI
Eberhart, Richard   Vol. I
Edwards, Jonathan   Vol. I
Eliot, T. S.   Vol. I
Eliot, T. S.   Retro. Supp. I
Elkin, Stanley   Supp. VI
Ellison, Ralph   Supp. II
Ellison, Ralph   Retro. Supp. II
Emerson, Ralph Waldo   Vol. II
Endore, Guy   Supp. XVII
Epstein, Joseph   Supp. XIV
Epstein, Leslie   Supp. XII
Erdrich, Louise   Supp. IV
Everwine, Peter   Supp. XV
Fante, John   Supp. XI
Farrell, James T.   Vol. II
Faulkner, William   Vol. II
Faulkner, William   Retro. Supp. I
Fiedler, Leslie   Supp. XIII
Finch, Annie   Supp. XVII
Fisher, M.F.K.   Supp. XVII
Fitzgerald, F. Scott   Vol. II
Fitzgerald, F. Scott   Retro. Supp. I
Fitzgerald, Zelda   Supp. IX
Ford, Richard   Supp. V
Francis, Robert   Supp. IX
Franklin, Benjamin   Vol. II
Frederic, Harold   Vol. II
Freneau, Philip   Supp. II
Frost, Carol   Supp. XV
Frost, Robert   Vol. II
Frost, Robert   Retro. Supp. I
Fuller, Margaret   Supp. II
Gaddis, William   Supp. IV

García, Cristina   Supp. XI
Gardner, John   Supp. VI
Garrett, George   Supp. VII
Gass, William   Supp. VI
Geisel, Theodor Seuss   Supp. XVI
Gibbons, Kaye   Supp. X
Gibson, William   Supp. XVI
Gilman, Charlotte Perkins   Supp. XI
Ginsberg, Allen   Supp. II
Gioia, Dana   Supp. XV
Glasgow, Ellen   Vol. II
Glaspell, Susan   Supp. III
Goldbarth, Albert   Supp. XII
Glück, Louise   Supp. V
Gordon, Caroline   Vol. II
Gordon, Mary   Supp. IV
Gunn Allen, Paula   Supp. IV
Gurney, A. R.   Supp. V
Haines, John   Supp. XII
Hammett, Dashiell   Supp. IV
Hansberry, Lorraine   Supp. IV
Hapgood, Hutchins   Supp. XVII
Hardwick, Elizabeth   Supp. III
Harjo, Joy   Supp. XII
Harrison, Jim   Supp. VIII
Harte, Bret   Supp. II
Hass, Robert   Supp. VI
Hawthorne, Nathaniel   Vol. II
Hawthorne, Nathaniel   Retro. Supp. I
Hay, Sara Henderson   Supp. XIV
Hayden, Robert   Supp. II
Hearon, Shelby   Supp. VIII
Hecht, Anthony   Supp. X
Heller, Joseph   Supp. IV
Hellman, Lillian   Supp. I
Hemingway, Ernest   Vol. II
Hemingway, Ernest   Retro. Supp. I
Henry, O.   Supp. II
Hijuelos, Oscar   Supp. VIII
Himes, Chester Bomar   Supp. XVI
Hoffman, Alice   Supp. X
Hoffman, Eva   Supp. XVI
Hogan, Linda   Supp. IV
Holmes, Oliver Wendell   Supp. I

Howe, Irving   Supp. VI
Howe, Susan   Supp. IV
Howells, William Dean   Vol. II
Hughes, Langston   Supp. I
Hughes, Langston   Retro. Supp. I
Hugo, Richard   Supp. VI
Humphrey, William   Supp. IX
Huncke, Herbert   Supp. XIV
Hurston, Zora Neale   Supp. VI
Irving, John   Supp. VI
Irving, Washington   Vol. II
Isherwood, Christopher   Supp. XIV
Jackson, Shirley   Supp. IX
James, Henry   Vol. II
James, Henry   Retro. Supp. I
James, William   Vol. II
Jarman, Mark   Supp. XVII
Jarrell, Randall   Vol. II
Jeffers, Robinson   Supp. II
Jewett, Sarah Orne   Vol. II
Jewett, Sarah Orne   Retro. Supp. II
Johnson, Charles   Supp. VI
Jones, James   Supp. XI
Jong, Erica   Supp. V
Justice, Donald   Supp. VII
Karr, Mary   Supp. XI
Kazin, Alfred   Supp. VIII
Kees, Weldon   Supp. XV
Keillor, Garrison   Supp. XVI
Kelly, Brigit Pegeen   Supp. XVII
Kennedy, William   Supp. VII
Kennedy, X. J.   Supp. XV
Kenyon, Jane   Supp. VII
Kerouac, Jack   Supp. III
Kincaid, Jamaica   Supp. VII
King, Stephen   Supp. V
Kingsolver, Barbara   Supp. VII
Kingston, Maxine Hong   Supp. V
Kinnell, Galway   Supp. III
Knowles, John   Supp. XII
Koch, Kenneth   Supp. XV
Komunyakaa, Yusef   Supp. XIII
Kosinski, Jerzy   Supp. VII
Kumin, Maxine   Supp. IV

Kunitz, Stanley   Supp. III
Kushner, Tony   Supp. IX
LaBastille, Anne   Supp. X
Lacy, Ed   Supp. XV
Lanier, Sidney   Supp. I
Larcom, Lucy   Supp. XIII
Lardner, Ring   Vol. II
Lee, Harper   Supp. VIII
Lee, Li-Young   Supp. XV
Leopold, Aldo   Supp. XIV
Levertov, Denise   Supp. III
Levine, Philip   Supp. V
Levis, Larry   Supp. XI
Lewis, Sinclair   Vol. II
Lindsay, Vachel   Supp. I
Locke, Alain   Supp. XIV
London, Jack   Vol. II
Longfellow, Henry Wadsworth   Vol. II
Longfellow, Henry Wadsworth   Retro. Supp. II
Loos, Anita   Supp. XVI
Lowell, Amy   Vol. II
Lowell, James Russell   Supp. I
Lowell, Robert   Vol. II
Lowell, Robert   Retro. Supp. II
Markson, David   Supp. XVII
McCarriston, Linda   Supp. XIV
McCarthy, Cormac   Supp. VIII
McCarthy, Mary   Vol. II
McClatchy, J. D.   Supp. XII
McCourt, Frank   Supp. XII
McCoy, Horace   Supp. XIII
McCullers, Carson   Vol. II
Macdonald, Ross   Supp. IV
McGrath, Thomas   Supp. X
McKay, Claude   Supp. X
Maclean, Norman   Supp. XIV
MacLeish, Archibald   Vol. III
McMillan, Terry   Supp. XIII
McMurty, Larry   Supp. V
McNally, Terrence   Supp. XIII
McPhee, John   Supp. III
Mailer, Norman   Vol. III
Mailer, Norman   Retro. Supp. II

Malamud, Bernard   Supp. I
Mamet, David   Supp. XIV
Marquand, John P.   Vol. III
Marshall, Paule   Supp. XI
Mason, Bobbie Ann   Supp. VIII
Masters, Edgar Lee   Supp. I
Mather, Cotton   Supp. II
Matthews, William   Supp. IX
Matthiessen, Peter   Supp. V
Maxwell, William   Supp. VIII
Melville, Herman   Vol. III
Melville, Herman   Retro. Supp. I
Mencken, H. L.   Vol. III
Merrill, James   Supp. III
Merton, Thomas   Supp. VIII
Merwin, W. S.   Supp. III
Michaels, Leonard   Supp. XVI
Millay, Edna St. Vincent   Vol. III
Miller, Arthur   Vol. III
Miller, Henry   Vol. III
Miller, Sue   Supp. XII
Minot, Susan   Supp. VI
Momaday, N. Scott   Supp. IV
Monette, Paul   Supp. X
Moore, Lorrie   Supp. X
Moore, Marianne   Vol. III
Mora, Pat   Supp. XIII
Morison, Samuel Eliot   Supp. I
Morris, Wright   Vol. III
Morrison, Toni   Supp. III
Mosley, Walter   Supp. XIII
Motley, Willard   Supp. XVII
Muir, John   Supp. IX
Mumford, Lewis   Supp. III
Nabokov, Vladimir   Vol. III
Nabokov, Vladimir   Retro. Supp. I
Naylor, Gloria   Supp. VIII
Nemerov, Howard   Vol. III
Neugeboren, Jay   Supp. XVI
Nichols, John   Supp. XIII
Niebuhr, Reinhold   Vol. III
Nin, Anaïs   Supp. X
Norris, Frank   Vol. III
Nye, Naomi Shihab   Supp. XIII

AUTHORS LIST / 561

Oates, Joyce Carol   Supp. II
O'Brien, Tim   Supp. V
O'Connor, Flannery   Vol. III
O'Connor, Flannery   Retro. Supp. II
Odets, Clifford   Supp. II
O'Hara, John   Vol. III
Olds, Sharon   Supp. X
Oliver, Mary   Supp. VII
Olsen, Tillie   Supp. XIII
Olson, Charles   Supp. II
O'Neill, Eugene   Vol. III
Ortiz, Simon J.   Supp. IV
Ozick, Cynthia   Supp. V
Paine, Thomas   Supp. I
Paley, Grace   Supp. VI
Parker, Dorothy   Supp. IX
Parkman, Francis   Supp. II
Patchett, Ann   Supp. XII
Percy, Walker   Supp. III
Pinsky, Robert   Supp. VI
Plath, Sylvia   Supp. I
Plath, Sylvia   Retro. Supp. II
Plimpton, George   Supp. XVI
Podhoretz, Norman   Supp. VIII
Poe, Edgar Allan   Vol. III
Poe, Edgar Allan   Retro. Supp. II
Porter, Katherine Anne   Vol. III
Pound, Ezra   Vol. III
Pound, Ezra   Retro. Supp. I
Powers, Richard   Supp. IX
Price, Reynolds   Supp. VI
Prose, Francine   Supp. XVI
Proulx, Annie   Supp. VII
Purdy, James   Supp. VII
Pynchon, Thomas   Supp. II
Quindlen, Anna   Supp. XVII
Rand, Ayn   Supp. IV
Ransom, John Crowe   Vol. III
Rawlings, Marjorie Kinnan   Supp. X
Reed, Ishmael   Supp. X
Reznikoff, Charles   Supp. XIV
Rice, Anne   Supp. VII
Rich, Adrienne   Supp. I
Rich, Adrienne   Retro. Supp. II

Ríos, Alberto Álvaro   Supp. IV
Robbins, Tom   Supp. X
Robinson, Edwin Arlington   Vol. III
Rodriguez, Richard   Supp. XIV
Roethke, Theodore   Vol. III
Roth, Henry   Supp. IX
Roth, Philip   Supp. III
Roth, Philip   Retro. Supp. II
Rowson, Susanna   Supp. XV
Rukeyser, Muriel   Supp. VI
Russo, Richard   Supp. XII
Salinas, Luis Omar   Supp. XIII
Salinger, J. D.   Vol. III
Salter, James   Supp. IX
Sandburg, Carl   Vol. III
Sanders, Scott Russell   Supp. XVI
Santayana, George   Vol. III
Sarton, May   Supp. VIII
Schnackenberg, Gjertrud   Supp. XV
Schwartz, Delmore   Supp. II
Scott, Joanna   Supp. XVII
Sexton, Anne   Supp. II
Shanley, John Patrick   Supp. XIV
Shapiro, Karl   Supp. II
Shepard, Sam   Supp. III
Shields, Carol   Supp. VII
Silko, Leslie Marmon   Supp. IV
Simic, Charles   Supp. VIII
Simon, Neil   Supp. IV
Simpson, Louis   Supp. IX
Sinclair, Upton   Supp. V
Singer, Isaac Bashevis   Vol. IV
Singer, Isaac Bashevis   Retro. Supp. II
Smiley, Jane   Supp. VI
Smith, Logan Pearsall   Supp. XIV
Smith, William Jay   Supp. XIII
Snodgrass, W. D.   Supp. VI
Snyder, Gary   Supp. VIII
Sobin, Gustaf   Supp. XVI
Sontag, Susan   Supp. III
Southern, Terry   Supp. XI
Stafford, William   Supp. XI
Stegner, Wallace   Supp. IV
Stein, Gertrude   Vol. IV

Steinbeck, John	Vol. IV
Stern, Gerald	Supp. IX
Stevens, Wallace	Vol. IV
Stevens, Wallace	Retro. Supp. I
Stoddard, Elizabeth	Supp. XV
Stone, Robert	Supp. V
Stowe, Harriet Beecher	Supp. I
Strand, Mark	Supp. IV
Styron, William	Vol. IV
Swenson, May	Supp. IV
Talese, Gay	Supp. XVII
Tan, Amy	Supp. X
Tate, Allen	Vol. IV
Taylor, Edward	Vol. IV
Taylor, Peter	Supp. V
Theroux, Paul	Supp. VIII
Thoreau, Henry David	Vol. IV
Thurber, James	Supp. I
Toomer, Jean	Supp. IX
Trilling, Lionel	Supp. III
Turow, Scott	Supp. XVII
Twain, Mark	Vol. IV
Tyler, Anne	Supp. IV
Untermeyer, Louis	Supp. XV
Updike, John	Vol. IV
Updike, John	Retro. Supp. I
Van Vechten, Carl	Supp. II
Veblen, Thorstein	Supp. I
Vidal, Gore	Supp. IV
Vollmann, William T.	Supp. XVII
Vonnegut, Kurt	Supp. II
Wagoner, David	Supp. IX
Walker, Alice	Supp. III
Wallace, David Foster	Supp. X
Warren, Robert Penn	Vol. IV
Wasserstein, Wendy	Supp. XV
Welty, Eudora	Vol. IV
Welty, Eudora	Retro. Supp. I
West, Nathanael	Vol. IV
West, Nathanael	Retro. Supp. II
Wharton, Edith	Vol. IV
Wharton, Edith	Retro. Supp. I
White, E. B.	Supp. I
Whitman, Walt	Vol. IV
Whitman, Walt	Retro. Supp. I
Whittier, John Greenleaf	Supp. I
Wilbur, Richard	Supp. III
Wideman, John Edgar	Supp. X
Wilder, Thornton	Vol. IV
Williams, Tennessee	Vol. IV
Williams, William Carlos	Vol. IV
Williams, William Carlos	Retro. Supp. I
Wilson, August	Supp. VIII
Wilson, Edmund	Vol. IV
Winters, Yvor	Supp. II
Wolfe, Thomas	Vol. IV
Wolfe, Tom	Supp. III
Wolff, Tobias	Supp. VII
Wright, C. D.	Supp. XV
Wright, Charles	Supp. V
Wright, Franz	Supp. XVII
Wright, James	Supp. III
Wright, Richard	Vol. IV
Wylie, Elinor	Supp. I
Yates, Richard	Supp. XI
Zukofsky, Louis	Supp. III

Brentwood Academy Library
Brentwood, TN 37027